A HISTORY OF THE MEDITERRANEAN AIR WAR 1940-1945
Volume One: North Africa
June 1940 – January 1942

A HISTORY OF THE
MEDITERRANEAN
AIR WAR
1940-1945

Volume One: North Africa
June 1940 – January 1942

Christopher Shores and Giovanni Massimello
with Russell Guest

GRUB STREET • LONDON

Published by
Grub Street
4 Rainham Close
London SW11 6SS

Reprinted 2012

British Library Cataloguing in Publication Data

Shores, Christopher F.
   Mediterranean air war, 1940-1945.
   Volume 1, North Africa, June 1940-January 1942.
   1. World War, 1939-1945 – Campaigns – Africa, North.
   2. World War, 1939-1945 – Aerial operations.
   I. Title
   940.5'4231-dc22

ISBN-13: 9781908117076

Cover design by Sarah Driver
Design by Roy Platten, Eclipse, Hemel Hempstead
roy.eclipse@btopenworld.com

Printed and bound by MPG Ltd, Bodmin Cornwall

Grub Street Publishing only uses FSC
(Forest Stewardship Council) paper for its books.

CONTENTS

INTRODUCTION

It is well over 40 years since Hans Ring and I worked on and produced *Fighters over the Desert*. This was followed six years later by *Fighters over Tunisia*. Both books have been out of print for many, many years, and I have been pressed frequently to allow them to be reprinted. This I have studiously avoided, since in the meantime it has become ever-more apparent to me that there was much more information that I would wish to include, or to use to rectify mistakes and misunderstandings in the original volumes. Particularly, while in those far-off days I had privileged access to records before these were released to the Public Records Office (now the National Archives), this was only at squadron level. The ability to research the documents of wings, groups, and command levels has made a considerable difference to my understanding of events.

After long thought and discussion, I have begun a major project. This involves, firstly, the re-writing of the Western Desert and Tunisian campaigns in such number of volumes as proves to be appropriate, but to include not just the fighters, but also the bombers, reconnaissance and transport aircraft, and their supporting units.

It will then be my intention, all things being equal, to continue the series with coverage of the Sicilian, Italian and Aegean campaigns, and the related Strategic Bombing Offensive launched by the US 15th Air Force and RAF 205 Group. The intention is, together with the other campaign histories in which I have been involved, ultimately to produce a full history of the whole Mediterranean area conflict between 1940-45.

In respect of the opening volumes relating to the Western Desert and Tunisia, these are designed essentially to form part of a series including *Malta: The Hurricane Years, 1940-41, Air War for Yugoslavia, Greece and Crete, 1940-41, Malta: The Spitfire Year, 1942* and *Dust Clouds in the Middle East*. Frequent cross-reference is being made to all areas where these earlier volumes impinge or relate to the subject matter of the current books.

It is also intended that, where appropriate, similar inter-relation may be achieved with volumes covering other campaigns, including *Fledgling Eagles, Bloody Shambles, Volumes 1 and 2, Air War for Burma* and *2nd Tactical Air Force, Volumes 1-4*. Indices included with each book will allow the progress of many individual pilots – and units – between these various theatres of operations. Those interested in following in more detail many of the pilots appearing in these volumes will be able to obtain further such information in *Aces High, Volumes 1 and 2*, and *Those Other Eagles*.

Readers of this volume will discover that I have employed first hand accounts on frequent occasions from the memoirs both of commanders and airmen. I have done so deliberately as I feel that these often encapsulate the attitudes and the knowledge prevailing at the time with a freshness and immediacy which latter-day reporting cannot always produce. I intend to continue to do this in the planned further volumes.

It will also become obvious that I have made considerable such inclusions where reference is made by those present (particularly at command level) to the inadequacies of the British Army at the time. I have done this because I believe that it has subsequently become accepted that the North African campaigns became mainly a battle for airfields, and that air power was increasingly the dominating and decisive factor. Indeed, the view of most of these commanders was that the Allied air force frequently saved the army from disaster. However, when one reads most of the accounts and memoirs of these battles from the army viewpoint, one is left with the impression that the air force hardly existed and played little part in the proceedings. My wish is to seek to remedy this perception.

Which brings me neatly to the coverage I have given to the land operations themselves. Far from being 'anti-army', I must begin by admitting that after military aviation, my other great passion is for tanks and other armoured fighting vehicles. Indeed, the temptation has been for me to write far more about these matters than space permits. I have therefore sought to limit the inclusion of such details to those which will allow the reader to try and understand just how the activities in the air related to what was happening on the ground below.

In the case of the Crusader operations which account for a considerable part of this volume, the battle was long, hard and complex. There have been numerous accounts of the fighting between mid November 1941 and the end of January 1942. I have sought to read them all, and they are included in the bibliography at the end of this book. In my opinion the best of the lot is Richard Humble's *Crusader; The Eighth Army's Forgotten Victory*, and I warmly recommend this book to those readers wishing to gain fuller knowledge and a wider understanding of this critical period of the war. Mr Humble's book is also considerably fairer to the involvement of the air forces than most!

When Hans Ring and I originally researched the Desert operations we found ourselves frequently baffled when we could not always find losses to relate to the claims of the fighter pilots involved. Many years of study of many air forces and campaigns have led me to understand just how prevalent over-claiming was in many circumstances, and to allow for this. To a greater or lesser extent, this is a phenomenon which is endemic in aerial combat.

I have in places been critical of the equipment provided to the Commonwealth air forces, and of the paucity of training being provided to those entering action for the first time from the beginning of 1941 onwards (and indeed such criticisms frequently apply just as much to the ground forces). That so much would be achieved by the end of 1942 with such undistinguished aircraft must surely result from truly heroic efforts.

I have found it necessary at times to indicate the sometimes malign influence of the British prime minister, Winston Churchill, in constantly pressing the commanders in the field to proceed before their forces were ready. Although often understandable in the circumstances prevailing, it did lead to the cruel and sometimes unfair damage to the careers of a number of gifted commanders whose main fault had been to try and bring home to the high command that which they did not wish to hear. I stress, however, that in referring to these matters I am straying into the areas of hindsight, and perhaps with a clearer knowledge of tactics and methods much better understood at a later date than was possible at the time. All too often it was a question not of what should have been done, but just what could be done, given the knowledge and resources available then. The reader should keep this in mind throughout.

Another major feature which I very much wish to stress is the fundamental role of the Dominions and colonies of the old British Empire. Without the support of the Australians, Canadians, Indians, New Zealanders, and in the air particularly the South Africans, one is led to the conclusion that without them the mother country would not have succeeded – certainly until well after the initial involvement of the United States of America in the war, had the United Kingdom still remained a free country by that time. Today it seems inconceivable that, in such circumstances, which heaven forbid, all, or indeed, any, of these great nations would rush immediately to Britain's aid at such grim cost and sacrifice. Even little Southern Rhodesia (as it then was) sent a squadron of aircraft to take part.

Whilst it is many years since I had the pleasure and excitement of working with Hans Ring (and I very much miss his frequently ascerbic comments!), I have been very fortunate to be joined in this case by my good friend, Giovanni Massimello, an Italian aviation historian of the first order, who has made possible a detailed inclusion of the operations of the Regia Aeronautica in a manner which had proved totally impossible in the original book. We have also been aided by Russell Guest, whose knowledge of the campaign and of the Luftwaffe fighter force is voluminous. We have also received considerable help and guidance from Winfried Bock which has always been most valuable to us. We would have loved to have included him in the research and editorial team, but his deep involvement in the vast study of the Luftwaffe fighter operations and units in which he has been, and remains, deeply involved, has prevented this – for reasons we well understand and respect.

I repeat the expression of thanks set out in *Fighters over the Desert* to pilots and fellow historians, all too many of whom are sadly no longer with us. I now add to the list of the former, Grp Capt Billy Drake and Col (previously Wg Cdr) J.F.'Stocky' Edwards. This list has also been greatly increased by other veterans who it has been my great pleasure and privilege to meet or correspond with. I also record gratitude for more recent help from friends and colleagues Sqn Ldr Andy Thomas, Chris Thomas, John 'Jack' Foreman, Frank Olynyk, Michel Lavigne and to my old 'sparring partner', Brian Cull.

In conclusion, it seems appropriate to include part of the preface with which *Fighters over the Desert* commenced back in 1969, but which remains as relevant today as it did then:

"Conditions in the Desert were, as will readily be appreciated, very different to those appertaining to the European area, and before the main narrative is commenced it is necessary to give a picture of some of the difficulties under which all the operations described in this book took place, and which were a common factor to both sides. The main trouble was sand – the fine desert dust being driven in clouds of stinging particles by every breath of wind. Great sandstorms would descend at any time, obliterating the landscape in a swirling fog which found its way into everything. This sand, if ingested into aero engines through the normal air intakes, could wear out the moving parts in a matter of hours, turning lubricating oil into an abrasive paste. For this reason all aircraft had to be fitted with special air filters which caused drag and resulted in reduced performance. Guns became jammed, perspex cockpit canopies scored and sratched, and food was ruined by the invasion of this menace, which also filled eyes, ears, noses and fingernails, making life at times a gritty nightmare.

"Due to the length of the lines of communication, and the lack of natural supply, water was strictly rationed, and that used for washing or shaving was carefully kept to fill the radiators of motor vehicles. Fresh food was virtually unobtainable, and tinned rations with hard biscuits were the staple diet. The violent heat of the day made most movement impossible during the hours around noon, and the metal parts of aircraft, tanks, etc, became so hot that to touch them was to risk a blistered hand. At night the temperature dropped rapidly, making the use of warm clothing essential. To add to these hardships, the troops were plagued by millions of persistent flies which settled on faces and on food continually. These conditions frequently caused 'Desert sores' which, aggravated by heat and sand, festered on for months. Being so lacking in landmarks, the great wastes of undulating sand, rock and scrub were difficult to navigate over; to be forced down in such circumstances was to risk a lingering death from starvation and dehydration.

"To set against these deprivations, the Desert was a place of great comradeship, and, due to the extreme temperature, germs could not flourish so that there was no infectious disease. Further to this the Desert was virtually uninhabited, so that the pitiful plight of refugees did not manifest itself, the opposing armies being able to get on with the fighting untroubled by the destruction of homes or the killing of women and children, and so far as it was possible to have a 'clean' war, it was in the Desert that it was fought."

Place Names
It has been the intention of the authors that place names mentioned should as far as possible be those as employed by the Commonwealth forces during the period covered. On occasions the interpretation of these names in German and Italian records differed somewhat, but while indicating these alternative spellings, British usage has been applied purely for the sake of clarity. While every effort has been made to keep to this basis, occasions may arise where our interpretation may not accord with current day spellings, particularly in regard to small and obscure locations which are not to be found in readily available atlases.

Illustrations
Photographs for this volume have been collected over more than 40 years, including some of those used in the original *Fighters over the Desert*. Many of them were received from people sadly no longer with us. It is likely, therefore, that I shall have forgotten from where some of them originally came. For any such lapses of my memory I apologise most profusely. Apart from those provided and acknowledged separately by my co-authors, particular thanks are due to Sqn Ldr Andy Thomas, the 33 Squadron, and 80 Squadron Associations, and Herr Jochen Prien and his team. Thanks also to Grp Capt B.Drake, Wg Cdrs A.C.Rawlinson and B.H.Gibbes, the Imperial War Museum and Bundesarchiv (for photos used in the original book), Clive Williams, Don Minterne, Brian Cull, Tony Holmes, Frank F.Smith, Robert C.Jones, Hans Ring, Gerhard Homuth, Ludwig Franzisket, Reiner Pöttgen, Rudi Sinner, Neil Mackenzie, F. Taylor, Giovanni Vitali and Herr Dettman.

Christopher Shores
Dorset, England 2012

Acknowledgements

The largest part of information regarding the Italian Regia Aeronautica presented in this volume comes from documents preserved by the Historical Branch of the Italian Air Force, in Rome. Therefore I wish to thank most sincerely all the personnel for the kind assistance provided to me during my frequent visits; in particular Tenente Colonnello Massimiliano Barlattani and Maresciallo Pasquale Rubertone.

I also wish to acknowledge the many historians and aviation fans that helped me to carry out this project through suggestions, advice and photographs. First of all my long-standing friends Giorgio Apostolo and Enrico Leproni, who generously gave me access to their archives, providing photographs and documents. Many useful details concerning naval activities were provided by the noted Italian navy historian, and dear friend, Erminio Bagnasco, while another precious photographic contribution was given by Luigi Ricci-Moretti. Many friends also provided encouragement and, quite often, the answers to my various questions. Among them I would like to cite especially Gianni Cattaneo, Uccio Catalanotto, Giancarlo Garello, Gregory Alegi, Paolo Varriale, Angelo Emiliani, Pierluigi Moncalvo, Umberto Bagatta, Gregorio Baschirotto, Gabriele Brancaccio, Gianandrea Bussi, Hans Werner Neulen, Frank McMeiken, James Oglethorpe, Andrea Fabianelli and Ludovico Slongo.

Finally, I wish to express my sincere gratitude to Chris Shores. Some years ago, when he invited me to take part in this demanding project, he broadened the horizons of my research on aviation history and, overall, laid the foundation of a solid and rewarding friendship.

Giovanni Massimello
Segrate, November 2011

N.B. All measurements in the book have been converted to imperial, for ease of reference.

CHAPTER 1

BACKGROUND

THE ROYAL AIR FORCE'S COMMAND STRUCTURE

Command of the RAF in the area termed 'the Middle East' divested from 11 June 1940 on the Air Officer Commanding-in-Chief (AOCinC), Air Chief Marshal Sir Arthur Longmore, GCB,DSO, who had taken up the appointment as commander of what was already known as 'Royal Air Force, Middle East' from Air Chief Marshal Sir William Mitchell as recently as 13 May 1940. At that time the command was essentially responsible only for Egypt, but Longmore's brief was clear from the start. On the outbreak of war with Italy, he would become liable not just for this country, but for units in Iraq, Aden and British Somaliland, the Sudan, Palestine and Trans-Jordan, and Malta. Additionally, his responsibility would encapsulate any operations which might occur in East Africa (Ethiopia, Eritrea and Kenya), Cyprus, Turkey, the Balkans (Yugoslavia, Greece, Bulgaria and Rumania), and over the Mediterranean Sea, Red Sea and Persian Gulf. This was a massive task, which would soon prove to be beyond the abilities of any single commander.

Royal Air Force, Middle East, thus covered potentially a vast area of some four and a half million square miles for which it fielded just 29 squadrons, equipped with around 300 aircraft, most of which were obsolescent if not actually obsolete. Nearly half of this force was based in Egypt for the primary duty of securing the Suez Canal, the main Mediterranean Fleet anchorage and base at Alexandria, and the route via the Red Sea to India and beyond. To aid Longmore in his new role were his Senior Air Staff Officer (SASO), Air Vice-Marshal R.M. 'Peter' Drummond, and his Air Officer i/c Administration, Air Vice-Marshal A.C.Maund. His fellow supreme commanders of the other services were, for the army, General Sir Archibald Wavell, who had a similarly wide-ranging area of command, and for the Royal Navy, Admiral Sir Andrew Cunningham, who was Commander-in-Chief Mediterranean and East Indies. Fortunately for the purposes of liaison, Longmore's headquarters were located in the same building in Cairo as were Wavell's; however, Cunningham insisted in carrying on the naval tradition of living aboard his flagship.

Just as Longmore took up his new and demanding position, the German breakthrough at Sedan was taking place, so soon to lead to the withdrawal of France from the war, and the entry of Italy into the conflict. The operations which followed the latter event and which affected those locations outside Egypt and Libya particularly, have been detailed in other titles in this series (see *Malta: the Hurricane Years, 1940-41; Malta: the Spitfire Year, 1942 ; Air War for Yugoslavia, Greece and Crete, 1940-41;* and *Dust Clouds in the Middle East*).

Within RAF, Middle East, Egypt Group had been formed on 18 April 1939 with headquarters at Heliopolis, controlling initially Advanced Wing which incorporated 33, 45, 208 and 211 Squadrons. In command of this very important unit was Air Cdr R.Collishaw, DSO, OBE, DSC, DFC, who had been one of the leading scout (or fighter) pilots of the First World War. Three days after its formation, Grp Capt L.O.Brown, DFC, AFC, arrived from London to become Collishaw's SASO.

Other units formed around this time were 1 (Bomber) Wing with 14, 30 and 55 Squadrons, 2 (Bomber) Wing with 60, 84 and 113 Squadrons, and the Bomber Transport Wing with 70 and 216 Squadrons. However, the majority of these units were based in Iraq or Trans-Jordan at this time; 60 Squadron was actually in India.

Not included within the establishments of any of these wings at the time the new group was being formed, and initially held for the defence of Alexandria and the Suez Canal, were 80 Squadron which

---

had reached Ishailia from England in May 1938, equipped with Gladiators, and a second fighter unit, 112 Squadron, which had disembarked on arrival from the UK during May 1939. However, once established, this unit would be required to despatch detachments southwards for the defence of Port Sudan.

On 4 August 1939, just prior to the outbreak of war in Europe, but with the threat very present, the units of Advanced Wing moved to their war stations. From Ismailia 33 Squadron went to Qasaba, 45 Squadron to Fuka and 211 Squadron to Daba, while 208 Squadron moved from Heliopolis to Mersa Matruh. All these new bases were on the Egyptian Mediterranean coastline, between the Delta and the frontier with Libya. A month later Grp Capt Brown moved from Heliopolis to HQ, Advanced Wing, at Maaten Bagush as commanding officer. His place as SASO of Egypt Group was taken by Wg Cdr E.B.Addison, OBE.

As the Advanced Wing units moved forward, those of 1 (Bomber) Wing began flying into Ismailia, 14, 30, 55 and 70 Squadrons all arriving there during the latter days of August.

Following the outbreak of war with Germany on 3 September 1939, a wholesale renumbering of units occurred. First, however, on the 18th of that month 201 Group was formed from elements of 86 Wing and the Hal Far (Malta) detachment of that wing. The genesis of this unit was somewhat complicated; originally formed in 1937 as 1 (General Reconnaissance) Wing aboard HMS *Cyclops*, the depot ship of the 1st Submarine Flotilla, it was shore-based at Kalafrana, Malta, to control flyingboat squadrons seeking to counter Italian submarines operating off the Spanish coast during the civil war in that country. It reformed in the UK on the RAF depot ship MV *Dumana* on 9 May 1939, and on the same day became 86 Wing for Mediterranean Command. It sailed for Malta, but after arrival there moved on to Alexandria at the start of June 1939. Here 201 Group was formed, but shortly thereafter *Dumana* and the balance of 86 Wing returned to Malta. Thus the new group was based upon Alexandria, to control all General Reconnaissance (GR) units in Egypt, including disembarked squadrons of the Royal Navy's Fleet Air Arm (FAA). Commanding officer was Grp Capt H.W.G.J.Penderel, who in practice initially had control of no squadrons pending the arrival of units equipped with Sunderland flyingboats.

Three days after the formation of 201 Group, HQ, Egypt, became 202 (Operations) Group, responsible for the control of all RAF operations over the Western Desert. This same date, 21 September 1939, saw the formation of four new wings. These were:

250 (Bomber) Wing – created by the re-numbering of 1 (Bomber) Wing at Ismailia. The wing was to control only 30 and 55 Squadrons, for 14 Squadron was about to depart for Amman in Trans-Jordan, and then for the Sudan.

251 (Bomber) Wing – similarly created by the re-numbering of 2 (Bomber) Wing at Heliopolis; initially this wing controlled only 70 Squadron, for 216 Squadron had been attached directly to HQ, RAF Middle East.

252 (Fighter) Wing – which formed at Fort Shafrakhana for the protection of Cairo, the Nile Delta and the Suez Canal. Initially it only incorporated 80 and 112 Squadrons, though in May 1940, 2 and 5 Squadrons of the Royal Egyptian Air Force also came under its control (at least nominally). Commanded by Wg Cdr C.B.S.Spackman, DFC & Bar, it would be taken over on 8 May 1940 by a notable fighter pilot of World War I, Wg Cdr J.S.T.Fall, DSC & 2 Bars, AFC. On 3 June 1940 a new improvised HQ would be set up at Seagull Camp, Mex, which was located just outside Alexandria.

253 (Bomber) Wing – which was formed by re-numbering Advanced Wing at Maaten Bagush, controlling 33, 45, 208 and 211 Squadrons. This wing would be absorbed into 202 Group on 10 June 1940, just as war was about to break out in the Middle East.

To operate effectively and on a continuing basis, an air force requires a solid back-up of equipment, training and administration, and in this way Egypt Group was already well-provided when war approached. 101 Maintenance Unit (MU) had been set up during 1938 as No 1 Ammunition and Petrol Depot, and was based at Tura. 102 MU, an aircraft storage unit, had been formed at Aboukir. It moved at the start of 1939 to Abu Sueir where it also operated the training and target towing flights. On 12 November 1939 this unit would be re-numbered 103 MU.

1 Middle East Air Stores Park (ASP) had formed at Fuka on 25 August 1939, but on 28 November became 31 ME ASP. A second ASP, No 12, was formed at the end of November 1939 and was attached to 103 MU. In June 1940 51 Repair & Salvage Unit (R & SU) was formed at Fuka to recover aircraft brought down in the Desert, while during the same month an intelligence photographic flight was set up at Heliopolis in great secrecy to undertake aerial surveillance duties. Two experienced reconnaissance

Hawker Hurricane I L1669 was the sole example of these relatively modern fighters available to 202 Group, RAF. Known as 'Colly's Battleship', it was employed by Air Cdr Raymond Collishaw to fly in and out of the frontier airfields to give the impression to the Italian intelligence service that he had many more of these aircraft than was in fact the case. It subsequently served with 80 Squadron and then with 274 Squadron.

officers, Sqn Ldr H.C.Macphail and Flt Lt Walker were despatched from 1 PRU in the UK with a Lockheed 14 fitted for such duties. Much initial work would be undertaken in the preparation photographically of target maps.

The services provided by these units became immediately apparent, leading to the formation of further such after the war had commenced. At the start of October 1940 32 ASP would form at Aboukir, together with 53 R & SU. In December 54 R & SU would also come into being at this base, but would accompany 32 ASP to Greece almost at once.

In one other way the command was well-served, and this was in the ready supply of trained aircrew. 4 Flying Training School had been formed at Abu Sueir as long ago as April 1921, many recruits from the UK being sent there to receive their training. This unit was by now producing about 300 new pilots each year. On 1 September 1939 it moved to Habbaniya in Iraq, becoming 4 Service Flying Training School (SFTS). Here it was still well-placed to supply RAF, Middle East, with replacement aircrew, many of them British nationals who had been working in the area at the outbreak of hostilities, or residents of the colonies of North and South Rhodesia, Kenya, Uganda or Tanganyika.

The increasing supply of pilots from this source and other training bases being set up around the world, would lead to the formation of the Middle East's own operational training unit (OTU), 70 (ME) OTU, at Ismailia on 10 December 1940. The unit was formed from a nucleus created by the incorporation of the Training and Reserve Pool (of which more later). At the same time as the new OTU was coming into operation, a Middle East Pool was also formed at Ismailia to hold fully-trained pilots arriving from the UK until they were allocated to squadrons.

This then was the structure with which RAF, Middle East, faced the onset of war in Egypt with Italy at dusk on 10 June 1940, or which developed from it during the remainder of that year.

Before progressing further, however, it is important to consider the command and control of the army alongside – and above – which the RAF would have to operate. Wavell's immediate deputy was Lt Gen Sir Henry Maitland Wilson, who was commander of British troops in Egypt. Two days before the Italian declaration of war, the headquarters of 6th Division in Palestine arrived in Egypt under the command of Maj Gen R.N.O'Connor who would take over command of the forces on the frontier, thereby relieving Wilson of the direct responsibility thereof. On 17 June HQ, 6th Division, became HQ, Western Desert Force. Richard O'Connor made a point of establishing an early rapport with Collishaw, whose HQ was located close to his own.

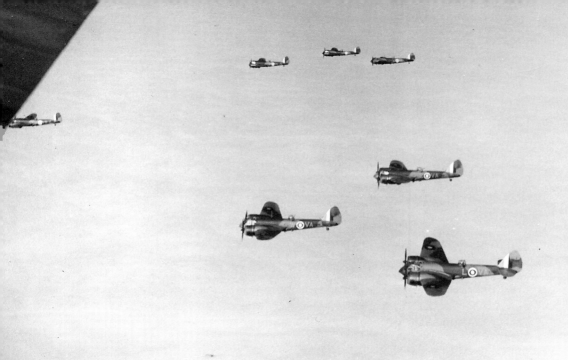

Above: At the outbreak of war in the Middle East, the RAF's main striking force was formed by four squadrons of Bristol Blenheim light bombers, mainly of the Mark I variety. A formation of nine of these aircraft from 113 Squadron is seen in flight.

Left: The defence of the Egyptian base areas in summer 1940 rested initially in the hands of 80 Squadron. Here Gloster Gladiator YK-K, K7882, of that unit is seen at Ismailia with a Blenheim I in the left background.

Bottom: The Bristol Bombays of 216 Squadron were employed both as transports and night bombers during the early days of the war. Unusually, this unit carried its squadron code letters SH and the individual aircraft letter L in one block on the rear fuselage, rather than divided by the roundel marking as was more usual.

CHAPTER 2

THE OPENING ROUNDS

As war broke out therefore, Collishaw's 202 Group had based in the area towards the frontier with Libya, a single squadron of Gladiators – 33 (Sqn Ldr D.V.Johnson), which was located at Mersa Matruh, about midway between El Alamein to the east and Sollum, on the frontier to the west. At nearby Qasaba was 208 Squadron (Sqn Ldr R.A.Sprague) with its army co-operation Lysanders, this unit maintaining detachments of these aircraft well forward at Sidi Barrani, out in the Desert at Bir Kanayis, and far to the south at Siwa Oasis. At Fuka and El Daba, on the coast back from Mersa Matruh, were the Blenheim I bombers of 45 (Sqn Ldr J.W.Dallamore) and 211 (Sqn Ldr J.W.B.Judge) Squadrons.

All other units were based well to the east in the inhabited areas of Egypt. Closest to the Desert was 80 Squadron (Sqn Ldr R.C.Jonas), its Gladiators located at Amiriya for the defence of the great naval base at Alexandria, home of the Royal Navy's Mediterranean Fleet. This unit also had on hand the single Hawker Hurricane fighter available in the Middle East at this time. This was L1669, an early Mark I which had been sent out from England by the Aircraft & Armament Experimental Establishment for Middle East trials; it was soon to gain the nickname 'Colly's Battleship'.

Alexandria was also the base of 230 Squadron, equipped with Sunderland flyingboats, commanded by Wg Cdr G.Francis. Here it would be joined by more of these big aircraft of 228 Squadron (Wg Cdr G.E.Nicholetts), this latter unit being posted out to the Mediterranean from Pembroke Dock in South Wales on 10 June, just as war was about to break out. Both these units would maintain detachments at Malta's Kalafrana seaplane base.

70 Squadron began the North African war still equipped with elderly Vickers Valentia transports. One of these is seen at Heliopolis following a fire which burned away much of the fabric covering of the aircraft's metal framework.

Gladiator RT-O, K7974, of 112 Squadron, the most recently-arrived fighter unit in Egypt. Initially this unit was required to despatch detachments both to the frontier and to the Sudan.

Well to the south and east was Heliopolis, located on the outskirts of Cairo, while some miles further south down the River Nile was Helwan. At the former base were the Blenheim IVs of 113 Squadron and the Bombay bomber-transports of 216 Squadron (Wg Cdr G.C.Gardiner, DSO, DFC). The latter airfield was home to 112 Squadron (Sqn Ldr D.M.Somerville) – a third Gladiator-equipped fighter unit – and the elderly Valentia transport biplanes of 70 Squadron. 113 Squadron (Sqn Ldr G.B.Keily, AFC) would move forward to Maaten Bagush on 10 June, while next day 70 Squadron would transfer to Heliopolis to join 216 Squadron.

Finally, at Ismailia on the Suez Canal to the north-east of Cairo, were 30 (Sqn Ldr U.Y.Shannon) and 55 (Sqn Ldr R.A.T.Stowell) Squadrons which were equipped with Blenheim Is. The former unit had converted a number of its aircraft to the 'F' (Fighter) configuration by the installation beneath the forward fuselage of a pack containing four .303in Browning machine guns. Detachments of these aircraft were located away from the parent unit at Amiriya, Helwan and Maaten Bagush.

At this stage only one other squadron was to be found throughout the Mediterranean area, 6 Squadron (Sqn Ldr W.N.McKechnie, EGM) and its Lysanders being located at Ramleh in Palestine, with detachments available to operate against local dissident elements, and to attempt to keep the peace between Arabs and Jews. No other units were closer than the Sudan and Iraq, areas from which no reinforcements could realistically be anticipated.

On the other side of the frontier in Libya was a considerably larger air force forming the Regia Aeronautica's Aeronautica della Libia. However, this force was divided between the two Libyan provinces of Cyrenaica in the east and Tripolitania in the west. At the commencement of hostilities, units in the latter area were being held ready for potential operations against French forces in neighbouring Tunisia, and were therefore not initially available for action against the RAF.

In Cyrenaica several units were based well to the east, not far from the frontier with Egypt. Around Tobruk on the coast was located 8° Gruppo CT, comprising three 12-aircraft squadriglie; the gruppo was still in the process of converting from the now rather elderly Fiat CR.32 to the more modern CR.42.

At El Adem, in the Desert to the south-east of Tobruk, were 44° and 45° Gruppo BT, each comprising two squadriglie of Savoia Marchetti S.79 tri-motor bombers, 73° Gruppo OA and 2° Gruppo APC, the former with two squadriglie of IMAM Ro.37bis and Caproni Ca.310 army co-operation aircraft, the latter with three squadriglie of Caproni Ca.309 Ghiblis.

208 Squadron was equipped with Westland Lysander army co-operation aircraft, a trio of which are seen flying over the Suez Canal. In practice these aircraft proved very vulnerable to opposing fighters and their front line service in North Africa would be relatively brief.

Well to the east at Benina, on the outskirts of the port/city of Benghazi, were two more S.79-equipped Gruppi, 30° and 32°. Also at Benghazi was 145° Gruppo comprising two squadriglie of S.75 tri-motor transport aircraft. On the coast between Derna and Tobruk was the seaplane anchorage of Menelao, where the Cant.Z.501 flyingboats of the autonomous 143ª Squadriglia were based.

The balance of the Aeronautica della Libia was located in Tripolitania, the main airfields being found around the major port of Tripoli. At Sorman, to the east of the city, were two specialized ground-attack units. 12° Gruppo Ass had two squadriglie equipped with a variety of Ca.310s, CR.42s and Breda Ba.65s, while 16° Gruppo Ass fielded Ca.310s, CR.32s and more Ba.65s. The latter was a single-engined, single-seat low-wing monoplane of fighter-like appearance, quite heavily armed with four 12.7mm Breda machine guns in the wings, and able also to carry a number of light bombs.

Nearby at Castel Benito were 10° Gruppo CT with three squadriglie of CR.42s and 13° Gruppo CT whose three squadriglie operated CR.32s and CR.42s. Two bomber gruppi, 46° and 47°, were located at Tarhuna, to the south-west of Sorman; the former had two squadriglie of S.79s, while the latter was equipped in the main with the older fixed-undercarriage S.81 trimotors, although supplies of S.79s were just beginning to arrive. This unit specialized in attacks on shipping at sea.

Also in the immediate area was 64° Gruppo OA, an army co-operation unit with two squadriglie of Ro.37bis, and 1° Gruppo APC with three squadriglie of Ca.309s. Another squadriglia of these aircraft, the autonomous 99ª Av Sahariana, was at Hon, deep in the Desert to the south. Finally, at Bir El Baheira, close to the Tunisian border, were two more bomber units, 35° and 36° Gruppo BT, with between them four more squadriglie of S.79s.

The units based in Libya provided an overall operational strength at the outbreak of war of 118 serviceable bombers (101 S.79s and 17 S.81s), 87 serviceable fighters (51 CR.42s and 36 CR.32s) and seven Ba.65 ground-attack aircraft. These figures did not include the various reconnaissance types – Ca.309 Ghibli and Ca.310 and Meridionali Ro.37, or the maritime Cant.Z.501 flyingboats.

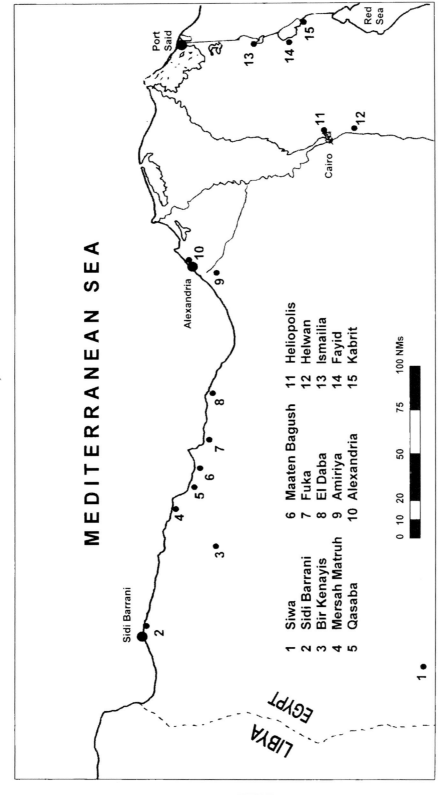

RAF Airfields, June 1940

MEDITERRANEAN SEA

Port Said

Red Sea

13 14 15

11 12

Cairo

10

9

Alexandria

8

7

6

5

4

3

2

Sidi Barrani

1

1 Siwa
2 Sidi Barrani
3 Bir Kenayis
4 Mersah Matruh
5 Qasaba
6 Maaten Bagush
7 Fuka
8 El Daba
9 Amiriya
10 Alexandria
11 Heliopolis
12 Helwan
13 Ismailia
14 Fayid
15 Kabrit

0 10 20   50   75   100 NMs

LIBYA
EGYPT

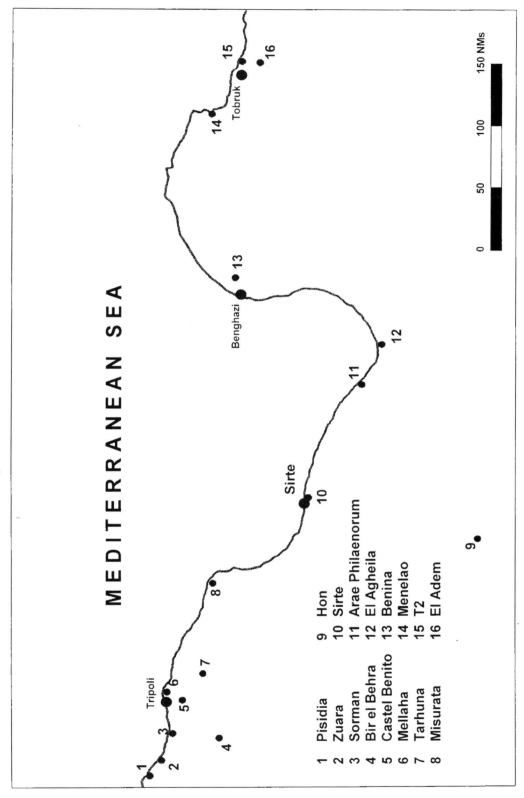

Regia Aeronautica, June 1940

MEDITERRANEAN SEA

Tripoli
Sirte
Benghazi
Tobruk

1 Pisidia   9 Hon
2 Zuara   10 Sirte
3 Sorman   11 Arae Philaenorum
4 Bir el Behra 12 El Agheila
5 Castel Benito 13 Benina
6 Mellaha   14 Menelao
7 Tarhuna   15 T2
8 Misurata   16 El Adem

0   50   100   150 NMs

AERONAUTICA DELLA LIBIA (Tripoli)   **Gen SA Felice Porro**

Comando Settore Ovest (Tripoli)   **Gen BA Raul di Barberino**

15° Stormo BT (Castel Benito) S.79/S.81	Col Silvio Napoli
46° Gruppo	Magg Bruno Cerne
20ª Squadriglia	Cap Sergio R. Guidorzi
21ª Squadriglia	Cap Daniele Zelè
47° Gruppo	Magg Angelo Tivegna
53ª Squadriglia	Cap Giuseppe Magrì
54ª Squadriglia	Cap Alberto Remorino
33° Stormo BT (Bir El Baheira) S.79	Col Giuseppe Leonardi
35° Gruppo	T.Col Michele Scattaglia
43ª Squadriglia	Cap Silvio Pugnali
44ª Squadriglia	Cap Giuseppe Pagliacci
36° Gruppo	Magg Pietro De Mattia
45ª Squadriglia	Cap Calcedonio Baculo
46ª Squadriglia	Cap Riccardo Folinea
50° Stormo Assalto (Sorman) Ca.310/Ba.65	Col Pietro Molino
12° Gruppo	Magg Bruno Cudugnello
159ª Squadriglia (Benina)	Cap Antonio Dell'Oro
160ª Squadriglia	Cap Duilio Fanali
16° Gruppo	Magg Spartaco Sella
167ª Squadriglia	Cap Alfredo Zanardi
168ª Squadriglia	Cap Luigi Lisardi

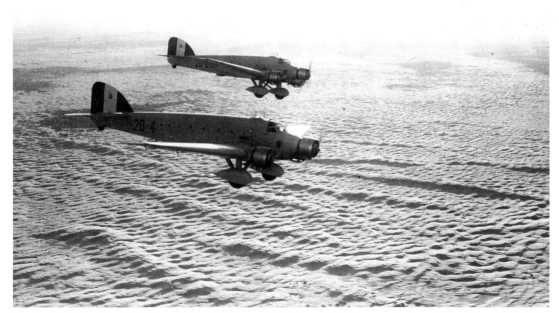

A pair of S.81 bombers of 20ª Squadriglia, 44° Gruppo, 15° Stormo BT, flying over the desert before the outbreak of war in North Africa.

A Caproni Ca. 309 Ghibli colonial aircraft painted with the pre-war anti-camouflage red stripes on its wings to make it conspicuous in case of emergency landing in the desert.

13° Gruppo CT (Castel Benito) CR.32/42	Magg Secondo Revetria
77ª Squadriglia	Cap Mario Fedele
78ª Squadriglia	Cap Giuseppe Dall'Aglio
82ª Squadriglia	Cap Guglielmo Arrabito
64° Gruppo OA (Mellaha) Ro.37	
122ª Squadriglia	
136ª Squadriglia	Cap Nicola Nicolai
1° Gruppo APC (Mellaha) Ghibli	T.Col Aristide Bagatta
12ª Squadriglia	Ten Mario Gulli
89ª Squadriglia (Sirte)	Cap Massimiliano Erasi
104ª Squadriglia	Cap Mario Pozzati
99ª Sq Av Sahariana (Hon) Ghibli	

Comando Settore Est (Tobruk)	**Gen DA Fernando Silvestri**
10° Stormo BT (Benina) S.79	Col Giovanni Benedetti
30° Gruppo	T.Col Giuseppe Rossi
55ª Squadriglia	Cap Luigi Bressanelli
56ª Squadriglia	Cap Gerardo Musch
32° Gruppo	T.Col Carlo Unia
57ª Squadriglia	Cap Arturo Mayer-Ziotti
58ª Squadriglia	Cap Ermine Bertelli
14° Stormo BT (El Adem) S.79/S.81	Col Giovanni Coppi
44° Gruppo	T.Col Enrico Maramaldo della Minerva
6ª Squadriglia	Cap Venanzio Brescianini
7ª Squadriglia	Cap Vincenzo Pitaluga
45° Gruppo	Magg Ezio Berni
2ª Squadriglia	Cap Fortunato Profumi
22ª Squadriglia	Cap Maurizio Niggi

A pilot climbs into the cockpit of his Ba.65 A.80 fighter-bomber of 12° Gruppo Assalto.

8° Gruppo CT (T2) CR.32	Magg Vincenzo La Carrubba
92ª Squadriglia	Cap Martino N. Zannier
93ª Squadriglia	Cap Mario Bacich
94ª Squadriglia	Cap Franco Lavelli
10° Gruppo CT (Benina) CR.42	T.Col Armando Piragino
84ª Squadriglia	Cap Luigi Monti
90ª Squadriglia	Cap Renzo Maggini
91ª Squadriglia	Cap Giuseppe D'Agostinis
73° Gruppo OA (T2/El Adem) Ro.37	Magg Adolfo Domenici
127ª Squadriglia	Cap Omero Giacomelli
137ª Squadriglia	Cap Giovanni Civale
2° Gruppo APC (El Adem) Ghibli	T.Col Oreste Andrei
16ª Squadriglia	Cap Mario Musumeci
23ª Squadriglia	Cap Sebastiano Baduel
Battaglione Sahariano (Hon etc.) Ghibli	**Magg Ottaviano Vimercati Sanseverino**
143ª Squadriglia RM (Menelao) Cant.Z.501	Cap Mario Bellotto

The obvious advantage enjoyed by the Regia Aeronautica in Cyrenaica was the ability to receive reinforcements rapidly both from Tripolitania, and from units based in Sicily and Italy, capable of flying directly across the Mediterranean. Indeed, on 12 June 10° Gruppo CT would move to Tobruk T2 airfield, while next day 47° Gruppo BT would fly in with its S.79s and S.81s to join 30° and 32° Gruppo at Benina. At the end of the month 12° Gruppo Ass would arrive at El Adem and 16° Gruppo Ass at Tobruk T2.

Reinforcement for 202 Group was considerably more problematical, but efforts were being made initially to take advantage of the air route across France while that country was still in the war. On 6 June, prior to the outbreak of war with Italy, six Hurricanes had been despatched from 10 Maintenance Unit to the Mediterranean. However, because of the grave danger in which the almost undefended island of Malta found itself, three were retained here, only three flying on to Mersa Matruh on 13 June. (For more details, see *Malta: The Hurricane Years*)

A further attempt to despatch more Hurricanes together with Blenheim IVs, commenced on 15 June, 12 of each leaving the UK in four flights, each comprising three of each type of aircraft. Most of these were lost en route to one cause or another, but by 20-22 June Malta's complement had risen to eight. The three which had reached Egypt were by then based at Alexandria for the defence of the naval base, and here they were soon to be joined by three more, which arrived in Egypt in company with three Blenheims on 24 June.

Cap Duilio Fanali, one of the most prominent Italian flyers during the early stages of air war in North Africa, in front of a Ba.65.K.14.

During July Longmore would receive some words of apparent comfort from the air ministry in London which advised him that he would be sent a dozen each of Hurricanes, Wellingtons and half a dozen Lysanders each month, while supplies of fighters and bombers built in the United States of America which were to be taken over from French orders, would start arriving in about November. Reference was also made to the re-opening by September of an air reinforcement route which had previously been tested, from Takoradi in the West African colony of Gold Coast, via Nigeria, Khartoum and Cairo.

Tuesday, 11 June 1940

Meanwhile, having been advised at midnight on 10 June that a state of war existed with Italy, Air Commodore Collishaw at once issued orders for 211 Squadron to despatch six Blenheims on an armed reconnaissance over the frontier at dawn, while two hours later 45 Squadron was to send eight more Blenheims on a low level attack on T3 airfield at El Adem. Here base personnel were seen formed up on the parade ground, apparently to hear a proclamation from Marshal Graziani announcing the outbreak of hostilities, read to them by the airfield commander.

The Blenheims swept in, bombing and strafing, reporting that L8476, flown by Sgt P.Bower, had been shot down by light AA, and had crashed burning into the sea with the loss of all the crew. One more, L8519, was damaged and crash-landed at Sidi Barrani where it was burnt out, again with the loss of the crew, while L8466 lagged when one engine failed due to damage. The other engine stopped after 100 miles had been covered, and this aircraft crash-landed at Buq Buq where the crew were picked up by the army; this aircraft was later recovered and repaired. Two more Blenheims suffered damage during this raid.

In fact the damage to all, or most, of these aircraft appears to have been inflicted by fighters, for as the raid was taking place six CR.32s had been scrambled from Tobruk and gave chase to the bombers as they departed El Adem. Cap Franco Lavelli, commanding officer of the 94ª Squadriglia, 8° Gruppo CT, and his pilots attacked together, claiming to have shot down two Blenheims and damaged four more, although two of the fighters suffered some damage from return fire.

More Blenheims of 55 and 113 Squadrons were ordered from Ismailia to Fuka, from where during the afternoon 18 of them launched a further attack on El Adem at 1903. The Tobruk-based fighters were up again on patrol led by Ten Gioacchino Bissoli of 93ª Squadriglia, and the pilots of these spotted six of the bombers as they were making their attack. Bissoli went for the last aircraft in the formation – L4823 of 113 Squadron – and shot this down near T3. Flt Lt D.Beauclair and his crew survived with burns, becoming the first PoWs of the new war, while a second Blenheim of 55 Squadron suffered some damage.

The bomber crews believed that they had inflicted considerable damage during these attacks, gaining hits on two hangars and leaving numerous aircraft on fire. The results were actually rather less impressive; three Ro.37bis of 73° Gruppo OA and two Ca.309s of 2° Gruppo APC were badly damaged, with two more Ro.37bis, five S.79s and six S.81s of 14° Stormo BT suffering slight damage.

Meanwhile, a substantial element of the Mediterranean Fleet had put to sea, HMS *Warspite* and *Malaya* being accompanied by HMS *Eagle*, plus five cruisers and nine destroyers. Two more cruisers from Port Said were to join the Fleet at sea, while a French force of four cruisers and three destroyers sortied from Beirut, Lebanon, to sweep into the Aegean and then sail to Alexandria.

The British vessels sailed along the Libyan coast for 12 hours, but little was seen.

British Casualties

45 Sqn	Blenheim I L8476 Sgt P.Bower and crew KiA; a/c in flames 10 miles off Tobruk
	Blenheim I L8519 Sgt M.Thurlow and crew KiA
	Blenheim I L8466 Flg Off A.Finch and crew safe after crash-landing
	Blenheim I L8469 damaged
	Blenheim I L8478 damaged
113 Sqn	Blenheim IV L4823 Flt Lt D.Beauclair and crew PoW
55 Sqn	Blenheim IV damaged

Italian Claims

94ª Sq/8° Gr CT	Cap Franco Lavelli & 5 other pilots	2 Blenheims
	Cap Franco Lavelli & 5 other pilots	4 Blenheims damaged
93ª Sq/8° Gr CT	Ten Gioacchino Bissoli	Blenheim

Wednesday, 12 June 1940

Intended to co-operate with the cruisers offshore, in the early hours of 12 June 29 Blenheims set off to attack the harbour at Tobruk, where a reconnaissance crew from 113 Squadron had reported many ships present. This operation was not a complete failure, but was certainly beset by problems. Aircraft taking part included six from 45 Squadron, five from 55 Squadron, nine from 211 Squadron and nine Mark IVs from 113 Squadron.

One of the 45 Squadron aircraft suffered engine trouble and returned early, followed by four more which failed to find the target and therefore brought their bombs back. One aircraft, L8524, had caught the tips of the propeller blades on the ground whilst taking off, which prevented the engines from synchronising. Undaunted, Flg Off D.F.Rixon continued, but he too failed to find Tobruk, releasing his bombs on troop concentrations near Bardia instead, before returning to force-land at Mersa Matruh.

Of the 55 Squadron aircraft, three suffered various technical problems and turned back, but two did manage to bomb the target area. Two of 211 Squadron's aircraft crashed on take-off and a third collided with a parked Bombay, L1481, suffering fairly minor damage. This left six aircraft to complete their mission. By the time they had done so it was dawn, and three CR.32s of 8° Gruppo CT had been scrambled, intercepting the Blenheims and claiming damage to one. The 211 Squadron crews identified their attackers as CR.42s, claiming to have shot down two of them; no losses were actually suffered by either side.

More successful was 113 Squadron, this unit's Blenheim IVs all bombing the target, obtaining a direct hit on the elderly cruiser *San Giorgio*. This vessel caught fire and was believed to have been beached, half-submerged, on a nearby sandbank. In fact she remained afloat in the Bay of Tobruk, acting as an AA battery until 22 January 1941, when she was scuttled.

As British patrols moved up to the frontier, Ten Adriano Visconti, a pilot in 23ª Squadriglia APC, reported strafing two armoured cars near Bir Shegga in his Ca.309. This pilot would later become one of Italy's most successful and famous fighter aces.

Over Alexandria three Gladiators of 80 Squadron undertook the RAF's first interception over Egypt, Flt Lt M.T.Pattle (K7910), Flg Off J.H.Lapsley (K7908) and Sgt C.E.Casbolt (K7892) discovering that their quarry was a friendly aircraft of MISR Airlines.

The Mediterranean Fleet suffered an important loss when the cruiser HMS *Calypso* was struck by a torpedo fired by the Italian submarine *Bagnolini*, commanded by Cap Corv Franco Tosoni Pittoni at 0058, 50 miles south-west of Gaudo; she sank 90 minutes later with the loss of 39 members of her crew.

British Claims

211 Sqn	Blenheim gunners	2 CR.42s

British Casualties

45 Sqn	Blenheim I L8524 force-landed at Mersa Matruh, slightly damaged
211 Sqn	2 Blenheims Damaged take-off crashes
211 Sqn	Blenheim Damaged taxying collision

Italian Claims

92ªSq/8°Gr CT	Ten Ranieri Piccolomini	Blenheim damaged

Thursday, 13 June 1940

Anticipating Italian reaction to the previous days' attacks, the RAF moved six Gladiators from 33 Squadron's B Flight forward to Sidi Barrani to undertake bomber escort duties. The Regia Aeronautica did now increase its activities, the newly-arrived 10° Gruppo CT CR.42s of 90ª Squadriglia undertaking their initial sorties from Tobruk, Cap Renzo Maggini, the squadriglia commander, leading three such fighters to provide cover for four S.79s raiding a convoy spotted off Bomba.

British patrols were now across the border, probing towards the Italian defences, notably forts at Capuzzo and Maddalena. 50° Stormo Ass had also arrived in eastern Cyrenaica during the day, and was at once in action, three Ca.310s strafing armoured cars in the Bir Shegga area, Ten Virgilio Corda's aircraft being hit by fire from these.

The first loss to the Italians occurred on this date, but not to hostile action. While two pilots from 82ª Squadriglia, 13° Gruppo CT, were undertaking a patrol over the frontier area, Serg Renato Giansante's CR.42 suffered an engine failure, causing him to undertake a force-landing. As the aircraft touched down, it caught fire and Giansante was killed.

Italian Casualties

159ªSq/12°Gr Assalto	Ca.310 Ten Virgilio Corda – a/c damaged by ground fire
82ª Sq/13° Gr CT	CR 42 Serg Renato Giansante KiFA

Friday, 14 June 1940

Activity became more pronounced on the 14th, a day on which mobile troops of the 7th Hussars captured the picturesque 'Foreign Legion' Fort Capuzzo. Four of 33 Squadron's Gladiators were off on patrol at 0735 in the hands of Flg Offs E.H.'Dixie' Dean and R.A.Couchman, and Plt Offs V.C.Woodward and A.R.Costello. They returned at 0925 reporting that they had made a low-flying attack on a Ghibli on the ground at Sidi Aziez, the damaged aircraft subsequently being captured by advancing British troops.

Regia Aeronautica records seem to indicate that in fact they had first encountered this aircraft whilst it was in the air. Ten Visconti had taken off from Monastir in his Ca. 309 Ghibli MM 11216 with an army officer, S.Ten Umberto Zolesi, aboard as observer, and 1° Av Luigi Moroso as crew. They had been attacked by Gladiators, and Visconti had force-landed near Sidi Aziez. Surviving unhurt, the trio removed the aircraft's machine guns to defend themselves, and were

The first aerial victories for RAF fighters over the desert were gained by pilots of 33 Squadron in their Gladiators. Flg Off Vernon Woodward, a Canadian, was the first pilot to make claims on 14 June 1940.

later rescued when another Ghibli flown by Serg Magg Oreste Speranza landed nearby. Visconti was decorated with the award of the Medaglia di Bronzo, and was allowed to transfer to 159ª Squadriglia, 12° Gruppo Ass. He had previously served with this unit until transferred to the APC following a dispute with a (presumably) senior colleague.

At 1000 hours Dean and Woodward were off again, followed a few minutes later by Sgt Craig. It seems that quite a few Italian units were in the air, for the RAF pilots reported meeting several Ca.310s escorted by CR.32s. Indeed, three Ca.310s of 159ª Squadriglia had taken off at 0930 to attack British vehicles in the Amseat area, while six CR.32s drawn equally from 92ª and 93ª Squadriglia of 8° Gruppo CT, were undertaking an escort when a reported nine Gladiators were seen.

The British fighters attacked at once, and whilst there is some question as to exactly what claims were made, it appears that Dean claimed one of the CR.32s shot down while Woodward claimed a Ca.310, then adding a CR.32 as a probable, shared with Sgt Craig. Woodward saw his Ca.310 crash-land amongst British armoured vehicles near Fort Capuzzo, returning to base with one bullet hole in his Gladiator, the projectile having missed his head by mere inches.

Two of the Ca.310s had been hit hard during the attack, that flown by Serg Magg Stefano Garrisi falling in flames, while Ten Virgilio Corda's aircraft was seriously damaged. Garrisi managed to bale out safely, but his gunner, Av.Sc Giuseppe Pascali, was killed.

Meanwhile, the CR.32 pilots had attacked the Gladiators, claiming three shot down for the loss of Serg Edoardo Azzaroni of 93ª Squadriglia, who crashed to his death.

It seems, however, that 10º Gruppo CT CR.42s were also in the area, for during a patrol Cap Renzo Maggini, Ten Giovanni Guiducci, Ten Franco Lucchini and Serg Giovanni Battista Ceoletta jointly claimed a Gladiator shot down over Buq Buq, which was recorded as being the first British fighter shot down by Italians during World War II. It was credited jointly to all four pilots, although it was agreed that it had been Guiducci who had fired the decisive burst.

In practice, no Gladiators were actually lost on this date, although a Blenheim of 45 Squadron was. 211 Squadron had despatched eight aircraft to bomb Fort Capuzzo, but there had been many failures of the 11 second delay fuses fitted to the 250lb bombs carried during this low level attack, and most bombers returned damaged by splinters from their own weapons, or by those dropped by other aircraft in the formation. During the day Blenheims of 45 Squadron had been out on several occasions. An initial raid on Sidi Aziez airfield, launched at 0700, failed to find any aircraft present, so motor vehicles were bombed instead. Half an hour later L8524, the aircraft which Flg Off Rixon had force-landed on the 12th, set off alone for Giarabub in the hands of Flg Off J.S.Davies, but it failed to return – apparently a victim of AA fire – Davies and his crew being listed as missing. Later in the day trios of aircraft made two attacks on Maddalena.

The day was also marked by the first offensive sorties to be flown by the Regia Aeronautica's bomber force. During the morning 12 S.79s of 15º Stormo BT undertook a raid on Sollum led by Col Silvio Napoli, while in the afternoon 17 more of these bombers from 10º Stormo BT, led by Col Giovanni Benedetti, bombed Sollum under escort by 10º Gruppo CT CR.42s.

British Claims			
Flg Off E.H.Dean	Gladiator L9046	CR 32	Capuzzo
Plt Off V.C.Woodward	Gladiator N5783	Ca 310	Capuzzo
		½ CR 32 Probable	
Sgt Craig	Gladiator N5768	½ CR 32 Probable	Capuzzo
British Casualties			
45 Sqn	Blenheim I L8524 Flg Off J.S.Davies and crew KiA, believed by AA fire at Giarabub		
Italian Claims			
92ª Sq/8º Gr CT	Cap Nino Zannier		
	Ten Ranieri Piccolomini		
	Serg Ernesto Pavan		
93ª Sq/8º Gr CT	Ten Gioacchino Bissoli	}	3 Gladiators
	Serg Edoardo Azzaroni		
	Serg Roberto Lendaro		
90ª Sq/10º Gr CT	Cap Renzo Maggini		
	Ten Giovanni Guiducci	}	Gladiator
	Ten Franco Lucchini		
	Serg Giovanni Battista Ceoletta		
Italian Casualties			
23ª Sq APC	Ca.309 MM11216 Ten Adriano Visconti – a/c shot-up on ground and subsequently captured		
159ª Sq/12º Gr Ass	Ca.310 Serg Magg Stefano Garrisi – a/c shot down; gunner KiA		
	Ca.310 Ten Virgilio Corda – a/c badly damaged		
93ª Sq/8º Gr CT	CR.32 Serg Edoardo Azzaroni KiA		

Saturday, 15 June 1940

The day was marked by the first operational sorties being made by the Breda Ba.65s when four 159ª Squadriglia aircraft led by Cap Antonio Dell'Oro, and escorted by 10º Gruppo CT CR.42s, strafed vehicles between Ponticelli and Amseat.

Sunday, 16 June 1940

At dawn El Adem and El Gobbi airfields were attacked by 15 Blenheims. Nine aircraft from each of 55 and 113 Squadrons had been despatched, but three of these from the former unit suffered engine troubles on the way to their target and were forced to withdraw. Those which arrived to bomb were intercepted by three 84ª Squadriglia, 10º Gruppo CT, CR.42s which upset the bomb-aimers' alignments, little damage being achieved despite bombs being seen to explode amongst parked aircraft. M.llo Mario Bandini, the Italian formation leader, claimed one Blenheim shot down, but was wounded by return fire; he was to receive a Medaglia d'Argento for his gallantry during this engagement.

Following the attack on T3 at El Adem, three Blenheims were pursued by four 91ª Squadriglia pilots, Ten Enzo Martissa, M.llo Vittorio Romandini, Serg Elio Miotto and Serg Alessandro Bladelli jointly claiming two shot down. During these attacks three of 113 Squadron's Blenheims suffered damage.

33 Squadron's Gladiators were repeatedly scrambled during the day as S.79s bombed forward troops, but ten of 12 such operations proved to be false alarms. However, during one such scramble in the morning, Flt Lt H.W.Bolingbroke DFC apparently became disorientated in heavy mist and crashed into the sea off Sidi Barrani, losing his life. The two pilots following him both made force-landings in the desert.

British Casualties				
33 Sqn	Gladiator N5759 Flt Lt H.W.Bolingbroke DFC, KiFA			
113 Sqn	3 Blenheims damaged			
Italian Claims				
84ª Sq/10º Gr CT	M.llo Mario Bandini	Blenheim	El Adem	Dawn
91ª Sq/10º Gr CT	Ten Enzo Martissa			
	M.llo Vittorio Romandini	2 Blenheims		
	Serg Elio Miotto			
	Serg Alessandro Bladelli			
Italian Casualties				
84ª Sq/10º Gr CT	CR.42 Damaged M.llo Mario Bandini wounded by return fire			

Wednesday, 19 June 1940

Following the initial border skirmishes, the Italians moved two divisions up to the frontier to retake Fort Capuzzo, commensurately increasing aerial activity. To be nearer to this area, 33 Squadron moved forward to Maaten Gerawla, where the unit was reinforced by two of 30 Squadron's Blenheim Ifs, and by Flg Off P.G.Wykeham-Barnes of 80 Squadron with one of the newly-arrived Hurricanes, P2638.

At 0745 the reinforcements, accompanied by four of 33's Gladiators, took off to patrol over the Sollum area. Here at 0940 the British pilots encountered five CR.42s of 84ª Squadriglia, led by their commanding officer, Cap Luigi Monti, and by the 10º Gruppo commander, T.Col Armando Piragino. These fighters were providing escort to five Ba.65s and nine CR.32s of 12º Gruppo Ass over the Sollum-Sidi Barrani area. The Italians recorded meeting the lone Hurricane and the Gladiators.

At the time of its publication, this English newspaper clipping, preserved in the Italian state archive, sheds some light on the capture of T.Col Armando Piragino, CO of 10º Gruppo CT, on 19 June 1940.

Peter Wykeham-Barnes in his Hurricane cut inside the turn of the leading CR.42 and shot it down into the sea, Serg Magg Ugo Corsi being killed. Reportedly, the Italian formation then commenced a gradual withdrawal into Libya, during which Wykeham-Barnes claimed a second CR.42, while two more were claimed by the 33 Squadron pilots. The 30 Squadron Blenheims had been patrolling out to sea when the engagement started, arriving too late to take part. In practice only one more CR.42 was lost, that flown by T.Col Piragino crash-landing after he had been hit and wounded; he became a PoW. Serg Giuseppe Scaglioni claimed one Gladiator shot down, and indeed Sgt R.Green* was shot down in N5888. Serg Narciso Pillepich claimed damage to two more, and Cap Luigi Monti to one. Subsequently, apparently a British communique admitted the loss of six aircraft – probably referring to all losses suffered since the war had commenced. 10° Gruppo CT believed that this referred purely to the 19th and in consequence increased its claims to six Gladiators, which were assigned collectively to all the pilots taking part.

Following the loss of Piragino, command of 10° Gruppo CT was provisionally assumed by Cap Giuseppe D'Agostinis, commander of 91ª Squadriglia. Serg Magg Corsi had been a veteran of the Spanish Civil War, and was considered an experienced and highly-regarded pilot.

British Claims

80 Sqn	Flg Off P.G.Wykeham-Barnes	Hurricane P2638	2 CR.42s
33 Sqn	Sqn Ldr D.V. Johnson	Gladiator N5782	½ CR.42
	Flt Lt G.E.Hawkins	Gladiator N5765	½ CR.42
	Flg Off A.H.Lynch	Gladiator N5764	½ CR.42
	Sgt R.L.Green	Gladiator N5888	½ CR.42

British Casualties

33 Sqn	Gladiator N5888 Sgt R.L.Green KiA

Italian Claims

10° Gr CT	T.Col Armando Piragino	
84ª Sq/10° Gr CT	Cap Luigi Monti	
	Serg Magg Ugo Corsi	6 Gladiators
	Serg Giuseppe Scaglioni	
	Serg Narciso Pillepich	

Italian Casualties

10° Gr CT	CR.42 T.Col Armando Piragino PoW
84ª Sq/10° Gr CT	CR.42 Serg Magg Ugo Corsi KiA

*It appears that Green's commission was just about to be granted at the time of his loss, for he is listed in the Commonwealth War Graves Commission records as a Plt Off.

Thursday, 20 June 1940

During the night of 20/21 June Italian bombers undertook their first nocturnal raids, Col Napoli leading 12 15° Stormo BT S.79s off at 0125 on the 22nd to bomb Mersa Matruh. Over the target AA fire struck the fuselage of M.llo Giovanni Lampugnani's 21ª Squadriglia, 46° Gruppo BT aircraft, causing it to dive out of control and collide with that flown by Cap Daniele Zelè, commanding officer of the squadriglia. Lampugnani and his crew were all killed when their aircraft hit the ground, but Zelè was able to crash-land his damaged bomber near Mersa Matruh, where the crew was captured. These were the first two S.79s lost in North Africa. Two days later an RAF aircraft would drop a bundle of letters written by Zelè's crew into Italian territory.

Italian Casualties

21ª Sq/46° Gr/15°St BT	S.79 M.llo Giovanni Lampugnani and crew KiA
	S.79 '21-1' Cap Daniele Zelè and crew PoW

Friday, 21 June 1940

230 Squadron despatched Sunderland L2160 'X' from Alexandria in the hands of the commanding officer, Wg Cdr G.Francis, on an early reconnaissance of Tobruk harbour. At dawn two 92ª Squadriglia, 8° Gruppo CT CR.32s flown by Ten Ranieri Piccolomini and Ten Giorgio Savoia, plus an 84ª Squadriglia, 10° Gruppo CT CR.42 flown by Serg Roberto Steppi, were scrambled to intercept the flyingboat, which they spotted over the coast to the north of the port. They were then joined by a 90ª Squadriglia CR.42, and it was the pilot of this, Ten Franco Lucchini, who was able to claim damage to the big four-engined aircraft, reporting that he left it with two of its engines on fire. The Sunderland had indeed been damaged, one explosive bullet tearing a hole in the hull some six by eight feet, while the fuel tanks were extensively holed. The latter were plugged successfully with plasticine by the crew, Francis landing back at base at

0830 where the aircraft was hauled up onto the slipway for repairs. The gunners claimed to have shot down one of their attackers into the sea, following which the others broke off after 15 minutes. However, no such loss was recorded.

This was not, however, the only engagement of the day involving a flyingboat. On this date HMAS *Sydney*'s catapult Seagull amphibian was attacked off Bardia by three biplane fighters while spotting for a bombardment operation. Flt Lt T.McBride Price managed to fly the badly damaged aircraft to Mersa Matruh, receiving a DFC for this action. The TAG reported that the attacking aircraft had been CR.42s, but in fact the aircraft had been attacked in error by 33 Squadron Gladiators. These were providing cover for the Mediterranean Fleet units involved in this bombardment of Bardia on this date, while Blenheims joined in attacking shipping.

During one such sortie later in the day two more 84ª Squadriglia CR.42 pilots intercepted a lone Blenheim as it approached Tobruk. Serg Giuseppe Scaglioni's fighter was hit by return fire, causing him to withdraw; Serg Corrado Patrizi's guns jammed, and he was unable to press home an attack.

During the day 8° Gruppo CT's 94ª Squadriglia began receiving CR.42s, then passing its CR.32s to 160ª Squadriglia of 12° Gruppo Ass, which was led by Cap Duilio Fanali.

British Claims		
230 Sqn	Gunners	Fighter shot down into sea
British Casualties		
216 Sqn	Bombay L5850 Flt Lt J.W.Smith & crew MiA at night over El Gobbi area	
230 Sqn	Sunderland L2160 'X' damaged; Wg Cdr G.Francis and crew returned safely	
HMAS *Sydney*	Seagull V amphibian A2-21 damaged; Flt Lt T.McBride Price returned safely with Lt J.Bacon, RN, aboard	
Italian Claims		
90ª Sq/10° Gr CT	Ten Franco Lucchini	Sunderland Damaged
Italian Casualties		
84ª Sq/10° Gr CT	CR.42 Damaged Serg Giuseppe Scaglioni – a/c damaged by return fire from Blenheim	

Night of Friday – Saturday, 21/22 June 1940
On this date a trio of 160ª Squadriglia CR.32s made a strafing attack on British armoured cars which were proceeding towards Garat el Berud, reportedly bringing two of them to a halt. During another sortie, M.llo Omero Alesi of 90ª Squadriglia, 10° Gruppo CT, undertook a reconnaissance over the Bardia-Amseat area. He reported encountering a number of Gladiators, claiming one of these shot down. No matching engagement has been discovered on the British side.

For the first time Italian bombers from the Dodecanese Islands raided Alexandria by night (see Chapter 13 'Blitz on Egypt').

Monday, 24 June 1940
An armistice between Italy and France was signed on 24 June, one day after the French had entered into a similar arrangement with Germany. This ended any worthwhile hopes the British had of receiving aid or reinforcement from Tunisia to the west or Syria to the east. On this very day the last three Hurricanes to make the flight across France before it became closed to them, arrived in Egypt and were issued to 80 Squadron.

Italian Claims		
90ª Sq/10° Gr CT	M.llo Omero Alesi	Gladiator	Bardia-Amseat area

Tuesday – Thursday, 25/27 June 1940
Next day Flt Lt M.T.StJ.Pattle of 80 Squadron flew another of the unit's Hurricanes up to Mersa Matruh to relieve Flg Off Wykeham-Barnes, who returned to Amiriya.

During a patrol flight carried out in the morning by five CR.42s of 13° Gruppo, S.Ten Italo Santavicca force-landed at Sidi Azeiz due to an engine failure. He set his aircraft on fire but was taken PoW.

Italian Casualties	
78ª Sq/13° Gr CT	CR.42 burnt out after force-landing S.Ten Italo Santavicca PoW

An arrangement was now put into effect between 33 and 112 Squadrons whereby some pilots from the latter unit would fly up from Helwan to Mersa Matruh for a few days, allowing a commensurate number of 33's pilots to replace them at the home base for a brief rest. Meanwhile, 30 Squadron moved its Blenheim IFs to Gerawla, located some miles south of Sidi Barrani, deep in the desert, but on the railway line to Sollum and beyond.

During 27 June two Morane 406 fighters arrived in Palestine from their unit, GC I/7, their pilots having absconded to join the Free French following the announcement of the armistice and the decision of the governor and his staff to espouse the new Vichy government. Next day 80 Squadron, which like 33 Squadron was organised on a three-flight basis at this time, concentrated all the Hurricanes now available (seven of them) into one flight, commanded by Flt Lt E.G.'Tap' Jones.

Due to personnel shortages amongst the bomber squadrons at this time, three of 45 Squadron's crews were attached to 113 Squadron, and subsequently four more crews with their aircraft were loaned to 211 Squadron.

Friday, 28 June 1940

During the middle of the morning four of 33 Squadron's Gladiators and a Blenheim IF were scrambled to intercept a raid on Mersa Matruh. The raiders were seen, but could not be caught. It appears that the Regia Aeronautica claimed to have destroyed 20 aircraft on the ground during this attack, but this is not confirmed from British records.

91ª Squadriglia's CR.42s were out strafing British armoured cars again. But at 1715 a formation of Blenheims, reported by Italian records to be 15 strong, attacked T2 airbase, catching the CR.42s of 10° Gruppo CT's 90ª Squadriglia on the ground there. One of these fighters was destroyed and several damaged, five mechanics and six soldiers also being killed.

A trio of pilots at readiness rushed to their aircraft, but Serg Amleto Monterumici was wounded as he climbed into the cockpit, while Serg Silvio Crociati was hit by splinters and also suffered burns; taken to hospital, he died that night.

Shortly after this raid, two S.79s appeared over Tobruk and prepared to land. The leading aircraft was carrying Marshal Italo Balbo, famous for having led formation flights of flyingboats on goodwill tours before the war, and after whom the word 'Balbo' had been applied to large formations of aircraft. Having been minister for air, he was now governor-general of Libya. In the second aircraft was General SAFelice Porro, commanding officer of the Aeronautica della Libia. The airfield's defences mistook the arrivals for more British raiders and opened fire at once. Balbo's aircraft was hit and crashed in flames, killing all aboard, although Porro's managed to escape. Upon learning of this, Collishaw arranged for a Blenheim to drop a wreath at the funeral when it took place.

Following this disastrous series of events, 10° Gruppo CT, badly affected by the losses suffered, withdrew to Benghazi to reorganise. It would be about three weeks before the unit had regained its full efficiency.

Italian Casualties	
90ª Sq/10° Gr CT	CR.42s 1 destroyed and several damaged on ground Serg Silvio Crociati KiA, Serg Amleto Monterumici WiA
	S.79 Mar Italo Balbo, the crew of Magg Ottavio Frailich and various passengers all killed – own AA

Saturday, 29 June 1940

At dawn seven CR.32s of 8° Gruppo and four CR.42s of 13° Gruppo were scrambled to intercept another attack, this time by nine Blenheims. Eight of these were fired on, and it was claimed that six had been shot down, two by S.Ten Torresi and one by S.Ten Zuccarini, the latter pilot and Serg Magg Fausti sharing three more. Zuccarini's aircraft was hit by return fire and he was wounded in one leg, force-landing. The whole combat had been seen from the ground, and all three pilots were later awarded the Medaglia d'Argento.

The reality was a little more prosaic, but damaging enough to 202 Group's limited availability of Blenheims. L8447 (Flg Off W.Mason) and L8522 (Flt Sgt R.Knott) were both shot down in flames by the fighters, all six members of the crews being killed. Although flown by 113 Squadron personnel, both these aircraft were in fact Mark I Blenheims, as was L8436, which ditched in the sea, reportedly after being hit by AA while attacking El Gobbi; Plt Off D.Pike and his crew were captured.

At much the same time as these events had been occurring, six Gladiators had been flown to Sidi

Two CR.42s of 92ª Squadriglia, 8° Gruppo, 2° Stormo CT. This unit was already based in Libya before the war and was most active in the early stages of the conflict.

Barrani to undertake patrols over Mersa Matruh. Soon after midday on one such patrol, one of the 112 Squadron pilots now attached to 33 Squadron, Plt Off P.R.W.Wickham (not to be confused with 80 Squadron's Flg Off P.G.Wykeham-Barnes – although frustratingly both were named Peter) attacked a Ro.37bis three miles west of Sidi Azeiz, which he forced to land in Italian-held territory. The squadron ORB recorded: "Rear gunner apparently hit."

Shortly after midday three more Gladiators engaged a trio of CR.32s over the Ridotta-Capuzzo area. Plt Off Vernon Woodward forced one down two-three miles north of Fort Capuzzo, near the Capuzzo-Bardia road. He then gave chase to a second which he claimed to have shot down after a long dogfight. His opponents would appear to have been aircraft of 50° Stormo Ass, in one of which S.Ten Antonino Weiss of 160ª Squadriglia was wounded in combat with a Gladiator, causing him to force-land east of Tobruk.

British Claims

112 Sqn	Plt Off P.R.W.Wickham	Gladiator K8031	Ro.37bis	3 miles W Sidi Azeiz
33 Sqn	Plt Off V.C.Woodward	Gladiator N5774	CR.32	2-3 miles N Capuzzo 1240 app.
			CR.32	Bardia

British Casualties

113 Sqn	Blenheim I L8436 Plt Off D.Pike and crew PoW
	Blenheim I L8447 Flg Off W.Mason and crew KiA
	Blenheim I L8522 Flg Off R.Knott and crew KiA

Italian Claims

77ª Sq/13° Gr CT	S.Ten Giulio Torresi	2 Blenheims
	S.Ten Gian Mario Zuccarini	Blenheim
		½ Blenheim
		½ Blenheim
		½ Blenheim
	Serg Magg Agostino Fausti	½ Blenheim
		½ Blenheim
		½ Blenheim
93ª Sq & 94ª Sq/8° Gr CT		2 Blenheims damaged

Italian Casualties

77ª Sq/13° Gr CT	CR.42 damaged S.Ten Gian Mario Zuccarini WiA and force-landed – Blenheim return fire
160ªSq/12°Gr Ass	CR.32 S.Ten Antonino Weiss – WiA and force-landed

Sunday, 30 June 1940

At 0610 six 160ª Squadriglia CR.32s attacked vehicles moving towards Ridotta-Capuzzo. Flg Off Dixie Dean and Plt Off Peter Wickham were patrolling over Bardia around this time, spotting three fighters taking off from the airfield here. Diving down, the two British pilots each claimed one of these shot down; the Italian aircraft were from 160ª Squadriglia Assalto on their way to escort a Ro.37 on a reconnaissance, Ten Ivano Vanni baling out while Serg Aldo Santucci force-landed, destroying his CR.32 in doing so. On this date also, a Ro.37 of 136ª Squadriglia was lost, flown by Serg Magg Gregorio Pecoraro, who was killed.

British Claims

33 Sqn	Flg Off E.H.Dean	Gladiator L9046	CR.32 or 42	Bardia 0805
112 Sqn	Plt Off P.R.W.Wickham	Gladiator N5783	CR.32	Bardia 0805

Italian Casualties

160ªSq/12°Gr Ass	CR.32 Ten Ivano Vanni baled – wounded
160ªSq/12°Gr Ass	CR.32 Serg Aldo Santucci – force-landed
136ª Sq Osservazione Aerea	Ro.37 Serg Magg Gregorio Pecoraro KiA

Monday, 1 July 1940

Plt Off W.Vale of 33 Squadron apparently claimed a CR.32 shot down on this date, although it is possible that this was recorded a day late in his logbook and related to the engagement on 30 June, recorded above. RAF records also indicate a claim on 28 June.

Flt Lt P.R.Woodward in Sunderland L5803 of 230 Squadron, who was patrolling over a convoy headed from the Bosphoros to Alexandria, was able to bomb an Italian destroyer. The crew reported achieving near misses close to the stern, following which the ship came to a standstill. No destroyers were in fact reported as having been damaged on this date, by Regia Marina.

British Claims

33 Sqn	Plt Off W.Vale	Gladiator N5766	CR.32	Fort Capuzzo

Wednesday, 3 July 1940

Three CR.42s of 94ª Squadriglia, 8° Gruppo CT were scrambled to intercept a Sunderland which was undertaking an anti-submarine patrol near Tobruk, Ten Giovanni Tadini and Serg Magg Trento Cecchi and Danilo Billi claiming to have shot this down near Bardia. In fact the flyingboat from the recently-arrived 228 Squadron returned to Alexandria, the crew reporting being attacked only by a single fighter which they believed they had successfully driven off.

Italian Claims

94ª Sq/8° Gr CT	Ten Giovanni Tadini		
	Serg Magg Trento Cecchi	}	Sunderland
	Serg Magg Danilo Billi		

Thursday, 4 July 1940

This proved to be the best day yet for 202 Group's fighters, commencing early in the morning when three of 33 Squadron's pilots encountered two CR.42s over Sollum. These were part of a flight of five such 8° Gruppo CT aircraft which had taken off from Menastir to escort a Ro.37bis to this area. Plt Off E.J.Woods and Flt Sgt L.Cottingham each claimed one shot down, Ten Giovanni Tadini baling out when his CR.42 burst into flames, while Serg Magg Arturo Cardano force-landed; both pilots were taken prisoner. Serg Magg Agostino Fausti, a 77ª Squadriglia pilot on loan to 8° Gruppo, returned to claim two Gladiators shot down, but the RAF formation actually suffered no loss.

Towards evening two sections of Gladiators, including four flown by attached pilots from 112 Squadron, patrolled over Menastir where they were able to attack five CR.42s which had just taken off – a formation which they identified as being nine strong. In quick succession nine were claimed shot down, four by Flg Off A.Gray Worcester, two by Flt Sgt Len Cottingham and one each by Flg Off Woods, Flg Off R.H.Smith and Plt Off R.J.Bennett.

Serg Magg Trento Cecchi had been first to fall, followed by S.Ten Nunzio De Fraia, who was wounded and baled out. Like Cecchi, Cap Franco Lavelli, who was shot down next, was killed, while Ten Domenico

Bevilacqua managed to regain the airfield in his badly damaged aircraft. Serg Magg Agostino Fausti fought on alone, but after some minutes was shot down and became the third pilot of the day to be killed. It may well have been him who managed to attack the Gladiator flown by Flg Off W.B.Price-Owen. The latter was reportedly attacked by one Fiat which had escaped the initial combat, the damage suffered by his aircraft causing him to bale out during the flight back to base. Fausti subsequently received a posthumous award of Italy's highest award for valour, the Medaglia d'Oro. It is possible that more CR.42s became engaged in this action, for the day's losses are recorded as including six of these fighters lost and four more badly damaged.

During a sortie by 113 Squadron Blenheims, one of the bombers was hit by AA fire, the pilot being wounded in both arms and legs. AC1 Albert A.Meadows, one of the 45 Squadron personnel on loan to the unit, left his gun turret to administer first aid, then managing to keep the pilot from passing out on the flight back to El Daba. There he operated the flaps and undercarriage before helping with the landing. For these acts he was awarded a DFM three days later, the first such award to be made in the area since the outbreak of hostilities.

Flt Sgt Len Cottingham of 33 Squadron claimed one CR.42 shot down during the morning ot 4 July 1940, adding two more that evening.

British Claims				
33 Sqn	Flg Off E.J. Woods	Gladiator N5781	CR.42	Sollum 0830
	Flt Sgt L.Cottingham	Gladiator N5765	CR.42	Sollum 0830
112 Sqn	Flg Off A.G.Worcester	Gladiator N5768	4 CR.42s	Menastir 1800
33 Sqn	Flg Off E.J.Woods	Gladiator N5781	CR.42	Menastir 1800
	Flt Sgt L.Cottingham	Gladiator N5765	2 CR.42s	Menastir 1800
112 Sqn	Flg Off R.H.Smith	Gladiator K7897	CR.42	Menastir 1800
	Plt Off R.J.Bennett	Gladiator N5779	CR.42	Menastir 1800

British Casualties	
112 Sqn	Gladiator N5751 Flg Off W.B.Price-Owen baled out over Buq Buq due to damage
113 Sqn	Blenheim damaged AA fire

Italian Claims		
77ª Sq/8º Gr CT	Serg Magg Agostino Fausti	2 Gladiators

Italian Casualties	
94ª Sq/8º Gr CT	CR.42 Ten Giovanni Tadini PoW
	CR.42 Serg Magg Arturo Cardano force-landed; PoW
	CR.42 Serg Magg Trento Cecchi KiA
	CR.42 S.Ten Nunzio De Fraia WiA
	CR.42 Cap Franco Lavelli KiA
93ª Sq/ 8º Gr CT	CR.42 Damaged Ten Domenico Bevilacqua
77ª Sq/13º Gr CT	CR.42 MM5543 Serg Magg Agostino Fausti KiA

Friday, 5 July 1940

12 of 33 Squadron's Gladiators were refuelling at Buq Buq when S.79s again struck. On this occasion although B Flight managed to get into the air, they were unable to engage. On the ground two of C Flight's Gladiators were damaged by bomb splinters.

British Casualties	
33 Sqn	2 Gladiators damaged on ground by bomb splinters

Prior to the outbreak of war in the Middle East, the aircraft carrier HMS *Eagle* had sailed from Singapore in May 1940 following a long and extensive re-fit. She was to take the place of HMS *Glorious* with the Mediterranean Fleet, following the departure of that vessel for operations off Norway in April. Aboard

Eagle were the 18 Fairey Swordfish torpedo-bombers of 813 and 824 Squadrons, but no fighters. On arrival at Alexandria, three Sea Gladiators which had been held in reserve for *Glorious*'s 802 Squadron, were taken aboard to provide a modicum of aerial defence in the hand of some of the 813 Squadron pilots and the ship's commander (flying), Lt Cdr Charles Keighly-Peach. (Details of most of the operations of this handful of fighters may be found in *Malta: The Hurricane Years, 1940-41* and *Air War for Yugoslavia, Greece and Crete, 1940-41*). While *Eagle* and the Mediterranean Fleet got ready for their first major sortie, 813 Squadron's aircraft prepared to launch an attack on the nearest ports in use by the Italians in North Africa.

The first such raid was to be undertaken on 5 July, with Tobruk the target. This was to be very much a combined operation with the RAF, the nine Swordfish flying from the naval airfield at Dekheila to Sidi Barrani. From here they flew to the target while 11 Blenheims of 211 Squadron bombed the nearby airfield and a dozen Gladiators of 33 Squadron patrolled overhead. Eight CR.42s of 8° Gruppo CT were damaged on the ground at Tobruk T.2 airfield by air attack.

The Swordfish crews reported sinking a destroyer and a merchant vessel, damaging one more destroyer and two merchant ships. In fact their attack had been extremely effective, sinking the 1,715-ton destroyer *Zeffiro* when the vessel's ammunition store exploded. The 3,955-ton *Manzoni* was also sunk, while the 15,354-ton Lloyd Triestino liner, *Liguria* and 5,171-ton *Serenitas* were hit and damaged to an extent whereby they were left stranded, to be refloated by the British a few months later when the port fell into their hands.

While the attack was in progress, two cruisers of the 3rd Cruiser Squadron (HMS *Capetown* and *Caledon*), together with four destroyers sailed to Bardia, commencing a bombardment of shipping in the harbour here at dawn on 6 July. Damage was claimed to two military supply vessels. The RN warships were then attacked by Regia Aeronautica bombers, but returned to Alexandria without any damage having been suffered.

The commander-in-chief issued a statement advising that the success of this operation had been due to the level of co-operation reached between the navy and air force.

Italian Casualties	
8° Gr CT	8 CR.42s damaged on the ground

Wednesday, 10 July 1940

Six S.79s from 10° Stormo BT bombed Sidi Barrani airfield, where one of 208 Squadron's Lysanders was destroyed. Two more of the 112 Squadron pilots attached to 33 Squadron, Flg Offs R.A.Acworth and E.T.Banks, attacked three of the bombers, but these jettisoned their bombs and flew out to sea, leaving the Gladiators behind. Although no claim was made on this occasion, the bomber flown by Ten Luigi Vicoli had been hit and damaged, and he was obliged to force-land near Tobruk with co-pilot Serg Pietro Angelin and another member of his crew dead.

The day also saw the arrival from Italy of 67° Gruppo OA, comprising 37ª and 115ª Squadriglia, both equipped with Ro.37bis, but this unit would soon be re-equipped with Ca.310Bs. Next day these units would be followed by 9° Gruppo CT from Sicily, (*see box*) which flew in to Berka. Comprising 73ª, 96ª, and 97ª Squadriglia, all equipped with CR.42s, the gruppo joined 10° Gruppo CT to bring 4° Stormo CT to its full strength in North Africa.

67° Gruppo OA (Mellaha) Ro.37bis	Cap Giusto Ebhardt
37ª Squadriglia	Ten Domenico Valsania
115ª Squadriglia	Cap Vittorio Falugi
9° Gruppo CT (Berka) CR.42	Magg Ernesto Botto
73ª Squadriglia	Ten Vittorio Pezzè
96ª Squadriglia	Cap Roberto Fassi
97ª Squadriglia	Cap Antonio Larsimont Pergameni

57ª Sq/32° Gr/10° St BTS.79   MM21405Ten Luigi Vicoli force-landed due to damage

Saturday, 13 July 1940

Early in July most of 30 Squadron's Blenheim IFs had moved to a new airfield which was still under construction at Ikingi Maryut, 20 miles south-west of Alexandria. From here on the 11th six aircraft had been despatched to Maaten Bagush for escort duties, and on the 13th three of these flew out to provide cover to units of the Mediterranean Fleet, arriving over the ships at a position 160 miles north of Mersa Matruh. As they arrived, a trio of S.79s from 20ª Squadriglia, 46° Gruppo, 15° Stormo BT was seen just about to attack, two of the Blenheims undertaking an interception while the third stayed close to the vessels in case a further raid should come in. An exchange of fire with the Savoias took place, one of the latter being seen diving away with smoke trailing from the starboard engine. The rear gunner in the leading Savoia then appeared to have been put out of action, but at this stage Plt Off I.C.Swann's Blenheim, K7181, VT-X, was hit by fire from 1° Av Dino Ornani's gun and went down in flames. Swann and his crew were seen to bale out, but were not found and were listed as missing in action.

During the day the CR.42s of 9° Gruppo CT of 4° Stormo, arrived at Berka airfield near Benghazi, having been operating briefly over Malta. The unit was led by Magg Ernesto Botto, a noted ace of the Spanish Civil War. Botto had lost a leg as a result of a combat there, and now flew with an artificial limb. As a result he had become known as 'Gamba di Ferro' (Iron Leg); a design of an armoured leg had become the unit emblem, and was now painted on all the gruppo's aircraft. Also arriving at this time was a new commanding officer for 10° Gruppo, the other component of 4° Stormo. This was Magg Carlo Romagnoli, who took over from the temporary command of Cap Giuseppe D'Agostinis following the loss of T.Col Piragino. Temporarily, Romagnoli, who had served in Ethiopia and during the Spanish Civil War, and who had already been decorated with two Medaglie d'Argento and two di Bronzo, took command of the whole Stormo, pending the arrival of Col Michele Grandinetti from Italy.

British Casualties

30 Sqn	Blenheim IF K7181 Flg Off I.C.Swann and crew KiA

Italian Claims

20ª Sq/46° Gr/15° St BT	1° Av Dino Ornani (gunner)	Blenheim

Blenheim L1491 of 211 Squadron flown by Plt Off E.Garrard-Cole force-landed near El Adem on 15 July 1940. The crew of three was captured but Garrard-Cole later escaped from his PoW camp in Italy.

Monday, 15 July 1940

It was Italian anti-aircraft fire which further reduced 202 Group's scarce assets on the 15th. Blenheim L1431 of 211 Squadron force-landed near El Adem after being damaged, Plt Off E.Garrard-Cole and his crew being captured. A second Blenheim, 55 Squadron's L4820, crashed at Buq Buq on return from a sortie to Gazala with the loss of Flg Off M.Fox and crew; the cause of this aircraft's demise is not known, although their aircraft was last seen to be on fire.

That night during a raid on Tobruk, another of 216 Squadron's Bombays (L5815) went down, again probably a victim of AA fire.

On this date, however, the personnel of 3 Squadron, Royal Australian Air Force, departed their homeland on SS *Orontes*, bound for the Middle East. They would change ship at Bombay, sailing then for Port Tewfic, Egypt, on SS *Dilwarra*, although it would be more than a month after their initial departure before their final destination would be reached.

The Regia Aeronautica was also further reinforced by the arrival from Italy of 54° Gruppo Autonomo BT. Formerly part of 37° Stormo BT, and comprised of 218ª and 219ª Squadriglia, the unit was equipped with S.81s, and these were to undertake a similar function to the Bombays of 216 Squadron – night bombing. Another new bomber unit, 33° Gruppo Autonomo BT, equipped with S.79s and recently transferred from Sicily, had also now arrived and was ready to operate (*see box*).

33° Gruppo Autonomo BT	T.Col Ferri Forte
59ª Squadriglia	Cap Luciano Guidoni
60ª Squadriglia	Cap Loris Bulgarelli
54° Gruppo Autonomo BT	Col Nicola Colavolpe
218ª Squadriglia	Cap Mario Casali
219ª Squadriglia	Cap Antonio Celotto

British Casualties

211 Sqn	Blenheim I L1491 Plt Off E.Garrard-Cole and two PoW
55 Sqn	Blenheim I L4820 Flg Off M.Fox and two KiA
216 Sqn	Bombay L5815 MiA Tobruk

Thursday, 18 July 1940

112 Squadron had now been ordered to join 33 Squadron at Maaten Gerawla, and had flown up the day before. Next day, Flg Off A.Gray Worcester, who had done so well on 4 July, flew into a hillside whilst leading a formation down through cloud, and was killed instantly.

During a night raid, an S.79 of 58ª Squadriglia, 32° Gruppo BT flown by Ten Giulio Cabassi was shot down by AA fire over Mersa Matruh and crashed to the ground, killing all the crew except the radio operator, 1° Av Fabozzi, who managed to bale out and became a PoW. This would appear to have been the aircraft claimed shot down by 33 Squadron 15 miles south of Mersa Matruh, although it was reported that only one member of the crew had been killed and the other five all became PoWs.

British Claims

33 Sqn	Gladiators	S.79 at night	15 miles S Mersa Matruh

British Casualties

112 Sqn	Gladiator K6130 Flg Off A.G.Worcester KiFA
216 Sqn	Bombay L5819 abandoned after force-landing in Western Desert

Italian Casualties

58ª Sq/32° Gr/10° St BT	S.79 MM 22333 Ten Giulio Cabassi and most of crew KiA; one PoW

Friday, 19 July 1940

On this date six CR.42s, three each from 93ª Squadriglia, 8° Gruppo CT, and 78ª Squadriglia, 13° Gruppo CT, scrambled to intercept four Blenheims, one of which was claimed shot down off the coast of Marsa

A couple of S.79s of 13ª Squadriglia, 26° Gruppo, 9° Stormo CT, ready to start the bombing run with the aimer already in the lower cabin.

Luch by all six pilots jointly. No loss of a Blenheim is recorded on this date by the RAF. However, records show that 55 and 211 Squadrons had taken off for a raid on Tobruk which was undertaken circa 1817-1830. One aircraft of 55 Squadron apparently force-landed near El Adem following attacks by three CR.42s, the crews being believed to have been captured. The rest of the formation was then attacked all the way to Bardia and on return one more Blenheim force-landed in Egyptian territory.

British Casualties (unconfirmed)	
55 Sqn	Blenheim force-landed near El Adem after fighter attack; crew possibly PoW
	Blenheim force-landed in Egypt on return from raid; cause unspecified

Italian Claims		
93ª Sq/8° Gr CT	S.Ten Orlando Mandolini	
	Serg Magg Italo Bertinelli	
	Serg Magg Roberto Lendaro	Blenheim
78ª Sq/13° Gr CT	Ten Ippolito Lalatta	
	S.Ten Natale Cima	
	Serg Salvatore Mechelli	

Saturday, 20 July 1940

While operating in the Tobruk area, spotting for the guns of the battleship HMS *Warspite*, the vessel's catapult Swordfish floatplane was shot down. Nonetheless, it was basically a good day for the Royal Navy. Having just returned to Alexandria from a convoy operation to Malta (see *Malta: The Hurricane Years, 1940-41*), HMS *Eagle's* two Swordfish squadrons had again gone ashore to Dekheila. On this occasion it was 824 Squadron which flew up to Sidi Barrani to launch a further attack on Tobruk, this time by moonlight. Here two 1,715-ton destroyers, *Nembo* and *Ostro*, were both sunk, while the 2,333-ton cargo vessel *Sereno* was left damaged and stranded to join the ships that might later be recovered. Claims were also submitted for hits on a second merchant vessel and an oiler. In support, Blenheims of 55 and 211 Squadrons also raided the port to distract the AA gunners.

The whole 50° Stormo Assalto (12° and 16° Gruppi) now relocated to T.2 airfield at Tobruk. By this date 2° Stormo CT was down to only 20 CR.42s serviceable in its six squadriglie.

British Casualties	
HMS *Warspite*	Swordfish floatplane Tobruk

Sunday, 21 July 1940

On this date six of 45 Squadron's Blenheims were detached to the Sudan to operate over East Africa (see *Dust Clouds in the Middle East*). They would return on 9 August.

Monday, 22 July 1940

8° Gruppo CT was now ordered to hand its remaining CR.42s to 13° Gruppo CT and move to Benghazi to re-equip. Meanwhile, 10° Gruppo CT, having returned from there to T3, El Adem, sent 15 CR.42s to escort ten 50° Stormo Ba.65s in an attack on British forces in the Bir Dignasc area. On this date 211 Squadron's Blenheim L6661 failed to return from a night attack on El Adem which it had undertaken from Qotaifiya. Sgt G.Smith and his crew were all killed.

British Casualties

211 Sqn	Blenheim I L6661 Sgt G.Smith & crew KiA; last seen over Sidi Barrani

Tuesday, 23 July 1940

33 Squadron was ordered to despatch three Gladiators to escort a Lysander on a reconnaissance sortie. Nine CR.42s of 13° Gruppo CT and nine more from 10° Gruppo CT were in the air and reported attacking a formation of Blenheims escorted by Gladiators between Sidi Azeiz and Bardia. Ten Guglielmo Chiarini of 82ª Squadriglia, 13° Gruppo, claimed one Gladiator shot down from which the pilot baled out. A second claim was submitted by S.Ten Giulio Torresi of the Gruppo's 77ª Squadriglia, while three pilots from 91ª Squadriglia, 10° Gruppo, claimed to have co-operated in the shooting down of one of these British fighters. Only one Gladiator was actually lost, Plt Off Preston baling out of N5774 south of Bardia.

During the day Cap Mario Fedele, commanding officer of 77ª Squadriglia, was scrambled to pursue a single Blenheim that had attacked his airfield. On catching up with his quarry he discovered that he had in fact been chasing a Ro.37bis, so turned to fly back to base. During his return flight his aircraft crashed into the ground for unexplained reasons and he was killed.

British Casualties

33 Sqn	Gladiator N5774 Plt Off Preston baled out

Italian Claims

82ª Sq/13° Gr CT	Ten Guglielmo Chiarini	Gladiator
77ª Sq/13° Gr CT	S.Ten Giulio Torresi	Gladiator
91ªSq/10° Gr CT	Ten Enzo Martissa	
	Serg Alessandro Bladelli	Share in one of the above
	Serg Elio Miotto	

Italian Casualties

77ª Sq/13° Gr CT	CR.42 Cap Mario Fedele KiFA

Wednesday, 24 July 1940

33 Squadron's time close to the frontier was drawing to a close by 24 July, 112 Squadron initially taking over. A and B Flights of the former unit had already withdrawn by this date, although B Flight remained active for the time being. The five pilots of this flight were to be heavily engaged during the next 48 hours; during the evening of the 24th they met 17 CR.42s (11 of 10° Gruppo CT and six of 13° Gruppo CT) which were on a sweep over the Sollum area. Here the Italian pilots encountered a formation which they reported to comprise nine Blenheims and 15 escorting Gladiators. Ten Giovanni Guiducci, S.Ten Giulio Torresi and Serg Magg Rovero Abbarchi each claimed one Gladiator shot down, Abbarchi pursuing his victim far into British-held territory. Ten Franco Lucchini meanwhile, reported obtaining hits on three Blenheims; while Ten Giuseppe Aurili claimed damage to another Gladiator and Ten Enzo Martissa forced one more to land in the desert. Cap Aldo Lanfranco was shot down by three Gladiators and baled out to become a PoW, while Serg Luigi Ferrario reached base in his badly damaged aircraft.

Certainly there were not 15 Gladiators involved in this engagement, and 33 Squadron's ORB recorded: "Five aircraft, B Flight, met 18 enemy aircraft over Sollum and shot down four and possibly one other. Sgt Shaw forced to land with engine trouble east of Buq Buq."

The five British pilots included Flg Off E.H.Dean, Plt Offs V.C.Woodward and A.R.Costello, and

Sgts R.L.Slater and Shaw. Costello and Slater each claimed one CR.42 shot down, while Woodward claimed one plus the 'possible'. Lack of evidence leads to the presumption that Dean made the fourth claim. Whether Shaw's "engine trouble" was caused by bullet damage is a moot point, but his would appear to have been the aircraft claimed both by Abbarchi and Martissa. The veracity of the latter's claim seems to be substantiated by the fact that next day he flew back to the location where the Gladiator had come down and destroyed it by strafing. 33 Squadron confirmed that Shaw's aircraft was indeed destroyed by air attack soon after it had come down, while he was able to return unharmed to his unit after a long walk through the desert. Martissa was awarded a Medaglia d'Argento "for his gallant behaviour".

British Claims

33 Sqn	possibly Flg Off E.H.Dean	Gladiator	CR.42	Sollum
	Plt Off V.C.Woodward	Gladiator N5768	CR.42	Sollum
		Gladiator N5768	CR.42 Probable	Sollum
	Plt Off A.R.Costello	Gladiator N5768	CR.42	Sollum
	Sgt R.L. Slater	Gladiator N5768	CR.42	Sollum

British Casualties

33 Sqn	Gladiator Sgt Shaw forced to land; a/c then destroyed on ground

Italian Claims

90ª Sq/10º Gr CT	Ten Giovanni Guiducci	Gladiator	Sollum
77ª Sq/13º Gr CT	S.Ten Giulio Torresi	Gladiator	Sollum
78ª Sq/13º Gr CT	Serg Magg Rovero Abbarchi	Gladiator	Sollum
90ª Sq/10º Gr CT	Ten Franco Lucchini	3 Blenheims Damaged	Sollum
84ª Sq/10º Gr CT	Ten Giuseppe Aurili	Gladiator Damaged	Sollum
91ª Sq/10º Gr CT	Ten Enzo Martissa	Gladiator forced to land	Sollum

Italian Casualties

84ª Sq/10º Gr CT	CR.42 Cap Aldo Lanfranco baled, safe and PoW
91ª Sq/10º Gr CT	CR.42 damaged Serg Luigi Ferrario

Thursday, 25 July 1940

Next day it was the turn of 33 Squadron to make a substantial number of claims for which commensurate losses have not been found. The same five pilots of B Flight escorted Blenheims of 55 Squadron over Bardia where they were intercepted by three CR.42s scrambled by 13º Gruppo CT. It was the British who overestimated the strength of the opposition on this occasion, the ORB recording: "B Flight aircraft had further successful encounter with the enemy shooting down five out of seven met over Bardia".

During a fierce fight, Woodward and Slater each claimed one shot down, Woodward's victim reportedly falling in flames. They then combined to share a third between them before coming under determined attack which shot down Slater's Gladiator and from which Woodward only escaped by weaving violently at an altitude of only 100 feet, where he found his Gladiator could turn more tightly than the pursuing CR.42. Costello claimed to have shared in the destruction of a fourth CR.42, and it is therefore assumed that this may have been with Dean. However, a claim for a CR.42 was also submitted on this date by Flg Off P.E.C.Strahan of 112 Squadron, who reported seeing eight such fighters over Bardia. His Gladiator was then hit and damaged, causing him to make a forced landing. It seems therefore that he may have been flying with B Flight on this date, or may have entered the engagement whilst involved in other duties. His claim is timed between 1010-1120, but unfortunately the time of the 33 Squadron encounter was not recorded.

Italian records indicate the target bombed as having been Derna, rather than Bardia, where two S.79s of 30º Gruppo, 10º Stormo BT, were destroyed on the ground. The three 8º Gruppo CT pilots all made claims, Serg Abbarchi for one Gladiator, while Ten Giovanni Beduz and Serg Leone Basso shared a second; no losses were recorded by the Italian unit.

During the day the move of A and C Flights of 112 Squadron to Maaten Bagush was completed – supporting the presence of Flg Off Strahan in the area. (B Flight had been detached to the Sudan at this time and would not ultimately return, being separated from the squadron to form an autonomous K Flight – see *Dust Clouds in the Middle East* for more details.)

On this date the 5ª Squadra Aerea was formed at Cirene under the command of Gen SA Felice Porro as a replacement for the Aeronautica della Libia, which had also been commanded by Porro. At the same time 175ª Squadriglia RST was formed at Tobruk T5 airfield for strategic reconnaissance duties.

British Claims

33 Sqn	Flg Off V.C.Woodward	Gladiator N5768	CR.42	Bardia
		Gladiator N5768	½ CR.42	
	Sgt R.L.Slater	Gladiator N5783	CR.42	Bardia
		Gladiator N5783	½ CR.42	Bardia
	Plt Off A.R.Costello		½ CR.42	Bardia
	u/k – possibly Flg Off E.H.Dean		CR.42	Bardia
			½ CR.42	Bardia
112 Sqn	Flg Off P.E.C.Strahan		CR.42	Bardia 1010-1120

British Casualties

33 Sqn	Gladiator N5783 Sgt R.L.Slater safe
112 Sqn	Gladiator damaged Flg Off P.E.C.Strahan force-landed

Italian Claims

78ª Sq/13º Gr CT	Serg Magg Rovero Abbarchi	Gladiator
	Ten Giovanni Beduz	½ Gladiator
77ª Sq/13º Gr CT	Serg Leone Basso	½ Gladiator

Italian Casualties

30º Gr/10º St BT	2 S.79s destroyed on the ground at Derna by bombing

Friday – Saturday, 26/27 July 1940

During the next two days CR 42s of 2º Stormo CT and of 91ª Squadriglia, 10º Gruppo CT, CR.32s of 160ª Squadriglia and Ba.65s of 159ª Squadriglia, 12º Gruppo Ass undertook strafing attacks on British armoured cars, while 33 Squadron's B Flight was involved in flying cover patrols for these vehicles. Throughout this 48-hour period the presence of the opposing aircraft failed to coincide, and no engagements occurred. Magg Bruno Cudugnello. commanding officer of 12º Gruppo, had to make a force-landing in his CR.32 (on the 27th) when it was hit in the oil and water tanks by fire from the ground. Cudugnello then walked until he reached the Via Balbia coast road, where he was picked up. By the end of these two days, however, 2º Stormo CT was down to a serviceable strength of only six aircraft, and in consequence would not operate again during the month that followed.

Italian Casualties

12º Gr Ass	CR.32 MM4660 Magg Bruno Cudugnello force-landed due to ground fire; aircraft subsequently destroyed by strafing

Sunday, 28 July 1940

Next day an attempt was made to recover Cudugnello's damaged aircraft but in the meanwhile it had been strafed and destroyed by British aircraft. A Ro.37bis flying nearby, in the hands of S.Ten Dario Brigadue of 136ª Squadriglia, was also shot down, and in the absence of any RAF claims for such an aircraft, it is assumed that this too fell to ground fire.

Eight Blenheim IFs from 30 Squadron had arrived at Maaten Bagush on the 27th, and from here early next morning two took off to escort a 113 Squadron Mark IV aircraft on a reconnaissance over the front, while three more carried out a separate reconnaissance. The Blenheim IV, flown by Sqn Ldr G.B.Keily, AFC, suffered some severe damage from AA fire, while at the same time three CR.42s of 10º Gruppo CT were scrambled, intercepting the other 30 Squadron aircraft south of El Adem. Ten Franco Lucchini of 90ª Squadriglia claimed one shot down, as did Serg Giuseppe Scaglioni of 84ª Squadriglia, while Serg Giovanni Battista Ceoletta, also on 90ª Squadriglia, claimed a probable.

Just one of the 30 Squadron aircraft was lost, K7178 last being seen by the crews of the other Blenheims diving away with three CR.42s in pursuit. Flt Sgt Innes-Smith and his gunner were killed. Whilst landing after this combat, Scaglioni crashed and his CR.42 had to be written off.

As a result of this action Sqn Ldr Keily was awarded a DFC during the following month. The citation stated:

"On 28 July 1940, Squadron Leader Keily was the pilot of an aircraft detailed to carry out a special reconnaissance over Libya. The reconnaissance had to be carried out at a low altitude owing to clouds. He was attacked by five enemy aircraft but, displaying great skill, he destroyed one of them. During the engagement the air observer was hit by a bullet. Notwithstanding the handicap of having the air observer's body leaning against him, Squadron Leader Keily continued with the reconnaissance, returning with information of great value. He has invariably displayed exceptional leadership, courage, and devotion to duty."

British Claims			
113 Sqn	Blenheim crew	CR.42	
British Casualties			
113 Sqn	Blenheim IV damaged by AA		
30 Sqn	Blenheim IF K7178 Flt Sgt Innes-Smith and gunner KiA		
Italian Claims			
90ª Sq/10º Gr CT	Ten Franco Lucchini	Blenheim	
	Serg Giovanni Battista Ceoletta	Blenheim Probable	
84ª Sq/10º Gr CT	Serg Giuseppe Scaglioni	Blenheim	
Italian Casualties			
84ª Sq/10º Gr CT	CR.42 Serg Giuseppe Scaglioni crashed on landing – safe		
136ª Sq OA	Ro.37bis S.Ten Dario Brigadue KiA		

Monday, 29 July 1940
An S.79 of 43ª Squadriglia, 33º Stormo, flown by Ten Francesco Casolla, was lost to AA fire north of Sidi Barrani on this date.

Italian Casualties	
43ª Sq/35º Gr/33º St BT	S.79 MM21629 Ten Francesco Casolla & crew MiA

Thursday, 1 August 1940
B Flight of 80 Squadron now moved its Gladiators to Sidi Barrani on a three-month detachment to take over from B Flight of 33 Squadron. The latter then rejoined the rest of the squadron at Helwan for refitting, and for two weeks' rest.

British Casualties	
33 Sqn	Gladiator N5775 struck off charge – reason unknown
80 Sqn	Gladiator L8010 abandoned near El Adem – reason unknown

Sunday, 4 August 1940
80 Squadron's first major engagement following B Flight's arrival at Sidi Barrani, occurred on 4 August, giving rise to a combat which in the past has been incorrectly recorded (for which this author was mainly responsible). Because two of the RAF's future leading fighter 'aces' were involved, coupled with a lack of detailed information regarding the Regia Aeronautica's operations, claims and losses, a degree of perhaps 'wishful thinking' crept into the account as originally written in *Fighters over the Desert* in 1969.

At 1650 a fairly large formation of 4º Stormo CT CR.42s took to the air, preparing to escort 50º Stormo Assalto ground-attack aircraft to raid a British garrison located some 20 miles (30 km) south-west of Sollum in the Bir Sheferzen area. At about 15,000 ft as top cover were nine CR.42s of 9º Gruppo CT led by Magg Botto, while at 11,500 ft was the main body of 21 CR.42s of 10º Gruppo CT, led by Magg Romagnoli. Beneath them at 3,000 ft were six CR.32s from 160ª Squadriglia Ass led by Cap Fanali, while at 1,000 ft were six Ba.65s from 159ª Squadriglia Ass, led by Cap Antonio Dell'Oro. By coincidence, all the four formation leaders were veterans of the Spanish Civil War.

At 1715 four of 80 Squadron's Gladiators took off to escort a Lysander over Bir Taieb el Esem. The pilots were Flt Lt Tom Pattle, Flg Off Peter Wykeham-Barnes, Plt Off J.H.Lancaster and Sgt K.G.R.Rew. Over the area to be reconnoitred the observer in the Lysander fired a Very cartridge, and leaving Wykeham-Barnes and Rew above, Pattle and Lancaster went to investigate, but initially saw nothing.

The Lysander crew had obviously spotted the Italian formation, and moments later the 12º Gruppo Ass pilots saw the small British formation. At the same time Wykeham-Barnes and Rew attacked the

Ba.65s, one of which Wykeham-Barnes claimed to have shot down in flames. They were then in their turn attacked by the CR.32s which shot down Rew's Gladiator (K7908) in flames. Wykeham-Barnes meanwhile, claimed one of these attackers shot down, but his own aircraft, L8009, was then badly damaged and he had to bale out.

Meanwhile Pattle and Lancaster had also dived on the Ba.65s, which were reportedly flying in a 'vic' of three plus two pairs (which is one more than were actually present). Pattle closed on two which jettisoned their bombs, and although two of his guns had ceased to function, he attacked one which he reported then force-landed.

Lancaster was also experiencing trouble with his guns and became involved with the Italian fighters. Their fire hit him, wounding him in one arm and shoulder, and seriously damaging his Gladiator. Nevertheless, he was able to shake off his pursuers, and made it back to Sidi Barrani.

During this 15-minute fight Cap Fanali claimed one Gladiator shot down, and M.llo Romolo Cantelli two more. No CR.32s were lost, although the Ba.65 flown by Serg Magg Paolo Perno was hit by about 50 bullets and the pilot was wounded in one leg.

Now alone, Flt Lt Pattle headed east for Egypt, but was then attacked by five CR.42s. He fought these for some while, finally believing that he had sent one spinning down, which he thought he had seen hit the ground. The others then broke away, and he once again turned for base, but it was not his day! Halfway to the frontier he found his way blocked by three Ba.65s and a dozen fighters, which he again identified as CR.42s, all these aircraft attacking his lone Gladiator. For a reported 15 minutes he managed to evade their attacks, but finally he flew right into the fire of one assailant and baled out of K7910.

During this eventful evening, the higher-flying CR.42 pilots reported meeting a formation of Blenheims near Ridotta Capuzzo, escorted by a reported seven Gladiators. The 4° Stormo pilots attacked, Cap Franco Lucchini claiming one Gladiator shot down, while three Blenheims and two Gladiators were credited to Lucchini and several other pilots jointly, with two more of these aircraft considered probably destroyed. Another trio of pilots from the top cover led by Cap Antonio Larsimont Pergameni chased three of the Blenheims and claimed to have inflicted damage on these.

Nine Blenheims had taken off at 2055, and were drawn from 55, 113 and 211 Squadrons, the crews reporting meeting 50 CR.42s. In a running fight gunners claimed four Italian fighters shot down and a fifth probably so, while four Blenheims suffered damage, although all were able to return to base. This engagement took place at much the same time as the fight with 80 Squadron was underway, but there was no note of any escorting Gladiators being present. It would seem therefore that some of the claims for Gladiators at this stage may have related to Pattle's lone aircraft.

Although Pattle and Wykeham-Barnes had both come down in hostile territory, they immediately made their separate ways towards Egypt, both being picked up safely by 11th Hussar patrols next day, while Lancaster was discovered in hospital in Alexandria. Next day B Flight received four more pilots as reinforcements – Flg Off G.F.Graham, Plt Off P.H.Stubbs DFM, Plt Off S.Linnard and Sgt E.W.F.Hewett.

British Claims

80 Sqn	Flg Off P.G.Wykeham-Barnes	Gladiator L8009	Ba.65	Bir Taieb el Esem 1715-1845
			CR.32	Bir Taieb el Esem 1715-1845
	Flt Lt M.T.StJ. Pattle	Gladiator K7910	Ba.65	Bir Taieb el Esem 1715-1845
			CR.42	Bir Taieb el Esem 1715-1845
113 Sqn	Bomber Gunners	Blenheims	2 CR.42s	Bir Taieb el Esem 1715-1845
55/211 Sqns	Bomber Gunners	Blenheims	2 CR.42s and one probable	Bir Taieb el Esem 1715-1845

British Casualties

80 Sqn	Gladiator K7908 Sgt K.G.R.Rew KiA
	Gladiator L8009 Flg Off P.G.Wykeham-Barnes baled out – safe
	Gladiator K7910 Flt Lt M.T.StJ.Pattle baled out – safe
	Gladiator damaged Plt Off J.H.Lancaster WiA
55,113/211 Sqns	4 Blenheims damaged

Italian Claims

160ª Sq/12° Gr Ass	Cap Duilio Fanali	Gladiator
	M.llo Romolo Cantelli	2 Gladiators

90ª Sq/10º Gr CT	Cap Franco Lucchini	Gladiator
	Cap Franco Lucchini	
	Serg Amleto Monterumici	3 Blenheims
	Ten Giuseppe Aurili	2 Gladiators
84ª Sq/10º Gr CT	Cap Luigi Monti	2 a/c Probably destroyed
	others	

Italian Casualties

| 159ª Sq/12º Gr Ass | Ba.65 damaged Serg Magg Paolo Perno WiA |
| | |

Tuesday, 6 August 1940

During the morning Ten Lucchini and Serg Monterumici were scrambled after a contact, but found nothing. On landing Lucchini's CR.42 (MM4384) flipped over, suffering so much damage that it had to be written off.

Success was obtained in the afternoon, however, when Cap Luigi Monti and Serg Alessandro Bladelli intercepted a 228 Squadron Sunderland (N9025) 20 miles (30 km) off the coast north-west of Tobruk. On this occasion they were successful in forcing it to land on the water. While Bladelli circled overhead, 'Gigi' Monti flew back to T.2 airfield to alert the Regia Marina command, who at once ordered out the torpedo-boat *Rosolino Pilo* to capture the prize. Meanwhile at 1820 a final message was received from Smith's crew reporting that one of their number had been killed, and that a destroyer was approaching.

Radio contact was maintained until the *Rosolino Pilo* had actually come alongside and taken the flyingboat in tow. LAC C.J.C.Jones, the flight rigger, had been the fatal casualty, while Sgt H.J.Baxter, LACs P.F.O.Davies and W.J.Pitt, and AC1 W.D.Price had all been wounded. They, together with Flt Lt M.W.T.Smith, Flg Off D.R.S.Bevan-John, Plt Off I.T.G.Stewart and LAC A.McWhinnie, all became PoWs. 228 Squadron recorded that it was subsequently learned from *"a reliable source"* that the aircraft had sunk under tow. However, during a reconnaissance over Tobruk later in the day, the crew of a 113 Squadron Blenheim reported seeing a Sunderland being towed into harbour. RAF records also indicated that the crew had scuttled the aircraft and taken to their dinghy prior to the arrival of the Italian warship, but clearly this was incorrect.

Meanwhile, a pair of 30 Squadron's fighter-Blenheims escorted three Swordfish torpedo-bombers from 824 Squadron to attack the tanker west of Tobruk. It appears that this was not found, for no such attack actually took place.

British Casualties		
228 Sqn	Sunderland N9025 Flg Off M.W.T.Smith and crew PoW	
Italian Claims		
10º Gr CT	Cap Luigi Monti	½ Sunderland
	Serg Alessandro Bladelli	½ Sunderland
Italian Casualties		
90ª Sq/10º Gr CT	CR.42 MM4384 Ten Franco Lucchini safe – landing crash	
96ª Sq/9º Gr CT	CR.42 damaged Serg Graziadio Rizzati safe – landing crash	

Thursday, 8 August 1940

Just after 1700 hours Magg Romagnoli set off at the head of 16 CR.42s (seven of 10º Gruppo and nine of 73ª Squadriglia, 9º Gruppo) to escort five S.79s and a lone Ro.37bis on a sortie to the frontier. During the day 80 Squadron's C Flight had flown up to join B Flight at Sidi Barrani, led by the commanding officer, Sqn Ldr P.H. 'Paddy' Dunn, as it was felt since the debacle of the 4th that rather larger formations were necessary to prevent a repetition of such losses. At about 1740 Dunn led a formation of 14 Gladiators to undertake an offensive patrol over the El Gubi area.

Over Gabr Saleh Ten Vittorio Pezzé spotted two patrols of Gladiators flying at about 8,000 ft (2,500 m), but as he led the 73ª Squadriglia formation to intercept these, the Fiats were attacked by more Gladiators from above. The confusion arising in such an engagement may be judged from the fact that each side identified the other as 27-strong, whereas in fact the two formations were actually of very comparable size.

In the combat which followed, the pilots of 80 Squadron felt that they had fully avenged the reverse of the 4th by a wide margin, claiming 15 CR.42s shot down, six of which appear subsequently to have

Sqn Ldr P.H.'Paddy' Dunn led 80 Squadron to a resounding victory on 8 August 1940. Claims were made for ten CR.42s shot down and five more probably so, Dunn personally claiming two. The Regia Aeronautica's 10° Gruppo CT actually lost eight fighters during this engagement.

Having been shot down by Italian fighters on 4 August 1940, Flt Lt M.T.Pattle, here in flight in his 80 Squadron Gladiator, was back in the air on the 8th, claiming two victories during his unit's very successful engagement on that date.

Another of the 80 Squadron Gladiator pilots who was able to claim two of the successes on 8 August 1940 was Flg Off Sid Linnard.

This wheel spat panel came from CR.42 MM 4306 flown by Ten Enzo Martissa who crash-landed in the desert on 8 August 1940. The griffin, emblem of 91ª Squadriglia, was hit in the head, while the pilot wrote on the white disc some farewell words, supposed to be his last, before being rescued by a Bersaglieri patrol two days later.

been classed as probables. On this occasion the degree of over-claiming was somewhat below average, for eight of the Italian fighters in fact went down.

Three Regia Aeronautica pilots baled out and were swiftly rescued by troops of 2ª Divisione Libica, and were back with their unit next day. Two more force-landed and were also rescued next day, while Ten Martissa force-landed about 10-12 miles (15 km) from T.3, having been wounded. He would be rescued by a Bersaglieri unit on the 10th when hope of his recovery had all but been given up. His CR.42 was recovered and repaired, and would later be put back into service with 84ª Squadriglia.

Serg Lido Poli had been hit early in the fight and severely wounded in one arm. He continued fighting, claiming to have shot down one Gladiator, but then force-landed. He was picked up and subsequently the injured arm had to be amputated; he became the first airman in North Africa to be awarded a Medaglia d'Oro whilst still alive. Of the pilots shot down, only M.llo Norino Renzi was killed. The members of 73ª Squadriglia were credited with three Gladiators shot down, and those of 10º Gruppo with two, but in fact only two such aircraft had been lost by 80 Squadron, Flt Sgt T.M. Vaughan being killed in K7903, while Flt Lt Evers-Swindell force-landed successfully and was picked up by the 11th Hussars, who took him to the casualty clearing station.

British Claims

80 Sqn				
	Sqn Ldr P.H.Dunn	Gladiator K8009	2 CR.42s	El Gubi 1740-1920
	Flt Lt M.T.St.J.Pattle	Gladiator K7971	2 CR.42s	El Gubi 740-1920
	Flt Lt R.V.Evers-Swindell	Gladiator L8010	2 CR.42s	El Gubi 1740-1920
	Flg Off S.Linnard	Gladiator K8017	2 CR.42s	El Gubi 1740-1920
	Flg Off P.G.Wykeham-Barnes	Gladiator K7916	CR.42	El Gubi 1740-1920
	Flg Off V.A.J.Stuckey	Gladiator K8022	CR.42	El Gubi 1740-1920
	Flg Off G.F.Graham	Gladiator L8008	CR.42 Probable	El Gubi 1740-1920
	Flg Off P.T.Dowding	Gladiator K7912	CR.42 Probable	El Gubi 1740-1920
	Flg Off H.D.Flower	Gladiator K8011	CR.42 Probable	El Gubi 1740-1920
	Flg Off H.U.Sykes	Gladiator K8003	2 CR.42 Probables	El Gubi 1740-1920

British Casualties

80 Sqn	
	Gladiator K7903 Flt Sgt T.M. Vaughan KiA
	Gladiator Flt Lt R.V.Evers-Swindell force-landed

Italian Claims

73ª Sq/9º Gr CT	Ten Vittorio Pezzé	
	Ten Valerio De Campo	
	Ten Carlo Battaglia	
	S.Ten Alvaro Querci	
	M.llo Norino Renzi	3 Gladiators
	Serg Magg Enrico Dallari	
	Serg Magg Antonio Valle	
	Serg Santo Gino	
	Serg Lido Poli	
10º Gr CT	Magg Carlo Romagnoli	
	Cap Giuseppe D'Agostinis	
91ª Sq/10º Gr CT	Ten Enzo Martissa	
	Serg Aldo Rosa	2 Gladiators
90ª Sq/10º Gr CT	Ten Giovanni Guiducci	
	Serg Magg Angelo Savini	
84ª Sq/10º Gr CT	Cap Luigi Monti	

Italian Casualties

73ª Sq/9º Gr CT	
	CR.42 Serg Lido Poli – force-landed, wounded
	CR.42 MM5652 M.llo Norino Renzi – KiA
	CR.42 Serg Magg Enrico Dallari – baled out, safe
	CR.42 Serg Magg Antonio Valle – baled out, safe
	CR.42 S.Ten Alvaro Querci – force-landed, safe
	CR.42 Serg Santo Gino – force-landed, safe
91ª Sq/10º Gr CT	CR.42 Serg Aldo Rosa – baled out, safe
	CR.42 MM4308 Ten Enzo Martissa – force-landed, WiA

Friday, 9 August 1940

13º Gruppo CT now moved westwards to Benghazi's Berka airfield to receive new deliveries of CR.42s. At Castel Benito 7º Gruppo Assalto arrived from Sicily, equipped with the Breda Ba.88 Lince – a new twin-engined ground-attack aircraft of very streamlined appearance, of which much was expected. The Gruppo's three squadriglie, 76ª, 86ª and 98ª, would soon move forward to Benina, but the aircraft was to prove a great disappointment. Somewhat underpowered by its 1,000 h.p. Piaggio P.XI R.C.40 engines, the fitting of sand filters to these caused them to overheat, and also slowed the aircraft by creating increased drag. Within two days only 13 of the 32 aircraft on strength were still serviceable.

An S.79 of 9º Stormo was set ablaze and destroyed on the ground by a British raid.

Monday, 12 August 1940

On this date A Flight of 80 Squadron which was still at Amiriya, now with the unit's Hurricanes on strength, was joined by a Free French flight which had been formed with the two ex-GC I/7 Morane 406s and two twin-engined Potez 63-11 reconnaissance-bomber aircraft, intended now to be employed in the long-range fighter role. The flight was commanded by Flt Lt Paul Jacquier, with Flg Off Antoine Peronne as his second in command.

During July 33° Gruppo BT (59ᵃ and 60ᵃ Squadriglia) had arrived in Tripolitania from Sicily, trained specifically for anti-shipping work with its S.79s. During August the unit moved to Benina for operations against British Egypt-based ships.

Italian Casualties

45ᵃ Sq/36°Gr/33° St BT   S.79 MM21684 Ten Gregorio Gregnanin and crew KiFA – crashed due to engine trouble on take-off from Benina

Thursday, 15 August 1940

30 Squadron put up six Blenheim Ifs as escort to 11 Blenheims from 55 Squadron which were to undertake an attack on the seaplane base at Bomba. Attacking from out to sea, the bombers released their bombs on the slipway and amongst anchored aircraft, while five minutes later the fighter-Blenheims strafed. One Cant.Z.506B was seen to tip onto its nose in the water and it was believed that all the aircraft seen there had been damaged by gunfire at least. A fuel dump was set on fire and flames spread to an equipment store. Burning fuel ran down the slipway and was seen to engulf two floatplanes. When the area fell into British hands some months later, 13 severely damaged flyingboats and floatplanes were counted. One 30 Squadron aircraft was hit in the wing by three bullets, probably fired from one of the rear guns in the moored aircraft.

Following nightfall, the first mission was undertaken by five Italian S.79 torpedo-bombers of the Reparto Sperimentale Aerosilurante; this small experimental unit had just arrived at El Adem from Sicily, having flown in to Benghazi three days earlier. Now four of these aircraft, led by Magg Vincenzo Dequal, took off at 1928, launching two torpedoes at vessels in Alexandria harbour at 2127 without observed results. During the return flight the aircraft flown by Magg Enrico Fusco ran out of fuel and force-landed in the desert; the entire crew was taken prisoner.

Five Italian pilots in front of an S.79 of Reparto Sperimentale Aerosiluranti; in the centre is Magg Vincenzo Dequal who led the first mission, on 15 August 1940. This experimental unit was destined to become the 278ᵃ Squadriglia AS.

Italian Casualties

RSA	S.79 MM22557 Magg E.Fusco force-landed in desert, crew PoW

Friday, 16 August 1940

Col Michele Grandinetti arrived at El Adem from Italy to take command of 4° Stormo CT. This unit despatched 39 CR.42s during the early morning hours to undertake a sweep and give cover to a Ro.37bis, the crew of which were directing artillery fire. During the sortie S.Ten Bruno Paolazzi's aircraft suffered an engine failure, causing him to force-land, but in doing so he damaged the Fiat so badly that it had to be written off.

Italian Casualties

96ª Sq/9° Gr/4° St CT	CR 42 S.Ten Bruno Paolazzi force-landed, safe – a/c W/O

Saturday, 17 August 1940

The Mediterranean Fleet had again sortied from Alexandria, this time to bombard Bardia again. By dawn it was on its way back, under regular fighter cover from 202 Group's units as Regia Aeronautica formations sought to attack.

At 0820 Flg Off Wykeham-Barnes' section spotted a Cant.Z.501 'shadower' (MM35459) from the base at Menelao, flown by S.Ten Cesare Como, which he, Flg Off 'Keg' Dowding and Plt Off Stubbs attacked twice, sending it plunging into the sea in flames.

10° Stormo BT was ordered to despatch ten S.79s to attack the warships, five from 58ª Squadriglia taking off at 0755, followed by five more from 57ª and 59ª Squadriglia led by Cap Gerardo Musch at 0830. At 0810 in the meantime, Cap Antonio Dell'Oro led four 159ª Squadriglia Ba.65s, escorted by 11 CR.32s from 12° and 16° Gruppo Ass on a similar mission, although nothing was to be seen by the Assalto pilots.

The first five S.79s were met by A Flight of 112 Squadron which attacked as the bombers were making their bombing run, the British pilots reporting that these were driven off.

The second flight of bombers was intercepted by more Gladiators and by a lone Hurricane flown by 80 Squadron's Flg Off John Lapsley, who had been sent up on detachment to Mersa Matruh for this particular operation. While Flt Lt L.G. Schwab and Plt Off P.R.W.Wickham each claimed one S.79 shot down, Lapsley attacked four more. It was the first time the Hurricane had met the S.79, and Lapsley found that the fire of the eight guns was most effective, shooting down three of the bombers, one of which crash-landed. Despite the two 112 Squadron claims, it does seem from Italian accounts that all these three fell to the Hurricane. First to go down was '57-9' flown by Ten Gino Visentin, followed by that piloted by Ten Camillo Mussi. A third bomber did indeed force-land, and the surviving crew members, 1st pilot Ten Arturo Lauchard, 2nd pilot Ten Vittorio Ceard and S.Ten Bruno Rossi were all taken prisoner. The aircraft, '56-9', was subsequently recovered and taken to Alexandria where it was put on display. The two surviving bombers, flown by Cap Gerardo Musch and S.Ten Luigi Venosta, both returned to base suffering severe damage – presumably caused by the attacks of the Gladiators.

Further raids followed by S.79s from 15° and 33° Stormo BT, and six more bombers were damaged. In total, 25 raiders were reported to

On 17 August 1940 Gladiators and a lone Hurricane of 80 Squadron intercepted S.79 of 10° Stormo BT attempting to raid units of the Mediterranean Fleet which had been bombarding Bardia. Five of the bombers were claimed shot down, three of them by Flg Off John Lapsley in the Hurricane. The Italian unit actually lost three of its aircraft with two more damaged. Lapsley would soon become the RAF's top-scoring fighter pilot in North Africa during the opening months of the war.

One of the S.79s shot down by John Lapsley on 17 August 1940 crash-landed, Ten Arturo Lauchard and his crew surviving to become PoWs. The aircraft, 56-9 of the 56 Squadriglia, 10° Stormo BT, was recovered and subsequently put on public display in Alexandria.

have made, or attempted to make, attacks during the day. In return the gunners aboard the S.79s claimed seven Gladiators shot down, two of them by the surviving 10° Stormo crews. In one of the ten 15° Stormo aircraft, gunner 1° Av Antonio Trevigni was credited with having shot down two Gladiators despite being badly wounded in his right leg. On return he was removed to Derna hospital where the leg was amputated. He was later awarded a Medaglia d'Oro. The only casualty recorded by the defending fighter units was one Gladiator damaged, in which Plt Off R.A.Acworth was slightly wounded.

British Claims

80 Sqn	Flg Off P.G.Wykeham-Barnes	Gladiator K8051	}		
	Flg Off P.T.Dowding	Gladiator K8021	}	Cant.Z.501	0905
	Plt Off P.H.Stubbs		}		
112 Sqn	Flt Lt L.G.Schwab	Gladiator		S.79	1050
	Plt Off P.R.W.Wickham	Gladiator		S.79	1050
80 Sqn	Flg Off J.Lapsley	Hurricane P2641		3 S.79s	1045

British Casualties

112 Sqn	Gladiator damaged Plt Off R.A.Acworth slightly wounded

Italian Claims

10° St BT	S.79 gunners	2 Gladiators
15° St BT	1° Av Antonio Trevigni (gunner)	2 Gladiators
15°& 33° St BT	S.79 gunners	3 Gladiators

Italian Casualties

57ª Sq/10° St BT	S.79 MM22331 57-9 Ten G.Visentin and crew KiA
56ª Sq/10° St BT	S.79 MM21351 56-7 Ten C.Mussi and crew KiA
56ª Sq/10° St BT	S.79 MM22313 56-9 Ten A.Lauchard and crew PoW
56ª Sq/10° St BT	S.79 MM21353 damaged Cap G.Musch and crew safe
	S.79 damaged S.Ten L.Venosta and crew safe
15° & 33° St BT	6 S.79s damaged
143ª Sq RM	Cant.Z.501 MM35459 S.Ten Cesare Como MiA

———

On arrival in Egypt from Australia, 3 RAAF Squadron was at first provided with a flight of elderly Gloster Gauntlet fighters to supplement its Lysanders until Gladiators became available. Four of these aircraft are seen here, the nearest being identified as K5268.

Monday, 19 August 1940

Following the air ministry's assurances as to reinforcements of aircraft which had been made during July, 24 Hurricanes had indeed been despatched by sea around the Cape and by mid August were approaching southern Egypt. 36 more would be delivered to Takoradi in crates where they would be erected and flown right across the continent. The first of these would arrive early in September.

Also promised were 75 US-built Martin 167F attack bombers, taken over from a French contract

Flg Off Peter Turnbull paints the name 'Ortago' on the nose of his 3 RAAF Squadron Gauntlet. These aircraft were sarcastically referred to by their pilots as 'The answer to the Stuka'.

following the fall of that country. On 1 August the promised deliveries were increased to 36 Blenheims and 18 Hurricanes a month as soon as this became possible. However, at this stage the Battle of Britain was at its height, and any further deliveries of fighters became impossible until the defence of the home country could be reasonably ensured.

The arrival of the first of these Hurricanes to supplement the few already to hand now allowed the formation of a full squadron of these aircraft, and during 19 August 274 Squadron came into existence at Amiriya with all available Hurricanes. Sqn Ldr Dunn was posted in from 80 Squadron to command the new unit, and with him came a number of 80 Squadron pilots including Flt Lt Evers-Swindell, Flg Offs Peter Wykeham-Barnes and John Lapsley, plus Plt Offs E.M.'Imshi' Mason, A.A.'Sam' Weller, Strang, Rankin and Crowther (the latter three all recent arrivals), as well as others from 33 and 112 Squadrons. The three older units were reformed on a two-flight basis, and were brought up to strength with Gladiator IIs. 80 Squadron's new commanding officer now became Sqn Ldr W.J.Hickey, who would arrive in September. Until then, command was temporarily taken by Flt Lt E.G.Jones. 274 Squadron was further reinforced by the attachment to it of the Free French Flight. Sqn Ldr Charles Ryley, who had been serving as a flight commander with 230 Squadron, flying Sunderland flyingboats, was posted to command 33 Squadron during the month, where he would find the Hurricane a somewhat different aircraft!

Four days later on the third, SS *Dilwarra* arrived at Port Tewfik, disembarking the personnel of 3 RAAF Squadron, who moved to Ismailia where the squadron was initially to begin equipping as an army co-operation unit with Lysanders. However, there was already considerable doubt as to the usefulness of this particular aircraft. Longmore recorded that he had discussed the matter with General Sir Thomas Blamey, commander of Australia's military contingent to the Middle East, indicating that he would prefer to turn the unit into a fighter squadron, initially with Gladiators, but when he had more Hurricanes available, with these aircraft. Blamey, he said, agreed and placed the unit under Longmore's direction. This differs somewhat from the Australian official history – but the result was the same. Within a few days the squadron was re-organised on a three-flight basis, with one flight of Lysanders, as planned, one to have Gladiators, and the third to be provided with the Gladiator's predecessor, the now very elderly Gloster Gauntlet biplane fighter with which the unit was to train for dive-bombing duties. "The answer to the Stuka!" was the unit's rather sarcastic response to this news.

At this time another new unit came into being when 267 Squadron was formed from the Heliopolis Communications Flight, its main duties being the delivery of mail and the transportation of VIPs around the Western Desert. Initial equipment included Avro Ansons, Miles Magisters and Percival Proctors. These were soon joined by larger transport types such as the Percival Q.6, and Lockheed Hudsons and 12As. Steadily an increasing variety of diverse aircraft would arrive with the unit.

Wednesday, 21 August 1940
As the result of a British raid on Tmimi, some S.79s were damaged, two so severely as to be written off.

Italian Casualties	
44ª Sq/35° Gr/33 °St	BT 2 S.79s MM 22100 and 22023 destroyed on ground

Thursday, 22 August 1940
80 Squadron now moved its headquarters from Amiriya to Shineifa, an airfield located 25 miles west of Mersa Matruh on the road to Sidi Barrani. B Flight was up at 1325, providing cover to Fleet Air Arm Swordfish torpedo-bombers returning from a raid on Tobruk.

In mid August 1940 pilots and Hurricanes detached from 33 and 80 Squadrons formed a new 274 Squadron. The first commanding officer was Sqn Ldr 'Paddy' Dunn (right, with puppy). Next to him is Plt Off E.M.'Imshi' Mason who would soon become the unit's outstanding pilot.

These were again aircraft from HMS *Eagle* which had gone ashore at Dekheila following a relatively uneventful convoy operation by the Fleet. From this airfield, three of the torpedo-bombers led by Capt Oliver Patch, RM, had flown forward to Maaten Bagush to operate by day once more, in co-operation with the RAF. In the Gulf of Bomba the submarine *Iride* (700 tons) had been spotted on the surface where she was embarking four SLC underwater assault craft ('human torpedoes' – dubbed 'maiali' [pigs] by their Italian crews) from the depot ship *Monte Gargano*. These were intended to be employed for a planned attack on RN vessels in harbour at Alexandria. In broad daylight the Fleet Air Arm crews pressed home their attacks, sinking the submarine *Iride* which broke in half, all aboard but five crewman being killed. The depot ship was also sunk. The third torpedo passed right beneath the torpedo-boat *Calipso*, which escaped destruction due to her shallow draught. Capt Patch subsequently received a mention in despatches for his leadership of this attack.

During the night of 22/23 August six Italian bombers (three from 10° Stormo and three from 15°) undertook a nocturnal raid on Alexandria.

Tuesday, 27 August 1940
British Casualties

216 Sqn	Bombay L5849

Thursday, 29 August 1940
British Casualties

208 Sqn	Lysander L4685 crashed during force-landing

Saturday, 31 August 1940
British Casualties

55 Sqn	Blenheim I L8397 Plt Off R.A.Smith and crew KIFA – a/c crashed out of control at Mersa Matruh due to engine failure during bombing sortie

CHAPTER 3

GRAZIANI MAKES A MOVE

By the start of September the situation for the Italians had changed considerably. France was no longer in the war, and so now presented no threat throughout the Italian sphere of influence. The United Kingdom was suffering the climax of the Luftwaffe's air attacks from its new bases in France and Belgium, and appeared to be in imminent danger of German invasion. There therefore appeared little likelihood of any substantial reinforcement of the British Imperial forces in Egypt in the foreseeable future.

However, the position of Italy's colonial empire and forces in East Africa was undoubtedly insecure. Initial operations there had not been without their successes – notably the occupation of British Somaliland – but the reinforcement and supply route was tenuous in the extreme. Britain controlled the Suez Canal, so any seaborne support would require a dangerous voyage right around the African continent, and was never to be attempted. By land, the way was blocked by the British presence in Egypt, the Sudan and Kenya. The latter colony was already receiving reinforcement from South Africa, and although Imperial forces throughout the region were very limited, their potential for future support and growth appeared more favourable than was the case for the Italian garrisons (see *Dust Clouds in the Middle East* for more details of actions here).

It was therefore extremely desirable to drive the British out of Egypt and the Sudan, thereby opening up a direct land route to Eritrea and Ethiopia – albeit a long one.

Following the death of Italo Balbo, Marshal Rodolfo Graziani had been appointed as the new governor and military Comandante Supremo in Libya. He was no stranger to the area, having governed Cyrenaica from 1930-34, when he had organised punitive operations against the local Senussi, gaining for himself the unenviable nickname 'Butcher of the Desert'. He had then commanded the southern front in Ethiopia during the invasion and conquest of that country, being appointed the first viceroy in 1936. In November 1939 he had become chief of the army staff, a position which he continued to hold after his posting back to Libya.

While the early months of the war had seen the Italian 10th Army fulfilling a defensive role, the changed circumstances now caused Il Duce, Benito Mussolini, to begin pressing Graziani to advance into Egypt and gain some military success before Britain was knocked out of the European war by his German ally. Graziani was acutely aware that his Libyan infantry divisions were critically deficient in motor transport, which would constrain their ability to operate other than along the route of the coastal highway. This shortage would also constrain the ability to supply and maintain any major force moving eastwards away from the coastal ports at Tobruk, Derna and Bardia – and of course, the main base at Benghazi.

Aware from good intelligence sources in Egypt that the British strength rested on the 7th Armoured Division and the Indian and New Zealand divisions, he remained ignorant of how under strength these formations were. Consequently, he continued to overestimate the capacity of the forces facing him. He therefore began a long and careful period of administrative build-up, while seeking to improve and strengthen the frontier defences which had been taking such a battering from the harassing attacks of the British mobile forces. Indeed, between 11 June-9 September 1940 Italian casualties would total some 3,500 compared with 150 suffered by the Imperial forces.

Meanwhile however, the weakness of those forces had been having a significant constraining effect on the operations being taken by General Wavell's forces – particularly the mobile armoured elements thereof. So worn had most of 7th Armoured Division's vehicles become from the constant movement, that he was obliged to advise London that presently his command would not be in a position to resist any major Italian offensive.

Consequently, harassing attacks on the increasingly strong defences were halted and the bulk of the armour withdrawn to the Matruh area for overhaul and repair. On 13 August Brigadier W.H.E.'Strafer' Gott was ordered to establish a flexible line of operations from Sollum southwards to Maddalena, to be manned only by 7th Armoured Division's Support Group, which was only to undertake delaying tactics should the anticipated offensive commence. Gott's force comprised three motorised infantry battalions, two batteries each of a dozen 25-pounder guns, two batteries of anti-tank guns, a section of medium artillery and detachments of engineers and machine gunners. Distant reconnaissance would continue to be undertaken by the armoured cars of the 11th Hussars.

While Graziani continued to resist pressure to launch an offensive for as long as possible, he simultaneously pressed ahead with his build-up; however, matters finally came to a head on 7 September. On that date Mussolini issued a direct order that an advance should begin two days hence whether the anticipated German invasion of Southern England had begun or not.

For the planned operation, Graziani had formed a mechanical group commanded by Generale Pietro Maletti, which was to operate in a sweeping flank attack to the south, although his infantry divisions were still generally inadequately mobile to be able to provide the full support desirable. Maletti's group would therefore open the drive over the frontier and initially along the coast road. With the British defences thereby breached, the 1ª Blackshirt (23 March) Division, which was fairly mobile, would take over the lead, Maletti then adopting his independent role on the southern flank.

Full support was planned from the Regia Aeronautica. Fighters would maintain patrols over the advancing troops, who would also be aided by the Assalto units. Bombers would concentrate on British forward airfields and landing grounds, and on troop concentrations preparing to resist the Italian moves.

Apart from the mechanised group and 1ª Blackshirts. Generale Mario Berti, commander of 10th Army, also had available the 62ª Marmarica and 63ª Cirene Divisions, giving him a front line strength of five divisions and a tank group of one medium, two mixed and four light tank battalions. In Tobruk was his immediate reserve formed by the 4ª Blackshirt and 64ª Catanzaro Divisions. 5ª Squadra Aerea's strength was about 300 serviceable bombers, fighters and ground-attack aircraft, plus reconnaissance, colonial, transport and coastal types.

Sunday – Tuesday, 1/3 September 1940
On 1 September 80 Squadron's B Flight moved from Sidi Barrani to Sidi Haneish, while two days later 112 Squadron despatched a flight to the former airfield.

Wednesday, 4 September 1940
On this date 2° Stormo CT, rested and re-equipped, returned to action. S.Ten Alfonso Notari and Serg Nadio Monti reported attacking two Blenheims over the frontier, leaving one with an engine on fire.

At 1330 Serg Ernesto Pavan, like the other two pilots a member of 92ª Squadriglia, was scrambled alone from Derna to intercept a pair of 211 Squadron Blenheims. He claimed both shot down, reportedly one member of the crew from one of these bombers baling out and becoming a PoW, whilst the other aircraft was pursued out to sea where Pavan reported that it ditched. He returned with his fighter damaged by return fire.

In fact 12 of 211 Squadron's aircraft had been out on a raid on Derna, joined by 12 from 55 Squadron and ten from 113 Squadron. One was lost, 211's commanding officer's L8376 was last seen heading for the coast with one engine stopped. Sqn Ldr Bax then force-landed in the desert in Italian-held territory, upon which the Blenheim was strafed by the attacking fighter. Bax and his crew escaped injury but were captured and became PoWs. A second bomber was forced to land, whilst in a third, a 113 Squadron machine, the pilot, Plt Off J.H.Reynolds, was killed instantly. Flt Sgt John Blair, the observer, grabbed the controls, and despite having had no training as a pilot, took evasive action while the air gunner fought off the attacking fighter. The pair of them then flew the aircraft back some 350 miles to base and landed it successfully; Blair was the recipient of an immediate award of the DFM. Bax's place would be taken a few days later by Sqn Ldr J.R.Gordon-Finlayson.

Elsewhere during the day one of 228 Squadron's Sunderlands was attacked by a pair of fighters, but escaped without damage.

British Casualties	
211 Squadron	Blenheim I L8376 Sqn Ldr A.R.G.Bax and crew force-landed; aircraft strafed on ground; crew safe
	Blenheim I L8471 damaged – forced to land with oil leak and several bullet holes in wing and tail; Flt Sgt Marpole and crew safe
113 Squadron	Blenheim IV damaged Pilot, Plt Off J.H.Reynolds KiA, but aircraft resumed base in hands of navigator, Flt Sgt J.Blair

Italian Claims		
92ª Sq/ 2° St CT	S.Ten Alfonso Notari	
	Serg Nadio Monti	Blenheim damaged
	Serg Ernesto Pavan	2 Blenheims
Italian Casualties		
92ª Sq/ 2° St CT	CR 42 damaged by return fire; Serg Ernesto Pavan safe	

Thursday – Friday, 5/6 September 1940

Ten S.79s of 10° Stormo BT raided Mersa Matruh on Thursday, but this was the unit's last operation in Africa. Next day it was learned that it was to be replaced by 9° Stormo BT (*see box for composition*). This unit landed at Castel Benito on the 6th, but remained there for three days before flying to Derna-El Feteiah on the 10th where on arrival it was bombed by British raiders. Next day the unit was finally operational. On 15 September, meanwhile, 10° Stormo returned to its home base at Viterbo, after having handed over its nine serviceable S.79s to 14°, 15° and 33° Stormi. On 6 September, meantime, an S.79 of 60ª Squadriglia, flown by Ten Pastorelli was hit by Gladiators over Mersa Matruh but managed to regain its base; two Gladiators were claimed shot down in return by 15° Stormo gunners.

9° Stormo BT (Derna) S.79	Col Mario Aramu
26° Gruppo	T.Col Italo Napoleoni
11ª Squadriglia	Ten Giovanni Ruggiero
13ª Squadriglia	Cap Edvige Pucci
29° Gruppo	T.Col Guglielmo Grandjacquet
62ª Squadriglia	Cap Vincenzo Tedeschi
63ª Squadriglia	Cap Victor Hugo Girolami

Italian Claims		
15° St BT	Bomber Gunners	2 Gladiators
Italian Casualties		
60ª Sq /33° Gr BT	S.79 damaged Ten Pastorelli, 5 crew wounded	

Sunday, 8 September 1940

5ª Squadra was reinforced by the arrival from Caselle of 30 CR.42s of 151° Gruppo CT, led by Magg Carlo Calosso, the new unit arriving at Castel Benito on this date. (*see box*) From here it moved forward to El Adem, ready for the offensive which was due to commence next day.

151° Gruppo CT (El Adem) CR.42	Magg Carlo Calosso
366ª Squadriglia	Cap Bernardino Serafini
367ª Squadriglia	Cap Simeone Marsan
368ª Squadriglia	Cap Bruno Locatelli

Monday, 9 September 1940

On 9 September the first movement of 10th Army's offensive began on the coastal road, although with a high degree of caution. Air activity at once increased, with large formations reported as up to 100 fighters appearing over the front, while raids on British airfields and troop positions were frequently made. In response the Blenheims of 55, 113 and 211 Squadrons were at once sent out to attack the Regia Aeronautica's airfields, together with transport groupings and supply dumps. 21 aircraft raided the main airfield at Tobruk, 27 CR 42s being seen over Buq Buq, although these did not engage.

The Imperial forces at once prepared to meet a sweeping turning movement from the south, but in doing so they over estimated the Italians' transport availability and desert worthiness, no such thrust developing. Indeed, when Generale Malettis's group moved up on the 11th to try something of this sort, its drivers became lost on their way to the assembly position at Sidi Omar. In consequence Graziani placed the group back under the control of Generale Berti, the force being ordered to co-operate instead with the coastal advance.

Tuesday, 10 September 1940

The first aerial clash following the start of the offensive occurred when S.79s bombed Sidi Barrani, Sollum and Mersa Matruh. 12 Gladiators from 80 Squadron, a pair of 274 Squadron Hurricanes, and two of 30 Squadron's Blenheim fighters intercepted at around 1400 hours. Flg Off John Lapsley in one of the Hurricanes claimed two S.79s shot down to add to his recent successes against these bombers, thus becoming the first RAF pilot to have claimed five aerial victories in the Middle East. He and another pilot had flown up for a brief attachment to 112 Squadron. This combat was certainly not without its excitements for him, for while making his attacks, a bullet from one of the bombers totally shattered the windscreen of his aircraft.

Meanwhile, a third S.79 was claimed by 80 Squadron's Flg Off Stukey, while Flt Lt Marlow of 30 Squadron claimed another bomber, Plt Off Jarvis of the same squadron adding claims for one more probably destroyed and one damaged over the sea to the north-west of Sidi Barrani.

Two S.79s from 33° Stormo BT were actually lost to the fighters, which appear to have indulged in some double-claiming on this occasion. These 46ª Squadriglia aircraft were flown by Ten Felice Scandone and S.Ten Alfonso Magliacane. Returning gunners in the surviving bombers claimed two Gladiators shot down and two more probably so.

Another S.79, this one the aircraft of the commanding officer of 9° Stormo BT, Col Mario Aramu, was destroyed on the ground at Derna by a British bombing attack immediately after it had landed.

British Claims

274 Squadron	Flg Off J.A.Lapsley	Hurricane	2 S.79s	Sidi Barrani
80 Squadron	Flg Off V.A.J.Stukey	Gladiator	S.79	Sidi Barrani
30 Squadron	Flt Lt F.A.Marlow	Blenheim IF K7906	S.79	Sidi Barrani
	Plt Off J.A.Jarvis	Blenheim IF K7105	S.79 probable	Sea NW Sidi Barrani
			S.79 damaged	Sea NW Sidi Barrani

Italian Claims

33° St BT	Bomber Gunners	2 Gladiators
	Bomber Gunners	2 Gladiators probable

Italian Casualties

46ª Sq/36° Gr/33° St BT	S.79 MM21730 Ten Felice Scandone and crew FTR
	S.79 MM21194 S.Ten Alfonso Magliacane and crew FTR
9° St BT	S.79 Aircraft of Col Aramu destroyed on the ground by bombs

Wednesday, 11 September 1940

8° Gruppo CT CR.42 pilots escorted three CR 32s over the Sidi Omar-Bir Sheferzen area. After 45 minutes in the air they reported spotting a lone Blenheim which was claimed to have been attacked by at least seven pilots and shot down. No British loss of such an aircraft has been found for this date.

Another single bomber, this one an S.79 of 175ª Squadriglia, a strategic reconnaissance unit which had just been formed at Gambut, had taken off from Tobruk at 0800 to undertake a sortie over Alexandria, flown by Ten Antonio Bilancia. Over the port it was intercepted by Plt Off S.N.Pearce of 30

Squadron who was patrolling in his Blenheim If, L1120. He made four attacks, shooting it down during the last of these at around noon.

The day was also marked by the start of operations by 9° Stormo, which had arrived a few days earlier. Another new arrival at this time was 63° Gruppo OA, its 41ª and 113ª Squadriglia bringing more Ro.37bis army co-operation aircraft to Cyrenaica.

British Claims					
30 Squadron	Plt Off S.N.Pearce	Blenheim IF L1120	S.79 0925-1245		at sea near Alexandria

Italian Claims			
10° Gr CT	Cap Vincenzo Vanni		
	Ten Giuseppe Aurili		
	Serg Magg Leonardo Ferrulli		
	M.llo Omero Alesi	Blenheim	
	Serg Roberto Steppi		
	Serg Narciso Pillepich		
	Serg Domenico Santonocito		

Italian Casualties	
175ª Sq	S.79 Ten Antonio Bilancia and crew FTR Alexandria

Thursday, 12 September 1940

By night Sqn Ldr Hickey, commanding officer of 80 Squadron, attempted to intercept a bomber which was attacking Mersa Matruh. He was able to fire two bursts before the aircraft became illuminated by searchlights, but was unable to ascertain the effect of these.

Friday, 13 September 1940

Early in the morning 10th Army opened a big artillery barrage on Musaid, then occupying the area. From here further heavy fire was then directed onto the airfield and barracks at Sollum (which were empty), troops on motorcycles and in trucks then moving down the highway as though on a ceremonial parade. Delaying fire was directed at the column head by 3rd Coldstream Guards, C and F Batteries of the Royal Horse Artillery, a section of 25/26 Medium Battery, Royal Artillery, a company from 1st King's Royal Rifle Regiment, and a machine-gun company of 1st Royal Northumberland Fusiliers.

As the British force withdrew eastwards, 1ª Blackshirt Division began trickling down the escarpment which marks the frontier, moving towards Sollum. At dusk Ten Emanuele Annoni, flying a 'hack' Caproni Ca.133 (MM60253) of 96ª Squadriglia from Benghazi to El Adem was fired on in error, being forced to land in the desert. However, he managed to get to El Adem next day after repairing the slight damage which his aircraft had suffered.

4° Stormo made two sorties providing cover for the advancing troops. During one of these missions, over the Sidi Omar-Bir Sheferzen area, a clash with Blenheims was reported and one Blenheim was claimed by Serg Magg Leonardo Ferrulli of 91ª Squadriglia (possibly shared with others).

By this date 80 Squadron had consolidated its flights at Sidi Haneish South, while 6 Squadron was ordered to Egypt from Palestine, arriving at Qasaba. In practice, a detachment from this unit had already been operating with 208 Squadron for several weeks.

Italian Claims		
91ª Sq/10° Gr/4° St CT	Serg Magg Leonardo Ferrulli	Blenheim destroyed

Saturday, 14 September 1940

During a fighter sweep Ten Franco Lucchini and Serg Bruno Bartoletti of 90ª Squadriglia CT intercepted a Blenheim which they claimed to have shot down. No RAF losses were recorded.

Returning from a mission over the Bir el Kreigat area in his CR.32, Serg Magg Corrado Sarti of 160ª Sq collided on landing with a Ba.65 parked at T.2. The pilot was injured and the two aircraft were damaged beyond repair.

The commanding officer of the recently-arrived 7° Gruppo Ass, Magg Marcello Fossetta, and M.llo Paolo Montanari took off in two of the new Ba.88s, but their mission failed due to the inadequate performance of these aircraft, which has already been mentioned. Consequently they would soon be withdrawn from front line service.

On the ground the holding operations continued until noon when the British force withdrew to a point just east of Buq Buq. Here reinforcements arrived, including a French motor mobile company. Withdrawals would continue next day to Alam Hamid, and on the 16th to Alam el Dab.

British Casualties

Unspecified unit	Blenheim Damaged

Italian Claims

90ª Sq/10°Gr/4° St CT	Ten Franco Lucchini	}	Blenheim
	Serg Bruno Bartoletti		

Italian Casualties

160ªSq/12°Gr	CR.32 MM4665 Ten Corrado Sarti, InjFA, hit a Ba.65 parked, both a/c W/O
159ªSq/12°Gr	Ba.65 MM75257 hit by Sarti's CR.32, W/O

Sunday, 15 September 1940

In England this was the day on which the greatest number of claims was made by the RAF against the Luftwaffe's attacks, marking the beginning of the end of the day bombing offensive against the country. It also marked the date which caused Adolf Hitler's planned invasion of the United Kingdom to be indefinitely postponed; it would later be chosen as 'Battle of Britain Day', an occasion still celebrated throughout the country.

In North Africa ten S.79s from 46° Gruppo, 10° Stormo BT raided Sidi Barrani where they were met by all available fighters. 80 Squadron had just moved to a landing ground identified by the letter 'Y', located 30 miles west of Shineifa, and from here had commenced a patrol south of Sidi Barrani at 1230. Spotting the approaching Italian bombers at about 1400, the unit's Gladiators attacked one formation of five, claiming damage to one of these. However, Plt Off Cholmeley's fighter was shot down into the sea by return fire and he lost his life when his aircraft sank at once without trace. Six of 112 Squadron's Gladiators were already on patrol at 16,000 feet, 30 miles out to sea when the bombers appeared. The sections of three each attacked a formation of five, two being claimed damaged.

274 Squadron's two Hurricanes were again present, Flg Off Lapsley and Sgt J.H.Clarke each claiming one bomber shot down near Maaten Bagush at 1315, although a bullet from one bomber shot away the mouthpiece of Clarke's flying helmet without injuring him. Flt Lt Marlow and Plt Off Jarvis of 30 Squadron spotted four more, pursuing these for 25 minutes before Marlow was able to claim one shot down north-west of Sidi Barrani, Jarvis adding claims for two more damaged, one of which he thought might possibly have been shot down.

Six S.79s had actually suffered damage during these various attacks, and three of these could not make it back to base. S.Ten Silvio De Francesco and M.llo Rinaldo Berghino of 20ª Squadriglia both landed at Tobruk with two dead and six wounded between them, while Cap Giovanni Masoero of 21ª Squadriglia force-landed at Ponticelli with two dead and two wounded aboard. Gunners claimed a Hurricane, a Blenheim IF and a Gladiator shot down, with a second Gladiator as a probable.

The Assalto units' Ba.65s were in evidence over the front during the day, but fell foul of ground fire. Ten Adriano Visconti of 12° Gruppo Ass had to force-land after his aircraft was hit by machine-gun fire whilst strafing tanks in the Bir Kuggat area. He had managed to regain Italian-held territory before coming down, and was picked up by an infantry unit, subsequently being flown back to Tobruk in a Ro.37.

Ten Mario Burroni of 16° Gruppo Ass also had his Ba.65 hit when attacking armoured cars. He came down in British territory, but was able to cross the lines on foot and regain his base. His damaged aircraft was later destroyed by Italian troops.

British Claims

274 Sqn	Flg Off J.A.Lapsley	Hurricane I	S.79	Maaten Bagush 1315
	Sgt J.H.Clarke	Hurricane I	S.79	Maaten Bagush 1315
80 Sqn	Flt Lt M.T.StJ.Pattle	Gladiator	S.79 damaged	Sidi Barrani 1400
112 Sqn	Plt Off E.T.Banks	Gladiator	S.79 damaged	Sidi Barrani 1400

	Plt Off R.H.Clarke	Gladiator	S.79 damaged	Sidi Barrani 1400
30 Sqn	Flt Lt F.A.Marlow	Blenheim IF K7096	S.79	1350
	Plt Off J.A.Jarvis	Blenheim IF K7105	S.79 probable	1350
	Plt Off J.A.Jarvis	Blenheim IF K7105	S.79 damaged	1350

British Casualties

80 Sqn	Gladiator Plt Off A.H.Cholmely FTR Sidi Barrani area 1400

Italian Claims

46º Gr/10º St BT	Bomber Gunners	Hurricane
	Bomber Gunners	Blenheim IF
	Bomber Gunners	Gladiator
	Bomber Gunners	Gladiator probable

Italian Casualties

21ª Sq/46º Gr/10º St BT	S.79 Damaged Cap Giovanni Masoero force-landed Ponticelli, 2 crew dead, 2 wounded
20ª Sq/46º Gr/10º St BT	2 S.79s Damaged S.Ten Silvio De Francesco and M.llo Rinaldo Berghino both force-landed at Tobruk; 2 crew dead and 6 wounded
46º Gr/10º St BT	3 S.79s damaged
159ª Sq/12º Gr Ass	Ba.65 MM75258 Ten Adriano Visconti force-landed due to ground fire
168ª Sq/16º Gr Ass	Ba 65 MM75148 Ten Mario Burroni force-landed due to ground fire; a/c later destroyed by own forces

Monday, 16 September 1940

During the afternoon a force of 50 tanks and lorried infantry began a more aggressive thrust, moving around the British left flank on the Alem el Dab position. This caused the latter's rearguard to withdraw at once to Sidi Barrani to avoid being cut off. However, the RHA 25-pounder guns then engaged, and the Italian thrust quickly petered out, no more such actions developing. Nonetheless, by nightfall Sidi Barrani had been entered by 1ª Blackshirts.

This clearly brought the first phase of the offensive to its conclusion, but a further move forward was anticipated when logistics had caught up. In the event this was not to happen. Graziani again commenced an administrative build-up, but a visiting German liaison officer reported back to Berlin that unless Mussolini were to issue further direct orders, it appeared unlikely that 10th Army would be ready to proceed further prior to mid December.

Now instead efforts were expended on constructing a string of forts southwards from Maktila and Sidi Barrani where the first two were prepared. Southwards from these locations were Tummar West, Tummar East, Point 90, Nibeiwa, Rabia, and finally Sofafi, 40 miles inland from the coast. Nibeiwa was typical, measuring 2,400 yards by 1,800 yards, and it was at this location that Generale Maletti's group was based.

As the British had withdrawn, they had destroyed much of the road from Sidi Barrani to the frontier, and had rendered the local water supply undrinkable. It had been realised that the Italians would be unlikely to move further east without ensuring that they had a metalled road from their base of operations, and a water pipeline in place. The unwillingness to operate in the open desert was readily admitted in 10th Army's subsequent intelligence summary detailing the recent offensive which was issued on 19 October. This stated: "As is well-known, the enemy has units more manoeuvrable in the desert than ours."

Two S.79s of 60ª Squadriglia of 33º Gruppo Autonomo were sent off on a strafing mission south-east of Sollum, flown by the commanding officer, Cap Loris Bulgarelli, and Ten Giovanni Roggero. Here they were mistakenly attacked by CR.42s which shot down Roggero's plane, killing the entire crew.

Italian Casualties

60ª Sq/33º Gr	S.79 MM21413 destroyed Ten Giovanni Roggero and crew killed by 'friendly fire'

Tuesday, 17 September 1940

The first of the Royal Navy's new generation of armoured aircraft carriers, HMS *Illustrious*, had arrived to join the Mediterranean Fleet at the start of September, initially undertaking a strike on Rhodes in company with HMS *Eagle* (see *Air War for Yugoslavia, Greece and Crete, 1940-41*). On return to Alexandria the air group began preparing for a strike to be launched in support of the forces ashore,

A successful torpedo action was carried out on 17 September 1940 by a couple of S.79s of 278ª Squadriglia AS flown by Ten Carlo Emanuele Buscaglia and Ten Guido Robone.

withdrawing before the Italian advance into Egypt. The group included the Fairey Fulmar fighters of 806 Squadron and two squadrons of the ubiquitous Swordfish, 815 and 819. On 15 September the ship sailed to launch a strike on Benghazi as a diversion to a planned bombardment of Bardia by cruisers. The attacking aircraft took off just after midnight on the night of the 16/17th.

Armed only with 250lb bombs instead of torpedoes on this occasion, nine 815 Squadron Swordfish dive-bombed the harbour while 819 Squadron's six aircraft all laid mines in the harbour entrance, apparently unobserved by the defenders whose attention was focussed on the dive-bombers. The latter, given the relatively small bombs they were carrying, were surprisingly successful, initially hitting the steamer *Gloriastella* (5,940 tons) and the torpedo-boat *Cigno*. The tug *Salvatore Primo* and the crane pontoon *Giuliana* were damaged, following which the destroyer *Borea* and the steamer *Maria Eugenia* (4,702 tons) were also hit, *Borea* being sunk and *Maria Eugenia* left ablaze. During the day which followed, a second Italian destroyer, *Aquilone*, struck one of the mines laid by 819 Squadron and sank as a result.

Meanwhile, Blenheims were also playing their part, bombing Benina airfield where three S.79s of 33° Stormo which were under repair, were destroyed. At the same time the gunboat HMS *Ladybird* shelled the escarpment road above Sollum from close range, while destroyers engaged targets in the Sidi Barrani area.

Attempts to bombard Bardia came to naught however, when the cruiser HMS *Kent* was struck on the stern by one of two air-launched torpedoes dropped by two S.79s of 278ª Squadriglia AS. This unit had been formed at El Adem as recently as 4 September from the nucleus provided by the Reparto Sperimentale Aerosilurante, which it will be recalled had arrived at this airfield during the previous month. The two S.79s, which took of at 2155 from El Adem, flown by Ten Carlo Emanuele Buscaglia (who would become one of most successful Italian torpedo-bomber pilots) and Ten Guido Robone, released their torpedoes almost simultaneously at the cruiser at 2245. In the dim moonlight they weren't able to ascertain which one actually hit the target. Three pilots of 4° Stormo (also based at El Adem) were aboard the torpedo-bombers as observers: Ten Giuseppe Aurili and Ten Ezio Viglione Borghese were on Buscaglia's plane and Ten Aldo Gon on Robone's.

Protected by RAF fighters, *Kent* made harbour two days later, but she had been so badly damaged that she was unfit for any further service in the Mediterranean. This was a blow as she was at the time the only eight-inch gun cruiser allocated to the Mediterranean Fleet, and a second such, HMS *York*, would not arrive for another week.

A patrol of Cant.Z.501s flying boats of 141ª Squadriglia RM. The upper wing surfaces had the red stripes that Sub Lt Stanley Orr described as like the rising sun.

Although Imperial losses had been kept very low during the withdrawal, being deprived of the forward airfields was to be felt by all the three services. With Sidi Barrani and its surrounding area now in Italian hands the RAF fighters were at bases 100 miles back, which significantly reduced the time they could spend over the front line area. To reach Benghazi, the Blenheims now had to operate at maximum range. Should Malta again have a desperate need for fighter reinforcement, Hurricanes with long-range tanks could no longer make the flight there from Egypt, and would have to go instead by ship from one end of the Mediterranean or the other.

Until now Royal Navy warships bombarding Bardia or Tobruk had been able to rely upon fighter cover. Now this could not realistically be provided even as far as Sidi Barrani, while Derna was too far for land-based Fleet Air Arm aircraft to attack. In contrast, however, Regia Aeronautica bombers could not expect fighter escort as far as the RAF's advanced bases at Mersa Matruh.

The problem of bombing Benghazi was about to be ameliorated, however, for during the month the first Vickers Wellington medium/heavy bombers arrived at Heliopolis to begin re-equipping 70 Squadron. Indeed, the first raid on Benghazi harbour was to be undertaken by these aircraft during the night of 18/19 September. 70's elderly Valentia transports were now all concentrated into the unit's C Flight and were moved to Habbaniyah in Iraq, where on 5 October the flight would become a part of 216 Squadron.

The increasingly successful defence of the United Kingdom at this time was in no small part due to the warning and control system, aided by radar. Now here in the Middle East air defence was beginning to prove an increasing problem with the Regia Aeronautica closer to Alexandria and the Canal Zone.

Until now the system had relied largely upon observation posts in the Western Desert, but these had now been driven back and were having to find new locations. Even by the end of September there were no fixed radar stations anywhere in the area, and only a few mobile sets. The latter were spread between Egypt, the Sudan, Palestine, Aden and Kenya. In Egypt they were too far apart and of too limited a performance to provide other than a general indication of incoming attacks. As a consequence, interceptions were infrequent and uncertain in their effect.

The defence of the very important naval base at Alexandria was in the hands of 252 (Fighter) Wing at Mex, with sector stations at Amiriya and Helwan. Here the biggest problem was obtaining warning of low-level torpedo, bombing or mining attacks. The wing's establishment of units was variable, depending very much on the requirements of the front. It also included two Gladiator squadrons of the Royal Egyptian Air Force, whose willingness to take part in interceptions remained extremely questionable. This was thus the situation as the war entered its next period of static operations.

The crew of Sqn Ldr G.L.Menzies' 228 Squadron Sunderland, engaged in a reconnaissance from Malta to Aboukir in Egypt, encountered and attacked a Cant. Z.501 midway through their flight, claiming this shot down. At 1100 on this date a trio of Fairey Fulmar fighters forming White Section of 806 Squadron from HMS *Illustrious*, also encountered such an aircraft, which was claimed shot down by Sub Lt Stanley Orr. He described it as being painted with "orange and red stripes like…rising sun", reporting that following his attack it started to climb and then slowly span down into the sea.

Two Cant.Z.501s were indeed lost on this date. The first, an aircraft of 145ª Squadriglia based at Benghazi, failed to return from a reconnaissance sortie during the morning, S.Ten Raniero Callori di Vignale and Serg Icaro Cappellini and their crew all being reported missing. The second, from 143ª Squadriglia based at Menelao, flown by S.Ten Renato Balestrero and Serg Giuseppe Borghese, was forced to land on the open sea by air attack. The crew were later picked up by a British ship and became PoWs. The latter aircraft would appear to have been that shot down by Stanley Orr.

British Claims

228 Sqn	Sqn Ldr G.L.Menzies and crew		Cant.Z.501	over sea between Malta and Egypt
806 Sqn	Sub Lt S.G.Orr	Fulmar N1879	Cant.Z.501	over sea

British Casualties

211 Sqn	Blenheim L6660 crash-landed at base after being hit by AA over Sidi Barrani

Italian Casualties

145ª Sq RM	Cant.Z.501 MM35454 S.Ten Raniero Callori di Vignale and crew MiA
143ª Sq RM	Cant.Z.501 MM35348 S.Ten Renato Balestrero and crew PoWs

Wednesday, 18 September 1940

Late in the afternoon three 13º Gruppo CT CR.42s flown by Ten Guglielmo Chiarini and Serg Franco Porta of 82ª Squadriglia, and Serg Magg Leone Basso of 77ª Squadriglia, took off from Tmimi en route for Gambut. After five minutes in the air they reported spotting nine Blenheims of 113 Squadron on their way to attack Tmimi. The latter released their bombs on the target, but were then engaged by the fighters, Chiarini and Basso claiming all three aircraft of the leading vic shot down. Porta then claimed a fourth from the next vic, and a fifth was considered to have been a probable shared among all participating pilots. The three victorious pilots then landed their Fiats, all of which had been damaged by return fire. They would all be awarded the Medaglia d'Argento.

RAF records indicate that only one loss was suffered during this engagement, a Blenheim IV going down in flames, from which Sqn Ldr Gerald Keily managed to bale out, although the other two members of his crew were killed; Keily survived as a PoW. Returning crews claimed one of their assailants shot down and a second possibly so. Two more Blenheims were damaged, but not seriously. A further pair which had been sent to the Benghazi area with orders to record the results of the attack on Benina, were chased off by fighters.

British Claims

113 Squadron	Bomber Gunners	CR.42 shot down and one more possibly	Tmimi

British Casualties

113 Squadron	Blenheim IV T2048 Sqn Ldr G.B.Keily, DFC AFC, baled out and PoW; two crew KIA Tmimi

Italian Claims

82ª Sq/13º Gr CT	Serg Franco Porta	Blenheim	Tmimi
	Ten Guglielmo Chiarini	Blenheim	Tmimi
77ª Sq/13º Gr CT	Ten Guglielmo Chiarini Serg Magg Leone Basso }	Blenheim	Tmimi
	Serg Magg Leone Basso	Blenheim	Tmimi
13º Gr CT		Blenheim Probable	Tmimi

Italian Casualties

82ª Sq/13º Gr CT	CR 42 damaged Ten Guglielmo Chiarini's aircraft hit by bombers' return fire, Tmimi
	CR 42 damaged Serg Franco Porta's aircraft hit by bombers' return fire, Tmimi
77ª Sq/ 13º Gr CT	CR 42 damaged Serg Magg Leone Basso's aircraft hit by bombers' return fire, Tmimi
Unspecified unit	S.81 under repair destroyed on the ground at Benina

Friday, 20 September 1940

8° Gruppo CT had now moved to Menastir, from where 37 CR.42s escorted S.79s to Mersa Matruh. Two pilots of 92ª Squadriglia reported attacking three Blenheims, S.Ten Vittorio Muratori claiming one probably shot down after two head-on attacks. During the return flight Serg Ernesto De Bellis claimed a Sunderland flyingboat shot down: no RAF losses relating to either type of aircraft have been discovered for this date.

Roald Dahl, later to become famous as an author of children's books, had just completed his training as a pilot and been posted to 80 Squadron. He was given the task of ferrying a replacement Gladiator, K7911, from 102 Maintenance Unit as he set out to join his new unit. Unfortunately, unfamiliar with flying over the desert, he became lost and had to make a force-landing two miles west of Mersa Matruh. The aircraft burst into flames and he was badly burned, being evacuated to an army field ambulance station. Consequently it would be April 1941 before he was again fit for operational flying, when he flew out a replacement Hurricane to 33 Squadron, then in Greece. (See *Air War for Yugoslavia, Greece and Crete*.)

Italian Claims

92ª Sq/8° Gr CT	S.Ten Vittorio Muratori	Blenheim probable	Mersa Matruh
	Serg Ernesto De Bellis	Sunderland	

Sunday, 22 September 1940

Strong Assalto patrols were undertaken by 50° Stormo Ass, five Ba.65s of 159ª Squadriglia, four of 168ª Squadriglia, six CR.32s of 160ª Squadriglia and six more from 167ª Squadriglia, strafing British vehicles and troops near Bir Shegga. 21 CR.42s from 8° Gruppo CT and 25 from 4° Stormo CT escorted 40 S.79s to attack Mersa Matruh, but during an RAF raid several of 2° Stormo CT's CR.42s were damaged on the ground at Menastir. Two days later 10° Gruppo CT withdrew to Berka airfield at Benghazi to rest and reorganise; the unit would remain there for nearly two months. Unfortunately, as the unit's motor convoy approached this destination a few days later, a trailer containing all the logbooks, diaries etc of 84ª Squadriglia, caught fire and all these records were lost.

This Ro.37bis reconnaissance plane of 137ª Squadriglia OA (MM 11236) was damaged by bombs at Sollum on 26 September 1940 and later repaired by the El Adem workshop.

Wednesday, 25 September 1940

Blenheims of 113 and 211 Squadrons raided Tobruk at 1420, but were intercepted by three CR.42s of 82ª Squadriglia, 13° Gruppo CT, S.Ten Gilberto Cerofolini, Serg Franco Porta and Serg Luigi Giannotti claiming two bombers shot down from the second section, with a third damaged. Again, all three pilots would receive the Medaglia d'Argento. Two Blenheims of 113 Squadron were damaged. Reportedly, 211

Squadron's L8523 suffered an engine fire during the return flight and subsequently crash-landed west of Qasaba, damaged beyond repair. Sqn Ldr J.Gordon-Finlayson, DFC, and his crew escaped unhurt.

British Casualties	
113 Sqn	2 Blenheims damaged over Tobruk by CR.42s
211 Squadron	Blenheim I L8523 crash-landed at Qasaba, damaged beyond repair; Sqn Ldr J.Gordon-Finlayson DFC, and crew safe
Italian Claims	
82ª Sq/13º Gr CT	S.Ten Gilberto Cerofolini
	Serg Franco Porta } 2 Blenheims shot down and one damaged
	Serg Luigi Giannotti

Thursday, 26 September 1940

The first four Blenheims and five Hurricanes to have completed the many stages of the flight from West Africa to Egypt, arrived at Abu Sueir on this date. Blenheims bombed Sollum airfield where a Ro.37bis was destroyed and two more damaged.

Italian Casualties	
137ª Sq OA	Ro 37bis destroyed on the ground by bombs
	2 Ro 37bis damaged on the ground by bombs

Friday, 27 September 1940

Blenheims undertook a raid on the Giarabub area during the day, 14 of these bombers being reported by the pilots of seven CR.42s which were providing cover to Italian troops. Six of the fighters were from 97ª Squadriglia, 9º Gruppo CT, the seventh being flown by Ten Mario Ferrero of 366ª Squadriglia, who was on a temporary attachment to 4º Stormo CT.

Serg Franco Sarasino, standing before his weary CR.42 of 82ª Squadriglia, 13º Gruppo, 2º Stormo CT. Sarasino (then transferred to 97ª Squadriglia) shared a Blenheim claim on 27 September 1940.

Cap Antonio Larsimont Pergameni, commanding officer of 97ª Squadriglia, with S.Ten Giovanni Barcaro and Serg Franco Sarasino, attacked an aircraft on the right of the British formation, seeing it crash into the ground. Ten Ezio Viglione Borghese, Ten Riccardo Vaccari and Serg Angelo Golino attacked one on the left, chasing it 50 miles deeper into Egypt and reporting that finally it was shot down. A third bomber was considered to be a probable, while the 'visitor', Ferrero, was also credited with sharing in the destruction of one of these aircraft.

Yet again, RAF records do not support this level of execution. It was reported that two Blenheims of 55 Squadron were strafing troops when one was shot down near Gambut, Plt Off Goodrich and his crew all being lost. The gunner, Sgt W.H.Thompson, managed to bale out, and his footprints were later discovered near the crash site, but he was not found; Goodrich and his navigator, Sgt W.C.Clarke, were killed in the crash. The crew of the returning aircraft claimed a CR.42 shot down.

British Claims			
55 Sqn	Bomber Gunners	Blenheim	CR.42 near Giarabub at 1345
British Casualties			
55 Sqn	Blenheim I L8394 Plt Off A.S.B.Goodrich and crew KIA/MiA, 43 miles NW Giarabub, 1345		
Italian Claims			
97ª Sq/9° Gr CT	Cap Antonio Larsimont Pergameni		
	S.Ten Giovanni Barcaro	} Blenheim	
	Serg Franco Sarasino		
	Ten Ezio Viglione Borghese		
	Ten Riccardo Vaccari	} Blenheim	
	Serg Angelo Golino		
366ª Sq CT	Ten Mario Ferrero	share in one of the above	
97ª Sq/9° Gr CT		Blenheim Probable	

Saturday, 28 September 1940
Blenheims of 55 Squadron attacked Sidi Barrani, escorted by three Gladiators and the two MS 406s of the Free French Flight attached to 274 Squadron. This was to be the only front line operation undertaken by these Moranes, for that evening the flight was ordered to Haifa in Palestine to commence training and re-equipment with Hurricanes.

Sunday, 29 September 1940
During the 28th the Mediterranean Fleet had sortied to escort a convoy to Malta. The battleships HMS *Warspite* and *Valiant* were accompanied by the recently-arrived new armoured Fleet aircraft carrier, HMS *Illustrious*, which had brought the Royal Navy's new fighter, the Fairey Fulmar, to the area. Also present were the cruisers HMS *Orion* and *York*, and HMAS *Sydney*, plus 11 destroyers. At sea the battlefleet was joined by two more cruisers, HMS *Liverpool* and *Glasgow*, and 1,200 troops, some airmen and RAF stores were carried to the island. There were frequent air raids, and aerial 'shadowing', the Fulmars disposing of three of the latter for one loss. (See *Malta: The Hurricane Years.*)

An S.79 of 14° Stormo BT, with an unusual locally-applied camouflage.

Four S.79s of 278ª Squadriglia AS (the whole strength of this unit) took off at 1425, led by commanding officer Magg Vincenzo Dequal. Torpedoes were launched by all the pilots, who claimed a hit on the convoy's last but one ship, but their claim wasn't confirmed.

Apparently the Regia Aeronautica also claimed three "carrier Hurricanes" shot down (clearly claims against attacking Fulmars). An S.79 of 62ª Squadriglia flown by Cap Antonio Caprini was lost to AA fire north of Sidi Barrani (i.e. over the sea), all members of the crew being killed. Gunners in other bombers in this formation claimed two British fighters in return. It seems that the third claim may have been made by the crew of a "shadowing" Cant.Z.501, and it was to such an aircraft that the only Fulmar actually to be lost during the day, fell. However, although Sub Lt Lowe's aircraft went down into the sea, the rest of Sub Lt G.A.Hogg's section reported sending down the Cant.Z.501 in flames at 1124. A second was claimed three hours later by Sub Lt Stanley Orr of White Section – both appear to have been aircraft of 143ª Squadriglia RM. Lowe and his observer, Ldg Air P.Douet, were picked up by the destroyer HMAS *Stuart*.

One of 208 Squadron's Lysanders whilst undertaking a TacR sortie over the Sofafi-Khamsa-Qatrani area attacked two columns of 60 open trucks with 20lb bombs, believing that four had been damaged. However, L4711 was then hit by AA fire (described by the unit as pom-pom fire), and was damaged. It seems the damage was severe enough to cause the aircraft to be written off, as it is listed as destroyed on that date.

British Claims

806 Sqn	Sub Lt G.A.Hogg	Fulmar	Cant.Z.501	over sea between Alexandria and Malta; 1124
	Sub Lt S.G.Orr	Fulmar N1879	Cant.Z.501	over sea between Alexandria and Malta; 1425

British Casualties

806 Sqn	Fulmar N1877 Sub Lt I.L.F.Lowe/L/A P.R.L.Douet shot down by return fire into sea; rescued safely
208 Sqn	Lysander L4711 hit and damaged by AA fire, and apparently written off; Flt Lt Black and Sgt Dixon safe

Italian Casualties

62ª Sq/29°Gr/9°St BT	S.79 MM22137 Cap Antonio Caprini, hit by AA fire
143ª Sq RM	Cant.Z.501 MM35473 Magg Nicola Covacovich, MiA
	Cant.Z.501 MM35504 S.Ten Ugo Leardi, MiA

Monday, 30 September 1940

Seven Blenheims from 113 Squadron raided Tobruk, but again this formation was intercepted by a trio of CR.42s from 78ª Squadriglia, 13° Gruppo CT as they turned for home. One bomber was claimed by Ten Giovanni Beduz, who then shared in claiming another with Serg Magg Ezio Masenti; a third was seen to leave trailing smoke.

Once more the damage was limited to one Blenheim, T2171 falling into the Mediterranean as it left the target at Maraua at 1345, Sgt L.Carter and his crew being lost. Other crews returned to claim one fighter shot down into the sea and two damaged from a reported 15 which they believed had attacked them!

Damage on the ground at Maraua had on this occasion been quite considerable. Two of 15° Stormo BT's S.79s were written off, two were badly damaged and had to be sent away for repair, and four more were damaged to a lesser degree. Additionally, four pilots and two airmen were mortally wounded. As a result, the unit was permitted a rest period in Tripoli.

During the day Sqn Ldr P.H.Alington and his crew of 230 Squadron while on patrol in Sunderland L2166, attacked and claimed to have sunk an Italian submarine. This appears to have been *Gondar*, which went down off Alexandria reportedly due to attack by both aircraft and ships. She was carrying SLC manned torpedoes ('maiali') intended for another attempt to attack Royal Navy Fleet units in harbour.

British Claims

113 Squadron	Bomber Gunners	1 CR.42 and 2 damaged

British Casualties

113 Squadron	Blenheim IV T2171 Sgt L.Carter and crew KiA, Maraua

78ª Sq/13° Gr CT	Ten Giovanni Beduz	Blenheim
	Ten Giovanni Beduz	} Blenheim
	Serg Magg Ezio Masenti	Blenheim damaged

Italian Casualties

| 53ª Sq/47° Gr/15° St BT | S.79 MM22192 destroyed on ground, four pilots and two airmen dead |
| | 4 S.79s MM22286, 22194, 22285, 22299 badly damaged on ground |

OCTOBER 1940

October was to see the beginnings of some fairly substantial re-equipment and reinforcement of Middle East Command generally. The RAF had been struck hard by a decision of 5 September to suspend all deliveries of Hurricanes due to the losses of these aircraft being suffered at that time in the UK. However, the improving situation there during October, and the reducing threat of imminent invasion as autumn approached with its adverse weather in the English Channel, meant that during the month deliveries were to recommence, and 33 Squadron was able to proceed with the programme of re-equipment begun during the previous month.

On 1 October Sqn Ldr Charles Ryley led nine Hurricanes up to Fuka, the other half of the unit then withdrawing to receive their new aircraft. This also allowed the Gladiators which were being cast off to be passed to 3 RAAF Squadron to augment that unit's elderly Gauntlets. By the 19th 33 Squadron had 16 operational Hurricanes on hand with four more in reserve, and on the 22nd four pilots flew up to Bir Kanayis to take part in a planned raid.

Plans were now afoot to increase overall RAF striking power without a commensurate increase in administrative personnel by the simple expedient of raising the establishment of the bomber squadrons from 12 to 16 aircraft, and of the Sunderland squadrons to six flyingboats each.

With the effective closure of the Mediterranean to most supply shipping, it had become vital to organise a massive reinforcement effort around the southern tip of Africa, and for this all available large liners were dedicated to the task. Because the speed of these vessels provided their greatest protection against U-Boat attacks – which were, of course, much more prevalent in the Atlantic than in the Indian Ocean – it became necessary to off-load their cargoes at Cape Town or Durban in South Africa. From there these had then to be re-shipped in such other merchant vessels as could be gathered in order to complete the voyages to East Africa, southern Egypt or Palestine.

Such slower vessels were also frequently required to sail between these countries and India, Australia or New Zealand, bringing reinforcements and supplies from these distant and diverse locations. This vast use of shipping tonnage was having an adverse effect upon the delivery of imports of vital materials to the UK, particularly from the western side of the Atlantic. Consequently it became very desirable to ensure that vessels returning from the Middle or Far East should carry whatever stores could be obtained from these areas, rather than simply making the return voyage in ballast.

The effect of this massive seaborne effort was to increase quite rapidly the available strength of army units in the area. By early December arriving units – or those about to arrive – would include 2nd Armoured Division, 5th Indian Division, 7th Australian Division and a further brigade group for the New Zealand Division, while 1st South African Division had been delivered to East Africa. With reinforcements for the existing units which were already present, plus necessary administrative troops, RAF and Royal Naval personnel, this amounted to a total of some 126,000 men plus a major part of their equipment, including vehicles, both armoured and 'soft skinned'.

October proved to be the month of the Wellington, for 23 more of these bombers flew out in the form of two existing squadrons from the UK. 37 Squadron came via Malta, where its aircraft were held until December, while 38 Squadron flew in to Ismailia.

Meanwhile the British Purchasing Commission which had been sent to the United States to acquire war materials, had commenced by taking over orders which had been placed by France and Belgium, but which the German occupation of those countries had rendered null and void. Of these, air ministry allocated to the Middle East in the first instance 227 Curtiss Mohawk fighters, while increasing the number of Glenn Martin 167F attack bombers from the initial 75 to 149.

Obviously, if these could be delivered directly to the Middle East by US shipping, the demands on the British Merchant Navy referred to above, could be ameliorated a little. However, due to the fighting in East Africa, the US president, Franklin D.Roosevelt, had designated the Red Sea and its approaches a war zone into which US shipping was not permitted to sail. Therefore, until the Italian presence in this area could be pacified, any such US deliveries had to be made to the West African ports. This would require the erection and testing of these aircraft to be undertaken there, followed by the long, arduous flight across the reinforcement route to Egypt via the Sudan. The latter had the double disadvantage of eating up flying hours also, reducing the period until overhaul was necessary.

In the event the first Glenn Martin – to be dubbed Maryland in RAF service – was not erected at Takoradi until 12 December. Therefore any deliveries of these aircraft would not occur until the new year in any event. Five days later came a big disappointment when the first four Mohawks became ready for testing. These proved to have such serious defects in their Wright Cyclone engines that it became impracticable to issue them to Middle East operational units. They were sent instead to India and South Africa for advanced training use, although a small number were to see some limited first line service in East Africa later in 1941 (see *Dust Clouds in the Middle East*). Use of American-built fighter aircraft would have to await the arrival of the Curtiss Hawk 81 – also from ex-French orders – when supplies of these could arrive.

The greatest concern of commanders in the Middle East at this time was that Germany might come to the aid of her ally, now that an early invasion of Southern England appeared less likely at least until late in the spring of 1941. Their concern was to prove all too well-founded in the event.

During recent weeks the RAF bomber force in Egypt had been further strengthened by the arrival from Shaibah in Iraq of 84 Squadron with Blenheim Is. This squadron had flown to Heliopolis during September, and would despatch its B Flight to Fuka and C Flight to Qotaifiya for operations during October and November. October was to see an increasing strength of attack by the Blenheim squadrons, sometimes now operating at wing strength.

Also at Heliopolis a new squadron had been formed on 19 August from the airfield's Communications Flight. 267 Squadron's main duties were to be the delivery of mail and the carriage of VIPs, and for these purposes its initial equipment included examples of the Proctor I, Anson I, Magister I, Hudson I, Hind, Vega Gull and Percival Q6.

Tuesday, 1 October 1940
During the day 80 Squadron's B Flight flew to Bir Kenayis on detachment with six Gladiators. This landing ground was located 40 miles south-west of Mersa Matruh on the road to Siwa. In the course of the month the squadron would exchange the remaining Gladiator Is still on strength, but now considerably worn, for Mark IIs, bringing the whole unit up to establishment on these fighters.

Wednesday, 2 October 1940

Italian Casualties

| 115ª Sq OA | Ca.310B MM20953 Serg Ido Baldasso crashed into the sea during transfer flight |
| | Ca.310B MM21767 written off due to flying accident |

Thursday, 3 October 1940
Within 252 Wing Wg Cdr J.S.T.Fall had been promoted Grp Capt on 23 September, and now in this more senior rank was posted to Helwan for other duties.

Saturday, 5 October 1940
20 S.79s from 9° Stormo BT, escorted by seven CR.42s, launched a raid on Mersa Matruh at 1350. Only Flg Off H.D.W. Flower of 80 Squadron was able to intercept, but while he expended all his ammunition at one formation of five bombers, he was unable to close the range and saw no results of his fire. 202 Group recorded that one S.79 was seen to leave the formation and was last sighted over the sea apparently badly damaged. The gunners aboard the speeding Savoias claimed to have probably shot down the Gladiator, but Flower's aircraft in fact escaped any damage.

Italian Claims

| 9° St BT | S.79s Bomber Gunners | Gladiator probable | Mersa Matruh |

———

Tuesday, 8 October 1940

At 0715 three CR.32s of 160ª Squadriglia and four Ba.65s of 159ª Squadriglia took off for a strafing attack on targets near Bir Khamsa, the Bredas being led by the commanding officer, Cap Antonio Dell'Oro. Covered by the CR.32s, the Ba.65 pilots dropped their 59 kg and 70 kg bombs on their designated targets, but Dell'Oro's aircraft was then seen to crash into the ground, it was thought a victim of AA fire. This was indeed the case, his aircraft being shot down by fire from a patrol of the 11th Hussars, members of which reported recovering one body from the burnt-out wreckage.

Cap Duilio Fanali, leading the CR.32s, returned later to the location and dropped a message, requesting news of the fallen pilot. A few days later a chivalrous message was delivered by an RAF aircraft, including a photograph of Dell'Oro's funeral with military honours.

After the death of Cap Antonio Dell'Oro on 8 October 1940, on every Ba.65 of 159ª Squadriglia was painted an inscription with his name.

Following the loss of its commander, 159ª Squadriglia was taken over by Ten Roberto Pastorelli. Thereafter each of the unit's aircraft had painted on it an inscription (see photo).

Elsewhere during the day Ten Ranieri Piccolomini of 92ª Squadriglia, 8º Gruppo CT, intercepted two bombers which he identified as Wellingtons, claiming one probably shot down; his CR.42 was hit by return fire and damaged. However the only Wellington unit operational at this time was 70 Squadron, which listed no actions during this period.

Italian Claims				
92ª Sq/8º Gr CT	Ten Ranieri Piccolomini	CR.42		Wellington probable
Italian Casualties				
159ª Sq/12º Gr Ass	Ba.65 MM75169 Cap Antonio Dell'Oro KiA Bir Khamsa			
92ª Sq/8º Gr CT	CR.42 damaged bomber gunners return fire; Ten Ranieri Piccolomini safe			
2ª Sq/45º Gr/14ºSt BT	S.79 MM21796 Ten Stefano Pelo and crew KiFA at Derna			

Wednesday, 9 October 1940

A further claim for a Ba.65 was made next day, this time by one of 80 Squadron's Gladiator pilots, Australian-born Flg Off R.N.Cullen, who had joined the unit on posting from 267 Squadron on 13 September. Cullen was engaged on a lone reconnaissance south of Sidi Barrani when he spotted what he thought to be six Ba.65s. Unseen, he climbed to 2,000 feet above these and then launched a diving attack on the leader's aircraft, which dived away pouring smoke from its engine. Cullen reported that the rest of the formation then turned on him, but he was able to make good his escape unscathed. He was credited with a probable victory, but no losses were recorded on the Italian side.

British Claims				
80 Sqn	Flg Off R.N.Cullen	Gladiator	Ba.65 probable	S Sidi Barrani

Saturday, 12 October 1940

Just before dusk Magg Ernesto Botto, commander of 9º Gruppo CT, and Ten Giulio Reiner of the gruppo's 73ª Squadriglia, spotted three Blenheims from 55 Squadron over El Adem. Botto attacked one bomber which he claimed ditched in the sea, while Reiner claimed a second, then attacking the third until his fuel ran out, claiming this as a probable. He then landed at Buq Buq, being transported back to El Adem by road; his aircraft would be collected next day. The Blenheims in fact all survived these attacks, but all three suffered damage. L8530 was so badly shot-up as to be a write-off. In one of the other aircraft the pilot, Flg Off G.E.P.Green, had been wounded. He was subsequently awarded a DFC for this sortie, having returned with the gun turret hydraulic system and the instrument panel out of action. However, Sgts W.H.Weller and J.McGarry baled out and were posted missing.

Another convoy was being run through to Malta at this time (see *Malta: the Hurricane Years, 1940-41*) and as reported therein HMS *Illustrious*'s Fulmar fighters had shot down a Cant.Z.501 flyingboat of 145ª Squadriglia which was undertaking a reconnaissance sortie east of Malta. Although no survivors had been seen, a message to 201 Group requested a search being instituted, and consequently a Sunderland was despatched to the area by 228 Squadron. After a two-hour search a dinghy was spotted containing three survivors, and a landing was made on the sea to pick them up. It transpired that the pilot had been killed and a gunner wounded; it had not proved possible to extricate the latter, and he had drowned when the aircraft went down. The occupants of the dinghy proved to be the co-pilot, a Serg Magg and a naval observer, all of whom were delivered to Kalafrana.

British Casualties			
55 Sqn	3 Blenheims damaged; L8530 damaged beyond repair and scrapped		
Italian Claims			
9° Gr CT	Magg Ernesto Botto CR.42	Blenheim	El Adem
73ª Sq/9° Gr CT	Ten Giulio Reiner CR.42	Blenheim	El Adem
		Blenheim probable	El Adem
Italian Casualties			
145ª Sq RM	Cant.Z.501 MM35308 MiA; S.Ten Giuseppe Di Giglio and two crew KiA; Serg Magg Firmino Donisotti and GM Oss Antonio Famigliulo survived as PoWs		

Monday, 14 October 1940

According to an Italian report, an S.79 of 63ª Squadriglia was intercepted by British fighters, and suffered severe damage.

During the preceding days the Mediterranean Fleet had been at sea, escorting a supply convoy to Malta, and in the hope of bringing units of the Regia Marina to battle. As the warships were heading back to Alexandria during the evening of the 14th, a single S.79 of 278ª Squadriglia Aerosiluranti flown by Cap Massimiliano Erasi (the new commander of the unit) struck, obtaining a direct hit with a torpedo on the cruiser HMS *Liverpool*, which damaged her severely, tearing off part of her bows. She survived, but had to be towed into harbour.

Italian Casualties	
63ª Sq/29° Gr/9° St BT	S.79 MM21445 seriously damaged by fighters

Tuesday, 15 October 1940

Three of 98ª Squadriglia Ass's Ba.88s took off to strafe armoured cars between Sidi Barrani and Bir Enba, led by Ten Saverio Gostini. En route Ten Luigi Proner's aircraft was shot down in error by the Italian DICAT (anti-aircraft artillery). The gunner, 1° Av Rossetti, managed to bale out, but Proner was killed in the crash.Plt Off D.B.M.Druce of 208 Squadron took off on a lone reconnaissance over

The wreck of a Ba.88 of 76ª Squadriglia, 7° Gruppo. The last action of this unfortunate type of aircraft was carried out on 15 October 1940.

Giarabub in Lysander L4714. The aircraft was spotted close to the ground by three CR.42 pilots of 92ª Squadriglia, 8° Gruppo CT, who were returning from a flight between Sollum and Giarabub. Ten Piccolomini, Serg Nadio Monti and Serg Magg Guglielmo Gorgone all attacked, Piccolomini delivering the 'coup de grace', whereupon the Lysander hit the ground and blew up.

British Casualties

208 Sqn	Lysander L4714* Plt Off D.B.M.Druce KiA Giarabub

Italian Claims

92ª Sq/8° Gr CT	Ten Ranieri Piccolomini CR.42		
	Serg Nadio Monti CR.42	Lysander	Giarabub
	Serg Magg Guglielmo Gorgone CR.42		

Italian Casualties

98ª Sq/7° Gr Ass	Ba.88 shot down by own AA fire; Ten Luigi Proner KiA; 1° av Rossetti baled out safe

*This aircraft has also been listed as L4717.

Wednesday, 16 October 1940
Sunderland P of 230 Squadron picked up the crew of a downed Swordfish.

Thursday, 17 October 1940
A Flight of 80 Squadron now relieved B Flight at Bir Kenayis.

Friday, 18 October 1940
216 Squadron, which was continuing its night attacks on Benghazi, lost another Bombay when L5816 failed to return from such a sortie.

British Casualties

216 Sqn	Bombay L5816 FTR from night raid on Benghazi

Saturday, 19 October 1940
33, 80 and 211 Squadrons set off to undertake a planned major strafing attack on Menastir airfield, but as they did so a heavy sandstorm blew up, and the target area was obscured, the attack having to be abandoned.

Monday, 21 October 1940
Gladiators from 80 Squadron's A Flight strafed motor transport in the Buq Buq-Sollum area with two vehicles being left in flames, damage to several others also being claimed.

Yet more reinforcements reached the Regia Aeronautica on this date, this time with the arrival at Benina from Sicily of 41° Stormo BT (*see box*). During the transfer flight one S.79 was lost in an accident.

During the month an autonomous unit, 114° Gruppo Autonomo BT, had also flown in. Formed from the Gruppo Speciale Bombardamento for long-range operations, it was equipped initially with three S.82s – large tri-motor transport aircraft. These had undertaken their first sorties against airfields in the Alexandria and Port Said areas during the night of 17 October.

41° Stormo BT (Benina) S.79	Col Enrico Pezzi
59° Gruppo	T.Col Emilio Draghelli
232ª Squadriglia	Cap Piero Padovani
233ª Squadriglia	Cap Valdo Meille
60° Gruppo	T.Col Pasquale D'Ippolito
234ª Squadriglia	Cap Mario Curto
235ª Squadriglia	Cap Athos Ammannato

235ª Sq/60º Gr/41º St BT   S.79 MM21097 Ten Carlo Capelli injured, two of crew KiFA

While 80 Squadron's Gladiators engaged in more strafing, three CR.42 pilots from 94ª Squadriglia, 8º Gruppo CT, intercepted a reconnaissance aircraft which they identified as a Wellington, and this was attacked, being credited as shot down by Serg Magg Danilo Billi.

Italian Claims

94ª Sq/8º Gr/2º St CT	Serg Magg Danilo Billi	CR.42	Wellington

CR.32 MM 4666 '160-10', usually flown by Cap Duilio Fanali, recovered on 20 October 1940, after a force-landing in the desert.

Thursday, 24 October 1940
When flying back from Berka airfield where a radio had been installed in his CR.42, S.Ten Carlo Battaglia crashed and was killed; the reason for his loss was not ascertained.

Italian Casualties

73ª Sq/13º Gr CT   CR.42 MM5650 S.Ten Carlo Battaglia KiFA

Friday, 25 October 1940
Blenheims of 55, 84 and 113 Squadrons were sent out to bomb Tobruk again. Three CR.42s were scrambled by 96ª Squadriglia, 9º Gruppo CT, led by Cap Roberto Fassi. Serg Magg Bruno Spitzl remained over El Adem to protect the airfield, while Fassi and S.Ten Carlo Agnelli made for Tobruk where they intercepted two of the bombers at 13,000 ft at 0825, claiming one of these shot down and the second as a probable. It seems that the former was an aircraft of 84 Squadron and the latter from 55 Squadron; 84's B Flight was operating from Fuka with 55 Squadron at this time. The 84 Squadron aircraft had one engine shot out, but the pilot, Sgt Alexander Gordon, and his gunner, Sgt George Furney, were able to fight off their attackers and subsequently to force-land when 45 miles west of Matruh at 0845. The aircraft was later repaired and flown back. The 55 Squadron aircraft had also been damaged, its crew claiming to have shot down one of the attacking CR.42s.

British Claims		
55 Sqn	Blenheim Bomber Gunners	CR.42
British Casualties		
84 Sqn	Blenheim I L8362 Sgt A.Gordon, pilot, forced to land; flown out later	
55 Sqn	Blenheim I damaged	
Italian Claims		
96ª Sq/9º Gr CT	Cap Roberto Fassi CR.42	
	S.Ten Carlo Agnelli CR.42	Blenheim shot down, Blenheim probable Tobruk

Sunday, 27 October 1940

While returning from a raid on Benghazi, Flg Off P.Squires of 113 Squadron became lost, he and his crew abandoning Blenheim T2068 by parachute near Amiriya.

British Casualties	
113 Sqn	Blenheim T2068 abandoned by Flg Off P.Squires and crew near Amiriya when becoming lost on return from a raid

Monday, 28 October 1940

The situation in the Middle East and Mediterranean area changed considerably on 28 October when Mussolini's forces from Albania crossed the border into north-western Greece following his declaration of war against this nation. For the Italians in North Africa this was, initially at least, to have little impact. For the British command however, it created a major dilemma and a completely new scenario of great importance – but one that could only be turned to any advantage at the expense of the Egyptian front.

Italian Casualties	
90ª Sq/10º Gr CT	CR.42 S.Ten Neri De Benedetti landing accident, injured

Tuesday, 29 October 1940

Italian Casualties

Unspecified unit	2 Ro.37bis destroyed on ground at Sollum by bombing

Thursday, 31 October 1940

Over Egypt aerial action erupted violently at the end of the month, seeing 33 Squadron introducing its new Hurricanes into combat with mixed results.

First, however, 80 Squadron's Gladiators escorted Blenheims to Menastir and to other targets 38 miles west of Bardia from 0915 onwards. Little was seen in the air, but the bombing results were considered to be good. It seems that during this attack three S.79s of 63ª Squadriglia, 29º Gruppo, 9º Stormo BT were destroyed on the ground by bombs in the Gambut area, a fourth of these aircraft being badly damaged.

A little later in the morning a major Italian raid began forming up for what was clearly intended to be a most punishing attack on the RAF bases at Mersa Matruh. Ten S.79s of 9º Stormo BT, led by T.Col Italo Napoleoni, commanding officer of 26º Gruppo, 11 of 14º Stormo BT, led by T.Col Alfonso Lidonnici, commander of 44º Gruppo, and five of 33º Gruppo Autonomo BT led by that unit's commander, T.Col Ferri Forte, were provided with an immediate escort of 19 CR.42s of 151º Gruppo Autonomo CT, led by Magg Carlo Calosso, while at higher altitude were 18 more of these fighters from 13º Gruppo CT, led by Cap Giuseppe Dall'Aglio.

Hurricanes of 33 Squadron and six Gladiators of 112 Squadron were scrambled to attack, intercepting the bombers at around 1315. The escorting CR.42 pilots fell on the defenders, making massive claims as they all piled in, many firing at the same British aircraft. Flg Off E.K.Leveille, one of 33 Squadron's Canadian pilots, was seen to shoot down two S.79s, but he was then attacked by four fighters and forced to bale out. Sadly, his parachute failed to open and he was killed instantly on impact with the ground. Flg Off Perry St Quintin, a Southern Rhodesian, claimed one bomber and a second as a probable, but he too was hit by the escorts and he had to carry out a force-landing. The third Hurricane pilot, Flg Off Frankie Holman, escaped, claiming one more S.79 shot down.

At the same time 112 Squadron's Gladiators were making their attack, but Plt Off Duff, who fired on a formation of ten S.79s was at once attacked and was shot down by six escorting CR.42s, and baled out. Flt Lt 'Algy' Schwab, another Canadian, and 2/Lt Smith, a SAAF pilot, turned on the escorts, Schwab

Hurricanes at a desert landing ground. At this stage these newly-arrived aircraft do not carry any squadron code letters, but the identity of that on the ground is either P3725 or P3729, either of which indicate that the unit in question was 33 Squadron.

claiming two of these shot down, but his engine then stopped and he force-landed. Smith was joined at that point by Plt Off Richard Acworth (who had just joined the fight in a seventh Gladiator), the latter claiming another CR.42 shot down. At this point Smith's Gladiator collided with Acworth's and both pilots had to bale out. Meanwhile Flg Offs J.F.Fraser and R.H.Clarke also attacked the bombers, but Clarke was at once shot down and killed by return fire from the three Savoias which he pursued. The engagement had thus cost the RAF seven of the ten fighters involved, with two of the pilots killed.

Regia Aeronautica fighter claims totalled six Gladiators and two probables, plus four Hurricanes (one identified as a 'Supermarine' or 'Spitfire'), plus two probables. The bomber gunners of 14° Stormo BT added further claims for two more Hurricanes, one Gladiator and one probable, for a grand total of 12 and five probables!

The top cover 13° Gruppo pilots appear to have engaged 112 Squadron in the first instance, Cap Domenico Bevilacqua, commander of 77ª Squadriglia, claiming two Gladiators shot down in quick succession. Ten Gianfranco Perversi of 82ª Squadriglia was reported to have rammed or collided with a Gladiator, both aircraft crashing to the ground. This raises the question, did fire from Schwab or Acworth – or both – cause him to come into collision with Smith's aircraft, and if so, did that cause the latter then to collide with Acworth? In the hectic conditions pertaining to this engagement this seems to be a fairly reasonable and logical proposition to advance.

Calosso's 151° Gruppo pilots also made high claims, Cap Bruno Serafini, commander of 366ª Squadriglia, Serg Magg Davide Colauzzi and Serg Mario Turchi each claiming a Hurricane, while Cap Bruno Locatelli, commander of 368ª Squadriglia claimed a Gladiator, two more pilots adding a second. With two more Hurricanes and a Gladiator as probables, 151° Gruppo's initial engagement in North African skies seemed to have been highly profitable.

Italian losses had been relatively modest, two S.79s being shot down and two crash-landing with dead and wounded aboard, both these aircraft subsequently being written off. Three more were seriously damaged, but fighter losses amounted only to the single CR.42.

British Claims

33 Sqn	Flg Off E.K.Leveille	Hurricane P3724	2 S.79s
	Flg Off P.R. St Quintin	Hurricane P3968	S.79
	Flg Off P.R. St Quintin	Hurricane P3968	S.79 probable
	Flg Off F.Holman	Hurricane P3725	S.79
112 Sqn	Flt Lt L.G.Schwab	Gladiator	2 CR.42s
	Plt Off R.A.Acworth	Gladiator	CR.42
	Flg Off J.F.Fraser	Gladiator	S.79 damaged

British Casualties

33 Sqn	2 Hurricanes P3724 & P3968 Flg Off E.K.Leveille KiA; Flg Off P.R.St Quintin force-landed, safe
112 Sqn	Gladiator Flt Lt L.G.Schwab force-landed, safe
	2 Gladiators L7608 & L7622 Plt Off R.A.Acworth and 2/Lt E.R.Smith collided, baled out, safe
	Gladiator Flg Off R.H.Clarke KiA
	Gladiator Plt Off B.B.E.Duff baled out, safe

Italian Claims

77ª Sq/13° Gr CT	Cap Domenico Bevilacqua	CR.42	2 Gladiators
	Serg Ernesto Paolini	CR.42	Gladiator damaged
	Serg Renato Gori	CR.42	Gladiator damaged
	Serg Mario Veronesi	CR.42	Hurricane damaged
	Serg Magg Dante Davico	CR.42	Hurricane damaged
78ª Sq/13° Gr CT	Serg Teresio Martinoli	CR.42	Gladiator
82ª Sq/13° Gr CT	Ten Guglielmo Chiarini	CR.42	} 'Spitfire'
	Serg Francesco Nanin	CR.42	
	Ten Gianfranco Perversi	CR.42	Gladiator (by collision)
366ª Sq/151° Gr CT	Cap Bruno Serafini	CR.42	Hurricane
	Cap Bruno Serafini	CR.42	}
	Serg Roberto Marchi	CR.42	} Gladiator
	S.Ten Carlo Albertini	CR.42	Gladiator probable
368ª Sq/151° Gr CT	Serg Magg Davide Colauzzi	CR.42	Hurricane
	Serg Magg Davide Colauzzi	CR.42	Hurricane probable
	Serg Mario Turchi	CR.42	Hurricane
	Cap Bruno Locatelli	CR.42	Hurricane
	Cap Bruno Locatelli	CR.42	Hurricane probable
14° St BT	Bomber Gunners	S.79s	2 Hurricanes
	Bomber Gunners	S.79s	Gladiator
	Bomber Gunners	S.79s	Gladiator probable

Italian Casualties

63ª Sq/29° Gr/9° St BT	S.79 MM21542	}
	S.79 MM20681	} destroyed on ground by bombs
	S.79 MM22111	}
	S.79 MM22199 damaged on ground by bombs	
82ª Sq/13° Gr CT	CR.42 MM4438 Ten Gianfranco Perversi KiA	
11ª Sq/26° Gr/9° St BT	S.79 MM21851 S.Ten Fulvio Fabiani and crew FTR	
	S.79 MM21437 Ten Roberto di Frassineto and crew FTR *	
14° St BT	2 S.79s crash-landed with dead and wounded aboard; written off	
	3 S.79s damaged	

*The only survivor from the two 9° Stormo bombers was Serg Magg Armando Zambelli, second pilot in di Frassineto's aircraft, who baled out and became a PoW.

As the result of growing concern regarding Italian intentions towards Greece, Anthony Eden, then the British war minister, arrived in the Middle East on 14 October to review the situation. Following his

A Hurricane, probably of 33 Squadron, tests its guns into a solidly-constructed firing butt.

return home, on 29 October Longmore learned of Mussolini's ultimatum to Greece, which had been immediately followed by the crossing of the border from Albania of his forces (see *Air War for Yugoslavia, Greece and Crete, 1940-41*).

November saw the first departures of RAF units from Egypt to Greece. General Wavell and his command were in a quandary. Morally, there was an imperative upon the British to go to the aid of the Greek nation, which had been an ally during the previous war. Always with his eyes open for an opportunity to gain a base for a drive into the so-called 'soft underbelly' of Europe from the south, Winston Churchill was extremely well-disposed to the point of insistence.

However, such an adventure would undoubtedly increase further the potential for a German intervention in the area. This latter threat was very clear to the Greek government, which was reluctant to accept the arrival of any British Empire troops onto their soil – although ready enough to welcome units of the RAF to bolster its own small and diverse air force. (The full story of the RAF's involvement in Greece, and the air war generally there and in Yugoslavia and over Crete, may be found in the companion volume *Air War for Yugoslavia, Greece and Crete, 1940-41*.)

The first unit to go was 30 Squadron with its Blenheim fighters, which flew to Eleusis on 3 November. It was followed three days later by a detachment of six of 70 Squadron's Wellingtons. These commenced operations by day, but immediately lost two of their number to fighters, the survivors flying back to Egypt on the 8th. They were replaced at once by six more – but these were to operate only by night.

Meanwhile the detached flights of the recently-arrived 84 Squadron were recalled to Heliopolis, allowing A Flight to be brought up to strength and despatched to Greece with six Blenheim Is. By the end of the month the whole squadron would be there, joined by 211 Squadron which arrived at Tatoi/Menidi on the 17th.

To provide escort for the Blenheims and defend the RAF's new bases, 80 Squadron with its full complement of Gladiator IIs, moved to Eleusis on 19 November. This, however, was but a start, and to service these far-off bases, 216 Squadron moved a detachment of its Bombays to Tatoi also.

The desert was not left totally denuded of support, however, for even as 80 Squadron was undertaking its final sorties before withdrawal and departure, 3 RAAF Squadron moved up to Gerawla on 2 November with its Gladiators, followed next day by the flight of Gauntlets. The Lysander flight remained

Hurricane I P2643/YK was the personal mount of 274 Squadron's CO, Sqn Ldr Paddy Dunn, as evidenced by the pennant under the cockpit, though he made no claims flying it.

at Helwan where it functioned primarily as a reinforcement pool. The squadron was now intended initially to operate in the close support, rather than the army co-operation role, and would commence undertaking tactical reconnaissance sorties on 13 November.

Meanwhile, far away in England the need both for more Hurricanes, but also for experienced and trained pilots to fly them, led to the despatch for the first time of a full operational fighter squadron to the Middle East. This was 73 Squadron, already with an outstanding record. One of the two original RAF fighter squadrons to be sent to France in September 1939, the unit had become a part of the Air Component there, and had seen action against the Luftwaffe both there, and subsequently over England during the summer of 1940.

The unit left its base at Castle Camps on 5 November, going aboard the aircraft carrier HMS *Furious* next day, and setting sail for Takoradi. All the unit's heavy equipment went by sea, however, travelling with that of the two Wellington squadrons, 37 and 38, which had also just been sent out. 34 pilots and Hurricanes aboard ship reached Freetown, Sierra Leone, on 25 November, and Takoradi two days later, where flying-off took place. The ground crews and other personnel were carried through the Mediterranean aboard the cruiser HMS *Manchester*, arriving at Alexandria on the 30th, from where they moved to Helwan to await the arrival of the air party. The long flight across Central Africa was undertaken by the latter, 27 of the Hurricanes arriving safely, although one pilot was killed in an accident en route. It would be some time before the unit had become sufficiently organised to operate as such, and initially some of its pilots would be attached to 274 Squadron.

In one important respect 73 Squadron had an inestimable advantage, for it brought with it a number of pilots who were already very experienced in aerial combat. The commanding officer, Sqn Ldr A.D.Murray, had only joined the unit in late September, but he had a strong team. Flt Lt J.D.'Smudger' Smith, a Canadian, had been with the squadron since May, as had Sgts E.A.Marshall and G.W.Garton; all three had seen considerable action and had several victory claims to their credit. Another experienced pilot, Flg Off M.L.ff.Beytagh, had joined in July, while the real 'stars' had both been posted in just before the squadron left the UK. Plt Off J.E.Storrar had claimed eight individual and two shared victories with 145 Squadron, and had been awarded a DFC, while Plt Off G.E.Goodman had been with 73's sister squadron, No 1, where he had claimed six and four shared; the award of a DFC would follow him to Africa.

Tuesday, 5 November 1940
A pilot of 33 Squadron claimed an S.79 destroyed on the ground at Sidi Barrani airfield. No such loss was reported by the Regia Aeronautica.

Thursday, 7 November 1940

18 CR.32s and six Ba.65s of 50° Stormo Assalto, led by Magg Bruno Cudugnello, flew south to strafe Siwa landing ground, where two Lysanders were claimed destroyed on the ground. A detached flight of 208 Squadron was based here and managed totally to mis-identify the attackers, recording them as 18 S.79s escorted by six CR.42s! Lysander L4721 was indeed destroyed during this raid.

British Casualties		
208 Sqn	Lysander L4721 destroyed on ground by air attack Siwa	
Italian Claims		
50° St Assalto	2 Lysanders on the ground	Siwa

Wednesday, 13 November 1940

In an effort to extend the range of their fighters, the Regia Aeronautica fitted additional fuel tanks to CR.42 MM4383 of 97ª Squadriglia, 9° Gruppo, 4° Stormo CT, and in this aircraft at dusk S.Ten Riccardo Vaccari undertook a strafing attack on Maaten Bagush airfield, destroying Valentia 'K' (Collishaw's personal aircraft – much to his annoyance). This would appear to have been K5605, reported as being struck off on 22 November.)

The date was also marked by three bombing raids on Alexandria. During the first two raiders bombed the Wardian area where 27 civilians were killed. The second and third attacks came in from the south to hit the harbour at 1933 and 2035 respectively, five Egyptians being killed as were eight British subjects aboard ships. Several more raids then followed, causing some damage and further casualties.

British Casualties	
Valentia ?	K5605, damaged beyond repair on ground

Saturday, 16 November 1940

Flg Off Benson of 208 Squadron undertook a photographic reconnaissance of Maktila camp from 18,000 feet in his Lysander, when CR.42s (reported by the crew subsequently as being six in number) attacked. Sgt Phillips, the gunner, was hit in one leg, but kept on firing until his gun jammed, and appears to have obtained some telling hits on one of the fighters. The engine of the Lysander stopped when the aircraft was down to 100 feet, and Benson carried out a crash-landing at the same moment that one of the CR.42s hit the ground.

Ten Mario Ferrero and Serg Cesare Chiarmetta of 366ª Squadriglia claimed to have forced the Lysander to land about 20 miles south-east of Sidi Barrani, but when Ten Raimondo Sacchetti of 368ª Squadriglia dived down to strafe the Lysander, his CR 42 crashed in flames nearby. Phillips subsequently received credit for having shot this aircraft down; both he and Benson survived, although the latter too was slightly wounded in one thigh.

British Claims			
208 Sqn	Sgt Phillips (air gunner) in Lysander CR.42		1415
British Casualties			
208 Sqn	Lysander L4717 Flg Off L.T.Benson/Sgt Phillips WiA but safe 1415		
Italian Claims			
366ª Sq/151° Gr CT	Ten Mario Ferrero Serg Cesare Chiarmetta }	Lysander forced to land	18m SE Sidi Barrani
Italian Casualties			
368ª Sq/151° Gr CT	CR.42 MM5580 Ten Raimondo Sacchetti KiA		

Sunday, 17 November 1940

An S.79 of 13ª Squadriglia, 26° Gruppo, 9° Stormo BT was returning from a night raid on Alexandria when it struck a tall radio mast while landing, and crashed. Ten Angelo Carabini and his crew were all killed.

Italian Casualties	
13ª Sq/26° Gr/9° St BT	S.79 MM22115 Ten Angelo Carabini and crew KiFA

Monday, 18 November 1940

112 Squadron's Flt Lt 'Algy' Schwab was scrambled to intercept a lone S.79, which he claimed to have shot down. No Italian loss for such an aircraft has been discovered, however.

British Claims

112 Sqn	Flt Lt L.G.Schwab	S.79

Tuesday, 19 November 1940

On this date the still relatively inexperienced pilots of 3 RAAF Squadron had their first encounter with hostile aircraft. It proved to be one of those days where in the confusion of combat both sides totally overestimated the results. Flt Lt B.R.Pelly was to undertake the reconnaissance sortie required, and was provided with cover by the commanding officer, Sqn Ldr P.R.Heath, and by Flg Offs A.C.Rawlinson and A.H.Boyd. When seven miles east of Rabia at about 1400 hours, 18 CR.42s appeared on the scene.

T.Col Revetria, commanding officer of 13° Gruppo CT, was indeed leading 18 CR.42s which had taken off at 1330 and were flying at 9,000 ft, while six more, led by Ten Chiarini were flying 4,500 ft above them. The main formation dived to strafe some British armoured cars when Chiarini reported sighting eight Gladiators which were attacking Revetria's formation, and at once engaged them.

The Australians later reported that the 18 fighters they had seen broke formation and nine of them attacked Pelly, the others going for his escorts. The fight lasted 25 minutes during which time Sqn Ldr Heath was shot down and killed. Pelly claimed one CR.42 shot down and a second damaged, while Boyd thought he saw four spin down out of control. Reportedly, army units later found three crashed Italian aircraft, and as the battle had extended into Italian-held territory, 202 Group considered that all six were actually destroyed, and credited the squadron accordingly.

The Italian pilots thought they had done just as well, claiming six Gladiators shot down and a seventh damaged – almost twice the number actually engaged! The actual result of the 12 claims made by the two sides appears to have been just a single Gladiator shot down!

British Claims

3 RAAF Sqn	Flt Lt B.R.Pelly	Gladiator II N5753	CR.42	7m E Rabia 400
	Flt Lt B.R.Pelly	Gladiator II N5753	CR.42 damaged	7m E Rabia 400
	Flg Off A.C.Rawlinson	Gladiator II L9044	CR.42	7m E Rabia 400
	Flg Off A.H.Boyd	N5752	4 CR.42s	7m E Rabia 400

N.B. In 1995 Grp Capt A.C.Rawlinson, commanding officer of 3 RAAF Squadron, 10 November 1941-1 January 1942, advised that a working party had resolved that an assessment of the unit's listed claims indicated that on 12 occasions during 1940-41 during which 55 claims were included, 25 of these were incorrect and should be deleted. This was the first occasion, when initially a total of seven claims were made. "It was later claimed that three enemy aircraft had been destroyed on our side of the lines but as the battle commenced over enemy territory and gradually moved eastwards it is probable that two other E/A were destroyed and possibly one other." Rawlinson denies that he personally made any claim on this date, while Boyd's claims can also be read as one and three probables. Seven claims on the squadron's list should therefore be changed to three.

British Casualties

3 RAAF Sqn	Gladiator N5750 Sqn Ldr P.R.Heath KiA

Italian Claims

77ª Sq/13° Gr/2° St CT	Ten Guglielmo Chiarini	Gladiator
	S.Ten Gilberto Cerofolini	Gladiator
	S.Ten Giuseppe Bottà	Gladiator
	S.Ten Giuseppe Timolina	Gladiator
82ª Sq/13° Gr/2° St CT	Serg Nino Campanini	Gladiator
	Serg Francesco Nanin	Gladiator
	?	Gladiator damaged

Wednesday, 20 November 1940

Next day 33 Squadron was ordered to despatch nine Hurricanes to escort a Lysander and a Blenheim which were to photograph the Italian dispositions at Sidi Barrani. Over the target area the formation was attacked by a reported 18 CR.42s, following which more of these fighters, estimated at 25-30 strong, appeared.

Magg Ernesto Botto had taken off at the head of a formation of 9° Gruppo CT CR.42s to sweep over the front near Bir Enba. After an hour in the air during the early afternoon, the Blenheim was seen below, escorted by the Hurricanes, Botto and his wingman going down to attack, but being bounced by some Gladiators as they did so. 33 Squadron recorded that there was a little skirmishing around their formation, but the Hurricane pilots stayed close to their charges, no claims or losses resulting.

Meanwhile, however, six 112 Squadron Gladiators had arrived on the scene and launched themselves at Botto's pilots, claiming eight shot down without loss. In return Italian pilots made a number of claims, but S.Ten Carlo Agnelli was shot down and killed, Serg Francesco Putzu failed to return and was classed as missing, while Ten Aldo Gon crash-landed but was safe. Serg Vittorio Pozzati was wounded in one foot, but managed to return to base.

British Claims

112 Sqn	Flt Lt R.J.Abrahams	CR.42	
	Flt Lt R.J.Abrahams	CR.42	
	Plt Off R.A.Acworth }		
	Plt Off R.A.Acworth	CR.42	
	Flg Off R.J.Bennett	CR.42	
	Plt Off A.R.Costello	CR.42	
	Plt Off L.L.Bartley	CR.42	
	Sgt G.M.Donaldson	CR.42	
33/112 Sqns	Unspecified pilots	3 CR.42s probable	

Italian Claims

96ª Sq/9º Gr CT	Cap Roberto Fassi	CR.42	Blenheim
	Cap Roberto Fassi	CR.42	2 Gladiators damaged
73ª Sq/9º Gr CT	Ten Aldo Gon	CR.42 MM5649	Gladiator
	Cap Mario Pluda	CR.42	Gladiator
96ª Sq/9º Gr CT	Serg Vittorio Pozzati	CR.42	Gladiator
	S.Ten Armando Moresi	CR.42	Gladiator probable
73ª & 96ª Sq/9º Gr CT	pilots shared		Gladiator
	pilots shared		2 Hurricanes

Italian Casualties

96ª Sq/9º Gr CT	CR.42 MM5649 S.Ten Carlo Agnelli KiA
97ª Sq/9º Gr CT	CR.42 MM5651 Serg Francesco Putzu MiA
73ª Sq/9º Gr CT	CR.42 MM5649 Ten Aldo Gon crash-landed, safe
96ª Sq/9º Gr CT	CR 42 Damaged Serg Vittorio Pozzati WiA

Friday, 22 November 1940

Italian Casualties

143ª Sq RM	Cant.Z.501 MM35296 destroyed at Menelao on ground by bombing

Sunday, 24 November 1940

S.Ten Amedeo Guidi of 366ª Squadriglia, 151º Gruppo Aut CT took off at 0630 to patrol over Bardia. Here he spotted and intercepted a lone Blenheim which he pursued for 20 minutes at sea level, last seeing it trailing smoke from its starboard engine; he landed at 0720. This was an aircraft of 55 Squadron, reported slightly damaged.

Marshal Graziani was by now under further pressure from Mussolini, who was demanding at least a move forward as far as Mersa Matruh to tie down British forces in Egypt and prevent them going to the aid of the Greeks. There the war was not going as anticipated, for the Greek army had shown a stubborn resistance in the mountains on the Albanian frontier. Indeed, they had thrown back the invaders just at a time when the onset of winter rendered further campaigning increasingly difficult.

British Casualties

55 Sqn	Blenheim slightly damaged by CR 42, but returned safely

Italian Claims

366ª Sq/151º Gr CT	S.Ten Amedeo Guidi	Blenheim Damaged	Bardia

The first engagement for 3 RAAF Squadron occurred on 19 November 1940 when four of the unit's pilots in their new Gladiators engaged CR.42s. The commanding officer, Sqn Ldr P.R.Heath, was shot down and killed, but army observers reported that the Australians had shot down many of their opponents. 202 Group therefore subsequently credited the surviving pilots with six victories. The Italians, who claimed six Gladiators in return, in fact suffered no loss. The three surviving Australians, seen here with one of the unit's fighters, are left to right: Flg Off A.C.Rawlinson, Flt Lt B.R.Pelly and Flg Off A.H.Boyd.

Tuesday, 26 November 1940

Blenheim T2067 of 113 Squadron failed to return from an early morning sortie to Bir Sofafi, the pilot being Flg Off D.S.Anderson, an Australian, who was reported killed with his crew. The cause of this loss is not known.

British Casualties

113 Sqn	Blenheim IV T2067 MiA; Flg Off D.S.Anderson and two KiA

CHAPTER 4

OPERATION COMPASS

On 4 October 1940, Adolf Hitler offered help to the Italian forces in North Africa in the form of mechanised and specialist troops. Anxious to remain totally independent of German aid at least until the third phase of the planned advance into Egypt had been accomplished with the advance on Alexandria about to be made, Mussolini refused. For that, he responded, he might well need heavy tanks, armoured cars and dive-bombers.

By this time Hitler had already ordered a study of the situation to be undertaken by General Wilhelm Ritter von Thoma, and had placed 3rd Panzer Division on standby should a move into the African theatre become desirable. In this he was prompted by the navy, which placed a considerable importance on the Suez route. In the event von Thoma reported that the position was very unsatisfactory, although efforts were underway to improve the situation. Sending troops at this juncture, in his opinion, could only make matters worse, at least until Mersa Matruh had been taken. Graziani pointed out that though works to the road and water supply were underway, resources were quite inadequate to allow the advance to be resumed at this stage. The British, he advised, enjoyed the great advantage of having a nearby railhead for their supplies and reinforcements.

Mussolini now advised Graziani that the Albanian front had become the priority, but that he should act to prevent British transfers of units to Greece. Indeed, British Intelligence were of the opinion that Graziani should be ready to advance again by mid November, and became increasingly mystified when no moves were made throughout this month.

Wavell and O'Connor now began to prepare for a counter-attack when an Italian move did occur. By now the bulk of O'Connor's forces were disposed in the Matruh area. 11th Hussars had been reinforced for their forward scouting duties by 2 Armoured Car Company of the RAF from Palestine, which became for the time being the Hussars' D Squadron.

When the whole of November had passed with no Italian offensive, Wavell decided that there was no longer any need to wait, and that an attack should be made to precipitate events. He decided that one of the new frontier fortified camps should be the subject of a short, swift assault. The attacking force should then withdraw, leaving a strong covering force in place to intercept and interrupt pursuit.

Valuable reinforcements were now available, the 7th Armoured and 4th Indian Divisions having been joined by 7th Royal Tank Regiment with heavy Matilda infantry tanks. The artillery had now received supplies of the new 25 lb gun/howitzer, which was proving to be excellent. In addition to these forces, there was the Matruh garrison.

O'Connor preferred to concentrate the initial attack on the central camps, keeping close watch meanwhile on those to south and north – and particularly on the water centre at Buq Buq. He also felt such an attack would prove to be a good way of drawing some of the pressure off the Greeks.

Consequently it was planned that 4th Indian and 7th Armoured Divisions would pass quietly through a gap between the Nibeiwa and Rabia camps, then turning north to attack Nibeiwa, Tummar East and Point 90 from the west. This assault would be made principally by 4th Indian and 7th RTR, while 7th Armoured provided cover against any interference from Buq Buq or Sofafi. The Matruh garrison would in the meantime pin down Italian forces in the Maktila camp, while the Royal Navy bombarded Maktila and Sidi Barrani from the sea.

In the event of success, 4th Indian should launch a second phase by striking north towards Sidi Barrani while 7th Armoured disrupted communications in the direction of Buq Buq. Exploitation in strength would then take place either north-west or south to Sofafi. The Royal Navy would then bombard coastal targets as far west as Sollum.

The RAF's part in this venture would begin with an intensifying of raids on Benghazi, Derna, Tobruk and Bardia, and on coastal shipping. Air Chief Marshal Longmore was very worried about the RAF's ability to sustain such a programme, given the recent withdrawals to Greece. He was also particularly concerned by the prospect of a sustained Italian air assault on the army's columns and bases.

In an effort to improve matters, on 21 November he ordered 11 and 39 Squadrons – both equipped with Blenheim Is – from Aden, and 45 Squadron from the Sudan, to Egypt. In the event the two former squadrons were not able to do more than provide detached flights to aid the squadrons already to hand. Longmore also ordered K Flight up from the Sudan with its handful of Gladiators. He also took the risk of ordering 274 Squadron from Amiriya to Sidi Haneish South (LG 13). 73 Squadron was due to be fully available at Dekheila by 12 December, but until that happened, this left the whole defence of the Delta in the hands of just two Fleet Air Arm Sea Gladiators from HMS *Eagle*'s small fighter flight, which came under 252 Wing's operational control while based at Dekheila. In the interim, however, the wing had been able to call on 806 Squadron's 16 Fulmars as long as these were ashore at Aboukir.

At this point however, Longmore's personal workload was considerably ameliorated by the arrival from England on 29 November as Deputy Air Officer Commanding-in-Chief, Air Marshal Arthur Tedder. In point of fact, Tedder was actually 'second choice'; six days earlier Air Marshal Owen T.Boyd, CB, OBE, MC, AFC, had been on his way out to take up this post when the Wellington in which he was travelling had become lost and was obliged to force-land in Sicily. Here the air marshal and the crew of the bomber all became PoWs (see *Malta: The Hurricane Years, 1940-41*).

Tedder had left England in an Imperial Airways flyingboat for Lagos, via Lisbon and Freetown, travelling as plain 'Mr Tedder'. Before his departure he had been advised by Air Chief Marshal Sir Wilfred Freeman, the vice chief of the air staff, who was a supporter of Tedder's, and with whom he would maintain a long and fruitful correspondence during the months ahead, that Longmore had originally asked for Tedder as his deputy, but that the prime minister had vetoed the posting. Following the loss of Boyd, he had rescinded his objections.

On reaching West Africa, Tedder had been very interested to inspect the arrangements which had been set up following the arrival there in mid-July of Grp Capt Thorold, to despatch reinforcements across the long overland route to the Sudan and on to Egypt. A few days prior to Tedder's arrival, Longmore had also received the welcome news of the significant damage inflicted on the Italian fleet at Taranto during the night of 11 November by aircraft of the Fleet Air Arm operating from HMS *Illustrious* (see also in *Malta: The Hurricane Years, 1940-41*).

Other changes were also in hand as the new offensive approached. On 1 December Air Headquarters, Egypt, was formed by 202 Group in Cairo. The Reinforcement and Reserve Pool at Ismailia had become the Training Unit and Reserve Pool on 21 September, while on 10 December this unit would metamorphose into 70 Operational Training Unit. Initially a general OTU for the Middle East, the unit swiftly set up a fighter flight with Gladiators and Hurricanes to prepare pilots due to join the fighter and army co-operation units.

On 20 December a new unit would be formed to control and administer the heavy bombers now available. 257 (Heavy Bomber) Wing would be set up at Shallufa with 37, 38 and 70 – the three Wellington squadrons. Advanced bases were quickly to be set up at Fuka and Daba as soon as the advance allowed.

Once this advance was fully underway, the need for closer and more intimate control of units at the front would lead to the formation of another new wing. This would be organised within 202 Group at 108 MU, Aboukir, on 1 January 1941 as 258 (Semi-mobile Advanced Fighter) Wing, and within three or four days it would move forward to Sollum to take over from HQ, AA Brigade, and initially to control 33, 73 and 274 Squadrons. The new unit would be commanded by Grp Capt C.B.S.Spackman, DFC & Bar, from 252 Wing, who would be replaced in the latter unit by Wg Cdr H.A.Simmons.

For the ground forces the distances for re-supply were likely to be very long and forward dumps, known as field supply depots, were created, one for each division, some 40 miles west of Mersa Matruh. Placed 14 miles apart and containing five days fuel and supplies each, they were very carefully set up, concealed and guarded, for their discovery and capture at this stage would jeopardise the whole undertaking.

Throughout the period of preparation 7th Armoured Division's Support Group carried out *"aggressive inquisitiveness"* of the camps, and of the Nibeiwa-Rabia gap. This led to an engagement on 19 November when the group's left column encountered a force of Italian tanks and lorry-borne infantry which emerged from the Nibeiwa camp. Another column then appeared from the Rabia camp, but turned back. The Support Group forces struck hard, destroying five medium tanks and damaging others. 11 prisoners were taken and about 100 casualties inflicted. The group's own losses amounted to three killed and two wounded – all inflicted by air attack.

Army units now commenced a major training exercise near Matruh during the night of 25/26 November. Replicas of Nibeiwa and Tummar camps had been marked out on the ground, and some very useful lessons were learned from this.

Encouraged by the lack of Italian aggression, on 28 November Wavell ordered that if the opportunity should offer itself to turn a local success into a major victory, the British forces should press ahead to achieve that goal. He stated to General Wilson: "I do not entertain extravagant hopes for this operation, but I do wish to make certain that if a big opportunity occurs we are prepared morally, mentally and administratively, to use it to the fullest." He also made a further bold decision at this point. As soon as the experienced 4th Indian Division had achieved its priority role here, it would be withdrawn and moved to Eritrea, the newly-arrived 6th Australian Division taking its place on the frontier.

It is now appropriate to consider the Italian 10th Army's dispositions as the British offensive approached. At Maktila in the north, and at Tummar and Sidi Barrani were the 1ª and 2ª Libyan Divisions and the 4ª Blackshirts. General Maletti's strong mixed group held the Nibeiwa camp, while at Rabia and Sofafi was the 63ª Cirene Division. The escarpment in the Sofafi/Halfaya area was held by the 62ª Marmarica Division. East of Buq Buq, opposite the Nibeiwa-Rabia gap, was the 64ª Catanzaro Division.

Thus a defending force of seven comparatively weak divisions faced an attacking force of one strong infantry division and one armoured division. The Regia Aeronautica by this time had available 140 bombers and 191 fighters and ground-attack aircraft. The former were predominantly based around Benghazi and Tmimi, the latter in the Tobruk, El Adem and Gambut area (see Order of Battle, see page 84).

During October and November 10th Army had been receiving conflicting reports of events in Egypt. Despite the outbreak of the war in Greece, Italian Intelligence believed that the British would greatly strengthen their forces in North and East Africa. Reports from Regia Aeronautica reconnaissance aircraft crews indicated the presence of vehicle concentrations and increased movement along the lines of communication. Nevertheless, until 5 December it was believed that this represented the relief of troops who had been in the forward area for some time, with fresh units. Chances of an offensive were not rated as being high.

The increase in aerial activity was noted on 5 December, while three days later 400 vehicles were spotted at midday 30-40 miles south-east of Nibeiwa. Graziani subsequently claimed that 10th Army was immediately notified, and interrogation of a prisoner captured on the 5th led to a warning that a strong British attack was likely in the next ten days. However, there is no note of this in 10th Army's Intelligence Summary. It does appear, however, that a strong warning was given to Graziani on 6 December that an attack was imminent.

For its part, 202 Group (which became AHQ, Egypt at the start of December) with its HQ now at Maaten Bagush, had available three squadrons each of fighters, Blenheim bombers and Wellington bombers, and one of Bombay bomber-transports. These units provided a total of 48 fighters and 116 bombers. Additionally, General O'Connor had been provided with an army/air component under his direct command for tactical reconnaissance and close support (see Order of Battle, see page 84).

Thus it was that on 5 December Wavell issued the final orders to O'Connor (and the only ones that he actually produced in writing, rather than by word of mouth). The latter sent out his own orders to his subordinate units next day. 31,000 men, 275 tanks, 120 guns and 60 armoured cars stood ready to advance. On 7 December O'Connor advised that this was not another exercise, but was "the real thing". By the 8th, 4th Indian Division had moved forward to within 15 miles of Nibeiwa – Operation Compass was about to commence.

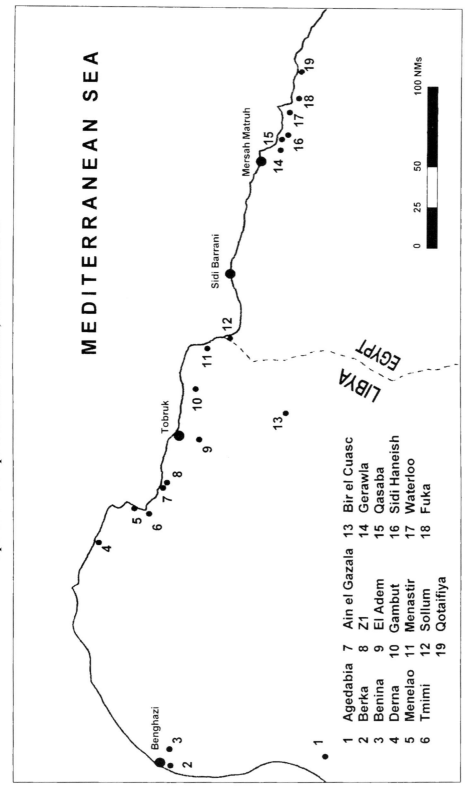

Operation Compass frontier airfields, December 1940

MEDITERRANEAN SEA

Benghazi
Tobruk
Derna
Sidi Barrani
Mersah Matruh
LIBYA
EGYPT

1	Agedabia	7	Ain el Gazala	13	Bir el Cuasc
2	Berka	8	Z1	14	Gerawla
3	Benina	9	El Adem	15	Qasaba
4	Derna	10	Gambut	16	Sidi Haneish
5	Menelao	11	Menastir	17	Waterloo
6	Tmimi	12	Sollum	18	Fuka
		19	Qotaifiya		

0 25 50 100 NMs

RAF Middle East Order of Battle at the start of December 1940

AHQ, Egypt

Fuka	33 Squadron	Hurricane Is
	55 Squadron	Blenheim Is
	11 Squadron Det	Blenheim Is (main squadron at Helwan)
Qotaifiya	45 Squadron	Blenheim Is
	9 Squadron Det	Blenheim Is (main squadron at Helwan)
Sidi Haneish	112 Squadron	Gladiators
	274 Squadron	Hurricane Is
LG 68 'Waterloo'	113 Squadron	Blenheim IVs
Fayid	37 Squadron	Wellingtons
	38 Squadron	Wellingtons
Kabrit	70 Squadron	Wellingtons
Heliopolis	216 Squadron	Bombays

Army/Air Component

Qasaba	208 Squadron	8 Lysanders
		4 Hurricanes
	6 Squadron Det	4 Lysanders
Gerawla	3 RAAF Squadron	8 Gladiators
		4 Gauntlets

Also available were the communications aircraft of 267 Squadron, the Sunderland flyingboats of the detachments of 228 and 230 Squadrons at Alexandria, and under 203 Group command, and various Fleet Air Arm aircraft at Dekheila; 73 Squadron with Hurricane Is was reforming here as swiftly as possible. Some assistance from bomber and reconnaissance units on Malta could also be expected.

Regia Aeronautica Order of Battle as at 9 December 1940

5ª Squadra Aerea (HQ at Tripoli)

Comando Settore Ovest

9° Stormo BT

26° Gruppo BT	S.79	**Castel Benito**
29° Gruppo BT	S.79	**Castel Benito**

15° Stormo BT (will move to **Benina** on 16 December)

46° Gruppo BT	S.79	**Castel Benito**
47° Gruppo BT	S.79	**Castel Benito**

41° Stormo BT

59° Gruppo BT	S.79	**Castel Benito**
60° Gruppo BT	S.79	**Castel Benito**
64° Gruppo OA	nil	**Mellaha**
67° Gruppo OA	Ro.37bis	**Mellaha**

The CR.42s of 151° Gruppo Autonomo CT were very active during the early phases of Operation Compass.

1° Gruppo APC	Ca.309	**Mellaha**
143ª Squadriglia RM	Cant.Z.501	**Caramanli** (part)
145ª Squadriglia RM	Cant.Z.501	**Caramanli** (part)

Comando Settore Est
 2° Stormo CT
  8° Gruppo CT — CR.42 — **Menastir**
  13° Gruppo CT — CR.42 — **Tmimi**

 4° Stormo CT
  9° Gruppo CT — CR.42 — **El Adem**
  10° Gruppo CT — CR.42 — **Berka**
  151° Gruppo CT — CR.42 — **El Adem/Agedabia**

 50° Stormo Assalto
  12° Gruppo Assalto — CR.32/Ba.65 — **Benina/El Adem**
  16° Gruppo Assalto — CR.32/Ba.65 — **Bir el Cuasc/Derna**
  33° Gruppo Autonomo BT — S.79 — **Z.1**

 14° Stormo BT
  44° Gruppo BT — S.79 — **Tmimi**
  45° Gruppo BT — S.79 — **Tmimi**

34° Stormo BT (will arrive at **Benina** on 16 December)
  52° Gruppo BT — S.79 — **Benina**
  53° Gruppo BT — S.79 — **Benina**
  54° Gruppo Autonomo BT — S.81 — **Benina**
  73° Gruppo OA — Ro.37bis — **Sollum/Benghazi**
  114° Gruppo Speciale BT — S.79 — **Ain el Gazala**
  145° Gruppo Autonomo — S.75 — **Benghazi**
  2° Gruppo APC — Ca.309/S.81 — **Benghazi**
   137ª Squadriglia OA — Ro.37 — **Berka**
   143ª Squadriglia RM — Cant.Z.501 — **Menelao** (part)
   145ª Squadriglia RM — Cant.Z.501 — **Benghazi** (part)
   175ª Squadriglia RST — S.79 — **Gambut**
   278ª Squadriglia AS — S.79sil — **El Adem/Benghazi**
   614ª Squadriglia Soccorso — Cant.Z.506S — **Benghazi**

———

Saturday, 7 December 1940

The RAF's first actions preceding the opening of the Operation Compass offensive in the Egyptian frontier area, began with attacks from Malta on Tripoli and its airfields, details of which may be found in Chapter 14 – 'In Defence of Tripoli'. Raids were also made on the Benghazi area, where substantial damage was reported, including the destruction of an S.79 of 33° Gruppo BT at Benina.

During the day meanwhile, 26 CR.42s of 2° Stormo CT strafed vehicle concentrations at Bir Khamsa and Bir Qatrani, claiming several trucks destroyed or damaged.

Italian Casualties	
33° Gr Aut BT	S.79 destroyed on ground

Sunday, 8 December 1940

Fighter patrols were maintained throughout the day over the British concentration areas. At about 1800 12 Blenheims attacked Benina airfield. Cap Giuseppe Aurili of 90ª Squadriglia intercepted the raiders, attacking the leading vic while it was making a second run over the target. He reported seeing one Blenheim crash not far from El Regina. Aurili, an ace of the Spanish Civil War, where he had operated under the cover name of 'Banchero', crashed while landing at dusk, damaging the undercarriage of his aircraft and suffering slight injuries himself. Cap Renzo Maggini at once took him in a Fiat 1100 car, heading for Benghazi Hospital for treatment, but on the way their vehicle collided with a van and both men were seriously hurt. Maggini would die next day as a result of multiple fractures while Aurili would require a long period of recovery before he was fit again.

By night 29 sorties were made by RAF Wellingtons and Blenheims, ten more aircraft being claimed destroyed or damaged at Benina, although no aircraft losses were reported here by the Italians. Bombays raided the defended camps.

British Claims		
	10 aircraft destroyed or damaged on ground	
Italian Claims		
90ª Sq/10° Gr CT	Cap Giuseppe Aurili	Blenheim

Monday, 9 December 1940

At 0700 Compass commenced as 4th Indian Division opened an attack on the camps at Nibeiwa. All Regia Aeronautica fighter and bomber units in Libya became involved at once in efforts to contain the British offensive. At about 0815 Ten Guglielmo Chiarini, who had been posted to 366ª Squadriglia, 151° Gruppo CT on 27 November, claimed a Blenheim shot down south-east of Alam Rabia; this was his fifth victory.

During a surveillance flight on this morning, S.Ten Giulio Torresi of 77ª Squadriglia intercepted two Blenheims and attacked them both. He reported that one ditched in the sea and the other force-landed and sank. These were his fifth and sixth victories, making him the top-scoring Italian pilot to date. Two Blenheims were lost and a third was written off on return to base.

Meanwhile, Hurricanes of 33 Squadron undertook a ground strafing mission during which the pilots reported encountering CR.42s, three of which were claimed shot down; one Hurricane force-landed. Their opponents seem to have been aircraft of 151° Gruppo, S.Ten Amedeo Guidi claiming one aircraft which had already been attacked by Serg Magg Cesare Chiarmetta. This was recorded as being either a Blenheim or a Spitfire, but was probably the missing Hurricane.

Just after midday Hurricanes from 274 Squadron intercepted five S.79s, claiming three shot down and two damaged; one of the latter was subsequently confirmed by the army on 15 December, who reported that it had crashed. Two of these bombers from 22ª Squadriglia, 45° Gruppo BT were actually lost, one of them flown by Ten Sergio Sartof, who was killed; he later received a posthumous Medaglia d'Oro.

Early in the afternoon 19 CR.42s of 9° Gruppo CT were led by Magg Ernesto Botto to escort a formation of S.79s in the Sidi Barrani-Bir Enba area. The rendezvous was missed, but Botto led his fighters on a freelance sweep, a formation of Gladiators being seen at lower altitude. Botto led a bounce on these, but the CR.42s were in their turn bounced by Hurricanes of 274 Squadron. In a confused fight, the Italian pilots claimed seven individual victories and three probables, plus a Hurricane collectively

Above: In preparation for a sortie over the front at the start of Operation Compass, Flg Off Vernon Woodward dons his parachute while 33 Squadron ground crew in their regulation issue pith helmets, prepare his brand-new Hurricane for flight.

Right: Pilots of B Flight, 33 Squadron prepare to man their Hurricanes at the start of Operation Compass in December 1940. They are led out by the unit commander, Sqn Ldr Charles Ryley, and are, left to right: Flg Off C.H.Dyson, DFC, Flg Off Perry St.Quintin, Flg Off Harry Starrett, Flt Lt G.E.Hawkins, Sgt J.Craig, Flg Off John Mackie and Flg Off Vernon Woodward.

assigned to all the pilots of 9° Gruppo. In return, four CR.42s were lost, three of which undertook crash-landings. The Gladiators they had attacked were presumably aircraft of 112 Squadron, but this unit recorded no losses and submitted no claims.

More CR.42s of 13° and 151° Gruppi were escorting S.79s when they too were engaged by Hurricanes. This seems to have taken place at the same time as the 9° Gruppo combat was underway, and probably also involved the Hurricanes of 274 Squadron. Three 368ª Squadriglia pilots claimed a single Hurricane between them, but Serg Francesco Nanin of 82ª Squadriglia, 13° Gruppo, was shot down and killed. During these fights the pilots of 274 Squadron claimed five CR.42s shot down and three more probably so, suffering no losses.

Of the day's activities, a rising 'star' in 274 Squadron, Plt Off E.M.Mason wrote home to his mother: "..we saw five S.79s. We got two, but although I shot at them I did not get one personally. I was probably too excited to aim deliberately enough. In the afternoon five of us met 27 CR.42s. We had a lovely dogfight and I personally accounted for one (confirmed). He went down with flames coming out but not properly blazing."

In the evening 33 Squadron lost a further Hurricane when Lt J.G.Fischer, SAAF, failed to return from a lone reconnaissance sortie. While driving to Comando Settore Est headquarters to report on the situation, Magg Botto was involved in a car accident and was taken to hospital with a serious head injury. Command of 9° Gruppo CT was assumed provisionally by Cap Larsimont Pergameni.

British Claims

33 Sqn	Flg Off V.C.Woodward		2 CR.42s	
	u/k		CR.42	
274 Sqn	Plt Off S.Godden	N2624	S.79	Sidi Barrani-Bir Zigdin el Hamra 1230
274 Sqn	Sqn Ldr P.H.Dunn	P372		Sidi Barrani-Bir Zigdin el Hamra 1230
	Flg Off P.G.Wykeham-Barnes	P2638		Sidi Barrani-Bir Zigdin el Hamra 1230
	Plt Off E.M.Mason	P3722	2 S.79s	Sidi Barrani-Bir Zigdin el Hamra 1230
	Plt Off Preston	P3720	2 S.79s damaged	Sidi Barrani-Bir Zigdin el Hamra 1230
	Flt Sgt T.C.Morris	V7300		Sidi Barrani-Bir Zigdin el Hamra 1230
	Sqn Ldr P.H.Dunn	P3723	CR.42	Sidi Barrani-Sofafi area 1608
			2 CR.42s probable	Sidi Barrani-Sofafi area 1608
274 Sqn	Flg Off P.G.Wykeham-Barnes	V7300	CR.42	Sidi Barrani-Sofafi area 1608
			CR.42 probable	Sidi Barrani-Sofafi area 1608
274 Sqn	Flg Off J.H.Lapsley	V7293	CR.42	Sidi Barrani-Sofafi area 1608
	Plt Off E.M.Mason	P3722	CR.42	Sidi Barrani-Sofafi area 1608
	Plt Off T.L.Patterson	P3720	CR.42	Sidi Barrani-Sofafi area 1608

British Casualties

33 Sqn	Hurricane force-landed
	Hurricane I 2/Lt J.G.Fischer MiA
45 Sqn	Blenheim I L1534 crash-landed; Flt Lt J.Paine & crew safe
	Blenheim I L6663 damaged, w/o on return; Flg Off C.W.S.Thomas & crew safe
113 Sqn	Blenheim IV T2073 crashed at Sidi Barrani; reason unknown. Plt Off J.N.Owen injured; two killed

Italian Claims

9º Gr CT	Magg Ernesto Botto	Gladiator
	Serg Magg Enrico Dallari	Gladiator
	Serg Magg Antonio Valle	Gladiator
	Serg Magg Otello Perotti	Gladiator
	S.Ten Riccado Vaccari	Hurricane
	Serg Magg Massimo Salvatore	Hurricane
	Unit victory	Hurricane
	Ten Valerio De Campo	Gladiator probable
	Ten Giulio Reiner	Gladiator probable
	Serg Santo Gino	Gladiator probable
366ª Sq/151º Gr CT	Ten Guglielmo Chiarini	Blenheim
	S.Ten Amedeo Guidi	Hurricane or Blenheim
368ª Sq/151º Gr CT	Cap Bruno Locatelli	
	S.Ten Furio Lauri	Hurricane
	Ten Orfeo Paroli	
77ª Sq/13º Gr CT	S.Ten Giulio Torresi	2 Blenheims

Italian Casualties

73ª Sq/9º Gr/4º St CT	CR.42 MM5599 Serg Magg Guglielmo Biffani PoW
	CR.42 Serg Santo Gino crash-landed
96ª Sq/9º Gr/4º St CT	CR.42 Ten Ezio Viglione Borghese crash-landed near Buq Buq
97ª Sq/9º Gr/4º St CT	CR.42 Ten Riccardo Vaccari crash-landed near Sollum; burned
82ª Sq/13º Gr/2º St CT	CR.42 Serg Francesco Nanin KiA
22 ªSq/45º Gr/14º St BT	S.79 Ten Sergio Sartof & crew KiA
	S.79 Ten Fortunato Del Dotto & crew KiA
6ª Sq/44º Gr/14º St BT	S.79 damaged and w/o; Ten Armando Toni & crew safe

Tuesday, 10 December 1940

During the day pilots of 9° Gruppo CT led by Ten Piero Bonfatti of 73ª Squadriglia claimed a Blenheim as a probable. One 45 Squadron Blenheim force-landed west of Menastir at 0700, but later took off again and returned to base.

On a lone reconnaissance to the south of Sidi Barrani Flt Lt C.B.Gaden of 3 RAAF Squadron intercepted an Ro.37 of 73° Gruppo OA flown by Cap Giacomelli, and shot this down.

In the afternoon T.Col Carlo Calosso led 21 CR.42s of 151° Gruppo CT to escort a formation of Ba.65s led by Cap Valentino Festa, to strafe British vehicles in the Bir Enba area. Over Tummar West at 1645 they were attacked by Gladiators of 3 RAAF Squadron, the pilots of which claimed three CR.42s shot down and two

A Ro.37 reconnaissance biplane; an aircraft of this type, flown by Cap Omero Giacomelli, was lost on 10 December 1940.

probables without loss. The Italian pilots claimed one Gladiator and a Hurricane, but lost one of their own fighters, the pilot becoming a PoW.

It seems that 33 Squadron may also have been involved in this engagement, for whilst again on a strafing sortie, this squadron's pilots claimed two CR.42s shot down and a third probable, but lost one Hurricane which crash-landed.

British Claims

3 RAAF Sqn	Flt Lt C.B.Gaden	Ro.37	South Sidi Barrani 0820
	Sqn Ldr I.D.McLachlan	CR.42	Tummar West 1645
	Flt Lt G.Steege	CR.42	Tummar West 1645
		CR.42 probable	Tummar West 1645
	Flg Off A.A.Gatward	CR.42	Tummar West 1645
		CR.42 probable	Tummar West 1645
33 Sqn	u/k	2 CR.42s	
		CR.42 probable	

British Casualties

33 Sqn	Hurricane I P3728 crash-landed		

Italian Claims

151° Gr CT	Unit victory	Gladiator	
		Hurricane	
73ª Sq/9° Gr CT	Ten Piero Bonfatti	Blenheim.probable	

Italian Casualties

127ª Sq/73° Gr OA	Ro.37 Cap Omero Giacomelli KiA	
367ª Sq/151° GR CT	CR.42 MM4444 Serg Gino Bogoni PoW	

Wednesday, 11 December 1940

274 Squadron undertook an early patrol during which a reconnaissance S.79 of 175ª Squadriglia RST flown by Ten Italo Caraffa was intercepted and shot down at 0740 by Plt Off Stanley Godden. However, during this sortie Flt Lt Evers-Swindell was obliged to force-land at Mersa Gargoub. Within minutes of this engagement one of two 8° Gruppo CT CR.42s which were on patrol over the front, was lost, Ten Vittorio Gnudi being reported missing.

16 more CR.42s, this time from 9° Gruppo CT, escorted Ba.65s south of Sidi Barrani at 0845, providing cover as the latter strafed armoured cars, some of which were claimed damaged. Whilst so engaged, a lone Hurricane entered the formation and was followed by the Italian fighters for some time, and was fired at, a probable being claimed.

At 1445 nine CR.42s from 151° Gruppo CT set off for a Ba.65 escort after vehicles in the Buq Buq area. While gaining height before heading for the front, one Hurricane bounced them and with a single long burst damaged MM4314 flown by Serg Eugenio Cicognani of 366ª Squadriglia, who was at the rear of the formation. Badly wounded in the arm and unable to continue, he baled out and was taken to Bardia Military Hospital where his right arm was amputated. The rest of the CR.42s followed this Hurricane to Buq Buq and claimed to have shot it down just before reaching this locality. This victory was credited to S.Ten Furio Lauri of 368ª Squadriglia, who was assisted by Serg Magg Ernesto De Bellis and Serg Stefano Fiore. A second Hurricane was claimed by S.Ten Amedeo Guidi of 366ª Squadriglia in co-operation with Cap Locatelli and Serg Magg Colauzzi.

At 1500 two Hurricanes bounced four Ba.65s of 16° Gruppo Assalto in the Buq Buq area, M.llo Antonio Gallerani of 168ª Squadriglia being shot down and a second Ba.65 badly damaged. During the afternoon four Ba.65s of 159ª Squadriglia, 12° Gruppo Assalto, were preparing to take off from Amseat for another sortie over the Buq Buq area when RAF bombers appeared overhead and dropped their bombs. The four pilots (Ten Adriano Visconti, M.llo Ennio Sagliaschi, Serg Magg Paolo Perno and Serg Magg Pietro Scaramucci) remained in their cockpits until the raid was over, then taking off to complete their mission. Over Buq Buq all four aircraft were damaged by AA fire.

Regia Aeronautica losses for the day had therefore been one S.79, two CR.42s with two more badly damaged, one Ba.65 and five damaged, two badly – four of them by ground fire. Claims had totalled two Hurricanes shot down and one probable.

During the day RAF pilots had claimed two S.79s, one each by 33 and 274 Squadrons. Claims for CR.42s totalled three and one probable, while one Ba.65 had been claimed plus a second probable. One of the CR.42s had been claimed by Plt Off Mason of 274 Squadron at 1540, and one each by Flt Lt J.M.Littler and Flt Sgt H.J.Goodchild of 33 Squadron, this unit also claiming one probable. Mason recorded:

"..late in the afternoon three of us were on patrol when I saw a speck on the horizon going towards Libya. I chased after it, the other two following, and eventually saw it was a lone CR.42 making for home (probably after ground strafing our own troops). I chased up behind him without him noticing me and waited until I was right behind him at point blank range and put a burst into him. The other two saw him go down burning."

One claim for a Ba.65 was made by Plt Off Perry St.Quintin, and a second was claimed as a probable – undoubtedly the 1500 hour combat with 168ª Squadriglia. 33 Squadron suffered the loss of one Hurricane shot down and three more damaged and forced to land.

As may be seen, RAF claims on this date were quite close to Italian losses, and British losses were much in line with those claimed by the Regia Aeronautica. The missing 33 Squadron pilot was Flg Off C.H.Dyson, DFC, who had been flying Hurricane P3726. He was to return on foot six days later,

in charge of a number of Italian PoWs. He proceeded to give an extraordinary account of his sortie on the 11th. Flying alone, he reported, he had come upon a formation of six CR.42s flying in two vics of three each, and escorting a lone S.79. He had fired a long burst at each of the vics in turn, and as a result all six Italian fighters had started to burn and fall. He was then attacked by other fighters and forced down near Sollum after, he claimed, probably shooting down a seventh CR.42.

At first this claim was treated with some scepticism, if not derision, but apparently a signal was then received from the army nearly a week later congratulating the pilot who on this date had brought down seven Italian aircraft. Ostensibly, this advised that one of the falling CR.42s had crashed into the S.79 and brought this down too. Why this signal should arrive six or more days after the event is not clear, and no evidence of it has been found by researchers. As may be seen above, lone Hurricanes had on two or three

Flg Off C.H.'Deadstick' Dyson, DFC, of 33 Squadron leans against the wing of a Hurricane a few days after a sortie on 11 December 1940 during which he claimed to have shot down six CR.42 fighters. This claim was confirmed at the time by another unreliable army report.

occasions attacked formations of CR.42s, and had been pursued by them and claimed shot down, or probably so, as was the case with Dyson. However, there is no evidence whatsoever that losses of this magnitude had been suffered by the Regia Aeronautica, and certainly not in the manner indicated.

Whatever the truth of this story, on the strength of it Dyson was awarded a Bar to the DFC which he had received before the war for service in Palestine.

By the end of the day 8° Gruppo CT had only one CR.42 still serviceable. Consequently this was handed over to 13° Gruppo CT and the unit withdrew to Benghazi. The gruppo's time in North Africa was at an end, although it would return to Libya a year later. Next day 13° Gruppo would move to Tobruk with its 13 serviceable aircraft.

British Claims

33 Sqn	Plt Off P.R.St.Quintin		Ba.65	
	Flt Lt J.M.Littler		CR.42	
	Flt Sgt H.J.Goodchild		CR.42	
	u/k		S.79	
	u/k		CR.42 probable	
	u/k		Ba.65 probable	
	Flg Off C.H.Dyson	P3726	6 CR.42s	
	Flg Off C.H.Dyson	P3726	CR.42 probable	
	Flg Off C.H.Dyson	P3726	S.79	
274 Sqn	Plt Off S.Godden	N2624	S.79	Sidi Barrani-Sofafi: Qur el Beid 0740
	Plt Off E.M.Mason	P3722	CR.42	Sidi Barrani-Sollum 1540

British Casualties

33 Sqn	Hurricane I P3726 Flg Off C.H.Dyson shot down; returned safe
	2 Hurricanes damaged and force-landed
274 Sqn	Hurricane P3824 Flt Lt Evers-Swindell force-landed; safe

Italian Claims

368ª Sq/151° Gr CT	S.Ten Furio Lauri		Hurricane
366ª Sq/151° Gr CT	S.Ten Amedeo Guidi	⎫	
	Cap Bruno Locatelli	⎬	Hurricane
	Serg Magg Davide Colauzzi	⎭	
9° Gr/4° St CT	Unit victory		Hurricane probable

Italian Casualties

175ª Sq RST	S.79 Ten Italo Caraffa and crew PoW
94ª Sq/8° Gr CT	CR.42 MM4309 Ten Vittorio Gnudi MiA
366ª Sq/151° Gr CT	CR.42 MM4314 Serg Eugenio Cicognani baled out, badly wounded
??	2 CR.42s badly damaged
168ª Sq/16° Gr/50° ST Ass	Ba.65 M.llo Antonio Gallerani KiA
	Ba.65 badly damaged
159ª Sq/12° Gr/50° St Ass	Ba.65 badly damaged by AA
	3 Ba.65s damaged by AA

Thursday, 12 December 1940

At 0745 a Blenheim of 45 Squadron took off for a raid on Sollum airfield. This was intercepted by five CR.42s of 82ª Squadriglia, 13° Gruppo, when over the target, and was shot down by Cap Guglielmo Arrabito. Arrabito's aircraft and that of Serg Luigi Giannotti were both hit by return fire and force-landed, although the pilots were later able to take off and fly back to T.3 airfield.

On this date 3 RAAF Squadron's venerable Gauntlets were withdrawn, having dive-bombed in the Sofafi area which 7th Armoured Division had cut off. No losses had been suffered, but it had become increasingly difficult to keep these elderly aircraft serviceable. The Australian unit was therefore brought up to full strength on Gladiators.

A few minutes later three pilots of 3 RAAF Squadron encountered CR.42s of 4° Stormo CT, reported as 17 strong. The Australians claimed two shot down and one probable without loss. The Italian pilots claimed two Gladiators shot down but lost Serg Onorino Crestani of 84ª Squadriglia, who became a PoW.

During the morning 14 CR.32s and Ba.65s of 50° Stormo Assalto had moved up to Sollum, but were bounced by Hurricanes, three Ba.65s of 159ª Squadriglia being hit. M.llo Ennio Sagliaschi crash-landed near Gambut, Serg Magg Giacomo Pappalepore was seriously wounded, and Serg Giuseppe Zardini wrote off his aircraft while crash-landing wheels-up at Tobruk.

Two engagements were recorded close to each other during the midday period. 33 and 274 Squadrons were engaged most of the day in strafing, but at 1200 Flt Sgt T.C.Morris of the latter unit claimed to have shot down two S.79s, then carrying out a force-landing west of Matruh.

There were no claims by the Hurricane units for Ba.65s, and no combats were recorded by the Italians involving S.79s. It therefore seems possible that Morris's two claims for the latter type had been incorrectly recorded and in fact related to the former.

More reinforcements for the Regia Aeronautica arrived on this date when 12 S.79s of 42° Gruppo BT flew in from Grottaglie to join 41° Stormo. At Alexandria 73 Squadron now had eight Hurricanes serviceable, ready for the defence of the port.

British Claims				
274 Sqn	Flt Sgt T.C.Morris	P3723	2 S.79s (possibly Ba.65s)	2-3m SSE Fort Capuzzo 1200
3 RAAF Sqn	Flg Off A.A.Gatward		CR.42 probable	6m NW Sofafi 1207
	Flg Off W.S.Arthur		CR.42	Pilot baled 1210
	Flg Off A.H.Boyd		CR.42	Pilot baled 1210
British Casualties				
45 Sqn	Blenheim I L8465 Plt Off P.C.Traill-Smith and crew KiA			
274 Sqn	Hurricane I P3723 force-landed; Flt Sgt T.C.Morris safe			
Italian Claims				
82ª Sq/13° Gr CT	Cap Guglielmo Arrabito		Blenheim	Sollum
96ª Sq/9° Gr/°4 St CT	Ten Aldo Gon	}	Gladiator	
	Serg Gustavo Minelli			
10° Gr/4° St CT	Cap Luigi Monti			
	S.Ten Luigi Prati	}	Gladiator	
	Serg Roberto Steppi			
Italian Casualties				
82ª Sq/13° Gr CT	CR.42 damaged Cap Guglielmo Arrabito force-landed; returned later			
	CR.42 damaged Serg Luigi Giannotti force-landed; returned later			
159ª S/12° Gr/50° St Ass	Ba.65 M.llo Ennio Sagliaschi crash-landed Gambut			
	Ba.65 Serg Magg Giacomo Pappalepore badly wounded			
	Ba.65 Serg Giuseppe Zardini crash-landed Tobruk; w/o			
84ªSq/10°Gr/4°St CT	CR.42 Serg Onorino Crestani PoW			

Friday, 13 December 1940

'Black Friday' proved to be a bad day for AHQ, Egypt's fighters. Early in the morning ten CR.42s led by Cap Antonio Larsimont Pergameni commenced an escort to S.79s of 33° Gruppo Autonomo BT to the Sidi Azeiz area. At about 0850 between Sidi Omar and Sollum, a formation of Gladiators from 3 RAAF Squadron were seen approaching. Unfortunately for the Australians, they failed to spot the covering fighters, and leaving no top cover for themselves, they dived on the bombers, Flt Lt Gordon Steege claiming one of these shot down and a second probably so (although other sources credit the confirmed victory to Chaz Gaden). The CR.42s were then upon them, pilots of 97ª Squadriglia engaging first, but at once Larsimont's Fiat collided with one of the Gladiators, which shed its wings and crashed to the ground. The rest of the Italian pilots believed that they had lost their commander, but Larsimont was actually able to regain control of his damaged aircraft and land at Menastir. Serg Magg Perotti attacked another Gladiator head-on and saw the pilot bale out, while Ten Viglione claimed another. Pilots of 73ª Squadriglia then also attacked, three more Gladiators being claimed destroyed and three more as probables.

Among the 3 RAAF pilots, Flt Lt C.B.Gaden was killed – probably in the collision with Larsimont – while Flg Offs W.S.Arthur and L.D.A.Winten both baled out, Winten slightly wounded; Flg Offs A.H.Boyd and A.A.Gatward both crash-landed. Boyd added claims for two CR.42s to those made by Steege, but on this occasion the only loss suffered by the Italians was Larsimont's damaged CR.42.

One Regia Aeronautica loss was suffered when Cap Loris Bulgarelli, commanding officer of 60ª Squadriglia, 33° Gruppo, was killed aboard his S.79 while strafing a column of British tanks at low altitude. T.Col Ferri Forte, commander of 33° Gruppo, who was flying as an observer, took over the controls of the badly damaged bomber and managed to get it back to base. It is possible that this aircraft had been attacked by Gordon Steege. Bulgarelli was later awarded a posthumous Medaglia d'Oro.

Later in the morning 274 Squadron's Hurricanes were intercepted by 151° Gruppo CR.42s led by T.Col Calosso, and while Flg Off John Lapsley claimed one shot down, 2/Lt F.J.Joubert, SAAF, was shot down and killed, the commanding officer, Sqn Ldr Paddy Dunn also being forced down. On this occasion the Italians, who suffered no losses, underestimated their success, claiming only a single Hurricane as a probable.

British Claims

3 RAAF Sqn	Flt Lt G.H.Steege (or Flg Off C.B.Gaden)	S.79
		S.79 probable
	Flg Off A.H.Boyd N5782	2 CR.42s

NB: 3 RAAF Squadron's list of claims originally included a total of six victories on this date, but was subsequently reduced to three)

274 Sqn	Flg Off J.H.Lapsley	P2641	CR.42

British Casualties

3 RAAF Sqn	Gladiator N5765 Flt Lt C.B.Gaden KiA
	Gladiator N5752 Flg Off W.S. Arthur baled out
	Gladiator N5766 Flg Off L.D.A.Winten baled out, slightly wounded
	Gladiator N5782 Flg Off A.H.Boyd crash-landed
	Gladiator N5764 Flg Off A.A.Gatward crash-landed
274 Sqn	Hurricane I P39762/Lt F.J.Joubert KiA
	Hurricane I damaged Sqn Ldr P.H.Dunn force-landed
3 RAAF Sqn	Gladiator badly damaged in landing accident – Plt Off J.F.Jackson

Italian Claims

9° Gr/4° St CT	Cap Antonio Larsimont Pergameni	Gladiator (by collision)
97ª Sq/9° Gr/4° St CT	Serg Magg Otello Perotti	Gladiator –
		pilot baled out
	Ten Ezio Viglione Borghese	Gladiator
73ª Sq/9° Gr/4° St CT	Ten Pietro Bonfatti	Gladiator
	S.Ten Giuseppe Oblach	Gladiator
	Serg Sergio Stauble	Gladiator
	Ten Valerio De Campo	Gladiator probable
	Ten Giulio Reiner	Gladiator probable
	Serg Magg Dallari	Gladiator probable
151°Gr CT	T.Col Carlo Calosso	}
366ª Sq/151° Gr CT	Ten Piero Veneziani	} Hurricane probable
	M.llo Giulio Cesare	}

Italian Casualties

9° Gr/4° St CT	CR.42 damaged by collision with Gladiator;
	Cap Antonio Larsimont Pergameni safe
60ª Sq/33° Gr Aut BT	S.79 damaged Pilot Cap Loris Bulgarelli KiA
	S.79 damaged, Pilot S.Ten Pierluigi Meroni slightly WiA

Two successful pilots of 9° Gruppo: Ten Ezio Viglione Borghese of 97ª Squadriglia, and S.Ten Alvaro Querci of 73ª.

Saturday, 14 December 1940

274 Squadron undertook two patrols over Bardia and Sollum. On the first of these eight Hurricanes met many S.79s at about 1030, claiming three shot down and two probables. Italian records show that at 0935 four S.79s of 15° Stormo heading for Sidi Azeiz to bomb motor vehicles encountered Gladiators, gunners claiming two shot down. However, RAF records do not indicate any major engagements involving Gladiators on this date.

At 1030 three S.79s encountered two Hurricanes, one bomber going down in flames and one crash-landing at Sidi Bu Amud. Three more then met fighters, one more S.79 being shot down in flames and one crash-landing at Gambut. These losses appear to relate to 274 Squadron's first patrol. One of those involved was Imshi Mason, who wrote:

"Two of us were on patrol well forward when I saw bomb bursts. I dived down and finally saw three S.79s. When they saw us they turned and made for home but I dived on the right hand man and taking my time, sat behind him and gave him a burst. Two chaps jumped out and floated down looking very miserable and then it burnt up and hit the ground and exploded with a terrific flash and blaze."

More Hurricanes were launched by 274 Squadron about an hour later, and at 1130 Flt Lt J.D.Smith, one of 73 Squadron's Canadian pilots who was flying on attachment to 274, claimed an S.79 over Gambut, a second being claimed by Sgt J.H.Clarke, who also added a probable.

Regia Aeronautica records identify one of the lost S.79s as an aircraft of 60ª Squadriglia, 33º Gruppo, flown by Ten Fulvio Gerardi and S.Ten Giorgio Moccheggiani, which fell in flames after an attack by Hurricanes. Gerardi managed to bale out, but Moccheggiani was killed in the crash, later receiving a posthumous Medaglia d'Oro.

Another S.79 from 234ª Squadriglia, 60º Gruppo, 41º Stormo BT, flown by S.Ten Dario Caiani was shot down by Hurricanes, while a second bomber from this unit flown by Cap Giovanni Scagliarini, was badly damaged and force-landed near Bu Amud where it was written off.

A 232ª Squadriglia, 59º Gruppo, 41º Stormo, aircraft flown by Ten Aramis Ammannato was forced to land in flames at Gambut and was destroyed, while another 41º Stormo bomber flown by S.Ten Sergio Cottarelli was also the victim of a Hurricane.

During the morning a formation of 151º Gruppo CT CR.42s led by T.Col Calosso engaged nine Blenheims over Bardia. Claims were listed as six shot down, although the 151º Gruppo records reveal a total for the day of only three, possibly indicating that the claims had been credited twice over to the two squadriglie involved, or that some claims were subsequently downgraded. However, a study of the British account of this combat provides the likely reason – that only three actually came down within Italian territory.

In his book *Wings over North Africa* AVM A.G. 'Tony' Dudgeon, who at this time was commanding officer of 55 Squadron, has described just what happened. Over the preceding three days AVM Collishaw had ordered attacks to be made on Bardia airfield in increasing strength, on each occasion at an hour earlier than on the preceding day (thus a few aircraft attacking at 1500 hours on 11th; the whole of 55 Squadron at 1400 hours on the 12th; the whole squadron again at 1300 hours on the 13th – a Friday !). On each occasion there had been no reaction by Italian fighters, but when the fourth attack was ordered for midday on the next day by a force of three squadrons, representations were made that this was pushing luck too far, and that a significant interception was likely to take place. Collishaw insisted, and Dudgeon led off eight aircraft of 55 Squadron and one from 11 Squadron.

Formations from 211 Squadron, led by Sqn Ldr J.R. 'Bishop' Gordon-Finlayson and 113 Squadron, led by Sqn Ldr R.N. 'Bob' Bateson, followed some way behind. Dudgeon had hoped

RAF fighter pilots claimed six S.79s shot down and three probables during a series of engagements on 14 December 1940. Italian losses actually amounted to five of these bombers. One and one probable were claimed by Flg Off A.A.P. 'Sam' Weller of 274 Squadron.

that the whole combined formation would attack at once, but the other two COs had decided to follow a few minutes later, apparently (according to Dudgeon) to allow 55 Squadron to draw away any opposition before they arrived. This is precisely what happened, the British crews believing that they were attacked by up to 50 CR.42s.

One of the 55 Squadron aircraft, flown by Flg Off 'Milly' Singleton, was shot down, crashing in flames into the sea. Of the remaining eight aircraft, only Dudgeon's returned to base undamaged, while a second limped in a little later on one engine, so badly damaged that it would not fly again. The other six all crash-landed or force-landed en route, two of them – the 11 Squadron machine included – within Italian-controlled territory. Dudgeon took off again and retraced the route, landing beside each of the two downed Blenheims on the wrong side of the lines; in each case he was able to take aboard the crew, flying all six back to the home airfield. Meanwhile, the crews of the other four aircraft down in friendly territory obtained lifts back to base. Thus the effective loss of eight aircraft had thankfully resulted in only three personnel casualties amongst 24 aircrew ! During this disastrous engagement for 55 Squadron, gunners claimed two CR.42s shot down in flames. The other two squadrons completed their attacks without sustaining any interceptions. In passing, it is noteworthy that all three commanding officers of these Blenheim units would be awarded DFCs within a month of each other at the start of 1941.

In the course of an afternoon patrol by nine 274 Squadron Hurricanes, five CR.42s were seen and all were claimed shot down, two each by Sqn Ldr Dunn and newly-promoted Flt Lt Lapsley; Dunn was again caused to force-land, although he returned safely next day. No losses of fighters were recorded by the Regia Aeronautica on this date.

Twelve CR.42s of 13° Gruppo had escorted S.79s of 9° Stormo over Sidi Aziez, splitting into two patrols each of six fighters. One of these, led by Ten Eduardo Sorvillo, stayed at 10,000 ft to cover the other, led by Cap Eduardo Travaglini, which dived down to strafe. During the third run, the top patrol spotted six Hurricanes below them and engaged, claiming four Hurricanes shot down. No losses were recorded by this unit.

Elsewhere, S.Ten Giuseppe Bottà of 82ª Squadriglia undertook three reconnaissance sorties during the day. During the third of these he clashed with four Hurricanes attacking S.79s, but saw no results. Another CR.42 pilot, Serg Graziadio Rizzati of 96ª Squadriglia, suffered a landing accident on return from a sortie and destroyed his aircraft, although he remained unhurt.

A 6 Squadron Lysander II failed to return from a sortie and was reported unofficially to have fallen to AA fire. The aircraft was subsequently found crashed in the Maddalena area with the crew buried alongside.

British Claims

274 Sqn	Plt Off E.M.Mason	P3722	S.79	Bir Chleba 1030
	Flg Off A.A.P.Weller	V7300	S.79	Bir Chleba 1030
	Flg Off A.A.P.Weller		S.79 probable	Bir Chleba 1030
	Plt Off T.L.Patterson	P3720	S.79	Bir Chleba 1030
	Plt Off T.L.Patterson	P3720	S.79 probable	Bir Chleba 1030
	Plt Off S.Godden	V7293	S.79	Bir Chleba 1030
	Flt Lt J.D.Smith	P5176	S.79	Gambut 1130
	(73 Sqn att)			
	Sgt J.H.Clarke	P2627	S.79	Gambut 1130
	Sgt J.H.Clarke	P2627	S.79 probable	Gambut 1130
	Sqn Ldr P.H.Dunn	P5175	2 CR.42s	25m W Bardia 1605
	Flt Lt J.H.Lapsley	V7293	2 CR.42s	30m W Bardia 1605
	Flg Off Greenhill	N2627	CR.42	25m W Bardia 1605
55 Sqn	Blenheim gunners		2 CR.42s	25m W Bardia 1605

British Casualties

55 Sqn	Blenheim I R3733 Flg Off M.S.Singleton and crew MiA
	Blenheim I T2049 force-landed; Plt Off P.G.Blignault and crew safe
	5 Blenheim Is damaged
11 Sqn	Blenheim I L8395 force-landed; Sgt Bailey and crew safe
274 Sqn	Hurricane I damaged Sqn Ldr P.H.Dunn force-landed; safe
6 Sqn	Lysander II L6877 Flt Lt D.T.StH.Dawes and Sgt R. Chantry KiA, Maddalena

41° St BT	S.79 gunners	2 Gladiators
	S.79 gunners	Gladiator probable
368ª Sq/151° Gr CT	Cap Bruno Locatelli	Blenheim
	Ten Giuseppe Zuffi	Blenheim
	M.llo Guido Paparatti	Blenheim
	Serg Piero Hosquet & others	Blenheim probable
366ª Sq/151° Gr CT	S.Ten Amedeo Guidi	2 Blenheims
367ª Sq/151° Gr CT	Serg Magg Francesco Spina	Blenheim
77ª Sq/13° Gr CT	Ten Eduardo Sorvillo	Hurricane
	Serg Renato Gori	Hurricane
82ª Sq/13° Gr CT	Serg Filippo Baldin	Hurricane
	Serg Filippo Baldin	
77ª Sq/13° Gr CT	Ten Eduardo Sorvillo	
	Serg Renato Gori	Hurricane
	3 other pilots	

Italian Casualties

60ª Sq/33° Gr Aut BT	S.79 Ten Fulvio Gerardi baled out; rest of crew KiA
234ª Sq/60° Gr/41° St BT	S.79 MM22221 S.Ten Dario Caiani and crew KiA except co-pilot Serg Magg Pasquale Spampinato, who baled out safely and was taken PoW
	S.79 MM22092 force-landed and w/o; Cap Giovanni Scagliarini and crew safe
232 ª Sq/59° Gr/41° St BT	S.79 MM22218 forced to land in flames at Gambut; Ten Aramis Ammannato and crew safe
	S.79 MM22230 S.Ten Sergio Cottarelli and crew KiA
366ª Sq/151° Gr	CR.42 MM 5646 on ground at Benina
37°St BT	S.81 on ground

Sunday, 15 December 1940

This proved to be a quieter day. All Italian forces in Egypt had now been driven across the border back into Libya. The best part of five out of seven divisions had been destroyed and 38,000 prisoners taken. During strafing operations 33 and 274 Squadrons each lost one Hurricane. Flg Off Peter Wykeham-Barnes of the latter unit made the day's only claim when he reported shooting down a CR.42 over Bir Chleba at 1040.

On this date four pilots of 73 Squadron flew their Hurricanes up to Sidi Haneish on attachment to 274 Squadron. However, following its recent loss of aircraft, 3 RAAF Squadron was temporarily withdrawn from operations. More reinforcements were on the way, for during the first week of December HMS *Furious* had landed 34 Hurricanes and their pilots at Takoradi. On 17 December would come the news that this carrier was sailing again with 40 more of these fighters for delivery in early January 1941.

British Claims

274 Sqn	Flg Off P.G.Wykeham-Barnes	V7300	CR.42	Bir Chleba 1040

British Casualties

33 Sqn	Hurricane u/k pilot and circumstances
274 Sqn	Hurricane u/k pilot and circumstances

Monday, 16 December 1940

Hurricanes from 33 and 274 Squadrons, the latter now joined by the attached pilots of 73 Squadron, flew defensive patrols over Bardia. Here during the afternoon S.79s and CR.42s were encountered, and between 1520-1545 claims were made for six S.79s, one CR.42 and one probable.

The first claim for the CR.42 was made at 1520 by Plt Off Mason, who recorded: "Later in the afternoon two of us met a CR.42 which attacked head-on, but I gave him a long burst and he went down in a spin. We didn't see him smoke or burn or hit the ground so he is unconfirmed." A second CR.42 was also claimed as a probable by Flt Lt J.D.Smith.

73 Squadron's Sgt Fred Marshall recorded: "After breakfast and meeting Flg Off Patterson of 274, we flew up to Sidi Barrani, where we refuelled and took off on an Offensive Patrol. I flew with Pat and

at 17,000 ft west of Sollum we spotted some 79s at about 5,000 ft. We dived and engaged them and I got two in flames, Pat two and Smithy one." At about the same time the sixth S.79 was claimed by Flg Off Peter Wykeham-Barnes, all these claims being made just to the south of Gambut.

Escorting CR.42s of 10° Gruppo CT engaged the Hurricanes, Ten Lucchini claiming one probably shot down. His opponent seems to have been Plt Off A.McFadden, another of the 73 Squadron pilots, who was pursued "up country" by two CR.42s, eventually force-landing due to lack of fuel; he returned next day, his aircraft subsequently being recovered undamaged.

The S.79s had indeed been six in number, and were from 29° Gruppo, 9° Stormo BT, briefed to attack Sidi Omar. Three bombers were shot down and three were damaged. The first to fall was flown by T.Col Guglielmo Grandjacquet, commander of the gruppo, followed by the lead bomber, which was in the hands of Cap Victor Hugo Girolami, commanding officer of 63ª Squadriglia; aboard this latter aircraft was the 9° Stormo commander, Col Mario Aramu, all aboard these two S.79s losing their lives. A third S.79 flown by S.Ten Amedeo Tonachella then crashed to the ground, although the pilot managed to bale out. Aramu, Grandjacquet and Girolami were all later awarded the Medaglia d'Oro.

An attack by Blenheims on Ain el Gazala set fire to a Ca.133 which was the 'hack' aircraft of 96ª Squadriglia. Two of the unit's pilots, Serg Spitzl and Minelli suffered burns, while all the pilots' logbooks were destroyed in the fire. This aircraft may have been that attacked during the morning by Flg Off H.C.Down and Plt Off T.B.Garland who reported attacking an S.79 circling to land at Menastir and causing considerable damage; they then strafed the aircraft on the ground.

British Claims

274 Sqn	Flg Off H.C.Down	P2652	}	S.79 damaged and strafed on ground; Menastir 0940	
	Plt Off T.B.Garland	P3721			
	Plt Off T.L.Patterson	P3544 YK-T		2 S.79s	5m S Gambut 1530-1545
	Flg Off P.G.Wykeham-Barnes	V7293		S.79	Gambut area 1535
	Plt Off E.M.Mason	P3720		CR.42 probable	5m S Gambut 1520
73 Sqn att 274 Sqn	Sgt A.E.Marshall	V7562 TP-A		2 S.79s	5m S Gambut 1530-1545
	Flt Lt J.D.Smith	V7553		S.79	
	Flt Lt J.D.Smith	V7553		CR.42 probable	

British Casualties

73 Sqn att 274 Sqn	Hurricane force-landed Plt Off A.McFadden; aircraft out of fuel; recovered next day

Italian Claims

90ª Sq/10° Gr CT	Ten Franco Lucchini	Hurricane probable

Italian Casualties

62ª Sq/29° Gr/9° St BT	S.79 T.Col Guglielmo Grandjacquet & crew KiA
63ª Sq/29° Gr/9° St BT	S.79 Cap Victor Hugo Girolami & crew KiA, including Col Mario Aramu
	S.79 S.Ten Amedeo Tonachella baled out; rest of crew KiA
96ª Sq/9° Gr CT	Ca.133 destroyed on ground; two suffered burns

Tuesday, 17 December 1940

During further patrols, pilots of 33 Squadron claimed a CR.42 shot down while strafing in the Bardia-Tobruk area. Their victim appears to have been S.Ten Natale Cima of 92ª Squadriglia; S.Ten Dario Magnabosco of 78ª Squadriglia claimed a Hurricane in flames.

Cap Larsimont Pergameni led 13 4° Stormo CR.42s to escort three S.79s attacking British shipping off the coast at Bardia, Gladiators reportedly being encountered. One of these was claimed by Ten Piero Bonfatti and Ten Giulio Reiner, and a second probable by Ten Valerio De Campo and Serg Mario Guerci. 15° Stormo BT gunners also claimed one Gladiator shot down.

Although 3 RAAF Squadron had resumed operations on this date, this unit does not appear to have been involved. The other remaining Gladiator-equipped unit, 112 Squadron, recorded undertaking patrols over the front throughout December, but during the month made no report of any engagements, claims or losses. 13° Gruppo CT now handed its remaining CR.42s to 4° Stormo and began preparing to return to Italy.

Pilots of 33 Squadron also claimed an aircraft which they identified as a Macchi 200 shot down on

An S.79 of 175ª Squadriglia RST. This unit was very active in reconnaissance missions from the last months of 1940, suffering a quite high attrition rate.

this date. As none of these aircraft were yet operating in North Africa, and the first Fiat G.50s would only reach Castel Benito on the 30th, it is surmised that this may have been an incorrectly identified Breda Ba.65 – although even this possibility is unlikely since the units equipped with these aircraft were at the time in the process of withdrawing.

British Claims

33 Sqn	u/k pilot		CR.42
	u/k pilot		MC.200

Italian Claims

78ª Sq/13° Gr /2° St CT	S.Ten Dario Magnabosco		Hurricane
73ª Sq/9° Gr/4° St CT	Ten Piero Bonfatti	}	Gladiator
	Ten Giulio Reiner		
	Ten Valerio De Campo	}	Gladiator probable
	Serg Mario Guerci		
15° St BT	S.79 gunners		Gladiator

Italian Casualties

92ª Sq/8° Gr/2°St	CR.42 S.Ten Natale Cima KiA

Wednesday, 18 December 1940

While patrolling in the Bardia-Gambut area, Flt Lt J.D.Smith, the 73 Squadron pilot, intercepted and shot down a reconnaissance S.79 of 175ª Squadriglia RST.

British Claim

73 Sqn att 274 Sqn	Flt Lt J.D.Smith	S.79	9 miles SSE Great Gambut 0830

Italian Casualties

175ª Sq RST	S.79 Ten Paolo Compagnone & crew KiA

Thursday, 19 December 1940

This seems to have been another day of over-optimism. 33 and 274 Squadrons appear to have operated at much the same times on this occasion. Around 1300-1330, 33 Squadron claimed two CR.42s, while 2/Lt Bob Talbot of 274 Squadron claimed a third, and Plt Off Greenhill added a fourth damaged. Somewhat more than two hours later 33 Squadron claimed two further CR.42s, and 274 Squadron's Flt Lt John Lapsley claimed another to bring the day's apparent 'bag' of these fighters to six and one damaged.

At the same time as the latter claims were recorded, other pilots of 33 Squadron intercepted S.79s, claiming three shot down, and 274 Squadron's Flg Off 'Sam' Weller found himself amongst seven of these bombers. Although his Hurricane was riddled by return fire, he managed to inflict damage on at least one before escaping and returning to base.

Twelve S.79s of 41° Stormo BT led by T.Col Emilio Draghelli, commander of the 59° Gruppo and T.Col Pasquale D'Ippolito, commander of 60° Gruppo, were escorted to Sollum by 21 CR.42s of 9° and

10° Gruppi. The former of these units, again led by Cap Larsimont Pergameni, was on its last mission before returning to Italy. When the Hurricanes attacked over the target, pilots of 73ª and 96ª Squadriglie and 10° Gruppo made a rather late interception, while 97ª Squadriglia stayed with the bombers. Serg Magg Ferrulli claimed one Hurricane shot down and a second damaged, but his CR.42 was hit in the engine and he had to make an emergency landing. Initially he was reported lost in action, but in fact he had managed to land within the fortified walls of Bardia, surviving unhurt.

Meanwhile Ten Pietro Bonfatti had claimed a second Hurricane shot down, and Serg Rossi one damaged; S.Ten Giuseppe Oblach claimed one probable. It seems that four other CR.42s also suffered damage during this combat. No bombers were lost during this attack, but seven were badly damaged with dead or wounded crew members aboard, although one flown by S.Ten Ferdinando Trolla did crash-land. Gunners in the S.79s claimed two Hurricanes shot down and three probables.

The earlier combat recorded by 33 Squadron may have been with 151° Gruppo. This unit was engaged in strafing when Hurricanes were encountered, one of which was claimed probably shot down by four of the Fiat pilots, their own unit suffering no loss.

British Claims

274 Sqn	2/Lt R.H.Talbot	P3721	CR.42	30m W Bardia 1305
73 Sqn	u/ks		2 CR.42s probable	Gzemi 1315
33 Sqn	Flg Off V.C.Woodward	P2499	2 CR.42s	1330
274 Sqn	Plt Off C.H.Greenhill	P3822	CR.42 damaged	Great Gambut 1330
	Plt Off A.A.P.Weller	V7300	S.79 damaged	Sollum-Bardia road 1545
	Flt Lt J.H.Lapsley	V7293	CR.42	Sollum-Gambut area 1550
33 Sqn	u/ks		S.79s	Bardia area 1550
	Flg Off C.H.Dyson		2 CR.42s	Bardia area 1550

British Casualties

274 Sqn	Hurricane I V7300 shot up by bombers' gunners, but returned

Italian Claims

73ª Sq/9° Gr/4° St CT	Ten Pietro Bonfatti	Hurricane
91ª Sq/10° Gr/4° St CT	Serg Magg Leonardo Ferrulli	Hurricane
73ª Sq/9° Gr/4° St CT	S.Ten Giuseppe Oblach	Hurricane probable
	S.Ten Giuseppe Oblach	Hurricane damaged
	Serg Pasquale Rossi	Hurricane damaged
368ª Sq/151° Gr CT	Cap Bruno Locatelli	
	Serg Magg Davide Colauzzi	Hurricane probable
	Serg Magg Annibale Ricotti	
367ª Sq/151° Gr CT	Cap Simeone Marsan	
41° St BT	S.79 gunners	2 Hurricanes and 3 probables

Italian Casualties

91ª Sq/10° Gr/4° St CT	CR.42 damaged Serg Magg Leonardo Ferrulli force-landed in Bardia
?	4 CR.42s damaged
233ª Sq/59° Gr/41° St BT	S.79 MM22268 damaged force-landed T.5; Cap Meille & S.Ten Bresciani wounded
	S.79 damaged crash-landed; S.Ten Ferdinando Trolla, pilot; 1° Av Luigi Favale KiA; 1°Av Nazzareno De Pascale & 1° Av Alfredo Palmieri wounded
	S.79 damaged emergency landing; Ten Vittorio Stancanelli and crew safe
	S.79 damaged T.Col Draghelli landed T.2bis; Ten Boris Premrù, M.llo mot Bruno Scagliarini, Serg arm Augusto Della Ciana & Serg RT Francesco Maurelli wounded
232ª Sq/59° Gr/41° St BT	S.79 damaged Ten Mario Persico last to land
235ª Sq/60° Gr/41° St BT	S.79 MM 21943 damaged Cap Athos Ammannato and crew safe

Thursday, 19 December 1940

During the night Blenheim T2059 of 113 Squadron failed to return from a raid on Gazala.

British Casualties

113 Sqn	Blenheim IV T2059 Plt Off V.Frith & crew MiA

Friday, 20 December 1940

This day was marked by the withdrawal from Libya of several Italian fighter gruppi. Leaving their CR.42s to the newly-arrived 23° Gruppo, 9° Gruppo departed for the homeland, followed by both gruppi of 2° Stormo CT, which was to re-equip with Macchi C.200s. Since 11 June this unit had flown 2,403 sorties and claimed 57 victories, this latter number subsequently being downgraded to 45. 13 CR.42s had been totally lost, not including force-landed or badly damaged aircraft, and 12 pilots were missing, two of them having become PoWs.

The day also saw the loss of a Ba.65 of 159ª Squadriglia in a landing accident in which the pilot was killed.

Italian Casualties

159ª Sq/12° Gr/50° St Ass	Ba.65 M.llo Francesco De Vivo KiFA

Saturday, 21 December 1940

33 and 274 Squadrons again patrolled over the Bardia-Sollum area, reporting encountering 30 S.79s and 40 CR.42s at 0645, 25 miles west of Bardia. Three of the bombers were claimed shot down, and from one of those claimed by 33 Squadron, three members of the crew were seen to bale out, but their parachutes did not open. An S.79 of 175ª Squadriglia, flown by Ten Brunetto Bruni, was actually lost.

Following the departure of 2° Stormo CT, a number of selected pilots from 13° Gruppo were retained and were posted to 4° Stormo for continued operations. One of these was Serg Teresio Martinoli, future top-scoring pilot of the Regia Aeronautica.

British Claims

33 Sqn	u/ks		2 S.79s	5m W Bardia
274 Sqn	Plt Off T.L.Patterson	P2544	S.79	

Italian Casualties

84ª Sq/10° Gr/4° St CT	CR.42 MM4332 landing accident; Serg Luciano Perdoni safe
175ª Sq Aut RST	S.79 Ten Brunetto Bruni and crew KiA

Sunday, 22 December 1940

33 Squadron pilots claimed two more S.79s. Two such aircraft were badly damaged, one of 53ª Squadriglia, 47° Gruppo, 15° Stormo reportedly being attacked by a 'Fairey Battle', which killed one gunner and wounded two other members of the crew; the bomber force-landed 18 miles south-east of Tobruk. A second S.79, this one from 41° Stormo, flown by Ten Bruno Pandolfi, returned to base with severe damage.

British Claims

33 Sqn	u/ks	2 S.79s

Italian Casualties

53ª Sq/47° Gr/15° St BT	S.79 MM21733 badly damaged. Force-landed 18 m SE Tobruk with one dead and two wounded; pilot Ten Federico Menon safe
235ª Sq/60° Gr/41° St BT	S.79 MM22232 badly damaged, Ten Bruno Pandolfi and crew safe

Monday, 23 December 1940

On an early morning patrol Plt Off Imshi Mason claimed two S.79s:

"The first one was well over Italian territory and was all alone making for home and only just off the ground. I got behind him and gave him a short burst. His port engine caught fire and he managed to get his aircraft down with wheels up. I didn't bother to fire again, but flew alongside and watched, as I hadn't seen one crash close to, yet. Out of the crew of five or six, only one got out. He stood looking at the wrecked machine so miserably that I hadn't the heart to machine gun him."

Some days later he wrote again:

"The machine I shot down and didn't machine gun the pilot (I thought) turned out to be a Caproni 310 and not a 79. The motors I saw rushing towards it turned out to be ours and all were taken prisoner. The two pilots had been both badly wounded and were taken to hospital, but the radio op and gunner were OK. I had a most interesting chat with the gunner afterwards at HQ. A very pleasant little chap – a photographer in civil life – just nearly finished his six years in the air force and going to start an art photography business at home. He said he fired 300 rounds at me!! He showed me a bullet hole in <u>and out</u> of his jacket that had not touched him."

His victim had been an aircraft of 67° Gruppo OA, S.Ten Gaetano Leporino and his crew failing to return from a reconnaissance.

Mason meanwhile had continued with his patrol:

"After this I climbed up and after a bit I saw a large formation below me of ten S.79s escorted by about 20 fighters (CR.42s). I dived past the escort and shot at one of the outside bombers and dived away. After climbing again I saw that although this chap had dropped back at first he had now got back in formation. I hung around above for about ten minutes and then whilst they were dropping their bombs (on our troops) I chose my opportunity and dived very steeply on this same fellow. As the escorting fighters saw me coming in plenty of time I had to continue my dive and away, closely pursued by extremely angry CR.42s. So I did not observe the result of my engagement, although I saw my bullets going into him. I was not going to claim this one. However, another pilot saw an S.79 burning on the ground near this encounter, so I have been told that I can have this as confirmed. Also, a later report from the army states that it was seen to go down in flames."

The formation attacked by Mason had comprised ten S.79s of 15° Stormo led by Col Napoli, escorted by 17 CR.42s of 10° Gruppo, led by Magg Romagnoli. An attack by five Hurricanes was reported by the fighters, 10° Gruppo pilots claiming one with another reportedly seen to force-land among armoured cars and a third was claimed as a probable. One CR.42, flown by Serg Luigi Ferrario of 91ª Squadriglia returned badly damaged. 2/Lt Bob Talbot had claimed one CR.42 shot down and an S.79 damaged, but Flg Off Greenhill's Hurricane was hit and he force-landed south of Taifa. The S.79 crews of 15° Stormo reported an attack by Hurricanes, but apparently the fighters were driven off by the escort and no damage was reported by them.

CR.42 MM 5544 '91-1' under repair at El Adem repair shop. It was damaged on 23 December 1940 while being flown by Serg Luigi Ferrario of 91ª Squadriglia, 10° Gruppo, 4° Stormo CT.

Plt Off Mason of 274 Squadron undertook a number of long-range sorties to attack Italian airfields during December 1940 and January 1941, claiming his fifth individual victory on 23 December.

British Claims

274 Sqn	Flg Off E.M.Mason	P3722	S.79 (actually Ca.310)	El Gobbi	0915
			S.79	W Capuzzo	0940
	2/Lt R.H.Talbot	P3721	CR.42		1000
			S.79 damaged		1000

3 RAAF Squadron's claim list originally indicated three victories on this date, but subsequently it was confirmed that no enemy aircraft were encountered by the unit.

British Casualties		
274 Sqn	Hurricane damaged force-landed S Taifa	

Italian Claims		
10° Gr/4° St CT	17 pilots	Hurricane
		Hurricane force-landed
		Hurricane probable

Italian Casualties		
67° Gr OA	Ca.310 MM21612 S.Ten Gaetano Leporino & crew PoW	
91ª Sq/10° Gr/4° St CT	CR.42 damaged Serg Luigi Ferrario safe	

Thursday, 26 December 1940

Eighteen CR.42s from 10° Gruppo and 12 from 23° Gruppo set out to escort ten S.79s of 34° Stormo on a raid. 3 RAAF Squadron Gladiator pilots reported meeting five S.79s with a close escort of six CR.42s, and with 18 more of these as top cover over Bardia. The Australian pilots claimed two CR.42s shot down, four probables and three damaged without loss. In return Magg Carlo Romagnoli and M.llo Leonardo Ferrulli claimed one Gladiator each, one more being claimed by 23° Gruppo. However, Cap Guido Bobba, commanding officer of 23° Gruppo's 74ª Squadriglia, was shot down and six more CR.42s were damaged. One of the S.79s force-landed near Ain el Gazala, reportedly hit by AA fire. Command of 74ª Squadriglia was taken over by Cap Mario Pinna.

Recorded 3 RAAF's Plt Off John Jackson of this encounter:

"My first fight on the patrol this afternoon, eight of us on the job saw ten bombers and goodness knows how many fighters up above us over Sollum Bay at about 15,000 to 18,000 ft. We went straight for them and I got into the middle of about a dozen at 17,000 ft but couldn't get a decent shot – fired 350 rounds but my fuselage guns were not working. Had my plane badly shot about, one bullet grazed my parachute straps and bruised my shoulder, a couple more whistled past my head and tore the cockpit cover edges and broke the glass, a few more tore a lot of the fabric off the starboard wings, a few more went through the lower mainplanes. Thanks to providence, I didn't get hit – the blighter must have got a good shot at me. There were too many of them for me to get a go at any one, quite a thrilling experience. Alan Rawlinson reckons he got one, also Jock Perrin, and there were three other possibles. Not bad work seeing how outnumbered we were. A few of the others also collected an odd bullet hole. It's a pity we haven't got better aircraft, the Gladiators are nowhere near as good as the CR.42s. Our air strength is about a tenth of theirs."

Cap Guido Bobba, commanding officer of 74ª Squadriglia, 23° Gruppo CT, who was shot down and killed on 26 December 1940.

British Claims				
3 RAAF Sqn	Flg Off W.S.Arthur	N5753	CR.42	off Bardia 1405-1430
	Flg Off W.S.Arthur	N5753	CR.42 damaged	off Bardia 1405-1430
	Flt Lt G.H.Steege		CR.42	
	Flt Lt G.H.Steege		CR.42 damaged	
	Flg Off A.C.Rawlinson	N5782	CR.42 probable	
	Flt Lt J.R.Perrin		CR.42 probable	
	Flg Off A.H.Boyd		CR.42 probable	
	Flg Off A.H.Boyd		CR,42 damaged	
	Flg Off P.StG.B.Turnbull		CR.42 probable	

British Casualties

3 RAAF Sqn	Gladiator N5756 damaged Plt Off J.F.Jackson safe 1405

Italian Claims

10° Gr/4° St CT	Magg Carlo Romagnoli	Gladiator
	Serg Magg Leonardo Ferrulli	Gladiator
23° Gr CT	?	Gladiator

Italian Casualties

74ª Sq/23° Gr CT	CR.42 Cap Guido Bobba MiA
23° Gr CT	6 CR.42s damaged
216ª Sq/53° Gr/34° St BT	S.79 force-landed S.Ten Bellini & crew safe

Friday, 27 December 1940

33 Squadron once again intercepted S.79s and escorting CR.42s, claiming three of the bombers shot down and two CR.42s probably so. In fact one S.79 of 216ª Squadriglia, 53° Gruppo, flown by S.Ten Aldo Peterlini, was shot down in flames over Sollum, two members of the crew baling out safely. CR.42 pilots of the 10° Gruppo escort claimed one Hurricane shot down and a second as a probable by three members of 70ª Squadriglia, 23° Gruppo. Gunners in the bombers were unable to offer any resistance on this occasion, as the lubricant in their machine guns had frozen.

British Claims

33 Sqn	u/k	3 S.79s
	u/k	2 CR.42s probable

Italian Claims

10° Gr/4° St CT	Cap Guiducci	
	Ten Lucchini	Hurricane
	& others	
70ª Sq/23° Gr CT	Ten Claudio Solaro	
	S.Ten Oscar Abello	Hurricane probable

Italian Casualties

216ª Sq/53° Gr/34° St BT	S.Ten Aldo Peterlini & crew KiA, apart from two who baled out

Saturday, 28 December 1940

Yet again 33 Squadron encountered a raiding formation composed of eight S.79s and seven CR.42s. This time one of each type were claimed shot down. The fighter may have been that flown by S.Ten Ruggero Caporali of 91ª Squadriglia, who was shot down and killed while strafing armoured cars near Sidi Rezegh. These claims brought 33 Squadron's total for December to 36 confirmed, 10 probables and 11 damaged.

British Claims

33 Sqn	u/k	S.79
	u/k	CR.42

Italian Casualties

91ª Sq/10° Gr/4° St BT	CR.42 MM4421 S.Ten Ruggero Caporali KiA

Sunday – Monday, 30/31 December 1940

On the 30th 73 Squadron, now fully up to strength, moved to Sidi Haneish to commence operations as an independent unit. Here it replaced 112 Squadron, which withdrew to Amiriya, temporarily to take over the defence of the Delta, but also to prepare for service in Greece.

The day also saw the arrival in Africa of 2° Gruppo CT led by Magg Giuseppe Baylon. This unit was equipped with Fiat G.50s, the first Italian monoplane fighters to reach Libya. However, no sooner had they arrived at Castel Benito than 27 of them suffered damage during a British bombing raid.

Next day – the last of the year – the Regia Aeronautica recorded the loss of another 67° Gruppo OA Ca.310, but no reason for its demise has been found.

Italian Casualties

67° Gr OA	Ca.310 MM21625 Ten Amelio Peri & crew MiA

By this date the Regia Aeronautica in North Africa had claimed 214 British aircraft destroyed and 64 more probably so since June. Of these, 157 destroyed and 46 probables were credited to the fighter units, which had lost 41 CR.42s in combat. Top-scoring unit had been 4° Stormo CT, with 95 of the confirmed victories.

RAF Middle East had been substantially reinforced by the end of the year. Since the start of September 41 Wellingtons, 87 Hurricanes and 85 Blenheim IVs had arrived. The completion of the re-equipment of 70 Squadron had ensured that three squadrons of heavy bombers had been available when needed throughout the offensive, while the number of Hurricane squadrons now stood at three. Three of the bomber squadrons were also now completely re-equipped with the Mark IV Blenheim. However, supply of these aircraft had still not been adequate to raise the strength of these units to the target of 16 aircraft; indeed, it was still proving quite difficult to maintain them at 12.

Here the reserves tell the story. Of the 19 Mark IV aircraft in reserve, only six were actually serviceable. The replacement of the earlier Mark Is did mean that 26 of these were in reserve, but of these only two were fully operational, all the rest being in the process of overhaul.

Wednesday, 1 January 1941

In the meantime the opening of the new year saw 20,000lbs of bombs dropped on Bardia by Wellingons and Swordfish by night, and by Blenheims by day, the latter undertaking 44 sorties. Next day another 30,000lbs were dropped, bringing the total tonnage to over 40 softening-up the port for assault and capture.

At 1320 on New Year's Day CR.42s intercepted a reported nine Blenheims, Serg Magg Fiorenzo Milella of 151° Gruppo's 366ª Squadriglia, claiming one shot down and a second as a probable, although on this occasion no losses were reported by the RAF. This gruppo had now been taken over by T.Col Raffaello Colacicchi, his predecessor, T.Col Calosso having departed for Italy on 29 December.

Italian Claims		
366ª Sq/151° Gr CT	Serg Magg Fiorenzo Milella	Blenheim
	Serg Magg Fiorenzo Milella	Blenheim probable
Italian Casualties		
Unspecified unit	S.79 with torpedo destroyed by bombs at Ain el Gazala	
	2 S.79s damaged on the ground by bombs	

Friday, 3 January 1941

On this date 6th Australian Division commenced an attack on Bardia, which brought out the Regia Aeronautica bombers in strength again. The day began badly for the RAF when at 0750 two Blenheims of 45 Squadron on their way to attack Gazala airfield were intercepted by a lone CR.42 flown by Serg Magg Mario Veronesi of 84ª Squadriglia, 10° Gruppo CT. Veronesi proceeded to claim both bombers shot down in flames, one of which he saw crash into the sea. He had in fact only managed to shoot down one, L8479, in which Flg Off P.Griffiths and his crew were lost. The returning crew of the other aircraft reported that Veronesi had been "most persistent" and appeared to be "a first-class pilot".

At 1310 Sgt Fred Marshall of 73 Squadron intercepted five S.79s of 52° Gruppo, 34° Stormo, which were attacking HMS *Terror*, nine miles north-east of Bardia, where the vessel had been supporting the Australian advance. The only British pilot to intercept, Marshall's attack was summarized in the 202 Group Intelligence Summary of 6 January:

"One of our Hurricanes engaged on offensive patrol at 1320 hours, 20 miles north of Ras Venner, and was at 15,000 ft when he observed heavy AA fire near Ras el Milh. On investigating he found that five S.79s in line abreast (almost a shallow vic) were bombing units of our fleet. Our aircraft gave chase and the enemy formation now turned due west. He closed in to 300 yards, and made a stern attack on the left hand aircraft of the formation which after a short burst caught fire and dived into the sea. Our aircraft then turned his fire onto the next aircraft and this also went down in flames after a burst of some 3-4 seconds. It was seen almost to explode before hitting the sea. Two of the crew were seen to bale out successfully. By this time his range was approximately 200 yards, and he fired at the third bomber. One burst stopped the starboard motor, the aircraft went into a long glide and some minutes later it was seen to land in the sea with a large splash. Our pilot then gave his attention to the fourth aircraft and soon silenced the return fire. Pieces of metal came away from the starboard motor. But at this moment his ammunition gave out and he broke away.

All the time our aircraft was in range the enemy air gunners kept up a fire until killed; the only evasive action taken being a gentle dive."

Three S.79s failed to return from this attack and the two remaining bombers crash-landed not far from Benghazi. Recorded Marshall: "The I.O.(intelligence officer) told me that with my score standing at five certs I would be put up for the DFM. I felt sorry for the two Ities who baled out; they were some 20 miles out to sea without a hope of being picked up." In the event it would be some considerable time and several actions later before Marshall's well-deserved decoration finally materialised. Soon after his return from this eventful sortie, Marshall was off again with Sqn Ldr A.D.Murray and Flg Off Jas Storrar to attack a landing ground, where they claimed to have strafed and destroyed eight aircraft.

55 Squadron despatched pairs of Blenheims throughout the day to attack Italian airfields in order to divert defending fighters away from strafing the advancing ground troops. One such attack on Derna at 0850 bombed 20-25 large aircraft without observed results. A second attack five minutes later was intercepted by two fighters identified as CR.32s. These made alternate attacks on the Blenheim flown by Sgt Dixon, trying to get beneath the bomber's tail. This they failed to do, and after ten minutes they broke away with steep turns to the right. The gunner could not ascertain whether he had been successful in hitting either, but the Blenheim returned undamaged.

Sgt A.E.Marshall of the newly-arrived 73 Squadron, had already seen action in France. On 3 January 1941 he matched John Lapsley's success by claiming three S.79 bombers during a single sortie.

Later in the afternoon at around 1600, two Blenheims of 55 Squadron were attacked over Derna by a single-engined monoplane fighter, but after three minutes this broke away without having inflicted any damage. The two bomber pilots then spotted a seaplane heading north-west just above the sea some 35 miles north of Tobruk. This was a Cant.Z.506B of 288ª Squadriglia RM, flown by S.Ten Roberto Colombo, who had aboard a naval officer, S.Ten Vasc Guerrino Galeazzi, as observer. Flg Off Walker dived from 10,000 feet to attack with the Blenheim's front gun from the starboard quarter. He then fell back before attacking again and apparently silencing the Italian aircraft's turret gunner. He then formated on the Cant, enabling his own turret gunner and that of Plt Off Wilson's aircraft to enfilade it. Following this attack one

Cant.Z.506 of 288ª Squadriglia RM; a floatplane of this unit was shot down in the Gulf of Sollum on 3 January 1941.

float was seen to fall off while the pilot appeared to be trying to make a water landing. However, a wing tip struck the water and also broke off as the aircraft crashed into the sea. It remained afloat for some time as the Blenheims circled above, but no-one was seen to get out. The whole engagement had lasted some 15 minutes, and on return to base Walker's aircraft was found to have suffered a number of hits by large calibre machine-gun bullets, one of which had punctured a fuel tank. Colombo and his crew were listed as missing in action. The bombers attacked, shooting down the floatplane which crash-landed off the coast near Sollum, the whole crew being reported missing.

During the day the Fiat G.50bis of 2° Gruppo CT undertook their first sorties over Libya, but reported no encounters. By dusk the Australian Division had taken 45,000 prisoners and had captured 500 guns, 100 light and 12 medium tanks – a tremendous coup.

British Claims

73 Sqn	Sgt A.E.Marshall	TP-D	3 S.79s	Ras Uenna – 20m out to sea 1310-1318
			S.79 damaged	20m out to sea 1310-1318
55 Sqn	Plt Off Walker & crew	T2243	} Cant.Z.506B	35m N Tobruk 1600
	Plt Off J.Wilson & crew	T2251		
73 Sqn	Sqn Ldr A.D.Murray		} 8 aircraft on the ground	
	Flg Off J.E.Storrar			
	Sgt A.E.Marshall			

British Casualties

45 Sqn	Blenheim L8479 Flg Off P.Griffiths & crew MiA 0750

Italian Claims

84ª Sq/10° Gr/4° St CT	Serg Mario Veronesi	2 Blenheims

Italian Casualties

215ª Sq/52° Gr/34° St BT	S.79 Ten Nunzio Mantegna & crew KiA
	S.79 S.Ten Giuseppe Canè & crew KiA
	S.79 S.Ten Vito Castro & crew PoW
	S.79 damaged crash-landed near Benghazi; S.Ten Maiani & crew safe
	S.79 damaged crash-landed near Benghazi; S.Ten Brombini & crew safe
288ª Sq RM	Cant.Z.506B MM45344 crash-landed in sea off Sollum; S.Ten Roberto Colombo & crew MiA

Saturday, 4 January 1941

At 0530 pilots of 33 Squadron claimed one CR.42 and a second probable over the Tobruk-Bardia area. Ten CR.42s of 23° Gruppo and 12 of 10° Gruppo were led by Magg Romagnoli to escort S.79s over Bardia at 0820. Two Blenheims of 45 Squadron were intercepted and were claimed probably shot down; both bombers suffered some damage, but returned to base.

Over Marsa Luch the Italians were bounced by Hurricanes, two of which they claimed to have shot down. One CR.42 was lost, S.Ten Ennio Grifoni of 91ª Squadriglia being killed, while S.Ten Bruno Devoto force-landed at T5 airfield. Their opponents would appear to have been from 274 Squadron, Plt Off Sidney Godden claiming two CR.42s shot down at 0935 and 0945 north of Great Gambut.

Pilots of 23° Gruppo again reported meeting Hurricanes over Bardia later in the morning, Cap Pietro Calistri, commander of 75ª Squadriglia, claiming one shot down. Ten Gino Battagion of 70ª Squadriglia was wounded and force-landed at Ain el Gazala. Battagion recalled:

"At 18,000 feet I saw two Hurricanes in front of me. I began shooting. They shot at me too. Suddenly, I felt a hit. An explosive bullet broke the windshield into many pieces and I was slightly wounded in the head. The explosion broke my goggles and wounded me in one eye. With blood oozing down my face, I lost consciousness for some seconds, perhaps ten or twenty. I recovered consciousness due to the air rushing into the cockpit and found that the aircraft was spinning. I managed to recover from the spin and when I was near the ground fired a burst at some trucks. My wingman signalled to me that one wheel of my aircraft was damaged but I managed to land at Ain el Gazala, near an ambulance. I landed at the slowest speed possible, holding the aircraft on the one serviceable wheel, and succeeded in stopping without overturning. The personnel near the ambulance recovered me and for three months I could not fly because my eye gave me a lot of trouble. Some splinters had been extracted from my head – some of them are still there!"

During this engagement Flt Sgt T.C.Morris of 274 Squadron claimed one CR.42 at 1245, north-west of Sidi Azeiz, but then carried out a force-landing as the radiator of his aircraft had been damaged.

That afternoon 10° Gruppo provided a further escort, one Hurricane being claimed shot down by four pilots in collaboration. It is likely that this was N2625 of 274 Squadron in which Sgt Hulbert was brought down by CR.42s in such circumstances.

British Claims

33 Sqn	u/k		CR.42	Tobruk-Bardia 0630
274 Sqn	Plt Off S.Godden	V7558	2 CR.42s	5m N Great Gambut 0935-0940
	Flt Sgt T.C.Morris	V7293	CR.42	5m NW Sidi Azeiz 1245

British Casualties

274 Sqn	Hurricane N2625 Sgt Hulbert
	Hurricane damaged V7293;Flt Sgt T.C.Morris force-landed
45 Sqn	Blenheim damaged; Flt Lt Rixson and crew returned safely
	Blenheim damaged; Sgt Harley and crew returned safely

Italian Claims

10° Gr/4° St CT	}	
23° Gr CT	}	2 Blenheims probably, one by Ten Claudio Solaro
10° Gr/4° St CT	Magg Carlo Romagnoli	Hurricane
91ª Sq/10° Gr/4° St CT	M.llo Leonardo Ferrulli	Hurricane
90ª Sq/10° Gr/4° St	Ten Franco Lucchini	
	Serg G.Battista Ceoletta	
91ª Sq/10° Gr/4° St	Serg Ambrogio Rusconi	Hurricane
	Serg Giovanni Casero	
75ª Sq/23° Gr CT	Cap Pietro Calistri	Hurricane
90ª Sq/10° Gr/4° St CT	Ten Giovanni Guiducci	
	S.Ten Neri De Benedetti	
	Ten Orlando Mandolini	Hurricane
	Serg Luigi Contarini	

Italian Casualties

91ª Sq/10° Gr/4° St CT	CR.42 S.Ten Ennio Grifoni KiA
	CR.42 damaged S.Ten Bruno Devoto force-landed
70ª Sq/23° Gr CT	CR.42 damaged Ten Gino Battagion WiA

Sunday, 5 January 1941

113 Squadron despatched three Blenheims to Tobruk at 0715. The crews reported being attacked by Macchi 200s; these were in fact six G.50bis of 2° Gruppo CT led by Magg Baylon. 10° Gruppo may have also become involved in this interception as Serg Teresio Martinoli claimed a Blenheim over Marsa Luch. One bomber was badly damaged, but managed to return to base.

Plt Off Mason and 2/Lt Talbot had been sent to a forward airfield, from where they set off to attack Gazala: "…I ground [strafed] some 42s and Bob shot down a 79 taking off." Talbot claimed an S.79 and a second damaged at 0820, and Mason claimed three CR.42s damaged on the ground. Regia Aeronautica records indicate two S.79s destroyed on the ground which would appear to relate to Talbot's claims.

The pair were off again four hours later:

"…in the afternoon we went there again and circled over the aerodrome. Suddenly I saw two CR.42s approaching to land. I dived down and came up behind. I gave the leader a burst and as I shot past him he turned slowly and dived straight into the middle of the aerodrome and exploded. In the meantime the other chap had turned and came for me head-on. I gave him a short burst and he did the same thing. This time on the edge of the aerodrome.

By then five more, also returning home, had seen me and were diving on me so Bob shot down the leader and they dispersed."

These three claims were all made at around 1220, and would appear to have related to 23° Gruppo CR.42s, this unit reporting that Ten Oscar Abello and Serg Pardino Pardini were both killed over Benina Z1 landing ground. Both members of 70ª Squadriglia, Abello had earlier claimed two victories over Malta, and would be awarded a posthumous Medaglia d'Oro (see also *Malta: the Hurricane Years 1940-41*).

Shortly after this engagement, pilots from 73 Squadron, who had been sent out singly at 15-minute intervals, began encountering hostile aircraft. Sgt Marshall claimed an S.79 south of Gambut, seeing the crew bale out. Around the same time Sgt H.G.Webster claimed a CR.42 and a damaged, Plt Off R.L.Goord also claiming a CR.42. Two more were claimed by 274 Squadron pilots at much the same time, one each by Sqn Ldr Paddy Dunn and Plt Off Wilson.

Seventeen CR.42s of 23° Gruppo were escorting 34° Stormo S.79s over Bardia, and were probably the aircraft encountered by these RAF pilots, S.Ten Sante Schiroli of 74ª Squadriglia being killed over Bardia, with S.Ten Leopoldo Marangoni of 75ª Squadriglia being shot down between Bardia and Tobruk. He baled out, having been wounded, and was taken to a British field hospital, but died there during the night. One Hurricane was claimed by Cap Mario Pinna, and a second was credited to the missing Marangoni, who would later be awarded a posthumous Medaglia d'Oro.

34° Stormo BT lost the S.79 flown by S.Ten Lino Salandin, while two more were forced to land in the desert and were destroyed. This latter pair were probably accounted for by newly-promoted Flt Lt Peter Wykeham-Barnes of 274 Squadron, who claimed one S.79 and one more as a probable in the Gambut area at around 1245. Another two S.79s were reported to have been damaged by AA.

Finally, at 1450 Flt Lt Mike Beytagh of 73 Squadron claimed another CR.42 near Massa Es Sahal, just west of Tobruk. Soon after this came news that Bardia had been captured with a further 20,000 prisoners.

British Claims

274 Sqn	Flg Off E.M.Mason	P3722	3 CR.42s damaged on ground	Gazala 0820
	2/Lt R.H.Talbot	P3721	S.79	Gazala 0820
	2/Lt R.H.Talbot	P3721	S.79 damaged	Gazala 0820
	Flg Off E.M.Mason	P3722	2 CR.42s	Gazala East 1220
	2/Lt R.H.Talbot	P3721	CR.42	Gazala East 1220
73 Sqn	Sgt A.E.Marshall	V7562	S.79	30m S Great Gambut 1240
	Plt Off R.L.Goord	TP-M	CR.42	25m SE Tobruk 1305
	Sgt H.G.Webster	V7551	CR.42	1300
	Sgt H.G.Webster	V7551	CR.42 damaged	1301
274 Sqn	Plt Off Wilson	N2624	CR.42	4-5m W Burg-el-Arab 1240
	Sqn Ldr P.H.Dunn	P3723	CR.42	5m NW Gambut 1245
	Flt Lt P.G.Wykeham-Barnes	V7558	S.79	12m SW Tobruk 1250
	Flt Lt P.G.Wykeham-Barnes		S.79 probable	12m SW Tobruk 1245
73 Sqn	Flt Lt M.ff.Beytagh	V7561	CR.42	near Massa Es Sahal, W Tobruk 1450

3 RAAF Squadron originally listed one victory on this date, but in fact the unit had not encountered any hostile aircraft during the day.

British Casualties

45 Sqn	Blenheim damaged

Italian Claims

73ª Sq/9° Gr/4° St CT	Serg Teresio Martinoli	Blenheim	Marsa Luch
75ª Sq/23° Gr CT	Cap Mario Pinna	Hurricane	
	S. Ten Leopoldo Marangoni	Hurricane	

Italian Casualties

70ª Sq/23° Gr CT	CR.42 Ten Oscar Abello KiA
	CR.42 Serg Pardino Pardini KiA
75ª Sq/23° Gr CT	CR.42 S.Ten Leopoldo Marangoni WiA, died of wounds
74ª Sq/23° Gr CT	CR.42 S.Ten Sante Schiroli KiA
217ª Sq/53° Gr/34° St BT	S.79 Ten Lino Salandin & crew KiA
34° St	2 S.79s destroyed in crash-landings

Two S.79s of 53° Gruppo BT in flight. An S.79 of 217ª Squadriglia, was lost on 5 January 1941.

Monday, 6 January 1941

Wt Off H.J.Goodchild of 33 Squadron became the first pilot to claim an Italian monoplane fighter in North Africa when at 1350 a patrol of three such aircraft from 2° Gruppo led again by Magg Baylon, were reported to have been attacked by Hurricanes between Sidi Rezegh and Bu Amud. Goodchild initially claimed one shot down and one damaged, although it appears that the second claim may also have been confirmed as destroyed later. Two G.50bis had indeed been hit, Baylon himself landing at Derna in his damaged machine, while Serg Magg Mario Muraro of 152ª Squadriglia, who had been wounded in one foot, got down at Tobruk T2. 2° Gruppo would be reinforced by the arrival of 358ª Squadriglia on this date, led by Cap Annibale Sterzi. Somewhat earlier in the day, Sgt R.I.Laing of 73 Squadron had claimed a CR.42 damaged south-east of Tobruk. Meanwhile, 4° Stormo CT withdrew to Benghazi.

At 1445 that afternoon Flg Off Jas Storrar of 73 Squadron claimed to have shot down a CR.42 west of Tobruk.

British Claims

73 Sqn	Sgt R.I.Laing	V7553	CR.42 damaged	10m SE Tobruk 1100
	Wt Off H.J.Goodchild		G.50	
	Wt Off H.J.Goodchild		G.50 damaged (possibly confirmed destroyed)	
	Flg Off J.E.Storrar	V7562	CR.42	W Tobruk 1445

Italian Casualties

2° Gr CT	G.50 damaged Magg Giuseppe Baylon force-landed at Derna
152ª Sq/2° Gr CT	G.50 damaged Serg Magg Mario Muraro force-landed at Tobruk, wounded

Tuesday, 7 January 1941

During the day 23° Gruppo CT moved from Derna to Benghazi. A G.50bis of 2° Gruppo force-landed and was badly damaged due to engine failure. These aircraft were not fitted with sand filters, and this omission was soon to cause a number of problems.

That morning at 1120 two Ba.65s and six CR.32s of 50° Stormo Assalto took off from Derna to strafe armoured cars in the Acroma area. Four vehicles were claimed destroyed, but Ten Italo Barbetta of 159ª Squadriglia had to force-land at Benina Z1. He was recovered by an S.81 flown by Ten Fioravante Montanari, the Ba.65 being set on fire before they left.

Italian Casualties

358ª Sq/2° Gr CT	G.50 damaged S.Ten Francesco Vichi force-landed due to engine failure
159ª Sq/12° Gr/50° St Ass	Ba.65 force-landed and destroyed to prevent capture; Ten Italo Barbetta safe

Wednesday, 8 January 1941

274 Squadron now began sending pairs of Hurricanes far behind Italian lines to strafe their airfields. On this date Sqn Ldr Dunn and Plt Off Mason attacked Gazala and Martuba, Dunn claiming two S.79s

destroyed on the former airfield; Mason fired at 11 of these bombers at the latter, claiming at least two destroyed. He explained:

"We devised this plan. We circled round until they fired at us. That meant that they had seen us. Then we waited for aircraft to take off or land and shot them in the air. If nothing appeared and we had to go home we would go down and machine-gun aircraft on the ground. We made a rule never to shoot at people or buildings like messes or tents, only at aircraft. So they got to know us and used to stand watching us set their machines on fire (except those who were using guns and pom poms at us)."

British Claims		
274 Sqn	Sqn Ldr P.H.Dunn	2 S.79s on ground
	Flg Off E.M.Mason	2 S.79s on ground at least

Italian Casualties	
Unspecified unit	2 S.81 transports destroyed by strafing on the ground at Martuba

In England Wg Cdr Kenneth B.B.'Bing' Cross, DFC, one of the two fighter pilots to survive the sinking of HMS *Glorious* at the conclusion of the Norwegian campaign (see *Fledgling Eagles*), received a signal in early December, posting him to the staff of the AOC-in-C, Mediterranean. Consequently, he went aboard HMS *Furious*, which was about to deliver a second batch of Hurricanes to Takoradi for the air supply route, the carrier sailing as part of Convoy WS5A. This time it was not an individual squadron which was being sent, but 40 aircraft and a group of pilots who, to Cross's surprise, were all of fairly junior rank and none of whom seemed to have obtained any experience during the Battle of Britain. Also aboard, he noted, was a flight of Fairey Fulmar fighters led by Lt L.A.'Skeets' Harris, destined for Alexandria and the Mediterranean Fleet, and six Blackburn Skua fighter/dive-bombers for defence of the convoy.

The convoy departed on 18 December, but on the 25th intelligence was received that the battle-cruiser *Admiral Scheer* was at sea, and the convoy scattered (it had, in fact, been *Admiral Hipper*). Next day *Furious* met Force H and was escorted into Gibraltar. She sailed again on the 29th, her cargo of Hurricanes being flown off to Takoradi on 8 January 1941. In leading the fly-off, Cross recalled that it was the first time he had flown a Hurricane since landing one on *Glorious* on 8 June 1940. He then accompanied one of the flights of these fighters in a Blenheim to Heliopolis. Here, on reporting to Peter Drummond, he learnt that he was to command 252 Air Defence Wing at Alexandria.

At this stage he found that his unit, based in a hutted camp by the sea to the west of the port, was still little more than a skeleton outfit. It comprised a thin screen of radar stations covering Alexandria and Cairo, a good reinforced concrete operations room and a filter room at Wing HQ. Also included was an as-yet empty airfield at Amiriya, ten miles south of Alexandria, on the edge of the Western Desert. AA defences locally were shared 50% around Alexandria, the balance at Cairo. Half of the Alexandria guns were manned by the Egyptian army, as were 100% of those around Cairo. Nonetheless, Cross soon found that those defending Alexandria quite willingly opened fire on raiders, while Cairo was never to be bombed, so the question never arose.

Meanwhile, during 7 and 8 January, Tedder had met Admiral Cunningham and General Auchinleck (then commander in India) for the first time – personalities with whom he would now frequently have to deal. Cross recorded at this time that he had met Tedder in 1932 and recognised him as a charismatic man.

Thursday, 9 January 1941
274 Squadron continued with its series of long-distance strafes. At 1120 2/Lt Bob Talbot claimed a CR.42 shot down over Martuba, and later at 1600 Plt Off Mason claimed another over Derna. He recorded:

"A single CR.42 took off and climbed up to engage me. We had a dogfight below the clouds and immediately over the aerodrome. It lasted a long time, about ten minutes. He was very good and much above the average Italian. We believe he is Major Ernesto Botti (sic) – a famous Italian ace who has a crack squadron of 42s. He has a Gold Medal for Valour and has an artificial leg from Spain. I am very glad to say that he managed to bale out successfully when I finally finished him off and I saw him down safely before we went home. A very good show."

It is clear that Mason's opponent cannot have been Ernesto Botto, for the latter was still in hospital as a result of his 9 December traffic accident. The identity of the pilot in question has not proved easy to ascertain, for 9º Gruppo had undertaken its last sorties in Libya on 19 December and 10º Gruppo was on its way back to Italy, having been ordered to repatriate on 5 January – so 4º Stormo CT cannot have been involved. 151º Gruppo would only resume operations on 22 January, having been rested at Agedabia prior to the date of this engagement. This leaves only 23º Gruppo, which apparently had just been ordered to withdraw from Derna to Benghazi in the wake of the retreating Italian forces. In fact one pilot of this unit's 74ª Squadriglia, Serg Magg Luigi Margutti, was reported to have been wounded on this date, although the circumstances are still unclear. On balance therefore, he would appear to have been the man shot down.

Elsewhere Cap Tullio De Prato, commanding officer of 150ª Squadriglia, 2º Gruppo CT led a patrol of three G.50bis which encountered a Hurricane. De Prato engaged this head-on, but his G.50bis was hit, obliging him to force-land near Z1, where he injured himself in leaping from the aircraft. 73 Squadron's Sgt Fred Marshall recorded: "Two patrols followed by the move to Bardia. I got bounced by three Fiat G.50s at 20,000 ft and was lucky to escape. I landed at Bardia after dark." He obviously had not realised that he had inflicted damage, for he made no claim, not even as a damaged.

At Z1 Ten Sergio Giacomello of 160ª Squadriglia, had been obliged to force-land his CR.32 when engaged in a sortie over Acroma. He rescued Cap De Prato after the latter's exit from his G.50bis, and both were picked up by the S.81 'hack', flown by Ten Fioravante Montanari. As this was returning to base it was encountered by 73 Squadron's Plt Off G.E.'Randy' Goodman, DFC, who, seeing it prominently marked with Red Crosses, flew alongside, receiving a cheerful wave from the pilot, which he reciprocated. As it appeared to be unarmed, he allowed it to proceed on its way. However, Giacomello's CR.32 was later destroyed by Flg Off Mason following his combat with the CR.42. He noted that six S.79s at Martuba which had been strafed the day before, all seemed to be burnt out.

British Claims				
274 Sqn	2/Lt R.H.Talbot	V7484	CR.42	Martuba 1120
	Flg Off E.M.Mason	P3722	CR.42	Derna 1600

Italian Casualties	
160ª Sq/12º Gr/50º St Ass	CR.32 destroyed on ground at Benina Z1; Ten Sergio Giacomello safe
150ª Sq/22º Gr CT	G.50 MM 6383 force-landed and destroyed at Benina Z1; Cap Tullio De Prato safe
74ª Sq/23º Gr Aut CT	CR.42 Serg Magg Luigi Margutti wounded during air combat
Unspecified unit	Ba.65 destroyed

Friday, 10 January 1941

Mason and Talbot were off again to the Derna area during the morning, where on arrival at 1000 they each claimed an S.79 shot down as these were going in to land. They were back for a second attack at 1400, when Mason again claimed a bomber shot down as it went in:

"…both shot down S.79s coming in to land. I got one in the morning and one in the afternoon. All crashed on the aerodrome. But they had set a trap for us. We were purposefully doing these shows at the same time for moral effect. When I saw this S.79 in the afternoon coming in to land and went screaming down on it and shot it down as it approached the boundary, a smoke fire was lit. Within five minutes five Fiat G.50s appeared. We were caught awkwardly because I was below them so we got mixed up. I got a long head-on attack on one and he should have gone, but of course is unconfirmed, and Bob got one who jumped out, also a possible. But we were late and had little petrol or ammunition so went home."

They each claimed one G.50 damaged, Talbot also claiming one destroyed.

It does not appear that a formal 'trap' had actually been set, but that G.50bis arrived at a propitious moment. Five such fighters had been out escorting a ground-attack formation. On return from this Serg Albino Fabbri of 152ª Squadriglia, 2º Gruppo CT claimed one Hurricane shot down near the Gulf of Bomba for the unit's first victory.

Also involved in this engagement were Magg Giuseppe Baylon, M.llo Giuseppe Alessandri and Serg Dino Cattani; the latter was hit and wounded. What the bombers attacked by Mason and Talbot were

On 10 January 1941 Cap Duilio Fanali, flying this CR.32, collided on landing with a Ba.65, destroying both aircraft.

has not been ascertained, for details of such losses have not been discovered in Italian records. A single S.83 transport (MM60408 I-AREM) flown by Cap Vittorio Suster with 12 passengers aboard was lost on this date, having taken off from Sirte at 0715, but failed to arrive at Rome. However, Sirte is a long way to the west of Derna.

While landing from a ground-attack sortie Cap Duilio Fanali of 160ª Squadriglia collided with a parked Ba.65. Both aircraft were destroyed, but he was unhurt.

British Claims				
274 Sqn	Flg Off E.M.Mason	P3722	S.79	Derna 1000
	2/Lt R.H.Talbot	V7484	S.79	Derna 1000
	Flg Off E.M.Mason	P3722	S.79	Derna 1605
	Flg Off E.M.Mason	P3722	G.50 damaged	Derna 1605
	2/Lt R.H.Talbot	V7484	G.50 damaged	Derna 1605
	2/Lt R.H.Talbot	V7484	G.50	Derna 1610

Italian Claims			
152ª Sq/2º Gr CT	Serg Albino Fabbri	Hurricane	nr Gulf of Bomba

Italian Casualties	
150ª Sq/2º Gr CT	G.50 Ten Lorenzo Pallavicini force-landed, engine failure; w/o
152ª Sq/2º Gr CT	G.50 damaged Serg Dino Cattani WiA
160ª Sq/12º Gr/50º St Ass	CR.32 Cap Duilio Fanali landing collision; safe
159ª Sq/12 ºGr/50º St Ass	Ba.65 destroyed on ground by collision of CR.32

Saturday, 11 January 1941

On 11 January G.50bis pilots reportedly scrambled over Derna, reporting engaging three Hurricanes. According to the logbook of S.Ten Francesco De Seta, he shared with others in shooting one down. However, there is no record of such an engagement from RAF sources, and it is possible that he was actually recording the action of the day before, dating this one day late.

Italian Claims			
2º Gr CT	S.Ten Francesco De Seta & others	Hurricane	Derna

Sunday, 12 January 1941

During the morning an S.79 of 175ª Squadriglia RST flown by S.Ten Giuseppe Anelli, crashed in flames during a flight to Barce. All the crew of eight were killed; the cause of their demise is not known. Other operations were made virtually impossible by a severe sandstorm which blocked out the whole of lower Egypt and the Western Desert.

Italian Casualties

175ª Sq RST	S.79 S.Ten Giuseppe Anelli & crew KiA

Monday, 13 January 1941

G.50bis undertook an escort to S.79s during the day, pilots reporting an engagement with three Hurricanes. Two were claimed shot down by Ten Francesco De Seta and others. Again there is no matching RAF report, and again the date in his logbook may have been incorrectly recorded.

Italian Claims

2° Gr CT	S.Ten Francesco De Seta & others	2 Hurricanes	

Tuesday, 14 January 1941

After several days when activity was greatly restricted by sandstorms, Plt Off Wilson of 274 Squadron undertook a sortie to Derna where he strafed five S.79s. On his return flight he force-landed at Sollum.

73 Squadron was ordered to undertake some low-level reconnaissances over the Italian lines, but during one such sortie Sgt Geoff Garton's aircraft was badly shot-up by light AA and he force-landed his Hurricane two miles inside British lines:

"I took off to patrol over Tobruk at 0900. After 45 minutes at 15,000 ft I went down to 2,000 or thereabouts, south of Tobruk, to have a recce of the troop positions. I found myself inside the Itie outer defence lines and was about to open fire on some troops when they started waving to me, so I held my fire and had another look, and was fired upon by the defences and hit. Their cannon shell hit the underside of the engine and damaged the cooling system which immediately filled the cockpit with white smoke. Thinking I was on fire, I pulled up to about 500 ft anticipating having to bale out, but finally discovered that the engine was merely shot up and that there was no fire. There was no engine either, as it had seized solid, and I pancaked, wheels up in the desert without knowing on which side of the lines I was. Fortunately I was greeted by an artillery officer of the 104th Brigade, Royal Horse Artillery, who gave me a whisky and some breakfast and provided transport to the nearest drome about 15 miles away. I then scrounged a lift back to base in a Lysander. The artillery wallahs had provided me with an up-to-date map of the Tobruk area showing the Itie defences and our own positions. This was what I had set out to obtain, but a badly damaged Hurricane seemed an inordinate price to pay. I shall keep clear of Tobruk in future."

British Casualties

73 Sqn	Hurricane V7561 Sgt G.W.Garton force-landed nr Tobruk 1000

Wednesday, 15 January 1941

An Italian steamship, *Città di Messina*, was torpedoed in the Gulf of Sirte by the submarine HMS *Regent* while sailing from Benghazi to Tripoli with hundreds of troops aboard. Among those lost were many airmen from the ground echelons of stormi which were being repatriated – namely those of 4°, 9° and 14°. Many documents were also lost in this disaster. Survivors were picked up by the Regia Marina destroyer *Centauro*.

Friday, 17 January 1941

During the morning Flt Lt Peter Wykeham-Barnes intercepted another Red Cross-marked S.81, this one an aircraft of 2° Gruppo APC, flown by S.Ten Augusto Masperi. He was not in as forgiving a mood as had been Randy Goodman, and he attacked it, forcing it to land ten miles west of Tobruk. The crew at once leapt out and set fire to the aircraft before British troops arrived to take the five of them prisoner.

British Claims

274 Sqn	Flt Lt P.G.Wykeham-Barnes	P2641	S.81	10m W Tobruk 1030

British Casualties

113 Sqn	Blenheim IV MiA to AA over Tobruk by night

Italian Casualties

2° Gr APC	S.81 forced to land and set on fire by crew; S.Ten Augusto Masperi & crew PoW

CHANGES IN MID JANUARY

On 14 January Longmore had received the dark news from Admiral Cunningham, advising of the loss of the cruiser HMS *Southampton* and serious damage inflicted on the carrier HMS *Illustrious* by German dive-bombers from Sicily which signalled the start of German involvement in the Mediterranean and Middle East generally. Longmore was ordered to send two more bomber squadrons to Greece, but resisted a suggestion from ACM Portal, chief of the air staff, that he should also despatch three Hurricane squadrons.

At this stage Longmore was becoming somewhat alarmed by the grandiose plans which Whitehall was developing for the area, He was concerned that a thorough over-estimate of Middle East air strength was being employed, a belief becoming apparent at that time that he had 1,000 aircraft, 1,000 pilots and 16,000 other personnel available to him. He was now being pressed to send more reinforcements to Greece and to supply instructors to Turkey in an effort to encourage that nation to join the Allied side.

Against this background he received the unhelpful news from air ministry that, due to a need to conserve shipping and to increase Bomber Command strength at home, six fighter squadrons and six medium bomber squadrons which had been promised were now unlikely to materialize. Longmore:

"Another signal reminded me of the great importance attached to maintenance of Greek morale and the necessity for me to consider additional fighter support. The following day one from the Prime Minister, himself, greatly admiring our brilliant support of Army operations and congratulations upon a victory over enemy Air Force achieved against heavy numerical odds. The signal went on to say that we should soon be, as usual, torn between conflicting needs. Support to the Greek Army to keep them in the field was of prime importance. Admiralty were being asked to send by carrier to Takoradi further air reinforcements. It was probable that four or five squadrons would be required for Greece and yet we would have to continue support to our Army in its Libyan offensive. I might count on being thoroughly re-equipped.

"This was followed immediately by another from CAS to the effect that anxiety about Greece was increasing and that Germans were assembling considerable land and air forces in Rumania. An early advance on Thrace through Bulgaria seemed probable. How much could I send to Greece and where should it go ? I was to consider with Wavell whether air units from Sudan could now be spared.

"On 9 January I sent a very full reply to Air Ministry stating that the Greek situation had been fully discussed with Dalbiac [AOC Greece] and that instructions had been given for 112 Fighter and 11 Bomber Squadrons with whatever Gladiators and Blenheims respectively could be made available to them. Some Gladiators might be taken from the Sudan but the other squadrons there, also those in Kenya, were waiting for re-equipment and in the meantime they were very fully occupied supporting Army operations with their obsolete aircraft. I pointed out that no more squadrons from Egypt could possibly be spared until the situation as a result of the Libyan offensive had become more stabilized. Hurricanes, Blenheims and Wellingtons were continuing to destroy the IAF and in the past three days over 75 had actually been burnt out or destroyed on their aerodromes. At the same time, Italian or German reinforcements to Libya might at any time increase resistance and produce a difficult situation for the armoured division then far forward in the area west and south of Tobruk. I again referred to the winter conditions in Greece and that Dalbiac had confirmed that until spring weather hardened up the forward airfields, Hurricanes could not be operated. Until Araxos and Agrinion were ready, possibly by the end of February, it was no use sending further Blenheims or Wellingtons even if they could be safely spared from Egypt. I had fully discussed the situation with Wavell, who was reluctant to abandon the Sudan offensive, just about to start, or curtail his successful advance into Libya and these operations would continue to entail the maximum support of the squadrons already engaged."

On 10 January the chiefs-of-staff advised Longmore that assistance to Greece must take priority over all in the Middle East once Tobruk was taken. Nonetheless, they did not believe this should prevent an advance on Benghazi if the going was good. Neither did they feel it was necessary to abandon the Sudan operation. Despite the apparent conflict that these latest views seemed to cause, Longmore found them:

"…very encouraging for it meant that I could still employ our small desert air force at maximum intensity in support of the Army in their continued successful offensive rather than plant squadrons on wet airfields in Greece where winter weather conditions were still restricting active air operations."

The reduction in Regia Aeronautica resistance was now allowing further reinforcement of the British air component in Greece to be undertaken. 39 Squadron had commenced re-equipping with Blenheim IVs at Helwan, but on 10 January it handed its new aircraft to 11 Squadron, called in its detachment at Qotaifiya, and on 23 January would withdraw to Helwan. Here three days later it would receive the first example of the Martin Maryland bomber to become available to an RAF squadron, beginning working up with these more potent US-built aircraft forthwith.

Having taken on its new Blenheim IVs, 11 Squadron left Egypt for Greece on 28 January, flying over to Larissa. It followed the Gladiators of 112 Squadron which had departed North Africa five days earlier for Eleusis. The place of this latter unit as defender of the Alexandria area had been taken by 33 Squadron, withdrawn from Fuka and the Cyrenaican front on 15 January; it too would soon begin preparations for a transfer to Greece.

It was while these moves were underway that the first Luftwaffe aircraft appeared over North Africa and Malta. During the night of 17/18 January Heinkel He 111 bombers from II.Gruppe of Kampfgeschwader 26 (II./KG 26) flew over from Sicily where the Luftwaffe was becoming established in some force, to undertake a raid on the Suez Canal (See Chapter 13 —'Blitz on Egypt'). This proved completely unsuccessful, and it would be some days yet before more machines carrying the black cross and swastika would be encountered.

Tuesday, 21 January 1941

On this date 6th Australian Division commenced its assault on Tobruk. 73 Squadron's pilots prepared to undertake an escort to Blenheims of 55 Squadron which were to bomb the port. As the first bomber took off at 0640, it was seen to be jettisoning its bombs, which exploded on the airfield. The Blenheim then crashed and burst into flames; one engine had failed on take-off.

The raid then got underway, but over Tobruk a pair of G.50bis were seen and pursued. Three more then intervened, and Plt Off Wainwright's Hurricane was shot down in flames by Serg Magg Antonio Patriarca of 358ª Squadriglia, 2° Gruppo CT. Plt Off Legge's Hurricane was also hit, but by ground fire, and the engine was set alight. He force-landed at El Adem where he was able to douse the flames with sand and water.

During the fight Sqn Ldr A.D.Murray claimed one G.50 shot down, while Legge claimed one damaged before being forced down. S.Ten Romano Pagliani was wounded in the left arm, but managed to get back to base as the only Italian casualty.

Two more British aircraft were lost to ground fire on this date, one of these a Hurricane of 274 Squadron. The pilot of this aircraft was fleeing from an attack by 73 Squadron's Flt Lt Beytagh at the time!

British Claims				
73 Sqn	Sqn Ldr A.D.Murray	V7560 TP-F	G.50	W Tobruk
	Plt Off B.P.Legge	TP-M	G.50 damaged	
British Casualties				
55 Sqn	Blenheim IV T1879 accidentally released bombs on take-off; Flg Off F.R.Bullot and crew KiA			
73 Sqn	Hurricane I P2639 TP-K Plt Off A.Wainwright KiA			
	Hurricane I Damaged TP-M hit by ground fire; force-landed; Plt Off B.P.Legge safe			
274 Sqn	Hurricane I Damaged V7213 hit by ground fire; force-landed; Flg Off C.J.Laubscher safe			
208 Sqn	Lysander hit by ground fire; crash-landed nr Tobruk; Flt Lt Webber safe			
Italian Claims				
358ª Sq/2° Gr CT	Serg Magg Antonio Patriarca		Hurricane	Tobruk
Italian Casualties				
358ª Sq/2° Gr CT	Fiat G.50 damaged S.Ten Romano Pagliani WiA			

Wednesday, 22 January 1941

Tobruk fell to the Australian assault, the Italian 61st Division surrendering. This allowed some 25,000-30,000 prisoners to be taken, together with circa 200 guns, 87 tanks and a huge number of 'soft-skinned' vehicles. The cost to the attacking force was 400 killed and wounded, of whom 250 were members of the Australian Division. As the port fell into Commonwealth hands, the damaged cruiser *San Giorgio* was scuttled.

After the taking of Tobruk, Collishaw's HQ moved to Sidi Mahmoud for the attack on Derna, 73 and 274 Squadrons moving to Gazala, 3 RAAF and 208 Squadrons to Tmimi, but at this stage 33 Squadron was now held back for despatch to Greece, providing cover for Alexandria for the time being.

Meanwhile the chiefs-of-staff had changed their views regarding Greece on 21 January when the Greek refusal to allow British ground forces into the country for fear of provoking German reaction, was altered. This, coupled with the arrival of the Luftwaffe in Sicily, resulted in their deciding that the fall of Benghazi was now a priority, and that the Dodecanese Islands, including Rhodes, should be captured as soon as possible – all while Malta continued to be firmly defended.

At this stage the British Air Attaché in Turkey quoted demands posed by that nation, that if it was to resist any German aggression it would require 500 first line aircraft from England and the USA, plus bombs, fuel, training and other support. Despite the German presence now in Sicily, the commanders-in-chief were ordered to prepare plans for the capture of this island, although it was accepted that the immediate chance of doing so had lessened, and would not in any case be possible until the Dodecanese had been taken.

On 27 January Longmore would signal the CAS in response to this latest directive, asking:

"Was it to be assumed that the RAF were still supporting Army operations on the Sudan and Kenya fronts, escorting convoys in the Red Sea, defending the naval base at Alexandria and the Canal area from Italian and German aircraft which were still using bases in the Dodecanese? Was it to be assumed that we were still supporting the British Army in Libya against German and Italian air opposition, perhaps defending Benghazi and its long line of sea communications, and lastly but by no means least should we take into consideration the fresh air commitments in Greece which would be inevitable in the spring? All the above considerations materially affected any estimate of total fresh air reinforcements required for the capture of Sicily. I asked whether Air Staff had attempted to work out what was the maximum number of squadrons of varying types which could be maintained in the Middle East, having regard to the limitations of existing air and sea lines of communication. With the Mediterranean practically closed and the German submarine campaign in full swing, there was definitely some limit and experience hitherto had shown it was a comparatively low one. I was still waiting for aircraft to equip No.39 Squadron, which had none. I was also waiting to form four fresh fighter squadrons and Nos. 47 and 223 Squadrons still had obsolete Wellesleys in the Sudan."

Thursday, 23 January 1941

While these high level events had been unfolding, back on the Libyan front on 23 January Serg Magg Ezio Masenti of 368ª Squadriglia had claimed a Blenheim shot down over Derna. It appears that a Blenheim of 55 Squadron crash-landed during this period, and this may well have been Masenti's victim. The raid on the airfield here caused serious damage to a Ba.65.

These unserviceable Ba.65s were left in Libya and found by British troops when they occupied Cyrenaica.

British Casualties		
55 Sqn	Blenheim possibly crash-landed on this date	
Italian Claims		
368ª Sq/151º Gr CT	Serg Magg Ezio Masenti	Blenheim Derna
Italian Casualties		
Unspecified unit	Ba.65 badly damaged on ground at Derna by bombing	

Friday, 24 January 1941

Flg Off Patterson force-landed unharmed in the Tobruk area, returning safely to 274 Squadron next day. A claim for a Blenheim probably shot down was made by an Italian fighter pilot; a CR.42 from the same unit was shot down, Serg Cesare Sironi being made a PoW. No losses or claims by RAF units have been found for this date, although records indicate that one Blenheim may have been damaged by fighters.

Italian Claims			
75ª Sq/23º Gr CT	Ten Giuseppe Vitali	Blenheim probable	Mechili
Italian Casualties			
70ª Sq/23º Gr CT	CR.42 badly damaged Serg Cesare Sironi PoW		
Unspecified unit	S.79 destroyed on the ground by bombs at Solluch		
	S.79 damaged on the ground by bombs at Solluch		

Saturday, 25 January 1941

Two days earlier six of 3 RAAF Squadron's pilots had been despatched to Abu Sueir to collect a pair of Hurricanes for the unit. These were picked up at the El Firdan Air Stores Park, and commented John Jackson: "…aren't they beauties ! The new type of mottled blue, grey and purple camouflage on the nose, leading edges of wings, and front surfaces, looks most peculiar." On the 25th however, it was still in Gladiators that the squadron undertook a patrol by four of its members. Flg Off Alan Rawlinson spotted five G.50bis approaching and called to Sqn Ldr Duncan Campbell: "Enemy aircraft", but the latter responded: "No, they are Hurricanes!" Rawlinson warned again "They are enemy aircraft".

During the opening months of 1941 Hurricanes arriving in Egypt were painted with a three-colour 'spaghetti' pattern on the noses and leading edges of the wings, giving rise to comment by Flg Off John Jackson, as 3 RAAF Squadron was currently converting to these aircraft. One such is seen here at Benina airfield. The big Vokes air filter beneath the nose of the aircraft – a tropical modification – may also be seen to advantage here.

Duncan ignored this, and next moment the G.50s were on the tails of the Gladiators. Rawlinson and Duncan both force-landed their badly damaged fighters, Flg Off P.StG.B.Turnbull got back with his aircraft shot to pieces, but Flg Off J.C.Campbell was shot down and killed. The Italian pilots were members of 358ª Squadriglia, out on a morning patrol over El Mechili, and they claimed four victories.

On this date the recently successful SAAF pilot, 2/Lt Bob Talbot, left 274 Squadron on posting home to South Africa.

British Claims				
3 RAAF Sqn	Flg Off P.StG.B.Turnbull	L9044	G.50 Damaged	Mechili area
British Casualties				
3 RAAF Sqn	Gladiator L8022 Flg Off J.C.Campbell KiA Mechili area			
	Gladiator N5857 Sqn Ldr D.Campbell force-landed; safe			
	Gladiator K7963 Flg Off A.C.Rawlinson force-landed; safe			
	Gladiator L9044 badly damaged; Flg Off P.StG.B.Turnbull safe			
Italian Claims				
358ª Sq/2º Gr CT	S.Ten Bruno Mondini MM6346	2 Gladiators		
	Cap Annibale Sterzi MM6335	Gladiator		
	M.llo Marco Aicardi MM5455	Gladiator		
368ª Sq/151º Gr CT	M.llo Giovanni Accorsi	Blenheim Probable	Maraua	

Sunday, 26 January 1941

Flg Offs Imshi Mason and T.L.Patterson were out on patrol again. Near Derna at 1510 CR.42s were spotted engaged in strafing Australian troops.

"…three of us were on patrol when we met more Italian aircraft. Patterson from Toronto, a great friend of mine, chased three G.50s and I saw seven CR 42s. I chased them and when they turned to attack me I had a quick dogfight with them all round me. The first one I fired at went down and crashed without burning. The second and third each turned slowly over and dived straight in and exploded. All this was over in two or three minutes. By the time the third one was down the others had disappeared which was very fortunate as my motor cut out and I had to force-land. All this took place very low over the top of the front line troops and I landed next to a blazing CR.42 amidst crowds of wildly enthusiastic Australians. Unfortunately the ground was very rough and I burst a tyre and went up on my nose, wrecking the poor old aircraft with which I had got all my victories. I removed the Blackpool crest and was given a lift to the Australian squadron [3 RAAF] who were quite near.

"The aerodrome where they were was the one where a few weeks previously I had ground strafed 11 S.79s and damaged them. Very interesting, to see them still there [these were probably aircraft of 9° Stormo], several burnt out. After I had force-landed I learnt that one of the CR.42 pilots had tried to bale out but his parachute had not opened. So I had a look at him. He was about 700 yards from his still blazing machine. I had got him in the right shoulder so he had not been able to open his chute. I went through his pockets and found a lot of interesting snapshots and a lot of letters. Before I left I covered him with his parachute and weighted it down with stones."

Mason's opponents on this occasion had been members of 368ª Squadriglia, 151° Gruppo, which recorded the loss of two CR.42s and their pilots, simultaneously claiming one Hurricane shot down and a probable. Patterson had been engaged with G.50bis of 358ª Squadriglia, 2° Gruppo, which had lost one G.50, the pilot of which, M.llo Ottorino Muscinelli, had been killed. His body fell near the wreck of his aircraft, but was not to be found until some months later.

During a ground-attack sortie, Ten Sergio Giacomello of 160ª Squadriglia, 12° Gruppo, 50° Stormo Assalto, force-landed in British-held territory after his CR.32 was hit by ground fire. Serg Magg Corrado Sarti landed nearby, jettisoning his parachute, and flew Giacomello back to base. On a later sortie during the afternoon S.Ten Giuseppe Mezzatesta of this unit was wounded in the head by shell splinters and force-landed near Derna. Taken to hospital, he died of his wounds on 1 February.

On this date the other gruppo in 50° Stormo, the 16°, left for Italy to join 54° Stormo CT, to become a fighter unit, re-equipping with MC 200s.

Five Hurricanes of 73 Squadron had taken off from Gazala to patrol over Mechili and Derna, but on the return flight spotted that one aircraft was not with them any more. The pilots, led by Flt Lt Beytagh, dived down to investigate a smoke column, but found only a crashed CR.42 – almost certainly one of Mason's victims. As they did so a machine gun mounted on a lorry hidden in a wadi, opened up, hitting V7559 flown by Sgt 'Jock' Stenhouse. At first it looked as if the aircraft was about to dive into the ground, but the pilot regained control, pulled up, and he baled out from 1,500 ft. Sgt Geoff Garton: "He was last seen lying face down on the ground with Itie transport converging on him from the west, and our own tanks from the east. Hope he has been found by someone as we believe he was hurt in his fall." He had indeed suffered a broken leg, but was rescued safely and removed to hospital. The 'missing' Hurricane had become separated and returned safely on its own.

During a British raid on Maraua, a 2° Gruppo G.50bis was destroyed and three ground personnel were killed. This unit now had only two G.50bis left serviceable and withdrew to Tripoli. Here it would be re-equipped with new G.50bis with sand filters and seat armour fitted.

British Claims

274 Sqn	Flg Off E.M.Mason	P3722	3 CR.42s	10m W Martuba 1510
	Flg Off T.L.Patterson	P3823	2 G.50s	1m S Derna 1510

British Casualties

274 Sqn	Hurricane I P3722 engine failure; crashed force-landing; Flg Off E.M.Mason safe
73 Sqn	Hurricane I V7559 shot down by ground fire; Sgt J.Stenhouse baled out, injured

368ª Sq/151º Gr CT	Serg Magg Annibale Ricotti	Hurricane
	Ten Giuseppe E.Zuffi	Hurricane probable

Italian Casualties

368ª Sq/151º Gr CT	CR.42 MM5564 S.Ten Alfonso Nuti KiA
	CR.42 MM6967 M.llo Guido Paparatti KiA
358ª Sq/2º Gr CT	G.50 MM6346 M.llo Ottorino Muscinelli KiA
160ª Sq/12º Gr/50º St Ass	CR.32 shot down by AA and force-landed; Ten Giacomello safe
	CR.32 S.Ten Giuseppe Mezzatesta WiA; force-landed, died of wounds
2º Gr CT	G.50 destroyed on ground at Maraua

Tuesday, 28 January 1941

50º Stormo's 12º Gruppo undertook its final operational missions on this date, Ten Sergio Giacomello, Ten Antonio D'Alessio, Serg Magg Natale Molteni and Ten Corrado Sarti undertaking a strafe in the Ummi Selima area. Thereafter, this unit also withdrew to convert to fighters. At the time of its withdrawal, 50º Stormo Assalto had, since 1 January, lost only two Ba.65s, three CR.32s and an S.81, and had claimed two probable victories.

Wednesday, 29 January 1941

At 0800 Flg Off L.T.Benson of 208 Squadron took off in Hurricane N2611 to undertake a reconnaissance sortie. One hour into the flight he was intercepted by Serg Giuseppe Sanguettoli of 74ª Squadriglia, 23º Gruppo, and was shot down and killed. Two of the gruppi's fighters had been scrambled from K2 airfield at Benghazi, but M.llo Carlo Dentis of 75ª Squadriglia had collided with a 'hack' Ca.133 as he took off, and he crashed. Both aircraft were destroyed, and Dentis would die of his injuries two days later. Meanwhile Benson was buried with full military honours, a message to this effect being dropped by an Italian aircraft on the day on which Dentis died.

Another CR.42 was lost when aircraft of 18º Gruppo CT began arriving at Castel Benito from Pantelleria. This unit had been operating over England from Belgium during the later stages of the Battle of Britain. S.Ten Eugenio Salvi badly damaged his fighter in a landing accident and it was written off.

British Casualties

208 Sqn	Hurricane I N2611 Plt Off L.T.Benson KiA

Italian Claims

74ª Sq/23º Gr CT	Serg Giuseppe Sanguettoli	Hurricane

Italian Casualties

75ª Sq/23º Gr CT	CR.42 collided with Ca.133 on take-off; M.llo Carlo Dentis died of injuries
23º Gr CT	Ca.133 destroyed on ground by collision with CR.42
95ª Sq/18º Gr CT	CR.42 S.Ten Eugenio Salvi safe

Thursday, 30 January 1941

Australian troops entered Derna, Italian forces abandoning all the Wadi Derna positions. Flg Offs Mason and Patterson carried out another of their strafing sorties, this time to Benina airfield. Here they became embroiled in a fierce dogfight with a lone CR.42. Both pilots were hit and slightly wounded before Mason managed to shoot it down:

"I decided to have a look at Benina, near Benghazi. Actually a hell of a way and much too far for a safe margin… I saw a single CR.42 on patrol and went for him. Where we boobed was that instead of taking our time Pat and myself were each scared the other would get there first. So we were going too fast. I attacked first and overshot him. By the time I had turned Pat had disappeared. We kept doing head-on attacks where we rush at each other head-on until point blank range and then each shoot past each other. Usually very successful. But this fellow wouldn't go down. On the fourth attack we went rushing at each other, each firing. But this time he didn't pull out but came straight on. I pulled up instinctively and as he passed underneath my wing I felt a crash and a bump. I thought we had collided. I had a glimpse of him going straight on and burning. I now realised that I had been hit and not collided. I felt a pain in my right side and saw a great hole in the side of the cockpit where an explosive bullet had come through and burst inside. Also the wing had had one explode and bits and pieces were flapping about. However, the aircraft seemed O.K.....Pat also got back and though his aircraft had no hole in it, the shrapnel had exploded in his left arm, really doing a lot of damage."

Mason thought he too had been badly hit, but on return discovered that his wounds were only superficial. However, this was to be the last of the run of successes that he and his wingmen had enjoyed since early December, this day's success bringing his total of confirmed claims to 14. Their doughty opponent had been Serg Magg Mario Turchi of 368ª Squadriglia, 151° Gruppo, who had force-landed, claiming that he had rammed his opponent. He was credited with one Hurricane destroyed and one probable.

British Claims			
274 Sqn	Flg Off E.M.Mason P3723	CR.42	Benina airfield 1145
British Casualties			
274 Sqn	Hurricane I P3723 badly damaged Flg Off E.M.Mason slightly wounded		
	Hurricane I damaged Flg Off T.L.Patterson seriously wounded		
Italian Claims			
368ª Sq/151° Gr CT	Serg Magg Mario Turchi	Hurricane	Benina
		Hurricane probable	Benina
Italian Casualties			
368ª Sq/151° Gr CT	CR.42 damaged force-landed; Serg Magg Mario Turchi safe.		

Even as Derna was taken, Longmore received yet another signal from London advising of a proposal to send between ten and 13 RAF squadrons into Turkey to counter any German invasion from Bulgaria. These, of course, would have to come entirely from the Middle East and could not be spared until the situation had stabilized in Cyrenaica, but would have to be at the expense of East Africa. Longmore was appalled, and made his feelings plain:

"Your message received. Quite frankly contents astound me…I cannot believe you fully appreciate present situation in Middle East, in which Libya drive in full career and Sudan offensive into Eritrea progressing satisfactorily. Neither show signs of immediate stabilisation. Arrival of aircraft in Middle East all routes hardly keeping pace with casualties."

Tedder: "Before I left London I had received a friendly tip that anything I could do to soften the acerbity of some signals from Middle East would be in the interest of all parties, and I did come to a gentlemen's agreement with Longmore that I would have a look at top level signals on those lines."

Friday, 31 January 1941
Over Libya Cap Bruno Locatelli, commanding officer of 368ª Squadriglia, 151° Gruppo CT, was shot down by ground fire near Mechili, baled out and became a PoW.

During the day 155° Gruppo CT landed at Castel Benito from Pantelleria; this was another G.50bis-equipped unit. Newly-formed, it comprised a new squadriglia, 360ª , and two squadriglie taken from other gruppi. From 20° Gruppo CT, still at this time based in Belgium as part of 56° Stormo CT, had come 351ª Squadriglia, while 378ª Squadriglia had been transferred from 22° Gruppo CT at Ciampino, Rome. The new gruppo would move forward to Benghazi over the next few days, but here the retreat of the Italian army from the area delayed deployment, and in the event the unit was not to commence operations until April. The day was also marked by the disbandment of 114° Gruppo and its two squadriglie, 272ª and 273ª.

The RAF was suffering similar problems. In preparation for more involvement in Greece, following the advance through Cyrenaica, 274 and 45 Squadrons were withdrawn into reserve, as were 37 and 38 Wellington Squadrons. By now only a trickle of fighter reinforcements were coming through the air route and hardly any crated Hurricanes were arriving by sea. The Mediterranean was almost closed due to the Luftwaffe presence. Longmore had by now been led to believe that supplies of fighter aircraft ordered in the USA would be sent directly to West Africa, including ex-French order Curtiss Mohawks and Tomahawks. Now came the depressing news that delivery of the Mohawks had been indefinitely held up due mainly to problems with the reliability of their Wright Cyclone radial engines, whilst "certain defects" had revealed themselves in the Tomahawk. The latter was a particular blow since Longmore had hoped to rearm the Gladiator units with these aircraft – as would eventually be done, but at a considerably later date.

CHAPTER 5

ENTER THE LUFTWAFFE

As mentioned earlier, He 111 bombers of II./KG 26 had already flown over to Benghazi in mid January to undertake a raid on Suez, which had proved unsuccessful, as had further occasional raids which had followed. Now, as Wehrmacht units began moving across the Mediterranean to Tripoli, more units of the Luftwaffe began arriving in North Africa on a more permanent basis. One of the first to arrive was Stukageschwader 1, equipped with Junkers Ju 87R dive-bombers which had gained a fearsome reputation for their performances in Poland and France, and which had been responsible for inflicting severe damage on HMS *Illustrious* on 10 January, coming close to sinking the aircraft carrier (see *Malta: the Hurricane Years, 1940-41*).

From February 1941 German planes started to be a common sight in Libya. Here a Ju 52/3m is seen in a typical North African environment.

Accompanying the Stukas were the Messerschmitt Bf 110C twin-engined long-range escort fighters of III Gruppe, Zerströrergeschwader 26 (III./ZG 26), joined by 2.Staffel of I./ZG 26. III.Gruppe was led by Maj Karl Kaschka, and the adjutant was Oblt Fritz Schulze-Dickow. The gruppe's three staffeln were commanded as follows:

7.Staffel	Oblt Matthes (soon to be replaced by Oblt George Christl)
8.Staffel	Oblt Prang
9.Staffel	Hptmn Bord

On transfer to Africa, these units set up at airfields at Castel Benito, Sirte and Arco Philenorum (soon to be known to the British as 'Marble Arch'). Both the Bf 110s and the Ju 87s had proved quite vulnerable to RAF single-engined fighters during the summer of 1940, and held no great terrors for the Hurricane

121

German and Italian airmen mix together for a picture. Their planes, an S.81 and a He 111 provide the background.

pilots unless met in overwhelming numbers. However, with RAF fighter strength so diminished by the withdrawals to Greece, these new arrivals at the least represented a considerable threat to the bomber squadrons and to the ground troops. Other Luftwaffe units arriving at this time included both tactical and strategic reconnaissance units. All these Luftwaffe units would prove capable of swift deployment between Sicily and Africa as the demands of current activities from these two locations had to be met. Their notable capacity for such deployments was greatly dependent upon a substantial fleet of Junkers Ju 52/3m transport aircraft, which shuttled between those locations and Germany itself on a very frequent basis.

Just prior to the despatch of units to Tripolitania, the operational units and strengths in Sicily forming X.Fliegerkorps as at 12 January 1941 had been:

Duty	Unit	Aircraft	On hand	Serviceable	Base
Long-Range Reconnaissance	1.(F)/121	Ju 88	12	(2)	Catania
Twin-engined Fighters (Zerstörer)	III./ZG 26	Bf 110	34	(16)	Palermo
Bombers	Stab/LG 1	Ju 88	4	(2)	Catania
	II./LG 1	Ju 88	38	(38)	Catania
	III./LG 1	Ju 88	38	(38)	Catania
	II./KG 26	He 111	37	(29)	Comiso
	2./KG 4	He 111	12	(12)	Comiso
Dive-Bomber (Stuka)	Stab/StG 3	Ju 87	9	(8)	Trapani
	I./StG 1	Ju 87	35	(11)	Trapani
	II./StG 2	Ju 87	36	(23)	Trapani

Saturday, 1 February 1941

Having moved to Gazala on 30 January, 73 Squadron sent forward a detachment to El Adem on 1 February. From here during the morning six Hurricanes set off to strafe Apollonia airfield, near Barce. Sqn Ldr Murray, Flg Off Storrar and Plt Off Wareham attacked the airfield, the commanding officer claiming the destruction of a Caproni Ghibli, while two more such aircraft and a Ca.310 were claimed by the other two pilots. In the meantime Flt Lt Beytagh's section strafed a nearby road, claiming several lorries destroyed.

In the afternoon Sgts Marshall and Wills encountered seven CR.42s south-west of Cirene, Wills claiming one of these shot down. Cap Bernardino Serafini, commander of 366ª Squadriglia, 151° Gruppo, claimed a Hurricane and a second probable, but in fact neither unit suffered any loss.

British Claims				
73 Sqn	Sqn Ldr A.D.Murray	V7560 TP-F	Ca.309 Ghibli on ground	Apollonia
	Flg Off J.E.Storrar	V7544 TP-S	2 Ca.309 Ghiblis on ground	
	Plt Off M.P.Wareham	V7299 TP-D	Ca.310 on ground	
	Sgt W.C.Wills	V7544 TP-S	CR.42	Cirene
				1605-1805

Italian Claims			
366ª Sq/151° Gr CT	Cap Bernardino Serafini	Hurricane	
	Cap Bernardino Serafini	Hurricane probable	

Italian Casualties	
23ª Sq APC	Ca 309 damaged by Blenheim's bombs, Soluch
Unspecified unit	2 Ca.310s damaged by bombs on the ground at Apollonia

Sunday, 2 February 1941

Six CR.42s of 151° Gruppo intercepted Blenheims of 55 Squadron, Cap Livio Ceccotti of 367ª Squadriglia pursuing one and firing several long bursts; he was credited with one probably shot down. However, on this occasion Blenheim T2240 was shot down, Plt Off P.Blignaut and his crew all being killed; a second Blenheim was damaged during a 20-minute fight, and crash-landed at Gazala on return. Bomber gunners claimed damage to two of the CR.42s.

Sunderland 'U' of 230 Squadron was reportedly attacked by two Cant.Z.506B floatplanes whilst on patrol over the Mediterranean. One of the Italian aircraft attacked for six minutes without inflicting any serious damage, but the RAF crew believed that they had gained hits on their opponent in return. It seems that only one floatplane was actually involved in this engagement, an aircraft of 288ª Squadriglia RM reportedly being attacked by a Sunderland when flying from Taranto to Benghazi. It was damaged sufficiently to require a crash-landing to be made on the sea a few miles from the Libyan coast. The crew were then rescued unscathed.

British Claims		
55 Sqn	Blenheim gunners	2 CR.42s Damaged

British Casualties	
55 Sqn	Blenheim T2240 Plt Off P.Blignaut & crew KiA
	Blenheim damaged Flt Lt Smyth crash-landed

Italian Claims			
367ª Sq/151° Gr CT	Cap Livio Ceccotti	Blenheim Probable	Gazala 1430

Italian Casualties	
288ª Sq RM	Cant.Z.506B MM45306 crash-landed on the sea after combat with a Sunderland; crew rescued
85ª Sq/18° Gr CT	CR.42 Serg Remo Pisetta collided with Ca.309 on ground; aircraft destroyed

Monday, 3 February 1941

Not yet familiar with the aircraft of their newly-arrived allies, Ten Gianfranco Galbiati of 378ª Squadriglia, 155° Gruppo, intercepted a twin-engined aircraft over Tripoli, which he took to be a Blenheim. He had in fact attacked a Junkers Ju 88 of long-range reconnaissance unit 1.(F)/121, which was damaged, one member of the crew being wounded.

Italian Claims		
378ª Sq/155° Gr CT	Ten Gianfranco Galbiati	Blenheim damaged (in fact it was a Ju 88)

German Casualties	
1.(F)/121	Ju 88D damaged By Italian fighter over Tripoli; one of crew wounded

---

Tuesday, 4 February 1941

7th Armoured Division was despatched on a long journey across a desert track from Mechili in an effort to cut off the Italian army as it retreated west and south from Benghazi and the 'bulge' of Cyrenaica. This was a real gamble, as the division was down to only 50 cruiser tanks and 95 light tanks. Most of which were now in a worn condition, all greatly in need of overhaul. Meanwhile, the pressure from behind the Italians was maintained by 6th Australian Division which pressed on round the coast route through Derna and Barce.

The results of the debacle now made themselves felt in the Regia Aeronautica's command structure. During the day the tactical command of 5ª Squadra moved from Benghazi to Tripoli where next day Gen SA Felice Porro was replaced by Gen SA Mario Aimone-Cat. A few days later Gen BA Fernando Silvestri replaced Gen DA Egisto Perino as chief of staff of the squadra.

In support of this latter advance a pair of Blenheims of 45 Squadron bombed the railway south-west of Barce, but were intercepted by CR.42s of 151° Gruppo, S.Ten Furio Lauri of 368ª Squadriglia shooting down L8538 30 miles west of Barce at 1120. Flt Lt J.Paine, the pilot, managed to bale out and evade capture, but the other two members of his crew were killed.

During the engagement Serg Ezio Masenti's CR.42 suffered engine trouble and he landed at Barce. Because of the imminent capture of the town and airfield, the unit's 'hack' Ca.133 was sent to pick him up, flown by M.llo Giovanni Accorsi and escorted by Cap Guglielmo Chiarini, both of 366ª Squadriglia. Three patrolling Hurricanes of 73 Squadron intercepted these two aircraft, Plt Off J.B.N.'Chips' McColl shooting down the Ca.133. As he did so, Chiarini dived on his tail, but was at once shot down by Plt Off Goodman. Other CR.42s then joined the fight, the third Hurricane, flown by Plt Off K.M.'Tiny' Millist, being shot down by Serg Antonio Camerini of 366ª Squadriglia.

Chiarini, one of the most successful of the Regia Aeronautica fighter pilots in North Africa, and Accorsi would both be awarded the Medaglia d'Oro; Masenti, however, remained unrescued at Barce and became a PoW.

A Ca.309 Ghibli of 26ª Squadriglia APC, failed to return on 4 February 1941.

Millist returned safely on 6 February, having crash-landed ten miles north-east of Benina, and walked until picked up by Australian troops. Recorded one of his fellow pilots: "…when he was shot down by a vintage biplane (CR.42) everyone laughed their bloody heads off. He went at it head-on, and of course the Itie had a cannon in the thing (sic). We were all told not to tackle them head-on, but Tiny did and got hit in the radiator for his pains."

A Ca.309 Ghibli of 26ª Squadriglia APC, flown by S.Ten Pietro Mazza, which had taken off from Berka airfield at 1015, failed to return.

Although 33 Squadron had departed from the Delta for Eleusis in Greece on 1 February, it appears that at least one of the unit's Hurricanes was still present at Amiriya on this date, for a claim was recorded for the squadron for an S.79 off Alexandria at 1333, the Italian aircraft reportedly last being seen on fire. No Regia Aeronautica casualty has been discovered. 252 Wing amplified the incident, recording that bullets from a Hurricane set the bomber's port engine on fire while large pieces were seen to fall off the fuselage. However a bullet through the engine pump of the fighter caused its pilot to have to break away without seeing any final conclusion to his attack.

British Claims				
73 Sqn	Plt Off J.B.McColl	V7372 TP-W	Ca.133	NE Derna 1333
	Plt Off G.E.Goodman	V7716 TP-U	CR.42	
33 Sqn	u/k		S.79 probable	off Alexandria

British Casualties	
45 Sqn	Blenheim IV L8538 Flt Lt J.Paine baled out; two of crew KiA
73 Sqn	Hurricane V7491 Plt Off K.M.Millist safe

Italian Claims		
368ª Sq/151º Gr CT	S.Ten Furio Lauri	Blenheim
366ª Sq/151º Gr CT	Serg Antonio Camerini	Hurricane

Italian Casualties	
368ª Sq/151º Gr CT	CR.42 MM6257 force-landed at Barce, engine failure; lost; Serg Ezio Masenti PoW
151ª Gr CT	Ca.133 MM60149 M.llo Giovanni Accorsi and 1º Av mot Aldo Gallerani, KiA
366ª Sq/155º Gr CT	CR.42 MM5602 Cap Guglielmo Chiarini KiA
26ª Sq APC	Ca.309 FTR; S.Ten Pietro Mazza and crew MiA

Wednesday, 5 February 1941

During the day Flt Sgt Morris of 274 Squadron force-landed in the desert due to shortage of fuel. British armoured cars spearheading 7th Armoured Division's rush across Cyrenaica, cut the coast road beyond Benghazi. In the afternoon tanks, artillery and anti-tank guns joined them, and when at dusk the vanguard of the Italian retreat arrived, they were so surprised to find themselves cut off that large numbers surrendered with barely a fight.

On this date Sqn Ldr Murray, Flg Off Storrar and Sgt Marshall of 73 Squadron undertook a strafe of Benina airfield, claiming to have destroyed about eight bombers on the ground. This attack was not recorded in Italian reports, and they may well have shot up aircraft which had already been destroyed in earlier 274 Squadron strafes, or abandoned, since the Regia Aeronautica bomber force in Libya was now virtually moribund.

British Claims		
73 Sqn	Sqn Ldr A.D.Murray	
	Flg Off J.E.Storrar	Approx 8 bombers on ground
	Sgt A.E.Marshall	

Thursday, 6 February 1941

At dawn Italian forces attacked desperately to try and clear the roadblock at Beda Fomm, a fierce battle commencing. This proved to be the most savage fight of the whole campaign and lasted all day. Behind them 6th Australian Division entered Benghazi.

Friday, 7 February 1941

The final Italian attack came in during the morning, following which their 10th Army ceased to exist. Another 20,000 men were lost, mainly as prisoners, together with 120 tanks and 190 guns. The commanding general, Generale Giuseppe Tellera, was killed, and his second-in-command, Generale Annibale 'Electric Whiskers' Bergonzoli, was captured. The First Libyan Campaign was effectively at an end.

Commonwealth units now took up positions in front of El Agheila, their communications and supply lines too far stretched to allow them to advance any further. Following the withdrawals to Greece, which were still continuing, they were by then in a parlous situation which only the collapse of the Italian forces appeared to make less serious than it in fact was.

In just two months this small force had utterly defeated an army more than four times its size, mainly due to brilliant leadership, real mobility, and great co-operation between land, air and naval forces. 130,000 prisoners had been taken, with 1,300 guns and 400 tanks captured or destroyed. Losses amounted to 500 killed, 1,373 wounded and 55 missing.

In fairness it should be pointed out that the Italian 10th Army had been organised for colonial operations and was totally unprepared, untrained and under-equipped to meet a modern mechanised force. However, six months had passed between the declaration of war and the British offensive, which should have given some time to at least partially remedy these faults. Next day, 8 February, Marshal Graziani resigned.

Saturday, 8 February 1941

Following the conclusion of the advance, 274 Squadron passed its Hurricanes to 3 RAAF Squadron to bring this unit fully up to strength on these aircraft. 274's pilots then flew the Australians' remaining Gladiators back to Amiriya, where personnel could enjoy a well-earned rest. This left 73 Squadron at Tobruk and 3 RAAF Squadron at Benina as the sole fighter defence of Cyrenaica.

During the closing days of this period, on the 7th while repairing the engine of S.79 MM22233 of 54[a] Squadriglia, Serg Ferruccio Morettin decided to try and save the aircraft which had force-landed in an open space 33 miles from Ara dei Fileni (Arco Philenorum). Although with no formal training as a pilot, he nonetheless took off in the newly-repaired aircraft and landed it safely at Misurata, then returning to his engineering duties.

Flg Off Alan Rawlinson of 3 RAAF Squadron with a newly-arrived Hurricane I at Amiriya. V7772 went to 73 Squadron first, however, only later serving with the Australian unit.

Three days later Ten Adriano Visconti, Ten Italo Barbetta, Serg Magg Umberto Bartolozzi and Serg Giuseppe Cardini ferried four Ba.65s of the disbanded 50° Stormo Assalto from Tripoli to Sicily, landing safely at Palermo-Boccadifalco airport. They were flown back to Africa next day to repeat the operation, following which all remaining 50° Stormo aircraft in Africa were demolished.

On 19 February 41° Stormo BT was ordered to repatriate its remaining 20 S.79s to Ciampino. Next day 13 of the bombers took off from Bir el Behra in very poor weather conditions. These gave much trouble, two aircraft returning to Bir el Behra and one ditching in the sea near Ischia island in the Gulf of Naples; the crew were recovered by ship. However, the aircraft flown by Cap Athos Ammannato, commander of 235[a] Squadriglia, 60° Gruppo, crashed into the sea west of Ischia with the loss of the entire crew. Ammannato was awarded a posthumous Medaglia d'Oro.

Finally, on 1 March T.Col Tito Falconi and Ten Claudio Solaro of 23° Gruppo CT flew two S.79s which they had found at Tripoli, to Ciampino, carrying most of the unit's pilots back to Italy. This brought to an end the withdrawal of the battered remnants of the units which had taken part in the retreat. It was now time to recommence operations with new units.

After the opening days of 1941 the Fiat CR.42 began to lose its fighter role with the Regia Aeronautica in North Africa. Initially they began to be replaced by growing numbers of G.50bis, and then by Macchi C.200s. By the end of the new year the Macchi C.202 would almost entirely take over. The CR.42s were gradually relegated to the ground-attack role, equipped with under-wing racks to allow carriage of two 50kg bombs.

Three S.79s of the newly-arrived 18ª Squadriglia in flight.

The SIAI S.79s were considered to have been ineffective as bombers, and while more would be despatched to Libya in the short term, in the near future they were to be employed in the main only as reconnaissance aircraft, or after conversion to become torpedo-bombers. They would soon be replaced in their bombing role by Fiat BR.20s, twin-engined bombers which would operate mainly by night.

Wednesday, 12 February 1941

As the Italians were regrouping and reinforcing their units, General Erwin Rommel, ex-Panzer commander in the French campaign, arrived at Tripoli to assume command of the German forces now in Africa. Two days later the reconnaissance and anti-tank elements of the 5th Light Division also arrived here.

German Casualties

6. (K)./LG 1	Ju 88A-5 WNr 6238 L1+IP shot down by AA SW Solluch; Obfw Max Schmadtke and 3 PoWs

PROBLEMS OF COMMAND

At this stage on 11 February Longmore flew to meet General Henry Maitland Wilson, newly appointed as governor of Cyrenaica, to discuss what would be the minimum air force presence necessary to protect the ports and the occupying forces – particularly now that German aircraft were dropping parachute mines into Tobruk harbour. It was decided that Grp Capt L.O.Brown should be i/c HQ, RAF Cyrenaica, headquartered at Barce, with 3 RAAF Squadron (now on Hurricanes) remaining at Benina for the defence of Benghazi; meanwhile 73 Squadron at Gazala should move to Bu Amud for the defence of Tobruk. 6 Squadron would now replace 208 Squadron at Barce, with one flight operating with the forward troops at Agedabia.

Longmore also visited General O'Connor, 13 Corps commander and the real victor of the Compass campaign, who had signalled 202 Group:

"I wish to record my very great appreciation of the wonderful work of the RAF units under your command, whose determination and fine fighting qualities have made this campaign possible.

Since the war began you have constantly attacked without intermission an enemy air force between five and ten times your strength, dealing him blow after blow, until finally he was driven out of the sky, and out of Libya, leaving hundreds of derelict aircraft on his aerodromes.

"In his recent retreat from Tobruk you gave his ground troops no rest, bombing their concentrations, and carrying out low-flying attacks on their MT columns. In addition to the above you have co-operated to the full in carrying out our many requests for special bombardments, reconnaissances, and protection against enemy air action, and I would like to say how much all this has contributed to our success.

It is my earnest hope that the XIIIth Corps will in future again have the co-operation of N.202 Group."

Wonderful praise indeed – but how the tone would soon alter when things began going badly for the army.

Unfortunately, receipt of this welcome signal coincided with another chiefs-of-staff direction to prepare maximum assistance by land and air from Africa to Greece should a German attack through Bulgaria materialize. Due to the good progress being made in East Africa at this stage (see *Dust Clouds in the Middle East*) it had become possible to despatch a South African division from there to Egypt, and at this stage 33 and 37 Squadrons were now ordered to Greece.

However, signals continued to flow from the fertile minds at air ministry, one proposing to allot sufficient Tomahawks to the Turks to equip and maintain two squadrons. Longmore's views were sought thereon, and he replied stressing the claims of Malta to the best fighters available, the desirability of re-equipping his two highly-trained, experienced and efficient Gladiator squadrons, and of the growing need for fighter cover for the long sea routes to Tobruk, Benghazi and Greece. All of these should take priority over any schemes for providing either Tomahawks or Hurricanes to Greece or Turkey.

To add to Longmore's problems, Admiral Cunningham took this opportunity to raise the possibility of a coastal group being formed similar to Coastal Command in the UK, to come under the operational control of the Royal Navy. His reasoning was that the RAF's commitments in the Middle East generally, and as planned, were far in excess of the capacity to meet them. Only by earmarking a proportion of RAF squadrons for co-operation with his command, could he ensure the support he felt the navy required. He did show Longmore the draft of his signal on these lines to the admiralty, and as the long-suffering airman felt that this could only be met by an increase in existing air strength, he raised no objections. It was to become an on-going and increasing demand from Cunningham in future months, exacerbated by forthcoming events in the Eastern Mediterranean.

On 16 February the chiefs of staff enquired whether an advance on Mogadishu in Somaliland was practicable following the rapid advance of General Cunningham's South African force to Kismayu (see *Dust Clouds in the Middle East*). He was able to acquiesce to this, and the city was taken swiftly.

On 19 February Anthony Eden, now secretary of state for foreign affairs, arrived in a Sunderland with Field Marshal Sir John Dill, chief of the imperial general staff, as representatives of the Defence Committee. It quickly became clear to Longmore that they had been given a rosier picture of the air situation than was in fact the case. Their arrival coincided with the Greek confirmation that they would resist a German invasion and would therefore accept the offer of three British divisions, an armoured brigade and additional RAF squadrons. This was to be disguised as further assistance against the Italians, requiring that disembarkations be made in the southern and western parts of the country, and not in the more appropriate Salonika area. Longmore's view was:

"We were now committed definitely to supporting the Greeks against the Germans and I came away from the conference with the conviction that, whatever transpired in the future, we were right in honouring our moral obligations to this brave little country to whatever extent was possible. We had systematically encouraged their spirit of resistance to aggression whether Italian or German and it will be left to historians to record whether, under the circumstances, we were right or whether we should have politely thanked them for what they had done in resisting the Italians, thus raking some of the load off us in North Africa, but that we must now leave them alone to do what they could to stem the impending German attack."

It may be recalled that during December Tedder had taken command of 202 Group during Collishaw's illness. From what he had seen, Tedder was now harbouring some reservations regarding this commander's abilities:

———

"There is no doubt that Collishaw had his points, but on the other hand he was a 'bull in a china shop' with little of the administration without which operations cannot function properly. Moreover, he had a tendency to go off half-cock. To listen to Collishaw while plans were being drawn up for the next advance, one would think that the advance would be to Tripoli non-stop ! I could not help feeling sorry for the staff at 202 Group. Collishaw did not know how to use them, which left them feeling frustrated and miserable, and I wondered whether the change in methods which I had introduced had any chance of surviving. Guest, the new SASO, had just taken over, and I had made him and his Wing Commander Ops draw up the operation orders for me. They managed to do the same for Collishaw – I only hoped that this would last.

I had been interested, looking back, to see that Longmore had had twice to enjoin on Collishaw a greater economy in the employment of his limited forces; on the other hand, I also knew that he felt – quite rightly up to a point – that the man on the spot should be given as free a hand as possible. What I hoped was that instead of the lucky-dip sort of planning which had been customary up till then, the Group's Staff was now properly employed, and the AOC would get put before him plans which were rational and economical. I also hoped that the squadron commanders would now have a much better understanding of the whole plan, and would adjust their operations in accordance with that plan."

Interestingly, further down the chain of command 'Bing' Cross recorded that somewhat later out of curiosity he had visited Collishaw's command (now 204 Group) which he hoped to join:

"Its commander was Air Commodore Raymond Collishaw, a Canadian and an ace from the First World War, and I had a talk with him in the summer of 1941. During the time I was in his office we were repeatedly interrupted by a succession of corporal clerks bearing signals from all and sundry. Collishaw would read the signals, dictate a reply, sign it and off went the corporal to despatch it. I thought it was a bit odd that none of his staff were consulted, and wondered how they knew what was going on. I heard later that Collishaw had conducted business this way whilst supporting the O'Connor advance earlier in the war, when 204 Group had very few squadrons, and had refused to change now even though the force had more than doubled."

Cross's colleague and close friend, Wg Cdr Fred Rosier, had similar, perhaps more forthright views: "'Collie' had initially done well against the Italians but when the Germans arrived he was soon out of his depth. His efforts to thwart them were amateur in the extreme and he lacked the professionalism needed for the job."

Despite all the problems landing on Longmore's shoulders at this time, not all was bad news and he was able to note that by March there were two new airfields available in the Canal Zone at Shallufa and Kabrit for use by the Wellington force which now stood at four squadrons in Grp Capt MacLean's 257 Wing. During the period from 1 January-15 March, actual deliveries of aircraft to Egypt and the Sudan had been as follows:

Wellingtons	12	Hurricanes	0
Blenheims	68	Fulmars	2 (for the Fleet Air Arm)
Marylands	7	Lockheed Lodestars	3 (from South Africa)

During February, consequent upon the great victory he had achieved, O'Connor received a knighthood and promotion to Lt Gen, taking over the post of commander, British troops in Egypt, from Lt Gen Wilson, who would become military governor and GOC-in-C in Cyrenaica. Since the start of 1941 Western Desert Force had been renamed XIII Corps, which was now disbanded, HQ, I Australian Corps, taking over under Gen Blamey. Before the end of the month, however, Wilson, Blamey and I Australian Corps had left for Greece, and what remained in Libya now became Cyrenaica Command under Lt Gen Phillip Neame, VC. O'Connor would later express his regret that he had not pressed on to Tripoli on his own initiative, forestalling the arrival of the Germans and Italian reinforcements while the gate was wide open. The desire to bolster up Greece would undoubtedly extend the fighting in North Africa by many months.

Friday, 14 February 1941

The first encounters with Luftwaffe aircraft were noted when a Bf 110 of III./ZG 26 force-landed in British-held territory, Uffz Lippki and his gunner becoming PoWs. A Ju 87R was also lost by I./StG 1, shot down over El Agheila by 11th Hussars. The pilot was killed, but the gunner became a prisoner.

German Casualties	
III./ZG 26	Bf 110E-1 WNr 3488 3U+FR Uffz Lippki & Uffz Matthies MiA
I./StG 1	Ju 87R-1 WNr 5427 A5+LH to AA, Agheila; Ofw Benker & Uffz Vollmarie KiA

Saturday, 15 February 1941

At 0745 Flg Off J.H.W.Saunders of 3 RAAF Squadron, flying Hurricane V5476, made the first claim for the Australian unit with their new aircraft, and also the first fighter claim in Africa for a Luftwaffe aircraft, when he intercepted and claimed a Ju 88 shot down. A Ju 88A-5 of III.(K)/LG 1 crash-landed at Tripoli, but reportedly due to damage caused by ground fire.

British Claims				
3 RAAF Sqn	Flg Off J.H.W.Saunders	V5476	Ju 88	6m W Benghazi 0745

German Casualties	
III.(K)/LG 1	Ju 88A-5 WNr 3214 L1+JR damaged crash-landed Tripoli

Sunday, 16 February 1941

It was again ground fire which inflicted the next loss on the Luftwaffe. Bren gun fire from D Company, 1st King's Royal Rifle Regiment hit the Bf 110 flown by Lt Hesterkamp of III./ZG 26, both he and Ogfr Bracht being killed when their aircraft crashed 30-40 miles beyond Agedabia.

At 1410 a Ju 52/3m, VB+VC, flown by Lt Emil Siess and carrying ten passengers, crash-landed at Mellaha. The aircraft was badly damaged, but all aboard escaped unhurt.

German Casualties	
III./ZG 26	Bf 110E-1 WNr 3896 3U+FS El Agheila; Lt Hesterkamp & Ogfr Bracht KiA
III.(K)/LG 1	Ju 88A-5 WNr 5118 crash-landing at Tripoli
III./LN Regt 40	Ju 52/3m WNr 6835 (?? VB+VC) damaged 80% at Tripoli due to sandstorm

Monday, 17 February 1941

On this date HQ, 258 Wing, moved forward to Benghazi. Grp Capt Spackman had left the wing a week earlier on posting to HQ, Middle East, Sqn Ldr D.V.Johnson taking over in his stead; he would be promoted Wg Cdr a few days later.

Italian Casualties	
129ª Sq	Ro.37bis destroyed in crash-landing during reconnaissance sortie, M.llo Giuseppe Badan KiFA

Tuesday, 18 February 1941

By this time German aircraft were beginning to appear in strength, and by 17 February were attacking convoys making for Benghazi. On the 18th 258 Wing reported that an afternoon raid was made on Benghazi harbour by 9-12 Ju 88s, while that evening Ju 87s and He 111s attacked this target. During the day 3 RAAF Squadron's pilots were to have their first major encounter with their new enemy, as John Jackson recalled:

"The Huns have been dive-bombing Agedabia, Agheila and other townships en route, and ground-strafing our forward troops, causing a number of casualties. We left here (Benina) and flew down south, about two hours ten minutes, and landed back at Agedabia to refuel. We went off again about 3 p.m. and on the return run sighted dead below us about 12 Ju 87s, though at first saw only three. I warned Gordon Steege and Johnny Saunders, who were in front of me. I was acting as swinger or hawk-eye, i.e. flying to and fro behind the main body of aircraft. You get good vision when you are flying nearly at right angles to the main flight, and can see all around, which the others cannot do. It's a great idea and I believe it is done by all squadrons in England. Anyway, I turned around and dived to attack, and as I turned I spotted the other nine or ten aircraft following up the first three. We were at about 4,000 ft, about 20 miles north-east of Agheila, near a place called Marsa Brega. I was very excited, as I realised we were unobserved. They were flying below at about 1,000 ft and had been dive-bombing and ground-strafing. They had actually dropped two bombs and shot up one of our trucks. Luckily, the driver and passenger, Driver Batten and Sgt Quinton, escaped injury by jumping out and taking shelter on the ground. The truck was badly damaged, bullet and shrapnel holes all over it – they had a miraculous escape.

"I did a diving attack on a Ju 87 and seemed to pepper it well and it eventually sheered away. I attacked another bloke by a shallow-dive quarter attack and peppered him until he also sheered away. Both looked as if they were going to land. Then I did a dead astern attack on a third bloke and followed and peppered him until he started to break up in front of me and eventually crashed in flames, and I had to pull up over him, as by this time we were only at about 200 ft. I then encountered fairly heavy ack-ack and machine-gun fire from our own troops and climbed like billyo to get away, and lost sight of the other Huns.

Flt Lt Gordon Steege, who led 3 RAAF Squadron on this date.

"Meanwhile, Gordon and John had chased a couple each, and thought they each got at least one, though did not actually see them go in. We have claimed: me one certain, two possibles; Gordon – one damaged, one probable; and John Saunders the same as Gordon. Hope we can get them all confirmed. I was a bit ahead of Gordon and John and lost sight of them and returned to Agedabia and landed, refuelled, and re-armed. The other two returned direct to Benina."

A British intercept of an Italian signal contained the information that nine Ju 87s had bombed the road 42 miles south of Agedabia, and were intercepted by Hurricanes. One Ju 87 was destroyed and two others failed to return; this probably means that they landed away from base, returning later.

British Claims

3 RAAF Sqn	Flg Off J.F.Jackson	P5176	Ju 87	Marsa Brega 1615
	Flg Off J.F.Jackson	P5176	Ju 87s probable*	
	Flt Lt G.H.Steege	V6737	Ju 87 probable*	1610
	Flt Lt G.H.Steege	V6737	Ju 87 damaged*	
	Flg Off J.H.W.Saunders	V7770	Ju 87 probable*	1605
	Flg Off J.H.W.Saunders	V7770	Ju 87 damaged*	

*The above claims all seem to have been credited as confirmed destroyed at a later date, according to the unit's total of victories

German Claims

I.StG 1	Hurricane	50m S Agedabia

German Casualties

1./StG 1	Ju 87 WNr 3351 Fw Hans Drolshagen & Uffz Wolfgang Schaefer KiA, Agedabia
	Ju 87 damaged Fw Erich Morgenstein, gunner, WiA

Wednesday, 19 February 1941

The Luftwaffe was able to submit its own first claims in Africa when Bf 110s of III./ZG 26 were escorting Ju 87s of II./StG 2 on a raid. They were intercepted by Hurricanes of 3 RAAF Squadron, Flt Lt Jock Perrin claiming one of the Stukas shot down. Uffz Kurt Steuber crash-landed his Ju 87R-1 near Nofilia; he and his gunner, Uffz Walter Neutwig were both wounded.

However, the escorting Zerstörer were upon the Hurricanes before the pilots of the latter had spotted them, and four were claimed shot down. Only two Hurricanes were actually lost, Flg Off Gatward's aircraft blowing up, while Perrin's was set on fire after he had hit one of the attackers. He

Newly-arrived Junkers Ju 87B dive-bombers – Stukas – of the Luftwaffe return from one of their first missions in North Africa. They are being greeted by ground crews who are gathered around one of the ubiquitous kübelwagens that would soon become very familiar in the area.

crash-landed and got out, somewhat burned and wounded in one eye. The 110s then completed the destruction of the blazing Hurricane on the ground. Recorded John Jackson:

"Jock Perrin, Gaty, and Boyd had gone ahead earlier and did a patrol down to Agheila. We were just waiting for them to return before taking off, when we heard bombs being dropped to the south, so we hopped into the air and made south. Passed several villages that had just been bombed and came across Boyd returning on his own, so realised something was wrong. He went back to Agedabia and we flew on and saw an aircraft in flames. We flew low and found it to be a Hurricane burning furiously, much to our sorrow. However, Jeffrey spotted Jock Perrin nearby, waving.

"We finished the patrol and got back to Agedabia and found out from Boyd that they had spotted a number of Ju 87s dive-bombing the village just near where we saw them yesterday and, before attacking, Jock had a good look around but could see no other aircraft, so he and Gaty dived to attack – Boyd held back. Jock got a Ju 87 and looked around to see three Messerschmitts on his tail. One came up from under him and set his gravity tank on fire. Anyway he turned and managed to shoot down an Me 110 and then had to force-land with his plane on fire, and luckily got out unhurt. Poor old Gaty was last seen by Boyd in flames, crashing onto the seashore, and evidently he went into the sea as no further trace of him has since been seen. The Me 110s were evidently sitting up above the dive-bombers – we were fortunate yesterday, as they either were not above the Ju 87s or did not see us. The Me 110 is much faster than a Hurricane, according to Boyd, and he reckons he held back because he could see it was just murder. I think he should have shared the fight."

Flg Off Jas Storrar, Plt Off Lamb and Plt Off R.L.Goord of 73 Squadron had been ordered to Benina to augment 3 RAAF in defence of Tobruk. Storrar encountered several Bf 110s over Benghazi, claiming damage to one of them, Lamb chasing a Ju 88 out to sea, using all his ammunition without obvious results. Actually he had managed to inflict damage on an aircraft of III.(K)/LG 1. 258 Wing noted that during one of the day's raids one He 111 had been claimed shot down by gunners on some small vessels out at sea. However, during the afternoon five Ju 88s had dive-bombed HMS *Terror*.

On this date HQ, RAF Cyrenaica was formed at Barce to take over command of all units in Cyrenaica. Commanded by Grp Capt L.O.Brown, DSC, AFC, with Wg Cdr J.W.B.Judge as SASO, its personnel were drawn from Advanced 202 Group, which was now disbanded. The new HQ was to take over control of:

Barce	208 Squadron (less one detached flight)
	6 Squadron (two flights)
	Advanced 31 ASP
Benina	3 RAAF Squadron
	Two Blenheims of 55 Squadron for reconnaissance duties
El Adem	Station HQ
	31 ASP
	51 RSU
	70 Squadron (one flight)
	Squadron (one flight)
Agedabia	208 Squadron (detached flight)
Benghazi	Sector HQ, 258 Wing
	216 AMES
Bu Amud	55 Squadron
Gazala	73 Squadron
Tobruk	235 AMES

British Claims

3 RAAF Sqn	Flt Lt J.R.Perrin	V7757	Ju 87	Marsa Brega area 1145
	Flt Lt J.R.Perrin	V7757	Bf 110 (Wehmeyer)	Marsa Brega area 1145

The squadron originally listed a third victory on this date, but this was later removed.

73 Sqn	Flg Off J.E.Storrar	V7553	Bf 110	Damaged Benghazi 1030
	Plt Off O.E.Lamb	V7371	Ju 88	Damaged Benghazi 1130

British Casualties

3 RAAF Sqn	Hurricane I V7314 Flg Off A.A.Gatward KiA
	Hurricane I V7757 Flt Lt J.R.Perrin slightly wounded and burned

---

German Claims

III./ZG 26	Uffz Hohmann	Hurricane	El Brega: at 1,000 ft altitude 1141
	Lt Alfred Wehmeyer	Hurricane (Gatward)	El Brega: 66 ft altitude 1142
	Fw Richard Heller	Hurricane (Perrin)	El Brega: 66 ft altitude 11148
	Oblt Richard Prang	Hurricane	El Brega: 1,000 ft altitude 1148
I.StG 1	unspecified	Hurricane	El Brega

German Casualties

5./StG 2	Ju 87R-1 crash-landed; Uffz Kurt Steuber & Uffz Walter Neutwig WiA
III./ZG 26	Bf 110E-1 WNr 3886 Lt Alfred Wehmeyer safe, Ogfr Wüst WiA; ditched in sea, picked up after 24 hours
III.(K)/LG 1	Ju 88 damaged by fighters over Benghazi
II./KG 26	He 111 WNr 3529 MiA to AA over Tobruk
	He 111 damaged by fighters; one of crew KiA, one WiA

The first Luftwaffe fighter aircraft to arrive in North Africa were the Messerschmitt Bf 110s of III./ZG 26, one of which is seen here taxiing in over a dusty desert airfield.

Thursday, 20 February 1941

On this date armoured cars of 2nd Armoured Division, which had relieved 7th Armoured Division in the forward area, encountered German troops for the first time between Agheila and Marsa Brega. During the day also the Italian Ariete Armoured and Trento Motorized Divisions reached Tripoli. These latter divisions were considerably better equipped and more formidable than had been most of those forming Graziani's 10th Army.

216 AMES, a mobile radar station, had arrived in Benghazi on 16 February, and was at last about to come into operation at this time to aid in the defence of Benghazi.

At Alexandria Paddy Dunn was posted to a staff job on promotion to Wg Cdr, command of 274 Squadron passing to the hands of John Lapsley.

German Casualties		
II./KG 26	He 111H-5 WNr 3771 1H+KN;Obfw Protsch and crew MiA Benghazi; claimed by Benghazi AA	

Night of Thursday – Friday 21/22 February 1941

German Casualties		
II.(K)/LG 1	Ju 88A-5 WNr 7128 L1+JM MiA Benghazi	
II./KG 26	He 111H-5 WNr 3847 1H+8M; Fw Woethe and crew MiA; claimed by Benghazi AA	

Saturday, 22 February 1941

Flying from Benina with 3 RAAF Squadron, 73 Squadron's commanding officer, Sqn Ldr A.D.Murray claimed a Ju 88 of II.(K)/LG 1 shot down three miles south of Benghazi at 0730.

During 22 and 23 February heavy bombing of Benghazi took place, involving both dive-bombers by day and level bombing by night. HMS *Terror*, the monitor which had supported the army for weeks with her two 15in and eight 4in guns, had arrived on 17 February, but was repeatedly hit and damaged. Admiral Cunningham ordered her to sail for Tobruk on the 22nd, but next day she was sunk by air attack. Meanwhile the fighter operations room which had been set up at Tobruk was closed on the 23rd, moving instead to El Adem.

British Claims				
73 Sqn	Sqn Ldr A.D.Murray	V7551	Ju 88	3m S Benghazi 0730

German Casualties				
II.(K)/LG 1	Ju 88A-5 WNr 2172 L1+JP; crew KiA			

Sunday, 23 February 1941

LG 1 Ju 88s were out in force again, 14 attacking Tobruk at night between 1842-1853. L1+ET was hit in one engine, Fw Egon Moritz managing to get his aircraft back over Axis-held territory where the crew baled out; only two survived, Moritz and one other being killed. The rest of the formation sank the destroyer HMS *Dainty*, also claiming damage to two large cargo vessels.

German Casualties		
9./LG 1	Ju 88A-5 WNr 3282 L1+ET shot down by AA; Fw Egon Moritz and one KiA; two baled out and safe	

Wednesday, 26 February 1941

On this date HQ, RAF Cyrenaica ordered 73 Squadron to send three more Hurricanes from Gazala to El Adem. Thereafter no further records appear to have been maintained (or to have survived the retreat) by this command prior to its disbandment in early April.

Friday, 28 February 1941

The recently-arrived radar station at Benghazi was able to pinpoint a Ju 88 and to guide a Hurricane flown by 3 RAAF Squadron's commanding officer to make a successful interception.

British Claims				
3 RAAF Sqn	Sqn Ldr D.Campbell	P3980	Ju 88	3m S Benghazi 0915

German Casualties				
III./KG 30	Ju 88A-1 WNr 6021 4D+HR; Fw Moritz and crew MiA			

A Spring of Mixed Fortunes

Saturday, 1 March 1941

At the start of March 6 Squadron, which was still maintaining its A Flight at Agedabia on detachment, received Hurricanes to replace this flight's Lysanders. Two days later 208 Squadron, the only other army co-operation unit still available, withdrew to Heliopolis to prepare for Greece, to where it would move a month later. 6 Squadron was preparing to move the balance of the unit to Libya from Palestine, but this too would take another four weeks. In preparation, A Flight began re-equipping with Hurricane Is with which it would move to Agedabia to work with 2nd Armoured Division, moving B Flight to Barce.

Despite the appearance of German troops and Italian reinforcements, the pressure to send more forces to Greece had been growing. The units so far despatched were now to be followed by a substantial expeditionary force, and to this end half of 2nd Armoured Division, the newly-arrived New Zealand Division, the 6th and 7th Australian Divisions and a recently-formed Polish Brigade Group were all sent across the Mediterranean to this destination.

Consequently, the defence of Cyrenaica now rested on a skeleton force, quite incapable of offering any sustained resistance to an Axis offensive. By 11 March all the tanks of a complete Panzer regiment would have arrived as part of 5th Light Division, and with this reinforcement to hand, Rommel now began to probe the Commonwealth defences.

Nonetheless, and partly due to the greatly reduced strength of AHQ, Egypt, there was to be remarkably little aerial activity throughout March. On 3 March a new unit came into existence when the Intelligence Photographic Flight at Heliopolis became the nucleus of 2 Photographic Reconnaissance Unit (PRU), equipped with three unarmed Hurricanes for this vital duty (V7428, V7423 and W9116) in addition to its existing Lockheed 10A, AX701. Commanding officer remained Sqn Ldr Macphail. The air ministry had decided as long ago as October that the Middle East should have its own PR, which involved mainly strategic photography for HQ, RAF Middle East, undertaken in the main from high altitude. The original intention had been to equip the unit with one flight of Hurricanes and one of Marylands, this subsequently being changed to two flights of Marylands. Non-availability of these latter aircraft led to the initial establishment now to hand. Initially one of the Hurricanes was fitted with three 14in lenses, and one with two 8in lenses. Besides Sqn Ldr Macphail and Flt Lt A.M.Brown as flight commander, three more pilots were also posted in and a photographic section was provided to develop and print the films.

One of most successful fighter pilots of 18° Gruppo CT was S.Ten Franco Bordoni-Bisleri, of 95ª Squadriglia. He claimed his first victory in Africa on 10 March 1941. On the cockpit fairing of his CR.42 (MM 5688) is painted his nickname 'Robur', taken from the advertisements for his family's well known liquor business.

Many of the unit's sorties would be carried out over Syria during June and July, and then over Iran. In September two further Hurricanes would arrive (W9353 and Z4182) and a Beaufighter (T3301), followed by a single Hurricane II (Z2412), all of these aircraft being painted overall blue for their high altitude role. It appears that, although Malta's Flg Off Adrian Warburton remained a member of 69 Squadron on that island, he also on occasion undertook sorties in 2 PRU's Beaufighter over Sicily and southern Italy.

Monday, 10 March 1941
S.Ten Franco Bordoni-Bisleri of 95ª Squadriglia, 18° Gruppo CT took off with his wingman, M.llo Felice Longhi from Wadi Tamet to intercept a Blenheim 70 miles from Benghazi. After a long chase Bordoni-Bisleri claimed this shot down, Longhi delivering the 'coup de grace'.

Italian Claims

95ª Sq/18° Gr CT	S.Ten Franco Bordoni-Bisleri	Blenheim	70m N Benghazi

Tuesday, 11 March 1941
With pressure building due to the forward movement of Rommel's forces, the main part of 258 Wing now began withdrawing towards Tobruk, although the unit's advanced elements were still at Benghazi next day. From there they would then move back to Benina.

Thursday, 13 March 1941
Fifteen Ju 87s undertook a concentrated attack on El Adem, as did nine Ju 88s of LG 1. This unit would be involved for the rest of the month in attacking shipping off Crete, then moving to the Balkans for the forthcoming invasion of Yugoslavia and Greece.

British Claims

55 Sqn	Flg Off Harries & crew	Ju 52/3m	3m from Bir el Gubi 1230 approx

Monday, 17 March 1941
One of 6 Squadron's new Hurricanes failed to return from a TacR sortie west of Agheila, Flg Off J.E.Wilson being shot down and becoming a PoW.

The wreckage of a burnt-out Gladiator at Mersa Matruh is inspected for possible recoverable items. The nose of a Hurricane may just be seen in the right background.

On this date 274 Squadron was required to despatch one of its flights to Malta to aid in the defence of the island which was now suffering sustained attack by Luftwaffe aircraft. Consequently seven aircraft and eight pilots were sent, led by Flg Off E.M.Mason, DFC. With him went Flg Offs C.J.Laubscher (a South African from the Transvaal) and J.S.Southwell, Plt Offs T.B.Garland, and D.F.Knight, and Sgts T.A.Quinn, M.P.Davies and R.J.Goode. The flight landed to refuel at El Abqar, but in doing so Garland crashed and suffered slight burns. Against advice he continued to the destination aboard a Wellington which navigated the Hurricanes across the sea to the island. They were not to return to the squadron. Southwell, Garland and Knight were all killed shortly after their arrival, Mason and Goode both being wounded. Mason, Laubscher and Quinn would return to North Africa with 261 Squadron, while Davies and Goode were posted elsewhere. Both Mason and Laubscher were later to return to action in the Western Desert, but of these eight pilots only Laubscher would survive the war.

On 11 March the first Fiat BR.20 bombers of 98° Gruppo BT (240ª and 241ª Squadriglie) had arrived at Bir Dufan from Italy, led by T.Col Ivo De Wittemberski. These undertook their first raid during the night of 17/18 March, attacking Benghazi harbour.

British Casualties		
6 Sqn	Hurricane Flg Off J.E.Wilson PoW	

Tuesday, 18 March 1941

A Blenheim from 55 Squadron departed at 0730 to reconnoitre airfields in the Sirte and Mechili area. The aircraft was last seen near Benina by the pilot of a Hurricane, but failed to return. The crew were later found to have been killed.

British Casualties		
55 Sqn	Blenheim IV T1995 FTR from airfield Flg Off T.Walker & crew KiA, reconnaissance; Benghazi	
German Claims		
Flak unit	Hurricane	15m ESE Arco Philenorum 1035

Thursday, 20 March 1941

Italian Casualties	
240ª Sq/98° Gr BT	BR.20 Ten Pietro Giardino-Roch & crew MiA, Benghazi

Friday, 21 March 1941

Elements of 5th Panzer Division began to move to Africa on 20 March, and next day the crew of a 55 Squadron Blenheim reported sighting a Messerschmitt Bf 109 in flight over Axis territory. This ominous report was not confirmed, but gave a foretaste of what was soon to occur. Three days later a small German armoured car detachment from the fort at El Agheila, drove British outposts back from Marsa Brega with considerable ease, fuelling Rommel's growing belief that he was 'pushing on an open door'.

45 Squadron received a new commanding officer, Sqn Ldr J.O.Willis taking over from Sqn Ldr V.Ray.

Saturday, 22 March 1941

Italian Casualties	
240ª Sq/98° Gr BT	BR.20 MM22265 destroyed in collision; S.Ten Vittorio Biagetti & all but one of crew KiFA
	BR.20 destroyed in collision; S.Ten Carlo Baj & all but one of crew KiFA
German Casualties	
Stab/StG 3	Ju 88A-5 WNr 0557 2F+XA shot down by AA, Giarabub Oasis; crew PoW

Sunday, 23 March 1941

German Casualties	
III./ZG 26	Bf 110E-1 WNr 3499 3U+NS shot down by AA at Marsa Brega; Uffz Macht & Uffz Leckebusch
	Bf 110E-1 WNr 3895 3U+AT crashed due to engine failure, Sidi Ahmed-el Magrun; Uffz Dehler & Gefr Milles

Tuesday, 25 March 1941

55 Squadron recorded that on this date the unit was supplied with six fighter Blenheims.

Thursday, 27 March 1941

84 Squadron, in which command had passed at the start of the month to Sqn Ldr H.D.Jones, recorded that Sqn Ldr Gordon-Finlayson, DSO, DFC, had taken up command of a new bomber wing. A general re-organisation began for these units during March, the commanding officer being promoted to Wg Cdr rank, while two flights were to be more formally created, each led by a Sqn Ldr. This would apply only to certain established units at first, but would steadily spread to all such squadrons during the year.

Friday, 28 March 1941

C Flight of 6 Squadron had flown in to Giarabub, but following its capture, moved back to Barce on this date.

Saturday, 29 March 1941

At 1325 a Bf 110 attacked a Sunderland of 230 Squadron, making four quarter attacks. The aim of the Luftwaffe pilot proved to be poor, achieving only a few hits on the tailplane and elevators which caused only slight damage to the big flyingboat. No claim appears to have been submitted by III./ZG 26.

British Casualties

230 Sqn	Sunderland Damaged

Sunday, 30 March – Sunday, 6 April 1941

German Casualties

2.(H)/14	Hs 126 hit by AA near El Agheila and force-landed by Lt Wolf

During the 30th Flg Off Holland of 267 Squadron took off in a Q.6 to take Air Marshal Tedder on a 'Cook's Tour' of Cyrenaica. While so engaged the aircraft suffered an oil pressure failure to its port engine, resulting in a force-landing on a camel track 15 miles north-west of Mechili. Unfortunately, the radio proved to have gone unserviceable, and those aboard had no idea that Barce was in the process of being evacuated due to German patrol activity. Tedder had been doing the navigating and was fairly certain of their location. It was decided therefore that all aboard would stay with the aircraft for the time being as they had sufficient water and supplies. Next day, however, efforts to attract the attention of a passing Wellington, a Lysander and then a Blenheim, proved fruitless, and it was decided that Holland and Sqn Ldr Bray, a member of Tedder's staff, should begin walking towards Barce.

No sooner had the pair departed than another Blenheim appeared, and this time the swift lighting of a fire and the firing of a couple of Very lights caught the eye of the pilot, who circled overhead and then landed reasonably successfully, although breaking the tailwheel of the aircraft in doing so. The pilot was Sgt Dixon who had been flying alone to deliver the aircraft, which had a damaged stern post, to the rear. Due to the damaged tailwheel it was not possible to take the party aboard, but having passed over two of the three water bottles he was carrying, Dixon successfully took off again and departed to raise the alarm.

Having spotted the Blenheim landing, and surmising that rescue by air was a better bet than walking, Holland and Bray returned. It was not until the early evening that Dixon came back, however. He had obtained a replacement aircraft for his unit after delivering the damaged machine. After

Pilots of 73 Squadron seen while visiting 3 RAAF Squadron at Benina; left to right: Plt Off R.L.Goord, Flg Off Jas Storrar and Flt Lt Donald Scott, DFC; Scott had seen considerable action over France and England during 1940, but shortly after arrival in North Africa he was posted to a training job.

three hours searching in vain, he had flown on to his own airfield, retracing from there the route he had taken earlier in the day. This allowed him to spot the downed Q.6 again, and he landed. This time he took Tedder and Bray aboard, flying them to Maraua, while help was sent out to collect Holland and LAC Gratwicke who had been left to guard the Q.6.

Meanwhile, General O'Connor and three other passengers were flown to Barce in an Anson, and from here next day Tedder was evacuated to Heliopolis in the Anson. On that day Flg Off Lydall flew to the Q.6 in 267's Lysander to fly the RAF pair out since, by that time, the Germans had already advanced to the east of their position.

Next morning Middle East Command, not being fully aware of the position, ordered the squadron to recover the Q.6, as a result of which Holland, Lydall and three LACs set off in an Anson, loaded with a good supply of food, water and armaments. Having spent the night at El Adem, they found the aircraft, landed alongside and posted guards while the Q.6 was worked on. At this stage an armoured patrol approached which fortunately proved to be British. The troops took over the defence, allowing work on the aircraft to progress speedily, and before the day was out both the Q.6 and the Anson had been flown back to Heliopolis. By this time the main German force had advanced 120 miles to the east of their location in the desert without spotting them.

While these events had been taking place,……

Monday, 31 March 1941

By the end of the month the Pavia, Brescia and Bologna Infantry Divisions of the Italian army had reached Tripolitania. On this final day of the month Rommel launched a reconnaissance in strength, similar to that made by Wavell and O'Connor nearly four months earlier. His force was already quite formidable, including 120 PzKw II and IV tanks of 5th Light Division and 80 M.13/40 tanks of the Ariete Division.

Between 0905 and 0919 ten BR.20s, led by T.Col Ivo De Wittemberski, set off on their first daylight raid, Agedabia being the target. One of the bombers was forced to return early

The 'business end' of a Bf 110, showing the armament of two 20mm cannon and four 7.9mm machine guns.

due to a technical malfunction. At 1058 the formation split into two vics, the first formed of four aircraft of 240ª Squadriglia, the second of five BR.20s of 241ª Squadriglia, at the same time arriving over Arae Philenorum to pick up an escort of five Luftwaffe Bf 110s. In the event only four of these fighters appeared, two providing the escort, the other pair heading off for Agheila.

At midday the formation had reached Agedabia where bombs were dropped on the town and airfield, two aircraft being claimed destroyed on the latter, and a third damaged. Just before bombs were released about ten Hurricanes were seen taking off from an airfield about six miles to the north, and as soon as these reached the requisite altitude they attacked the rear formation of five.

These were aircraft of 3 RAAF Squadron, the pilots of which knew exactly what they were after. John Jackson: "Acting on secret information received at HQ, 12 Hurricanes were off today to patrol over Agedabia. We had been told to expect ten bombers and five fighters at a certain time and we went off in three formations of four, the lower formation at 3,000 ft, middle at 7,000 ft, and top at 10,000 ft. I was in the middle formation." The escorting Zerstörer engaged, but one was shot down almost immediately.

"We had patrolled the area for about one hour when the lower formation spotted two Me 110s and the four of them pounced onto one and brought it down in flames. Duncan Campbell got credit for it, though Pete Jeffrey (CO) and Kloster also got very good bursts into it." They had shot down a 7./ZG 26 aircraft flown by Obfw Josef Bracum, with Uffz Kasper as his gunner.

Meanwhile all five BR.20s were hit and damaged, some crew members were wounded and 1º Av Luigi Ambrosino, gunner in the bomber flown by Ten Francesco La Ganga, was killed. The engagement lasted

Hurricanes of 3 RAAF Squadron at Amiriya in March 1941. In the foreground is Flt Lt Pelly's aircraft named 'Pamela'.

about five minutes, when at 1205 the pilot of the only remaining Bf 110, Hpt Steinberger in a 9.Staffel machine, claimed a Hurricane shot down. A second was claimed hit by a burst fired by 1° Av Renato Anselmino, rear turret gunner in Ten Angelo Tucceri's aircraft, and he reported seeing the pilot of this Hurricane baling out. Whatever it was that he thought he had seen, in fact no Hurricanes were lost during this combat.

Four of the BR.20s were so badly damaged that they were forced to land at Arae Philenorum, but Ten Augusto Grassi, flying the fifth, managed to join up with the four 240ª Squadriglia aircraft and landed safely at Tamet with these. Once again, the Australians appear later to have had claims confirmed as destroyed for three of the bombers, but this does not seem to be how they saw it at the time. John Jackson recorded:

> "Found out when I got back to Benina that John Saunders and Lindsay Knowles had got in attacks on the bombers and John had badly damaged one, Knowles probably two. They were the only two to attack the bombers – good work. Actually, we all should have been able to attack the bombers but, through breaking formation and milling about, the squadron lost its effectiveness and a lot of chaps had gone off home singly or in pairs and didn't even see the bombers. Mort Edwards and Knowles had Me 110s on their tails during the mêlée but managed to shake them off. I didn't even see an Me 110. The CO gave us a sound talk on our bad airmanship. I think everybody realises what a rotten display we made – we should have got those bombers. Our RT seems very inefficient and practically hopeless – most unreliable, and is continually breaking down in different aircraft, and as a result, leads to muddles and misunderstandings in the air, and seriously interferes with our efficiency in combat."

Jackson's own experience in this regard seems to have been fairly typical:

> "The top and middle formations got mixed up and Hurricanes milled about, going hell west and crooked for about ten minutes, and then started to leave the area. Most of us were some miles north of Agedabia and I had just called over RT that I was going to go back, land and refuel as my aircraft was using a lot of juice, when someone called up to look behind and we saw a huge stick of bombs

go off over Agedabia drome. I turned and flew up-sun but could not see the bombers, but eventually spotted some flying seawards. I started to chase them but lost sight of them again, they were too far away when I spotted them. I then flew east of Agedabia up-sun for about ten minutes, looking for enemy aircraft, and then landed to refuel. Found the drome full of craters, about 25 in all, and a lot of incendiary bombs were still burning, but I found a strip and landed. One gun post had been hit badly – one gunner killed, one officer and three men badly wounded. The Me 110 brought down by Duncan had crashed in flames and nothing was left of it. I found that 6 Squadron had done a Tac R and the pilot had spotted 150 to 200 enemy tanks and armoured vehicles moving east in a big column from Agheila – looks as if they are on the warpath."

British Claims

3 RAAF Sqn	Sqn Ldr D.Campbell	P3980	Bf 110*	Agedabia 1145
	Flg Off J.H.W.Saunders	V6737	BR.20	Agedabia 1145
	Flg Off W.G.Kloster	V7253	BR.20	Agedabia 1145
	Flg Off L.E.S.Knowles	V7556	BR.20	Agedabia 1145

*Initially this victory was credited to Campbell, Kloster and Sqn Ldr Peter Jeffrey (V7567) jointly; it was subsequently credited to Campbell alone since it was he who had set it on fire.

German Claims

9./ZG 26	Hptm Theodore Steinberger	Hurricane	NW Agedabia 1205

German Casualties

7./ZG 26	Bf 110E-1 WNr 3948 3U+PR Ofw Josef Bracum/ Uffz Kasper KiA
III./ZG 26	Bf 110E-1 WNr 3919 60% damaged; possibly on 1 April

Italian Claims

241ª Sq/98° Gr BT	1° Av Renato Anselmino (gunner)	Hurricane

Italian Casualties

241ª Sq/98° Gr BT	BR.20 MM21910 badly damaged; Ten Francesco La Ganga pilot; one crew dead and two wounded
	BR.20 MM22619 badly damaged; Cap Alfredo Sordini pilot
	BR.20 MM22245 badly damaged; S.Ten Amedeo Piazza and crew wounded
	BR.20 MM21914 badly damaged; Ten Angelo Tucceri pilot
	BR.20 MM21921 damaged; Ten Augusto Grassi pilot; gunner wounded

Rommel was now in a position similar to that which Wavell had been in the previous December. Believing himself only to have weak forces available when compared with those facing him, he commenced his advance on a limited scale, prepared however, to exploit any favourable situation that arose.

It is of interest here to note that following the downgrading of the S.79 as a bomber and its replacement by the BR.20s, Italian multi-engined bomber formations were never again to appear over the Western Desert. Bombers were seen in strength on rear airfields on several occasions, and certainly were involved by night, but failed to put in an appearance over the battlefield by day.

Tuesday, 1 April 1941

On the opening day of April Ten Italo Larese and Serg Elio Cesaro of 152ª Squadriglia, 2° Gruppo CT, claimed a Blenheim probably shot down. An aircraft of 55 Squadron had taken off at 1525 on a reconnaissance towards Tripoli, but this subsequently ditched south-west of Benghazi. The crew were later spotted in their dinghy, but could not be found again and were lost. This squadron had been commanded by Sqn Ldr A.S.Dudgeon since October 1940, but ill health had kept him in hospital for some time and at the start of the new month his place was taken by Sqn Ldr R.S.Darbyshire, who was promoted from Flt Lt.

By this date the HQ of 258 Wing had become fully established at Tobruk.

British Casualties

55 Sqn	Blenheim V5423 ditched SW Benghazi; Flg Off M.S.Ferguson and crew MiA

Italian Claims

152ª Sq/2° Gr CT	Ten Italo Larese	}	Blenheim probable
	Serg Elio Cesaro		

Wednesday, 2 April 1941

Two Hurricane pilots from 3 RAAF Squadron claimed an aircraft probably shot down west of Benghazi at 1830. This was intercepted at 20,000 feet, identified as an S.79, and was last seen at 2,000 feet with the starboard engine pouring smoke. Their incorrect recognition of the trimotor at this stage of the war is understandable, but what they had actually encountered was a Cant.Z.1007bis, some of which had been on the strength of 175ª Squadriglia RST since early March. The aircraft was badly shot-up, but managed to get back to Castel Benito, the crew claiming to have shot down a Hurricane but with the observer, Ten Ugo Del Curto, and a gunner dead; Del Curto was awarded the Medaglia d'Oro.

On this date Rommel decided that the British were in full retreat, and pushed forward a two-pronged advance. His German forces with the Italian Brescia Division advanced on Benghazi, while Ariete Armoured Division set off through the desert towards Mechili. 2nd Armoured Division with about 50 tanks remaining made for Msus during the day to cover the supply dump there from a reported armoured thrust. They arrived to find the dump blown up, and were then in a perilous position as there was no petrol available for refuelling. Benghazi was ordered to be evacuated, and a general retreat to Mechili began. Meanwhile, 73 Squadron sent a flight forward to Benina again to assist 3 RAAF Squadron.

On return from his sojourn out in the desert, Tedder had discovered a situation close to chaos arising within the command of the army. Wavell felt initially that both Neame and Maj Gen Gambier-Parry, commander of the 2nd Armoured Division, were failing to handle the situation well. Wavell later recorded:

"In view of his greater experience of this type of warfare I yesterday sent for O'Connor with the intention of putting him in command, but on his arrival today the situation was so serious I considered change of command undesirable as Neame was doing well in a difficult situation; also found O'Connor had not been well lately and might become ill, so left Neame in command with O'Connor to help and advise him. This will work satisfactorily, and is agreeable to both."

It was hardly ideal, and was an uncomfortable situation for O'Connor, having to 'peer over his colleague's shoulder' all the time. Fortunately, the pair were old friends which somewhat ameliorated the situation – for the moment.

British Claims					
3 RAAF Sqn	Flg Off M.D.Ellerton	V7353	}	S.79 probable	nr Benghazi 1830
	Flg Off A.M.Edwards	V7556			

Italian Claims		
175ª Sq RST	Gunners in Cant.Z.1007bis	Hurricane

Italian Casualties	
175ª Sq Aut RST	Cant.Z.1007bis MM33372 damaged (subsequently w/o); Observer, Ten Ugo Del Curto, and gunner 1°Av Anceschi KiA
368ª Sq/151° Gr CT	CR.42 MM6915 badly damaged; hit a hut on landing, killing an airman; Serg Magg Giacinto Fiascaris safe

Thursday, 3 April 1941

Consequent upon the retreat of the ground forces the Hurricanes of 73 and 3 RAAF Squadrons now fell back to Maraua. While patrolling over forward troops from this base, the Australians intercepted eight Ju 87s of II./StG 2 escorted by an equal number of Bf 110s from III./ZG 26.

There is some confusion regarding the 3 RAAF Squadron claims and subsequent confirmations, as these bore little relationship to actual Luftwaffe losses. Flg Off Peter Turnbull appears to have claimed two Bf 110s shot down and two more as probables initially, but subsequently was credited with all four destroyed, Flt Lt Gordon Steege adding one more and three damaged. III./ZG 26 actually suffered only one loss, noting that the gunner in this Bf 110 had been wounded.

However, Hptmn Christl of the Zerstörer unit claimed two Hurricanes shot down south-west of Solluch, Ofw Sander adding a third; 3 RAAF Squadron also actually escaped without loss, but with some aircraft damaged. Meanwhile, Flt Lt Alan Rawlinson had claimed (or was credited with) three Ju 87s shot down, Lt G.K.Smith adding a fourth, while other pilots claimed two probables and two damaged. II./StG 2 lost two dive-bombers during this fight.

———

Plt Off John Jackson:

"About noon we went off on another patrol, about ten of us. We now have four or five pilots from 73 Squadron attached to us. We need them too, as some of our chaps are very war-weary and showing the effects of the strain. We got no distance south of Sceleidima when somebody spotted enemy aircraft. We were in three flights, Gordon Steege leading the bottom flight with me, John Saunders, and Pete Turnbull, and Alan Rawlinson leading the middle flight about 1,000 ft above us. The top flight did a wild-goose chase after one of our Blenheims they spotted out on our starboard side, which happened to be returning from a reconnaissance trip, and they did not see the enemy.

"They turned out to be about ten Me 110s escorting about 15 Ju 87s, which were dive-bombing and ground-strafing our retreating ground forces. I only spotted two Me 110s and didn't see any of the other enemy aircraft. I followed Gordon Steege into the attack and got on the tail of an Me 110, just after he had fired a few bursts at it and sheered away from it. I fired two bursts and my guns stopped – rotten luck. Just as I was getting very close, I saw a few bits and pieces and sparks flying from the Me 110. Pete Turnbull followed me into the same Me 110, and gave it a burst also. Gordon Steege got credit for this kite, as he attacked first and probably got in the best attack. Immediately my guns stopped I did a steep spiral to gain speed and went like hell to get out of the area as I reckoned it was useless to remain without guns firing. I flew back to Benina, where I knew the CO was still waiting, and gave him news of the fight.

"Pete Turnbull had a go at two more Me 110s and blew an engine out of one and bits off another and fired at a couple of others. Smith, one of three South African pilots attached to us, attacked the Ju 87s and blew the tail clean off one and sent it down in flames. Jimmy Davidson also claimed one Ju 87 and Alan Rawlinson sent two 87s down in flames. Wish my guns hadn't stopped, I was feeling very fit and enjoyed the bit I had. I'm satisfied Me 110s are no match for a Hurricane – at low heights we can catch them and out-turn them without too much trouble. All our chaps returned safely to Sultan though some had some nasty bullet holes – both Pete Turnbull and Jimmy Davidson had holes through their ailerons and both were jamming badly – they were very fortunate to get back. Pete also had a bullet through one of his tyres and landed nicely with one flat tyre. The boys are awfully bucked about this show. Three Me 110s and five Ju 87s, about five of them down in flames, and possibly others damaged."

6 Squadron, which had been supporting 2nd Armoured Division, found itself deserted at Antelat and flew to Msus. From here the armoured units were making for the coast, desperately seeking fuel.

British Claims

3 RAAF Sqn	Flg Off P.StG.B.Turnbull	V7492	4 Bf 110s*	Sceleidima 1300
	Flt Lt G.H.Steege	V3937 OS-P	Bf 110	Sceleidima 1300"
			3 Bf 110s damaged	Sceleidima 1300
	Flt Lt A.C.Rawlinson	V7772	3 Ju 87s damaged	Sceleidima 1300
	Flt Lt A.C.Rawlinson	V7772	Ju 87 damaged	
	Lt G.K.Smith	P3980	Ju 87	
	Flg Off J.M.Davidson	V7566	Ju 87 probable	
	Flg Off J.H.Jackson	V76770	Ju 87 probable	
	Flg Off J.H.W.Saunders		Ju 87 damaged	

*Initial claims appeared to be no more than 2 destroyed, but credited ultimately with four in squadron records

British Casualties

3 RAAF Sqn	Hurricane I V7492 damaged Flg Off P.StG.B.Turnbull safe
	Hurricane I V7566 damaged Flg Off J.M.Davidson safe

German Claims

III./ZG 26	Hpt Georg Christl	2 Hurricanes	SW Solluch
	Ofw Franz Sander	Hurricane	

German Casualties

III./ZG 26	Bf 110E-1 WNr 3885 Uffz Stirnweis safe; Uffz Bock WiA
6./StG 2	Ju 87R-2 WNr 6034 crash-landed; Uffz Erwin Dyerr WiA, died later
5./StG 2	Ju 87R-2 WNr 5885 Uffz Christian Appmann baled out, WiA; Uffz Peter Ott KiA

Friday, 4 April 1941

Despite the downgrading of the S.79, on 4 April more of these bombers arrived in Tripolitania. 27° Gruppo of 8° Stormo (18ª and 52ª Squadriglie) flew in to Misurata despite the loss in a crash of one 18ª Squadriglia aircraft en route. Another S.79 crash-landed near Homs and had to be written off. Its sister unit, 28° Gruppo (10ª and 19ª Squadriglie) would follow by the end of May.

On the ground, under constant attack, 2nd Armoured Division's columns made for Mechili, the Division HQ losing contact with the rest of its units. The remainder of the British forces in the forward area now fell back on Benina and Msus.

Italian Casualties

18ª Sq/27° Gr/8° St BT	S.79 S.Ten Arcadio Vergna & crew KiFA near Tripoli
18ª Sq/27° Gr/8° St BT	S.79 MM21475 badly damaged; S.Ten Francesco Belloni and crew WiFA near Homs

Saturday, 5 April 1941

The Hurricanes enjoyed something of a 'field day' against the Stukas which were attempting to play havoc with the retreating columns. Weather was fine when at 1405 two of 73 Squadron's aircraft and three of 3 RAAF Squadron took off on patrol. Within half an hour a formation of Ju 87s from 6./StG 2 were spotted and the Commonwealth pilot waded in, claiming five shot down and two damaged. 6.Staffel actually lost three aircraft. Recalled Plt Off Bill Eiby: "By now the bloody army was in full flight. They retreated and the Jerries were knocking hell out of our convoys. We got scrambled and ran into this mob, I dived at this bastard and hit him and he caught fire. He went straight in. I should have shot down another but he eluded me. Soon after that they withdrew the Stukas as the Hurricanes could shoot them down like flies."

Hurricane I TP-K, P2646, of 73 Squadron. This aircraft has the tri-colour 'spaghetti' paint scheme to the underside of the nose and the wing leading edges. Although clearly carrying 73 Squadron code letters, aircraft records do not show it to have served with that unit.

Flg Off Edwards had to force-land when his Hurricane was hit by return fire, but he was unhurt. He would be picked up by elements of 2nd Armoured Division, but would subsequently be captured with his rescuers.

Sqn Ldr Duncan Campbell led off another patrol to the Barce Pass area at 1635, this time nine aircraft taking part. Once again Ju 87s were seen, estimated at about 12 strong. These were from 4./StG 2, and suffered heavily. Nine were believed to have been shot down, five actually failing to return. High claims or not, eight losses by the single gruppe in one day represented an unsustainable rate of attrition.

Plt Off John Jackson:

"We decided to do another patrol immediately, led by Duncan Campbell, to search for Mort Edwards and at the same time protect our retreating troops from enemy dive-bombers. We had gone no distance before we bumped into a large number of Ju 87s, unescorted by fighters. We attacked immediately and I saw Jock Perrin send one down in flames. I then attacked another and gave it a good burst and reckoned I had damaged it badly, when another Hurricane came at it from my starboard and, doing a beam attack, sent it down in flames. I then attacked two others, damaging them, and got on the tail of a fourth and gave it a couple of bursts and silenced its rear guns, when my guns ceased to fire. I then had the enemy at about 100 ft and felt enraged that he looked like escaping, and his rear gunner appeared to be dead, so I thought I might dive at him and clip him with my wing, I decided it was too low to get away with this, so I made a couple of dummy attacks at him, and much to my delight and surprise, he crash-landed in a Bedouin cultivated wadi and his aircraft hit the side of the wadi and spun around in a cloud of dust. I flew around a few times and eventually the pilot got out looking a bit dazed. I gave him a wave and returned to Maraua but pinpointed the spot in case I ever get back over the area and will ground-strafe the aircraft and completely destroy same, though I doubt if it could ever be flown out of the wadi.

Hurricane I P3967/OS-B of 3 RAAF was flown by Jock Perrin when he claimed 3 Ju87s of II/StG 2 on 5 April 1941. Two days earlier, Flt Lt Gordon Steege had used it to claim a Bf 110.

"Score this patrol was Jock Perrin three, self one and two possibles, Jewell three, and I forget the rest. Jewell saw Duncan Campbell losing height with a stream of white smoke pouring from his aircraft and he has not been seen since. I feel confident that both Mort and Duncan force-landed safely, though they may be taken prisoners."

While Edwards would indeed become a PoW as already described, Duncan Campbell was in fact killed.

Sgt Geoff Garton of 73 Squadron added: "I went off on a late patrol and we met about 12 Ju 87s. I got one destroyed, and chased another for miles without being able to take him and knock him out of the air."

As soon as all the Hurricanes were on the ground again, they were ordered to evacuate Maraua and fly to Derna instead, which they did without even waiting to refuel. Everything left behind was destroyed by the ground party. On arrival at Derna it was found that six Bf 110s of 7./ZG 26 had just carried out a strafing attack on the airfield. They had managed to hit five Blenheims, two Lysanders and a Hurricane. Two of the Blenheims and the Lysanders were unflyable and had to be burnt. All was chaos, panic and confusion. AA gunners claimed to have shot down one of the Bf 110s, but none were actually lost or damaged.

73 Squadron was reinforced on this date by three Hurricanes and their pilots from Egypt, one of the latter being Flg Off R.F.Martin, DFC, who had served with the unit in France a year earlier. At this time, however, Plt Off J.B.'Chips' McColl was posted back to the UK.

British Claims

73 Sqn	Flt Lt M.L.ff.Beytagh	V7810 TP-W	Ju 87	1445
	Plt Off W.T.Eiby	V7550 TP-O	Ju 87	1445
3 RAAF Sqn	Flg Off W.G.Kloster	P5176	Ju 87	Maraua 1445
	Flg Off M.D.Ellerton	V7353	2 Ju 87s	Maraua 1445
73 Sqn	Plt Off R.M.Millist	V7766 TP-Z	Ju 87	1700
			Ju 87 damaged	1700
	Sgt G.H.Garton	V7716 TP-U	Ju 87	1700
3 RAAF Sqn	Flt Lt J.R.Perrin	P3967	3 Ju 87s	Bu Cassal 1700
	Flg Off W.E.Jewell		3 Ju 87s	20m S Maraua 1700
	Flg Off J.F.Jackson	V7772	Ju 87	20m S Maraua 1700

As a detached flight from 73 Squadron was operating with 3 RAAF Squadron, the latter originally included the four victories claimed by the pilots of the former unit in the latter's total. These were subsequently deleted.

British Casualties

3 RAAF Sqn	Hurricane I V7347 Flg Off A.M.Edwards force-landed; PoW
	Hurricane I V7567 Sqn Ldr D.Campbell KiA
55 Sqn	Blenheim IV L6657 ⎫
	Blenheim IV T2180 ⎬ destroyed or damaged beyond repair in strafe and w/o
	Blenheim IV T2344 ⎪
	Blenheim IV T2383 ⎭
	Lysander
	Lysander
	Hurricane

German Casualties

6./StG 2	Ju 87R-2 WNr 6044 Oblt Peter Riedinger & Gefr Heinz Wilke KiA
	Ju 87 damaged force-landed; Gefr Heinz Orlowski, gunner, WiA
	Ju 87R-2 WNr 6031 damaged 40%; force-landed; Ogfr Kurt Loos, gunner, WiA
4./StG 2	Ju 87R-2 WNr 6046 Oblt Hans Sonntag & Fw Heinrich Kieselhorst KiA
	Ju 87R-2 WNr 5951 T6+GH Ofw Heinz Gragert PoW; Uffz Heinrich Ehlers, gunner, KiA
	Ju 87 damaged force-landed; Ogfr Kurt Heinrich, gunner, WiA
	Ju 87 damaged force-landed; Fw Günther Stulken WiA
	Ju 87 damaged force-landed; Ogfr Walter Rauer, gunner, WiA
KurierSt.Afrika	He 111 N6+IA shot down by AA near El Adem; crew PoW, including Hpt Baudissin, chief intelligence officer to Gen Rommel

Sunday – Monday, 6/7 April 1941

Sunday proved to be a disastrous day for the army, for General Sir Richard O'Connor, architect of Operation Compass, and General Neame were captured when their car was intercepted by a German motorcycle patrol near Derna. O'Connor's loss was of particular significance, as with his flare for mobile operations; he would probably have proved a worthy opponent to Rommel in the campaigns to come. He would be released from captivity following the fall of Italy in 1943, and would return to the UK in time to command a corps during the campaign in Western Europe. Following the loss of these two critical commanders, Lt Gen Sir Noel Beresford-Peirse was appointed to command a reconsituted Western Desert Force a week later.

At this point, with the conclusion of the main fighting in East Africa and the securing of the Red Sea route for the arrival of reinforcements by sea from both the UK and the USA, Longmore had flown to Khartoum on 3 April to discuss the withdrawal of many of the units there to Libya or Greece. Two days later he had received a signal from Drummond of the bad news relating to German successes in Cyrenaica which had caused the withdrawal of troops from Benghazi. Longmore at once flew straight back, having agreed that two squadrons, 47 and 237, should remain in Ethiopia for mopping-up duties, but two SAAF squadrons and all units with all but the oldest aircraft, should move to Egypt. Similarly, Aden was denuded of everything but Vincent biplanes (see *Dust Clouds in the Middle East*).

Worse was to come, for on arrival in Cairo on 6 April the news was received that German forces had attacked Yugoslavia and Greece. Signals from London once again proliferated. On the 4th Cyrenaica was to be treated as absolute priority, but within 48 hours the Balkans had become the critical theatre, the minimum necessary being retained in Egypt to secure the western flank of that country. Longmore recorded:

"A rather subdued C-in-C's conference in the afternoon attended by Eden and Dill discussed the question of priorities and what we should hold. The Admiral and I were most anxious to keep some depth for the air defence of Alexandria thus giving at least some cover to convoys both coastal and to Malta. We both hoped that Tobruk could be held. The operation for taking the Dodecanese would have to wait."

During the day Axis forces reached the coast road at Derna and their tanks got to Msus. The Australian infantry now began falling back on Tobruk, while 2nd Armoured Division arrived at Mechili. At this stage, and in the circumstances arising, General Wavell took direct command and was able to halt the movement of 7th Australian Division to Greece, just as its troops were about to embark. His order of the day was to hold Tobruk at all costs. However, these actions coincided with the deeply unwelcome news that on the other side of the Mediterranean, German forces had invaded both Yugoslavia and northern Greece.

The retained Australian division at once went aboard ship, but sailed now for Tobruk, where they began landing to form a defensive garrison next day, based upon the quite extensive defences which had been built by the Italians. In Egypt meanwhile, 7th Armoured Division began reforming as rapidly as possible. By now most British forces were back at Derna, and the RAF component at Sidi Mahmoud and Gambut. However, an undeserved but extremely welcome lull fell upon the frontal area, since Rommel had temporarily lost track of his armour, which had itself become disoriented on the way to Mechili during a violent sandstorm.

All forces not now heading for Tobruk were ordered to fall right back to the defences at Mersa Matruh, on the frontier. This would mean a return almost to the point at which the First Libyan Campaign advance had got fully underway.

Back at Amiriya 274 Squadron was reinforced by the arrival of eight new pilots, three of whom were seasoned veterans of the Battle of Britain. These latter were Flt Lt Dudley Honor, Flg Off Owen Tracey and Plt Off Noel Agazarian. Honor, a Fairey Battle pilot at the outbreak of war, had been flying Hurricanes with 145 Squadron, but had so far only been able to claim a single shared victory. Tracey, however, had flown with 79 Squadron (also on Hurricanes), and had already claimed three shot down and three more probably so. Agazarian had been flying Spitfires with 609 Squadron, and had claimed six and two more shared destroyed, plus a number damaged. All would soon have the opportunity to add to these totals.

At Bu Amud two of 73 Squadron's Hurricanes had just landed when a plot appeared on the radar. Sgt Ken Souter was scrambled at 0740 and 20 minutes later intercepted a Ju 88A-5 of 2.(F)/123 from Sicily as it passed Tobruk. He engaged, firing all his ammunition and claiming a probable. His attack had been effective, however, and the aircraft crashed into the sea off Bardia.

During the afternoon a number of strafing sorties were undertaken by both fighter squadrons, several motor vehicles being claimed destroyed or damaged on the Gazala-Tobruk road. One pair of Hurricanes took off at 1400, but 73 Squadron's Plt Off K.Millist failed to return for a second time, on this occasion shot down by ground fire just outside the Tobruk perimeter. He had just been advised of the award of a DFC, though for some reason this was not to be gazetted until the following November. This time his luck had run out however, and he did not return.

Flg Off Scott and Sgt Marshall were off five minutes later at 1405, joining Flt Lt Alan Rawlinson and Flg Off Lindsey Knowles of 3 RAAF Squadron on a further patrol. A pair of Ju 52/3ms of III./KGrzbV 1 were seen on the ground about ten miles south of Mechili, and were strafed. Marshall claimed to have destroyed both, but the two Australian pilots also each claimed one destroyed. Marshall's Hurricane was hit by ground fire but he managed to return. Knowles, however, was obliged to land at Gazala due to lack of fuel. Everyone was leaving, and on the advice of the retreating troops, he set fire to P3980 and departed with them. When a truckload of volunteers from the squadron arrived to deal with the problem, it was only to find the burnt-out Hurricane and no sign of its pilot.

During the day Flg Off Pike of 6 Squadron had spotted hostile armour nearly cutting off British units in Derna. Upon receiving his warning, the unit withdrew at once to El Adem. A Flight then went to Gazala to continue operations from there, but part of the flight's ground personnel, led by Flt Lt C.O.Sanders, were cut off and captured.

Following his special duties at HQ, RAF, Middle East, Grp Capt Spackman now returned to command 258 Wing; he had been commanding an organisation identified as Z Wing, which had been formed in Cairo for service on Crete.

British Claims

73 Sqn	Sgt K.Souter	V7553 TP-E	Ju 88 probable	off Tobruk 0800
	Sgt A.E.Marshall	V7560 TP-F	2 Ju 52/3ms on ground	10m S Mechili
3 RAAF Sqn	Flt Lt A.C.Rawlinson		Ju 52/3m on ground	10m S Mechili
	Flg Off L.E.S.Knowles	P3980	Ju 52/3m on ground	10m S Mechili

3 RAAF Sqn	Hurricane I P3980 abandoned out of fuel at Gazala; Flg Off L.E.S.Knowles safe
73 Sqn	Hurricane I V7550 Plt Off K.M.Millist KiA by ground fire
	Hurricane I V7560 TP-F damaged; Sgt A.E.Marshall safe

German Claims

| III./KGbV 1 | unspecified crew | Hurricane | Mechili area 1440 |

German Casualties

| 2.(F)/123 | Ju 88A-5 WNr 0491 4U+FK Ofw Werner Reinicke & crew KiA |
| III./KGrzbV 1 | 2 Ju 52/3ms destroyed on ground near Mechili |

Tuesday, 8 April 1941

This was another bad day for the British, 2nd Armoured Division being cut off at Derna and largely overwhelmed. At the same time the separated headquarters, together with the Indian motor brigade, were overrun at Mechili, where these forces had been surrounded. 5th Light Division and the Ariete Division were now at Mechili, the Brescia Division at Derna, and the first elements of 15th Panzer Division were arriving in Tripolitania. Commonwealth troops finished their withdrawal into Tobruk, and during the day 3 RAAF Squadron flew offensive patrols over Mechili. Flg Off Jewell was forced to land due to engine failure during this sortie.

The Axis air forces were quick off the mark. Within hours of the fall of Derna five G.50bis fighters from 155° Gruppo CT (four from 378ª Squadriglia led by Cap Bruno Tattanelli, and one from 351ª Squadriglia, flown by Ten Carlo Cugnasca) flew in to the airfield there to provide cover for the arrival of formations of Ju 52/3m transports. The Italian fighters were rapidly followed by a Ca.133 carrying a servicing party and two more pilots. Next day two more G.50bis would arrive, one in the hands of the gruppo commander, Magg Luigi Bianchi. They were joined during the afternoon by Cap Gino Callieri's 360ª Squadriglia, and subsequently two days later by 351ª Squadriglia under a new commanding officer, Cap Angelo Fanello. Immediately upon their arrival these units were called on to provide escort for formations of Luftwaffe Ju 87s.

Uffz Wolfgang Schwerzel of III./ZG 26 intercepted and shot down a Blenheim of 55 Squadron in the Benghazi area during the day, following which this latter unit and 45 Squadron began withdrawing to Egypt, as did 3 RAAF Squadron; the latter had been advised that re-equipment with Curtiss Tomahawk aircraft would follow imminently.

Thus 6 Squadron was left within the fortified perimeter of Tobruk at El Gobbi West to act as the 'eyes' of the army, while 73 Squadron remained for the moment at Bu Amud to provide some degree of local air defence. At the same time HQ Cyrenaica handed over control of the fighters here to 258 Wing and departed for Egypt. During the day Flt Lt Storrar of 73 Squadron carried message bags which he dropped in the Bomba area. On his return flight he spotted a lone Ju 87 near Derna, which he claimed to have shot down. He then noted a Lockheed Lodestar which had force-landed in the desert, and landed alongside. This proved to be AX682 of 267 Squadron, the personal aircraft of General Wavell which had been giving increasing problems. On taxying out at Tobruk to head back to Egypt, one of the wheel brakes seized, requiring immediate temporary repairs. It had then taken off, but after about a quarter of an hour the oil pressure

Lockheed Lodestar AX 682 of 267 Squadron, forced to crash-land, ten miles north-west of Sollum. The aircraft had been carrying Field Marshal Wavell and his staff and was later strafed on 15 April by Flt Lt John Jackson.

began to fall on one of the engines and the pilot was forced to turn back and land on a strip near the port, which is where the aircraft had been spotted by Storrar when one member of the crew fired a Very light to attract his attention.

He aided the crew in clearing sand from a filter, then draining some oil from his Hurricane to allow the Lodestar to take off again. This it did, although after 20 minutes the pressure again began to drop. The pilot kept the aircraft flying on the remaining engine for as long as possible, but it began to overheat and again he had to force-land. This time the brakes seized again, making the aircraft swing wildly, then tip over, causing the port wing and part of the tail to be torn off. Fortunately, it was not long before the party and the wreck were found by a patrolling armoured car which carried Wavell and his staff, and the crew of the aircraft to Sollum, where they arrived just after 0100. With daylight, Wavell was then flown back to Cairo where his headquarters were in a state of near-panic over his non-appearance.

Meanwhile Storrar had been unable to restart the engine of his Hurricane. Knowing that he was just south of Tobruk, but was faced with a 32-mile walk back to the squadron:

Flg Off Jas Storrar of 73 Squadron. After claiming a Ju 87B of II./StG 2 shot down near Derna on 8 April 1941, he spotted the Wavell Lodestar on the ground and landed to give aid.

".....I walked at night, hiding in the shade during the day. I had to get past a German Panzer encampment until I reached the road near Tobruk and I had to use the stars to get direction. It took me two nights, and I was grateful for my Boy Scout training as I headed directly at the Pole Star. The worst part of the trip was that I was wearing flying boots which kept filling with sand and did my feet no good at all. Just before dawn on the second night I heard voices – Aussie voices, from troops guarding the Tobruk perimeter. I had walked into a minefield being laid to close the perimeter. The Australians led me safely through and took me back by truck to the squadron."

By a strange coincidence Erwin Rommel had also suffered a problem whilst being flown in a Storch light aircraft in the Mechili area. Here Italian troops fired on his aircraft as it flew low above them, causing him to order the pilot to climb to about 3,000 feet where they were out of range of small arms fire, but could still observe the action on the ground. On going in to land to consult with the 5th Panzer Regiment, the Storch struck a sand dune and nosed in. He was rescued by a truck provided by the regiment's gunners.

During the day the first move was made to reinforce the RAF fighters since the withdrawals to Greece had got underway. The campaign in East Africa was now moving to a satisfactory conclusion and air supremacy was almost complete. It was thus possible for the Hurricane-equipped and experienced 1 SAAF Squadron to be released for service in the Western Desert, the South African government having agreed to allow its forces to operate as far north as this. Consequently, the squadron began its move to Egypt forthwith.

British Claims

73 Sqn	Flt Lt J.E.Storrar	P3818	Ju 87	Markha, SE Derna

British Casualties

55 Sqn	Blenheim T2381 Flt Sgt E.Vigneaux & crew KiA, Benghazi
3 RAAF Sqn	Hurricane I force-landed due to engine failure; Flg Off W.E.Jewell safe
73 Sqn	Hurricane I P3818 abandoned; Flt Lt J.E.Storrar safe
267 Sqn	Lodestar AX682 badly damaged in force-landing; Gen Wavell and all aboard, safe

German Claims

7./ZG 26	Uffz Wolfgang Schwerzel	Blenheim	NE Mechili 1715

German Casualties

II./StG 2	Ju 87 forced down by Hurricane; crew unhurt
2.(H)/14	Fi 156 WNr 0687 force-landed Mechili and destroyed; Gen Erwin Rommel and pilot safe

Wednesday, 9 April 1941

To replace the now almost defunct HQ, RAF Cyrenaica, the advanced party of a new group arrived at Maaten Bagush on this date to set up a command structure for the defence of Egypt as opposed to that of Tobruk, where 258 Wing continued to direct the defence of that port. The initial arrivals included Wg Cdrs McKechnie who was to command Fuka Satellite and McLaughlin whose 'parish' was to be Sidi Haneish North. These initial personnel were from the Rear HQ of 202 Group, withdrawn from Tobruk and incorporated into a new 204 Group which officially formed on 12 April, initially under Grp Capt Guest and Wg Cdr M.W.Baker, Air Cdr Raymond Collishaw arriving later that day to take over. Grp Capt L.O.Brown and Wg Cdr J.W.Judge from HQ, RAF Cyrenaica would arrive from Tobruk on the 13th and would depart for Cairo next day on the absorption of their unit into 204 Group. The RAF contingent remaining within the Tobruk perimeter was commanded by Wg Cdr E.R.F.Black, RAAF formerly commanding officer of 3 RAAF Squadron, who was now air liaison officer to the army HQ there.

Pilots of 73 Squadron with a Hurricane shortly before the unit's involvement at Tobruk. Left to right: Plt Off P.Holdenby, Plt Off C.C.O.Joubert, Plt Off W.T.Eiby, Plt Off K.M.Millist, DFC, Sqn Ldr A.D.Murray, DFC, Plt Off P.C.Humphreys, Plt Off M.P.Wareham and Plt Off O.E.Lamb. Holdenby, Millist and Lamb were all later killed whilst operating over the port/fortress.

To provide the air defence of the port/fortress, 73 Squadron was now ordered to fly in to El Gobbi, one of the four airstrips inside the perimeter defences. While the ground party commenced the move to this new base, all the flyable but unserviceable Hurricanes were flown to Buq Buq for overhaul; some of the longer-serving pilots were despatched eastwards for a well-earned rest.

At 0730 A Flight sent off two Hurricanes, the pilots of these coming upon a lone G.50bis, flown by Ten Cugnasca of 351ª Squadriglia, and upon a single Hurricane which proved to be that flown by Plt Off Eiby of B Flight on his way in from Bu Amud. Cugnasca attacked, believing that he had shot down one Hurricane before his guns jammed. Sgt Marshall and Eiby gave chase, pursuing the Italian aircraft to Derna, where as Cugnasca landed, his G.50bis swerved off the runway and was damaged. It seems that the two English pilots believed that their attacks had been the cause of this, returning to El Gobbi to claim the probable destruction of this aircraft.

Three more Hurricanes were off at 1030 to intercept a raid by He 111s of II./KG 26 and Bf 110s of 7./ZG 26. Flg Off Goodman shot down one of the escort, the pilot being killed and the gunner seriously wounded. He was then attacked by Hptmn Christl, the staffelkapitän, and his Hurricane was damaged, causing him to force-land within the outer defences from where he was driven back to El Gobbi. A second Bf 110, flown by Lt Heinrich Schultz, was shot down by AA and his gunner was killed, one of the He 111s also being brought down in the same way.

Luftwaffe reconnaissance staffel 2(H)./14 initially operated the Henschel Hs, an army co-operation aircraft similar to the RAF's Lysander. They proved equally vulnerable to fighter attack, although this particular aircraft had been on the ground.

The squadron was ordered to strafe Axis columns advancing on Tobruk soon after midday, four aircraft taking off at 1240 for the Mechili area. En route the four pilots spotted an Hs 126 one mile south of Gadd el-Ahmar: "…used all our ammunition on Hs 126 which was shot down." The Henschel was reported to have force-landed rather than crashed, but was a total write-off, the pilot being killed and his observer, Oblt Kurt Weith, being wounded.

Flg Off Goodman, undaunted by his earlier force-landing, Flt Lt Beytagh and a third pilot took off to patrol over the harbour at 1450, landing again just as seven Hurricanes of A Flight were preparing to take off for an attack on Derna, where the crews of Blenheims on reconnaissance had reported a number of Bf 110s on the ground. The intention was that Flt Lt Smith should lead five to strafe these aircraft on the ground, with Flg Off Martin and Sgt Marshall providing cover.

As the formation neared its target, a Ju 52/3m was seen taking off to the west, this being pursued and claimed shot down by Martin and Marshall. The rest undertook their strafing pass, Sgt Bob Laing recalling:

"I don't really remember how many we fired at and, of course, one couldn't tell if they were really badly damaged as very few caught fire, but I would say about 20 to 30 could well have been shot up. There was not much ground fire, so we had it all our own way and returned to Tobruk well pleased with ourselves."

Sgt Geoff Garton arrived in North Africa with 73 Squadron in late December 1940, subsequently seeing long service there. During April 1941 he was much in action over Tobruk, claiming several victories in the fortress area.

In fact they were credited with the destruction of six Bf 110s, an S.79 and an unidentified aircraft. The 'S.79' was actually an S.81 transport of 96° Gruppo BaT, which was damaged, as was one G.50bis of 378ª Squadriglia. The damage to III./ZG 26's aircraft is not known. However, the Hurricane flown by Sgt Elsworth (Rhodesian) crashed into a small hill at Marsa Jahal, probably hit by ground fire; the pilot was killed.

A final dusk attack on vehicles and troop concentrations in the Derna area by Flt Lt Smith and Flg Off Martin brought a very busy day for 73 Squadron to a close.

A further success was credited to 6 Squadron, however, when one of the unit's Lysanders, undertaking a low level reconnaissance flown by Flg Off J.E.McFall, DFC, spotted a trimotor aircraft on the ground near Mechili, tentatively identified as an S.82. The gunner, Cpl Copley opened fire on this with his rear seat Vickers K gun, reporting that it burst into flames. During the day this unit moved across to Tobruk West landing ground, also known as Crum-el-Chel.

British Claims

73 Sqn	Sgt A.E.Marshall	7562 TP-A	}	G.50 probable	
	Plt Off W.T.Eiby	V7810 TP-W			
	Flg Off G.E.Goodman	V7546 TP-Q		Bf 110	nr Derna 1030-1050
	Flg Off R.F.Martin	V7553 TP-E	}	Hs 126	
	Sgt G.W.Garton	V7766 TP-Z			
	Sgt H.G.Webster	V7716 TP-U			
	Sgt A.E.Marshall	V7562 TP-A		Ju 52/3m	
	Flt Lt J.D.Smith	V7371 TP-C	}		
	Plt Off R.McDougall	V7560 TP-F			
	Sgt R.I.Laing	P2646 TP-K		6 Bf 110s on the ground	Derna
	Sgt J.E.Elsworth	V7552 TP-J		S.79 on the ground	
	Sgt W.C.Wills			u/i e/a on the ground	
	Flg Off R.F.Martin	V7553 TP-E			
	Sgt A.E.Marshall	V7562 TP-A	}		
6 Sqn	Plt Off J.E.McFall, DFC/ Cpl D.G.Copley			S.82 (or Ju 52/3m) on the ground	

British Casualties

73 Sqn	Hurricane I V7552 TP-J crashed into hill; Sgt J.P.Elsworth KiA
	Hurricane I V7546 TP-Q damaged and force-landed; Flg Off G.E.Goodman safe

Italian Claims

351ª Sq/155º Gr CT	Ten Carlo Cugnasca	Hurricane

Italian Casualties

351ª Sq/155º Gr CT	G.50bis damaged on landing after combat; Ten Carlo Cugnasca safe
96º Gr BaT	S.81 damaged on ground by strafing
378ª Sq/155 º5Gr CT	G.50bis damaged on ground by strafing

German Claims

7./ZG 26	Hptmn Georg Christl	Hurricane

German Casualties

7./ZG 26	Bf 110E WNr 3874 3U+CR shot down; Lt Heinrich Schultz and Gfr Pier KiA
	Bf 110E shot down by AA; Fw Helmut Jaculi KiA; Uffz Johann Wala MiA
II./KG 26	He 111 shot down by AA, Tobruk
2(H)./14	Hs 126 WNr 4372 shot down; Uffz Heinrich Straeten KiA, Oblt Kurt Weith WiA
III./KGrzbV 1	Ju 52/3m shot down in flames on coast at Derna; Fw Schneider and crew KiA

Bf 110 of III./ZG 26 at rest. It is fitted with long-range tanks beneath the wings to allow escort sorties far across the Mediterranean to be undertaken.

Thursday, 10 April 1941

The Axis forces now reached the Tobruk perimeter, four brigades of Australian infantry, supported by artillery and an improvised tank regiment, being cut off as the port/fortress became fully invested. With dawn seven more Hurricanes flew in led by Flt Lt G.E.Ball, DFC, a Battle of Britain veteran who was to take over leadership of B Flight from Flt Lt Beytagh. The rest of the pilots with him were all Frenchmen, forming the 1ere Escadrille de Chasse, under the command of Sous Lt James Denis, a 35-year-old of considerable experience. His pilots were Sous Lts Albert Littolf, Louis Ferrant, Noel Castelain and Sgt Chefs René Guédon and Xavier de Scitivaux. Littolf had seen action during the fighting in France in 1940, and already had several claims to his credit. On arrival the unit temporarily formed C Flight of 73 Squadron (see *Air War for Yugoslavia, Greece and Crete, 1940-41* for more details of some of these pilots).

The day began for the fighters at El Gobbi with a number of strafing attacks on Axis transport in the Derna-Gazala area. On one such early mission at 0905, Sgt Chef de Scitivaux's Hurricane was hit by ground fire, causing him to crash-land on the beach at Umm Ghene Gniah, about 25 miles from Tobruk. He was seen to be walking in the direction of the port, and although slightly injured, he subsequently reached the defences safely.

Meanwhile, the standby section of C Flight was scrambled to engage a number of Ju 87s escorted by CR.42s. James Denis: "…I was lucky to shoot down a CR.42, for it was our first sortie, and the first victory for Free French Fighter Flight 1."

Axis aircraft now began attacking the British columns withdrawing into Tobruk, six Italian Ju 87s of 96° Gruppo being led to the area by their newly-promoted commanding officer, Magg Ercolano Ercolani, escorted by nine 155° Gruppo G.50bis and three Bf 110s of III./ZG 26; this raid was the operational debut for Italian-flown Stukas in North Africa, the crews claiming to have inflicted considerable damage to their targets.

From 1330 73 Squadron despatched aircraft at five-minute intervals, but swirling sandstorms reduced visibility and nothing was seen. 1715 brought an alarm as Ju 87s attacked gun positions on the defence perimeter, but although three Hurricanes were scrambled, some wild AA fire from the ground once again prevented any decisive engagements.

At 1759, however, the crews of six Bf 110s from 8./ZG 26 spotted a lone Hurricane near Bardia. This was flown by Sgt Webster on his way back from a strafing sortie in this area, and he was shot down by Lt Alfred Wehmeyer, crash-landing at Bu Amud without suffering any injury.

The strafing during the day amounting to 36 sorties, seems to have been quite effective, and indeed during one such attack the commanding officer of the 5th Light Division, General Major Heinrich Kirchheim, had been wounded. However, 73 Squadron's diarist noted: "All the pilots seemed browned off with this ground strafing – we are losing too many machines which we can ill afford to do and the ultimate result puts us very much on the debit side."

British Claims				
73 Sqn	Sous Lt J.Denis	V7716 TP-U	CR.42	Tobruk area
British Casualties				
73 Sqn	Hurricane I crash-landed, damaged by ground fire; Sgt Chef X.de Scitivaux returned safe			
	Hurricane I W9195 shot down, crash-landed near Bardia; Sgt Webster safe			
German Claims				
8./ZG 26	Lt Alfred Wehmeyer		Hurricane	near Bardia 1750
German Casualties				
IV./KGrzbV 1	Ju 52/3m struck a mine at Derna			

Friday, 11 April 1941

Despite 73 Squadron's disquiet, 23 more strafing sorties were undertaken, leading to claims for 11 MT destroyed and other vehicles damaged. Sous Lt Denis led four aircraft from his C Flight to the Gazala area at 0945, Bf 110s being encountered in the vicinity, one of which Sous Lt Castelain and Sgt Chef Guédon claimed to have shot down. One of the Luftwaffe pilots believed that he had possibly brought down a Hurricane in return, but in fact neither unit suffered any loss or damage.

Flt Lt Ball on his first sortie from El Gobbi, led three Hurricanes to strafe MT at 1135. As the trio returned two more fighters were scrambled to cover their landings, followed ten minutes later by a further pair as an incoming raid had been reported. This formation was composed of both German and Italian

Stukas, six of the latter from 236ª Squadriglia being led by Ten Ettore Marcozzi. They were escorted once more by nine G.50bis led by Magg Bianchi and by Bf 110s of III./ZG 26. Two of those scrambled at once made contact with the raiders, Sgt Marshall recording:

"Destroyed one G.50 which crashed on beach west of Tobruk. This enemy aircraft was one of four which had attacked me. Confirmed by gun battery in vicinity." Sgt Garton, who was flying with him, added: "Met 15 Me 110s and three G.50s, who jumped me from a great height. Tried to do a bit of dogfighting but superior numbers forced me to evacuate that part of the sky mighty quickly – pretty tough."

At that point Flt Lt Ball's section arrived back from their strafing, Sgt Laing firing at two Stukas, one of which was claimed damaged. One Ju 87 of 236ª Squadriglia failed to return, M.llo Enrico Bassi and his gunner being seen to be shot down by a Hurricane. Bassi managed to bale out to become a PoW, but Colombo, his gunner, was killed.

The escorting G.50bis pilots claimed one Hurricane shot down and a second probably so, but the narrative recorded in the 155° Gruppo CT records indicate that Bassi's Ju 87 had probably fallen to Marshall, mis-identified while under attack by four of the Italian fighters:

"At the end of the Stukas' dive, a Hurricane attacked one and shot it down. Cap Tattanelli shot at the Hurricane, and also Ten Biccolini managed a hit. In the meantime the aircraft of M.llo Serafino had been hit with one shot in the left wing from a Hurricane coming from the rear. While manoeuvring in order to disengage, Serafino saw a third Hurricane and shot at him; the English fighter went down trailing black smoke and went out of sight of the Italian pilot. Then, during the manoeuvre in order to get his place in the formation, he saw another enemy fighter and gave him a burst. In the meantime, Cap Tattanelli got nearer to the first fighter and gave him many bursts, making him dive until he crashed."

Despite these claims, none of the four Hurricanes involved suffered any serious damage, and all were operating again later in the afternoon.

The returning dive-bomber crews claimed to have damaged the freighter *Draco* in the harbour. The day had also seen the first major attack on the Tobruk defences which was mounted by the Wehrmacht's 5th Light Division, joined by elements of the Italian Brescia and Trento Divisions, the Axis troops advancing behind a Stuka 'bomb carpet'. However, the attack was beaten back after some hard fighting.

British Claims

73 Sqn	Sous Lt N.Castelain	V7853	}	Bf 110	Tobruk
	Sgt Chef R.Guédon	V7859			
	Sgt A.E.Marshall	V7560 TP-F		G.50	Tobruk
	Sgt R.I.Laing	V7371 TO-C		Ju 87 damaged	Tobruk

German Claims

III./ZG 26	unspecified pilots		Hurricane possible	Tobruk

German Casualties

2(F)./123	Bf 110E-3 WNr 2307 4U+ZK lost

Italian Claims

378ª Sq/155° Gr CT	Cap Bruno Tattanelli	}	Hurricane	
	Ten Manlio Biccolini			Tobruk
	M.llo Lorenzo Serafino		Hurricane probable	Tobruk
360ª Sq/155° Gr CT	Ten Dino Lombardi		Hurricane probable	Tobruk

Italian Casualties

236ª Sq/96° Gr BaT	Ju 87R shot down; M.llo Enrico Bassi baled and PoW; 1° Av Giacomo Colombo KiA
378ªSq/155° Gr CT	G.50bis MM6330 badly damaged and written off on return to base; pilot Cap Tattanelli
	G.50bis MM 6339 slightly damaged; M.llo Lorenzo Serafino safe

Saturday, 12 April 1941

During the day the aircraft and advanced party of 3 RAAF Squadron arrived back at Mersa Matruh

An Italian photo of Hurricane I TP-U, V7716, of 73 Squadron in which Flt Lt G.E.Ball, DFC force-landed outside the Tobruk perimeter, becoming a PoW.

where they were joined by 31 ASP. The squadron's main party would arrive next day. Meanwhile, 10,000 gallons of petrol at Kilo 8 from Sollum, together with all other petrol and RAF stores at Sollum, were all destroyed to prevent them falling into Axis hands. Sidi Barrani was now established as an advanced landing ground, covered by RAF armoured cars and a battalion of infantry.

At Tobruk Hurricanes were out on reconnaissance flights from early in the morning. One pair went off at 0730, but Sgt Wills was shot down by ground fire while strafing, his Hurricane crashing near El Adem. He had been critically injured, and although removed from his cockpit by German soldiers, he died shortly afterwards. Later in the morning three C Flight pilots undertook another strafing sortie, attacking a convoy near Gadd el-Ahmar, then becoming separated in worsening weather. Two returned, but Sgt Chef Guédon was not with them; hit by ground fire, he had crash-landed his Hurricane and was taken prisoner.

By mid morning sandstorms were causing visibility to reduce considerably, catching one pair of Hurricanes in the air. They could be heard circling overhead, searching for El Gobbi, but could not be seen. Finally, Sgt Ellis managed to force-land at Tobruk West where all three tyres of his undercarriage were punctured. However, the newly-arrived Flt Lt Ball was not seen again. He had run out of fuel and force-landed outside the perimeter, where he was captured by Axis troops.

A sandstorm then prevented any further operations until later in the afternoon when it cleared and six Ju 87s attacked the harbour. These were aircraft of III./StG 1 which had just arrived at Derna to replace I./StG 1 which was being withdrawn for operations over Greece. The Stuka crews found the defences at Tobruk ready for them, losing half of their number in quick succession. J9+JH came down in the sea, victim of gunfire from the ships, two more aircraft being brought down on land where both crews became PoWs. An Hs 126 of 2(H)./14 was also hit by AA when seeking to spot for the Axis artillery over the perimeter defences, the observer being wounded and the aircraft damaged.

British Casualties	
73 Sqn	Hurricane I V7560 TP-F shot down by ground fire; Sgt W.C.Wills died of wounds
	Hurricane I V7853 crash-landed due to ground fire; Sgt Chef René Guédon PoW
	Hurricane I V7716 TP-U force-landed due to fuel shortage and lost; Flt Lt G.E.Ball, DFC, PoW
German Casualties	
7./StG 1	Ju 87R-1 WNr 5436 J9+PH Fw Franz Holzinger/Gefr Rudolf Anwaud PoW
	Ju 87R-1 WNr 5549 J9+JH Obfw Karl Buchholz/Gefr David Kerchbaumsteiner KiA
8./StG 1	Ju 87R-1 WNr5672 6G+HS Uffz Anton Wegscheider/Uffz Horst Henz PoW
2(H)./14	Hs 126 WNr 4228 5% damaged by machine-gun fire over Tobruk; Oblt Siegfried Abel WiA

Sunday, 13 April 1941

Sandstorms again greatly reduced aerial activity in the Tobruk area during the morning. Following the loss of three aircraft on the previous day an urgent request for reinforcements had been sent out. Now six more Hurricanes were flown in, led by Flt Lt H.A.Olivier who was to take over the vacant flight commander position in B Flight. He brought with him one more Free French pilot, Wt Off André Ballatore, the other aircraft being flown by squadron pilots who had taken out aircraft in need of repair or overhaul. This arrival allowed further Hurricanes to be flown to Bu Amud for similar purposes.

One raid by Regia Aeronautica Ju 87s with G.50bis and Bf 110 escort did take place during the early afternoon, but the four Hurricanes which were scrambled failed to make contact.

To the east of Tobruk some 45 Axis heavy tanks were reported to be well on their way towards Sollum, whilst transport aircraft were seen to be using El Adem to discharge maintenance personnel and fuel; it was thought that these might also be landing at Great Gambut by night for similar purposes.

During the day 3 RAAF Squadron undertook an offensive patrol over the Tobruk area, whilst Blenheims of 45 and 55 Squadrons attacked MT convoys on the Msus-Sollum road. These raids proved costly, the latter unit reportedly losing two of its aircraft.

British Casualties	
55 Sqn	Blenheim IV L8664 MiA
	Blenheim IV L4819 MiA
6 Sqn	Lysander R1996 overshot landing at Tobruk in sandstorm and crashed

German Casualties	
2(H)./14	Hs 126 crashed in sandstorm at Zliten; Oblt Martin/Lt Uebele KiA

With disaster piling upon disaster, Tobruk invested, Axis forces at Sollum and Capuzzo and Malta struggling to survive, (see *Malta: the Hurricane Years, 1940-41*), it cannot have been much recompense to Longmore next day to receive a signal from air ministry detailing a resolution which had been adopted by the House of Commons on 9 April, which read: "That this House on the occasion of the recent victories by sea, land and air in North Africa, Greece and Mediterranean records with gratitude its high appreciation of the service of all ranks of His Majesty's Forces in these brilliant operations, and also of those who by their labour and fortitude at HQ, ME, have furnished the means which made these successes possible." The secretary of state for air added his best wishes to the RAF.

Much better news was the arrival of the first 12 Tomahawks, together with advice that 17 more were underway and another 145 were in crates at Takoradi, being assembled as rapidly as possible. Unfortunately, these aircraft were suffering problems both with engines and armament. A few more Hurricanes also arrived, but at this stage Middle East could only count something less than 50 of these fighters serviceable (not including Malta).

Monday, 14 April 1941

For 73 Squadron the relatively quiet hours of the past day or two came to an abrupt halt when at 0730 a major attack on the port was launched by an estimated 70 aircraft. These included Ju 87s from III./StG 1 and II./StG 2, with seven from 96° Gruppo. The escort included eight G.50bis of 155° Gruppo, four CR.42s of 18° Gruppo and five Bf 110s of III./ZG 26.

To face this onslaught, 73 Squadron had serviceable just eight Hurricanes, two of which were just on their way back from a patrol during which Flg Off Goodman and Sgt Webster had claimed the destruction of a lone Hs 126. They had just landed when Webster was ordered off again with Sgt Ellis and two of the French pilots to assist Flt Lt Smith, who had taken off alone five minutes earlier to investigate reports of bombing at the harbour.

Webster and Ellis at once spotted a number of Stukas over the harbour and attacked, Ellis claiming two shot down at once. As Webster got on the tail of another, however, he was attacked by a pair of G.50bis flown by Ten Carlo Cugnasca and M.llo Angelo Marinelli, and was shot down in flames at 0743, falling within the perimeter to his death. It would appear that the 18° Gruppo CR.42s may also have joined this combat, for claims for Hurricanes shot down were also submitted by S.Ten Franco Bordoni-Bisleri and M.llo Guido Fibbia.

Observers on the ground then saw a Hurricane which was obviously that flown by Flt Lt Smith, shoot down two Italian fighters and inflict damage on a third before being shot down and killed by the 351[a]

Squadriglia commander, Cap Angelo Fanello, who had lost sight of Cugnasca's and Marinelli's G.50s after seeing them shooting down Webster's aircraft. These were clearly Smith's victims, and both were killed. Recorded the 351ª Squadriglia diary: "Cap Fanello came back over the place of the combat and he saw, near the Hurricane in flames, two G.50s; one had flames near the engine and the other one, which perhaps had tried to land without undercarriage, was hidden by a cloud of sand." These were the aircraft of Ten Cugnasca and M.llo Marinelli, who were posted missing.

The air defence of Tobruk was considerably enhanced by the arrival to fly with 73 Squadron of a group of experienced French pilots who then operated as the unit's C Flight. The two most successful were Lts Albert Littolf (left) and James Denis (right). They are seen here somewhat later in the year when Group de Chasse n.1 was formed in which they were to become the flight commanders. Between them is the commanding officer of that unit, Capt Jean Tulasne.

Two experienced pilots had been lost in this engagement, one from each side. The 27-year-old Canadian, J.D.'Smudger' Smith, was a very popular member of the squadron. Carlo Cugnasca, born in Switzerland, had been well-known in Italian aviation circles as a gifted aerobatic pilot pre-war. He had served in the Spanish Civil War, and had later flown over England during the autumn of 1940. He was also a close friend of the film actress Alida Valli, who would later have a starring role in the iconic film 'The Third Man'.

While these events had been unfolding, the two French pilots had each claimed a Stuka shot down, Albert Littolf also claiming two more as probables. Out of ammunition, Sgt Ellis had landed and leapt into another Hurricane which was armed and ready, taking off to rejoin the battle and claim his third Ju 87 of the day. Apparently Ellis's former aircraft was rapidly re-armed, allowing Flg Off Martin to take off in it; he met a Bf 110 which he claimed to have damaged. Claims had been quite accurate on this occasion, four Ju 87s being lost.

Learning of the attack, Sqn Ldr Jeffrey, who had taken over command of 3 RAAF Squadron following the loss of Sqn Ldr Campbell, despatched two Hurricanes to investigate. At 1045, ten miles east of the port and while flying at 1,000 feet, Flg Off Arthur and Lt Tennant, SAAF, spotted a trio of Bf 110s which they attacked. Although each claimed one Bf 110 probably shot down, it seems likely that they both fired at the same aircraft, since the reports of each man mentioned that his opponent dived away steeply towards the sea, blue smoke issuing from the fuselage. Each pilot was awarded a probable victory, but it seems that these claims were later re-classified as destroyed, according to 204 Group records. III./ZG 26 reported the loss of only one Bf 110 on this date, the crew of which survived. The two Hurricane pilots then continued their patrol, seeing a Ju 52/3m on the landing ground at Menastir. Each carried out two strafing runs, seeing their bullets hit the transport, but it did not burn.

Meanwhile at El Gobbi Flg Off Goodman led four Hurricanes to investigate activity reported to the east, but failed to see anything. Further patrols and scrambles followed until 1715 when four aircraft scrambled on the approach of a further raid. Once more it was Ju 87s, G.50bis and Bf 110s, but in smaller numbers than in the morning. Sous Lts Littolf and Castelain attacked the Stukas, Littolf claiming one shot down, but the escort then intervened and shot down Plt Off Lamb's aircraft which was seen to dive straight into the ground from 3,000 feet, the New Zealander being killed. Two claims for Hurricanes shot down were submitted by pilots of 7./ZG 26 – as with the 3 RAAF Squadron pilots it is likely that they 'double-claimed' on the same aircraft.

Two G.50bis from 378ª Squadriglia, led by Cap Tattanelli and three from 360ª Squadriglia, led by Ten Vittorio Galfetti, had provided close escort for the Stukas, Tattanelli reporting engaging one Hurricane which was attacking a Ju 87, and which he had seen diving towards the ground. This may have been

Castelain's aircraft, which landed again only ten minutes after taking off, and which may have suffered some damage.

Geoff Garton summarized the day's events:

"Flt Lt Smith bravely tackled five G.50s single-handed and succeeded in destroying two before being shot down himself. He and his victims all crashed within a few hundred yards of each other, all burnt out. Another tragedy was Webby, who was shot down in flames while attempting to force-land. Thus, in one engagement, two of the very best types were lost. B Flight, in Webby, lost one of the oldest members and an amazing personality who will be greatly missed. Later on today, Lamb was shot down and killed. Thus ended a very black day for the Squadron, with a firm resolve that new tactics must be evolved, as to carry on any longer operating singly is approaching suicide."

British Claims

73 Sqn	Flg Off G.E.Goodman	Hurricane I V7673 TP-P	Hs 126	Tobruk 0650-0730
	Sgt H.G.Webster	Hurricane I V7553 TP-E		
	Flt Lt J.D.Smith	Hurricane I P2652	2 G.50s	Tobruk 0725-
	Flt Lt J.D.Smith	Hurricane I P2652	2 G.50s damaged	Tobruk 0725-
	Sgt R.W.Ellis	Hurricane I V7299 TP-D	2 Ju 87s	Tobruk 0735-0750
	Sgt R.W.Ellis	Hurricane I V7673 TP-W	Ju 87	Tobruk 0750-0805
	Sous Lt A.Littolf	Hurricane I V7856	2 Ju 87s	Tobruk 0750-0805
	Sous Lt A.Littolf	Hurricane I V7856	2 Ju 87 probables	Tobruk 0750-0805
	Sous Lt J.Denis	Hurricane I W9198	Ju 87	Tobruk 0750-0805
3 RAAF Sqn	Flg Off W.S.Arthur	Hurricane I P3725	Bf 110 probable	Tobruk 1045
	Lt A.A.Tennant	Hurricane I V7728	Bf 110 probable	Tobruk 1045

3 RAAF Squadron originally listed three victories on this date. On review "Two of the enemy aircraft were severely damaged and last seen diving steeply towards the sea. Later confirmed by army in Tobruk." Thus these two probables are listed in the unit's total as confirmed victories.

73 Sqn	Sous Lt A.Littolf	Hurricane I W9198	Ju 87	Tobruk 1715-

British Casualties

73 Sqn	Hurricane I V7553 shot down by Bf 110s; Sgt H.G.Webster KiA
	Hurricane I V2652 shot down by G.50bis; Flt Lt J.D.Smith KiA
	Hurricane I V7766 TP-Z shot down by Bf 110s; Plt Off O.E.Lamb KiA

German Claims

7./ZG 26	Lt Karl-Heinz Bittner	Hurricane	Tobruk 1045
	Fw Werner Reiner	Hurricane	Tobruk 1045

German Casualties

Stab III./StG 1	Ju 87R2 J9+CH WNr 5874 shot down; Lt Hans Martinez and Uffz Helmut Pohl PoW
4./StG 2	Ju 87 T6+JM shot down; Fw Heinrich Russ and Uffz Fritz Weber PoW
	Ju 87 force-landed outside Tobruk perimeter; pilot safe; gunner, Lt Erich Hummel baled out over British lines and PoW
	Ju 87 crash-landed in Axis-held territory; gunner, Uffz Heinrich Kroll WiA
III./ZG 26	Bf 110 WNr 3418 shot down; crew safe

Italian Claims

351ª Sq/155º Gr CT	Ten Carlo Cugnasca }	Hurricane	Tobruk 0725-
	M.llo Angelo Marinelli }		
	Cap Angelo Fanello	Hurricane	Tobruk 0725-
95ª Sq/18º Gr CT	S.Ten Franco Bordoni-Bisleri	Hurricane	Tobruk 0725-
	M.llo Guido Fibbia	Hurricane	Tobruk 0725-

Italian Casualties

351ª Sq/155º Gr CT	G.50bis MM6362 shot down, Ten Carlo Cugnasca KiA
	G.50bis MM6370 shot down, M.llo Angelo Marinelli KiA

Tuesday, 15 April 1941

Down now to only seven serviceable Hurricanes, 73 Squadron ceased to operate as separate flights, amalgamating its remaining pilots and aircraft into a single entity. However, the next four days were very quiet, in the main due to the frequent sandstorms persisting at this time. Attacks on the ground continued to be beaten off meanwhile.

Although 3 RAAF Squadron was now close to ceasing to operate, during the day Sqn Ldr Peter Jeffrey managed to undertake a special sortie, as recalled by John Jackson:

"The CO did a great job today. A TacR report stated there were two enemy aircraft on Menastir aerodrome near Fort Capuzzo, and they had to be ground strafed – not a nice job as it was probable the Huns had some ack-ack guns covering same, so CO decided to do the job himself and went off alone. He found the aircraft had gone but on another drome near Fort Capuzzo spotted four Ju 52s just about to land, evidently loaded with supplies for Fort Capuzzo and Bardia garrisons. It

A CR.42 of 83ª Squadriglia, 18° Gruppo, in flight.

seemed most unlikely that there was no fighter escort with them but the CO couldn't see any, so waded into them and shot down one whilst the other three were landing. One of them evidently saw him and crash-landed. The CO then ground strafed them, setting two on fire and burning them up completely. He ran out of ammunition on the other one and had to leave it just riddled with bullets, but not on fire – a magnificent piece of work. All the time one of our photographic-reconnaissance Hurricanes was watching from about 15,000 feet and saw the whole thing.

"Six of us went back in the afternoon. Lindsey Knowles and Donati dived down and strafed the fourth Ju 52 and it went up in a heck of a blaze – must have been loaded with petrol. I spotted an aircraft on the ground a few miles away and identified it as a Lockheed Hudson, one of our own which had force-landed a few days previously with the AOC and had to be abandoned as it was in enemy territory. I decided it would be best to burn it so I dived down and strafed it and set it on fire – 30,000 quids (£) worth."

The Ju 52/3ms were aircraft of 1./KGrzbV 9, one such being recorded as shot down on this date. From the details given above, it is assumed that the other three aircraft were indeed all destroyed on the ground. The aircraft strafed by Jackson was, of course, the Lodestar of 267 Squadron, which had force-landed and been abandoned on April 14 whilst carrying the commander-in-chief, Field Marshal Wavell.

British Claims

3 RAAF Sqn	Sqn Ldr P.Jeffrey	Hurricane I	Ju 52/3m	airfield N. Fort Capuzzo 1200
	Sqn Ldr P.Jeffrey	Hurricane I	2 Ju 52/3ms	on ground airfield N. Fort Capuzzo 1200
	Sqn Ldr P.Jeffrey	Hurricane I	Ju 52/3m	damaged on ground airfield N. Fort Capuzzo 1200
	Flg Off L.E.S.Knowles	Hurricane I		
	Flg Off R.F.Donati	Hurricane I	Ju 52/3m	on ground p.m.
	Flt Lt J.Jackson	Hurricane I	Lockheed Hudson	on ground p.m.

British Casualties

ME	Lysander P9192 lost
14 Sqn	Blenheim IV Z5863 FTR from reconnaissance Halfaya-Sollum; Plt Off J.Ormiston and one KiA, one WiA and baled out to become PoW

Italian Casualties

Unspecified unit	CR.42 destroyed on the ground by bombs at Derna

Wednesday, 16 April 1941

Hurricanes of 3 RAAF Squadron undertook patrols providing cover to a Walrus amphibian catapulted from HMS *Gloucester*, spotting for the guns of this cruiser which were bombarding Bardia and Capuzzo. The Australians reported an inconclusive engagement with a Messerschmitt, but one such aircraft was in fact lost during the day.

———

However, in the Derna area a CR.42 from 85ª Squadriglia, 18° Gruppo CT was in the air in the hands of Serg Luigi Gorrini, who reported attacking an aircraft identified as a Blenheim or Beaufighter in this vicinity. He watched as this flew off trailing smoke from its starboard engine, subsequently crashing not far from the southern boundary of the airfield after the crew had baled out. The identity of this aircraft has not been definitely ascertained, but III./ZG 26 lost a Bf 110 near Derna and the question must be asked, had Gorrini mistaken the twin-engined Messerschmitt fighter for the similarly twin-engined Beaufighter?

It was at this time that his unit began receiving its first CR.42s fitted with bomb racks, and would soon begin a gradual transfer to the ground-attack role.

German Casualties			
III./ZG 26	Bf 110E-1 WNr 3884 3U+ZR destroyed; Ofw Reimann/Gefr Grzik		
Italian Claims			
85ª Sq/18° Gr CT	Serg Luigi Gorrini	Blenheim/Beaufighter	Derna

Thursday, 17 April 1941

3 RAAF Squadron and 39 Squadron undertook tactical and strategic reconnaissance sorties during the day, the Australian fighters and 274 Squadron also engaging in offensive patrols to protect bombers. The latter were Blenheims of 45 and 55 Squadron which attacked the airfield at Derna. S.Ten Franco Bordoni-Bisleri of 18° Gruppo CT's 95ª Squadriglia, attacked one of these, claiming to have caused it to force-land 30 miles from the target area. 204 Group recorded only that one air gunner was slightly wounded by fire from a CR.42, but in fact one aircraft from 55 Squadron was lost.

During the day Ju 87s of III./StG 1 attacked the Tobruk defences, but no contact was made by those Hurricanes which managed to get off the ground. At this stage 274 Squadron moved up to Sidi Haneish to replace 3 RAAF Squadron which began to withdraw to commence the promised re-equipment with Tomahawks. The unit's remaining Hurricanes were handed to 73 and 274 Squadrons.

Four of the Australian pilots remained on temporary detachment at El Gobbi, joined by three from 274 Squadron, led by Sqn Ldr Lapsley, but they were not called upon. When the Australians flew back to Maaten Bagush they were joined by four Lysanders and a Magister of 6 Squadron. This latter unit left its A Flight at Tobruk West with five TacR Hurricanes and two Lysanders, together with the commanding officer, Sqn Ldr Weld.

British Casualties			
55 Sqn	Blenheim IV V5574 shot-up by CR.42 off Derna at 1000; Flg Off Blackmore and crew MiA		
Italian Claims			
95ª Sq/18° Gr CT	S.Ten Franco Bordoni-Bisleri	Blenheim	Reported force-landed 30m from Derna

Friday, 18 April 1941

During the day, 204 Group fighters again flew cover patrols in support of the spotter Walrus from HMS *Gloucester*. In Tobruk, however, 73 Squadron was down to only four serviceable Hurricanes, but three of the aircraft released by 3 RAAF Squadron, flew into the surrounded port as reinforcements during the day.

When further attacks on Axis airfields were made, a 45 Squadron Blenheim was intercepted and shot down by a Bf 110 of III./ZG 26, Flg Off Collins and his crew all being killed. On a reconnaissance sortie one of 6 Squadron's Hurricanes was slightly damaged by Flak.

During the day the first Italian fighter unit equipped with Macchi C.200 aircraft (374ª Squadriglia of 153° Gruppo Autonomo CT) arrived at Castel Benito from Italy.

British Casualties			
45 Sqn	Blenheim IV V5438 shot down; Flg Off E.G.Collins and crew KiA		
6 Sqn	Hurricane I V7814 slightly damaged by Flak; Plt Off M.Moulding safe		
German Claims			
7./ZG 26	Lt Ferdinand Glanz	Blenheim	N Sidi Barrani 1100

CHAPTER 6

REVERSES AND REINFORCEMENTS

Just as the situation in Cyrenaica was approaching its nadir came the bad news that on 6 April German forces had launched a powerful 'Blitzkrieg' thrust into Yugoslavia and northern Greece. This raised the spectre of a possible overriding need to despatch yet more reinforcements to what quickly became a 'meat-grinder' for Allied aircraft.

Meanwhile, however, as already mentioned better news was at hand from the front in East Africa where the successful conclusion of the main campaign freed forces for service further north. It also allowed safe access through the Red Sea to the southern end of the Suez Canal. Whilst this route had already been employed by British shipping with relative impunity, this latter advantage would prove particularly helpful with the delivery of US-built aircraft. President Roosevelt had been unable to relax the prohibition on his nation's vessels venturing into what had until this point been a war zone, but now this could be done. In Ethiopia itself only a relatively marginal numbers of troops and units of second-line aircraft needed to be retained for the mopping-up of the remaining Italian garrisons deep in the hinterland. (For details of this campaign see *Dust Clouds in the Middle East*.)

May 1941 saw the entry into operations over North Africa of the US-built Martin Maryland bomber. This aircraft was to serve with three squadrons of the SAAF, 12, 21 and 24, and with the RAF's 39 Squadron. In the latter unit the aircraft was employed mainly in the reconnaissance role.

Consequently, on 5 April 94 Squadron at Aden handed over its remaining Gladiators to one of the units which was to remain in the area for the time being, and departed for Egypt to re-equip with Hurricanes. Next day 1 SAAF Squadron, the premier Hurricane-equipped fighter squadron amongst those which had been operating over the Eritrean-Ethiopian areas in the north of the region, followed 94, but bringing their aircraft with them. Later in the month several other South African pilots from the recently very successful 3 SAAF Squadron, would be posted to reinforce 1 SAAF.

Three days later 14 Squadron with Blenheim IVs and 203 Squadron, a coastal reconnaissance unit equipped with the fighter version of this aircraft, the Mark IVf, also set off for Egypt, soon followed by the pilots of K Flight and 1430 Flight. The former, it may be recalled, had originated as a detached flight from 112 Squadron which had been sent south to the Sudan where it had subsequently become a small independent unit. The pilots, who had been operating Gladiators there, now formed the nucleus of a new fighter unit, 250 Squadron, on their arrival in Egypt, and before April was out had collected nine examples of the new Curtiss Tomahawk – the first of these US-built fighters to be issued to a unit in the Middle East.

At this stage as well, 223 Squadron handed its surviving Vickers Wellesley bombers to 47 Squadron, which was remaining in Ethiopia, and it too soon reached Egypt. However, it would be many months before the unit became operational again, as it settled into Shandur to act as an operational training unit for Blenheim and Maryland crews.

SAAF bomber units in East Africa had already begun receiving small numbers of Marylands before the fighting there had effectively ended, and these too were to reinforce the RAF in the desert. On 24 April 14 SAAF Squadron set off for Egypt to reform with a full establishment of these aircraft. At the same time the unit was renumbered to avoid confusion with the RAF's 14 Squadron, becoming instead 24 SAAF Squadron. It was accompanied to the new theatre of operations by 60 SAAF Squadron, a specialist photographic-reconnaissance unit, which had also received the fast Maryland for these duties. Between 8-12 May 12 SAAF Squadron also re-equipped with Marylands and departed for Egypt.

In the meantime on 17 April the commanding officer and 16 pilots of 2 SAAF Squadron also moved to Egypt. It was intended that theirs would be one of the first squadrons to re-equip with Tomahawks, but in the first instance they were temporarily equipped with Hurricanes on their arrival.

Despite this growing influx of reinforcements to North Africa, the benefit was about to be greatly reduced due to the arrival on 14 April of the first elements of I Gruppe, Jagdgeschwader 27, equipped with the Messerschmitt Bf 109E. While the Hurricane Is may well have got the measure of the twin-engined Bf 110s and the Ju 87 dive-bombers, as well as the Italian monoplane fighters now arriving in growing numbers, the excellent Bf 109E was without question superior to the Hurricane in many ways – notably in speed, altitude performance and armament. Only in manoeuvrability did the British fighter retain an edge. Indeed, the Hurricane in the Middle East was also fitted with a large Vokes air filter under the nose to reduce the impact of the ingestion of sand and dust. This had the effect of degrading the performance below that which had been achievable at home. The Messerschmitt on the other hand was fitted with a considerably smaller, neater and less drag-inducing filter, which did not have a similar detrimental effect. The Bf 109E was soon to become the scourge of 204 Group's units.

During the period February-May 1941 Malta's defenders had already experienced the malign effect of the Bf 109E, a single staffel of which had come close to wiping out the resident Hurricanes at one point. I./JG 27 had reached Sicily in early March, but had flown only two operations there, claiming a single victory over Malta. It had then operated over Yugoslavia during the opening days of April before flying on to Africa. 1.Staffel flew in to Ain el Gazala first, and very shortly the whole gruppe of three staffeln were established here, on most occasions just one staffel flying up to Gambut each day to operate. On occasions of importance the entire gruppe would move forward to this advanced base.

The pilots of this newly-arrived unit were experienced and confident. They had flown during the Battle of France, claiming 64 victories, and in the Battle of Britain, where they had claimed 32 more. The gruppe carried as the unit emblem, a map of Africa, superimposed on which was a panther's head and the face of a negro. This had been carried since spring 1940 and had no connection with the gruppe's posting to Africa, but this strange coincidence was looked on as a good omen by the personnel. The gruppe arrived without any tropical clothing due to all the recent moves which had occurred. A variety of multi-coloured outfits had to be acquired from a Jewish peddler in Tripoli in the first instance!

The commanding officer was Hauptmann Eduard 'Edu' Neumann, a fine leader who was to have a penchant for desert operations. He had flown in Spain with the Legion Condor, claiming two victories there to which he had added seven more over Western Europe in 1940. He had brought with him a circus caravan, captured in France, in which he lived, and which was to become a familiar sight to Axis troops who referred to it as 'Neumann's Bunte Buhne' (Neumann's Chequered Stage).

The three staffeln, with a strength of some 30-40 aircraft, were commanded by experienced pilots, 1.Staffel by Oblt Wolfgang Redlich, who at this time was credited with ten victories; 2.Staffel by Hptmn Erich Gerlitz (three victories) and 3.Staffel by Oblt Gerhard Homuth (15 victories). Several of the other pilots had already distinguished themselves; Oblt Ludwig Franzisket had 14 victories and Lt Willi Kothmann seven (the last of these claimed over Malta during a brief stay in Sicily during March); Obfw Hermann Förster had six victories and had been the first German pilot to shoot down an aircraft at night.

Edu Neumann, the commanding officer, later recalled:

"The Gruppe was equipped with the Bf 109E type; the 'Emil' was superior to all enemy fighter aircraft then operating in North Africa and the initial successes gave the pilots the feeling of safety and superiority in numbers – quite considerably so in the later stages of the campaign.

"The main strength of the Bf 109E lay in its excellent performance, high diving speed and good armament. The aircraft was allowed to fly 'Freie Jagd' in the smallest formations (Rotte or Schwarm) and through this offered ideal chances for gifted and aggressive fighter pilots to show their qualities. Some pilots, like Marseille, Homuth and others, took advantage of this situation to a large degree."

Probably the most interesting and colourful of the new pilots was a young man destined to become one of the most contentious fighter pilots of all time, Oberfahnrich (Ensign) Hans-Joachim Marseille. Although he had claimed seven Spitfires shot down already, he was viewed by his superiors and his fellow pilots with suspicion and reserve. He had a long list of punishments for breaches of discipline, and was reputed to be the 'black sheep' of the Luftwaffe. He was an intolerable boaster, proudly displaying his publicized adventures with famous actresses. He was also identified by his long hair, a scarf which he always wore, and by a predeliction for jazz, a form of music considered decadent and therefore frowned upon by the authorities at that time. He had been awaiting promotion to officer for many months while serving with other units, and was unfortunate on posting to JG 27 to be assigned to the staffel commanded by Oblt Homuth, a strict, duty-bound Prussian, one of the most disciplined officers in the Luftwaffe, who was unlikely to look with favour on the escapades of 'Jochen', as this 'enfant terrible' was known. Once he had been given the chance to prove himself fully, it would become obvious that his behaviour had been mainly due to an over-sized inferiority complex, but until that time he was closely watched by his commanders.

"109s ABOVE !"

Saturday, 19 April 1941
Plt Off 'Sam' Weller of 274 Squadron set off in a Hurricane converted for long-range operations to strafe Gazala airfield. Here he spotted a line of parked CR.42s and S.79s, claiming to have damaged six of the fighters and to have destroyed at least one of the bombers during his six-hour flight.

The main event of the day, however, and which was to have a profound effect on the Allied fighter squadrons, occurred soon after midday. Hurricanes from 274 Squadron had returned to El Gobbi early in the morning from where Sqn Ldr Lapsley and two other pilots commenced a patrol over Tobruk, followed by three more of the unit's aircraft 30 minutes later. It was the intention that refuelling should take place as necessary at Sidi Barrani to allow extended patrol times to be flown over the area.

As the second section arrived on station, 20 Ju 88s of III./KG 30 sought to raid the harbour, escorted by Bf 109Es of 1./JG 27 on their first sorties over Africa. Attacking Lapsley's section, the Messerschmitt pilots at once shot down Plt Off Baker's Hurricane which fell in flames near El Adem; Baker baled out and became a PoW. Lapsley, meanwhile, had pursued one of the bombers, but was attacked by two Messerschmitts, causing him to crash-land near El Gobbi, where the damaged aircraft was strafed and he was wounded in one leg and in a shoulder. Only Sgt George Kerr managed to escape at low level and return to Sidi Haneish.

At this point the second section of Hurricanes arrived, but only Flg Off D.J.Spence spotted the bombers, one of which had been shot down by the harbour defences. Spence attacked, shooting down one more and damaging a second. He then saw Lt Werner Schroer's Bf 109 below, which had just been involved in the strafing of Lapsley's Hurricane, and attacked this also. Schroer reported: "I was attacked by a Hurricane from out of the sun and had 48 bullet holes in my aircraft, but was able to force-land close to our airfield at Gazala."

1./JG 27 gained a further success later in the afternoon when Uffz Sippel intercepted one of 6 Squadron's TacR Hurricanes over Gazala and shot this down in flames. The pilot was the unit's commanding officer, Sqn Ldr Rowland Weld, who was killed.

John Lapsley, after his run of successes early in the Desert war, was a great loss to his squadron. He later recalled:

"The impact of the Messerschmitt 109s was very great. These aircraft had a very significantly better performance than the Hurricane in climbing, diving and level speed. The manoeuvrability of the two aircraft was comparable. Our results against the Italians had been so good that perhaps we were a little over-confident and had not sufficiently absorbed the tactical lessons of the war in Europe. This all combined to give us a very rough time for the first few weeks after the Messerschmitts arrived."

This fact now allowed 155° Gruppo CT to begin withdrawing its G.50bis fighters to Benghazi where they were to have air filters fitted. Many problems had been experienced due to sand ingestion into the engines. Consequently, the unit's 360ª Squadriglia flew back on this date, its place being taken by 150ª Squadriglia from 2° Gruppo. 152ª Squadriglia would follow next day, replaced by 378ª Squadriglia, while 358ª Squadriglia would follow on the 22nd, relieved by 351ª Squadriglia.

British Claims				
274 Sqn	Flg Off A.A.P.Weller	Hurricane I P3977	S.79 destroyed and 6 CR.42s on the ground at Gazala.	
	Plt Off D.J.Spence	Hurricane I V7354	Ju 88	Ras el Mehata 1100-1245
	Plt Off D.J.Spence	Hurricane I V7354	Ju 88 damaged	Ras el Mehata 1100-1245
	Plt Off D.J.Spence	Hurricane I V7354	Bf 109	W Tobruk 1100-1245

British Casualties	
274 Sqn	Hurricane I W9296 shot down; Plt Off H.J.Baker PoW Tobruk area 1100-1245
	Hurricane I V7811 crash-landed from combat and strafed; Sqn Ldr J.H.Lapsley, DFC, WiA El Gobbi 1100-1245
6 Sqn	Hurricane I shot down in Gazala area; Sqn Ldr R.Weld KiA 1530

German Claims			
1./JG 27	Oblt Wolfgang Redlich	Hurricane	SE Tobruk 1350
		Hurricane	W Tobruk 1400
	Lt Werner Schroer	Hurricane	W Tobruk 1100-1245
	Uffz Hans Sippel	Hurricane	Ain el Gazala 1530

German Casualties	
1./JG 27	Bf 109E-7 WNr 3790 crash-landed Gazala, damaged 60% in combat, Lt Werner Schroer safe
8./KG 30	Ju 88A-5 WNr 3214 4D+GS destroyed over Tobruk in combat with fighters; Obfw Kurt Distel and crew KiA
	Ju 88A-5 WNr 3293 4D+KS destroyed over Tobruk in combat with fighters; Hptmn Alfred Neumann, StKap and crew KiA
9./KG 30	Ju 88A-5 damaged in combat over Tobruk; one of crew WiA
2(H)./14	Ju 52/3m WNr 2965 destroyed on the ground at Ain el Gazala in strafing attack
	Hs 126 WNr 3277 destroyed on the ground at Ain el Gazala in strafing attack
	Hs 126 WNr 3434 destroyed 80% on the ground at Ain el Gazala in strafing attack
	Hs 126 WNr 4227 destroyed 80% on the ground at Ain el Gazala in strafing attack

Sunday, 20 April 1941

Over Derna a Blenheim IV of 55 Squadron was pursued by a G.50bis flown by Serg Magg Luigi Caroli of 351ª Squadriglia, 155° Gruppo, but was shot down by the airfield's AA gunners. Only two crew were aboard, but both were killed. The stricken bomber crashed onto a III./ZG 26 Bf 110, seriously damaging it.

Uffz Hans Sippel of 1./JG 27 made a claim for a Wellington at 0525 to the west of Tobruk. It seems unlikely that he had attacked the Blenheim intercepted by Caroli, but no loss for a Wellington has been found. Given the early hour recorded, it could well be a late-returning night bomber that he had attacked. recorded in Chapter 12, 'The Bomber Offensive', an aircraft of 38 Squadron, T2993 flown by Plt Off Slatter, set out to bomber Benghazi, but attacked Burre instead – well to the west of Tobruk. The aircraft is then recorded as having been written off, reason unknown. All this is indicated as having occurred one day later on 21 April. However, had the aircraft returned badly enough damaged to require writing off, the decision to do so might possibly have occurred a day after its return, resulting in its sortie also being recorded 24 hours late. No other explanation has been found.

Otherwise, the day was fairly quiet in the Tobruk area, 73 Squadron undertaking patrols but without any hostile aircraft being seen. During the day Erwin Rommel experienced another lucky escape when his armoured control vehicle was strafed by low-flying Hurricanes; his driver was badly wounded while a truck driver and a despatch rider were both killed and the radio truck was destroyed. His attackers were probably a trio of 73 Squadron pilots led by Flg Off Goodman.

At this stage the 73 Squadron commanding officer, Sqn Ldr Murray, who had recently been advised of the award of a DFC (gazetted on 28 March), but who was now sick and exhausted, was flown out in a Blenheim with four of his pilots to Sidi Haneish; the latter four were to fly new Hurricanes back to El Gobbi next day, led by the replacement commander, Sqn Ldr Peter Wykeham-Barnes, DFC, from 274 Squadron. Geoff Garton recorded: "At midday the CO, Griff, 'Monty'(Ellis) and myself left El Gobbi per Blenheim for Sidi Haneish to bring back replacement kites. Landed at Maaten Bagush where the AOC had a quiet chat with us and gave us all the gen. Things don't appear to be very good. Stayed the night at Haneish where our advanced party is stationed."

Meanwhile, underway from Alexandria via Crete to undertake a bombardment of Tripoli, (see *Air War for Yugoslavia, Greece and Crete, 1940-41* and Chapter 14, – 'In Defence of Tripoli' in this volume), the Mediterranean Fleet sailed into the area between the North African coast and Sicily. At 1043 an unidentified plot appeared on HMS *Formidable*'s radar to which a section of 806 Squadron Fulmars were directed. These fighters were flown by two of the unit's most experienced pilots, Lt Cdr Charles Evans and Sub Lt Jackie Sewell, and they intercepted a trimotor identified as a Cant.Z.1007bis, apparently on its way from Cyrenaica to Sicily. This aircraft was claimed shot down at 1115. It seems that the aircraft in question was actually an S.82 transport of 607ª Squadriglia which had taken off from Benghazi and which was lost with the whole crew. Two hours later a small formation was reported at a distance of 25 miles, two more sections of Fulmars (four aircraft) rapidly taking off to intercept these new intruders. These proved to be five Ju 52/3m transports from I./KGrzbV 9 en route for Africa. Brown Section (Lt J.H.Shears and Sub Lt P.D.J.Sparke – the latter a former Swordfish pilot with a DSC and Bar) made the first attack, followed by Grey Section, led by Lt R.S.Henley.

One of the transports escaped northwards, but the other four were all claimed shot down, two of them exploding in the air, suggesting that they were loaded with fuel. It appeared that one of these had fallen to Lt Shears, but his aircraft was hit by return fire and spun into the sea; he and his observer, Sub Lt Dixon, were killed. Robert Henley recalled: "…after I had made my first attack (on a lone Ju 52) I pulled into the sun and watched Johnny Shears close from dead astern to within 50 yards or so when he was obviously hit and nosed vertically into the sea. I made another pass and claimed a possible, then returned to where Johnny had gone in, to search for him in vain."

As four Ju 52/3ms were officially credited to the Fulmars, it would seem that Lt Henley received credit for one, as did Lt Shears, whilst it is believed that Sub Lt Sparke claimed the other two. In the event, it appears that only two Luftwaffe aircraft were actually lost, Obfw Josef Kastl and Fw Walter Heyer and their crews being reported missing.

British Claims

806 Sqn					
	Lt Cdr C.L.G.Evans		}	Cant.Z.1007bis	over sea
	Sub Lt A.J.Sewell				
	Lt J.H.Shears	Fulmar		Ju 52/3m *	over sea
	Lt R.S.Henley	Fulmar		Ju 52/3m *	over sea
	Sub Lt P.D.J.Sparke	Fulmar		2 Ju 52/3ms *	over sea

*Official confirmation aboard *Formidable* simply credited the four pilots involved with four victories; this is an estimate of how the individual claims were submitted.

British Casualties

806 Sqn	Fulmar I shot down by return fire from Ju 52/3m; Lt J.H.Shears/Sub Lt E.J.H.Dixon KiA		
55 Sqn	Blenheim IV T2383 shot down; Sgt D.Rawlings and Sgt P.Huxstep KiA		

German Claims

1./JG 27	Uffz Hans Sippel	Wellington	W Tobruk 0525

German Casualties

I./KGr.zbV 9	Ju 52/3m exploded over sea from fighter attack; Obfw Josef Kastl and crew MiA
	Ju 52/3m exploded over sea from fighter attack; Fw Walter Heyer and crew MiA
III./ZG 26	Bf 110 WNr 3860 60% damaged on ground by crashing Blenheim

Italian Casualties

607ª Sq	S.82 MM60325 MiA en route to Sicily from Benghazi; Ten Loris Pivetti and crew KiA

Monday, 21 April 1941

Having completed its attack on the Tripoli area during the early hours, and achieved complete surprise, the Mediterranean Fleet was well on the way back to Egypt by mid morning when at 1110 a 'shadower' at last appeared. This was intercepted by Orange Section of 803 Squadron from *Formidable*, again being recognised as a Cant.Z.1007bis. Half an hour after this sighting had been reported, Orange 2 (Sub Lt W.C.Simpson) returned, reporting that the Italian aircraft had been damaged, but the section leader, Lt Wright, and his observer, Sub Lt F.W.Ponting, had lost contact. At last at 1340 contact was restored and White Section of 806 Squadron (Sub Lts Stanley Orr and G.A.Hogg), two more of this unit's very experienced pilots, were despatched to find Wright and lead him back to the carrier. After flying 20 miles, this latter pair spotted a Do 24N flyingboat from Seenotstaffel 6, heading south from Syracuse, Sicily, at 1,000 feet, too low for the ships' radars to have picked it up.

The two fighter pilots attacked at once and forced it down onto the sea with its port engine on fire. The flyingboat's pilot made two attempts to take off again but on each occasion was attacked by the Fulmars until it settled in the water, streaming a trail of petrol and oil; it was then claimed destroyed. Meanwhile, Lt Wright had found his own way back to

Obfw Albert Espenlaub of 1./JG 27 who was one of the early successful pilots of I Gruppe in Africa. The nose of his Bf 109E is painted yellow and carries the gruppe emblem – a map of Africa surmounted by a leopard and the head of a negro.

Formidable, reporting that the aircraft he and Simpson had targeted, had also in fact been shot down.

Two S.79 torpedo-bombers of the 278ª Squadriglia took off from Benghazi's Berka airfield to attack a British convoy sighted south-west of Crete. The first, flown by Ten Guido Robone, left at 1650, spotting the convoy and launching a torpedo which Robone's crew claimed had hit a large vessel (possibly the oiler *British Lord*). Of the second aircraft, which had departed at 1725 in the hands of Cap Oscar Cimolini, there was no news. Subsequently, many years later in 1960, its wreck was found south-west of Giarabub by an oil company exploration team. The remains of five crew members were found nearby, whilst those of a sixth, the gunner 1°Av Gianni Romanini were discovered about 55 miles away, not far from the Gialo-Giarabub trail, which he had obviously been trying to reach in an effort to seek assistance.

At Tobruk the five replacement Hurricanes which had arrived at El Gobbi early on the 21st were joined by three more during the day. Patrols were then flown by 274 Squadron Hurricanes over warships which had landed a force of Royal Marine commandos to attack certain coastal targets, and over the forward

Messerschmitt Bf 109Es of I./JG 27 on their way from Sicily to Tripoli in April 1941.

area. Six were off at 0800, these encountering JG 27 Bf 109Es. Flg Off Spence attacked one so closely that he collided with it. Although both aircraft were damaged, each managed to reach territory in the hands of the respective forces before force-landing. It seems that the pilot of the Messerschmitt was Lt Schroer, who had been slightly wounded. It is therefore very possible that Spence had brought down the same pilot twice in three days. He was flown back to his squadron in a Blenheim, believing that the Messerschmitt he had rammed, had dived into the ground.

The squadron made a further patrol, led by Flt Lt Dudley Honor, who had temporarily assumed command of the unit following the departure to hospital of the wounded Sqn Ldr Lapsley. Sqn Ldr G.E.Hawkins, previously a flight commander with 33 Squadron, would arrive next day to take over. After less than three weeks in command of 55 Squadron, Sqn Ldr Darbyshire was posted to 204 Group on 19 April, his place being taken on a temporary basis by Sqn Ldr F.A.Marlow. The squadron noted that it had been provided with a Blenheim I (short-nosed) fitted with a 20mm cannon, but that as at 21 April little had been done with it.

73 Squadron also undertook a number of patrols on this date during one of which five Bf 109Es attacked and Sous Lt Castelain's aircraft was badly damaged – almost certainly the victim of Obfw Alfred Espenlaub, who was awarded a probable victory. Castelain attempted a force-landing but his aircraft flipped over on its back at El Gobbi and he suffered a broken arm.

Dive-bombers returned to the attack on the harbour at 1900, four 73 Squadron Hurricanes being scrambled to intercept. The engine of Sgt Ellis's aircraft cut as he attempted to take off, and by the time he had restarted it, he was too late to rejoin the other three: "This evening we scrambled after 60 Ju 87s and 20 ME 110s did a fierce attack on the harbour. We three immediately got split up and I engaged and managed to shoot down one Ju 87, while Benny (Goodman) and the Frenchman (Denis) got one each. I was then attacked by an overwhelming number of 110s and had to retire gracefully into the AA barrage for safety." 1./JG 27 was also present, and Denis was successful in shooting down one of the Bf 109Es, Uffz Sippel failing to return.

It was not a good day for the German unit, for one of the 2.Staffel pilots, Obfhr Heinrich Pompsch, had shot down an Italian bomber in error, although no Italian loss appears to have been recorded. Werner Schroer recalled that this depressed Pompsch very severely.

———

Air Marshal Arthur Tedder visits 73 Squadron at Tobruk. The tall, fair-haired officer in the dark pullover is the squadron commander, Sqn Ldr Peter Wykeham-Barnes. At the extreme left the officer dressed in overalls is one of the unit's attached Frenchmen, identifiable by his service cap.

British Claims

274 Sqn	Flg Off D.J.Spence	Hurricane I V7354	Bf 109	Forward area; by collision 0800-1245.
803 Sqn	Lt A.J.Wright	Fulmar I		
	Sub Lt W.C.Simpson	Fulmar I	Cant.Z.1007bis	Over sea circa midday
806 Sqn	Sub Lt S.G.Orr	Fulmar I		
	Sub Lt G.A.Hogg	Fulmar I N1988	Do 24N	Over sea, S Sicily circa 1350
73 Sqn	Sous Lt J.Denis	Hurricane I V7834	½ Ju 87	Tobruk 1900-1920
	Sous Lt J.Denis	Hurricane I V7673	Ju 87	Tobruk 1900-1920
	Flg Off G.E.Goodman	Hurricane I AS990	½ Ju 87	Tobruk 1900-1920
	Flg Off G.E.Goodman	Hurricane I AS990	Ju 87	Tobruk 1900-1920
	Sgt G.W.Garton	Hurricane I V7673	Ju 87	Tobruk 1900-1915

British Casualties

274 Sqn   Hurricane I V7354 crash-landed El Gobbi after collision with Bf 109; Flg Off D.J.Spence safe

German Claims

1./JG 27   Obfw Albert Espenlaub   Hurricane   Tobruk

German Casualties

1./JG 27   Bf 109E-7 WNr 3777 shot down over Tobruk; Uffz Hans Sippel KiA

Bf 109E-7 WNr 4170 'White 3'; crash-landed Ain-el-Gazala 40% damaged; Lt Werner Schroer MiA (returned)

Seen'tst 6 Do 24N forced down on sea and destroyed, S Sicily

Italian Casualties

278ª Sq AS   S.79 MM23881 FTR; Cap Oscar Cimolini and crew MiA

Tuesday, 22 April 1941

Better weather allowed a heavy raid to be launched against Tobruk at dawn by around 30 Ju 87s, including five from 236ª Squadriglia, six Bf 110s plus about a dozen Bf 109Es and G.50bis providing escort. Four Hurricanes got off, their pilots claiming one Ju 87 shot down, one probable and one damaged. Gunners in the Luftwaffe bombers claimed to have shot down a Hurricane, but none of the British fighters suffered any notable damage.

The same four fighters intercepted another incursion at 1050, Flg Off Martin claiming a Bf 109E shot down. Then half an hour later five more Hurricanes were scrambled, Sous Lt Littolf also claiming a Messerschmitt. It seems likely that he and Martin had in fact attacked the same aircraft, for JG 27's only loss was the ill-fated Obfhr Pompsch, who apparently managed to bale out, but died of his wounds next day. Sgt Marshall had encountered the Italian fighters, meanwhile, shooting down a 358ª Squadriglia aircraft for his 13th victory. Cap Salvatore Teja, commander of 152ª Squadriglia, claimed a Hurricane in return, shared with one of his pilots, and a second was claimed by Cap Annibale Sterzi, but no 73 Squadron aircraft were lost or damaged. Luftwaffe records indicate that a Ju 88 of 6./LG 1 fell to fighters over the harbour, but no such claims were made, and it is possible that the aircraft was shot down by the AA defences.

The Mediterranean Fleet was nearing Alexandria by evening, having maintained anti-'shadower' patrols all day, many being reported but without interceptions being made. At 1724 a raid was finally plotted closing with the ships, and two sections of Fulmars were scrambled; these were Ju 88s of III./LG 1 out searching in the area north of Tobruk. Two such bombers were spotted 30 miles from the fleet and at once every available fighter was launched until 14 were in the air by the time that the intruders got close. The first pair, from 8.Staffel, were attacked by Green Section of 803 Squadron (Lt J.M.Bruen and Sub Lt D.H.Richards) and Grey Section of 806 Squadron (Lt Henley and Sub Lt Sparke). Bruen's section forced one bomber to jettison its load and make off into clouds, possibly damaged. The second, flown by Uffz Gerhart Pfeil, was also seen to jettison its bombs, but was then shot down into the sea by Julian Sparke, Henley's guns having failed to operate. Lt Jasper Godden, the observer in Bruen's 6A, N1951, recalled: "We saw nothing until the Fleet was well on its way back to Alexandria – at about 1700 hours we spent 30 minutes in combat with two Ju 88s. One was shot down – not by us – all I had was a Thompson sub-machine gun – you could see the .45 inch bullets trickling out of the muzzle – the muzzle velocity was so low !"

Black and White Sections of 806 Squadron also intercepted a lone Ju 88, reported to be a shadower, and this was claimed probably destroyed by Lt Cdr Evans, Sub Lt Sewell and Sub Lt Orr. No damage was caused to the fleet.

British Claims

73 Sqn	Sous Lt J.Denis	Hurricane I	Bf 109	Gazala
	Sous Lt J.Denis	Hurricane I	G.50	
	Sous Lt J.Denis	Hurricane I	Ju 87	
	Flg Off G.E.Goodman	Hurricane I	G.50	
	Sous Lt A.Littolf	Hurricane I V7357	Bf 109	SW Tobruk 1125
	Sgt A.E.Marshall	Hurricane I V7353	G.50	
	Flg Off R.F.Martin	Hurricane I V7372	Bf 109	Tobruk c. 1130
	Plt Off M.P.Wareham	Hurricane I V7837	Ju 87	SW Tobruk 1135
806 Sqn	Sub Lt P.D.J.Sparke	Fulmar I	Ju 88	Over sea
	Lt Cdr C.L.G.Evans	Fulmar I		
	Sub Lt A.J.Sewell	Fulmar I	Ju 88 probable	
	Sub Lt S.G.Orr	Fulmar I N1988		

British Casualties

45 Sqn	Blenheim IV L1481 shot down over Benghazi, reportedly by Flak; Flt Sgt WE.Beverley and crew KiA
208 Sqn	3 Lysanders, L4707, L4722 and P9195 destroyed by own forces during evacuation of El Adem

German Casualties

2./JG 27	Bf 109E-7 WNr 4112 shot down SE Tobruk. Obfhr Heinrich Pompsch died of wounds next day
8./LG 1	Ju 88A-10 WNr 2209 shot down over sea; Uffz Gerhart Pfeil and crew MiA

Italian Claims

358ª Sq/2° Gr CT	Cap Annibale Sterzi	Hurricane	0940-1110
152ª Sq/2° Gr CT	Cap Salvatore Teja	} Hurricane	
	Serg Rino Ricci		

Italian Casualties

358ª Sq/2° Gr CT	G.50 MM5455 Serg Enzo Falcinelli KiA

Wednesday, 23 April 1941

The day was marked by further raids on Tobruk. Following an abortive initial scramble, probably after a lone reconnaissance aircraft, four Hurricanes took off at 1000 to intercept 20 Ju 87s (again five from 236ª Squadriglia), 30 Bf 109s and ten Bf 110s. Sqn Ldr Wykeham-Barnes claimed a Ju 87 and a Bf 109, but was shot down by three more Messerschmitts, coming down on the edge of the harbour wall, suffering only a strain to one leg.

However, the JG 27 pilots were vigilant. Plt Off Peter Haldenby was shot down and killed, and Flg Off Martin baled out of his damaged aircraft, wounded in one arm. Three more Hurricanes had also taken off following the initial four, the surviving pilots claiming three Ju 87s shot down, Sgt Marshall seeing his crash 15 miles west of Tobruk. Plt Off Chatfield returned with the rudder of his Hurricane damaged, while Sous Lt Littolf only escaped a pursuing Messerschmitt when it was driven off his tail by the Tobruk AA gunners. Nonetheless, his Hurricane had been badly damaged and he crash-landed at El Gobbi, but the Bf 109 was hit by Bofors guns and crashed, Fw Werner Lange being killed. Sgt Laing: "We watched a ME 109 roar past at about 150 feet and the Bofors gunner got his deflection right with the fifth or sixth shot and blew the plane to pieces. In what wreckage we saw close by the field, all we found was a boot."

Oblt Wolfgang Redlich, staffelkapitän of 1./JG 27, would be one of the first Luftwaffe pilots in North Africa to be awarded the Ritterkreuz.

A few minutes later Sgt Marshall's Hurricane was attacked on the ground by Lt Eugen von Moller, who had already claimed one Hurricane shot down; Marshall: "I was strafed in the cockpit by a ME 109, wounded in head and shoulder. LAC Webster and another [LAC 'Jock' Boyd], who was hit nine times but survived] seriously injured at wing tips."

The dive-bomber attack on the harbour had been very successful, the freighters *Urania* and *Draco* being hit; bomb splinters and debris hit the corvette *Gloxinia*, mine-dredger *Fareham* and an anti-submarine vessel previously the South African whaler *Southern Sea*.

A further raid followed at 1500, again comprising Ju 87s and about 20 escorting Bf 109s. Four Hurricanes went up again, but were driven off the bombers by the Messerschmitts. During this engagement the only success was claimed by Sous Lt Denis:

"I was well-trained and a confirmed fighter. What's more I was considered an elite shot. I knew my job well, and it explains why during my fight with this pilot, presumably Marseille, I was patient enough to act as if I hadn't seen him, wait until the last second and skid, avoiding his bullets which passed very close to my right. I watched them carefully."

The Bf 109, flown by newly-arrived Obfhr Marseille, shot past him and he opened fire, hitting the engine. The Messerschmitt then crash-landed in no-man's land with 30 bullet hits; Marseille was able to get out and make his way to German lines, however. Here he recalled how, as he leaned forward, two bullets passed behind his head, two more going by just in front of his face.

This day's action effectively brought an end to 73 Squadron's defence of Tobruk. That evening Air Cdr Collishaw wrote to Air Marshal Tedder:

"I am of the opinion that the air situation at Tobruk is critical for the following reasons. The enemy has concentrated two new fighter wings at Derna and Gazala which permits him to escort his bombers over Tobruk with ME 110s at approximately 15,000 feet with ME 109s flying a good deal higher. The striking forces arrive in overwhelming numbers over Tobruk within ten minutes of the warning being received so that our comparatively few fighters at Tobruk are still well beneath the

Obfr Hans-Joachim Marseille, initially considered the 'enfant terrible' of 3./JG 27, but soon to become one of the most successful fighter pilots of the war, is seen here with an early victim. While originally thought possibly to have been an aircraft of 213 Squadron, there is just sufficient left of the squadron code letters on the fuselage side of this Hurricane I to suggest that it was from 274 Squadron (code letters NH). The scimitar on a triangle marking beneath the cockpit is noteworthy.

escorting enemy fighters when the bombing commences. In these circumstances the enemy fighters will always have a great advantage over our fighters as they retain the initiative. During recent days the enemy has acted aggressively in the Tobruk area, both against our fighters and against our ground forces in the Tobruk defended area. Enemy fighters have ground-strafed our troops some two or three miles inside the Tobruk defences and have taken the initiative in every way possible and a serious reduction has occurred in our fighter force.

"I sent all available Hurricanes to Tobruk so that on 21.4.41 they had 15 serviceable aircraft. On 23.4.41 the enemy made a succession of attacks on Tobruk which caused our pilots to be continuously on the alert and engaged in combat from daybreak until noon. Group Captain Spackman decided that the pilots must be given a rest and they were instructed to stand off for the afternoon. A succession of enemy raids developed during the afternoon without fighter protection and the enemy bombed and ground-strafed El Gobbi aerodrome. Several of the 73 Squadron pilots took off during the enemy attacks but the ME 109s assaulted them as they were taking off and landing with the result that Sqn Ldr Wykeham-Barnes was wounded and several other pilots killed and wounded. The result was that out of 15 serviceable Hurricanes which were available at 21.4.41 only five remain serviceable on 23.4.41. Group Captain Spackman considers that we ought to produce a minimum of nine aircraft on patrol at a time which means that we must have at least 18 serviceable Hurricanes at El Gobbi continuously.

"No.274 Squadron have approximately 13 aircraft available but, I understand that these represent a major part of the Hurricanes available in Egypt at the present time and I am loathe to send them to Tobruk as the Hurricane casualties in fights and ground-strafing at Tobruk would obviously reduce our available Hurricane fighter force in Egypt to a more dangerous level. It is for consideration therefore, whether we ought to continue to send large numbers of Hurricanes to El Gobbi where we shall obviously lose some, or whether some alternative plan must be adopted. This is, of course, a matter for the AOC-in-C's decision. On the one hand it is vital that we must maintain our air protection of Tobruk, while on the other hand we must not lose what available Hurricanes we have for the defence of Egypt in readiness should the enemy continue his advance in the Western Desert.

"I am sending this letter by an officer early on 24.4.41 and request that I may be informed early as to what decision is taken in this matter."

British Claims

73 Sqn	Sqn Ldr P.G. Wykeham-Barnes	Hurricane I V7837	Bf 109	Tobruk 1130-1205
	Sqn Ldr P.G. Wykeham-Barnes	Hurricane I V7837	Ju 87	Tobruk 1130-1205
	Sgt A.E.Marshall	Hurricane I V7353	Ju 87	Tobruk 1130-1205
	Plt Off Chatfield	Hurricane I W9299	Ju 87	Tobruk 1130-1205
	Sous Lt A.Littolf	Hurricane I V7728	Ju 87	Tobruk 1130-1205
	Sous Lt A.Littolf	Hurricane I V7728	Bf 109	Tobruk 1130-1205
	Sous Lt J.Denis	Hurricane I AS990	Bf 109	Tobruk 1505-1520
	Sous Lt J.Denis	Hurricane I AS990	Bf 109 probable	Tobruk 1505-1520

British Casualties

73 Sqn	Hurricane I V7837 shot down; Sqn Ldr P.G.Wykeham-Barnes baled out safe
	Hurricane I V7834 shot down; Plt Off P.Haldenby KiA
	Hurricane I W9299 slightly damaged; Plt Off P.M.Chatfield safe
	Hurricane I V7728 badly damaged and crash-landed; Sous Lt A.Littolf safe
	Hurricane I V7353 strafed on ground; Sgt A.E.Marshall WiA
	Hurricane shot down; Flg Off R.F.Martin baled out, WiA
55 Sqn	Blenheim IV T1873 shot down in flames by Bf 109 20m W Tobruk; Sgt T.Fullarton and two KiA
	Blenheim IV crash-landed at base; Sgt Rann and crew safe

German Claims

Stab I./JG 27	Oblt Ludwig Franzisket	Hurricane	Tobruk 1040
1./JG 27	Lt Hans-Jurgen von Moller	Hurricane	Tobruk airfield 1045
1./JG 27	Lt Hans-Jurgen von Moller	Hurricane	(on ground) E Tobruk 1055
Stab I./JG 27	Oblt Ludwig Franzisket	Hurricane	Tobruk 1105
3./JG 27	Obfhr Hans-Joachim Marseille	Hurricane	Tobruk 1250
1./JG 27	Oblt Wolfgang Redlich	Blenheim	NE Tobruk 1250
	Oblt Wolfgang Redlich	Blenheim	N Tobruk 1255

German Casualties

1./JG 27	Bf 109E-7 WNr 4163 shot down over Tobruk; Fw Werner Lange KiA
3./JG 27	Bf 109E-7 WNr 5160 crash-landed and destroyed Tobruk area; Ogfhr Hans-Joachim Marseille MiA (returned)

Thursday, 24 April 1941

RAF bombers raided Derna airfield, their attack wounding five Italian fighter pilots, all of whom were taken to Derna Hospital. At Tobruk only one patrol went up during the morning, but nothing was seen. Only in the evening did 18 escorted Ju 87s appear to renew the attack on the vessels damaged during the previous day. AA claimed one shot down, but the Hurricanes were not scrambled.

Italian Casualties

360ª Sq/155° Gr CT	Ten Gianni Caracciolo wounded by bombs at Derna airfield
152ª Sq/2° Gr CT	Cap Salvatore Teja wounded by bombs at Derna airfield
	S.Ten Giovanni Mancini wounded by bombs at Derna airfield
	Serg Alfredo Di Spezio wounded by bombs at Derna airfield
	Serg Alvino Marinucci wounded by bombs at Derna airfield

Friday, 25 April 1941

HQ 258 Wing now requested a nominal roll of 73 Squadron pilots and aircraft at El Gobbi. This showed only five Hurricanes serviceable, and the unit was ordered to prepare to withdraw to Sidi Haneish. First, however, four of these aircraft were scrambled after another raid early in the morning, comprised of 20 Bf 109s and some Italian Ju 87s. Flt Lt Olivier decided that the odds were too great, and ordered the pilots to return to base.

By evening eight Hurricanes were flyable of which only half were operationally serviceable, and these left at 1800, landing initially at Gerawla. The commanding officer with Flg Off Goodman, Plt Off Humphreys and the intelligence officer, had already gone ahead in a Blenheim. Of his short time at El Gobbi, Peter Wykeham-Barnes later wrote:

" I was commanding officer of 73 Squadron in the spring of 1941, first inside Tobruk and later at Sidi Haneish. It was a very bad time, as we were outclassed by the 109s, heavily outnumbered, and hopelessly placed tactically. Our losses were very heavy, both inside and outside Tobruk. During my six months in command I lost 120% of my pilot strength, including four Flight Commanders.
        We shot down a number of Stukas and 109s. Few of these were confirmed as the battles were always over enemy territory, or over the small Tobruk perimeter. On the whole I think our losses were about the same as our victories, or somewhat more. The poor profit/loss ratio was increased by the fact that we did a lot of ground attacks on airfields, where we lost heavily to German light Flak. Our role was to keep up some appearance of participation, so that the Army should not feel deserted by the Air Force, but the heavy cost of this was known, and we were urged to hold out until the Desert Air Force could be reinforced with new fighter squadrons."

Part of the squadron's servicing party remained to recover such spares as could be salvaged from the wrecked Hurricanes; however at Tobruk West 6 Squadron's A Flight remained, now with two Hurricanes and four Lysanders under Flg Off Fletcher, although it appears that Flt Lt Mike Beytagh had managed to attach himself to this unit.
        Since flying in on 9 April, 73 Squadron had claimed 31 aircraft shot down plus five probables in the air, and eight aircraft together with many motor vehicles of various types destroyed on the ground. This had been achieved with the loss of circa 25 Hurricanes, 15 of which had been shot down. Six pilots had been killed, two had become PoWs and four had been wounded. Since their arrival as C Flight, Escadrille de Chasse N.1's share of the total included ten confirmed and two probable claims in the air.
        Air Chief Marshal Longmore now cabled the air ministry in London:

"We have to maintain periodic offensive patrols over Tobruk by refuelling at Sidi Barrani. Fully realise that this will give enemy, which you must remember are both German and Italian, far too free hand over Tobruk but am convinced that at the moment there is no alternative. 73 Squadron losses in personnel and aircraft when operating from Tobruk were prohibitive. Under those conditions they were being outnumbered in their encounters with large formations up to the tune of seven or eight to one. They have had three squadron commanders in two weeks. Tedder has seen the remnants of them in the desert today and reports that the majority of pilots will have to be replaced at once. Including four operational/serviceable aircraft left in 73, total immediately available Hurricanes in the Western Desert today was 14. We are taking every possible step to re-establish the position but I am sure you will agree that when our fighters do engage the enemy they must do it with reasonable strength – i.e. we must employ occasional strong patrols instead of trying to cover long periods with penny packets. When we have sufficient Hurricanes to maintain air cover of refuelling at Tobruk, we shall resume refuelling and rearming there. Without such cover, aircraft on the ground at Tobruk are a hostage to fortune we cannot afford."

Italian Casualties

241ª Sq/98° Gr BT	BR.20 '241-6'lost in flying accident; Ten Augusto Grassi and crew safe

Saturday, 26 April 1941

At Gerawla, 274 Squadron continued to operate, being effectively the only fighter squadron now available in the Western Desert. For the time being the unit's main duties included TacR sorties and attacks on transport aircraft and other ground targets. From one such sortie the Canadian pilot Flg Off Patterson who had done so well during the later stages of Operation Compass, failed to return. It was subsequently discovered that whilst west of Bardia at about 1630, he had encountered three Bf 110s of 8./ZG 26. He had at once shot down Lt Oskar Lemke's aircraft, but then collided with that flown by Uffz Max Hohmann, who carried out a crash-landing near Sollum. Hohmann and his gunner, Uffz Wünsche, both survived and walked back to their base, but Patterson and both the crew of Lemke's aircraft were killed.

———

Sgt F.H.Dean was sent off to attack tanker vehicles reported operating from Derna to the forward area. He returned to claim one bowser in flames and four shot-up.

British Claims				
274 Sqn	Flg Off T.L.Patterson	Hurricane I V7763	2 Bf 110s	
British Casualties				
274 Sqn	Hurricane I V7763 shot down; Flg Off T.L.Patterson KiA			
German Casualties				
8./ZG 26	Bf 110E-1 WNr 3870 shot down by Hurricane, Bardia; Lt Oskar Lemke/Uffz Rudi Petters			
	Bf 110D-2 JU+JS WNr 3404 collided with Hurricane and crash-landed; Uffz Max Hohmann/Uffz Wünsche returned safe			

Sunday, 27 April 1941

While flying a TacR sortie at dawn, Plt Off Godden spotted a Bf 110 strafing troops at Buq Buq. He attacked this and it was seen to force-land near the escarpment south of Sollum. A further long-range sortie was then flown by Flg Off Weller during which he strafed ten Ju 52/3m transports at Benina. One of these aircraft was seen to burst into flames, and he claimed a further seven damaged. He was awarded an immediate DFC in recognition of the two special missions he had undertaken.

Prior to his attack, the Ju 52/3ms had been spotted by the crew of a reconnaissance Maryland of 39 Squadron. The Canadian pilot, Flt Lt W.M.'Butch' Lewis, recorded:

"We had completed our recce and were coming back over Benina when we were confronted by a sight of what looked like a hundred Ju 52s lined up wingtip to wingtip. It was too good to miss, but it was not our job to attack, so I called up the crew and asked them what they thought about it. 'Let's wreck them, sir', they said. So from about two and a half miles up in the air I pointed the nose down in a steep dive. It looked as if the Junkers had just landed, for there were groups of soldiers gathered about the landing ground. We dived right down to about 50 feet, and flashed along the line of German aircraft giving them all we had. One of the aircraft burst into flames immediately, and smoke poured from others. The soldiers were too startled to raise their rifles. They just closed up like penknives and toppled to the ground. As we mowed through them at the bottom of our dive, the belly of our aircraft must have almost been skimming the ground. My observer told me afterwards that we had done a good job. My other gunner fired a burst into a CR.42 which was standing away from the line of German aircraft."

British Claims				
274 Sqn	Plt Off S. Godden	Hurricane I V7825	Bf 110	
	Flg Off A.A.P.Weller	Hurricane I P3971	Ju 52/3m	on ground Benina
	Flg Off A.A.P.Weller	Hurricane I P3971	7 Ju 52/3ms	damaged on ground
39 Sqn	Flt Lt W.M.Lewis and		Ju 52/3m	in flames on ground
	crew of Maryland		Ju 52/3ms (several)	damaged on ground
German Casualties				
KGrzbV 104	4 Ju 52/3ms WNrs 6163, 5582, 6848, 6793 destroyed on ground at Benina			

Monday, 28 April 1941

Next day a Blenheim of 45 Squadron flew into Tobruk to collect a number of passengers, including Wg Cdr D.V.Johnson, 258 Wing's commanding officer, Sqn Ldr The Reverend J.E.Cox, RAF chaplain in the Western Desert, Sqn Ldr D.P.Barclay, Plt Off S.E.Belse and Capt R.W.Plowwright. While taking off, a patrol of Bf 109Es from I./JG 27 flew over the area at a considerable height and distance from Tobruk. Obfhr Marseille here demonstrated his fantastic eyesight, which was later to become legendary, spotting the Blenheim as it moved along the runway long before any of his comrades had seen it. Leaving the formation, he dived out of the sun as it took off, and shot it down into the sea. There were no survivors. This combat was witnessed by Jan Yindrich, a Polish soldier in Tobruk, who described it thus:

"....when a Blenheim came roaring down over our heads at about 50 feet. There was a terrific rattle of machine-gun fire and at first I thought the Blenheim had made a mistake and was firing at us, or choosing an awkward spot to clear her guns. Bullets whistled around, so we dived into the slit trench. A Messerschmitt, hot on the tail of the Blenheim, was responsible for the bullets. The Blenheim roared down the wadi, out to sea, trying to escape from the Messerschmitt, but the Messerschmitt was too close. The Blenheim fell out of the sky and crashed into the sea. The plane disappeared completely not leaving a trace. The Messerschmitt banked and flew inland again."

British Casualties			
45 Sqn	Blenheim IV Z5898 shot down over Tobruk during communications flight; Plt Off B.C.de G.Allan and crew, and five passengers all KiA		

German Claims			
3./JG 27	Obfhr Hans-Joachim Marseille	Blenheim	N Tobruk 0925

Tuesday, 29 April 1941

Ju 87s and Bf 110s again attacked Tobruk, on this date an army transport vessel, HMT *Chalka* being sunk in the harbour. However, one Stuka of 236ª Squadriglia was hit by AA and crash-landed in the desert. Italian DICAT gunners claimed to have shot down a raiding aircraft over Benghazi.

Italian Casualties	
236ª Sq/96º Gr BaT	Ju 87 MM 5799 hit by AA and crash-landed; crew safe

Wednesday, 30 April 1941

Rommel now commenced a new attack on Tobruk during the evening. Although short of aircraft, 73 and 274 Squadrons flew many ground-strafing sorties in the Sollum-Gazala-Gambut area throughout the day prior to this new assault commencing. Sous Lt Littolf shot up a large convoy, the only one to be found on this date, while another Frenchman, Plt Off Jean Pompei, who had recently joined 274 Squadron, but who had been detached to 73 Squadron to join his fellow countrymen there, spotted an Hs 126 of 2(H)./14 near Gambut which he shot down, reporting that it attempted a landing, but turned over as it did so.

274 Squadron sent off single Hurricanes at 15-minute intervals. During one such sortie Plt Off Godden spotted four Bf 110s strafing British troops, attacking and claiming one of these shot down and a second damaged. However, Flg Off Charles Greenhill's aircraft was seen to spin in while strafing an abandoned fuel dump near Buq Buq, while the recently-successful Flg Off Spence was shot down and killed near Tobruk. It seems probable that he had been attacked while strafing in the Gazala-Sollum area by Oblt Redlich of I./JG 27 and his wingman, and had been pursued towards Tobruk, Redlich claiming to have shot a Hurricane down. However, Lt K.Rankin, an artillery officer within the fortress, later recalled:

"…saw a dogfight between a Hurricane and two ME 109s. The Hurricane put up a marvellous show and must have been a most experienced pilot. Then the most awful thing happened – he finished his fight and came away, ammunition expended, to land at the emergency landing ground. Some mad LAA gunners started shooting at him, and to my horror, shot him down in a great burst of black smoke from only about 300 feet. This was one of the worst things I had yet seen in the war and Oh, how I cursed and swore at those complete idiots !"

Over the harbour another Ju 87 was hit by AA, this time a Luftwaffe aircraft of Stab II./StG 2, the crew of which was lost.

On this day seven S.79s of 19ª Squadriglia BT, led by Cap Francesco Possemato, arrived at Castel Benito from Villacidro, in Sardinia. The unit would become mainly devoted to reconnaissance duties.

British Claims				
73 Sqn	Plt Off J.Pompei		Hs 126	0820-1200
274 Sqn	Plt Off S.Godden	V7825	Bf 110	30m S Sollum
	Plt Off S.Godden	V7825	Bf 110 damaged	

British Casualties	
274 Sqn	Hurricane I V7734 crashed while strafing; Flg Off C.H.Greenhill KiA
	Hurricane I V7555 shot down by Bf 109s and/or British light AA at Tobruk; Flg Off D.J.Spence KiA

Thursday, 1 May 1941

Shortly after midnight a further assault on Tobruk commenced, but was held off by the defenders. Dawn brought a heavy Axis air raid on the perimeter positions, for which, of course, there was no immediate defence. However, on learning of this latest attack, patrols of Hurricanes were sent off by 73 and 274 Squadrons. Six aircraft from the latter unit reached the area to find eight 3./JG 27 Bf 109s patrolling overhead. In fact only four were seen initially, these being led by Oblt Homuth at medium altitude to provide escort for some Bf 110s, while four more at higher level were being led by Obfhr Marseille.

The 274 Squadron pilots attacked Homuth's schwarm from out of the sun and with the advantage of height, Flt Lt Honor, who was leading the flight, and Flg Off Agazarian each claimed one Messerschmitt shot down, Plt Off Hutt claiming a probable. At that point the Hurricanes were hit by Marseille's schwarm which had dived to the rescue. Marseille shot one Hurricane down which he reported crashed at once. He then attacked its wingman as it tried to evade him, seeing this crash-land at Tobruk on fire. Homuth, meanwhile, turned into the British attack, claiming to have hit one Hurricane from which the pilot baled out, and then claimed a second which he reported crashed near Tobruk, red flames being observed.

There is little doubt that Marseille's first victim was Plt Off Stan Godden, victor of seven previous engagements, who was seen to crash in flames and was killed. Plt Off Hutt's aircraft was then hit and he had to undertake an emergency landing at El Gobbi; Sgt Milburn's aircraft also suffered severe damage, causing him to crash-land at the same airfield.

The identity of Homuth's first claim is less certain as none of the British pilots are believed to have baled out. However, it would appear that he had caught the aircraft flown by Flg Off Pike of 6 Squadron, who was just returning from a TacR sortie. Recorded Plt Off Moulding of the same unit subsequently:

"The Messerschmitts seemed to take off when we took off – they were only 20 miles outside the perimeter. You could see them take off and you could only fly round for about 20 minutes, otherwise they'd get you. That's what happened to 'Pat' Pike – he didn't get down quick enough. I saw him coming into land and was hoping he wouldn't because I could see what was going to happen – a Messerschmitt was following him on his approach. A two-second burst, and that was that. He managed to pull up but got a couple of bullets in his backside. Everybody including the padre went out to help in case the Hurricane caught fire, and got him out."

The wounded Pike was taken to hospital where Capt J.Devine, the medical officer who treated his wounds, wrote in his diary:

"[He] told me how four Messerschmitts had waited until his landing flaps were down and his wheels had touched the ground before shooting him up. His was one of the last remaining Hurricanes here, and he had been told to stay out to sea until 12 Messerschmitts circling the drome area had gone away. When the wireless people gave him the all-clear, he came in to land. Then the wireless suddenly warned him there were four Messerschmitts a few hundred yards behind, on his tail. His plane was shot to pieces. He was furious that they had bothered to warn him when it was too late to be of use, for he said the few seconds of suspense before the cannons opened fire on him were the worst. In fact he seemed angrier with the wireless people than with the enemy."

Apart from the claims submitted by Honor and Agazarian, the army reported seeing two more Messerschmitts crash, though only Hutt's claim for a probable was outstanding. Honor: "We were patrolling the area when we saw four ME110s engaged in bombing. We dived down and as we did so we became involved with the escort of ME109s. There was a hectic dogfight. The combat was, however, of short duration and three ME109s, one of them in flames, were seen crashing away to the ground a few minutes later. The other German aircraft scattered." In fact only one Bf 109 had been seriously hit in which Gefr Köhne was wounded, although he was able to get back to Derna where he force-landed. It seems very likely – as was to happen quite often – the soldiers had actually seen and counted Hurricanes going down. As regards the demise of Pike's aircraft, 204 Group noted that a Hurricane of 6 Squadron had been shot down "accidentally" by AA at Tobruk. This, however, is in contradiction of Moulding's and Devine's reports, and would seem to have been an error which should have related to the loss of Doug Spence and his aircraft on the previous day.

A week later on 8 May the last four aircraft of 6 Squadron would depart Tobruk. It was at this point that the squadron recorded that Flg Off Pike had been slightly wounded by a Bf 109 when stepping out of his aircraft at Tobruk. Presumably this was a late report of what had apparently occurred on 1 May.

204 Group did report that during other sorties 274 Squadron aircraft shot-up 14 MT, and later another two trucks full of troops, all to the south-west of Sidi Aziez. It was also noted that the day saw the first sortie by a special 'strafer' Blenheim IV, fitted with a 20mm cannon in the nose. Apparently the crew of this aircraft undertook a successful attack during which ten vehicles were claimed destroyed.

British Claims				
274 Sqn	Flg Off D.G.S.Honor	W9269	Bf 109	Tobruk area 0630-
	Flg Off N.leC. Agazarian	V7829	Bf 109	Tobruk area 0630-
	Plt Off P.H.V.Hutt	V7755	Bf 109 probable	Tobruk area 0630-
British Casualties				
274 Sqn	Hurricane I V7825 shot down in flames; Plt Off S.Godden Tobruk area 0630-			
	Hurricane I V7755 damaged and made emergency landing; Plt Off P.H.V.Hutt safe			
	Hurricane I crash-landed; Sgt Milburn safe			
6 Sqn	Hurricane I V7814 shot-up on landing; Flg Off P.E.R. Pike WiA			
German Claims				
3./JG 27	Oblt Gerhard Homuth		Hurricane	12m S Tobruk 0915
	Obfhr Hans-Joachim Marseille		Hurricane*	11m S.Tobruk 0915
	Oblt Gerhard Homuth		Hurricane	Tobruk airfield 0920
	Obfhr Hans-Joachim Marseille		Hurricane*	3m SE Tobruk 0925

*It appears that one of these claims was treated as a probable.

German Casualties	
3./JG 27	Bf 109E-7 WNr 3805 damaged 40%; force-landed S Tobruk;Gefr Hermann Köhne WiA

Friday, 2 May 1941

Rommel's renewed assault on Tobruk was abandoned, although other Axis forces re-occupied Sollum, Capuzzo and the Halfaya Pass – in British hands since the previous December. While supporting these operations, III./ZG 26 suffered several losses to AA and other ground fire, three Bf 110s being shot down, and a fourth badly damaged; one of the former came down within the Tobruk perimeter, the other three all force-landing in the area held by Axis troops.

274 Squadron, now under the command of Sqn Ldr G.E.Hawkins, an ex-33 Squadron flight commander, undertook strafing attacks between Tobruk and Sollum, reportedly in conjunction with a Blenheim fitted with a four-gun 'pack' under the fuselage. Whether or not this was the same cannon-armed aircraft which had operated on the previous day, is not clear. However a further 20 MT and two staff cars were attacked on the El Adem-Sidi Aziez road.

Whilst engaged on one such sortie the pilot of one Hurricane reported seeing a Bf 110 crash after engaging a Blenheim, but no corresponding report has been found from any of the bomber crews operating in the area. Probably the pilot had seen one of the AA-hit aircraft retreating from the area at the time the strafer Blenheim was operating. However, during the day one Blenheim was claimed shot down by Italian fighter pilots, with a second damaged, but no such loss has been found.

German Casualties	
8./ZG 26	Bf 110E WNr 3877 damaged 50% by AA W Tobruk; Uffz Heinz Richter WiA; gunner safe
	shot down by AA Tobruk; Gefr Arthur Krelle and Gefr Walter Wohlert PoW

Italian Claims		
366ª Sq/151° Gr CT	Serg Arturo Imberti	Blenheim
	Ten Amedeo Guidi	Blenheim damaged

Saturday, 3 May 1941

Both sides now paused to re-group and build up supplies with the result that little occurred in the air for the next few days. On the 3rd Blenheims of 45 and 55 Squadrons bombed an estimated 75 plus Ju 52/3ms on Benina airfield, believing that a substantial number had been damaged.

The campaign in Greece was also at a close at this time, and by 30 April the British Commonwealth forces there had been evacuated (see *Air War for Yugoslavia, Greece and Crete, 1940-41*). Wavell now wrote to Longmore on 1 May: "On behalf of the Army I should like to thank you for the great effort made by the Royal Air Force in Greece to support the Army in spite of the enemy's overwhelming superiority. The gallantry and skill of the Royal Air Force in accomplishing so much against such numbers and in fighting to the end whatever the odds against them has won the admiration of all who were in Greece."

At this very critical moment, on 30 April Longmore was ordered to return to England for discussions on all aspects of future air operations at the express wishes of the prime minister. Tedder was to be appointed acting AOC-in-C during his absence, with AVM Drummond as deputy. In the light of the situation, exacerbated by an attack on the training base at Habbaniya by Raschid Ali's Iraqi forces which began on 2 May (see *Dust Clouds in the Middle East*), Longmore suggested that his return be postponed until the latter had been dealt with. An immediate reply, which he felt to be "ominous", required his immediate departure none the less.

On 3 May, therefore, he boarded a Sunderland of 10 RAAF Squadron for home, refuelling at Malta en route. Expecting to be returning as soon as possible, he did not take his leave of Wavell, Cunningham or of the British Ambassador in Egypt, nor of the officers and men of RAF Middle East.

The Sunderland landed at Plymouth early on 5 May and he was soon deeply involved in discussions concerning the rate of reinforcement, the need for new specialist squadrons, for better mobility of units, improvements in maintenance, etc. He also attended two late night meetings of the Defence Committee where he felt some of the regular members looked very tired, many having already spent all day in their offices. The same could not be said of Churchill, who "seemed in excellent form, very much in charge of proceedings and apparently relishing his vast responsibilities in framing future war plans."

Sunday, 4 May 1941

Two S.79s of 52ª Squadriglia, 27° Gruppo BT, made night attacks on Tobruk – the first nocturnal mission for 8° Stormo BT. During the same night a lone BR 20 of 240ª Squadriglia, 98° Gruppo BT, flown by the unit commander, T.Col De Wittemberski, took off from Barce at 0320, also to bomb Tobruk harbour and shipping. On the way back the crew reported being attacked by a night fighter over Apollonia. The port engine was hit and set ablaze, following which the crew baled out, but the wireless operator, 1° Av Italico Marchini died in the crash. No record of any fighters operating at night at this time have been discovered in British records, and no claim of any sort has been found. What had attacked the Italian bomber remains a mystery.

Italian Casualties	
240ª Sq/98 °Gr BT	BR.20M MM22622 shot down near Tobruk; T.Col De Wittemberski and crew baled out; one KiA

Monday, 5 May 1941

The main event of the day was a claim by Oblt Homuth of 3./JG 27 for a 'Martin 167' shot down east of Acroma during the early part of the morning. This was a reconnoitring aircraft from 39 Squadron.

On the Allied side of the lines 258 Wing recorded that a temporary fighter operations room had been dug out alongside the 204 Group HQ at Maaten Bagush. Directed from there was the mobile radar unit, 216 AMES, at Mersa Matruh, where 1 SAAF, 73 and 274 Squadrons were also to be based. Control of all fighters was allocated to the defence of the Matruh area and the 204 Group landing grounds.

British Casaulties			
39 Sqn	Martin 167 AH 285 Sqn Ldr G O Mills and crew MIA		
German Claims			
3./JG 27	Oblt Gerhard Homuth	Martin 167	6m E Fort Acroma 0832

Wednesday, 7 May 1941

The Regia Aeronautica now ordered the Ju 87-equipped 96° Gruppo BaT to return to Italy. The unit was to be replaced by 97° Gruppo from which 239ª Squadriglia was due to arrive first to operate as an autonomo unit, until joined by 209ª Squadriglia later.

By night a naval bombardment of the Benghazi area inflicted severe damage on two G.50bis fighters of 155° Gruppo CT.

Italian Casualties	
351ª Sq/155° Gr CT	G.50 MM6348 badly damaged on ground at Benghazi by naval gunfire
360ª Sq/155° Gr CT	G.50 MM6343 badly damaged on ground at Benghazi by naval gunfire

While the influx of new units reaching RAF, Middle East, appeared promising, in Greece the situation had deteriorated with remarkable rapidity. The final reinforcement had been the despatch there of 208 Squadron from Palestine which had occurred during March. Thereafter, the German advance proved to be so rapid that there was no time to send further units before those already there had been driven back with heavy losses. Within two weeks the fighting had reached the Athens area, and by the end of the month the remaining squadrons – now little more than tattered remnants – had departed the south of the country for Egypt, or to try and formulate an effective air defence for the island of Crete.

Already by 1 May what remained of 80 Squadron had reached Aqir; during the rest of that month 11, 30, 33, 84, 112, 113 and 208 Squadrons all reached North Africa; all, however, were in need of almost complete reformation and re-equipment. Following its arrival in Egypt, 203 Squadron had been despatched to Crete on 30 April to join 30 Squadron in long-range maritime patrols in support of the Royal Navy. The latter part of the month was to require quite substantial involvement from 204 Group's over-stretched forces as the withdrawal from Crete followed German airborne landings on that island. (See *Air War for Yugoslavia, Greece and Crete, 1940-41* for the full story.)

As if that were not enough, at the start of May an insurrection in Iraq threatened British interests there, including particularly the RAF's major training base at Habbaniya. This also offered the Germans and Italians a potential base in the rear of the British forces in Egypt and Palestine. The situation required urgent attention, and while the more advanced pupils at 4 Service Flying Training School formed and operated an air striking force at Habbaniya, sections of Wellingtons from 37 and 70 Squadrons, and a detachment of Blenheim IVs from 203 Squadron were despatched to help.

These were followed by 11 and 84 Squadrons as soon as they had been brought up to strength with Blenheims following their return from Greece, and ultimately Hurricanes of 94 Squadron arrived from Egypt. By the end of the month matters had been stabilised, but what had happened led to a further distraction in regard to Syria, as will be described shortly.

Anxious to improve the situation in the Middle East, Winston Churchill, the British prime minister, had ordered reinforcements to be despatched to Egypt urgently, and a convoy code-named Tiger had sailed. This had been precipitated by receipt of a message from Wavell to the effect that British forces in the Western Desert were gravely inferior to the Axis in terms of armoured strength, and that this situation was likely to worsen towards the end of the month. It was decided to be worth the risk to push the faster elements of this vital convoy straight through the Mediterranean, thereby saving some 40 days going round the Cape route. Five 15-knot transports – *Clan Chattan, Clan Lamont, Clan Campbell, Empire Song* and *New Zealand Star* were to carry 295 tanks and 53 Hurricanes through to Egypt. These vessels were to be escorted by an enhanced Force H from Gibraltar which was to include the battleships HMS *Renown* and *Queen Elizabeth*, aircraft carrier HMS *Ark Royal*, cruisers HMS *Sheffield, Naiad* and *Fiji*, plus nine destroyers. The cruiser HMS *Gloucester* and all available destroyers of the 5th Destroyer Flotilla were to sail west from Malta to join this escort.

It was decided to combine this with the running of vital supplies and fuel to the beleaguered island of Malta from the eastern end of the Mediterranean. Consequently, on 6 May the battleships HMS *Warspite, Barham* and *Valiant*, five cruisers of the 1st Battle Squadron, the aircraft carrier HMS *Formidable*, and a force of covering destroyers put to sea from Alexandria to escort four large merchant vessels and two tankers to the island. Here the naval escort was to take over the protection of the Tiger convoy, which was approaching from the west, Force H having turned back south of Sardinia.

The bigger warships had each to be led out of harbour by a tug due to aerial mining undertaken during the previous night, which 'degaussing' Wellingtons of 1 GRU (see Chapter 13 – Blitz on Egypt) were seeking to explode harmlessly (n.b. the actions which followed have been described in *Malta: the Hurricane Years, 1940-41* and *Air War for Yugoslavia, Greece and Crete, 1940-41*, but are so pertinent to the Desert war that they are repeated here for the sake of clarity and continuity).

Thursday, 8 May 1941

The Tiger convoy, which had passed through the Straits of Gibraltar during the night of 5/6 May, now came within range of air attack, and for the next four days activity in the air tended to centre around it. The convoy had escaped discovery until now due to bad weather and poor visibility, but this was not to continue, and a series of hard-fought combats now ensued. *Ark Royal* had embarked a second squadron of Fulmars to supplement its resident 808 Squadron (Lt R.C.Tillard). This additional unit was under the command of Lt Cdr J.Sholto Douglas; however the two units had between them only 12 aircraft fully serviceable on this morning.

FORCE H OPERATIONS ON 8 MAY

The early morning patrol had been vectored towards a 'shadower' and although this was spotted it could not be intercepted, so all now knew that the assault would soon commence. The first incoming raid appeared on the radar screens at about 1345, still 32 miles from the ships. This comprised five S.79s of 280ª Squadriglia Aerosiluranti which had taken off from Elmas airfield near Cagliari, Sardinia. These were flown by Cap Dante Magagnoli, Cap Amedeo Moioli, Cap Ugo Rivoli, Ten Marino Marini and S.Ten Francesco Cappa. They were escorted by 15 CR.42s of 3° Gruppo CT, eight from 153ª Squadriglia and seven from 154ª Squadriglia, all led by the gruppo commander, T.Col Innocenzo Monti; these fighters departed Monserrato (also near Cagliari) at 1205, nine providing close escort with the other six as top cover. Weather conditions were very poor, with a low cloud ceiling and limited visibility. Nonetheless, the British ships were sighted at 1340, some 120 miles south of Sardinia.

Two sections (four Fulmars) of 807 Squadron were scrambled to join the four Fulmars of 808 Squadron on patrol, these latter aircraft intercepting the incoming S.79s, but as Lt Tillard led the attack they were themselves bounced by a dozen of the escorting CR.42s. Almost immediately Tillard's Fulmar was shot down, he and his observer, Lt M.F.Somerville, being killed. The three other Fulmars were also hit, the aircraft of both Lt G.C.McE.Guthrie and Pty Off (A) R.E.Dubber sustaining damage to their tail units, while in Lt Taylour's aircraft the TAG, Pty Off(A) L.G.T.Howard received a severe leg wound, an explosive bullet shattering both tibia and fibula. One CR.42 overshot their aircraft and Taylour managed to score hits on it, forcing it into a spin from which he considered it would not be able to recover. Having evaded the other Fiats, Taylour headed for the carrier with his wounded TAG, where only prompt and skilful action by the Ark's surgeon prevented the loss of Howard's leg.

The Italian pilots claimed five Fulmars shot down, two more being claimed by the gunners in the S.79s. Five further Fulmars were credited to the fighter unit as probables. All but two of the CR.42s would return to base between 1340 and 1440, but Ten Massimino Mancini's aircraft had been damaged and he had to crash-land, as did Serg Magg Guerrino Cavalca, who had run out of fuel. The S.79 pilots all managed to release their torpedoes, Moioli and Magagnoli claiming to have hit a cruiser. However, all five torpedo-bombers had been badly damaged during the attack, and although three got back to Elmas, Marini had to crash-land in the sea near Galite Island, while Ten Cappa's aircraft was seen to crash into the water with the loss of all the crew. Marini and his crew got ashore in their dinghy from where they were later rescued. Cappa would subsequently be awarded a Medaglia d'Oro posthumously.

Meanwhile, a further formation of five S.79 bombers from 32° Stormo had taken off from Decimomannu some time after the initial raiding force, covered by ten more 3° Gruppo CT CR.42s led by Cap Giorgio Tugnoli (five from each of the squadriglie). It would seem to be with this formation that the four 807 Squadron Fulmars made contact, Lt N.G.Hallett and his No.2 – Pty Off(A) A.G.Johnson – hitting one bomber; however, the gunner returned fire, hitting Hallett's engine, forcing him to ditch. Both he and his Australian observer, Lt V.A.Smith, managed to scramble out and were both soon picked up by the destroyer HMS *Foresight*. Meanwhile the two Blue Section aircraft flown by Lt R.E.Gardner and South African Lt K.Firth attacked the same Savoia, which was probably that flown by Cap Armando Boetto, commanding officer of the 49ª Squadriglia; Blue 1 got in the final burst before it disintegrated and fell into the sea. A second S.79 flown by S.Ten Michele Fonseca of 228ª Squadriglia was also lost. Eight of the bombers broke through the defences to launch torpedoes at the Ark and at the battlecruiser *Renown*, but without obtaining hits. There followed a short lull, but from 1620 onwards a succession of attacks by small formations of S.79s commenced although all were successfully beaten off, mainly by the intense gunfire of the ships. Additionally, Yellow Section of 808 Squadron, two Fulmars flown by Lt A.T.J.Kindersley and Lt R.C.Hay, RM, caught one bomber at 1710 and claimed it shot down.

An S.79 of 175ª Squadriglia RST in flight. This unit provided the HQ with daily reports on the movements of British troops.

Just before dusk, at 1930, a further raid was detected when a full 70 miles distant. Three Fulmars were already up – Red Section of 807 Squadron – and four more (all that were now immediately available) were scrambled, the incoming attack proving to comprise 28 Ju 87s of I./StG 1 from Cagliari, in two formations, with a top cover of six Bf 110s of 9./ZG 26, these being led by Hptmn Thomas Steinberger. The three Fulmars of Red Section engaged the escort, as the other four, two each from 807 and 808, attacked the dive-bombers and broke them up. Lt Cdr Sholto Douglas engaged two Bf 110s, but these turned on the Fulmar, gaining hits on both its wings which caused damage to the hydraulic system. Red 2, Pty Off(A) R.T.Leggot, dived to attack a Ju 87 but was himself targetted by a Bf 110. He managed to turn inside his assailant and opened fire from 200 yards, seeing white vapour trail from the Messerschmitt as it pulled away. Lt Taylour, flying as Yellow 1 and now with Pty Off(A) F.A.Barnes in the rear seat, claimed one Ju 87 shot down, but they too were then attacked by a Bf 110, the starboard wing and hydraulic system therein being hit, with the result that the undercarriage leg on this side dropped down. Blue Leader, Lt 'Jimmie' Gardner, claimed another Ju 87 shot down with a second as probably destroyed – the latter subsequently being confirmed by cine gun-camera. However, the windscreen of his aircraft was shattered by crossfire from other Stukas, and with the radiator damaged, he crash-landed the badly damaged Fulmar on the carrier's deck; neither he nor his TAG, Pty Off(A) R.Carlisle, suffered injuries. One other Fulmar pilot, Sub Lt R.F.Walker flying No 2 to Gardner, reported seeing his fire hit a Bf 110, following which he attacked a Ju 87 which disappeared into cloud pouring smoke.

All seven Fulmars had landed back on the carrier by 2015 but two were again scrambled almost immediately on the approach of three more S.79s. Lts Guthrie and Hay were unable to prevent the attack, two of the Savoias releasing torpedoes at *Ark Royal* and *Renown*, narrowly missing the carrier. The attackers on this occasion seem to have been Cap Mario Spezzaferri, Ten Mario Laguercia and Ten Carlo Copello, all from 278ª Squadriglia AS, based on the island of Pantelleria; they all reported launching torpedoes at *Ark Royal*, but were unable to ascertain the results.

The returning Zerstörer pilots of 9./ZG 26 claimed three of the Fulmars shot down, identifying their victims as 'Hurricanes', the first of these claims being made by Oblt Bergfleth – probably Lt Cdr Sholto Douglas's aircraft – the subsequent two by Hptmn Steinberger. However, the Messerschmitts did not get away unscathed – indeed Fw Hans Hufnagel and his gunner were both wounded and crash-landed their badly damaged aircraft at Comiso, a second badly damaged Bf 110 crash-landing at Trapani, whilst a third returned with minor damage. At least one Ju 87 was damaged during the attack, both Lt Neuber and his gunner returning to Cagliari wounded.

At last darkness arrived and with it respite for the fleet and convoy, and welcome rest for the aircrews. However, at midnight one of the transports – *New Zealand Star* – was slightly damaged by a mine exploding in its paravane, following which *Empire Song* hit two mines. A fire broke out in her ammunition hold and the crew were taken off by an attendant destroyer. At 0400 she blew up with the loss of 57 of the precious tanks and ten of the even more precious Hurricanes. During the hours of darkness, and around midnight, a lone torpedo-bomber from 278ª Squadriglia AS, attempted a daring attack on HMS *Queen Elizabeth*, the torpedo only narrowly being avoided. Ten Guido Robone returned to Pantelleria claiming a probable hit on the battleship.

MEDITERRANEAN FLEET OPERATIONS ON 8 MAY

Meanwhile, the Mediterranean Fleet and its fighters had also been heavily engaged. En route to the rendezvous point HMS *Ajax* and three destroyers had been detached to bombard Benghazi during the night of 7/8th. Harbour installations and shipping were claimed to have been successfully shot up, while as the vessels sailed north to rejoin the main force they encountered two Axis transports, one of which blew up violently when attacked, the second running ashore and being left in flames.

As had been the case in the Western Basin of the Mediterranean, very poor visibility and occasional rain had frustrated the Luftwaffe's reconnaissance aircraft in finding the fleet. Frequent radar plots on the 8th showed the presence of the searchers, radio intercepts indicating the occasional fleeting sightings which were achieved. As had *Ark Royal* to the west, HMS *Formidable* had also taken aboard two fighter squadrons for this important operation, in this case 803 and 806 Squadrons. During the early part of the morning Blue Section of 803 Squadron was vectored onto two Italian bombers, identified as Cant.Z.1007s. Both were engaged and believed shot down. Recorded Leading Airman Tim Dooley, TAG in Sub Lt A.C.Wallace's N1913: "We circled round and watched our target dive into the sea; there was no sign of our leader (Lt C.W.R.Peever/Pty Off(A) F.Coston) – the last I saw of them they were following their target down, still knocking pieces off it." This Fulmar failed to return and was assumed to have been shot down by return fire from its victim.

Early in the afternoon radar indicated that a number of hostile aircraft were approaching and two sections of Fulmars were scrambled to join 806 Squadron's White Section (Lt R.MacDonald-Hall and his TAF, L/Air Harry Phillips, in N1990, with Lt P.S.Touchbourne flying as White 2 in N1865) which was already airborne. MacDonald-Hall recalled:

"We came across two He 111s. The first of which I rather stupidly flew in formation with some 50 yards behind, but managed to blow up the Heinkel's starboard engine, the debris of which being glycol and fuel, smothered my cockpit and I watched it cartwheel down and hit the sea. I then rejoined Touchbourne and we harassed, attacked and shot down the other Heinkel prior to returning to *Formidable*. My hydraulics had been damaged and the starboard wheel would not come down, and the port wing was badly damaged by the rear gunner's fire, as was the port tyre. I landed with one leg down, the other retracted and the wheel deflated."

Meanwhile Green Section of 803 Squadron (Lt J.M.Bruen and Lt D.J.Godden in N1951, with Sub Lt D.H.Richards flying Green 2) intercepted another He 111 which Bruen shot down. A fourth Heinkel was claimed by another 806 Squadron section, shot down into the sea by Lt L.S.Hill; his No 2, Lt G.B.Davie (late of 805 Squadron) crashed into the sea on returning to the carrier, only the TAG surviving. The claims made were very accurate, and it appears that White Section's victims were probably both aircraft of 6.Staffel, KG 26 – 1H+AP flown by Obfw Willy Kleinknecht and 1H+FB (Oblt Hermann Pfeil). There were no survivors. One of the other Heinkels was from 4.Staffel (Oblt Eberhard Stüwe's 1H+BC), the other from 5.Staffel, 1H+FN flown by Oblt Max Voigt; the crews perished. These bombers had been despatched to attack the Suez area.

Later in the afternoon two sections from 806 Squadron encountered Ju 88 snoopers, Lts R.S.Henley and P.D.J.Sparke believing they had shot down an aircraft of 2(F)./123 off Cap Passero. In fact they had damaged it, wounding two members of the crew, but it regained its base at Catania. Lts MacDonald-

Hall and Touchbourne were up again towards the end of the day and they too engaged a lone Ju 88, reporting that it had crashed into the sea with no survivors following their attack.

The bad weather which had saved the fleet from sustained air attack also had tragic consequences for a number of *Formidable*'s aircraft. Two Albacores on anti-submarine and reconnaissance patrols were lost, only one crew being rescued, while a Fulmar crewed by Pty Off(A) W.T.Chatfield and L/Air C.F.Norman crashed into the sea with the loss of both men. During the day Marylands of 39 Squadron at Fuka undertook a number of maritime reconnaissance sorties to the south and north of the fleet, but two were lost. On a sortie south of the fleet, AH296, flown by Lt A.U.M.Campbell, SAAF, was intercepted by a Bf 109E of 3./JG 27 from Gazala while flying near the North African coast between Bardia and Tobruk, and was shot down into the sea off Derna with the loss of all aboard. It would appear that this aircraft fell to Hpt Gerhard Homuth, although on this occasion, having claimed a Martin 167 on the 5th, he now identified his victim as a Blenheim. Meanwhile, Plt Off J.W.Best had instructions to land AH281 at Malta on completion of his sortie to the north of the ships, but due to technical difficulties, he was forced to come down at Methone on the southern tip of the Peloponnese, near Cape Akritas, where the crew were captured. (One gunner, Sgt J.A.Quitzow, later escaped from the PoW camp at Salonika and got back to Egypt.)

British Claims

808 Sqn	Lt E.W.T.Taylour/Pty Off(A) L.G.T.Howard	CR.42 probable	Western Mediterranean
	Lt A.T.J.Kindersley		
	Lt R.C.Hay, RM }	S.79	Western Mediterranean
807 Sqn	Lt N.G.Hallett/Lt V.A.Smith		
	Pty Off(A) A.G.Johnson		
	Lt R.E.Gardner	S.79	Western Mediterranean
	Lt K.Firth }		
	Pty Off(A) R.T.Leggot	Bf 110 damaged	Western Mediterranean
	Lt R.E.Gardner/Pty Off(A) R.Carlisle 2 Ju 87s	Western Mediterranean	
	Sub Lt R.F.Walker	Ju 87 damaged	Western Mediterranean
808 Sqn	Lt E.W.T.Taylour/Pty Off(A) F.A.Barnes	Ju 87	Western Mediterranean
	Lt E.W.T.Taylour/Pty Off(A) F.A.Barnes	Ju 87 damaged	Western Mediterranean
803 Sqn	Lt C.W.R.Peever/Pty Off(A) F.Coston Cant.Z.1007bis	Eastern Mediterranean	
	Sub Lt A.C.Wallace/L/Air T.Dooley Cant.Z.1007bis	Eastern Mediterranean	
806 Sqn	Lt R.MacDonald-Hall/L/Air H.Phillips	He 111	Eastern Mediterranean
	Lt P.S.Touchbourne	He 111	Eastern Mediterranean
803 Sqn	Lt J.M.Bruen/Lt D.J.Godden N1951 He 111	Eastern Mediterranean	
806 Sqn	Lt L.S.Hill		
	Sub Lt G.B.Davie/Pty Off(A) W.T.Chatfield N1870	He 111	Eastern Mediterranean
	Lt R.S.Henley		
	Lt P.D.J.Sparke }	Ju 88	Cap Passero
	Lt R.MacDonald-Hall		
	Lt P.S.Touchbourne }	Ju 88	

British Casualties

808 Sqn	Fulmar Lt R.C.Tillard/Lt M.F.Somerville MiA Western Mediterranean
	Fulmar damaged Lt Cdr J.Sholto Douglas and observer safe Western Mediterranean
	Fulmar damaged Lt G.C.McE.Guthrie and observer safe Western Mediterranean
	Fulmar damaged Lt E.W.T.Taylour safe; Pty Off(A) L.G.T.Howard WiA Western Mediterranean
	Fulmar damaged Pty Off(A) R.E.Dubber and observer safe Western Mediterranean
	Fulmar damaged Lt.E.W.T.Taylour/Pty Off(A) Barnes safe Western Mediterranean
807 Sqn	Fulmar damaged and crash-landed Lt R.E.Gardner/Pty Off(A) R.Carlisle safe Western Mediterranean
	Fulmar damaged Lt N.G.Hallett/Lt V.A.Smith safe Western Mediterranean
803 Sqn	Fulmar Lt C.W.R.Peever/Pty Off(A) F.Coston MiA Eastern Mediterranean
806 Sqn	Fulmar N1870 crashed on return Sub Lt G.B.Davie/Pty Off(A) W.T.Chatfield KiA Eastern Mediterranean FAA
	2 Albacores MiA
39 Sqn	Maryland AH296 Lt A.U.Campbell, SAAF, and crew MiA on ferry flight to Malta
	Maryland AH281 force-landed Methone, Peloponnese, Greece; Plt Off J.W.Best and crew PoW

Italian Claims

153ª Sq/3° Gr CT	Cap Giorgio Tugnoli CR.42	Fulmar	Western Mediterranean
	Ten Massimino Mancini CR.42	Fulmar	Western Mediterranean
154ª Sq/3° Gr CT	Ten Elio Broganelli	Fulmar	Western Mediterranean
	S.Ten Cesare Ciapetti	Fulmar	Western Mediterranean
3° Gr	S.Ten Cesare Ciapetti		
	Serg Angelo Zanaria	Fulmar	Western Mediterranean
	unidentified pilot		
	unit claim	5 Fulmars probable	Western Mediterranean
280ª Sq/130° Gr	S.79 gunners	2 Fulmars	Western Mediterranean

Italian Casualties

280ª Sq/130° Gr	S.79 MM23872 S.Ten Franco Cappa and crew killed
	S.79 Ten Marino Marini and crew rescued
49ª Sq/38° Gr/32° St BT	S.79 Cap Armando Boetto and crew killed
228ª Sq/89° Gr/32° St BT	S.79 S.Ten Michele Fonseca and crew killed
153ª Sq/3° Gr CT	CR.42 MM7203 Serg Giuseppe Zani MiA
153ª Sq/3° Gr CT	CR.42 Ten Massimino Mancini crash-landed

German Claims

9./ZG 26	Oblt Johannes Bergfleth	Hurricane	W Trapani 18.50
	Hptmn Fritz Steinberger	2 Hurricanes	W Trapani 18.53 & 19.01
3./JG 27	Oblt Gerhard Homuth	Blenheim	60m east-north-east Tobruk, 1010

German Casualties

2(F)./123	Ju 88A-5 4U+LK WNr 0643 lost; Konrad Heyde (pilot) safe;Uffz Karl Holst WiA; both rescued
4./StG 3	Ju 87 damaged Lt Alexander Neuber/Gefr Heinz Lepplin WiA 24m west Sicily
6./KG 26	He 111H-5 WNr 3850 1H+AP Obfw Willy Kleinknecht and crew MiA
	He 111H-5 WNr 3887 1H+FP Oblt Hermann Pfeil and crew MiA
4./KG 26	He 111H-5 WNr 3870 1H+BC Oblt Eberhard Stüwe and crew MiA
5./KG 26	He 111H-5 WNr 3885 1H+FN Oblt Max Voigt and crew MiA
9./ZG 26	Bf 110 damaged, crash-landed Comiso Fw Hans Hufnagel and gunner WiA
	Bf 110 damaged, crash-landed Trapani crew safe
	Bf 110 damaged crew safe

Friday. 9 May 1941

By 0800 1st Battle Squadron was 120 miles to the south of Malta, with the Tiger convoy 90 miles to the west. The weather remained uncertain, with many fog patches and visibility less than two miles. By early afternoon the supply convoy from Alexandria had reached the island safely, and at 1515 the convoy and escorting destroyers joined forces with the Battle Squadron some 40 miles off Malta. Axis aircraft searched all day, but the only contact came when Lts Henley and Sparke of 806 Squadron again caught a reconnaissance Ju 88, this time a machine from 1(F)./121, which they attacked and badly damaged; the Junkers crashed on return to Catania and was totally destroyed, although the crew survived. At 1600 one of the searchers at last located the ships, but no attack developed before darkness fell.

British Claims

806 Sqn	Lt R.S.Henley	Ju 88
	Lt P.D.J.Sparke	

German Casualties

1(F)./121	Ju 88 damaged crashed on return to Catania
2(F)./123	Ju 88A-5 WNr 0647 shot down 50m W Malta; Lt Eduard Geissler and crew rescued

Saturday, 10 May 1941

The snoopers were out in force next morning, but in variable visibility they experienced trouble in maintaining contact when sightings were made. Similarly, patrolling Fulmars were unable to achieve any effective interceptions. An He 111 sighted and pursued by Lts MacDonald-Hall and Touchbourne disappeared into the murk before they could get within range. A little later the approach of another hostile caused a scramble to be ordered, but as Lt Touchbourne's N1865 was boosted off by catapult the aircraft crashed over the starboard side, both the pilot and his TAG, L/Air C.H.Thompson, perishing. As a result of this fatal accident the remaining crews were not keen to make use of the booster in spite of assurances from engineers. In an effort to raise morale and restore confidence, the commander (flying), Cdr C.J.N.Atkinson, allowed himself to be boosted off even though he had not flown a Fulmar before.

Not long after this there was warning of enemy aircraft in the area and three sections of Fulmars were ranged for take-off, the booster being used. In the last aircraft was newly-attached Sub Lt Basil Sinclair (ex 805 Squadron) and his TAG, L/Air Freddy de Frias, who recalled:

"I asked him (Sinclair) if we were to be boosted – 'Shouldn't think so I've only got eight hours on Fulmars and I've never done a booster. They'll probably shoot off the others and then we'll do a normal take-off.' I relaxed but was soon shaken when we were waved up to the loading position. Sinclair must have made some frantic signals because he throttled back and the Flight Deck Officer hopped up on to the stub plane. I heard everything through the intercom which Sinclair had left on. 'What's the snag?' (enquired the FDO). 'None except I've never been boosted or even had a briefing' (replied Sinclair) 'No time to argue, there's a gaggle (of enemy aircraft) on that plot. Listen, when you are on the trolley I'll wind you up. Get your straps as tight as you can. Normal take-off flaps and coarse pitch. Let the stick centre itself, put your hand behind it and tuck your elbow into your guts. Open the throttle to full take-off power and tighten up the screw. Then lift your left hand and put your head back against the pad. When you drop your hand I'll give you a moment to put it at the back of the throttle so it won't close, then off you go.' I sat there horrified. In my mind I still had the picture of the Fulmar which had pranged off the booster floating down the starboard side with the TAG strapped in the rear seat, which had come adrift, with his head at an odd angle and obviously dead. The pilot had slumped forward but appeared to be moving a bit. Then it sank as it reached the stern and the planeguard hadn't picked up anything. We were now mounted on the booster carriage and the engine roared. I saw the operator push the lever and felt the usual rush of blood to my face. There was a yell from up front and my hand flew to the canopy-jettison handle. But it was only Sinclair yelling 'It works ! It works !'"

Elsewhere on this date Sgt Glover of 274 Squadron undertook a long-range reconnaissance sortie during which he reported strafing Gazala South airfield. Here he claimed to have shot down a Bf 109 as it was taking off, following which he shot-up four or five more on the ground. Luftwaffe records, while noting his attack, reported that in fact no serious damage was caused.

Meanwhile Blenheim IV T2274 of 14 Squadron, a unit which had just arrived in North Africa from the Sudan, was heading for Derna when intercepted near Sollum by Serg Magg Felice Squassoni of 18° Gruppo in a CR 42. Squassoni attacked, seeing hits, but was only able to claim a probable. However, the bomber had suffered fatal damage and subsequently crash-landed east of Sollum, although Sgt Taylor and his crew survived unhurt. The day also saw the arrival at Sidi Haneish of 1 SAAF Squadron to join 73 and 274 Squadrons.

British Claims				
274 Sqn	Sgt C.Glover	Hurricane I P3469	Bf 109	Gazala South airfield 0730-1040
British Casualties				
806 Sqn	Fulmar N1865 crashed in sea on boosted take-off; Lt E.W.T. Touchbourne/L/Air C.H.Thompson KiFA			
14 Sqn	Blenheim IV T2274 crash-landed near Sollum Flt Sgt J.R.Taylor and crew safe			
German Claims				
Flak unit	Hurricane		nr Gazala	
Italian Claims				
85ª Sq/18° Gr CT	Serg Magg Felice Squassoni		Blenheim probable	near Sollum

Sunday, 11 May 1941

Still bad visibility continued to protect the fleet, and only one further engagement was to occur as the vessels neared Alexandria on 11 May. Once again Lts Henley and Sparke were involved, this intrepid pair attacking a formation of Ju 88s from II. and III./LG 1. Each selected a target, Henley attacking an aircraft from 5.Staffel, his fire wounding the gunner, Ogfr Horst Goldner. Sparke meanwhile closed to very short range on Ofw Otto Engel's L1+IR from 7.Staffel, but either collided with, or was simultaneously shot down by, the bomber, the two aircraft falling together into the sea. Only one parachute was seen by Henley who then failed to locate its occupant in the sea.

According to reports, Lt Cdr Charles 'Crash' Evans, volatile commander of 806 Squadron, demanded that a search be made as sea conditions were very slight and oily calm. He considered that if Julian Sparke or his TAG, L/Air Arthur Rush, had baled out, or if their aircraft had force-landed, there was a very good chance that they would be found. Captain Bisset, however, refused to allow such a search as it was already late in the afternoon, and the dangers inherent in allowing the carrier to slow down while a search was made, required him to put the safety of the ship, its escorts and the convoy first. The morale of the aircrew aboard was badly affected by this ruling.

British Claims			
806 Sqn	Lt R.S.Henley		Ju 88
	Lt P.D.J.Sparke	N1990	Ju 88
	L/Air A.Rush		
British Casualties			
806 Sqn	Fulmar N1990 Lt P.D.J.Sparke/L/Air A.Rush MiA		
German Claims			
2.(H)/14	Fw Herbert Schädlich (pilot)		Hurricane
German Casualties			
5./LG 1	Ju 88A-5 WNr 2209 damaged 50% crash-landed on Crete after combat; gunner Ogfr Horst Goldner WiA		
7./LG 1	Ju 88A-5 WNr 2296 L1+IR collision with Fulmar during combat; Obfw Otto Engel and crew MiA		

Monday, 12 May 1941

Late in the morning Tiger convoy and the 1st Battle Squadron steamed into Alexandria, carrying 238 tanks and 43 Hurricanes for Wavell's forces. Ten of the fighters would be flown to Crete during the following week for issue to 33 and 112 Squadrons.

The relatively heavy attrition suffered by the Fulmars during this operation left only a few serviceable aboard the carriers, and until others could be rendered so, *Formidable* would be unable to put to sea to escort warships and convoys between Egypt and Crete. On arrival in port Charles Evans was rested from his spell as commanding officer of 806 Squadron, this unit being taken over by Lt Cdr J.N.Garnett, a former Swordfish pilot with 830 Squadron on Malta, who had recently commanded the Sea Gladiator Flight aboard HMS *Eagle*.

1 SAAF Squadron undertook its first offensive action in North Africa, making a strafing attack. Lt Uys force-landed during this sortie due to lack of fuel. 274 Squadron, however, suffered a more serious loss when Flg Off English failed to return from an afternoon sortie; Italian sources claimed that two Hurricanes had been shot down by anti-aircraft fire near Sollum.

British Casualties	
1 SAAF Sqn	Hurricane I Lt D.C. Uys force-landed due to fuel shortage
274 Sqn	Hurricane I Flg Off K.P.English KiA
German Casualties	
St.Fl.Ber.X.Fl.	Ju 52/3m in combat with fighter; one man killed, Benghazi area

Thursday, 15 May 1941

Although it would still be some time before the first of the tanks and aircraft to be off-loaded from the Tiger vessels could be pressed into service, the British command concluded that Axis strength in the forward area was not great. The small number of tanks available were gathered to allow the first British offensive against the Germans in Africa to be launched under the code-name Brevity. The aim was limited to recovering Sollum and Capuzzo as a 'jumping-off' area for a larger action once the Tiger supplies were to hand.

Thus it was that on 15 May 7th Armoured Division with 24 new I tanks (Matildas) and 29 cruiser tanks, 7th Support Group and 22nd Guards Brigade, commenced an advance towards the top of the escarpment at Halfaya Pass, on Bir Waer, Musaid and Capuzzo, and from Bir Hafid towards Sidi Aziez. They were supported by Hurricanes of 73, 274 and 1 SAAF Squadrons, and by Blenheims of 14, 45 and 55 Squadrons, the two latter units both having recently added a few Blenheim IVf aircraft modified to carry a forward-firing 20mm cannon for ground strafing. However, the operation was doomed to immediate failure.

The advancing troops quickly captured the Halfaya Pass, and the fortresses of Capuzzo and Sollum, while the fighters patrolled overhead. 274 Squadron, covering the line Sofafi-Halfaya-Sidi Aziez, reported meeting Luftwaffe bombers with fighter escort, Flt Lt Dudley Honor claiming one Bf 109 shot down and shared and damage to three more; Flt Sgt Dean failed to return, shot down by Oblt Homuth of I./JG 27.

During the day the British armour reached a point 20 miles south-west of Bardia, when Rommel launched a counter-attack with forces from the 5th Light and 15th Panzer Divisions. The armoured strength of these forces proved to be unexpectedly strong, and the British troops were driven back next day, losing all their gains with the exception of the Halfaya Pass. Brevity had been – brief!

British Claims

274 Sqn	Flt Lt D.S.G.Honor	Hurricane I W9269	Bf 109	Tobruk area 1000-1220
	Flt Lt D.S.G.Honor	Hurricane I W9269		Tobruk area 1000-1220
	Plt Off P.L.V.Hutt	Hurricane I	3 Bf 109s damaged	Tobruk area 1000-1220
208 Sqn	Flg Off R.J.Hardiman	Hurricane I V7710	Hs 126 damaged	nr Sollum 1300

British Casualties

274 Sqn	Hurricane I V7827 Flt Sgt F.H.Dean			

German Claims

3./JG 27	Oblt Gerhard Homuth	Hurricane	Sollum 1215

Friday, 16 May 1941

All RAF units were kept extremely busy ground-strafing in support of the retreating British forces. Hurricanes of 274 Squadron undertook strafing sorties, and during an early operation two were intercepted over Gambut by Bf 109s, Flg Off Agazarian, the Battle of Britain veteran, being shot down while Flg Off Clostre failed to return. Sgt Glover spotted a Bf 109 south of Gambut and claimed to have shot this down in flames. Only one claim was submitted by Fw Elles of 2./JG 27, so it would appear that one of the British fighters probably fell to ground fire.

At much the same time Lt Talbot and Lt Uys of 1 SAAF Squadron encountered a lone Ju 87 over El Adem, which Talbot claimed to have shot down. During a later strafing sortie, Lt Burger of this unit crash-landed after his Hurricane sustained damage from ground fire. Capt M.Quirk at once landed alongside and flew Burger back to base in the cockpit of his aircraft. He was later awarded a DSO for this exploit.

In the afternoon two of 45 Squadron's strafer Blenheims were attacked by a trio of Bf 109s when engaged in strafing vehicles on the Tobruk-Bardia road, Flt Lt Haines' aircraft being shot down by Oblt Redlich of 1./JG 27. A Blenheim was also claimed by Serg Mario Lingua of 95ª Squadriglia, 18° Gruppo CT, but near Benghazi, and no such further loss has been found. (Squadron records noted that this had been Haines' 76th operational sortie.)

British Claims

1 SAAF Sqn	Lt R.H.Talbot	Hurricane I	Ju 87	Bir Bellafan, W El Adem 0930
274 Sqn	Sgt C.Glover	Hurricane I P3469	Bf 109	S Gambut 1520-1800

British Casualties

274 Sqn	Hurricane I Flg Off N. le C.Agazarian KiA			
	Hurricane I Flg Off D.H.J.Clostre KiA			
1 SAAF	Hurricane I V7862 Lt H.J.P.Burger crash-landed, AA fire			
45 Sqn	Blenheim IV V5817 shot down into sea off Tobruk by three Bf 109s; Flt Lt A.C.Haines and Sgt S.Cordy KiA;			
	Observer baled out and rescued			

German Claims

2./JG 27	Fw Franz Elles	Hurricane	Tobruk 0937
1./JG 27	Oblt Wolfgang Redlich	Blenheim	1655

Italian Claims

95ª Sq/18° Gr CT	Serg Magg Mario Lingua	Blenheim	5m off coast at Benghazi

In London, meanwhile, by 18 May Longmore was finding that the results of the conferences and discussions he had attended seemed to have given promise of a goodly supply of aircraft and equipment to the Middle East, and he prepared to return to Cairo. Passage was arranged for him to fly to Takoradi to take the overland route from there. Next day, however, he was informed by Sir Archibald Sinclair, secretary of state for air, that he was not to go, and that Tedder was to be appointed in his place.

Poor, baffled Longmore was obviously desperately hurt. In his memoirs he simply records: "My personal feeling are better left to the imagination. It seemed that the change had already been planned when the signal recalling me to England for consultations had been sent. I received my GCB from His Majesty and retired to the obscurity of my home at Grantham to await the next throw of the dice whilst the situation in Crete went from bad to worse." At least he was not 'put out to grass', for at the end of May he was offered the post of inspector-general of the RAF. There is little doubt that the acerbic nature of some of his signals had upset a number of influential people, but one is left with a deep feeling of distaste at the dishonourable and unkind manner in which this gallant commander, who had served his country so well under such adverse conditions, had been treated – by Churchill as much as anyone.

Tedder records that Longmore had sent a particularly vituperative signal, which he admitted the latter had "slipped past" him, and which had he known, he would have prevented him sending.

"I hoped it did not mean that the prime minister had lost his temper with Longmore and proposed to send someone else to relieve him.

Longmore departed for London before lunch on 3 May. I felt very sorry for him, for I had come to like him and to appreciate his steadiness, honesty, decency and thoughtfulness for others. As he climbed into his aircraft, his grip on my elbow and his 'Good luck, Ted' were almost affectionate. I wondered whether he would be back. I had a feeling he would not."

And so Tedder became the overall air commander in the area – a post he was to hold for the rest of the African war as the Allied air forces there grew and grew in strength. Bing Cross recorded:

"Tedder had many problems to solve when he succeeded Longmore as AOC-in-C, not least of which the fact that his aircraft were numerically and qualitatively much inferior to those of the enemy. In this situation both the Navy and the Army suffered at the hands of the Regia Aeronautica and the Luftwaffe and loud and often were the complaints. In addition to his command responsibilities, Tedder also had the task of 'educating' his fellow C-in-Cs in the ways of air warfare. His philosophy that the presence of the Air was essential in making combined operations effective, found a ready recipient in Auchinleck but less so in Admiral Cunningham; as the commander of the historic Mediterranean Fleet, he valued his individual freedom of action. Quite often from my camp at Alexandria, situated a mile or so from the Great Pass, the entrance channel to the harbour, we would see this massive fleet of destroyers, cruisers, aircraft carriers and battleships silently putting to sea, mostly at dusk. In my 'scrambler' telephone conversation with Middle East Air Headquarters in Cairo, I used to mention that I had observed this Fleet movement and was surprised that Tedder knew nothing of it! Needless to say with the arrival of the Luftwaffe in Greece and Sicily, the Mediterranean Fleet got some awful shocks and despite the triumphs of Taranto and Matapan the Luftwaffe closed the Gibraltar-Suez route for two whole years from 21 May 1941 until May 1943. Tedder's inability through lack of resources to cope with the Luftwaffe was not appreciated by Admiral Cunningham and complaints continued, but nevertheless as modern aircraft reached the command and our operations increased, Tedder did succeed in gaining the confidence of both the Navy and the Army. Later when the Americans entered the war and Tedder was appointed Air C-in-C under Eisenhower, he was to display a mastery of all aspects of air warfare.

"He was always a welcome visitor to the squadrons and the aircrew, and his informal talks on the wider aspects of the war were greatly appreciated by those actually doing the fighting. Tedder never sought popularity from those he commanded but he always had their universal respect."

As Longmore had hoped, prior to his dismissal, yet more reinforcements were arriving from a variety of locations at this time. From Australia came the personnel of 450 and 451 RAAF Squadrons, the former reaching Abu Sueir and the latter Aboukir, both on 12 May. It was the intention that both these units should be equipped with Hurricanes, 451 to undertake an army co-operation role. In the event only this latter unit was to be ready for operational duties in the shorter term, and it would be the rest of the year before 450 became available.

———

The resident RAAF unit in the Middle East, 3 RAAF Squadron, had passed its remaining Hurricanes to 274 Squadron on 20 April and withdrawn to Aboukir where it was to follow the newly-formed 250 Squadron in receiving Tomahawks. In the event it took the Australians longer than expected to become fully converted to their new fighters, and not until the start of June would they be ready to resume operations.

Following the despatch of the Tiger convoy, efforts were then concentrated on getting a number of further Hurricane units from the UK to Malta and North Africa as quickly as possible. This entailed launching them from aircraft carriers to Malta in the first instance. Code-named Splice, the first such operation occurred on 21 May, when the carriers HMS *Ark Royal* and *Furious* sent off 48 Hurricanes forming the air parties of 213 and 249 Squadrons, and part of 229 Squadron (six aircraft). All but two reached the island safely, from where the aircraft of 213 and 229 Squadrons were led in flights to Egypt by four Beaufighters of 252 Squadron. One section of seven 213 Squadron aircraft lost their Beaufighter and returned to Malta, but were to complete the flight safely two days later. 249 Squadron remained as part of the island's defences, allowing the very tired pilots of the resident 261 Squadron to fly out to Egypt also, taking with them some very worn Hurricanes.

The two carriers returned on 6 June (Operation Rocket) to fly off 44 more Hurricanes, all but one of which arrived. These were from 46 Squadron which was to stay on the island, and the rest of 229 Squadron which had remained at Gibraltar pending transport since the Splice operation. The pilots of the latter unit were less than impressed when their brand new Hurricane IIbs were retained by the defenders and they were obliged to fly on to Africa in older Mark Is which the resident units gladly released. Once again those flying on were led by Beaufighters, two undertaking this navigational role on this occasion.

Eight days later on 14 June Operation Tracer brought *Ark Royal* towards Malta again, this time to launch 20 Hurricanes of 260 Squadron; on this occasion she was accompanied by the new armoured carrier HMS *Victorious*, which sent off 28 more aircraft of 238 Squadron; 45 of the 48 launched were to make it, although not all safely. To lead the fighters onward on this occasion four Lockheed Hudson maritime patrol bombers of 200 Squadron from Gibraltar joined the convoy, each leading 12 of the Hurricanes.

One Hurricane failed to take off; one suffered engine trouble en route and was last seen heading for the African coast; one crashed into the sea; one overshot the runway on arrival and crash-landed, and one spun-in on arrival, Sgt R.MacPherson, the 260 Squadron pilot, being killed in the crash; 43 landed safely. Following this flight, a signal from HQ, RAF Middle East, to air ministry in London, stated:

"Report that four Hudsons escorting Hurricanes were flown by completely inexperienced crews who were unable to look after themselves much less escort 12 Hurricanes. Some of these crews were apparently on their first flight ex-OTU. Three out of four Hurricanes lost due entirely to faulty navigation by one Hudson. The squadron commanders (of 238 and 260 Squadrons) further state that Admiral Somerville was with difficulty dissuaded from sending off all aircraft at night despite the fact that Hurricane pilots had not operated from carrier before, even by day. Consider it fortunate under circumstances that only four Hurricanes lost."

The Hudson mentioned in this signal had first flown 60 miles north of Malta, then south, missing the island by ten miles. The pilot then asked for a course when 70 miles away south-east. On being given a course, he still flew for 15 minutes on a reciprocal bearing until given direct orders over the R/T in clear to turn about. The Hudson pilot was put under arrest on arrival on the island.

Meanwhile, Fulmars, rescue boats and Hurricanes from the resident 249 Squadron were sent out to search for the missing pilots, Flt Lt T.F. 'Ginger' Neil finding 238 Squadron's Sgt Campbell in the sea 40 miles from Kalafrana, where he was safely picked up, as was Sgt A.D.Saunders of 260 Squadron, the other missing pilot.

The pilots of the two squadrons were soon on their way to Africa, 21 undertaking the seven-hour flight to LG.07 on the 15th, eight next day and five the day after. The remainder stayed behind as reinforcements for the island's defenders. Two further deliveries were to follow later in June as Operations Tracer I and Tracer II, but the 64 Hurricanes flown off were all retained by Malta.

The problem facing the four new squadrons which had now reached Egypt was that in all cases the arrivals represented only the air parties – pilots and aircraft. The core of each squadron – ground crews, administration, medical officer, etc – were all despatched by sea via the Cape, and it would be several weeks at least before any of them arrived. Consequently, these units were unable to operate as individual entities until that time, and effectively for the time being were little more than a pool of temporary reinforcements for the existing squadrons. 213, 229 and 238 Squadrons had all played important parts in the defence of the United Kingdom during 1940, and all still retained a number of experienced pilots, several of whom would enjoy considerable success in the Middle East. However, the circumstances of their arrival prevented them being able to make best use of their skills initially.

These three squadrons had all been involved both in the fighting over France during May-June 1940, and then in the Battle of Britain. Commanding officers were:

213 Squadron	Sqn Ldr D.S.MacDonald, DFC
229 Squadron	Sqn Ldr F.E.Rosier
238 Squadron	Sqn Ldr H.A.Fenton

Amongst the more experienced and battle-hardened members of these units, who already had some substantial degree of success in aerial combat, were:

213 Squadron	Flg Off D.L.Gould and Plt Off G.H.Westlake.
229 Squadron	Plt Offs R.E.Bary, D.F.K.Edghill and W.A.Smith.
238 Squadron	Flt Lt E.J.Morris and Plt Off J.R.Urwin-Mann, DFC.

There was, however, an interesting aside connected with certain pilots in 238 Squadron which is worthy of note. During 1940 one of the flight commanders had been Flt Lt John Anthony O'Neill, DFC, previously a bomber pilot with 58 Squadron. He was posted in mid-December to command 601 Squadron. During 1941 O'Neill, DFC, was shown in 238 Squadron's operations record book first as a Flg Off and then as a Flt Lt, before becoming commanding officer during September. Identification was not helped by the squadron being one of those where no initials were recorded for pilots and others.

As a result, J.A.O'Neill has for long been identified as being both officers. In fact, shortly before the departure of 238 Squadron for the Middle East, J.A.'s elder brother had been posted to the unit as a Flg Off, having previously served as a Coastal Command pilot with 224 Squadron. Even more confusingly, both brothers had been awarded DFCs on the same date – 30 July 1940. However, it can now be confirmed that the O'Neill with 238 Squadron in 1941 was not J.A.'Peggy' O'Neill, who later served as a night fighter in India, but Hugh Francis O'Neill.

The fourth unit, 260 Squadron, had not yet seen any action, but was led by Sqn Ldr C.J.Mount, DFC, who did enjoy experience of action with another unit, as did ex-Spitfire pilot Plt Off O.V.Hanbury.

In the event it was to be 260 Squadron, the least experienced, which was the first to have the opportunity to operate as an individual unit in North Africa when it was paired with the ground party of 450 Squadron, RAAF, which at the time had no air party. As 260/450 Squadron the unit was to see action during the latter part of the operations which took place over Syria during June and July. (See *Dust Clouds in the Middle East*.)

It should also be mentioned that every squadron flying Hurricanes in the Middle East at this time were equipped with the Mark I version of the aircraft. This was at a time when Fighter Command in the UK was operating Mark II Hurricanes which were already considered to be outclassed by the opposition, and which were rapidly being phased out in favour of the Spitfire II and V. On Malta too, the Mark II was the predominant type in use.

At this time however, 201 Group, which still had received but few reinforcements, was bolstered by some welcome, if unusual, additions to its establishment. As described in *Air War for Yugoslavia, Greece and Crete, 1940-41*, eight Dornier Do 22s, a Sim XIV and an elderly Heinkel He 8 – all floatplanes of the Yugoslav Naval Air Arm's 1, 2 and 3 Hidroplanska Komanda – had reached Crete following the fall of their nation to German invasion, and these had subsequently made their way to Egypt where they were available with their crews for anti-submarine operations. They had been followed by five Avro Ansons of the Greek 13 Mira, which also formed a flight for similar purposes. Indeed, by the midsummer these two small units would have become 2 (Yugoslav) and 13 (Hellenic) Squadrons.

Sunday, 18 May 1941
Two Blenheims of 45 Squadron took off from LG.17 (Fuka Main) at 0400, briefed to attack the airfield at Derna. Heavy ground fire was experienced, causing the two aircraft to separate, one failing to return. Italian records indicate that the pilot of a Bf 110 claimed to have shot down a Wellington over Derna on this date,

and given the hour at which the British aircraft had departed, he may well have mis-identified his victim.

British Claims				
274 Sqn	Plt Off Hamilton	Hurricane I P3469	Bf 109	damaged on ground E El Adem
British Casualties				
45 Sqn	Blenheim IV T2056 MiA near Derna; Flg Off J.Beveridge and two KiA			
German Claims				
Unspecified Bf 110 unit and pilot		Wellington		Derna

Monday, 19 May 1941

Five Blenheims were despatched by 45 Squadron to attack motor transport, but one aircraft was seen to crash and burst into flames. The crew was lost, including the pilot Plt Off G.H.Reuter, a Belgian operating under the 'nom de guerre' D.Carter, who was on his first operational sortie with the unit.

Even at this late stage, 6 Squadron was still undertaking some reconnaissances in its remaining Lysanders. On this date Flg Off McFall landed by some forward troops to discuss the situation, then taking up the brigade major to observe this for himself.

British Casualties	
45 Sqn	Blenheim IV T2179 crashed near Capuzzo; Plt Off G.H.Reuter and one KiA; one PoW

Tuesday, 20 May 1941

An S.79 of 19ª Squadriglia, 28° Gruppo, 8° Stormo BT, flown by Serg Magg Giulio Calzolari, crashed into the sea, killing all aboard – reason unknown. The day was also marked by the disbandment of 53° Gruppo and its two squadriglie, 216ª and 217ª.

Two S.79s from 281ª Squadriglia AS, flown by Magg Vittorio Cannaviello and Magg Guglielmo Di Luise, attacked the Royal Navy's Force D with torpedoes, claiming a hit on a cruiser.

While strafing Mechili during the afternoon, Flt Lt Honor claimed to have shot down a Bf 110 which had just taken off, and to have destroyed a Ju 52/3m on the ground. However, when two of this squadron's pilots later took off in a Magister to fly back to the rear areas, they disappeared and were never traced.

Flying a patrol to the north of Crete, the commanding officer of 39 Squadron, Wg Cdr A.McD.Bowman, DFC, and his crew encountered a single Ju 52/3m heading for the island which they shot down into the sea.

Whilst flying from Sidi Haneish to Sidi Barrani in the 274 Squadron Miles Magister liaison aircraft, Flt Lt Ross and Plt Off Hutt failed to arrive at their destination. This occasioned a quite widespread search next day in which Lysanders joined the squadron's Hurricanes, but no signs of the missing pair or their aircraft were ever found.

British Claims				
274 Sqn	Flt Lt D.S.G.Honor	Hurricane I P3469	Bf 110	S Gambut 1520-1800
39 Sqn	Wg Cdr A.McD. Bowman	Maryland	Ju 52/3m	
British Casualties				
274 Sqn	Magister MiA; Flt Lt A.M.Ross and Plt Off P.L.V.Hutt MiA			
German Casualties				
KGrzbV 40	Ju 52/3m 9P+FK shot down into sea by Maryland; Fw Alfred Timme and crew KiA			
Italian Casualties				
19ª Sq/28° Gr/8° St	S.79MM 21841 Serg Magg Giulio Calzolari and crew KiA			

Wednesday, 21 May 1941

The morning again began with a series of strafing attacks, Hurricanes of 73, 274 and 1 SAAF Squadrons all shooting up MT columns on the Trigh [road] Capuzzo. Large numbers were claimed destroyed, including one ammunition lorry, which blew up violently. French pilots Sous Lt Denis and Plt Off Pompei encountered six Bf 109s while so engaged, Denis claiming one shot down in flames, although Pompei failed to return; although no claim was submitted by any of I./JG 27's pilots. Denis's victim appears to have been Obfhr Marseille of 3.Staffel, who crash-landed in the Tobruk area following combat with fighters. He survived unhurt, his aircraft suffering 40% damage.

———

Other aircraft of 3./JG 27 were certainly in evidence, however, for at much the same time Blenheims of 14 Squadron, which had moved to LG.2 (Qotaifiya III) from Heliopolis at the start of the month, appeared in the area. Two of these followed the Hurricanes in strafing MT, but five others had been sent off individually in swift succession for similar attacks along the Tobruk-Capuzzo road, and these ran into Messerschmitts from this same unit which shot them all down in a period of less than ten minutes, Oblt Gerhard Homuth and Obfw Herbert Kowalski claiming two apiece; not one member of any of the crews survived.

Also during the morning, five Cant.Z.1007s from 50° Gruppo Autonomo BT, led by Ten Mario Morassutti, bombed Force D, reportedly hitting and sinking the destroyer HMS *Juno*.

No news was received regarding Pompei's fate for a month, but on 20 June he would be reported alive at Liva, having covered 300 miles from the spot where his Hurricane had gone down. Subsequently, he wrote:

"I tried to make for the coast with three Jerries on my tail, with a badly crippled plane. By the time I reached the coast at 2,000 feet the engine packed up completely and I crash-landed, wheels up, on a piece of flat rock. I managed to get out and began limping in an easterly direction, when some Arabs called to me. They were armed, and I thought it prudent to stop. They asked 'Italiano ?', and I shook my head. 'Germani ?' 'No.' 'Ingress ?' 'Yes'. This pleased them no end, and they carried me to their tent a few hundred yards away where they dug out of my leg some sixty pieces of shell splinters, using a needle which was normally used for sewing their tents.

"I stayed with them for about three weeks, and there was never any attempt to give me away – they hated the Italians, and took potshots at them whenever they felt they could get away with it. Eventually a caravan of camels passed through going east, and they took the opportunity to send me along. On the journey we passed within 200 yards of a German patrol which was clearly visible in the moonlight. The caravan left me at a vault in the desert while an old shepherd took a message to our lines, travelling some 90 miles in two days. He met up with a British armoured car which took him to an intelligence officer, and a motorised patrol was sent out to collect me. Needless to say, I had long been given up for dead."

British Claims

73 Sqn	Sous Lt J.Denis	V7859	Bf 109	in flames Tobruk-Capuzzo road 0615-0850

British Casualties

73 Sqn	Hurricane I V7813 Plt Off J.Pompei MiA; returned on foot 20 June 1941
14 Sqn	Blenheim IV T2173 shot down Tobruk-Capuzzo road area; Plt Off R.Johnson and crew KiA
	Blenheim IV Z5979 shot down Tobruk-Capuzzo road area; Sgt N.Hoskins and crew KiA
	Blenheim IV T2346 shot down Tobruk-Capuzzo road area; Sgt J.Taylor and crew KiA
	Blenheim IV L8874 shot down Tobruk-Capuzzo road area; Sgt J.F.Matetich and crew KiA
	Blenheim IV V5511 shot down Tobruk-Capuzzo road area; Plt Off R.Gilmour and crew KiA
6 Sqn	Hurricane I Plt Off R.A.Griffith killed in landing accident, Burg el Arab

German Claims

3./JG 27	Obfw Herbert Kowalski	Blenheim	SE Fort Capuzzo 0750
	Lt Heinz Schmidt	Blenheim	SE Fort Capuzzo 0756
	Oblt Gerhard Homuth	Blenheim	SE Fort Capuzzo 0757
	Obfw Herbert Kowalski	Blenheim	SE Fort Capuzzo 0757
	Oblt Gerhard Homuth	Blenheim	SE Fort Capuzzo 0758

German Casualties

3./JG 27	Bf 109E-4 WNr 1567 Obfhr Hans-Joachim Marseille crash-landed Tobruk area after combat with fighter; aircraft 40% damaged

Thursday, 22 May 1941

1 SAAF Squadron was ordered to send all available aircraft to Sidi Barrani East to undertake standing patrols over the gunboat HMS *Aphis* which was shelling targets along the coast, and to cover a number of small steamers sailing between here and Tobruk. Unfortunately, only three Hurricanes were available,

but these went forward to do the best they could. During the early afternoon, Lt A.J.Botha was flying out to take over one such patrol when he saw: "ahead of him, six or seven Ju 87s flying in echelon starboard in a westerly direction. As soon as they saw him they broke formation and dived towards the sea. Botha attacked the nearest…the dive-bomber went down steeply, crashing into the sea. Botha had lost considerable height and found himself below another…he delivered a belly attack and the aircraft burst into flames. The remaining Stukas made off without molesting the gunboat."

An Italian claim was made for a Blenheim over Benghazi during the morning, but no British loss was recorded.

British Claims			
1 SAAF Sqn	Lt A.J.Botha	2 Ju 87s	20m N Sidi Barrani 1425
German Casualties			
1./JG 27	Bf 109E-1 WNr 3588 60% damage due to engine failure, Sollum		
StG 2	Ju 87 WNr 6098 T6+GS shot down; Kohls Kitzrow MiA		
Italian Claims			
95ª Sq/18° Gr CT	M.llo Cesare Accomazzo	Blenheim	Benghazi 1035

CHAPTER 7

CRETAN DIVERSION

Friday, 23 May 1941
On Crete at this time the German invasion which had been launched on 15 May was beginning to get established and the first unit of Bf 109E fighters, III./JG 77 was in the process of moving to the island where Maleme airfield was now considered secure enough for such a move. Churchill pressed Wavell to send any aid that could be spared, and in particular 204 Group was requested to provide all the help possible to supplement the efforts already being made by night by the Egyptian-based Wellington bomber units (see Chapter 12 – The RAF's Night Bombing Offensive for their activities).

A word of explanation here. A full account of air and naval operations associated with the German invasion of Crete is given in *Air War for Yugoslavia, Greece and Crete, 1940-41* in this series. To maintain the 'flow' of the narrative relating to the units of 204 Group and of the Wellington squadrons in Egypt, details of the operations of these units over Crete are repeated here. However, all actions performed by units not a part of these two elements, and of the aircraft carrier-borne squadrons of the Fleet Air Arm have not been included.

AVM Collishaw had little enough available, but the Blenheim squadrons and Grp Capt Spackman's 258 (Fighter) Wing were ordered to do all that they could. Initially, 14 Squadron prepared five Blenheims to raid Maleme, accompanied by three Hurricanes from 274 Squadron, fitted with long-range tanks. As the formation set off, the lead Blenheim was forced to turn back due to a technical fault, and in consequence the operation was called off.

From Sidi Haneish airfield 73 Squadron was ordered to despatch six Hurricanes to land at Heraklion, from where they were to operate against the unescorted transport aircraft flying in to Maleme, and to strafe the troops there and those around Heraklion. At departure time, 1135, a Blenheim arrived to undertake the navigating, the formation setting out over the sea, Flg Off G.E.Goodman leading the fighters. Two hours later five Hurricanes returned; Goodman reported that they had flown over a number of British naval vessels which had put up such a tremendous barrage that the formation had been scattered. He feared that the Blenheim and one of the Hurricanes – V7424 flown by Sgt Bob Laing, a Tasmanian in the RNZAF – might have been shot down into the sea. In the circumstances, he had decided to return with the surviving aircraft of his flight.

At 1300, meanwhile, seven of 24 SAAF Squadron's new Marylands set off, and although two had to return early, the other five bombed and strafed the mass of transport aircraft on and around Maleme airfield. They were followed by four Blenheims of 45 Squadron which also bombed, although one was intercepted and shot down, probably by Lt Gunther Hannak from the southern Greece-based 2.(J)/LG 2 in a Bf 109E. Finally, two Beaufighters of 252 Squadron – the only aircraft of this type available – strafed, Sqn Ldr Yaxley and Sub Lt Fraser claiming four Ju 52/3ms destroyed. Indeed, the total result of these three attacks was believed to have been ten of these transports written off; Luftwaffe records confirm a total of six, mainly from KGrzbV 106 and I./LLG 1.

73 Squadron was ordered to try once more, and at 1520 the same five pilots, plus one replacement, set off again, led this time by a 24 SAAF Squadron Maryland. Soon after their departure the 'missing' Blenheim appeared and landed at Sidi Haneish, the pilot reporting that after becoming separated during the barrage, he met up with Sgt Laing's Hurricane, and that the pair had continued towards Crete, where he presumed Laing had landed at Heraklion. And indeed he had, as he later recalled:

———

"Having passed over the bleak-looking slopes of the mountain range I soon sighted the crossed runways of Heraklion, close by the township of Canea. Having circled the landing strip I noticed some good-sized bomb craters in the runway but as the place seemed deserted I decided to land. I made a good landing, running down to the south-east towards the beach. The propeller clanked to a standstill and there was not a sound, which to say the least was most eerie ! I stepped out of the aircraft and decided to walk to the nearest building, a stone hut some 300 yards away. Having gone a few yards a machine-gun opened up on the aircraft and myself, with some degree of accuracy, and I realised I was not alone. To return to the Hurricane would have been of little use as it was merely a sitting duck and I decided to run for it. Bullets began to whistle round and I dived for a small depression in the ground, which gave me a little cover. I remained there lying with my head towards the direction of the machine-gunfire to make a smaller target; also my dark blue tunic against the runway was quite fair camouflage. They gave the Hurricane and myself the works for quite a time and I tried to pluck up courage to make a bolt for it – luckily my mind was made up for me by the approach of a British Matilda tank, which rumbled up and shielded me from the fire of the machine-gun. The tank commander, and Army major, lifted up the trap door of the tank, greeted me with a smile and apologised for the reception I had got. Having exchanged views on the situation and the Bosch in particular, he suggested I taxi the aircraft down to the revetment area, about half a mile down the runway, where I would find some shelter. Apparently he wanted to save the aircraft, as in those days pilots were more easily replaced than aircraft. Fortunately the engine was not damaged and I was able to taxi down at high speed, helped along with bursts of fire from the Bosch machine-guns, who were very active at this time."

Within half an hour six Bf 110s arrived and commenced strafing the gun positions. The Hurricane was soon sighted and was reduced to a blazing wreck. Bob Laing sheltered with others as the airfield was constantly bombed and strafed, and he adds: "We could do nothing about it, except the Aussie-manned guns accounted for several aircraft but at a very high cost to themselves. Without my plane I was a mere spectator of the operation in progress, and one experienced a terrible feeling of frustration to witness Heraklion being reduced to a shambles."

Just about dusk in the midst of yet another raid by about a dozen Ju 88s, 73 Squadron's six Hurricanes arrived. Despite being low on fuel, the fighters attempted to intercept, both Flg Off Goodman and Plt Off J.H.Ward claiming damage to bombers during a brief skirmish as they pursued them over Canea and out to sea, before being obliged to break away and head back to Heraklion. The airfield had been pitted with craters, two Hurricanes suffering broken tailwheels as a result. The airfield was still under small-arms fire from paratroops positioned on a ridge and behind rocks on the perimeter, and as the pilots headed for shelter, they had constantly to throw themselves flat for cover. Two Hurricanes were rapidly refuelled and were sent up to patrol until dusk, but nothing more was seen. After a hurried consultation with the OC Land Forces, Goodman learned that there was no stock of .303in ammunition for the Hurricanes and only limited fuel available. It was decided that as the Hurricanes could offer little assistance they should return to Egypt in the morning.

British Claims				
73 Sqn	Flg Off G.E.Goodman	W9198	Ju 88 damaged	
	Plt Off J.H.Ward	V7816	Ju 88 damaged	
British Casualties				
45 Sqn	Blenheim IV V5624 shot down over Maleme; Plt Off P.J.Vincent and crew KiA			
73 Sqn	Hurricane I V7424 destroyed on the ground by strafing Bf 110s			
German Claims				
2.(J)/ LG 2	Lt Gunther Hannak	Blenheim	S Maleme	
9./JG 77	Obfw Georg Bergmann	Blenheim	S Maleme 15.00	
German Casualties				
KGrzbV 106	} 6 Ju 52/3ms destroyed on the ground by RAF attack			
I./LLG 1				

Saturday, 24 May 1941

Following a night's desultory sleep for the pilots, the six Hurricanes prepared to depart, Laing and Goodman squeezing into the cockpit of W9198, Goodman using his companion's knees as a seat, the parachute pack having been discarded and stowed into the fuselage. Before heading for Egypt all pilots were to use up their remaining ammunition by strafing enemy positions around the airfield, which they did. Bob Laing continues:

> "Our journey back across the Mediterranean was uneventful from an enemy point of view but we struck a head wind during the last 100 miles and with petrol low, we were feeling anything but comfortable. We finally landed at Sidi Haneish in a sandstorm with our petrol gauges registering zero. Surely Allah had been with us and my only complaint was that I was so stiff and numbed after sitting for three hours in a cramped cockpit and used as a cushion for the pilot. However, I gave the flight commander a big hand and said 'Thanks Benny – a lot.'"

Goodman and Laing were the first to arrive, landing at 0830, but were followed by Plt Off Ward; no others returned to base. It was later learned that Flg Off R.F.Donati had run out of fuel and force-landed V7802 at Fuka, Plt Off Frank Moss coming down just inside Ras el Kanayis with V7879 also out of fuel. Of the other two – Plt Off Bob Goord (V7736) and Plt Off Bob Likeman (V7764) – nothing was ever heard. It was assumed that both had come down in the water, the severe sandstorm over the coast and out to sea probably contributing to their loss.

Earlier on this date two destroyers, HMS *Jaguar* and *Defender*, had departed Suda Bay, Crete, carrying a number of naval personnel no longer required on the island. These included a Fleet Air Arm contingent commanded by Lt L.K.Keith and Sub Lt R.V.Hinton of the land-based 805 Squadron, which would now begin to reform in Egypt.

British Casualties

73 Sqn	Hurricane I V7736 lost on flight between Crete and N Africa; Plt Off R.L.Goord MiA
	Hurricane I V7764 lost on flight between Crete and N Africa; Plt Off R.H.Likeman MiA

Sunday, 25 May 1941

During the day, however, 204 Group's involvement was much increased. Already during the night 37 Squadron Wellingtons had again set out to raid Maleme, when at dawn four Marylands of 24 SAAF Squadron appeared overhead, bombing and machine-gunning the airfield and surrounding troop positions. They were followed by six 14 Squadron Blenheims, led by Sqn Ldr D.C.Stapleton, the crews of which saw a number of Ju 52/3ms already on fire as a result of the South African attack, and added their light bombs to the carnage. An estimated 24 aircraft were considered to have been destroyed or badly damaged, although many of those hit were almost certainly already wrecked. One Blenheim was slightly damaged by Flak splinters in return, the gunner of this aircraft being wounded in one foot.

At Gerawla 274 Squadron had by now received four Hurricanes fitted with long-range tanks. The pilots were not happy, however, for not only did the tanks slow the Hurricanes down and make them less manoeuvrable, but also the armour plating behind the seats had to be removed and ammunition reduced to compensate for the weight of the extra fuel. One commented:

> "The additional tanks gave the Hurricane a range of 900 miles compared with the normal range of 600 miles. There were two additional tanks – one port, one starboard. The port tank emptied first, then the starboard tank. Air locks were liable to develop owing to bad refuelling or severe bumps in the air and throw the system out of commission. You never knew when the port tank emptied if the starboard tank was going to feed through. If your starboard tank refused to work over the sea, that was the end."

Nonetheless, the four Hurricanes prepared to leave for Maleme at 0530 accompanying two Blenheims of 45 Squadron. One fighter burst its tailwheel on take-off and aborted, but the other three rendezvoused with one of the Blenheims, the other having crashed on take-off from Sidi Barrani. Near Crete the little formation entered dense, low-lying cloud and became separated, all but one Hurricane abandoning the strike and returning separately to Egypt. Plt Off A.J.C.Hamilton continued alone in V7562 towards

Maleme. Over Suda Bay he encountered an aircraft identified as a Ju 88, claiming this shot down into the sea. (No Luftwaffe loss of such an aircraft has been found for this date, however.) His Hurricane now developed the feared fuel problems, and he landed at Heraklion where the undercarriage suffered severe damage on the cratered runway. He would subsequently be captured when the island fell, spending the rest of the war as a PoW.

The next strike was carried out by six more Blenheims from 45 Squadron, which dropped 20lb and 40lb bombs from 14,000 feet, the crews seeing them fall amongst the clutter of transports, causing two explosions and three fires; they believed that about 12 Junkers had been hit. Three 55 Squadron Blenheims then attacked, all crews returning to report only light Flak, and apparently no fighters. Just after midday three further Blenheims set out, this time from 14 Squadron, but these did encounter Bf 109s of II./JG 77 on patrol and ready for them over Suda Bay, and within minutes Flt Lt R.A.Green's aircraft had been shot down into the sea, followed by those flown by Lt S.R.E.Forrester, SAAF, and Sgt H.P.Jeudwine, all nine men aboard perishing. Two of the Blenheims fell to Uffz Rudolf Schmidt of 5.Staffel, a third was claimed by Oblt Hans Brockmann of 6.Staffel, and a fourth claim appears to have been made by Fw Otto Kohler, another 5.Staffel pilot (although this may actually have been for a Hurricane later in the day). It would appear that fire from the gunners struck the Messerschmitt flown by the gruppe's recently promoted kommandeur, Hptmn Helmut Henz, who was killed when his aircraft crashed into the sea off Antikythera Island during this combat. Three 55 Squadron Blenheims which arrived shortly afterwards escaped interception and returned unscathed. They were followed during the afternoon by yet another four Blenheims from 45 Squadron, but three turned back with minor defects, Lt Jones, SAAF, attacking alone, reporting near-misses with his 44 20lb bombs.

The final strike of the day against Maleme was to be made by three South African Marylands and two Hurricanes from 274 Squadron. Off at 1530, one Maryland soon developed a fault, turned back, and force-landed at Sidi Barrani. The two remaining bombers went in first, bombing and strafing the area. As they headed away over the mountains, Lt E.G.Ford's aircraft was seen trailing smoke from one engine; clearing the peaks, he crash-landed the stricken bomber near Tymbaki on the south coast. The crew were unhurt, but pursuing German fighters strafed the damaged aircraft and set it on fire.

Meanwhile the two Hurricanes, W9266 flown by Flt Lt Dudley Honor and P3469 in the hands of Flt Lt Hubert Down, had followed the Marylands in, as Honor later recalled:

"As we crossed the mountains there were so many enemy aircraft in the sky that I was undecided whether to have a crack at the ones in the air or carry out my original orders. Down and I dived along the river valley. As we approached, we saw two transport aircraft circling to land. There were so many aircraft on Maleme that it was just a congested mess. Some were on their noses, some obviously burnt out. It was difficult to decide in that mass which of the aircraft on the ground to attack. I decided to have a crack at the two which were landing. I thought they were probably full of troops and equipment. They came in too fast for us. We were still about 2,000 yards away as the second one started to touch down. I opened fire at this range and continued firing as I approached the aerodrome. I passed over at about 50 feet, spraying everything I could see. Down's aircraft was about 300 yards astern of me.

I saw three 109Fs (sic) taking-off from the aerodrome, going in an easterly direction. I thought they were going after the Marylands. I got to the north boundary, still at about 50 feet and noticed some troop-carriers, German and Italian [however, there is no evidence to suggest that Italian transport aircraft were involved in these ferrying operations – Ed], coming into the aerodrome along the line of the Cape Spada peninsula; they were at about 1,000 feet. As I passed over the northern boundary the AA guns opened up; the sky was black around me with ack-ack bursts. I pulled up to the line of troop-carriers, head on. They stretched right along the peninsula, with about half a mile between each. There was an endless line of them, away to sea. I managed to get up to the same height as the leading aircraft – it was an Italian S.29 (sic) – and gave it a very short burst at dead range. It made no attempt at evasion and burst into flames and went straight down into the sea. I carried straight on and had a crack at a second, a Ju 52 loaded with troops. He half-turned away from me and went down. I saw him as he turned over on his back, and hit the water."

The two transports attacked were probably both Ju 52/3ms of KGrzbV 106.

Meantime, Flt Lt Down was being pursued out to sea by Bf 109Es of II./JG 77 – possibly those seen taking off by Honor; he did not return. Other German pilots then gave chase to Honor, apparently joined by at least one Bf 110, as he recalled:

"Suddenly there was a series of explosions and my control was gone. A 110 had attacked me from underneath and behind. I did not observe it before the attack. I started to take what evasive action I could. My controls were very badly damaged. I could only try to dodge him. The chase lasted about 15 minutes and I got closer and closer to the sea. I worked in as close to the cliffs as possible, watching him in the mirror. Each time I saw a white puff coming from the front of him I did a skidding turn.

"I saw the cannon shells bursting in the sea alongside. He must have used up all his ammunition without hitting me again because he sheered off. A 109F (sic) then took up the fight. He employed the usual tactics on me, diving and then climbing. I was unable to turn with him but managed to get him round the north of the peninsula, out of sight of the aerodrome. There was cloud at 2,500 feet but I could not climb to get up there. After about five minutes a burst of fire hit my engine; there was a horrible bang and an awful smell of cordite in the cockpit. I was about 20 feet from the sea when I was hit. I could not pull out so I steered straight ahead to make a landing on the water at high speed, at about 220 mph. I reduced speed in order not to hit the water too hard and touched down at about 120 mph. After about 15 seconds the aircraft began to sink. I still had the cockpit hood closed and my safety harness was still fastened. I went down 40 feet before I realised what was happening. I noticed the sea turning from blue to dark green...I opened the hood, which luckily had not jammed...and turned the knob of my Mae West. I was wearing a German Mae West [taken from a Ju 87 gunner who had been shot down during the Battle of Britain, during which time Honor had served with 145 Squadron] which inflates automatically, whereas the RAF type had to be blown up by mouth. I drifted to the surface slowly, noticing the water grow lighter and lighter. It seemed a long time. I broke surface to find the 109F still circling overhead at about 50 feet. Fortunately the pilot did not appear to see me and after a couple of circuits made off round the peninsula towards Maleme."

Sqn Ldr Dudley Honor of 274 Squadron after his adventures over and around Crete, described in this chapter. The tip of the lightning bolt marking carried on this unit's aircraft may just be seen on the fuselage of his Hurricane.

In this engagement the II./JG 77 pilot claimed two Hurricanes shot down, one by Uffz Schmidt, who had earlier in the day shot down two of 14 Squadron's Blenheims, and one by FjGefr Gunther Marschhausen, both of 5.Staffel. Dudley Honor, meanwhile, continued to float in the water:

"The sea was very rough; I was about half a mile from the cliff and after swimming for about a couple of minutes, I realised I was floating stern upwards. I still had my parachute on...I jettisoned it and my trousers, which were hampering me. I carried on swimming for about three hours until I was just about 20 yards from the cliffs, which were about 100 feet high, not only sheer but overhanging. Each time I tried to get a handhold I was dragged away again by the suction of the retreating wave. My nails and flesh were torn by the rocks...I found it impossible to get to the shore so I relaxed and allowed myself to drift round into a small cave. By this time it was nearly nightfall. I saw a German seaplane fly along the cliffs very near me...I thought he might be searching for me. Eventually I was washed into another cave and although smashed up against the end by the drive of the sea, managed to hang on by grabbing a thick stalagmite and crawled up onto a little ledge."

Further north during the day, a patrolling reconnaissance Maryland from 39 Squadron encountered a number of Ju 52/3ms between Crete and Greece, which are believed to have been aircraft of KGrzbV 60. Flt Lt R.A.'Butch' Lewis and his crew claimed to have shot down one and to have damaged two others; their victim would seem to have been Lt Ralf Billerbeck's aircraft, which crashed near Corinth, killing him and injuring three of his crew. Returning from their sortie, the Maryland crew reported seeing transports in formations of ten crossing the sea, each formation escorted by a single Bf 109 or Bf 110.

In Egypt, ready for the morrow, 274 Squadron received a further six long-range Hurricanes, flown up to Gerawla by newly-arrived pilots of 229 Squadron. At Sidi Haneish 73 Squadron received six reinforcement pilots from 213 Squadron, who had also just arrived, together with six non-tropicalised Hurricanes, attached "for special duties over Crete". How these units came to be present will be explained below.

During the afternoon trios of Hurricanes from Egypt which had been undertaking patrols over shipping along the African coast were directed instead to provide cover for the carrier HMS *Formidable*, which had been badly damaged by air attack and was making for Alexandria. On the third such patrol, this one by aircraft of 73 Squadron, a reconnaissance Ju 88 being engaged, Sqn Ldr Peter Wykeham-Barnes claimed damage to this before his reflector gunsight failed, saving the German aircraft from probable destruction.

The absence of the escorting fighters over the coastal shipping proved costly however. On this date the Luftwaffe's Ju 87s were joined by similar aircraft from the Regia Aeronautica's 239ª Squadriglia BaT which undertook their first operation since their arrival. Seven Ju 87Rs led by Cap Giuseppe Cenni and escorted by eight CR.42s of 18° Gruppo CT, attacked transport vessels off the coast near Marsa Luch, claiming to have sunk one vessel of about 4,000 tons. They had in fact sent down the 3,741-ton *Helka* and had damaged the sloop HMS *Grimsby*. More Stukas from I./StG 1 finished off the latter vessel later in the evening, but in doing so lost one dive-bomber apparently to the AA defences.

British Claims

274 Sqn	Plt Off A.J.C.Hamilton	V7562	Ju 88	Suda Bay 0530-1000
	Flt Lt D.G.S.Honor	W9266	S.79	Maleme area 1530-
	Flt Lt D.G.S.Honor	W9266	Ju 52	3m Maleme area 1530-
73 Sqn	Sqn Ldr P.G. Wykeham-Barnes	V7012	Ju 88	damaged over ships 1430-
39 Sqn	Flt Lt R.A.Lewis & crew		Ju 52/3m	over sea between Crete and Greece
			2 Ju 52/3ms	damaged over sea between Crete and Greece
Benheim squadrons				24 transport aircraft on ground Maleme

British Casualties

45 Sqn	Blenheim IV Z5766 destroyed in a crash-landing while preparing to take off for Maleme; Sgt E.McClelland and crew safe
14 Sqn	Blenheim IV slightly damaged by Flak over Maleme; gunner slightly wounded
	Blenheim IV T2065 shot down over Maleme; Flt Lt R.A.Green and crew KiA
	Blenheim IV V5510 shot down over Maleme; Lt R.E.Forrester, SAAF, and crew KiA
	Blenheim IV T2003 shot down over Maleme; Sgt H.P.Jeudwine and crew KiA
24 SAAF Sqn	Maryland ccrash-landed due to Flak damage and destroyed on ground by strafing Bf 109s; Lt E.G.Ford and crew safe
274 Sqn	Hurricane I P3469 shot down over Maleme; Flt Lt H.C.Down KiA
	Hurricane I W9266 shot down in sea near Maleme; Flt Lt D.G.S.Honor survived

German Claims

6./JG 77	Oblt Hans Brockmann		Blenheim	Maleme 1115
5./JG 77	Uffz Rudolf Schmidt		Hurricane	Maleme 1706
	Gefr Gunther Marschhausen		Hurricane	
	Uffz Rudolf Schmidt		Blenheim	Maleme 1715
	Fw Otto Kohler		Blenheim	Maleme 1718
	Uffz Rudolf Schmidt		Blenheim	Maleme 1722

German Casualties

3./StG 1	Ju 87R-2 WNr 6069 destroyed in combat NE Tobruk; Ofhr Hans Wimmer/ Gefr Friedrich Lein KiA
Stab II./JG 77	Bf 109E-7 WNr 1271 Hptmn Helmut Henz KiA in combat with Blenheims over Maleme
KGrzbV 106	2 Ju 52/3ms shot down into sea near Maleme
KGrzbV 60	Ju 52/3m lost near Corinth; Lt Ralf Billerbeck KiA; three of crew injured

---

Monday, 26 May 1941

Throughout 26 May aircraft of 204 Group were once more very active over Crete, the first strike of the day being made by six 24 SAAF Squadron Marylands. Four of these were to bomb and strafe Maleme, while two dropped medical supplies and ammunition to the garrison at Retimo. Three of the bombers returned with Flak damage, but the two supply droppers met stiffer opposition. One was crewed by volunteer Free Frenchmen under Cmdt Georges Goumin. The intention had been to skim the waves on approach, climb to 2,000 feet when about ten miles out, then dive to sea level and break through any defending fighters at high speed. The objective was reached without either aircraft being hit, and Capt K.S.P.Jones, SAAF, flying the leading Maryland, reported: "…the German fighter screen was like a swarm of bees overhead. About half way across the island we saw them get the French Maryland. The pity was no effort could really help." Apparently Cmdt Goumin, having completed his supply dropping task, had decided to strafe Maleme, as one of his crew – Adj Chef Albert Marteau, the WOP/AG – recalled:

"We noticed Canea on the way in and then arrived at Maleme; there was a crowd on the beach. The pilot sprayed the Ju 52s with his machine-guns and I joined in with my two machine-guns in turn. The reaction soon came – tracers arrived from all sides – above, below, right, left. Sgt Roger Lefevre, the other gunner, stated later that a German fighter had been attacking us [This was a Bf 109E of III./JG 77, flown by Lt Emil Omert, who claimed his third victory against the Maryland although he identified it as a Blenheim]. Brutally the plane sideslipped. I fell and Lefevre fell from his turret, landing on me with his knees in my back. In falling he pulled out his intercom wire; there was total silence and we became entangled in our parachute harnesses. The plane flew on but through the machine-gun holes I saw the ground rapidly approaching. I waited for the crash and I braced myself, then… a void. On touching the ground the barrels of my machine-guns had pivoted on their axis and the sight had hit me on the head. When I regained my senses I saw that the plane was resting on its belly along the ditch, broken by the banking – an incredible chance. The engines were on fire and the heat revived me. No question of escaping from below so I detached my parachute and Lefevre struggled to free the hatch near the turret. I helped pull him out but the moment we reached the ground, a patrol of Austrian mountain troops appeared and captured us. I tried to indicate by gestures that there had been four of us in the burning plane."

Cmdt Goumin, however, was dead, having been hit in the chest by a bullet whilst still at the controls of the Maryland (1697, ex AH307). The observer, Lt Pierre Courcot, had not had time to take over before the crash; he was seriously injured, but would survive as a prisoner of war, as would the two gunners.

At Gerawla 274 Squadron also had a number of French airmen attached, all of whom had absconded from Syria when France capitulated. Initially they had been formed into 2 Free French Flight under Flt Lt Paul Jacquier, and had operated the various aircraft in which they had fled – Morane 406s and Potez 63-11s – until re-equipped with Hurricanes and attached to 274 Squadron. Having not so far seen any action, they were now about to be well and truly 'blooded'.

Six long-range Hurricanes were to go after the transports flying into Maleme, three setting out at 15-minute intervals commencing at 1310, followed by the other three at 1415. New Zealander Flg Off Ower Tracey, a former Battle of Britain pilot with three victories to his credit, was first to arrive over Maleme. Here he promptly claimed a Ju 52/3m shot down, but a Bf 109 then fastened onto his tail, and he dived towards the steep cliffs, his Hurricane (Z4511) taking several hits in the fuselage, in the fuel tanks and in the propeller. Reaching sea level, Tracey pulled clear at the last moment, believing that the pursuing Bf 109 had plunged straight into the sea behind him. Having nursed his damaged aircraft back across the sea to Sidi Barrani, he force-landed; he claimed both the Ju 52 and the Bf 109 as destroyed.

Whilst Tracey was fighting for his life, a second Hurricane (Z4312), flown by Sgt George Kerr, had arrived off Maleme, and he too at once claimed a Ju 52 shot down in flames into the sea. Like Tracey, he was also pounced upon by a Messerschmitt, and soon followed his victim into the sea. Kerr survived the crash and managed to get ashore; next day he would by chance meet his flight commander, Flt Lt Honor, shot down the previous day. In fact Honor had witnessed the fight in which Kerr had sent the Junkers into the sea. It seems probable that the German pilots involved in these engagements were Oblt Walter Höckner of II./JG 77 and Lt Fritz Geisshardt of Stab I.(J)/LG 2, each of whom claimed Hurricanes on this date over Crete, Geisshardt's claim being his 18th.

The next lone Hurricane, Z4250 flown by Frenchman Flt Sgt Marcel Lebois, evaded the now-alerted

Messerschmitts but did encounter the Junkers transports, one of which he claimed shot down. He arrived safely back at Gerawla at 1800, where he awaited news of two of his fellow countrymen flying in the final section to Maleme. On nearing the island these three Hurricanes separated and hunted for the transports individually, Flt Lt Jacquier soon encountering one making for Maleme. He recalled:

"I was flying at approximately 10,000 feet about 20 kilometres north of Maleme when I noticed a single Ju 52 flying very low (100-200 metres) heading for Crete. I attacked from the rear, made a single pass, disengaged above and banked upwards to the right. I saw it disappear into the sea. Some minutes later I saw a second lone Ju 52, at the same altitude. Again I attacked from the rear and broke away upwards and this also went into the sea. In both attacks the Ju 52s only returned fire at the last moment. I regained altitude and continued to Maleme to strafe. While I was attacking, five Bf 109s and two Bf 110s on aerial defence were circling at about 500-1,000 metres, at slow speeds – with undercarriages down – no doubt for identification by German airfield defences. I dived at great speed from 3,000 metres, going west to east (sun behind me). I shot a Ju 52, which blew up, and levelled out some metres above the ground. On the eastern edge of the airfield I received a shock – the engine was hit – it cut and petrol flooded the cockpit. Using my speed I glided along the beach between Maleme and La Canee [Canea] and landed (Z4632) wheels-up amongst the German forward positions. I was captured immediately. Apart from rough handling by Austrian mountain troops on capture, I was treated well in accordance with the Geneva Convention. I was wearing the badges of my rank in the RAF and at my first interrogation by the Germans at Maleme, I indicated that I was a French-Canadian. Some time later I met, in the PoW camp, Lt Courcot and two others (Marteau and Lefevre) in French uniform – surviving crew of the Glenn Martin – and I decided that I would share the same fate as my compatriots. Thus, at my second interrogation, in Athens, I stated that I was French."

From this second trio of Hurricanes, only Flg Off Antoine Peronne (the other Frenchman) was to return, landing Z4538 back at Gerawla at 1915. During his five-hour sortie he too had met a Ju 52/3m and claimed this shot down. The third pilot, Sgt Colin Glover, had been killed when his Z4606 was intercepted and shot down into the sea; whether he encountered any transports before his demise is not known. At least six Junkers had been claimed by the Hurricane pilots; records indicate that three from KGrzbV 172 were shot down – those flown by Fw Gerhard Kraus (4V+DW) and Obfw Hans Möckel – and one from KGrzbV 105. One each of KGrzbV 60, 106 and Stab XI FlK were damaged, and all obliged to crash-land at Maleme.

Six Blenheims drawn equally from 45 and 55 Squadrons were then briefed to make a dusk attack on Maleme, but just prior to their take-off at 1700, two more 274 Squadron Hurricanes flown by Sgt P.B.Nicolson and Wt Off Charles Coudray, another of the French pilots, were sent off to strafe, both carrying out their missions and returning safely. The Blenheims arrived however, to find the defences alerted, and while the three 55 Squadron aircraft again escaped interception, those of 45 Squadron were caught by patrolling JG 77 Bf 109Es of 6.Staffel, led by Oblt Höckner. This pilot first attacked Sgt N.H.Thomas' T2339 and shot it down in flames with the loss of all the crew. He then attacked the leader, T2350, and severely damaged it. Flg Off T.F.Churcher and his crew all baled out, he and the observer, Plt Off R.D.May, being captured at once. The gunner, Sgt H.G.Langrish, was more fortunate in that he evaded capture and wandered for two days and three nights until he reached the south coast, where he was picked up by a destroyer. The third Blenheim (V5592) meanwhile escaped the slaughter and returned across the sea, but became lost over the desert. When fuel ran out Plt Off J.Robinson ordered a bale out. The three men gathered on the ground, but the observer, Sgt W.B.Longstaff, then wandered off on his own and was never seen again. Robinson and his gunner (Sgt A.F.Crosby) walked for four days and five nights without food and water before they were spotted and picked up.

Over the desert during the day Flt Lt F.E.G.Hayter of 6 Squadron was reconnoitring east of Halfaya in a Lysander when intercepted by five Bf 109s of 2./JG 27. He undertook avoiding action which allowed his gunner, Sgt E.Hodge, to get hits on one Messerschmitt which was seen to break away with smoke pouring from the engine. Hayter was ultimately forced to crash-land the Lysander, which was then strafed on the ground, its destruction being credited to Oblt Ernst Maack. However, the crew survived unhurt and were subsequently picked up by the army. Lt Fritz Schröder of this unit crash-landed in the sea on this date, reportedly due to fuel shortage during an attack on ships off Bardia. Schröder became a PoW, while his aircraft was recovered virtually intact and was brought in to headquarters, 204 Group, for a full inspection. Another Ju 87 was also lost by II./StG 2, Obfw Ewald Kruger's aircraft being reported shot down near Sollum.

British Casualties

274 Sqn   Hurricane I Z4511 Flg Off O.V.Tracey damaged over Crete; force-landed on return

Hurricane I Z4312 Sgt G.Kerr shot down over Crete; pilot safe

Hurricane I Z4606 Sgt C.R.Glover KiA

Hurricane I Z4632 Flt Lt P.J.F.Jacquier shot down by Flak and PoW

24 SAAF Sqn   Maryland 1607 (ex AH307) shot down on Crete. Pilot, Cmdr G.Goumin KiA; Lt P.Courcot wounded and PoW; Adj Chef A.Marteau & Adj Chef R.Lefevre PoWs

45 Sqn   Blenheim IV T2339 shot down over Crete; Flt Sgt N.Thomas and crew KiA

Blenheim IV V5592 shot down over Crete:Flg Off T.Churcher & observer PoW; WoP/AG evaded and returned

Blenheim IV T2350 lost on return; abandoned; Plt Off J.Robinson and one safe; one missing

6 Sqn   Lysander P1740 crash-landed and strafed on ground; crew safe

*actually Maryland

German Casualties

I./JG 27   Bf 109E-4 WNr Lt Fritz Schröder crash-landed in sea nr Bardia; PoW

II./StG 2   Ju 87 Obfw Ewald Kruger lost in combat nr Sollum

I./KGrzbV 172   Ju 52/3m 4V+DW shot down, Crete; Fw Gerhard Kraus

Ju 52/3m shot down, Crete; Obfw Hans Möckel

Ju 52/3m shot down, Crete

KGrzbV 105   Ju 52/3m shot down, Crete

KGrzbV 60   Ju 52/3m damaged and crash-landed, Crete

Stab/FlK   Ju 52/3m damaged and crash-landed, Crete

Tuesday, 27 May 1941

By now there were almost 27,000 German troops in Crete and the German high command was now convinced of victory as was Wavell of defeat. Early in the day he signalled the prime minister that Crete was no longer tenable and that troops must be withdrawn. He acknowledged the enemy's overwhelming air superiority, which made reinforcement impossible. The chiefs of staff reluctantly signalled their agreement. The RAF would largely be blamed for the loss of Crete, but lack of secure air bases was the prime reason, combined with the numerical strength of the Luftwaffe and the costly but daring use of their airborne forces.

     Despite the approaching evacuation, Air Commodore Collishaw considered 204 Group should continue to do what it could to frustrate the German advance, both by night and day. At 0300 therefore, three Blenheims of 45 Squadron prepared to take off from Fuka to repeat attacks made during the hours of darkness by the Wellingtons. However, the leading aircraft – Z5896 – crashed just after getting into the air and burst into flames. Flg Off N.W.Pinnington and his observer were killed although the gunner was thrown clear, though suffering from severe burns. He would succumb to his injuries three weeks later. The operation, during which spikes and small bombs were to have been dropped on the airfield, was cancelled.

Early in the morning,when two of 39 Squadron's Marylands were out making reconnaissances along the coastline of Crete, a photo-reconnaissance Hurricane (V7423) of 2 PRU made a sortie over Rhodes in the hands of an ex-30 Squadron pilot, Flg Off S.N.Pearce. This was claimed probably shot down by Serg Magg Gastone De Portis of 162ª Squadriglia, but in fact returned undamaged. In Egypt further Blenheims were readied for an afternoon attack on Maleme. 14 Squadron made available just three aircraft at Qotaifiya landing ground (seven miles south-west of El Daba), while at Maaten Bagush six of 55 Squadron were prepared. Just after 1430 the first Blenheims began lifting off at the latter base.

The first pair collided as they became airborne, Flg Off Harris managing to belly-land his aircraft without casualties, but Sgt W.L.Martin's T2051 spun in with the loss of all aboard. The other four got off and raided Maleme successfully, believing that several of the estimated 100 Ju 52/3ms seen on the ground were probably destroyed by their bombing. In rapidly failing light the bombers became separated during the return flight, and only two landed at their base. The other two had become lost over the desert, both crashing. The wreck of Sgt J.H.Cheesman's T2175 and the bodies of the crew were found by a 6 Squadron Lysander. The skipper of the other missing Blenheim, Sgt Bale, had ordered his crew to bale out when their fuel was exhausted; all three arrived back at their base two days later.

The 14 Squadron section fared no better. One aircraft returned early with engine trouble; the other two, which were to bomb troop concentrations between Maleme and Suda Bay, could not find their target, so attacked the airfield instead. On return, in darkness, they became separated, both becoming lost and also crashing in the desert. Z5593 came down 30 miles south-west of Mersa Matruh; the French-Canadian pilot, Flg Off Jean Le Cavalier, was killed, while the other two managed to bale out, although only the gunner was found alive. The other Blenheim (T2338) crashed 60 miles south of El Daba, the all-New Zealand crew having baled out. Three days of air searches were necessary before the wreck was located, and three more before the observer, Sgt M.B.Fearn, and the gunner, Sgt J.N.McConnel, were found; of the pilot, Flg Off M.Mackenzie, no sign was ever discovered.

The Blenheim strike had achieved little. Six of the nine participating bombers had been totally lost – none due to enemy action – and nine crew members had perished. 204 Group's Blenheim Wing could ill-afford such a rate of attrition.

The final operation of the day was launched at 1530 when two Hurricanes of 274 Squadron rendezvoused with a Blenheim IVf of 45 Squadron, directed to attempt further interception of the Ju 52/3m air convoy, still streaming into Maleme. As the trio headed towards the south coast of Crete however, they encountered six Ju 88s of II./LG 1 and attacked at once. The Blenheim pilot, South African Lt D.Thorne, made a port beam attack on one low-flying bomber, the crew claiming that considerable damage had been inflicted and that the Junkers had probably been destroyed, although they did not see it hit the sea. Both Hurricane pilots, Flg Off Weller (Z4250) and Sgt Nicolson (Z4536) also engaged, each believing that they had shot one down, and indeed the Blenheim crew reported seeing one Ju 88 falling in flames and two others hit the sea. In fact only one was lost, Lt George Freysoldt and his crew perishing in L1+EW; presumably all three fighters had attacked the same aircraft, each unaware of the others' involvement. Following the fight the Hurricanes became split up from the Blenheim, and after an uneventful patrol hunting for transport aircraft, both landed at Heraklion, from where they returned next day, at daybreak. Meanwhile the Blenheim had returned direct to its base.

British Claims

274 Sqn	Flg Off A.A.P.Weller	Z4250	Ju 88	Over sea 1520-
	Sgt P.B.Nicolson	Z4536	Ju 88	Over sea 1520-
45 Sqn	Crew of Blenheim IVf		Ju 88 probable	Over sea 1520-

British Casualties

45 Sqn	Blenheim IV Z5896 crashed on take-off at Fuka; Flg Off N.Pinnington and crew KiFA
55 Sqn	Blenheim IV T2051 collided on take-off at LG 15; Flt Sgt W.Martin and crew KiFA
	Blenheim IV collided on take-off at LG 15; crash-landed; Flg Off J.Harris and crew safe
	Blenheim IV T2175 crashed out of fuel after raid on Maleme; Sgt J.Cheesman and crew KiFA
	Blenheim IV L9319 crashed in desert after raid on Maleme; Sgt R.Bale and crew baled & safe
14 Sqn	Blenheim IV V5593 crashed in desert after raid on Maleme; Flg Off J.Le Cavalier and one KiFA; one survived
	Blenheim IV T2338 abandoned over desert after raid on Maleme; Flt Lt.M.Mackenzie lost; two found safe later

German Casualties

II./LG 1	Ju 88 L1+EW lost to fighter attack; Lt George Freysoldt and crew KiA		
9./JG 77	Bf 109E-7 WNr 59958 shot down by ground fire and 85% destroyed, Maleme area		

Italian claims

162ª Sq CT	Serg Magg Gastone De Portis	Hurricane probable	Rhodes

Wednesday, 28 May 1941

On this date an Italian convoy, sailing from Rhodes to Crete under the command of Cap Vasc Aldo Cocchia, disembarked in Sitia Bay (north-east Crete) a force of about 2,700 troops, formed mainly from the 9th Infantry Regiment 'Regina' and other minor units, and accompanied by 13 L.35 light tanks.

Following the losses suffered during the previous day, few sorties were made by 204 Group aircraft, only two Blenheims of 55 Squadron undertaking a strike on Maleme and returning without incident. With the onset of evening two South African Marylands were scrambled from Fuka to cover returning warships, but saw nothing. Patrols were carried out by two 45 Squadron Blenheims, each escorted by a 274 Squadron Hurricane, but saw no enemy activity. At Gerawla 274 Squadron was reinforced by five pilots on attachment from 73 Squadron, for operations over Crete, and at Abu Sueir three more Beaufighters arrived from Malta. Two of these were from 272 Squadron, including that flown by the commanding officer, Sqn Ldr A.W.Fletcher, while the third was piloted by Flt Lt Bill Riley of 252 Squadron, who had just been released from brief hospitalisation following an incident over Malta when his Beaufighter had been shot down in error by a Hurricane pilot. He was a most experienced pilot, having flown Gladiators in Norway and Hurricanes during the Battle of Britain; he was credited with four and two shared air victories.

At this time 1 SAAF Squadron at Sidi Haneish was joined by ten pilots and Hurricanes from 2 SAAF Squadron, led by Capt D.H.Loftus. This latter squadron was now based at Amiriya where it was working up on Tomahawks, so this detachment was a temporary measure as regards aircraft as well. 24 SAAF Squadron now had two flights at Fuka under Maj C.E.Morton, while 12 SAAF Squadron had arrived at Shandur on 26 May having already converted to Marylands in East Africa, but was not yet ready to enter operations.

The day was also marked by the award of a Bar to his DFC for Flg Off McFall of 6 Squadron, who was also promoted Flt Lt. By the end of the month this unit was undertaking virtually all its sorties on Hurricanes, although its nine aircraft of this type were still augmented by five Lysander IIs.

German Casualties

2.(F)/123	Ju 88 lost over the Mediterranean; Lt Fritz Gortan KiA; Uffz Herbert Nispel WiA; one other KiA and one PoW

Thursday, 29 May 1941

Rather more success was achieved during daylight hours when 21 protective sorties were undertaken over various returning warships during the morning and early afternoon by Hurricanes of 274 Squadron. These patrols consisted of two or three aircraft at a time, usually accompanied by a single South African Maryland or a Blenheim IV of 45 Squadron. At 1200 a Maryland flown by Lt Miles Barnby was circling over ships of the Royal Navy's Force B when the crew spotted a lone aircraft at 13,000 feet. Barnby turned in behind to investigate and saw that it was a Ju 88 – a reconnaissance aircraft of 2.(F)/123, which at once dived away. Barnby followed, firing several times with his front guns, but breaking off at 6,000 feet when an explosive bullet struck the Maryland and filled the cockpit with smoke. As the Junkers disappeared from the South African's view, pouring black smoke from its damaged starboard engine, it was attacked by one of the escorting Hurricanes, Flg Off Tracey in V7830 shooting 4U+EK down into the sea with the loss of Fw Ernst Chlebowitz and his crew. Meanwhile another of the Hurricane pilots, Plt Off Arthur Sumner (V7855), reported engaging an aircraft which he believed to be a Do 17, which he claimed to have damaged before it evaded his attack and disappeared.

During one of the earlier escort sorties, Sgt Peter Nicolson was detailed to break away and make a dash over central Crete to the Retimo area, where he was to drop a message bag to the besieged garrison. This contained orders for a withdrawal to Plaka for evacuation, "phrased in slang so as to make it unintelligible if picked up by the Germans". As Nicolson attempted to carry out this duty, his Hurricane (Z4634) was intercepted at about 0900 by Oblt Erich Friedrich of Stab/JG 77, and was shot down into the sea with the loss of the pilot. Whether or not he ever got to drop the message bag is not known, but it certainly never reached Lt Col J.R.Campbell, the officer commanding at Retimo.

Throughout the day CR.42s of 85ª Squadriglia, 18° Gruppo CT were involved in patrols. During one of these Serg Luigi Gorrini claimed a Blenheim shot down about 12 miles north-west of Benghazi, and a second damaged, while on another sortie Serg Spartaco Petrignani claimed one more of these bombers. No corresponding RAF losses have been found.

British Claims

274 Sqn	Flg Off O.V.Tracey	Z4536	}	Ju 88	over sea 1040-1355
24 SAAF Sqn	Lt M.Barnby	V7890			
274 Sqn	Plt Off A.Sumner	V7855		Do 17	damaged over sea 1040-1355

British Casualties

274 Sqn	Hurricane I Z4634 Sgt P.B.Nicolson KiA over Crete

German Claims

Stab/JG 77	Oblt Erich Friedrich	Hurricane	Rethymnon, Crete 0900

German Casualties

2.(F)/123	Ju 88D-2 WNr 0802 4U+EK MiA Alexandria; combat with Hurricane S Crete. Fw Ernst Chlebowitz and crew KiA
III./ZG 26	Bf 110D-2 WNr 3407 destroyed by fire at Castel Benito
III.(K)/LG 1	Ju 88A-5 WNr 3353 crash-landed Sollum due to engine trouble; 70% destroyed

Italian Claims

85ª Sq/18° Gr CT	Serg Luigi Gorrini	Blenheim
	Serg Luigi Gorrini	Blenheim damaged
	Serg Spartaco Petrignani	Blenheim

Friday, 30 May 1941

Throughout the day 274 Squadron's Hurricanes flew 30 sorties over two naval forces which were heading south, again sometimes accompanied by a single Blenheim or Beaufighter. Their first contact with the opposition was made just after 0800 when Sqn Ldr G.E.Hawkins's section of three Hurricanes encountered three bombers which were identified as He 111s. Despite the identification – at this stage of the war all German aircraft were relatively new and uncommon to RAF pilots in Africa – these would seem to have been Do 17s of I./KG 2. One of the aircraft intercepted was claimed shot down by Hawkins's two wingmen, the Free Frenchmen Flg Off Peronne and Wt Off Ballatore, the aircraft being seen to crash into the sea. Their victim would appear to have been U5+GL, flown by Uffz Heinz Hövel.

Late in the afternoon Plt Off G.A.Tovey (in W9329) was accompanying a Beaufighter flown by Flt Lt Riley of 252 Squadron when they came across Lt Walter Fischer's He 111 (1H+KN) of II./KG 26, which was on a ferry flight to Cyrenaica. Bill Riley attacked first, but closed so rapidly that his Beaufighter collided with the bomber, although both aircraft seemed to escape serious damage. This did, however, allow Tovey the opportunity to nip in and shoot the Heinkel down into the sea.

As dusk approached the final sorties were being flown by three Hurricanes and a Beaufighter, the latter by Sub Lt I.F.Fraser, FAA. In the fading light a reconnaissance Ju 88 (7A+HM) of 4.(F)/121 was seen, and was apparently attacked by both Fraser and Plt Off Sumner (Z7855) although each was ignorant of the other's presence. Fraser claimed a probable, Sumner a definite victory; whoever fired the telling burst, the Junkers crashed into the sea with the loss of Oblt Franz Schwarz-Tramper and his crew. On return to Fuka in darkness, the Beaufighter pilot had difficulty finding the airfield, and after circling a couple of times, crash-landed T3230 two miles south of his base, without seriously injuring himself or his observer.

Ready for the morrow, and whatever action it might bring, 274 Squadron at Gerawla now received a further influx of pilots to aid in the long patrol sorties. Three South Africans from 1 SAAF Squadron included the highly experienced pair Capt K.W.Driver DFC, with a score of 11 victories, and Lt R.H.Talbot, DFC, with eight. 73 Squadron sent over three pilots, all Frenchmen, and these included another highly skilled pilot, Sous Lt Albert Littolf. A veteran of the fighting in France the previous year, he had been credited with two victories and a third shared while flying with the Armée de l'Air, then escaping to join the RAF and had been posted to join 73 Squadron in the desert as part of Free French Fighter Flight No 1 in the past month. During the squadron's heroic defence of the Tobruk garrison, Littolf had claimed a further five victories.

274 Sqn	Flg Off A.D.M.Peronne	Z4536			
	Wt Off A.Ballatore	W9303	}	He 111*	S Crete 0800+
	Plt Off G.A.Tovey	W9329		He 111	S Crete 1805
	Plt Off A.Sumner	V7855		Ju 88	S Crete 2010-2040
252 Sqn	Sub Lt I.F.Fraser			Ju 88 probable	S Crete

*Believed to be a Do 17

German Casualties

I./KG 2	Do 17 U5+GL Uffz Heinz Hövel & crew KiA
II./KG 26	He 111 WNr 3950 1H+KN Lt Walter Fischer & crew KiA 110 m S Crete
4.(F)/121	Ju 88A-5 WNr 2356 7A+HM MiA S Crete at 1645; Oblt Franz Schwarz-Tramper & crew KiA

Saturday, 31 May 1941

Two destroyers, HMS *Napier* and *Nizam* had departed southern Crete during the early hours of the day, crammed with troops being evacuated. Despite searches for these vessels by the Luftwaffe, they suffered only one attack when 12 Ju 88s of II./LG 1 dived on them at 0850, *Napier* being damaged by near misses. The ship's gunners claimed one of these bombers shot down and a second damaged, while overhead a patrolling Maryland of 24 SAAF Squadron and three 274 Squadron Hurricanes flown by the attached SAAF pilots, arrived on the scene and gave chase to two of the raiders. Lt Talbot (Z4510) fired two bursts at one bomber, but it evaded him. Then Capt Driver (Z4614) and Lt A.J.B.Bester (P2646) made beam and stern attacks on the other, which dived into the sea. Talbot and the Maryland pilot, Lt C.S.Kearney, gave chase for some 70 miles before Talbot succeeded in getting in a burst which hit an engine. Kearney, with his engines at full boost, overhauled the Hurricane, closed in on the damaged Junkers and poured all his remaining ammunition into it. The same engine appeared to have been hit again, for it now stopped and the bomber was last seen flying just ten feet above the sea. It was assumed to have crashed, Kearney and Talbot being credited with its destruction, but in fact the pilot managed to nurse it back to Heraklion, where he crash-landed the badly damaged bomber. It was subsequently written-off, reportedly due to severe AA damage. Meanwhile, Capt Driver reported meeting three or four other Ju 88s and claimed to have shot one of these down into the sea; no other Ju 88s were recorded lost.

It would seem that the relieving section of Hurricanes from 274 Squadron which arrived to take over from the South Africans, also met the Ju 88s noted by Driver. Flown by three of the attached French pilots, these engaged the bombers, Sous Lt Littolf in W9329 claiming one shot down. He then reported meeting a lone Cant. Z.1007bis, apparently a reconnaissance machine out from Libya, claiming this damaged before it escaped. However, one of the Hurricanes, W9273 flown by Sgt Auguste Guillou, failed to return; it may either have been hit by return fire from the Ju 88s, or shot down by an escorting Bf 110, for during the day the Germans were to claim four Hurricanes shot down south of Crete.

While these actions were underway Force D comprising the cruiser HMS *Phoebe* and four destroyers, left Alexandria to make a last run to Sphakia in southern Crete. No opposition was met until the ships were nearing the Cretan coast. Here between 1825 and 1905 three attacks were made by Ju 88s, but all bombs fell wide and it was believed that one bomber was hit by AA fire. By now the vessels were out of effective range of protecting Hurricanes, but some cover was still being provided by a few Marylands and Blenheims. On arrival over the British force, Lt Jim Williams of 24 SAAF Squadron saw two aircraft circling nearby, one of these another Maryland, the other a Bf 110 which was apparently too involved in stalking this other Maryland to notice the approach of the new arrival. Closing to 150 yards range, Williams fired two bursts into the Zerstörer with his front guns, reporting that it burst into flames and spiralled down into the sea. This may have been Hptmn Karl Heindorf's aircraft from 2./ZG 26, the loss of which was recorded next day – though reportedly to AA fire.

Later in the day Lt Bob Talbot, in the air for a second time, intercepted a Cant flyingboat which was attempting to shadow British shipping, pursuing this for about 100 miles until he reported that he had brought it down in the sea 50 miles off Tobruk. No such loss has been discovered, however.

During the day Hurricanes of 274, 73 and 1 SAAF Squadrons had flown 44 sorties, Fulmars of 806 Squadron, Blenheims of 45 and 55 Squadrons, and Marylands of 24 SAAF Squadron each contributing another six, with Beaufighters, strengthened by the arrival of six more of these powerful aircraft, adding another eight. The Marylands of 39 Squadron also continued their daily maritime reconnaissance duties, joined on this day by another such aircraft from 69 Squadron, out from Malta.

That night Flt Lt Dudley Honor of 274 Squadron was able to attract the attention of the crew of a 228 Squadron Sunderland, and was picked up and flown back to Egypt. He and Sgt Kerr had made their way to the Cretan coast, but Kerr's feet had been so badly lacerated during the walk that he was not able to make it to the boat going out to the Sunderland, and he had to be left behind, becoming a PoW.

British Claims

274 Sqn	Lt R.H.Talbot	Z4510	⎫	Ju 88	S Crete 0700-0915
24 SAAF Sqn	Lt C.S.Kearney		⎬		
274 Sqn	Capt K.W.Driver	Z4614	⎭	Ju 88	S Crete 0700-1000
	Sous Lt A.Littolf	W9527		Ju 88	S Crete 0850
	Sous Lt A.Littolf	W9527		Cant.Z.1007bis	damaged S Crete 0920
	Lt R.H.Talbot	W9322		Cant.Z.501	50m off Tobruk 1330-1800
24 SAAF Sqn	Lt J.A.Williams			Bf 110	S Crete

British Casualties

274 Sqn	Hurricane I W9273 Sgt A.J.P.Guillou MiA

The fall of Crete at the end of May brought a further problem for RAF, Middle East. From this island and from airfields in southern Greece, Luftwaffe bomber units were now in a position to undertake a much more sustained attack on targets in Egypt – particularly at Alexandria and around the Suez Canal. Consequently, it became necessary to enhance the fighter defence of this area. Fortunately, however, the range was rather too great to allow fighter escorts to be flown, German activities here therefore being confined mainly to the hours of darkness for other than high-flying individual reconnaissance aircraft. Details of the operations associated with this area will be found in Chapter 13 – Blitz on Egypt.

CHAPTER 8

MIDSUMMER CRISIS

At the beginning of June there was an element of slightly greater stability in the Mediterranean area generally. Following the Axis occupations of Yugoslavia, Greece and Crete, much of the Luftwaffe – and, indeed, the Wehrmacht – had withdrawn northwards for reasons that would soon become abundantly clear. While there had been no diminution in Axis dispositions in North Africa, much of X.Fliegerkorps had departed Sicily, leaving Malta facing relatively desultory attacks by the Regia Aeronautica. This left the island's defenders able to concentrate once again on building up offensive forces to interdict the vital supply routes between Southern Europe and Libya (see *Malta: The Hurricane Years, 1940-1941*).

During June 1941 AVM G.G.Dawson was sent out to the Middle East due to "Churchill's legitimate dissatisfaction with the rate of serviceability the RAF was achieving". He proposed drastic changes in organisation, wholeheartedly approved by Tedder, taking the post of chief maintenance and supply officer, directly under Tedder. A maintenance group to superintend maintenance and repair work and organise salvage units was formed.

There was initially some argument with air ministry as to whether this was the way to proceed, or if the maintenance group should be placed under the administration air officer. Tedder at once made the point that circumstances were not at all the same with the position and way of doing things in the UK. Middle East had no air ministry, ministry of aircraft production, or maintenance command to rely on; his point was taken.

Tedder initially doubted that he would last long in this new position following the fall of Crete, but was assured that his stock in the air ministry was rising. Freeman wrote to him:

"I am afraid you are always getting telegrams from us saying you must attack ships, you must relieve Habbaniya, you must hold on to Crete, you must defend convoys, you must advance in Libya. All this must be maddening to you, and make it difficult to know what priorities really matter. I sometimes feel that we might end the next telegram by saying 'You must win the war.' I hope it is unnecessary for me to tell you that I joined with the C.A.S.' handsome vote of confidence in you. We both know what you and Drummond have to put up with."

He therefore wrote in his personal journal: "I do not think this is a time to be mealy-mouthed. If Whitehall does not like what I say, then it is too bad !" He was advised by Air Chief Marshal Sir Charles Portal, chief of the air staff, that the Defence Committee had approved his proposal to reinforce Middle East by 15 July to an effective strength of 40 and a half squadrons of modern aircraft, later to be increased to 50. The problem, however, remained delivery.

Following the fall of Crete, the Middle East commanders were now beginning to receive a barrage of demands from the prime minister to undertake a new offensive in Cyrenaica, both to relieve Tobruk and to make full use of what Churchill viewed as the generous reinforcements of tanks and aircraft which had been sent during recent weeks. He seems to have become fixated by the 'numbers game' and failed to grasp fully the time required to prepare and train units for desert operations. In doing so, he allowed pressure to placate both parliament and the various commonwealth governments to override military advice. This was to become a constant theme of the North African campaigns by which the British commanders there were to be constrained during the next 18 months. Certainly he had many problems, not least with parliament, but he does seem almost wilfully to have failed to accept or to understand that numbers alone meant little in modern warfare if the personnel were not fully trained for the theatre in which they were to operate, and the duties they were to fulfil there.

Tedder himself appeared initially to have been swayed by this approach, but increasingly he and the other air commanders began to realise that this was something of a 'red herring'. Following the pilot wastage of the Battles of France and Britain, experienced, fully trained fighter pilots were in gravely short supply. Aircrew were now being rushed through the new Commonwealth Air Training Plan in rapidly increasing numbers. However, the amount of time spent at operational training units was at an absolute minimum, training in tactics before reaching squadrons was brief, and above all, training in aerial gunnery was woefully inadequate. Exactly the same situation was affecting Fighter Command in the UK, where losses in cross-Channel operations during 1941 were worryingly high. At least, however, most squadrons there had Spitfires. Air ministry remained resolutely unwilling to release these fighters for overseas service throughout 1941 in case the Luftwaffe should return to the full-scale attack on the home island. It was not until the parlous state of Malta's desperate defence – now fully perceived as vital to the whole Middle Eastern strategy – demanded that better aircraft be sent. Even then, it was March 1942 before the first Spitfire fighter (as opposed to the odd unarmed photographic reconnaissance version) was allowed to operate anywhere outside the UK, and longer than that before the first squadron became operational over the Western Desert.

It seemed to take the RAF a long time to realise and accept that a fighter aircraft was not in the first instance an aircraft which happened to carry guns, but a flying gun which required effective marksmanship above all to be of proper use. Shooting at a slow bomber, progressing along a steady course was in no way comparable with trying to keep the sight on a weaving, jinking fighter aircraft; this required special skills. Without the necessary in-depth training, the allowances for deflection could usually only be mastered by someone who had already gained considerable experience of bringing down birds on the wing – or at the least, clay pigeons.

Simply to send quantities of aircraft inferior to such opposition as was likely to be met, together with inadequately trained pilots, and expect them to achieve the desired results was unrealistic. Against the experienced, superbly trained Luftwaffe pilots and their superior Messerschmitt Bf 109s, it was little more than an invitation to those pilots to increase their personal tallies of victories and for the German medal manufacturers to cast additional quantities of Ritterkreuz (Knights' Crosses) to award to them.

Against this background, the recent hostile actions of the Vichy French authorities in Syria in allowing German and Italian aircraft to transit their territory to reach Iraq, together with other actions considered to be adverse to British interests, caused commanders concern regarding this situation at their backs. The neutralisation and occupation of Syria to secure the position at the eastern end of the Mediterranean appeared necessary. It would also provide an immediate frontier with Turkey, whose involvement in the war on the British side was still considered to be a desirable possibility.

There were the hopes that such an undertaking might not result in too great an adverse reaction from the French, but in the event that this did not prove to be the case, it was necessary to earmark adequate forces for this undertaking. This proved to be a wise and necessary precaution, as considerable resistance was in fact offered, which resulted in a fratricidal battle of campaign proportions which was to take more than a month to resolve.

Prior to an invasion being commenced, actions against Vichy airfields near the borders had seen the initial operational involvement of two new types entering service in RAF, Middle East's domain. 250 Squadron had become operational on 11 May at Aqir (Palestine), and three days later two of its aircraft were involved in the first sorties by Middle East Tomahawks to strafe aircraft on Palmyra airfield. This attack was repeated next day, but due to lack of French reaction in the air, the squadron was released on the 16th, and a few days later began the move to Egypt.

On 5 June a detachment of Beaufighters of 252/272 Squadron from Edcu operated from Lydda in Palestine, strafing the Royal Dutch Shell fuel oil depot at Beirut. (Details of the involvements of aircraft of this type during the summer and early autumn of 1941 may be found in Chapter 15 – In Support of the Royal Navy, and in *Malta: The Hurricane Years, 1940-41*.)

On 8 June the invasion of Lebanon and Syria commenced. Support in the air was provided by Hurricanes of 80 Squadron and the newly-operational Tomahawks of 3 RAAF Squadron in the fighter role, plus 208 Squadron, also with Hurricanes, but in the tactical reconnaissance role, and the Blenheim IV bombers of 11 and 84 Squadrons. Blenheim IVf fighters of 203 Squadron were also committed, as was a new small unit known as X Flight, equipped with eight Gladiators.

Further support was provided in the coastal area by several Fleet Air Arm squadrons including 803 Squadron with Fulmars and 806 with borrowed RAF Hurricanes, plus 815 Squadron with Swordfish. French resistance was strong, as considerable reinforcement of the Armée de l'Air had occurred immediately before the invasion, involving a considerable number of modern bombers and Dewoitine 520 fighters. The latter proved superior to the Hurricane Is and Fulmars, inflicting some quite considerable casualties. However, they were ultimately countered effectively by the Australian Tomahawks, and – surprisingly – by X Flight's Gladiators.

As fighting progressed, reinforcements to the British forces included 260/450 Squadron (which has already been mentioned earlier) and by the Blenheims of 45 Squadron. A section of 33 Squadron joined 806 Squadron, but was not called upon, while X Flight, reinforced by some of the pilots who had served with 261 Squadron on Malta earlier, was expanded into a new 127 Squadron. Fleet Air Arm reinforcements included Fairey Albacore torpedo-bombers of 826 and 829 Squadrons operating from Cyprus against French shipping, with Wellingtons drawn from 37, 38, 70 and 148 Squadrons making a number of night raids from the Canal Zone. The campaign ended on 12 July with the capitulation of the Vichy authorities, followed by the departure for metropolitan France of the majority of their armed forces. (Details of the Syrian Campaign may be found in *Dust Clouds in the Middle East*.)

For the British, their backs were now secured, most of the units involved being freed to return to the main front in the Western Desert. Here, even as the Syrian invasion was underway, the prime minister's desires had been acceded to – prematurely, it must be said, as the local commanders were well aware. Operation Battleaxe was launched on 14 June, but did little better than the previously ill-fated Brevity, and would be called off three days later after heavy losses, as will be described.

Meanwhile, re-equipment and reformation of the units which had served in Greece and Crete was fully underway, and may be summarized as follows:

11 Squadron:	departed Greece for Ramleh on 16 May. Brought up to strength on Blenheim IVs. Operations over Syria 8 June-12 July.
30 Squadron:	departed Crete for Amiriya on 28 May and re-equipped with Hurricane Is. Moved to Edcu on 22 June.
33 Squadron:	departed Crete for Amiriya on 1 June and brought up to strength on Hurricane Is. Detachments sent to Heliopolis, Gerawla, El Gamil and Fuka during the next two months.
80 Squadron:	departed Crete for Palestine on 29 April. Brought up to strength on Hurricane Is. Operations over Syria 8 June-12 July.
84 Squadron:	departed Greece for Heliopolis during April. Brought up to strength on Blenheim IVs. Operations over Iraq in May and Syria 30 June-12 July.
112 Squadron:	departed Crete for Fayid on 31 May. Converted to Tomahawks during September.
113 Squadron:	departed Crete for Ramleh on 15 May. Brought up to strength on Blenheim IVs. To Maaten Bagush for operations in the Western Desert on 31 May.
208 Squadron;	departed Crete for Aboukir on 28 April. To Gaza 1 May and operations over Iraq and Syria until 12 July.
211 Squadron;	departed Crete for Heliopolis on 23 April as echelon. Re-equipped with Blenheim IVs in May.

Greece had cost the RAF 72 aircraft in combat and 55 destroyed on the ground, with a further 82 abandoned during the retreat. 148 aircrew had been killed and 15 had become PoWs. Fleet Air Arm casualties to its 815 Squadron had been two Swordfish lost on operations, three ditched in the sea and two force-landed; one crewman had been killed and five had become PoWs.

Additionally, Crete had been defended for some months by 805 Squadron, Fleet Air Arm, this unit withdrawing to Dekheila on 19 May. The unit had operated a heterogeneous collection of Fulmars, Sea Gladiators, Brewster Buffaloes and Hurricanes (the latter borrowed from the RAF). On 16 June the unit moved to Mersa Matruh to undertake coastal defence fighter operations.

The Greek government had ordered 30 Grumman F4F-3A Wildcat fighters during August 1940, but these had arrived at Suez only in April 1941, just too late for delivery. Their presence was indicated to the British authorities and they were to be diverted to the Royal Navy as a Lend-Lease transfer at the end of the month. These aircraft were then used to re-equip 805 Squadron during July and August.

East Africa also provided further reinforcements during this period. 237 Squadron – the sole operational unit of the Royal Southern Rhodesian Air Force – arrived at Wadi Halfa on 30 May, equipped with Gladiator IIs which were mainly ex-94 Squadron machines; a detachment was then despatched to Kufra Oasis. Another unit to arrive was 40 SAAF Squadron which like the Rhodesian squadron undertook a tactical reconnaissance role.

Against this background, the start of June 1941 had still found both the air and ground forces of the British Commonwealth in North Africa available in less strength and to a lower level of preparedness than the commander-in-chief and his subordinate commanders could have wished when planning a new offensive.

Sunday, 1 June 1941

With the need to divert action over Crete and the returning vessels ended, June 1941 now presented a different set of challenges to RAF, Middle East. For the coming six months sustaining the Tobruk garrison was to become a priority which placed considerable demands on both the air force and the navy. At the same time pressure from Churchill grew to resume the offensive following the despatch of the Tiger convoy reinforcements and other forces which were on their way by the longer Cape route.

The first day of the new month provided evidence of what lay ahead as the meagre resources of 204 Group involved in naval protection sorties along the North African coast to the beleaguered port amounted to 35 by Hurricanes, seven by Marylands, six by Beaufighters and one by a lone Blenheim fighter. Notable here was the effort by the Beaufighters of 252 Squadron, which had just flown in to Abu Sueir after a period based on Malta.

73 and 274 Squadrons took part in the shipping patrols for which the latter's remaining long-range Hurricanes proved particularly useful. However, the patrols were unable to prevent an attack on the AA cruiser HMS *Calcutta*, which was sunk by a pair of Ju 88s with the loss of 117 men; 255 more were picked up from the sea.

1 SAAF Squadron meanwhile, patrolled inland where during the afternoon Lt A.J.Botha intercepted an Hs 126 of 2.(H)/14 flying low over the desert about 15 miles east of Sidi Rezegh. Botha approached from head-on as the 'spotter' dived even lower in an effort to evade the Hurricane. This, however, allowed Botha to attack from the beam and the German aircraft went down to crash in flames, the crew failing to survive.

204 Group's striking power was hardly aided by the need on this date to withdraw 45 and 55 Squadrons for rest and re-equipment following the heavy losses these two light bomber units had recently suffered.

As if these vital issues were not enough to cope with, a dispute arose as to whether victories claimed by pilots when they were attached to other squadrons than their own – as had happened to a considerable degree recently – should be credited to the unit with which they were temporarily flying, or to their parent unit. The decision was taken that such claims would be credited to the parent unit, at least insofar as the pilots who had just been attached to 274 Squadron were concerned.

As has been described earlier, the strength of RAF, Middle East, was showing signs of a potential rapid growth following the arrival of recent reinforcements and the withdrawal of units from the Greece/Crete fiasco, but the Luftwaffe too was to welcome an important new arrival in Africa on this date. The unit in question was no more than a single staffel of Bf 109E fighters, but a staffel of considerable virtuosity. 7./JG 26 flew in to Gazala with just six of the Messerschmitt fighters to hand. The unit had taken part in the fighting over England during the previous summer, and had then spent nearly five months in Sicily, operating over Malta. Here its commanding officer, Oblt Joachim Müncheberg had personally claimed 19 of the island's defenders shot down (plus one Yugoslav aircraft during a brief move to the Adriatic coast of Italy during April). This had brought his own tally to 43 for which he had received the award of the prestigious Ritterkreuz (Knight's Cross to the Iron Cross), followed by the Eichenlaube (Oak Leaves) to this award.

His pilots had claimed an additional 23 victories during their relatively brief period over Malta, during which time the island had been rendered nearly defenceless by their depredations for a time; not a single Bf 109 had been lost in combat during this period (see *Malta: the Hurricane Years, 1940-41* for more details of 7./JG 26's operations to the end of May 1941). Although subordinate to Neumann of JG 27, Müncheberg was treated by the latter as an honoured guest in the best oriental fashion. The resident Luftwaffe fighter unit, I./JG 27, recorded at this time that from the beginning of June British bombers attacked the Gazala airfields and the surrounding tented camps at frequent intervals, forcing the gruppe to break camp and pitch their tents between the dunes and the beach. Many ideas were tried to mislead the bombers, mock fires being lit on dull days a couple of miles away on which the bombers unloaded, making a fine job of killing local vermin! During the month a schwarm from 2.Staffel (Lts Willi Kothmann and Stahlschmidt. Obfw Hermann Förster and Fw Franz Elles) strafed a sailing ship of 200 tons and set it on fire. It was maliciously suggested in the unit that the captain of the ship had overturned the lamp in his cabin in the excitement, while others said that Lt Stahlschmidt had hit the petrol cooking stove in the galley. However, the crew of eight Englishmen and six Greeks were forced to abandon ship before it blew up, and landed in German-held territory, becoming prisoners. The captain was a small, fair-haired, moustachioed character by the name of Chessney, who after the war became a notorious smuggler and pirate in the Mediterranean, until he committed suicide in February 1954. Stahlschmidt described the 'Sea Battle of Bomba Bay' that evening for a radio war correspondent.

British Claims			
1 SAAF Sqn	Lt A.J.Botha	Hs 126	15m E Sidi Rezegh 1500
German Casualties			
2.(H)/14	Hs 126 Fw Josef Haase & Uffz Georg Scholtern KiA		
I./StG 1	Ju 87R-2 WNr 6051 20% damaged		
II./StG 2	Ju 87R-2 WNr 5876 90% destroyed in crash-landing at El Adem due to engine trouble		

Monday, 2 June 1941
On this date those pilots of 73 and 1 SAAF Squadrons still attached to 274 Squadron, returned to their own units.

During the day Tobruk's AA gunners claimed two Ju 87s shot down from a force of eight Italian-flown Stukas escorted by three Bf 110s. One of 239ª Squadriglia's dive-bombers was shot down with the loss of the crew, while two of III./ZG 26's Bf 110s were very seriously damaged.

Further west 18° Gruppo CT's S.Ten Bordoni-Bisleri claimed two Blenheims shot down over Benghazi though his CR.42 was hit by return fire which shattered the windscreen and damaged the upper wing. It seems probable that he had actually managed to bring down a long-range reconnaissance Blenheim IV of 203 Squadron. These were Bordoni's fourth and fifth claims, credited to a pilot who would ultimately become one of the Regia Aeronautica's top-scorers with 19 victories.

British Casualties			
203 Sqn	Blenheim IV L9318 MiA		
German Casualties			
III./ZG 26	Bf 110E-1 WNr 3902 70% Marsa Luch		
	Bf 110E-1 WNr 3983 70% Ras Azaz		
Italian Claims			
95ª Sq/18° Gr CT	S.Ten Franco Bordoni-Bisleri	2 Blenheims	Benghazi
Italian Casualties			
239ª Sq BaT	Ju 87R shot down by AA over Tobruk; Ten Paolo Livio/Av. Sc Giuseppe Tempo KiA		

Tuesday, 3 June 1941
Reconnaissance on this date reported that 17 German fighters (13 Bf 109s and four Bf 110s) were present on Great Gambut airfield. Consequently, 1 SAAF Squadron, which was engaged in escorting a small convoy to Tobruk, was called in and ordered to undertake an immediate attack with all available aircraft. Six Hurricanes were despatched, led by Lt Bob Talbot, who knew the airfield from earlier attacks. The formation refuelled at Sidi Barrani, then flew along the coast over the sea until reaching a point between Bardia and Tobruk. As two pilots stayed above at 6,000 feet to give cover, the other four dived down to strafe. The attacking pilots could identify only two Bf 110s, six Ju 87s and a few miscellaneous aircraft, but were able to claim three of the Stukas and one unidentified type destroyed – three of them in flames – and ten more believed to have been damaged.

As the Hurricanes departed the target area, one was seen to be trailing smoke, apparently hit by fire from the ground. Reported one of the returning pilots: "About half a mile from the aerodrome the nose of the aircraft suddenly dropped. The Hurricane struck the ground almost vertically and burst into flames immediately." The pilot had been Lt Talbot, until then the SAAF's most successful fighter pilot in North

A convoy winds its way through the hairpin bends of the Halfaya Pass.

Africa, who had claimed nine and one shared aerial victories; his Hurricane had been hit during its third strafing pass. The general officer commanding Western Desert Force, Lt Gen Sir Noel Beresford-Peirse, subsequently signalled his regrets to the squadron on the loss of "one of your most gallant officers".

32 more Hurricane sorties were expended on shipping patrols on 3 June. Three of 274 Squadron's long-range aircraft flown by C Flight pilots – attached 229 Squadron personnel – engaged Ju 87s of II./StG 2 and six escorting Bf 109Es of 2./JG 27 over two ships at around 1500. A brief dogfight between the fighters ensued, during which Flg Off Ron Bary shot down Uffz Reichenstein, and Fw Franz Elles brought down Sgt Peter Crump's aircraft, which crashed into the sea at 1750. Reichenstein crash-landed between Gambut and Gazala, his aircraft being totally destroyed, although he escaped unhurt himself. Two of the Ju 87s were brought down by the ships' AA, crashing at Gambut as virtually total wrecks, although again the crews survived.

British Claims			
229/274 Sqn	Flg Off R.E.Bary	Bf 109	over coast
British Casualties			
1 SAAF Sqn	Hurricane I Z4515 Lt R.H.Talbot KiA Great Gambut area		
229/274 Sqn	Hurricane I Z4369 Sgt P.Crump KiA over coast		
German Claims			
2./JG 27	Fw Franz Elles	Hurricane	Gambut 1750
German Casualties			
2./JG 27	Bf 109E-7 WNr 4127 crash-landed after combat, 100% destroyed; Uffz Egon Reichenstein safe		
8./ZG 26	Bf 110E-1 WNr 3950 80% destroyed at Gambut		
II./StG 2	Ju 87R-1 WNr 5678 90% destroyed at Gambut		
	Ju 87R-1 WNr 6042 90% destroyed at Gambut		

Wednesday – Saturday, 4/7 June 1941

During 4th 73 Squadron was reinforced with six new pilots, while Flt Lt Dudley Honor rejoined 274 Squadron following his adventures on Crete; he was awarded a Bar to his DFC. As already recounted, ten more 229 Squadron pilots arrived at Mersa Matruh on 7 June, having completed their journey from Gibraltar where they had been awaiting transport.

———

Saturday, 7 June 1940

Italian Casualties

279ª Sq AS   S.79 badly damaged on the ground at Derna by bombs

Sunday, 8 June 1941

Tobruk remained the main focus of Axis attention, and on this date another of 239ª Squadriglia's Ju 87Rs was shot down in flames here when eight of the unit's aircraft attacked troops in the Fort Pilastrino area; the crew were killed.

German Casualties

Unspecified unit   Ju 88 destroyed on the ground at Derna by bombs

Italian Casualties

239ª Sq BaT   Ju 87R shot down by AA over Tobruk; S.Ten Mario Daverio/ 1ª Av Italo Masi KiA

Monday, 9 June 1941

Following a period of patrolling but little action, a quite major series of strafing attacks were organised by 204 Group in an effort to reduce the perceived air strength of the Axis prior to the commencement of a new offensive on the ground. Reconnaissance indicated the following Axis strength:

Derna South   70 bombers and other aircraft
Gazala South   40 fighters (mainly Bf 109s)
Gazala North   Approximately 30 fighters (largely CR.42s)
Martuba   15 long-range bombers and other aircraft

Four Marylands from 24 SAAF Squadron were to be escorted by 14 Hurricanes from 73 and 274 Squadrons, each of the bombers leading a group of fighters to a different airfield.

    All aircraft took off in moonlight prior to dawn on what was a rather poorly and hastily-planned operation. Confusion prevented the four individual formations forming up as had been ordered, and some Hurricane pilots turned back. One Maryland crew then jettisoned their bombs before arriving over Derna due to heavy Flak, but two bombed as briefed. The fighters strafed two of the fields at dawn, claiming 14 aircraft burnt and ten shot-up.

    The operation proved something of a disaster for 73 Squadron, however, four of which unit's aircraft formated on one of the Marylands making for Gazala North, while Flt Lt Oliver Green's flight of four which had been ordered to attack Gazala South (the hotbed of Messerschmitts) failed to formate on their Maryland. Despite this, Green decided to head on, leading his section some 200 miles directly to their target – an inspired piece of navigation. At Gazala South Bf 109s and G.50s were identified and strafed, six being claimed on fire. Other Bf 109s scrambled to intercept as the airfield's Flak defences put up a warm welcome.

    Following the attack, Green led his trio out to sea, but as he was doing so, spotted a Messerschmitt on the tail of Sgt Bob Laing's aircraft. He fired at this, but saw no result, returning to land at 0650. Meanwhile Oblt Redlich and Uffz Steinhausen of I./JG 27 shot down two of the Hurricanes, Plt Off Greville Tovey's aircraft going into the sea in flames; that flown by Sgt Laing crash-landed within the Tobruk defences having been hit by Flak and then by a fighter. He later described his ordeal:

New arrivals in the Western Desert were the **Hurricanes of 1 SAAF Squadron, two of which are seen here.**

"We were ordered off early in the morning to fly the 30 or 40 miles west to Gazala, to try and knock out any 109s we could find on the ground. It was not a good idea because it was just before dawn and you could not see enough to get yourself into position for a decent burst. I found two 109s but could not get a decent squirt at them although a Storch lit up quite nicely – not that it would bring the end of the war much closer! One of the Jerry ground gunners managed to hit my radiator; I felt a solid bang underneath which gave rise to a steady leak of steam and glycol, leaving a distinctive trail as I set off east. I was quite happy that I could at least reach Tobruk, but rather stupidly forgot that I made an excellent target against the dawn sky to which I was heading. I began to relax a little when I got a solid burst from a 109 up the tail, and I found it quite startling to hear the banging on the armour plate behind my seat, while the instruments on the top and sides of the panel disintegrated. I found myself thinking thank God that armour plating really works. Perhaps they were not using armour-piercing ammo. Some of the firing must have hit the control surfaces as the Hurricane grew steadily more nose-heavy. Just to add to my predicament the ether in the glycol was rising up from the floor and causing me to become anaesthetised. Anyway she hit the ground more or less level, with a bounce or two. My straps were none too tight and I banged my face on the

June 1941 saw the arrival from a defensive role at Maryut of 250 Squadron, thus bringing the Curtiss Tomahawk to the desert. The commanding officer, Sqn Ldr John Scoular, who had seen action in France with 73 Squadron a year earlier, led the unit in this new environment.

gunsight, doing wonders to my natural beauty. She began to burn so I jumped out and started to walk a few miles towards Tobruk, feeling none too chipper. A small cave came into view and I laid down in it to recover a bit. I realised later that I had been concussed in the crash, and that I was not in any condition to do any steady thinking or walking. After an hour or two I was found by an Indian patrol and taken into Tobruk, and to hospital."

Five of 274 Squadron's aircraft managed to reach Derna where four Ju 87s were identified and strafed. An accompanying Wellington crew reported seeing eight fires on the ground as a result of the attack; all these Hurricanes returned safely.

British Casualties			
73 Sqn	Hurricane I Plt Off G.Tovey KiA		
	Hurricane I Sgt R.I.Laing crash-landed at Tobruk, safe		
German Claims			
1./JG 27	Oblt Wolfgang Redlich	Hurricane	N Tobruk 0500
	Uffz Gunther Steinhausen	Hurricane	N Tobruk 0505

Tuesday, 10 June 1941

A Ju 87 of II./StG 2 was lost, reportedly in combat with fighters, but no Allied claim for such an aircraft has been recorded on this date.

German Casualties	
II./StG 2	Ju 87R-2 WNr 5881 75% destroyed at Gambut due to combat with fighters
I./JG 27	Bf 109E-1 WNr 6201 100% destroyed in crash-landing at Gambut

Wednesday, 11 June 1941

An important addition to 204 Group's establishment occurred with the arrival at Sidi Haneish of 250 Squadron, equipped with Curtiss Tomahawks. This unit had recently commenced operations in defence of Alexandria (see Chapter 13 – Blitz on Egypt), and now moved into the forward area to take part in forthcoming offensive operations. The Tomahawk was a US-built fighter, with a top speed of 352 mph and an armament of two .50in Browning machine guns mounted in the nose, above the engine, and four .303in guns in the wings. It performed best at lower altitudes, being a fairly manoeuvrable machine, and in this respect was better-suited to desert conditions of aerial warfare than to those over Western Europe, where combat was generally at high levels. Although plagued at first with teething troubles, it was an improvement on the Hurricane II in many ways, and much better than the Mark I which still equipped North African units. Certainly, it was sufficient of a match for the Bf 109E to set the German fighter pilots pressing for the early arrival of the improved F model.

Ten of the newly-arrived 229 Squadron pilots were attached to 73 Squadron's C Flight on this date, while four more went to 6 Squadron and four to 208 Squadron, the two latter groups to undertake tactical reconnaissance duties in the meantime. During the day fighter Blenheims of 113 Squadron resumed operations, strafing MT and also attacking Berka airfield where three large aircraft were claimed destroyed on the ground.

Thursday, 12 June 1941

As further reinforcement prior to the forthcoming offensive, seven of 33 Squadron's more experienced pilots who had been attached to 30 Squadron for defensive duties, were led by Flt Lt Vernon Woodward to join 274 Squadron at Gerawla on attachment.

Early in the day eight of 239ª Squadriglia's Ju 87s again set off to bomb Tobruk, targeting gun batteries at Fort Perrone. Here one was shot down by AA with the loss of the crew. Several Luftwaffe aircraft were damaged on the ground, either by air attack or in accidents.

III./LG 1 had despatched four Ju 88s from its base in Sicily to attack Fuka airfield during the early hours. With full daylight, I Gruppe of this geschwader moved from Gaddura to Eleusis in southern Greece from where it could also operate over North Africa.

German Casualties	
Kdo.Fl.H Ber Afrika	Kl 32 crashed Ain el Gazala; Fw Pförtner/Gefr Schmid
I./JG 27	Bf 109E-4 WNr 3480 35% damaged in take-off crash at Gambut
	Bf 109E-1 WNr 3549 30% damaged by air raid, Ain el Gazala
	Bf 109E-1 WNr 5431 15% damaged by air raid, Ain el Gazala
Italian Casualties	
239ª Sq BaT	Ju 87R shot down by AA at Tobruk; Ten Cesare Gallo/Serg Magg Florindo Gondolo KiA

On this, the eve of the new offensive code-named Operation Battleaxe, the strengths of the allied air forces which would be committed to action were:

204 Group

73 Squadron	Hurricane I	Sqn Ldr P.G.Wykeham-Barnes, DFC
plus Det 213 Squadron	Hurricane I	Flg Off C.B.Temlett, DFC
274 Squadron	Hurricane I	Sqn Ldr G.E.Hawkins
plus Det 229 Squadron	Hurricane I	Flt Lt W.A.Smith
plus Det 33 Squadron	Hurricane I	Flt Lt V.C.Woodward, DFC
1 SAAF Squadron	Hurricane I	Maj T.Ross Theron
plus Det 2 SAAF Squadron	Hurricane I	Capt D.H.Loftus
250 Squadron	Tomahawk IIb	Sqn Ldr J.E.Scoular, DFC
6 Squadron	Hurricane I	Sqn Ldr P.Legge
14 Squadron	Blenheim IV	Sqn Ldr D.C.Stapleton, DFC, AFC
45 Squadron	Blenheim IV	Wg Cdr J.O.Willis, DFC
113 Squadron	Blenheim IV and IVf	Sqn Ldr R.H.Spencer
39 Squadron	Maryland	Sqn Ldr A.McD.Bowman, DFC
24 SAAF Squadron	Maryland	Maj C.E.Martin, DFC

Totals included 98 Hurricanes and Tomahawks, while altogether 105 Blenheims, Maryland and Wellingtons could be called upon for bombing assistance. The recently-arrived Beaufighters of 272 Squadron had left again, this time to take part in the fighting in Syria, but as mentioned, 113 Squadron had just arrived back in the desert, now with some of the 20mm-armed strafer Blenheim IVfs. First mention was also made of the arrival with 274 Squadron of a cannon-armed Hurricane. 238 Squadron, another Battle of Britain Hurricane unit, began arriving in Egypt also, but like 213 Squadron, most of its star performers in 1940 had left the unit during the previous six months. 250 Squadron moved to Sidi Haneish from Lake Maryut with its Tomahawks.

The new offensive was to be marked by the first really large participation of the SAAF in the Western Desert fighting, and the next week was to see some of the heaviest aerial action to date in African skies. It would also set the pattern for much that would transpire in the actions both on the ground and in the air for the next 12 months or so.

CHAPTER 9

OPERATION BATTLEAXE

Saturday, 14 June 1941

Battleaxe began for the air force before dawn, for three of 24 SAAF's Marylands had been briefed to take off while it was still dark to lead flights of Hurricanes to undertake a further pre-emptive attack on the Lutwaffe's forward airfields. One bomber was to lead six Hurricanes of 1 SAAF Squadron to Gazala South. One was to take six of 73 Squadron's fighters to Gazala North, and the third was to guide six more long-range Hurricanes of 274 Squadron to Derna.

At 0439 hours Flg Off George 'Randy' Goodman, DFC, of 73 Squadron took off with Flt Sgt J.White, DFM, another Battle of Britain veteran, and Plt Offs Chatfield, Ward, Moss and Logan, led by Lt C.S.Kearny. Flak was intense, Roy Chatfield force-landing his damaged Hurricane at Capuzzo where he became a PoW. Ward, Moss and Logan all returned, but of Goodman there was no news, and he was presumed shot down. He had indeed fallen and was buried at El Mrassas cemetery. John White had run short of fuel, but as he came in to land at Sidi Barrani, he crashed, dying of his injuries. Both he and Goodman were serious losses to the squadron. Goodman had claimed ten individual and six shared victories, four of the former and two of the latter since arriving in Africa. White had flown with 72 Squadron in England where he had been credited with three and two shared, plus five probables.

These, however, were not to be the only experienced and decorated fighter pilots to be lost on this opening morning of the offensive. Hardly had the 73 Squadron aircraft departed, than the six 1 SAAF Squadron Hurricanes followed them off from Sidi Barrani at 0515, to Gazala South airfield. Poor visibility caused the formation to break up until only the leader of the Hurricanes, Capt K.W.Driver, DFC, and the Maryland remained. They were also on different radio frequencies, and unable to contact it, Driver watched in frustration as it sailed past the target area, flying on for a further 20 miles before the pilot realised his mistake and turned back. It then passed over Gazala at about 3,000 ft, with Driver providing cover from a further 3,000 ft above. Heavy Flak opened up, and I./JG 27's Oblt Franzisket rapidly took off.

On 14 June 1941 the leading South African fighter pilot, Capt Ken Driver, DFC, was shot down over Gazala by Oblt Ludwig Franzisket of 2./JG 27. The slightly wounded Driver was then entertained by his victors. He is seen here with, left to right, Hptmn Eduard Neumann, the gruppenkommandeur, Franzisket, and at right, Hptmn Springorum.

Seeing the Messerschmitt approaching, Driver made a frontal attack, both pilots opening fire. Driver's burst missed, but Franzisket's hit the Hurricane's fuel tank which exploded, the flames burning the back of Driver's neck.

Franzisket had now got too close, the left wing of his fighter striking the tail of Driver's, cutting it off. At that point Driver baled out. Not realising that his aircraft had lost its wingtip, Franzisket carried on and shot down the Maryland from which the pilot baled out, although the other members of the crew were killed. Both Driver and the Maryland pilot, Lt E.C.Newborn, were captured and were initially entertained by the JG 27 personnel, Franzisket showing his damaged Messerschmitt to the former.

Hptmn Springorum, who had lived for many years in the USA and who spoke fluent English, was annoyed at being disturbed so early in the morning, and angrily asked Newborn:

"By the hell, what do you English want here in Africa?" Smiling, Newborn responded: "The same that the Germans want here, sir !"

Both then burst out laughing.

Ludwig Franzisket leads Driver into his tent for breakfast.

Ken Driver was as great a loss to his unit as was Goodman to his. During the recent fighting in East Africa (see *Dust Clouds in the Middle East*) he had claimed nine Italian aircraft shot down, and had added one further against the Luftwaffe since his unit had arrived in the Western Desert. Ludwig Franzisket provided a most detailed account of the events of this day:

"The 14 June 1941 started a few minutes before dawn with bombs dropping and ground attacks being made on the south-east corner of the landing ground at Ain el Gazala, where 3.Staffel of JG 27 was stationed [This clearly relates to the attack by the 73 Squadron aircraft a few minutes earlier]. At that time 1.Staffel were on alert. One alert Rotte scrambled from the western edge of the airfield and pursued the low-flying Hurricanes in a westerly direction towards Tobruk where they caught them up. In the few minutes between the first and second waves of the attack, I jumped out of my bed and took off from the southern edge of the airfield. While closing the roof of my cockpit the mechanic showed me a twin-engined aircraft approaching from an easterly direction. I took off and closed in a right-hand turn, at which I was fired on very violently by our own Flak. While still climbing at 1500 metres a single Hurricane closed in on me from in front, and somewhat higher. As my aircraft was climbing very slowly I had no other choice than to point my Bf 109 at the Hurricane, approaching 'Schnauze-auf-Schnauze' (head-on), and to fire. The Hurricane fired likewise, but his bursts were too high, as I could see very clearly by the tracer. We both fired until the last second, and the aircraft touched each other. Just before this I had seen hits on the engine of the Hurricane, and Captain Driver told me afterwards that a cannon hit had set on fire the gravity tank of his Hurricane. This tank was in front of the seat, and the darting flame burned his neck. When both aircraft collided, my airscrew touched the right wingtip of the Hurricane and Driver's airscrew smashed the right wingtip of my Bf 109. I saw the Hurricane going down in a steep dive, and watched the pilot bale out. The Hurricane crashed some hundred metres south of the airfield, and Driver landed nearby. I turned and flew back to the airfield in a northerly direction when suddenly I observed a Martin Maryland some hundred metres north-east of Gazala airfield at 1500 metres. Although my aircraft was flying with one wing slightly low because of the damaged wingtip, I closed in and fired. The Maryland made a slight right-hand turn. I fired again, my burst going from the right engine along the whole fuselage to the tail. This engine caught fire, the Maryland went into a flat spin and one man baled out, the bomber diving steeply and crashing some hundreds of metres north of the Via Balbia.

219

"During the whole action there was no other Bf 109 in the sky over Ain el Gazala. Driver fired until the last second before the collision. Afterwards he told me that he had not seen the ramming, his aircraft already being on fire, he was preparing to bale out. I breakfasted with him in my tent and later we visited my Bf 109, whose right wing was being removed by the mechanics. Driver was very quiet and reserved, and we chatted for about two hours in my tent. He showed me a photo of his wife and a blonde curl that he carried. I promised to drop a container over Sidi Barrani with a message for her, as she was in Cairo at the time, having come to visit him. He was very glad about this."

Meanwhile, back at Sidi Barrani the third Maryland, flown by Lt C.L.Clarkson, had crashed on take-off. Without their guide the 274 Squadron pilots set off alone but failed to find their target in heavy mist. About three hours later another pilot of 3./JG 27, Lt Friedrich Hoffmann, made another claim for a Martin 167 about 20 miles south-east of Gambut. This would appear to have been a reconnaissance Maryland of 39 Squadron, which failed to return, Lt Coetzee and his crew being reported missing. As the Western Desert Force advance got underway, much effort was expended in providing standing patrols of fighters over the army at 5,000, 9,000 and 13,000 ft. This was known to be enormously wasteful of the available fighters, but was the result of the express demands of the ground forces. Not only was it frequently to place aircraft at a tactical disadvantage, but it also tied up potential escorts for the medium bombers which were consequently hardly used during the opening days of the operation.

During one such patrol by a trio of 2 SAAF Squadron pilots led by Capt D.H.Loftus, who were flying at the least favourable 6,000 ft level, a reconnaissance Bf 110 of 2(H)./14 was spotted near Halfaya. This was the first such sighting for the squadron, and following a long stern chase the Messerschmitt was shot down about 30 miles south-west of Sofafi for the unit's first victory in North Africa. The crew of two became PoWs.

During the last patrol of the day, commencing at 1910, three 1 SAAF Squadron Hurricanes were passing over Rabia at 2005 when a formation of Ju 87s was spotted passing nearby, and were at once attacked. Immediately, three escorting Bf 109s of I./JG 27 dropped on the attackers, Oblts Redlich and Schneider each shooting down one Hurricane. Lt A.A.Webb returned to report that he had seen Lt R.V.Christie's aircraft burst into flames and crash; Lt Botha also failed to return. News of him was received on 23 June when units of 7th Armoured Division found his crashed aircraft. On 5 July came an army report that he had shot down two of the dive-bombers before his demise and these were posthumously credited to him. Sadly, this would appear to have been a piece of wishful thinking.

British Claims

2 SAAF Sqn	Capt D.H.Loftus	⎫		
	Lt J.R.R.Wells	⎬	Bf 110	30m NW Sofafi
	Lt L.A.Stone	⎭		
1 SAAF Sqn	Lt A.J.Botha	V7809	2 Ju 87s	S Bir Hacheim 1945

British Casualties

73 Sqn	Hurricane I Z4507; Flg Off G.E.Goodman, DFC, KiA
	Hurricane I V7383; Flt Sgt J.White, DFM, KiFA
	Hurricane I Z4384; Plt Off R.Chatfield PoW
1 SAAF Sqn	Hurricane I V7831; Capt K.W.Driver, DFC, PoW
24 SAAF Sqn	Maryland II 1609; Lt E.C.Newborn PoW; 3 KiA
1 SAAF Sqn	Hurricane I V7809; Lt A.J.Botha KiA
	Hurricane I V7818; Lt R.V.Christie KiA
39 Sqn	Maryland II AH299; Lt Coetzee and crew FTR (Pilot believed to be I.M.Coetzee, later reported to be a PoW)

German Claims

3./JG 27	Oblt Ludwig Franzisket	Hurricane	S Ain el Gazala 0505
	Oblt Ludwig Franzisket	Martin 167	SE Ain el Gazala 0506
	Lt Friedrich Hoffmann	Martin 167	18m SE Gambut 0756
1./JG 27	Oblt Hugo Schneider	Hurricane	SE Halfaya Pass 1842
	Oblt Wolfgang Redlich	Hurricane	SE Halfaya Pass 1845

German Casualties

2(H)./14	Bf 110 Uffz Otto Unger & Lt Friedrich Giessalmann PoW
3./JG 27	Bf 109E 10% damaged in collision; Oblt Ludwig Franzisket unhurt

---

Sunday, 15 June 1941

11th Indian Brigade Group advanced along the coast road towards Halfaya and Sollum, while the 'I' tanks of 7th Armoured Division together with 22nd Guards Brigade set off through the desert and turned north on the Capuzzo-Sollum defences, a detachment making for Halfaya. At the same time 7th Armoured's cruiser tanks, accompanied by the division's support group, moved in a sweep further to the south. It was, in effect, a similar thrust to that employed at the start of Operation Compass six months earlier. It was not to enjoy any similar success, however, and although Capuzzo was taken, little other progress was made, in particular the defences at the Halfaya Pass resisting strongly.

Senior pilots of I./JG 27 in 1941; left to right: Oblt Ludwig Franzisket, adjutant of the gruppe, Hptmn Karl-Wolfgang Redlich, 1 Staffel, and Hptmn Gerhard Homuth, 3 Staffel.

274 Squadron undertook an early sortie to strafe Sidi Aziez airfield; on returning from this, the pilots reported meeting a CR.42, the first Italian fighters seen in some weeks, and this was claimed shot down by Plt Off Briggs; no corresponding Italian loss has been discovered for this date. This unit made first use of its cannon-armed Hurricane when at 0600 Plt Off Sumner was despatched in this to attack a field gun position between Fort Capuzzo and Halfaya. He was led to this target by Plt Off McBarnet in one of 6 Squadron's TacR Hurricanes. However, the pair were intercepted by a trio of Bf 109s from I./JG 27 and were both shot down; Sumner was killed, but McBarnet survived with slight wounds.

Somewhat later 6 Squadron's Flt Lt McFall was undertaking a TacR sortie when he was pursued by a trio of Bf 109s from Fort Capuzzo to Sidi Barrani where he crash-landed. He was strafed as he got out of the cockpit and was very badly wounded, dying soon afterwards.

M.llo Luigi Jellici, 150ª Squadriglia, 2° Gruppo, scrambled in his G.50bis to intercept a Blenheim over Derna, with no results, but one of these bombers was claimed by 2./JG 27's Uffz Stöckler, who was himself to be shot down and killed during the day.

A crash-landed Bf 109E 'Schwarze 5' is inspected by British troops. The identity of the pilot of this aircraft or the cause of the crash have not been ascertained.

At 1000 Flg Off Sowrey and his section from C Flight (the 213 Squadron pilots), of 73 Squadron, took off, encountering a pair of Bf 109s, one of which he claimed to have shot down.

At 1655 ten Hurricanes of 274 Squadron strafed the Acroma-Capuzzo road, an Hs 126 of 2(H)./14 flown by Fw Herbert Schädlich being spotted in this area and shot down by Flg Off Hobbs. Once again the strafing fighters were intercepted by JG 27 Bf 109s, three being shot down while Flg Off Antoine Peronne force-landed a fourth in enemy-held territory. One of the missing pilots, Flt Sgt Lebois, reached Allied territory on foot several days later. Meanwhile, at around the same time Flg Off Sowrey's section from 73 Squadron again became engaged with Messerschmitts, Sowrey claiming his second Bf 109 of the day plus one more damaged, Plt Off Leach claiming a probable. Sowrey's claim may have originally been submitted as a probable as well, but has widely been reported as his second confirmed victory of the day.

British Claims

274 Sqn	Plt Off J.L.Briggs	Hurricane I Z4612	CR.42	Gazala-Tobruk road	0540-0840
213 Sqn	Flg Off J.A.Sowrey	Hurricane I W9293	Bf 109	Sollum area 0815-1010	
73 Sqn	Flt Lt P.O.V.Green	Hurricane I	Bf 110	damaged Sollum 1230	
213 Sqn	Flg Off C.B.Temlett	Hurricane I	Bf 109	damaged Capuzzo 1235	
274 Sqn	Flg Off J.B.Hobbs	Hurricane I W9268	Hs 126	Acroma-Capuzzo 1655-2015	
73 Sqn	Plt Off S.J.Leach	Hurricane I	Bf 109 probable	Sollum 1810	
213 Sqn	Flg Off J.A.Sowrey	Hurricane I	Bf 109 probable	Sollum 1845	
	Flg Off J.A.Sowrey	Hurricane I	Bf 109 damaged	Sollum 1845	
	Flg Off C.B.Temlett	Hurricane I	Bf 110 damaged	Sollum 1930	

British Casualties

274 Sqn	Hurricane (cannon) shot down; Plt Off A.Sumner KiA 0600-
6 Sqn	Hurricane I shot down; Plt Off A.W.J.McBarnet slightly wounded 0600-
73 Sqn	Hurricane I Z4559 shot down; Plt Off P.Pound wounded by British AA 1130
	Hurricane I badly damaged in combat 1130
	Hurricane I badly damaged in combat 1130
6 Sqn	Hurricane I shot down; Flt Lt J.E.McFall, DFC*, critically wounded – died later
274 Sqn	Hurricane I shot down; Wt Off C.Coudray KiA 1655
	Hurricane I shot down; Flt Sgt Lebois returned several days later 1655
	Hurricane I shot down; Sgt M.K.Daniels KiA 1655
	Hurricane I Z7827 force-landed in enemy territory; Flg Off A.M.D. Peronne PoW 1655
73 Sqn	Hurricane I shot down; Plt Off J.S.Logan KiA
2 SAAF	Hurricane I Z4243 shot down 2/Lt B Guest returned on the 17th, force-landed W Capuzzo c 1845
39 Sqn	Maryland AH 283 shot down Plt Off W E Brine, RAAF, shot down by 109s near Gambut

German Claims

2./JG 27	Uffz Rudolf Stöckler	Blenheim	0655
	Fw Franz Elles	Hurricane	0705
1./JG 27	Oblt Wolfgang Redlich	Hurricane	Sollum 1140
2./JG 27	Obfhr Hans-Arnold Stahlschmidt	Hurricane	Sollum 1140
3./JG 27	Lt Friedrich Hoffmann	Martin 167	12m NW Bardia 1152
	Oblt Ludwig Franzisket	Hurricane	18m SE Gambut 1630
	Lt Friedrich Hoffmann	Hurricane	18m SE Gambut 1640
7./JG 26	Fw Karl-Heinz Ehlen	Hurricane n.b.	1655
2./JG 27	Lt Willi Kothmann	Hurricane	NW Fort Capuzzo 1727
Stab I./JG 27	Hptmn Eduard Neumann	Hurricane	6m W Fort Capuzzo 1730
1./JG 27	Oblt Wolfgang Redlich	Hurricane	SE Fort Capuzzo 1735
2.(H)/14	Lt Karl-Otto Holzapfel (observer)	Hurricane	

German Casualties

1./JG 27	Bf 109E-7 WNr 4128 shot down; Uffz Heinz Greuel KiA
	Bf 109E-7 WNr 2943 shot down in combat; pilot safe
2./JG 27	Bf 109E-7 WNr 4123 shot down in combat; Uffz Rudolf Stöckler KiA
2(H).14	Hs 126 shot down 12m SW El Adem; Fw Herbert Schädlich KiA, observer Oblt Karl Münch WiA – baled out

Monday, 16 June 1941

The Western Desert Force continued its advance from Capuzzo towards Sollum during the morning, but became engaged with a large force of all arms as the 15th Panzer and 5th Light Divisions launched a counter-attack. This caused the British forces to fall back, despite 4th Indian Division occupying Halfaya and starting to press on towards Sollum.

These activities resulted in a considerable increase in Axis air activity, and at 0953 204 Group ordered 3, 73, 229, 250, 274, 1 SAAF and 2 SAAF Squadrons to operate in strength at 18,000 feet. By this time an early claim had been made at 0915 for a Bf 109 shot down by Plt Off Edghill of the 229 Squadron detachment flying with 73 Squadron. A claim for a Hurricane had been made by Lt Friedrich Hoffmann of 3./JG 27 at 0752, but as with Edghill's claim, no corresponding engagement has been discovered. Despite the time differential, it is possible that these two units may have encountered each other. It appears that Hoffmann had been flying alone over British lines and had experienced some difficulty in getting his claim confirmed.

The two South African units were ordered to fly together, but by this time these units were only able to put up a joint formation of seven Hurricanes. From 1 SAAF, Maj Theron led Capt Quirk and Lts Burger and Tatham; 2 SAAF's Capt Kok led Lts Wells and Rushmere, these pilots taking off mid morning. At around 1140 Ju 87s of I./StG 1, escorted by 14 G.50bis of 2° Gruppo CT led by T.Col Giuseppe Baylon, were seen heading for the Sidi Omar area, nine Bf 109s flying top cover. Over the Sollum-Capuzzo-Bardia area a warning was shouted just before a Messerschmitt appeared on Kok's tail and his aircraft went down in flames. Wounded, he crash-landed within British-held territory, five miles east of Sollum. Theron at once gave chase to the fighter which he believed had just shot down Kok, reporting that this dived into the ground in a cloud of flame, smoke and dust.

As Theron sought to regain altitude, he spotted six G.50bis approaching him, and went into a tight turn. In trying to follow him, the Italian fighters stalled out one after another until only two remained. At that point he came out of his turn and attacked the second G.50, claiming that it fell away in flames. Heading east from Sollum, his Hurricane was then hit by a tremendous burst of AA fire (which proved to have been British!), which broke the back of his Hurricane. He baled out, but had been hit in the left arm by shell fragments. "I gave a violent kick to the joystick to force myself out of the smoke-filled cockpit," he recalled. Falling head first from 7,000 feet he dropped through the harness as his parachute opened, but his legs caught so that he went down "by my ankles ....my left arm broken and swinging loose past my head." As he approached the ground, he tried to hunch up, landing on his right thigh. Wind then caught the canopy, dragging him across the rough, stony desert surface with his thigh dislocated, until some nearby troops managed to collapse the parachute and rescue him.

Meanwhile, as Theron had pursued the Bf 109, Capt Quirk and Lt Tatham had spotted the bombers with fighter escort attacking troops near Capuzzo and Rucheibit. Further away were six more bombers escorted by a further pair of Messerschmitts. Splitting away from each other before attacking, Quirk then claimed to have shot down the second and third Ju 87s in the formation. However, the cockpit of his Hurricane was then hit by fire from a Messerschmitt and he was slightly wounded. With his aircraft on fire, he also baled out, fortunately wind carrying him into territory south of Capuzzo, still in friendly hands.

On the Axis side, one Ju 87 and one Bf 109 had been lost, while Lt Hoffmann of 3./JG 27 had made his second claim of the day at 1146, Fw Elles of 1.Staffel adding a further Hurricane at 1155, with Cap Annibale Sterzi, commanding officer of 2° Gruppo's 358ª Squadriglia, also claiming a Hurricane during this engagement, firing only 36 rounds in doing so.

Somewhat later, a further claim for a Bf 109 was submitted by 213 Squadron's Sgt P.P.Wilson, but again no such loss appears to have been recorded.

During the mid afternoon at 1500, the pilots of eight Tomahawks of 250 Squadron reported the unit's first combat over the desert when five Bf 109s were met at 22,000 feet over Bardia. Sqn Ldr J.E.Scoular and Flt Lt R.F.Martin, both of whom had served with distinction with 73 Squadron in France in 1940, each claimed damage to one of the German aircraft. It is interesting to note that the Luftwaffe pilots initially identified these new opponents as 'Brewsters'.

Although the RAF reported that 204 Group's fighters had caused the Axis bombers to jettison their bombs when attacked for the third day in succession, 73 Squadron received orders at the close of operations, that patrols by sections of aircraft should be discontinued due to the large opposing formations now being encountered. Future sorties of this nature should be undertaken only at squadron strength.

It had indeed been another torrid day for the SAAF units, highlighted perhaps by the comment of one pilot:

"…our ignorance of German tactics and the superiority of the 109 still had us in trouble."

With evening, ten III./LG 1 Ju 88s raided the Sollum area. The unit would repeat the attacks during two raids next day, attacking Sollum in the afternoon and Capuzzo a few hours later.

British Claims

229 Sqn	Plt Off D.F.K.Edghill	Hurricane I	Bf 109	E Sollum, over sea 0915
1 SAAF Sqn	Maj T.R.Theron	Hurricane I Z4090	Bf 109	Sollum-Capuzzo-Bardia 1140-
	Maj T.R.Theron	Hurricane I Z4090	G.50	Sollum-Capuzzo-Bardia 1140-
	Capt K.A.Quirk	Hurricane I V7756	2 Ju 87s	Sollum-Capuzzo-Bardia 1140-
	Capt K.A.Quirk	Hurricane I V7756	Ju 87 damaged	Sollum-Capuzzo-Bardia 1140-
213 Sqn	Sgt P.P.Wilson	Hurricane I	Bf 109	Capuzzo 1220
250 Sqn	Sqn Ldr J.E.Scoular	Tomahawk AK416	Bf 109 damaged	Bardia area 1500
	Flt Lt R.F.Martin	Tomahawk AK419	Bf 109 damaged	Bardia area 1510

British Casualties

2 SAAF Sqn	Hurricane I shot down; Capt J.A.Kok crash-landed, WiA
1 SAAF Sqn	Hurricane I Z4090 shot down; Maj T.R.Theron baled out, safe
	Hurricane I V7756; Capt K.A.Quirk baled out, WiA

German Claims

3./JG 27	Lt Friedrich Hoffmann	Hurricane	6m WBuq Buq 0752
	Lt Friedrich Hoffmann	Hurricane	6m S Bardia 1146
2./JG 27	Fw Franz Elles	Hurricane	S Bardia 1155

German Casualties

1./JG 27	Bf 109E-7 WNr 6428 shot down; Oblt Hugo Schneider missing but returned
1./StG 1	Ju 87 WNr 6042 shot down W Sollum; Uffz Karl Steinmann/Gefr Erwin Helmrich PoWs

Italian Claims

358ª Sq/2° Gr CT	Cap Annibale Sterzi	Hurricane	Sidi Omar area 1515-

Italian Casualties

20° Gr CT	G.50bis badly damaged on the ground at Martuba by bombs
	Ca.133 'hack' badly damaged on the ground at Martuba by bombs

Tuesday, 17 June 1941

By now the Western Desert Force armoured units had been seriously weakened, having lost some 150 tanks during the past three days. Rommel meanwhile, had lost only 50, and still had about 200 panzers of various types available. With only some 20 cruisers and even less 'I' tanks to hand, it was clear that little more could be achieved by the British. Consequently, a withdrawal began, and by late afternoon the Commonwealth forces had crossed the frontier again, this time back into Egypt where by nightfall they had re-occupied the Sidi Barrani-Sofafi line.

Faced with the task of protecting the army's withdrawing forces, Air Cdr Collishaw had available still his Hurricane squadrons, also considerably weakened, and the new Tomahawks of 250 Squadron. He could also call on the South African Marylands which had been standing idle due to the inability to provide adequate fighter escort as a result of the demands of other duties – mainly patrolling the front area.

At 1100 seven Hurricanes from 1 and 2 SAAF Squadrons took off, briefed to attack Axis transport columns. These fighters had reached Sidi Omar when they were attacked by an equal number of Bf 109s from 3./JG 27 (and, apparently, elements of the newly-arrived 7./JG 26), which were on a bomber escort mission. In moments two Hurricanes had gone down in flames, with a third disappeared; a fourth, flown by Lt Durose, was reportedly hit by a heavy burst of Flak, and he crash-landed at Sidi Barrani. Amongst the successful Messerschmitt pilots, Lt Heinz Schmidt claimed two of the aircraft shot down.

Following this early debacle, the bombers were despatched under fairly minimal fighter protection. Blenheims of 14 and 113 Squadrons, joined by 24 SAAF Squadron Marylands, bombed the vehicles of the advancing German columns near Sollum with some effect. During a second attack in the same area some 22 tanks and other vehicles were counted by observers as having been destroyed or disabled.

At the same time the other RAF Hurricane squadrons were heavily involved in combats with escorted formations of Ju 87 dive-bombers. 14 G.50bis from 2° Gruppo CT took off mid afternoon led by T.Col Baylon to escort Stukas attacking armoured columns south of Halfaya. Hurricanes were engaged and three of these were claimed shot down without loss to the Italians. Somewhat later 3./JG 27 also encountered Hurricanes again, three more being claimed – two by Lt Schmidt to bring his total on this personally very successful day to four. In the course of this late afternoon period, 73 Squadron lost one aircraft, apparently to ground fire when Plt Off Reynolds was strafing a road. Two of the attached 229 Squadron pilots failed to return, last being seen engaged with Bf 109s. 274 Squadron also lost two aircraft during a strafing operation, in the course of which Flt Lt Dudley Honor claimed to have damaged a Messerschmitt.

33 Squadron, on the unit's first encounter with the opposition since its return from Crete, was able to submit claims for six Axis aircraft shot down, to which would be added two further claims by 229 Squadron's Plt Off Edghill. One 33 Squadron pilot was shot down and killed.

The claims made on this occasion seem to have been somewhat optimistic, for they amounted to four Ju 87s, three G.50bis and a Bf 109. On this date, however, only one dive-bomber was lost. No German or Italian fighters failed to return.

Finally, during the last hour of daylight, the two SAAF fighter squadrons were again sent off at 1800 as the Luftwaffe appeared to be making a major air effort. The six pilots, four from 1 SAAF and two from 2 SAAF, spotted a formation of Ju 87s and Ju 88s near Sollum, these being followed by at least two further formations. Lts Bester and Webb made for the bombers, the other four Hurricanes remaining above to give cover against the escorts which had to be there. They were, and 15 or 16 Bf 110s plus Bf 109s dived to the attack. Bester and Webb became involved with the Bf 110s of III./ZG 26, Bester claiming to have hit the engine of one: "The 110 reared-up. Stalled and fell over towards the ground...........its pilot could never gain control at that altitude." It seems that the German pilot did however. The other four pilots were now also involved, Lt Conradie, who was hit and wounded in the head, reporting that he "poured a stream of machine-gun bullets into a Me 110. Smoke streamed from both its engines." He had no time to see it all before being hit and wounded again, but his claim was confirmed as 'destroyed', as was Bester's. Once

While the majority of the victories claimed by pilots of 7./JG 26 accrued to its commander, Oblt Müncheberg, Lt Klaus Mietusch, seen here hatless, also achieved some success.

again, the Luftwaffe aircraft appears to have escaped serious damage – did he see black exhaust smoke from the two Daimler Benz engines being boosted to avoid his attack? However, all six South Africans returned despite claims for two of them shot down by the Zerstörer pilots, and a final claim by Obfhr Marseille for his second of the day. Nearly half an hour later a claim was made by Obfw Förster of 2./JG 27 for a Brewster. Subsequent claims for aircraft thus identified over the following days proved to relate to engagements with 250 Squadron's Tomahawks. On this occasion, however, Förster's recognition was not at fault. Sgt Demoulin of 272 Squadron, undertaking a convoy patrol in one of the unit's Beaufighters, reported being relieved by a Brewster Buffalo. This was an aircraft of 805 Squadron from Dekheila, flown by Lt Lloyd Keith, a Canadian Fleet Air Arm pilot who had gained experience of fighter aircraft when he joined an 'ad hoc' flight of Sea Gladiators formed on HMS *Eagle* earlier in the war, although normally a Swordfish pilot (see *Air War for Yugoslavia, Greece and Crete, 1940-41* for more details of this pilot and his activities). Operating from Mersa Matruh on this date, he was undertaking this patrol sortie alone when attacked and shot down by Förster, and he crashed north-west of Sidi Barrani. Badly hurt, he was picked up by a German patrol, but died of his injuries ten days later.

By the end of the day, therefore, Axis fighter pilots had claimed at least 13 Hurricanes and one Buffalo shot down against the loss of a single Ju 87. Nine Hurricanes had been lost with a tenth crash-landing, although not necessarily all had fallen to fighter aircraft. However, the ten claims for Axis aircraft shot down had clearly been extortionate – and possibly indicative of the pressure under which the Commonwealth pilots had been operating.

Perhaps the really important result of this virtual blood-letting was the level of cover provided to the army which brought forth a heart-felt congratulation from Sir Noel Beresford-Peirse, Western Desert Force GOC, to Air Cdr Collishaw. Tedder also signalled Collishaw a few days later:

"Please express to all your fighter squadrons the deep admiration I feel for their magnificent work during the recent operations. During the initial stages… they had to operate under conditions which exposed them to attack by superior numbers whenever the enemy chose to concentrate. Only in this way could continuous cover be ensured for the army. It was a hard job but it was done and the cover was completely successful….relentless low attacks before the land operation….and the final stages….were a potent factor in preventing the enemy from concentrating or maintaining large forces in battle…."

Following the very heavy SAAF losses during Battleaxe, the dominion undertook its own wash-up investigation. The inability to release sufficient fighters to allow full and effective use of the bombers was confirmed. This was a weakness which would continue almost unabated, and would take most of the rest of the year to resolve.

More pertinent, the commanding officer of 233 Squadron, now employed as a light bomber operational training unit, made clear that the aircrews had not received sufficient training to render them fully effective in the bombing role. The 30 hours of what should have been a 50-hour course, had prepared them only for reconnaissance work, not for tactical bombing. Indeed, by this time the situation was arising where more aircraft were becoming available than properly trained crews to fly them. (It is worth mentioning at this point that until later in 1941 the light bombers – notably Blenheims and Marylands at this time – were still referred to as medium bombers, the change in terminology only occurring some months later.)

A further example of the problems being encountered at this stage occurred within 6 Squadron, one of the tactical reconnaissance units. In order to resolve a shortage of properly-trained pilots for this role six of 229 Squadron's personnel were attached, including Flt Lt J.B.Holderness and Plt Off J.A.F.Sowrey Recorded the unit: "They are fighter pilots but can carry out simple tactical reconnaissances." However behind this somewhat bland and optimistic statement lay the seeds of disaster for this group of young men.

In the desert the Axis forces had now also halted, making no attempt to press their advantage and advance further into Egypt. Claims were made at the time that the air resistance offered had brought them to a halt, but in practice Rommel had received firm orders to proceed no further at this stage. Although he was unlikely to have been privy to the reasons for this, in fact no further supplies or reinforcements for the Afrika Korps could be anticipated at this point since within a few days the massive German attack on the Soviet Union would commence.

British Claims

33 Sqn	Flt Lt V.C.Woodward	Hurricane I Z4377	G.50	Bir Sofafi-Sidi Omar 1640-1850
	Flt Lt V.C.Woodward	Hurricane I Z4377	G.50 damaged	Bir Sofafi-Sidi Omar 1640-1850
	Sgt G.E.C.Genders	Hurricane I Z4174	2 G.50s	Bir Sofafi-Sidi Omar 1640-1850
	Flg Off D.T.Moir	Hurricane I Z4175	Ju 87	Bir Sofafi-Sidi Omar 1650-1850
	2/Lt D.C.Dove	Hurricane I W9298	Bf 109	Bir Sofafi-Sidi Omar 1650-1850
229 Sqn	Plt Off R.R.Mitchell	Hurricane I	Ju 87	Bir Sofafi-Sidi Omar 1730-1745
	Plt Off D.F.K.Edghill	Hurricane I	2 Ju 87s	Sofafi-Halfaya area
1 SAAF Sqn	Lt A.J.P.Bester	Hurricane I	Bf 110	Sofafi-Halfaya area 1930
	Lt J.Conradie	Hurricane I Z4347	Bf 110	Sofafi-Halfaya area 1930
	Lt J.Conradie	Hurricane I Z4347	Bf 110 damaged	Sofafi-Halfaya area 1930

British Casualties

1 SAAF Sqn	Hurricane I Z4422 shot down; Lt J.B.White MiA ESE Sidi Omar 1215
	Hurricane W9269 shot down; Lt G.K.Smith PoW, died of wounds Sidi Omar 1215
	Hurricane V7689 shot down; Lt K.K.Mitchell PoW Sidi Omar 1215
	Hurricane Z4510 shot down by Flak; Lt R.A.Durose crash-landed, safe
73 Sqn	Hurricane I shot down by ground fire; Plt Off H.G.Reynolds returned on 19 June 1941
229 Sqn	Hurricane I P3977 shot down; Sgt G.K.Wooller KiA
33 Sqn	Hurricane I Z4509 shot down; Flg Off E.J.Woods KiA
274 Sqn	Hurricane I Z4110 shot down; Plt Off Grassett MiA
	Hurricane I Z4533 shot down; Plt Off T.L.W.E.Officer MiA
1 SAAF Sqn	Hurricane I damaged; Lt J.Conradie wounded
805 Sqn	Brewster Buffalo AX813 shot down; Pty Off L.K Keith, DSC, PoW, died of wounds 26 June 1941

German Claims

7./JG 26	Oblt Klaus Mietusch	Hurricane	SE Sidi Omar 1030
	Oblt Klaus Mietusch	Hurricane n.b.	
3./JG 27	Lt Heinz Schmidt	2 Hurricanes	SE Sidi Omar 1115, 1133
	Lt Heinz Schmidt	2 Hurricanes	NE Gambut 1710, 1712
	Obfhr Hans-Joachim Marseille	Hurricane	NE Gambut 1715
	Fw Karl Mentnich	Hurricane	NE Gambut 1720
	Obfhr Hans-Joachim Marseille	Hurricane	NE Gambut 1845
Stab III./ZG 26	Maj Karl Kaschka	Hurricane	S Suleimann 1832
8./ZG 26	Lt Fritz Schulze-Dickow	Hurricane	SE Sollum 1836
2./JG 27	Obfw Hermann Förster	Brewster	1910
I.StG 2	Oblt Hans-Joachim Warnicke and crew	Hurricane	

German Casualties

6./StG 2	Ju 87 WNr 6047 shot down; Lt Franz Lauberger/Uffz Thomas Mantsch KiA 6m SE Halfaya Pass

Italian Claims

150ª Sq/2° Gr CT	S.Ten Agostino Celentano	Hurricane	S Halfaya 1530-
	M.llo Olindo Simioniato	Hurricane	S Halfaya 1530-
358ª Sq/2° Gr CT	Serg Magg Antonio Patriarca	Hurricane	S Halfaya 1530-

Wednesday, 18 June 1941

The Tomahawks suffered their first losses when eight aircraft of 250 Squadron set off at 0550 to strafe the Capuzzo-Tobruk-El Adem road. Here Flg Off Hamlyn's aircraft was hit by Flak and he had to undertake a force-landing 40 miles east of Tobruk. The other seven pilots turned for home, but over the Sollum-Sidi Barrani area they were jumped by four 1./JG 27 Bf 109s, three of the German pilots each claiming one fighter shot down – although again they identified their victims as Brewsters. It proved to be the last time such a mistake would occur. One of the pilots shot down, Plt Off Munro, had managed to bale out, but was discovered to have been dead on reaching the ground – either from wounds suffered before he could vacate the aircraft, or from hits while he was falling through the engagement. Jack Hamlyn, meanwhile, had made contact with a group of Arabs who proved to be friendly, and joining them, he finally arrived at Sidi Barrani 15 days later with badly blistered feet, rejoining 250 Squadron on 4 July.

During the day Lt J.M.Bruen, RN, led five Fleet Air Arm pilots to Sidi Haneish to form a composite RN/RAF squadron, 806/33. However, it was on this date that it was finally accepted by the British command that Operation Battleaxe had failed, and next day the naval pilots returned to Palestine while 33 Squadron's detachment would fly back to Amiriya. 73 Squadron were happy to welcome back to the fold, Flg Off Reynolds, who had been shot down the previous day. The Luftwaffe presence was briefly strengthened by the arrival at Derna early in the day of II./LG 1. However, after attacking British tanks in the Sollum-Sidi Omar area, the unit's Ju 88s then returned to Eleusis. From Sicily, meanwhile, III Gruppe's bombers raided Fort Maddalena.

British Casualties			
250 Sqn	Tomahawk AK412 hit by Flak, force-landed; Flg Off J.Hamlyn safe, returned 4 July 1941		
	Tomahawk AK383 shot down; Plt Off D.A.R.Munro RAAF, KiA		
	Tomahawk AK399 shot down; Sgt J.Morton KiA		
	Tomahawk AK403 shot down; Sgt C.M.Sumner KiA		
German Claims			
1./JG 27	Lt Karl Remmer	Brewster	E Sollum 0600
	Oblt Wolfgang Redlich	Brewster	E Sollum 0600
	Uffz Günther Steinhausen	Brewster	Buq Buq 0605
German Casualties			
7./JG 26	Bf 109E WNr 2016 Gambut 40% damaged		
Italian Casualties			
376ª Sq Aut	CR.42 crashed at El Adem, pilot S.Ten Luigi Prati killed		

Thursday, 19 June 1941

Following the failure of this ill-fated offensive, both sides settled down once more to a period of recoupment, and the race to build up supplies for the next offensive re-commenced. The Axis lines of communication were severely stretched, and with Tobruk still in Allied hands, every item of equipment, rations, fuel, etc had to come overland across the desert from Benghazi and Tripoli – journeys of several hundred miles. Rommel appreciated that before he could advance further into Egypt he would have to capture Tobruk's port facilities. On the British side it was now appreciated that much stronger forces and a much greater quantity of supplies would be required before any future offensive could be considered that had any reasonable chance of success. Consequently there was to be little activity by the ground forces, other than isolated raids and patrols, for several months. In the air, although each side carried out some sweeps and bombing raids, the main scene of activity during the summer of 1941 was once again above the convoys making their way to and from Tobruk with supplies, reinforcements and replacements. Strong fighter patrols were flown over these by the RAF, and the Axis air forces launched frequent bombing raids on the ships, while fighter sweeps sought to try and dispose of the air cover.

The day also saw the arrival of four new properly-trained army co-operation pilots with 6 Squadron; in addition 274 Squadron was reinforced by the attachment of the flying personnel of 238 Squadron.

Friday, 20 June 1941

It was on this date that Oblt Joachim Müncheberg, commanding officer of the recently-arrived 7./JG 26, submitted his first claim in North Africa, for a Hurricane shot down south-east of Buq Buq, the pilot of which was reported to have been killed. The identity of this aircraft has not been established. An RAF intelligence summary noted that a 6 Squadron Hurricane had crash-landed, but that the pilot was safe. This would appear to have been Müncheberg's victim.

British Casualties			
6 Sqn	Hurricane crash-landed; pilot safe		
German Claims			
7./JG 26	Oblt Joachim Müncheberg	Hurricane	0755

Sunday, 22 June 1941

204 Group recorded that one Tomahawk from a formation of six such aircraft of 250 Squadron, left the formation apparently due to engine failure when ten miles north-west of Sidi Barrani, and failed to return.

The day was also marked by the almost incredible news that Germany had launched an undeclared attack on the Soviet Union on a massive front. Now at last the Commonwealth no longer stood alone against the continental power of Germany and Italy. Clearly this would greatly constrain the ability of the Germans strongly to reinforce their units serving in North Africa. For the British, however, the need to send all possible aid and supplies to the new ally would all too soon begin to impact upon that nation's potential to increase the size and improve the equipment of the Commonwealth's own forces in North Africa. Indeed, before long the reverses initially suffered by the Russian armies would

The Luftwaffe fighters were joined during mid June 1941 by the Bf 109Es of 7./JG 26, led by Oblt Joachim Müncheberg. This unit had been operating over Malta from Sicily with great success since February, and would remain in North Africa until the latter part of September.

also begin to affect the planning of further Middle Eastern operations. The perception had now arisen that a German advance from the southern end of this new Eastern Front through the Caucasus and into Iran could conceivably present a major new threat to the whole area of the Middle East.

A Bf 109E of 7./JG 26 carrying beneath the cockpit the schlageter marking of the geschwader, while on the noses of the unit's aircraft, which were painted yellow, was the red heart of 7 Staffel.

Tuesday, 24 June 1941

Plt Off James Sowrey who had arrived in North Africa as a fighter pilot with 229 Squadron, and who had received brief training in tactical reconnaissance duties, had joined 6 Squadron on 14 June to undertake such sorties. His brother, John Sowrey, had come out to the Middle East at the same time with 213 Squadron. At this point James was now serving on attachment to 73 Squadron. He set off on an early morning reconnaissance flight, and was flying from Mersa Matruh towards Sidi Barrani when he was suddenly attacked by a trio of Bf 109s and was shot down and killed by Oblt Müncheberg.

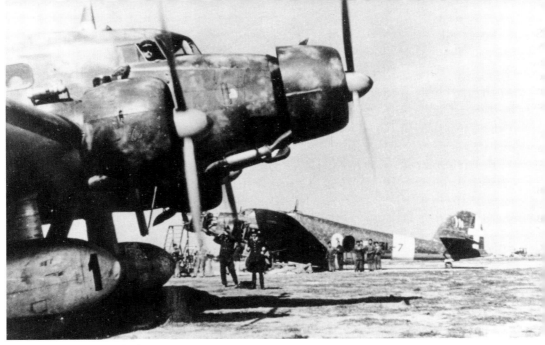

An S.81 and a Cant.Z.1007bis.

Shortly after this loss, Flg Off Hobbs of 274 Squadron was engaged in providing cover to HMS *Auckland* and *Parramatta*, and to MV *Pass of Halmata*, when a trio of S.79 torpedo-bombers from 279ª Squadriglia swept in to attack. Hobbs at once shot down that flown by Cap Orazio Bernardini, which crashed into the sea. Bernardini and his co-pilot, Serg Magg Urbano Gentilini, were both wounded, but the whole crew managed to get aboard an inflatable dinghy which the aircraft had been carrying. However, Serg Magg Riccardo Bolagna, the radio operator, and M.llo Vito Sinisi, one of the gunners, then both died of the injuries they had sustained. The survivors were picked up by a Cant.Z.506B floatplane 19 hours later, the dead members of the crew subsequently being awarded the Medaglia d'Oro.

Also during the day a Cant.Z.1007bis of the 'Sezione cinematografica' was intercepted over a convoy in the Gulf of Sollum by a Hurricane of 274 Squadron, the pilot of which identified his opponent as an S.79. The intruder was shot down, the camera man Cap Mario Anelli being killed.

113 Squadron's cannon-armed fighter-Blenheims were active during the day, strafing motor transport concentrations; returning crews claimed to have destroyed 16 vehicles.

British Claims

274 Sqn	Flg Off J.B.Hobbs	Hurricane I Z4704	S.79	over ships 0920-1300

British Casualties

6 Sqn   Hurricane I P3967 shot down; Plt Off J.A.F.Sowrey KiA

German Claims

7./JG 26	Oblt Joachim Müncheberg	Hurricane	0800

Italian Casualties

279ª Sq/131°Gr Aut AS   S.79 MM23860 shot down in sea; Cap Orazio Bernardini and Serg Magg Urbano Gentilini picked up next day; two died of injuries; Sez cinematografica Cant.Z.1007bis MM23314 down over Gulf of Sollum. Pilot Serg Giuseppe Farina PoW, photographer Cap Mario Anelli KiA

Wednesday, 25 June 1941

In a repeat of the previous day's events, another of 6 Squadron's Tac R Hurricanes, again flown by an ex-229 Squadron pilot, Plt Off Grosvenor, was intercepted by Bf 109s near Sidi Barrani and shot down by Hptmn Gerlitz of 2./JG 27, the British aircraft crashing in flames with the loss of the pilot.

Marylands of 12 and 24 SAAF Squadrons joined Blenheims of 113 Squadron to undertake a wing-strength attack on the Gazala airfields. While they were so engaged, fighters of 1 SAAF, 73, 250 and 274

Squadrons carried out a wing sweep over the area. While flying between Bardia and Tobruk, Sqn Ldr Scoular, 250 Squadron's commanding officer, suffered engine trouble with his Tomahawk and headed away towards the coast to force-land. He actually had the wheels of his aircraft down when at a height of 1,000 ft he reported meeting a lone G.50bis. Reacting swiftly, he claimed to have shot this down, then managing to fly back to base feeding petrol to the faltering engine with the hand pump. No trace of this engagement has been found in Italian records.

An S.79 of 19ª Squadriglia searched the area around Sidi Barrani, seeking survivors of the cinematagraphic Cant.Z.1007bis lost on the previous day. This aircraft was then itself shot down – apparently by ground fire – S.Ten Luigi Gentile and his crew all being wounded and subsequently being captured.

British Claims				
250 Sqn	Sqn Ldr J.E.Scoular	Tomahawk	G.50	Tobruk-Bardia 1505
British Casualties				
? Sqn	Hurricane I Z4263 shot down; Plt Off B.A.Grosvenor KiA			
German Claims				
?./JG 27	Hptmn Erich Gerlitz		Hurricane	1025
?./JG 27	Lt Werner Schroer		Hurricane	1420
Italian Casualties				
19ª Sq	S.79 shot down near Sidi Barrani; S.Ten Gentile and crew WiA and PoW			

Thursday, 26 June 1941

12 SAAF, 24 SAAF and 113 Squadrons again formed a wing of 27 bombers to attack Gazala No 5 airfield where 17 Ju 52/3ms and 31 fighters had been spotted. At least five aircraft were claimed destroyed in this attack, one of the transports being seen to blow up as it was taking off. Meanwhile the five available fighter squadrons again swept over the area, having put up 64 aircraft between them. 250 Squadron was engaged by a reported 30 fighters between Capuzzo and Tobruk. At 1410 Plt Off Kent claimed damage to a Bf 109 at 21,000 ft, and 20 minutes later he claimed to have shot down a G.50 to the north-west of Capuzzo. As he was doing so a fiery Australian, Plt Off Clive Caldwell, claimed a Bf 109 to the west of Capuzzo, while two of his fellow countrymen, Sgts Coward and Paxton, also made claims against Messerschmitts. However, two of the squadron's aircraft were shot down a few minutes later by pilots of 3./JG 27.

At much the same time 73 Squadron's pilots had spotted some Ju 87s, one of which Flg Off Temlett claimed to have damaged, but at this point the unit's Hurricanes were attacked by six Bf 109s and Plt Off Derek Ward was shot down by Obfw Förster of 2./JG 27. On return, pilots from this unit reported seeing two Messerschmitts being shot down by the 250 Squadron Tomahawks.

Yet another of 6 Squadron's ex-229 Squadron pilots was shot down on this date, but on this occasion it was

With 250 Squadron came an Australian pilot who was quickly to make quite a name for himself, although not initially greatly impressing his commanding officer; this was Plt Off (but soon to be promoted) Clive 'Killer' Caldwell.

flak from the Axis Halfaya Pass defences that struck Plt Off Maslen's Hurricane and he was able to glide his damaged aircraft to a safe force-landing. Following this, he then had to undertake a 30-mile walk back to friendly territory.

204 Group noted that during the day five Bf 109s made a strafing attack on Sidi Barrani airfield, where two RAF lorries and a bowser were destroyed, and one airman killed.

British Claims

73 Sqn	Flg Off C.B.Temlett	Hurricane I	Ju 87 damaged	Sidi Omar-Tobruk 1430
250 Sqn	Plt Off C.R.Caldwell	Tomahawk AK419	Bf 109	3m W Capuzzo 1430
	Sgt G.C.Coward	Tomahawk AK447	Bf 109	15m W Sidi Omar 1430
	Plt Off J.F.S.Kent	Tomahawk AK376	G.50 damaged	Gazala 1410
	Plt Off J.F.S.Kent	Tomahawk AK376	G.50	6m NW Capuzzo 1430
	Sgt T.G.Paxton	Tomahawk AK446	Bf 109 probable	S.Tobruk, convoy patrol 1430

British Casualties

250 Sqn	Tomahawk shot down; Flg Off Monteith
	AK398 shot down; Sgt D.R. Gale, RAAF, KiA
73 Sqn	Hurricane I Z4190 shot down; Plt Off D.H.Ward safe
6 Sqn	Hurricane I P3721 shot down by Flak; Plt Off A.V.Maslen safe

German Claims

2./JG 27	Obfw Hermann Förster	Hurricane	Gambut 1330
3./JG 27	Oblt Ludwig Franzisket	P-40	Ain el Gazala 1345
	Obfw Herbert Kowalski	P-40	Ain el Gazala 1355
II(K)/LG1	Crew of Hptm Joachim Helbig	P-40	
Unspecified unit		2 Blenheims	Gazala area

German Casualties

7./JG 26	Bf 109E WNr 5917 crash-landed Gambut 30% damaged
3./JG 27	Bf 109E-7 WNr 3799 crashed, unknown reason; Lt Heinz Schmidt KiA
1./JG 27	Bf 109E-7 WNr 3773 force-landed Gambut, 25% damaged; pilot safe
	Bf 109E-7 4925 30% damaged by bombs at Ain el Gazala
	Bf 109E-7 WNr 4107 30% damaged by bombs at Ain el Gazala

Sunday, 29 June 1941

I and II./LG 1 despatched Ju 88s to raid Alexandria during the early hours. On the way, whilst near Tobruk, the MV *Pass of Halmata* (758 tons) was spotted, attacked, and sunk. The destroyer HMAS *Waterhen* was also seen and was claimed 'probably sunk'. However, during the evening seven Ju 87Rs of 239ª Squadriglia also attacked shipping off the Libyan coast near Bardia. Two 500 kg bombs dropped by Serg Magg Ennio Tarantola and Serg Dino Fabbri found *Waterhen* still afloat at that time, hitting her astern, and she sank during the night soon after midnight.

Serg Magg Ennio 'Banana' Tarantola climbing into the cockpit of his Ju 87 dive-bomber. Tarantola was credited with having hit the destroyer HMAS *Waterhen* on 29 June 1941.

Serg Luigi Gorrini of 85ª Squadriglia, 18° Gruppo, during a patrol over Benghazi sighted two Blenheims, attacking the leading aircraft at 16.000 ft altitude. As he sought to press home his attack, he passed out – probably due to oxygen starvation – his CR.42 falling towards the ground. He recovered just in time to pull it out of its dive and landed safely.

Monday, 30 June 1941

The last day of the month proved to be very busy as 204 Group launched a maximum fighter effort to provide cover to HMS *Flamingo* and the transports MV *Antiklion*, *Miranda Tiberio* and *South Isles*. During the day six major attacks were launched against these vessels, between 20 and 45 bombers, plus Bf 109s, B 110s and G.50s being reported. At least 12 defending fighters were kept on patrol between 1500-2015, but these were frequently overwhelmed by superior forces. In a morning sortie Oblt Gunther Hoffmann-Lörze of 7./LG 1 claimed to have hit a freighter; in the early afternoon aircraft from III./LG 1 repeated the attack claiming damage to *Flamingo* and HMS *Cricket*.

A Cant.Z.501 flyingboat of this Benghazi-based unit, 196ª Squadriglia RM, rescued Tarantola on 30 June 1941.

During one of the earliest clashes, pilots of 1 SAAF Squadron encountered eight Ju 87s which were attacked at once, two claims being made before the escorts could interfere. Lt Russell was then shot down and killed, it would appear the victim of a Bf 110 of 8./ZG 26. Somewhat later 274 Squadron submitted a claim for one of this unit's aircraft plus a second damaged. Towards evening it was the turn of 250 Squadron when seven of this unit's Tomahawks engaged a formation comprising 29 Ju 87s, 12 G.50bis, ten Bf 109s and five Bf 110s. Plt Off Caldwell claimed two of the dive-bombers and shared a Bf 110 with Sgt Bob Whittle; Flt Lt Dickie Martin claimed two Italian fighters identified either as a G.50 and an MC.200, or as two G.50s.

The escorting G.50bis were from 20° Gruppo CT, one of this unit's pilots, Cap Furio Niclot Doglio of 353ª Squadriglia, claiming a Hurricane while 3./JG 27's Oblt Ludwig Franzisket claimed a P-40. Plt Off Kent, another of 250 Squadron's Australians, was shot down and killed while Sgt Ryan's Tomahawk was badly damaged, resulting in a force-landing. The attack force included four Ju 87Rs from 239ª Squadriglia, and one of these, flown by Serg Magg Ennio Tarantola with 1° Av Ruggero Pittini as gunner was reportedly hit by AA fire when diving on the ships. Tarantola released his bomb and managed initially to keep the aircraft in the air. As the engine began to fail, Pittini baled out, but was not seen again. Tarantola spent 18 hours drifting in his dinghy before being rescued by a 196ª Squadriglia Cant.Z.501. Following this eventful sortie, Tarantola sought to transfer to fighters, subsequently joining 151ª Squadriglia CT and ultimately becoming a fairly successful fighter ace.

A smiling Cap Furio Niclot Doglio, of 353ª Squadriglia. Niclot Doglio claimed his first victory on 30 June 1941. He would add six more victories over Malta on July 1942, before being shot down and killed by George Beurling of 249 Squadron on 27 July 1942.

On one occasion during the day CR.42s of 18° Gruppo CT provided escort to Ju 88s bombing the ships when they were some 30 miles south of Ras Azzaz. Here Ten Enrico Manfredini of 83ª Squadriglia reported encountering three Hurricanes, one of which he claimed to have probably shot down.

1 SAAF Sqn	Capt M.S.Osler	Hurricane I	Ju 87	65m NW Sidi Barrani 1240-
	Capt M.S.Osler	Hurricane I	Bf 109 damaged	65m NW Sidi Barrani 1240-
	Lt R.W.Simpson	Hurricane I	Ju 87	65m NW Sidi Barrani 1240-
274 Sqn	Lt J.A.Hoffe	Hurricane I W9359	Bf 110	over ships 1430-1725
	Sgt Parbury	Hurricane IZ4641	Bf 110 damaged	over ships 1430-1725
250 Sqn	Flt Lt R.F.Martin	Tomahawk AK419	G.50	50m NE Tobruk 1735
	Flt Lt R.F.Martin	Tomahawk AK419	MC.200	50m NE Tobruk 1735
	Plt Off C.R.Caldwell	Tomahawk AK346	2 Ju 87s	50m NE Tobruk 1735
	Plt Off C.R.Caldwell	Tomahawk AK346	½ Bf 110	50m NE Tobruk 1735
	Sgt R.J.C.Whittle	Tomahawk AK423	½ 110	50m NE Tobruk 1735
	Sgt R.J.C.Whittle	Tomahawk AK423	G.50 probable	50m NE Tobruk 1735

British Casualties

1 SAAF Sqn	Hurricane I Z4112 shot down; Lt A.S.Russell KiA
Unspecified unit	2 Hurricanes damaged
250 Sqn	Tomahawk AK37 shot down; Plt Off J.F.S.Kent, RAAF, KiA
	Tomahawk AK37 badly damaged and force-landed; Sgt T.G.Ryan safe

German Claims

8./ZG 26	Obfw Heinz Swoboda		Hurricane	N Marsa Luch 1540
3./JG 27	Oblt Ludwig Franzisket		P-40	Marsa Luch 1635

German Casualties

8./ZG 26	Bf 110E-2 WNr 3311 shot down; Uffz Friedrich Wiesböck and Gefr Wolfgang Otto MiA
	Bf 110E-1 WNr 3459 shot down; Fw Walter Schöne and Fw Karl Rohde MiA
II./StG 2	Ju 87R-2 WNr 6019 30% damaged in combat

Italian Claims

83ª Sq/18° Gr CT	Ten Enrico Manfredini		Hurricane probable	30m N Ras Azzaz
353ª Sq/20° Gr CT	Cap Furio Niclot Doglio		Hurricane	1545-

Italian Casualties

239ª Sq BaT	Ju 87R hit by AA over Tobruk; force-landed in sea; Gunner baled out and MiA; Serg Magg Ennio Tarantola rescued

The end of June also saw the departure from 73 Squadron of Flg Off Temlett and Plt Offs Chatfield and Sowrey who left Sidi Haneish for Abu Sueir and from there travelled to Lydda in Palestine where they were attached to 80 Squadron. At the same time 6 Squadron moved to Tel Aviv, also in Palestine, the unit's place in Egypt being taken by 451 Squadron.

Friday, 4 July 1941

Sidi Barrani was strafed by a reported 14 Axis fighters during the afternoon, one unserviceable Tomahawk being destroyed and a Miles Magister communications aircraft was badly damaged. Two officers, one RAF, the other army, were wounded. Other aircraft bombed 113 Squadron's airfield, slightly damaging one Blenheim. Involved in this attack, actually, were only five G.50bis of 151ª Squadriglia, 20° Gruppo CT, which apparently made three passes, allowing the over-assessment of their numbers to occur. During one such pass, Cap Mario Montefusco, the commanding officer of the unit, was hit and wounded by AA fire; assisted by his wingman Serg Magg Donato Mancini, Montefusco tried to stay in the air and make for his base but after a few miles he crashed and was killed. He was awarded a posthumous Medaglia d'Oro.

With evening, Ju 88s of III./LG 1 and He 111s of II./KG 26 raided Tobruk, claiming hits on two vessels. At Benghazi Flak gunners claimed two aircraft shot down, but no British losses have been found.

British Casualties

Unspecified unit	Tomahawk destroyed on ground
	Miles Magister badly damaged on ground
113 Sqn	Blenheim slightly damaged on ground

Italian Casualties

151ª Sq/ 20° Gr CT	G.50 MM 6405 hit by AA at Sidi Barrani, Cap Mario Montefusco KiA

German Casualties

3./StG 1	Ju 87 hit by AA E Tobruk; Gunner Uffz Otto Hoppe KiA

Saturday, 5 July 1941

153 ° Gruppo Autonomo CT arrived at Castel Benito from Italy, with 22 MC.200s. Unfortunately, one fighter flown by Ten Piero Arangino crashed, not far from the airfield due to an engine failure; the pilot was killed. This unit would eventually move to Derna, where it would arrive on 12 July.

During the day a Wellington which had force-landed 25 miles south of Sidi Barrani during the previous night (see Chapter 12 – The RAF's Night Bombing Offensive) was repaired sufficiently to be flown to base after an attack by Bf 109s had been beaten off from the ground.

Italian Casualties	
196ª Sq RM	Cant.Z.501 MM35078 lost in a flying accident; S.Ten Vito Maderno and crew KiFA
372ª Sq/153° Gr CT	MC.200 Ten Piero Arangino KiFA

Monday, 7 July 1941

Following the loss of G.E.Goodman as 73 Squadron's A Flight commander, he had been rather unsatisfactorily replaced. Recalled Oliver Green in his autobiography, *Mezze*:

"Johnny Goodman's replacement … was Aidan Crawley, about whom little was known except that he had been a member of 601 Auxiliary Squadron at Hendon on the outskirts of London back in 1936.....
Aidan had come to the Middle East theatre from the Balkans where it was said he had been the assistant RAF Attaché in Sofia, the Bulgarian capital. He was out of flying practice and it was pretty obvious to us that he should have been posted to a staff job.

"Square pegs are seldom fitted in to round holes and we had as a fighter commander at a fairly desperate time someone who would require all the training he could get while we were hard pushed to train the younger replacements. At 34, Aidan was considerably older than the rest of us who averaged about 21 years. He had done very little recent flying and had only limited experience of flying modern aircraft. In short, through no fault of his own, he was a bit of a liability and a worry to us. Peter Wykeham-Barnes was

After service in East Africa, Flt Lt Oliver Green became a flight commander in 73 Squadron. He was shot down by Italian fighters whilst undertaking a strafing attack on Gambut airfield on 7 July 1941, becoming a prisoner for the rest of the war.

aware of this and asked me to take him in hand and train him. It was not easy to spare the time for him while flying my own operational sorties and working up my own boys in B Flight.

"By a stroke of luck, an experienced Hurricane squadron, No. 229, was on the way to Egypt and the vanguard flight had just arrived after flying off an aircraft carrier in the western Mediterranean and staging through Malta. The Flight Commander, Bill Smith (W.A.Smith), was an exceptional fighter pilot who had taken part in the Battle of Britain. He virtually took Johnny Goodman's place and we alternated in leading the squadron sorties and sweeps."

Thus it was that on 7 July six Hurricanes from 73 Squadron took off, led by Flt Lt Aidan Crawley, to strafe various airfields. First attacked was Sidi Aziez, but on leaving this location Flg Off M.P.Wareham noted that only three other aircraft were with him, and that there were several columns of smoke rising from the Axis base. The four remaining pilots then attacked Gambut, but from here they encountered heavy Flak during their return journey. Wareham saw one Hurricane go down 15 miles east of Gambut, but when he landed, he did so quite alone. Flt Lts Crawley and Green, Plt Offs Leach and White, and Sgt Jupp all failed to return. Oliver Green recalled what had happened:

"We positioned at Sidi Barrani, our forward refuelling strip, where we could also rendezvous with our top cover. Bill Smith was leading the 229 contingent so I felt assured of good support, particularly as I had won some money from him at poker the night before and I knew he was keen to get it back. The other squadrons were also there and they took off first so that they could climb to height and be in position. We went off in loose tactical formation, giving us freedom to manoeuvre, and maintained tactical radio silence. Our course to Greater Gambut from Sidi Barrani was in a rough west-north-west direction and I was surprised that Aidan led us on a northerly course roughly parallel to the enemy coast, knowing that he would have to turn west towards Gambut and that he was increasing our chances of being spotted and reported by their listening posts as we crossed the coast.

"Looking back on our ill-fated sortie, I realised that Aidan had not actually flown over enemy territory before. Nevertheless, it was surprising when he crossed right over the top of the coastal town of Bardia which was the main German garrison and forward base for their tank forces. We sailed over the town at 2,000 feet, just as if giving a flying demonstration. I knew that we were bound to have been spotted and reported to their fighter organisation and that our only hope lay in dropping to ground level immediately and flying south in the hope of gaining some tactical advantage before turning west for the attack on Gambut.

"The only way to do this was to break radio silence to tell him that I would lead him to the target at low level. To my consternation my radio set was not functioning. I could neither transmit nor receive. This was not an unusual fault and we normally overcame it by using hand signals but from my position on the right flank with another pair of aircraft between us, there was no way I could signal to him. I could only hope we would not be picked up and, if we were, that Bill and his boys could give us protection. However Aidan carried on at 2,000 feet before descending in a shallow dive on Lesser Gambut, the wrong airfield. Now surely, I thought, we must turn south and do a deep diversion before heading north for a very low level run from a different direction on the right airfield.

"Aidan however had different ideas and climbed up slowly to 1,000 feet searching for Greater Gambut which lay about ten miles to the south. I should explain that airstrips in the desert were hard to pick up as they consisted of an area of level sand with no runways or buildings and only a few tents and refuelling bowsers. In short, they looked like any other stretch of sand. After doing a leisurely circuit Aidan saw Greater Gambut and went into another shallow dive attack. I had no option but to follow him although it was a recipe for disaster and compounded when I got my first glimpse of the target and saw there were no aircraft there. The birds had flown and our trip had been in vain. Just as I realised this I saw tracer bullets, looking like red ping pong balls, zipping past me. I immediately broke hard left, away from Rod [Plt Off R.W.K.White], who was close in on my right, and behind the formation hoping that he would be able to stick with me.

"We were flying at ground level by then and although he turned with me, tragically he hit the ground and exploded in flames. The attacking formation was a mix of 109s, G.50s and what looked like Macchi 200s but I was too busy taking evasive action to look closely or even care for it was obvious that they had made me their principal target. My last sight of Aidan was of him sailing along with his boys apparently unaware of what was happening behind him. I knew that against these superior odds, my only chance of survival was to keep twisting and turning at ground level to make it as difficult as possible for them to get a clear shot at me and to keep heading for home. I could see the bullets hitting the ground alongside and ahead of me and knew I would have to be very lucky to get away.

"Sure enough, after a short, desperate series of evasive turns the oil tank was hit and exploded. Oil sprayed all over the windscreen, effectively blinding me, and the engine seized and stopped with a bang. I hit the ground at about 180 mph and, although my straps were done up tightly, my head snapped forward and hit the gyro gunsight which protruded from the windscreen. We rocketed along the ground. Bouncing about in a cloud of dust, my greatest fear was that my Hurricane would burst into flames and I would be trapped inside.

"My luck was in. As we came to a halt, I was able to scramble out and run from the wreckage before they strafed it and me. I got far enough away to be a spectator to their attacks. Curiously, the Hurricane did not burn, perhaps due to the recently fitted self-sealing tanks. After a short time and several attacks each, they flew away and I was left alone to contemplate that loneliest of all feelings, total isolation in the desert, one of the most unfriendly and harshest of places on earth. As I collected my thoughts and tried to work out what to do next, I heard the noise of an aircraft overhead and looked up to see a Blenheim flying home. There could not have been a more poignant reminder of my isolated predicament."

Three casualties were recorded among Regia Aeronautica personnel at Gambut after the attack – a young car driver, killed, a fitter, Av.Sc Ugo Giacomazzi, and a pilot, Serg Magg Francesco Visentin, both wounded. Also some G.50bis suffered minor damage.

While two claims were made by Regia Aeronautica fighter pilots for Hurricanes shot down during the 73 Squadron attack, two more such claims were also submitted by pilots of I./JG 27 next day. These would also seem to fit Oliver Green's narrative almost perfectly – particularly as there are no matching RAF losses on that date. It seems very likely therefore that the claims of Hptmn Eduard Neumann and Lt Werner Schroer were incorrectly listed a day late; two of the five Hurricanes lost were indeed their victims. Anti-aircraft defences at Bardia claimed to have caused two Hurricanes to crash-land, reporting that one of the pilots was captured but the other got away.

Later in the day 250 Squadron, in company with several other squadrons, carried out a large-scale sweep over Bardia, but nothing was seen. Plt Off Clive Caldwell became separated from the formation, and at 1845 reported encountering a pair of G.50bis west of El Adem. one of which he claimed to have shot down. He then shot up various targets on his way back to base. The day did, however, see the departure from Egypt of 14 Squadron which now withdrew to Petah Tiqva, near Tel Aviv in Palestine.

British Claims

250 Sqn	Plt Off C.R.Caldwell	Tomahawk AK346	G.50	25m W El Adem 1845

British Casualties

73 Sqn	Hurricane I V7802 MiA; Flt Lt A.Crawley PoW
	Hurricane I Z4173 shot down; Flt Lt P.O.V.Green PoW
	Hurricane I Z4649 MiA; Plt Off S.J.Leach KiA
	Hurricane I V7757 MiA; Plt Off R.W.K.White KiA
	Hurricane I M9197 MiA; Sgt G.A.Jupp KiA
	Hurricane I Z4773 damaged by Flak; Plt Off M.P.Wareham returned

Italian Claims

153ª Sq/20° Gr CT	Ten Vittorio Merlo	Hurricane
	Serg Bruno Baldacci	Hurricane

A pair of Bf 110s of III./ZG 26 over supply shipping off the Mediterranean coast.

Tuesday, 8 July 1941

At 0817 a number of Bf 110s from III./ZG 26 strafed Bagush Satellite airfield without their approach having been spotted on the radar. Fortunately for 113 Squadron the unit's aircraft had moved to the forward landing ground, and all that remained at the home base was a single unserviceable Blenheim, which was indeed destroyed. However, one airman was killed during the attack, and two others were seriously wounded, the attacking aircraft also strafing a train spotted in the neighbourhood. 204 Group noted that a tactical reconnaissance Hurricane of 451 Squadron was shot down by Flak near the Halfaya Pass, the army successfully recovering the pilot, Plt Off K.E.Whalley, and bringing him to safety. A Luftwaffe aircraft also fell victim to AA fire over Tobruk on this date, a Ju 87 of I./StG 3 suffering 65% damage.

A kübelwagen and a Bf 110 jointly experience a sandstorm at Derna.

British Casualties

113 Sqn	Blenheim IV V5793 destroyed on ground Maaten Bagush (LG.15) by Bf 110s
451 Sqn	Hurricane force-landed and destroyed by army. PO K E Whalley safe

German Claims

1./JG 27	Lt Werner Schroer	Hurricane	W Bardia 0700
Stab I./JG 27	Hptmn Eduard Neumann	Hurricane	3m E Halfaya Pass 0755

(It is suspected that there was a mistake on dates here and that these claims relate to the losses of the 7th)

Wednesday, 9 July 1941

During the early hours Ju 88s of III./LG 1 attacked HMS *Defender* 60 miles north of Sollum, claiming hits amidships with three SC 250 and one SC 50 bombs, with three more SC 250s being seen to fall alongside the vessel. That afternoon the gruppe returned to the area to bomb Tobruk again.

Friday, 11 July 1941

Hurricanes from 274, 73/229 and 1 SAAF Squadrons flew defensive patrols over HMS *Defender*, which had been damaged by bombing and was being towed by HMS *Vendetta* towards Mersa Matruh; however, the damaged vessel began to list heavily and had to be sunk by gunfire. Her loss was also claimed by the Ju 88 crews of III./LG 1 who attacked after dawn, reporting hits by a further four SC 250s. Hits were also claimed on *Flamingo* and *Cricket*.

Saturday, 12 July 1941

British Claims

250 Sqn	Plt Off C.R.Caldwell	Tomahawk AK367	Bf 109 damaged	42m NW Sidi Barrani 1745-1935

Tuesday, 15 July 1941

73 Squadron with the attached pilots from 229 Squadron undertook an evening patrol over lighters on the way to Tobruk, during which a Bf 110 was spotted. The Hurricane pilots at once gave chase and were led to a formation of 15 Ju 87s from II./StG 2 and five from 239ª Squadriglia, escorted by Bf 110s and Bf 109s. Attacking at once, five of the dive-bombers and one Bf 110 were claimed shot down, together with a probable and a couple believed to have been damaged. Plt Off Johns had remained above as top cover and was thus able to spot a Bf 110 about to attack the British fighters and was able to drive it off. He then spotted eight Ju 87s, one of which he claimed to have shot down in flames.

Meanwhile, Oblt Müncheberg of 7./JG 26 had joined the fight to the south-west of Ras Azzaz, though he thought he was encountering Tomahawks. He fired at one fighter from among 12 he had counted, but had no time to note results as he was targetted by two more. These, however, then attacked the Ju 87s and Bf 110s, allowing him to turn his attention onto one fighter which was on the tail of the Bf 110 flown by Obfw Heller, and this he claimed to have shot down in flames, seeing it fall within British-held territory – his 46th victory. The Bf 110 pilots also claimed four victories, which they too identified as P-40s (Tomahawks), three of these being credited to Richard Heller. This led directly to the award to him of the Knights' Cross, the citation also reciting that none of the Ju 87s in his care had been lost. This was certainly not correct, for at least two of the dive-bombers were missing, and some sources record that three pilots were killed during this engagement. 2 SAAF Squadron's new Tomahawks were involved in combat for the first time, Capt A.Q.Masson claiming damage to a Bf 110; Lt.J.R.R.Wells' aircraft was shot-up by one of the German fighters.

One Bf 109 was reported lost by I./JG 27 during the day, reportedly coming down in the Gambut-Ras Azzaz area following combat with a Hurricane. The pilot survived unhurt although the aircraft was a total loss. However, no claim for such a victory was submitted by any of the RAF and SAAF pilots on this date. It is assumed that if it was indeed attacked by a British fighter, the pilot of the latter had no opportunity to watch the results of his fire. Alternatively, the successful pilot may have been one of those who failed to return on this date.

Joachim Müncheberg was by now becoming disenamoured of his brief sojourn in North Africa. He complained that the heat was getting him down, and that the only chances for combat were now over the ships entering Tobruk. While the identification of his opponents had on this occasion been faulty, he nonetheless added that more and more Curtiss fighters were arriving and that it was high time the F model of the Bf 109 arrived.

British Claims

73 Sqn	Plt Off N.P.Wareham	Hurricane I	Ju 87	50m NW Sidi Barrani 1930
	Plt Off N.P.Wareham	Hurricane I	Bf 110	50m NW Sidi Barrani 1930
	Plt Off R.McDougal	Hurricane I	2 Ju 87s	50m NW Sidi Barrani 1930
	Plt Off R.McDougal	Hurricane I	Bf 110 probable	50m NW Sidi Barrani 1930
229 Sqn	Flt Lt W.A.Smith	Hurricane I	Ju 87	50m NW Sidi Barrani 1930
	Flt Lt W.A.Smith	Hurricane I	Ju 87 damaged	50m NW Sidi Barrani 1930
	Plt Off G.B.Johns	Hurricane I	Ju 87	50m NW Sidi Barrani 1930
	Plt Off D.F.K.Edghill	Hurricane I	Ju 87	50m NW Sidi Barrani 1940
	Plt Off D.F.K.Edghill	Hurricane I	Ju 87 damaged	50m NW Sidi Barrani 1940
2 SAAF Sqn	Capt A.Q.Masson	Tomahawk	Bf 110 damaged	Sidi Barrani area c.1915

British Casualties

73 Sqn	Hurricane I Z4347 MiA; Plt Off F.M.Moss KiA
229 Sqn	Hurricane I P3729 MiA; Plt Off R.G.Lauder KiA
	Hurricane badly damaged; Sqn Ldr F.E.Rosier unhurt
2 SAAF Sqn	Tomahawk AK/AN455 badly damaged; Lt J.R.Wells safe
	Tomahawk slightly damaged; Capt A.Q.Masson safe
	Tomahawk slightly damaged; Lt N.J.Cullum safe

German Claims

8./ZG 26	Uffz Heinz Bövers		P-40	N Ras Azzaz : 6,000 ft altitude 1833
	Obfw Richard Heller		P-40	N Ras Azzaz : 330 ft altitude 1835
			P-40	N Ras Azzaz : 150 ft altitude 1836
			P-40	N Ras Azzaz : 100 ft altitude 1837
7./JG 26	Oblt Joachim Müncheberg		P-40	SW Ras-el-Milh 1840

German Casualties

I./JG 27	Bf 109E-7 WNr 4150 shot down in combat N Ras Azzaz; pilot safe
5./StG 2	Ju 87R-2 WNr 6053 shot down 30m N Ras Azzaz; Uffz Heinz Scheel/Gefr Heinz Mehling KiA
6./StG 2	Ju 87R-2 WNr 5994 shot down 30m N Ras Azzaz; Oblt Hans-Joachim Warncke/ Uffz Albert Wolf KiA
5./StG 2	Ju 87R-2 WNr 5940 shot down 30m N Ras Azzaz; gunner Fw Wilhelm Bornhieff WiA

Thursday, 17 July 1941

Italian Casualties

153° Gr CT	MC.200 crash-landed near Sidi Omar during transfer flight from Derna to Gambut, cause unknown; pilot baled out safely.

Saturday, 19 July 1941

Hurricanes were again mistaken for Tomahawks, this time by pilots of I./JG 27, when 12 Bf 109s bounced 73 Squadron north-east of Ras Azzaz at 1,800 feet while 12 aircraft of this unit were patrolling over 'A' lighters making for Tobruk.Three victories were claimed by the German pilots, one Hurricane actually being shot down and one damaged. 48 sorties were expended by RAF fighters on defending the vessels during the day.

British Casualties

73 Sqn	Hurricane I W9270 shot down; Plt Off H.G.Reynolds KiA
	Hurricane I damaged; Sous Lt A.Littolf safe

German Claims

1./JG 27	Fw Peter Werfft	P-40	Sollum Bay 1805
3./JG 27	Oblt Ludwig Franzisket	P-40	N Ras Azzaz 1815
1./JG 27	Lt Werner Schroer	P-40	NE Ras Azzaz 1817

Wednesday, 23 July 1941

Another new shape made its appearance in desert skies when nine Grumman Martlets of 805 Squadron, Fleet Air Arm, joined ten Tomahawks of 250 Squadron in escorting four Marylands of 24 SAAF Squadron on shipping patrol. Unfortunately, two of these new aircraft gave chase to a suspected enemy prowler, consequently running out of fuel in doing so. Both were forced to ditch in the sea, but only one of the pilots was rescued. The Martlet, another American aircraft, was the export version of the Grumman F4F Wildcat fighter, in service with the US Navy.

British Casualties

805 Sqn	Martlet 3890 out of fuel chasing e/a and ditched; Lt P.R.E. Woods KiA
	Martlet out of fuel chasing e/a and ditched; pilot rescued

Monday, 28 July 1941

During take-off for an early morning patrol, Lt Conradie's 1 SAAF Squadron Hurricane suddenly dived from 500 feet and he was killed instantly.

British Casualties

1 SAAF Sqn	Hurricane I V7359 crashed into sea – no apparent reason; Lt J.J.Conradie KiFA

Tuesday, 29 July 1941

24 MC.200s of 153° Gruppo were on patrol over the Gambut-Derna area between 1315 and 1400. During this sortie the MC.200 flown by S.Ten Giulio Binetti of 372ª Squadriglia crashed to the ground for no apparent reason, killing the pilot. S.Ten Aldo Conti of 353ª Squadriglia, 20° Gruppo was forced to land his G.50bis in enemy-controlled territory and was taken PoW.

For the RAF, patrols over two 'A' lighters were again the order of the day, 36 sorties being undertaken for this purpose. 2 SAAF Squadron was by now so low on serviceable aircraft that it was only able to put up eight to take over from 250 Squadron during the evening, by which time the two lighters being protected were 40 miles from Sidi Barrani. As the South African Tomahawks approached, the vessels were seen to be under attack by about a dozen Stukas. In fact there were 12 Luftwaffe Ju 87s and six from the Regia Aeronautica's 209ª Squadriglia taking part in the raid.

Six of the Tomahawk pilots made for the bombers, two more remaining overhead to offer some cover. At that point ten escorting Bf 109s suddenly appeared and attacked these two, a general dogfight commencing. The 2 SAAF Squadron pilots subsequently reported that when under attack, the Ju 87s throttled back, lowered their flaps and made stall turns "emitting black smoke to give the appearance of damage". Captains Loftus and Masson were credited with one apiece, a third being claimed by Lt J.R.R.Wells, while Lts Alexander, Field and Pannell each claimed a probable, Pannell adding two damaged. However, 'Kolo' Masson, another veteran of East Africa, failed to return and Capt J.A.Kok was shot down, becoming a PoW. Three more Tomahawks were damaged by the Messerschmitts, which were from 7./JG 26, but Lt Whelehan claimed two of these shot down as well as another Ju 87 as a probable. As so often happened, Axis losses were lighter than appeared from the claims made. Two Ju 87s (one German and one Italian) were shot down, and a third damaged; the escorting fighters suffered no loss.

The Italian Stuka pilots returned to report that the ships had been bombed before the Tomahawks attacked them, one tanker being claimed sunk. Indeed, one of the A lighters was sunk and the second was badly damaged. From the aircraft of this unit which had been shot down, S.Ten Antonio Longoni, and his gunner Av.Sc Alberto Petrellese, managed to force-land on the sea 18 miles east of Ras Azzaz. Both were seen climbing into their dinghy, but when the rescue aircraft arrived, no trace of any survivors was to be found.

Until the arrival of Bristol Beaufighters, the most potent aircraft for attacking Axis ground targets was the Blenheim IVf fitted with a fixed 20mm cannon in the nose, supplementing the under-fuselage pack containing four .303in Browning machine guns. Very little detail of these aircraft survived, but they were used in small numbers by several units, including in this case 113 Squadron.

Cap Gino Callieri, commander of 360ª Squadriglia, was undertaking a convoy escort off Benghazi in his G.50bis, when at 1750 he sighted a periscope about six miles north of Ghemines. Landing, he immediately notified HQ of Settore Centrale, this command at once sending out five Ju 87s of 239ª Squadriglia and two CR.42s of 18° Gruppo to hunt the British submarine. This was HMS *Cachalot*, commanded by Lt H R B Newton, DSO, which was cruising north of Benghazi. At 1940 Ten Vladimiro De Nunzio sighted the vessel and dive-bombed her, claiming a direct hit. *Cachalot* was eventually rammed and sunk by the torpedo-boat *Achille Papa*, commanded by Ten Vasc Gino Rosica at 0343 on 30 July. The crew of 71, with the exception of only one sailor, were rescued by *Achille Papa* and taken PoW.

British Claims

2 SAAF Sqn	Capt D.H.Loftus	Tomahawk	Ju 87	40m from Sidi Barrani 1905
	Capt A.Q.Masson	Tomahawk AK485	Ju 87	40m from Sidi Barrani 1905
	Lt J.R.R.Wells	Tomahawk	Ju 87	40m from Sidi Barrani 1905
	Lt A.Alexander	Tomahawk	Ju 87 probable*	40m from Sidi Barrani 1905
	Lt D.D.Pannell	Tomahawk	Ju 87 probable	40m from Sidi Barrani 1910
	Lt D.D.Pannell	Tomahawk	2 Ju 87s damaged	40m from Sidi Barrani 1910
	Lt V.P.Field	Tomahawk	Ju 87 probable	40m from Sidi Barrani 1910
	Lt T.B.Whelehan	Tomahawk AK394	2 Bf 109s	40m from Sidi Barrani 1910
	Lt T.B.Whelehan	Tomahawk AK394	Ju 87 probable	40m from Sidi Barrani 1910

*This claim may have been confirmed

British Casualties

2 SAAF Sqn	Tomahawk AK485 shot down; Capt A.Q.Masson KiA
	Tomahawk shot down; Capt J.A.Kok PoW
	3 Tomahawks damaged

German Claims

7./JG 26	Fw Karl-Heinz Ehlen	P-40	30m E Bardia 1747
	Oblt Joachim Müncheberg	P-40	24m E Bardia 1748
	Lt Hans Johannsen	P-40	12m S Sidi Barrani 1750
	Oblt Joachim Müncheberg	P-40	24m E Bardia 1752

German Casualties

2./StG 1	Ju 87R-2 WNr 6140 shot down in combat 50m N Sidi Barrani; Fw Ewald Hentsch/ Uffz Karl Steinfeld KiA
	Ju 87 damaged in combat; gunner Uffz Fritz Klose WiA

Italian Casualties

372ª Sq/153º Gr CT	MC.200 MM5082 crashed; S.Ten Giulio Binetti KiFA
353ª Sq/20º Gr CT	G.50 force-landed; S.Ten Aldo Conti PoW
209ª Sq Aut BaT	Ju 87R WNr 5976 shot down; S.Ten Longoni and gunner Av.Sc Petrellese MiA

Friday, 1 August 1941

Three S.79s of 279ª Squadriglia AS took off from Derna at 1850 to attack British shipping. Two returned without having seen anything, but the third crash-landed between Marsa Luch and Bardia. It was subsequently written off, although the crew survived unhurt.

Italian Casualties

279ª Sq AS	S.79 MM23963 crash-landed and written off; Ten Guglielmo Ranieri and crew safe

Saturday, 2 August 1941

At 1830 a dozen Hurricanes of 1 SAAF Squadron commenced a patrol over the destroyers *Vendetta* and *Havoc* to the north-west of Sidi Barrani as dusk approached. At about 1950 a formation of 15-20 Ju 87s of I./StG 1 was spotted approaching at 16,000 ft, escorted by 20 Bf 109s and MC.200s, flying some 3-4,000 ft higher. The Hurricane pilots at once attacked the dive-bombers, four being claimed shot down, two each by Capts Osler and van Vliet. They were immediately engaged by Bf 109s from 1./JG 27 and 7./JG 26, the pilots of these claiming five fighters shot down (three of them mis-identified as P-40s); three were actually lost, while Maj Wilmot, 1 SAAF's commanding officer claimed one Messerschmitt shot down. It seems he may have hit one of the JG 26 aircraft, which subsequently crash-landed at Gazala, suffering 50% damage; two of the dive-bombers were lost. Observers aboard the ships of the convoy reported that they had seen five Ju 87s and a Bf 109 crashing into the sea – but such reports could be notoriously misleading. The escorts to the dive-bombers had included 12 MC.200s of 153° Gruppo, their pilots reporting an engagement with Hurricanes which led to claims for two of these probably shot down. One of the missing South African pilots was Lt Ruffel, a new member of the unit. He had baled out having been wounded, and came down 40 miles out to sea. Inflating his life jacket, he swam for a night and a day, often lapsing into unconsciousness, but finally reached the coast – only to be taken prisoner by German troops.

British Claims

1 SAAF Sqn	Maj L.A.Wilmot	Hurricane I	Bf 109	35m from Sidi Barrani 1950
	Capt M.S.Osler	Hurricane I	2 Ju 87s	35m from Sidi Barrani 1950
	Capt C.A.van Vliet	Hurricane I W9239	2 Ju 87s	25m from Sidi Barrani 1955

British Casualties

1 SAAF Sqn	Hurricane I Z4699 shot down; Lt A.A.L.Tatham KiA
	Hurricane I V7717 Lt A.S.Ruffel swam to shore; PoW
	Hurricane I Z4506 Lt A.A.Tennant KiA

German Claims

1./JG 27	Fw Günther Steinhausen	2 Hurricanes	24m NW Mersa Matruh 1850
7./JG 26	Lt Hans Johannsen	P-40	NW Mersa Matruh 1855
1./JG 27	Uffz Gerhard Keppler	P-40	24m NW Mersa Matruh1855
	Obgw Albert Espenlaub	P-40	24m NW Mersa Matruh1857

German Casualties

7./JG 26	Bf 109E-7 WNr 6467 crash-landed Ain el Gazala, 50% damaged
3./StG 1	Ju 87R-2 WNr 6971 shot down 30m N Bardia; Lt Hans Wagner/Fw Alfons Grechler KiA
	Ju 87R-2 WNr 6050 shot down 30m N Bardia; Ofhr Bruno Kalch/Gefr Franz Hudler KiA

Italian Claims

374ª Sq/153º Gr CT	M.llo Egeo Pardi	Hurricane Probable
372ª Sq/153º Gr CT	S.Ten Mario Peselli	Hurricane Probable

During the day 250 Squadron collected two Tomahawks from Wadi Natrun which had been painted in a new desert camouflage scheme of dark earth and mid stone on the upper surfaces, and azure blue below. This scheme was now to be applied to all aircraft in the theatre; until this date aircraft had been finished in the standard temperate land scheme of green and brown, with sky undersurfaces.

Sunday, 3 August 1941

A raid on gun emplacements east of Tobruk was undertaken by 21 Marylands as escorting fighters patrolled above. No interceptions occurred, but one Italian fighter was lost whilst returning from a strafing attack in the Habat-Buq Buq area. During the day 272 Squadron returned to Edcu following its detachment to Malta.

British Claims				
250 Sqn	Plt Off C.R.Caldwell	Tomahawk AK416	Bf 109 damaged	Capuzzo 0840-1025
German Casualties				
7./JG 26	Bf 109E-7 WNr 5821 75% destroyed by bombs at Ain el Gazala			
1./JG 27	Bf 109E-7 WNr 4889 destroyed by bombs at Ain el Gazala			
Italian Casualties				
353ª Sq/20° Gr CT	G.50 MM5961 MiA; Serg Magg Michele Simonetti MiA			

Tuesday, 5 August 1941

Over the coastal area 11 patrolling Hurricane pilots from 73 Squadron encountered two Bf 110s of 8./ZG 26, one of which dived on them from above, the pilot, Lt Bidlingmair, claiming two of them shot down. As the formation crossed the coast near Bardia, one Hurricane was hit in the lubrication system, obliging the pilot to force-land on the beach two miles north of Sidi Barrani. Other members of the squadron claimed to have inflicted damage on one of the attackers.

By night an S.79 from 10ª Squadriglia flown by S.Ten Gioacchino Rossini, was reported to have been shot down by a British fighter. Pilot, co-pilot and one member of the crew were able to bale out, but the others aboard were lost.

British Claims				
73 Sqn	Unspecified pilot(s)	Bf 110	damaged nr Bardia	
British Casualties				
24 SAAF Sqn	Maryland II AH354 MiA from raid on Derna. Lt C.Clarkson and crew found buried later			
73 Sqn	Hurricane I force-landed on beach due to damage; pilot safe			
German Claims				
8./ZG 26	Lt Dieter Bidlingmair	2 Hurricanes	N Sidi Barrani 1535-1536	
Italian Casualties				
10ª Sq/28° Gr/8° St BT	S.79 MM21486 shot down by fighters during night mission; S.Ten Rossini, the co-pilot and one member of the crew baled out			

Friday, 8 August 1941

Seven Hurricanes of 73 Squadron took off at 0730 to commence a day of patrolling over coastal shipping. Once in the air they were attacked by a trio of Bf 110s which dived on them from above. The RAF pilots dodged these, although one of the German pilots thought he had been successful in shooting down two of the British fighters – one of which he (or his gunner) mis-identified as a P-40. In practice the Hurricanes all escaped damage and four gave chase to their attackers, claiming to have silenced all the rear gunners and inflicted serious damage on all three. Subsequently, two were claimed as probably shot down.

British Claims				
229 Sqn	Sgt L.Luck	Hurricane I	Bf 110 probable	over sea off Sidi Barrani 0730
73 Sqn	Plt Off R.McDougal	Hurricane I	Bf 110 probable	20m N Sidi Barrani 0740
German Claims				
8./ZG 26	Ofw Richard Heller	Hurricane	N Sidi Barrani 0655	
	Ofw Richard Heller	P-40	N Sidi Barrani 0656	

Saturday, 9 August 1941

The night of 8/9 August proved to be one of mixed fortunes for 73 Squadron and its attached 229 Squadron pilots. Off at 0325 two pilots, aided by searchlights, shot down a bomber which was not showing IFF (identification friend or foe); it turned out to be a 113 Squadron Blenheim, one of eight which had been attacking Gazala No. 2 airfield and gunnery workshops at Bardia; two members of the crew were killed. However, the bomber brought down near Lake Maryut by Plt Off Johns proved to be an LG 1 machine, which had flown from Athens to undertake its attack. However, this seems to have been the same Ju 88 which was intercepted and claimed shot down by a number of pilots from 30 Squadron (see Chapter 13 – Blitz on Egypt).

By day a new commander for the RAF in North Africa arrived in the person of Air Vice-Marshal Arthur Coningham, DSO, MC, DFC, AFC, who took over from Venn. A successful and experienced fighter pilot during the First World War, Coningham, a New Zealander, had been commanding 4 Group of Bomber Command in the UK. 15 years earlier he had pioneered the air reinforcement route from Takoradi to Cairo, which was now in regular use much as he had undertaken it all those years before. The day was also marked by the first sorties to be undertaken by the new Tac R squadron, 451.

British Claims				
229 Sqn	Plt Off G.B.Johns	Hurricane I Z4262	He 111 (or Ju 88)	4-5m out to sea from Mersa Matruh 0330
British Casualties				
113 Sqn	Blenheim IV V5990, shot down in error off Mersa Matruh; Sgt W.R.Sands, RAAF, survived but the other two members of the crew were KiA			

Sunday, 10 August 1941

451 Squadron gained an early success when Plt Off R.T.Hudson, who was undertaking a reconnaissance sortie near Bardia, happened upon an Hs 126 of 2.(H)/14 on a similar mission, and shot it down.

During the day eight Marylands of 24 SAAF Squadron carried out a raid escorted by Tomahawks, Hurricanes and Martlets, the latter from the RN Fighter Squadron. No opposition was encountered in the air, but Flak damaged Lt Hedley's 1 SAAF Squadron Hurricane, causing him to crash-land.

The day also saw the arrival in Libya of 160° Gruppo CT (375ª, 393ª and 394ª Squadriglie) at Tamet with CR.42s to replace 18° Gruppo. At the same time 12° Gruppo CT (159ª, 160ª, 165ª Squadriglie) – equipped with G.50bis – took the place of 2° Gruppo, the two relieved units returning to Italy.

British Claims				
451 Sqn	Plt Off R.T.Hudson	Hurricane I	Hs 126	10m NNW Fort Maddalena 1150
British Casualties				
1 SAAF Sqn	Hurricane I crash-landed due to Flak damage; Lt P.M.Hedley safe			
German Casualties				
2.(H)/14	Hs 126 shot down; Oblt Heymer survived			

Monday, 11 August 1941

Fighter sorties over RN ships amounted to 48 during the day. Between 1415-1525 a dozen 2 SAAF Squadron Tomahawks undertook a patrol during which four Bf 110s were encountered, one of these being claimed shot down. However, during an earlier operation that afternoon, one of the unit's Tomahawks had crashed only 700 yards from the edge of 12 SAAF Squadron's airfield, the pilot being killed. It was reported that the pilot was believed to have been undertaking a shoot-up of the area. During a further patrol by 1 SAAF Squadron's Hurricanes, six Ju 88s and two Bf 110s were seen, but were not engaged.

British Claims				
2 SAAF Sqn	Lt L.A.Stone	Tomahawk	Bf 110	50m N Sidi Barrani 1050
German Casualties				
I./NJG 3	Bf 110E-1 WNr 3944 shot down; Gefr Reinhold/Gefr Stark			
Italian Casualties				
Unspecified unit	S.81 Red Cross aircraft destroyed on the ground at Berka by bombs			

During the month the first Luftwaffe night fighters reached North Africa when Hptmn Peters led the Bf 110s of I./NJG 3 from Greece to Derna. Although these presented an obvious threat to the night-operating Wellingtons, in the event the newly-arrived Messerschmitts were to be employed mainly by day in the first instance, undertaking reconnaissance, patrol and strafing sorties.

At this stage 112 Squadron arrived at Maryut from Palestine to become the third Tomahawk unit in the desert; it was the first time that the squadron had returned to operations since its Gladiators had been withdrawn from Crete in early May.

At the same time the Fleet Air Arm made a positive reinforcement of the fighter strength of the Allied air forces, forming the RN Fighter Unit (also referred to as the RN Fighter Squadron, or RNFS) to carry out shipping patrol duties and occasionally to assist in land operations. This unit was initially formed with Hurricanes flown by the pilots of 803 and 806 Squadrons who had been in Syria. They were joined by the Grumman Martlets of 805 Squadron, producing a unit which was actually of about two squadrons strength.

Tuesday, 12 August 1941
German Casualties

JG 27	Bf 109 crash-landed Gambut, 70% damaged
III./ZG 26	Bf 110E-1 WNr 3453 shot down by AA; Uffz Seiler/Ogfr Schmidt

Thursday, 14 August 1941
A pilot of the newly-arrived 160° Gruppo CT was killed when he crashed when undertaking an engine test at Got Bersis.

Italian Casualties

394ª Sq/160° Gr CT	CR.42 MM7541 crashed during engine test; S.Ten Dario Magnabosco KiFA

Saturday, 16 August 1941
Whilst on a diversionary patrol north of Gambut, Sgts McDonnell and Cash of 274 Squadron intercepted a lone S.79 which they claimed to have damaged. However, Cash's fighter was hit by return fire and crashed into the sea.

55 Squadron was now taken over by Wg Cdr R.D.Welland, who arrived on posting from Jerusalem.

British Claims

274 Sqn	Sgt J.F. Cash	Hurricane I V4578	} S.79 damaged	Great Gambut 0815-1025
	Sgt McDonnell	Hurricane I Z4770		

British Casualties

274 Sqn	Hurricane I V4578 hit by return fire and crashed in sea; Sgt J.F.Cash KiA

Sunday, 17 August 1941
Six Luftwaffe Ju 87s and six from 209ª Squadriglia set out to bomb ships in Tobruk harbour, escorted by 13 G.50bis of 20° Gruppo, but encountered very heavy AA fire which damaged many of the dive-bombers. One gunner, 1° Av Oscar Ricci, was killed in one of the Italian aircraft, and in another Ju 87 S.Ten Antonio Ragonese force-landed near El Adem.

Following recent substantial reinforcements of Hurricanes to Malta, and the departure of Luftwaffe aircraft from Sicily, it had become possible to spare a few for the North African front. Consequently, on this date four such fighters, flown by Plt Off G.D.Marshall and three Sgt pilots, set off for Cyrenaica. Three of these failed to arrive and were assumed to have been lost. Italian records indicate that two of them landed at Bardia due to engine trouble where the pilots were captured by German troops.

British Claims

250 Sqn	Plt Off C.R.Caldwell	Tomahawk AK504	G.50	Convoy patrol 0710-0920

British Casualties

In transit	3 Hurricanes MiA, flown by Plt Off G.D.Marshall and two Sgts. Two force-landed at Bardia due to engine failure; two pilots PoW; 1 pilot MiA

Italian Casualties

209ª Sq Aut BaT	2 Ju 87s hit by AA during attack on Tobruk; one force-landed near El Adem; S.Ten Ragonese safe; Cap Romanese safe, gunner 1° Av Ricci killed

Monday, 18 August 1941

The day was again marked by a substantial number of sorties flown over shipping. On one such sortie at 1815 12 Tomahawks from 250 Squadron were off Ras-el-Mil when 13-20 Bf 109s escorting three-six Bf 110s were seen, the latter jettisoning bombs five miles from the ships. The former attacked, one Tomahawk being shot down and a second so badly damaged that it crashed on landing.

According to Italian records, a Blenheim made an emergency landing south of Ras Azzaz where it was captured by German troops. No loss of such an aircraft is listed by the RAF on this date. However, a Malta-based aircraft, Z6160 (unit unknown) is listed as being struck off charge for unspecified reason, and it is possible that this may be the aircraft in question.

British Claims

250 Sqn	Plt Off C.R.Caldwell	Tomahawk AK504	Bf 109 damaged	Convoy patrol 1930-2015
	Sgt R.T.C.Whittle	Tomahawk AK380	Bf 109 probable	Convoy patrol 1930-2015

British Casualties

250 Sqn	Tomahawk AK 554 shot down; Sgt G.M.McCullough KiA			
	Tomahawk badly damaged and crashed on landing			

German Claims

2./JG 27	Obfw Hermann Förster	P-40	E Ras Azzaz	1830

Following the brief respite which had commenced at the start of July, 6 Squadron now began moving to Wadi Halfa where the unit would become fully established by the 26th. With it went three Lysander Is and three Mark IIs, five Gladiator Is and six Mark IIs. From here four of the Lysanders and four Gladiator IIs moved to Kufra to provide defence and local reconnaissance.

A crash-landed Tomahawk of 250 Squadron within Commonwealth lines.

Tuesday, 19 August 1941

Operation Treacle commenced, involving the replacement in the Tobruk defences of the 18th Australian Infantry Brigade and 18th Cavalry (Indian Army) by the 1st Polish Carpathian Brigade. A month earlier General Sir Thomas Blamey, commander of Australian troops in the Middle East, had proposed to General Auchinleck that the Australian elements of the garrison in Tobruk be replaced. At the same time the Australian government approached the British War Cabinet on similar lines. The Syrian operation being over, there was a strong desire that all Australian troops be brought under one command, while concern existed for the physical condition of the men of these units following their long exposure to the front line.

Auchinleck was instructed to co-operate effectively and sympathetically, but Tedder was less than overjoyed, later recording that he doubted whether such a relief operation would have been undertaken had the main part of the garrison been British troops, rather than Australian.

From the start it was clear that any such operation would have to be carried out by fast warships and during the moonless period of the calendar. Codenamed Treacle (probably because it appeared to be a 'sticky' operation), the operation was to be carried out during the period 19-29 August. Typically, two destroyers and a fast minelayer would undertake the actual transfer of troops, accompanied by cruisers to provide anti-aircraft cover, and by squadrons of fighters by day.

During the next 11 nights, approximately one third of the garrison was exchanged, 6,116 men and 1,297 tons of supplies being carried in and 5,040 men taken out. This was a very different task to the transportation of reinforcements and supplies, and the withdrawal of wounded, placing a considerably increased burden on the fighter units involved.

S.79s of 10° Stormo BT escorted by Messerschmitt Bf 110s.

Thursday, 21 August 1941

This proved to be the defining day of the Treacle operation. An early morning fighter sweep over the shipping lines arrived five minutes late, HMS *Kipling* radioing that she was under attack but that no defending aircraft were in sight. Hearing this message, the pilots of 2 SAAF Squadron took off at 0740 to go to the rescue. Meanwhile, 1 SAAF had arrived on the scene to find only a damaged destroyer and no sign of the Axis bombers, which had departed. As the Tomahawks followed, Maj St E. 'Saint' Truter's aircraft developed oil trouble and he turned back for repairs. Taking off again with Lt R.K.Stephenson, he attempted to catch up with the rest of the squadron, but in so doing the pair were attacked by eight Bf 109s from 2./JG 27. Stephenson's fighter was hit and he was slightly wounded, but in trying to formate on Truter, his aircraft fell away temporarily out of control. The last he saw of Truter's Tomahawk was of it being heavily attacked; Truter was shot down and killed. The Luftwaffe pilots involved submitted claims for three shot down, two identified as P-40s and one as a Hurricane.

The numbers of Axis fighters observed during the morning patrols led 204 Group to believe that more such aircraft had been brought up, threatening heavier raids during the forthcoming evening sailing. Consequently, the SAAF Maryland units were ordered to bomb airfields in the area at Bardia, Menastir and Capuzzo. Thus at around 1200 a dozen bombers from 12 SAAF and 24 SAAF Squadrons set off for these targets. It appears that full fighter escort was not provided, but 12 Hurricanes of 229/73 Squadron did seek to cover those bombers heading for Menastir, while a pair of such aircraft from the RNFS climbed to 20,000 feet over the area. Somewhat later, but when some of the units mentioned were still in the air, seven Hurricanes of 1 SAAF Squadron and eight Tomahawks of 2 SAAF, set off at 1820 to provide high cover.

As the Marylands approached their targets, dust trails were seen on the airfields ahead as German fighters took off in preparation to intercept. The 73 Squadron formation patrolled north of Bardia at 15,000 feet, but were attacked by seven Bf 109s and went into a defensive circle. Messerschmitts attacked again as the British fighters headed for the coast, and once more when they were between Bardia and Sidi Barrani. One Hurricane was shot down into the sea and two more failed to return.(73 Squadron's records for this period seem to be incomplete, no details of these losses being provided therein; however, it is known that one of the pilots involved was Sgt, or Plt Off, P.J.Horniman, one of those attached from 229 Squadron.) It seems likely that these had fallen to pilots of 7./JG 26 and 2./JG 27. The pair of naval pilots, meantime, spotted ten Bf 110s at 10,000 feet, Lt H.P.Allingham firing on one which dived away shedding pieces, although he did not follow. It appears that he was subsequently credited with a victory during this engagement, although his victim was recorded as being a Bf 109. He had almost certainly attacked a formation of eight Bf 110s of 8./ZG 26 which had taken off to intercept the bombers, led by

Oblt Schulze-Dickow, and in company with nine Bf 109s.

The Zerstörer crews spotted 1 SAAF Squadron over the three destroyers *Kandahar*, *Griffin* and *Jackal*, the German crews diving down to attack these. As they did so they were themselves attacked by the Tomahawks, which were flying at a higher level. Schulze-Dickow reported that he had attacked the leading fighter which zoomed up at the last second to avoid a collision and crashed into the sea beside one of the destroyers, the pilot being rescued. Lt W.P.Stanford later recorded that "...the leading 110 appeared to aim at Captain D.H.Loftus who was leading the 2 SAAF formation, but it hit Lt R.C.Yeats with a full broadside of cannon fire and sent him spinning down in flames."

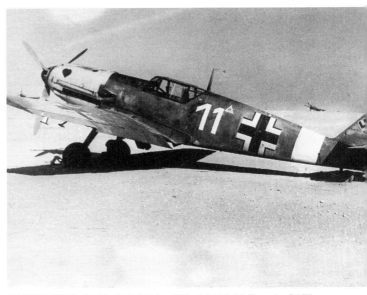

Bf 109E/7N Werke Nr 4139 'Weisse 11' of 7./JG 26 flown by Lt Theo Lindemann in which he claimed a Martin Maryland shot down on 21 August 1941.

Following Schulze-Dickow, another ZG 26 pilot claimed to have shot down the leading aircraft of a flight which crashed near the warships, and a third was claimed during this initial pass, this one crashing on one of the destroyers on fire. It would appear that all three had actually claimed against Yeats's Tomahawk, which was the only one lost at this point. On a further pass a fourth fighter was claimed by one of these German pilots, identified as a Hurricane which lost a wing and crashed into the sea. The other Tomahawk pilots then attacked the big Messerschmitts, Lt D.D.Pannell claiming one shot down, he and two other pilots claiming others damaged or as probables. One Bf 110 flown by Lt Heinz Plumek was shot down with the loss of the crew. It also appears that one of 1 SAAF Squadron's Hurricanes was badly damaged during this combat. Lt Yeats had managed to bale out of his stricken Tomahawk, despite suffering severe burns. He fell into the sea close to one of the destroyers. Although under orders not to stop, this vessel reversed its engines vigorously to bring it to a halt, thereby sucking Yeats below the water and nearly drowning him. Nevertheless, he was pulled out of the sea to face many months in hospital.

While this dogfight had been underway, the Marylands had completed their bombing and turned for home. In doing so, they flew right through the swirling fighters and came under attack. 12 SAAF Squadron's Lt J.E.M. Goodwin's aircraft was shot down in flames three miles east of Sidi Barrani. As the bomber went down, two parachutes were seen to open, but no survivors were subsequently found. Maj O.W.B. van Ginkel, DFC, brought his Maryland home, shot-up so badly that it was written off as beyond repair, and with the rear gunner, Air Sgt A.W.Graham, wounded.

The pair of bombers which had attacked Menastir were also targetted, Lt L.F.Leisegang's aircraft being hard hit, losing one engine. However, he was able to dive away so fast that his attackers, which followed for 50 miles, could not catch him. Capt G.Bateman and his crew were less fortunate. Their Maryland was also hit and set afire, but Bateman was able to hold it level so that the crew might bale out. What then transpired was graphically described in the citation to a DFM for Air Sgt Francois Joubert, who was:

"acting as bottom gunner on Maryland 1623 at 1905 hours on 21 August 1941, whilst returning from a bombing raid on Menster (sic) aerodrome. The aircraft was intercepted by six Me 109s off the Gulf of Salum (sic) and, in the ensuing fight, the top gunner was seriously wounded and put out of action. The aircraft was set on fire, the flames spreading through the top turret. Sergeant Joubert attempted to extinguish the fire but the fire extinguisher proved ineffective. By this time, Captain Bateman, the pilot, had brought his aircraft over land and ordered his crew to abandon it.

The intercommunication at this stage was out of action and neither of the Sergeants heard the pilot's instructions. On seeing the pilot and observer leaving the aircraft, Sergeant Joubert realised that the aircraft was being abandoned. He immediately, with great difficulty, assisted the badly wounded Sergeant from his turret towards the bottom escape hatch. Sergeant Wiggills' parachute harness got hung up on the rear sight of the bottom gun and Sergeant Joubert lifted the gun from its mounting and dropped the gun and gunner through the hatch. While doing so, the fore-sight of the gun caught Sergeant Joubert's ripcord causing the parachute to open inside the aircraft. Joubert gathered up the parachute in his arms and jumped in his turn but had considerable difficulty in getting it open and was only about 1,000 feet from the ground when it did open. The canopy of the parachute also had several holes burnt through it by the fire in the rear compartment. Throughout, Sergeant Joubert showed remarkable coolness and great gallantry in assisting his comrade to escape from a badly burnt aircraft."

The Battleaxe offensive of June 1941 proved costly for the Commonwealth forces both in terms of aircraft and tanks. One of the latter, an A-13 cruiser, has been abandoned and captured by Axis forces.

Successful I./JG 27 pilots Oblt Hugo Schneider (left) and Obfw Albert Espenlaub.

Three claims were made against the Marylands by pilots of 1./JG 27, while Lt Werner Schroer of that unit made a final claim for a Hurricane at 1820 to bring the evening's action to a close. Army observers reported that a Bf 110 had been seen to fall in flames near Sidi Barrani (obviously Lt Plume's aircraft), and a Ju 88 was also reported down in this area, the crew apparently becoming prisoners. No claims for such an aircraft by any of the Allied fighter units involved have been found. Radio Cairo subsequently reported that the formation leader shot down by Schultze-Dickow had been one of the most successful South African fighter pilots. It is assumed that the pilot referred to was 'Saint' Truter, who had actually fallen several hours earlier during the morning engagement.

British Claims

2 SAAF Sqn	Lt C.A.Whaites	Tomahawk AK524	Bf 110	damaged 20m N Sidi Barrani 1905
	Lt W.P.Stanford	Tomahawk AK442	Bf 110	damaged 20m N Sidi Barrani 1905
	Lt D.D.Pannell	Tomahawk	Bf 110	20m N Sidi Barrani 1905
	Lt D.D.Pannell	Tomahawk	Bf 110	damaged 20m N Sidi Barrani 1905
RNFS	Lt H.P.Allingham	Hurricane I W4245'H'	Bf 109	10m WNW Sidi Barrani 1700

British Casualties

229/73 Sqn	Hurricane I V7492 MiA from patrol NE Bardia; Plt Off P.J.Horniman KiA		
	Hurricane I Z4511 MiA from patrol NE Bardia; Plt Off J.Shelley MiA 1920		
	Hurricane I apparently MiA; pilot's name not recorded		
12 SAAF Sqn	Maryland II 1636 shot down off Sidi Barrani by Bf 109s; Maj O.W.B.van Ginkel, DFC, and two safe; air gunner badly wounded		
	Maryland II 1662 shot down by Bf 109s E Sidi Barrani; Lt J.E.M.Goodwin and crew KiA		
24 SAAF Sqn	Maryland II 1623 shot down by Bf 109s over Bay of Sollum; Capt G.L.Bateman and crew baled; air gunner wounded		
	Maryland II damaged by fighters; Lt L.F.Leisegang and crew safe		
2 SAAF Sqn	Tomahawk AK375 shot down; Maj St E.Truter KiA 20m NE Sidi Barrani 0815		
	Tomahawk AK372 damaged; Lt R.K.Stephenson slightly WiA 20m NE Sidi Barrani 0815		
	Tomahawk AK370 shot down; Lt R.C.Yeats baled out, WiA W Sidi Barrani 1905		

German Claims

2./JG 27	Lt Willi Kothmann	P-40	0714
	Hptmn Erich Gerlitz	P-40	0715
	Oblt Ernst Maack	Hurricane	0715
	Obfw Hermann Förster	Hurricane	W Gambut 1745
7./JG 26	Lt Theo Lindemann	Martin 167	W Sidi Barrani 1755
	Oblt Klaus Mietusch	Martin 167	n.b.
8./ZG 26	Obfw Richard Heller	P-40	NE Sidi Barrani 1756
	Oblt Kurt Rosenkranz	P-40	NE Sidi Barrani 1756
	Oblt Fritz Schulze-Dickow	P-40	NE Sidi Barrani 1756
	Oblt Kurt Rosenkranz	Hurricane	NE Sidi Barrani 1803
1./JG 27	Hptmn Wolfgang Redlich	Martin 167	W Sidi Barrani 1755
	Oblt Hugo Schneider	Martin 167	E Sidi Barrani 1803
	Obfw Albert Espenlaub	Martin 167	Sidi Barrani 1807
	Lt Werner Schroer	Hurricane	NE Bardia 1820

German Casualties

8./ZG 26	Bf 110 WNr 3919 Lt Heinz Plumek KiA, Fw Gerhard Weist WiA 20m SE Sidi Barrani
	3U+AS WNr 3453 Uffz Werner safe, Ogfr Hermann Schmidt KiA

Friday, 22 August 1941

A reconnaissance aircraft from 39 Squadron on a sortie over the coastal area of the Axis lines between Tobruk and the Egyptian frontier, was intercepted and shot down by an Italian G.50bis. Although the squadron was now equipped in the main with Marylands, and the identity of the missing aircraft has in the past been recorded as such, more recent research indicates that it was in fact a Blenheim, which was believed to have been shot down into Sollum Bay.

A G.50bis of 155° Gruppo CT. The unit emblem is barely visible below the cockpit.

British Casualties

39 Sqn	Blenheim IV AH361 MiA, Sollum Bay; Sgt C.K.Berriman, RAAF, and crew KiA		

Italian Claims

352ª Sq/155° Gr CT	S.Ten Vittorio Muratori	Blenheim	Tobruk

Saturday, 23 August 1941

At 0555 12 250 Squadron and 2 SAAF Squadron Tomahawks took off to commence the first of what would amount to 110 individual sorties over the ships during the day. A Ju 88 was seen and pursued through cloud by Capt Pannell of the South African unit and Flg Off Thornton of 250 Squadron. With the port engine on fire, it was seen to crash into the sea and sink, ten miles north of Sidi Barrani. One Tomahawk returned at once having been slightly damaged during this engagement, the pilot reporting that a member of the German crew had been seen in the water. A Walrus, escorted by a pair of fighters, at once set out, but only an empty dinghy was to be found. Meanwhile, five more pilots attacked a further Ju 88, reporting silencing the rear gunner following which the aircraft was last seen diving towards the sea, pouring smoke.

More 250 Squadron aircraft were on their way to Sidi Barrani to undertake another patrol at 1345, when three more Ju 88s were seen, one of these being claimed shot down between Taifa and Ishailia Rocks by the commanding officer, Sqn Ldr Scoular.

British Claims

250 Sqn	Plt Off F.C.Thornton	Tomahawk AK430	Ju 88 damaged	0600
2 SAAF Sqn	Lt D.D.Pannell	Tomahawk AK432	} Ju 88	N Sidi Barrani 0615
250 Sqn	Plt Off F.C.Thornton	Tomahawk AK430		
	Sqn Ldr J.E.Scoular	Tomahawk AK555	Ju 88	Ishailia, 16m off Taifa Rocks 1500-1700

German Casualties

7./LG 1	Ju 88A-5 WNr 3317 L1+CR shot down by Curtiss P-40 north of Benghazi; Lt Sigismund Kloss KiA, two of crew MiA, one PoW

Monday, 25 August 1941

A Luftwaffe reconnaissance crew spotted six RN destroyers to the north of Ras Azzaz during the day. On receipt of this news, two S.79 torpedo-bombers from 279ª Squadriglia AS were sent off from Derna to attack, flown by Cap Giulio Marini and Ten Mario Frongia. Both pilots released their torpedoes at 1930, claiming a probable hit on a destroyer. No damage was reported by the Royal Navy. On this date, however, Flg Off Munro of 272 Squadron had trouble starting the engines of his 272 Squadron Beaufighter, taking off late as a result. The aircraft did not return, and his body was later washed ashore; of his observer, Sgt McAdam, there was no sign.

British Casualties

272 Sqn	Beaufighter Ic FTR; Flg Off D.N.R.Munro and observer, Sgt McAdam, MiA

Tuesday, 26 August 1941

49 shipping patrols were undertaken by fighters during the day, while six Marylands attacked tank concentrations at Marsa Luch. Off at 1730 to cover a minelayer, three destroyers and three cruisers, a dozen fighters each from 250 and 274 Squadrons, were followed at 1850 by ten Tomahawks of 2 SAAF Squadron and 12 Hurricanes of the RNFS. At 1830 a reported 11 Bf 109s dived on 250 Squadron out of the sun, Plt Off S.A.Wells claiming to have shot down one as the unit went into a defensive circle, gaining height as it did so. The Messerschmitts attacked twice more without result, and then a third time when Wells claimed a second shot down and Sgt M.S.Hards a third. However, Hards' aircraft was hit and damaged, and he force-landed halfway between Maaten Bagush and Sidi Barrani, suffering a broken ankle.

The second formation was then also attacked out of the sun, the RNFS weaver Sub Lt Pudney, being shot down into the sea. Three claims were made by 1./JG 27 pilots, but none of their Messerschmitts appear actually to have been shot down or even badly damaged during this encounter. Bruce Pudney was reported to have been rescued by the crew of a cruiser, but in fact he had been killed.

6 Squadron, duly rested, was now posted to Wadi Halfa with three Lysander Is, three Mark IIs, six Gladiator IIs and five Mark Is. From here a flight was detached to Kufra Oasis, comprising four pilots with four Lysander IIs and four Gladiator IIs.

British Claims

250 Sqn	Plt Off S.A.Wells	Tomahawk AK416	Bf 109	5m N Sidi Barrani 1830
	Sgt M.S.Hards	Tomahawk AK374	Bf 109	5m N Sidi Barrani 1830

British Casualties

250 Sqn	Tomahawk AK374; Sgt M.S.Hards force-landed, slightly WiA			
RNFS	Hurricane I Z4052 Sub Lt G.B.Pudney (806 Sqn) KiA			

German Claims

1./JG 27	Fw Günther Steinhausen	P-40	N Sidi Barrani
	Lt Hans Remmer	Hurricane	15m N Sidi Barrani
	Fw Peter Werfft	Hurricane	Sidi Barrani

Wednesday, 27 August 1941

During the evening two more of 279ª Squadriglia's S.79 torpedo-bombers were again despatched from Derna to hunt for British shipping, Cap Marini on this occasion leading Ten Umberto Barbani to the area during the early evening. The latter was forced to turn back due to a failure with his torpedo, but Marini pushed on and released at 2015, claiming to have probably damaged a light cruiser. This appears to have been HMS *Phoebe*, which did indeed suffer damage from an air-launched torpedo.

Whilst on patrol, Sgt Green of 272 Squadron spotted a hostile aircraft and broke away from his section, claiming to have destroyed the intruder before rejoining formation. What it was, was not recorded.

British Claims

250 Sqn	Plt Off C.R.Caldwell	Tomahawk AK493	Bf 109 probable	off coast 1815
272 Sqn	Sgt Green	Beaufighter Ic 'L'	E/a	0927

Thursday, 28 August 1941

A dozen 1 SAAF Squadron Hurricanes and nine 250 Squadron Tomahawks set off to patrol over shipping at 1840, the former at 6,000 feet, the latter at 15,000. At 1915 the South Africans spotted ten Bf 109s at 10,000 feet as the ships' AA opened up. Lt Marseille dived, his fire hitting Lt Williams' aircraft, the pilot suffering slight wounds and crash-landing at Sidi Barrani. 2/Lt Herbert's fighter also suffered some fairly severe damage.

On this date 261 Medium Bomber Wing was formed at Maaten Bagush under the command of Col H.S.Willmott. Initially, it was to command 12 and 24 SAAF Squadrons, 39, 113 and 21 SAAF Squadrons, but due to its mainly maritime and reconnaissance function, 39 was then withdrawn. Resting from recent activities, 12 SAAF would undertake the wing's first operation on 11 September with an attack on Gazala and Gambut, but 24 SAAF would not be engaged in any further operational sorties until it had been re-equipped with Douglas Bostons; 21 SAAF would commence its first such activities on 22 September.

British Casualties

1 SAAF Sqn	Hurricane I Z4697 damaged and crash-landed; Lt V.F.Williams WiA			
	Hurricane I Z4704 badly damaged; 2/Lt W.L.Herbert safe			

German Claims

3./JG 27	Lt Hans-Joachim Marseille	Hurricane	2m NW Sidi Barrani 1800

Friday, 29 August 1941

31 sorties were flown over the shipping on this date, ten 250 Squadron Tomahawks patrolling over two destroyers north-west of Ishailia Rocks from 1800 hours. Here they were attacked by a small flight of Bf 109s. One Tomahawk, flown by Plt Off Clive Caldwell, was attacked and damaged by Lt Werner Schroer as the Australian was acting as weaver to the formation. With his aircraft alight, Caldwell prepared to bale out, Schroer returning to base to claim a victory. As he left, however, the fire died down, and Caldwell settled back into the cockpit. Spotting several other aircraft, despite the wounds he had suffered, he claimed a Bf 109 shot down – although none appear to have been lost on this date.

British Claims				
250 Sqn	Plt Off C.R.Caldwell	Tomahawk AK493	Bf 109	N Sidi Barrani 1905

British Casualties	
250 Sqn	Tomahawk AK493 damaged; Plt Off C.R.Caldwell slightly WiA

German Claims				
4./JG 27	Lt Werner Schroer	P-40		NW Sidi Barrani 1810

German Casualties	
Stab/StG 3	Ju 88 shot down by AA Tobruk; Fw Franz Rogosch and three KiA, including Oblt Hans-Georg Stopka; one PoW
5./LG 1	Ju 88A-5 Trop WNr 4340 L1+SC shot down by AA; Fw Herbert Schelm and crew MiA

Saturday, 30 August 1941

During the evening Oblt Homuth of 3./JG 27 claimed a Blenheim shot down near Sollum, but no commensurate loss has been found. A Maryland of 39 Squadron was lost on this date (see Chapter 15 – In Support of the Royal Navy).

German Claims			
3./JG 27	Oblt Gerhard Homuth	Blenheim	Sollum 1730

Sunday, 31 August 1941

At dusk two Italian fighter pilots from 360ª Squadriglia, Ten Gianni Caracciolo and M.llo Francesco Fagiolo, spotted an intruder when patrolling over Benghazi harbour. They attacked and forced it to land near K.2 airfield where it proved to be a Luftwaffe Ju 88. Damaged beyond repair, it had to be written off, with the pilot and gunner both wounded. Poor visibility was claimed to have been the reason for this mistaken interception.

During this same evening three Blenheims of 113 Squadron were despatched to bomb the very harbour where the unfortunate German crew had already been attacked. No further interceptions seem to have taken place, but two of the British bombers failed to return, all members of both crew being lost; it was thought that both had succumbed to Flak over the target area, one being seen to fall in flames. The formation's bombs missed the ship which it had been sent out to attack.

In another change of command, 84 Squadron was taken over by Wg Cdr C.D.C.Boyce.

British Casualties	
113 Sqn	Blenheim IV T2066 MiA; Sgt G.L.R.Sulman and crew KiA
	Blenheim IV V6136 MiA; Wg Cdr R.H.Spencer, DFC, and crew KiA

German Casualties	
5./LG 1	Ju 88A-5 WNr 3280 damaged beyond repair by Italian fighter at Benghazi; Fw Eduard Ott and one WiA, two safe

As August drew to a close there was a lull in operations. At this point 73 Squadron which was now down to only three serviceable Hurricanes, withdrew to Amiriya to re-equip. 229 Squadron ended its long attachment to that unit and began re-establishing as an independent unit at LG.93, where it would be re-equipped with Mark IIc Hurricanes before resuming operational flying. To take 73's place in the forward area, 33 Squadron now departed Amiriya for Sidi Haneish – still, however, retaining its Hurricane Is.

Monday, 1 September 1941

By the end of August the airfields at Sidi Barrani had virtually ceased to be used as squadrons withdrew to rebuild their strengths. Although they were very vulnerable to surprise attack by Axis aircraft, it was decided that the risk should be taken to re-utilise them – particularly in the provision of shipping patrols. However, it would be necessary to employ the costly and relatively inefficient business of maintaining standing defensive patrols to try and ensure their security. Consequently, 1 SAAF Squadron was moved forward to LG.05, 2 SAAF went to LG.03 and 250 Squadron to LG.07 further back at Mersa Matruh.

German Casualties	
2./JG 27	Bf 109E-7 WNr 4161 95% destroyed by bombs, Ain el Gazala

Wednesday, 3 September 1941

At 1000 (Axis time) 23 G.50bis of 20° Gruppo CT took off, led by T.Col Mario Bonzano, to make a strafing attack in the Sidi Barrani area. They arrived over LG.05 at 1135 (GMT), strafing 1 SAAF Squadron's Hurricanes and damaging three of these, also riddling every tent with machine-gun fire. The Italian pilots believed that they had destroyed eight aircraft and many vehicles on the ground here. As quickly as possible six Hurricanes were got off but were too late to engage the raiders.

Ten miles away at LG.02, 2 SAAF Squadron had four aircraft up on standing patrol and seven on immediate readiness. A telephoned warning sent the latter Tomahawks into the air within 90 seconds, the last of these hardly being airborne before the raiders swept in, some of them as low as 150 ft. The South African pilots identified the attackers as 27 in number, and at once attacked. Lt Whaites made the first claim for one G.50 which he saw spin into the ground two miles from the camp. The second claim was made by Lt Cullum, who witnessed his target go into the ground at high speed, while a third was "shot to pieces" by fire from five Tomahawks before being given the 'coup de grace' by Lts Stanford and Wells, who reported that it had crashed five miles west of Sidi Barrani. All these were seen by ground personnel on the airfields. Further claims were made by Lts Sayers and Gernecke who each claimed one shot down onto an escarpment to the west, while Lt Farrell's claimed victim reportedly fell into the sea. The only casualty to the squadron was Lt Stones' aircraft which was hit by Bofors AA fire from the airfields, and was forced to crash-land.

The Italian pilots reported being engaged by Tomahawks and Hurricanes following completion of their strafing attack and became involved in a 25-minute combat during which claims were made for 14 of the intercepting fighters shot down, plus three more probables and a number damaged for the loss of four G.50s. It appears that six more G.50s suffered fairly severe damage during this engagement. In consequence

T.Col Mario Bonzano, CO of 20° Gruppo Autonomo, in front of his G.20bis.

of this action, T.Col Bonzano received the immediate award of the Medaglia d'Argento.

During the day a pair of Tac R Hurricanes from 451 Squadron were intercepted near Sollum by three aircraft identified as Bf 110s which shot down that flown by Sgt Readett, who was killed. The identity of these attackers has not been ascertained.

On this date a second Beaufighter squadron began forming at Fayid when personnel of 252 Squadron who had been attached to 272 Squadron for some weeks, left the latter unit. (For the background stories to these two units, see Chapter 15 – In Support of the Royal Navy.)

British Claims

2 SAAF Sqn	Lt C.A.Whaites	Tomahawk	G.50	2m S Sidi Barrani North 1000-1240
	Lt N.J.Cullum	Tomahawk	G.50	nr Sidi Barrani 1000-1240
	Lt A.D.Farrell	Tomahawk	G.50	in sea E Sidi Barrani 1000-1240
	Lt R.A.Gernecke	Tomahawk	G.50	W Sidi Barrani 1000-1240
	Lt J.W.Sayers	Tomahawk	G.50	W Sidi Barrani 1000-1240
	Lt W.P.Stanford	Tomahawk AK442	} G.50	5m W Sidi Barrani 1000-1240
	Lt J.R.R.Wells	Tomahawk		

British Casualties

1 SAAF Sqn	3 Hurricane Is damaged on ground
2 SAAF Sqn	Tomahawk AM 376 hit by 'friendly' AA and crash-landed; Lt L.A.Stone safe
451 Sqn	Hurricane I V7774 shot down; Sgt L.M.Readett, RAAF, KiA

German Claims

Unidentified unit	Hurricane

Italian Claims

20° Gr CT	T Col Mario Bonzano	Tomahawk
	T Col Mario Bonzano	Hurricane
	T Col Mario Bonzano	Hurricane probable
353ª Sq/20° Gr CT	Cap Riccardo Roveda	Hurricane
	Serg Magg Tullio Covre	Hurricane
	Serg Magg Ersio Caponigro	Hurricane
	Serg Magg Ersio Caponigro	Hurricane probable
	Serg Spiridione Guiducci	Hurricane
352ª Sq/20° Gr CT	Serg Magg Francesco Pecchiari	Hurricane
	Serg Magg Otello Bonelli	Hurricane
	Serg Giuseppe Mirrione	Hurricane
151ª Sq/20° Gr CT	Cap Giampiero Del Prete	Hurricane
	Cap Giampiero Del Prete	Hurricane shared
	M.llo Federico Tassinari	Tomahawk
	Serg Magg Alberto Porcarelli	Tomahawk
	Serg Magg Guglielmo Gorgone	Tomahawk
352ª Sq/20° Gr CT	Serg Magg Francesco Visentin	Hurricane probable
353ª Sq/20° Gr CT	Serg Alcide Leoni	Hurricane shared
151ª Sq/20° Gr CT	S.Ten Pietro Menaldi	Hurricane shared
352ª Sq/20° Gr CT	Cap Luigi Borgogno	Hurricane damaged
	S.Ten Giorgio Oberwerger	Hurricane damaged
	M.llo Maurizio Iannucci	Hurricane damaged
	Serg Magg Renato De Silvestri	Hurricane damaged

Italian Casualties

353ª Sq/20° Gr CT	G.50 MM5939 shot down; Serg Magg Bruno Baldacci KiA
352ª Sq/20° Gr CT	G.50 MM5933 shot down, crash-landed; S.Ten Vittorio Muratori KiA
	G.50 MM5947 shot down, crash-landed; Serg Giovanni Vescovi KiA
	G.50 shot down, crash-landed; Serg Magg Renato De Silvestri PoW

Thursday, 4 September 1941

An RAF attack on Barce airfield destroyed two MC.200s of 153° Gruppo CT.

Italian Casualties

153° Gr CT	MC.200s MM6532 and MM 5190 destroyed on ground at Barce

Friday, 5 September 1941

In the very early hours eight Albacores of 826 Squadron, FAA, dive-bombed Tmimi landing ground, claiming direct hits on six Ju 87s.

Dust storms by day had rendered the use of the Sidi Barrani airfields rather difficult during this period, although patrols were launched as often as possible. One break occurred during the late afternoon, allowing 2 SAAF Squadron to send off a flight of Tomahawks. Capt Pannell, a veteran of the East African campaign, was first off and disappeared before the rest of the formation could join up with him. Seeing nothing, these pilots returned, but Pannell did not. An AA unit reported seeing two unidentified aircraft crash into the sea, and a member of the squadron hopefully recorded: "We are certain that he shot down a Ju 88 but must have been wounded himself and both aircraft came down together." This would appear to have been a piece of wishful thinking, for it seems certain that Pannell had actually fallen foul of a 1./JG 27 Bf 109 flown by Fw Kaiser, who claimed a P-40 shot down north-west of Sidi Barrani.

Battle of Britain Hurricane pilot Teddy Morris arrived in North Africa with 238 Squadron in May 1941, but in September took over command of 250 Squadron from John Scoular.

British Casualties			
2 SAAF Sqn	Tomahawk AN223 shot down; Capt D.D.Pannell KiA		
272 Sqn	Beaufighter T3310 lost to enemy action		
German Claims			
1./JG 27	Fw Emil Kaiser	P-40	NW Sidi Barrani 1750

Saturday, 6 September 1941
British Casualties

229 Sqn   Hurricane I crashed and overturned on landing; Plt Off D.F.K.Edghill very seriously injured

Sunday, 7 September 1941

Two further strafing attacks hit the Sidi Barrani landing grounds during the day. The first such raid was made by 15 G.50bis of 155° Gruppo, joined by 22 MC.200s of 153° Gruppo which all took off from Gars El Ahrad at 0600. The British were caught unawares on this occasion. 2 SAAF Squadron had been given a day's rest and had just dispersed their Tomahawks when at 0745 the Italian fighters arrived and commenced a 20-minute strafing attack. Two Tomahawks went up in flames and five aircraft on adjacent strips were also seen to burn. 1 SAAF Squadron reported that attacking Fiats and Macchis destroyed one of the unit's Hurricanes and damaged four more while the

A close-up of G.50bis '351-4' of 155° Gruppo CT.

RNFS lost one Hurricane burnt plus two more damaged. The returning 153° Gruppo pilots claimed to have strafed a bomber (identified as a Baltimore), five Hurricanes (two of which were left burning), three Gladiators and a large biplane. 155° Gruppo claimed two Hurricanes on fire and four more – plus a bomber – strafed.

On return 378ª Squadriglia recorded that two G.50bis had been hit by fire from Hurricanes, but Ten Ugo Palli and Serg Roberto Gaucci got back safely. Pilots reported that steel cables attached to small parachutes had been launched into the air as they attacked, the G.50bis flown by Serg Giovanni Del Fabbro of this unit suffering damage to the right wing and tail from these.

There can be little doubt that what Del Fabbro had encountered was the low-level defensive weapon known as the parachute-and-cable device (PAC). This had been developed rapidly during the early summer of 1940 in an effort to bolster the inadequate AA defences of many targets in southern England. Typically, a battery consisting of some 25 launching tubes would be inserted in the ground in three rows each of eight or nine, ostensibly across the route which a low-level attacker might be anticipated to follow. In each tube was a rocket attached to a light steel cable of some 480 feet in length. At each end of this cable a small parachute was attached.

Upon the approach of low-flying raiders, an intrepid airman – usually of the lowest rank – would press an electronic actuator which caused the rockets to ascend to a height of some 600 feet. On arrival of this initial upwards flight, the top parachute would open, allowing the cable to drop slowly to the ground, in the path (it was hoped) of the oncoming aircraft. Should a wing or other part of such an aircraft strike the cable, the force of the collision would activate the lower cable so that the two parachutes pulled it backwards to the line of flight, one above the victim and one below. It was the intention that the drag of the two parachutes and the weight of the cable might thereby pull the aircraft out of the air and cause it to crash.

These devices were quite easily and swiftly produced, and were supplied in the main for the defence of aircraft factories. They were, however, also installed in three-battery strength at RAF Kenley, where they were fired on 18 August 1940 when that airfield suffered a low-level attack by Dornier Do 17s. One of these bombers was thought to have struck such a cable, subsequently crashing. On subsequent investigation there remained some doubt as to whether the bomber had either actually been damaged by the PAC device, or whether this device had singly, or in conjunction with other elements of the defence, caused it to crash.

Clearly, the possibilities of success with such a haphazard device were slight, and the secretary of state for air, Sir Archibald Sinclair, had already expressed scepticism as to its effectiveness, recommending that production should be ceased within the next four to six weeks; Churchill, it seems, agreed. It happened, however, that the prime minister visited Kenley the day after Sinclair's views had been expressed. Having had the device demonstrated to him, and the fate of the Dornier explained, he changed his mind, allowing the PAC to continue in production, albeit on a much reduced scale.

In *With Prejudice*, Tedder states that as Sidi Barrani was so close to Axis territory and so vulnerable to attack, Mersa Matruh was stripped to allow strong defences to be built up in the former area. "We also installed radar, which was of limited value as far as low-flying aircraft were concerned, the PAC rocket (parachute cable) and machine guns." Despite much research, this has proved to be the only reference to the use of the device in North Africa, over a year after its appearance at home. Similarly, no evidence has been found as to how sets had arrived in the Middle East, or of them ever being employed again.

During the day three Hurricanes from each of 33 Squadron's flights undertook standing patrols over Sidi Barrani and Sidi Barrani East airfields. (Part of the unit remained at Giarabub at this time.) During the afternoon the squadron maintained six Hurricanes at readiness, joined by two more of the RNFS. At 1730 the pilots of these aircraft were ordered to scramble, but by the time they had reached their aircraft and strapped in, six more G.50s had appeared overhead and strafed them. Two Hurricanes were badly damaged and a third, which caught fire, then blew up and was destroyed. The pilots all survived, but Sgt MacDonnell was wounded in six places. It appears that all but one of the aircraft were damaged to some extent, for headquarters listed casualties during this late afternoon raid as one destroyed and six damaged. The day's depredations had cost 21 fighters burnt out or badly shot-up.

Following this disastrous series of attacks, 258 Wing at once ordered the Sidi Barrani airfields to be abandoned. That same evening 1 SAAF Squadron withdrew to Maaten Bagush, and 2 SAAF Squadron to Sidi Haneish, where 33 Squadron and the RNFS consolidated. The Sidi Barrani landing grounds were, for the time being, to be employed only as forward refuelling bases. At Sidi Haneish the withdrawn units were joined by 112 Squadron which began moving in to LG.92; two days later 3 RAAF Squadron flew in to LG.102 from metropolitan Egypt to become the fourth Tomahawk unit in the Western Desert.

British Casualties	
2 SAAF Sqn	2 Tomahawks AK497 &AN227 destroyed on ground
1 SAAF Sqn	Hurricane I destroyed on ground
	4 Hurricane Is damaged on ground
33 Sqn	Hurricane I destroyed on ground
	2 Hurricane Is damaged on ground
33 Sqn/RNFS	3 Hurricanes damaged on ground
Italian Casualties	
378ª Sq/155° Gr CT	3 G.50s damaged; all pilots safe
Unspecified units	CR.42 destroyed on the ground at Berka by bombs
	2 Ro.37bis badly damaged on the ground at Berka by bombs
	Ca.133 badly damaged on the ground at Berka by bombs

It was at around this time that Winston Churchill issued a directive clarifying the economical use of air power in the future. Tedder expressed considerable satisfaction with this, since its effect was to corroborate the line he himself had frequently taken with Wavell and Admiral Cunningham. In so doing, it removed from his shoulders a great deal of the unhelpful demands, requests, suggestions and (to some extent) complaints of many of the senior officers in the other services.

Directed Churchill:

"Never more must the ground troops expect, as a matter of course, to be protected against the air by aircraft. If this can be done, it must only be as a happy make-weight and a piece of good luck. Above all, the idea of keeping standing patrols of aircraft over moving columns should be abandoned. It is unsound to 'distribute' aircraft in this way, and no air superiority will stand any large application of such a mischievous practice. Upon the military Commander-in-Chief in the Middle East announcing that a battle is in prospect, the Air Officer Commanding-in-Chief will give him all possible aid irrespective of other targets, however attractive. Victory in the battle makes amends for all, and creates new favourable situations of a decisive character. The Army Commander-in-Chief will specify to the Air Officer Commanding-in-Chief the targets and tasks which he requires to be performed both in the preparatory attack on the rearward installations of the enemy and for air action during the progress of the battle......As the interests of the two C-in-Cs are identical it is not thought any difficulty should arise. The AOC-in-C would naturally lay aside all routine programmes and concentrate on bombing the rearward services of the enemy in the preparatory period. This he would do not only by night, but by day attacks with fighter protection. In this process he will bring about a trial of strength with the enemy fighters and has the best chance of obtaining local command of the air."

Monday, 8 September 1941

At 1305 a 12 SAAF Squadron Maryland took off to undertake a high altitude reconnaissance over Sollum Bay, searching for a submarine believed to be in the area. An attack was then made on a secondary target at Bardia during which the aircraft was hit and badly damaged by Flak. Lt Aitchison managed to get back to the unit's home airfield, LG.105 at Daba where he ordered the crew to bale out. The pilotless aircraft then executed two perfect turns before diving into the ground near LG.24.

British Casualties	
12 SAAF Sqn	Maryland II 1644 shot down by Flak; Lt R.H.Aitchison and crew baled out; one injured

Tuesday, 9 September 1941

48 shipping protection sorties were undertaken; during one of the evening patrols by seven Hurricanes of 33 Squadron, a dozen Bf 109s of Stab, 1. and 3./JG 27 attacked, claiming five of the British fighters shot down within the space of six minutes. Three Hurricanes were actually lost, two pilots being killed while the commanding officer, Sqn Ldr J.W.Marsden (who had recently taken over the unit after serving as a flight commander in 94 Squadron) managed to bale out without suffering any injury; he was picked up and taken into Tobruk. Flg Off Crockett had been delayed in taking off due to difficulty in starting the engine of his Hurricane. As a result he had got off late and had not been seen to join the other six aircraft before the attack by the Messerschmitts commenced. When he failed to return it was assumed that he had been shot down just before reaching the patrol area. Lt Dove had been pursued by three Bf 109s for nearly 20 minutes, but managed ultimately to escape them.

British Casualties			
33 Sqn	Hurricane I Z4505 shot down; Sqn Ldr J.W.Marsden baled and safe		
	Hurricane I Z4547 shot down; 2/Lt F.B.M.Bodmer KiA		
	Hurricane I shot down; Flg Off A.G.Crockett KiA		
German Claims			
3./JG 27	Lt Hans-Joachim Marseille	Hurricane	SE Bardia 1712
	Lt Friedrich Hoffmann	Hurricane	30m E Sidi Barrani 1712
Stab I./JG 27	Oblt Ludwig Franzisket	Hurricane	18m E Sidi Barrani 1715
1./JG 27	Fw Peter Werfft	Hurricane	Sollum Bay 1717
3./JG 27	Lt Hans-Joachim Marseille	Hurricane	SE Bardia 1718

Thursday, 11 September 1941

A night attack by British bombers on the Martuba airfields destroyed a G.50bis and damaged five S.79s.

Italian Casualties	
20° Gr CT	G.50 MM6531 destroyed on ground at night at Martuba
52ª Sq BT	2 S.79s MM22112 and MM21469 damaged on ground at night
8° St BT	3 S.79s MM21473, MM21474 and MM22280 damaged on ground at nigh

Uffz Reiner Pöttgen of 3./JG 27 was usually the rottenflieger (wingman) of Jochen Marseille. Here he is climbing into the cockpit of his Bf 109E.

Friday, 12 September 1941

In the early hours, a Blenheim fighter of 113 Squadron was sent up to patrol the Bagush-Fuka area where an S.79 of 28° Gruppo BT was engaged and shot down in flames. The Blenheim was slightly damaged by return of fire and the observer was wounded.

All available pilots of 238 Squadron were now despatched to Takoradi to collect and fly back Hurricane IIs via the cross-Africa route. Next day 229 Squadron would begin receiving aircraft of this mark also, while 3 RAAF Squadron noted that practice had begun on flying a new 'fluid pairs' formation which it was anticipated would be able to cope with the diving attacks of the Messerschmitts.

British Claims

113 Sqn	Flg Off Lydall	Blenheim IVf R3919	S.79	in flames near Fuka Satellite during night of 11/12th; aircraft slightly damaged and observer wounded 0235-0535

Italian Casualties

10ª Sq/28° Gr/8° St BT   S.79 MM 22093 MiA S Mersa Matruh at 0310; Ten Cesare Piccaretta and crew KiA

Saturday, 13 September 1941

Lt Marseille intercepted a lone 451 Squadron TacR Hurricane during the evening, shooting this down. Flt Lt Byers was wounded and was taken prisoner, but was to die of his wounds a week later.

Four days earlier 14 Hurricanes had flown off the aircraft carrier *Ark Royal* to Malta, but after refuelling all these fighters had carried on to North Africa. Now the Ark returned, joined on this occasion by HMS *Furious*, the two vessels launching a further 46 Hurricanes. One crashed on take-off, but the others all reached Malta. Here 22 were retained for the defending squadrons, but the other 23 flew on to Cyrenaica, bringing the number of reinforcements in these two operations – codenamed Status I and Status II – to 37. Amongst the pilots were several who would soon begin to make their mark in the desert, including an American citizen, Plt Off Lance Wade, and two Canadians, Wally Conrad and George Keefer. Amongst the bomber squadrons, command of 55 Squadron now passed to Sqn Ldr C.J.K.Hutchins, who was promoted Wg Cdr.

British Casualties				
451 Sqn	Hurricane I V7775 shot down; Flt Lt P.J.A.Byers PoW,WiA, died 20th			
German Claims				
3./JG 27	Lt Hans-Joachim Marseille		Hurricane	S Bardia 1725
Italian Casualties				
10ª Sq/28°Gr/8°St BT	S.79 MM 21482 crashed near base at Martuba in early hours. Cap Aurelio Baisi and crew baled out; Baisi KiA – probably hit tail of aircraft when baling			

Sunday, 14 September 1941 –Rommel's Mid Summer Dream

On 14th Rommel launched an end-of-training exercise with live ammunition for 21st Panzer Division code-named Operation Midsummer Night's Dream. This took the form of a reconnaissance-in-force seeking to find and destroy British supply dumps which German intelligence had indicated were being built up preparatory to a repeat of the Battleaxe offensive. At this stage such dumps did not exist (although they soon would). Rommel was clearly thirsting for action following a lengthy period of supervising training and dispositions, and he accompanied the operation personally.

The day therefore proved to be one of heavy combat, as the powerful force of Axis troops, including about 100 tanks and armoured cars, crossed the Egyptian frontier. Two columns then headed in the direction of Sidi Barrani, covered by Luftwaffe and Regia Aeronautica fighters, operating from forward landing grounds.

During the mid afternoon a pair of reconnaissance Hurricanes from 451 Squadron were intercepted by 1./JG 27 and both were shot down, the pilots both crash-landed and both survived, although Sgt Rowlands did suffer wounds.

At much the same time an S.79 of 19ª Squadriglia was undertaking a reconnaissance over the Derna Mersa Matruh-Sidi Barrani area when it was intercepted by Plt Off Bowker of 112 Squadron, who shot it down in the Sidi Rezegh area; Cap Sergio Fonsili and his crew were lost.

Given the inadequacies of the training of SAAF Maryland crews which had been highlighted following the Battleaxe losses, a number of the personnel from the units operating these aircraft had been given some special additional training in what was referred to as the army bombing scheme, designed to provide closer support and co-operation for the forces on the ground.

Now, faced with this new Axis threat, 12 SAAF and 24 SAAF Squadrons were ordered into the attack during the midday period, Lt Col J.T.Durrant leading 23 Marylands to attack a column between El Qara and El Hama, which appeared to be making for the Quattara Depression. Meanwhile, a force of 11 Italian Ju 87s from 209ª Squadriglia BaT had been ordered to bomb Fort Maddalena.

Unopposed, the Marylands released 26 250lb bombs from 7,000 feet onto dispersed vehicles, crews claiming that direct hits had been obtained and two fires started. The panzers had already run up against the 25-pounder guns of 7th Armoured Division's Support Group, but now came close to losing their commander himself. During the course of this first raid Rommel was out of his armoured command vehicle when a bomb splinter ripped the heel off his left boot, another seriously wounding his driver.

Following this promising start, a second attack was launched towards the end of the afternoon, an escort of Hurricanes from 33 Squadron being provided. This raid went in south-west of Sofafi from only 1,800 feet, the numbers of vehicles present being noted to have increased. This time, however, defending fighters struck hard, three of the escorting Hurricanes being shot down by pilots of 3./JG 27 with the unit's commander, Oblt Homuth, attacking Lt Hamm's Maryland. His fire struck the bomb bay and the port engine, both of which began to burn. Hamm at once gave the order to bale out, but received no response. He flew on for three minutes in order to give the gunners time to bale out as the flames reached the cockpit. Suddenly the aircraft blew up and he found himself blown clear at 1,000 feet, managing to get his parachute open and landing within 200 feet of a part of his wrecked bomber. He was picked up by a British armoured car, but was the sole survivor of the crew. Meanwhile, the surviving 33 Squadron pilots had been fighting back, returning to claim a Bf 109 and a G.50bis shot down – although no Axis fighter losses were actually suffered.

In the meantime disaster had struck the Italian dive-bombers. 13 Ju 87Rs of 209ª Squadriglia Autonoma had lost their escorts over Sidi Barrani, and 11 of these ran out of fuel – presumably while awaiting the arrival of the fighters. The result was that all 11 force-landed near Fort Maddalena subsequently to be captured by the British together with nine of the crews who all became PoWs. One of these aircraft, MM5763, was later recovered by 39 Squadron, eventually being allocated the British serial

One of the 11 Ju 87Bs of 209ª Squadriglia BaT which failed to return on 14 September 1941, is inspected by British personnel.

HK827. Two crews made early returns to their base (Cap Marco Romanese, the commanding officer, and S.Ten Antonio Ragonese); two more pilots, Cap Cesare Zanazzo and Ten Ezio Quarantelli, with one gunner, Av.Sc Flavio Penzo, evaded capture and walked for three days until picked up by the crews of some German tanks.

As a consequence of these losses, 209ª Squadriglia would be out of action for eight weeks, not flying another operational sortie until 24 November. Cap Romanese at once commenced a search for his missing comrades, eventually being wounded when a Bf 110 in which he was being flown by a Luftwaffe pilot was apparently attacked by a British fighter identified as a Hurricane. Perhaps not surprisingly, he was held responsible for the loss of virtually his whole unit and was at once replaced in command by Ten Quarantelli, and later by Cap Giacomo Ragazzini.

Finally, towards evening five Tomahawks of 3 RAAF Squadron were despatched to undertake a low-lying attack on Gambut where 50-60 aircraft, including many Ju 87s, had been spotted. "Many destroyed" claimed 204 Group, but the only claim which the Australian pilots submitted on their return appears to have been for a single Ju 88 damaged there. John Jackson, on his first sortie over the desert since April, recorded:

"Sixty-odd Ju 52s were reported to be on Gambut drome and we six were to strafe them, and 2 SAAF were to act as top cover at about 10,000 ft, to fire off their guns and generally distract the enemy ground forces, whilst we sneaked in low from the west up-sun and surprised and strafed them.

"No. 2 SAAF, Capt Loftus in charge, took off and we six then took off, followed underneath them, and flew out to sea over Sollum Bay past Bardia Point (none of our six had life jackets). At a point out to sea due north of Gambut, 2 SAAF headed inland and flew north-east of Gambut at 10,000 ft and headed south-west, crossing the Bardia-Tobruk road and then, flying with the sun dead behind us, formed a right echelon and headed for Gambut. No. 2 SAAF stirred up a hornets' nest and fighters started to take off and, just as we arrived at Gambut, we struck three of them in the air. I turned to attack one 109 and got a couple of bursts at it and as I did so one of our chaps sheered across me, missing collision by inches only. I then turned and strafed the western side of the drome and along the north side – sprayed a lot of aircraft, think I must have damaged at least four pretty well. There were lots of aircraft, and close together – couldn't help doing a fair bit of damage. As I swept down the north side I could see fighters taking off under me and a Ju 88 flashed under me smoking, and looked to have been damaged. We took them completely by surprise and the ack-ack was negligible and all to the north-west.

Another of the 11 Ju 87s of 209ª Squadriglia BaT lost in the desert on 14 September 1941.

"The three fighters in the air as we approached upset our attack and our chaps got out of formation, but Bruce Evans managed to stick to me and just as we left the drome I saw Plt Off Roberts out to my left. He had attacked the Ju 88, hitting it, and had done some strafing. Our strict orders were to make one dive straight through and away. We could see no sign of our other three chaps, Bothwell, Burbury and Lees.

"The South Africans were supposed to cover us on the way back but lost sight of us after we strafed and flew south at a low height, zigzagging to and fro dodging Hun ground forces. Now and again we got ack-ack fire, very close and accurate. After passing out of Libya into Egypt, we could see a lot of Hun stuff heading east – it was obvious they were making a push. Anyway, it was dark when we three, myself, Evans and Roberts, arrived at Barrani and landed safely. The other three didn't turn up. All the 11 SAAF chaps got back OK just before dark. They struck no enemy fighters though one of them reported two Me 110s climbing up to them over Gambut but did not see them again.

"It appears Roy Bothwell attacked a 109 over Gambut, was unable to do any strafing, and got separated from everybody else, so he headed south low across the desert and landed back at Sidi Barrani North drome, a few miles from Barrani East, about the same time as we got back. When he landed he was told they were evacuating Barrani as the Huns were pushing up and he would have to burn his aircraft or fly it out, so he rang up Barrani East, got a flare path out, and flew his aircraft across – a good effort."

Both 1./JG 27 and 153° Gruppo CT reported intercepting the Tomahawks, each unit claiming two sho down, although only two were actually lost. 18 MC.200s from the Italian unit had been patrolling ove Bir Habata when the Tomahawks were spotted, but during the engagement Cap Egeo Pittoni was hit an badly wounded, causing him to force-land near Gambut. From there he was rushed to a German fiel hospital before being flown to the main hospital in Derna in a Ca.133 next day.

By now Rommel had already ordered a withdrawal to Axis-held territory, the raid having gaine nothing save the capture of two soldiers in a truck who had with them documents which appeared t contain codes. The main result of the operation, however, was to persuade Rommel that the British were far from ready to launch any new offensive and that he therefore had adequate time to complete the planning and preparation for the attack on Tobruk.

With nightfall, meanwhile, four Fleet Air Arm Albacores were out over Gambut, claiming eight aircraft destroyed on fire or blowing up and at least four more damaged. Three 205 Group Wellingtons, diverted from their usual long-range duties, also attacked this target, claiming a further two aircraft destroyed or damaged. It seems that the Regia Aeronautica's units had been the main recipients of these attacks, two MC.200s being reported destroyed on the ground at Gambut in the following day's records. RAF assessors believed that at least 36 Axis aircraft had been destroyed during the preceding two days – a considerable over-estimate.

Next day the Axis force withdrew, having lost ten tanks and 15 other vehicles. The attacks, particularly those of the South African Marylands, had undoubtedly done much to achieve this, but once again in providing the support needed by the army, the Commonwealth units had paid a high price. It would be some time before such tactical use of the light bombers would be repeated.

Wg Cdr H.A.'Jimmy' Fenton, a Battle of Britain pilot with 238 Squadron, in North Africa in May 1941. In September he became wing leader of 243 Wing.

A trio of MC.200s of 374ª Squadriglia, 153° Gruppo Autonomo CT, flying over the desert. This was the first Macchi-equipped unit to reach Libya.

British Claims

112 Sqn	Plt Off N.Bowker	Tomahawk AN218	S.79	Sidi Rezegh 1625-1910
33 Sqn	Flg Off G.D.N. Noel-Johnson	Hurricane I Z4189	Bf 109 probable	50m SW Buq Buq 1730-1910
	Plt Off D.S.F. Winsland	Hurricane I Z4024	Bf 109	50m SW Buq Buq 1730-1920
	Sgt Stroud	Hurricane I Z4040	G.50	50m SW Buq Buq 1730-1920
3 RAAF Sqn	Flg Off H.G.H.Roberts	Tomahawk AK439	Ju 88 damaged	Gambut airfield 1900
24 SAAF Sqn	Maj J.F.Britz and crew of Maryland		2 Bf 109s	one with front guns, one by turret gunner

British Casualties

33 Sqn	Hurricane I Z4503 shot down; Flg Off L.R.Marshall badly burned and died three days later
	Hurricane I W9298 shot down; Sgt Nourse survived and returned later
	Hurricane I V7106 shot down; Sgt C.L.Rogers, RAAF, KiA
24 SAAF Sqn	Maryland II 1654 shot down by Bf 109; Lt M.Hamm baled out; rest of crew KiA
3 RAAF Sqn	Tomahawk AK456 shot down; Flg Off Burbery, RAAF
	Tomahawk AK464 Plt Off Lees, RAAF, crash-landed; returned on 18th
451 Sqn	Hurricane I shot down, crash-landed; Flg Off W.D. Hutley, RAAF
	Hurricane I V7485 crash-landed; Sgt H.R.Rowlands, RAAF, WiA

German Claims

1./JG 27	Lt Werner Schroer	Hurricane	S El Hambra 1555
	Fw Thomas Osswald	Hurricane	SE Habat
3./JG 27	Oblt Gerhard Homuth	Martin 167	S El Sofafi 1745
	Lt Hans-Joachim Marseille	Hurricane	SE El Sofafi 1746
	Lt Friedrich Hoffmann	Hurricane	5m SE Habat 1747
	Oblt Gerhard Homuth	Hurricane	SE El Sofafi 1748
1./JG 27	Oblt Wolfgang Redlich	P-40	SSE Sidi Aziez 1815
	Fw Günther Steinhausen	P-40	SE Gasr el Ahrid 1815

German Casualties

Stab/StG 3	Bf 110 in combat over Gambut at 1615; force-landed Cap Romanese; pilot, Oblt Gerd Kleedehn WiA

Italian Claims

372ª Sq/153° Gr CT	Ten Luciano Gamba	Tomahawk	Bir Habat p.m.
	Serg Magg Secondo Tassinari	Tomahawk	Bir Habat p.m.

Italian Casualties

374ª Sq/153° Gr CT	MC.200 MM5111 damaged and force-lands; Cap Egeo Pittoni badly wounded
209ª Sq Aut	11 Ju 87Rs force-land out of fuel in hostile territory; MM5763, 5766, 5772, 5797, 5794, 5801, 5805, 5831, 5924 5944, 5947; nine crews PoW; Ten Laerte Crivellini, Ten Erio Domizioli, S.Ten Alessandro Palamidessi, M.llo Giulio Giunta, Ten Alfredo Brambilla, Serg Magg Riccardo Pivetti, Serg Luciano Cainero and Serg Renzo Bartolomasi and their gunners. Two pilots made early return: Cap Mario Romanese and S.Ten Antonio Ragonese; two days later Cap Zanazzo, Ten Quarantelli and Av Sc Flavio Penzo were rescued by German troops, 1° Av Giovanni Pozzi by a Ju 52
19ª Sq/28° Gr/8° St	S.79 MM21751 MiA on early afternoon reconnaissance; Cap Sergio Fonsili and crew MiA

At this time there was considerable re-organisation taking place on both sides of the line. At last, staffeln from I./JG 27 were being withdrawn one at a time to return to Germany to re-equip with the new Bf 109F. This aircraft was a considerably cleaned-up development of the E model, with a more powerful engine offering an enhanced maximum speed of 390 mph at altitude, and having an armament of one engine-mounted cannon of either 15mm or 20mm calibre, plus a pair of 7.9mm machine guns above the engine. Although this appeared to be a reduction in armament from the E's two wing-mounted MG FF 20mm cannon, the new guns featured a considerably higher muzzle velocity. Coupled with this, the presence of the main weapons on the centre line of the aircraft allowed for more accurate firing at all distances from the target. Generally, the aircraft was a great improvement over its predecessor, and increased further the advantage of the German fighter pilots. The aircraft was to be queen of the desert skies for the next nine months at least.

On the British side squadrons now began to be grouped into operational wings for the first time, while several more bomber squadrons also arrived. 11, 45 and 55 Squadrons with Blenheims, all returned to Fuka, and 21 SAAF Squadron with Marylands began operations from LG.21. 2 SAAF Squadron was ested at this time, receiving many reinforcements when the existing personnel were on leave. 39 Squadron exchanged some of its Marylands for Beauforts. The Imperial ground forces in the Western Desert were now given a new and illustrious title – 8th Army.

Monday, 15 September 1941

During the night of 14/15 September British bombers achieved success when attacking Gambut, the Germans attributing the raid to ten aircraft of the Fleet Air Arm, which dropped 33 bombs, four failing to explode. The others destroyed two Bf 110s of 8./ZG 26, damaged three more seriously together with I./JG 27 Bf 109, and caused slight damage to another two. Two Italian fighters were also destroyed.

During the day the versatile role being undertaken by the Bf 110 night fighters of I./NJG 3 was demonstrated when three of the unit's aircraft took off at 0600 to make strafing attacks on Giarabub and Siwa where the crews claimed to have damaged ten lorries.

German Casualties	
./ZG 26	2 Bf 110s destroyed, with three more badly and two more slightly damaged on ground at Gambut
/JG 27	1 Bf 109 badly damaged on ground at Gambut
Italian Casualties	
72ª Sq/153° Gr CT	2 MC.200s MM5084 and MM6717 destroyed on ground at Gambut

Tuesday, 16 September 1941

The small 6 Squadron detachment at Kufra was allocated two Hurricanes at this stage to improve its chances of surviving any interceptions during forthcoming operations.

At 0710 on this morning a Bf 110 of 1./NJG 3 undertook a convoy escort. At 1308 three Ju 88s of II./LG 1 set out to look for the missing Italian Stukas. One of these was sighted at 1430, the aircraft and one man being seen in grid square 5139.

Thursday, 18 September 1941

British Casualties	
4 Sqn	Hurricane I P2641 destroyed on ground in air raid

Friday, 19 September 1941

German Casualties	
Unspecified unit	2 Bf 110s destroyed on ground by bombing
	5 Bf 110s damaged on ground by bombing

Sunday, 21 September 1941

Far away at Kufra Oasis, 6 Squadron's detached C Flight suffered an attack at noon by a single He 111. One Lysander was destroyed on the ground and eight personnel casualties were suffered. Two Gladiators attempted to intercept, but were outrun, whilst the raider dropped 40 bombs which destroyed one Lysander.

British Casualties	
Sqn	Lysander destroyed on ground

Monday, 22 September 1941

A new SAAF bomber unit, 21 Squadron, arrived at El Daba during the day, led by Lt Col J.D.Pretorius, who had commanded 3 SAAF Squadron on Hurricanes in East Africa. The unit had arrived in Egypt without full equipment, but had taken over all possible from 24 SAAF Squadron as the latter withdrew to re-equip. This had allowed 21 to move forward swiftly to commence operations.

II./JG 27 arrived in Libya with new Bf 109F aircraft on 23 September 1941 to join I Gruppe. One of this unit's most successful pilots at this time was Hptmn Gustav Rödel, staffelkapitän of 4 Staffel. He had recently been awarded the Ritterkreuz and had brought his personal tally of victories to 21.

Tuesday, 23 September 1941

The Marylands of 21 SAAF Squadron made their first sorties over Axis territory. Crews in the nine bombers attacking Gambut reported seeing one aircraft on fire on the ground.

However, the most important event of the day was the arrival from Doberitz in Germany of a second complete gruppe of Bf 109s – II./JG 27. This unit of three staffeln had claimed 25 victories in the Battle of France, 60 in the Battle of Britain, 17 in Greece the previous April, and a further 39 in ten days in Russia. The insignia carried by the gruppe depicted the bear of Berlin, the unit being very proud to be the godchild of the capital city. The commanding officer was Hptmn Wolfgang Lippert, holder of the Knights' Cross, who had a personal score of 24 at this time, four of which had been gained during the Spanish Civil War. 4., 5. and 6.Staffeln were led respectively by Hptmn Gustav Rödel, Hptmn Ernst Düllberg and Oblt Rolf Strössner. Rödel was also a Knights' Cross holder with 21 victories to his credit and other successful pilots included Obfw Otto Schulz (nine), Hptmn Düllberg (seven), Fw Herbert Krenz and Obfw Karl-Heinz Bendert (six each) and Obfw Emmerich Fluder (five). Schulz in particular was to shine here, and he would be second only to Marseille in number of victories at the time of his death. The gruppe brought with it, as well as more Bf 109Fs, two lion cubs, Simba and Caesar, presents from the Berlin Zoo; these were soon returned as it proved impossible to provide sufficient food for them. The newly-arrived unit would undertake its first operational sorties three days later.

German Casualties

2.(H)/14	Hs 126 WNr 4228 5F+AK crashed; Lt Karl Keller/Fw Ernst Mäuser KiFA

Wednesday, 24 September 1941

Nine Marylands attacked dumps north of Gambut where they did not report any interception. However, at 1330 (Axis time) Lt Marseille of 3./JG 27 claimed to have shot down a 'Martin 167'.

During the day 31 fighter patrols were flown over coastal shipping by RAF fighters, and 45 more over the forward area. One such was undertaken by 3 RAAF Squadron from 1245, over the Sofafi-Sidi Sulman-Sidi Omar area, nothing of note being seen. On return, however, Flg Off Saunders and Sgt Hiller broke away to attack a Ju 88. Hiller lost sight of both the bomber and Saunders, but the latter caught the Junkers and claimed to have shot it down in flames – although it appears to have been credited as a probable, possibly due to lack of witnesses. Ultra intercepted a message that this aircraft had bellied in between Gazala and Tobruk after an attack by Curtiss fighters. Immediately after attacking the bomber, Saunders was himself targetted by a reported six Bf 109s of 3./JG 27, and was shot down by Oblt Homuth; the Australian survived with only slight wounds. Actually, only four German fighters had been involved, having taken off at 1303 (Central European Time).

One of the Messerchmitt pilots involved was Lt Marseille, who was mentioned in the daily report which Ultra intercepted on this date. Herein it was stated that the five claims he had recently made had brought his personal tally to 17 confirmed and six unconfirmed. This, however, is correct only if all the seven claims he had made during 1940, before joining JG 27, are included. Ultra also noted that one staffel of II./JG 27 had been due to arrive at Gazala on the 23rd, which indeed it had.

Lt Hendrik Liebenberg (right) of 1 SAAF Squadron on 24 September 1941 landed to pick up Lt Melville McRobert, who had been shot down, flying him back in the cockpit of his Hurricane – a practice soon to be discouraged as it endangered two pilots rather then just one.

Later in the afternoon Capt P.J.Robbertse led nine 1 SAAF Squadron Hurricanes over the front where they were bounced by more 3./JG 27 Messerschmitts. Four of the South African pilots at once formed a defensive circle, but the German fighters concentrated on the other five, shooting down three of these – and claiming six, four of them by Marseille. Lt McRobert baled out as his aircraft fell in flames; Capt van Vliet, attacked several times, also baled out as his Hurricane went into a spin. Capt Osler and Lt Liebenberg both thought they had inflicted some damage on their attackers, but as Lt Dold sought to cover van Vliet as he fell, his aircraft also was badly hit and he was wounded, crash-landing at 250 mph. He then sheltered under the wing of his burning aircraft as the Bf 109 swept in to strafe the downed aircraft.

Not realising that he had come down in British-held territory, he continued to hide from troops which appeared until after dark, when he made his way to safety. Liebenberg spotted trucks moving towards where McRobert could be seen, struggling to free himself of his parachute. As infantry spilled from these vehicles, Liebenberg flew over them to allow the roundels on the underside of his wings to be seen in an effort to ascertain whether they were friendly or not. The answer came, as they opened fire on him. At once, he turned to strafe them, later reporting: "I opened fire on them………the nearest was only 50 yards off when he dropped." Nevertheless, he then landed close to McRobert and helped the wounded pilot into his own aircraft. Twice McRobert fell from the wing, after which Liebenberg discarded his own parachute and took off with McRobert perched on his knees, operating the control stick and throttle, while Liebenberg dealt with the rudder during the 100 miles back to Bagush. Although being greatly congratulated for this selfless feat, Liebenberg received no decoration, for the authorities were now seeking to discourage such dangerous and potentially costly escapades.

During the day seven of 113 Squadron's fighter Blenheims were detached to Malta.

British Claims

3 RAAF Sqn	Flg Off J.H.W.Saunders	Tomahawk AK539	Ju 88 probable	Sofafi-Sidi Sulman-Sidi Omar 1445
1 SAAF Sqn	Capt M.S.Osler	Hurricane I	Bf 109 damaged	5m NW Halfaya Pass 1700
	Lt H.C.W.Liebenberg	Hurricane I	Bf 109 damaged	5m NW Halfaya Pass 1700

British Casualties

3 RAAF Sqn	Tomahawk AK539 shot down; Flt Lt J.H.W.Saunders, RAAF, slt WiA
1 SAAF Sqn	Hurricane I Z4241 shot down; Capt C.A.van Vliet rescued by forward troops, returned on 27th
	Hurricane I Z4241 shot down; Lt B.E.Dold WiA, picked up by troops, returned 28th
	Hurricane I Z4241 shot down; 2/Lt J.McRobert WiA, picked up by Hurricane and flown back

German Claims

3./JG 27	Lt Hans-Joachim Marseille	Martin 167	Gambut 1330
	Oblt Gerhard Homuth	P-40	Sidi Omar 1340
	Lt Hans-Joachim Marseille	2 Hurricanes	Buq Buq 1645-47
	Oblt Gerhard Homuth	Hurricane	Buq Buq 1647
	Lt Hans-Joachim Marseille	2 Hurricanes	Buq Buq 1651-1700
	Obfw Herbert Kowalski	Hurricane	Buq Buq 1710

Having been in North Africa for a little over three months, 7./JG 26 now departed for Sicily on the start of the long journey home to rejoin the parent gruppe in France. During that time the staffel had claimed some 13 victories, ten of which had been confirmed. Five of these were credited to Joachim Münchenberg, bringing his personal tally to 48, with two each being claimed by Lt Theo Lindemann and Fw Karl-Heinz Ehlen; Oblt Klaus Mietusch had made three claims, but two of these had not been confirmed.

Thursday, 25 September 1941

98 sorties were flown over Royal Navy warships during the day, but hostile fighters were only encountered once when ten Tomahawks of 112 Squadron were returning from a patrol as top cover to the RNFS when they were attacked out of the sun by two fighters identified as Bf 109s. Plt Off Gerry Westenra, part of the highest-flying section, took evasive action and called a warning which was not heard. About ten minutes later he was attacked again, the tip of his starboard wing and aileron being shot off. He managed to fly his damaged aircraft as far as the Sidi Barrani area, where he baled out when his aircraft began to smoke and the ammunition for his engine-mounted .5in guns began to explode. No Axis claim has been found.

112 Sqn	Tomahawk AK495 damaged by fighter attack; Plt Off D.F.Westenra subsequently baled out, safe

Italian Claims

393ª Sq/160º Gr CT	Serg Vittorio Ghini	Blenheim probable	Benghazi

Friday, 26 September 1941

This date saw the first sorties over North Africa by the new Bf 109Fs, aircraft of 4./JG 27 being involved. However, no contact with British aircraft occurred.

6 Squadron's detachment at Kufra suffered a further Axis incursion by an Italian reconnaissance aircraft identified as an S.81; it was in fact an S.79 of 174ª Squadriglia RST. Sgt Walter took off in one of the Gladiators and gave chase, but never managed to get closer than 400 yards. He pursued the Savoia for 90 miles, gradually forcing it down from 7,000 ft to 1,500 ft, although he remained unable to see the results of his fire. The crew of the Italian aircraft reported being attacked by two Gladiators, claiming to have shot one of them down. Whatever the results of this action, it was the last engagement in which an RAF-flown Gladiator would ever take part.

British Claims

6 Sqn	Sgt Walter	Gladiator N5851	S.81 possibly damaged	Kufra Oasis

Italian Claims

174ª Sq RST	Gunners	Gladiator	Kufra Oasis

Another unit active in the reconnaissance role was 174ª Squadriglia, also equipped with S.79s.

Saturday, 27 September 1941

A tactical reconnaissance Hurricane of 451 Squadron commenced a sortie to the Bardia area in the hands of Flg Off Graeme-Evans during the early morning, escorted by a 33 Squadron aircraft, flown by Plt Off Lowther. At around 1000 (Axis time) the pair were intercepted by six I./JG 27 Bf 109Es, both aircraft being shot down, one by the gruppenkommandeur, Hptmn Neumann, the other by the 3.Staffel commander, Oblt Homuth. Lowther was reported to have shot down one of the attackers, but was himself killed. There were no Luftwaffe losses.

As both sides prepared for their planned offensives during the autumn months of 1941, a group of I./JG 27's leading pilots relax. Left to right: Lts Karl Kügelbauer, Hans-Joachim Marseille, both of 3 Staffel, Lt Werner Schroer of 1 Staffel and Lt Hans-Arnold Stahlschmidt of the Gruppenstab.

Whilst on another early morning reconnaissance, the crew of a Maryland of 12 SAAF Squadron spotted one large (est. 6,000 tons) and three smaller ships in Bardia harbour, unloading supplies. An initial bombing attack was frustrated by cloud, a second raid being sent off at 1506 when Maj J.F.Britz led nine 21 SAAF aircraft to this target, escorted by Tomahawks of 250 and 3 RAAF Squadrons. Britz later recorded spotting several fighters climbing towards the formation and others taking off and patrolling over the harbour.

As he dived to attack, he saw tracers flying past his starboard wing and looking in that direction, he observed Lt Louw's aircraft on fire with members of the crew in the process of baling out. The aircraft, containing a crew on their first sortie, had been attacked by a pair of Bf 109s from 3./JG 27. Britz was heard to call: "Look out, I'm going to fire my front guns." Surrounded by Flak bursts, he opened fire on the two fighters which had just despatched Louw's aircraft, following which one Messerschmitt pulled up in an inverted position, and reportedly the pilot dropped out "in a ball of flames", his parachute failing to open. This all occurred as Louw's Maryland was falling towards the sea, blazing furiously. As Britz pressed on through the Flak, one of his gunners, Air Sgt M.H.Petterson, reportedly sent a second fighter down trailing smoke, while Air Sgt P.Earnshaw fired short bursts at long range at a third which had now appeared.

Two 'Martin 167s' were claimed by pilots of the German unit, but despite the details recorded, no Messerschmitts appear to have been lost or badly damaged. A few minutes later, however, Hpt Redlich, staffelkapitän of 1.Staffel, shot down one of the escorting Tomahawks, Plt Off P.C.Wells being killed. In return two claims for Bf 109s were submitted by Plt Off Caldwell and Sgt Humphries, but again, no German losses were recorded.

Of this operation, 3 RAAF Squadron's John Jackson wrote;

"We escorted eight Maryland bombers on their job of bombing Bardia. No.250 Squadron were escorts also. The bombers were at 18,000 ft, we at 20,000 ft, and 250 Squadron about the same height. All went well until we got over the target area and the bombers split up. We kept over a section of three bombers and they were OK. One of the other bombers was shot down either by ack-ack or by an Me 109 – we saw the splash it made. One of the 250 Squadron pilots was shot down in flames, Flg Off Wells. The bombing didn't seem very effective and I am very dubious about the value of bombing unless on a very big and concentrated target like an industrial area, or big concentration of MT or aircraft. We noticed several Me 110s low down over Bardia, but our job was purely protective, so did not go down after them.

"Results in the air war in the desert recently have not been very satisfactory. The Hun has been getting more of our fighters than we are getting of his. We need better aircraft as he can outspeed and outclimb us easily, and his armament is superior – we must at least have equal armament. So far our .3 ammunition in the Tommies has been ball, just useless against armour plating. I heard today that armour-piercing ammunition has now arrived – about time too. We will have to get aircraft equal to the 109; the Hun now is using a later model 109, the Me 109F.

"Hear I am to go on leave tomorrow – have had a lot of boils for about a fortnight and have been feeling very off colour, and Doc has decided I will clear up quicker and better if I go back to Alex where I can have a couple of hot baths every day; evidently my skin does not react too well to dirt, dust and sand. Ed reckons I'm soft !'"

It proved in fact John Jackson's last operational flight in North Africa. After his leave, he was posted home to Australia. There, sadly, he would be shot down and killed on 28 April 1942 while flying in defence of New Guinea; by that time he had received the award of a DFC for his service in Egypt, Libya and Syria.

Later in the afternoon two 12 SAAF Squadron Marylands took off, led by Lt Col S.L.Bosch, AFC, one to attack dumps and the other to the Bardia area. Both were reported to have been badly damaged, and in each aircraft one of the gunners was wounded. These may have been hit by Flak, as no other Axis fighter claims seem to have been made.

British Claims

33 Sqn	Plt Off Lowther	Hurricane I W9325	Bf 109	Tac R escort, Qasaba Barrani
250 Sqn	Sgt A.Humphries	Tomahawk AK221	Bf 109	off Bardia 1535-1745
	Plt Off C.R.Caldwell	AK324	Bf 109	15m S Buq Buq 1635
21 SAAF Sqn	Maj J.F.Britz	Maryland	Bf 109	15m S Buq Buq 1635
	Air Sgt M.H.Petterson (Maryland gunner)		Bf 109	Bardia area 1635

British Casualties

451 Sqn	Hurricane I shot down; Flg Off Graeme-Evans
33 Sqn	Hurricane I shot down; Plt Off C.C. Lowther KiA
250 Sqn	Tomahawk shot down; Plt Off P.C.Wells KiA
21 SAAF Sqn	Maryland II 1650 'G' ; Lt A.Louw, pilot, PoW; three crew KiA
12 SAAF Sqn	2 Maryland IIs damaged; 2 gunners wounded; cause uncertain

German Claims

Stab I./JG 27	Hptmn Eduard Neumann		Hurricane	W Bardia 1000
3./JG 27	Oblt Gerhard Homuth		Hurricane	4m SE Ras Azzaz 1010
	Lt Friedrich Hoffmann		Martin 167	5m SE Bardia 1638
	Obfhr Karl Kugelbauer		Martin 167	4m SE Bardia 1638
1./JG 27	Hptmn Wolfgang Redlich		P-40	SW Sidi Barrani 1650

Sunday, 28 September 1941

In the early hours 55 Squadron lost two of three Blenheims to Flak during a raid on the ships in Bardia harbour, claimed shot down at 0335, by Flak units coded Karnevall and Ituna. No damage having been inflicted on these ships so far, around midday a force of 18 Marylands drawn from both SAAF squadrons sought to attack again, led by Lt Col Bosch. This time the bombers were covered by a very large fighter escort, including aircraft from 33 and 112 Squadrons, six Tomahawks of 250 Squadron acting as top cover; these fighters were also joined by six Hurricanes and six Martlets from the RNFS. At 1320 the 33 Squadron pilots cut across in front of the Martlets, causing two of the latter to fall behind. The other four Martlet pilots then saw three G.50s turning in front of the two trailing aircraft, Sub Lt R.W.M.Walsh claiming one of these shot down. His opponents seem to have been aircraft of 155° Gruppo CT, the pilots of this unit reporting seeing 17 aircraft described as 'twin-engined American bombers' with 12-18 fighters as escort. However, this unit did not report any casualties. Meanwhile, Plt Off Caldwell of 250 Squadron claimed a Bf 109 probably destroyed; no German loss has been found either, although South African bomber crews reported seeing one enemy aircraft gliding down.

| 250 Sqn | Plt Off C.R.Caldwell | Tomahawk AK324 | Bf 109E | 15m NW Bardia 1300 |
| 805 Sqn | Sub Lt R.W.M.Walsh | Martlet | G.50 | 1320 |

British Casualties

| 55 Sqn | Blenheim IV Z7374 shot down in sea by Flak; Flt Lt J.H.Wilson and one KiA; one PoW |
| | Blenheim IV V5560 shot down near target by Flak; Sgt W.A.Ross and two KiA |

Tuesday, 30 September 1941

As another month came to an end the 113 Squadron fighter-Blenheims detached to Malta, returned less one of their number (see *Malta: the Hurricane Years, 1940-41*). On this date 1 SAAF Squadron at last began to receive some Hurricane IIs to replace their worn Mark Is, while command of 73 Squadron passed to Sqn Ldr D.H.Ward.

British Claims

| 250 Sqn | Plt Off C.R.Caldwell | Tomahawk AK324 | Bf 109 damaged | convoy patrol 1330-1610 |

Wednesday – Thursday,1/2 October 1941

Following night raids by Wellingtons, six Blenheims bombed landing grounds at Gambut on the 1st. Next day nine Marylands raided dumps alongside the Bardia-Tobruk road which had been bombed during the previous night by Royal Navy Albacores.

250 Squadron recorded a visit from WWI ace, Grp Capt G.W.Murlis-Green, DSO & Bar, MC & Bar, who was now commanding 71 OTU at Gordon's Tree, to discuss training requirements.

According to an Axis report, during the 2nd a Hurricane of an unidentified unit landed at El Hania airfield at 1200 due to an engine failure, the pilot being captured. It seems clear, however, that an error recording the date on which this occured was made in this case, and that the aircraft in question was an all-pale blue Mark 1(PR) Hurricane of 2 Photographic Reconnaissance Unit which is listed as having failed to return from a sortie over Benghazi, but apparently on the 3rd. The pilot, Flt Lt Brown, one of the unit's flight commanders, became a PoW.

British Casualties

| 2 PRU | Hurricane I W9116 force-landed at El Hania due to engine failure; Flt Lt A.M.Brown PoW |

Friday, 3 October 1941

It was on this date that the first encounter with the new Bf 109Fs of II./JG 27 occurred. During the morning six Hurricanes from 33 Squadron escorted a TacR aircraft of 451 Squadron over the front. Near Buq Buq they were attacked by seven of the new fighters, Sgt Lowry being shot down by Uffz Reuter, baling out when his Hurricane burst into flames.

Around noon 12 Tomahawks of 2 SAAF Squadron had landed at Sidi Barrani to refuel following a sweep over Sidi Omar. This was a slow process on this dangerously exposed landing ground, and the pilots were anxious to be off again as quickly as possible. Nine had got into the air as the formation leader, Capt G.C.Krummeck recalled:

"Three held up by the bowsers were still taxying out when three Bf 109Fs attacked. Lt A.George and Lt D.V.D.Lacey and I got off under attack. The Germans came in so fast that they overshot. Lacey, just airborne, his wheels still down, lifted his nose and fired a burst....The German crash-landed and was found dead with a bullet through him.... First 109F victim to fall in the desert to superb gunnery by a skilled pilot..."

Again, despite these details, no Luftwaffe aircraft was actually reported lost. (It is suspected that the wreckage found by personnel of B Squadron, Kings Dragoon Guards, some time later which appeared to confirm Lacey's success, had actually found that shot down several days later on the 7th, in which Lt Langanke had been killed [see below]).

33 Squadron was off again at 1400, five Hurricanes once more to protect a TacR aircraft, although this time also provided with a top cover of 112 Squadron Tomahawks. On the return flight 4./JG 27 pilots attacked, shooting down Sgt Stirrat's Tomahawk which appears to have been claimed by two pilots at

the same time. Flg Off Groves targetted one Messerschmitt, claiming damage (it will be noted that it had now become necessary to provide much stronger escorts for TacR aircraft due to the heavy losses the latter had been suffering to the Bf 109s).

British Claims				
2 SAAF Sqn	Lt D.V.D.Lacey	Tomahawk	Bf 109F	Sidi Barrani
112 Sqn	Flg Off J.L.Groves	Tomahawk AK457	Bf 109 damaged	1400-1630
British Casualties				
451 Sqn	Hurricane I Z4325 shot down; Sgt R S Lowry, RAAF, baled out			
112 Sqn	Tomahawk AK502 shot down; Sgt I.H.Stirrat, RAAF, KiA			
German Claims				
5./JG 27	Uffz Horst Reuter	Hurricane		E Buq Buq 1052
4./JG 27	Oblt Gustav Rödel	Hurricane		SW Sidi Barrani 1555
	Lt Arthur Schacht	Hurricane		SW Sidi Barrani 1555

Sunday, 5 October 1941

II./JG 27 was again successful two days later when three Bf 109Fs took off at 0910, intercepting four Hurricanes of 33 Squadron over Sidi Omar where they were again escorting a Lysander of 451 Squadron. Two Hurricanes were shot down by Oblt Düllberg and Uffz Reuter, both Commonwealth pilots becoming PoWs.

During the day a BR.20M bomber of 13° Stormo BT crashed in the desert near El Mechili whilst on its way to bomb Tobruk; the reason for its loss is not known, but one member of the crew managed to bale out and survived; he was picked up next day by a Ca.133.

British Casualties			
33 Sqn	Hurricane I Z4188 shot down; Plt Off D.R.Lush, RCAF, PoW		
	Hurricane I Z4768 shot down; Sgt F.Seamer, RAAF, PoW		
	Lysander P1676 crashed at Giarabub – cause unknown		
German Claims			
5./JG 27	Uffz Horst Reuter	Hurricane	S Sidi Omar 0939
	Oblt Ernst Düllberg	Hurricane	0940
Italian Casualties			
1ª Sq/11° Gr/13° St BT	BR.20 MM22710 crashes near El Mechili; S.Ten Stanislao Pretto and most of crew KiA;		
	one baled out and picked up next day		

Monday, 6 October 1941

During the early morning 14 fighters were despatched to escort a PR Hurricane over Tobruk, while a dozen 2 SAAF Squadron Tomahawks flew a diversionary patrol over the Sidi Omar area. Here the latter were surprised by 14 Bf 109Fs of II./JG 27, Oblt Rödel and Obfw Schulz shooting down two of the South African pilots, both of whom were killed. Lt Whaites claimed one shot down, although his own aircraft was damaged, with Lt Lacey claiming a probable – although no German losses were suffered. Moments later the two successful pilots claimed three Hurricanes shot down in the same area, but no losses of such aircraft have been found for this date, no mention of such a loss being included in the 204 Group or Air Headquarters, Western Desert, records. During the day six Blenheims bombed MT workshops at Bardia.

British Claims				
2 SAAF Sqn	Lt D.V.D.Lacey	Tomahawk	Bf 109F probable	Sidi Omar area
	Lt C.A.Whaites	Tomahawk AN319	Bf 109F	Sidi Omar area
British Casualties				
2 SAAF Sqn	Tomahawk AN251 shot down; Lt R.C.W.Miller KiA			
	Tomahawk AK513 shot down; Lt C.A.N.McGarr KiA			
	Tomahawk AN319 damaged; Lt C.A Whaites unhurt			
12 SAAF Sqn	Maryland damaged			

German Claims

4./JG 27	Oblt Gustav Rödel	P-40	SE Sidi Omar 0910
	Obfw Otto Schulz	P-40	SE Sidi Omar 0910
	Obfw Otto Schulz	2 Hurricanes	SE Sidi Omar 0915-0920
	Oblt Gustav Rödel	2 Hurricanes	SE Sidi Omar 0920

Tuesday, 7 October 1941

Ten Blenheims raided Bardia and nine Marylands of 12 SAAF Squadron took off at 0940 to attack ammunition dumps at Gazala. Ten minutes after the latter aircraft had departed the target, four Bf 109Fs of 5./JG 27 intercepted, concentrating their attack on Lt A.M.C. Smith's aircraft, inflicting considerable damage and wounding two members of the crew. However, Air Sgts Thom and Stead in Lt J.A.van Rooyen's Maryland, claimed to have sent down two of the Messerschmitts. Their fire had indeed shot down Lt Langanke's aircraft which crashed south of Sidi Omar, the pilot being killed. Meanwhile, Smith was subsequently able to land on return to LG.07, where his aircraft ground-looped. One of his wounded gunners, Air Mech L.Soloman later died of his wounds.

The day also saw 38 fighter sorties flown on escort duties, four more being undertaken as a diversion for a TacR Hurricane. Air HQ, Western Desert was joined by Grp Capt K.B.B.Cross, DFC.

The rising 'star' of the recently-arrived II./JG 27 was Obfw Otto Schulz, seen here in a Gruppenstab Bf 109F-4 trop. He claimed three victories over British fighters on 6 October 1941 to open his North African scoring, these representing his victories 10-12.

British Casualties	
12 SAAF Sqn	Maryland II 1638 damaged; Lt A.M.C.Smith and one safe; radio operator died of wounds; air gunner wounded

German Casualties	
5./JG 27	Bf 109F-4 trop WNr 8440 shot down S Sidi Omar in combat with Maryland; Lt Gustaf-Adolf Langanke MiA

Wednesday, 8 October 1941

A very heavy dust storm rendered operations impossible. At this time a number of Hurricane pilots from 274 and 1 SAAF Squadron were rested by being attached to 73 Squadron at Gamil for routine patrol duties.

Thursday, 9 October 1941

A BR.20M of 4ª Squadriglia, 11º Gruppo BT returned from a night raid and landed with one bomb hung-up in the bomb bay. Following an inspection, this was accidentally released and exploded, destroying the aircraft and killing one armourer.

At 1239 a Bf 110 of Stab St G 3 took off for a coastal reconnaissance as far as El Daba. At 1457 the crew claimed a reconnaissance aircraft shot down.

Later in the day Cap Gino Callieri, commander of 360ª Squadriglia, fired on a Blenheim over Benghazi, but without result. On this date 204 Group was re-titled Air HQ, Western Desert, and Grp Capt G.R.Beamish was ordered to form a new bomber wing. At LG.10 a fifth Tomahawk squadron came into the line with the arrival of 4 SAAF Squadron so equipped.

German Claims

Stab St G 3		Maryland?	Unknown crew 1457

Italian Claims

360ª Sq/155º Gr CT	Cap Gino Callieri	Blenheim damaged	Benghazi

Italian Casualties

4ª Sq/11° Gr/13° St BT	BR.20 MM22178 destroyed on ground by own bomb; one armourer killed
Unspecified Unit	CR.42 destroyed on ground by bombs at Benghazi by night
	CR.42 badly damaged on ground by bombs at Benghazi at night
	G.50bis badly damaged on ground by bombs at Benghazi at night
	S.79 badly damaged on ground by bombs at Benghazi at night
	S.81 badly damaged on ground by bombs at Benghazi at night

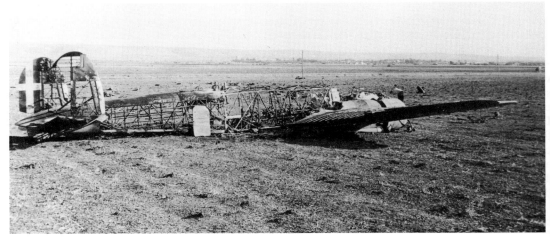

The remains of a BR.20 destroyed on the ground.

A G.50bis of 360ª Squadriglia flown by M.llo Francesco Fagiolo. From April this unit had been devoted to the defence of Benghazi.

Friday, 10 October 1941

Twelve Hurricanes of 33 Squadron on a shipping escort operation during the morning were attacked by Bf 109s of 2./JG 27, one being shot down by Obfw Förster and a second sustaining damage. Towards the latter part of the afternoon Förster gained a further success when he shot down a 451 Squadron TacR aircraft. During the day 2 SAAF Squadron lost two Tomahawks when these collided during a sweep. One pilot managed to bale out, but Lt Cullum was killed. During this quite active day the fighters had undertaken 83 sorties over a convoy bound for Tobruk, and 34 more covered a trio of TacR aircraft, each over a different area.

14 Squadron's long-serving commanding officer, Wg Cdr D.C. Stapleton, DFC, AFC, completed his tour and was replaced by the very experienced Wg Cdr J.K.Buchanan, DFC, who was promoted from flight commander.

Flt Lt Peter Turnbull bids farewell to 3 RAAF Squadron at Sidi Haneish during October 1941 as he prepares to return to Australia, having suffered a broken arm in a car accident. Left to right: Turnbull, Flt Lt Lindsay Knowles, Flt Lt 'Woof' Arthur and Sqn Ldr Peter Jeffery in front of Tomahawk AN335.

British Casualties			
33 Sqn	Hurricane shot down; Plt Off T.C.Patterson		
	Hurricane damaged		
451 Sqn	Hurricane shot down; Flt Lt L F Malone DFC KIA		
2 SAAF Sqn	Tomahawk AN284 lost in mid-air collision; Lt N.J.Cullum KiFA		
	Tomahawk AM456 lost in mid-air collision; 2/Lt D A Hinde baled out		
German Claims			
2./JG 27	Obfw Hermann Förster	Hurricane	0950
	Obfw Hermann Förster	Hurricane	1600

Saturday, 11 October 1941

In 250 Squadron Clive Caldwell was now appointed flight commander.

Sunday, 12 October 1941

By this date the RAF's fighter units had been grouped into three wings for future operations. 258 Wing comprised 112, 250, 2 SAAF and 3 RAAF Squadrons, all, it will be noted, equipped with Tomahawks, for offensive action over Cyrenaica, and to provide escort to bombers and reconnaissance aircraft. 269 Wing controlled those Hurricane squadrons tasked with the interception of hostile aircraft over the units of 8th Army, while 262 Wing retained responsibility for the defence of the delta area and Alexandria, and for providing reinforcement for the two forward wings when necessary.

The morning saw considerable action, commencing with a dawn sortie by Plt Off Russell of 229 Squadron during which he intercepted a Ju 88 near Mersa Matruh, claiming to have damaged it. This seems to have been a reconnaissance aircraft of 2.(F)/123 in which Lt Gessler and his crew were lost. Between 0730-0945, 12 Tomahawks of 2 SAAF Squadron and 12 of 3 RAAF Squadron took off to carry out a protective sweep over the army in the Sheferzen area. Bf 109Es of 3./JG 27 attacked and a general dogfight commenced. Lt Whaites, who was acting as weaver to the South African unit, was hit, his aircraft gliding down trailing white smoke, but he was found dead in the cockpit when help got to him. Lt D.S.Rogan's aircraft was also shot-up, one of three Tomahawks which returned in a damaged condition.

The Australians took the brunt of the attack, Flg Off Roberts crash-landing within friendly territory, while Sgt Scott crash-landed at LG.05. These losses all seem to have accrued to Oblt Franzisket and Lt Marseille of 3./JG 27, who claimed three 'P-40s' in the opening minutes of the action.

Subsequently, Sgt Parker was shot out of a defensive circle, apparently by 2./JG 27's Lt Sinner. The latter's burst of fire hit the cockpit of the Tomahawk on the port side, cannon shells setting the fuel tank behind this ablaze at which Parker baled out. Possibly he was already critically wounded, or else fell through a burst of fire, for when he reached the ground he was dead. It was thought at the time that he had been shot on his parachute, but it is most unlikely that in the heat of a dogfight any pilot would have been able to leave the fight and concentrate on such a difficult target as a man swinging beneath a parachute.

Immediately after seeing Parker bale, Sinner was targetted by two Tomahawks at which time he pulled his Messerschmitt nearly vertical and stalled. Pulling out of the ensuing dive when he reached a lower defensive circle of Hurricanes, he nosed down at top speed and made for Gambut where he was the first back.

Amongst the Tomahawk pilots engaged, Sgt Cameron claimed one Bf 109 shot down and Flg Off Jewell a second as a probable. Shortly behind the first Tomahawks to reach the area, ten more of these aircraft from 112 Squadron appeared, encountering a reported ten G.50s and 15 Bf 109s. Two more 2./JG 27 pilots, Hptmn Gerlitz and Lt Körner, at once shot down Plt Off Parker (the second pilot of this name to fall on this date) and Sgt Leu, while three more Tomahawks were damaged and one pilot wounded. A single claim for a Bf 109 was submitted by Plt Off Jeffries, and on this occasion one 1.Staffel aircraft did suffer 40% damage in combat, but probably inflicted by the 3 RAAF Squadron pilots. That evening Parker and Leu, both having been slightly wounded, were found by troops of the Coldstream Guards, and were back with the unit by the 14th.

Air HQ, Western Desert, reported that during these clashes up to 35 Bf 109Es and Fs, plus ten G.50s had been reported involved. Claims were listed as having included one Bf 109F, two Bf 109Es, a G.50 and an unidentified fighter, plus four more Messerschmitts damaged. This total considerably exceeds those claims actually listed by the units involved. It seems the number of Tomahawks suffering damage were also discounted, for the total of losses suffered was recorded as six, with one pilot killed and three missing, two of whom returned later, as recorded above. Apparently one of the Tomahawks was subsequently repaired and flown out two days later.

British Claims

229 Sqn	Plt Off W.C.Russell	Hurricane IIb Z4967	Ju 88 damaged	Mersa Matruh 0455-0615
112 Sqn	Plt Off R.J.Jeffries	Tomahawk AM410	Bf 109F	Bir Sheferzen-Sofafi 0620-0900
3 RAAF Sqn	Sgt A.C.Cameron	Tomahawk AK506	Bf 109F	Sheferzen area 0910
	Flg Off W.E.Jewell	Tomahawk AK476	Bf 109 probable	Sheferzen area 0915
	Flg Off P.R.Bothwell	Tomahawk	Bf 109 damaged	Sheferzen area 0925
2 SAAF Sqn	Lt D.V.D.Lacey	Tomahawk	Bf 109 probable	
	Lt D.S.Rogan	Tomahawk	Bf 109 damaged	

British Casualties

2 SAAF Sqn	Tomahawk AK551 shot down; Lt C.A.Whaites KiA
	Tomahawk badly damaged; Lt D.S.Rogan unhurt
	2 Tomahawks damaged, pilots unspecified
3 RAAF Sqn	Tomahawk crash-landed; Flg Off H G H Roberts safe
	Tomahawk crash-landed; Sgt D.Scott safe
	Tomahawk shot down; Sgt T.D.Parker baled out but KiA
112 Sqn	Tomahawk AN220 shot down; Plt Off F.E.Parker slt WiA, rescued by army returned 14th
	Tomahawk AM396 shot down; Sgt R.M.Leu rescued by army returned 14th
	Tomahawk AM444 badly damaged; Flg Off J.L.Groves unhurt
	Tomahawk AM481 badly damaged; Sgt C.F.McWilliams unhurt
	Tomahawk damaged; Plt Off P.C.F.Brunton WiA

German Claims

3./JG 27	Oblt Ludwig Franzisket	P-40	Bir Sheferzen 0808
	Lt Hans-Joachim Marseille	2 P-40s	Bir Sheferzen 0812-15
2./JG 27	Lt Rudolf Sinner	P-40	Sidi Omar 0905
	Hptmn Erich Gerlitz	Hurricane	50m SSE Sollum 0930
	Lt Friedrich Körner	P-40	SE Sollum 0934

German Casualties

| 1./JG 27 | Bf 109E-7 WNr 6001 40% damaged in combat, Capuzzo area |
| 2(F)./123 | Ju 88 4U+1K WNr 0441 MiA; Lt Eduard Gessler and three KiA |

Monday, 13 October 1941

2 SAAF Squadron moved to LG.110 on this date. During the day three Blenheims raided the Gazala landing grounds and five more were targeted with Bardia harbour. Two Marylands undertook a reconnaissance to the north of Ras el Milh, searching for survivors of two A lighters which had been lost during the night of 11/12, but nothing was to be seen.

Tuesday, 14 October 1941

The air plans for the forthcoming offensive were now put in hand. Commonwealth forces were now almost ready to strike again, and the operation was planned to begin the following month under the codename Crusader. Now 261 Wing became the Medium Bomber Group, with 11, 45, 55 and 113 Blenheim squadrons to hand. Bombing operations both by night and day were intensified against Axis airfields, supply dumps, and on targets in and around Benghazi.

Thursday, 16 October 1941

During an early morning photographic reconnaissance mission over Sidi Barrani by four MC.200s of 374ª Squadriglia, 153° Gruppo CT, two of the aircraft failed to return, both pilots being lost. It was thought that their demise was due to a mid-air collision.

Sqn Ldr Yaxley now took over command of 272 Squadron as Sqn Ldr Fletcher was posted to HQ, Middle East. The unit suffered an unexpected and unnecessary loss on this date when Flt Lt Wordsworth took up the squadron's senior medical officer to make a mock attack on the Mediterranean Fleet. Taken by surprise, some of the ships opened fire, and after colliding with the mast on a destroyer, the Beaufighter went straight into the sea with the loss of both aboard. Following this, Flg Off Bartlett took over command of Wordsworth's A Flight.

British Casualties

| 272 Sqn | Beaufighter Ic collided with destroyer's mast after being fired on by units of the Mediterranean Fleet; |
| | Flt Lt Wordsworth and squadron SMO both KiFA |

Italian Casualties

| 374ª Sq/153° Gr CT | MC.200s MM5193 and MM5899, destroyed, possibly collision; Ten Albino Gizzi and M.llo Riccardo Tamanini MiA |

Friday, 17 October 1941

One of the recently-arrived Bf 109Fs was lost on this date, the reason not being known.

German Casualties

| 6./JG 27 | Bf 109F-4 trop WNr 8471 lost in Sollum-Sidi Barrani area; Oblt Franz Schulz MiA |

Saturday, 18 October 1941

I./JG 27's airfield was raided by six Blenheims which dropped bombs and many wire barbs, designed to puncture aircraft tyres. These were christened 'English Hedgehogs', the aircrews swiftly walking round the airfield picking them all up before any aircraft took off.

Sunday, 19 October 1941

At the start of the morning 1 SAAF Squadron with its new Hurricane IIs, joined 2 SAAF and 3 RAAF Squadrons at LG.110 to sweep over the forward area, providing escort for a TacR aircraft. While still forming up, six Bf 109s of 2./JG 27 attacked, shooting down Lt Hedley's Hurricane. He baled out, but his parachute snagged on the tail of his aircraft, tearing it apart, causing him to fall to his death.

Later in the day a 55 Squadron Blenheim from LG.17 undertook a sweep north-west of Derna from which it failed to return. A dozen more Blenheims in two formations of six each, attacked landing grounds. 208 Squadron moved to LG.10. At Air HQ, Western Desert, Grp Capt C.E.N.Guest, OBE, departed from the post of SASO, and Grp Capt Beamish was posted to take command of a new fighter wing.

British Casualties

1 SAAF Sqn	Hurricane II Z2898 shot down; Lt P.M.Hedley KiA
55 Sqn	Blenheim IV Z7416 W Derna; 2/Lt J.N.Murphy, SAAF, and two KiA

German Claims

2./JG 27	Hptmn Erich Gerlitz	Hurricane 60m SE Sidi Barrani 0935

Flt Lt Alan Rawlinson with Sqn Ldr Peter Jeffery at Sidi Haneish in October 1941 at the time when the former was about to take over command of 3 RAAF Squadron from the latter.

Monday, 20 October 1941

238 and 1 SAAF Squadrons flew forward to LG.109 in order to escort three Blenheims of 55 Squadron and six of 113 Squadron which were to attack the Gambut landing grounds. In the event the bombers arrived over their target early, 15 minutes ahead of their escorts, so that they had no fighter protection when four Bf 109s attacked as they were heading out to sea to commence their return flight.

The leading 55 Squadron aircraft was hit and gradually lost height and speed before ditching in the sea 30 miles north of Gambut; the crew was not found. Behind them, one of the 113 Squadron bombers was also targetted as it departed the target and was last seen falling away. On this occasion only one claim was made by Lt Körner of 2./JG 27.

When the 23 Hurricanes arrived on the scene they too were attacked as the approached Gambut. Sgt Savy and Sgt Knappett of 238 Squadron were both shot down, the latter crash-landing and the former baling out. However, Savy was killed and Knappett reportedly died on 26 November, possibly from wounds suffered at this time. 1 SAAF Squadron's Lt Evans also failed to

During October 1941 80 became the first Hurricane squadron in North Africa to carry bombs. At this stage the unit's Hurricane Is were loaded with 40lb bombs as seen here. As soon as Mark II Hurricanes became available to the unit, this role ceased, although it was later to become widespread practice for fighter squadrons – albeit with considerably heavier and more potent weapons.

return, subsequently being reported a PoW. Despite the loss of three Hurricanes, only one claim was made by Oblt Rolf Strössner of 6./JG 27 in one of the new Bf 109Fs.

Also during the day 66 sorties had been flown over the shipping lanes by aircraft from 33, 229 and 250 Squadrons and the RNFS. On this date as well, 80 Squadron arrived at LG.103 from Palestine, now equipped with Hurribombers – Mark Is fitted with underwing racks to carry eight 40lb bombs. The pilots of such an illustrious fighter unit were not best pleased at this change of role. At the same time 274 Squadron received six Hurricane IIs, followed by three more next day. The unit's old Mark Is were flown away by pilots of 30 and 94 Squadrons, as at this stage the former unit was provided with 18 Hurricane Is and ordered to move up to the desert again for night-fighting duties.

British codebreakers were closely following I./JG 27's practice of sending a staffel at a time to Germany to re-fit with Bf 109Fs. On this date they reported that 1. Staffel was at Erding, collecting the following Bf 109F4s:- WNrs 8472, 8474, 8476, 8477, 8478, 8480, 8481, 8482, 8484, 8487, 8494, 8506, and 8519.

British Casualties

55 Sqn	Blenheim IV V6228 shot down; Sqn Ldr H.G.P.Blackmore and crew KiA
113 Sqn	Blenheim IV V5641 shot down; 2/Lt E.H.Burr and crew KiA
238 Sqn	Hurricane I shot down; Sgt F.V.Savy baled out but KiA
	Hurricane I crash-landed; Sgt R.A.Knappett WiA; died 26 November
1 SAAF Sqn	Hurricane II Z2566; Lt C.H.Evans PoW SE Sollum 1030

German Claims

6./JG 27	Oblt Rolf Strössner	Hurricane	N Sidi Omar 0940
2./JG 27	Lt Friedrich Körner	Blenheim	60m N Marsa Luch 0945

Tuesday, 21 October 1941

Nine Marylands from 12 SAAF Squadron and nine from 21 SAAF Squadron raided Benghazi without interception. During the day a notable ex-bomber pilot, Air Cdr B.E.Embry, DFC, AFC, arrived at Air HQ to become the new SASO.

German Casualties

4./LG 1	Ju 88A-5 WNr 8263 MiA Benghazi area; Lt Hans Sauer and crew MiA

Wednesday, 22 October 1941

There were 38 fighter sorties by RAF fighter units incorporating shipping protection, fighter sweeps and an escort to Blenheims. On the latter, ten Tomahawks of 2 SAAF Squadron covered 45 Squadron Blenheims over Gasr El Ahrad. Whilst returning from this raid, the formation was attacked by Bf 109s from II./JG 27, Lt Sturman of the South African unit being shot down and killed. Lt Rogan claimed to have shot down one of the attackers, but no Luftwaffe loss was actually suffered. Air HQ recorded that the unit also submitted a claim for a second Messerschmitt damaged, or possibly a probable.

At 1710 (Axis time) four S.79 torpedo-bombers from 279ª Squadriglia Aut AS set off from Derna on an armed reconnaissance sortie; one aircraft, flown by Ten Umberto Barbani, failed to return.

Following the recent formation of the Medium Bomber Group, 45 and 55 Squadrons were now removed from its control at which it reverted to being 261 Wing.

British Claims

2 SAAF Sqn	Lt D.S.Rogan	Tomahawk	Bf 109F	Gasr El Ahrad
	U/k pilot	Tomahawk	Bf 109F damaged	

British Casualties

2 SAAF Sqn	Tomahawk AN230 shot down; Lt D.H.B.Sturman KiA

German Claims

5./JG 27	Oblt Ernst Düllberg	P-40	E Sidi Omar 1200

Italian Casualties

279ª Sq Aut AS	S.79 MM23950 MiA; Ten Umberto Barbani and crew FTR

Thursday, 23 October 1941

Six Hurricane IIs of 1 SAAF Squadron took off at 0930 for a wing sweep with 3 RAAF Squadron's Tomahawks below them and 238 Squadron's Hurricanes above. The latter unit was three miles behind them when Flak bursts caused two of the South African pilots to scatter out of formation. Six Messerschmitts from II./JG 27 appeared, and in moments the stragglers were picked off. Lt Milner was wounded and crash-landed, while Lt McKenzie was initially pinned into his cockpit by the slipstream, finally managing to bale out. He fell many thousands of feet before pulling the ripcord, his parachute finally opening just 1,000 feet above a minefield. With breakages to bones in both an ankle and an arm, his only complaint was that he had lost a shoe!

Lt Liebenberg, who had been leading the squadron, had called out "Pas op, Kerels, 109s above!" as the Bf 109Fs attacked, and he claimed one shot down and a second damaged, further claims being made by

2/Lts Penberthy and Waugh. This gave the squadron a boost in morale, since a couple of 'green' pilots had been able, apparently, to shoot down Bf 109Fs in their new 12-gun Hurricane IIbs – although in practice all three South African pilots appear to have identified their opponents as Bf 109Es. As so often at this time, however, no losses had actually been suffered by the German unit – and indeed, only one claim for a Hurricane had been made by Hptmn Lippert, the gruppenkommandeur. Air HQ seem to have subsequently down-graded these claims somewhat, recording the total as two shot down and one damaged.

Later in the day a Maryland of the newly-arrived 60 SAAF Squadron flown by the commanding officer, Maj S.B.F.Scott, failed to return. This may have been the aircraft claimed during the afternoon by 3./JG 27's Obfw Kowalski as a Blenheim. His had been one of two 109s scrambled at 1224 to intercept a lone reconnaissance aircraft.

A mystery claim was made in the same general area by Serg Magg Luigi Mannelli of 353ª Squadriglia, 20° Gruppo CT, who was scrambled at 1330. He spotted a single-engined aircraft which had landed at Tobruk and was just taking off again. He attacked this and reported that he saw the pilot bale out. His claim was logged as a 'Spitfire'. This is thought to be an attack on one of 451 Squadron's Hurricanes, as the unit was operating a small detached flight in Tobruk during this period. It is not known if any aircraft was actually lost.

Other Marylands were involved in an attack on Derna airfields, causing "considerable material damage" as intercepted by Ultra. The SAAF unit involved reported the presence of some 50 Axis aircraft on the port's main and satellite landing grounds.

British Claims				
1 SAAF Sqn	2/Lt L.R.S.Waugh	Hurricane IIb	Bf 109F	Halfaya Pass 1045
	Lt H.C.W.Liebenberg	Hurricane IIb	Bf 109F	Halfaya Pass 1045
	Lt H.C.W.Liebenberg	Hurricane IIb	Bf 109F damaged	Halfaya Pass 1045
	2/Lt V.A.Penberthy	Hurricane IIb	Bf 109F	Halfaya Pass
British Casualties				
1 SAAF Sqn	Hurricane BD829 shot down; Lt K.M.McKenzie baled out, WiA			
	Hurricane II Z2314; 2/Lt W.S. Milner WiA			
60 SAAF Sqn	Maryland MiA, Maj S.B.F.Scott and crew KiA			
German Claims				
Stab II./JG 27	Hptmn Wolfgang Lippert		Hurricane	S Buq Buq 0930
3./JG 27	Obfw Herbert Kowalski		Blenheim	50m S Tobruk 1240
Italian Claims				
353ª Sq/20° Gr CT	Serg Luigi Mannelli		Spitfire	Tobruk

Friday, 24 October 1941
During the previous day 14 Squadron had arrived in Palestine, with 84 Squadron due to follow on the 27th. These two Blenheim units would become part of 265 Wing, which at this date had not yet formed. At the same time 264 Wing was forming at Sidi Haneish North under Wg Cdr H.A.Fenton. This unit would take control of 30, 33 and the RNF squadrons for shipping and lines of communication defensive patrol duties. At the end of October it would be renumbered 269 Wing, 265 becoming 270 Wing. By night six Albacore crews had dropped flares over the Bardia area in co-operation with Royal Navy warships which were undertaking a bombardment.

Saturday, 25 October 1941
During the evening three of 279ª Squadriglia's S.79s, flown by Cap Giulio Marini, Ten Guglielmo Ranieri and S.Ten Aligi Strani, left Derna to attack warships spotted 12 miles north of Ras Azzaz. Two of the pilots released torpedoes, Strani claiming a hit on a cruiser; he had in fact caused damage to the minelayer HMS *Latona*.

Sunday, 26 October 1941
Nine Marylands targetted Benghazi during which the bombers were intercepted by two fighters identified as Bf 109s. These, however, did not press home their attacks and it was believed that one was hit by fire from the rear gunners. 261 Wing despatched six of 113 Squadron's fighter Blenheims to strafe traffic along the Agedabia-El Agheila road, the crews reporting firing on about 60 motor vehicles.

The air party of 260 Squadron saw action during the closing stages of the Syrian campaign. With the whole unit reunited, it then moved forward to LG.115 to commence operations over the Western Desert. Seen here is one of the unit's Hurricanes at this time. Although clearly carrying 260 Squadron's ME code letters, official records do not appear to show P2466 ever having served with this unit.

Wednesday, 29 October 1941

On this date 265 Wing was finally formed to incorporate 14, 45, 55 and 84 Squadrons and the Free French GRB 1. Initially, however, 84 Squadron was not to operate as a complete unit, but was to provide flights which would be attached to 14 and 45 Squadrons; the commanding officer of the wing was to be Grp Capt G.R.Beamish. Immediately, however, the new unit was retitled 270 Wing, as already indicated above.

That very evening nine 55 Squadron Blenheims set off from LG.53 (Fuka Point) to bomb Tmimi landing ground and dumps thereon. Attacking in the dark, Lt G.C.Reid's R3660 was reportedly seen to be hit, either by Flak or a night fighter, part of the empennage being shot away, with the

One of the best-known and most colourful bomber pilots in North Africa was Wg Cdr J.K.Buchanan of 14 Squadron, seen here with his crew in front of the tail of one of the unit's Blenheim IVs at Gambut; 'Teddy' Ford (left) and Geoff Whittard (right). Note the line of bombs laid out on the ground behind, waiting to be loaded on this and other aircraft.

elevators also damaged. Despite experiencing great difficulty in controlling the aircraft, Reid got back to the Alexandria area, but shortly after spotting the lights of the port, both engines failed due to shortage of fuel, and at 0055 he ditched the aircraft in the sea about 200 yards offshore, 50 miles from El Alamein. Although both other members of his crew suffered some injury, all three managed to swim ashore. A second Blenheim failed to return, the crew having reported very bad weather conditions.

British Casualties

55 Sqn	Blenheim IV R3660 damaged over target and ditched in the sea on return. Lt G.C.Reid, SAAF, and two crew swam ashore, the latter pair having been injured
55 Sqn	Blenheim IV Z7683 MiA Tmimi area; Lt D.H.Blair, SAAF, and crew KiA

Subsequently, during the opening days of November, a flight of Blenheims from 8 Squadron arrived to be attached to 55 Squadron. 84 Squadron was by then on its way from Iraq as a full squadron and would reform at Amiriya on 12 November, the Free French unit being due to arrive at much the same time. Unit commanding officers were:

14 Squadron	Wg Cdr J.K.Buchanan DFC
45 Squadron	Wg Cdr J.O.Willis, DFC
55 Squadron	Wg Cdr C.J.K.Hutchins
84 Squadron	Wg Cdr C.D.C.Boyce

113 Squadron (Sqn Ldr R.N.Stidolph) now also joined the wing, to be involved mainly in night operations during early November.

As the war progressed the turret on the Blenheim IV was up-gunned from a single Vickers 'K' gun to a pair of Brownings – a much more effective armament. Manning such a battery here is Sgt S.W.Lee of 113 Squadron.

Thursday, 30 October 1941

Fighters flew 34 sorties to cover TacR aircraft during the day, part of this effort being provided by 238 and 250 Squadrons when 11 aircraft from each unit swept over Gambut and Bardia. Six Bf 109Fs were encountered and Plt Off McInnes, the 238 Squadron weaver, was at once shot down. The Tomahawk pilots engaged, Sgts Whittle and Creighton each claiming a Messerschmitt shot down. However, Sgt Cornall's aircraft fell in return and Plt Off Coles's was badly damaged; Cornall managed to crash-land within friendly territory, suffering only slight wounds. Three pilots from II./JG 27's 4.Staffel claimed four fighters between them (all identified as Hurricanes) during this engagement – on this occasion a substantial over-assessment.

During the day nine 21 SAAF Squadron Marylands set off to attack Benghazi, but were prevented from reaching their target by adverse weather in which two of the bombers collided. While one managed to limp home, the other crashed in the Barce area, two members of the crew being seen to bale out. In fact all on board survived to become PoWs. The whole sequence of events was observed by S.Ten Mario Proserpio of 374ª Squadriglia, who did not open fire.

British Claims

250 Sqn	Sgt R.J.C.Whittle	Tomahawk AM392	Bf 109F	15m SW Sollum 0945
	Sgt F.A.Creighton	Tomahawk AM274	Bf 109	20m SW Bardia 0945
	Sgt F.A.Creighton	Tomahawk AM274	Bf 109 damaged	20m SW Bardia 0945

British Casualties

238 Sqn	Hurricane I shot down; Plt Off McInnes
250 Sqn	Tomahawk shot down; Sgt Cornall
	Tomahawk badly damaged; Plt Off Coles unhurt
21 SAAF Sqn	Maryland II 1672 'B' collided and crash-landed; Lt D.L.Lamont and crew PoWs
	Maryland II 1661 'D' collided, damaged, but returned

German Claims

4./JG 27	Obfw Otto Schulz	2 Hurricanes	S & SW Bardia 0930-0935
	Lt Arthur Schacht	2 Hurricanes	6m E Sidi Omar 0935
	Obfw Otto Schulz	2 Hurricanes	15m SW Sollum 0943

During October further efforts had been expended by the Commonwealth fighter squadrons to devise a suitable formation for ongoing operations over the front. Several units were now employing a basis whereby a complete squadron weaved as an alternative to keeping one or two highly vulnerable weavers above and behind the main formation where so many had been picked off by marauding Messerschmitts. Additionally, with the growing number of units becoming available, squadrons were operating together in pairs, or even trios.

Amongst the other units, 24 SAAF Squadron was re-equipped with the first Douglas Boston III light bombers to arrive in North Africa, moving forward to LG.21 with these new aircraft, ready to commence operations. 272 Squadron's Beaufighters also returned to Egypt from Malta, while a special strategic reconnaissance flight of Marylands was formed from 223 Squadron, which was still at Shandur, acting as a bomber OTU. Based initially at Fuka, this operational flight now took over the duties which had been carried out by 39 Squadron. Here they were joined at the Fuka Satellite airfield by a further trio of Marylands of 60 SAAF Squadron (as

Armourers prepare guns and ammunition for Hurricanes of 274 Squadron. The aircraft in the background carries the lightning flash painted on the sides of this unit's aircraft at the time. Careful examination of the photograph indicates that the nose appears to be carrying the multi-colour 'spaghetti' camouflage applied here during the opening months of 1941.

the Survey Flight had become) which were to undertake photographic reconnaissance sorties. Fuka also became the base for a new RN Fulmar Flight, formed for shipping protection. The opposing forces saw a small reduction in the units available, when the night-fighter Bf 110s of I./NJG 3 returned to Europe.

73 Squadron also carried a colourful spearhead marking (although the colours used varied widely) on the unit's Hurricanes during 1941. This is clearly illustrated here with a group of the ground crew in attendance.

Saturday, 1 November 1941

Nine Marylands of 21 SAAF Squadron were off again two days later, this time briefed to attack Derna airfield. Here the bombers were attacked by two fighters identified as a Bf 109 and a G.50, and three Marylands were damaged before the attackers were driven off. Their attackers had actually both been Italian aircraft, Serg Magg Giovanni Tonello of the 374ª Squadriglia claiming to have probably shot down one bomber. However, his MC.200 was hit by return fire and he was wounded, subsequently force-landing near Bir Temrad, near Gazala at 1435.

This raid had been successful in destroying four Ju 87s and damaged ten more, plus an Italian liaison aircraft. Six German soldiers were also killed and a further four wounded.

British Casualties			
21 SAAF Sqn	3 Marylands damaged by fighters		
German Casualties			
Unspecified Stuka Gruppe	4 Ju 87s destroyed and ten damaged on the ground at Derna		
Italian Claims			
374ª Sq/153° Gr CT	Serg Magg Giovanni Tonello	Bomber probable	Derna 1355
Italian Casualties			
374ª Sq/153° Gr CT	MC.200 MM5188 damaged and force-lands; Serg Magg Giovanni Tonello WiA ; Derna 1435		
Unspecified unit	Ca.309 MM11273 destroyed on ground at Derna		

Sunday, 2 November 1941

253 Wing despatched fighter cover for two TacR sorties over the Gambut area, one Tomahawk failing to return. During the day 274 Squadron moved up to LG.110.

Five Blenheims of 45 Squadron set off to attack a supply dump on the Tobruk-Bardia road. On return, while attempting to land at LG.53 in dense fog, the wing of one aircraft hit the ground and a hung-up 250 lb bomb fell off and exploded. The crew were thrown clear by the blast, but both the observer and the radio operator died of the injuries they had suffered.

British Casualties	
250 Sqn	Tomahawk failed to return – not due to enemy action. Plt Off Thornton ditched due to engine trouble
45 Sqn	Blenheim IV V6143 'T' destroyed by own bomb dropping off on landing; Sgt F.Scott survived but crew of two died of injuries

Monday, 3 November 1941

In 258 Wing the squadrons were now ordered to fly regularly in pairs, 112 and 3 RAAF Squadrons and 2 and 4 SAAF Squadrons being 'paired-off'. 2 SAAF Squadron pilots now began flying a formation of pairs of aircraft in line astern, squadrons in line abreast, all weaving. This was undoubtedly a somewhat unwieldy formation. For some reason the Western Desert squadrons were still reluctant to adopt the classic German 'finger-four' formation, which had been in use by many squadrons in the UK for some months.

Tuesday, 4 November 1941

Marylands were again out over the front on 4th, nine of 12 SAAF Squadron raiding dumps. At Berka fires were started, crews claiming that one aircraft had been destroyed and several others damaged on the ground. As the formation turned for home it was attacked by CR.42s from 393ª and 394ª Squadriglie. Serg Bernardi of the former unit identified the raiders as Blenheims, claiming two shot down over Benghazi for which he was later awarded the Medaglia d'Argento; 394ª Squadriglia's Serg Malavasi claimed to have obtained hits on another. During the attack Lt Parsons's Maryland fell behind the formation due to drag caused by the jamming of the bomb doors. The top gunner claimed to have driven off the two Italian biplanes. Lt T.E.Ryan, who had also dropped back in order to make a photographic run over the target, attempted to attack, but found that his front guns failed to operate. He therefore drew abreast of the remaining CR.42, which his gunners then claimed to have shot down in flames. Initially, the 12 SAAF Squadron gunners claimed two CR.42s shot down in flames, but Air HQ reported their apparent success as one in flames and one damaged.

Another Maryland suffered damage during the day when the crew of an aircraft of a strategic

---

reconnaissance unit which had been provided by 223 Squadron in the Sudan, reported being attacked by a Bf 109 when flying between Bir Tegeder and Hachei. The gunners claimed to have shot their assailant down; this was in fact an MC.200 of 372ª Squadriglia flown by Ten Italo Palli, who attacked an aircraft over Derna but ran out of fuel and force-landed south of Tmimi.

British Claims

12 SAAF Sqn	Gunners in Maryland	CR.42	
	Gunners in Maryland	CR.42 Damaged	
223 Sqn det.	Gunners in Maryland	Bf 109	

British Casualties

223 Sqn	Maryland of special strategic reccennaissace unit, damaged by fighter

Italian Claims

393ª Sq/160° Gr CT	Serg Duilio Bernardi	2 Blenheims	Benghazi
394ª Sq/160° Gr CT	Serg Antonio Malavasi	Blenheim damaged	Benghazi
372ª Sq/153° Gr CT	Ten Italo Palli	u/i reconnaissance a/c damaged	Derna 1310

Wednesday, 5 November 1941

Marylands were once again engaged by Italian fighters when six bombers from 21 SAAF Squadron repeated the attack on Berka airfield, where once more fires were started on the ground. Three CR.42s and three monoplanes – again identified as Bf 109s – reportedly intercepted, pursuing the raiders for about 12 miles. 2/Lt Blake's aircraft was seen to have its port engine and the rear gunner's position on fire, following which it crashed near the target, all the crew being killed. Returning crews reported that it was one of the monoplanes which had shot the Maryland down. Four Italian pilots of 160° Gruppo had actually intercepted and although this unit was equipped with CR.42s, it is highly likely that Fissore, who made a claim for an individual victory, was actually flying a G.50bis borrowed from 360ª Squadriglia which had also been based at Benghazi since July.

Elsewhere during the day four fighter-Blenheims of 113 Squadron attacked MT and troops on the Agedabia-el Agheila road, firing on about a dozen vehicles and a troop concentration. By night six of 11 Squadron's Blenheims took off to attack the motor workshops at Derna. One aircraft suffered an engine failure as it set out, force-landing in the sea near Alexandria. 80 Squadron moved its Hurri-bombers forward to LG.111.

British Casualties

21 SAAF Sqn	Maryland II AH392 'K' shot down; 2/Lt N.C.Blake and crew KiA
11 Sqn	Blenheim IV T2343 force-landed in sea after engine failure; Sgt F.E.Turner, RAAF unhurt; crew of two both injured; rescued by Royal Navy

Italian Claims

393ª Sq/160°Gr CT	Ten Giuliano Fissore	Blenheim	Benghazi 1510
	Ten Giuliano Fissore		
	S.Ten Renato Baroni		
394ª Sq/160° Gr CT	S.Ten Carlo Piccone	Blenheims	Benghazi 1510
375ª Sq/160° Gr CT	M.llo Giuseppe Desideri		

Italian Casualties

129ª Sq OA	Ro 37bis destroyed on ground
151ª Sq/20° Gr CT	G.50 MM6383 collided with S.79 on landing; a/c w/o; Serg Magg Guglielmo Gorgone injured
Unspecified	S.79 MM22188 badly damaged in collision with landing G.50. A/c w/o

Thursday, 6 November 1941

Six Tomahawks of 2 SAAF Squadron from LG.110 intercepted a photo-reconnaissance S.79 during the morning, all six pilots obtaining hits on the unfortunate aircraft before it was finally finished off by Lt Rogan.

The South African unit was joined at LG.110 during the day by 3 RAAF Squadron, while A Flight of 94 Squadron arrived at LG.100.

2 SAAF Sqn	Lt D.S.Rogan	Tomahawk	S.79	Matruh area 1040

Italian Casualties

19ª Sq/28° Gr /8° St BT   S.79 MM22325 shot down; S.Ten Celestino Tomelleri and crew MiA

Friday, 7 November 1941

Taking off in the early hours, a fighter Blenheim of 113 Squadron strafed dispersed aircraft on Martuba West airfield, where the crew claimed to have hit two Ju 88s. It seems that they had actually been successful in destroying a single S.79 there.

Somewhat later nine Marylands were despatched to Derna by 12 SAAF Squadron, three of these aircraft returning early. The other six encountered two fighters identified as G.50s and heavy AA fire, two of the bombers suffering damage. There seems little doubt that they had actually been intercepted by a pair of 153° Gruppo MC.200s flown by Cap Natale Veronesi, commander of 374ª Squadriglia and Ten Bruno Zavadlal of 372ª Squadriglia, these pilots reporting repeated attacks without visible result.

About an hour and a half later six more Marylands, this time from 21 SAAF Squadron, approached. These had taken off from LG.21 at Qotaifiya to attack the motor depot and repair shops at Derna. Just after the bombing the formation was attacked by three fighters which were once again identified as Bf 109s. They were in fact two MC.200s from 372ª Squadriglia of 153° Gruppo CT. One, flown by M.llo Marino Mariani, was shot down by the combined return fire from the leading trio of Marylands, but the other pilot, S.Ten Mario Peselli, then concentrated his attack on aircraft 'G' in the second flight. This was last seen going down trailing smoke but with the gunners still returning fire. Observing smoke from one engine, Peselli had continued to pursue his quarry, seeing two members of the crew bale out. He then struck the bomber's wingtip with that of his aircraft whereupon it belly-landed near Tmimi. Serg Donato Mancini of 151ª Squadriglia, 20° Gruppo, also took part in this interception flying a G.50bis; he reported firing on a Baltimore which crash-landed near the Gulf of Bomba. It seems very probable that he had attacked the same bomber as that brought down by Peselli. The returning bomber crews once again claimed to have shot down one of the attacking fighters in flames and damaged another.

It is interesting to note that in both cases the Italian pilots identified the bombers as Baltimores – a development of the Maryland which had yet to see service in North Africa.

By November 1941 3 RAAF Squadron was back in the Western Desert, now equipped with Tomahawks. At this stage the unit's aircraft carried only a single individual aircraft identity letter, but a two-letter squadron code (CV) would soon be applied. W was AN325.

British Claims

2 SAAF Sqn	Maryland gunners	Bf 109 damaged	Derna a.m.
1 SAAF Sqn	Maryland gunners	Bf 109	Derna a.m.

British Casualties

2 SAAF Sqn	2 Marylands damaged by fighters and AA Derna a.m.
1 SAAF Sqn	Maryland II AH415 'G' shot down; Capt G.W. Parsons and one PoW; two gunners KiA

German Casualties

(F)/123	Ju 88 in combat with MC.200 over Derna; one of crew KiA and one WiA

Italian Claims

72ª Sq/153° Gr CT	S.Ten Mario Peselli	Baltimore forced to land	Derna 1100-1220
51ª Sq/20° Gr CT	Serg Magg Donato Mancini	Baltimore crash-landed	Near Gulf of Bomba 1130

Italian Casualties

72ª Sq/153° Gr CT	MC.200 MM5887 shot down; M.llo Marino Mariani KiA
Unspecified unit	S.79 destroyed on ground at night at Martuba

Saturday, 8 November 1941

Six fighter Blenheims of 113 Squadron again attacked the Agedabia-El Agheila road, claiming two aircraft destroyed on the ground together with many vehicles. One Blenheim failed to return, and was believed to have suffered engine trouble.

MC.200s of 357ª and 385ª Squadriglie of 157° Gruppo CT arrived at Castel Benito from Italy on its way to the front.

British Casualties

13 Sqn	Blenheim IVf Z5867 MiA; Sgt J.H.Moody and crew KiA

During the month four early-model Boeing B-17C Flying Fortresses arrived at Shallufa in the Canal Zone where they were attached to 220 Squadron. These aircraft initially flew some night raids on Benghazi with 37 and 38 Squadrons (see Chapter 12 – The RAF's Night Bombing Offensive), but were not to prove very successful in this role. On 8 November two of these aircraft undertook their first daylight raid on a target in the Tobruk area. One suffered an engine failure, causing the pilot to force-land in Axis territory. This created something of a panic in case the new aircraft might fall into enemy hands, and this was to lead to a spate of special fighter operations next day, as will be recounted. Following this misadventure, only one more raid would be flown over the desert, Derna being the target on this occasion. Bf 109s sought to intercept on this occasion, but without success. Subsequently, several attacks would be launched against Italian Fleet bases during one of which one Fortress was intercepted by a pair of Bf 110s, but the pilot found that he was easily able to out-turn these opponents.

Sunday, 9 November 1941

Wg Cdr Hutchins, 55 Squadron's commanding officer, was posted to HQ, ME, being replaced by Wg Cdr A.Foord-Kelsey.

German Casualties

I./JG 27	Bf 109F damaged 25% by bombs on the ground

Monday, 10 November 1941

237 Squadron [the Royal Rhodesian Air Force's only unit, which had been taking part in operations in East Africa (see *Dust Clouds in the Middle East*)] arrived at LG.10 on this date to commence TacR activities, equipped with Hurricanes.

After two days of searching, the crew of one of ten Marylands sent out on this date, spotted the missing Fortress, the crew of which were safe. An army patrol was sent out to pick them up.

German Casualties

I./LG 1	Ju 88A-5 WNr 2285 destroyed in strafing attack

Regia Aeronautica Savoia S.79 in flight over the Mediterranean in company with Bf 110 of III./ZG 26.

Soon to be very active over the Axis front-line airfields were the Beaufighter Ics of 272 Squadron, a trio of which are seen here on a sortie.

CHAPTER 10

OPERATION CRUSADER

THE PREPARATORY PHASE

With the inflow of reinforcements and programme of expansion and re-equipment, the command structure and support elements of HQ, RAF Middle East, required some considerable readjustment and growth prior to the date being set for the new major offensive.

To deal with the initial issues of supply, maintenance and administration, Maintenance Group had been set up at Heliopolis in June 1941, becoming 206 (Maintenance) Group on 1 September. This group already had available 31, 32 and 33 Air Stores Parks (the last of these having returned from Greece), but more had been set up. 34 and 37 ASPs were both formed in the UK and shipped out to Egypt, snd 36 and 38 ASPs were formed within the group locally. By early September they were based as follows:

31 ASP	Abu Sueir	36 ASP	Amiriya
32 ASP	Burg el Arab	37 ASP	Shallufa
33 ASP	Fuka	38 ASP	Qassassin
34 ASP	El Firdan		

The all-important repair & salvage units had also been increased in number. As with the ASPs, two had been formed in the UK and shipped out, while two more had been formed locally. 54 R & SU had returned from Greece during April, so that the units available by September were:

51 R & SU	Fuka	57 R & SU	Shallufa
52 R & SU	Khartoum (Sudan)	58 R & SU	Abu Sueir
53 R & SU	Wadi Natrun	59 R & SU	Amiriya
54 R & SU	Gaza (Palestine)	61 R & SU	Amiriya
55 R & SU	Ismailia		

(56 R & SU would be formed at Habbaniya, Iraq, on 5 January 1942)

The number of maintenance units had been greatly increased throughout the Middle East, in Iraq and Sudan as well as in Egypt, and also at Takoradi in West Africa. A number of these new MUs were in fact re-numbered aircraft assembly units or air ammunition parks, and by the start of November 1941 at least 19 of them would be operating throughout the area.

New flying units had also come into being. On 1 June 71 (Middle East) OTU had been formed at Ismailia to take over 70 OTU's duties for the training of fighter and army co-operation pilots. The following month 70 OTU moved to Nakuru in Kenya. 71 OTU also changed base two months later, transferring its activities to the Sudan during September. The following month its C Flight was taken to form the nucleus of a new 74 OTU at Aqir, Palestine. This new unit was to specialise in the training of tactical reconnaissance pilots, leaving 71 clear to concentrate on fighters. Another OTU, 73, was formed at Sheik Othman, Aden, on 20 November, and this too was to concentrate on fighter training.

To deal with the growing influx of reinforcements reaching the area, four personnel transit camps had been set up, 21 PTC at Kasfareet, 22 PTC at Almaza, 23 PTC at Helwan and 24 PTC at Aboukir. The old Middle East Pool had been disbanded on 1 September and reformed as the Middle East Reserve Unit, but this too would be disbanded at the start of 1942.

Several flights were also formed for specific duties. The first of these was 1411 (Meteorological) Flight at Heliopolis, formed on 14 April from the existing Met Flight for weather investigation duties, for which it was equipped with a trio of Gladiators.

During October 1437 (Strategic Reconnaissance) Flight was formed at Fuka with Marylands to augment the role of 60 SAAF Squadron (which was actually only of flight size). On 13 August the Sea Rescue Flight had been formed at Kabrit with 201 Group, using three Wellingtons.

On the administrative side, 204 Group had continued to command all units in the Western Desert, including 253, 257 and 258 Wings, with its Advanced HQ at Maaten Bagush and Rear HQ at Burg el Arab. On 21 October 1941, however, in recognition of its greatly increased range of responsibilities, it was renamed AHQ, Western Desert.

As described in Chapter 12, 205 Group had come into existence on 23 October by the expansion of 257 Wing at Shallufa to control the growing force of heavy bombers by then available. By the end of 1941 this new group would have its Advanced HQ established at LG.20, Qotaifiya. A few days later 211 Group was formed as 'Nucleus Group Western Desert' becoming 211 (Medium Bomber) Group only in December, to control local units in Cyrenaica. It would reform on 15 January 1942 at Tobruk, but its continued existence in this format was to be brief.

With so many new squadrons now present, numbers of further wings were formed to control groups of these units. However, the system of numbering seemed convoluted in the extreme, and it was to be several weeks before a degree of permanence crept into the situation.

Western Desert Air Force's two key wing leaders confer; Grp Capt Bing Cross (left) and Wg Cdr Fred Rosier.

The process had commenced at the start of May when 253 Wing was formed as the Air Component or Army Co-operation Wing under AHQ, Western Desert. In this role it commanded initially 1 SAAF, 45, 113 and 274 Squadrons, moving its HQ to Sidi Haneish in late July. Here it had available 229 Squadron with fighters, 451 Squadron for tactical reconnaissance, and 113 Squadron for bombing. On 17 November it was disbanded into HQ, AHQ, Western Desert, now with the three tactical reconnaissance squadrons – 208, 237 and 451.

Meanwhile, earlier in 1941 the two wings controlling units in the desert had been 258 (Semi-mobile Advanced Fighter) Wing and 259 (Medium Bomber) Wing. In early October 261 (Medium Bomber) Wing and 263 (Fighter) Wing were formed. The former initially commanded 12 SAAF, 21 SAAF and 24 SAAF Squadrons; not unreasonably, it was re-christened 3 SAAF Wing on 13 November. 263 Wing was to remain in Palestine and Trans-Jordan for the next three years and therefore to all intents and purposes disappears from our story at this point.

On 11 October 262 (Fighter) Wing was established, taking over the 258 Wing squadrons, which initially left this new unit with an indigestible 13 squadrons! These were at this stage 80, 94, 112, 229, 238, 250, 260, 274, 1 SAAF, 2 SAAF, 3 RAAF, 4 SAAF and the Royal Navy Fighter Squadron.

Two weeks later 264 and 265 Wings were set up. 264 was a fighter wing, 'mopping up' the rest of the fighter units in the area. It would be responsible for providing cover to coastal shipping and lines of communication, for which purpose it was to incorporate 30, 33 and 805 (FAA) Squadrons. On 31 October it was renumbered 269 Wing.

265 (Medium Bomber) Wing controlled the Blenheims in 14, 55, 84 and the Free French Lorraine squadron. It lasted a little longer than 264 Wing, being renumbered 272 Wing on 3 December. The so-recently incorporated 269 Wing, having been increased in value to include 229 Squadron and an RN Fulmar flight, but having lost 33 Squadron, would again change name on 5 December when it became 234 Wing.

Are you now thoroughly confused? *They* surely must have been, but the numbering 'feast' had by no means ended. During November 270 (Light Bomber) Wing came into being at Fuka, taking on 265 Wing's units as well as others. It was to incorporate detachments of 8 Squadron from Aden, 11 Squadron, plus 14, 55, 84 and the Lorraine.

On the first day of December 268 Wing would be formed, but two days later became 273 Wing. On 16 December 273 became 233 Wing, while on the same date 272 Wing became 232 Wing.

By mid December this plethora of numbers would resolve itself into:

232	(Medium Bomber) Wing
233	(Fighter) Wing
234	(Fighter) Wing
235	(Medium Bomber) Wing
258	(Fighter) Wing
262	(Fighter) Wing
3 SAAF	(Medium Bomber) Wing

At the start of 1942 several more wings would be formed within 201 and 205 Groups – but more of that later.

By late summer 1941 the newer types of aircraft to be received – notably the Tomahawk fighters and Maryland bombers – had been 'bedded down' into service. At this stage a number of Mark II Hurricanes at last became available for issue to some of the units still operating the elderly Mark Is. First to re-equip were 229 and 238 Squadrons which received Mark IIbs, while 73 Squadron was to operate some of each mark. The pilots were delighted to receive the higher-performing aircraft, but it does need to be kept in mind that the Hurricane II was still no match for the Messerschmitt Bf 109F, nor was it for the new Italian Macchi C.202 which was also about to appear over the front.

Thus it was that on 11 November 1941, just prior to the launching of Operation Crusader, the Order of Battle for RAF, Middle East, insofar as the Western Desert and Egypt were concerned, was as follows:

HQ, RAF Middle East (Cairo)

67 Squadron	Lodestar/Audax/Proctor	Heliopolis (Wg Cdr C.S.Wynne-Eaton, DSO)
PRU	L.R. Hurricane I/	Heliopolis (Sqn Ldr H.C.Macphail, DFC)
	Beaufighter IPR	

201 Group (Naval Co-operation) (Alexandria)

2 (Yugoslav) Squadron	Dornier Do 22	Aboukir
13 (Hellenic) Squadron	Anson, Fulmar	Dekheila
272 Squadron	Beaufighter Ic	Edcu (Sqn Ldr A.W.Fletcher,DFC*)
(Less detachment to WDAF)		
Sea Rescue Flight	Wellington Ic	

Advanced GR Base, Fuka (would become Advanced HQ,
201 Group on 7 December 1941, and 235 Wing on 15 January 1942)

39 Squadron	Beaufort I/Maryland	Maryut, Alexandria (Wg Cdr R.B.Cox)
(Less detachment to WDAF)		
203 Squadron	Blenheim IV	Burg el Arab (Wg Cdr A.F.Johnson)
(Less detachment to WDAF)		
230 Squadron	Sunderland	Kasfareet (Wg Cdr M.C.Collins)

202 Group (would become AHQ, Egypt, on 1 December 1941) (Cairo)

117 Squadron	Wellesley	Bilbeis (Wg Cdr W.E.Rankin)
(Less detachment to WDAF)		
216 Squadron	Bombay	Khanka (Wg Cdr G.R.Howie)
(Less detachment to WDAF)		
223 Squadron	Maryland	Shandur
(Acting as temporary OTU)		

250 Wing (Ismailia)

73 Squadron	Hurricane I	Port Said (Sqn Ldr D.H.Ward, DFC)
(Less detachment to WDAF)		
1 GRU	Wellington I/Ic	Ismailia

252 Wing (Alexandria)

73 Squadron detachment	Hurricane I	Amiriya
213 Squadron detachment		
from Cyprus	Hurricane I	Amiriya, Heliopolis (Sqn Ldr R.Lockhart)

205 Group (Shallufa)

37 Squadron	Wellington Ic	Shallufa
38 Squadron	Wellington Ic	Shallufa
70 Squadron	Wellington Ic/II	Kabrit
148 Squadron	Wellington Ic/II	Kabrit
108 Squadron	Wellington Ic	Fayid

AHQ, Western Desert
(Advanced HQ, Bir Khamsa; Rear HQ, Maaten Bagush)

1 (RAAF) Air Ambulance Unit	DH 86	Fuka (Flt Lt J.G.MacDonald)
60 SAAF Squadron	Maryland	Fuka (Maj E.U.Brierley)
1437 Flight	Maryland	Fuka
39 Squadron detachment	Beaufort I/Maryland	Fuka
(from 201 Group)		
203 Squadron detachment	Blenheim IV	Fuka
(from 201 Group)		
31 Squadron detachment	DC 2	Maaten Bagush
(from Lahore, India)		
117 Squadron detachment	DC 2	Maaten Bagush
(from 202 Group – operated with 31 Squadron detachment as a single squadron)		
216 Squadron detachment	Bombay	Maaten Bagush
(from 202 Group)		

Communications Flight	Various	Maaten Bagush
826 Squadron (FAA)	Swordfish/Albacore	Maaten Bagush (Lt Cdr J.W.S.Corbett)
33 Squadron	LR Hurricane I	Giarabub (Sqn Ldr J.W.Marsden)
113 Squadron	Blenheim IVf	Giarabub (Wg Cdr R.N.Stidolph)
272 Squadron detachment (from 201 Group)	Beaufighter Ic	Gerawla

253 (Army Co-operation) Wing (Ghot Wahas)

208 Squadron	Hurricane I	Sidi Barrani (Sqn Ldr L.G.Burnand, DFC)
451 Squadron	Hurricane I	Sidi Barrani (Sqn Ldr D.Williams)
237 Squadron	Hurricane I	Gerawla

258 (Fighter) Wing (Bir Khamsa)

2 SAAF Squadron	Hurricane IIa/IIb/I	Maaten Bagush (Maj J.I.N.E.Baxter)
2 SAAF Squadron	Tomahawk	Sidi Haneish (Maj C.Gey van Pittius)
3 RAAF Squadron	Tomahawk	Sidi Haneish (Sqn Ldr A.C.Rawlinson, DFC)
94 Squadron	Hurricane I	Sidi Haneish (Sqn Ldr H.C.Mayers, DFC)
238 Squadron	Hurricane IIa/IIb	Sidi Haneish (Sqn Ldr H.F.O'Neill, DFC)
274 Squadron	Hurricane IIa/IIb	Fuka (Sqn Ldr D.S.G.Honor, DFC*)

263 (Fighter) Wing (Sidi Haneish)

4 SAAF Squadron	Tomahawk	Sidi Haneish (Maj A.C.Barrett)
112 Squadron	Tomahawk	Sidi Haneish (Sqn Ldr F.V.Morello)
250 Squadron	Tomahawk	Sidi Haneish (Sqn Ldr E.J.Morris)
229 Squadron	Hurricane IIa/IIb	Sidi Haneish (Sqn Ldr W.A.Smith)
260 Squadron (operational from 20 November)	Hurricane I	Fuka (Sqn Ldr T.M.Horgan, DFC)
260 Squadron	Hurricane I	Maaten Bagush (Sqn Ldr D.R.Walker)

269 (Fighter) Wing (Sidi Haneish)

80 Squadron	Hurricane I/IIa/IIb	Sidi Haneish (Sqn Ldr F.A.Marlow)
RN Fighter Squadron	Hurricane I/Martlet	Sidi Haneish (Lt D.C.E.F.Gibson/ Lt Cdr A.F.Black/ Lt Cdr J.N.Garnett)

3 SAAF (Medium Bomber) Wing (Maaten Bagush)

12 SAAF Squadron	Maryland	El Daba (Lt Col R.H.Preller, DFC)
21 SAAF Squadron	Maryland	Qotaifiya (Lt Col J.D.Pretorius)
24 SAAF Squadron	Maryland	Fuka (Lt Col J.T.Durrant, DFC)
21 Squadron	Blenheim IV	Maaten Bagush (Wg Cdr R.Kellett, DFC, AFC)

270 (Medium Bomber) Wing (Fuka)

Squadron detachment (from Aden)	Blenheim IV	Fuka
15 Squadron	Blenheim IV	Fuka (Wg Cdr J.O.Willis, DFC)
45 Squadron	Blenheim IV	Fuka (Wg Cdr A.Foord-Kelsey)
14 Squadron	Blenheim IV	Maaten Bagush (Wg Cdr J.K.Buchanan, DFC)
84 Squadron	Blenheim IV	Maaten Bagush (Wg Cdr C.D.C.Boyce)
Lorraine Squadron	Blenheim IV	Abu Sueir (Cdt E.Corniglion-Molinier)

N.B. Just before the launch of Operation Crusader, the fighter wings were re-organised so that 262 Wing became entirely composed of Hurricane squadrons (1 SAAF, 94, 229, 238, 260 and 274) while 258 Wing controlled all the Tomahawks (2 SAAF, 3 RAAF, 4 SAAF, 112, and 250, plus the RN Fighter Squadron). 30 and 80 squadrons were transferred to the direct command of AHQ, Western Desert.

_____

HQ, RAF Middle East also controlled 203 Group at Khartoum, Sudan, RAF Palestine and Trans-Jordan (AHQ Levant from 11 December 1941), AHQ Aden, AHQ Iraq, AHQ East Africa and AHQ Mediterranean at Malta. Other than being available potentially to provide reinforcements, none of these commands impact upon the actions dealt with herein. Indeed, where they became involved in any operational activities, these have already been dealt with in other books in this series – notably *Malta: The Hurricane Years, 1940-41*, *Malta: The Spitfire Year, 1942*, and *Dust Clouds in the Middle East*.

At this point in the war the United Kingdom had, of course, gained an ally in the Soviet Union following the German invasion in June 1941. However, in November 1941 that nation appeared to be in grave danger of imminent defeat, and certainly of assistance only in ensuring that the greater part of the Wehrmacht and Luftwaffe were prevented from further major involvement in the Mediterranean area.

Indeed, the possibility of a German thrust through the Caucasus and Black Sea into Iran, and thence to Iraq, Syria and Palestine in the rear of the Commonwealth forces, should Russia collapse, was becoming a matter of some concern to Middle East commanders. The worry was already looming that substantial reinforcements of these areas might well become necessary in the foreseeable future. In the event this threat – which did not evaporate until well into 1943 – would not come to pass. Of much more immediate impact would be the actions of Japan – and in a very much shorter timescale.

THE REGIA AERONAUTICA AND LUFTWAFFE

It is now appropriate to consider the Orders of Battle pertaining to the Axis forces on the eve of the first major British offensive in nearly six months.

Regia Aeronautica

5ª Squadra Aerea (Tripoli)   Gen SA Vittorio Marchesi

Comando Settore Ovest (Tripoli)   Gen BA Raul di Barberino

98° Gruppo Aut BT (Castel Benito) BR.20	T.Col Ivo De Wittemberski
240ª Squadriglia	Cap Ugo Machieraldo
241ª Squadriglia	Cap Alfredo Sordini
3° Gruppo Aut CT (Sorman/Misurata) CR.42	T.Col Innocenzo Monti
153ª Squadriglia	Cap Giorgio Tugnoli
154ª Squadriglia	Cap Giuseppe Tovazzi
155ª Squadriglia	Cap Bruno Alessandrini
12° Gruppo Aut CT (Castel Benito) G.50	Magg Bruno Cudugnello
159ª Squadriglia	Cap Roberto Pastorelli
160ª Squadriglia	Cap Vincenzo Sant'Andrea
165ª Squadriglia	Cap Corrado Ceccacci
236ª Sq Aut BaT (Castel Benito) CR.42	Cap Alessandro Cerutti
175ª Sq Aut RST (Castel Benito) S.79	Cap Raffaele Cantarella
145° Gruppo Aut T (Castel Benito)	T.Col Felice Mazzetti
600ª Squadriglia (S.82)	
604ª Squadriglia (S.74/S.75)	Cap Bruno Trocca
610ª Squadriglia (S.82)	Ten Umberto Allevi

Airfields in use during Operation Crusader, November 1941 – January 1942

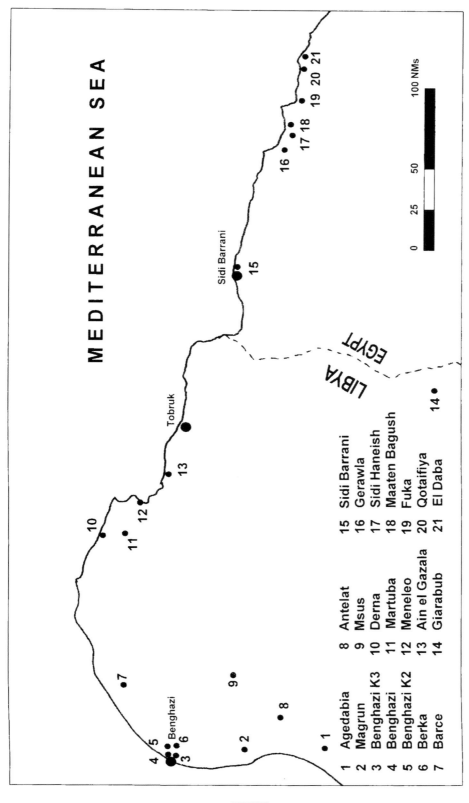

MEDITERRANEAN SEA

Sidi Barrani

Tobruk

LIBYA
EGYPT

1	Agedabia	8	Antelat	15	Sidi Barrani
2	Magrun	9	Msus	16	Gerawla
3	Benghazi K3	10	Derna	17	Sidi Haneish
4	Benghazi	11	Martuba	18	Maaten Bagush
5	Benghazi K2	12	Meneleo	19	Fuka
6	Berka	13	Ain el Gazala	20	Qotaifiya
7	Barce	14	Giarabub	21	El Daba

0   25   50   100 NMs

Comando Settore Centrale (Benghazi)	Gen BA Venceslao D'Aurelio

160° Gruppo Aut CT (Benghazi K2) CR.42	T.Col Fernando Zanni
375ª Squadriglia	Cap Massimiliano Langosco
393ª Squadriglia	Cap Paolo Arcangeletti
394ª Squadriglia	Cap Giovanni Giannini
360ª Squadriglia CT (Benghazi K2) G.50	Cap Gino Callieri
174ª Sq Aut RST (Berka) S.79	Cap Ferruccio Ronzi
209ª Sq Aut BaT (Benghazi K2) Ju 87	Cap Cesare Zanazzo
244ª Sq Aut BT (Benghazi K2) S.81	Cap Mario Casali

Comando Settore Est (Derna)	Gen BA Ferdinando Raffaelli

13° Stormo BT (Barce) BR.20	Col Antonio Pirino
11° Gruppo (Barce)	T.Col Giuseppe Aini
1ª Squadriglia	Cap Riccardo Piovano
4ª Squadriglia	Cap Giovanni Lazzarini
43° Gruppo (Martuba)	T.Col Roberto Pagliocchini
3ª Squadriglia	Cap Francesco Bassi
5ª Squadriglia	Cap Mario Persico
8° Stormo BT (Martuba) S.79	Col Fernando Accardo
27° Gruppo	T.Col Pietro Morino
18ª Squadriglia	Cap Felice Terracciano
52ª Squadriglia	Cap Duilio Piacentini
28° Gruppo	T.Col Aditeo Guidi
10ª Squadriglia	Cap Pietro Galassi
19ª Squadriglia (Derna)	Cap Giuseppe La Penna
20° Gruppo CT (Martuba) G.50	T.Col Mario Bonzano
151ª Squadriglia	Cap Furio Niclot Doglio
352ª Squadriglia	Cap Luigi Borgogno
353ª Squadriglia	Cap Riccardo Roveda

Late November 1941; a Macchi C.202 just assigned to 81ª Squadriglia, 6° Gruppo, 1° Stormo, at Ciampino airport. Before leaving for Libya all the 'tropical' equipment, including primarily the sand filter, had to be installed. The camouflage also had to be adapted, from the uniform dark green colour to a mottled sand and green.

An MC.202 of 71ᵃ Squadriglia, 17° Gruppo, 1° Stormo, already finished to the colonial standard.

153° Gruppo CT (Derna) MC.200	Magg Andrea Favini
372ᵃ Squadriglia	Cap Armando Farina
373ᵃ Squadriglia	Cap Piero Raimondi
374ᵃ Squadriglia	Cap Natale Veronesi
155° Gruppo Aut CT (Ain el Gazala) G.50	T.Col Luigi Bianchi
352ᵃ Squadriglia	Cap Riccardo Spagnolini
378ᵃ Squadriglia	Cap Bruno Tattanelli
376ᵃ Sq Aut CT (Derna) CR.42	Cap Ippolito Lalatta
279ᵃ Sq Aut AS (Derna) S.79	Cap Giulio Marini

The total number of operational aircraft available to 5ᵃ Squadra Aerea was 441, 304 of which were serviceable. In addition there were some units of general and maritime reconnaissance:

15° Gruppo OA Ca.311	Magg Bruno Cerne
32ᵃ Squadriglia (Agedabia)	Cap Carlo Gautier
125ᵃ Squadriglia (Benghazi/Berka)	Cap Aldo Regnoli
67° Gr OA Ro.37/Ca.311	Cap Giovanni Minervino
129ᵃ Squadriglia (Ain el Gazala)	Cap Ercole Giordanengo
132ᵃ Squadriglia (Benghazi/Berka)	Cap Vezio Vernesi
69° Gruppo OA (Zuara) Ca.311	Magg Ettore Zambaldi
118ᵃ Squadriglia	Cap Giuseppe Gaggi
123ᵃ Squadriglia	Cap Vittorio Falugi
145ᵃ Sq RM (Pisidia/Menelao) Cant.Z.501	Cap Nicolò Albanese
196ᵃ Sq RM (Benghazi) Cant.Z.501	Cap Massimo Giovannozzi
Sez. Soccorso (Benghazi) Cant.Z.506	Ten Gaetano Mastrodicasa

At this time command of 5ª Squadra had just changed, General Vittorio Marchesi having taken over from Generale Mario Aimone-Cat on 6 November.

Reinforcements were soon conveyed to Libya; by 25 November the following had arrived:

9° Gruppo CT (Martuba) MC.202	Cap Antonio Larsimont-Pergameni
96ª Squadriglia	Cap Ezio Viglione-Borghese
97ª Squadriglia	S.Ten Jacopo Frigerio
17° Gruppo CT (Martuba) MC.202	T.Col Bruno Brambilla
71ª Squadriglia	Cap Pericle Baruffi
72ª Squadriglia	Cap Pio Tomaselli
80ª Squadriglia	Cap Clizio Nioi
8° Gruppo CT (Benghazi K3) MC.202	Magg Mario Bacich
92ª Squadriglia	Cap Nino Zannier
93ª Squadriglia	Cap Riccardo Marcovich
94ª Squadriglia	Cap Mario D'Agostini
151° Gruppo CT (Benghazi K2) CR.42	Magg Antonio Giachino
366ª Squadriglia	Cap Bernardino Serafini
367ª Squadriglia	Cap Giuseppe Costantini
368ª Squadriglia	Cap Giuseppe E. Zuffi
157° Gruppo CT (Benghazi) MC.200	Magg Luigi Filippi
357ª Squadriglia	Cap Oreste Minuto-Rizzo
384ª Squadriglia	Cap Piergiuseppe Scarpetta
385ª Squadriglia	Cap Elio Fiacchino

By early December arrived:

6° Gruppo CT (Martuba) MC.202	T.Col Vezio Mezzetti
79ª Squadriglia	Cap Domenico Camarda
81ª Squadriglia	Cap Giuliano Giacomelli
88ª Squadriglia	Cap Dante Ocarso
150° Gruppo CT (Martuba) MC.200	T.Col Antonio Vizzotto
363ª Squadriglia	Cap Luigi Mariotti
364ª Squadriglia	Ten Mario Bellagambi
365ª Squadriglia	Cap Domenico Bevilacqua

By year end some of these reinforcements would have been repatriated (9°, 151°, 157° Gruppi) together with some war-weary units (20°, 153°, 155° Gruppi).

Most relevant units to arrive in North Africa would be 9° and 17° Gruppi with new MC.202s. 9° Gruppo had replaced its CR.42s at the start of 1941, but had been flying MC.200s since. In June it had been the first unit to receive MC.202s and after training, had moved to Comiso (Sicily) in late September to operate over Malta where the first successes with the new fighter were gained (see *Malta: The Spitfire Year, 1942*). In late November 73ª Squadriglia would be left at Comiso while 96ª and 97ª Squadriglie would be rushed to Libya following the outbreak of the new offensive, arriving at Castel Benito on 23 November. From here they would move forward to Martuba during the late afternoon of the 25th.

17° Gruppo, the second unit to re-equip with MC.202s, was held for three weeks at Ciampino airfield while sand filters and other tropical equipment was fitted. The first squadriglia to reach Castel Benito would be 71ª on 23 November, which would also move to Martuba two days later. It would soon be joined here by 72ª and 80ª Squadriglie. The other Gruppo forming 1° Stormo CT (6° Gruppo with 79ª, 81ª and

88ª Squadriglia) would join 17° Gruppo early in December, the whole 1° Stormo reuniting at Martuba on 14 December.

Meanwhile, 151° Gruppo CT which had left Libya at the end of July, would be urgently recalled from Sardinia, arriving with its CR.42s at Castel Benito on 22 November.

LUFTWAFFE

It is not so easy to prepare a meaningful Order of Battle for the Luftwaffe in North Africa as at 10 November (or close to that date), as very little had changed since the Battleaxe operation. However, a great deal was just about to happen which would completely change the strength and composition of the Luftwaffe in the Mediterannean generally.

Since the early summer of 1941, the offensive against the Soviet Union had been a major pre-occupation of the German command at most levels. Those who had served in the Mediterranean at this time have subsequently complained that it was hard to get Adolf Hitler's attention focussed on this area, since he clearly saw it as a sideshow of little importance compared with Operation Barbarossa and its subsequent actions. In fairness, when looking at the vast resources employed in that conflict, he was essentially correct, certainly in the context of 1941.

However, by November the attrition to the supply convoys crossing the Mediterranean from southern Europe was so severe that it was becoming increasingly apparent that something had to be done if a disaster was to be avoided. This was particularly so as Erwin Rommel's plans for an assault to capture Tobruk were approaching completion – and Rommel's 'star' was still high in the political firmament in Germany. During November alone (which was to be the worst month of the year) 63% of all cargoes for Libya were lost – mainly to destroyer and submarine flotillas and to torpedo aircraft, all of which were operating from Malta (see *Malta: The Hurricane Years, 1940-41*).

Fortuitously for the Germans this coincided with the onset of autumn and winter conditions on the Eastern Front which would allow both an opportunity to rest and re-equip many of the Luftwaffe's units there, and to redirect some of them to southern Europe without major dislocation to the very restricted operations now taking place on the major front.

Until now, the main Luftwaffe command in the Mediterranean had remained X.Fliegerkorps, commanded by Gen Hans-Ferdinand Geisler. As when it had first been sent to Sicily during early 1941, his command was essentially one specializing in anti-shipping activities, and this remained his main preoccupation. The elements of X.Fliegerkorps which had been subtracted from the establishment and despatched to North Africa as Fliegerführer Afrika remained in the hands of GenMaj Stefan Fröhlich, who was subordinate to Geisler and had to date received little further support from the latter's command which was much involved in actions in the eastern Mediterranean and along the Egyptian coast, designed to retain the Luftwaffe's hegemony here over the Royal Navy.

As at 15 November, therefore, the only new unit to have reached the area had been II./JG 27, which had indeed arrived to shore-up Fliegerführer Afrika's fighter force, bringing with it the Bf 109Fs which it had only recently received in Germany. It had been one of the first units to withdraw from the east, departing Russia for Germany at the start of July 1941. However, the rest of the geschwader – the Stab and III.Gruppe – had also come out of the line during October, and were under orders to follow II.Gruppe to North Africa when re-equipment had been completed. Although these units were not yet physically present, they were nonetheless included in the Order of Battle, raising the figures of establishment and strength of the forces available to the Luftwaffe in the Mediterranean, but at this point not the numbers of aircraft immediately ready:

Units	Establishment	Actual Strength	Immediately Available
Stab, I., II. and III./JG 27 (Bf 109Fs) I./StG 1,	124	108	22
II./StG 2, Stab and I./StG 3 (Ju 87Bs and Rs)	129	107	86
III./ZG 26 (Bf 110Ds and Es) II./KG 26	39	39	26
Stab, I., II., and III./LG 1 (Ju 88As) (He 111s)	151	139	61
1.(F)/121 and 2.(F)/123 (Ju 88Ds and Bf 110s)	21	17	9
Totals	464	410	204

To this total should be added several short-range TacR staffeln equipped with Hs 126s and (increasingly) Bf 110s, an air/sea rescue staffel with Do 24 flyingboats, and some liaison units with Fi 156s. At this stage of the war large numbers of Ju 52/3m transports could be made available from home-based units at short notice, despite the losses which had been suffered during the Cretan invasion.

To command and direct the much larger forces now being prepared to move to the area, the first priority was perceived to be an overall commander. The job was offered to Feldmarschall Albert Kesselring – 'Smiling Albert' to his subordinates – who was to take up the position of Oberbefelshaber Süd (Commander-in-Chief South). As such he would have precedence over all other German commanders in the area of (almost) all forces – and his appointment came as a not altogether welcome surprise to his Italian allies.

Albert Kesselring had served in World War I as an artillery man and was not an airman. However, he was perceived to be an excellent organiser, being qualified as a staff officer. Recruited into the clandestine air staff in 1933, he served initially as a GenMaj i/c administrative services. When Gen Walter Wever, the Luftwaffe's 'prophet' of strategic air power was killed in a flying accident in June 1936, Kesselring replaced him as chief of air staff. As an ex-soldier, he did not espouse the same views as Wever, and was amongst those who were instrumental in redirecting the Luftwaffe as an essentially tactical force.

In 1937 he took command of the new Luftflotte 1 as a GenOberst, leading this force during the invasion of Poland in September 1939, where he became enthused by the apparent efficacy of the Stuka dive-bomber as an instrument of air power. He then moved to command Luftlotte 2, which he led throughout the Western European campaign of May-June 1940, the Battle of Britain during the summer of that year, and then the Operation Barbarossa invasion of the Soviet Union. By that time he had been promoted feldmarschall.

Taking up his new post on 28 November 1941, Kesselring soon found that his life would not necessarily be an easy one. He was to be followed in early December by II.Fliegerkorps under GenOberst Bruno Lörzer, which had been part of his command in Luftflotte 2, although its composition would differ somewhat from that appertaining to its service in Russia.

Kesselring would now command both II. and X.Fliegerkorps, and Fliegerführer Afrika, which would now come under the former. Initially he instructed Geisler to become responsible for the neutralisation of Malta until the new command could arrive. Lörzer had been one of the more successful fighter pilots of the Great War, ending that conflict as a hauptmann in command of the elite JG III, equipped with BMW-engined Fokker D.VIIs – arguably the best, and certainly one of the best fighter aircraft of that war. He had been credited with 44 aerial victories and remained a close personal friend of Hermann Göring, who had been an immediate contemporary. Lörzer had been in command of II.Fliegerkorps both during the Battle of Britain and Barbarossa, and had been awarded the Ritterkreuz on 29 May 1940.

Kesselring quickly found that his subordinate Fröhlich had one of the most difficult jobs as Fliegerführer Afrika. He had to try and satisfy Rommel's persistent demands for air support, but whilst junior in rank to Rommel, was subordinate not to him, but to Kesselring. Similarly, due to Rommel's high standing at home, he was in no way subordinate to Kesselring, despite the latter's apparently senior position. With the Italians, his position depended upon a liaison system known as Italuft, which had been set up in 1940 to co-ordinate the activities of 5ª Squadra Aerea and X.Fliegerkorps. Rommel theoretically was responsible to Marshal Ettore Bastico, C-in-C, Italian Armed Forces in North Africa, but in practice frequently disagreed with him and when it suited him, simply ignored his colleague.

Immediately upon taking up his new role, Kesselring had already diagnosed that if Axis fortunes were to prosper in North Africa, the correct strategic move would be to invade and take control of Malta, which was the main base of the British forces strangling the supply routes to Libya. He was rapidly disabused of this possibility for which, he was advised, sufficient troops were not available. Clearly, the painful lessons of Crete were still much to the fore in the minds of the High Command.

What then of II.Fliegerkorps, now due to become the strongest element of Kesselring's armoury? Stab and I./JG 53 had left Russia in early August, but already being equipped with Bf 109Fs, these units moved initially to the North Sea coast where they undertook defensive duties until ordered to Sicily in mid December. Here they joined II. and III.Gruppen which had left the Soviet Union at the start of October, arriving via Germany in Sicily at the same time. As will be recounted later, III.Gruppe moved across to Africa, its stay would be brief and it soon rejoined the rest of the geschwader in the assault on Malta. These units were supplemented by II./JG 3 in early January 1942.

November saw the arrival in Sicily of I./NJG 2 with Ju 88C long-range night fighters. This unit had been operating in the intruder role over eastern England, and in the Mediterranean would expand its night-fighting role to allow for day convoy escort duties between Crete and Libya on occasions.

Similarly, a sizeable bombing force began arriving in Sicily co-terminously. From Holland two coastal bomber gruppen, KGr 606 and 806, reached the island where they came under the control of Stab/KG 54, which arrived at much the same time with I./KG 54, both units after service on the Eastern Front. They were followed at the turn of the year by Stab, II. and III./KG 77. All these units were equipped with Ju 88s, and all would operate only over Malta and the sea lanes around. They did, however, free up the elements of II. and III./LG 1, and those of the Stuka gruppen which had been operating over Malta, allowing them to return to North Africa during this period.

Thus one month after the situation indicated with the 15 November Order of Battle, the forces available to II. and X.Fliegerkorps and Fliegerführer Afrika had almost doubled – although most of the increase was nonetheless based in Sicily and operating almost entirely against Malta in order to ameliorate the supply position of the Axis forces in Libya:

Units	Establishment	Strength	Immediately Available
Stab, I., II. and III./JG 27 Stab, I., II. and III./JG 53)	248	217	180
(Bf 109Fs) I./NJG 2 (Ju 88Cs)	82	58	4
I./StG 1, II./StG 2, Stab and I./StG 3 (Ju 87s)	129	85	43
III./ZG 26 (Bf 110Ds and Es) Stab, I., II.and III./LG 1	39	26	18
(Ju 88As) II./KG 26 (He 111s)			
KGr 606, 806 (Stab and I/KG 54 not yet arrived). (Ju 88As)	276	232	9
Totals	774	618	334

Of perhaps even greater danger to the Allied cause than this increase in strength of the Luftwaffe, was the ordering to the Mediterranean at the start of December of a substantial part of the Kriegsmarine's U-Boat fleet. Ten were ordered to prepare for operations in the eastern basin, while 15 were to place themselves to the east and west of the Straits of Gibraltar.

Tedder was by now becoming fully au fait with what was necessary for Western Desert Air Force to try and achieve. On the eve of the battle he wrote to ACM Portal: "The key to air superiority is the comparatively small number of German fighters, and apart from the maintenance of pressure on enemy supplies, every effort is being directed towards ensuring an effective knock-out of the Hun in the air."

Operations meanwhile, were continuing:

Tuesday, 11 November 1941
21 SAAF Squadron sent off six Marylands to attack Benina, but as these approached the target they were engaged by ten fighters which caused the formation to turn back without making the planned attack. Six more then raided Benina, but these too were intercepted, reportedly by Bf 109s, three of the bombers being hit.

During the day a third SAAF fighter unit undertook its first operations in the desert, flying top cover for 2 SAAF Squadron which was itself escorting a TacR sortie. The flight commanders and senior pilots of 4 SAAF Squadron had actually been attached to 1 SAAF and 2 SAAF Squadrons since early October to gain prior experience. Now the unit had moved up to the forward area on 26 October, led by Maj A.C.Barrett. Here it joined 112 and 250 Squadrons in 262 Wing.

Wednesday, 12 November 1941
Four claims were made by the pilots of JG 27 on this date. Oblt Düllberg and two of his 5.Staffel men each claimed a 'P-40' around 1540, with 1.Staffel recording a single victory at an unrecorded time. Actual losses have not proved so easy to set against these claims on this occasion. The newly-arrived 4 SAAF Squadron scrambled five Tomahawks which were on stand-by, to engage nine Messerschmitts. In a 30-minute dogfight the unit suffered its first casualty, Lt A.W.Alder being shot down and killed. As these were identified as being the E version of the Bf 109, they may well have been from I.Gruppe.

Tactical reconnaissance Hurricane pilots also suffered interception; one aircraft of 451 Squadron and one of the detachment of 40 SAAF Squadron serving with the Australian unit, were shot down when engaged in a photographic sortie over the frontier wire; both pilots were killed and would appear possibly to have been the victims of the 5./JG 27 fighters.

British Casualties			
40 SAAF Sqn/	Hurricane I MiA; Lt G.D.K.Thomas KiA		
451 Sqn			
451 Sqn	Hurricane I MiA; Plt Off K.E.Whalley KiA		
4 SAAF Sqn	Tomahawk AN 438 shot down; 2/Lt A.W.Alder KiA		
2 PRU	Hurricane I 2665; pilot baled out over sea near Gazala due to engine failure; Flg Off White		
German Claims			
5./JG 27	Obfw Erich Krenzke	P-40	ESE Sollum 1540
	Uffz Horst Reuter	P-40	E Bardia 1542
	Oblt Ernst Düllberg	P-40	ENE Bardia 1544
1./JG 27	Staffel victory	P-40	

274 Squadron bade farewell to their commanding officer, Sqn Ldr Dudley Honor, who was posted as wing leader of 258 Wing on Hurricane IIs. Ex-80 Squadron Sid Linnard took over in his stead. This coincided with the arrival as commander of the wing of Grp Capt Bing Cross from Egypt, who flew in a new Hurricane II, BD884. Cross explained in his autobiography:

"Coningham had planned a new organisation for the fighter force in the anticipated advance of some 800 miles to Tripoli. He expected movement to be rapid once the enemy land forces had been destroyed south of Tobruk and was therefore forming a second Wing, 263, to add to that presently at Sidi Barrani and making both mobile by providing a generous establishment of MT. The intention was that the second Wing Headquarters would remain alongside that controlling the fighters, then move forward with the Army and install themselves on the next set of airfields constructed by the Royal Engineers as the advance proceeded. As soon as they were installed they would call the fighters forward and so remain well within range of our forward troops. To prevent confusion as to who was in command, the CO of 258 Wing was to be a Group Captain and 263 a Wing Commander. The Group Captain would decide for himself which HQ he would command from. The officers nominated for these key posts were Wg Cdr 'Bull' Halahan (to be made an acting Grp Capt) and command 258 Wing while 263 Wing was to be commanded by an old friend from Digby days, Wg Cdr Fred Rosier.

"The two men were contrasting figures. Halahan was a burly man who strode about the place with an arrogant air which plainly said: 'I am the boss around here and make no mistake about it.' He had commanded a squadron in France in the early days and had done a short stint in Malta (see *Malta: The Hurricane Years, 1940-41*). Rosier had been a Flight Commander in 229 Squadron at the time of Dunkirk and in the days before self-sealing tanks were standard equipment in the Hurricane. He had been hit and when his plane caught fire, baled out but was badly burned about the face in the process and still bore the scars. He was a most intelligent man, a great character and trusted by everyone from top to bottom. Halahan on the other hand was a man who it was difficult to get to know. He was a loner. He made grandiose plans for sweeps with Big Wings and indicated that he would always lead when a Big Wing operation was ordered. When he said this to all the fighter pilots gathered for a conference to discuss Crusader, a pilot who had been with Halahan in France was heard to remark, 'I will give 500 piastres for every time that man crosses the wire.'

"Halahan's idea, an absurd legacy from the Big Wing sweeps at home by Fighter Command across the Channel which achieved nothing at great cost and retained Spitfires in England which were desperately needed elsewhere, was quickly quashed with the arrival in October of Air Commodore Basil Embry as the Senior Air Staff Officer to Coningham. He was, in my opinion, the most outstanding leader in the air up to the rank of Air Vice-Marshal that the Royal Air Force produced during the war. Starting in 1939 as a Blenheim squadron commander, he continued to fly on operations in each rank from Squadron Leader to Air Vice-Marshal. He was a most dynamic personality and quickly took a grip on the fighter organisation, pronouncing that even if Big Wings were an advantage, which he doubted, the difficulty of mass assembly and take-off from desert strips with their attendant clouds of dust made them impossible. Moreover having three different

Air Vice-Marshal Arthur 'Mary' Coningham discusses tactics with Grp Capt Bing Cross at WDAF headquarters at LG.122 during November 1941.

types, the Hurricane I and II and the Tomahawk, with different characteristics would make manoeuvre and control in the air too difficult to put into practice. He consequently paired the squadrons by type of aircraft into Small Wings which certainly proved to be a very satisfactory tactic during Crusader.

"Of course nothing made up for the inferiority in performance of all the fighters used in the Middle East in comparison with the Messerschmitt 109F. Neither of our best, the Hurricane II and the American Tomahawk, could compete and the Hurricane I was quite outclassed. Even the Italian Macchi 202 was better than anything we had. Well might our Commander-in-Chief, Air Marshal Tedder have written in his journal 'One Squadron of Spitfire Vs would have meant a lot.'

"In the end Halahan was not even to have the opportunity of 'crossing the wire'. The request to the Air Ministry to promote Halahan to Acting Grp Capt was refused and Coningham had to think again. He sent for me on 11 November and explained again his planned organisation for the command and control of the fighters through the two Wing HQs, 258 and 263, then said – rather reluctantly I thought – 'I want you to command 258 Wing'. I was surprised at first and then delighted, even though I thought that Coningham wasn't all that certain that I was the right man for the job."

Cross went on to describe his arrival at Sidi Barrani where he found Halahan had been in command of the wing for some time, and had received no notice of his being replaced. Having taken over:

"...we decided to operate over the battle area in the largest manageable formations which after trials we found to be two squadrons, a total of 24 aircraft. Maintenance was not a problem and serviceability high. The Tomahawk was beautifully built but both it and the Hurricane were short of performance compared to the 109F.

"At this time in the desert, we had four Hurricane squadrons, four of Tomahawks, plus a naval squadron of Hurricanes and Grumman Martlets....Though I was not aware of it at the time, I learned later that Tedder had to contend with numerous suggestions for the organisation and operation of the air forces under his command, particularly those in the desert. The 8th Army Commander, Lt Gen Sir Alan Cunningham and Gen Sir Thomas Blamey, the Australian, were foremost in their 'requirements'. Mostly the demands were for squadrons to be allocated directly to Army formation, mostly to Corps and Divisions, but even Brigades were to have their quotas. The Squadron Commanders would receive their operating orders direct from the Generals concerned. That none of these gentlemen had ever flown an aeroplane or had the slightest knowledge of the training, operational or logistic aspects of Air Forces, did not appear to concern them at all. Fortunately, in Gen Sir Claude Auchinleck, Tedder had as a colleague one of the most intelligent Generals on the British side in the entire war. He saw very early on the virtues of centralised control of the air forces by the Air Officer Commanding located alongside the Army Commander. Tedder and his subordinate Air Vice-Marshal Coningham made their arrangements accordingly.

"We airmen, who had been fighting the Germans in France, Norway, the Battle of Britain and over Germany itself, had no illusions about the formidable prowess of our opponents and consequently were not often surprised by the operations of the Luftwaffe during Crusader. Operationally, we were more experienced than the Army and despite the inferiority of our aircraft we seized the initiative from the beginning and held on to it throughout. Our surprise was caused by growing realisation of the incompetence of large parts of the 8th Army. I had assumed that having chased the Italians out of Egypt and Cyrenaica, met the Germans, however briefly, in Greece and Crete and faced them for some months recently on the Egyptian frontier, the Army's organisation would be adequate to absorb inexperienced formations fresh out from the United Kingdom. I could not have made a more incorrect assumption. The first shock was the realisation that, like ours, much of the soldier's equipment was inferior to the enemy's but unlike the airmen, lack of continuous operational experience meant the Army had not learnt how to minimise these deficiencies. Many of the commanders at all levels had not fought the Germans at all in this war. This led to a crucial lack of appreciation of the importance of the most elementary essentials when facing so formidable an enemy. Nowhere was this more apparent than in the area of communications.

"W/T communication from forward formations to Army HQ and vice-versa simply did not work. The result was that even the location of friendly formations was often unknown and this made planning bomber operations difficult and sometimes impossible. Despite this almost complete absence of information on the locations of our troops, mercifully few mistakes in identity occurred. The most serious result to us was the under-utilisation of the light bomber force which waited hour after hour bombed up and ready to go, but no information about targets came from the Army. Army intelligence did not pass on to us accurate locations of enemy formations even with the air reconnaissance squadron working directly under Corps HQ, as had been agreed before the battle began. But this proved to be immaterial. With our fighter sweeps and bombers continuously over the battle area the reports we received often gave us a more up-to-date and accurate picture of what was going on than was available at 8th Army HQ. This was quickly recognised and the exchange of information between Operations Rooms became rapid and extensive and benefited all."

GIARABUB (JARABUB)

About 15 miles north of the far southern end of the wire erected by the Italians on the frontier with Egypt, lay the oasis of Giarabub, originally a Regia Aeronautica airfield. By late 1941 this was firmly in British hands and became the location of two landing grounds originally Giarabub Nos 1 and 2, subsequently known as LGs.107 and 108.

While XIII and XXX Corps prepared for the main offensive, a relatively small body known as Oasis Force, comprising 29th Indian Infantry Brigade Group and 6th South African Armoured Car Regiment, commanded by Brigadier D.W.Reid, was formed at Giarabub. This was to advance on Gialo (Jalo) to give protection to a new airfield (LG.125) to be constructed in the open desert 100 miles north-west of Giarabub from which air attacks could be made on the coastal area south of Benghazi. Oasis Force itself was to harass the Axis forces as opportunity offered, thereby helping to create the impression that a major attack was developing from the south. To aid in this impression, a bogus concentration was established at Giarabub of camps, dumps and dummy tanks, appropriate volumes of spurious radio traffic being carried out. These activities aided considerably in diverting attention from the real work going on further north.

In preparation for the planned movement of RAF units to LG.125, 33 Squadron, with its long-range Hurricane Is, moved to Giarabub from Gerawala on 8 November, followed on the 14th by 113 Squadron. The latter unit had now had its Blenheim IVs converted to an enhanced fighter configuration by incorporation of the usual under-fuselage pack of four .303 in machine-guns plus a long-barrelled Hispano 20mm cannon which was fitted on the floor of the observer's position in the nose, extending through the bomb-aiming window. These aircraft had already undertaken a number of strafing attacks on the Agedabia-El Agheila road at maximum range; the availability of the Giarabub landing ground, and particularly that at LG.125 subsequently, would greatly facilitate these attacks. Command of 33 Squadron had just changed at this point, Sqn Ldr Marsden being in need of a rest following his recent traumatic experiences; he was replaced by Sqn Ldr Derrick Gould, an ex-274 Squadron pilot who had recently joined 33 as a flight commander.

Although deep in the Cyrenaican desert, Giarabub was easy to find from the air. Plt Off Don Edy:

"Giarabub was a deadly hole. The landing ground was the bed of an ancient lake and all around it there were cliffs and gullies. The boys drove the vehicles up one of the waddies just off the plateau and here we proceeded to make camp. I found that the wind had scooped out neat places about four feet deep under the cliffs. They made ideal places for our cots. We strung netting from the overhang and soon had fly-resistant bedrooms.

"From the air Giarabub was fairly easy to find once you got used to the place. As the scrubby northern desert ended and the true sand sea began, there was a strip of black land beginning at the oasis and stretching 200 miles west before it turned south to the Gialo Oasis. It was comparatively simple to find the black strip. As the wire passed through Giarabub, all we had to do in theory was to find the place where the wire and the black strip joined. Mostly it was easy, but there were times when sandstorms or haze made it difficult to be sure where you were.

"Even though we were behind the enemy lines there was little danger of attack from their ground forces. The only thing we would have to contend with was an attack from the air. The difficulties in supplying such a force as ours were considerable. Bombay aircraft flew in most of the gasoline and food. Once a week a convoy of trucks made its way south with extra supplies of everything from spare parts for the aircraft to cigarettes and razor blades."

Thursday, 13 November 1941

Eight night/dawn patrols were flown by Hurricanes of 30 Squadron during one of which Sgt Ovens intercepted a Ju 88 over Maaten Bagush at 5,700 ft, his fire setting the port engine alight. The bomber was last seen going out to sea, and Ovens was awarded a probable.

During the morning an S.79 from 19ª Squadriglia took off from Derna in the hands of S.Ten Walter Montanari to undertake a reconnaissance over Giarabub and Siwa. Over the former area he reported being attacked repeatedly by two fighters, but although his aircraft was damaged, he escaped, returning to claim one of his attackers shot down. 33 Squadron's Sgt Kelsall made eight attacks on the Savoia, no second fighter being involved. He overestimated the damage he had inflicted, claiming the Savoia probably shot down. However, this rather tortuous engagement indicates how restricted was the performance of the unit's long-range Mark Is.

Changes continued to take place amongst the Air HQ, Western Desert, units. 261 Wing was renumbered 3 (SAAF) Wing on this date, responsible for the operation of the South African light bombers.

British Claims

30 Sqn	Sgt L.A.Ovens	Hurricane I	Ju 88 probable	Maaten Bagush- Fuka area 0525
33 Sqn	Sgt A Kelsall	Hurricane I Z4505	S.79 probable	Giarabub area 1200-1255

Italian Claims

19ª Sq/28° Gr/8° St BT	S.Ten Walter Montanari and crew	Fighter damaged	Giarabub

Italian Casualties

19ª Sq/28° Gr/8° St BT	S.79 damaged by fighters over Giarabub; S.Ten Walter Montanari and crew safe

In preparation for the approaching British offensive, several units moved up closer to the front line area. 238 Squadron moved to LG.123 via LG.111, and next day 260 Squadron flew to LG.109 where it was joined by the rest of 94 Squadron. 274 Squadron, meanwhile, bade farewell to their commanding officer, Dudley Honor, who was promoted to lead the wing which this unit was to form with 1 SAAF Squadron. Honor's place at the head of 274 was taken by Sqn Ldr Sidney Linnard, who had been serving with 80 Squadron as a flight commander. At this stage as well, the Tac E squadrons were allocated specific duties, 208 Squadron being ordered to undertake sorties on behalf of XXX Corps, 451 Squadron similarly serving XIII Corps.

Friday, 14 November 1941

Nine Marylands bombed dispersed aircraft on Derna airfield, two aircraft being reported as receiving direct hits. Intense Flak was encountered and one bomber was badly damaged, last being seen losing height near Ras Azzaz. An Italian radio broadcast reported that the aircraft had crashed near the target area and that the crew had been captured. In fact one member of the crew had been killed. The pilot, Lt Stevens, who later took part in the Great Escape from Stalag Luft III, but was captured again and was one of those shot on 29 March 1944.

British Casualties	
12 SAAF Sqn	Maryland II AH287 shot down by Flak off Marsa Luch; Lt R.J.Stevens and two PoWs, one KiA appr 1345
German Casualties	
Unspecified unit	Ju 87 destroyed on the ground at Derna by bombs
Italian Casualties	
129ª Sq OA	Ro.37bis flown by Ten Carlo Codignola FTR

112 Squadron pilots in the Western Desert. Back row left to right: Sgt Rudolf Leu RAAF, Plt Off Neville Duke, Plt Off J.F.Soden, Flg Off A Humphreys, Sqn Ldr Tony Morello, Flt Lt C.F.Ambrose, Plt Off E.Dickinson, Sgt H.G.Burney, FO J.Westenra. Front row: Plt Off J.J. Sabourin, Plt Off N. Bowker, Flg Off J.P.Bartle, Sgt K.F.Carson RAAF.

112 Squadron quickly adopted a shark's tooth emblem for its Tomahawks. This can be seen on the forward nose panel which has been removed and laid on the ground to allow access to the engine and air filters. Even at this early stage, the aircraft already carries the unit code letters GA as well as the aircraft's own J.

Saturday, 15 November 1941

There was a substantial increase in activity pending the big attack. The move of 33 and 113 Squadrons to Giarabub had clearly concerned the Axis, for following the reports of the Italian reconnaissance on the 13th, the Luftwaffe now launched an attack on the airfield there at around 0905. A force reported as comprising nine Ju 88s and six Bf 110s approached at high level, six Hurricanes taking off to intercept. As they did so, seven more 110s and four Bf 109s, the latter fitted with long-range drop tanks, came in at low level. The Bf 110s went down to strafe, but as the Hurricanes dived on these, they were themselves attacked by the 109s, two being shot down. Sgt Price was killed, while Plt Off Anderson managed to crash-land suffering only a small gash to his head. Only one claim was made by the Luftwaffe by Obfw Espenlaub of 1./JG 27. However, one Blenheim was destroyed on the ground and two Hurricanes were damaged. III./ZG 26 suffered the loss of at least one Bf 110, reportedly to AA fire. Oblt Schulze-Dickow crash-landed, having suffered slight wounds to his face, his aircraft coming down on a dry salt lake. At once Obfw Swoboda landed alongside to pick up the crew and fly them back to base. Air HQ recorded that one Bf 110 had been shot down by a Hurricane, others inflicting damage on three Ju 88s. No claims of such a nature have been discovered in 33 Squadron's records.

On return the German crews incorrectly reported that two squadrons of Tomahawks and one of Marylands were now based at Giarabub.

Throughout the day British fighters undertook 48 sorties during sweeps over the forward area and 34 more on local defence flights. It was the bombers which were to see some of the toughest action of the day whilst attacking Axis landing grounds. Before dawn nine Albacores raided Gambut, and nine Marylands followed to hit Tmimi at 0920. Six more Marylands raided Gazala at 0910, while at 1435 nine returned to Tmimi, followed at 1500 by a further eight to Gazala again.

The second attack involved aircraft of 12 SAAF Squadron, the crews reporting some 40 Axis aircraft in blast pens and on the runway. Many bombs were seen to fall amongst these, and claims for five damaged were made. One Maryland returned with two bombs hung-up, but landed safely. However, when maintenance work was being carried out on this aircraft, it caught fire which caused these bombs to explode – probably as a result of a cigarette or match setting off petrol vapour in the bomb bay; six members of the ground crew lost their lives and two more were injured.

During the mid afternoon period five MC.200s from 153° Gruppo CT escorted an S.79 of 19ª Squadriglia flown by S.Ten Guido Giancarlo on a reconnaissance mission. Over Bir Khamsa they were intercepted by a pair of 1 SAAF Squadron Hurricanes which were undertaking a local defensive patrol. The two South African pilots incorrectly identified the Macchis as G.50s which they thought to be eight strong, and attacking, they claimed one shot down each. They had in fact shot down one, the Italians returning to base to claim one of their attackers probably shot down in return; in fact neither Hurricane suffered any damage.

The third of the raids bombed store dumps east of the landing ground at Gazala, but ten minutes after leaving the target, heading out to sea, the bomber crews found fighters waiting for them. Maj Fowler at once turned into the attack but as he did so Lt Roulston's aircraft was hit and was last seen diving for the coast, pursued by one of the Messerschmitts and with the starboard engine streaming smoke. The aircraft fell about 30 miles north of Tobruk with the loss of the whole crew. Meanwhile other fighters concentrated their attack on Maj Fowler's aircraft. He fired his rearward-mounted 'scatter guns' at these, and his top gunner, Sgt T.J.Hatting, claimed to have shot one of the Bf 109s down into the sea (no such loss was actually recorded). Two pilots of JG 27's 1.Staffel each claimed one Martin 167 shot down as a result of this engagement.

Ground-strafing operations were flown by six of 113 Squadron's fighter Blenheims to attack traffic on the Agedabia road, while four Beaufighters from 272 Squadron on their first ground-strafing attack in the frontal area, targetted Barce-Giorani-Berka road where 20 MT were claimed destroyed.

British Claims

1 SAAF Sqn	Capt M.S.Osler	Hurricane II	G.50	25m W LG.130 1610
	2/Lt J.T.Seccombe	Hurricane II	G.50	20-30m from LG.130 1610
21 SAAF Sqn	Maj Fowler	Maryland	Bf 109	

British Casualties

33 Sqn	Hurricane I 3980 shot down; Sgt R.B.Price KiA
	Hurricane I 4505 crash-landed; Flg Off Anderson slightly injured
113 Sqn	Blenheim IV destroyed on ground at Giarabub
Unspecified unit(s)	Hurricanes damaged on ground at Giarabub
21 SAAF	Maryland II AH403 'W' shot down; Lt F.H.Roulston and crew KiA
12 SAAF Sqn	Maryland II AH350 blew up on ground on return from sortie; six ground crew killed and two injured

German Claims

1./JG 27	Obfw Albert Espenlaub	Hurricane	0930
	Oblt Hugo Schneider	Martin 167	Marsa Luch
	Fw Günther Hillert	Martin 167	Marsa Luch

German Casualties

III./ZG 26	Bf 110E-2 3U+DS WNr 4413 crash-landed; Oblt Schulze-Dickow slt WiA, rescued
7./LG 1	Ju 88A-5 WNr 8277 35% damaged by fighters at Tobruk

Italian Claims

153° Gr CT Unspecified pilot(s)		Hurricane probable	Bir Khamsa 1545-

Italian Casualties

373ª Sq/153° Gr CT	MC.200 shot down; Serg Aldo Villa KiA
Unspecified unit	MC.200 destroyed on the ground at Gambut by bombs
	MC.200 damaged on the ground at Gambut by bombs

Sunday, 16 November 1941

Twelve Tomahawks of 2 SAAF Squadron were scrambled, eight patrolling over their own airfield as four searched for an approaching aircraft. A Bf 110 was spotted over Sidi Barrani and this was pursued, but at this point a Bf 109 attacked Lt Lacey's aircraft. This was driven off by Lt Coetzee, Lacey reporting that he had silenced the rear gunner in the 110, stopped one engine and set the other afire, the German aircraft last being seen spinning into clouds below. It is thought that this may have been a reconnaissance version of the Messerschmitt which was lost on a ferry flight from Martuba on the way to Germany, the crew of which were reported killed in an accident.

Nine Marylands attacked Gazala No 2 landing ground, crews reporting having set one aircraft on fire on the ground. Two fighters attempted to intercept, one being claimed to have crashed. Four Beaufighters were sent off to patrol over the seas between Derna and Crete. Here a single Ju 87 was spotted and attacked, being claimed damaged, but was lost in cloud. Three more of the squadron's aircraft strafed the Derna-Tmimi road, two Ju 87s being claimed destroyed on the ground at Tmimi, together with a mobile W/T post. Whilst engaged in this strafe, one Beaufighter struck a pole, but survived to return. The same target was also attacked by six Blenheims. Meanwhile 272 Squadron was bringing its aircraft forward to Gerawla for further such operations. On this date also, 265 Wing moved to LG.75.

British Claims

272 Sqn	Flg Off A.A.Salter	Beaufighter Ic 'H'			
	Plt Off H.H.Crawford	Beaufighter 'K'		Ju 87 damaged	25m from Derna 0800
	Plt Off J.Watters	Beaufighter 'B'			
	Sgt R.J.G.Demoulin	Beaufighter 'E'			
2 SAAF Sqn	Lt D.V.D.Lacey	Tomahawk		Bf 110	S Sidi Barrani 1315

German Casualties

2.(H)/14	Bf 110 crashed; Fw Herbert Flohr, Oblt Fritz Strassner and gunner lost on ferry flight

Monday, 17 November 1941

Recently a new specialist unit had been formed of commando-trained troops at the suggestion of Capt David Stirling, named Special Air Service (SAS). The initial intention behind the unit's formation was to drop small parties of troops by parachute deep behind Axis lines to undertake sabotage attacks on aircraft standing on airfields. Now the first such attack was to be attempted, a force of 55 men and seven officers moving from their base at Kabrit to Maaten Bagush to be transported on their sortie by five Bombays of 216 Squadron. This would be the first parachute drop in Middle East Command. Although warned by the RAF's meteorological service that weather conditions were likely to be far from ideal, Stirling decided that the raid would proceed, and consequently during the previous evening the Bombays took off to fly the commandos to the Gazala and Tmimi area. In the very bad weather prevailing, the drop went badly wrong; 46 men were dropped, but the containers of bombs, food etc could not be found and a number of personnel were injured. The raids had to be aborted. Arrangements had been made for each group to picked up at pre-agreed spots by the vehicles of the Long Range Desert Group (LRDG). In the event only four officers and 18 men got back, although included amongst them were Capt Stirling and his deputy, Lt Robert Blair 'Paddy' Mayne. They were transported to Siwa Oasis, the LRDG HQ, from where they were flown back to Kabrit by transport aircraft.

One Bombay, however, flown by Flt Sgt West and carrying aboard 16 men commanded by a Capt Thompson, had landed in the desert to await the dawn. At first light the crew found that they were only some half mile from Gazala airfield. An Italian soldier walked over to inspect the aircraft and was immediately captured and taken aboard, West then taking off. Two Bf 109s were seen to take off from Gazala, and two attacks were made before the Bombay crash-landed in some dunes, shot down by 4./JG 27's Obfw Otto Schulz. Thompson and his second-in-command, Lt Bonnington, were taken prisoner, along with those of their men who were not killed, and had a long conversation with the pilots of JG 27 in Hptmn Lippert's tent.

Thompson was then flown to the rear in a Fieseler Storch, but en route this force-landed due to lack of fuel. The pilot then went off on foot in search of aid, leaving the tough commando under the guard of the Fliegerführer Afrika meteorologist, who was also a passenger. Waiting until the pilot was out of sight, Thompson made short work of knocking out this unfortunate man, and then set off for the British lines. By very bad luck he walked straight into the crew of a Ju 52/3m who had also force-landed, and was recaptured. That evening he rejoined the meteorologist ('wetterfrosch') and had a drink with him in the Fliegerführer Afrika bar!

Meanwhile some of the troops from the other Bombays had been able to attack I./JG 27's dispersals, but were driven off. With daylight two Bf 109s from 2.Staffel took off, the pilots following the tyre tracks of some of the LRDG vehicles sent to pick the raiders up. These vehicles were claimed destroyed by the German fighters when they caught up with the remains of the raiding party.

Further movements preparatory to the offensive continued to take place during the day. 24 SAAF Squadron moved up to a forward base at LG.112 with its new Douglas Bostons for reconnaissance sorties, two aircraft going out at once to report on four Axis landing grounds and a concentration of tanks seen near Sidi Aziez. 260 Squadron moved to LG.124 at Fort Maddalena, while 73 Squadron at Gamil sent forward its battle flight composed of seven pilots and aircraft to operate in the forward area. By this time 30 Squadron and the RNFS had also advanced into the area, leaving just the Martlets of 805 Squadron's part of the RNFS for the defence of the Alexandria area. 30 Squadron was now ordered to carry out shipping protection patrols as well as its more specialized nocturnal defensive duties.

272 Squadron's Beaufighters were out again during the day, one trio strafing many vehicles as three more attacked an airfield at Gadd el Ahmar, claiming two S.79s damaged on the ground here.

British Claims

272 Sqn	Three unnamed pilots	2 S.79s	Damaged on ground at Gadd el Ahmar

British Casualties

216 Sqn	Bombay L58347 crash-landed; Flt Sgt West, crew, and 16 SAS officers and other personnel PoWs		

German Claims

4./JG 27	Obfw Otto Schulz	Bombay	NE Ain el Gazala 0710

After 17 months of war in the Western Desert, the Allied forces were about to carry out the biggest offensive operation so far. Not only was it the largest offensive in the Desert War, but indeed, the greatest to date by the British Commonwealth since the start of the war. Great hopes were pinned on this adventure, which if successful, would ease the pressure on Russia, still staggering under the initial Axis blows, raise the siege of Malta, and give Britain back control of the Mediterranean.

As 8th Army's XIII and XXX Corps prepared to launch the new offensive, the Axis forces remained substantially unaware. Rommel was in Greece, but was about to return to supervise the final preparations for the attack on Tobruk which was due to commence only five days hence. Air reconnaissance by the Luftwaffe, however, had become impossible, for on 16 November the weather over the Jebel Akhdar area of Cyrenaica had deteriorated to an extraordinary degree, violent rainstorms turning every Axis airfield into a sea of clinging mud. It presaged what was probably the worst winter conditions in living memory. These conditions, of course, extended eastwards, soaking the troops waiting to launch Crusader, but to the great advantage of Desert Air Force, these conditions reached only so far as a point about midway between Sollum and Sidi Barrani. Hence, unknown to their opponents, the British squadrons faced no similar constraint upon their initial operations.

On this occasion the weather could even be a deadly enemy for the Axis. An Ultra intercept noted a report that one man of I./St G 1 and four men of a signals detachment at Tmimi, had been drowned in flash floods!

The final pre-Crusader sorties involved an escort to Blenheims attacking Bir el Baheira, by Tomahawks of 3 RAAF and 112 Squadrons, followed by a strafing attack on this target by Hurricanes of the RNFS. At this time, however, the Luftwaffe had received more of the excellent Bf 109Fs when 1.Staffel returned from Germany re-equipped. III./ZG 26 now re-assembled as a full gruppe at Derna, 7.Staffel from Sicily and 9.Staffel from Crete joining 8.Staffel there. However, when the Axis forces began to withdraw from the area some days later, two of these staffeln went over to Crete again to escort Ju 52/3ms flying in supplies.

THE BATTLE BEGINS

Tuesday, 18 November 1941

Following fierce electrical storms during the night to the north and west of the RAF's airfields, the opening of the great offensive commenced in the face of only the most limited Axis resistance in the air. 3 SAAF Wing sent off 17 Marylands to attack Tmimi and Gazala, but the driving rain and 10/10th cloud cover which was experienced in the Tmimi area ensured that 12 SAAF Squadron could not find the target. At Gazala at 0915 nine 21 SAAF Squadron aircraft found eight Axis fighters up and waiting for them. The crews jettisoned their bombs and sought cloud cover. However, Lt Reid's aircraft was shot down in flames. By now the bombers were down to 1,000 ft, and in another Maryland Air Sgt M.Jack fired on one Bf 109F, claiming that it spun into the ground, trailing smoke. A second bomber was damaged, crash-landing at Sidi Barrani in a recoverable condition. Two Martin 167s were claimed by Hptmn Redlich and Obfw Espenlaub of 1./JG 27, though two Italian pilots of 155° Gruppo CT claimed to have shared with the German pilots in the destruction of one of these.

Western Desert Air Force fighter commanders consult with the AOC in the shadow of a typical command caravan. Left to right: Grp Capt Guy Carter, Air Vice-Marshal Arthur Coningham, Wg Cdr F.E.Rosier and Wg Cdrs T.B.de la P.Beresford, H.C.Mayers and H.A.Fenton (the latter sitting in the doorway).

About an hour behind the Marylands, Blenheims raided Bir el Baheira airfield (LG.140), attacking 12 aircraft on the ground here. From this attack Plt Off Loughlin's aircraft failed to return, all members of the crew being killed.

Later in the day 11 Blenheims and six Marylands, this time escorted by two squadrons of Tomahawks, bombed some 200-300 armoured vehicles and supporting motor transport bogged in at Bir el Gubi. At midday the Beaufighters of 272 Squadron were despatched in two flights, one of six aircraft and one of three, to attack Axis airfields. These aircraft achieved the greatest success of the day, involving the first confirmed claims for aircraft destroyed in the air for this unit. At 1415 the formation of six swept in over Tmimi airfield just as five Ju 52/3m transports had taken off, all of which were claimed shot down, to which Flg Off Salter then added a claim for an Hs 126. Aircraft on the ground were then strafed, four S.79s being claimed (Italian records show that two S.79s were actually damaged during this attack); a Fi 156 was also claimed, and it appears that this may have been shot down by Flg Off Bartlett, rather than being destroyed on the ground. During their return flight, the pilots strafed Gadd el Ahmar airfield again, firing on ten Italian soldiers there. As the Beaufighters left the area a Bf 109F gave chase, but Bartlett opened up his engines, reaching a speed of 260 knots and leaving the fighter behind; all six landed safely.

At much the same time, the other three Beaufighter crews headed for Barce, but as they approached this airfield they encountered two more Ju 52/3ms, claiming both shot down in flames. Transport vehicles were then seen on the road east from Barce and were attacked, following which a pass was made over the airfield, a large number of tents being fired on. Again, all aircraft returned safely. Aside from these important operations, the squadron continued to send out pairs of aircraft on convoy escort sorties along the coast.

During the day five offensive sweeps were made by a total of 11 squadrons of Hurricanes and Tomahawks, but in no case were any opposing aircraft seen.

Bristol Beaufighters had been operating as long-range coastal fighters over the Mediterranean for some months. In November 1941, however, they moved forward to support Operation Crusader with a number of low-flying strikes on Axis airfields and concentrations. These heavily-armed aircraft proved admirably suited for this task.

An Axis convoy on the coastal highway in western Cyrenaica being strafed by Beaufighters.

While these activities had been occurring to the north, from Giarabub 33 Squadron undertook its first long-range strafing attack on the Italian airfield at Gialo (identified by the RAF pilots as El Eng). Recorded Plt Off Lance Wade: "Strassing (sic)was a success but we were attacked by CR.42s. I shot down two, other fellows got one in the air and several on the ground." Air HQ concurred with this claim, crediting the squadron with three shot down at Gialo (220 miles south-east of Benghazi), plus one CR.42 and one Caproni Ghibli destroyed on the ground at Gasr el Shabi (60 miles south-east of Agedabia). Regia Aeronautica records show that two CR.42s engaged the Hurricanes over Gialo, but both were shot down, one pilot being killed and one wounded. The latter, Serg Magg Tarantini, claimed to have damaged one of the attackers; a third CR.42 was damaged on the ground.

British Claims

33 Sqn	Plt Off L.C.Wade	Hurricane I Z4360	2 CR.42s	El Eng (Gialo) airfield
	Squadron victory	Hurricane Is	CR.42	El Eng (Gialo) airfield
272 Sqn	Plt Off J. Watters	Beaufighter Ic 'R'		
	Plt Off W.G.Snow	Beaufighter Ic'J'		
	Flg Off A.A.Salter	Beaufighter Ic'H'	5 Ju 52/3ms	Tmimi airfield 1415
	Plt Off K.B. Orr	Beaufighter Ic'A'		
	Sgt R.J.G.Demoulin	Beaufighter Ic'E'		
	Flg Off M.L.P.Bartlett	Beaufighter Ic 'B'		
	Flg Off A.A.Salter	Beaufighter Ic'H'	Hs 126	Tmimi 1415+
	Flg Off M.L.P.Bartlett	Beaufighter Ic 'B'		
	Plt Off W.G.Snow	Beaufighter Ic 'J'	4 S.79s	on ground Tmimi
	Sgt R.J.G.Demoulin	Beaufighter Ic		
	Flg Off M.L.P.Bartlett	Beaufighter Ic'B'	Fi 156	on return flight from Tmimi 1415
	Sgt J.S.Ross	Beaufighter Ic'N'		
	Plt Off N.K.Lee	Beaufighter Ic'V'	2 Ju 52/3ms	S. Barce 1220
	Plt Off H.H.Crawford	Beaufighter Ic'K'		

British Casualties

21 SAAF Sqn	Maryland II AH396 'U' shot down; Lt H.D.Reid and crew KiA
	Maryland II damaged and crash-landed
14 Sqn	Blenheim IV Z9543 MiA; Plt Off C.D.Loughlin and crew KiA

German Claims

1./JG 27	Hpt Wolfgang Redlich	Martin 167	S Ain el Gazala 0930
	Obfw Albert Espenlaub	Martin 167	E Bir Hacheim

Italian Claims

393ª Sq/160° Gr CT	Serg Magg Luciano Tarantini	Hurricane Damaged	Gialo
155° Gr CT	Two unspecified pilots	Bomber shared with German fighters	Gazala

Italian Casualties

393ª Sq/160° Gr CT	CR.42 MM7756 shot down over Gialo airfield; Serg Alberto Gardelli KiA
	CR.42 MM7551 shot down over Gialo airfield; Serg Magg Luciano Tarantini WiA
	CR.42 MM7554 damaged on ground
Unspecified unit	2 S.79s damaged on ground at Tmimi

Wednesday, 19 November 1941

With little Axis reaction on the ground since Rommel was still insisting that no British offensive was underway, little was achieved. By early afternoon XXX Corps armour had reached a position east of Sidi Rezegh. 7th Armoured Division moved onto Sidi Rezegh airfield from which Axis aircraft were still taking off, capturing 16 G.50bis and a Ca.133 of 20° Gruppo CT on the ground there. By the time darkness fell, 7th Armoured was only about 15 miles from the Tobruk perimeter, and established on the Sidi Rezegh escarpment.

25 miles to the south, 22nd Armoured Brigade had attempted to unseat the Ariete Armoured Division in the Bir el Gubi area, but had been seen off with the loss of 25 tanks destroyed and 45 more damaged. The Italians had been well dug-in and had fought with considerable resolution. This had been helped by the lack of infantry to support the British tanks, which also had little artillery support.

4th Armoured Brigade pursued various targets – both real and non-existent – the day ending with

XXX Corps' armour spread widely across the desert, without any of the concentration which would have been so desirable. To the north XIII Corps continued its movement up the coast towards Halfaya, where the garrison had been bombarded during the night by HMS *Euryalis* and *Naiad*.

In a day of stormy weather, low cloud and occasional rain showers, the Axis air forces were again unable to operate more than a handful of their fighters. Taking full advantage of this situation, 272 Squadron Beaufighters were off again at 0640, arriving over Tmimi two hours later where four crews found a number of Ju 87s and some Bf 109s on the ground. Flg Off Morris and Sgt Price went in first, shooting up a number of aircraft, each leaving two Ju 87s burning, to which Price added two Bf 109s, 'blazing furiously'. He then fired on a number of tents. The other three then made their attack, Flt Lt Campbell shooting up a Ju 87. At this stage Flak was experienced and Campbell's aircraft was hit, causing him to return on one engine. Sgt Haylock's aircraft was also hit and quite badly damaged, while he was wounded in the foot. In order to ensure early medical attention, he flew all the way back to Edcu, where he belly-landed his aircraft. In the event his wound proved not to be too bad. The others all landed safely at LG.10 at 1145. Three of the pilots were able to claim five dive-bombers and two fighters destroyed before making good their escape.

The medium bombers were out in force as were the fighters of 262 Wing which undertook 11 sweeps over the XXX Corps tanks during the day. On one such operation 24 Tomahawks – apparently from 2 and 4 SAAF Squadrons – reported attacks on 15 Italian fighters on Sidi Rezegh airfield, claiming two destroyed and three damaged; these were probably counted amongst those captured when 7th Armoured Brigade subsequently overran the field, as already recounted.

Six 45 Squadron Blenheims took off at 1120 to bomb targets in the battle area. Here Plt Off Hughes' aircraft was hit by Flak, causing him to crash-land in the middle of an armoured engagement near Sidi Omar. The crew safely reached British lines and were returned to their unit two days later. Of Plt Off Magor's aircraft there was no sign; he had fallen foul of one of the few Luftwaffe fighters to get into the air, the Blenheim being claimed shot down at 1250 by Uffz Reuter.

During the day 451 Squadron with the attached aircraft and pilots from 40 SAAF Squadron, moved forward to LG.132, located 20 miles north of Maddalena and a similar distance south of Bir Sheferzen, to operate in support of XIII Corps. II./JG 27 had again managed to get some Bf 109s into the air, and reportedly eight of these strafed the Tac R Hurricanes on the ground. Air HQ reported that two of the latter were destroyed, but other sources list three as being damaged; it seems that all but one of the aircraft there were hit to some extent.

Tomahawks of 3 RAAF Squadron were on their way to undertake a sweep at this time, when the aircraft flown by Flg Off Fischer developed a problem with its oil supply. He broke away to return to LG.110, but whilst on the way there, he spotted four of the Messerschmitts strafing LG.132, and at once attacked, claiming to have shot one down. The others turned on him, Uffz Reuter inflicting damage on his aircraft which obliged him to crash-land south of Sidi Omar. Fischer, slightly wounded, got out of his Tomahawk whereupon Reuter proceeded to strafe and destroy it. II./JG 27 did not, in fact, record the loss of one of its aircraft during this operation.

During the afternoon 3 SAAF Wing despatched 12 Blenheims from 11 Squadron, nine Marylands from 12 SAAF Squadron and eight from 21 SAAF Squadron to attack a big force of transports on the Bardia-Tobruk road. These were noted to be moving west, giving the impression of a withdrawal by the Axis forces. Considerable Flak was encountered and one Maryland was hit, being seen to spin down towards the coast. Lt Braithwaite and one member of his crew were killed, the other two surviving to become PoWs.

Later in the day 451 Squadron's Lt W.Andrew was flying cover for another of the unit's aircraft undertaking a reconnaissance, when he was forced down at dusk, apparently by an unidentified German aircraft. He began walking back, arriving after two days and nights.

Far to the south at Giarabub, one of 113 Squadron's fighter Blenheims was lost during the day when it crashed on take-off without apparent reason, the crew of three all being killed. From here during the day 33 Squadron began to move its aircraft and equipment to LG.125.

During the day a flight from 237 Squadron moved up to reinforce 451/40 SAAF Squadron after that unit's recent losses, while 1 SAAF Squadron transferred to LG.124 at Fort Maddalena. At Derna three Cant.Z.1007bis reconnaissance-bombers of 176ª Squadriglia RST arrived from Italy to undertake strategic reconnaissance sorties. Towards the end of the day II./JG 27's Oblt Rödel, engaged on a reconnaissance sortie, spotting a strong British armoured car column advancing from a southerly direction 60 miles from Tobruk. At first he was not believed, so Edu Neumann took off and found the column. He set his stop-watch and flew along the length of the column for nearly ten minutes.

British Claims				
272 Sqn	Flt Lt G.L.Campbell	Beaufighter Ic 'U'	Ju 87	on ground Tmimi 0840
	Flg Off G.W.Morris	Beaufighter Ic 'R'	2 Ju 87s	on ground Tmimi 0840
	Sgt N.A.J.Price	Beaufighter Ic 'J'	2 Ju 87s	on ground Tmimi 0840
	Sgt N.A.J.Price	Beaufighter Ic 'J'	2 Bf 109	on ground Tmimi 0840"
3 RAAF Sqn	Flg Off F.Fischer	Tomahawk AK407	Bf 109F	20m N Maddalena 1420*

*When compiling a list of their claims in September 1942, 3 RAAF Squadron originally listed four victories on this date. It was subsequently realised during the 1990s that three of these were credited to Flt Lt Pelly and Flg Off Boyd, who were no longer with the unit; these were therefore an incorrect repeat of the claims made a year earlier on 19 November 1940. This difficulty was due to the original records having been burnt early in 1941 when a brew-up for tea went awry, causing the operations truck carrying the records to be burnt out.

British Casualties	
272 Sqn	Beaufighter Ic 'U' damaged by Flak; Flt Lt G.L.Campbell safe
	Beaufighter Ic 'Q' damaged by Flak and crash-landed at base; Sgt Haylock WiA
3 RAAF Sqn	Tomahawk AK407 crash-landed; Flg Off F.Fischer slt WiA
45 Sqn	Blenheim IV Z7510 'C' shot down; Plt Off E.A.Magor and crew KiA
	Blenheim IV V5943 shot down by Flak, crash-landed; Sqn Ldr A.Hughes and crew safe, returned 21st
12 SAAF Sqn	Maryland II AX319 shot down by Flak; Lt T.L.Braithwaite and one KiA; two PoW
113 Sqn	Blenheim IVf V5866 crashed on take-off; Sgt J.F.Hemus and crew KiFA
451 Sqn	Hurricane I shot down; Lt W.Andrew returned on foot two days later

German Claims			
5./JG 27	Uffz Horst Reuter	Blenheim	5m SW Gasr el Ahrid 1250
	Uffz Horst Reuter	P-40	S Sidi Omar 1415

Italian Casualties	
20°Gr CT	16 G.50s destroyed on ground at Sidi Rezegh
	Ca. 133 destroyed on ground at Sidi Rezegh

Thursday, 20 November 1941

Realising the threat to the proposed offensive on Tobruk posed by the arrival of British armour in the forward area, the Afrika Korps began to respond on this date, initial actions giving the British command the mistaken impression that things were going well. In fact, confusion was multiplying rapidly, and decisions were taken to depart from the original Crusader plan with near-catastrophic results.

In the air activity now increased significantly as the Axis air forces were able to get into the air in greater numbers. At 0620 ten Tomahawks of 112 Squadron and ten of 3 RAAF Squadron, led by Wg Cdr P.Jeffrey, took off on an offensive sweep. Between El Adem and Acroma five or six Bf 110s were seen and were attacked at once. Between them, the Tomahawk pilots claimed four shot down, two probably so and one damaged. However, 112 Squadron's Plt Off Jeffries' aircraft was hit and badly damaged after he had claimed one of the probables; 3 RAAF's Flg Off Bobby Gibbes' aircraft was also hit, although he managed to get back to base before crash-landing. 8./ZG 26 lost three aircraft, but only one member of each crew was wounded – basically a lucky day for the unit, despite the equipment losses.

At 1100 12 more Tomahawks, this time from 250 Squadron, took off to provide cover to 11 Hurricanes of the RNFS on a sweep over the Gambut-El Adem area. Five miles south of Bir el Gubi at 1210, a dozen Ju 87s of I./StG 1 were spotted, covered by 15 JG 27 Bf 109s. Both British squadrons attacked the Stukas at once; Sub Lt P.N.Charlton ('Fearless Freddie' to his compatriots) claimed to have shot down three, then seeing a Tomahawk which had just attacked a Ju 87, now firing at his aircraft. Hit by this, he had to crash-land at once. Sgt Whittle of 250 Squadron also claimed three Ju 87s, while other pilots of the combined formation added five more as probables and one damaged, with Sgt Nitschke claiming two more Ju 87s and Flt Lt Bary a Bf 109.

The Messerschmitts had immediately come to the defence of their charges, two Tomahawks being shot down with the loss of one pilot, and two more damaged, both crash-landing. Despite these losses only two claims were submitted by 1./JG 27, while the only losses recorded by the Germans were those of two Ju 87s, the crews of both of which were killed.

Even as this fight was coming to a close, a disaster was about to occur. During the morning 12 SAAF Squadron had been ordered off to bomb 50 tanks and motor vehicles near Gabr Saleh. The formation

An RNFS Hurricane showing similar white-painted code OL and a darker individual letter, as illustrated in the crash-landed example on page 320.

took off later, received no signals, and the raid was called off. 3 SAAF Wing was then ordered to attack a similar target 40 miles west of Gabr Saleh on the road which by-passed Tobruk. This raid was to follow an assault launched 30 minutes earlier by 21 Blenheims and Marylands. This first strike was covered by the Tomahawks of the two South African squadrons, and returned unscathed.

Now nine unescorted Marylands of 21 SAAF Squadron flew into the area to encounter the I./JG 27 Bf 109s which attacked the rear sub flight, the bomber crews later reporting being "raked from front to stern by a withering hail of cannon and machine-gun fire". The middle bomber, flown by Lt E.S.Corbett, went down with a wing on fire, all the crew being killed; it was believed by those in other aircraft that the gunners had managed to shoot down one Messerschmitt as they fell, but this was not the case. The middle flight was then attacked, Capt J.H.Eccles' aircraft going down; he was the only survivor. The attack then shifted to the leading flight, Lt R.S.Haines' aircraft falling and being seen to crash. At this stage the remaining six aircraft were still holding together and firing back, a second Bf 109 being claimed in flames at this stage. By now the Marylands were fleeing at zero feet as the Messerschmitts kept after them, bringing down the aircraft of the formation leader, Maj R.J.Stewart. Finally the "yellow-nosed demon" as Lt MacDonald referred to his attacker, poured a "hellish raking fire" into that pilot's bomber, pursuing him for 60 miles. Air Sgt du Pre, his guns jammed, managed to save Air Sgt Russell, who had been badly wounded in both legs, from falling out of an open hatch, and bound up his wounds. MacDonald, who with du Pre would be recommended for an immediate gallantry award, finally got his badly shot-up aircraft back to base, although the Maryland was a complete write-off.

Air Sgt Thompson-Brundidge, an American top turret gunner attached to the unit and in one of the surviving aircraft, claimed to have shot down a third Messerschmitt, and reported subsequently that the leader of the yellow-nosed 109s was definitely a master pilot, and confirmed that he was responsible for at least three of the bombers destroyed. Although four Marylands had been shot down and a fifth significantly damaged, the only claims submitted by JG 27 were for three of the bombers destroyed by

Lt Hans-Arnold Stahlschmidt; as so often, despite the SAAF crews' claims, none of the Bf 109s were lost or badly damaged. Lt Michael MacDonald was subsequently awarded a DFC, but du Pre remained undecorated.

Five of 272 Squadron's Beaufighters again managed to catch the Luftwaffe unawares at Tmimi during the early afternoon. Having received intelligence information that more German aircraft were at this airfield, the Beaufighters took off at 1145, arriving over the target area at 1355. Three aircraft attacked in line abreast, followed by the other two in line astern, making four passes. 14 Ju 87s were claimed destroyed on the ground during these attacks, together with a lone Bf 109. A fuel dump was also reported to have been destroyed, the fire from this being seen from 30 miles away. The aircraft flown by Plt Off Snow was hit in the port wing, the aileron control being damaged, but again all the aircraft returned to LG.10 at 1510.

Six of 80 Squadron's newly-converted Hurricane fighter-bombers escorted by two fighters, flew the unit's first sorties over the desert since 1940, attacking vehicles on the road north of Bir el Baheira. A dozen Hurricane IIs of 1 SAAF Squadron targetted camps and vehicles in the Marsa Luch-Bir Micail area, but in the face of heavy ground fire 2/Lt Currin was shot down, becoming a PoW, while Lt Kershaw force-landed his damaged aircraft at LG.132.

At 1445 Blenheims of 11 Squadron took off, tasked to bomb aircraft and MT. Two Ju 52/3m transports were claimed destroyed on the ground at Gasr El Ahrid, but two Blenheims were hard hit by Flak, one returning damaged beyond repair; the second crash-landed on return to LG.75 with a wounded gunner aboard.

From Giarabub, 33 Squadron sent six long-range Hurricanes to strafe 30 aircraft on Benina airfield, including 'tropicalised gliders'. Claims were made for four aircraft destroyed and at least eight damaged. Flg Off Jewell landed on an enemy airfield due to lack of fuel, but Sgt Stammers failed to return, although

Sergeant pilots of 250 Squadron who did very well during the opening days of Crusader. Left to right: Bob Whittle, Maurice Hards and R.H. 'Slinger' Nitschke. Whittle and Nitschke were each credited with shooting down three Ju 87s on 21 November, while Hards claimed two Bf 109s, plus one probable and two damaged on the 23rd.

he reached the squadron, unhurt, later. In the event none of the Hurricanes involved made it back to LG.125, though most flew in next day from other locations. Nonetheless, this attack may have been one of the most successful on this costly day, III./LG 1 reporting the loss of three Ju 88s due to strafing fighters at Benina, with three more damaged. An Ultra intercept regarding this attack, noted that initially it had been reported as involving six Hurricanes at 1320. A further intercepted report refined this to five Hurricanes at 1319; this also mentioned that a Ju 52/3m was also shot-up and three men wounded, while Flak gunners claimed one Hurricane probably shot down.

During the day a single claim was submitted by Uffz Niederhöfer of 5./JG 27 for a Hurricane shot down south of El Adem, but this was not confirmed and was treated as a probable. Eight MC.200s of 153° Gruppo and three G.50bis of 155° Gruppo took off at 1650 to strafe British forces in the Bir el Gubi area. One of the latter, flown by Serg Italo Abrami of 378ª Squadriglia, was hit by AA fire and crash-landed, the aircraft being abandoned.

On the ground 15th and 21st Panzer Divisions disengaged and pushed north to Sidi Rezegh, where only 7th Armoured Brigade and 7th Support Group were situated. The Afrika Korps put in an immediate attack, but the out-numbered British managed to hold on until 22nd Armoured Brigade arrived just before dark.

Tac R squadrons flew many sorties for the army during one of which Plt Off Lomas of 208 Squadron crash-landed after his Hurricane had been hit by Flak. The Tobruk garrison was ordered to break out on the following day, and with this in prospect, 451 Squadron sent a detachment of four Hurricanes to operate from within the perimeter. 4 SAAF Squadron during the day, moved their Tomahawks to LG.122. This had been a costly and rather unsatisfactory day for the RAF, substantial losses not being matched by Axis attrition which had been generally considerably over-estimated.

British Claims

Sqn	Pilot	Aircraft	Claim	Location/Time
112 Sqn	Flg Off J.F.Soden	Tomahawk AN242	Bf 110 damaged	Sidi Rezegh 0630-0800
	Plt Off R.J.Jeffries	Tomahawk AN410	Bf 110 probable	Sidi Rezegh 0630-0800
	Plt Off N.Bowker	Tomahawk AN415	}	
	Sgt A.H.Christie	Tomahawk AK503	} Bf 110	Sidi Rezegh 0630-0800
	Sgt R.M.Leu	Tomahawk AK509	}	
	Plt Off N.Bowker	Tomahawk AN415	Bf 110 probable	Sidi Rezegh 0630-0800
	Sgt K.F.Carson	Tomahawk AN303	Bf 110	Sidi Rezegh 0630-0800"
258 Wg	Wg Cdr P.Jeffrey	Tomahawk AN224	}	
3 RAAF Sqn	Flg Off R.H.Gibbes	Tomahawk AN465	} Bf 110	El Adem-Acroma 0720
	Flt Lt L.E.S.Knowles	Tomahawk AN410	}	
	Flt Lt J.G.Manford	Tomahawk AK390	}	
3 RAAF Sqn	Sgt R.H.Simes	Tomahawk AM507	Bf 110	20m S Tobruk 0730
250 Sqn	Flt Lt R.E.Bary	Tomahawk	Ju 87 probable	S Bir el Gubi 1210
	Flt Lt R.E.Bary	Tomahawk	Bf 109	
	Sgt R.H.Nitschke	Tomahawk	2 Ju 87s	
	Sgt R.H.Nitschke	Tomahawk	Bf 109 damaged	
	Sgt R.J.C.Whittle	Tomahawk AM313	3 Ju 87s	
	Sgt R.J.C.Whittle	Tomahawk AM313	Ju 87 damaged	
	Unspecified pilots	Tomahawk	2 Ju 87s probable	
RNFS	Sub Lt P.N.Charlton	Hurricane I W9327 'M'	3 Ju 87s	S Bir el Gubi
	Sub Lt P.N.Charlton	Hurricane I W9327	Ju 87 probable	
	Sub Lt R.L.Johnston	Hurricane I	Ju 87 probable	El Adem 1215
272 Sqn	Flg Off A.A.Salter	Beaufighter Ic 'H'	}	
	Plt Off W.G.Snow	Beaufighter 'J'	}	
	Plt Off K.B.Orr	Beaufighter 'A'	} 14 Ju 87s	on ground Tmimi 1355
	Plt Off D.H.Hammond	Beaufighter 'B'	} Bf 109	on ground Tmimi 1355
	Sgt R.J.G.Demoulin	Beaufighter 'E'	}	
21 SAAF Sqn	Maryland gunners		Bf 109s	
11 Sqn	Blenheim gunners		2 Ju 52/3ms	on ground

British Casualties

12 Sqn	Tomahawk badly damaged; Plt Off R.J.O.Jeffries unhurt
RAAF Sqn	Tomahawk damaged, crash-landed at base; Flg Of R.H.Gibbes unhurt
250 Sqn	Tomahawk shot down; Plt Off W.W.Swinnerton unhurt
	Tomahawk down; Plt Off R.S.Masters KiA
	Tomahawk badly damaged, crash-landed at base; Flt Lt Rose unhurt
	Tomahawk; Sgt R.H.Nitschke unhurt
NFS	Hurricane I crash-landed; Sub Lt P.N.Charlton unhurt
SAAF Sqn	Hurricane II shot down by Flak; 2/Lt H.P.Currin PoW
	Hurricane II damaged, force-landed at base; Lt R.H.C.Kershaw safe
3 Sqn	Hurricane I MiA; Flg Off Jewell
	Hurricane I 7561 FTR; Sgt Stammers returned later unhurt
208 Sqn	Hurricane I shot down by ground fire, crash-landed; Plt Off F.L.Lomas safe
1 Sqn	Blenheim IV V6268 damaged beyond repair by Flak; Plt Off P.F.Smith and crew safe
	Blenheim IV Z5866 badly damaged; crash-landed on return. Plt Off J.L.Loam and one safe; one gunner WiA
21 SAAF Sqn	Maryland II AH302 'V' shot down; Lt R.S.Haines and crew KiA
	Maryland II AH305 'E' shot down; Lt E.S.Corbett and crew KiA
	Maryland II AH387 badly damaged; Lt M.C.E.MacDonald and two unhurt, one WiA
	Maryland II AH407 'M' shot down; Maj R.J.Stewart and two KiA, Lt D.Duffus, DFC, PoW
	Maryland II AH409 'X' shot down; pilot, Capt J.H.Eccles baled out and PoW; three KiA

German Claims

./JG 27	Hptmn Wolfgang Redlich	P-40	Bir el Gubi 1215
	Obfw Albert Espenlaub	P-40	S Bir el Gubi 1220
Stab I./JG 27	Lt Hans-Arnold Stahlschmidt	3 Martin 167s	S Tobruk 1220-1230
./JG 27	Uffz Hans Niederhöfer	Hurricane n.b.	S El Adem

German Casualties (Note: Ultra provided all the details regarding St G 1 and 8 ZG 26 losses.)

./StG 1	Ju 87 R-2 trop WNr 6072 shot down 60m S Tobruk by fighters; Lt Jochen Hiddessen/Gefr Franz Schaffranek KiA
./StG 2	Ju 87 shot down S Bir el Gubi; Uffz Friedrich Figge/Gefr Alfred Heinse KiA
./ZG 26	Bf 110E-2N WNr 4005 shot down on armed recce south of El Adem, by fighters 100% loss
	Fw Werner Ludwig slightly wounded
	Bf 110 E-1N WNr 3457 shot down on armed recce south of El Adem, by fighters. 100% loss, damaged;
	gunner Ogfr Rolf Shön WiA
	Bf 110E-1N Trop WNr 3879 shot down on armed recce south of El Adem, by fighters 100% loss; Ogfr Martin Graf WiA
	Bf 110-E-1N WNr 4009 shot down on armed reconnaisance S El Adem by fighters, 100% loss; crew safe
(H)./14	Bf 110E-3 WNr 2370 missing on ferry flight; Oblt Strassner and crew MIA
I./LG 1	3 Ju 88A-5s WNr 2322, 8223 and 8224 destroyed at Benina in fighter strafe
	3 Ju 88A-5s WNr 3347, 4339 and 5275 75% damaged at Benina in fighter strafe

Italian Casualties

78ª Sq/155° Gr CT	G.50 MM6025 hit by AA, crash-landed at Bir el Gubi and abandoned; Serg Italo Abrami safe

Friday, 21 November 1941

During the night Rommel had finally accepted that 7th Armoured Division was about to break through to the Tobruk garrison at just the point where he had intended to launch his own offensive. At once he ordered a counter-attack on Sidi Rezegh which by evening would bring XXX Corps' advance to a halt.

Meanwhile to the east XIII Corps had sent the New Zealand Division swinging north from the frontier wire at Bir Sheferzen, to outflank the Italo-German forces at Sidi Omar and Halfaya.

Prior to the launch of Crusader, 109 Squadron had been formed hastily with six Wellingtons for the special task of jamming the radios in German tanks (despite a squadron of this number already existing in the United Kingdom at this time). For this role the Wellingtons had been fitted with a three-inch diameter tube, seven feet long, which was lowered beneath the fuselage in flight. The unit had been ready since the end of October and had undertaken its first sorties on the preceding day. During the 21st the unit operated in the Fort Capuzzo area in support of the New Zealanders, but when they had been in the air for some time, two were attacked by JG 27 Bf 109s, one being claimed shot down by Lt Hans Remmer of 1.Staffel east of Sidi Omar at 0950, and one by Obfw Otto Schulz of 4.Staffel five minutes later south-west of El Adem. One Wellington was actually lost, a second being damaged beyond repair. Of those aboard the

Carrying the name 'Kiwi' beneath the cockpit, Hurricane I Z4932 was an aircraft of the Royal Naval Fighter Squadron. Although photographed by German personnel, it seems later to have been recovered, repaired and put back into service. Despite the fuselage side panel having been removed, the top of the white-painted unit code OL can be made out. The individual aircraft letter B has been added in a much darker colour.

missing aircraft, Flt Sgt Wolf, the pilot, and four members of the crew were killed, as was Lt Co R.P.G.Denman, a senior war office radio counter-measures expert, who was aboard; only one man survived

For the fourth day in succession 272 Squadron sent Beaufighters to attack Tmimi. Taking off at 1000 the four aircraft involved spotted an airfield at 1155 which was believed to be Martuba Satellite. Here three Ju 87s, a Ju 88 and a high wing monoplane (possibly an Hs 126) were shot-up. Six lorries were then seen on a road to the north and were also strafed, some being left in flames. A Ju 87 was then observed in the air to the north of the airfield, and was targetted by Flg Off Bartlett and Sgt Price, who both claimed hit on it. During the return flight Plt Off Watters was pursued by two Bf 109s which made six attacks on the Beaufighter, but aided by his observer who gave warning as each Messerschmitt approached to attack, he evaded their fire, his aircraft suffering only slight damage. Meanwhile, Sgt Price inadvertently flew over a big concentration of troops and tanks, being fired on very heavily. With his observer, Sgt Hobbis, wounded in the thigh and with 24 holes in his aircraft, he got back to base. Here it transpired that one of the undercarriage tyres had been hit and this caused the Beaufighter to swing violently on landing.

During the day eight Western Desert Air Force fighter squadrons carried out frequent sweeps over the battle area. The Hurricane squadrons were particularly heavily committed, flying many sorties. At 1030 12 of 229 Squadron's aircraft swept over the Sidi Rezegh area, meeting only a single Bf 109, and that without result. Sgt Boyde's aircraft was seen to be hit by Flak and he did not return. In the early afternoon the unit suffered a further casualty to the ground defences, on this occasion Plt Off Russell being forced down at Tobruk. 80 Squadron Hurricanes were sent to escort Blenheims, but lost their commanding officer when Sqn Ldr T.M.Horgan, DFC's aircraft was also hit by Flak, causing him to crash-land seriously injured.

During the early afternoon Tomahawks from 112 Squadron patrolled near El Adem, two CR.42s of 376ª Squadriglia Aut CT being encountered at a height of 500 feet as the British fighters were returning to their base. One was at once shot down by Sgt Leu and the other was despatched after a chase by three of the unit's pilots. Recorded one of these, Plt Off Neville Duke:

Lt Eric Saville's first encounter with enemy aircraft occurred on 21 November when he collided with a Macchi C.200. He discusses the damaged wingtip of his 2 SAAF Squadron Tomahawk, TA-C, AN311, with US war correspondent Quentin Reynolds. For Saville it was the start of an illustrious career as a fighter pilot.

"Encountered two Fiat CR.42s south of El Adem. Attacked same with Plt Off 'Butch' Jefferies and Sgt Carson. Did three attacks on one which was flying at about 500 ft. He did a few turns and then went in to land. Turned over, after running a few yards, onto its back and the pilot was out like a shot. Butch and Cameron started to shoot the poor devil up but I couldn't do it, so I set the machine on fire.

"I went down to look at the pilot who was running with his hands up. His face was full of fear and the next time I saw him he was lying on the ground. There was no need to murder the poor devil as our troops were coming up, and as we came back from patrol we came over the crash and the army had his parachute in pieces."

The Italian pilot had not, in fact, been hit and survived to be taken PoW.

On an earlier patrol a Bf 109E was claimed damaged by Plt Off Cole of 250 Squadron, while at much the same time 5./JG 27's Obfw Woidich claimed a P-40 south of Gazala. Neither unit recorded any loss or damage. Lt J.A.Smith of 40 SAAF Squadron, attached to 451 Squadron, was shot down in flames by Flak three miles short of the unit's airfield whilst engaged on a Tac R sortie for XIII Corps in the Sidi Omar area.

It was to this area that Free French Blenheims were sent to attack a target near Menastir in response to a call from the New Zealanders. The bombers were escorted by ten Tomahawks of 4 SAAF Squadron, which themselves had a top cover of 12 more such fighters of 2 SAAF Squadron. The pilots of the latter unit encountered three MC.200s of 153° Gruppo CT on a reconnaissance, the Italian pilots identifying the South African formation as Hurricanes. Lt Stone at once shot down the aircraft of the squadriglia commander, Cap Pietro Raimondi, who became a PoW. Meanwhile Lt Saville passed another so closely that in breaking off his attack, his starboard wingtip caught the Macchi's fuselage, close to the cockpit, sending the Tomahawk spinning round in a 90 degree turn. The result of this collision to the Italian aircraft was not observed, but Saville returned with several feet of the wingtip bent at a right angle, and was credited with having damaged his opponent. Lt Hinde was seen eight miles south of Gasr El Ahrid, his Tomahawk trailing smoke. Too low to bale out, he landed his burning aircraft and was picked up by a British armoured car. The surviving Macchi pilots claimed one of their attackers shot down – almost certainly Hinde's aircraft.

During the day the remaining serviceable B-17 Fortress joined nine Marylands in bombing Gazala airfield. One of three Bostons of 24 SAAF Squadron was lost during a morning reconnaissance over Sidi Rezegh, Gambut and Maddalena, crashing near Gambut at 1030 with the loss of the whole crew. Bombers from both sides were out by night. At Ain el Gazala a G.50bis and an MC.200 were destroyed by bombs, and nine G.50s were slightly damaged, while at LG.75 two more of 109 Squadron's special Wellingtons were badly damaged. 270 Wing noted that the Blenheims of 8 Squadron attached to 55 Squadron, should move forward as an independent unit. On the other side of the lines 384ª Squadriglia of 157° Gruppo CT joined its sister squadriglie at Derna.

British Claims

272 Sqn	Flg Off M.L.P.Bartlett	Beaufighter Ic 'S'	3 Ju 87s	on ground Martuba 1115
	Plt Off J.Watters	Beaufighter Ic 'H'	Ju 88	on ground Martuba 1115
	Sgt J.S.Ross	Beaufighter Ic 'R'	Hs 126	on ground Martuba 1115
	Sgt N.A.J..Price	Beaufighter Ic 'N'		
	Flg Off M.L.P.Bartlett	Beaufighter Ic 'S'	Ju 87 damaged	Martuba area 1115
	Sgt N.A.J.Price	Beaufighter Ic 'N'		
250 Sqn	Plt Off R.B.Cole	Tomahawk	Bf 109E damaged	S El Adem 1400-1505
112 Sqn	Sgt R.M.Leu	Tomahawk AK509	CR.42	Sidi Rezegh 1535-1705
	Plt Off R.J.Jeffries	Tomahawk AK541		
	Plt Off N.F.Duke	Tomahawk AK402 'F'	CR.42	Tobruk, nr El Adem 1535-1705
	Sgt K.F.Carson	Tomahawk AN436		
2 SAAF Sqn	Lt E.C.Saville	Tomahawk AN311	MC.200 damaged	W Tobruk 1645
	Lt L.A.Stone	Tomahawk	MC.200	W Tobruk 1645

British Casualties

229 Sqn	Hurricane IIc Z5141 shot down; Sgt A.L.Boyde KiA
	Hurricane IIc Z4967 forced down; Plt Off W.Russell safe
	Hurricane IIc crash-landed; Plt Off W.Persse safe
80 Sqn	Hurricane I crash-landed; Sqn Ldr T.M.Horgan, DFC, WiA
451 Sqn	Hurricane I shot down; Lt J.A.Smith KiA
2 SAAF Sqn	Tomahawk AN311 'TA-C' damaged by collision; Lt E.C.Saville (40 SAAF Sqn attached) unhurt
	Tomahawk MiA; Lt D.A.Hinde safe
4 SAAF Sqn	Tomahawk shot down; Lt J.G.Ereaut KIA Flak
109 Sqn	Wellington Ic Z8907 shot down; Flt Sgt H.I.Wolf, RCAF, and six KiA; one survivor
	Wellington Ic damaged beyond repair
	2 Wellington Ics damaged on the ground at night
24 SAAF Sqn	Boston III W8375 'P' crashed; Lt G.A.Chalkley and crew KiA
223 Sqn	Maryland II AH368 damaged beyond repair
272 Sqn	Beaufighter Ic 'N' damaged by ground fire; observer, Sgt Hobbis, WiA

German Claims

1./JG 27	Lt Hans Remmer	Wellington	E Sidi Omar 0950
4./JG 27	Obfw Otto Schulz	Wellington	SW El Adem 0955
5./JG 27	Obfw Franz Woidich	P-40	7 km S Gazala 1500

German Casualties

9./ZG 26	Bf 110 W Nr 4028 100% to Flak, which hit the bombs under a wing which exploded, and after force-landing the crew was picked up by another 110
2(H),/14	Hs 126 WNr 3397 80% damaged by strafing attack
Kourier Stafel Trop	He 111 WNr 1626 NV+1G destroyed on ground by strafing attack; Fi 156 WNr 5114 70 % damaged by strafing attack

Italian Claims

153° Gr CT	Unspecified pilots	Hurricane	1630

Italian Casualties

376ª Sq Aut CT	2 CR.42s, MM5036 and MM7942, shot down: Ten Aldo Marchetti and Serg Luigi Bagato PoW
373ª Sq/153° Gr CT	MC.200 shot down; Cap Piero Raimondi PoW
155° Gr CT	G.50 on ground at Ain el Gazala by bombers at night
	G.50s slightly damaged on ground at Ain el Gazala by bombers at night
153° Gr CT	MC.200 destroyed on ground by bombers at night

Dawn heralded a day of unprecedentedly heavy air combat, a day on which the opposing fighters clashed head-on in a violent fight for air superiority which was to cause unusually heavy casualties on each side. On the ground XXX Corps came under increasingly heavy attack by Rommel's armour, although in the coastal area XIII Corps continued to make good progress.

Five of 109 Squadron's special Wellingtons were again out over the battle area where one was attacked by nine fighters identified as Bf 109s. Sgt Nicholson's aircraft was shot down with the loss of the whole crew, but a second escaped into cloud after sustaining damage. Their attackers had actually been MC.200s of 153° Gruppo, pilots from this unit claiming a Wellington probably shot down in the Bir Hacheim area.

Amongst the WDAF fighters, first off at 0945 were 12 Tomahawks of 3 RAAF Squadron which were to escort Blenheims of 45 Squadron on a raid on the Acroma-El Adem road. Bobby Gibbes:

Flg Off Bobby Gibbes of 3 RAAF Squadron was one of the first successful Tomahawk pilots of the Crusader campaign. His personal narrative has been drawn on heavily here.

"I was on the morning operation in which B flight was to escort six Blenheims to bomb Bir el Gubi. After take-off we rendezvoused with five Blenheims instead of the expected six. We split into two sixes close cover, flying three aircraft on either side of the bombers. I flew in number one position on the port.

The Blenheims were very much slower than our Tomahawks and we had to weave in order to stay alongside them. This actually was advantageous as it enabled us to scan the skies well, in search of enemy aircraft. We had arranged with the bomber crews for their rear gunners to fire into the air above if they saw enemy aircraft, and this would alert us if we hadn't already spotted them. Our radio frequencies were different to those which the bomber radios were tuned to, and this was always a great disadvantage to all pilots and crews.

"On the way to the target area, we passed a few miles to the port of enemy aircraft which were busily bombing our troop positions, with their fighter escort weaving above. We passed without much apparent notice of each other, as both lots of protective fighters were obliged to remain with their charges.

"Shortly before reaching our target, a line of single black ack-ack bursts was seen above the broken cloud layer, and these, we knew, were to indicate to the German fighter pilots our position and heading. A few minutes later, a force of about 15 109s appeared above, and this formation split into two sections and started to attack our top cover. The top cover was free to mix it with the enemy, but we pilots giving close cover were obliged to remain with our five Blenheims.

"Our top six did a wonderful, but terribly costly job in engaging the enemy and preventing them from attacking the Blenheims. Only two got through in an attempt to attack the bombers, and only one of these actually fired a quick burst at one of the rear aircraft. Two of us attacked it, driving it off. I was able to get into a very close position behind it, and only broke off my attack when I was in danger of running through the curtain of fire from the rear gunners of the bomber formation. I know that I was hitting it and I doubt if it did any real damage to the bomber, nor was I able to claim having damaged it as I did not see any bits fly off.

"A second 109 dived onto the tail of my number three, Malcolm Watson. I saw it coming and I called a desperate warning to him, but again, our poor radio communication resulted in him not hearing me and he continued his weave. It hit him hard, and he half rolled, and went into a lazy spiral dive, evidently having been killed in the attack. I pulled around onto the 109 and fired at it as it dived away, but whether I damaged it or not, I do not know.

"On two or three occasions during the combat, I felt my aircraft being hit and the strong smell of cordite permeated the cockpit. Each time my heart nearly stopped as I hadn't seen an attacking aircraft. I took wild evasive action, but could not see the aircraft which had hit me. After suffering terrific fear on each occasion, I suddenly realized that I had been firing my own guns, and the point fives, being in the cockpit, accounted for the vibration and the smell of gunpowder. It was the first time that I had worn gloves when flying, and I wasn't conscious that, without the normal feel of my finger on the trigger, I had been tensing my grip without being aware of doing so. I threw the gloves onto the floor of the cockpit and never wore them again.

"The fighters up above slowly disappeared behind us and the plumes of dense black smoke from the desert below, bore mute testimony to the gallant action of our top cover. How many of the fires were enemy, and how many ours, we didn't know. The bombers had done a good job. They ran up steadily on their target and dropped their bombs, I believe with great accuracy but unseen by us. It was enough for us to see the bombs leave their aircraft and to see them turn for home, while we wondered the while if we would ever make it. How slow those bombers were, and how slowly the desert passed below! How we wished that we could open our throttles and dive for home and safety, but this could not be! After landing back with our five bombers intact, our remaining top cover landed. We had lost three of our pilots, Malcolm Watson who I saw go down, and Johnny Saunders and Eric Lane. The three were killed. I have told how Malcolm went and later I learned that Eric Lane had been seen battling with three 109s. He got on the tail of one of these and had it smoking badly when another 109 jumped him from behind and shot him down in a mass of flames.

We never did hear how Johnny died."

Luftwaffe claims were very precise on this occasion, three P-40s being claimed shot down between 1020-1040. A Bf 109 of 1./JG 27 force-landed north-west of El Gubi and another was reported missing, an Ultra intercept confirming that both were as a result of this combat.

As the Australian Tomahawks landed, 112 Squadron took off, 13 fighters strafing columns near El Adem. Plt Off Sabourin was shot down by Flak, taking to his parachute and landing in the Indian Division's lines; he returned to the squadron two days later. Around 1330 13 Hurricanes of 238 Squadron took off to sweep over the Baheira-Gambut area where Flg Off Morgan and Sgt Mathews were shot down by Flak.

At much the same time five MC.200s of 153° Gruppo patrolling in the Capuzzo-Gambut area, became engaged with two Hurricanes, the Italians claiming one shot down and one probable. These were probably Tac R aircraft of the newly-arrived 237 Squadron which reported that Flt Lt Hutchinson, who was engaged in a sortie to the Capuzzo-Gambut area with Flg Off Olver as his protective weaver, was shot down in flames by Italian fighters, managing to bale out. A second Hurricane from this unit flown by Flg Off Sindall, also failed to return from a mission over Tobruk, but was later reported safe.

229 Squadron Hurricanes then escorted five Blenheims of 11 Squadron over the front, two fighters being reported south of Tobruk (Bf 109s or Bf 110s), one of which was claimed to have been damaged. The bomber unit recorded that two Bf 109s from a force of ten, attacked the rear of the formation. One pulled up at close range, exposing its belly to Sgt Fisher, the gunner in Plt Off Rechner's aircraft. He was then able to get a good burst into it, following which it went down pouring black smoke and was reportedly seen to crash.

At 1105 I./StG 1 and II./StG 2 attacked columns near Ain El Gubi, but reported the loss of three aircraft – one crashed and burnt, one force-landed and one missing. The first of these was reported to have fallen to fighters, while one of the others appears to have returned subsequently. On this occasion, however, no claims for Stukas were submitted by WDAF pilots on this date, and the losses would therefore have been caused to 8th Army AA defences.

Soon after midday 80 Squadron, escorted by three other fighter squadrons, made a successful fighter-bombing attack on a large column of MT on the Acroma-El Adem road. Following them came 12 Blenheims of 45 Squadron in two formations. These attacks were estimated to have destroyed about 100 vehicles including ten petrol tankers, and to have so damaged the road as to temporarily block it in several places. However, the second formation of six Blenheims was attacked over the target area by an estimated

The individual letter on Z5469 appears to have been applied in a rather amateurish and freehand manner. This Hurricane II served initially with 274 Squadron.

20 Bf 109s and four were shot down in rapid succession, the other two both sustaining considerable damage. Six Blenheims were claimed by JG 27 pilots between 1400-1406, and then a seventh at 1415. Subsequently, nine Marylands of 21 SAAF Squadron, escorted by SAAF Tomahawks, raided columns in the Bir Hacheim area. Amongst those lost was the squadron's commanding officer, J.O.Willis, who had been leading the unit since March. Temporarily he was replaced by Sqn Ldr F.J.Hustin, but on the 26th the new commander arrived – and by one of those coincidences, his name was C.B.B.Wallis.

At 1540 nine Tomahawks from 112 Squadron and 13 from 3 RAAF Squadron took off for an offensive sweep over the Tobruk-El Adem area. Bobby Gibbes:

"In order to ensure a full squadron strength of 12 aircraft, we would have one and sometimes two extra machines standing by, or taking off with the formation. If an aircraft turned back, the extra aircraft would take its place.

"On the afternoon of the 22nd I foolishly volunteered to be the thirteenth man, and when one aircraft turned back I took its place and became number two to Lin Knowles. I was to regret having made this stupid decision. The operation was to be an offensive patrol of the forward area by two squadrons, number 3 and 112, with 3 leading, led by Peter Jeffrey. We were escorting Wing Commander Freddie Rosier who was flying a Hurricane Mark 2. He wanted to get into Tobruk and it was planned that he would drop down there on the homeward leg of the patrol. Fred did not make Tobruk. We crossed the wire on Egypt's boundary and climbed on a westerly heading weaving our way towards Bir el Gubi. Shortly after passing this landmark, and about to turn onto a northerly heading towards Tobruk, aircraft were seen and reported above our level, coming towards us. They passed about 3 or 4,000 feet above us on our port. Peter turned the wing to the left in a gentle turn behind the 20 plus 109s which climbed up into the sun and started to dive down and vigorously attack us. A fierce fight commenced. After a short time, the enemy started to form a circle about 2,000 feet above us, and they then started coming down in twos and threes from all directions.

"After their attacks they would climb up again or sometimes, continue their dive through our formation and pull away before climbing up for further attacks. Ultimately, we ourselves somehow formed a defensive circle, when the lead aircraft caught up with the end machines. This circle was a recommended tactic and supposedly provided great protection to all aircraft in it. When enemy aircraft attacked, they would be subject to the firepower of one or more aeroplanes flying behind the machine being attacked. What a dreadful fallacy this theory really was. All it did with certainty, was to ensure that the leader was no longer recognisable, and virtually this made all aircraft leaderless. As the pairs were broken up by repeated attacks, we became a gaggle of single aircraft.

"The Messerschmitts had the advantage of height and when they dived on us they proved to be difficult targets due to the great speed which they had built up in their dive. It was hard to get more than a fleeting shot at them as they flashed past.

One of our pilots, Wilfred Arthur, at the time a Flight Lieutenant, tried breaking upwards after each attack on him, meaning to play the Germans at their own game. He gained quite a lot of altitude before a number of the enemy made a concerted attack on him forcing him to make a hurried diving retreat back to us. From memory, I believe that one or two of our more twitchy pilots took a pot at him as he rejoined the circle. They had become used to seeing only enemy aircraft come down from above.

"Eddie Jackson's Tomahawk was hit by an explosive 20mm shell in the starboard wing root. A big section of the wing was blown off and it was quite amazing that the aircraft still flew. He remained aggressive and continued to use his aircraft to the full. This spoke well for the rugged construction of the Curtiss aircraft which was still able to take high G forces without the wing collapsing.

"As I mentioned earlier, I was flying as Lin Knowles's number 2. When the first attacks started, Lin pulled up to fire at a 109 which was diving onto our formation. I followed him up until a second 109 pulled in behind us. I called out a warning and broke out of its way. From then on I was not able to locate him again and indeed was kept too busy to really try. The intensity of the attacks was quite horrendous and we were all fully occupied in trying to stay alive and fighting back when possible.

"At one stage I pulled up after a 109 which dived from south to north across the formation and I managed to get a full deflection shot at it. There was a vivid flash from his cockpit area on the starboard side, and the aircraft which had been climbing, fell off to starboard and started diving away. I felt that it had 'had it', but I was not able to watch further as I was myself attacked and by the time I got clear, there was nothing to be seen of my possible victim.

"During the combat I fired at several aircraft but was unable to claim any results although I must have scored the odd hit. I only saw the definite strike. At one time I pulled up to have a shot at a 109 which was pulling away after an attack. I noticed a 109 shooting at me from extreme range, but he had to allow full deflection to hit me and as I didn't think he was laying off enough lead, I kept on with my attack on the escaping aircraft. I completely overlooked my diminishing speed and when near the stall, I was startled to hear the sound of bullets striking my aircraft and saw my starboard wing start to look like the family colander. In an agony of fear, I kicked on full left rudder and rammed the stick forward in a desperate attempt to get clear of the hail of bullets. The next moment, I was being thrown violently around the cockpit. I thought for a moment that my controls had been shot away but then realised that I was in an inverted spin. I thought of opening my canopy and releasing my harness and dropping clear, but as I had 4,000 feet I decided to stay with it and to see if I could regain control. Due to having my harness fairly loose, I had terrific difficulty in getting my feet onto the rudders. I was completely clear of the cockpit seat because of the outward inertia of the spin and my head was hard up against the canopy. By a supreme effort I manage to get on some opposite rudder and came out inverted. It was a simple matter to roll out. I tightened my harness. A short time later, while flying almost on the deck after diving out of the defensive circle to shoot at a 109, I pulled up fairly hard to rejoin my friends. I must have hit a slipstream as I flipped onto my back at about 300 feet above the desert. I had long practiced low aerobatics, but never this low. My reaction was automatic and I pushed the stick forward and rolled out. I was amazed to be still alive and I was shaking even more than before, if this was possible. Afterwards, one of the surviving pilots discussing the combat in the safety of the mess, said, 'Did you see that bloke flick onto his back right on the deck and go in.' So positive had he been of my fate that he hadn't bothered to watch me actually hit. He was amazed when I finished the story for him.

"A 109 carried out an attack on one of our aircraft and as it started pulling away and I was trying to get a shot at it, a Tomahawk dived from somewhere above with a lot of speed and firing

---

from about a hundred yards, hit it cleanly in about the cockpit area. The Messerschmitt disintegrated in a ball of flames. As I watched the wings and bits falling down I could only admire such magnificent shooting. I think the Tomahawk was flown by Alan Rawlinson.

"A 109 dived in to attack. A Tomahawk pulled up and carried out a head-on attack on it, both aircraft shooting furiously. Each held his attack until the last moment before breaking. They left it too long, clipped their starboard wings and each flew in a gentle but steepening dive away from each other to the desert below and hit almost simultaneously. A wing from each aircraft fluttered down almost together like falling leaves, hitting the ground about half way between the crashed aircraft. I watched and prayed that our pilot would bale out but he did not open his canopy, and was probably knocked out by the impact. The 109 pilot also went in with his aircraft. We later confirmed that the Tomahawk was flown by Lindsay Knowles.

"The fight raged on and gradually we were forced lower and lower. Some of the lowest planes were literally skimming the desert. This gave some measure of relief as the 109s were no longer able to dive straight down through us and away. Instead they had to pull up after their attacks. Again, it stopped them diving as steeply which resulted in less speed and gave us a fraction more time to shoot at them as they flashed past. On the debit side, due to wind effect, our circle was gradually drifting to the south-east and this was carrying us over various German and Italian concentrations of troops, guns and tanks with a resulting hail of fire coming up at us from below to add to our worries. Some of the more aggressive pilots aimed an occasional burst at ground targets as they passed over, but I for one, was content to save my ammunition for use against the Luftwaffe. It seemed unlikely that any of us would survive, but I wanted to at least be able to shoot back until I was killed. The numbers of 109s would sometimes seem to dwindle, but just as we were starting to have some faint hope, a fresh batch would arrive, keen to be in at the kill. We were 150 miles from our base and they were a mere few miles from theirs. As they used up their supply of ammunition and petrol, they would land back, hurriedly re-arm, refuel and return to this combat.

"Time passed and the fight went on. I looked at my watch, at my gauges and noting the way my petrol was diminishing, eased back my throttle a little, leaned my mixture as much as possible, probably more than I should have. Would my petrol last until darkness? If so, how far would we be able to fly before being forced to land, still miles inside enemy territory? Would we survive a landing in darkness away from an aerodrome? It would be unlikely.

"At last the sun sank below the horizon and in the east a slight bluish tinge told of approaching night. There are fewer 109s now. There might be a hope, if only the leader would make a break for home. But where is the leader? Perhaps he is dead. Would it be possible for me to lead this team out of the circle where we were like a mob of sheep. I called up the CO. I called up Lin. Dead silence. I called up the mob and told them that I was going to make a break for home and broke away waggling my wings. Not a soul followed. I hurriedly rejoined the circle. The 109s looked as if they were leaving us. I called up again and again broke towards home waggling my wings. The circle broke almost to a man and followed. 'Woof' Arthur flew up alongside me and took over the lead. It was a great relief to see him as I had doubts about my ability to find my way back to base. The little enemy dots were fading into the darkness.

"Woof's navigation was good and he led us into a newly captured aerodrome. We landed in approaching darkness, most of us very low in fuel and morale. The combat had lasted for one hour and five minutes. During this time we were under constant attack from above and for a fairly long period, from below as well.

"I landed with only ten gallons of petrol left and I was practically right out of ammunition. The other pilots were also suffering from fuel shortage, and on reaching the aerodrome there was no pansy flying and of carrying out a normal circuit; no time to take precautions. Wheels went down and we went straight in praying that the runway was clear, and that we would be able to see the ground when the time came to hold off and put the aircraft down. A couple of the pilots had to make dead-stick landings when their motors cut on final and another had his motor cut when taxying in to disperse his aircraft.

"We assembled, those who were left, at the mess tent of the squadron which had just moved up to this newly captured aerodrome. Word was passed to our squadron that we had landed. The relief of the squadron people must have been quite considerable, as only Alan Rawlinson had landed back and he had only been able to report having shot down two 109s (credited as one and one probable).

———

"Word came through that Peter Jeffrey was safe but that Freddie Rosier was missing. Fred was not seen after the fight started. Also missing from the operation were Lin Knowles, Sammy Lees, Robbie Roberts, Ron Simes and Bill Kloster. Peter had been the sixth pilot missing. Sammy Lees and Lin Knowles were later confirmed to have been killed and Bill Kloster and Robbie Roberts had become prisoners of war. Ron Simes walked back.

"When the combat started, Fred Rosier was flying just below the Tomahawks in his Hurricane. He tried to keep up with the climbing squadrons but his machine was not capable of doing so. He saw one of the Tomahawks get shot down and the pilot land and get out of his aircraft. As he couldn't get up to the fight and as this pilot was miles behind enemy lines, he decided to do the next best thing and pick him up."

Rosier himself recorded later:

"...I decided to fly to the besieged fortress of Tobruk to organise the airfield facilities for fighter operations and to find out why the post (radar) there was failing to give us early warning of the approach of aircraft from the west.

"That afternoon with an escort of two Tomahawk squadrons, 112 (Shark) Squadron and 3 Squadron of the Royal Australian Air Force, I set off in my Hurricane II for Tobruk. We were well on the way when at 1615 hrs, south-east of El Adem, we were intercepted by a group of perhaps 20 Bf 109s. Bobby Gibbes wrote in his diary that day: 'They straight away climbed up into the sun and came down onto us and started to dogfight. Soon got sick of that and formed a big circle about 2,000 feet above us and came down in twos and threes from all directions.'

"After about 20 minutes, on breaking away, I saw a Tomahawk of 112 Squadron, diving down streaming smoke. I followed it down. He lowered his undercarriage and force-landed, only a few miles away from an enemy column which I had noticed. In order to prevent the pilot falling into the 'bag' I decided to attempt to rescue him. I landed the Hurricane alongside the Tomahawk and the pilot, Sgt Burney, an Australian, ran across to me. I jumped out, discarded my parachute and he climbed into my cockpit. I sat on top of him, opened the throttle and started to take off. Then disaster struck, just as I started my take-off run my right tyre burst. I accelerated but the wheel dug into the sand and we ground to a halt. There was nothing to do but abandon the plane.

"At that time it was nearly dusk and, as there was an Italian armoured column about two miles away, we ran to the shelter of a nearby wadi. After some time as there was no sign of the enemy, we returned to the aircraft and I quickly removed all my possessions from the Hurricane, including my wife's photograph....and hid them under some nearby brushwood. Taking some food and water we returned to our hiding place where we planned to spend the night. A little later, trucks arrived and Italian soldiers began to search for us. They found all my possessions but although they came within yards of where we were hiding behind some rocks, they did not see us.

"The next morning, anxious to get as far away as possible from the scene of our landings, we set off in an easterly direction to walk the 30 miles or so back to our lines. That night, using the Pole star to navigate, we found ourselves in the middle of some German tanks and lorries. We started crawling on our hands and knees and I thought the game was up when lights came on and we were twice challenged by sentries. Eventually, when all became quiet we continued walking. As dawn was breaking we found ourselves still close to the enemy force who were searching for us on motorcycles. We therefore made for the shelter of some brushwood surrounding a dry well which was the only bit of cover for miles around.

"At about 0800 that morning (24 November) we found ourselves in the middle of an artillery battle with shells falling on and around the enemy force close to us, which immediately began to disperse and withdraw. We then heard unmistakable orders being barked out in English. I decided that the best thing to do was to make a dash for it, so we ran until we eventually reached the artillery unit. We were at first greeted with suspicion but we were soon given some tea and food and sent on to an armoured brigade headquarters not far away.

"They welcomed us and provided us with a truck and driver to take us to Fort Maddalena. En-route, as we approached a South African armoured car unit, shells started falling around us and a number of enemy tanks coming straight towards us appeared about two miles away. The enemy force which we had encountered had broken through and was heading east towards the Egyptian frontier. The South African major's last words to us were. 'I think we are the last line of defence before the wire.' So we turned round and went like the wind, heading east. Later we were strafed by 110s but our fighters appeared and shot down four of them. Again, we passed a most uncomfortable night not knowing the position of the Hun tanks but got back to Maddalena the next morning – 25th.

Neville Duke (112 Squadron):

"I got on the tail of one and followed him up. Got in a burst from stern quarter and its hood and pieces of fuselage disintegrated. Machine went into a vertical dive and the pilot baled out. Flew round and round the pilot until he landed, then went down to look at him. I waved to him and he waved back. Poor devil thought I was going to strafe him as he initially dived behind a bush and lay flat.

"Rejoined Squadron which was going round and round in a defensive circle. The 109s kept diving down on us and I saw a Tomahawk go in with half its wing off after colliding with a 109. The fight lasted about 40 minutes. Longest ever! Force-landed after breaking away from circle by myself, at an advanced landing ground (LG.134)."

Claims by the two Tomahawk squadrons during the two engagements on this day amounted only to four Bf 109s shot down, to which were added four probables and seven damaged. German losses totalled six shot down, though not a single pilot was killed. However, Lt Scheppa, who was wounded, was taken to an Italian hospital where he and 24 Italians would lose their lives next day during a bombing attack. Two pilots were captured, one of them – Obfhr Weskott – clearly having been shot down by Neville Duke. Hpt Düllberg was also wounded, crash-landing at II.Gruppe's airfield at Bir el Gubi. He had seen a single Tomahawk closing in on him in a wide turn, but had thought it was too far away to be dangerous. It opened fire from what he called an "olympic distance" and hit his fighter twice, one shot going through his life jacket, the other hitting the cockpit and wounding him in the left foot. On this occasion the German pilots had substantially over-estimated their own results, claiming no less than 11 P-40s plus one unconfirmed, during the period between 1625-1700 against actual losses of seven – all but one from 3 RAAF Squadron.

Despite the fact that the Luftwaffe had clearly come off best from the day's actions, the cost was obviously considered too high, as it was to be the last occasion on which the 109s met Commonwealth fighters in force and dog-fought them. From this time onwards they returned to their normal tactics of utilizing their superior speed and altitude performance to undertake dive-shoot-and-climb tactics, these negating the Tomahawk's superior manoeuvrability and saving the Messerschmitt pilots from further heavy losses.

Bobby Gibbes:

"22 November 1941 proved to be a day of disaster for 3 Squadron. By dusk our pilot strength had been depleted by almost 50%. In the morning battle we lost three pilots, all killed, and in the afternoon, a further four, two of whom were killed and the other two became prisoners of war. Al Rawlinson had been the only pilot of our 11 to land back at base. A further five surviving pilots had landed at a forward aerodrome, and two others arrived back the following day.

"My morale was at bedrock and I thought that I would not be able to take it any more, and I spent the whole (next) morning mooching around in a state of funk and dreaded bring asked to fly again. I was ashamed of my fear and frightened that my friends might see it. I kept to myself as much as possible, but occasionally I would go to the operations tent, pretending that I wanted to have another go at the Huns, but frightened that if I was given a job I would not be able to force myself into getting into my aeroplane. It would have to be a new aircraft too. My aircraft was in the workshops and would be there for quite a while being patched up."

During the previous day 33 Squadron had moved from Giarabub to the new landing ground LG.125. Aware, and alarmed, by the possibility of an Allied thrust from this area, several Axis raids were undertaken during the day against the forces here. 11 Bf 110s bombed and strafed a column of armoured cars 90 miles north-west of Giarabub, one car and four tenders being destroyed. Then around 1300 12 Ju 88s from LG 1 attacked the new airfield, where two Hurricanes and two Blenheims (apparently visiting aircraft from 11 Squadron) were destroyed on the ground. Some of 33 Squadron's aircraft got off, Lance Wade reporting:

"Nine bombers (Ju 88s) bombed the drome. Six of us went up to meet them. I destroyed one 88. Another was shared by two Sgts [actually Flg Off Winsland and Sgt Genders.]. One 88 turned back and strafed the drome. We lost two a/c on the ground. None in the air."

Two more claims were made for Ju 88s damaged. Don Edy:

"All six Hurricanes climbed to 10,000 feet and formed a loose patrol formation of three pairs. For 20 minutes we flew back and forth, up-sun from the landing ground, expecting almost anything.
"Winnie (Winsland) spotted the enemy first and peeled off to attack. As I caught up to Winnie's plane I could see first three, then six, then nine, and finally 12 Ju 88s diving on our base from all four points of the compass. Their bombs were already exploding by the time we mixed with them. In seconds the air was full of wheeling and diving planes.
"This was my first scrap with enemy bombers and I was really excited. I followed Winnie as closely as possible as he manoeuvred to get on the tail of a Ju 88. We both gave it a good squirt as we shot past.
"All this action happened within a few seconds. The next thing I knew I was alone in the air with two bombers. While trying to catch them up I looked back and could see six black pillars of smoke over the base, but no other planes. It took quite a while to get near the Junkers and I tried to figure out the best method of attack. They were flying in close formation for mutual protection so I attempted to get above and ahead of them for a frontal attack. Each time I pulled up they just turned and presented their tails. I gave up that idea and went into a dive, gaining speed enough to come up under one of them.
"I gave it a good burst of bullets, with no real results, so I climbed again and this time came in from above and behind. The two rear gunners in the 88s returned my fire but missed. I got one of them as he didn't fire again. By now my guns were almost empty and the gas was getting low. I pulled up in front of them and came in, head on, leaving my finger on the trigger button until all the guns stopped firing. Although black smoke came from the engine of one I don't think I did much damage. It was most disappointing to see them fly off merrily for home.
"I was angry at myself for making such a poor showing on this first fight and to add to the misery, I didn't have the faintest idea where I was. The fight had taken us a good distance away from the base, so I headed south-east, hoping to strike either the wire or the black strip. Luckily I spotted the smoke from a burning plane on the ground and by the time I reached that, there were more pillars of smoke on the horizon marking the base. The aircraft below was an 88 and the four crew members were standing forlornly in the desert nearby. We never did find out what happened to them. By the time one of our trucks got there, they were gone. Possibly a German plane came out to pick them up, or even one of our Army units from the north."

1./LG 1 lost one Ju 88, with one killed and three captured, while in a second lost by 4.Staffel, there were no survivors.
During the morning at 1014 the crew of a Stab/StG 3 Bf 110 observed a Ju 88 crashing in flames whereupon the pilot landed alongside, taking off with seven aboard. The bomber unit involved is not known, but despite the time differential, it is perhaps possible that this rescue related to the German crew mentioned by Don Edy.
Towards evening one S.79 and four Bf 110s approached, reportedly five Hurricanes being scrambled. According to Don Edy, however, only two Hurricanes took off, finding just the S.79 which "must have been lost, as it circled the landing ground twice as though trying to decide where it was. By the time the pilot realized his mistake, Lance and Genders were on it." Wade added: "Sgt Genders and I contacted and shot down one S.79 reco machine. Two of the crew baled out and were made PoWs." This accords with Regia Aeronautica records which indicate that a single Savoia of 18ª Squadriglia, 27° Gruppo BT flown by S.Ten Piero Ravizza, took off at 1315 from Martuba on reconnaissance to the south, where it

was shot down by British fighters. Ravizza baled out and became a PoW.

Elsewhere during the day six Fiat BR.20s of 1ª Squadriglia, 11° Gruppo BT bombed British columns north of Gialo where two of the bombers were shot down and another badly damaged by AA. Another Italian aircraft to be lost on this date was a 372ª Squadriglia MC.200 in which Ten Italo Palli took off from Barce at 1310, but failed to return. A Luftwaffe Ju 87 was also lost to the south of Bir el Gubi by II./StG 2 – probably another victim of ground fire. The Regia Aeronautica was further reinforced by the arrival at Derna of three more Cant.Z.1007bis for 176ª Squadriglia RST.

Sqn Ldr Yaxley, formerly commanding officer of 252 Squadron, received news that he was to be promoted Wg Cdr and given command of 272 Squadron. He led off his first attack by this active unit on this date, eight Beaufighters making for Benina airfield. As they approached, however, it was noted that a fighter screen was waiting and that a very effective Flak barrage was being put up. After making two attempts to get through this safely, Yaxley decided not to proceed with the attack and led his formation away to the north. Vehicles were strafed instead, four lorries and three petrol tankers being claimed destroyed. The weather was very bad, however, and the formation broke up, two aircraft then landing at Kilo 75 due to fuel shortage.

British Claims

3 RAAF Sqn	Flt Lt W.S.Arthur	Tomahawk AN389	Bf 109F damaged	Bir el Gubi 1030
	Sqn Ldr A.C.Rawlinson	Tomahawk	Bf 109F damaged	
	Sgt D.Scott	Tomahawk AN305	2 Bf 109Fs probable	Bir el Gubi
	Sgt R.H.Simes	Tomahawk	Bf 109F	W Bir el Gubi
11 Sqn	Bomber gunners		Bf 109	
33 Sqn	Plt Off L.C.Wade	Hurricane I V7828 ⎫	Ju 88	LG.125 1300
	Flg Off Winsland	Hurricane I ⎬		
	Sgt G.E.C.Genders	Hurricane I	Ju 88	
	Unspecified pilots	Hurricane I	3 Ju 88s damaged	
112 Sqn	Plt Off N.F.Duke	Tomahaw AK402 'F'	Bf 109F	S El Adem 1615
	Plt Off J.P.Bartle	Tomahaw AK538	Bf 109F	El Adem 1545-1720
3 RAAF Sqn	Flt Lt W.S.Arthur	Tomahaw AN224	3 Bf 109s damaged	SE El Adem 1615
	Sqn Ldr A.C.Rawlinson	Tomahaw AN365	Bf 109	
	Sqn Ldr A.C.Rawlinson	Tomahaw AN365	Bf 109 probable	
	Sqn Ldr A.C.Rawlinson	Tomahaw AN365	Bf 109 damaged	
	Flg Off R.H.Gibbes	Tomahaw AN224	Bf 109 probable	
	Flg Off E.H.B.Jackson	Tomahaw AN441	Bf 109 damaged	
33 Sqn	Plt Off L.C.Wade	Hurricane I V7828 ⎫	S.79	LG.125 Late p.m.
	Sgt G.E.C.Genders	Hurricane I Z4633 ⎬		
229 Sqn	Unspecified pilot		Bf 109 damaged	S.Tobruk

3 RAAF Squadron originally listed six victories for this date. This was subsequently altered as follows: "AM Escort to 11 Squadron Blenheims who later confirmed that two ME 109s claimed by Sgt Scott as probables were destroyed. PM Sqn Ldr Rawlinson 2 ME 109s destroyed. F/O Knowles or F/O Lees collided head on with a ME 109 which was destroyed." Thus the squadron considered that three of the claims for probables in the above listing were subsequently confirmed.

British Casualties

45 Sqn	Blenheim IV T2318 shot down; Sgt C.Melly and one of crew PoW, one KiA
	Blenheim IV Z6439 'Y' shot down; Wg Cdr J.O.Willis DFC and crew KiA
	Blenheim IV Z9609 shot down; Sgt R.Wood and one of crew PoW; one returned
	Blenheim IV Z7686 shot down; Plt Off C.E.O'Neill and crew KiA
109 Sqn	Wellington Ic X9988 shot down; Sgt R.E.Nicholson and five crew KiA; Wellington, damaged
3 RAAF Sqn	Tomahawk AM378 shot down; Plt Off E.H.Lane KiA
	Tomahawk AN 416 FTR; Flt Lt J.H.W.Saunders KiA
	Tomahawk FTR; Flg Off M.Watson KiA
112 Sqn	Tomahawk AN330 shot down by Flak; Plt Off J.J.P.Sabourin baled out
238 Sqn	Hurricane IIc shot down by Flak; Flg Off Morgan unhurt
	Hurricane IIc shot down by Flak; Sgt Mathews
33 Sqn	2 Hurricanes destroyed on ground at LG.125
11 Sqn	2 Blenheim IVs destroyed on ground

British Casualties

258 Wg	Tomahawk force-landed; Wg Cdr P.Jeffrey picked up by ground troops and returned 24th
3 RAAF Sqn	Tomahawk AM 507 shot down; Sgt Simes picked up by ground troops and returned 26th
	Tomahawk AN410 shot down; Flt Lt L.E.S.Knowles KiA, wreck later found at 7miles at 055 degrees from Bir Hacheim aerodrome
	Tomahawk AN373 shot down; Flg Off H G H Roberts PoW
	Tomahawk AK390 shot down; Flg Off W.G.Kloster PoW
	Tomahawk AN 305 shot down; Plt Off L.Lees KiA; wreck later found at 7miles at 055 degrees from BirHacheim aerodrome
	Tomahawk badly damaged; Flg Off R.H.Gibbes safe
112 Sqn	Tomahawk AM390 shot down; Sgt H.G.Burney picked up by ground troops and returned 25th
262 Wg	Hurricane II damaged landing to pick up Sgt Burney and abandoned by Wg Cdr Rosier; picked up by ground troops and returned 25th
237 Sqn	Hurricane shot down; Flt Lt Hutchinson baled out
	Hurricane MiA; Flg Off C.L.Sindall later reported safe

German Claims

1./JG 27	Oblt Hugo Schneider	P-40	E Bir el Gubi 1035
Stab II./JG 27	Hptmn Wolfgang Lippert	P-40	SE Ain el Gazala 1020
	Hptmn Wolfgang Redlich	P-40	SE Ain el Gazala 1040
	Hptmn Wolfgang Redlich	Blenheim	SE Ain el Gazala 1400
	Uffz Josef Grimm	Blenheim	SE Ain el Gazala 1405
Stab II./JG 27	Lt Hans Doye	Blenheim	SE Ain el Gazala 1405
4./JG 27	Oblt Gustav Rödel	Blenheim	50m SE Ain el Gazala 1405
1./JG 27	Obfw Albert Espenlaub	Blenheim	NW Bir el Gubi 1406
4./JG 27	Obfw Fritz Rockel	Blenheim	SE Ain el Gazala 1406
1./JG 27	Hptmn Wolfgang Redlich	Blenheim	NE Bir Hacheim 1415
4./JG 27	Oblt Emmerich Fluder	P-40	NW Bir Hacheim 1625
	Oblt Emmerich Fluder	P-40	Bir Hacheim 1628
Stab II./JG 27	Hptmn Wolfgang Lippert	P-40	NW Bir Hacheim 1630
5./JG 27	Fw Hans Glessinger	P-40	Bir Hacheim 1631
	Obfw Franz Woidich	P-40	NW Bir Hacheim 635
4./JG 27	Oblt Gustav Rödel	P-40	SE Bir Hacheim 1640
1./JG 27	Hptmn Wolfgang Redlich	P-40	SE Bir Hacheim 1645
Stab II./JG 27	Hptmn Wolfgang Lippert	P-40	NW Bir Hacheim 1645
	Fw Karl-Heinz Bendert	P-40	SE Bir Hacheim 1646
4./JG 27	Obfw Otto Schulz	P-40	12m SE Bir Hacheim 1655
5./JG 27	Uffz Hans Niederhöfer	P-40 o.Zg.	n.b. 1700
1./JG 27	Oblt Hugo Schneider	P-40	S Bir Hacheim

N.B. In addition Ultra intercepts reported that LG 1's Ju 88 crews claimed 2 Hurricanes shot down on this date.

German Casualties

1./JG 27	Bf 109F-4 trop WNr 8479 shot down; Obfhr Josef Weskott baled out PoW
1./JG 27	Bf 109F-4 trop WNr 8494 crash-landed; Fw Günther Hillert PoW
5./JG 27	Bf 109F-4 trop WNr 8444 shot down Bir Hacheim; Lt Kurt Scheppa wounded; died in bombing attack on Bir Hacheim hospital next day
5./JG 27	Bf 109F-4 trop WNr 8466 shot down, crash-landed Bir el Gubi; Oblt Ernst Düllberg WiA
5./JG 27	Bf 109F-4 trop WNr 8461 shot down Bir el Gubi; Uffz Horst Reuter safe
5./JG 27	Bf 109F-4 trop WNr 8459, down Bir el Gubi; Uffz Karl-Heinz Panier safe
1./LG 1	Ju 88A-4 WNr 5581 L1+JH shot down; Lt Rolf Dräger and two PoW, one KiA
4./LG 1	Ju 88A-5 WNr 4338 shot down 110m E Agedabia; Uffz Berthold Borndcheim and three MiA
I./StG 1	Ju87R2 trop WNr 6072 shot down by fighters Ain El Gubi
II./StG 2	Ju 87 MiA S Bir el Gubi

On 23 rd Lt Schulz of Sonderkommando Jung – a detachment of I./NJG 2 in Afrika, flying recce sorties – reported the following casualties, the message being intercepted by the British:

R4+NK Oblt Harms bellied in at Catania as hydraulics had been shot-up at 1147

R4+RK Lt Voight Fw Wolf shot down at 0815 probably making a low level attack on a British landing ground

Another intercept reported 6 Ju 88s (R4+HK, NK, MK, LK, RK and WK) had left Catania for Benina between 0920 to 0934 pm on the 22nd.

153° Gr CT	Unspecified pilots	Hurricane	Ridotta Capuzzo-Gambut area 1030
	Unspecified pilots	Hurricane probable	Ridotta Capuzzo-Gambut area 1030
	Unspecified pilots	Wellington probable	Bir Hacheim area

Italian Casualties

8ª Sq/27° Gr/8° St BT	S.79 shot down; S.Ten Piero Ravizza and one baled out, PoW
1ª Sq/11° Gr/13° St BT	2 BR 20s MM22747 and MM21892 MiA; Ten Giuseppe Cigerza and crew, S.Ten Edoardo Ottaviani and crew MiA
	BR.20 badly damaged by AA, Ten Ambrogio Vercesi and crew safe
372ª Sq/153° Gr CT	MC.200 FTR; Ten Italo Palli MiA

Sunday, 23 November 1941

Another day of heavy combat with XXX Corps' armour forced into retreat. First off at 0730 were 229 and 238 Squadrons, 11 and 12 Hurricanes respectively being led by Wg Cdr M.J.Louden to sweep over the forces around El Adem. Here 18 Ju 87s of I./ StG 1 and 15 of II./StG 2 with some 20 Bf 109s and G.50s (the latter being 13 aircraft of 155° Gruppo CT) escorting were identified. The British squadrons attacked near Sidi Rezegh where six Stukas were claimed shot down plus three probables and eight damaged, while against the escorts one G.50 of 378ª Squadriglia was shot down and one Bf 109 claimed damaged.

Escorting Bf 109s pilots claimed three victories – one identified as a Hurricane and two as P-40s, but on this occasion it was the Italians who inflicted the most damage, claiming eight fighters – three identified as Tomahawks, the rest as Hurricanes. At much the same time as this engagement was taking place, five pilots of 153° Gruppo CT, who had taken off to escort a reconnaissance S.79, claimed a Hurricane north of El Cuasc – possibly having strayed into the area of the big engagement.

The two RAF squadrons were quite hard-hit, losing seven aircraft, although three of the pilots returned to their units on foot fairly soon. Next day an Ultra intercept of the after-action report was able to ascertain the Stuka casualties as involving 2.and 3./StG 1 which each lost one Ju 87, while a further I./StG 1 crew force-landed and was rescued by another of the unit's aircraft. In StG 2, II.Gruppe reported three crews missing and one force-landed, whilst one more crew baled out over their base on return. Two of these casualties would appear to have related to 6.Staffel, which recorded two of its aircraft shot down or badly damaged with members of the crews wounded. Two StG 3 aircraft suffered similarly, involving one from the Stab and one of 6.Staffel.

More Hurricanes were off at 0830, ten of 94 Squadron joining others of 260 Squadron on a further wing sweep over Sidi Rezegh, El Adem and Gabr Saleh. Over El Adem the formation was jumped by two Bf 109s, Wg Cdr Howard Mayers claiming damage to one of these. At 1130 ten Tomahawks of 250

The fifth unit to enter action with the Tomahawk was 4 SAAF Squadron, KJ-P serving with this unit.

One flight of the Royal Naval Fighter Squadron which operated in the Western Desert in support of the RAF during late 1941, was formed from 805 Squadron with Grumman Martlet fighters, two of which are seen here taking off.

Squadron provided cover for 11 RNFS Hurricanes patrolling over South African troops in the Sidi Rezegh area. Here six Ju 88s escorted by 12 Bf 109s and 12 G.50bis were encountered. The Messerschmitts attacked the Hurricanes, Sub Lt Willis being shot down and killed. Sub Lt Henderson fired at a Bf 109 which was on the tail of a Tomahawk, claiming it as a probable, and Sub Lt Astin claimed another damaged which was later confirmed to have been destroyed. Two other aircraft damaged were also claimed by the naval Hurricane pilots.

Meanwhile, the 250 Squadron pilots fought the Messerschmitts for 12 minutes, three being claimed shot down plus one probable and 11(!) damaged. However, Sqn Ldr Morris's aircraft was damaged and Sgt Palethorpe was shot down and killed.

Between 1440-1640 15 Tomahawks from 2 SAAF and 4 SAAF Squadrons were attacked by ten Bf 109s which dived out of the sun. The South Africans turned through 180 degrees to meet them, but one passed so close that it collided with Lt Golding's aircraft and apparently spun into the ground; Golding was able to land his badly damaged aircraft safely. Meanwhile, Capt Bosman found two directly above him at one of which he fired three bursts, reporting that it disintegrated. Wt Off Jackson claimed a probable. However, Lt du Plessis did not return, having been shot down and killed. Two P-40s were claimed by pilots of II./JG 27 at this time.

While this fight had been underway, 18 Marylands had attacked vehicles of the Italian Ariete Division as they were heading north, dropping 16 tons of bombs on them, though with little effect. One 21 SAAF Squadron bomber was hit by Flak and force-landed in an area occupied by 1st South African Division.

Two Bostons of 24 SAAF Squadron had set off on a reconnaissance of the Bir el Gubi-Bir Hacheim area, but one had been shot down by a Bf 109 flown by Obfw Espenlaub between El Adem and Gazala at around 1400. Lt Blake crash-landed the burning aircraft, then rescuing the observer who was trapped in the nose, by kicking in the perspex screen. The two of them then pulled out the wounded gunner, Sgt Atkinson. The second gunner had managed to bale out before the crash, all four becoming PoWs. Lt Blake would later escape from Italian prison camp and was subsequently awarded an MC for work with the Italian partisans later in the war.

At 1530 another big raid set out, nine Blenheims being escorted by ten Hurricanes of the RNFS, four from 229 Squadron and four from 238 Squadron, with a top cover of five Tomahawks of 250 Squadron. The formation was attacked by Bf 109s all the way to Sidi Rezegh and several aircraft were shot down. One of these was a naval Hurricane from which Lt Cox baled out, while Plt Off Sellar of 238 Squadron was shot down and killed. This unit's Flt Lt Jack Urwin-Mann got back despite damage inflicted on his Hurricane, and one pilot from this unit was able to claim damage to a Bf 109. Amongst the Tomahawks, Sgt Coward's aircraft was hit by Flak and he had to carry out a crash-landing.

1./JG 27's Hptmn Redlich claimed a Hurricane shot down during this engagement; this was his third success of the day, having claimed another Hurricane either during the first morning combat or during this fight. Thus during the three engagements between Tomahawks and Bf 109s on this date, five

Messerschmitts had been claimed destroyed plus one more by the naval Hurricane pilots, most of which had been identified as Bf 109Es. In fact II./JG 27 lost two aircraft – both of the F version. This gruppe's commanding officer, the 12-victory Ritterkreuzträger Hptmn Wolfgang Lippert, on baling out over British-held territory, had struck the tailplane of his aircraft which broke both his legs. The medical officer who treated him initially, was subsequently captured and reported that the fractures had been uncomplicated. However, on reaching hospital gangrene set in and he was advised that it would be necessary to amputate both limbs. In desperation he refused this for several days, although finally he had to agree. Ten minutes after the operation he suffered an embolism and died. Having previously received the news given by the captured medic, his death came as a great shock to JG 27.

In the LG.125 area during the day 33 Squadron was again in action early in the day when two pilots were scrambled to intercept a reconnaissance Bf 110 from 2.(H)/14. Don Edy: "Early in the morning Winnie and Andy scrambled and intercepted a Messerschmitt 110 before it got near us. They attacked it several times and soon had the satisfaction of seeing it go down in flames. We could see the whole fight from the ground. It was one of the most intensely interesting spectacles I have ever witnessed. It wasn't often we were able to watch such a show." Later two Ju 88s bombed Giarabub, both being claimed damaged by AA and Hurricanes, one of which was reportedly found to have crashed 15 miles away – though no such loss was listed by the Luftwaffe on this date. On a later operation Plt Off Anderson's aircraft was shot down by Flak, but he survived and returned safely.

Meanwhile, four 272 Squadron Beaufighters had attacked landing grounds in the Barce area, where a line of S.79s were strafed, one being left in flames; it was believed that the rest had all been hit and three of them destroyed. In fact one S.81, one S.79 and a BR.20 were damaged here, where the explosion of a bomb killed a 13° Stormo BT pilot, M.llo Vasco Bosi, and seven airman. One Beaufighter flown by Plt Off Lee was hit by Flak and crashed at Bir el Gubi, where the aircraft was completely burnt out. However, Lee and his observer, Sgt Gowing, suffered only minor cuts and bruises, returning on foot two days later. Light Flak also hit Flg Off Salter's aircraft, damaging the hydraulic system which caused him to crash on landing.

To the east at 1605 two Martlets of 805 Squadron were patrolling over ships when two S.79s were spotted. The two naval pilots attacked, reporting that they had set fire to one engine, but had been unable to see the results before the intruders escaped.

The question should perhaps be asked at this stage as to why the RAF pilots were frequently continuing to identify Bf 109s as E models when such aircraft had practically disappeared from the Luftwaffe's establishment in North Africa. The F models generally had the wingtips painted white at this time, and possibly when seen against the blue sky from which these aircraft were on most occasions appearing, might well have given the impression that the wings were squared-off.

A pair of Martlets of 805 Squadron (one almost hidden behind the tail of that in the foreground) immediately after ceasing to undertake operations over the desert. The squadron was then bound for East Africa.

British Claims

Unit	Pilot	Aircraft	Claim	Location/Time
229 Sqn	Sqn Ldr W.A.Smith	Hurricane IIc BD774	Ju 87	SW Sidi Rezegh 0720-0905
	Sqn Ldr W.A.Smith	Hurricane IIc BD774	Ju 87 probable	SW Sidi Rezegh 0720-0905
	Sgt Wesson	Hurricane IIb Z3146	Ju 87	SE Tobruk 0720-0905
	Sgt Wesson	Hurricane IIb Z3146	Ju 87s damaged	SE Tobruk 0720-0905
	Plt Off H.Ravn	Hurricane IIb Z5269	Ju 87	Tobruk area 0720-0905
	Plt Off H.Ravn	Hurricane IIb Z5269	Ju 87 damaged	Tobruk area 0720-0905
	Flt Lt G.B.Johns	Hurricane IIb Z5311	Ju 87 probable	Tobruk area 0720-0905
	Wt Off N.C.Hoare	Hurricane IIb Z5328	Ju 87 probable	Tobruk area 0720-0905
	Wt Off N.C.Hoare	Hurricane IIb Z5328	Ju 87 damaged	Tobruk area 0720-0905
	Wg Cdr M.J.Louden	Hurricane IIb Z5270	Bf 109 damaged	SE Tobruk 0720-0905
	Plt Off R.G.Marland	Hurricane IIb Z4955	Ju 87 probable	SE Tobruk 0720-0905
238 Sqn	Plt Off Collenette	Hurricane IIc 'T'	Ju 87	El Adem 0730-0900
	Flg Off C.R.Forsyth	Hurricane IIc 'J'	G.50	El Adem 0730-0915
	Flt Lt Wolsey	Hurricane IIc 'A'	Ju 87	El Adem 0730-0902
	Flt Lt Wolsey	Hurricane IIc 'A'	Ju 87 damaged	El Adem 0730-0902
	Flg Off Morgan	Hurricane IIc 'Y'	2 Ju 87s damaged	El Adem 0730-0915
	Plt Off Jenkins	Hurricane IIc 'D'	Bf 109 probable	El Adem 0730-0915
	Plt Off Sellar	Hurricane IIc 'M'	Ju 87	El Adem 0730-0904
	Plt Off Sellar	Hurricane IIc 'M'	Ju 87 damaged	El Adem 0730-0904
33 Sqn	Plt Off D.F.Winsland	Hurricane I Z4251 }	Bf 110	LG.125 area 0820-0900
	Flg Off Anderson	Hurricane I Z4633 }		
94 Sqn	Wg Cdr H.C.Mayers	Hurricane I Z4719	Bf 109 damaged	El Adem area 0830-1000
	Lt A.H.Moolman	Hurricane I Z4427	Bf 109 damaged	El Adem area 0830-1000
33 Sqn	Plt Off Edy	Hurricane I Z4565 }		
	Sgt Davidson	Hurricane I V7772 }	Ju 88 probable	LG.125 area 1000
	Sgt Kelsall	Hurricane I W9351 }		
RNFS	Sub Lt G.R.Henderson	Hurricane I	Bf 109 probable	W Gabr Saleh 1130-
	Sub Lt A.R.Astin	Hurricane I Z4177 'Q'	Bf 109	SE Gubi
	Sub Lt A.R.Astin	Hurricane I Z4177 'Q'	Bf 109 damaged	
	Sub Lt P.Fell	Hurricane I Z4189	G.50 probable	20m SE Gubi 1640
	Sub Lt J.F.Kee	Hurricane I	G.50 damaged	20m SE Gubi 1640
250 Sqn	Sqn Ldr E.J.Morris	Tomahawk	Bf 109s damaged	S El Adem 1230
	Flt Lt C.R.Caldwell	Tomahawk AK498	Bf 109E	Tobruk 1230
	2/Lt D.L.Norton, SAAF	Tomahawk	Bf 109 damaged	Tobruk 1230
	Sgt R.J.C.Whittle	Tomahawk	Bf 109E	Tobruk 1230
	Sgt R.J.C.Whittle	Tomahawk	2 Bf 109Es damaged	Tobruk 1230
	Sgt McWilliam	Tomahawk	Bf 109 damaged	S El Adem 1230
	Sgt W.O.Cable	Tomahawk	Bf 109 damaged	S El Adem 1230
	Plt Off R.B.Cole	Tomahawk	3 Bf 109s damaged	S El Adem 1230
	Sgt M.S.Hards	Tomahawk	2 Bf 109s	Tobruk 1230
	Sgt M.S.Hards	Tomahawk	Bf 109 probable	Tobruk 1230
	Sgt M.S.Hards	Tomahawk	Bf 109s damaged	Tobruk 1230
	Flt Lt C.R.Caldwell	Tomahawk AK498	Bf 109E	W Capuzzo 1600
	Sgt W.O.Cable	Tomahawk	Bf 109E	W Capuzzo 1600
	Sgt R.H.Nitschke		Bf 109E damaged	W Capuzzo 1600
238 Sqn	Sgt Fairbairn	Hurricane IIc 'E'	Bf 109 damaged	LG.122 1530-1705
4 SAAF Sqn	Capt A.C.Bosman	Tomahawk	Bf 109	LG.122 1600
	Lt D.W.Golding	Tomahawk	Bf 109	LG.122 1600
	Wt.Off.II R.E.Jackson	Tomahawk	Bf 109 probable	LG.122 1600
272 Sqn	Flt Lt G.L.Campbell	Beaufighter Ic 'S' }		
	Flg Off A.A.Salter	Beaufighter Ic 'R' }	4 S.79s on ground	Barce mid p.m.
	Plt Off N.K.Lee	Beaufighter Ic 'P' }		
	Sgt R.J.G.Demoulin	Beaufighter Ic 'E' }		

805 Sqn	Sub Lt J.R.Routley	Martlet	}	S.79 damaged	over convoy 1605
	Sub Lt R.W.M.Walsh	Martlet			

British Casualties

229 Sqn	Hurricane IIc shot down; Plt Off J.R. Stideford KiA
	Hurricane IIb Z5269 shot down; Plt Off H.Ravn returned immediately
238 Sqn	Hurricane IIc FTR; Flg Off J.E.Sulman KiA
	Hurricane IIc Z5062 FTR; Plt Off W.G.R. Outhwaite RAAF MIA, died 28th 0845?
	Hurricane IIc FTR; Sgt D.W.Pike KiA
	Hurricane IIc 'T' shot down; Plt Off Collenette returned
	Hurricane IIc crash-landed; Plt Off E.M. Frost returned
RNFS	Hurricane I V7308 shot down at Bir el Gubi; Sub Lt A.J.C.Willis KiA 1125
	Hurricane 1 W9359 crash-landed; Sub Lt K.G.Talbot returned safely
250 Sqn	Tomahawk damaged; Sqn Ldr E.J.Morris unhurt
	Tomahawk shot down; Sgt D.M.Palethorpe KiA
	Tomahawk AN435 FTL LG.123 at 1730; Sgt G C Coward WIA 1730
4 SAAF Sqn	Tomahawk MiA; Lt P.A.du Plessis KiA
272 Sqn	Beaufighter Ic 'P' shot down by Flak; Plt Off N.K.Lee and observer, Sgt Gowing, returned on 25th
	Beaufighter Ic 'R' damaged by Flak and crashed at LG.10 on return; Flg Off A.A.Salter safe
RNFS	Hurricane I shot down; Lt D.P.Z.Cox baled out
238 Sqn	Hurricane IIc FTR; Plt Off R.E.Sellar KiA
	Hurricane IIc damaged; Flt Lt J.R.Urwin-Mann unhurt
33 Sqn	Hurricane I FTR; Flg Off Anderson; force-landed in dark – returned next day
24 SAAF Sqn	Boston III W8378 shot down; Lt C.W.E.Blake and crew PoW

German Claims

1./JG 27	Hptmn Wolfgang Redlich	Hurricane	SE El Adem 0835
	Obfw Albert Espenlaub	2 P-40s	S Bir el Gubi 0840-0845
Stab II./JG 27	Hptmn Wolfgang Lippert	Hurricane	E Bir Hacheim 1225
Stab I./JG 27	Hptmn Eduard Neumann	Hurricane	Sid Rezegh 1244
1./JG 27	Obfw Albert Espenlaub	Boston	SW El Adem
5./JG 27	Oblt Emmerich Fluder	P-40	SE Sidi Rezegh 1555
4./JG 27	Oblt Ferdinand Vögl	P-40	S Tobruk 1605
1./JG 27	Hptmn Wolfgang Redlich	Hurricane	SE El Adem
	Hptmn Wolfgang Redlich	Hurricane	S Bir el Gubi 1635

German Casualties

Stab II./JG 27	Bf 109F-4 trop WNr 8469 shot down Bir el Gubi; Hptmn Wolfgang Lippert baled out, PoW
5./JG 27	Bf 109F-4 trop WNr 8446 shot down SE Bir el Gubi; Fw Hans Glessinger MiA
2./StG 1	Ju 87 shot down 60m S Tobruk; Oblt Eberhard Keidel/Gefr Werner Keller KiA at 0840
3./StG 1	Ju 87 shot down 60m S Tobruk; Fw Rudolf Vetter/Gefr Rudolf Kihr KiA at 0840
I St G 1	Ju 87 crash-landed in combat SE Bir el Gubi, crew rescued
6./StG 2	Ju 87 crash-landed in combat SE Bir el Gubi; pilot, Oblt Fritz Eyer WiA
6./StG 2	Ju 87 crash-landed in combat 15m S El Adem; Fw Karl Polka/Uffz Robert Reinelt WiA
Stab/StG 3	Ju 87 combat 100m SSE Derna; Oblt Edmund Kraus safe; gunner Fw Helmut Bartels WiA
6./StG 3	Ju 87 in combat Bir el Gubi; Ogefr Heinrich Steindl; Ogefr Georg Peters WiA
2.(H)/14	Bf 110 down; Oblt Hans Dietrich Budde/Gefr Reinhold PoWs
III./LG 1	Ju 88A-5 trop WNr 4363 destroyed at Benina by bombs; Uffz August Neumann and one KiA
I./NJG 2	Ju 88C-6 shot-up over Africa, crash-landed on return to Sicily 50% damaged; Lt Voight safe

Italian Claims

155° Gr CT	T.Col Luigi Bianchi	2 Tomahawks	Bir el Gubi 0745-
351ª Sq/155° Gr CT	S.Ten Giuseppe Riccardi	2 Hurricanes	Bir el Gubi 0745-
378ª Sq/155° Gr CT	Ten Tullio Martinelli	Tomahawk	Bir el Gubi 0745-
378ª Sq/155° Gr CT	Ten Vittorio Galfetti	Hurricane	Bir el Gubi 0745-
378ª Sq/155° Gr CT	Serg Magg Luigi Caroli	Hurricane	Bir el Gubi 0745-
153° Gr CT	Unspecified pilot	Hurricane	N El Cuasc 0725-
159ª Sq/12° Gr CT	Serg Giuseppe Zardini	Blenheim	Castel Benito 1315

Italian Casualties

378ª Sq/155° Gr CT	G.50 MM6388 down;
	Cap Bruno Tattanelli baled out safely
Governor of Libya	S.81 destroyed on ground at Barce
Unspecified unit	S.79 on ground at Barce
1ª Sq/11° Gr/13° St BT	BR.20 damaged on ground at Barce,
	pilot M.llo Vasco Bosi 4ªSq and
	7 airmen killed

Monday, 24 November 1941

An early morning patrol over Gialo by Plt Off
Wade and Sgt Inglesby proved successful when an
S.79 was encountered and claimed shot down by
the two pilots. This pair then engaged eight-ten
CR.42s, each pilot claiming to have damaged one.
Wade: "Sgt Inglesby and self attacked and
destroyed one S.79 bombing El Eng. Encountered
8-10 CR.42s. Damaged one. Later confirmed by
ALO Moet as destroyed." Although this aircraft
was then credited to Wade, it seems that the ALO
had been mistaken, for the only Italian fighter
casualty was an aircraft of 160° Gruppo CT

Cap Bruno Tattanelli, CO of 378ª Squadriglia, 155°
Gruppo CT. He was shot down on 23 November but baled
out safely.

which was damaged, S.Ten Ivo Pizzini being
wounded. Similarly, the S.79, an aircraft of 174ª Squadriglia had escaped destruction, returning to base
with a wounded crew member aboard.

A second early operation involved three Bostons of 24 SAAF Squadron which set out to undertake a
reconnaissance of the area Bir el Gubi-Bir Hacheim-Acroma-El Gobbi. Off at 0800, these aircraft were
attacked about an hour and a half later over Gazala by Obfw Espenlaub of 1./JG 27, who concentrated
his fire on Lt Roxburgh's aircraft, setting both engines on fire, shooting the guns out of the hands of Air
Sgt B.van den Berg, and wounding both gunners. The crew then baled out, subsequently being picked
up by two Luftwaffe aircraft and flown to Gazala as prisoners.

Shortly after midday a lone Bf 110 bombed Giarabub landing ground, but inflicted no damage. Two
Hurricanes were scrambled to intercept, Flg Off Noel-Johnson and Sgt MacDonald claiming to have
inflicted damage on the intruder.

During the afternoon nine of 80 Squadron's Hurribombers set off to attack tanks heading for
Maddelena, but as they approached the Sidi Rezegh area, about a dozen Bf 110s suddenly streaked
beneath them at "an incredible speed", flying in the same direction. Both sides were clearly surprised by
this turn of events, but the British pilots at once attacked, joined by escorting Tomahawks from 4 SAAF
Squadron. The South African pilots claimed two shot down and shared two more with Hurricane pilots;
only one of the latter, Sgt Comfort, was identified and it is possible that the second was shared with Flg
Off Tulloch, whose Hurricane was seen to dive into the ground in flames. One of the South African
Tomahawks was hard hit, the pilot, Lt Rogan, having his leg almost severed. Loosing blood heavily, he
managed to apply a form of tourniquet and got back to base. Despite his efforts, he subsequently lost
the leg by amputation. (He would later return to operational flying with an artificial limb.) Four more
claims for aircraft damaged were submitted by the 80 Squadron pilots, but initially Flt Sgt Ekiel (Z4801)
and Sgt Foskett failed to return. Both were safely back next day, having landed at Sidi Barrani. Foskett
reported that he had shot down one of the Bf 110s, noting that these aircraft appeared to have a
European-style camouflage paint scheme, and that his victim had crash-landed, following which four
people climbed out. This led the squadron to the view that they might have intercepted a formation in
the process of arriving from the other side of the Mediterranean.

This seems unlikely, since it was undoubtedly III./ZG 26; 17 aircraft from this unit, escorted by 15 Bf
109s, were ground-strafing when the WDAF was encountered, the German pilots claiming three
Hurricanes and four 'P-40s' shot down, but losing three of their own aircraft, the crews of two of which
became PoWs. One of the successful pilots, Obfw Richard Heller of 8.Staffel, was also shot down as
described by his gunner, Uffz Mühlbrodt:

"The sun was just rising but already the Bf 110s were hovering over the British columns. Our Rotte has discovered a new column on the march. Suddenly I see one, two, three, four black dots on the right. They are approaching. I shout: 'Fighters !' My pilot curves in and at the same moment the fighters zoom over us and we can see the blue rings of their cockades. They turn in again. The sky above is full of black specks and I count 12 or more fighters. It seems as if we have fallen right into the midst of a strong formation.

"We try to escape in a frantic dive, because it is hopeless to fight such an overwhelming crowd, but we cannot escape. The Curtiss are too high and overtake us in the dive. Our engines scream and I shout to the pilot: 'First attack !' Exactly behind us appears the snout of a Curtiss; a right turn is useless because to left and right of the attacking fighter two more Curtiss are flying. Out of the wings of the Curtiss come flashes of all colours. Then it rattles in our aircraft as if someone were knocking a milk churn. The next Curtiss is attacking, while the first is hovering over us like a satisfied bird. Second attack, so quickly, that I can scarcely warn the pilot. The hail of bullets comes down like a shower. There is no escape. We are in the trap. The fighters relieve each other as if on a shooting range. Both engines stutter, the right one is smoking. We have only one chance; a belly-landing in the desert ! I see the ground approaching. At the same moment a Curtiss is closing in for an attack. The Bf 110 glides towards the ground very softly, but the Curtiss is diving at us like a meteor. The cannon and gun burst are whistling around us, splinters whizz through the cabin. Heller holds the stick with the left, and with the right hand holds the gunsight. I myself seize the machine gun, because we will touch down at any moment. While gliding the Bf 110 hits a heap of stones, there is a mighty jerk, and I land between the drum magazines. For a moment I sit benumbed in the cockpit, but then I jump up. It is high time, as from both sides flames are blazing into the cabin. I jump out and run for cover. The Curtiss disappears. Heller's left hand is bleeding, it was hit between thumb and forefinger. I tie up his arm and make a sling. After a short march we are found by German soldiers who take us to the next airfield. We ask about our wingman, but he had more luck and has landed safely at home despite some damage."

A few minutes later 94 Squadron attacked a column of vehicles south of El Adem where Lt Palm, after shooting-up three lorries, encountered three G.50bis, claiming one of these shot down. At this point the air force was about to face a crisis not of its own making.

Kenneth Cross:

"Rommel sent an armoured column supported by motorised infantry behind our forward troops and made a dash eastwards to the frontier wire aiming at a point near Sidi Omar. The route was right across the Army's communications from Fort Maddalena. This move was not reported by the Army, but by mid-morning our fighter leaders were reporting a column going east 'lickety spit behind our forward troops'. 8th Army HQ at first refuted the idea that any enemy could be in such a position 'behind our troops' and asserted 'RAF mis-identification'. I quizzed the next Wing Leader to land, personally. It was Pete Jeffrey, a very experienced and hard-headed Australian. I said, 'The Army say it can't be an enemy column in that location.' 'Well tell them the tanks have big black crosses on them and no British column possesses flak like this one!' The next sweep due over the battlefield was by two South African squadrons who were quickly re-briefed to attack the 'soft' part of the column (ie. the transport vehicles) because their machine-guns were useless against 'hard' tanks. I decided to go along with them to see things for myself. It was mid-afternoon and before I left I gave instructions that all squadrons were to attack the column until darkness made further attacks impossible, but unfortunately there was only about two and a half hours of daylight left.

"We found the column without difficulty because of the enormous cloud of dust it was kicking up by its high speed. It was led by 30 or 40 tanks followed closely by some 200 MT. Up came the light flak as we approached and for some apparent reason the entire column stopped. The squadrons made their attack while I watched, and then I flew quickly back to base on my own. It was plain to me that Rommel was headed for the wire and the key question in my mind was, would he turn north to help his troops surrounded at Halfaya and Bardia, or would he turn south to attack our Headquarters and airfield area? From his present position he could reach us to the south during the night. I landed and hurried off to Western Desert Headquarters to see Coningham. He had already anticipated my fears and had asked the Army to alert the brigade assigned to airfield defence, only to be told that it had been sent elsewhere.

"Of course there is nothing more vulnerable than an airfield with its aeroplanes on the ground. The vast perimeter dictated by the length of the runways makes defence an impossibility for the airmen ground crew, hence the need for ground troops to attack the enemy before he reached the airfield area. Also, airmen ground crews were neither trained nor equipped for soldier duties. Without any defence, there were only two things to do; evacuate the aircraft to safe bases and when they had gone, send the ground crews off into the desert and hope the enemy wouldn't find them. We had no weapons for defence except rifles and pistols. Back at Wing Headquarters I sent an order for all squadrons to return to their original airfields in the rear at Sidi Haneish 'before last light'. There was just about an hour and a half of daylight left and it was a measure of our operational efficiency that despite the complete surprise of my orders, all serviceable aircraft left promptly and were safe at Sidi Haneish before dark.

"The next step was to disperse the ground crew and equipment away from the airfields and orders were sent to proceed south for some ten miles and to camp there for the night. This move, though unprecedented, quite unexpected and at very short notice, was satisfactorily completed but the officers and airmen spent a most uncomfortable winter's night on 24/25 November, sleeping under their lorries. No fires were allowed, not even a cup of chlorinated tea to lessen their misery.

Russ Foskett, who, as a sergeant with 80 Squadron, shot down a Bf 110 on 24 November 1941. Here he is later in the war as commanding officer of 94 Squadron.

"During the night, which I spent in the operations truck, we were full of apprehension. Would Rommel turn north or south when he reached the wire? There were no troops between us and him now. Worse still, as darkness fell, our only source of reliable information, air reconnaissance, ceased. Suddenly there came the sound of armour close to where we were and it took me a moment or two to realise that not even Rommel could have covered the distance from the point of last light sighting to our location in such a short time. I went outside to see a collection of Honey (M3A Stuart) light reconnaissance tanks going by with David Belchem (a pre-war friend now serving with the Royal Tank Regiment) in the leading tank. 'My, my,' I thought, 'we really are scraping the barrel if this is our only defence against Rommel's formidable column!' Sitting through the long night with my Wing staff, it was inevitable that the deficiencies of the 8th Army was a topic of conversation, and it was pretty critical conversation at that. Many sarcastically reminded us of the Army's queries before the start of Crusader as to the Air Force's ability to fulfil its role! The general conclusion amongst these battle-hardened airmen was that our Army partners in Crusader were a very amateur lot, particularly their Commanders. We were grateful that in Tedder and Coningham we had experienced leaders and that their subordinates had been thoroughly tested in combat against Germans and Italians in Europe and the Mediterranean. True the South Africans were new to it all but when teamed up with the British and Australians they learned fast, and when it came to air firing they were above average already."

It had been a close-run thing. One hour before sunset the Axis ground forces had attacked LGs.123 and 124 from where Cross had organised the hasty evacuations to LGs.122 and 128. Here, consequently, large numbers of aircraft ended up congregated together, presenting an incredible target for the advancing Germans, should they spot them. In fact during the night Rommel's tanks passed within ten miles of LG.122, missing a golden opportunity to destroy some 175 British aircraft on the ground. Next morning they passed within five miles of LG.132 at Sidi Omar. Kenneth Cross continued: "When dawn came, pre-arranged reconnaissance aircraft from Sidi Haneish were already over the area of the enemy column's last sighting and quickly located it on the wire south of Sidi Omar and going north. Sighs of relief all round and then, after consultation with Coningham I ordered the squadrons and ground crews to return to their airfields."

Late in the day the seven Hurricanes of the 73 Squadron Battle Flight arrived at Giarabub to take over from 33 Squadron. Three more of the latter unit's aircraft moved up to LG.125. From LG.10 three Beaufighters of 272 Squadron strafed roads north and south of Barce, about 15 vehicles being strafed.

The day was also marked by the transfer of Italian troops in North Africa to Rommel's direct command.

British Claims

33 Sqn	Plt Off L.C.Wade	Hurricane I Z4311	CR.42	LG.125 area a.m.
	Plt Off L.C.Wade	Hurricane I Z4311	} S.79	LG.125 area a.m.
	Sgt Inglesby	Hurricane I V7711		
	Sgt Inglesby	Hurricane I V7711	CR.42 damaged	LG.125 area a.m.
	Flg Off G.D.N.Noel-Johnson	Hurricane I Z4040	} Bf 110 damaged	1300
	Sgt MacDonald	Hurricane I Z4633		
80 Sqn	Sgt R.G.Foskett	Hurricane I Z4744	Bf 110	NW Maddalena 1530-1710
	Flt Lt Hon D.A.Coke	Hurricane I Z4833	Bf 110 damaged	NW Maddalena 1530-1710
	Flg Off P.T.Dowding	Hurricane I Z4931	Bf 110 damaged	NW Maddalena 1530-1710
	Flt Sgt P.W.Wintersdorf	Hurricane I Z4426	Bf 110 damaged	NW Maddalena 1530-1710
	Sgt A.C.Comfort	Hurricane I Z4764	} Bf 110	LG.122, NW Maddalena 1615
4 SAAF Sqn	Lt R.Chadwick	Tomahawk		
	Lt Y.Visser	Tomahawk	} Bf 110	LG.122 1615
	Lt V.A.Greenberg	Tomahawk		
	2/ Lt R.A.B.Thorpe	Tomahawk AN369	½ Bf 110	
	Capt D.D.Moodie	Tomahawk AN376	½ Bf 110	1615
	Lt M.Duff-Richardson	Tomahawk	½ Bf 110	1620
94 Sqn	Lt R.B.Palm	Hurricane I Z4856	G.50	SW Sidi Omar 1700

British Casualties

24 SAAF Sqn	Boston III W8384 shot down; Lt B.G.Roxburgh and crew baled out and PoWs
12 SAAF Sqn	Maryland II destroyed on ground at LG.76
237 Sqn	Hurricane shot down by Flak; Flt Lt Spence
80 Sqn	Hurricane I shot down; Flg Off C.H.L.Tulloch KiA
	Hurricane I force-landed Tobruk; Sgt N.Crouch safe
2 SAAF Sqn	Tomahawk AN369 FTR; 2/Lt R.A.B. Thorpe unhurt, picked up by ground troops, returned 26th
4 SAAF Sqn	Tomahawk AK518 damaged; Lt D.S.Rogan seriously wounded, but managed to return to base

German Claims

1./JG 27	Obfw Albert Espenlaub	Boston	S Ain el Gazala 0935
8./ZG 26	Lt Dieter Bridlingmaier	Hurricane	El Gubi 1600
9./ZG 26	Lt Alfred Wehmeyer	Hurricane	Bu Malitza 1608
8./ZG 26	Obfw Richard Heller	Hurricane	20m S Gobi 1609
7./ZG 26	Uffz Karl Emsbach	P-40	S Bir El Hacheim 1612
	Obfw Helmut Haugk	2 P-40s	Trigh el Abd 1613-1616
	Uffz Heinz Golisch	P-40	Trigh el Abd 1618

German Casualties

II./JG 27	Ju W 34 destroyed by bombs at Ain el Gazala
8./ZG 26	Bf 110 WNr 3410 shot down; Lt Herbert Gassner/ Gefr Reddig PoWs
9./ZG 26	Bf 110 WNr 3326 shot down; Oblt Hans Kolle/Ogfr Jurgen Luckmann PoWs
8./ZG 26	Bf 110 crash-landed; Obfw Richard Heller/ Uffz Mühlbrodt; Heller WiA; picked up by ground troops and returned

Italian Claims

13° St BT	BR.20 gunners	Fighter Probable	Wadi el Mra area

Italian Casualties

375ª Sq/160° Gr CT	CR.42 damaged; S.Ten Ivo Pizzini WiA
32ª Sq OA	Ca.311 MM11499 FTR; Cap Carlo Gautier and crew MiA
174ª Sq RST	S.79 damaged; returned with wounded crewman on board

Tuesday, 25 November 1941

The main duty of the WDAF during this day was to strafe the advancing Axis columns. However, at 0630 five Beaufighters of 272 Squadron were again the first aircraft in the air, strafing Jedabia airfield where two CR.42s and a Ca.310 were claimed damaged on the ground. The former of these would appear to have been aircraft of 160° Gruppo CT, which reported that three of the unit's fighters were damaged at Agedabia. The Beaufighter crews also reported seeing a transport aircraft crash-land 'in a hurry' some 30 miles east of the airfield, although none of the pilots fired at it until after it had crashed. During this sortie Flt Lt Bartlett's aircraft collided with a telegraph pole which tore off three feet and six inches from the wingtip of the starboard wing. It required the assistance of his observer to hold the aircraft steady on the way back to base. A large fuel tanker was also claimed to have been destroyed during this sortie.

At 0815 12 Tomahawks of 112 Squadron strafed troops; despite two aircraft being hit by ground fire, all returned. Surprise had been lost, however, and when 12 more Tomahawks, this time from 3 RAAF Squadron, appeared ten minutes later, they flew into a furious barrage. Flg Off Jewell was shot down, as was Flg Off Bothwell, who was wounded, dying next day. Flt Lt Manford was forced to crash-land, but survived unhurt, as did Flt Lt Arthur, who managed to nurse his damaged aircraft back to base. Jewell, meanwhile, had come down between two columns of Axis transports and hid. He was discovered and captured, being asked for directions to Sidi Omar. Taking the risky course of giving his captors incorrect directions, he caused them to drive straight into a New Zealand patrol where he took the opportunity to leap from the vehicle in which he was a passenger, as the Germans made off at high speed.

During the morning 262 Wing arrived at LG.110, ready to move on to LG.122. On arrival at the former airfield the welcome news was received that Wg Cdr Fred Rosier was safe (see 22 November).

A mid afternoon encounter proved heavy and confused, a plethora of claims being made by the Commonwealth pilots. Twelve 112 Squadron Tomahawks and seven from 3 RAAF Squadron undertook a sweep over Sidi Rezegh, encountering a mixed force of 60-70 Axis aircraft which had just attacked the ground forces. This force included 17 Ju 87s of I./StG 3, 15 of II./StG 2, 12 Bf 110s and 12 Bf 109s. Pilots reported Bf 110s at 1,300 feet, Ju 87s at 6,000 feet, Bf 110s at 10,000 feet, then Ju 88s, CR.42s and a top cover of Bf 109Es, Bf 109Fs and G.50bis. Claims were submitted for four Bf 110s, plus one probable and two damaged, one Bf 109, one probable and two damaged, two G.50bis, one probable and three damaged, two Fi 156s and a single CR.42 – all around 1540. Each unit lost one Tomahawk, both pilots being killed.

It was during this same mid afternoon period that JG 27's Bf 109F pilots claimed one Hurricane and four P-40s, while Bf 110 pilot Lt Hans Hufnagel also claimed one of the latter, as did Regia Aeronautica pilots for two more; in total this was well over the actual losses inflicted. Axis losses were, as so often, considerably lower than the claims of the Tomahawk pilots appeared to indicate. III./ZG 26 suffered the loss of two Bf 110 crews, all reported missing, although one pilot, Lt Joern Scharf was later reported to be a PoW. The two Fi 156s shot down by Rex Wilson were both aircraft of II./JG 27 which had been unlucky in flying into the combat area when on the way to attend the funeral of Lt Scheppa. They were flown by Lt Gorny and Oberarzt Heydenreich, who subsequently reported that after crashing, their aircraft were strafed on the ground, Gorny suffering wounds.

The aircraft claimed as a CR.42 by 112 Squadron's Flg Off Humphreys, appears actually to have been a Ro 37bis of 129ª Squadriglia. This was attacked by a fighter and forced to crash-land at El Adem, and while Ten Antonio Grillo and Giuseppe Conti survived unhurt, the biplane was a complete write-off.

Of this hectic combat, Bobby Gibbes later recorded:

"The Wing Leader led the squadrons down after the enemy aircraft as they dived out to sea, slightly east of Tobruk. I started to follow, but noticed quite a lot of fighters above us, so I changed my mind and climbed up alone after them. Luck was with me. They proved to be mainly Italians in G.50s and Macchi 200s who were flying in line astern, in groups of five aircraft, in each formation. They had watched our wing dive down after the bombers, and this appeared to have absorbed their interest, as I seemed to be almost unobserved. On each occasion, they had almost passed by me before I was seen, and the leader, by then, was so committed to his dive, that he was not able to do much about dealing with me, and I found that I was able to get good bursts at numerous machines, without once leaving myself open.

"One team of five aircraft came down in a gentle dive, noticed me at the last moment, and the leader tried to pull round onto me. This put me into a very favourable position as I came in at them

---

342

from the opposite direction, on the inside of their turn, and I was able to have a crack at each of the five as they swept by, in line astern. The same thing happened three or four times, and although I didn't do much noticeable damage, I did however, succeed in breaking up their formation considerably. Without doubt, I prevented a few co-ordinated attacks on the squadrons below.

"A G.50 came at me shooting madly. I returned his fire, crouching low behind the engine and feeling the size of a house. He made the mistake of breaking his attack too early, and turned away to starboard. I pulled off a little lead, and saw bits and pieces fly from his cockpit area. The aircraft rolled onto its back to the right and went into an uncontrolled spin, pouring black smoke. I turned my aircraft and watched it plummet down towards the sea below, and then with a jerk, realising my foolishness, I kicked on hard rudder and looked behind. I was just in time. Macchis and G.50s were coming at me from all directions. I gave the old Tommy everything, weaving my way through them, and climbed above. Suddenly, they all seemed to be so very harmless, like clueless children out on a Sunday jaunt, whose aunt had temporarily left them. My morale was terrific, and for the first time, no residue of fear remained. I saw a line of G.50s below my level and dived to attack. They were doing a gentle turn to port when I joined them, making the formation six, but only for a moment. My bullets concentrated around the tail-end aircraft and I don't think he would have known what hit him. His aircraft shuddered, hesitated in its turn, bunted outwards, pulled up into a half loop, then fell away, obviously completely out of control leaving a spiral trail of black smoke behind it. It was probably flown by a dead pilot. I pulled around onto the next aircraft, and when I fired, it flicked onto its back and dived away, but it appeared to be under control. Maybe I didn't damage it too much, but I certainly frightened hell out of the pilot.

"The remainder of the flight broke up in all directions, and taking advantage of the superior performance of my aircraft, I climbed up above them, to avoid any tests of manoeuvrability, and to take stock of proceedings, and try to get my machine guns working again, as some had given up the ghost. I noticed a splash in the sea below, but didn't know if it was my G.50 or not, but supposed that it was.

"The fight went on and I am afraid that I was now behaving in a childish manner and I was whooping like a wild Indian on the warpath. I do not believe that I shot anything down after this, but things were moving at too fast and furious a rate to get time to observe the results of further attacks. Without doubt I hit the further odd machine as I was able to get into infallible positions. The air-space which had been full of stunting Italians, suddenly cleared like magic as seems to happen in air combat. I looked around and the only aircraft which I could see was a 109 below me. I chased after it at full throttle, climbed up into the sun and positioned myself for an attack. I then saw why the 109 was not more alert. His eyes were fastened on another prey in the form of two unsuspecting Tomahawks cruising in formation below him. He put his aircraft into a gentle dive heading south-west and behind the Tomahawks and I started my dive from the north to north-east, out of the sun, heading him off, coming in at right angles. I called a warning to the two Tommys, and on a converging course, I rapidly closed on the 109 which had now dropped slightly below them in order to stay out of sight. At last I had a complete drop on a 109.

"My dreams had materialised and I had one exactly where I wanted it. At high speed, in range, fire. I pressed the trigger and my guns barked in response. By almost a sixth sense my German friend saw me at the last moment, and pulled his stick back making my fire pass below him. He then proceeded to pump-handle his joystick rapidly backwards and forwards, as if following the track of the switchback rail at Luna Park, and I didn't have a hope in hell of hitting him in my first attack. I overshot, pulled around, washing a lot of speed off, and got in an attack from the port rear quarter, which I believe hit him, but did not stop him. I fired again and again, but although he looked a bit sick in the end, he was nevertheless still flying and gradually pulled out of range. I had lost what should have been a certain kill. The Hun beat me by fast thinking and a trick which was too good for me. Full credit to him. I noted this trick and added it to my limited repertoire, and it was later to prove useful in getting out of a similar jam."

Shortly after this big fight, 258 Wing's Lt Col L.A.Wilmot claimed a Bf 110 shot down, while at an unspecified time another such aircraft was claimed by Sgt Comfort of 80 Squadron. One of these claims (or possibly both) relate to a reconnaissance aircraft from 2.(H)/14 which was reportedly lost to fighters over Sidi Omar; Wilmot had indeed claimed his victim in this area when leading the South African

Tomahawk squadrons on a sweep. He reported that this aircraft fell in flames, its crash setting two vehicles alight and colliding with a third. The German pilot, Lt Eberhard Kuhnt, was rushed to Bardia hospital, and from there was put on an Italian torpedo-boat bound for Taranto. On the way this vessel was itself torpedoed and he became a PoW.

Elsewhere during the day Lt Johnston of the RNFS was shot down by Flak whilst undertaking a lone reconnaissance. He became a PoW, but escaped three hours later during a raid by Blenheims, returning to his unit next day. During the 25th 109 Squadron flew five sorties with its special Wellingtons, but by the end of the day the unit had only one serviceable and two damaged but repairable aircraft left. Consequently, operations ceased and the unit was stood down. Near Tobruk a Ju 87 of I./StG 3 was shot down by AA, the crew becoming prisoners. The day also saw the arrival at Derna from Tripoli of the MC.202s of 9° and 17° Gruppi CT, which then moved to Martuba during the afternoon. Ten Bf 110s of III./ZG 26 arrived at Derna between 1630 and 1636, an Ultra intercept noting the aircraft involved as being coded 3U+BR, GR, HS, XS, DD, AT, CT, ET, FT,and NT. Initially, LS and BS were reported as being overdue.

After commanding 1 SAAF Squadron, Lt Col Laurie Wilmot took over 2 SAAF Squadron on 12 November 1941, also acting as sweep leader with 258 Wing.

British Claims

272 Sqn	Wg Cdr R.G.Yaxley	Beaufighter Ic 'A'		
	Flt Lt M.L.P.Bartlett	Beaufighter Ic 'B'		
	Plt Off D.H. Hammond	Beaufighter Ic 'S'	CR.42s damaged on ground	Agedabia
	Plt Off H.H.Crawford	Beaufighter Ic 'C'	Ca.310 damaged on ground	Agedabia
	Plt Off J.Watters	Beaufighter Ic 'T'		
112 Sqn	Plt Off N.Bowker	Tomahawk AK503	Bf 110	Sidi Rezegh area 1525-1710
	Flg Off P.H.Humphreys	Tomahawk AK405	CR.42	Sidi Rezegh area 1525-1710
	Flg Off P.H.Humphreys	Tomahawk AK405	Bf 109F probable	Sidi Rezegh area 1525-1710
	Flt Lt D.F.Westenra	Tomahawk AN303	G.50 probable	Sidi Rezegh area 1525-1710
3 RAAF Sqn	Flg Off R.H.Gibbes	Tomahawk AN374	2 G.50s	Sidi Rezegh area 1540
	Flg Off R.H.Gibbes	Tomahawk AN374	3 G.50s damaged	Sidi Rezegh area 1540
	Sgt M.J.Baillie	Tomahawk AK378	Bf 109E	Sidi Rezegh area 1540
	Sgt F.B.Reid	Tomahawk AN408	Bf 110	Sidi Rezegh area 1540
	Sgt R.K.Wilson	Tomahawk AK506	Bf 110	Sidi Rezegh area 1540
	Sgt R.K.Wilson	Tomahawk AK506	2 Bf 110s damaged	Sidi Rezegh area 1540
	Sgt R.K.Wilson	Tomahawk AK506	2 Fi 156s	Sidi Rezegh area 1540
	Sgt R.K.Wilson	Tomahawk AK506	Bf 109 damaged	Sidi Rezegh area 1540
	Flg Off E.H.B.Jackson	Tomahawk AM406	Bf 110 damaged	Sidi Rezegh area 1540
258 Wg	Wg Cdr P.Jeffrey	Tomahawk	Bf 110	Sidi Rezegh area 1540
	Wg Cdr P.Jeffrey	Tomahawk	Bf 110 damaged	Sidi Rezegh area 1540
258 Wg	Lt Col L.A.Wilmot	Tomahawk	Bf 110	Bir Sheferzen 1645
80 Sqn	Sgt A.C.Comfort	Hurricane I	Bf 110	

British Casualties

3 RAAF Sqn	Tomahawk AN406 shot down; Flg Off W.E.Jewell captured but escaped and returned
	Tomahawk AM398 shot down; Flg Off P.R.Bothwell KiA – died 26th
	Tomahawk crash-landed; Flt Lt Manford unhurt
	Tomahawk damaged; Flt Lt W.S.Arthur unhurt
	Tomahawk shot down; Flg Off B.A.Evans KiA
RNFS	Hurricane I shot down by Flak; Lt.R.L.Johnston captured but escaped and returned
112 Sqn	Tomahawk AK461 'A' shot down; Sgt F.D.Glasgow KiA

German Claims

4./JG 27	Oblt Gustav Rödel	Hurricane		N Tobruk 1555
	Oblt Gustav Rödel	P-40		N Tobruk 1557
	Obfw Otto Schulz	P-40		N Tobruk 1600
	Obfhr Gerhard Endmann	P-40		N Tobruk 1605
1./JG 27	Obfw Albert Espenlaub	P-40		S Tobruk 1605
9./ZG 26	Lt Hans Hufnagel	P-40		1601

German Casualties

1./JG 27	Bf 109F-4 trop WNr 8494 crash-landed at Gazala after combat
3./StG 3	Ju 87 WNr 6315 shot down by AA W Tobruk; Uffz Hans-Joachim Schäfer/Uffz Anton Herrmann PoWs
2.(H)/14	Bf 110 shot down Sidi Omar; Lt Eberhard Kuhnt/ Obfw Karl Rabannser PoWs; gunner Ogefr Paul Oeser KiA
8./ZG26	Bf 110 WNr 3985 FTR; Oblt Dieter Bidlingmaier/Uffz Gerhard Becker MiA
	Bf 110 WNr 3181 FTR; Lt Joern Scharf/Uffz Hermann Bogler MiA; Scharf later reported to be PoW
II./JG 27	Fi 156 shot down; Lt Gorny WiA
	Fi 156 shot down; Oberarzt Heydenreich unhurt
Unspecified unit	Ju.W.34 destroyed on ground at Ain el Gazala
	2 Bf 109s damaged on ground by bombs at Ain el Gazala
I./StG 3	Ju 87R2 WNr 6068 destroyed at Gambut; Oblt Alfred Kauschke safe

N.B.: One of the Fi 156s lost was WNr 5072 of the Desert Rescue staffel. The two 8./ZG26 aircraft were WNr 3985 and 3181.

Italian Claims

353ª Sq/20° Gr CT	Cap Riccardo Roveda	Tomahawk		Gambut mid p.m.
	Serg Alcide Leoni	Tomahawk		Gambut mid p.m.

Italian Casualties

129° Sq OA	Ro 37bis shot down, crash-landed, w/o; Ten Antonio Grillo and Ten Giuseppe Conti safe
160° Gr CT	3 CR.42s damaged at Agedabia
Unspecified unit	S.82 damaged on ground at Benghazi
	G.50bis damaged on ground at Benghazi
	Ca.133 damaged on ground at Benghazi

Wednesday, 26 November 1941

At dawn German troops thrust towards Sidi Aziez and Bir el Hariga, four Hurricanes of 451 Squadron just getting away in time. During the day German tanks entered Bardia, and to the east the New Zealanders captured Belhamed. The Tobruk garrison now reached Ed Duda, but on this date General Cunningham was replaced by Maj Gen Ritchie as OC 8th Army.

At 1145 a dozen Hurricanes of 229 Squadron and 11 of 238 Squadron swept over Sidi Rezegh, pilots reporting meeting 12 Bf 109s. Two of these were claimed by pilots of 229 Squadron, but 238 Squadron suffered heavily; Sgt Knappett and Sgt Kay were both shot down, the former killed but the latter making his way back on foot, while Flg Off Kings and Plt Off Currie both crash-landed. Currie came down within the Tobruk defences, while Kings removed the overcoat from a dead Italian soldier, then driving an abandoned tank all through the night to reach Tobruk as well.

MC.202 pilots of 9° Gruppo had undertaken their first sorties, 11 of them claiming eight fighters shot down and a ninth probably so. One Macchi was hit and damaged, but the pilot, Cap Antonio Larsimont Pergameni, was unhurt. There seems little doubt that it was the 229 and 238 Squadron Hurricanes that the Italian pilots had engaged.

At much the same time six Beaufighters of 272 Squadron again strafed Agedabia, claiming a Caproni aircraft shot down before strafing Ju 87s and CR.42s on the ground. Sgt Price's aircraft failed to return and was believed to have been shot down by Flak. In fact S.Ten Giuseppe Cantù of 375ª Squadriglia,

A Ghibli of 12ª Squadriglia APC. An aircraft of this unit was forced to land in the desert, probably by Beaufighters, on 16 November 1941.

160° Gruppo, had shot this aircraft down, the crew becoming PoWs. Four CR.42s were then seen over a convoy, one of these being attacked and claimed damaged by Flt Lt Campbell.

Mid afternoon 151° Gruppo CT sent off nine CR.42s to escort other fighters of this type, strafing armoured cars in the Agila area. Two of 33 Squadron's Hurricanes were patrolling over the Gialo area – the last of several such sorties during the day. Plt Off Bill Winsland and Flg Off Clostre spotted the Italian formation and Winsland at once dived to attack, but was shot down and baled out. Cap Bernadino Serafini and Serg Magg Antonio Camerini claimed one each, both reporting that the pilot had baled out; they had obviously double-claimed on Winsland's aircraft. A third Hurricane was claimed by two other pilots. Winsland was later picked up and flown back to his unit in a Blenheim from El Eng.

At the time this engagement was taking place, nine Tomahawks of 3 RAAF Squadron with others from 112 Squadron patrolled over the Sidi Rezegh area from 1530. Six Bf 109s of I./JG 27 attacked, Hptmn Redlich shooting down one Australian Tomahawk from which Sgt Hiller baled out to become a PoW. Sgt Cameron claimed one Messerschmitt shot down in return, but none were actually lost or damaged.

Neville Duke was less than impressed with the day's operations:

By the end of November two MC.202-equipped gruppi joined the Regia Aeronautica units in North Africa. These were 9° Gruppo of 4° Stormo and 17° Gruppo of 1° Stormo. Ten Emanuele Annoni of 96ª Squadriglia, 9° Gruppo, made his first claim in Libya for a Hurricane on 26 November. By the end of the war he had reached a score of ten individual victories.

"Wing sweep in the afternoon with 3 RAAF and 229's Hurricanes. The cloud was low, about 6,000 feet, and over the Sidi Rezegh area we saw about six Bf 109s through a break in the clouds. Immediately all three squadrons went into a defensive circle ! Disgusting show. No. 3 RAAF lost two more chaps. That makes about 14 in four days. I think Tomahawks are shooting at each other as a Tommy looks very much like a 109."

Earlier in the day Hptmn Steinberger of 9./ZG 26 had also claimed a P-40, but no matching loss has been found. However, another 2.(H)/14 Bf 110 was lost, falling to AA fire; the crew became prisoners. During the day seven squadrons of Marylands and Blenheims operated over the battle area. At Ed Duda a column of 30 AFVs was partially destroyed and completely dispersed by an attack by Blenheims.

British Claims

229 Sqn	Sgt Warminger	Hurricane IIb Z3146	Bf 109	Sidi Rezegh area 1145-1330
	Plt Off J.H.Penny	Z5302	Bf 109	Sidi Rezegh area 1145-1330
33 Sqn	Flt Lt D.F.Winsland	Hurricane IIc	S.79	Gialo Oasis 1515
272 Sqn	Flt Lt G.L.Campbell	Beaufighter Ic 'O'		
	Flg Off G.W.Morris	Beaufighter Ic 'S'		
	Plt Off K.B.Orr	Beaufighter Ic 'A'	Caproni shot down	Jedabia 1215
	Plt Off W.G.Snow	Beaufighter Ic 'C'	4 CR.42s on ground	Jedabia 1215
	Plt Off J.H.Baker	Beaufighter Ic 'K'		
	Sgt N.A.J.Price	Beaufighter Ic 'E'		
	Flt Lt G.L.Campbell	Beaufighter Ic 'O'	CR.42 damaged	over convoy in Agedabia area
3 RAAF Sqn	Sgt A.C.Cameron	Tomahawk AN294	Bf 109	near Tobruk 1600
250 Sqn	Flt Lt C.R.Caldwell	Tomahawk AK498	Bf 109 damaged	

British Casualties

272 Sqn	Beaufighter Ic 'E' shot down by Flak; Sgt N.A.J.Price/ Sgt F.Southern PoWs
3 RAAF Sqn	Tomahawk AM413 shot down; Sgt G.E.Hiller PoW
238 Sqn	Hurricane IIc BV170 shot down; Sgt Kay returned on foot
	Hurricane IIc crash-landed; Flg Off Kings evaded capture and reached Tobruk
	Hurricane IIc Z5222 crash-landed; Plt Off H.G. Currie unhurt at Tobruk
	Hurricane IIc Z2355 shot down; Sgt R A Knappett, RAAF, KIA 1315
229 Sqn	Hurricane IIc 2/Lt N.C.Hoare KiA c. 0900*
451 Sqn	Hurricane I Z4308 crash-landed Gasr El Ahrad; Flt Lt A.D.Ferguson safe
33 Sqn	Hurricane IIc shot down by CR.42s Jalo Oasis/Agheila; Flt Lt D.S.F.Winsland PoW

* Variously listed as killed 22nd or 26th. Believed crashed during delivery flight of Hurrcane Z 5144 or Z 5328 50m SSW Sollum

German Claims

9./ZG 26	Hptmn Fritz Steinberger	P-40	1448
1./JG 27	Hptmn Wolfgang Redlich	P-40	W Bu Amud 1615

German Casualties

2.(H)/14	Bf 110 shot down by AA; Fw Eberhard Kurz PoW; Gefr Karl Harms WiA

Italian Claims

96ª Sq/9° Gr CT	Cap Ezio Viglione Borghese	Tomahawk	Sidi Rezegh 1150-
	Ten Emanuele Annoni	Tomahawk	Sidi Rezegh 1150-
	Ten Fernando Malvezzi	Tomahawk	Sidi Rezegh 1150-
	M.llo Manlio Olivetti	Tomahawk	Sidi Rezegh 1150-
97ª Sq/9° Gr CT	M.llo Raffaele Novelli	Fighter	Sidi Rezegh 1150-
	S.Ten Gianni Barcaro	Tomahawk	Sidi Rezegh 1150-
	Serg Magg Massimo Salvatore	2 Fighters	Sidi Rezegh 1150-
96ª Sq/9° Gr CT	M.llo Dante Labanti	Hurricane probable	Sidi Rezegh 1150-
375ª Sq/160° Gr CT	S.Ten Giuseppe Cantù	Beaufighter	Agedabia 1230
	S.Ten Giuseppe Cantù	Beaufighter probable	
	Serg Aurelio Munich		
366ª Sq/151° Gr CT	Cap Bernardino Serafini	Hurricane	Agheila area 1515
	Serg Magg Antonio Camerini	Hurricane	Agheila area 1515
	Ten Amedeo Guidi		
	M.llo Paolo Monanari	Hurricane	Agheila area 1515

Italian Casualties

125ª Sq OA	Ca.311 FTR from sortie over Msus-Antelat area
12ª Sq APC	Ca.309 Ghibli MM11270 flown by Serg Guido Degli Esposti, forced to land 25m off Sidi Magrun, probably by Beaufighters
9° Gr CT	MC.202 damaged; Cap Antonio Larsimont Pergameni safe

Thursday, 27 November 1941

Deteriorating weather reduced aerial activity as the Axis armour began to withdraw towards Tobruk, but the New Zealanders captured Sidi Rezegh and at last joined hands with the Tobruk garrison at Ed Duda.

Seven Hurricanes of 238 Squadron escorted Blenheims of 84 Squadron over El Adem, but here one of the bombers was shot down by Flak and a second so damaged that it crash-landed on return to base.

94 Squadron undertook a number of strafing sorties during the second of which Flg Off Vos shot-up an S.79 on the ground and then claimed to have set fire to a Bf 109F being transported on a trailer some 12 miles from El Adem. However, Plt Off J.M.Wylie of 260 Squadron failed to return from a freelance pairs sortie, and 2 SAAF Squadron's Lt Hinde was shot down, reportedly by an MC.200. There were no claims recorded by Italian pilots on this date, but during the afternoon two claims for Hurricanes were made by I./JG 27 pilots, Oblt Hugo Schneider of this unit also claiming a 'Martin 167' at the same time. During an afternoon operation Blenheims of 11 Squadron and Marylands of 24 SAAF Squadron made an attack on a column of armour and other vehicles south-east of Fort Capuzzo, just before this column was attacked by British armour. Flak was heavy, one Maryland being badly damaged and six more to a lesser extent, but no fighter attack was reported.

Three pilots of 73 Squadron's Battle Flight, covered by two aircraft of 33 Squadron, strafed Agedabia airfield, claims being made for one CR.42 destroyed and three damaged, plus nine other aircraft damaged. The Regia Aeronautica reported that a raid on Derna had inflicted serious damage to buildings and equipment, the Ju 87s of 239ª Squadriglia being flown out of this airfield to Sicily. However, in the opposite direction three torpedo-carrying S.79 AS of 284ª Squadriglia arrived at Derna, led by Cap Massimiliano Erasi. At LG.128 80 Squadron welcomed a new commanding officer; Sqn Ldr M.M.Stephens, DFC & Bar, was a veteran of the fighting over France and England in 1940, having already claimed about 14 victories – two of them Italian reconnaissance aircraft over western Turkey when on attachment to the air force of that country. Regia Aeronautica records indicate that some aircraft from Rhodes were indeed lost over Western Turkey during 1941, but these were S.81s, not S.84s, which had only recently gone into service for the first time.

Four 272 Squadron Beaufighters were ordered off again at 1045, Tmimi once again being their target. However, they arrived over Martuba by mistake and finding no aircraft there, strafed tents instead. The weather was again bad in the area, and many of the cannons in the aircraft failed to fire. Two aircraft force-landed at Mersa Matruh due to failing light. During the day, however, came the welcome news of an award of the DSO to Wg Cdr Yaxley.

British Claims

94 Sqn	Flg Off V.Vos	Hurricane I	S.79	shot-up on ground
	Flg Off V.Vos		Bf 109F	shot-up on ground whilst on towed trailer

British Casualties

84 Sqn	Blenheim IV N3532 shot down by Flak; Sgt T.Ingham-Brown and one PoWs; one KiA
	Blenheim IV Z9538 damaged by Flak and crash-landed at base; Sgt J.D.McKillop and crew unhurt
260 Sqn	Hurricane I FTR; Plt Off J.M.Wylie
2 SAAF Sqn	Tomahawk shot down; Lt D.A.Hinde safe
24 SAAF Sqn	Maryland badly damaged by Flak
	6 Marylands slightly damaged by Flak

German Claims

Stab I./JG 27	Lt Hans-Arnold Stahlschmidt	Hurricane	S El Adem 1620
1./JG 27	Lt Hans Remmer	Hurricane	S El Adem 1620"
1./JG 27	Oblt Hugo Schneider	Martin 167	El Adem

German Casualties

Unspecified unit	3 Bf 109s damaged on ground by bombs at Ain el Gazala

Friday, 28 November 1941

The weather was worse, but on the ground fighting was very heavy as Axis tanks counter-attacked near Tobruk, re-opening a corridor between the port and Sidi Rezegh, and inflicting heavy losses on 7th Armoured Division.

At 0935 1 SAAF Squadron sent 12 Hurricanes to escort Blenheims of 11 Squadron to the Trigh Capuzzo, other fighters of 274 Squadron providing top cover. Heavy Flak was again encountered and

Blenheim Z7703 was shot down in flames, crashing near the Tobruk-Bardia road where the bomb load exploded, the whole crew being killed. Z5906 was also shot down and crashed in the same area. At this point one of the South African Hurricanes, flown by Capt Liebenberg, who had just claimed a Bf 110 shot down, was also hit and came down.

These complementary photographs from German sources were originally thought to have been of RAF aircraft lost during the Battleaxe offensive. Recent research indicates that their demises occurred considerably later, on 28 November 1941. The Blenheim IV in the foreground of the first photo is believed to have been Z5906 flown by Flt Lt J.Pringle-Wood of 11 Squadron. Beyond it is a crash-landed Hurricane, featured in close-up in the second photo. This is now known to have been X-K, Z4965 of 1 SAAF Squadron, and carried the name 'Laura'. (The normal code for this unit was AX, but in this case the A seems to be missing.) The aircraft had been flown by Capt Hendrik Liebenberg, who became a PoW following a rescue attempt detailed in the text.

At once Lt S.Patterson in Blenheim L1317 landed to pick up both Flt Lt Pringle-Wood and the crew of Z5906, and Liebenberg. Reportedly, this Blenheim was spotted by the pilot of a Bf 109 as it took off again, and was attacked; however, Patterson managed to shake the fighter off, but then flew over a Flak position at low level, fire from this hitting the nose and the starboard engine, causing him to come down near a German encampment close to the road and about eight miles east of Gambut. No claim by any German or Italian fighter pilot was made for this aircraft.

All aboard survived the crash, although Patterson's gunner, Sgt J.F.M.Bennett, RAAF, was injured. The others were all captured, although Plt Off G.S.Burgan, RAAF, Patterson's navigator, was able to escape that night and made the long walk back, reaching LG.76 on 4 December, where apparently he reported Liebenberg's victory over the Bf 110. Liebenberg subsequently managed to escape from a train taking him to Germany from Italy at the end of 1943, reaching Allied lines and returning to his squadron during 1944. Sgt Bennett was killed when Mustangs strafed a train in which he was travelling on 19 February 1945, and one other crewman from Z5906 escaped from PoW camp in Italy in September 1943 when Italy capitulated. Burgan was still with 11 Squadron nearly five months later, but was killed on 9 April 1943.

During the day one Maryland squadron and three Blenheim units (including the Free French GRB 1) sent out aircraft to operate singly, relying on the poor visibility for protection from interception. However, at 1500 Lt Hans Remmer of 1./JG 27 intercepted one of the French Blenheims and shot this down in flames east of Gazala. The crew survived to become PoWs, the injured pilot and observer being taken to hospital; there the latter, Flg Off C.Pougin de la Maisonneube, died two days later. The pilot, Flt Sgt Jabin, was flown to Italy where he recovered from his injuries, then escaping to join the Italian resistance later in the war.

During the afternoon at 1450 12 Hurricanes of 94 Squadron took off to strafe targets around El Adem, where Lt Moolman encountered another lone Bf 110 and claimed this shot down. The formation was attacked by Bf 109Fs of II./JG 27, however, and three Hurricanes were shot down in rapid succession by Obfw Schulz – who claimed the first as a P-40, and then two Hurricanes. Plt Off Muhart crashed near Tobruk and was taken to hospital, suffering from burns and shock, but of the other two pilots there was at first no news. Flg Off Vos had been captured and hospitalised at Derna, but he would be released when this port fell to the 8th Army. Lt Palm had also been wounded, but was evacuated to Italy where he made numerous escape attempts while a PoW. He was subsequently moved to Stalag VIIA from where he finally got away, reaching Gibraltar in November 1943 – one of the few to escape in Germany and evade recapture. He received a DSO.

Meanwhile during the morning a Cant.Z.1007bis of 176ª Squadriglia had undertaken a reconnaissance in the hands of Ten Renato Limiti, when it was attacked and shot down over Gazala by a Bf 109. The crew all suffered wounds but managed to bale out. Subsequently the Fliegerführer Afrika, Gen Fröhlich, presented personal excuses and apologies to Gen Ferdinando Raffaelli, commander of the Regia Aeronautica's eastern sector.

British Claims

1 SAAF Sqn	Capt H.C.W.Liebenberg	Hurricane II Z4965	Bf 110	10m E Gambut	0935-0955
94 Sqn	Lt A.H.M.Moolman	Hurricane I Z4779	Bf 110	15-20m W El Adem 1450-1630	
250 Sqn	Flt Lt C.R.Caldwell	Tomahawk AK498	Bf 109 probable	Trigh Capuzzo	

British Casualties

11 Sqn	Blenheim IV Z5906 shot down by ground fire; Flt Lt J.Pringle-Wood and crew picked up by L1317
1 SAAF Sqn	Hurricane II Z4965 shot down; Capt H.C.W.Liebenberg picked up by Blenheim L1317
11 Sqn	Blenheim IV L1317 shot down; Lt S.Patterson and crew, rescued crew of Z5906 and Capt Liebenberg all PoW
	Blenheim IV Z7703 shot down; Flt Sgt R.Enticknap and crew KiA
Lorraine Sqn	Blenheim IV V6142 shot down; Wt Off R.Jabin and one PoWs; one (GRB 1) KiA
94 Sqn	Hurricane I Z4427 shot down; Plt Off S.N.Muhart WiA
	Hurricane I Z4614 shot down; Flg Off V.Vos
	Hurricane I Z4930 shot down; Lt R.B.Palm POW W El Adem 1600

German Claims

1./JG 27	Lt Hans Remmer	Blenheim	12m SE Ain el Gazala 1420
4./JG 27	Obfw Otto Schulz	P-40	N El Adem 1600
		2 Hurricanes	SW and over El Adem 1610-1612

Unspecified units	Ju 52/3m destroyed on ground by bombs at Derna
	2 Ju 88s damaged on ground by bombs at Derna
	6 Bf 110s damaged on ground by bombs at Derna
	3 Ju 87s damaged on ground by bombs at Derna

Italian Casualties

76ª Sq RST	Cant.Z.1007bis shot down by Bf 109; crew all WiA, but all bale out
53° Gr CT	MC.200 destroyed on ground at Derna
Unspecified unit	4 S.79s damaged on ground at Derna
	Cant.Z.1007bis damaged on ground at Derna

Saturday, 29 November 1941

With morning eight Hurricanes of 229 Squadron and ten of 238 Squadron swept over Tobruk, meeting five fighters identified as G.50bis at 1015. Sqn Ldr O'Neill and Sgt Pearson claimed one of these shot down, the latter then adding claims for one probable and one damaged; Sqn Ldr Smith of 229 Squadron claimed damage to another. It would seem that their opponents were MC.200s of 373ª Squadriglia, 153° Gruppo, which reported one aircraft damaged and its pilot wounded, while a claim was made for one British fighter damaged, identified as a Tomahawk.

Hurricanes and Tomahawks operated as pairs of squadrons all day; meanwhile five Blenheim and Maryland units and their escorts attacked MT. On one such operation 260 Squadron was attacked by Bf 109s and MC.202s while escorting Marylands. The Axis fighters were followed back to their base where one was claimed shot down by Sqn Ldr Walker, the commanding officer.

On another escort to nine Marylands by 250 Squadron and the RNFS, Ju 87s were seen bombing near Bir el Gubi. However, Bf 109s were also spotted in the vicinity, requiring the British fighters to remain close to their charges.

During the early afternoon Uffz Gromotka of 6./JG 27 with another pilot from this unit, pursued a TacR Hurricane of 208 Squadron in which Flg Off Cotton was undertaking a sortie. The reconnaissance pilot managed to ward off attacks for 30 minutes until both the Germans were out of ammunition, whereupon he crash-landed only 15 miles from LG.134 when his engine finally failed. He was awarded an immediate DFC, and Gromotka was credited with shooting down his Hurricane.

At evening six Hurricanes of 30 Squadron were in the air when ordered to investigate a possible intruder near LG.75. An attack was intended on the railhead south of Sidi Barrani, and here Plt Off Ratlidge intercepted a Ju 88 which he claimed to have shot down in the area of LG.74. It was subsequently confirmed that this had crashed in flames, the crew of three being captured.

From Giarabub the Hurricanes of 73 Squadron's Battle Flight departed to the unit's main base for servicing, there being no facilities for them at the forward airfield. The day also saw the formation of 265 (Light Bomber) Wing, which would come under the command of Grp Capt G.Y.Tyrell from 1 December. It was then retitled 272 Wing, and would ultimately become 232 Wing on 10 December.

British Claims

238 Sqn	Sqn Ldr O'Neill	Hurricane IIc 'B'	} G.50	Tobruk 0940-1120
	Sgt P.Pearson	Hurricane IIc 'H'		
	Sgt P.Pearson	Hurricane IIc 'H'	G.50 probable	Tobruk 0940-1120
	Sgt P.Pearson	Hurricane IIc 'H'	u/i e/a damaged	Tobruk 0940-1120
229 Sqn	Sqn Ldr W.A.Smith	Hurricane IIc BD785	G.50 damaged	SE Tobruk 1015
260 Sqn	Sqn Ldr D.R.Walker	Hurricane I Z4792	Bf 109	El Adem a.m.
30 Sqn	Plt Off G.W.Ratlidge	Hurricane I Z4230	Ju 88	LG.75 area 1810

British Casualties

208 Sqn	Hurricane crash-landed; Flg Off P.T.Cotton unhurt

German Claims

6./JG 27	Uffz Fritz Gromotka	Hurricane	SW El Adem 1432

German Casualties

6./LG 1	Ju 88A-5 WNr 6239 L1+CM shot down; Obfw Max Haun and two PoW, one KiA

Italian Claims

53° Gr CT	Unspecified pilot(s)	Tomahawk damaged	S El Adem 1000-1130

Sunday, 30 November 1941

Heavy fighting continued throughout the day as the Afrika Korps attacked British infantry at Sidi Rezegh. By evening the area was once more in Axis hands and Tobruk was again isolated. During an early sweep over the El Adem area by Hurricanes of 238 Squadron, pilots submitted claims for a Bf 109 probable and a Bf 110 damaged for no loss.

Squadrons again undertook sweeps in pairs, 112 and 3 RAAF Squadrons locating about 50 Axis aircraft near Bir el Gubi just after 0900. These included Ju 87s of II./StG 2 plus numbers of Bf 109s, MC.202s, MC.200s and G.50bis – mainly from Italian units – which were preparing to attack troops of the New Zealand Division. The Tomahawk pilots attacked at once, claiming 16 aircraft shot down and 16 damaged, forcing most of the others to jettison

Wg Cdr Peter Jeffrey with Sgt Alan Cameron on 30 November 1941. Jeffery had landed to pick up the downed Cameron and had flown back to base with this very large fellow-Australian crammed into the cockpit of his Tomahawk with him. In the background Sgt Derek Scott is looking out of a tent.

their bombs – all at a cost of three fighters shot down. Claims included three Ju 87s and 12 damaged; 4./StG 2 reported that gunners were wounded in two Stukas during this engagement.

Sgt 'Tiny' Cameron of 3 RAAF Squadron was shot down, apparently by Obfw Schulz of II./JG 27, and baled out, but was later picked up and flown back to base by Wg Cdr Jeffrey – this was quite a feat as Cameron was easily the tallest man in the squadron. Flt Lt 'Woof' Arthur failed to return with the squadron but arrived safely a little later, having force-landed due to a faulty distributor. He had put up the day's outstanding performance, claiming two fighters and two Ju 87s.

112 Squadron was able only to contribute three of the claims for aircraft destroyed, but accounted for two of the losses. Plt Off Bowker was shot down by one of the Italian fighters, crash-landing at LG.112, while Plt Off Neville Duke was caught on the way back to base by the indefatigable Schulz and was shot down near Tobruk. He crash-landed and leapt clear, sprinting to cover in some nearby scrub, whereupon Schulz, in his usual manner, thoroughly shot-up the Tomahawk, setting it on fire. Both British pilots were back with their squadron safely next day.

Neville Duke:

"Got into the middle of things, and onto a G.50 chasing him west down to ground level where he crash-landed after pumping tons of lead into him.

"Jumped on by two-three 109s and a G.50. Damaged a 109. Ran for home and was chased by a 109F; dodged four-five attacks and got in a few shots at him but he was too fast. Finally he hit me in the port wing and, I think, the petrol tank. Machine turned on its back at about 500 ft, out of control. Saw the ground rushing up and then I kicked the rudder and pushed the stick and prayed. Got control just in time and the machine hit the ground on its belly. Hopped out jolly quick and then darted behind some scrub and lay on my belly about 20 yards from the crash.

"The Hun came down and shot-up my machine, which was already smoking and set it on fire. Horrible crack and whistle of bullets near me and I thought I was going to be strafed but the Hun cleared off. Started off to walk across the desert home but saw a lorry coming my way. Lay down behind another bush thinking they were Huns but as they went past I recognised the uniforms and popped up and gave 'em a yell.

The 30 November 1941 party to celebrate 3 RAAF Squadron's (incorrectly assessed) 100th victory was enlivened by the news of the award of the DSO to old squadron commander, Wg Cdr Peter Jeffrey. Left to right: Flg Off Tommy Trimble, Flg Off Bobby Gibbes, Sgts Walt Mailey and Rex Wilson, Plt Off Fred Eggleton, Flg Off Lou Spence and Plt Off Les Bradbury. Note the dirty trouser legs – a give-away sign of a Tomahawk pilot, since the nose-mounted .50in machine guns dripped oil onto the pilots' legs whenever fired.

"A Lysander came over and after much waving, landed. Got a lift in the back seat with a General and flew over to battle H'Qtrs with them. Later returned in Lysander to my own aerodrome. Feel very lucky to be alive and a bit browned off with the war!"

Apart from the two claims submitted by Otto Schulz, Italian G.50bis pilots of 155° Gruppo claimed three British fighters plus one probable and two damaged, one victory also being claimed by the pilots of 20° Gruppo while the MC.200 pilots of 153° Gruppo claimed one and one probable. Against the multitude of British claims, only two G.50bis went down as did one MC.200, two more of the latter suffering damage.

Following this engagement, four of 272 Squadron's Beaufighters, which had moved forward to LG.122 for operations, were sent to strafe Martuba East and West airfields at 1140. Here the pilots claimed to have damaged eight aircraft on the ground, two of which were seen to catch fire. In fact six S.79s suffered damage during this attack and one airman was killed. During this attack Flt Lt Bartlett's

Sgt Walt Mailey was one of those to enjoy success on 30 November, claiming two Italian fighters shot down and three dive-bombers damaged.

Sgt Alan Cameron, Flg Off Bill Kloster, Plt Off Lawton Lees and Sgt Derek Scott stand in front of Wg Cdr Peter Jeffery's Tomahawk, named 'Hepsa Bah' after his black MG sportscar. By the end of January 1942 all those illustrated here would be dead, or have become PoWs.

Beaufighter was hit in the tail by Flak, returning with two thirds of the rudder blown away, and with the stern post and elevator damaged. The aircraft were then flown back to LG.10.

Elsewhere during the day two claims for Hurricanes were submitted by JG 27, including one in the afternoon by the kommandeur of I.Gruppe, Hptmn Eduard Neumann, but no commensurate losses have been found. On the ground 4th South African Armoured Car Regiment claimed to have forced down and destroyed two Ju 87s on this date; two such aircraft of 239ª Squadriglia were hit by AA fire, but in fact both managed to return.

Hptmn Joachim Helbig of 4./LG 1 was wounded by bomb splinters during a raid on the unit's airfield at Benina.

Thus November ended, having seen the heaviest fighting in the air and on the ground in the Western Desert since the start of the war. The campaign still had far to go however, and December opened as another month of fierce fighting began.

British Claims

238 Sqn	Plt Off Jenkins	Hurricane II 'D'	Bf 109 probable	El Adem 0730-0915
	Sgt T.Wolstenholme	Hurricane II 'R'	Bf 110 damaged	0730-0850
3 RAAF Sqn	Sgt A.C.Cameron	Tomahawk AK506	G.50	El Gubi 0900
	Sgt A.C.Cameron	Tomahawk AK506	4 Ju 87s damaged	El Gubi 0900
	Flg Off R.H.Gibbes	Tomahawk AN499	G.50	El Adem area 0910
	Sgt D.Scott	Tomahawk AN374	G.50	El Adem area 0910
	Sgt D.Scott	Tomahawk AN374	Ju 87	El Adem area 0910
	Sgt D.Scott	Tomahawk AN374	Ju 87 damaged	El Adem area 0910
	Sgt R.K.Wilson	Tomahawk AM392	MC.200 damaged	El Adem area 0910
	Sgt R.K.Wilson	Tomahawk AM392	Ju 87 damaged	El Adem area 0910

RAAF Sqn	Sgt R.K.Wilson	Tomahawk AM392	Bf 109 damaged	El Adem area 0910
	Sqn Ldr A.C.Rawlinson	Tomahawk AN408	MC.200	El Adem area 0915
	Flt Lt W.S.Arthur	Tomahawk AN224	2 Ju 87s	Bir el Gubi 0915
	Flt Lt W.S.Arthur	Tomahawk AN224	2 G.50s	Bir el Gubi 0915
	Sgt W.H.A.Mailey	Tomahawk AK446	MC.200	El Adem area 0915
	Sgt W.H.A.Mailey	Tomahawk AK446	G.50	El Adem area 0915
	Sgt W.H.A.Mailey	Tomahawk AK446	3 Ju 87s damaged	El Adem area 0915
	Flg Off T.Trimble	Tomahawk AM384	2 MC.200s	El Adem area 0915
	Flg Off T.Trimble	Tomahawk AM384	3 Ju 87s damaged	El Adem area 0915
12 Sqn	Plt Off N.F.Duke	Tomahawk AN402 'F'	G.50	Bir el Gubi 0915
	Plt Off N.F.Duke	Tomahawk AN402 'F'	Bf 109 damaged	Bir el Gubi 0915
	Plt Off N.Bowker	Tomahawk AN338	MC.200	Bir el Gubi 0915
	Sgt R.M.Leu	Tomahawk AK509	G.50	Bir el Gubi 0915
	Plt Off K.R.Sands	Tomahawk AK377	G.50 damaged	Bir el Gubi 0915
50 Sqn	Flt Lt C.R.Caldwell	Tomahawk AK498	Bf 109 probable	Trigh Capuzzo
72 Sqn	Wg Cdr R.G.Yaxley	Beaufighter Ic 'Q'	⎫	
	Flt Lt M.L.P.Bartlett	Beaufighter Ic 'V'	⎬ Aircraft damaged on ground, two in flames,	
	Plt Off H.H.Crawford	Beaufighter Ic 'S'	Martuba	
	Plt Off J.Watters	Beaufighter Ic 'O'	⎭	

British Casualties

RAAF Sqn	Tomahawk AK506 shot down; Sgt A.C.Cameron baled out; picked up by Wg Cdr Jeffrey
	Tomahawk AN224 force-landed due to technical trouble; Flt Lt W.S.Arthur safe
12 Sqn	Tomahawk AK402 'F' crash-landed; Plt Off N.F.Duke returned next day
	Tomahawk AN338 crash-landed; Plt Off N.Bowker returned next day
72 Sqn	Beaufighter Ic V damaged by Flak; Flt Lt M.L.P.Bartlett safe

German Claims

I./JG 27	Obfw Otto Schulz	P-40	NE Bir el Gubi 0910
			SW El Adem 0920
I./JG 27	Uffz Hans Niederhöfer	Hurricane	Ain el Gazala 1035
Stab I./JG 27	Hptmn Eduard Neumann		Bir el Gubi 1600

German Casualties

I./StG 2	Ju 87 in combat E Bir el Gubi; gunner Uffz Otto Herbert WiA
	Ju 87 in combat E Bir el Gubi; gunner Gefr Manfred Spiegelberg WiA

Italian Claims

155° Gr CT	T.Col Luigi Bianchi	Hurricane	Bir el Gubi 0820-
	T.Col Luigi Bianchi	Tomahawk probable	Bir el Gubi 0820-
351ª Sq/155° Gr CT	S.Ten Pietro Zanello	Tomahawk	Bir el Gubi 0820-
378ª Sq/155° Gr CT	Serg Italo Abrami	Tomahawk	Bir el Gubi 0820-
352ª Sq/20° Gr CT	S.Ten Giorgio Oberwerger	Tomahawk	Bir el Gubi 0820-
374ª Sq/153° Gr CT	M.llo Egeo Pardi	Tomahawk	Bir el Gubi 0820-
	M.llo Egeo Pardi	Tomahawk probable	Bir el Gubi 0820-
55° Gr	Ten Tullio Martinelli	⎫	
	Ten Giuseppe Bonfiglio	⎬ 2 Fighters damaged	Bir el Gubi 0820-
	Ten Vittorio Galfetti	⎭	

Italian Casualties

378ª Sq/155° Gr CT	G.50 MM5967 shot down; S.Ten Eugenio Giunta PoW
	G.50 MM6023 shot down; Serg Girolamo Monaldi KiA
374ª Sq/153° Gr CT	MC.200 damaged; M.llo Egeo Pardi WiA
	MC.200 damaged; Ten Mario Mauro WiA
153° Gr CT	MC.200 crash-landed
39ª Sq BaT	2 Ju 87Rs damaged; Cap Riccardo Piovano and S.Ten De Seta unhurt
unspecified unit	S.79 severely damaged on ground at Derna at night
	6 S.79s damaged on ground at Martuba

Due to a miss-counting of the 1940 claims, 3 RAAF Squadron's pilots believed that the unit's 100th victory had fallen to them on 30 November 1941. A party was held that evening and was attended by: back row, left to right – Tom Briggs, Sgt Walt Mailey, Flg Off Harry Schaeffer and Lance Threlkeld; front row, left to right – Sgt Frank 'Bev' Reid, Flg Offs Bobby Gibbes, Ed Jackson and Nicky Barr (marked with X), Wg Cdr Peter Jeffrey. Flg Off Lou Spence, Sqn Ldr Alan Rawlinson, Robin Gray and Flg Off Les Bradbury.

Monday, 1 December 1941

The Afrika Korps renewed a most violent attack on the New Zealand Division in force near Tobruk striking the escarpment area at Belhamed. This cut the division into two halves, forcing a withdrawal to the frontier when nightfall came.

Against this background at 0800 eight MC.200s of 153° Gruppo CT escorted a Bf 110 south-east of Bir el Gubi –presumably a reconnaissance aircraft. The Italian pilots reported encountering Tomahawks two of which were claimed shot down, although Ten Renzo Sappa of 373ª Squadriglia was shot down and killed. A claim for a Bf 110 probably shot down in this area was made by Sgt MacDonnell of 274 Squadron.

However, at much the same time 12 Tomahawks of 250 Squadron and eight Hurricanes of the RNFS undertook a sweep over the El Duda-Bir el Gubi-Gabr Saleh area, reporting meeting a formation of bombers, identified as Ju 88s, nine-20 strong, escorted by numbers of fighters believed to have been G.50s MC.202s and Bf 109s. The bombers immediately jettisoned their bombs and dived for the ground, turning west. They were attacked at once by the naval pilots who reported what appeared to have been their most

uccessful combat to date, while the Tomahawks engaged the high-flying top cover. Lt Allingham made
a long chase after one of the bombers, gaining hits on this aircraft which he reported then dug its wingtip
into the ground and crashed. Allingham then attacked a G.50, claiming this shot down as well. Sub Lt
H.S.Diggins claimed to have shot down an Italian fighter near the ground, and Sub Lt Dennison reported
that on turning sharply, a G.50 which was trying to attack him, went into a spin and crashed. Probables
were claimed against a Ju 88, a G.50 and a Bf 109.

At higher altitude while engaging the top cover, Plt Off J.L.Waddy, a young Australian pilot in 250
Squadron who was soon to make a big name for himself, also claimed a Messerschmitt probably
destroyed. One of the Tomahawks was shot down, but Plt Off Adams survived to return next day. The
RNFS suffered no losses. It appears at least possible that one of the fighters assumed to be a G.50 was
the missing MC.200, and was one of the aircraft claimed in this engagement by Waddy or one of the
naval pilots.

A little later at 1025 two Tomahawks of 3 RAAF Squadron were scrambled to intercept a
reconnaissance Ju 88 of 2.(F)/123 which was caught and shot down by Sgt Wilson. An hour later 12
MC.202s, six each from 96ª and 97ª Squadriglia of 9° Gruppo CT escorted German and Italian Stukas
over Bir el Gubi. During the return flight Hurricanes and Tomahawks attacked.

Within minutes of the Italian fighters taking off, 12 Hurricanes of 1 SAAF Squadron set out to escort
Blenheims from the Free French Lorraine unit which were seeking to bomb targets at El Duda; 12 more
Hurricanes from 274 Squadron provided top cover. A brisk dogfight ensued, into which it appears that
Bf 109s of JG 27 waded. The German pilots claimed three Hurricanes shot down with the Italians adding
two Tomahawks and six Hurricanes, plus a further five Hurricanes as probables. 274 Squadron lost three
aircraft while one of the South African fighters was hit in the glycol tank, causing the engine to blow up.
Lt Hoffe force-landed in 'no-man's land' whereupon Flt Lt Owen Tracey, one of the 274 Squadron flight
commanders, landed and picked him up, flying him back to base in BD821. Of the other downed pilots,
Plt Off Weeks was picked up by British armoured cars and returned safely two days later; Sgt Perse, who
had been wounded, was taken into hospital at Tobruk.

In return for these casualties, 274 Squadron's remaining pilots claimed three Bf 109s shot down and
a fourth damaged. One MC.202 of 97ª Squadriglia was hit in the radiator and force-landed, the pilot
unhurt. It had really been 'one of those days'.

During the early afternoon one of 109 Squadron's special Wellingtons operated again, being attacked
by a Bf 110. The pilot used cloud cover to avoid this, but was pursued by it for some 20 minutes. When
it finally broke away, the rear gunner appeared to have been silenced; the Wellington suffered no damage.

Between 1900-2000 three trios of Albacores from 826 Squadron searched for Axis MT, finding clusters
of these at intervals when flares were dropped and bombs were released on them.

British Claims

4 Sqn	Sgt MacDonnell	Hurricane IIb BD885	Bf 110 probable	El Duda-El Gubi-Tobruk 0720-0900
RNFS	Lt H.P.Allingham	Hurricane I Z4245	Ju 88	El Duda-Gabr Saleh 0910
	Lt H.P.Allingham	Hurricane I Z4245	G.50	El Duda-Gabr Saleh 0910
	Sub Lt H.S.Diggens	Hurricane I V7107	G.50 or MC.202	10m S Duda 0915
	Sub Lt G.Dennison	Hurricane I 'C'	G.50	10m S Duda 0915
	Sub Lt P.N.Charlton	Hurricane I Z4177	Bf 109 probable	10m S Duda 0915
	Sub Lt P.N.Charlton	Hurricane I Z4177	Bf 109 damaged	10m S Duda 0915
	Sub Lt K.L.Wood	Hurricane I 'E'	Ju 88 probable	10m S El Duda 0910-1915
	Sub Lt K.L.Wood	Hurricane I 'E'	G.50 probable	10m S El Duda 0910-1915
	Sub Lt G.D.Dick	Hurricane I 'Y'	Bf 109 probable	10m S El Duda 0915
250 Sqn	Plt Off J. Waddy	Tomahawk AN347	Bf 109 probable	Bir el Gubi 0910
	Sgt F.M.Twemlow	Tomahawk	Bf 109 damaged	Bir el Gubi 0910
3 RAAF Sqn	Sgt R.K.Wilson	Tomahawk AN457	Ju 88	over LG.122 1100
274 Sqn	Plt Off W.A.G.Conrad	Hurricane IIb Z5064	Bf 109	W El Adem 1145-1315
	Sgt J.Dodds	Hurricane IIb Z5117	Bf 109	W El Adem 1145-1315
	Plt Off R.N.Weeks	Hurricane IIb Z4008	Bf 109 damaged	W El Adem 1145-1315
	Sgt Harrington	Hurricane IIb Z5347	Bf 109	W El Adem 1145-1315
			Bf 109 damaged	W El Adem 1145-1315

British Casualties

250 Sqn	Tomahawk FTR; Plt Off Adams returned next day	
	Tomahawk crash-landed; Plt Off Swinnerton back next day	
274 Sqn	Hurricane IIb Z4008 shot down; Plt Off R.N.Weeks picked up by ground troops and returned	
	Hurricane IIb Z2817 shot down; 25m SW El Adem at 1300; Sgt G.W.F. Perse WiA; returned 3 December	
	Hurricane IIb Z2510 shot down; Sgt Alman MiA	
	Hurricane II Z5310 force-landed; Lt W.H.Hoffe picked up by Hurricane and returned	

German Claims

5./JG 27	Uffz Hans Niederhöfer	Hurricane	SW Sidi Rezegh 1230
4./JG 27	Oblt Gustav Rödel	Hurricane	El Adem 1240
1./JG 27	Hptmn Wolfgang Redlich	Hurricane	Bir el Gubi 1255

German Casualties

2(F)./123	Ju 88 4U+JK WNr 1541 shot down 30m SE Fort Maddalena; Lt Franz-Heinrich von Gablenz and one PoWs; one KiA

Italian Claims

153° Gr CT	Unspecified pilots	Tomahawks damaged	SE Bir el Gubi 0800-0950
96ª Sq/9° Gr CT	Cap Ezio Viglione Borghese	Hurricane	Bir el Gubi 1135-
	Ten Fernando Malvezzi	Tomahawk	Bir el Gubi 1135-
	Ten Emanuele Annoni	Tomahawk	Bir el Gubi 1135-
	M.llo Dante Labanti	Hurricane	Bir el Gubi 1135-
	Serg Magg Bruno Spitzl	Tomahawk damaged	Bir el Gubi 1135-
97ª Sq/9° Gr CT	S.Ten Gianni Barcaro	Hurricane	Bir el Gubi 1135-
	S.Ten Gianni Barcaro	Hurricane probable	Bir el Gubi 1135-
	M.llo Rinaldo Damiani	2 Hurricanes	Bir el Gubi 1135-
	S.Ten Jacopo Frigerio	Hurricane	Bir el Gubi 1135-
	Serg Alfredo Bombardini	2 Hurricanes probable	Bir el Gubi 1135-
	Cap Antonio Larsimont Pergameni	Hurricane probable	Bir el Gubi 1135-
	M.llo Otello Perotti	Hurricane probable	Bir el Gubi 1135-

Italian Casualties

373ª Sq/153° Gr CT	MC.200 shot down;
	Ten Renzo Sappa KiA
97ª Sq/9° Gr CT	MC.202 hit and force-landed;
	S. Ten Jacopo Frigerio unhurt

Tuesday, 2 December 1941

The weather proved poor on this date, reducing the amount of aerial activity taking place. Early in the day Sqn Ldr O'Neill, commanding officer of 238 Squadron, intercepted a Bf 110 west of Sollum, claiming to have inflicted some damage on this. Two pilots of 2 SAAF Squadron flew in to a sandstorm and were both lost, while a stripped Hurricane of 2 PRU at Heliopolis also failed to return from a sortie west of Bardia. Two Hurricanes of 237 Squadron carried out a TacR sortie over Menastir and Bardia during the morning, but Flg Off Sindall was shot down by Flak; he survived to return to the squadron later.

33 Squadron, still at LG.125, strafed airfields around Agedabia during the morning. Flg Off Charles claimed damage to three CR.42s and an S.79 on the ground. Six Hurricanes returned for a repeat attack during the afternoon, this time damage being claimed to a Ju 87, three S.79s and six CR.42s. During this attack Sgt Challis flew so low that the wingtip of his fighter struck a CR.42,

Fw Hans Niederhöfer of 5./JG 27 with his desert 'shades' on. He made his first claim on 1 December 1941, for a Hurricane south-west of Sidi Rezegh.

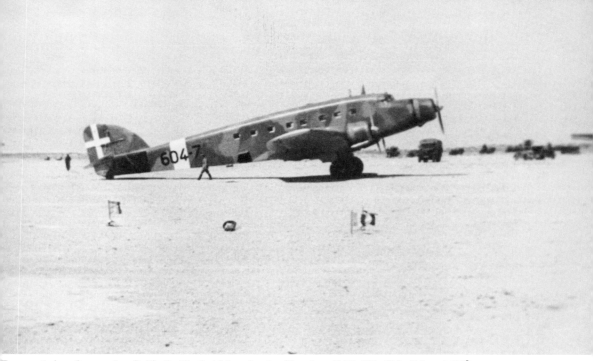

Transport aircraft were also vital in the North African theatre. Here is an S.75 of the Tripoli-based 604[a] Squadriglia T.

damaging both aircraft. Italian records confirm losses here as four CR.42s destroyed, seven damaged and one S.81 damaged – all aircraft of 151° Gruppo CT. Another CR.42 was lost on this date during a force-landing by a pilot of 160° Gruppo; an MC.200 of 157° Gruppo failed to return from a sortie, its pilot being reported missing – probably another victim of the weather.

Five 272 Squadron Beaufighters took off from LG.10, but one landed again at once and a second force-landed with engine trouble. The remaining three strafed Barce airfield, where seven aircraft thought to be BR.20 bombers were strafed, crews claiming to have destroyed an unidentified aircraft and damaged six. Actual losses were somewhat more prosaic, amounting to a single S.75 transport destroyed and two BR.20s damaged, one of them seriously. However, aircraft 'J' flown by Flg Off A.A.Salter was hit by Flak and crash-landed near the target area. This Beaufighter was T4665, on loan from 252 Squadron. Salter and his observer, Sgt A.G.Glover, became PoWs.

During the day the RNFS moved to LG.123 with 18 Hurricane Is and nine Martlets. The RN Fulmar Flight moved to Fuka Satellite with 12 Mark II Fulmars.

Amongst the Italian units, 155° Gruppo CT was now ordered to repatriate to Italy, handing over its remaining equipment to 20° Gruppo. 376ª Squadriglia Autonoma also departed, passing its equipment to 153° Gruppo. T.Col Luigi Bianchi, commanding officer of 155° Gruppo did not accompany his unit to their homeland, however, remaining in Libya as liaison officer with Fliegerführer Afrika to co-ordinate Regia Aeronautica missions with those of the Luftwaffe.

British Claims

238 Sqn	Sqn Ldr O'Neill	Hurricane IIc 'B'	Bf 110 damaged	W Sollum 0630-9810

British Casualties

2 SAAF Sqn	Tomahawk AN396 lost in sandstorm; Lt D.A.Hinde KiA
	Tomahawk AN370 lost in sandstorm; Lt L.D.Wood KiA
2 PRU	Hurricane V7423 FTR; Flg Off Wade MiA
237 Sqn	Hurricane shot down by Flak; Flg Off Sindall returned
33 Sqn	Hurricane I damaged colliding with CR.42 on ground; Sgt B.W. Challis unhurt
272 Sqn	Beaufighter Ic T4665 'Q' shot down by Flak; Flg Off A.A.Salter and observer, Sgt A.G.Glover PoWs

German Casualties

Unspecified unit(s)	6 Ju 52/3ms destroyed on ground at Derna

Italian Casualties

151° Gr CT	4 CR.42s destroyed on ground at Agedabia
	7 CR.42s damaged on ground at Agedabia
	S.81 damaged on ground at Agedabia
384ª Sq/157° Gr CT	MC.200 FTR; Serg Elio Carmignani MiA
394ª Sq/160° Gr CT	CR.42 forced to land and destroyed on ground; S.Ten Roberto Gentile safe
604ª Sq T	S.75 I-LUSS destroyed on ground at Barce
13° St	2 BR.20s damaged on ground at Barce, one severely

Wednesday, 3 December 1941

Rommel despatched strong patrols towards the Egyptian frontier again, one along the coast road and one on the Trigh Capuzzo. Maximum efforts were expended by the RAF and the army against these thrusts, which on this occasion were driven back with heavy losses. During these operations virtually nothing was seen of the Axis air forces and the only engagement occurred around midday when Sqn Ldr Smith and Sgt Burns of 229 Squadron intercepted a reconnaissance aircraft in the Solluch area. Smith identified this as an S.84 – a rare recognition – which he claimed to have damaged. This was in fact one of 176ª Squadriglia RST's Cant.Z.1007bis trimotors, which actually failed to return, the crew being lost. The growing Axis problems with fuel supply came to a head during the day, the Regia Aeronautica being ordered to stop bombing raids both by day and night due to shortage of this critical resource. Following this order, 98° Gruppo BT departed for Italy next day, its BR.20s being left to the remaining units of 13° Stormo. The Italian fighter force was further reinforced, however, when 16 MC.200s of 8° Gruppo CT flew in from the homeland.

British Claims

229 Sqn	Sqn Ldr W.A.Smith	Hurricane IIc BD785	S.84 damaged	Gabri-Solluch area 1120-1315

Italian Casualties

176ª Sq RST	Cant.Z.1007bis FTR; Ten Terzo Tenchini (pilot), Cap Guido Panante (observer) and crew MiA

Thursday, 4 December 1941

Again the morning erupted with a massive battle over the El Adem area into which various formations would seem to have strayed. Italian fighters were out in strength escorting formations of Ju 87s (16 German and six Italian); 17° Gruppo with 11 of its new MC.202s, ten of 153° Gruppo with MC.200s, and more MC.200s of 157° Gruppo. Overhead patrolled JG 27 Bf 109s, seeking to pick off stragglers as usual.

Another 17 German Stukas were escorted by 11 G.50bis from 20° Gruppo, this formation having taken off by 0745, and these aircraft were surprised by 2 SAAF Squadron which had arrived over the battle area first. The South African Tomahawk pilots claimed five Ju 87s and a probable, plus a G.50bis. As the unit turned for home, Lt Dodson collided with Ten Giuseppe Vitali's G.50bis and both went down; Vitali survived to become a PoW, but Dodson did not. Lt Lipawski's Tomahawk was badly hit during the fighting and he force-landed – although he was able to get his undercarriage down.

12 Hurricanes of 274 Squadron, providing top cover for nine more from 1 SAAF Squadron, swept over the area. The South Africans again took the lion's share of the fight, Lt Penberthy claiming that he had shot the tail off one MC.202 at the top of a loop, while 2/Lt Waugh claimed one which he saw crash plus one probable and one damaged. Other pilots claimed two more probables and two damaged. One straggling Hurricane was shot down, but its pilot, 2/Lt Meek, returned safely next day. Sgt MacDonnel of 274 Squadron, following the main part of his unit in order to break away and escort a TacR aircraft over El Adem-Tobruk, encountered a mass of Ju 87s and fighters, claiming one Macchi damaged.

With 2 SAAF Squadron had come 112 and 250 Squadrons, and as the South Africans sought to break through to the bombers, 112 Squadron took on the fighter escort while 250 Squadron sought to hold off the top cover. The 'Shark' Squadron pilots claimed three G.50bis and an MC.200, plus a Ju 87, with another of the latter and a Bf 109 as probables, suffering no more than one badly damaged Tomahawk in return. 250 Squadron was able to add two probables, one for a Bf 109, the other identified as either a G.50bis or an MC.200.

From this confused combat the Regia Aeronautica pilots returned to claim ten Tomahawks and two Hurricanes shot down with two more Tomahawks probably so. Three pilots of 5./JG 27 claimed three 'P-40s' between 1016-1020. Italian losses were relatively heavy on this occasion, and apart from the 20° Gruppo G.50bis already mentioned, two MC.200s were shot down, one more force-landed with a wounded pilot, and another was damaged, the pilot of this also being wounded. These aircraft had almost certainly been misidentified by their opponents as G.50bis. Two MC.202s crash-landed, and six more were damaged. Amongst the Luftwaffe units involved, only one Ju 87 of Stab II./StG 2 has been identified as being shot down or badly damaged, both members of the crew being wounded. The pilot was Hptmn Leonhard Busselt, kommandeur of II./StG 2.

This crash-landed MC.200 belonged to 387ª Squadriglia of 157° Gruppo Autonomo; this unit was repatriated to Italy by the year end.

Neville Duke obviously was left feeling rather 'chipper' after this combat, recording:

"Oh, Boy, another! Encountered the Hun Circus of Ju 87s, 109s, Macchi 200s and G.50s. Got stuck into them. Came across five Ju 87s flying in close formation and sprayed them all. One broke away and went down in a gentle dive, smoking a bit. Couldn't watch him as some 109s appeared and I don't like them!

"Pounced on a Macchi 200 and had a pretty good dog-fight. He started beetling off home and I chased him. Once he did a complete roll in front of me. My guns were all haywire and in the end only one cannon was going and I had to keep cocking that. Finally that stopped just as we came roaring over Tobruk at nought feet. The Macchi was still showing fight however, but he suddenly spun in off a steep turn and crashed. I was hoping he would land on the aerodrome as he had put up a good fight – nearly always at ground level, and once we went chasing out to sea. I was making dummy attacks on him as my guns had packed up.

"I landed at Tobruk and had lunch. It had bucked the boys up no end to see the fight."

On 4 December 1941 S.Ten Giuseppe Vitali's Fiat G.50bis of 352ª Squadriglia, 20° Gruppo CT, collided with the Tomahawk flown by Lt F.R.Dodson of 2 Squadron. Both aircraft crashed, but only Vitali (above) survived to become a PoW.

At 1400 12 Hurricanes of 274 Squadron escorted Marylands over the Trigh Capuzzo. During the return flight Sgt Dodds attacked a Bf 110 and set both engines on fire. Unfortunately, he then lost his goggles and failed to see its fate, being credited only with a probable. However, on this day Maj Karl Kaschka kommandeur of III./ZG 26, was shot down in the area, and since Dodd's claim was the only one made for such an aircraft, it seems reasonably certain that Kaschka was his victim. Oblt Wehmeyer landed alongside the wreck in another of the unit's aircraft, but found Kaschka dying, and his gunner, Uffz Mühlhauser, dead.

During the day there was a tragic accident when three Blenheims of the Lorraine Squadron took off from one end of their airfield at the same time as three from 45 Squadron took off in the opposite direction from the other end. A hump in the centre of the field prevented them from seeing each other until they met head-on just after becoming airborne. The number ones missed each other and the number twos pulled up, although the French aircraft stalled and crashed. The number threes met head-on, all members of both crews being killed.

One of 109 Squadron's Wellingtons, X9986, was operating again to the south-west of LG.05 when it was intercepted and fired on in error by a Hurricane.

British Claims

2 SAAF Sqn	Lt J.F.R.Dodson	Tomahawk	G.50 by collision	Bir el Gubi 0830
	Lt D.V.D.Lacey	Tomahawk	2 Ju 87s	NW Bir el Gubi 0830
	Lt D.V.D.Lacey	Tomahawk	3 Ju 87s damaged	NW Bir el Gubi 0830
	Lt G.B.Lipawski	Tomahawk	Ju 87	NW Bir el Gubi 0830
	Lt G.B.Lipawski	Tomahawk	Ju 87 damaged	NW Bir el Gubi 0830
	Lt E.C.Saville	Tomahawk	Ju 87	Bir el Gubi 0830
	Lt E.C.Saville	Tomahawk	Ju 87 probable	Bir el Gubi 0830
	Capt P.J.Robbertse	Tomahawk	G.50	Bir el Gubi 0830
	Capt P.J.Robbertse	Tomahawk	Ju 87	Bir el Gubi 0830
274 Sqn	Sgt MacDonnell	Hurricane IIb BD821	MC 202 damaged	S Trigh Capuzzo 0920-1105
112 Sqn	Flt Lt D.F.Westenra	Tomahawk	G.50s	El Adem-Sidi Rezegh 0935-1055
	Plt Off N.Bowker	Tomahawk AN372	G.50	El Adem-Sidi Rezegh 0935-1055
	Plt Off N.Bowker	Tomahawk AN372	Ju 87	El Adem-Sidi Rezegh 0935-1055
	Plt Off N.F.Duke	Tomahawk AN337 'F'	MC.200	E Sidi Rezegh 1935-1055
	Plt Off N.F.Duke	Tomahawk AN337 'F'	Ju 87 probable	E Sidi Rezegh 1935-1055
	Sgt R.H.Christie	Tomahawk AK354	Bf 109F probable	Sidi Rezegh area
	Flg Off P.J.Humphreys	Tomahawk AN415	Bf 109 damaged	El Adem- Sidi Rezegh
1 SAAF Sqn	2/Lt L.R.S.Waugh	Hurricane II	MC.202	12m SW El Adem 1020
	2/Lt L.R.S.Waugh	Hurricane II	MC.202 probable	12m SW El Adem 1020
	2/Lt L.R.S.Waugh	Hurricane II	MC.202 damaged	12m SW El Adem 1020
	Lt. V.A.Penberthy	Hurricane II	MC.202	12m SW El Adem 1020
	2/Lt C.B.Willson	Hurricane II	MC.202 probable	12m SW El Adem 1020
	Lt R.H.C.Kershaw	Hurricane II	MC.202 probable	12m SW El Adem 1020
	Lt R.H.C.Kershaw	Hurricane II	MC.202 damaged	12m SW El Adem 1020
	2/Lt A.D.Maclean	Hurricane II BD779	MC.202 damaged	12m SW El Adem 1020
250 Sqn	Flt Lt I.F.Rose	Tomahawk	Bf 109 damaged	5-10m S Bir el Gubi 1030
	Flt Lt R.E.Bary	Tomahawk	Bf 110 probable	SE Tobruk 1030
	Plt Off K.G.Hart	Tomahawk	G.50 or MC.200	SE Tobruk 1030
274 Sqn	Sgt J.Dodds	Hurricane IIb Z2835	Bf 110 probable	Trigh Capuzzo area 1355-1525

British Casualties

1 SAAF Sqn	Hurricane II shot down by a MC. 202, force-landed; 2/Lt T.A.Meek returned next day
2 SAAF Sqn	Tomahawk collided with G.50, then FTR; Lt F.R.Dodson KiA
	Tomahawk force-landed; Lt G.B.Lipawsky unhurt
112 Sqn	Tomahawk badly damaged; Sgt A.H.Ferguson unhurt
45 Sqn	Blenheim IV V5991 collided head-on with Z9572 on take-off; Plt Off J.H.Tolman and crew KiFA
Lorraine Sqn	Blenheim IV Z9572 collided head-on with V5991 on take-off; Sgt G.Fifre and crew KiFA

German Claims

4./JG 27	Obfw Otto Schulz	P-40	Bir el Gubi 1016
	Oblt Gustav Rödel	P-40	NE Bir el Gubi 1018
	Uffz Alfred Heidel	P-40	Bir el Gubi 1020

German Casualties

Stab II./StG 2	Ju 87 in combat E Bir el Gubi; Hptmn Leonhard Busselt/Gefr Horst Aktories WiA
III./ZG 26	Bf 110 shot down; Maj Karl Kaschka and Uffz Mühlhausen KiA

Italian Claims

151ª Sq/20° Gr CT	Ten Lanfranco Baschiera		
	Serg Luigi Mannelli	Tomahawk	SE Bir el Gubi 0745-0915
	M.llo Ennio Tarantola	Tomahawk probable	SE Bir el Gubi 0745-0915
17° Gr CT	T.Col Bruno Brambilla	Hurricane	Bir el Gubi - El Adem 10.20
71ª Sq/17° Gr CT	Cap Pericle Baruffi	Tomahawk	Bir el Gubi - El Adem 10.20
	Ten Pierfrancesco Conti	Tomahawk	Bir el Gubi - El Adem 10.20
	S.Ten Ottorino Capellini	Tomahawk	Bir el Gubi - El Adem 10.20
	Serg Egidio Buogo	Tomahawk	Bir el Gubi - El Adem 10.20
80ª Sq/17° Gr CT	S.Ten Renato Bagnoli	Hurricane	Bir el Gubi - El Adem 10.20
72ª Sq/17° Gr CT	Cap Pio Tomaselli	Hurricane	Bir el Gubi - El Adem 10.20
	Serg Magg Gabriele Romagna	Tomahawk	Bir el Gubi - El Adem 10.20
71ª Sq/17° Gr CT	Serg Carlo Ermo	Tomahawk probable	Bir el Gubi - El Adem 10.20
352ª Sq/20° Gr CT	Serg Aldo Bonazza	Tomahawk	Bir el Gubi - El Adem
353ª Sq/20° Gr CT	Serg Spiridione Guiducci	2 Tomahawks	Bir el Gubi - El Adem

Italian Casualties

373ª Sq/153° Gr CT	MC.200 force-landed; Ten Felice Mezzetti WiA
153° Gr CT	4 MC.202s damaged
384ª Sq/157° Gr CT	MC.200 shot down; S.Ten Arrigo Zancristoforo KiA
385ª Sq/157° Gr CT	MC.200 shot down; Ten Vittorio Conti PoW
157° Gr CT	MC.200 damaged; pilot WiA
72ª Sq/17° Gr CT	MC.202 MM7866 destroyed in crash landing; S.Ten Lorenzo Chellini rescued
71ª Sq/17° Gr CT	MC.202 MM 7874 force-landed due to engine failure, M.llo Marcello Lui safe
	2 MC.202s damaged; T.Col Bruno Brambilla and Ten Pierfrancesco Conti returned
352ª Sq/20° Gr CT	G.50 crash-landed after collision; Ten Giuseppe Vitali PoW

Friday, 5 December 1941

The day saw another 'Stuka Party' (or 'Hun Circus' as Neville Duke recorded it in his diary) to the south-east of El Adem. On this occasion 250 Squadron, which had recorded a single claim for a Bf 109 about an hour earlier, put up a dozen Tomahawks, with top cover provided by ten more from 112 Squadron. Around mid morning some 35 Luftwaffe and Regia Aeronautica Ju 87s were seen, covered by Bf 109Fs of JG 27, and by 13 MC.200s of 153° Gruppo, 14 G.50bis of 20° Gruppo and two MC.200s of 157° Gruppo.

The majority of the Stukas were forced to jettison their bombs, and claims then included 16 Ju 87s and four fighters shot down, four Ju 87s and four fighters probably so, plus one Ju 87 and four fighters damaged. The cost was five Tomahawks. 250 Squadron had concentrated on the bombers as 112 Squadron held off the fighters, this allowing Flt Lt Clive Caldwell at the head of the former unit to claim five Stukas shot down, while Sgts Whittle and Cable each claimed two; Sgt Twemlow claimed one, but was able to add two more as probables. Although engaged mainly with the escorts, 112 Squadron nevertheless included six Ju 87s amongst their claims, three of them by Plt Off Neville Bowker, who also claimed damage to one fighter. The unit's star was Plt Off Sabourin, who claimed two fighters and two damaged, plus one Stuka.

Bf 109F pilots of I. and II./JG 27 claimed five P-40s, to which the G.50bis pilots of 20° Gruppo added claims for nine more. The MC.200 pilots of 153° Gruppo reported firing at many British fighters but without being able to ascertain result. Two G.50bis were damaged, causing T.Col Mario Bonzano and his wingman to make force-landings, while an MC.200 of 153° Gruppo was also brought down. 239ª Squadriglia BaT recorded the loss of one Ju 87 in which the crew were killed, one more crash-landed and a third force-landed with the pilot wounded.

Personnel of a South African Maryland squadron pause in the preparation of one of the unit's aircraft for a raid, to watch as five of the unit's aircraft set off to attack another target.

Amongst the British fighters, 250 Squadron reported being hit by Bf 109s which severely mauled the unit, four Tomahawks being shot down with two of the pilots killed and one wounded. 112 Squadron's Plt Off Duke also subsequently having to crash-land. Duke:

"Oh dear, shot down again. Met the Hun Circus again and all the types piled in and got ten down. I stayed up to stave the 109s off but got hit in the right elevator which was carried away, and in the starboard wing where all the trailing edge up to the aileron was shot off.

"Spun down from 10,000 ft to about 2-3,000. Undid the straps, etc, preparatory to baling out, but it seemed to fly OK. Made north for Tobruk at ground level. Crash-landed at 150 mph as I could not keep nose up at slower speed; got thrown about the cockpit, and found I'd been hit in the right leg by cannon shell splinters. Hopped out pretty quick. Pinched the compass and clock from the machine as spoils of war!

"The chaps were pretty surprised to see me again at Tobruk. I was whisked off to the hospital and X-rayed but the wounds were not very bad. Lucky enough to get a lift back in a Blenheim same evening. Shot down twice within five days – so flying down to Cairo for a few days' leave."

At 1415 ten Hurricanes of 1 SAAF Squadron were covered by 274 Squadron on a wing sweep over El Adem. Here they were attacked by German and Italian fighters, Lt Sandilands of the South African unit being shot down, claimed by Lt Marseille and Oblt Homuth of 3./JG 27 around 1530. A Hurricane was also claimed during the afternoon by M.llo Salvatore in a 9° Gruppo MC.202 – but at the earlier time of 1410. In return the SAAF pilots claimed one Bf 109 probably shot down and four fighters damaged. Somewhat later a further claim for a Bf 109 damaged was submitted by Capt Doherty of 2 SAAF

Squadron in the Bir el Gubi area. During the day one of II./JG 27's Bf 109Fs was reported lost in combat, but during which engagement is not clear, the pilot apparently suffering no injury.

Led by Lt Col Wilmot, 2 and 4 SAAF Squadrons then escorted a Blenheim to Tobruk carrying the army commander. They then patrolled to the south until over El Adem Bf 109s began attacking 4 SAAF Squadron. As one of these attackers shot past him, Capt Bosman got a shot at it and reported that it went straight into the ground. One pass was then made against 2 SAAF Squadron, Capt Doherty claiming to have inflicted some damage on one, but Lt Loffhagen returned with bullet holes in the tail of his Tomahawk.

During the day six Hurricanes from 33 Squadron with two more acting as top cover, strafed Agedabia again. Claims were made for three CR.42s destroyed on the ground there, with three more damaged, while two S.79s parked around the airfield were also claimed damaged. Two CR.42s were actually destroyed – aircraft of 366ª Squadriglia, 151° Gruppo, and four more suffered damage. An S.81 which had been damaged during an earlier raid was also set on fire. This would appear to have been the aircraft which 33 Squadron recorded to have blown up as Plt Off Lance Wade passed over it, damaging his aircraft. This caused him to have to force-land 20 miles east of the target. Sgt Wooler landed to pick him up, but in doing so his aircraft suffered a broken tailwheel and had to be abandoned. Both pilots began walking towards safety and were successfully picked up by a Blenheim next day.

The day also saw 94 Squadron re-equipped with 18 new Hurricane IIs, the unit's old Mark Is then being handed to the RNFS.

British Claims

250 Sqn	Plt Off F.A.Creighton	Tomahawk	Bf 109	20m SW Bardia 0945
112 Sqn	Flt Lt C.F.Ambrose	Tomahawk AK475	MC.200 probable	Tobruk-El Adem 1050-1220
	Flt Lt C.F.Ambrose	Tomahawk AK475	G.50 probable	Tobruk-El Adem 1050-1220
	Plt Off J.P.Bartle	Tomahawk AN372	Ju 87	Tobruk-El Adem 1050-1220
	Plt Off J.P.Bartle	Tomahawk AN372	G.50	Tobruk-El Adem 1050-1220
	Plt Off N.Bowker	Tomahawk AK509	3 Ju 87s	Tobruk-El Adem 1050-1220
	Plt Off N.Bowker	Tomahawk AK509	G.50 damaged	Tobruk-El Adem 1050-1220
	Sgt R.M.Leu	Tomahawk AK354	MC.200	Tobruk-El Adem 1050-1220
	Sgt R.M.Leu	Tomahawk AK354	Bf 109F probable	Tobruk-El Adem 1050-1220
	Plt Off J.J.P.Sabourin	Tomahawk AK457	G.50	Tobruk-El Adem 1050-1220
	Plt Off J.J.P.Sabourin	Tomahawk AK457	Ju 87	Tobruk-El Adem 1050-1220
	Plt Off J.J.P.Sabourin	Tomahawk AK457	Bf 109E	Tobruk-El Adem 1050-1220
	Plt Off J.J.P.Sabourin	Tomahawk AK457	Bf 109F damaged	Tobruk-El Adem 1050-1220
	Plt Off J.J.P.Sabourin	Tomahawk AK457	G.50 damaged	Tobruk-El Adem 1050-1220
	Flg Off J.F.Soden	Tomahawk AK377	Ju 87	Tobruk-El Adem 1050-1220
	Flg Off J.F.Soden	Tomahawk AK377	Bf 109F probable	Tobruk-El Adem 1050-1220
250 Sqn	Flt Lt C.R.Caldwell	Tomahawk AK498	5 Ju 87s	15m S El Adem 1145
	Flt Lt C.R.Caldwell	Tomahawk AK498	MC.200 damaged	15m S El Adem 1145
	Sgt W.O.Cable	Tomahawk	2 Ju 87s	15m S El Adem 1145
	Sgt W.O.Cable	Tomahawk	Ju 87 damaged	15m S El Adem 1145
	Flt Lt I.F.Rose	Tomahawk	Ju 87 probable	15m S El Adem 1145
	Sgt F.M.Twemlow	Tomahawk	Ju 87	15m S El Adem 1145
	Sgt F.M.Twemlow	Tomahawk	2 Ju 87s probable	15m S El Adem 1145
	Sgt R.J.C.Whittle	Tomahawk AM313	2 Ju 87s	15m S El Adem 1145
	Sgt R.J.C.Whittle	Tomahawk AM313	Ju 87 probable	15m S El Adem 1145
1 SAAF Sqn	Plt Off J.H.Galyer	Hurricane II	MC.202 damaged	10m NE El Adem 1510
	2/Lt G.R.Connell	Hurricane II	2 Bf 109Fs damaged	El Adem area 1510
	Lt W.L.Herbert	Hurricane II	Bf 109F probable	El Adem area 1515
	Lt W.L.Herbert	Hurricane II	Bf 109F damaged	El Adem area 1515
4 SAAF Sqn	Capt A.C.Bosman	Tomahawk	Bf 109F	Bir el Gubi area 1535-1735
2 SAAF Sqn	Capt V.P.J.Doherty	Tomahawk	Bf 109F damaged	Bir el Gubi area 1535-1735
33 Sqn	Six pilots	Hurricane Is	3 CR.42s	Agedabia on ground
	Six pilots	Hurricane Is	3 CR.42s damaged	Agedabia on ground
	Six pilots	Hurricane Is	2 S.79s damaged	Agedabia on ground

British Casualties

250 Sqn	Tomahawk shot down; Plt Off Coles WiA
	Tomahawk shot down; Sgt McWilliam returned next day
	Tomahawk shot down; Sgt E.P.Greenhow KiA
	Tomahawk shot down; Sgt J.R.Gilmour KiA
112 Sqn	Tomahawk AN337 'F' crash-landed; Plt Off N.F.Duke slt WiA
1 SAAF Sqn	Hurricane II Z5119 shot down; Lt N.M.Sandilands KiA
1 SAAF Sqn	Hurricane II force-landed due to lack of fuel; Lt W.L.Herbert unhurt
2 SAAF Sqn	Tomahawk AK or AN275 slightly damaged; Lt R.F.Loffhagen safe
33 Sqn	Hurricane I force-landed due to damage; Plt Off L.C.Wade picked up next day
	Hurricane I damaged trying to pick up Plt Off Wade and abandoned; Sgt Wooler picked up next day

German Claims

5./JG 27	Uffz Horst Reuter	P-40	SE Bir el Gubi 1143
6./JG 27	Lt Franz Külp	P-40	Bir el Gubi 1145
4./JG 27	Oblt Gustav Rödel	P-40	NW Bir el Gubi 1155
1./JG 27	Hptmn Wolfgang Redlich	P-40	S Bir el Gubi 1205
	Uffz Josef Grimm	P-40	S Bir el Gubi
3./JG 27	Lt Hans-Joachim Marseille	Hurricane	1525
	Oblt Gerhard Homuth	Hurricane	1535

German Casualties

II./JG 27	Bf 109F-4 trop WNr 8429 lost in combat, details unknown
3./StG 3	Ju 87 WNr 6153 destroyed by the explosion of its own bomb, Bir el Gubi; Fw Hans Bremkamp/Uffz Wilhelm Heger KiA
III./JG 53	2 Bf 109F-4/Zs WNr 7398 and damaged by bombing at Tmimi WNr 7364 605

Italian Claims

20° Gr CT	T Col Mario Bonzano	Tomahawk	
353ª Sq/20° Gr CT	Cap Riccardo Roveda	Tomahawk	
	Serg Magg Tullio Covre	Tomahawk	
	Serg Spiridione Guiducci	Tomahawk	
352ª Sq/20° Gr CT	Cap Luigi Borgogno	Tomahawk	
	M.llo Otello Bonelli	Tomahawk	
	Serg Magg Francesco Pecchiari	Tomahawk	
151ª Sq/20° Gr CT	M.llo Ennio Tarantola	Tomahawk	
	Serg Luigi Mannelli	Tomahawk	
96ª Sq/9° Gr CT	M.llo Massimo Salvatore	Hurricane	EL Adem-Gambut-Bir el Gubi 1410

Italian Casualties

20° Gr CT	G.50s damaged and force-landed; T.Col Mario Bonzano and his wingman safe
153° Gr CT	MC.200 damaged and force-landed; pilot safe
239ª Sq BaT	Ju 87R shot down; Serg Giovanni Mangano/Av.Sc Martino Spada KiA
	Ju 87R crash-landed; S.Ten Luigi Steffanina/1° Av Arduino Faienza PoW
	Ju 87R force-landed; Serg Franco Lanfredi WiA
366ª Sq/151° Gr CT	2 CR.42s destroyed on ground
	4 CR.42s damaged on ground
	S.81 (already damaged) destroyed on ground

Saturday, 6 December 1941

Beaufighters of 272 Squadron were again active, four setting out at 0950 to target Tmimi. During this raid Bf 109s attacked and Plt Off Snow's aircraft was shot down, being seen to crash-land two miles north of Tmimi with the port engine on fire. Four Messerschmitts attacked Flg Off Roman's 'A1' and inflicted severe damage before he was able to elude them. Sgt Lowes' 'N' was also damaged, but both he and Roman managed to return to LG.10. It seems that Snow's aircraft fell to Oblt Rödel of 4./JG 27, who claimed a Beaufighter at 1155 near Tobruk.

Four more Beaufighters repeated the attack at 1115, damage to five Ju 87s on the ground being claimed. Considerable light Flak was encountered and this time Flt Lt Campbell's aircraft was hit, causing him to force-land 40 miles to the south. Plt Off Hammond at once landed alongside, and after the latter's

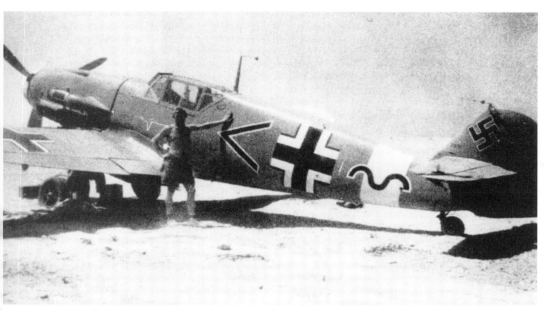

III./JG 27 arrived at Tmimi on 6 December 1941 to join the other two gruppen of the geschwader in North Africa. This is the adjutant's aircraft, Werke Nr 7077.

assistance in making some repairs to his damaged Beaufighter, Campbell was able to take off again. Unfortunately, before he could reach base the aircraft crash-landed 90 miles inside Egypt with the engine bearers broken. Hammond once again landed to pick up Campbell and his observer, but this time in doing so his own aircraft suffered some damage, the tailwheel oleo leg collapsing. Nevertheless, he was able to take off again with Campbell and his observer aboard after fuel and other equipment had been jettisoned to lighten the aircraft. Once back in the air, Hammond strafed the crashed aircraft to complete its destruction before flying back to base. Over the target, meanwhile, Plt Off Stephenson's aircraft had also been hit, this pilot suffering wounds to his legs, while his observer, Sgt Olive, was mortally wounded. With one damaged engine and a seriously damaged aircraft, Stephenson flew direct back to Edcu where he crash-landed. Despite this effort, Oliver was never to regain consciousness.

Whilst the second 272 Squadron attack on Tmimi was in progress, 24 Hurricanes of 229 and 238 Squadrons undertook a protective wing sweep over El Gubi where nine Ju 87s, escorted by fighters identified as G.50bis, MC.200s and Bf 109s, were met. At the same time four squadrons of Blenheims, including the Free French Lorraine unit, appeared in the area escorted by two more squadrons of Hurricanes, 274 and 1 SAAF. The bombers' target was MT south-west of El Adem. Bf 109s and MC.202s at once attacked the French aircraft, Obfw Otto Schulz shooting down two of them at once. All four squadrons of Hurricanes then became involved, Wg Cdr Dudley Honor in one of the 274 Squadron aircraft claiming an MC.202 shot down; other pilots claimed a Bf 109 as a probable, plus three Bf 109s, three MC.202s and one MC.200 damaged. However, 229 Squadron lost two aircraft, although both pilots returned later, while 238 Squadron lost three more, one of which crash-landed with the pilot unhurt. Two Hurricanes were claimed during this engagement by Lt Marseille, and a third was claimed by Uffz Horst Reuter of 5./JG 27, though apparently at an earlier time – possibly mis-recorded. The only Axis losses on this date were two 9° Gruppo MC.202s which collided whilst escorting Ju 87s to Bir el Gubi, one pilot being killed while the other baled out.

On 6 December III./JG 27 began arriving at Tmimi from Doberitz. It would be followed four days later by the Geschwader Stab to bring the whole geschwader together for the first time since 1940. With the Stab came Geschwader Kommodore, Maj Bernhard Woldenga. To date III.Gruppe had been the star performer and was one of the oldest in the Luftwaffe. It had originally formed in April 1937 as I./JG 131, becoming I./JG 1 during 1939. Having claimed 80 victories during the French campaign, the unit was retitled III./JG 27 in time for the Battle of Britain. During this fighting 54 more victories had been added, following five during a brief period of action over Malta in May 1941. In Russia the unit had gained a further 220 victories. The gruppenkommandeur was Hptmn Erhard Braune, who had personally claimed 12 victories to date, while the three staffeln, 7., 8., and 9. were led by Oblt Hermann Tangerding (eight victories), Oblt Hans Lass (14 victories) and Oblt Erbo Graf von Kageneck. This latter was at the time the top-scoring pilot of the whole geschwader, and indeed one of the highest scorers in the entire Luftwaffe with 65 victories credited at the time of his arrival in Africa. He was also a holder of the Knights' Cross with Oak Leaves. Other successful pilots were Oblt Ludwig Bauer (nine), Uffz Hans Fahrenberger (seven), and Fw Emil Clade and Walter Hillgruber (six each). Kommodore Bernhard Woldenga, was also a Knights' Cross holder; he had claimed three victories to date.

Also from Sicily came Feldmarschall Kesselring on a visit to assess the overall situation. During the day he engaged in meetings with Rommel, Geisler, Fröhlich and Marchesi.

British Claims

238 Sqn	Flg Off Aldridge	Hurricane IIc 'F'	Bf 109E probable	E Bir el Gubi 1115-1245
	Flg Off Aldridge	Hurricane IIc 'F'	Bf 109 damaged	E Bir el Gubi 1115-1245
	Flg Off C.R.Forsyth	Hurricane IIc 'K'	2 MC.202s damaged	
274 Sqn	Wg Cdr D.S.G.Honor	Hurricane IIb Z5435	MC.202	8m from Tobruk 1120-1305
	Plt Off Weeks	Hurricane IIb Z4000	MC.200 damaged	SW Tobruk
	Sgt J.Dodds	Hurricane IIb Z2835	MC.202 damaged	
1 SAAF Sqn	2/Lt A.D.Maclean	Hurricane II BD779	Bf 109F damaged	20m SE El Adem 1230
	2/Lt J.T.Seccombe	Hurricane IIb	Bf 109F damaged	
272 Sqn	Flt Lt G.L.Campbell	Beaufighter Ic ⎫		
	Plt Off D.H.Hammond	Beaufighter Ic ⎬ 5 Ju 87s damaged	on ground Tmimi	
	Plt Off A.P.Stephenson	Beaufighter Ic ⎪		
	fourth pilot	Beaufighter Ic ⎭		

British Casualties

272 Sqn	Beaufighter Ic T3246 'J' shot down; Plt Off W.G.Snow RAAF and observer, Sgt J.Dalton, PoWs
	Beaufighter Ic 'A1' badly damaged; Flg Off C.L.Roman and observer safe
	Beaufighter Ic 'N' damaged; Sgt D.C.Lowes and observer safe
	Beaufighter Ic crash-landed; Flt Lt G.L.Campbell picked up safely
	Beaufighter Ic damaged; Plt Off A.P.Stevenson WiA, observer Sgt Olive mortally WiA
229 Sqn	Hurricane IIc shot down; Plt Off Ruffhead returned
	Hurricane IIc shot down; Sgt Roy returned
238 Sqn	Hurricane IIc shot down; Flg Off Zabaiski
	Hurricane IIc shot down; Plt Off Omerod WiA
	Hurricane IIc shot down; Sgt Mathews crash-landed, returned next day
GRB 1	Blenheim IV V6495 shot down; crew apparently survived unharmed
	Blenheim IV V6503 shot down; Flg Off R.Sandre and crew KiA

German Claims

5./JG 27	Uffz Horst Reuter	Hurricane	N Sidi Daud 1020
4./JG 27	Oblt Gustav Rödel	Beaufighter	Tobruk 1155
3./JG 27	Lt Hans-Joachim Marseille	Hurricane	SE El Adem 1210
	Lt Hans-Joachim Marseille	Hurricane	S El Adem 1225
4./JG 27	Obfw Otto Schulz	2 Blenheims	SE El Adem 1228-1230

Italian Casualties

97ª Sq/9° Gr CT	MC.202 MM7738 destroyed in midair collision; M.llo Raffaele Novelli KiFA
	MC.202 MM7745 destroyed in midair collision; Serg Magg Anselmo Andraghetti baled out

Sunday, 7 December 1941

The first action of the day occurred when two TacR Hurricanes of 237 Squadron which had taken off at 0730, were intercepted by Lt Marseille of 3./JG 27 12 miles west of Sidi Omar at 0930. He claimed one of these aircraft shot down, Flg Off B.White's aircraft falling in flames in precisely the area identified by the German pilot. 237 Squadron recorded its loss as being due to Flak (not an unusual mistake given the Luftwaffe's rapid dive and climb tactics).

Two days earlier 24 SAAF Squadron had returned to the control of 3 SAAF Wing at LG.130 to commence bombing operations with its new Bostons, following a period when these had been restricted to reconnaissance duties. Three remained at Fort Maddalena, however, to continue the latter role. One of these was now despatched to El Adem to photograph the road from there to Acroma, and to report on weather conditions. Near Gazala the aircraft was intercepted and attacked by 4./JG 27's Obfw Otto Schulz at 0950, one engine being set on fire and the wing beginning to burn. Lt Kingon ordered the crew to bale out, but as he then learned that the gunners were too badly wounded to escape, he returned to his seat and undertook a successful crash-landing. Despite flames and exploding ammunition, he then carried the wounded from the wreck, returning for water and a first aid kit. All were subsequently captured, including the observer who had managed to bale out. The two gunners were later liberated when Derna hospital fell into Allied hands, but Kingon and the observer, Air Sgt C.J.Rudge, were sent to Italy. Kingon, known in the squadron as 'the fighting padre', escaped after the Italian capitulation in September 1943, and was awarded an MBE for his subsequent activities behind enemy lines.

Meanwhile, a second Boston, Z2181, was despatched at 0720 on a similar sortie, but this too was shot down in the El Adem area, reportedly by Flak, only one member of the crew surviving to become a PoW. Again, the cause of the loss of this aircraft appears to have been incorrectly recorded, for in just this area at 1015 a Boston was claimed shot down by 1./JG 27's Lt Hans Remmer.

It was now possible to employ the airfield at Tobruk as an advanced landing ground, and at once 274 and 1 SAAF Squadrons had been

In November 1941 Sid Linnard was posted to command 274 Squadron. During a fight over Tobruk on 7 December the unit enjoyed a number of successes, the new commanding officer claiming a Macchi C.202, a second probable and a third damaged.

ordered to land there to refuel after undertaking an early morning sweep. The South Africans had just completed refuelling when the unit was scrambled around 1000 after an enemy formation over El Adem, leaving 274 Squadron still undertaking this necessary exercise. They encountered nine Ju 87s with a large fighter escort ten miles south-west of El Adem and attacked at once. Maj Osler and Plt Off Galyer each claimed one fighter shot down, but three of the unit's Hurricanes were shot down in return, Lt Penberthy as he was pursuing a Messerschmitt to the ground; he survived as a PoW. However, Lt Kershaw's wingman, 2/Lt C.B.Willson, was shot down in flames and he was killed, while Kershaw's aircraft was badly damaged by cannon fire. He and Lt Hojem, whose aircraft had also been hard hit, made it back to base. Capt van Vliet crash-landed his damaged aircraft 20 miles south of base, but survived unhurt.

Somewhat behind 1 SAAF Squadron, 274 Squadron had followed from Tobruk, and this unit's pilots reported 15 Ju 87s, also with a large fighter escort – almost certainly the same formation as that attacked by the South Africans. According to the squadron, Bf 109s made their usual dive-and-climb attacks, but the Italian fighters present appeared to be badly organised, allowing three to be claimed shot down as well as one of the Stukas, while two more were added as probables and one damaged. Sgt Parbury dived down to claim the destruction of a Ju 87 which had force-landed, and damaged a second.

As with the South Africans, losses to the unit were not light, three pilots being shot down, two of whom were killed. During this fighting Luftwaffe pilots claimed three fighters shot down, two of them incorrectly identified as P-40s. One Bf 109F of 5./JG 27 was shot down over Tobruk – the unit reporting this as another victim of AA fire. The pilot, Lt Külp (actually a member of 6.Staffel), who had just claimed one of the Hurricanes before being brought down, managed to walk to El Adem where he lunched with the doctor in charge of a hospital for British PoWs.

The balance of the Hurricane losses were undoubtedly due to the efforts of the MC.200 pilots of 153° Gruppo CT – perhaps not so disorganised as had appeared to their opponents, since the pilots of this unit claimed six British fighters shot down. However, the unit lost four of its own aircraft shot down with three pilots killed and a fourth captured. One more of this unit's aircraft was damaged, and one further MC.200 of 157° Gruppo which had also been taking part in the Stuka escort, force-landed. Both the pilots of these latter two aircraft were reported safe. The Italians recorded that the British attacks were made at around 1155, after the Stukas had completed their dive-bombing. It is interesting to note that the British and South African pilots all claimed MC.202s on this occasion despite all the Italian aircraft involved in fact having been MC.200s.

Towards the end of the day Axis forces began withdrawing towards Gazala, and JG 27's gruppen were forced to leave the complex of airfields there, where they had been based since their arrival in April and thereafter. The Regia Aeronautica had to cease all reconnaissance sorties over the sea due to the growing fuel crisis. Next day the Regia Aeronautica commenced a wholesale evacuation of units following orders issued by Generale Vittorio Marchesi. The Gazala airfields were to be evacuated at once, with the command HQ of 5ª Squadra going to Benghazi in preparation for a further move to Misurata.

On the other side of the lines 270 Wing now received a new commanding officer in the person of Grp Capt R.Kellett, DFC, AFC, formerly commander of 11 Squadron. Grp Capt Beamish departed to Advanced Air HQ as grp capt fighters and senior plans staff officer. 272 Squadron despatched two Beaufighters to strafe vehicles on the Benghazi-Cirene road. They were followed by a second pair, but one of these, flown by Flt Lt Bartlett, was badly damaged by Flak, although the pilot was able to get the aircraft back to base.

British Claims

250 Sqn	Plt Off K.G.Hart	Tomahawk	⎫		
	Plt Off W.W.Swinnerton	Tomahawk	⎬	Ju 88 damaged	SW LG.123 0930-0945
	Unspecified pilot	Tomahawk	⎭		
274 Sqn	Sqn Ldr S.Linnard	Hurricane IIb Z5064		MC.202	W El Adem 110-1240
	Sqn Ldr S.Linnard	Hurricane IIb Z5064		MC.202 probable	W El Adem 110-1240
	Sqn Ldr S.Linnard	Hurricane IIb Z5064		MC.202 damaged	W El Adem 110-1240
	Plt Off G.C.Keefer	Hurricane IIb BD880		MC.202	W El Adem 110-1240
	Plt Off G.C.Keefer	Hurricane IIb BD880		MC.202 damaged	W El Adem 110-1240
	Plt Off Moriarty	Hurricane IIb Z4015		G.50	W El Adem 110-1240
	Plt Off Moriarty	Hurricane IIb Z4015		Ju 87	W El Adem 110-1240
	Plt Off Weeks	Hurricane IIb Z4000		MC.202 probable	W El Adem 110-1240
	Sgt C.R.Parbury	Hurricane IIb Z5117		Ju 87 on ground, which had force-landed	W El Adem 110-1240
	Sgt C.R.Parbury	Hurricane IIb Z5117		Ju 87 damaged	W El Adem 110-12401
1 SAAF Sqn	Maj M.S.Osler	Hurricane II		MC.202	10m SW El Adem 1150
	Plt Off J.H.Galyer	Hurricane II		Bf 109F	10m SW El Adem 1145
	Lt W.L.Herbert	Hurricane II		G.50 damaged	10m SW El Adem 1150

British Casualties

237 Sqn	Hurricane shot down; Flg Off B.D.White KiA
24 SAAF Sqn	Boston III Z2202 'V' shot down; Lt A.M.Kingon and crew PoW
	Boston III Z2181 'R' shot down; Lt W.N.Hollenbach and two KiA; one PoW
1 SAAF Sqn	Hurricane II Z5338 shot down; 2/Lt C.B.Willson
	Hurricane II crash-landed; Capt C.A.van Vliet unhurt
	Hurricane II BD626 shot down; Lt V.A.Penberthy PoW
	Hurricane II damaged; Lt R.H.C.Kershaw unhurt
	Hurricane II Z4009 shot down; G.C.Lt Hojem unhurt
274 Sqn	Hurricane IIb BD783 shot down; Flt Lt J.B.Hobbs KiA
	Hurricane IIb Z5260 shot down; Plt Off F.H.Sutton KiA
	Hurricane IIb Z2395 shot down; Plt Off Gain MiA
272 Sqn	Beaufighter Ic badly damaged by Flak; Flt Lt M.L.P.Bartlett and observer safe

German Claims

3./JG 27	Lt Hans-Joachim Marseille	Hurricane	12m W Sidi Omar 0930
4./JG 27	Obfw Otto Schulz	Boston	S Ain el Gazala 0950
1./JG 27	Lt Hans Remmer	Boston	S El Adem 1015
	Obfw Albert Espenlaub	P-40	SE El Adem 1155
	Uffz Josef Grimm	P-40	W El Adem 1205
6./JG 27	Lt Franz Külp	Hurricane	Tobruk 1205

German Casualties

5./JG 27	Bf 109F-4 trop WNr 8425 shot down by AA over Tobruk; Lt Franz Külp MiA, returned
5./StG 2	Ju 87 in combat E Bir el Gubi; pilot Uffz Walter Krug WiA

Italian Claims

153° Gr CT	Unspecified pilots	6 Fighters + 8 probables	Tobruk area	1155

Italian Casualties

372ª Sq/153° Gr CT	MC.200 shot down; Cap Armando Farina KiA
	MC.200 shot down; S.Ten Guido Sturla KiA
	MC.200 shot down; M.llo Rino Lupetti KiA
157° Gr CT	MC 200 shot down; Serg Ernesto Revello PoW
373ª Sq/153° Gr CT	MC.200 force-landed; Cap Cesare Marchesi safe
	MC.200 damaged; M.llo Erberto Rocchetta safe

Monday, 8 December 1941

British troops now again made contact with the Tobruk garrison and Rommel withdrew his forces into prepared positions at Gazala. Very early in the morning four Hurricanes of 33 Squadron strafed Agedabia once more, claiming damage to five CR.42s and a twin-engined aircraft on the ground. It is presumed that most of these were dummies or aircraft which had already been destroyed, for actual casualties amounted to only one 151° Gruppo aircraft. Flg Off Charles's aircraft was hit in the glycol system by fire from the ground – reportedly the machine gun in a Ca.311, manned during the attack and probably the twin-engined aircraft claimed by the unit. Charles force-landed five miles to the east of the airfield, where Flt Lt Gould landed and picked him up. The fourth Hurricane's pilot who had failed to find the target, instead strafed some MT. 113 Squadron's cannon Blenheims were also out during the day, four of these attacking and claiming damage to 18 vehicles on the El Faidia-Narawa road.

At 0950 12 Hurricanes of 94 Squadron providing top cover for 260 Squadron, swept over the Bir el Gubi-El Adem area where they were jumped by four Bf 109s, but without result. A single claim for a P-40 had been made in the same general area by Lt Marseille an hour or so earlier, but no corresponding loss for this claim has been found.

At 1040 eight MC.202s of 9° Gruppo commenced a patrol of the Gazala-Tobruk area, followed 50 minutes later by 11 more such aircraft

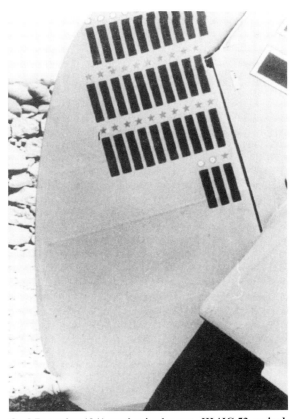

On 8 December 1941 another jagdgruppe, III./JG 53, arrived in Africa from the Eastern Front. At this time one of the unit's most successful pilots was Obfw Hermann Neuhoff, the victory-marked rudder of whose Bf 109F is seen here. He was to claim four victories over the desert in as many days before the unit departed again, this time for Sicily to operate over Malta.

De Havilland 86 A31-7 of the RAAF's 1 Air Ambulance Unit, was one of two such aircraft attacked over LG.138 on 8 December 1941; it survived after suffering some damage, but its fellow aircraft, A31-8, did not.

from 17° Gruppo. It seems that both formations encountered the same Allied formation which comprised 18 Blenheims drawn from two squadrons, escorted by Hurricanes of 274 and 1 SAAF Squadrons, the pilots of the former unit identifying their opponents as Bf 109s, MC.202s and MC.200s. These were engaged as the bombers sought to attack some 250 vehicles to the south-west of El Adem. However, they had only been spotted by the 274 Squadron pilots, the South Africans continuing on their way with the bombers, leaving the other unit heavily outnumbered.

The 9° Gruppo Macchis attacked first, claiming two fighters shot down and nine damaged for the loss of one of their aircraft force-landed. As the British unit sought to return to base, they were hit by 17° Gruppo whose pilots claimed six shot down plus two probables in return for damage to just two MC.202s. Sqn Ldr Linnard, while engaged with one aircraft which he took to be a Messerschmitt, saw what he identified as an MC.200 attacking a Hurricane, both aircraft making steep turns and losing height. Linnard shook free from his own combat and tried to shoot the Macchi off the other Hurricane's tail, but he was too late, bullets from the Italian fighter, which was turning inside the Hurricane, striking the area of the cockpit. The stricken aircraft then turned over at low level and dived into the ground several miles south of El Adem, bursting into flames. One other Hurricane was seen to go down vertically, while a third, flown by Sgt MacDonnell, crash-landed at Tobruk. The two missing pilots were Flt Lt Owen Tracey and Sgt Haines; subsequently, squadron personnel met South African soldiers who reported that they had found a grave beside a wrecked Hurricane, and that on this was a flying helmet and the identity disc of Tracey. One of the original Battle of Britain pilots, he was a great loss who had claimed six victories at the time of his death, three of them in Africa and over Crete.

In return for these losses Sgt Dodds claimed two fighters shot down – identified as one Bf 109 and one MC.202 – while claims were also made for two more probables and five damaged. However, it seems that 80 Squadron also became engaged in this mêlée. Six of this unit's fighter-bombers attacked a section of the coast road, cover being provided by four more Hurricanes. These latter four reported beating off an attack by 12 Bf 109s and MC.202s without loss, claiming two shot down, one probable and two damaged.

Amongst the reinforcements sent to North Africa by the RAAF was 1 Air Ambulance. This useful little unit had moved from Gaza (Palestine) to Fuka in mid October, commencing casualty evacuations at once. On 17 November it moved to LG.10 for the forthcoming Crusader operations with its three De Havilland DH 86 four-engined biplanes, A31-3, A31-7 and A31-8.

On this date, A31-7 flew up to LG.138 at 1230, taking off for LG.134 three minutes later, heading for this latter airfield at 60 feet. When within six miles of the destination the pilot, Capt Nel, a SAAF airman who usually flew a Lodestar for the South African Air Ambulance, but who had been attached to the Australian unit, heard gunfire. He then saw two Bf 110s which overshot his aircraft, about 30 feet above.

One of the DH 86s of 1 Air Ambulance Unit, RAAF, used for casualty evacuation from forward air strips.

At once he turned sharp left and went down to minimum altitude. Here he found he was flying across the line of fire of five Bf 110s, all formating on A31-7 at a range of 150 yards. Continuing to fly at full throttle, he landed at LG.138 at 1305.

As soon as possible he took off again for LG.10 where he arrived at 1445. Inspection showed bullet holes in the tailplane and rudder, and in the cabin. It was felt that it was the clear, cool-headed thinking of the pilot that had prevented the aircraft being shot down. Meanwhile, A31-3 had evacuated eight patients to Mersa Matruh by 1050, where Flg Off B.D.Bates took over from Plt Off E.B.Annear, leaving LG.134 at 1140 when advised that it was safe to proceed to LG.138. As he approached this landing ground he saw bombs bursting and flames about two miles off, but did not see any other aircraft until a Bf 110 passed him at low level and at right angles to his line of flight. He at once did a steep turn at low level and landed as Hurricanes of 73 Squadron chased off the attackers. At 1620 he was able to report that A31-8 had been shot down two miles south of LG.138 but the crew of Flt Lt MacDonald, the unit commander, were all safe.

The Bf 110s had been part of a force from III./ZG 26, escorted by Bf 109s, which had shot-up the road at 1300, close to the airfield where 2 SAAF Squadron was based. Several Tomahawks were scrambled, their pilots managing to keep the attackers away from their base, but as they did so, they saw the DH 86 being shot down. Lt Saville claimed one Bf 110 possibly shot down, while pilots of 73 Squadron's Battle Flight also joined the fight, claiming one destroyed and one probable.

DH 86 A31-8 in flames after being shot down over LG.138 by Obfw Helmut Haugk of 7./ZG 26 on 8 December 1941. The Luftwaffe pilot identified his unusual victim as a 'Valentia'.

The Bf 110s attacking LG.138 on 8 December 1941 were intercepted by Hurricane pilots of 73 Squadron's 'Battle Flight', formed for the Crusader offensive. Including the unit's more experienced pilots, the flight was formed with left to right – Lt D.Barlow, Plt Off R.Laing, Sqn Ldr Derek Ward, Flg Off R.McDougal, Flg Off T.P.K.Scade and Flt Lt G.R.A.McG. 'Robin' Johnston.

At 1230, very much the same time as this fighting was taking place, eleven more Tomahawks of 3 RAAF Squadron and ten of 112 Squadron were patrolling the forward area, but were attacked by six Bf 109s and two Bf 110s over Gusier, Sgt Alves' fighter being badly shot-up.

During this attack three Bf 110s were actually lost, one of them a 9.Staffel aircraft which had suffered damage, crashing while landing at Derna. The crews of the other two aircraft came down in the area, at least three of them becoming prisoners. The German pilots completely mis-identified the ambulance aircraft, Obfw Haugk claiming A31-8 as a Valentia; one claim was also made for a Hurricane, it being very likely that the aircraft attacked was in fact Alves' Tomahawk. HQ, Western Desert, recorded that six Bf 110s and six Bf 109s strafed three airfields in the Maddalena area at this time.

Now down to only two aircraft, 1 RAAF Air Ambulance would nonetheless move to El Adem on 28 December, but would return to Mersa Matruh on 28 January, and then back to LG.10 three days later.

We now come to one of those problems which almost defy the historian's efforts. At 1310, just after the claims made by both the British and German pilots operating over the LG.138 area, the usually reliable Obfw Schulz of 4./JG 27 was credited with a Boston shot down. No Boston was involved in an engagement on this date; however, a possible explanation for this claim exists. Since October 1941, 31 Squadron, a transport unit based at Lahore in India, had been maintaining a detachment at Bilbeis equipped with ex-airline DC-2s. These were employed in flying supplies up to the desert and bringing back casualties. The unit's operations record book is very lacking in detail for this period, but describes how DC-2 DG475 'X', flown by Flt Lt Howell and Wt Off D.S.Lord (later in the war to be awarded a Victoria Cross for conduct during the Arnhem airborne operation) was attacked ten miles north-east of LG.138 by three fighters identified as Bf 109s or Bf 110s. Badly damaged, the aircraft crash-landed, one of the nine passengers aboard being killed.

The loss of DG475 has been recorded elsewhere (notably in aircraft serial lists by 'Air-Britain') as having occurred on 25 December, while other sources have indicated the 8th or the 25th. However, by 25 December the front lines were well to the west of the LG.138 area coupled with which the Axis air forces had become very short of fuel, and no claim appears to have been made by any of their units for a victory of this nature.

Thus both the time and the location of Schulz's claim would fit quite neatly into the circumstances of

8 December. Possibly Schulz claimed a 'Douglas', and because the Boston was a product of that manufacturer – and he had shot one down only the day before – it seems possible that the unit records identified this aircraft as another of the same type. This is clearly an assumption and a hypothesis, but it is one which the authors have decided to employ on this occasion. This basis does appear to be confirmed by an Ultra intercept of a report which noted that on 8 December Luftwaffe claims had amounted to two Tomahawks and three aircraft identified as Valentias shot down for the loss of four Bf 110s and two Bf 109s.

At very much the same time as these events were taking place a British raid on Derna left a Cant.Z.1007bis and five Ju 52/3ms in flames – but perhaps more importantly, also destroyed 9,000 litres of precious fuel.

British Claims

80 Sqn	Sgt F.Mason	Hurricane IIb Z4786	Bf 109F	1045-1235
	Plt Off R.Reynolds	Hurricane IIb Z4801	Bf 109F	1045-1235
	Sgt G.H.Whyte	Hurricane IIb Z4714	MC.202 probable	1045-1235
			MC.202 damaged	1045-1235
94 Sqn	Sqn Ldr H.C.Mayers	Hurricane	Bf 109F damaged	1145
2 SAAF Sqn	Capt V.P.J.Doherty	Tomahawk	Bf 109 damaged	Tobruk-El Adem area 1125-1415
274 Sqn	Sqn Ldr S.Linnard	Hurricane IIb Z5064	2 MC.202s damaged	SW El Adem 1125-1300
	Plt Off Moriarty	Hurricane IIb Z4015	2 MC.202s damaged	SW El Adem 1125-1300
	Plt Off G.C.Keefer	Hurricane IIb BD880	Bf 109 damaged	SW El Adem 1125-1300
	Sgt J.Dodds	Hurricane IIb Z2835	Bf 109F	SW El Adem 1125-1300
	Sgt J.Dodds	Hurricane IIb Z2835	MC.202	SW El Adem 1125-1300
	Sgt R.W.Henderson	Hurricane IIb Z5367	MC.202 probable	SW El Adem 1125-1300
	Sgt R.H.N.Walsh	Hurricane IIb Z5435	Bf 109E probable	SW El Adem 1125-1300
73 Sqn	Flg Off T.P.K.Scade	Hurricane I	Bf 110	1250
	Flg Off R.McDougal	Hurricane I	Bf 110 probable	1250
2 SAAF Sqn	Lt E.C.Saville	Tomahawk	Bf 110 probable	LG.122 1300
			MC.202 damaged	W Mechili 1540
	Marylands units		5 Ju 52/3ms destroyed by bombing at Derna	
	Marylands units		3 u/i aircraft destroyed by bombing at Derna	

British Casualties

33 Sqn	Hurricane I force-landed; Flg Off Charles picked up by Hurricane
274 Sqn	Hurricane IIb BD885 shot down; Flt Lt O.V.Tracey KiA
	Hurricane IIb Z5066 shot down; Sgt Haines KiA
	Hurricane IIb BE347 crash-landed; Sgt J.P.MacDonnell safe
	Hurricane IIb Z5130 force-landed; Plt Off Thompson unhurt
3 RAAF Sqn	Tomahawk damaged; Sgt Alves unhurt
1 RAAF Air Ambulance	DH 86 A-31-8 shot down; Flt Lt J.G.MacDonald and crew safe
	DH 86 A-31-7 slightly damaged; Capt D.U.Nel and crew safe
31 Sqn	DC-2K DG475 'X' crash-landed due to combat damage; Flt Lt Howell, Wt Off D.S.Lord and eight passengers safe, one passenger KiA
216 Sqn	Bombay slightly damaged on ground at LG.138

German Claims

3./JG 27	Lt Hans-Joachim Marseille	P-40	15m SE El Adem 0815
7./ZG 26	Obfw Helmut Haugk	Valentia	1242
	Lt Helmut Scheid	Hurricane	1247
4./JG 27	Obfw Otto Schulz	Boston	N Ridotto 1310

German Casualties

7./ZG 26	Bf 110 WNr 3662 shot down; Lt Winfried Foldtt and Ogfr Berchner PoW
8./ZG 26	Bf 110 WNr 2153 shot down; Oblt Otto Reitsperger PoW
9./ZG 26	Bf 110 WNr 3452 damaged and crashed on landing at Derna; Lt Hermann Weber and Uffz Welledorf KiA
4./JG 27	Bf 109F-4 trop WNr 8431 force-landed S El Adem out of fuel; Obfw Fritz Rockel PoW
	Bf 109F-4 trop WNr 8430 force-landed S El Adem out of fuel; Gefr Heinz Kleinert PoW
KGrzbV 102	Ju 52/3m WNr 6543 100% destroyed
	Ju 52/3m WNr 6579 80% destroyed
Unspecified unit	5 Ju 52/3ms destroyed on the ground at Derna

32ª Sq	Air gunner in Ca.311 on ground	Hurricane	Agedabia early a.m.
96ª Sq/9° Gr CT	Cap Ezio Viglione Borghese	Hurricane	Ain el Gazala -Tobruk 1040-
97ª Sq/9° Gr CT	S.Ten Gianni Barcaro		
	S.Ten Gianni Barcaro	3 Hurricanes damaged	Ain el Gazala -Tobruk 1040-
	Serg Alfredo Bombardini	Hurricane	Ain el Gazala -Tobruk 1040-
	M.llo Otello Perotti	2 Hurricanes damaged	Ain el Gazala -Tobruk 1040-
	S.Ten Jacopo Frigerio	4 Hurricanes damaged	Ain el Gazala -Tobruk 1040-
80ª Sq/17° Gr CT	Ten Renato Talamini	Hurricane	Ain el Gazala -Tobruk 1130-
	S.Ten Renato Bagnoli	Tomahawk	Ain el Gazala -Tobruk 1130-
72ª Sq/17° Gr CT	Ten Mario Carini	Hurricane	Ain el Gazala -Tobruk 1130-
	S.Ten Guido Modiano	Hurricane	Ain el Gazala -Tobruk 1130-
71ª Sq/17° Gr CT	S.Ten Vittorio Bacchi Andreoli	Tomahawk	Ain el Gazala -Tobruk 1130-
	M.llo Achille Martina	Tomahawk	Ain el Gazala -Tobruk 1130-
	S.Ten Ottorino Capellini	Tomahawk probable	Ain el Gazala -Tobruk 1130-
80ª Sq/17° Gr CT	Serg Magg Mario Host	Tomahawk probable	Ain el Gazala -Tobruk 1130-

Italian Casualties

Unspecified unit	Cant..Z.1007bis destroyed by bombing at Derna
	2 MC.200s damaged on ground at Derna by bombing
	3 S.79s damaged on ground at Derna by bombing
151° Gr CT	CR.42 damaged on ground at Agedabia
97ª Sq/9° Gr	MC.202 MM 7739 damaged, force-landed and destroyed on ground by own forces; Serg Alfredo Bombardini safe
72ª Sq/17° Gr CT	MC.202 MM 7758 damaged; Ten Mario Carini safe, crash-landed
80ª Sq/17° Gr CT	MC.202 damaged; Ten Renato Talamini safe

The day had also seen the arrival at Tmimi of the main body of III.Gruppe of JG 53 'Pikas' with a reinforcement for the Luftwaffe fighters of 21 more Bf 109Fs. Led by Hptmn Wolf-Dietrich Wilcke, the unit had taken part in the fighting of the French campaign and over England during 1940, then serving in the east from June to October 1941. It had then been withdrawn to Germany to re-equip, having built up a tally of 587 victories. The three staffeln, 7., 8., and 9 were led respectively by Oblt Heinz Altendorf, Oblt Hans-Joachim Heinecke and Oblt Franz Götz. The unit included many experienced and successful pilots, two of whom – Wilke and Lt Herbert Schramm – had received the award of the Knights' Cross. At the time of the unit's arrival in Africa Schramm had already claimed 37 victories, Wilke 34 and Götz 31. Additionally, Lt Hermann Neuhoff had 32, Obfw Werner Stumpf 25, Altendorf and Heinecke 15 each, Lt Hermann Munzert 13, and three other pilots had claimed eight or more.

Two of the unit's aircraft which had arrived early on 5 December had already been severely damaged on the ground in a bombing attack. No sooner had the gruppe arrived at this airfield than it was prepared to move again, going to Derna on the 11th from where it commenced operations. III./JG 27 also departed Tmimi next day, moving to Martuba.

News now began to filter through that there had been a major attack by Japanese forces on British and US bases in the Far East. Whilst this brought the USA into the war on the side of the British Commonwealth and the Soviet Union, it also became quickly obvious to the Middle East commands that many of the supplies now reaching Africa would have to be diverted to this new war zone – exactly the same problem as that which had arisen during the previous British advance through Cyrenaica, then due to the Italian and German invasions of Greece and Yugoslavia.

Tuesday, 9 December 1941

The pressure in the desert was beginning to tell on Rommel's forces at last, and they now began to withdraw. It was to be a day of heavy activity for the WDAF, many sweeps by pairs of squadrons being flown over the Bir el Gubi/El Adem/Tobruk area, during which several formations of German fighters would be encountered.

First, however, fighters engaged on these operations intercepted a succession of Luftwaffe reconnaissance aircraft. At 0830 Flg Off 'Robin' Johnston of 73 Squadron's Battle Flight claimed a Ju 88 over Sidi Omar. Nine Tomahawks of 250 Squadron had taken off to join Hurricanes of the RNFS on a sweep over the El Adem-Bir el Gubi area at 0720, reporting meeting five Bf 110s and ten Bf 109s at

0845, one of the former being claimed shot down by Flt Lt Bary and Plt Off Waddy, this aircraft being seen to crash in flames. This appears to have been from 2.(H)/14 which lost a Bf 110 in which the pilot was killed but the gunner survived, to become a PoW.

Shortly after this engagement, two Hurricanes of 274 Squadron with two from the 73 Squadron detachment, patrolled over LGs. 122, 123 and 124, where another Ju 88 was claimed shot down by Plt Off Kuhle of the former unit. At much the same time Tomahawks of 2 SAAF Squadron patrolling over Bir el Gubi also intercepted a lone Ju 88. Practically every pilot in the squadron fired at this, whereupon reportedly it crashed in flames. Thus apart from the Bf 110, three claims for Ju 88s had been made in close proximity both in time and location. At least two such aircraft were lost by 2(F)./123, one being reported over Bir el Gubi in combat with P-40s, while one fell to Hurricanes over Fort Maddalena.

At 1035 nine Tomahawks of 3 RAAF Squadron and ten of 112 Squadron carried out a sweep over the Tobruk-El Adem area. Whilst south of El Adem the formation was surprised by six Bf 109s of I./JG 27 which attacked out of the sun, Oblt Hugo Schneider and Uffz Grimm each claiming one P-40 shot down. On this occasion the German pilots had underestimated the damage they had inflicted, as Sgt Rex Wilson, and Flg Off Rutter were both shot down and killed, while Sgt Cameron force-landed, all these pilots being members of the Australian squadron. Wg Cdr Peter Jeffrey claimed one Messerschmitt shot down, but his aircraft was damaged and he force-landed at Tobruk. Two more Bf 109s were claimed by Sgt Mailey.

In 112 Squadron's formation Sgt Carson's Tomahawk was badly shot-up as well. 'Tiny' Cameron survived unhurt, and would return to the squadron three days later. But Rex Wilson was a considerable loss to his unit. He had claimed eight aircraft shot down since his arrival in North Africa, and had just been recommended for the award of a DFM, which would be gazetted during January.

Hurricanes from 80 Squadron attacked MT and a blockhouse south-west of El Adem with bombs, but were attacked in turn out of cloud by a trio of Bf 109s. The squadron's new commanding officer, Sqn Ldr Mike Stephens's Hurricane was set on fire and he was wounded in both feet. He was in the act of baling out when the attacking fighter overshot him. Quickly, he slipped back into the cockpit, took aim and thought he had shot his assailant down; he then did bale out and was picked up by Polish troops who carried him into Tobruk and confirmed his victory (although it seems likely that it was his own Hurricane which they had observed crashing in flames).

However, three more Hurricanes failed to return, Flt Lt The Honourable David Coke, Flt Sgt Rivalant and Sgt McVeen all being reported missing. Rivalant returned safely several days later, but two days later David Coke was found dead beside his Hurricane four miles west of Acroma. On 12 December the squadron's previous commander, Sqn Ldr Tommy Horgan, was discovered by the unit, badly wounded and in Tobruk hospital. Just a few beds away was his replacement, Mike Stephens, for whom the award of a DSO would be gazetted on 20 January 1942. Unfortunately, it transpired that his wounds were rather more serious than had at first appeared, and there was therefore no question of his return to the unit; 80 Squadron was again without a leader. It seems that the squadron had been attacked by pilots of 5./JG 27 around midday, but this staffel too only claimed two Hurricanes shot down on this occasion.

250 Squadron undertook a further operation escorting Blenheims over Derna. Here three pilots, Sgts Nitschke, Twemlow and Whittle, became involved in a fight with a reported six Bf 109s and MC.202s, Nitschke and Twemlow each claiming one of the Italian fighters shot down. During the mid afternoon period Plt Off Usher of 94 Squadron claimed damage to a Bf 109, and at 1545 ten Hurricanes of 238 Squadron swept to the south-west of El Adem. Five Bf 109s were seen at 9,000 feet and Flt Lt Urwin-Mann led an attack on these, he and Sgt Pearson each claiming one damaged. However, Sgt Lloyd was shot down, baling out over Tobruk, while Pearson and Sgt Boreham force-landed there. All three returned safely to the unit next day.

Despite all the claims made, only one Bf 109 was lost on this date, but a second was badly damaged during a force-landing and no Italian fighters failed to return, nor suffered any damage in combat. One further claim for a P-40 was made by Oblt Homuth of 3./ JG 27, recorded at 1415, while in the evening Uffz Hans Niederhöfer, who had claimed one of the successes in the engagement with 80 Squadron, added a Lysander to his tally, claimed to the south-east of El Adem.

During the day Marylands of 21 SAAF Squadron attacked Derna, where two Axis aircraft were claimed destroyed on the ground. Fighters identified as three Bf 109s and two G.50bis attacked the bombers during their return flight when they were near Martuba. Two Marylands were damaged, but gunners claimed one G.50bis shot down. Attacks were also made on Tmimi by one squadron of Marylands and one of Blenheims. Blenheims of 14 Squadron were briefed to attack MT on the Derna-

Mersa Matruh road, but in poor visibility the target was not found and the crew of 'Z', T2064, released their bombs on a Flak position instead. During the return flight the observer in this aircraft was unable to find LG.75 and consequently the aircraft was abandoned when it ran out of fuel. Sgt J.H.Pilley, DFM, was killed, but Sgt Grimsey and the other two members of his crew walked back to the home airfield which proved to be quite close.

WDAF fighter units now began moving forward closer to the battle area; 260 Squadron flew in to Sidi Rezegh, with 112 Squadron going to El Adem. However, at the same time the strength of the Regia Aeronautica's fighter force in Libya was further enhanced with the arrival at Martuba of 6° Gruppo CT, led by T.Col Vezio Mezzetti. Joining 17° Gruppo to complete the arrival of 1° Stormo CT in North Africa, the unit flew in with 32 more MC.202s. One rather bizarre event occurred on this date, however, when an Italian fighter pilot reportedly 'went wild', shooting down two Luftwaffe transport aircraft in flames as they were about to land at Tmimi. An Ultra intercept also picked up on this piece of news, adding the (slightly incorrect) information that the Italian fighter was an MC.200 and that the two transports fell on the edge of the airfield, two Luftwaffe personnel being seriously wounded and two less so.

Reportedly, Obfw Schulz of II./JG 27 took off rapidly and shot the offender down, but no formal report of this matter was recorded in the daily logs of either air force. However, an account in an Italian aviation magazine (*Volare* of May 1984), while mentioning no names or units, provided sufficient information to allow a reconstruction of this 'friendly fire' action to be undertaken. At 1010 on 9 December three MC.202s of 71ª Squadriglia, 17° Gruppo CT, based at Martuba were preparing to take off for a patrol (the second of the day for this unit) over the Ain el Gazala-Tobruk area. The leader was the gruppo commander, T.Col Bruno Brambilla, a Spanish Civil War veteran who had claimed three victories there, and who had added a claim for a Hurricane a few days earlier on 4 December. His wingmen were Ten Glauco Vatta and Serg Remo Broilo.

Just before taking off, they received advice of a British incursion towards Derna, and consequently Ten Pierfrancesco Conti was also scrambled to intercept the bombers which were supposedly already on their return course to their base. At about 1030 Brambilla spotted two multi-engined aircraft over Tmimi, flying at low level, which he incorrectly identified as Wellingtons. He dived to attack them at once, firing most of his ammunition at them and setting both on fire. His victims were in fact Ju 52/3ms carrying men and material to JG 27 which had just recently arrived at Tmimi. Recalling this accident after the war, Edu Neumann, then gruppenkommandeur of I./JG 27, described it as " a true disaster".

Meanwhile, Schulz had indeed rapidly taken off, chasing and attacking Brambilla's Macchi, one 20mm shell hitting the tail and severely damaging the rudder. Brambilla, taken completely by surprise by this attack which to him was totally inexplicable, actually managed to escape and return safely to Martuba.

Within two hours of landing he fully understood what had transpired following the arrival of a cable reporting that an MC.202 had shot down two German Junkers landing at Tmimi. Many years later Remo Broillo, one of the wingmen, recalled that when his commanding officer realized the gravity of his mistaken identification, he "had a nervous breakdown and burst into tears." An inquiry followed that established the good faith of the pilot.

During the day a Grumman Amphibian of 1 RAAF Air Ambulance Unit crashed on landing to the north-north-east of Benghazi at 1515. Passengers Flt Lt J.P. Bartle, Plt Off S.D. O'Donnell amd Sgt McWilliam all suffered injury, shock and exposure. RAAF records indicate that the serial number of this aircraft was AK882, but this number seems in fact to have been allocated to a Kittyhawk. No record of a Grumman Amphibian being allocated an RAF serial has been discovered.

British Claims

73 Sqn	Flg Off G.R.A.McG.Johnston	Hurricane II	Ju 88	Sidi Omar 0830
250 Sqn	Flt Lt R.E.Bary	Tomahawk	} Bf 110	Bir el Gubi 0845
	Plt Off J.L.Waddy	Tomahawk AK498		
274 Sqn	Plt Off van der Kuhle	Hurricane IIb Z5064	Ju 88	5m S Sollum 0900-1100
2 SAAF Sqn	Squadron Victory	Tomahawks	Ju 88	NE El Adem 0900
80 Sqn	Sqn Ldr M.M.Stephens	Hurricane I Z4415	Bf 109F	Acroma road 1050-1200
258 Wg	Wg Cdr P.Jeffrey	Tomahawk AN408	Bf 109F	S El Adem 1115
3 RAAF Sqn	Sgt W.H.A.Mailey	Tomahawk AN374	2 Bf 109Fs	S El Adem 1120
250 Sqn	Sgt R.H.Nitschke	Tomahawk	MC.202	Derna
	Sgt F.M.Twemlow	Tomahawk	MC.202	Derna

In 3 RAAF Squadron's mess tent at El Adem, December 1941. Left to right: Sgt Walt Mailey, Flg Off R.H.S.Gray, Flg Off Bobby Gibbes, Sgt Bev Reid, Flg Offs Harry Schaeffer and Lance Threlkeld.

94 Sqn	Plt Off G.L.Usher	Hurricane IIc BD856	Bf 109 damaged	Sidi Rezegh-El Adem 1325-1500
	Sgt D.A.Forder	Hurricane IIc	Bf 109 damaged	Sidi Rezegh
	Sgt T.Hindle	Hurricane IIc	Bf 109 damaged	Sidi Rezegh
238 Sqn	Flt Lt J.R.Urwin-Mann	Hurricane IIc 'F'	Bf 109 damaged	NE El Adem 1545-1700
	Sgt P.Pearson	Hurricane IIc 'H'	Bf 109F damaged	NE El Adem 1545-1700

British Casualties

3 RAAF Sqn	Tomahawk AN437 shot down; Sgt R.K.Wilson KiA
	Tomahawk AK178 shot down; Flg Off D.Rutter KiA
	Tomahawk AK499 crash-landed; Sgt A.C.Cameron returned three days later
258 Wg	Tomahawk force-landed; Wg Cdr P.Jeffrey unhurt
112 Sqn	Tomahawk AK533 badly damaged; Sgt K.F.Carson unhurt
238 Sqn	Hurricane IIc shot down; Sgt Lloyd baled out
	Hurricane IIc force-landed; Sgt Pearson returned next day
	Hurricane IIc force-landed; Sgt Boreham returned next day
80 Sqn	Hurricane I Z4415 shot down; Sqn Ldr M.M.Stephens, DFC *, baled out, WiA
	Hurricane I FTR; Flt Lt Hon D.A.Coke KiA
	Hurricane I FTR; Sgt McVean MiA
	Hurricane I Z4786 FTR; Flt Sgt J.N.Rivalant returned several days later
94 Sqn	Hurricane IIc shot down SE El Adem by six Bf 109s; Sgt T.Hindle baled out safe
14 Sqn	Blenheim IV T2064 Z abandoned out of fuel near LG.75; Sgt J.H.Pilley, DFM, KiFA; Sgt H.S.Grimsey and rest of crew safe

German Claims

1./JG 27	Uffz Josef Grimm	P-40	W Bir el Gubi 1140
	Oblt Hugo Schneider	P-40	W Bir el Gubi 1143
5./JG 27	Uffz Hans Niederhöfer	Hurricane	S Tobruk 1155
	Uffz Horst Reuter	Hurricane	Sidi Rezegh 1210
3./JG 27	Oblt Gerhard Homuth	P-40	S Gambut 1415
5./JG 27	Uffz Hans Niederhöfer	Lysander	SE El Adem 1710

German Casualties

II./JG 27	Bf 109F-4 trop WNr 8441 lost on operations, reason unknown
III./JG 53	Bf 109F-4/Z crash-landed at Tmimi; 60% damaged; reason unknown
2(F)./123	Ju 88A-5 4U+FK WNr 0523 shot down in combat with P-40s over Bir el Gubi; Lt Gerhard Schulz and two KiA
1.(F)/121	Ju 88D-2 7A+AH WNr 0826 shot down over Fort Maddalena by Hurricanes; Lt Bailer and crew KiA
2.(H)/14	Bf 110 E-3 WNr 2502 shot down; Fw Günther Ursinus, pilot, KiA; Fw Karl-Heinz Schulze PoW, Oblt Herbert Lüdderrsen MIA
Unspecified unit	2 Ju 52/3m shot down in error by Italian fighter over Tmimi 1030

Italian Casualties

Unspecified unit	4 G.50bis destroyed on ground at Martuba by bombs
	2 G.50bis badly damaged on ground at Martuba by bombs

Wednesday, 10 December 1941

This proved to be a costly and harrowing day for the SAAF. Initially at 0715 Tomahawks of 2 and 4 SAAF Squadrons took off to patrol over the Tobruk area. It was a cloudy day and when over El Adem towards the end of the sortie, 12 Bf 109s emerged out of the overcast, making three dive-and-climb attacks during which Lt Marseille hit Lt Enslin's aircraft, causing him to bale out. Enslin, afraid of being shot-up on his parachute, fell from 10,000 feet to 4,000 feet before pulling the ripcord. When he reached the ground, Lt Lipawsky landed alongside and flew him back to base. One 4 SAAF Tomahawk was damaged, Lt Chadwick subsequently crash-landing at base as a result. According to AHQ, claims were made for one Bf 109 probable and one damaged.

Several bomber formations were sent out to attack a column retreating westwards between Taieb el Esem and Mechili, but bad weather and sandstorms prevented most finding their target. One of the formations despatched comprised six Bostons of 24 SAAF Squadron, led by Maj E.N.Donnelly on his first such operation. On their way to the target, flying in two vics each of three aircraft, the bombers passed through heavy cloudbanks, but were suddenly confronted by a formation of Ju 87s, escorted by a dozen Bf 109s. At once the Messerschmitt pilots – from 2./JG 27 – broke away to attack the Bostons which were flying at about 7,000 feet.

Attacking from above and from the rear quarter, Lt Willi Kothmann shot down the third aircraft of the rear vic, flown by Lt J.A.Williams. Both gunners were badly wounded, and Williams's instrument panel was shattered by a cannon shell, both engines cut and the aircraft began to burn. Williams ordered abandonment, but a second attack prevented this, causing him to resume his seat, fighting to keep the aircraft from going into a vertical dive. Again he ordered the crew to bale out, but then saw that one of the wounded gunners had not got clear, so once more resumed his seat. Finally, with the aircraft down to 1,500 feet and blazing fiercely, he managed to get out before the Boston hit the ground; the observer, Lt B.G.Alexander, failed to escape.

However, fire from the gunners had hit Kothmann's Bf 109, damaging it and wounding him seriously. He was forced to break away and land at his airfield at Tmimi as quickly as possible. In *Eagles Strike*, James Ambrose Brown quotes the words of Colonel P.M.J.McGregor regarding the rest of the engagement (of the first vic).

"It was set on fire. Though wounded, Genis managed to fly in perfect formation into a protective cloud layer to give his crew sufficient time to bale out. The observer, Lt D.McPherson, parachuted safely down, but the pilot and the two RAF gunners, Sgts R.E.Bowerman and D.C.M.Ross, were too severely wounded to leave the aircraft, which spun down and exploded on striking the ground."

This aircraft had fallen to Fw Elles. The No.1 aircraft of the rear vic was the next to go, catching fire from Hptmn Gerlitz's shells.

"The Boston commanded by Capt F.W.Goch, the leader of the second flight, also went down in flames, but the pilot and observer, Lt H.Raw, reached the ground by parachute. Capt Goch died two hours later from bullet wounds and head injuries. The two gunners, Sgts B.A.S.Delaney and M.V.Clulee, failed to bale out. The second aircraft in the rear flight also went down in flames. The intercommunication failed and only the pilot, Lt B.Middleton-Stewart, left the machine which exploded shortly afterwards in mid-air. The remainder of the crew, Flg Off E.M.Harding and Air Sgt J.H.van Dyk and Flt Sgt J.Handley, were killed."

This aircraft was shot down by Obfw Förster. Lt Körner caught the No.3 aircraft of the leading vic, and this too crashed in flames.

"The third Boston of the leading flight, under Lt D.R.Haupt, had an engine and wing set on fire. The pilot and two gunners, Air Sgts V.StG. Black and L.E. Venter, baled out shortly before the wing fell off. The pilot was injured when he struck the tailplane and Sgt Venter was wounded. Sgt Black fell through the fire of an attacking fighter and his body reached the ground riddled with bullets. The observer, Lt L.B.Bensimmon, was not seen to leave the aircraft.

The sixth Boston, that of the leader of the formation, alone escaped. It jettisoned its bombs and severely damaged made a force-landing near LG.76. Of the 20 officers and men making up the five crews that were shot down, 12 were killed and only eight got back. What made the losses even more tragic was that the majority of the men involved.....had survived eight months of hard operations and were due for return to the Union very soon."

During that time the squadron had lost 19 aircraft in action, 12 during unescorted missions. Col H.G.Willmott, the 3 SAAF Wing commander, protested at the use of Bostons unescorted, but AHQ felt there was little alternative as at this point most targets were beyond fighter escort range. From that day onwards this fiasco was known to the South Africans as 'The Boston Tea Party'. It was also the last occasion on which Bostons were sent out unescorted on daylight bombing raids. However, more painful losses were soon to follow for the SAAF units.

During a raid on Martuba, Maryland crews claimed one aircraft destroyed on the ground and a petrol dump on fire. The attack on this airfield had been more effective then realised, however, 20° Gruppo CT reporting that four of the unit's G.50bis fighters were destroyed on the ground here, and six more suffered damage.

The only other action of the day occurred when Lt Bromwich of 805 Squadron (part of the RNFS) attacked a Bf 110 north of Ras el Kanayas, Bromwick engaging it for 15 minutes in his Martlet. Despite one cylinder of his engine being shot away early in the combat, he managed to claim his opponent as probably destroyed. One Ju 87 of I./StG 1 was shot down by AA fire when attacking a cruiser near Derna.

British Claims

805 Sqn	Lt H.F.Bromwich	Martlet	Bf 110 probable	N Ras el Kanayas

3 RAAF Squadron originally listed one victory for this date. This was subsequently realised to be a repeat of a claim made by Flg Off Gaden a year earlier, on 10 December 1940.

British Casualties

2 SAAF Sqn	Tomahawk shot down; Lt B.G.S.Enslin baled out and picked up by Tomahawk
4 SAAF Sqn	Tomahawk damaged, crash-landed at base; Lt R.E.Chadwick unhurt
24 SAAF Sqn	Boston III Z2170 shot down; Lt G.Genis and two KiA; one WiA
	Boston III Z2182 shot down; Capt F.W.Goch and two KiA; one survived
	Boston III Z2187 shot down; Lt J.A.Williams survived; one KiA, two WiA
	Boston III Z2191 shot down; Lt B.Middleton-Stewart survived; three KiA
	Boston III Z2201 shot down; Lt D.R.Haupt and one WiA; two KiA
805 Sqn	Martlet damaged; Lt H.F.Bromwich unhurt

German Claims

3./JG 27	Lt Hans-Joachim Marseille	P-40	SE El Adem 0850
2./JG 27	Lt Willi Kothmann	Boston	Bir Hacheim 1400
	Hptmn Erich Gerlitz	Boston	10m E Bir Hacheim
	Fw Franz Elles	Boston	E Bir Hacheim 1401

| 2./JG 27 | Obfw Hermann Förster | Boston | 10m E Bir Hacheim 1402 |
| | Lt Friedrich Körner | Boston | 10m E Bir Hacheim 1403 |

German Casualties

| 3./StG 1 | Ju 87 shot down by ships' AA NE Derna; Oblt Heiko Steinhagen/Gefr Hans Lerch KiA |
| 2./JG 27 | Bf 109F-4 trop damaged 10% by Bostons; Lt Willi Kothmann WiA |

Italian Casualties

| 20° Gr CT | 4 G.50bis destroyed on ground at Martuba |
| | 6 G.50bis damaged on ground at Martuba |

Thursday, 11 December 1941

Six Tomahawks of 250 Squadron with the Hurricane Is of the RNFS, patrolled over the Gazala area during the early morning. Here a formation assessed as 24 Bf 109s, three Bf 110s and 24 Ju 88s were engaged. Two fighters and two bombers were claimed shot down, although Sgt Malcolm Canty was brought down by Lt Marseille of 3./JG 27, and was killed. This patrol reported that subsequent to this action, six more Bf 109s attacked and three of these were also claimed shot down, plus one probable. From these engagements the only loss actually suffered by the Luftwaffe fighters was the Bf 109F of 2./JG 27 flown by Fw Franz Elles, which was hit in the oil cooler. Elles crash-landed and became a PoW. Four Ju 88s of I./LG 1 had taken off at 1030 to bomb targets in the Bir Hacheim area where a reported six Tomahawks or Hurricanes attacked, shooting down L1+HH; Oblt Heinrich Paulus and his crew were captured. The unit had flown over from Eleusis early in the morning to Tmimi, but here during the day a second of the gruppe's aircraft was destroyed on the ground in a strafing attack. A further move to Derna was then made, and at the end of the day I., II. and III. Gruppen departed from Derna, Tmimi and Benina respectively to return home to Eleusis.

Patrols over Tobruk continued all day, one such by Hurricanes reportedly engaging nine Bf 110s and Bf 109s near Acroma, the former being forced to jettison bombs and climb into clouds. One Hurricane was lost during a patrol over Sidi Omar. This may have been an aircraft claimed damaged by T.Col Brambilla of 17° Gruppo CT whilst he and nine of his pilots were involved in escorting Bf 110s in the Acroma area, his claim being timed at 1235.

94 Squadron sent off Hurricanes during the morning in pairs on 'rhubarb' low level strafing sorties. Sgt Wincote, one of two off at 0900, failed to return, as did Lt Moolman and Sgt Thompson who set off a little over two hours later. Moolman baled out, wounded in arm and legs, becoming a PoW. He was later to report that he had shot down a Bf 109 before falling to another himself. Confusingly, AHQ noted that during an early patrol three Hurricanes failed to return and the pilot of a fourth was wounded by Flak. However, those returning reported having spotted 40 enemy aircraft on the ground ten miles south-east of Gazala. Other Hurricanes, operating in pairs, strafed traffic south of Benghazi, claiming to have destroyed a staff car, a petrol tanker and another large vehicle, whilst inflicting damage on numerous other such targets.

Three Blenheims of 11 Squadron were despatched to bomb Derna airfield, but two returned early due to lack of cloud cover, and the third was lost. This latter aircraft had been intercepted over Bomba Bay by Obfw Espenlaub of 1./JG 27, and shot down with the loss of the crew.

Soon after midday ten Tomahawks of 4 SAAF Squadron escorted the GOC, Gen Ritchie, to Tobruk. Bf 109s attacked, shooting down one Tomahawk flown by Lt Taylor.

As can be seen from the schedule of claims and losses, this was a rather confused day during which the times allocated to several of the Luftwaffe claims do not appear to coincide with the Allied losses recorded, while AHQ records indicate that there may have been one or two additional losses of Hurricanes. What is clear is that claims for three fighters – all identified as P-40s – were submitted by pilots of 7./JG 53 as that unit's first successes over Africa, while a fourth was made by a pilot of 4./JG 27. It is very likely that most of these claims related in fact to the 94 Squadron Hurricanes and to the Tomahawk flown by Lt Taylor of 4 SAAF Squadron.

AHQ also recorded that sea reconnaissance aircraft had reported that Ju 52/3ms were flying between Crete and Derna, obviously bringing in desperately needed fuel for the Luftwaffe which was now suffering a serious decline in supplies arriving from the usual route from Tripoli. It was also reported that ground forces had spotted 13 such transports which appeared to have lost their way and strayed over the lines, AA gunners claiming one of these shot down and a second damaged. In fact some of these reports had

been received earlier, and a substantial effort was being planned to intercept these aircraft, using Beaufighters, Marylands, Blenheim fighters and Martlets, all operating in pairs.

With this in mind Air Marshal Tedder and AVM Coningham had attended a meeting with Col Willmott and his 3 SAAF Wing staff, since it was Coningham's view that the speed and front-gun armament of the Maryland rendered it suitable to operate as a makeshift fighter in such circumstances. To this Lt Col Pretorius, commanding officer of 21 SAAF Squadron, enthusiastically agreed, although Willmott and the other unit commanders felt that "it was sheer lunacy". However, Tedder was apparently impressed by Pretorius's views, protests were overruled, and the first such operations were planned on the 11th. Each of the Maryland squadrons was to send out four pairs of aircraft, 12 SAAF to cover an area 15-20 miles on either side of a course 210 degrees from Maleme to Apollonia, with 21 SAAF patrolling 40-60 miles north of Derna.

During an early patrol by a pair from 12 SAAF Squadron, four transports were spotted flying towards Apollonia and were attacked, each Maryland pilot shooting down a Ju 52/3m into the sea in flames. Lt Ross attacked another which fell back trailing smoke, but he then ran out of ammunition. Lt van Breda meanwhile, sought to attack the fourth but his aircraft was hit by return fire from a top gunner, damaging his aircraft. He broke away and with oil leaking, just made it to base, where he force-landed at dusk.

The four pairs from 21 SAAF Squadron all intercepted transports, which the crews were surprised to find appeared to have been modified to carry top-gun positions. These aircraft flew just above the waves, rendering attack from below impossible, and a series of running fights followed. Lt D.Long-Innes' aircraft had one engine knocked out and the cockpit became flooded with fuel. Breaking off, he headed for land, but on arrival passed over two Axis airfields from where small arms fire inflicted further damage, preventing the undercarriage being lowered, resulting in a crash-landing on arrival at LG.76.

The second pair met three transports, Lt A.L.Thackwray shooting down one with his front guns, while his rear gunner claimed a second. The gunner in this continued to return fire even as the trimotor came down in the sea, his fire apparently striking Lt W.L.Wood's aircraft, which failed to return, all the crew being lost. (Strangely, Lt A.H.M.Moolman, the SAAF pilot with 94 Squadron who was shot down and became a PoW on this date, subsequently was added to the list of those missing from Wood's Maryland – clearly an administrative error relating to his membership of the same service.)

Another such interception was made when Sgt J.S.Ross of 272 Squadron patrolling between Crete and Derna, encountered two aircraft which were unidentified, but which he reported each to have four engines. Attacking, he claimed to have inflicted damage on both.

British Claims

250 Sqn	Sqn Ldr E.J.Morris	Tomahawk	Bf 109 probable	Gazala 0800-
	Plt Off K.G.Hart	Tomahawk	Bf 109	Gazala 0800-
	Sgt R.H.Nitschke	Tomahawk	Bf 109	Gazala 0800-
	Plt Off G.H.Ranger	Tomahawk	Bf 109	Gazala 0800-
	Plt Off G.H.Ranger	Tomahawk	Ju 88	Gazala 0800-
	Sgt M.S.Hards	Tomahawk	Bf 109	Gazala 0800-
	Sgt M.S.Hards	Tomahawk	Ju 88	Gazala 0800-
	Plt Off W.W.Swinnerton	Tomahawk	Bf 109	Gazala 0800-
94 Sqn	Lt A.H.M.Moolman	Hurricane IIb	Bf 109	
12 SAAF Sqn	Lt G.N.Ross	Maryland	Ju 52/3m	over sea
	Lt G.N.Ross	Maryland	Ju 52/3m damaged	over sea
	Lt R.H.van Breda	Maryland	Ju 52/3m	over sea
21 SAAF Sqn	Capt A.L.Thackwray	Maryland	2 Ju 52/3ms	over sea
272 Sqn	Sgt J.S.Ross	Beaufighter Ic	2 four-engined aircraft damaged over sea	

British Casualties

11 Sqn	Blenheim IV Z7797 shot down; Sqn Ldr C.F.Darbishire and crew KiA
12 SAAF Sqn	Maryland II damaged and crash-landed on return; Lt R.H.van Breda and crew safe
21 SAAF Sqn	Maryland II AH344 'Y' shot down; Lt W.L.Wood and three KiA
250 Sqn	Tomahawk AN344 shot down; Sgt M.A.Conty, RCAF, KiA
94 Sqn	Hurricane IIb MiA; Sgt Wincote
	Hurricane IIb MiA; Z5342 Lt A.H.M.Moolman baled out WiA, PoW
	Hurricane IIb MiA; Sgt W.J.C.Thompson KIA
4 SAAF Sqn	Tomahawk shot down Tobruk area; Lt D.L.Taylor FTR

German Claims

3./JG 27	Lt Hans-Joachim Marseille	P-40		NW Tmimi 0930
Stab III./JG 53	Hptmn Wolf-Dietrich Wilcke	Hurricane		1100
4./JG 27	Obfhr Gerhard Endmann	P-40		W Tobruk 1115
7./JG 53	Lt Ernst Klager	P-40		W Tobruk 1120
	Uffz August Nieland	P-40		W Tobruk 1120
	Obfw Hermann Neuhoff	P-40		W Tobruk 1130
1./JG 27	Obfw Albert Espenlaub	Blenheim		Bomba Bay 1145

German Casualties

2./JG 27	Bf 109F-4 trop WNr8537 shot down S Gazala; Fw Franz Elles PoW
I./LG 1	Ju 88A-5 WNr 5555 destroyed on ground at Tmimi during strafing attack
	Ju 88A-5 L1+HH shot down near Bir Hacheim; Oblt Heinrich Paulus and crew PoW
II./KGrzbV 1	Ju 52/3m WNr 1321 shot down between Derna-Maleme, Crete; Fw Hans Laufer and crew KiA
KGrzbV 300	Ju 52/3m TA+QA WNr 5205 lost Derna; Uffz Helmet Jung and crew KiA
	Ju 52/3m HB+HO WNr 5591 lost Derna; Fw Heinz Mende and crew MiA
KGrzbV 400	Ju 52/3m SI+MS WNr 7274 lost to AA; Fw Heinz Richter and crew MiA
	Ju 52/3m WNr 6167 40% damaged: force-landed at Derna

Italian Claims

17° Gr CT	T.Col Bruno Brambilla	Fighter Damaged	Acroma area	1235

Friday, 12 December 1941

3 SAAF Wing was asked to continue the oversea patrols next day, and many fuel-carrying aircraft were observed, on occasion up to 11 in a group; Do 24 flyingboats were also seen. There no doubt to rescue any crews brought down into the water. The Maryland crews attempted to break up the German formations by dropping bombs onto the surface of the sea before attacking with guns when these attempts proved fruitless. One pair of 21 SAAF Squadron aircraft took off at 0800, followed by a further pair at 0900.

Capt Ramsay, one of the 0800 pair, his Maryland shot-up by a trio of Ju 52/3ms, made for Tobruk, his observer unconscious from petrol fumes which were slowly overcoming him as well. Hardly aware of his return, he landed amidst a dump of artillery shells, a bomb still on its rack and the cockpit flooded in fuel. Meantime Lt F.A.Rouse had claimed two Ju 52/3ms shot down from a formation of 11, reporting seeing men jumping from the burning transports into the water as he shot the elevators from a third and his gunner saw flames from a fourth as a result of his fire. At that stage Bf 110s, which had obviously been ordered to

Gruppenkommandeur of III./JG 53 was Hptmn Wolf-Dietrich Wilcke, who claimed his 35th victory on 11 December 1941, immediately after arriving at Derna.

escort the transports following the previous day's attacks, appeared on the scene and shot down Lt T.L.Parry's aircraft. Another Maryland, flown by Maj M.H.Fowler who had departed at 0900, was last seen heading for Tobruk pursued by two Messerschmitts. Claims for Marylands were submitted by Oblt Schulze-Dickow and Uffz Günther Wegmann, who had taken off at 0850, the former pilot claiming another about an hour later; this was almost certainly Fowler's aircraft.

Two more 12 SAAF Squadron Marylands set off later than had those from 21 SAAF, but both failed to return, the aircraft flown by Maj T.S.Fisher and Lt W.G.Parsons both being lost with their crews. Both appear to have been shot down at about 1330 by Obfw Otto Polenz of 8./ZG 26. From the 14 Marylands operating, the two SAAF squadrons lost a total of 13 aircrew missing or killed. Recorded the 21 SAAF Squadron diarist: "To us older members the strain of seeing our old comrades fall in battle is becoming almost unbearable." Wing medical officers ordered immediate rest for older members of the aircrews suffering severe strain. Four crews were relieved as 13 were kept intact for further operations.

Beaufighters of 272 Squadron had also been active during these operations. Wg Cdr Yaxley and Plt Off Hammond set off at 0850, spotting five Ju 52/3ms heading for Derna. Hammond claimed one shot down in flames and one damaged, while Yaxley claimed damage to three more. Both Beaufighters were hit by return fire, however, the observer in Yaxley's aircraft being wounded in both lungs; Hammond headed for Edcu where he crash-landed, deciding that the home base was a better place to get repairs undertaken than at the forward airfield. Later in the morning about six more Ju 52/3ms were claimed damaged by the squadron, Plt Off Orr and Sgt Lowes claiming to have shot the undercarriage off one transport.

During this same period 55 Squadron had despatched a Blenheim at 0635 to look for an Axis transport ship with a cruiser escort. It was followed at 0700 by two more aircraft, detailed to undertake an anti-shipping sweep over the Derna area. The first aircraft, flown by Flt Sgt Thompson, was reportedly attacked by a Bf 110 at 0900 and was hit by its first burst of fire, crashing into the sea 15 miles north of Apollonia with the loss of all the crew. The other pair were attacked several times by a Bf 110, but at 1024 when 12 miles north of Cape Aamer, Flg Off Anderson broke away and made as if to land, but crashed into the sea 40 miles north-east of Derna; again, all the crew were lost. It is possible that these aircraft were attacked by night fighters of I./NJG 2, Lt Haas and Lt Laufs claiming Beaufighters over the sea. At 1000 another Blenheim, this one from 11 Squadron, had set off to bomb Derna airfield if sufficient cloud cover existed; this aircraft also failed to return, 2/Lt Burrage's crew being killed.

While these oversea operations were taking place, the main body of the air forces were again involved in extensive activities over the armies. 4th Armoured Brigade, supported by infantry, had opened an attack on the Gazala positions, and at midday nine Tomahawks of 250 Squadron provided cover for the Hurricanes of 80 Squadron and the RNFS to the Martuba area, strafing and bombing motorized columns. They were attacked after their strafe by Bf 109s and MC.202s, 80 Squadron losing Flg Off Dowding, who had been with the unit in Greece, Plt Off Reynolds, Sgt Whyte and Sgt Halliwell. 250 Squadron lost 2/Lt Norton, who was wounded and ended up in Tobruk hospital, but Plt Off Ranger claimed a Bf 109 and Sgt Nitschke an MC.202 in return. It seems probable that two of these British losses were attributable to Oblt Erbo Graf von Kageneck, who claimed one P-40 and one Hurricane shot down during the early afternoon.

6° Gruppo undertook a sweep of the Gazala-Tobruk-El Adem area with 10 MC.202s from 1310. At 1330 50 British fighters were encountered at an altitude of 9,000ft, and all the Italian pilots were involved in multiple combats, during which 1603 rounds of ammunition were expended. This resulted in claims for one P-40 and one Hurricane, with hits being claimed on 12 of the former and eight of the latter. Serg Saiani made an emergency landing, but due to the presence of enemy forces nearby, he set fire to his aircraft. Cap Camarda's Macchi was damaged seriously enough for it to be written off on return.

An hour later 11 Hurricanes from 1 SAAF Squadron encountered six Bf 109s over Gazala, losing Lt Seccombe. It was the turn of 4 SAAF Squadron at 1515, the unit's Tomahawks providing top cover to bombers attacking the Derna road, as 2 SAAF Squadron flew close escort. The formation was jumped by Axis fighters, Capt Robbertse of 2 SAAF and Lt Player of 4 SAAF being shot down. 2 SAAF also lost Lt Verster who reportedly was shot down by heavy Flak and killed. 4 SAAF's pilots turned into the attack, when Capt Bosman claimed two Messerschmitts shot down and two damaged, Lt Golding adding one more destroyed.

15 minutes behind the South Africans, 18 more Tomahawks from 112 and 3 RAAF Squadrons set out to sweep over the Derna area. Over Tmimi a large Axis formation was spotted and attacked, but during the initial turn two Tomahawks collided, Flg Off Fred Eggleton's aircraft going into an uncontrolled spin. With his aircraft damaged, Flg Off Robin Gray turned for base. Flg Off Nicky Barr broke off to escort him, and while so involved gained his own first success, claiming a Bf 110 shot down. Meanwhile, Eggleton had regained control of his aircraft:

"We took off from El Adem at 1530 hours. I was leading Blue flight with Robin Gray on my left and Nick Barr on my right. Woof Arthur was leading the squadron. I was flying Tomahawk AN335 which was in excellent condition though we had some trouble with the 0.5inch guns in the cockpit which were inclined to jam, due to the desert dust ingested during taxiing.

"We were climbing into the sun at 10,000 feet, near the Gulf of Bomba, when we saw a number of Me 109s taking off from the German base at Tmimi directly beneath us. There was a lot of chatter on the intercom. Suddenly, I felt my aircraft lurch and looked round to see Robin Gray's aircraft had drifted towards mine and his airscrew was chewing off my port wingtip. With the extra drag from the damaged wingtip, I couldn't keep up with the squadron and dropped away.

"I soon found that the aircraft responded reasonably well to the controls and, seeing three Tomahawks of 112 Squadron chasing up after five Me 109s climbing after 3 Squadron, I decided to join the attack. With my height advantage, I was able to dive down and come up to make a quarter attack from below. I was the first to open fire and, though the range was a bit long, I succeeded in breaking up the Messerschmitt formation.

"The Messerschmitts turned to join battle and a good old fashioned dog-fight ensued. There seemed to be Me 109s and Tomahawks everywhere! I made two further quarter attacks from below at Me 109s circling to attack. I could see glycol streaming behind each of them but could not claim to have shot them down. I managed to get close behind a third Me 109 but, due to the absence of one wingtip, my aircraft flicked on its back just before I pressed the trigger. Meanwhile, I was having continual trouble clearing my 0.50 in guns which were jamming.

"I got close behind another Messerschmitt and put a long burst into him. I was surprised to see tracer streaming from my wings towards him. I didn't think we had tracer! Suddenly I realised there was another Messerschmitt close behind me and pumping bullets at me. I flicked into a steep turn and got away from him unscathed but, by this time, I had lost a lot of height and the friendly Tomahawks had vanished.

"I was at 1,500 feet and could see three Messerschmitts circling above me waiting for the kill.

There were no clouds and I was at least 60 miles into enemy territory, so I decided to make the best of the situation and try to get at least one of them. One made a head-on attack at me and I pulled up toward him staring at the yawning hole in his airscrew boss through which his cannon was pointing towards me. My 0.5 guns jammed again but he too seemed to be having trouble with his guns as he did not open fire. I tipped the joystick slightly forward and went under him with what seemed inches to spare.

"The net result was that I lost further height and found myself at 1,000 feet with my Messerschmitt friends still above me. I could see two of them and was clearing my 0.5 in guns saying to myself, 'I'll get at least one of you bastards', when I heard a dull 'plop' near my feet.

"The third Messerschmitt had come up behind me and lobbed an explosive shell into the oil cooler beneath my engine.

"I flicked into a steep turn and shook him off but the damage was done and my aircraft was on fire. I was now flying east with a thick trail of black smoke behind me and the Me 109 in close pursuit. I opened the cockpit canopy to get a better look but flames and smoke came up around me and I quickly closed it again. This was it! I had to get out fast! I undid my safety belt and disconnected my oxygen line but forgot about my intercom cord.

"I flung open the cockpit, eased the stick forward – and floated up out of the cockpit into the slip-stream, which swept me back against the tail fin. My intercom cord came adrift and luckily it was my parachute pack which took the brunt of the blow from the tail fin. I found myself spinning like a top but threw out my arms and legs in a spread-eagled position which had the immediate effect of stopping the spin. I was facing down with my arms and legs stretched out and, out of the corner of my eye, I could see my aircraft with its smoke trail fading into the distance with the Me 109 close behind.

"The land below stretched out like a coloured map and I could see the Gulf of Bomba to the north. I reached for the rip cord with my right hand but remembering Sgt Parker's fate over Tobruk, decided to make a delayed drop, even though I had baled out at only 1,000 feet. I clutched the handle of the rip cord whilst falling freely towards the land below. It was quite exhilarating, and I was fascinated with the view but, all of a sudden, I could see stones and tufts of grass and I realised I was getting very close to the ground.

"I yanked at the rip cord and the parachute opened immediately.

"I was relieved to feel the support of the shroud lines. I floated for about ten seconds and noted that there was a strong drift towards the east. The terrain was undulating, with rock outcrops but, fortunately, I was drifting towards a flat grassy patch. Fortunately also, I was facing the direction I was drifting. In textbook style, I pulled hard on the shroud lines just before my feet touched the ground. Although this helped to cushion my landing, my feet hit the ground with a jar and I turned several somersaults, finally being dragged along on my head by my still-inflated parachute. I was glad at the time that my flying helmet was well padded, otherwise I would have sustained severe head injuries.

"After a struggle, I finally managed to release my parachute harness and halt my undignified progress across the ground. With no weight on the shroud lines, the parachute collapsed and lay on the ground near me. I stood up to take stock of the position. By a miracle, I was not wounded and seemed to be uninjured by the fall. A couple of weeks later, I suffered acute back pain, but felt nothing when shot down.

"I looked around and immediately saw the Me 109 returning at low altitude from the east. He saw my parachute and then saw me and went into a steep left hand turn with the obvious intention of strafing me. I sprinted a hundred yards in eight seconds to take cover behind some rocks just as the Messerschmitt began its dive. He didn't open fire as my cover was good and, as soon as he passed over, I ran to some bushes a few yards away where I had better all-round cover. He did not come back and I assumed that he and his companions had landed at Tmimi, their base nearby, and that a search party might soon come out to find me. It was 1630 hrs and there were several hours of daylight left. I drew my pistol determined to defend myself.

"I was completely transformed! A few minutes ago, in the air, where I had been trained to fight, I had faced certain death with detached calm. I was now on the ground with the chance of survival and was completely scared. I realised I would have no chance of resisting a search party and I dared not move before nightfall for fear of being spotted.

"Some years ago, I borrowed from Clive Caldwell a book entitled *Fighters over the Desert – The Air Battles in the Western Desert June 1940 to December 1942*……. I was able to deduce …that the German pilot who shot me down was a fighter ace – Erbo Graf von Kageneck."

Following the sweep by 112 and 3 RAAF Squadrons, 250 Squadron then flew a second such operation meeting Ju 87s with fighter escort, claims being made for two Stukas, two Bf 109s and one probable – although one of the claims for a Messerschmitt submitted by Plt Off Waddy may have been made during the earlier operation. There were no losses on this occasion. Luftwaffe sources record that three British fighter-bombers crash-landed near Tmimi, two of the pilots being captured, and it is probable that these were Hurricanes of 80 Squadron.

WDAF fighter losses for the day had thus amounted to some 14 aircraft – two of them apparently by collision and one to Flak – plus one damaged. As recorded, it is likely that two were claimed in the early afternoon by von Kageneck of 9./JG 27. But during the mid afternoon period seven fighters were claimed by the newly-arrived III./JG 53. The Germans were on this occasion clearly operating in conjunction with Italian MC.202s, 11 of which had taken off at 1555 drawn from two squadriglie of 17° Gruppo straight away encountering 30 Tomahawks at only 4,500ft claiming eight fighters shot down. The only Axis loss appears to have been three 1° Stormo MC.202s which force-landed plus one damaged when two pilots were wounded. The day had clearly been much to the advantage of the Axis fighters.

It also saw 176ª Squadriglia RST depart from Derna for Barce, as from the latter airfield 284ª Squadriglia AS moved to Benghazi (K.2).

At Fliegerführer Afrika command headquarters, an important meeting was held during the day attended by Kesselring, Rommel, Gen Gambara (chief of staff of the Italian army), and Generals Geisler Fröhlich, Marchesi and Raffaelli during which a quick evacuation of all the advanced airfields was agreed coupled with actions to try and ensure that the British did not thereby acquire complete aerial superiority.

British Claims

Sqn	Pilot	Aircraft		Claim	Location/Time
272 Sqn	Wg Cdr R.G.Yaxley	Beaufighter Ic 'D'	}	4 Ju 52/3ms damaged	Derna 0850-
	Plt Off D.H.Hammond	Beaufighter Ic 'V'			
	Plt Off D.H.Hammond	Beaufighter Ic 'V'		Ju 52/3m	Derna 0850-
	Flt Lt M.L.P.Bartlett	Beaufighter Ic		Ju 52/3m damaged	
	Plt Off H.H.Crawford	Beaufighter Ic		Ju 52/3m damaged	
	Plt Off K.B.Orr	Beaufighter Ic 'T'	}	5 Ju 52/3ms damaged	40m from Derna 1145
	Sgt D.C.Lowes	Beaufighter Ic 'Y'			
250 Sqn	Sgt R.H.Nitschke	Tomahawk		MC.202	Martuba 1300
	Plt Off G.H.Ranger	Tomahawk		Bf 109F	Martuba 1300
	Sgt F.M.Twemlow	Tomahawk		Ju 87	
	Plt Off J.L.Waddy	Tomahawk AN290		Bf 109	
	Sgt G.C.Coward	Tomahawk		Ju 87	
	Sgt G.C.Coward	Tomahawk		Bf 109 probable	
	Flt Lt C.R.Caldwell	Tomahawk AK498		Bf 109	
1 SAAF Sqn	2/Lt R.J.P.Collingwood	Hurricane II		Bf 109F probable	SE Gazala 1330
	Lt R.H.C.Kershaw	Hurricane II		Bf 109F probable	10m S Gazala 1340
	Maj M.S.Osler	Hurricane II		Bf 109F	
	2/Lt T.A.Meek	Hurricane II		Bf 109F damaged	
112 Sqn	Plt Off J.P.Bartle	Tomahawk AN372		Bf 109F probable	Tmimi 1525-1630
	Plt Off J.P.Bartle	Tomahawk		MC.202 damaged	Tmimi 1525-1630
	Plt Off E.Dickinson	Tomahawk AM459		MC.202 damaged	Tmimi 1525-1630
	Sgt D.N.McQueen	Tomahawk AN303		Bf 109F damaged	Tmimi 1525-1630
4 SAAF Sqn	Capt A.C.Bosman	Tomahawk		2 Bf 109s	Gazala 1530
	Capt A.C.Bosman	Tomahawk		2 Bf 109s damaged	Gazala 1530
	Lt D.W.Golding	Tomahawk		Bf 109F	Gazala 1530
3 RAAF Sqn	Flg Off A.W.Barr	Tomahawk AN336		Bf 110	Martuba area 1600
	Flg Off R.H.Gibbes	Tomahawk AM374		Ju 88 probable	Martuba area 1600
1 SAAF Sqn	Lt J.T.Seccombe	Hurricane II		G.50	W LG.130 1610
12 SAAF Sqn	Lt F.A.Ruse	Maryland		2 Ju 52/3ms	

British Casualties

Squadron	Casualty
272 Sqn	Beaufighter Ic damaged and crash-landed at base; Plt Off D.H.Hammond unhurt
	Beaufighter Ic damaged; Wg Cdr R.G.Yaxley safe, observer WiA
12 SAAF Sqn	Maryland II 1622 shot down; Lt W.G.Parsons and crew KiA
	Maryland II AH405 shot down; Maj T.S.Fisher and crew KiA
21 SAAF Sqn	Maryland II AH289 'B' shot down; Lt T.L.Parry and crew KiA
	Maryland II 1614 'G' damaged beyond repair; Capt F.C.Ramsay and two unhurt; one WiA
	Maryland II 1661 'D' shot down; Maj M.H.Fowler and crew KiA
11 Sqn	Blenheim IV Z7909 FTR; 2/Lt R.I.Burrage and crew KiA
15 Sqn	Blenheim IV Z5908 shot down; Flt Sgt J.H.L.Thompson and crew KiA
	Blenheim IV Z9595 shot down; Flg Off C.H.Anderson and crew KiA
13 Sqn	Blenheim IV V5588 crashed, unknown reason: 2/Lt C.N.Summersgill and crew KiA
30 Sqn	Hurricane I Z4931 FTR; Flg Off P.T.Dowding PoW
	Hurricane I Z4501 FTR; Plt Off Reynolds PoW
	Hurricane I Z4776 FTR; Sgt R.Whyte PoW
	Hurricane I Z4031 FTR; Sgt G.F.Halliwell PoW
250 Sqn	Tomahawk AN290 shot down; 2/Lt D.L.Norton WiA
1 SAAF Sqn	Hurricane II shot down; Lt J.T.Seccombe baled out
2 SAAF Sqn	Tomahawk AN422 shot down; Capt P.J.Robbertse PoW
	Tomahawk AN353? shot down; Lt J.R.Verster PoW. Rescued by Army on 24th
4 SAAF Sqn	Tomahawk AN351 shot down; Lt L.O.B.Player
	Tomahawk slightly damaged; Capt A.C.Bosman safe
3 RAAF Sqn	Tomahawk AN335 in collision, then shot down; Flg Off F.F.H.Eggleton PoW
	Tomahawk collided with AN335 and damaged, but returned to base; Flg Off R.Gray safe
112 Sqn	Tomahawk AN413 GA-K MiA; Plt Off R.J.D.Jeffries KiA
	Tomahawk AK457 MiA; Sgt W.E.Houston KiA
	Tomahawk AK476 MiA; Sgt J.Alves KiA
	Tomahawk damaged; Flt Lt P.H.Humphreys safe

German Claims

Unit	Claimant	Aircraft	Time/Location
III./ZG 26	Oblt Schulze-Dickow	Maryland	0850-
	Uffz Günther Wegmann	Maryland	0850-
	Oblt Schulze-Dickow	e/a	over sea 1010
./NJG 2	Lt Haas	Beaufighter	
./ZG 26	Obfw Otto Polenz	2 Marylands	1330
./JG 27	Oblt Erbo Graf von Kageneck	P-40	Tmimi 1346
	Oblt Erbo Graf von Kageneck	Hurricane	Tmimi 1346
?./JG 53	Obfw Hermann Neuhoff	Hurricane	1600
	Uffz Rudolf Schmidt	Hurricane	1600
	Lt Siegfried Hosnedl	Hurricane	1600
./JG 53	Obfw Werner Stumpf	2 Hurricanes	1603-1605
	Lt Wolf Schaller	Hurricane	1610
?./JG 53	Obfw Hermann Neuhoff	P-40	1610

German Casualties

KGrzbV 102	Ju 52/3m G6+KS WNr 2958 lost; Lt Himmler and crew MiA Crete-Derna
	Ju 52/3m G6+CR WNr 6721 lost; Uffz Sander and crew MiA Crete-Derna
KGrzbV 400	Ju52/3m CE+EH WNr 7210 shot down near Derna; Obfw Max Busko and crew
3./KGrzbV 400	Ju52/3m 9G+HH WNr 6583 lost; Uffz Josef Bordlein and crew MiA Crete

Italian Claims

Unit	Claimant	Aircraft	Time/Location
80ª Sq/17° Gr CT	Cap Clizio Nioi	Tomahawk	Martuba area 1600
	Cap Clizio Nioi	Tomahawk probable	Martuba area 1600
	S.Ten Renato Bagnoli	Tomahawk	
	M.llo Pio Marsilli	Tomahawk	
	Serg Magg Mario Host	Tomahawk	
	Ten Emilio Marchi	Tomahawk probable	
71ª Sq/17° Gr CT	Ten Glauco Vatta	Tomahawk	

71ª Sq/17° Gr CT	M.llo Marcello Lui	Tomahawk	
	Serg Remo Broilo	Tomahawk	
	Serg Egidio Buogo	Tomahawk	
81ª Sq/6° Gr CT	Ten Guido Beggiato	Hurricane	Gazala area 1330
88ª Sq/6° Gr CT	M.llo Natalino Stabile	Tomahawk	

Italian Casualties

79ª Sq/6° Gr CT	MC.202 MM7767 damaged; Cap Domenico Camarda returns	
79ª Sq/6° Gr CT	MC.202 MM7880 force-lands near Ain el Gazala; Serg Renato Saiani WiA	
71ª Sq/17° Gr CT	MC.202 MM7871 damaged and force-landed; Ten Glauco Vatta safe	
71ª Sq/17° Gr CT	MC.202 MM 7861 damaged and belly-landed; Ten Pierfrancesco Conti slighty wounded	

We had left Fred Eggleton lying hidden amongst desert thorn bushes near Tmimi, waiting for nightfall

"The adrenaline was coursing through my system and my heart was pumping like a steam engine. To the north, behind undulating landscape, I could hear aircraft landing and taxiing at Tmimi. To the south, behind a low ridge, I could hear motorised transports travelling along an east-west road which I judged to be Trigh Capuzzo. I had a good map and was able to pinpoint my position fairly accurately. I was about 60 miles west-north-west of El Adem and at least 50 miles into enemy territory. I had a field service water bottle full of water but no emergency ration. However, I had a couple of dozen tablets of malted milk in my pocket to make up in a small way for this deficiency. I also had a neck stud magnetic compass which proved to be invaluable for travel by night. I was wearing battle dress over khaki shorts and shirt with long socks and a battered pair of desert boots.

"I was left alone for the rest of the day and set out toward the east an hour after nightfall. I decided to keep away from made roads and tracks for fear of being spotted by passing traffic. The surface was undulating, hard and stony with wadis criss-crossing here and there. I fell flat on my face a couple of times when, in the faint moonlight, I failed to notice that the ground dropped away in front of me. The moon was in its last quarter and set towards midnight. After that, I had to rely on the light of the stars to pick my way. At 2200 hrs, I saw a motor cycle headlight, north of my position, bobbing along towards the east. I judged it must have been on a made track as it would not have been possible for a wheeled vehicle to travel across the terrain I was traversing. It seemed quite close but I could hear no sound so it must have been at least two miles away.

"I maintained my walking directions by using the luminous dial of the compass to pick a star in the direction I wanted to go and walked towards that star. In the early hours, when it was very dark, I found myself within a couple of yards of a camel. I seriously contemplated shooting it for food but thought better of it.

"Towards dawn, I found the terrain had changed to stony desert country somewhat like inland Australia. By this time, I had found it necessary to rest after an hour's walk and lay down on the ground until wakened by the cold an hour later. Before daylight, I took cover in some low bushes and did not move for the rest of the day. Every couple of hours, I would suck a malted milk tablet and moisten my lips with water. I refrained from urinating or defecating, with the idea of deriving the maximum benefit from the food and fluid in my body. My nerves were shattered and I was scared every time I heard gunfire from aircraft dog-fighting overhead.

"I set off again an hour after dark – following the same routine of one hour walking and one hour rest. The going was easier than on the first night with a much flatter surface. After a couple of hours walking, I came on a fairly wide east-west track and, since there seemed to be no traffic, I decided to walk along it for a while. At midnight, I heard a man's voice quite close to me and immediately dropped to the ground to see several human figures silhouetted against the starry sky. My desert boots with their crepe rubber soles were completely silent and I had not been seen or heard. I crawled away into the darkness and made my escape. My impression was that it had been an Italian army unit, camped for the night. I decided that I had better stick to my original plan and avoid all tracks as I continued in a south-easterly direction.

"At 0100 hrs, I began to see Verey Lights rising slowly into the sky ahead of me. My only means of judging how far away they were was the slowness with which they rose up. This indicated to me that they might be as much as ten miles away. I judged them to mark enemy strong posts, and altered course when one rose ahead of me, only to find that I was walking toward another stronghold when a Verey Light went off ahead of me a few minutes later. By the early hours, I was becoming confused – there seemed to be strong posts strung outright across my path and, to add to my disquiet, there were tank tracks criss-crossing the desert around me.

"I decided I should try to find a good hiding place for the coming day as it seemed likely I might find myself in the middle of a tank battle. I was in luck! Just before first light, I found a shallow hole about six feet long, two feet wide, and eighteen inches deep in the middle of a flat area. I lay down in it, determined to stay there for the day. I heard a truck whirring close by to the north-west of my hide-out. Soon after that, I heard a loud whirring further away to the south-east. I lay perfectly still, not daring to put my head up to have a look. I just had to wait developments without revealing my presence. I had not long to wait. Bullets began to zip in bursts right over my hole. I could hear them zipping just before the noise of the distant machine gun reached me. After the firing had been going on for a minute or two, I heard a cry from the truck to the north-west, and then complete silence for a few minutes. There was a further whirring sound to the south-east which slowly faded into the distance.

"All this time, I had been petrified with fear and, to add to my horror, a desert rat had crawled into my hide and was sniffing around my feet – no doubt thinking I was a corpse. At least, I thought, the rat would be edible, so I carefully aimed my pistol at the rodent just six inches from my foot. I fired, and missed! The rat beat a hasty retreat and I took comfort that, at least, I had not shot myself in the foot. I stayed in my hole for the rest of the day, without moving. After dark I got up and walked towards the truck to the north-west. It was an open military lorry and there were two dead Italian soldiers lying beside it. They had been the targets of the zipping bullets! One had an aluminium pannikin attached to his belt. There was a piece of parmesan cheese in it but, although I was weak with hunger, I did not feel like eating it.

"I found I was fairly close to a road and decided it would be too risky to continue in the direction I had been walking for fear of blundering into a minefield. The area in which I found myself had obviously been closely fought-over and it would have been foolish to remain there. I was weak and demoralised from lack of food and even wondered if I should give myself up.

"Eventually, I made up my mind to try and retrace my steps for a few miles and then turn south, in an attempt to reach the front line at a place where the opposing forces were more dispersed and there would be less risk of walking into a minefield.

"I set off toward the west, filled with doubts as to whether I could last the extra couple of days which I would need to reach the front line by the route I had now chosen. After walking for a little more than an hour, I heard a voice challenge me from near-by. Since I could not see my challenger and, since it seemed he could see me, I put up my hands, called 'kamerad' and waited to be captured. It was an Italian anti-tank battery and I was promptly disarmed, two Italian soldiers struggling with each other to take my pistol as a souvenir."

Eggleton was captured during the night of 14 December. He had walked about 20 miles during the past three nights and had reached a spot about five miles south-west of Gazala. Subsequently shipped to prison camp in Italy, he escaped from a train carrying himself and other prisoners to Germany, and reached neutral Switzerland where he remained in internment until the end of the war. Whilst there, he met and married a Swiss girl.

Saturday, 13 December 1941

Dawn heralded yet another day of heavy combat as 8th Army battered at the Gazala line. During an early sortie by 5./JG 53, Lt Hermann Münzert claimed a twin-engined aircraft identified as a Beaufort. At the same time Obfw Heller of 8./ZG 26 claimed a Blenheim. Five Blenheims of 18 Squadron and six from 107 Squadron from Malta had been sent out from Luqa to attack shipping in Argostoli harbour, Cephalonia, where three merchant vessels and five *Navigatori*-class destroyers were bombed. Z7858 'M' of 18 Squadron was pursued by a Bf 109 (? was it actually a Ju 88C flown by Lt Herbert Haas of I./NJG 2) for nearly 45 miles, finally ditching near Malta with the port engine on fire. The crew were rescued by a Maltese fishing boat. Two more aircraft from 107 Squadron were shot down, the crew of Z7368 all being killed while that of Z7800 survived as prisoners. In the absence of other German claims or of any by Italian fighter units, these appear to have been the aircraft claimed by the Luftwaffe units mentioned.

Sqn Ldrs Beresford and Walker, the commanding officers of 94 and 260 Squadrons respectively, flew to El Adem for a briefing. As they took off to return they were jumped by two Bf 109s while flying at 50

Some of I./JG 27's successful pilots in December 1941.Left to right: Fw Emil Kaiser, Oblt Hans-Joachim Marseille and far right, Lt Hans-Arnold Stahlschmidt. Marseille had claimed two P-40s on the 13th of the month as his 33rd and 34th victories.

feet; between them, they fired at one of the Messerschmitts which had overshot, hitting it from extremely long range which nonetheless caused it to force-land near Tobruk. Their victim was a 1./JG 27 aircraft flown by Obfw Albert Espenlaub who since his arrival in North Africa had claimed 14 victories. He was taken prisoner, but he would be shot and killed on 25 February 1942 whilst attempting to escape.

At 1130 they led their squadrons to escort Blenheims raiding the Martuba road. East of Tmimi a number of Bf 109s were encountered, Lt Gibson of 94 Squadron claiming one shot down with Flt Sgt Dunwoodie claiming a second damaged. During this fight Sqn Ldr Walker was wounded, but he managed to return to base.

In the meantime there had been considerable action during the late morning/midday period. 272 Squadron Beaufighters swept out to sea again to seek more of the fuel-carrying transports flying in from Crete. Flg Off Roman, one of the unit's Belgian pilots, attacked a Do 24 escorted by Bf 110s, claiming to have damaged the flyingboat and probably shot down a Bf 110, his own aircraft suffering only a single large hole in the tail. However, Flg Off Morris's Beaufighter was shot down to the south of Crete by Obfw Sommer of I./NJG 2, he and his observer being killed.

The afternoon was busy and somewhat confused. At 1245 14 Ju 87Rs of 209ª and 239ª Squadriglie took off with a number of Luftwaffe Stukas to attack armoured cars in the Gazala area. They were escorted by 14 MC.200s of 153° Gruppo and 19 G.50bis of 20° Gruppo. The latter unit engaged British fighters, claiming five shot down "in co-operation with German fighters". Hptmn Gerlitz of 2./JG 27 had claimed one P-40 east of Tmimi at 1400, but between 1600-1640, pilots from 3. and 5./JG 27, and from 8./JG 53, claimed five fighters (two of them by Lt Marseille).

At 1510 ten Tomahawks from 3 RAAF Squadron had taken off to carry out a sweep, at 1600 spotting a reported eight bombers and eight escorting fighters in the Tmimi area. Three Bf 109s were claimed shot down, with one more probable and three damaged, plus a Ju 87 damaged. Flg Off Tommy Trimble was shot down, but survived and returned to the unit a week later. During the return flight, Flg Off Barr, who had already claimed one of the Messerschmitts, spotted a lone Ju 88 and claimed to have destroyed this too.

The South African Tomahawks had been out ahead of the sweep by the Australians, escorting a formation of Blenheims from 84 Squadron over El Adem and Derna. Fighters attacked, one of which Lt D.W.Golding claimed as shot down at about 1400, but Lt Lorentz was shot down and baled out, while Capt Bosman's aircraft was damaged; Lorentz was probably the victim of Hptmn Gerlitz. Lt E.C.Saville of 2 SAAF Squadron then claimed a Ju 88 shot down over Derna and a second damaged at 1430.

At the time that the 3 RAAF Squadron sweep was underway, 274 and 1 SAAF Squadrons had commenced sending out pairs of Hurricanes at short intervals on 'rhubarbs', and some of these met the formation the Australians had been battling with. Sqn Ldr Linnard and Plt Off Wally Conrad of 274

Squadron had been first off at 1600, and between them claimed a Ju 87. At 1610 Plt Offs Thompson and Kuhle took off at the same time as Maj Osler and 2/Lt Connell of 1 SAAF. The 274 Squadron pair met two Bf 109s and two MC.200s, Thompson claiming one of the former shot down, reporting that his crashed 20 miles south of Bomba. Maj Osler became separated from his wingman in cloud, attacking several aircraft and claiming an MC.200 shot down. Connell, meanwhile, also found a number of Axis aircraft, claiming damage to several before being shot-up by hostile fighters and crash-landing. At 1615 Plt Off Halliday and Lt Meek of 1 SAAF Squadron took off, but Halliday was rapidly shot down. Baling out, he was taken to Tobruk hospital with slight injuries.

AHQ recorded that during the day 20 attacks had been made on the forward troops, but few casualties had been suffered. Four Stukas had been claimed shot down, as had a Ju 88 in the Gazala area. One Italian Ju 87 had force-landed after being hit by AA, Cap Ragazzini and his gunner becoming PoWs; moreover at least two German Stukas were also lost, one reportedly another victim of AA fire. A 1./JG 27 Bf 109 also force-landed and was destroyed after being hit by AA, the pilot escaping unhurt. An aircraft of 7./JG 53 was also shot down in which Lt Karl Vockelmann was wounded.

Flg Off A.W.'Nicky' Barr joined 3 RAAF Squadron on 26 November 1941, quickly becoming the unit's outstanding pilot. He claimed his first victory on 12 December.

One further Hurricane was also lost when Flg Off Miles-Johnson of 237 Squadron took off at 1530 to undertake a TacR sortie over El Adem-Acroma-Tmimi-Gazala. He was shot down, but returned later. Flt Lt Derek Gould, who had joined 33 Squadron during October, flying a lone reconnaissance sortie over Agedabia, happened upon three CR.42s over Sabchet el Ghanesh (53 miles south-east of Agedabia), claiming to have inflicted damage on two of these.

Nine Blenheims of 55 Squadron had been ordered off for a combined high and low level attack on destroyers and cargo vessels in Navarin Bay. Following a long flight, V6291 was intercepted by a Bf 109 when north-east of Tmimi on the return flight, being shot down at 1655 by Obfw Bendert of Stab II./JG 27, Flt Lt G.Pelling and his crew being killed.

At this stage the Regia Aeronautica decided to pull back all its fighter units in the Martuba area. 6° Gruppo and 20° Gruppo moved to Derna, 9° Gruppo to Barce and 17° Gruppo to Benghazi K.2. On 15 December 8° and 13° Stormi BT would move from Barce to Misurata.

British Claims

74 Sqn	Sqn Ldr T.B.de la P.Beresford	Hurricane IIc BD919	}	Bf 109	near Tobruk 1145-1200
260 Sqn	Sqn Ldr D.R.Walker	Hurricane I			
272 Sqn	Flg Off C.L.Roman	Beaufighter Ic 'K'		Do 24 damaged	40m from Derna 1150-1500
	Flg Off C.L.Roman	Beaufighter Ic 'K'		Bf 110 probable	40m from Derna 1150-1500
5 SAAF Sqn	Maj A.X.Kriel	Tomahawk		Bf 109F	Gazala, on beach 1400
	Lt D.W.Golding	Tomahawk		Bf 109F	Gazala, off beach
2 SAAF Sqn	Lt E.C.Saville	Tomahawk		Ju 88	Derna 1430
	Lt E.C.Saville	Tomahawk		Ju 88 damaged	Derna 1430
94 Sqn	Sgt W.H.Dunwoodie	Hurricane IIc		Bf 109 damaged	Tmimi-Martuba road 1510
	Lt D.Gibson	Hurricane IIc BD706		Bf 109	15m E Tmimi 1515
3 RAAF Sqn	Sgt R.H.Simes	Tomahawk AN291		Bf 109 probable	W Tmimi 1545
	Sgt R.H.Simes	Tomahawk AN291		Bf 109 damaged	W Tmimi 1545
	Flg Off E.H.B.Jackson	Tomahawk AN270		Bf 109F damaged	W Tmimi 1600

3 RAAF Sqn	Flg Off A.W.Barr	Tomahawk AN336	Bf 109	W Tmimi 1600
	Sgt A.C.Cameron	Tomahawk AN274	Bf 109	
	Sgt A.C.Cameron	Tomahawk AN274 ⎫	Bf 109F	W Tmimi 1600
	Flg Off P.J.Briggs	Tomahawk AK438 ⎭		
	Flg Off R.H.Gibbes	Tomahawk AM374	Bf 109s damaged	W Tmimi 1600
	Flg Off R.H.Gibbes	Tomahawk AM374	Ju 87 damaged (? Conf)	W Tmimi 1600
	Flg Off A.W.Barr	Tomahawk AN336	Ju 88	30m S Gazala 1615
1 SAAF Sqn	Capt M.S.Osler	Hurricane II	MC.202	Gazala area, SSE Tmimi 1640
	2/Lt G.R.Connell	Hurricane II	2 u/i e/as	Gazala area 1645
274 Sqn	Sqn Ldr S.Linnard	Hurricane IIb Z5064 ⎫	Ju 87	Gazala-Tmimi area 1645-1750
	Plt Off W.A.G.Conrad	Hurricane IIb Z4000 ⎭		
	Plt Off Thompson	Hurricane IIb Z5130	Bf 109F	20 m SW Benghazi 1615-1715
250 Sqn	Sgt R.J.C.Whittle	Tomahawk AM313	MC.202	
		Tomahawk	Ju 88	
33 Sqn	Flt Lt D.L. Gould	Hurricane	2 CR.42s damaged	

British Casualties

18 Sqn	Blenheim IV Z7858 'M' ditched near Malta after fighter attack; Sgt F.W.Jury and crew picked up by Maltese fishing boat
107 Sqn	Blenheim IV Z7368 shot down by fighters; Sgt R.D.Gracie and crew KiA
	Blenheim IV Z7800 shot down; Sgt A.J.Lee and crew PoW
260 Sqn	Hurricane I damaged; Sqn Ldr D.R.Walker WiA
55 Sqn	Blenheim IV V6291 shot down: Flt Lt G.Pelling and crew KiA
4 SAAF Sqn	Tomahawk AK516 shot down; Lt F.C.Lorentz baled out
	Tomahawk damaged; Capt A.C.Bosman unhurt
272 Sqn	Beaufighter Ic T3250 shot down; Flg Off G.W.Morris and navigator KiA
3 RAAF Sqn	Tomahawk AM 384 shot down; Flg Off T.H.Trimble returned on 20th
1 SAAF Sqn	Hurricane II crash-landed; 2/Lt G.R.C.Connell unhurt
	Hurricane II shot down; Plt Off Halliday baled out, slt WiA; returned to unit 27 January 1942
237 Sqn	Hurricane shot down; Flg Off Miles-Johnson returned later
272 Sqn	Beaufighter Ic T3250 MiA; Flg Off G.W.Morris and observer KiA
	Beaufighter Ic 'K' slightly damaged; Flg Off C.L.Roman and observer safe

German Claims

8./ZG 26	Obfw Heller	Blenheim	0903
9./JG 53	Lt Hermann Münzert	Beaufort	0905
III./ZG 26	Uffz Biern	Blenheim	NE Derna 1245
I./NJG 2	Obfw Hermann Sommer	Beaufighter	S Crete, into sea 1330
2./JG 27	Hptmn Erich Gerlitz	P-40	E Tmimi 1400
3./JG 27	Lt Hans-Joachim Marseille	P-40	NE Martuba 1600
8./JG 53	Oblt Hans-Joachim Heinecke	Hurricane	1603
3./JG 27	Lt Hans-Joachim Marseille	P-40	3m NE Tmimi 1610
3./JG 27	Oblt Gerhard Homuth	P-40	SW Tmimi 1615
5./JG 27	Obfw Erich Krenzke	P-40	SE Ain el Gazala 1640
Stab II./JG 27	Obfw Karl-Heinz Bendert	Blenheim	7m NE Tmimi 1655

German Casualties

1./JG 27	Bf 109F-4 trop WNr 8477 shot down at El Adem; Obfw Albert Espenlaub PoW
1./JG 27	Bf 109F-4 trop WNr 8472 force-landed due to AA, 100% destroyed; pilot safe
7./JG 53	Bf 109F-4/Z WNr 7357 shot down; Lt Karl Vockelmann WiA
1./StG 1	Ju 87 crashed landing at Derna; Obfw Ernst Fleischmann/Fw Max Wagner KiFA
1./StG 3	Ju 87 shot down 15m SE Ain el Gazala by AA; Fw Eberhard Vos/Uffz Lorenz Lermer KiA
6./LG 1	Ju 88A-5 WNr 4333 10% damaged by fighters in Bir Hacheim area; two members of crew KiA

Italian Claims

| 20° Gr CT | Unspecified pilots | 5 Hurricanes in co-operation with Luftwaffe fighters |

Italian Casualties

209ª Sq B a'T	Ju 87R Wnr 5848 hit by AA and force-landed; Cap Giacomo Ragazzini, 1°Av Guido Vanz PoW
19ª Sq/28° Gr/8° St	S.79 destroyed on ground at night
Unspecified unit	5 MC.202s damaged by strafing on ground at Martuba

---

Bf 109F-4 trop 'Weisse 11' of I./JG 27 which was shot down on 13 December 1941. The pilot, Obfw Albert Espenlaub, was captured but was shot and killed while attempting to escape.

Sunday, 14 December 1941

WDAF units repeated the 'rhubarb' operations of the previous day, and during an early sortie of this type by Plt Off Moriarty and Sgt Dodds of 274 Squadron, a twin-engined Italian bomber was spotted 30 miles west of Gazala. Identifying this as a Ca.135, Dodds claimed to have shot it down into the sea. Whatever he had attacked, it was not a Ca.135 which was an export aircraft built in Italy for the Hungarian air force and never in Italian service. It is tempting to speculate that the aircraft in question might have been the basically similar BR.20, on the way back to Italy. However, records indicate that no Italian bombers of any kind were in the air on this date.

Six Tomahawks from 3 RAAF Squadron then undertook a rhubarb to the Martuba area, where seven Ju 87s and eight Bf 109s were engaged. This was probably part of a formation of 13 Italian Ju 87Rs which had joined Luftwaffe Stukas to repeat the previous day's raid. One 209ª Squadriglia aircraft was shot down, reportedly by AA, the crew being killed. During this engagement two Tomahawks were shot down, one of the pilots being killed.

Ten Hurricanes of 260 Squadron also flew rhubarbs, operating over the Gazala area, where Flg Off Hanbury claimed a Ju 88 of III./LG 1 shot down and a Bf 109 damaged, but Flt Lt Bandinell failed to return.

During the early afternoon 229, 238 and 250 Squadrons also flew rhubarbs during one of which Sqn Ldr W.A.Smith of 229 Squadron claimed a Bf 109 shot down, other members of this unit claiming damage to both a Bf 109 and a Bf 110. 238 Squadron's commanding officer, Sqn Ldr O'Neill, claimed an He 111 damaged over Bu Amud airfield. Eight of 250 Squadron's Tomahawks intercepted 12 Ju 88s and just two Bf 109s, Plt Off Ranger claiming one of the latter north-west of Gazala.

AHQ recorded that during considerable strafing by the Hurricane squadrons, two lorries had been claimed destroyed and 35 damaged, with heavy casualties. Four British aircraft were reported to have been lost, although only three such have been identified unless the fourth related to a 14 Squadron Blenheim. This aircraft had departed early for LG.144 at El Adem to collect a fighter escort. This never materialised and at 1100 the aircraft took off again to bomb targets of opportunity, from which sortie it failed to return, the crew all perishing. No Axis fighter claim for such an aircraft has been found, so it is assumed to have fallen to Flak.

Hermann Neuhoff of III./JG53, now commissioned as a Lt, is sitting on the tail of his Bf 109F a few weeks later in Sicily. He had claimed his fourth North African victory on 14 December 1941.

During the day Luftwaffe fighters had made claims for five British aircraft shot down, three during the morning and two in the afternoon. On this occasion WDAF claims for Bf 109s had been closer to reflecting the actuality, for three were lost, one being an aircraft of 2./JG 27 in which the previously successful Obfw Hermann Förster was killed, the other two being aircraft from 7./JG 53, both the pilots being lost.

British Claims

274 Sqn	Sgt J.Dodds	Hurricane IIb Z5130	Ca.135	20m W Gazala 0830-1010
3 RAAF Sqn	Sgt F.B.Reid	Tomahawk	Ju 87 damaged	Martuba, 50m S El Gazala 1000-1015
	Sgt W.H.A.Mailey	Tomahawk	Bf 109 damaged	SE Martuba 1010
112 Sqn	Sgt S.C.Johnson	Tomahawk AN303	Bf 109 damaged	near Tmimi 1100
250 Sqn	Plt Off G.H.Ranger	Tomahawk	Bf 109F	Martuba 1300
229 Sqn	Plt Off M.A.Beatty	Hurricane IIc BE205	Bf 109 damaged	SE Tmimi 1450-1545
	Sqn Ldr W.A.Smith	Hurricane II BD785	Bf 109	SE Tmimi 1450-1545
	Sgt Tiffin	Hurricane IIb Z4955	Bf 110 damaged	7-8m NW Gazala 1450-1545
238 Sqn	Sqn Ldr O'Neill	Hurricane IIc	He 111 damaged	Bu Amud airfield 1750-1815
260 Sqn	Flg Off O.V.Hanbury	Hurricane I	Ju 88	Gazala area
	Flg Off O.V.Hanbury	Hurricane I	Bf 109 damaged	Gazala area
	Plt Off T.R.Hawthorne	Hurricane I	Bf 109F damaged	Gazala area
	Plt Off T.R.Hawthorne	Hurricane I	Ju 88 probable	Gazala area
250 Sqn	Flt Lt C.R.Caldwell	Tomahawk AK498	4 Bf 109s damaged	

British Casualties

3 RAAF Sqn	Tomahawk AN285 shot down; Flg Off D.E.Knight KiA
	Tomahawk AN 270 shot down; Sgt D. Scott PoW
260 Sqn	Hurricane I FTR; Flt Lt J.H.Bandinell FTR
14 Sqn	Blenheim IV Z5860 'O' FTR; Sgt F.W.Dennis, RAAF, and crew KiA

German Claims

2./JG 27	Oblt Josef Unterberger	P-40		E Tmimi 1010
9./JG 53	Lt Erich Beckmann			1020
Stab I./JG 27	Lt Hans-Arnold Stahlschmidt			S Tmimi 1120

| 7./JG 53 | Obfw Hermann Neuhoff | Hurricane | 1545 |
| 9./JG 53 | Obfw Werner Stumpf | P-40 | 1550 |

German Casualties

2./JG 27	Bf 109F-4 trop shot down E Tmimi; Obfw Hermann Förster KiA		
7./JG 53	Bf 109F-4/Z WNr 7360 shot down; Uffz August Nieland KiA		
	Bf 109F-4/Z WNr 7381 shot down; Lt Wolfgang Ihrig MiA		
7./LG 1	Ju 88A-5 WNr 2310 L1+DR shot down over Tobruk; Ofw Helmut Grude and three KiA		

Italian Casualties

| 209ª Sq BaT | Ju 87R Wnr 5923 shot down by AA; Serg Gino Lipparini, 1° Av Augusto Passini KiA | | |

Monday, 15 December 1941

Following their unsuccessful attempt to raid Axis airfields in November, the SAS had now moved to Gialo, 150 miles south of the Mediterranean coast, where they were joined by elements of the LRDG. It was now planned that they would be taken to the vicinity of their targets in the latter organisation's trucks, rather than attempting to go in by air and parachute. Raids had now been planned against Sirte on 14th, Agheila on the 16th and Agedabia on 21 December. 39 commandos and their transport had thus set off on 8 December to drive the 280 miles to the planned area, fortunately without being spotted. On arrival at the coast road Axis patrols were spotted and a reorganisation was planned. Now Lt Paddy Mayne, a notoriously large and tough Northern Irishman, was to lead part of the force to attack Tamet airfield, 30 miles to the west of Sirte, where it was apparent many aircraft were evacuating to, while David Stirling led the rest to Sirte. Separate groups were led to Agheila by Lt 'Jock' Lewis and to Agedabia by Lt W.Fraser.

Stirling's party found Sirte now deserted. With no targets available, they mined the road nearby and withdrew. Agheila similarly proved to be empty, Lewis and his team attacking a roadhouse which was thought to be a meeting place for senior Axis officers. Having shot-up this target, this group also departed without loss.

Mayne's attack on Tamet airfield resulted in three CR.42s, an MC.200 and a Ju 87 being destroyed, and other aircraft damaged. Mayne later recorded his account of the night, subsequently included in his biography (*Colonel Paddy: The Man Who Dared* by Patrick Marrinan, Pretani Press, 1983):

"It was just after ten o'clock when we left the truck. An ideal night for the job. No moon, and pleasantly cool for walking. There were four of us, keyed-up, tense. A little nervous. We moved quietly, heading slightly to the right of the North Star. The desert finished, and we crossed a tarmac road – the one Mussolini built to carry his men to the Delta. We were neither expected, nor invited, and we had the initiative. I began to feel happy, we could hear the sea, and after about a hundred yards we came across two wooden huts in a dip. The sound of sleeping came from inside. From the look of them they were not Arabs, so we put some time-bombs on the roof and left. Back up the path we heard voices and hid till they came abreast. I guessed they would lead us to the airfield, and they did. They disappeared in to a building rather like a Nissen hut with a door at each end. The sound of singing and talking came from inside. I kicked open the door and stood there with my Colt 45, the others at my side with a tommy-gun and another automatic. The Germans stared at us. We were a peculiar and frightening sight, bearded and with long, unkept hair. For what seemed an age we just stood there looking at each other in complete silence. I said 'Good Evening'. At that a young German arose and moved slowly backwards. I shot him, and as he fell, he knocked glasses to the ground from his table. I turned and fired at another some six feet away. He was standing beside the wall as he sagged.

"Hawkins, a Londoner, opened up with his tommy-gun....The room was by now in pandemonium. So we left, throwing hand grenades to add to the confusion. The dozen or so enemy that we had killed or wounded did not matter much numerically. But we hoped to create a feeling of insecurity and anxiety among the Axis, and to make them waste men on sentry duty. For the same reason we mined the road, forcing their drivers to move cautiously.

"The night was livening up. Quite a bit of firing, but none in our direction. We found two dumps of forty gallon petrol drums covered with camouflage netting and placed sufficient bombs in to destroy the lot.

"Then came the greatest thrill. They looked beautiful. Low, sleek, deadly in the air, but strangely impotent now. Thousands of pounds worth of craftsmanship waiting to be destroyed by a little plastic high explosive. As grateful as children on Christmas morning we moved from plane to plane, placing our bombs in the cockpits or petrol tanks.

"The bombs were composed of high explosive mixed with thermite, a detonator and a time pencil. These pencils were ingenious devices consisting of a spring, a striker, a capsule of acid, and a retaining wire. When the capsule was broken the acid burned through the wire, released the spring and striker, and so detonated the bomb. The time lag between setting and detonation depended on the thickness of the wire. That night, we decided on thirty minutes. The thermite was mixed with the explosive to ensure burning.

"The planes silhouetted against the night sky were a mixed bag of Stuka bombers, Messerschmidt (sic) fighters and transports dispersed in a rough circle at intervals of about twenty yards. As I approached one I saw a glow of light in the cockpit. I thought someone was sitting there smoking. So I quietly moved round the rear of the plane and up to the cockpit. I clambered on to the wing and peered inside. Someone had neglected to switch off the panel lights, and the dashboard was softly illuminated. A sharp tug, then a heave, and I had ripped out the dashboard for a souvenir.

"We were now running short of bombs. We had wasted too many on telegraph poles, and had been too generous at the petrol hut and around the dumps. But we each had a hand grenade left, so before leaving we tossed them into the cockpits of the last two planes.

"Happy and contented, and with empty haversacks, we set off, back to our trucks and the Long Range Desert Group. We hadn't gone far, possibly a quarter of a mile, when there was an explosion. A terrific sheet of flame shot upwards, lighting the area. Feeling slightly naked in the light, we turned and got down in the sand to watch our handiwork. It was magnificent and terribly satisfying to watch the petrol dump ablaze.

"One by one the German planes joined in the flames. There would be an explosion, a flash of light, then a steady fire. I produced cigarettes and a flask of rum, and we relaxed.

"Since our attack on the hut, there had been spasmodic firing, but now everything opened up in a great crescendo. Towards the sea we heard heavy guns, the sky was criss-crossed with anti-aircraft tracer, and there were bursts of ground defence fire as some imaginative gunner started to see shadows moving. We learned later from Army headquarters that they had intercepted a message from the Italian commander of the local garrison to his headquarters in Tripoli to the effect that unless urgent reinforcements were sent they would not be able to hold out. I don't think our little force could have held the area against anything more formidable than a donkey and cart!

"The glare from the petrol fire was lessening. So, stubbing our cigarettes in the sand, we continued to walk to the rendezvous point. I had not been too certain of my ability to pinpoint the trucks on our return march, and as I was scared of overshooting, I asked the LRDG to flash a torch every three minutes from two o'clock.

"Just when we began to get worried we saw the welcoming light directly in front. There was a great reception awaiting us. The LRDG were just as pleased at our success as we were. We climbed aboard the trucks, settled ourselves among the petrol, rations and ammunition, and left it to them to get as many miles away as possible to a safe hiding place before the enemy fighters came looking for us at dawn."

Mayne, of course, had incorrectly identified both aircraft and enemy personnel as Germans, whereas they were Italians. He was right in other respects, however. These raids greatly unsettled air force personnel at the bases behind the lines, and caused much reinforcement and patrolling activity to be undertaken in the following days. Considerable scarce fuel was burned by aircraft reconnoitring the area looking for the perpetrators and seeking other possible raiders. They also found it difficult to ascertain how the bombs were detonated and how they might be defused in the future if further attacks were to take place – as indeed, they did. While the other raids on Sirte and Agheila had found nothing worthy of attack, that was not the case with Lt Fraser's group, which would attack Agedabia on the 21st as will be related.

The two remaining Regia Aeronautica bomber units, 8° and 13° Stormi BT, now withdrew from Barce to Misurata. For the RAF, the day involved mainly defensive patrols over the battle area which resulted in little aerial action.

272 Squadron now moved from LG.10 to Bu Amud to operate, the former airfield having been flooded when high winds brought heavy rain, rendering it unserviceable. 50 tents and temporary offices were

blown down and a considerable amount of kit was destroyed by the flooding; a rum ration was issued due to these abnormal circumstances. From Bu Amud meanwhile, the squadron's Beaufighters undertook a sweep to the west of Derna, attacking a convoy of 60 MT near El Gobbi. Flt Lt Lydall and Sgt Ross then claimed to have probably shot down a Ju 52/3m and damaged a second 15 miles to the west of Derna. However, Ross's aircraft was hit and damaged and he was slightly wounded, causing him to crash-land on return to base. He reported that the aircraft he and Lydall had attacked appeared to have Italian markings.

At 1130 Obfw Otto Schulz of 4./JG27 claimed a P-40 south-west of Gezireh. It seems that he may have shot down 250 Squadron's Plt Off G.H.Ranger, who was killed; other reports, including log book entries by other pilots at the airfield, indicate that Ranger was killed when he crashed whilst taking off. It is quite conceivable, of course, that Schulz made a low-level attack on Ranger's Tomahawk as it was leaving the ground. At the time of his death Ranger had claimed four victories in three combats since his arrival in Africa, to add to a couple he had claimed over France during the previous summer whilst flying Spitfires. He died only a few days before the award of a DFC to him was announced.

Following his brief leave in Cairo, Plt Off Neville Duke rejoined 112 Squadron on this date:

"The Squadron is in a very poor state of morale. Everybody has had enough of the war. I know I have…….. Sat at stand-by in the cockpit this afternoon in a hell of a dust storm; no fun at all……
…Got a bit tight tonight – nothing else to do and it helps the old nerve."

British Claims

272 Sqn	Flt Lt J.E.Lydall	Beaufighter IC		
	Flt Lt J.E.Lydall	Beaufighter IC	Ju 52/3m probable	15m W Derna
	Sgt J.S.Ross	Beaufighter IC 'S'	Ju 52/3m damaged	
	Sgt J.S.Ross	Beaufighter IC 'S'		

British Casualties

250 Sqn	Tomahawk crashed taking off or shot down; Plt Off G.H.Ranger KiA SW Gezireh
272 Sqn	Beaufighter Ic 'S' damaged, crash-landed at base; Sgt J.S.Ross slightly WiA
80 Sqn	Hurricane Z4859 Sgt H.J.Cross, RAAF, baled out Tobruk 1900
	Hurricane Z4764 Sgt V.B.Handyside, RAAF, crash-landed Tobruk 1900 and then shot in the arm by a truck driver

German Claims

4./JG 27	Obfw Otto Schulz	P-40	SW Gezireh 1130

German Casualties

II./JG 27	Bf 109F-4 trop WNr 8564 shot down; pilot safe

Italian Casualties

Unspecified unit	MC.200 destroyed on ground by SAS at Tamet
	3 CR.42s destroyed on ground by SAS at Tamet
	Ju 87R destroyed on ground by SAS at Tamet

Tuesday, 16 December 1941

2 SAAF and 4 SAAF Squadrons undertook a wing sweep by 17 Tomahawks over Gazala providing cover to British armour. This had commenced a flanking movement three days earlier, but had been slowed by delayed deliveries of supplies occasioned by soft sand which had prevented 7th Armoured Division from completing the envelopment that had been planned.

Around the middle of the afternoon a lone Bf 110 attacked the South African Tomahawks, shooting down Capt Moodie of 4 SAAF, who took to his parachute. Both squadrons turned on the intrepid attacker and shot the aircraft down between them, although the identity of the German pilot has not been discovered, or of his fate.

Five Marylands of 21 SAAF Squadron bombed Benina, claiming to have destroyed at least nine aircraft on the ground there. Operating from LG.125, Flg Off Charles of 33 Squadron flew close to his target during a strafing attack and crashed into it, his aircraft bursting into flames.

During the day 7./JG 53 lost two Bf 109s, Oblt Altendorf becoming a PoW after crash-landing, although Gefr Klötzer, who came to earth in a similar manner, avoided capture and returned safely a day later. Both had been brought down by AA. Immediately following these losses, III./JG 53 returned to Sicily to resume operations from there over Malta.

On this date 3 RAAF Squadron was withdrawn from operations to re-equip with the first of the new Curtiss Kittyhawks to become available. Although in many ways similar to the Tomahawk, the new aircraft incorporated a number of improvements. Visually, the main difference was the enlarged radiator air intake, a modified cockpit canopy and the radio aerial. The Allison V-1710-39 engine was shorter than the Tomahawk's V-1710-33, which raised the thrust line, allowing the length of the fuselage to be reduced by six inches and the undercarriage to be shortened. The new engine did offer only a small increase in horse power, from 1,040 to 1,150; however, the weight had increased by some 75 lbs, and while top speed remained virtually unchanged, the climb rate was slightly degraded. Of particular significance, the fuselage guns had been removed and replaced by six wing-mounted .50in Brownings, three in each wing with 281 rounds per gun. This substantially enhanced the aircraft's 'punch', but it did not make for such accurate gunnery as the nose-mounted weapons. Importantly, the aircraft had provision to carry a drop tank beneath the fuselage and small bomb racks beneath the wings. This considerably increased the versatility of the aircraft when compared with its predecessor. With a maximum speed of 354 mph it was certainly not the equal of the Bf 109F other than perhaps at low altitudes, or of the MC.202 in the hands of a determined and experienced Italian pilot. As these aircraft became available, the squadron passed four of its remaining Tomahawks to 112 Squadron, two to 2 SAAF Squadron and two to 4 SAAF Squadron. The Australian pilots then left for Geneifa to collect their new machines.

British Claims

2 SAAF Sqn	unit shared claim	}	Bf 110
4 SAAF Sqn			

British Casualties

4 SAAF Sqn	Tomahawk AN376 shot down; Capt D.D.Moodie baled out, returned on 19th
33 Sqn	Hurricane I collided with target and crashed; Flg Off P.S.Charles KiA
272 Sqn	Beaufighter T4702 MiA

German Casualties

7./JG 53	Bf 109F-4/Z WNr 7348 crash-landed, AA; Oblt Heinz Altendorf PoW
	Bf 109F-4/Z WNr7408 crash-landed, AA; Gefr Hartmut Klötzer MiA – returned
1.(F)/121	Ju 88A-5 WNr 503 destroyed by bombs at Benina
	Bf 110E-3 WNr 2300 destroyed by bombs at Benina

Wednesday, 17 December 1941

Three days of intensive air attack on the retreating Axis forces commenced on this date. Mid morning 11 Hurricanes of 80, 94 and 260 Squadrons strafed north-east of Martuba, losing Sgt Cross of 80 Squadron. Eight Hurricanes of 1 SAAF Squadron escorted five Blenheims from 84 Squadron and three of 14 Squadron on a raid on Derna where 12 Bf 109s attacked the formation. The top cover had disappeared as the German pilots kept up a steady assault, Lt Sinner of 2./JG 27 and Lt Marseille of 3.Staffel each claiming a fighter shot down at 1110, Oblt Franzisket adding two more a few minutes later, and Marseille a fifth at 1128; both he and Franzisket incorrectly identified their victims as P-40s. Four of the South African aircraft were lost, with three of the pilots killed, while two more were badly damaged. In return two Messerschmitts were claimed shot down and a third damaged. Lt MacRobert crash-landed west of Tmimi, then walking for five hours until he met troops of the Indian Brigade. As these were about to attack Derna, he accompanied them before returning to his unit, where he arrived on the 20th.

Five Macchis from 6° Gruppo were also scrambled at 1100, three from 79ª Squadriglia and two from 81ª Squadriglia, nine bombers and 15 fighters being encountered between 1110 and 1120 at 6,000ft over Gazala. During this engagement the MC.202 pilots claimed three fighters, identified as Tomahawks, and three bombers damaged, for one loss, Ten Polizzy's aircraft being hit in the cooling system causing him to force-land, his Macchi being written off.

During the late morning or early afternoon eight of 80 Squadron's Hurribombers were escorted by 229 and 238 Squadrons to attack vehicles near Mechili. The attack was not carried out as both Bf 109s and MC.202s intercepted the formation over the target area, causing the 80 Squadron pilots to jettison their bombs. Sgt Comfort of this unit was shot-up and badly wounded, though he managed to get back to base. However, 229 Squadron's Plt Off D.Allcock was shot down and killed, and a second Hurricane

This Macchi C.200 of 153° Gruppo Autonomo '373-9' was the personal mount of Gen BA Ferdinando Raffaelli, commanding officer of Settore Est (Eastern Sector).

was damaged, Sgt Browne having to force-land at El Adem, 3./JG 27's Lt Friedrich Hoffmann claiming a Hurricane east of Mechili. In return, Sgt Carson claimed to have shot down a Bf 109, although his opponent may have been an MC.202 – either Polizzy's aircraft (unlikely, given the time difference), or another from this unit which was lost during the afternoon – possibly in rather unusual circumstances.

Here there was another event of some mystery. Generale BA Ferdinando Raffaelli, commander of the Regia Aeronautica's eastern sector, had arrived at Martuba to visit the newly arrived 6° Gruppo CT, where he asked the unit commander, T.Col Mezzetti to join him in a visual reconnaissance over the enemy columns moving south-east of Mechili. The two officers took off at 1620 in MC.202s of 81ª Squadriglia, with six others but not far from Mechili they encountered and became engaged with a flight of hostile

This Bf 109F carries the markings of the adjutant of I./JG 27, Lt Rudi Sinner, who claimed his second victory over a Hurricane on 17 December 1941.

fighters. From a confused fight Mezzetti failed to return, but when Raffaelli landed at 1710 his report of the action failed to shed much light on the details of the clash. This caused rumours to grow amongst 6° Gruppo's pilots to the effect that Mezzetti may have been a victim of 'friendly fire'. Nevertheless, given the recorded time of the engagement, it does seem more probable that the opponents had been from 229 Squadron and that Sgt Carson had been the successful British pilot.

During the same period an attack by South African Marylands on Barce was underway, and one of 9° Gruppo CT's MC.202s was destroyed on the ground and two of the unit's pilots were wounded, one of them, Ten Giuseppe Deanna, fatally. A Cant. Z.1007bis was also destroyed and 12 other aircraft were damaged. The returning bomber crews believed that they had destroyed 15 Ju 52/3ms by this raid.

From LG.125 Hurricanes strafed 40 vehicles south of Agedabia, claiming 16 trucks and two petrol tankers damaged. Reportedly, four Bf 109s and MC.200s were encountered, and claims made for two damaged, but no details of these claims have been found.

Two attacks were made during the day by Italian torpedo-bombers. The first was launched at 1300 by three S.79s of 281ª Squadriglia AS, flown by Cap Carlo Emanuele Buscaglia, Ten Aldo Forzinetti and Ten Carlo Faggioni. A probable hit on a cruiser was claimed, but Forzinetti's aircraft was shot down and ditched in the sea with the loss of the whole crew. The second attack was carried out at 1755 by three more S.79s, this time from 279ª Squadriglia AS, flown by Cap Giulio Marini, Ten Guglielmo Ranieri and Ten Mario Frongia. This trio also thought that at least two of their torpedoes struck home, but in neither case was any damage actually reported by the Royal Navy.

From 269 Wing, Wg Cdr Jimmie Fenton was posted to command 258 Wing due to Grp Capt Cross having been injured. Fenton's place as wing leader was taken by Sqn Ldr Troughton-Smith, commanding officer of 234 Wing which 269 Wing would metamorphise into at the end of the month. Three days later on 20 December, Wg Cdr Mermagen arrived as commanding officer of the wing.

As darkness fell, Flt Lt Davidson of 30 Squadron on a late convoy patrol, intercepted an unidentified aircraft which he thought might have been an He 111, and claimed this as probably shot down.

British Claims

1 SAAF Sqn	Capt C.A.van Vliet	Hurricane II Z5304	Bf 109F	E Derna and Gazala 1130-1200

	Capt C.A.van Vliet	Hurricane II Z5304	Bf 109F damaged	E Derna and Gazala 1130-1200
	2/Lt R.J.P.Collingwood	Hurricane II Z5304	Bf 109F	10m E Derna, 15m E Gazala 1130
229 Sqn	Sgt Carson	Hurricane IIc BE116	Bf 109F	El Mechili area 1550-1715
250 Sqn	Flt Lt C.R.Caldwell	Tomahawk AK498	Bf 109 probable	(poss He 111) convoy patrol - 1955
451/40 SAAF Sqn	Capt C.J.Gardiner	Hurricane	Ju 87	

British Casualties

80 Sqn	Hurricane I Z4168 FTR; Sgt H.J. Cross MiA S Derna road 1245
	Hurricane I shot down; Plt Off B.R.S.Williams KiA
1 SAAF Sqn	Hurricane II Z5156 shot down; Lt G.C.Hojem, KiA
	Hurricane II Z5456 shot down; Lt K.J.O'Reilly KiA
	Hurricane II BD619 shot down; Lt J.M.R.Barclay KiA
	Hurricane II Z5117 shot down; Lt M.MacRobert crash-landed and later returned
	Hurricane II Z5304 badly damaged; Capt C.A.van Vliet unhurt
	Hurricane II BD779 badly damaged; Lt A.J.Biden unhurt
80 Sqn	Hurricane I damaged; Sgt A.Comfort WiA
229 Sqn	Hurricane IIc shot down; Plt Off P.O.D.Allcock KiA
	Hurricane IIc damaged and force-landed; Sgt Browne unhurt

German Claims

2./JG 27	Lt Rudolf Sinner	Hurricane	SE Martuba 1110
3./JG 27	Lt Hans-Joachim Marseille	P-40	WNW Martuba 1./JG 27
	Oblt Ludwig Franzisket	P-40	Martuba 1112
	Oblt Ludwig Franzisket	P-40	SE Tmimi 1120
3./JG 27	Lt Hans-Joachim Marseille	P-40	S Bay of Gazala 1128
	Lt Freidrich Hoffmann	Hurricane	6m E Mechili 1648

German Casualties

II./JG 27	Bf 109F-4 WNr 7377 shot down; pilot safe
Erg.Gr/LG1	Ju 88A-5 WNr 2313 L1+KW shot down by AA on reconnaissance sortie; Obfw Heinz Betken and three MiA

Italian Claims

81ª Sq/6° Gr CT	Ten Antonio Palazzeschi	Tomahawk	Ain el Gazala 11.10-11.20
79ª Sq/6° Gr CT	Ten Piero Polizzy	Tomahawk	Ain el Gazala 11.10-11.20
	Serg Magg Mario Tozzi	Tomahawk	Ain el Gazala 11.10-11.20
6° Gr CT	Unspecified pilots	3 bombers damaged	Ain el Gazala 11.10-11.20

Italian Casualties

96ª Sq/9° Gr CT	MC.202 MM7750 destroyed on ground at Barce
97ª Sq/9° Gr CT	Ten Giuseppe Deanna and M.llo Otello Perotti WiA on ground by bombing, Deanna fatally
Unspecified unit	Cant.Z.1007bis destroyed on ground at Barce
Unspecified unit(s)	12 aircraft damaged on ground at Barce
79ª Sq/6° Gr CT	MC.202 MM7770 written off after crash-landing; Ten Piero Polizzy safe
6° Gr CT	MC.202 MM7765 MiA; T.Col Vezio Mezzetti MiA; grave subsequently found 25 April 1942
281ª Sq AS	S.79 MM23960 shot down in sea; Ten Aldo Forzinetti and crew KiA

Thursday, 18 December 1941

Considerable bombing and ground strafing took place throughout the day, 262 Wing carrying out 140 sorties, 66 of them in low level attacks. Marylands of the two SAAF squadrons raided Benina where at least five aircraft were believed to have been destroyed. In a repeat attack in the afternoon, seven more were claimed plus nine believed to have been damaged. 24 SAAF Squadron's Bostons raided Axis vehicle columns to the west of Maktila, the bombers being escorted by Tomahawks of 2 and 4 SAAF Squadrons. At Derna 17° Gruppo CT suffered a very damaging raid by seven bombers at 1000. This attack killed four airmen, wounded three more, and wrote off ten Macchis.

During one operation at 1600, 2 SAAF Squadron's Lt Stone was shot down and killed near Maraua by Lt Saar of 9./JG 27, Lt Copeland of 4 SAAF claiming a Bf 109 in return, and damaging a second. 40 minutes later a further Messerschmitt was claimed by Lt Golding of this same squadron. This second engagement may have been with MC.202s of 6° Gruppo, this unit's 81ª Squadriglia submitting claims for three Tomahawks shot down plus one probable, with two of its own aircraft damaged.

Returning from an attack on MT in the Mechili area, 250 Squadron encountered two Bf 109s attacking ground forces near Gazala, one of these being claimed damaged by Flt Lt Caldwell. Attacks on El Agheila airfield by Hurricanes and Tomahawks also brought claims for a Ju 52/3m and a number of vehicles destroyed.

By this time, however, Western Desert Air Force was becoming very short of serviceable aircraft. On this date for instance, 1 SAAF Squadron had been unable to operate and would only be able to do so a day or two later by borrowing Hurricanes from 274 Squadron. 12 SAAF and 21 SAAF operated jointly, virtually as a single unit, and bombing raids on Axis airfields were having to be undertaken once again without adequate fighter escort. 269 Wing also reported that its units were suffering from a shortage of oil and petrol. The wing now moved to Gambut, bringing with it its Communications Flight, equipped with Hawker Hart biplanes.

That the Axis were in little better condition was demonstrated when Martuba airfield was occupied. Here were found, destroyed or unserviceable, many German and Italian aircraft. These were later counted to include:

Ju 87s	3	G.50s	7
Bf 110s	3	S.79s	8
He 111	1	MC.202 (or Bf 109)	1
Bf 109s	5	3-engined monoplanes	2
Hs 126	1	S.79s believed to be relics of	4
Fi 156s	9	earlier campaigns	

Additionally, large quantities of German bombs, some of very heavy types, were also found.

As the day neared its close, JG 27 evacuated Derna airfield after Lt Sinner had spotted three British columns approaching the town from the south. Before he could get back to the airfield, his Messerschmitt was hit by AA and he had to crash-land at Martuba. Portenteously, Fw Reiner Pötgen wrote in crayon on the door of the Derna control room, "We come back! Happy Christmas!" The Germans were joined in the evacuation by their Italian allies.

British Claims

4 SAAF Sqn	Lt W.M.Copeland	Tomahawk	Bf 109F	Mechili 1600
	Lt W.M.Copeland	Tomahawk	Bf 109F damaged	Mechili 1600
	Lt D.W.Golding	Tomahawk	Bf 109F	Mechili 1640
250 Sqn	Flt Lt C.R.Caldwell	Tomahawk AK498	Bf 109 damaged	

British Casualties

2 SAAF Sqn	Tomahawk AN353 shot down; Lt L.A.Stone KiA
260 Sqn	Hurricane shot down by Flak; Plt Off Cidman returned safely

German Claims

9./JG 27	Lt Oskar Saar	P-40	SE Maraua 1600

German Casualties

8./LG 1	Ju 88A-5 WNr 5222 destroyed by bombs at Benina
3./KGrzbV 500	Ju 52/3m WNr 7035 destroyed on ground by bombs at Benina
	Ju 52/3m WNr 7209 destroyed on ground by bombs at Benina

Italian Claims

81ª Sq/6°Gr CT	Cap Giuliano Giacomelli	Tomahawk	Maraua 1600
	M.llo Giovanni Collovini	Tomahawk	
	Serg Magg Nello Meneghetti	Tomahawk	
	Ten Giorgio Falchi	Tomahawk probable	

Italian Casualties

81ª Sq/6° Gr CT	2 MC.202s damaged; Serg Magg Nello Meneghetti and Ten Giorgio Falchi unharmed

Friday, 19 December 1941

During the night of 18/19 December Benghazi was heavily raided (see Chapter 12 – The RAF's Night Bombing Offensive). At midday nine Marylands of 12 and 21 SAAF Squadrons were out again to raid Benina where 50-60 aircraft were counted on the ground. As the bombers headed for home Lt Stanford's aircraft was shot down by Hptmn Gerlitz of 2./JG 27, the crew of three being seen to bale out, although in the event only the pilot survived. Other Bf 109s then attacked the rear vic of bombers, two of the rear gunners being wounded and the engine of one Maryland being set on fire. On return three Messerschmitts were claimed to have been shot down, but it seems that once again the bomber crews had been misled by the typical Luftwaffe evasive tactics, the casualties of the latter amounting to slight (5%) damage to one JG 53 aircraft, which did inflict wounds on the pilot, Fw Alfred Seidl. The 24 SAAF Squadron Bostons again enjoyed an escort by the South African Tomahawks, attacking Maraua airfield, where considerable damage was claimed.

Five Beaufighters of 272 Squadron strafed vehicles and troops on the Tocra-Benghazi road, then attacking many more on the road south of Barce. Here fire from the ground hit Plt Off Crawford's aircraft, rendering the starboard engine u/s. Accompanied by Flt Lt Bartlett, he turned for home but was unable to maintain height and crash-landed 35 miles south-west of Barce. Bartlett at once landed alongside to pick up the downed crew, but in doing so his aircraft came under fire from two tanks and two armoured cars. Although his Beaufighter was damaged, he managed to get off the ground and flew back to base.

Sgt Whittle of 250 Squadron was less fortunate. When his Tomahawk was shot down by ground fire he had to walk 30 miles before reaching the safety of British-held territory. II./JG 27 reported that Oblt Otto Schulz of 4.Staffel was shot down by an Italian fighter, force-landing without suffering any injury. It is interesting to note that this was the same Luftwaffe pilot who reportedly had been forced to shoot down an Italian fighter pilot who appeared to have 'gone berserk'. One is left speculating about the possible cause.

From LG.125 11 Hurricanes in two flights strafed the Agedabia-El Agheila road, claiming six vehicles destroyed and 60 damaged. The aircraft, from 33 Squadron, became separated during their return flight and only Flg Off Cloete landed back at LG.125. Flg Off Wade came down at Giarabub, and Flt Lt Rumsey and Flg Off Dallas force-landed in the desert; there had been no news of Dallas by the end of the following day. A further loss was suffered when Wt Off Lamour of 80 Squadron, taking off to fly to Gazala, crash-landed. The bombs beneath the wings exploded and he was badly injured, necessitating the amputation of his legs.

262 Wing now moved to Mechili, while away to the east 269 Wing shifted to Maaten Bagush, were it would come under the control of HQ, Egypt.

During the day, under continuing pressure from the advancing British forces, 9° Gruppo CT now withdrew from Barce to Bir el Merduna; three unserviceable MC.202s were set on fire by their ground crews to prevent their capture.

British Claims			
250 Sqn	Flt Lt C.R.Caldwell	Tomahawk AK498	Bf 109 probable
12 SAAF Sqn	Bomber gunners		2 Bf 109s
21 SAAF Sqn	Bomber gunners		Bf 109
British Casualties			
12 SAAF Sqn	Maryland II 1630 shot down; pilot Lt R.E.Stanford PoW; rest of crew KiA		
	Maryland II damaged		
21 SAAF Sqn	Maryland II damaged		
272 Sqn	Beaufighter Ic T4783 'E' hit by ground fire, crash-landed; Plt Off H.H.Crawford and navigator burned aircraft then		
	PoWs;Beaufighter Ic 'P'; Flt Lt M.L.P.Bartlett landed to try and pick up downed crews; aircraft damaged by tank fire		
	and took off again		
250 Sqn	Tomahawk shot down by ground fire; Sgt R.J.C.Whittle walked back		
80 Sqn	Hurricane I crash-landed and bombs exploded; Wt Off Lamour badly injured		
German Claims			
2./JG 27	Hptmn Erich Gerlitz	Maryland	SE Benina 1240
German Casualties			
4./JG 27	Bf 109F-4 trop shot down by Italian fighter and force-landed. Oblt Otto Schulz safe		
8./JG 53	Bf 109F-4/Z damaged 5% in combat with Marylands; Fw Alfred Seidl WiA		
Italian Casualties			
9° Gr CT	3 MC.202s, MM7729, 7722 and 7713, burnt on withdrawal from Bir el Merduna		

Saturday, 20 December 1941

The night of 19/20 again saw heavy raids on Axis targets – this time the airfield at Benina where fires were seen amongst dispersed aircraft on the ground (see Chapter 12 – The RAF's Night Bombing Offensive). British commando forces launched an attack 30 miles west of Sirte, claiming to have destroyed 22 aircraft and other targets. Later it was recorded that the airfield attacked had been Tamet, where actual destruction had included four Ju 87s, four CR.42s and six MC.202s.

Early on 20 December eight Blenheims of 45 Squadron and six of the Lorraine unit took off to attack an armoured column at Ghemines, near Benghazi. They were escorted by 19 Tomahawks drawn from 112 and 250 Squadrons. South of Barce the formation came under attack by an estimated 12-20 Bf 109s, and was at once badly split up. The defending Tomahawk pilots claimed three Bf 109s shot down plus one probable, while the gunners in the French Blenheims added one further claim, although on this occasion the Messerschmitts actually suffered no loss. Their own claims were modest and undoubtedly accurate, for five Tomahawks were lost as were four Blenheims, with a sixth fighter and a fifth bomber badly damaged. Indeed, only one claim for a Blenheim was submitted by Lt Pietsch. Returning Lorraine crews reported that one of their missing aircraft had blown up, the Messerschmitt responsible then flying through the wreckage to shoot down a Tomahawk. It appears that Obfw Otto Schulz may have claimed a Blenheim which was not confirmed, also accounting for two of the escorting fighters, so he may have been the German pilot involved. One of the 112 Squadron Tomahawks flown by Plt Off Ken Sands force-landed in the Maraua area, some 20 miles north-north-west of Cheruba. Sands was picked up by some Senussi tribesmen and remained with them until rescued by an armoured car patrol of the King's Dragoon Guards, returning to his unit on 23 December to report that he had gone down because his aircraft had suffered engine trouble. Following this experience, he was rested from operations. Sgt Bennett and his crew from 45 Squadron managed, with the aid of some Arabs, to walk to Derna after carrying out a force-landing near Barce; they returned to the unit on the 27th.

A further Blenheim was lost when an aircraft of 84 Squadron briefed to attack motor transport, flew into the escarpment in a sandstorm near Gambut when trying to land, and blew up. The whole crew, including a passenger, were killed.

At around the same time as the bombers and their escorts had gone out, 33 Squadron despatched a pair of Hurricanes from LG.125 on an early patrol along the El Agheila-Agedabia road. Here Plt Off MacKenzie encountered a lone CR.42, which he reported shooting down into the sea. A second pair followed, these being attacked by two 157° Gruppo MC.200s, Serg Alfredo Rosso from the unit's 357ª Squadriglia claiming one of the Hurricanes shot down; Sgt Greene's aircraft actually escaped with slight damage occasioned by a bullet in the fuel tank.

Somewhat later a further pair of Hurricanes came across a transport aircraft, which the pilots at once attacked. This was a Ca.133 'hack' aircraft of 153° Gruppo which was being flown by Ten Felice Mezzetti of the 373ª Squadriglia, transporting a number of the unit's personnel. As a result of the attack Mezzetti had to crash-land this aircraft 17 miles from Agedabia at 0915, but he accomplished this successfully, all aboard surviving unscathed, despite the two British pilots reporting that they had strafed the occupants after they left the aircraft. 33 Squadron subsequently reported that the Ca.133 had been damaged rather than destroyed. During the afternoon 112 and 250 Squadrons undertook a further bomber escort mission during which Sgt Burney of the former unit shot down a Ju 88 of II./(K)LG 1.

Air HQ now reported that adverse weather and the enemy withdrawal from airfields within range of fighter-escorted raids were again causing the main targets to become MT convoys.

Following recent losses, 239ª Squadriglia BaT now passed its remaining Ju 87s to 209ª Squadriglia and returned to Italy. JG 27 evacuated Maraua airfield as well as Derna, moving to Got Bersis and Magrun. Very large numbers of Axis aircraft were now being discovered abandoned on the various airfields as they fell into British hands. At Gambut 39 aircraft were discovered, all of which were write-offs. These included 16 Bf 109s and Bf 110s, five Ju 87s, four MC.200s, three S.79s, an Fi 156 Storch, a CR.42 and a Hurricane painted with German markings,

British Claims

250 Sqn	Flt Lt C.R.Caldwell	Tomahawk AK498	Bf 109F	S Barce 0815
	Sgt G.C.Coward	Tomahawk	Bf 109F probable	S Barce 0815
	Plt Off J.L.Waddy	Tomahawk AM399	Bf 109F	S Barce 0815
112 Sqn	Plt Off K.R.Sands	Tomahawk AN372	Bf 109F	near Maraua 0820-0950
Lorraine Sqn	Bomber gunners		Bf 109	S Barce 0820-0950
33 Sqn	Plt Off MacKenzie	Hurricane I Z4572	CR.42	Marsa Brega early a.m.

---

33 Sqn	Sgt B.W.Challis	}	Hurricane I V7649	Italian transport a/c	a.m.
	Sgt R.V.Kierath	}	Hurricane I Z4499		
112 Sqn	Sgt H.G.Burney		Tomahawk AN289	Ju 88	1310-1430

British Casualties

33 Sqn	Hurricane I slightly damaged; Sgt Greene safe
112 Sqn	Tomahawk AN372 engine trouble; Plt Off K.R.Sands force-landed at Maraua; returned
	Tomahawk AK418 shot down; Sgt A.H.Ferguson KiA
	Tomahawk AN340 'N' badly damaged; Sqn Ldr A.V.Morello unhurt
250 Sqn	Tomahawk shot down; Plt Off W.W.Swinnerton returned
	Tomahawk AK452 shot down; Sgt R.H.Nitschke KiA
	Tomahawk shot down; Sgt P.C.Bell KiA – reportedly on 21st
45 Sqn	Blenheim IV V5948 'X' shot down; Sgt G.T.Bennett and crew returned on 27th
	Blenheim IV V613 'R' shot down; Flt Sgt J.Burns and crew KiA
GRB 1	Blenheim IV V6505 shot down; Lt Col C.Pijeaud and one KiA; one baled out
	Blenheim IV L8832 shot down; Flt Sgt J.Redor and crew KiA
	Blenheim IV badly damaged
84 Sqn	Blenheim IV T2394 flew into ground and exploded; Flt Sgt C.S.Bayford and 3 KiA

German Claims

2./JG 27	Lt Hans Remmer	P-40		W Maraua 0935
4./JG 27	Obfw Otto Schulz	2 P-40s		W Maraua 0940-0943
7./JG 27	Lt Heinz Pietzsch	Blenheim		W Barce

German Casualties

4./LG 1	Ju 88A-5 WNr 5258 L1+GM shot down; Oblt Bernhard Wiessmann and two KiA, one MiA
2.(F)/123	Ju 88A-5 WNr 0693 lost to strafing attack on ground at Magrun

Italian Claims

357ª Sq/157° Gr CT	Serg Alfredo Rosso	Hurricane	0650

Italian Casualties

153° Gr CT	Ca.133 crash-landed; Ten Felice Mezzetti and all aboard safe
19ª Sq/28° Gr/8° St BT	S.79 lost, Ten Andrea Silvestri and crew KiA
Unspecified unit	4 MC.202s under repair at Barce destroyed on ground by bombs

Sunday, 21 December 1941

During the night of 21/22 December the SAS troops led by Lt Fraser staged another successful sabotage attack, this time on Agedabia airfield, where they claimed to have destroyed 37 assorted Italian aircraft. As had been the case with the attack by 'Paddy' Mayne's group on the 15th, the results, though impressive, had been somewhat over-estimated, their total of aircraft destroyed being put at 61 in the one week. It had in fact been a somewhat more modest 29, but others had suffered varying degrees of damage.

Two pairs of 33 Squadron Hurricanes patrolled over roads. The second pair spotted a Ju 52/3m escorted closely by two Bf 109s, with three more of the latter flying above. Although this appeared to be the transport of some important personage, the Junkers was too heavily escorted to get at. However, an attack was made on the Messerschmitts and one was claimed damaged by Plt Off Wade.

Immediately following the latest SAS attack, 151° and 160° Gruppi CT moved to Arae Philenorum, 153° Gruppo going to Misurata, 6° and 17° Gruppi taking their MC.202s to Tamet. Here two days later 9° Gruppo, the first of the MC.202 units to reach Libya, would pass its serviceable aircraft to the two 1° Stormo units and repatriate.

British Claims

33 Sqn	Plt Off L.Wade	Hurricane I BD774	Bf 109 damaged	Agedabia-Agheila road
274 Sqn	Plt Off G.C.Keefer	Hurricane IIb BD880	Ju 88	Gulf of Bomba 1430-1605

German Claims

5./JG 27	Oblt Ernst Börngen	Blenheim	2m SW El Agheila 1502

German Casualties

1(F)/121	Ju 88 hit by AA E Msus; Lt Werner Bock and one PoWs
5./LG 1	Ju 88A-5 WNr 2303 L1+IN shot down in the Tobruk area; Lt Hans Peter and three MiA

Italian Casualties

151° Gr CT	8 CR.42s destroyed on ground at Agedabia by SAS troops night 21/22nd
160° Gr CT	5 G.50bis destroyed on ground at Agedabia by SAS troops night 21/22nd
8° Gr CT	6 MC.200s destroyed on ground at Agedabia by SAS troops night 21/22nd
Unspecified unit	2 Ca.311s destroyed on ground at Agedabia by SAS troops night 21/22nd
	S.79 destroyed on ground at Agedabia by SAS troops night 21/22nd
	2 Ca.164s destroyed on ground at Agedabia by SAS troops night 21/22nd

Monday, 22 December 1941

By now Air HQ Western Desert, had established itself at Bu Amud, about ten miles north of Sidi Rezegh. With several fighter units now based at Mechili it was possible to attack Magrun where the airfield had become very congested with Axis aircraft, their units all desperate for fuel. The day bombers were now located at Gambut, Sidi Rezegh and Bu Amud, which rendered it impossible for the Marylands to take part in such raids, but the Bostons of 24 SAAF Squadron were in range.

A dozen Tomahawks from 2 SAAF and 4 SAAF Squadrons were ordered to provide cover for 13 RAF Tomahawks from 112 and 250 Squadrons, led by Lt Col Wilmott. On arrival about 25 Axis aircraft were seen landing and taking off, the Commonwealth pilots claiming four Ju 87s, a Ju 88, a Bf 109 and an MC.202 shot down, with a Ju 52/3m and two more Ju 87s claimed as probables, plus several others damaged. Just as the formation, all ammunition exhausted, prepared to leave the area, 16 more Ju 52/3ms were seen coming in to land, about which nothing could be done. These were loaded with barrels of fuel which allowed the evacuation of aircraft to Sirte and Arae Philenorum to commence. The only loss was a single 4 SAAF Squadron Tomahawk, the pilot of which returned later.

The South African fighters then escorted 24 SAAF Squadron's Bostons to the same target in the afternoon when four more aircraft were claimed to have been destroyed. Finally, Blenheims escorted by Tomahawks, renewed the attack, claiming two more Ju 52/3ms, two probables and two damaged, again all on the ground. Flt Lt Caldwell in one of the escorting Tomahawks of 250 Squadron, claimed a Bf 109 shot down.

Bf 109Fs of 7./JG 53, showing the famous 'Pik As' (Ace of Spades) marking of III Gruppe on their noses.

During a strafing attack along the Agedabia road, two Beaufighters of 272 Squadron were hit, Plt Off Orr's aircraft being shot down while in the other Sgt Lowes was badly wounded in the foot and twice fainted from loss of blood during the return flight, making for Tobruk. His observer, Sgt C.F.Cutting: "...took over the controls – a difficult task in a Beaufighter – on both occasions, navigated the aircraft and revived the pilot, eventually bringing him back across 300 miles of desert to one of our landing grounds where the pilot was able to make a landing." These words were from the citation for an immediate award of the DFM to Cutting for this performance.

British Claims

250 Sqn	Sgt G.C.Coward	Tomahawk	Ju 87 damaged	Magrun 0940
	Sgt F.M.Twemlow	Tomahawk	Ju 87	Magrun 0940
112 Sqn	Flt Lt D.F.Westenra	Tomahawk AN303	} Ju 87 damaged	Magrun 0945-1130
	Flt Lt D.F.Westenra	Tomahawk AN303	} Ju 87	Magrun 0945-1130
	Plt Off J.P.Bartle	Tomahawk AN274		
	Sgt K.F.Carson	Tomahawk AK531	} Ju 87 probable	Magrun 1030-1100
	Sgt K.F.Carson	Tomahawk AK531	} Ju 87 probable	Magrun
	Plt Off N.F.Duke	Tomahawk AK354		
	Plt Off N.F.Duke	Tomahawk	Bf 109F	W Magrun, near coast 1030-1100
	Plt Off N.F.Duke	Tomahawk	Ju 52/3m probable	S Benghazi 1030-1100
4 SAAF Sqn	Capt A.C.Bosman	Tomahawk	Ju 87	Magrun airfield 1030
	Capt A.C.Bosman	Tomahawk	Ju 87 damaged	Magrun airfield 1030
	Lt D.W.Golding	Tomahawk	MC.202	Magrun airfield 1030
	Lt W.M.Langerman	Tomahawk AN247	Bf 109 damaged	Magrun airfield 1030
2 SAAF Sqn	Capt V.P.J.Doherty	Tomahawk	Ju 87	Magrun airfield 1410-1610
	Lt E.C.Saville	Tomahawk	Ju 88	on ground and one Damaged Magrun airfield 1030
	Lt R.P.Lofhagen	Tomahawk	Ju 52/3m on ground	Magrun airfield 1410-1610
	Col L.A.Wilmott	Tomahawk	Ju 52/3m on ground	Magrun airfield 1410-1610
	Maj G.C.Krummek	Tomahawk	Do 17 or Do 215	on ground Magrun airfield
Bomber unit		Blenheim crews	2 Ju 52/3ms	on ground Magrun airfield
		Blenheim crews	2 Ju 52/3ms probable	on ground Magrun airfield
		Blenheim crews	2 Ju 52/3ms damaged	on ground Magrun airfield
24 SAAF Sqn		Boston crews	4 e/a	on ground Magrun airfield
250 Sqn	Flt Lt C.R.Caldwell	Tomahawk AK498	Bf 109	

British Casualties

4 SAAF Sqn	Tomahawk AN247 DX- M FTR; Lt W.M. Langerman MiA, returned later
272 Sqn	Beaufighter Ic FTR; Plt Off K.B.Orr/Sgt Jackson PoWs
	Beaufighter I damaged; Sgt Lowes WiA, observer Sgt C.F.Cutting, safe

German Casualties

4./StG 2	Ju 87 shot down S Agedabia; pilot Gefr Willi Becker KiA
	Ju 87 in combat Sidi Ahmed el Magrun; gunner Uffz Georg Claus WiA

Tuesday, 23 December 1941

The air forces on both sides were suffering severely from fuel and spare parts shortages following a month of concentrated operations. Indeed, JG 27 would be reduced to no more than six serviceable Bf 109s by the end of the day. 3 SAAF Wing was in no better shape. It had already been decided a few days earlier that 24 SAAF Squadron should be withdrawn due to oil consumption problems with the engines of its Bostons, and that 12 SAAF Squadron should hand over its remaining Marylands to 21 SAAF Squadron and itself withdraw for re-equipment.

Thus it was that when called upon to attack targets in the Agedabia-Agheila area on this date, 12 Squadron could put up just four Marylands for its last operation before withdrawing. These were joined by two more aircraft from 21 Squadron, all taking off from LG.147 at 0920 to attack the airfield at Arae (or Arco) Philenorum (Marble Arch to the British forces) from high altitude. Having bombed the objective, the South Africans were attacked by two 1./JG 27 Bf 109s as they departed, two of the 12 Squadron aircraft being shot down over Msus. The crew of AH382 were all killed, but Lt Morgan managed to crash-land 'J', the crew being picked up by tank crews of 7th Armoured Division. Some time later Morgan and one of his crew returned to the unit, the other two being delivered to hospital in Tobruk, where they were retained.

Shortly after these events, five Beaufighters of 272 Squadron commenced a sortie towards the same target, but as they approached they were intercepted by Oblt Gerhard Homuth of 3./JG 27, who was engaged in a sortie to Agheila, and who at once shot down two of these aircraft flown by Flg Offs Baker and Lee.

British Claims

272 Sqn	Sgt R.J.G.Demoulin	Beaufighter Ic 'N'	Ju 52/3m probable	Agedabia airfield 1055-
	Flg Off J.H.Baker	Beaufighter Ic	Ju 52/3m	

British Casualties

12 SAAF Sqn	Maryland II 1618 'J' crash-landed; Lt C.J.Morgan and three WiA but rescued
	Maryland II AH382 shot down; Lt H.C.Lotz and crew KiA
272 Sqn	Beaufighter Ic shot down; Flg Off J.H.Baker and navigator KiA
	Beaufighter Ic shot down; Flg Off N.K.Lee and navigator survived

German Claims

1./JG 27	Oblt Ludwig Franzisket	Maryland	NE Agedabia 1224
	Lt Hans Remmer	Martin 167	NE Agedabia 1225
3./JG 27	Oblt Gerhard Homuth	2 Beaufighters	E Arco Philenorum 1400-1410

Bf 109Fs of II./JG 27 carrying the unit's 'Berliner Bäer' (Berlin Bear) marking on their noses. They are seen here at new year 1942.

Wednesday, 24 December 1941

The Tomahawks of 112, 250, 2 SAAF and 4 SAAF Squadrons again operated together from Msus, strafing the El Agheila-Agedabia road and the Agheila airfield where Sgt McQueen of 112 Squadron claimed to have destroyed a Ju 52/3m on the ground. Meanwhile the advanced party of the wing also arrived here, the rest still being at Antelat. Ten Hurricanes from 94 Squadron then provided cover for others of 260 Squadron on a sweep over the area south-east of Agedabia. Here they were attacked by JG 27 Bf 109s, reported as being four to six in number, and the pilots at once went into a defensive circle. From this Plt Off Thompson claimed a Messerschmitt as a probable "going down pouring black smoke" – possibly the usual exhaust from the 109's booster in a getaway dive. Meanwhile, Sgt Maxwell claimed another damaged, although his own aircraft was badly shot-up. What does seem certain, however, is that one or other of these pilots had hit the aircraft flown by Oblt Graf von Kageneck of III./JG 27. During this engagement this pilot was hit and wounded in the stomach by a fighter which broke out of a defensive circle to fire at him – although the Germans identified them as Tomahawks. Kageneck managed to struggle back to base, but would die of this wound on 12 January.

It was a black day for the Luftwaffe, for not only was the top-scoring pilot of JG 27 mortally wounded, but the commanding officer of III./ZG 26, Hptmn Thomas Steinberger, was lost over the sea near Crete together with a Bf 110 of 9.Staffel flown by Fw Max Hohmann, during a ferry flight from Athens to the island.

It had been a bad day for the Regia Aeronautica also, but for a different reason. Italian fighter units at Nofilia and Arae Philenorum were grounded for lack of fuel, because, they reported "…the amount sent to refuel them was taken by the Germans along the road".

That afternoon two Beaufighters of 272 Squadron carried out a sweep over the Agheila road during which they were attacked by Bf 109s. Flg Off Roman claimed to have shot one of these down, while Lt Nitzsche of 8./JG 27 claimed to have destroyed both Beaufighters. In practice, both sides seem to have escaped unscathed on this occasion.

British Claims

250 Sqn	Flt Lt CR.Caldwell	Tomahawk AK498	Bf 109 damaged	Msus
272 Sqn	Flg Off C.L.Roman	Beaufighter Ic 'H'	Bf 109	Ras Lanuf 1405
94 Sqn	Sgt M.M.Maxwell	Hurricane IIb BD899	Bf 109F probable	SE Agedabia 1600
	Plt Off W.J.C.Thompson		Bf 109 probable	

British Casualties

94 Sqn	Hurricane IIb badly damaged; Sgt M.M.Maxwell unhurt

German Claims

8./JG 27	Lt Hans Nitzsche	2 Beaufighters	Gulf of El Agheila

German Casualties

9./JG 27	Bf 109F-4 trop damaged 60%; Oblt Erbo Graf von Kageneck WiA, died 12 January 1942
III./ZG 26	Bf 110 MiA; Hptmn Thomas Steinberger and crew lost over sea near Crete
9./ZG 26	Bf 110 MiA; Fw Max Hohmann and crew lost over sea near Crete

Thursday, 25 December 1941

Further strafing sorties were undertaken by British units during the day, but without encountering either the Luftwaffe or the Regia Aeronautica. Ground fire remained as dangerous as ever, and when the Tomahawk squadrons swept along the Agedabia-Beda Fomm-Antelat road, Sgt Creighton's 250 Squadron Tomahawk was shot down, though he was able to return safely. They were followed by 94 and 260 Squadrons to the same area, and here Sgt McKay's Hurricane was also shot down. Wg Cdr Howard Mayers landed his Hurricane nearby, allowing McKay to climb aboard and be flown back to base.

British Casualties

250 Sqn	Tomahawk FTR; Sgt F.A.Creighton MiA
260 Sqn	Hurricane I shot down by ground fire; Sgt W.R.McKay picked up by Hurricane and returned

German Casualties

1./JG 27	Bf 109F-4 trop damaged 45% by AA; Oblt Ludwig Franzisket WiA

Friday, 26 December 1941

Flg Off Patterson, a tactical reconnaissance pilot with 208 Squadron but who was attached to 33 Squadron, set off for a long-range sortie at 1030 to reconnoitre the coastal area. When near Agheila at 1140 his Hurricane was intercepted by II./JG 27's Hptmn Gerlitz, who shot it down.

80 Squadron's airfield at El Adem was accurately bombed by Ju 88s which destroyed one Hurricane and damaged two more.

On this date 803 Squadron welcomed a new commanding officer when Lt Cdr A.F.Black who had distinguished himself on Crete, was replaced by Lt B.S.McEwen. The Regia Aeronautica's Settore Est was now disbanded due to the loss of all its airfields, command of the remaining Italian units being handed over to Settore Centrale.

British Claims				
238 Sqn	Sqn Ldr O'Neill	Hurricane IIc	He 111 damaged	Gazala
British Casualties				
208 Sqn	Hurricane shot down; Flg Off Patterson			
80 Sqn	Hurricane I destroyed on ground by bombs			
	2 Hurricane Is damaged on ground by bombs			
German Claims				
Stab II./JG 27	Hptmn Erich Gerlitz		Hurricane	E El Agheila 1140

Saturday, 27 December 1941

An LG 1 Ju 88 raided Gazala during the afternoon, but was intercepted and shot down by Sqn Ldr Smith of 229 Squadron, the crew becoming PoWs. Tomahawks from 112, 250, 2 SAAF and 4 SAAF Squadrons machine-gunned MT between Agedabia and El Agheila, pilots claiming three destroyed and 50 damaged. Return fire from the ground damaged four of the British fighters and shot down a fifth. Flg Off Neville Bowker, one of 112 Squadron's star performers, crash-landed and was seen running from his aircraft; he was later reported to be a PoW. He had originally joined the unit in Greece where he had claimed his first two victories (see *Air War for Yugoslavia, Greece and Crete, 1940-41*). He had subsequently claimed the squadron's first victory with the Tomahawk on its return to North Africa, and when shot down his total had risen to ten and one shared. Later in the war (1 October 1943) the award of a DFC was gazetted, back-dated to January 1942.

During the day a Tac R Hurricane of 208 Squadron had been intercepted and shot down by Gefr Kasten of 8./JG 27. However, the day also saw the arrival at Msus of 3 RAAF Squadron, rested and re-equipped with their new Kittyhawks.

British Claims				
229 Sqn	Sqn Ldr W.A.Smith	Hurricane IIc BD785	Ju 88	Gazala 3 airfield area 1525
British Casualties				
112 Sqn	Tomahawk AN283 shot down by ground fire; Flg Off N.Bowker PoW			
208 Sqn	Hurricane shot down; Flt Lt E.W.Seymour-Horsley safe			
Unspecified	4 Tomahawks damaged by ground fire			
2 SAAF Sqn	Tomahawk AN 375? shot down by Flak Lt B.R.McFarlane PoW			
German Claims				
8./JG 27	Gefr Klaus Kasten		Hurricane	SE Agedabia
German Casualties				
8./LG 1	Ju 88A-5 WNr 4371 L1+KS shot down Derna-Gazala; Uffz Karl Keibl and three KiA			

Sunday, 28 December 1941

Following the successful attacks on Tamet and Agedabia by the SAS, Capt Stirling had decided to 'strike while the iron was hot' and undertake a further series of raids before withdrawing to reform and re-equip. Setting out as before from Gialo, Stirling himself was to head for Sirte again, and Mayne for Tamet, while Fraser targeted Arae Philenorum (Marble Arch) and Lewis Nofilia, all having departed for these destinations on the 23rd. In the early hours of Sunday Mayne's group was again successful in launching their attack on Tamet, this time with even more significant success. Although actually more profitable than their first visit to this airfield, things did not go so smoothly. They had found 27 aircraft present, but as they were setting the bombs, one went off ten minutes early, raising the alarm. In a brief fire-fight they managed to get clear without loss and reach their rendezvous with the LRDG, making a safe return to Gialo. It had been 1° Stormo CT's recently-arrived MC.202s which they had been able to blow up this time, nine 17° Gruppo fighters being destroyed.

None of the other three attacks proved successful, however. Trying to get to Sirte, Stirling's group became mixed up on the coast road with a column of Axis armour assessed as being of division strength. They finally got clear, but only reached the airfield an hour before dawn to find it now surrounded by considerable concentrations of barbed wire. They withdrew, although Stirling was able to persuade their LRDG drivers to join them in shooting up some 'soft skin' vehicles on the road as they departed.

At Nofilia Lewis's raid went badly wrong, his group being driven off after being able to claim only two aircraft destroyed. On this occasion the Regia Aeronautica did not list any losses at Nofilia, and it appears likely that the aircraft blown up were two which had already been abandoned due to previous damage. This group then set off for Arae Philenorum to pick up Lewis and his team. On the way they were attacked from the air, Lewis being killed and all the trucks put out of action. One vehicle was cannibalized from the rest, and this then drove on to meet Fraser, of whom there was no sign. In these circumstances the driver than made for Gialo, where they arrived in due course. Fraser's group had found nothing to attack at Arae Philenorum and had then reached an incorrect rendezvous point. Having laid up for a time to rest, they then began the long trek to Gialo, attacking two Axis vehicles en route to obtain food and water. They were finally picked up safely by a British armoured column and returned to base.

In the morning, 3 RAAF Squadron undertook its first sorties with its new Kittyhawks, accompanied by Tomahawks of 112 and 250 Squadrons. Meanwhile, Hurricanes from 260 and 274 Squadrons swept over Agedabia where Sgt McKay of the former unit claimed a Ju 88 shot down. Some time earlier a single claim for a Hurricane was submitted by 2./JG 27, but no loss has been found to account for this. During the day Fleet Air Arm fighters were active whilst escorting coastal shipping. Sub Lt Griffin intercepted four torpedo-carrying S.79s of 281ª Squadriglia AS 50 miles north of Ras el Milh, shooting down the aircraft flown by Ten Luigi Rovelli and forcing two more crews to jettison their torpedoes. Whilst so engaged, his Martlet was hit by return fire and crashed into the sea. Near Tobruk Sub Lt P.Fell of 806 Squadron spotted an He 111 which he claimed as probably destroyed. Further east near Sidi Barrani two Fulmars from the RN Fulmar Flight became engaged with a Ju 88, but Lt Sanderson's aircraft was hit in the engine by return fire, forcing him to come down in the sea from which he was subsequently rescued. A second S.79 was lost by the Regia Aeronautica when S.Ten Pasquale Marzuoli's reconnaissance aircraft of 174ª Squadriglia RST failed to return.

At 1730 Sgt Paxton led 11 of 30 Squadron's Hurricanes on an evening strafe of enemy positions in rather hazy conditions. Considerable light Flak, machine-gun and rifle fire was put up by the troops under attack, and Plt Off Theobald's aircraft failed to return, being presumed shot down over the target.

With 33 Squadron the commanding officer, Sqn Ldr Marsden, now left for the UK, his place being taken by Flt Lt Gould, who had effectively been leading the squadron throughout most of the month and who was now promoted. On the same day Sgt Wooler, who had been shot down on the 20th, returned to the unit on an RASC lorry. He had walked for five days, finally being picked up on Christmas Day. Next day the squadron would move to Msus.

The day was also marked by the return from hospital of Grp Capt Cross, who resumed command of 258 Wing from Wg Cdr Fenton. Fenton brought him up to date: "…our Wing was now working directly with XIII Corps commanded by Lt Gen Godwin-Austen with Brig John Harding as his BGS. Their HQ was located about 40 miles south-west of Msus at a place called Antelat where three new airfields were being constructed for us and to which we would move as soon as they were ready."

British Claims

260 Sqn	Sgt W.R.McKay	Hurricane I	Ju 88	15m SW Agedabia 1100-1240
238 Sqn	Flt Lt J.R.Urwin-Mann	Hurricane IIc	Bf 110 damaged	NE El Adem 1625-1714
805 Sqn	Sub Lt R.Griffin	Martlet 3895	S.79	N Ras el Milh
806 Sqn	Sub Lt P.Fell	Hurricane	He 111 probable	nr Tobruk

British Casualties

805 Sqn	Martlet 3895 shot down by return fire; Sub Lt R.Griffin KiA
RN Fulmar Flt	Fulmar crashed in sea when hit by return fire; Lt F.P.Sanderson rescued
30 Sqn	Hurricane I Z4709 FTR; Plt Off E.H.C. Theobald KiA

German Claims

2./JG 27	Lt Friedrich Körner	Hurricane	NE El Hasseiat 0855

Italian Casualties

281ª Sq AS	S.79 MM24089 shot down; Ten Luigi Rovelli, Serg Magg Ugo Scardapane and crew KiA
174ª Sq RST	S.79 FTR; S.Ten Pasquale Marzuoli WiA, co-pilot Serg Eraldo Cirillo and crew KiA
71ª Sq/17° Gr CT	MC.202 MM7759 destroyed on ground by SAS
72ª Sq/17° Gr CT	4 MC.202s, MM7868, 7869, 7755 and 7719 destroyed on ground by SAS
80ª Sq/17° Gr CT	4 MC.202s, MM7730, 7749, 7756 and 7760 destroyed on ground by SAS

Tuesday, 30 December 1941

4 SAAF Squadron's Tomahawks began taking off at 1220 for a wing sweep over the Agedabia-Agheila-El Hasseiat area. Six aircraft had got into the air when a reconnaissance Ju 88 from 2(F)./123 appeared overhead; these at once gave chase, two pilots catching it and shooting it down near Msus.

The day also saw the departure for Kasfareit of 112 Squadron as this unit passed its remaining Tomahawks to 250 Squadron in readiness to become the second unit to receive Kittyhawks. 33 Squadron moved to Msus.

British Claims

4 SAAF Sqn	Capt A.C.Bosman	Tomahawk	}	Ju 88	Msus airfield 1245
	Lt D.W.Golding	Tomahawk			
RNFS	Sub Lt D.W.Langdon	Hurricane I		Ju 88 Poss damaged	10m N Ras Redud

German Casualties

2(F)./123	Ju 88 D1 4U+HK WNr1529 shot down in combat; Lt Karl-Heinz Renner and two KiA; two baled out, one PoW, one evaded and safe

Italian Claims

165ª Sq/12° Gr CT	M.llo Romolo Cantelli		2 Beaufighters

Wednesday, 31 December 1941

Eleven Hurricanes of 229 Squadron escorted Blenheims of 14 Squadron to the Agedabia area during the morning, but here they were bounced by III./JG 27 Bf 109s, the pilots of which claimed three of the Hurricanes shot down; 229 Squadron in fact lost two, one pilot being killed. 2/Lt Jones, the pilot of the other aircraft, was initially reported to be safe with the Guards, but subsequently he was captured before he could return to the unit.

Hurricanes, Tomahawks and Kittyhawks patrolled over the battle area where during the afternoon Sgt Reid of 3 RAAF Squadron made the first claim for the Kittyhawks when he reported inflicting damage on a Bf 109 from a formation of eight.

Four Beaufighters attacked MT west of El Agheila, crews claiming to have destroyed a petrol tanker and two trucks and damaged 60 more vehicles as well as inflicting heavy casualties. An Fi 156 was also seen and claimed shot down, and a small tug spotted off the coast at Nofilia was claimed damaged.

Later in the day Plt Off Thompson and Sgt James Dodds of 274 Squadron scrambled after an intruder, but neither returned intially. Dodds had made several attacks on a Ju 88, seeing pieces falling off and an explosion in the port engine before it dived away steeply. Not having seen it crash, he was able only to claim a probable, but it would appear that he had in fact shot down a reconnaissance aircraft from 2.(F)/123. He then landed 30 miles west of Msus from where he finally returned to his unit two days later. Thompson, meanwhile, had returned safely, having also landed away at the end of the sortie.

British Claims

3 RAAF Sqn	Sgt F.B.Reid	Kittyhawk AK604		Bf 109 Damaged	15m SE Agedabia 1415-1430
272 Sqn	Flg Off C.L.Roman	Beaufighter Ic 'N'	}		
	Plt Off D.H.Hammond	Beaufighter Ic 'P'		Fi 156	Ras Lanuf 1425
	Sgt Y.Tedesco	Beaufighter Ic			
274 Sqn	Sgt J.Dodds	Hurricane IIb Z2831		Ju 88 Probable	Scramble 1645-1730

British Casualties

229 Sqn	Hurricane IIc BD726 shot down; 2/Lt S.V.Jones PoW
	Hurricane IIc shot down; Sgt C.W.McL.Burns KiA

An MC.200 of 364ª Squadriglia, 150° Gruppo Autonomo CT. This unit, led by Magg Antonio Vizzotto, had replaced the similarly-equipped 153° Gruppo by mid-December 1941.

German Claims

Stab III./JG 27	Oblt Erhard Braune	Hurricane	E Agedabia
./JG 27	Lt Heinz Pietzsch	Hurricane	E Agedabia 1125
	Lt Erich Schöfbeck	Hurricane	E Agedabia 1125

German Casualties

.(F)/123	Ju 88 shot down

So 1941 came to a close, although the Crusader battle was to continue for several more days into the new year. Before continuing the narrative, it is opportune to consider the more general events regarding the air forces which had taken place during December. As already mentioned, III./JG 27 and the Geschwaderstab had now arrived from Russia, but during the early days of the month, the remainder of .Gruppe had also returned after re-equipping in Germany. However, the now formidably big number of Bf 109Fs had in practice been considerably restricted in the number of sorties they could put up due to the overriding shortage of fuel. By the close of the year III./ZG 26 had flown 2,862 sorties in North Africa, 483 of them as ground-attack missions. Eleven aircrew had been killed in action, six killed in accidents, 27 were missing, nine had been captured and 16 wounded.

At the end of the year the Regia Aeronautica's Order of Battle had undergone considerable change. During mid December 153° and 157° Gruppi CT and the autonomous 376ª Squadriglia, had returned to Italy. These units were replaced by 8° Gruppo from 2° Stormo CT and 150° Gruppo Autonomo, all being equipped with MC.200s. Meanwhile 10° Gruppo of 4° Stormo (not yet in Libya) was in the process of exchanging its MC.200s for 202s. At the time of its departure, the active 153° Gruppo had claimed 19 opposing aircraft shot down, 12 probables and 35 destroyed on the ground. Much reduced in strength, 5ª Squadra would commence the new year with 31 S.79s, 24 BR.20s, 14 G.50bis, 34 CR.42s. 24 MC.200s, 35 MC.202s and just three Ju 87s serviceable.

As recorded on 18 December, the number of destroyed and damaged Axis aircraft at Martuba had been considerable. Since then the count at other airfields as they fell into British hands had yielded so far to less than 458 deserted or wrecked aircraft, about half of which were German. On Gambut were 42, on the Martuba strips were 37, at El Adem were 78, at Derna 75, on the Gazala strips 71 and at Benina 64.

Specific counts at Benina and other fields were subsequently undertaken and amounted to:

A Hurricane II of an unidentified unit at one of the airfields captured from the Axis during the Crusader advance. In the foreground is the wreckage of a Bf 110, the unit marking on the nose identifying this as belonging to III./ZG 26.

Derna		El Tmimi		Berka landing ground and satellite		Benina	
Bf 109s	11	Ju 87s	7	G.50bis	15	Bf 110s	5
Bf 110s	8	Bf 109s	4	S.79s	4	He 111s	4
Ju 87s	7	Ju 88s	3	Ro 37bis	2	Goelands	1
Ju 52/3ms	18	Ju 52/3ms	2	BR.20s	1	Ba.88s	1
Ju 88s	4	S.81s	3				
Fi 156s	6	**Barce**		Ro.63s	1	*Damaged*	
He 111s	3	MC.202s	5	Ca.310s	1	Ju 52/3ms	12
Goelands	1	Bf 109s	1	Ca.133s	2	Bf 109s	6
Gliders	6	Ca.311s	2	Bf 109Fs	4		
G.50bis	3	**Nofilia**				Ju 87s	7
MC.200s	4	u/i e/a	2	Damaged		Ju 88s	22
MC.202s	1			CR.42s	20	u/i e/a	1
S.79s	?						

Agedabia		Tamet		Benghazi Harbour	
u/i e/a	37	u/i e/a	27	Cant.Z.501s	3

This amounted to circa 203 aircraft destroyed and 72 damaged and abandoned. These figures were clearly provisional, and the numbers subsequently recorded have had a tendency to change from time to time. They may, however, be taken as representing a fairly accurate assessment of actual Axis losses up to this date.

This captured Hurricane I, V7670, is being inspected by personnel of 14 Squadron on Gambut airfield after the capture of this base and the recapture of the aircraft. Again the aircraft records are somewhat unhelpful, indicating that this machine served with 261 Squadron (Malta-based) and then 208 Squadron (TacR). It appears to have been put back into RAF service (probably with 208 Squadron), for it is reported to have been lost during a reconnaissance sortie over the sea on 18 July 1942.

The work of the RAF repair and salvage units aided greatly in maintaining the strength of the squadrons by recovering many repairable aircraft and returning them to service. This convoy of Queen Mary trailers show each vehicle to be loaded with a Hurricane.

For the British Commonwealth air force the bomber strength was weakened when the Blenheim-equipped 45 and 113 Squadrons left for the Far East; further squadrons were to follow them during January. During December the Fleet Air Arm's land-based fighters, which had taken such a valuable part in the early stages of the offensive, began reverting to their normal duties, first the Martlets and then the Hurricanes returning to shipping protection sorties once more. Some slight RAF reinforcement was received when B Flight of 213 Squadron moved from Cyprus to Edcu to assist in the night defence of the Nile Delta area.

CHAPTER 11

A NEW YEAR DAWNS – DARKLY

Thursday, 1 January 1942

The new year commenced with a number of fighter sweeps. From their base at Antelat, Hurricanes of 229 and 238 Squadrons undertook two such missions, during the first of which they encountered seven Bf 109s south-east of Agedabia where Sgt Case of the former unit was shot down. He returned two days later, claiming to have shot down one of the Messerschmitts eight miles north of Agedabia; he was awarded a probable. He had been wounded in the arm and nose whilst hiding under his aircraft which was strafed after he had crash-landed.

Blenheims of 11 and 14 Squadrons took off just before midday to attack MT south-east of Agedabia, escorted by Hurricanes. About 2,000 vehicles were seen, widely dispersed, south-east of Agedabia, and several were claimed to have been hit. However, one 11 Squadron bomber was hit by Flak as it was leaving the target area, and fell in flames with the loss of the crew.

It seems that the escorting fighters were again from 229 and 238 Squadrons, Flt Lt Johns and Sgt Metherall from the former unit each claiming to have damaged a Bf 109, while a third such claim was made by Sgt Waddell of the latter. However, Metherall force-landed two miles west of Solluch having been slightly wounded. Only one claim was made by JG 27 on this date, and it was possibly Metherall's aircraft which was claimed shot down by II.Gruppe's Hptmn Gerlitz during the early afternoon.

Bf 109F-4 trop 'Gelbe 2' of 6./JG 27 with an LG 1 Ju 88A-4.

The end of 1941 brought deliveries of Curtiss Kittyhawks to supplement, and ultimately replace, the Tomahawks. Before January 1942 was out both 112 and 3 RAAF Squadrons had been re-equipped with these aircraft. Here a number of newly-delivered aircraft are seen in flight prior to joining a squadron.

Shortly after this engagement nine Kittyhawks of 3 RAAF Squadron took off to patrol and strafe south of Agedabia. Fifteen miles to the east they encountered 16 Ju 87s and six Bf 109s about to attack Allied troops. At least three of the dive-bombers were Italian-flown aircraft of 209ª Sq BaT, led by Cap Gualtiero Pilot. The Stukas at once went into a defensive circle and jettisoned their bombs as the Kittyhawks dived down for their first major combat, the Australians claiming three or four shot down, one probable and three damaged. However, the unit's new commanding officer, Sqn Ldr 'Dixie' Chapman, who had taken over on New Year's Day, was shot down in the first Kittyhawk to be lost; he survived to return to the unit, but on 26 February would be replaced by Bobby Gibbes, it is assumed due to his lack of operational experience. Some months later he would be posted to command 451 Squadron instead. One of the Italian Ju 87 pilots, Ten Ezio Quarantelli, claimed a P-40 shot down. He and two other pilots then had to force-land near Arae Philenorum, having run out of fuel. Two of the aircraft would be recovered next day, but the third, in which Serg Vinicio Capriata had been slightly wounded, had to be written off.

Flt Lt Bartlett of 272 Squadron, who had escaped from Axis armoured vehicles in his Beaufighter in such dashing fashion whilst rescuing another downed crew during the previous month, was killed when his tent caught fire. Four of the unit's Beaufighter crews strafed a reported 60 MT in the El Agheila-Sirte area, claiming 12 and one fuel tanker destroyed and three damaged.

Bardia now fell to Commonwealth troops, 7,982 prisoners being taken, of whom about 1,000 were Germans. At the same time 1,000 British PoWs were freed.

British Claims

229 Sqn	Sgt Case	Hurricane IIc	Bf 109 probable	8m N Agedabia 0715-0835
	Flt Lt G.B.Johns	Hurricane IIc BD634	Bf 109 damaged	20m S Agedabia 400-1500
238 Sqn	Sgt Waddell	Hurricane IIc 'G'	Bf 109 damaged	Agedabia 1400-1535
3 RAAF Sqn	Flg Off F.Fischer	Kittyhawk AK610	Ju 87	15m E Agedabia 1555
	Flg Off F.Fischer	Kittyhawk AK610	Bf 109 damaged	15m E Agedabia 1555
	Sqn Ldr D.R.Chapman	Kittyhawk	3 Ju 87s damaged	15m E Agedabia 1600
	Flg Off L.T.Spence	Kittyhawk AK698	Ju 87	15m E Agedabia 1600
	Flg Off A.W.Barr	Kittyhawk AK599	Ju 87	15m E Agedabia 1600
	Flg Off A.W.Barr	Kittyhawk AK599	Ju 87 probable	15m E Agedabia 1600
	Sgt A.C.Cameron	Kittyhawk AK597	Bf 109	15m E Agedabia 1600
	Sgt A.C.Cameron	Kittyhawk AK597	Bf 109 probable	15m E Agedabia 1600
	Sgt A.C.Cameron	Kittyhawk AK597	Bf 109 damaged	15m E Agedabia 1600
	Sgt A.C.Cameron	Kittyhawk AK597	Ju 87	15m E Agedabia 1600
	Sgt A.C.Cameron	Kittyhawk AK597	Ju 87 damaged	15m E Agedabia 1600

British Casualties

29 Sqn	Hurricane IIc crash-landed; Sgt Case WiA, returned on 3rd	
38 Sqn	Hurricane IIc force-landed; Sgt Metherall WiA	
1 Sqn	Blenheim IV T2226 shot down by Flak; Flg Off A.J.W.Froggatt and crew KiA	
RAAF Sqn	Kittyhawk AK597 shot down; Sqn Ldr D.R.Chapman safe	
72 Sqn	Flt Lt M.L.P.Bartlett K on ground	

German Claims

Stab II./JG 27	Hptmn Erich Gerlitz	Hurricane	NE Agedabia 1520

Italian Claims

209ª Sq BaT	Ten Ezio Quarantelli	Curtiss P-40

Italian Casualties

209ª Sq BaT	Ju 87 Wnr 5798 damaged and force-landed; Serg Vinicio Capriata wounded
	2 Ju 87s damaged

Friday, 2 January 1942

At 1100 Hurricanes of 94 and 260 Squadron made a wing sweep over the area south-west of Agedabia, six pilots from the former unit providing cover for ten from the latter. When about 12 miles from the target area, the top cover was bounced by Bf 109s, Plt Off Thompson being shot down by Oblt Braune. Fortunately, he was able to bale out into territory in British hands, and was back next day. Four pilots managed to get bursts at the attackers, all claiming to have inflicted damage – but all the Messerschmitts returned unscathed. The day also saw the departure of another Blenheim unit as 84 Squadron left for the Far East. 80 Squadron rather exultantly noted that the first batch of the unit's pilots had been despatched to Heliopolis to collect new Hurricane IIc aircraft, armed with four 20mm cannon, to replace their ageing Mark I Hurribombers.

British Claims

50 Sqn	Flt Lt A.R.Hall	Hurricane I	Bf 109 damaged	12m S Agedabia 1055-1210
	Flg Off H.J.Mann	Hurricane I	Bf 109 damaged	12m S Agedabia 1055-1210
	Plt Off N.V.Glew	Hurricane I	Bf 109 damaged	12m S Agedabia 1055-1210
4 Sqn	Sgt Forder	Hurricane IIb Z5433	Bf 109F damaged	SE Agedabia 1105-1205

British Casualties

4 Sqn	Hurricane I shot down; Plt Off C.K.T.Thompson baled out and returned next day

German Claims

Stab III./JG 27	Oblt Erhard Braune	Hurricane	20m N Agedabia 1135

Saturday, 3 January 1942

Ordered to undertake a reconnaissance over the Agedabia-Hasseiat-Chonfus area, 2/Lt J.S.Iddeson of 208 Squadron took off at 0715, escorted by 3 RAAF Squadron Kittyhawks. At 0815 the formation was attacked by Bf 109s and Iddeson's Hurricane was seen to go down in flames, victim of Oblt Homuth of ./JG 27.

Around midday another sweep by Hurricanes was made over Agedabia, this time 229 and 238 Squadrons taking part. A reported four or five Bf 109s were encountered, two being claimed damaged, both British units returning without loss. The day also saw 80 Squadron at last collect the first Mark IIc Hurricanes for the unit.

British Claims

229 Sqn	Plt Off W.C.Russell	Hurricane IIc DG634	Bf 109 damaged	E-SE Agedabia 1200-1315
238 Sqn	Plt Off C.R.Forsyth	Hurricane IIc 'W'	Bf 109 damaged	N Agedabia

British Casualties

208 Sqn	Hurricane shot down; 2/Lt J.S.Iddeson KiA

German Claims

./JG 27	Oblt Gerhard Homuth	P-40	NE Agedabia 0820

———

Sunday, 4 January 1942

During the morning at 0840, Oblt Rödel and Gefr Monska of II./JG 27 each claimed a Hurricane sho[t] down, although Monska's claim was not confirmed. One of the gruppe's aircraft was reported to hav[e] been shot down in combat on this date, and presumably during the same engagement. HQ, Wester[n] Desert, recorded that during sweeps over Agedabia Bf 109s were met on three occasions, one of thes[e] being claimed damaged. The identity of the squadron involved has not been found, but may well hav[e] caused this Luftwaffe loss.

Three Ju 87s of 209ª Sq then took off at 0920 to bomb armoured vehicles in the El Hasseiat area. Th[e] aircraft flown by Ten Mendes Ceccaroni was hit by AA and crashed to the ground not far from Agedabi[a] killing the pilot; the gunner Av.Sc Guido Venturi was seriously wounded.

During the day heavy British artillery fire forced JG 27 to evacuate Agedabia and withdraw to Agheila while on the other side of the lines 1 SAAF Squadron moved up to Martuba to resume operations.

In the course of an evening convoy patrol in worsening weather conditions, Plt Off Scott of 3[?] Squadron was seen to break away and disappear. A search for him and his aircraft proved abortive, bu[t] his body was later picked up from the sea by the navy and he was then properly buried at sea.

British Claims				
274 Sqn	Plt Off C.D.A.Browne	Hurricane IIb BD821	Bf 110 damaged	Antelat area 1030-1100
2 SAAF Sqn	Lt. R.F.Loffhagen	Tomahawk AN294	Bf 109 damaged	0700-0920
British Casualties				
30 Sqn	Hurricane I MiA; Plt Off F.A.Scott KiA			
German Claims				
4./JG 27	Oblt Gustav Rödel		Hurricane	12m SE Agedabia 0840
6./JG 27	Gefr Otto Monska		Hurricane n.e.	SE Agedabia 0840
German Casualties				
6./JG 27	Bf 109F-4 trop WNr 8464 shot down Agedabia; Fw Wolfgang Gerecke MiA, returned			
Italian Casualties				
209ª Sq BaT	Ju 87 MM8031 Ten Mendes Ceccaroni killed, gunner wounded			

Monday, 5 January 1942

Five BR.20s from 3ª Squadriglia of 43° Gruppo BT took off from Arae Philenorum on a night sortie t[o] bomb Benghazi. During the return flight the bomber flown by Ten Costanzo Montazzoli crash-lande[d] in the desert 42 miles south of El Merduna. Three crew members managed to reach El Merduna on foo[t] after a two-day walk; two others who had been seriously wounded, were then picked up by a Luftwaf[f] Storch, but one of them, Av.Sc Sante Briguglio, later died of his injuries.

During the day an important convoy of war material for the Axis forces arrived unscathed at Tripo[li] – the second to do so in three weeks. Over Benghazi harbour, now in British hands, Hurricanes wer[e] scrambled to intercept raiders. Sgt Kelsall of 33 Squadron claimed one Ju 88 shot down and a Bf 1[10] damaged, while Plt Off Browne of 274 Squadron claimed damage to another Bf 110.

British Claims				
33 Sqn	Sgt A Kelsall	Hurricane I V7431	Ju 88	Benghazi harbour
	Sgt A Kelsall	Hurricane I V7431	Bf 110 damaged	Benghazi harbour
274 Sqn	Plt Off C.D.A.Browne	Hurricane IIb BD821	Bf 110 damaged	Antelat area 1030-1100
Italian Casualties				
3ª Sq/43° Gr/13° St	BR.20 Ten Costanzo Montazzoli and crew returned after crash-landing, one died of injuries			

Tuesday, 6 January 1942

On this date the Axis forces withdrew from their line at Agedabia before a heavy frontal assault could b[e] launched. Early in the morning five Ju 88s and three He 111s raided Bu Amud bomber airfield, bu[t] without causing any serious damage. One Heinkel was believed to have been hit by AA fire.

Later in the morning an S.79 of 174ª Squadriglia flown by S.Ten Filippo Milazzotto undertook reconnaissance sortie over Benghazi. Here his aircraft was attacked by a reported five Hurricanes. Durin[g] 20 minutes of attacks it was damaged, returning with several members of the crew wounded, althoug[h] they claimed to have shot down one of the fighters. The only RAF claim discovered was for a Bf 11[0] damaged, but the time and location indicate that the 33 Squadron pilot had seriously misidentified his opponent.

British Claims					
33 Sqn	Plt Off MacKenzie	Hurricane I Z4572	Bf 110 damaged	road W El Agheila	0945-1235
Italian Claims					
174ª q RST	S.79 gunner		Hurricane	over Benghazi 0945-1330	
Italian Casualties					
174ª Sq RST	S.79 damaged; S.Ten Filippo Milazzotto safe; Cap Mario Raimondo (observer) and Serg Angelo Zaccaria (co-pilot) WiA				

Wednesday, 7 January 1942

33 Squadron was ordered to undertake a TacR sortie over Agheila, to be escorted by 20 Tomahawks from the South African units. The latter were accompanied on this occasion by Col J.E.O.Marais, the air staff officer from Training HQ in South Africa, where he had been much involved in setting up the Joint Air Training Scheme. He had been in the Middle East since November, visiting the squadrons and undertaking an operational course. He had been attached to 2 SAAF Squadron on 21 December to gain front line experience.

Over Agedabia at 1300, 4 SAAF, which was providing the top cover, encountered six Bf 109s and Lt Copeland, who was straggling badly, was at once shot down. Flt Lt Christmas, Lt Clarkson and Lt Thorpe were then attacked, Christmas (who had been attached to the squadron) baling out. At that point Capt Bosman managed to fire at one Messerschmitt which made off belching smoke, for which he would be awarded a probable, while Lt Golding also claimed a probable. As the formation turned for home, 2 SAAF Squadron was attacked and was badly broken up, Lts Halliday, Reilly and Loffhagen all being shot down. Halliday and Loffhagen were both killed, but Reilly, on his first operational sortie, managed to bale out of his burning aircraft, but had great difficulty in pulling his parachute ripcord due to seriously burned hands. The chute finally deployed when he was down to only 800 feet.

Meanwhile, four Messerschmitts attacked Marais' aircraft. Lt B.R.Garner shouted a warning, but thought Marais could not have heard him, as no evasive action was taken. After the initial attack, Marais tried to force-land, but three of the German pilots attacked again when he was down to about 200 feet, and his Tomahawk crashed out of control. Garner claimed to have inflicted some damage on one of the opposing aircraft, Lt Lipawsky also claiming one as a probable. As the formation got closer to their base, a seventh Tomahawk went down, Lt Baker of 4 SAAF belly-landing due to engine trouble. He and Flt Lt Christmas would both rejoin the unit next day, while Lt Copeland, who had been slightly wounded, arrived back two days later.

The Luftwaffe pilots from I and II./JG 27 claimed five of the fighters which had been lost, their own aircraft actually escaping any damage despite the claims made by the South African pilots.

MC.200s of 92ª Squadriglia, 8° Gruppo escorted seven CR.42s of 3° Gruppo on a strafing mission. Serg Magg Nadio Monti, one of the Macchi pilots, suffered an engine failure and force-landed within Axis lines near El Merduna. He was able to get back to his unit on foot, two days later returning to his aircraft in an effort to get it back. However, a second engine failure occurred and he had to crash-land, this time seriously damaging the aircraft.

Headquarters, Western Desert, noted that until an airfield near Benghazi became serviceable, allowing Sector Control and RDF (radar) to be established, the port could only be defended by standing fighter patrols from Zt Msus, 70 miles to the south-east. 4 SAAF Squadron had already been tasked with this duty, but next day 2 SAAF Squadron would move to Antelat with its six remaining serviceable Tomahawks, to join their fellow unit in this role.

British Claims				
33 Sqn	Plt Off G Edy	Hurricane I V7649	S.79 damaged	Benghazi harbour
250 Sqn	Flg Off K.G.Hart	Tomahawk	S.79 damaged	1010-1200
4 SAAF Sqn	Capt A.C.Bosman	Tomahawk	Bf 109 probable	Agedabia 1300
	Lt D.W.Golding	Tomahawk	Bf 109 probable	Agedabia 1300
2 SAAF Sqn	Lt G.B.Lipawsky	Tomahawk	Bf 109F probable	Agheila area 1215
	Lt B.R.Garner	Tomahawk	Bf 109F probable	10m NW Agheila 1330

4 SAAF Sqn	Tomahawk AK406 crash-landed; Lt K.Copeland slt WiA and returned
	Tomahawk shot down; Flt Lt B.E.Christmas baled out
2 SAAF Sqn	Tomahawk AK518? shot down; Lt E.B.M.Halliday KiA
	Tomahawk AK525 shot down; Lt G.Reilly WiA
	Tomahawk AN380? shot down; Lt R.P.Loffhagen KiA
SASO Training	Tomahawk AN294 shot down; Col J.E.O. Marais KiA
4 SAAF Sqn	Tomahawk AN411? crash-landed due to engine trouble; Lt R.G. Baker unhurt

German Claims

3./JG 27	Oblt Gerhard Homuth	2 P-40s	NE Agedabia 1215-1220
5./JG 27	Uffz Horst Reuter	P-40	SW Gasr el Brega 1240
1./JG 27	Oblt Hugo Schneider	P-40	SW Gasr el Brega 1300
	Fw Günter Steinhausen	P-40	SW Gasr el Brega 1302

Italian Casualties

| 92ª Sq/8° Gr CT | MC.200 MM6520 force-landed due to engine failure; attempted to recover on 9 January, but crash-landed and badly damaged after further engine failure; on both occasions Serg Magg Nadio Monti safe |

Thursday, 8 January 1942

During the morning 21 CR.42s fighter-bombers of 3° Gruppo CT led by T.Col Innocenzo Monti, were escorted by 11 MC.200s of 150° Gr CT (Magg Antonio Vizzotto), with eight MC.202s from 88ª Sq, 6° Gr CT, led by Cap Dante Ocarso, as indirect support, to strafe units of XIII Corps to the south-east of Agedabia. Ten Kittyhawks from 3 RAAF Squadron had taken off for a sweep over the Agedabia-Agheila area and their pilots spotted the Italian formation, incorrectly identifying the top cover MC.202s as Bf 109s. The Australians attacked at once, claiming seven shot down, three probables and a damaged, for the loss of one Kittyhawk. By this point the CR.42 pilots had already claimed one Blenheim and two motor vehicles destroyed on the ground. Although 3 RAAF's claims included two of the biplanes shot down and a third probably so, no casualties were actually suffered by 3° Gruppo. The escorting fighters clashed with the attackers, pilots of 150° Gruppo claiming two Kittyhawks shot down and 6° Gruppo adding one more plus one probable. Italian losses amounted to two MC.200s shot down and six more damaged. Following this combat the Australian pilots reported that the MC.200s could out-turn their Kittyhawks.

A small mystery now intrudes into events. Having received both a DFC and Bar, Clive Caldwell flew his last Tomahawk sorties with 250 Squadron on 30 December at which point his commanding officer, Sqn Ldr E.J.Morris, wrote in his logbook: "An exceptional fighter pilot

Cap Domenico Bevilacqua, commanding officer of 365ª Squadriglia, 150° Gruppo Autonomo CT. He claimed his third (shared) victory in North Africa on 8 January 1942, having already claimed two Gladiators shot down on 31 October 1940, while in command of 77ª Squadriglia.

whose leadership and skill in combat have been of the highest order." – a rather more enthusiastic assessment than that made by the previous CO some months back. By this time Caldwell had claimed some 16 individual and two shared victories, plus numerous probables and damaged, making him by a fair margin, the most successful fighter pilot with the WDAF. In January Caldwell was posted to command 112 Squadron, which was just in the process of re-equipping with Kittyhawks. *Clive Caldwell Air Ace* by Kristen Alexander states "Caldwell took command of 112 Squadron on 6 January 1942"; Neville Duke's diary records on the 5th: "Heard today that Flt Lt Caldwell of 250 Squadron is to be our new CO." However he then indicates that on 9 January: "The Squadron is about operational now and we are standing by for a show at any time." On the 12th he recorded: "The new CO….came back from leave today…" *Shark Squadron; The History of 112 Squadron 1917-1975* by Robin Brown indicates that the first sorties were flown with the new Kittyhawks on 9 January, and lists Caldwell as joining the unit on the 13th.

In his logbook, however, Caldwell lists flying Kittyhawk AK658 from 5 January onwards, and certainly taking part in a sweep on 8 January when he claimed damage to a Bf 109. He claimed another possible damaged on the 13th, and one more on the 25th. It would then be nearly a month before he made any further claims. This may be a small anomaly, but possibly a significant one.

British Claims

Squadron	Pilot	Aircraft	Claim	Location
3 RAAF Sqn	Flg Off R.C.Hart	Kittyhawk AK617	CR.42 probable	Agedabia area 0845-0915
	Flg Off R.C.Hart	Kittyhawk AK617	Bf 109E probable	Agedabia area 0845-0915
	Flt Lt E.H.B.Jackson	Kittyhawk AK650	MC.200	Agedabia area 0850
	Flt Lt E.H.B.Jackson	Kittyhawk AK650	3 MC.200s damaged	Agedabia area 0850
	Flg Off H.H.Schaeffer	Kittyhawk AK645	CR.42	Agedabia area 0850
	Flg Off H.H.Schaeffer	Kittyhawk AK645	MC.200 probable	Agedabia area 0850
	Sgt R.V.Pfeiffer	Kittyhawk AK619	2 MC.200s	Agedabia area 0850
	Sgt R.H.Simes	Kittyhawk AK610	CR.42	Agedabia area 0850
	Sgt R.H.Simes	Kittyhawk AK610	2 MC.200s	Agedabia area 0850
112 Sqn	Sqn Ldr D.R.Caldwell	Kittyhawk AK658	Bf 109 damaged	

British Casualties

3 RAAF Sqn	Kittyhawk AK656 MiA; Flg Off A.R.Baster KiA
252 Sqn	Beaufighter T4149 on ferry flight, ditched off Cyrene

Italian Claims

Unit	Pilot	Claim	Location
8° Gr CT		Blenheim on ground	Agedabia 0900
8° Gr CT	Serg Adriano Vezzi	P-40	Agedabia 0900
150° Gr CT	Magg Antonio Vizzotto		
363ª/150° Gr CT	Ten Enea Atti	2 P-40s	Agedabia 0900
365ª/150° Gr	Cap Domenico Bevilacqua		
	S.Ten Fausto Filippi		
88ª Sq/6° Gr CT	Cap Dante Ocarso		
	Ten Raffaele Giannuzzi Savelli		
	S.Ten Alfredo Civetta		
	S.Ten Giuseppe Sparapani	P-40 plus a probable	Agedabia 0900
	S.Ten Roberto Sgorbati		
	M.llo Gian Lino Baschirotto		
	Serg Magg Anano Borreo		
	Serg Luigi Bartesaghi		

Italian Casualties

150° Gr CT	2 MC.200s MM6668 and MM 5342 shot down; pilot baled out and returned two days later
	MC.200 crash-landed
	6 MC.200s damaged

Friday, 9 January 1942

The tables were firmly turned next day, however, when eight Kittyhawks of the newly-equipped 112 Squadron and 11 from 3 RAAF Squadron escorted seven Marylands to bomb Marsa Brega. Oblt Homuth of 3./JG 27 dived alone on the Australians, shooting down Flg Off Chinchen's aircraft, which the pilot crash-landed at Msus, and that flown by Sgt Simes, who was killed. Ron Simes had just brought his score to five and one probable during the previous day's engagement, having been one of the more successful Australian pilots. The award of a DFM was gazetted some three months after his death, the citation crediting him with six victories plus one shared; details of only five of these claims have been found.

About an hour later 229 Squadron despatched ten Hurricanes on another bomber escort, this time over the Agedabia area. This unit was also intercepted by Bf 109s of I./JG 27, three 1.Staffel pilots claiming four British fighters shot down (three of them identified as 'P-40s'), and indeed four Hurricanes were lost. Two of the pilots survived unhurt, returning to the unit, but Sgt Browne was killed and Sqn Ldr Smith was wounded. Bill Smith was a very experienced ex-Battles of France and Britain pilot, who had claimed five or six victories by this time, together with a substantial 'bag' of claims for probables and damaged enemy aircraft. He would be awarded a DFC in March 1942, and recover to return to operational flying.

112 Squadron carried out a second escort mission during the day, eight of the unit's Kittyhawks providing cover for six Tomahawks of 250 Squadron which were themselves escorting seven Blenheims to bomb north of El Agheila. During the return flight Sgt 'Kit' Carson was attacked by a lone Bf 109 his aircraft being damaged, requiring a force-landing; however, no claim was submitted by any of the German pilots on this occasion. He returned safely, the second Sgt Carson to be shot down on this date one of the surviving 229 Squadron Hurricane pilots having the same name. Earlier in the day nine MC.202s of 88ª Squadriglia had been led by Cap Ocarso on a free sweep starting at 0830. The Italian pilots dived down to strafe Agedabia landing ground, where an aircraft and some vehicles were claimed damaged. Also on this date 79ª Squadriglia moved to Arae Philenorum.

British Casualties

3 RAAF Sqn	Kittyhawk shot down; Flg Off Chinchen
	Kittyhawk shot down; Sgt R.H.Simes
229 Sqn	Hurricane IIc DG634 shot down; Sqn Ldr W.A.Smith WiA
	Hurricane IIc Z5063 shot down; Sgt Carson returned
	Hurricane IIc BE116 shot down; Sgt Foulger returned
	Hurricane IIc Z5588 shot down; Sgt A.G.Browne KiA
112 Sqn	Kittyhawk AK672 force-landed ; Sgt K.Carson unhurt

German Claims

3./JG 27	Oblt Gerhard Homuth	P-40	Marsa Brega 1415
	Oblt Gerhard Homuth	P-40	10m N Gadd el Ahmar 1420
1./JG 27	Fw Günter Steinhausen	P-40	E Agedabia 1505
	Oblt Hugo Schneider	Hurricane	E Agedabia 1507
	Uffz Josef Grimm	P-40	E Agedabia 1515
	Fw Günter Steinhausen	P-40	E Agedabia 1530

Saturday, 10 January 1942

Severe sandstorms considerably reduced flying on this date, dust clouds reaching heights of many thousand feet and extending several miles out to sea. However, 94 and 260 Squadrons managed to undertake a sweep during which Sgt Weightman of the latter unit spotted a Bf 110 – probably a TacR aircraft of 2.(H)/14 – which he chased almost as far as Agheila, claiming to have probably destroyed it. The Luftwaffe unit did in fact lose one of its aircraft, reportedly to a P-40 north-west of Marsa Brega, the crew of three being killed.

Italian fighters had also succeeded in getting airborne, five MC.202s of 88ª Squadriglia led by Ten Giannuzzi-Savelli, took off at 0820 to escort CR.42s of 3° Gruppo. Diving down to strafe Agedabia airfield, the pilots claimed damage to three aircraft identified as 'Bristols'.

British Claim

94 Sqn	Sgt Weightman	Hurricane IIb BE117	Bf 110 probable	El Agheila

German Casualties

2.(H)/14	Bf 110 shot down by P-40 NW Marsa Brega; Lt Walter Scheller, and Uffz Johannes Engelke KiA

Italian Claims

88ª Sq/6° Gr/1° St CT	3 'Bristols' damaged on ground at Agedabia

Sunday, 11 January 1942

During the early part of the morning Hurricanes from 94 and 260 Squadrons, making a sweep similar to that flown the day before, encountered nine Ju 87s and six escorting Bf 109s attacking ground forces at

Bettaful, 25 miles south-east of Marsa Brega. Plt Off Crosbie and Sgt Stone of 94 Squadron each claimed one Bf 109 shot down, and it appears that the latter had brought down the 7./JG 27 aircraft flown by Lt Pietzsch, who baled out to become a PoW.

Around midday ten Kittyhawks of 3 RAAF Squadron and ten of 112 Squadron, escorted six Blenheims of 14 Squadron to attack 250 MT west of El Agheila, where a large oil fire was ignited during the attack. Six of the Australian-flown aircraft flying as extra top cover, were attacked by I./JG 27 Bf 109s which at once shot down Flg Off Jones and Sgt Cameron in the Agedabia-El Brega area. Flg Off Nicky Barr attacked two Italian fighters which he identified as G.50s, claiming one shot down, but then saw a Messerschmitt cause a Kittyhawk to crash-land. He attacked this aircraft and claimed to have shot it down as well, then preparing to land to pick up the downed Australian pilot. At that point he was attacked by two more Bf 109s, one flown by Obfw Schulz of II./JG 27. Turning into these, he claimed to have shot down one, and to have damaged the other (apparently Schulz's aircraft), but was then shot down himself by his opponent, crash-landing. Schulz, as was his way, at once strafed the Kittyhawk thoroughly, completing its destruction. Barr had been slightly wounded, but would be back with the unit three days later. He had now claimed seven victories in only two weeks – a most unusual feat for a WDAF pilot at this time – and was awarded an immediate DFC. During this combat another Bf 109 was claimed as a probable and one as damaged.

There is little doubt that one of the Messerschmitts which Barr had shot down was that flown by 1./JG 27's Oblt Hugo Schneider (himself victor of nine combats) who was killed. However, no Regia Aeronautica losses of G.50bis or MC.200s have been found on this date. Sgt Alan 'Tiny' Cameron had twice before returned to the squadron after being shot down, and he too had claimed seven victories and been awarded a DFM. On this occasion he was not so lucky, however. Taken prisoner, he escaped on the 17th, but was betrayed by Arabs and recaptured, then being sent to a PoW camp in Italy. Probably during this engagement Italian AA gunners claimed two aircraft shot down over El Agheila.

During the day 6° Gruppo headquarters moved to Arae Philenorum where it would be joined by 81ª Squadriglia on 15 January. HQ, Western Desert, reported that in the Benghazi area an Italian bomber was claimed shot down by the port defences immediately before being intercepted by a Tomahawk.

British Claims

94 Sqn	Plt Off J.A.Crosbie	Hurricane IIb Z5453	Bf 109	10m S Agedabia 0900
	Sgt R.Stone	Hurricane IIb Z5330	Bf 109	10m S Agedabia 0900
3 RAAF Sqn	Flg Off H.G.Pace	Kittyhawk AK690	Bf 109 probable	El Agheila 1240
	Flg Off A.W.Barr	Kittyhawk AK645	G.50	El Agheila 1245
	Flg Off A.W.Barr	Kittyhawk AK645	2 Bf 109s	El Agheila 1245
	Flg Off A.W.Barr	Kittyhawk AK645	Bf 109 probable	El Agheila 1245
	Flg Off P.J.Briggs	Kittyhawk AK643	Bf 109 damaged	8m S El Agheila 1505

British Casualties

3 RAAF Sqn	Kittyhawk shot down; Flg Off R.S.Jones PoW
	AK617 shot down; Sgt A.C.Cameron PoW
	AK645 crash-landed; Flg Off A.W.Barr WiA but returned

German Claims

Stab I./JG 27	Lt Hans-Arnold Stahlschmidt	P-40	NE Agedabia 1248
2./JG 27	Lt Friedrich Körner	P-40	N Marsa Brega 1250
4./JG 27	Obfw Otto Schulz	P-40	Antelat 1310

German Casualties

1./JG 27	Bf 109F-4 trop WNr 8488 shot down; Oblt Hugo Schneider KiA
7./JG 27	Bf 109F-4 WNr 8299 shot down; Lt Heinz Pietzsch baled, PoW

Monday, 12 January 1942

Hurricanes were engaged on two sweeps south-east of Agedabia and over shipping. Attacks on the Axis garrison at Halfaya continued, many of the sorties being undertaken by Wellingtons. Hurricanes patrolled here, seeking Ju 52/3ms attempting to drop supplies to the defenders, but while engaged on one such sortie, a 30 Squadron aircraft failed to return, last being seen apparently firing at a target close to the sea – presumably a Ju 52/3m. One such aircraft was reported missing in the area, indicating a possibility that the two aircraft collided or were mutually shot down.

During the day 94 and 260 Squadrons moved forward from Msus to Antelat. But now Axis troops were taking up strong positions between Maaten Giofer and Maaten Belchei, and from there to the coast.

British Casualties	
30 Sqn	Hurricane I; G.W.Ratlidge MiA
German Casualties	
II./KGrzbV 1	Ju 52/3m 1Z+LV WNr 6564 lost; Obfw Kohla and crew MiA, Sollum

Tuesday, 13 January 1942

Before dawn another 30 Squadron pilot intercepted one of the supply-dropping Ju 52/3ms in the Halfaya Pass area, but Flt Lt Davidson was able only to claim damage.

With daylight the Allied ground forces came under quite sustained air attack, nine CR.42s of 3° Gruppo escorted by seven MC.200s of 150° Gruppo being followed by eight Bf 109s. At 1330 seven Kittyhawks from 3 RAAF Squadron, operating from Antelat, carried out a sweep. Whilst returning from this sortie, four Bf 109s attacked, Lt Körner of I./JG 27 shooting down Flg Off Schaeffer's aircraft, the pilot force-landing at Msus. Here he was able to effect repairs to the Kittyhawk, allowing him to fly back next day.

Later in the day four Bf 109s dived out of clouds above 208 Squadron's airfield in the Antelat area just after the XIII Corps air adviser, Wg Cdr Charles, had taken off on a radio test. Several attacks were made on his aircraft which burst into flames. Charles baled out but was only at 50 feet and hit the ground before his parachute could open; as a result, he was killed. On this occasion no Luftwaffe or Regia Aeronautica claims for his demise have been found and it is assumed that the pilots attacking his Hurricane had lost sight of it in the clouds prevailing. However, II./JG 27's successful Obfw Otto Schulz was shot down by AA, but survived to return to his unit next day.

British Claims				
30 Sqn	Flt Lt R.T.P.Davidson	Hurricane I	Ju 52/3m damaged	Halfaya Pass area 0430-0640
3 RAAF Sqn	Flg Off R.H.Gibbes	Kittyhawk AK600	Bf 109F damaged	8m S El Agheila 1450
British Casualties				
3 RAAF Sqn	Kittyhawk AK699 force-landed; Flg Off H.H.Schaeffer repaired aircraft and returned next day			
208 Sqn	Hurricane shot down; Wg Cdr G.P.Charles XIII Corps air adviser, KiA			
German Claims				
2./JG 27	Lt Friedrich Körner	P-40		Antelat 1435
German Casualties				
4./JG 27	Bf 109F-4 trop WNr 8437 shot down by AA Agedabia; Obfw Otto Schulz MiA, returned			
Italian Casualties				
364ª Sq/150° Gr CT	MC.200 damaged by AA, Ten Alberto Spigaglia returned			

Wednesday, 14 January 1942

Whilst most Axis bomber activity was occurring over Benghazi harbour at this time, 80 Squadron launched a pre-dawn patrol over Tobruk, where a Ju 88 was spotted. Before the fighters could open fire, the bomber was blown to pieces by a direct hit by naval AA gunners at the port.

During the day command of 80 Squadron was taken over by J.R.Urwin-Mann, DFC, who had been serving as a flight commander with 238 Squadron. 112 Squadron now moved to Antelat where this unit also welcomed a new commanding officer; this was the newly-promoted Sqn Ldr C.R.Caldwell, DFC & Bar, from 250 Squadron.

During an early morning Tac R sortie, Flg Off Fortune of 208 Squadron failed to return from the Bir Suera-Giofer area. Initially he was reported missing, believed killed, but in May news would arrive that he had survived and was a PoW. There being no Axis fighter claims at this time, he is assumed to have fallen to ground fire.

At 1305 94 and 260 Squadrons took off, led by Wg Cdr Beresford, on a defensive sweep south-west of Agedabia. 94 Squadron provided top cover, flying a new formation of stepped-up fours. The top flight of this unit was jumped over Bir el Ginn by two Bf 109s of II./JG 27, flown by Hptmn Gerlitz and his rottenflieger, Uffz Horst Reuter. Sgt Phillips was picked off first, and Sgt Forder of the lower flight, who was straggling, was also shot down and killed. One of these was Gerlitz's victim, the other falling to Reuter. The former then returned to base with engine trouble but the latter tore into the rest of the top

On 14 January 1942, 94 Squadron's Hurricanes were hard hit by a pair of Bf 109Fs from II./JG 27, seven of the British fighters being shot down, six of them by Uffz Horst Reuter. Hurricane FZ-P, here being inspected by German troops after crash-landing, may have been one of these.

flight, Sgt Maxwell and Sgt Harvey baling out, and Flt Sgt Wood, Sgt Weightman and Sgt Stone crash-landing. Unaware of the extent of his victory, he claimed four on his return, but although he was able to confirm Gerlitz's victory, Gerlitz, due to his early return, was unable to see any of Reuter's, and his four claims were not confirmed. In fact he had shot down no less than six Hurricanes. All the pilots with the exception of Forder, returned safely.

Reuter's report of the action gives a very good description of the typical tactics of the Bf 109 pilots:

"We met some 30 Hurricanes flying below us. Hptmn Gerlitz selected the last aircraft of the formation which was weaving violently and this was mortally hit, disappearing downwards. Gerlitz then reported over the R/T that he had engine trouble and must return. I was not willing to miss such an opportunity and decided to stay. In the meantime the Hurricanes had formed a defensive circle, but one left this for a few seconds. I dived at high speed out of the sun, fired, and pulled up, back into the sun. The pilot baled out, and the plane crashed, burning. The British formation was now very agitated and confused. Again I dived into the whirling crowd and shot the wing and rudder of a second Hurricane to pieces; the aircraft crashed down almost vertically. I climbed again into the sun and next second dived vertically down again, pulling out for a burst, and climbing back into the sun from where I noticed a big cloud of smoke rising from the ground. My next attack failed and I hid in the sun, waiting my chance. After five minutes the formation calmed down and started on the homeward trip. I came down at very high speed, pulled out behind a Hurricane and zoomed sharply over it into higher and safer regions; the Hurricane went down like a torch. Once more I picked out a Hurricane and attacked, pieces of his tail unit just missing my cockpit, and again I climbed into the sun; the pilot baled out and the aircraft went down like a fireball. On the next attack, just before I could fire, the Hurricane zoomed up in a high and very sharp turn. I was close behind, and tried to jump over him. But my aircraft was as sluggish as a plank of wood. I covered my head with my arms and waited for the grinding crash, but nothing happened – somehow we had missed each other. Now I was finished and weaved home at low level."

A newcomer to 94 Squadron in January 1942 was Flt Sgt J.F.Edwards. He was soon to become one of the most successful Kittyhawk pilots of the North African war. He is about to undertake an early flight with the unit while it was still operating Hurricane IIs.

On this occasion the British realised that all the damage had been inflicted by only two Bf 109s and reported this in the squadron diary. 260 Squadron, lower down, were involved with two or three other Bf 109s, Flt Lt Hall claiming one of these shot down and Sgt McKay damage to another.

A little later 250 Squadron despatched ten Tomahawks with Kittyhawks of 3 RAAF and 112 Squadrons to provide cover to a Tac R Hurricane over El Agheila. Four Bf 109s attacked, inflicting slight damage on one Tomahawk. Flg Off Swinnerton then spotted two G.50bis or MC.200s, claiming one of these shot down on the coast. In fact there were no losses recorded by the Regia Aeronautica on this date.

British Claims

260 Sqn	Flt Lt A.R.Hall	Hurricane I	Bf 109	Suera
	Sgt W.R.McKay	Hurricane I	Bf 109 damaged	Suera 1430-
250 Sqn	Plt Off W.W.Swinnerton	Tomahawk	G.50	E Marsa Brega 1630

British Casualties

94 Sqn	Hurricane IIb shot down; Sgt R.H.Phillips returned safely
	Hurricane IIb shot down; Sgt D.A.Forder KiA
	Hurricane IIb shot down; Sgt M.M.Maxwell baled out, returned safely
	Hurricane IIb shot down; Sgt Harvey baled out, returned safely
	Hurricane IIb shot down; crash-landed; Flt Sgt Wood returned safely
	Hurricane IIb shot down; Sgt Weightman returned safely
	Hurricane IIb shot down; Sgt R.Stone returned safely
208 Sqn	Hurricane MiA; Flg Off J.Fortune PoW
250 Sqn	Tomahawk slightly damaged; Sgt Stewart safe

German Claims

Stab II./JG 27	Hptmn Erich Gerlitz	Hurricane	W Bir el Ginn 1533
5./JG 27	Uffz Horst Reuter	Hurricane	Bir el Ginn 1535
	Uffz Horst Reuter	Hurricane	Bir el Ginn 1541
	Uffz Horst Reuter	Hurricane	N Bir el Ginn 1545
	Uffz Horst Reuter	Hurricane	E Antelat 1550

Thursday, 15 January 1942

Lts Baker and Duff-Richardson of 4 SAAF Squadron whilst undertaking a patrol over a convoy approaching Benghazi at midday, intercepted one of 176ª Squadriglia Aut RST's Cant.Z.1007bis reconnaissance aircraft flown by S.Ten Renato Tobia, and shot this down. Following this engagement, the squadron was ordered to exchange its Tomahawks for Hurricane Is while engaged on harbour defence.

British Claims

272 Sqn	Flt Lt J.E.Lydall			Bf 110 damaged
4 SAAF Sqn	Lt R.G.Baker	Tomahawk	}	Cant.Z.1007bis
	Lt M.Duff-Richardson	Tomahawk		

Italian Casualties

176ª Sq/ Aut RST	Cant.Z.1007bis MiA; S.Ten Renato Tobia and crew MiA; co-pilot Serg Sabato Elia PoW

Friday, 16 January 1942

260 Squadron was now ordered to Benina to exchange the unit's Hurricanes for 4 SAAF Squadron's Tomahawks, but at the last moment this order was cancelled and the unit returned to LG.109. The South African squadron again put up patrols over Benghazi during the day, on one of which Capt Bosman and Lt Jackson intercepted a Ju 88 of I./LG 1 which was shot down into the sea.

Tobruk was raided three times during the day, but no significant damage was caused. HQ, WD, recorded that the pilot of one Hurricane (Sgt Foskett of 80 Squadron) shot down an aircraft believed to be a Bf 110 into the sea, then driving off a complete formation of 12 hostile aircraft; 80 and 803 Squadrons had actually launched a total of five Hurricanes between them in dissuading this attack.

At this point WDAF reported that it still had available 97 fighters, plus 25 more which could be made serviceable within 48 hours, plus 28 bombers with an equal number potentially available in the same two-day period. Coincidentally, Luftwaffe fighter strength in North Africa was:

Stab/JG 27	3 Bf 109s	of which	2 serviceable
I./JG 27	23 Bf 109s	of which	6 serviceable
II./JG 27	25 Bf 109s	of which	7 serviceable
III./JG 27	19 Bf 109s	of which	3 serviceable
JaboStaffel./JG 53	5 Bf 109s	of which	4 serviceable
III/ZG 26	8 Bf110s	of which	4 serviceable
TOTAL	83	of which	26 serviceable

On this same date Regia Aeronautica fighter strength (serviceable or otherwise) was:

G.50bis	26
MC.200	16
MC.202	30

British Claims

4 SAAF Sqn	Capt A.C.Bosman	Tomahawk AN315	Ju 88	Benghazi area 1000-1200
80 Sqn	Sgt R.G.Foskett	Hurricane I Z4420	Bf 110	Tobruk area 1500-1535

German Casualties

8./LG 1	Ju 88A-5 WNr 4353 L1+LS shot down over sea; Ogefr Rudolf Bösch and one MiA, one WiA,one KiA
2./LG 1	Ju 88A-4 WNr 5546 L1+BK shot down over El Daba; Gefr Paul Eising and three MiA

Saturday, 17 January 1942

Three Hurricanes attacked MT on the Nofilia-Marsa el Ameyia road, claiming 14 damaged. Other Hurricanes, joined by RN Martlets, provided cover for a convoy during which Sgt Paxton of 30 Squadron (an ex-250 Squadron Tomahawk pilot) shot down a Ju 88, the demise of which was confirmed by the crew of HMS *Carlisle*.

The day saw the occupation of Bardia by British troops; moreover, at Halfaya the garrison surrendered unconditionally, and without destroying the remaining stores or spiking their guns. 5,500 PoWs were taken and 76 Allied troops were released from captivity. 2 SAAF Squadron now moved to Martuba, while a number of changes took place within the staff of RAF, Middle East. Wg Cdr Peter Wykeham-Barnes arrived at the main HQ, while Sqn Ldr C.E.G.Wyckham was attached to Rear HQ. Wg Cdr Howard Mayers arrived from Antelat to the same HQ, and HQ, RAFME welcomed Wg Cdr J.A.'Prof' Leathart, DSO (a notable fighter pilot of the Dunkirk evacuation period, when he commanded 54 Squadron in Fighter Command) as Wg Cdr Tactics.

By this time Commonwealth forces had reached the limit of the Crusader offensive, and lines of communication and supply were extremely stretched, despite the occupation of Benghazi. Several major units had now to be pulled out of the line for rest and re-equipment, and these included the veteran 7th Armoured Division. Equipment of all types was in short supply due to the situation in the Far East, which would soon be greatly exacerbated.

Amongst the flying units, movements continued. On 18 January 3 RAAF Squadron would move to Antelat, with 238 Squadron going to El Gobbi. Following the capture of so many Axis aircraft during the advance, 1 SAAF Squadron had become the first to repair a Bf 109F to the point where the engine could be started, this example having been found on Derna airfield.

After the attachment of some of its pilots and aircraft to 451 Squadron, 40 SAAF Squadron had now been readied for operations as an autonomous unit with both Hurricanes and Tomahawks. However, 21 SAAF Squadron had been withdrawn for re-equipment, bringing to an end the service life of the Maryland as a bomber. To join the night defence of Egypt and the base areas, the first squadron of radar-equipped Beaufighter night fighters had arrived at Abu Sueir (See Chapter 13 – Blitz on Egypt). For the time being the RNFS remained available to the RAF as a reinforcement, maintaining at this time 18 Hurricanes at Tobruk and nine Martlets at Sidi Haneish.

The Free French fighter unit, GC N.1 Alsace arrived at LG.X, Ismailia, from Palestine, the unit's Morane 406s now replaced by Hurricanes. The unit was commanded by Cdt Jean Tulasne, its two escadrilles led by Capitaine James Denis and Lt Albert Littolf, who had both achieved considerable success during the fighting over Tobruk in the previous April.

It was also at this time that 80 Squadron received a letter from Flg Off 'Keg' Dowding, who had been shot down several weeks earlier and had become a PoW. This missive had been entrusted to an escaping army officer, and had safely reached its destination. He advised that he believed he had shot down a Bf 109, and that Plt Off Reynolds and Sgts Halliwell and White were all also PoWs. He had no news of Flt Lt Coke (whose body had been found in the meantime) or of Sgt McVean.

Thus, although much ground had been occupied by 8th Army, no overwhelming victory had been gained, and Rommel's forces were still basically complete and ready to take up the fight again at any time – as they were very quickly to do. Indeed, the Axis in North Africa were now receiving considerable reinforcement and re-supply via the much shorter lines of communication with Tripoli. At the same time the convoys despatched from Southern Europe were beginning to get through with substantially lighter losses due to the renewed Axis attacks on Malta. These had practically destroyed that island's continued ability to interdict these vital supply lines from sea and air (see *Malta: The Hurricane Years, 1940-41* and *Malta: The Spitfire Year, 1942*).

British Claims				
30 Sqn	Sgt T.G.Paxton	Hurricane I	Ju 88	convoy patrol 1000
Italian Casualties				
81ª Sq/6° Gr CT	MC.202 MM 7879 badly damaged at Arae Philenorum by incoming Bf 109			

Sunday, 18 January 1942

Meanwhile, throughout the day Beaufighters provided cover for two convoys, 272 Squadron being joined by a detachment from 252 Squadron which had flown up to Berka for this purpose during the previous day. The convoys were attacked repeatedly, six Ju 88s and two unidentified aircraft being engaged, four of which were claimed to have been hit before escaping into cloud. 272 Squadron's Flt Lt Lydall attacked one bomber, but this disappeared into clouds, while Sgt France in 'F' attacked one twice, claiming damage. Over convoy Boxer in the afternoon Plt Off Gunnis of 252 Squadron claimed a Ju 88 shot down and two unidentified types as probables. The latter would appear to have been torpedo-carrying S.79s of 284ª Squadriglia AS, one of which crashed near Nofilia with the loss of the crew, while all those aboard Cap Putti's aircraft were wounded. During these operations one Beaufighter failed to return, Plt Off Beet and his navigator being lost during an attack on raiding Ju 88s.

British Claims

272 Sqn	Sgt France	Beaufighter Ic 'F'	Ju 88 damaged	over convoy
252 Sqn	Plt Off H.H.K.Gunnis	Beaufighter Ic T4834 'F'	Ju 88	over convoy Boxer; 1420-1800
			2 u/i e/a probables	

British Casualties

252 Sqn	Beaufighter Ic T4833 MiA; Plt Off C.H.Beet and navigator KiA from attack on Ju 88s on convoy patrol off Cyrenaica

Italian Casualties

284ª Sq/ 131° Gr AS	S.79 MM 24083, crashed near Nofilia, Cap Elio Bellocchi and crew KiA
284ª Sq/ 131° Gr AS	S.79, Cap Carlo Putti and crew WiA

Monday, 19 January 1942
One vessel was obliged to drop out of one of the convoys due to engine trouble, and was out of range of fighter cover when Ju 88s attacked and sank her before Beaufighters could come to the rescue.

Tuesday, 20 January 1942
Bing Cross:

"It was terribly cold in the desert at this time and by some freak to do with sun-spots, wireless communication with Western Desert HQ was interrupted for long spells each lasting 24 hours. Since 13 Corps HQ found the same difficulty in communicating with 8th Army HQ, we were largely left to ourselves in conducting operations. I discussed with Fred Rosier our prospects for the advance into Tripolitania and we agreed that as soon as it started we should be prepared for greatly increased opposition in the air, and the inevitable losses we would suffer since there had been no change in the situation whereby all our fighters were inferior to the latest models of the Me 109. Because the distances to our base areas in Egypt were so great and the communications so poor, we decided to bring up before the advance started the two reserve aircraft per squadron that were held in the rear supply unit way back at Maaten Bagush. With these additional aircraft we would have just over 100 fighters on the four airstrips at Antelat and this comprised the major part of the fighter force in the Middle East at this time. Then on 20 January it started to rain.

"We had no meteorological staff in the desert since forecasting was unnecessary, the weather always being flyable. Now it rained and how it rained! Most downpours lasted for about half-an-hour and the rain was heavier than anything I had experienced anywhere before. The graded dirt runways were rapidly turned to mud and unfit for take-off or landing. Many of the tracks from the Wing HQ to the airstrips became bogs and impassable for vehicles. This was a very serious situation. On the Antelat airstrips the fighter force was quite helpless, and unable to lift a finger in its own defence, let alone defend the Army. The Luftwaffe were operating from sandy strips near the coast which we knew from previous experience dried quite quickly after even the heaviest of rain. When the enemy discovered our plight, as they were bound to do sooner or later from our complete absence from the skies over the front line, we could expect our airstrips to be attacked and our aircraft destroyed. The gun defences of the airstrips were provided by the Army was then, and the light ack-ack of Bofors guns, our main defence against low-flying fighters, though good, was far from sufficient to prevent any determined attack. The long term effects of the destruction of the fighter force, if this were to happen, were appalling to contemplate. The Army, though superior in numbers to the enemy, was only just a match for him if left alone to get on with the job. If it was to suffer air attack by an unfettered Luftwaffe as well as by the enemy land forces, then defeat as in Greece and Crete could be expected. To my great surprise, however, XIII Corps was not particularly worried when the situation was explained over the field telephone. They said that the front at Agedabia was quiet and it was believed that the first movement there would be our offensive to start the advance into Tripolitania.

"During the afternoon of 20 January the rain mercifully eased and in discussion with Rosier and the Squadron Commanders we decided that if we could make the strips serviceable by filling the soft spots with bushes and stones, we could at least provide a token presence in the air over the front and hopefully conceal our predicament from the Luftwaffe. When I went to bed that night I prayed that the dry weather of the afternoon and evening would continue during the night. My prayers were in vain. All through the night at irregular intervals the heavens opened and down came the rain. The noise of the downpour on the metal roof of my trailer was deafening. Then it would stop and the silence of the desert would return and after a bit I would fall asleep, only to be wakened shortly afterwards by the next deluge.

"When dawn came at last on 21 January I dressed quickly and went outside. My first step on what looked like firm ground resulted in my leg descending up to my upper thigh in mud the colour and consistency of chocolate blancmange. Water was lying in puddles everywhere. Because there was no lasting vegetation and therefore no root structure to hold the soil together or provide any form of drainage, the desert was waterlogged. By carefully probing the ground with a stick I reached the Mess tent 50 yards away. The cooks were busy making breakfast but were late because, like me, they had encountered problems moving from their sleeping tents to the Mess.

"Fortunately the field telephones continued to function despite the lines being laid on the surface. I checked with the Squadron Commanders and found that conditions with them were the same as at my Headquarters, so that all our airstrips were unserviceable. It had stopped raining, however. I called a meeting of the Commanding Officers at once. They made their way on foot as best they could, and when they were all gathered, I told them that it was imperative that we move from the Antelat area just as soon as we were able. I explained that there was an ex-German airstrip south of Benghazi, which seemed to have escaped the worst of the rain and which we would use temporarily, and we could cover the front from there. It would be a bit congested with all six squadrons on the one strip but we would have to accept that. The next problem was how we were to fly off our waterlogged strips. One of the Squadron Commanders said that his strip, though pretty bad, was not as wet as the others because it had been built on a slight ridge, and we all staggered off to look at it. It was certainly better than the others but even here, there was still the problem of the apparently bottomless holes filled with mud. There was only one thing for it – we would have to fill these holes with whatever we could find nearby, which in practice meant little scrub bushes and stones.

"We set about the task, some 2,000 men, everyone except the Bofors crews and the wireless operators on watch. In no time all were coated in mud from head to toe but everyone was cheerful, glad to be getting on with something constructive at last. By mid-day a strip, 800 yards long and 40 feet wide, had been prepared and was tested by manhandling a lorry on to it and sending it up and down a couple of times. We were ready to go. Fortunately, the rain still held off and the desert was beginning to dry. Then a signal arrived from the coast that the airstrip south of Benghazi was unsuitable because parts of it had been mined by the Germans. There was no alternative now but to return to the strips we had left some days before at Msus. We knew they were dry. I sent a 'Most Immediate' signal to Beamish telling him of the change, and got a reply within the hour saying that he did not understand the reasons for going to Msus but nevertheless agreed with the change. In the meantime the order of take-off by the six squadrons had been arranged and then began the most extraordinary take-off operation witnessed in the Desert up to that time.

"First, the Hurricanes. Each one was manhandled to the take-off point by 30 or more airmen under the wings and some on the tail. Then with the engine going full bore and amidst clouds of mud and water the aeroplane progressed slowly towards the end of the strip. I watched with some anxiety as the first Hurricane opened up for take-off. It went lurching down the narrow strip, the pilot rightly keeping the tail down until he had enough speed to give him some fore and aft control and then tail up and he was airborne. I breathed a sigh of relief. One after another the Hurricanes left the ground and then it was the turn of the Tomahawks. These aeroplanes were heavier than the Hurricanes but surprisingly did not sink into the mud as much; probably because they had larger diameter wheels. By nightfall we had despatched three of the six squadrons. In the meantime, my

Wing HQ and the advanced ground parties of the squadrons had packed up and were ready to move back on the main desert track from Antelat to Msus. It was to take them 24 hours to cover the 40 miles to Msus, many bogged vehicles having to be winched out by the winding gear of the accompanying ack-ack gunners. There was no rain that night and at first light on 22 January the remaining aircraft were manhandled to the strip and despatched. The ground crews left in their vehicles immediately the last aircraft was airborne.

"We had decided that Fred Rosier and a skeleton Wing HQ would remain at Antelat, keep in close touch with XIII Corps HQ and brief the fighters in the air by R/T as they passed overhead on their way to the operating area at Agedabia. My own Hurricane was at the end of the strip, but before leaving I went over to Corps HQ to tell them of the arrangements I had made. When I got there I sensed a certain uneasiness and John Harding told me that the Germans had attacked towards Agedabia during the night. He believed that the enemy move was 'only a reconnaissance in force and wouldn't get far'. I was startled: we had enough problems without having to cope with an enemy advance. However, the measures I had taken of moving the squadrons back to Msus, entirely because of the unserviceability of the airstrips at Antelat, proved so fortuitous a move that in the event saved all six squadrons and 258 Wing HQ from being overrun by the enemy.

"I hurried back to the airstrip, saw Fred Rosier, briefed him on the situation, warned him to watch closely with Corps HQ the enemy's movements and to let us know at Msus, by point-to-point R/T, of any developments. I then took off in my Hurricane and landed on a good hard strip at Msus half an hour later. My HQ had arrived some hours previously and had set up camp in its former location. I joined them there and was regaled with the story of their horrific journey through the night, with the frequent bogging of vehicles. However, all had arrived eventually at Msus together with the ground parties. With the ground drying rapidly, I hoped that the rear parties (those that had departed after the last aircraft had left) would travel quicker. This proved to be the case and we were all complete by mid-afternoon on 22 January. The ground at Msus was quite dry and despite the exhaustion caused by our journey from Antelat, the squadrons would be operational for first light next day, 23 January."

Wednesday, 21 January 1942

Occasioned by the weather, there were two days of aerial inactivity for the reasons just described. The line at this point had been established approximately from Marsa Brega to Bir el Ginn (ten miles south-east of Marsa Brega) - Maaten Balcheis - Maaten Giofer - Morada. On Wednesday, however, as Cross had sensed, had come somewhat alarming reports of three Axis columns moving eastwards. One of these, comprising 33 tanks, some other AFVs and about 200 MT was approaching Marsa Brega. The other two columns were five miles south of Bir es Suara, the northerly of these including 26 tanks and the southerly containing 60-80 MT and a few tanks. Overhead, Allied ground forces claimed to have shot down "one reconnoitring Axis aircraft".

However, XIII Corps, which had moved up after their successful operations in the Halfaya and coastal area, were not in a strong state, and would rapidly fall back on the Agedabia-El Hasseiat line in an effort to consolidate and stabilise the defence.

Although this Axis force had only three days rations and possessed less than 100 tanks, Rommel had decided not to inform either Rome or Berlin of this typically intuitive probing advance which he was launching. His reasons were that the higher commands were insisting on a period of rest and recoupment before any new offensive action was attempted. He, as always, sought to capitalize on any thinning of the Allied forces facing him – occasioned presently by their lack of further advance.

Thursday, 22 January 1942

At once Axis aerial activity increased. The Axis forces were now reported to be advancing in strength north towards Agedabia, while an Allied column was seen to be withdrawing to a line Agedabia - El Hasseiat. At Antelat 33 and 112 Squadrons were the last to go, the final aircraft to leave the ground doing so under fire from German artillery. Squadrons made for Msus, where they were joined by 229 Squadron from Gazala. Despite the precipitate flight from Antelat, only two Hurricanes and four Kittyhawks – all of which were unserviceable – had to be abandoned.

At noon 12 Kittyhawks of 3 RAAF Squadron undertook a sweep over the Agedabia-Getafia-Bettaful-El Hasseiat line where 30 Ju 87s escorted by 12 G.50bis, MC.200s and six Bf 109s were seen attacking 1st

Armoured Division. Two G.50bis, an MC.200 and a Ju 87 were claimed shot down, with two more G.50s damaged. Their opponents included three Italian-flown Ju 87s of 209ª Squadriglia, flying with German Stukas and escorted by MC.200s of 150° Gruppo, led by Magg Vizzotto, which had been attacking British vehicles in the Wadi el Faregh area. When the Kittyhawks attacked, the 150° Gruppo pilots claimed one probable and three damaged, but Serg Renato Carrari of 364ª Squadriglia was shot down and killed. As the Australian pilots commenced their return flight, they were bounced by a pair of Bf 109s, and although only one claim was made by Lt Stahlschmidt of I./JG 27, two Kittyhawks were shot down; Plt Off Giddy claimed one of these attackers damaged.

Under cover of the Kittyhawk sweep, Blenheims had attacked about 400 closely-packed MT north of Wadi el Faregh (15 miles south-south-east of El Agheila), bombs being seen bursting amongst these vehicles, appearing to cause damage and starting two fires. Later reconnaissance indicated that serious damage had been caused.

At 1430 ten Tomahawks of 250 Squadron escorted nine more Blenheims to the Bir es Suera area, west of Marsa Brega, to attack about 700 MT on the road south-west of Agedabia. This time the bombers undershot, and no particular damage was caused. The escort, meanwhile, saw two Bf 110s and four Bf 109s, attacking these and claiming one Bf 110 shot down by the commanding officer and three other pilots jointly. Meanwhile Sgt Twemlow saw three of the Bf 109s about to attack the bombers and reported driving these off, claiming damage to one. However, Sqn Ldr Morris and Flg Off Beresford both failed to return and were believed to have fallen to Italian Breda AA fire, gunners of such weapons claiming two aircraft shot down on this date.

At much the same time as this raid had got underway, eight MC.202s of 6° Gruppo led by Magg Marco Larcher, had taken off for a sweep over El Ahmar-Agedabia. 12 British bombers and escorting fighters were engaged – almost certainly the formation being escorted by 250 Squadron. The Italian pilots reported that they had 'strafed' five P-40s and some bombers, but submitted no claims and suffered no losses. Later, ten CR.42s of 3° Gruppo, escorted by 150° Gruppo MC.200s led again by Magg Antonio Vizzotto, attacked MT in the El Hasseiat area, leaving two trucks in flames and others damaged.

British Claims

3 RAAF Sqn	Flg Off R.H.Gibbes	Kittyhawk AK612	Ju 87	W Getafia 1245
	Flg Off R.H.Gibbes	Kittyhawk AK612	2 G.50s damaged	W Getafia 1245
	Flg Off P.R.Giddy	Kittyhawk AK604	MC.200	W Getafia 1245
	Flg Off P.R.Giddy	Kittyhawk AK604	Bf 109F damaged	W Getafia 1245
	Flg Off R.C.Hart	Kittyhawk AK691	MC.200	W Getafia 1245
	Flg Off R.C.Hart	Kittyhawk AK691	Bf 110 damaged	W Getafia 1245
250 Sqn	Sqn Ldr E.J.Morris	Tomahawk	}	
	Flg Off K.G.Hart	Tomahawk	} Bf 110	W Marsa Brega 1430-1630
	Plt Off C.W.Harris	Tomahawk	}	
	Flg Off Beresford	Tomahawk	}	
	Plt Off J.L.Waddy	Tomahawk AN444	Bf 109 probable	W Marsa Brega 1430-1630
	Sgt F.M.Twemlow	Tomahawk	Bf 109 damaged	W Marsa Brega 1430-1630

British Casualties

3 RAAF Sqn	Kittyhawk shot down; Flg Off E. Bradbury returned on 25th, shell shocked, having been shot down by the gunner in a Ju 87
	Kittyhawk AK736 shot down; Flg Off J.A.McIntosh KiA
250 Sqn	Tomahawk AN444 shot down; Sqn Ldr E.J.Morris returned on foot later
	Tomahawk shot down; Flg Off Beresford returned on foot on 28th

German Claims

Stab I./JG 27	Lt Hans-Arnold Stahlschmidt	P-40	E Getafia 1250

German Casualties

2(H)./14	Bf 110 shot down; Oblt Freudenberger and one PoW

Italian Claims

150ª Gr CT	Unidentified pilots	P-40 probable plus one damaged

Italian Casualties

364ª Sq/150° Gr CT	MC.200 MM 5156 Serg Renato Carrari KiA

Bing Cross:

"My station wagon had survived the move and during the afternoon I went round the squadrons. Everyone was in good heart and looking forward to resuming full operations the next morning. When I returned to the Wing HQ in the late afternoon I found the operations caravan functioning fully and contact with WDAF HQ established. I therefore sent a brief situation report to Beamish and then asked the Operations Officer if Wg Cdr Rosier had reported anything from Antelat. He said he had been unable to contact him on R/T or W/T. This was odd because I had impressed on Fred the need to keep us informed about the ground situation as interpreted by XIII Corps. No contact having been made with Rosier by 1600 hours, I decided to make a quick trip back to Antelat before dark to see if I could raise Fred by R/T from there.

"The wintry sun was low in the sky as I flew and was directly ahead of me, making forward visibility difficult. I was over the top of Antelat almost before I realised I was there, and overshot the airfield a little. Looking back down sun, the visibility was better and I saw that the site of Rosier's HQ was now empty. I was flying at 2,000 ft and I saw a column of vehicles headed by a few tanks approaching the now empty airstrips on the track from Agedabia. At the same moment the column opened up on me with a volume of light flak and I realized at once that it was the enemy. Reconnaissance in force it certainly was! It had moved fast to reach its present position. I sheered off and headed for Msus. On the way back the truth struck me. There was no Army presence between Antelat and the squadrons on the ground at Msus. What's more the desert was drying rapidly and it wouldn't take long for the enemy to cover the 40 miles, which it had taken our ground parties 24 hours to negotiate. I was fairly certain though, that they couldn't do it during the night. I called Wing on the R/T and told the operator to summon the Squadron Commanders and Wing staff to a meeting at the operations caravan right away. I landed just before dark and drove straight there to find that they were already assembled. I told them of my experience over Antelat. In the meantime, I was informed that we had received no replies from our frequent calls to XIII Corps and Rosier.

"There was no need for me to stress our extreme vulnerability at Msus. We would have to move further back until the Army stabilised a front somewhere. Mechili was the next airfield about 80 miles to the north-east and that was where we would have to go. There were long faces amongst the Squadron Commanders when I said the ground parties and aircraft must leave at first light, whilst the aircraft would operate forward to the Antelat area and land back at Mechili. One CO said, 'Some of my chaps have only just pulled in from that dreadful march from Antelat and have had no sleep for 48 hours.' 'Well,' I replied 'If we don't leave at first light we may well be in the bag by mid-day!' They all knew the truth of what I said and hurried off back to their squadrons. Though the men were near exhaustion, preparations for the departure started straightaway and then, sometime after midnight, all was quiet as everyone snatched a few hours sleep. I sent a signal to Coningham's HQ telling them what I intended. By this time I was pretty certain the situation at Antelat would be known at Tmimi, where the joint Army-Air HQ were located and they would fully appreciate the need for a hasty withdrawal to Mechili. Long before dawn I was awakened by the noise of vehicles and having dressed I went outside. All around were the lights of trucks forming themselves in columns and more and more joining from the airstrips every minute.

"We had a Flt Lt Young, a 'hostilities only' officer, who was something of an expert in desert navigation and he had been given the task and great responsibility of leading the convoy to Mechili. At the first sign of light in the east he came across to my trailer and asked permission to start. I gave it to him and wished him luck. He went back to his vehicle, pulled out a Very pistol, fired a green light high in the air, mounted his vehicle and started off eastwards at the head of his 400 truck convoy. As it grew lighter, the first of the squadrons was airborne and the ground crews who stayed behind to see the aircraft off, then ran to their trucks and set off to catch up with the convoy. When all the squadrons had gone I went over to my Hurricane, the airmen starting the engine as I approached. We changed mounts, the ground crew in my station wagon and me to the aeroplane. They were confident that they would soon catch the convoy up and I waved to them as I took off, setting a course for Tmimi, for it was high time I found out exactly what my superior HQ knew about what was going on.

"At Tmimi I saw George Beamish in his office trailer and gave him an account of the events at Antelat and the reasons for my ordering the move to Mechili after such a short stay at Msus. He appreciated that there had been no time to consult Coningham by signal and said that both he and Coningham were very relieved when they heard that I had extricated the fighter force from such a predicament. I emphasised that it was the rain soaking the airstrips that had dictated my decision to withdraw from Antelat and that if I had depended on XIII Corps and their belief that the enemy's advance was 'just a reconnaissance in force that won't get far', all six squadrons with over 100 aircraft and the Wing HQ would have been overrun and captured. Beamish said that word had come through that XIII Corps HQ at Antelat had very nearly suffered that fate themselves and were now on their way to Msus.

"When Coningham subsequently signalled Tedder regarding the debacle, he reported that the enemy advance to Agedabia and Antelat was "…quite unopposed and due to serious blunder of Guards Brigade which opened road". The first warning 258 Wing had (finally) received had come from Godwin-Austen's HQ at 1300 hours on the 22nd and was limited to the words: "Move back at once, enemy coming."

Friday, 23 January 1942

By this date Rommel had realized that the Allied forward area was only very lightly held, and consequently his forces were able to seize Agedabia. A column of 30 tanks and 400 MT was sent through Antelat and then south-south-eastwards to Maaten el Grara (45 miles east of Agedabia). A second column made for Antelat itself.

Hurricanes and Kittyhawks flew protective sweeps over Allied troops in the Antelat-Agedabia-El Hasseiat area, but only a few Bf 109s were seen. During an afternoon sweep Sgts Dodds and Wildy spotted five Messerschmitts below, Dodds at once diving on these and getting two good bursts into one. He saw pieces fly off this as it rolled over and dived away with smoke pouring from it. He did not see the final result, and was credited with a probable. Wildy had lost sight of the German aircraft almost as soon as he had spotted them, and as a result was unable to make contact.

Four Hurricanes of 33 Squadron were despatched on a strafing sortie led by Plt Off Lance Wade to machine-gun 100 MT and 17 tanks on the Agedabia-Antelat road, 25 vehicles being claimed badly damaged and three fires started. Canadian Don Edy recalled in his book *Goon in the Block*:

"Lance took off with me as his number two, and climbed to 500 feet before heading for the front. I almost screwed my head off keeping a lookout for enemy aircraft and nearly missed Lance when he headed for the deck after 20 minutes flying. He had spotted small dust clouds ahead, indicating vehicles on the move and gone down low to avoid detection.

"We hadn't flown more than two minutes when we saw a much larger dust cloud rise up on our right. This looked like enemy fighters taking off from Agedabia, so Lance wheeled around and headed for home. A minute before the turn I was scared silly about something unknown and a minute after I was happy as a lark. We still had orders not to tangle with the 109s if it could be avoided and Lance was doing the right thing in turning back. We could always come out again when there were no fighters around. I figured we would land at Msus, the raid I had worried about would be over and therefore all my fears were senseless. With this in mind I started to sing at the top of my voice.

"Suddenly Lance climbed to 1,000 feet and started to circle. I didn't gather what his plan was at first. After circling for five minutes, he headed for the deck, this time towards the German lines. My heart leaped into my throat and stayed there. Lance, instead of letting a few 109s get the better of him, had circled until he was sure we were not the intended prey and then headed in to finish the job. All my fears returned in full strength. Strangely enough they then disappeared the moment we climbed for the attack. Our dive was a complete surprise to the Huns and the excitement made me forget to be afraid.

"I can remember the first target very clearly. I was flying too low really and when the bullets left the guns some of them were hitting the sand well before the others reached the truck in my sights. A German, who was lying in the sand well out of the line of fire, suddenly jumped up and ran right into the cone of fire from the eight machine guns. This was the first time I fully realized the full impact of bullets striking. It seemed as though an invisible force smacked him and rolled him over and over like tumbleweed. As I pulled up over the truck, I could see a lick of flames coming from the back and out of the corner of my eye I saw a gas truck explode from Lance's attack.

"We made three passes at that column. By that time the Germans had their 20mm cannons unlimbered and were firing at us from all directions. There were four or five lorries with these ack ack guns mounted in the back. The sky was thick with little black puffs of smoke, but I was too busy and excited to pay any attention to them. I kept turning and weaving to make as difficult a target as possible.

"In the split second I was going to turn and dive on the last truck in line, two shells hit my Hurricane in quick succession, one in the engine and one in the radiator. The noise was terrific from the explosions. Then the engine ran down like a huge busted alarm clock and stopped dead.

"The cockpit filled with spraying oil and white smoke. My first thoughts were 'FIRE, the plane's on fire, get the hell out.' I pulled the seat harness and started to climb out of the cockpit to jump, then realized that the aircraft was only 100 feet up and a parachute wouldn't have time to open. I slumped back in the bucket seat and turned off the switches. The situation seemed hopeless, and pictures flashed through my mind of the plane burning, with me in it.

"All this happened in a matter of seconds. As no flames appeared and some of the smoke cleared, I began to automatically guide the plane. A Hurricane drops pretty quickly with a dead engine and I subconsciously pulled the stick back into my stomach. The aircraft ricocheted off the sand like a skipping stone. As it was travelling about 200 mph, it skimmed up in the air again. This gave me time and height enough to bring it down straight and level. The smoke was actually escaping glycol from the radiator. It cleared a bit so I could see the ground a few feet below. With one hand braced on top of the instrument panel and the other on the stick, I held the plane level. It hit the soft sand, skidded for several hundred feet and then dug its nose into the ground.

"I couldn't have been luckier. When I first hit, the cockpit canopy slammed forward and nearly took off the top of my head. The plane didn't ground-loop, or throw me around and the skid slowed it down to a point where it didn't flip over on its back. The pressure forced me forward hard enough to crack my head on the gun sight, but I wasn't knocked out. Blood gushed out over my eyes and I thought at first that I was badly hurt, but it turned out to be just a bad cut. It only took a second to jump out and run like a hare in case the poor old Hurricane exploded.

"I ran about 100 yards, then began to feel sick, and sat down. My head was throbbing and blood was all over the place. All of a sudden an aircraft circled overhead and I could see Lance waving to me. He had his wheels and flaps down and was trying to land to pick me up. The ground was too rough there, so a landing or take-off would have been impossible. After circling three times, trying to find a smooth spot, Lance had to wave again and fly off for the base. I waved back, but when he was gone I sat down, feeling more sick and discouraged than before. The most amazing part of Lance's attempt to pick me up, and the proof of just what kind of a man he was, was that all the time he circled my position, every gun in the German column was trained on him, pumping shells in his direction as fast as they could. He paid no attention to them and not one shell hit him. I'm certain Lance was truly sorry he couldn't pick me up and save me from what we always considered would be certain death. Strafing seemed to be such a dirty trick in a way; we figured we would be shot if we were unlucky enough to be caught by the people we were actually strafing.

"This was very much in my mind when an armoured car came across the sand in my direction. There was a German Officer standing in the front with a Tommy gun pointed straight at me. I started to run. Then saw how useless this was and stood there waiting to see what would happen next.

"When the car was 100 yards away the Officer lowered the gun and I had a flicker of hope. When he got closer he aimed it again and my heart sank right down in my boots. All I could think was, 'The bastard, he's going to shoot'. I could see a picture in my mind of a forlorn little figure standing out in a waste land, as though I was above looking down, on myself, with the German and the gun bearing inexorably down on me.

"Before I could recover from the scare, the car pulled up in a cloud of dust and the Germans jumped out, laughing at the joke they had played on me. They were highly pleased with themselves for having shot the plane down. The Officer, a very young fellow, came up with a pistol in his hand and said: 'You are my prisoner. If you try to escape you will be shot. For you the war is over.'

"I doubt if there is a lonelier feeling in the world than when one is first taken Prisoner of War...."

The day was also marked by the move of 94 Squadron to Zt Msus, but 229 Squadron, which had arrived there on the previous day, moved to Mechili. In the Msus area a Bombay of 216 Squadron, assisting with these moves, strayed over Axis columns and was shot down by Flak.

Saturday, 24 January 1942

Two Hurricanes of 208 Squadron took off on a dawn TacR, but were intercepted by a pair of Bf 109s from I./JG 27 which were scrambled from Belandah. Plt Off Stephens was then shot down by Uffz Walchhofer west of Agedabia, and was killed.

Bing Cross:

"When I arrived overhead Mechili (this) morning, it looked very crowded with over 100 aircraft on the airfield. Fortunately, the Luftwaffe had been left far behind by the Wehrmacht and were out of range for we certainly were an excellent target. I landed and was met by my driver full of tales of the convoy's experiences on the way from Msus. He drove me over to Wing HQ located on a small knoll about half a mile from the edge of the airfield. Here all was functioning well. A programme of armed reconnaissance had been arranged for the fighters and had been going on since dawn. Another squadron was standing by to escort Blenheims who were expected overhead by mid-morning. I was told that reconnaissance of the Antelat/Msus area showed that the enemy was in small numbers at the former but they had not progressed further east. Rosier's 263 Wing HQ was now set up at Msus and had been in contact with the recce aircraft.

"It was a relief to know that Fred was safe and during the day we exchanged signals. We agreed that he would stay at Msus as long as he could to perform the same role as at Antelat – always supposing XIII Corps established themselves at Msus and had any information worth passing on to our fighters. At present our situation map at Mechili, based entirely on air force recce and reports from the fighter leaders, seemed to be the only one in the desert painting the whole picture. During our operations that day we saw nothing of the enemy air force. The absence was fortunate because the Desert east of Msus and up to and beyond Mechili was full of straggling army units heading east who plainly could not defend themselves against air attack. We were using all our aircraft forward and couldn't possibly have looked after such widely dispersed motor transport. Many of these stragglers stopped at Wing HQ asking for information about what was going on. Many had no orders and were just following the general movement eastwards."

Early in the afternoon eight MC.202s of 6° Gruppo and ten MC.200s of 150° Gruppo escorted three Ju 87s of 209ª Squadriglia, Luftwaffe Ju 87s and seven CR.42s of 3° Gruppo to attack Msus; one Italian Ju 87 returned early due to engine trouble. At 1415 six Hurricanes of 274 Squadron had taken off to fly to Msus, the pilots reporting meeting 30 Axis aircraft including Ju 87s and various Italian fighter types, which they engaged despite being heavily outnumbered. Claims were made for two Ju 87s plus a probable, a CR.42 shot down and an MC.200 damaged. Plt Off Moriarty had to crash-land 15 miles west of Msus when his aircraft was hit, but he was able to return to the squadron next day, claiming two more victories over a Ju 87 and a CR.42, plus two more Stukas as probables.

Having completed their attacks when the Hurricanes appeared, both returning Italian Ju 87s were hit, one force-landing in British-held territory where the crew destroyed their aircraft before becoming PoWs. At least two German Stukas were also lost, one crew being killed and the other captured. According to StG 3's records a third aircraft was also shot down, the crew being reported missing, although it would appear that they subsequently returned on foot since they were not listed as casualties.

Meanwhile, the remaining Italian Ju 87 managed to limp back to El Merduna. Two of the CR.42s were also lost (though Italian records listed these as falling to AA fire), the pilots of these both also becoming prisoners. The escorting pilots of 150° Gruppo claimed hits on several P-40s, but made no specific claims.

The Luftwaffe's Stuka force in the Mediterranean area had recently undergone a series of rationalisation re-designations. The Stab and I./StG 3 had been serving in the area since the early months of 1941, as had I./StG 1 and II./StG 2. On 13 January 1942 the two latter gruppen had been renamed II. and III./StG 3, so that now all Stuka units in the area formed a single Stukageschwader 3, led by Oberstlt Karl Christ, kommandeur of I.Gruppe remained Ritterkreuzträger Maj Walter Sigel, while kommandeur of the retitled II.Gruppe was Hptmn Kurt Kuhlmey, who had taken part in the attack on HMS *Illustrious* in January 1941, and who would receive the Ritterkreuz later in 1942. All these three units continued to operate the long-range Ju 87R, although the new III./StG 3 – ex II./StG 2 – also received some of the first of the new Ju 87D. Commanded by Maj Walter Ennecerus, who had led the successful attacks on both *Illustrious* and HMS *Formidable*, as well as that on the cruiser HMS *Southampton*, this gruppe's kommandeur had been holder of the Ritterkreuz since July 1940, and was without doubt one of the truly outstanding Stuka leaders and exponents in the Luftwaffe. For the time being, however, his III.Gruppe remained in Sicily, undertaking attacks on Malta.

As Axis lines moved rapidly eastwards, Arae Philenorum became too far distant for operational purposes, 6° Gruppo CT being forced to use El Agheila as a forward landing ground.

During the day 4 SAAF Squadron, ordered now to El Adem, resumed flying their Tomahawks again. 1 SAAF Squadron flew their captured Bf 109F for the first time, Maj Osler being the pilot. He complained that, despite the high performance of the aircraft, he found visibility from its narrow cockpit to be poor.

British Claims

274 Sqn	Sqn Ldr S.Linnard	Hurricane IIb Z5316	Ju 87 between Mechili and Msus 1415-1525
	Sqn Ldr S.Linnard	Hurricane IIb Z5316	MC.200 damaged between Mechili and Msus 1415-1525
	Flt Lt A.J.Smith	Hurricane IIb DG631	MC.200 between Mechili and Msus 1415-1525
	Flt Lt A.J.Smith	Hurricane IIb DG631	MC.200 damaged between Mechili and Msus 1415-1525
	Flt Lt B.H.A.Playford	Hurricane IIb Z5446	Ju 87 probable between Mechili and Msus 1415-1525
	Plt Off P.D.Moriarty	Hurricane IIb Z4015	Ju 87 between Mechili and Msus 1415-1525
	Plt Off P.D.Moriarty	Hurricane IIb Z4015	2 Ju 87s probable between Mechili and Msus 1415-1525
	Plt Off P.D.Moriarty	Hurricane IIb Z4015	CR.42 between Mechili and Msus 1415-1525
	Sgt J.Dodds	Hurricane IIb Z5435	Ju 87 between Mechili and Msus 1415-1525
	Sgt J.Dodds	Hurricane IIb Z5435	CR.42 between Mechili and Msus 1415-1525
	Sgt Worthington	Hurricane IIb Z5381	Ju 87 between Mechili and Msus 1415-1525
	Sgt Worthington	Hurricane IIb Z5381	Ju 87 probable between Mechili and Msus 1415-1525
2 SAAF Sqn	Lt E.C.Saville	Tomahawk	Ju 88 damaged Gazala area

British Casualties

274 Sqn	Hurricane IIb crash-landed; Plt Off P.D.Moriarty, returned later
208 Sqn	Hurricane Z4539 shot down; Plt Off O.C.Stephens, RAAF, KiA, left 0720 for Agedabia

German Claims

6./JG 27	Uffz Johann Walchhofer	Hurricane	W Agedabia 0830

German Casualties

3./StG 3	Ju 87 shot down by AA 27m N Agedabia; Fw Karl-Heinz Hübner/Uffz Heinz Kosbab KiA
	Ju 87R-2 WNr 6115 shot down in combat 15m S Msus; Obfw Werner Clock/ Uffz Nicholas Lumbers PoWs
	Ju 87 shot down. Crew MiA

Italian Casualties

209ª Sq/ BaT	Ju 87 WNr 5927 crash-landed and destroyed, Cap Gualtiero Pilot and gunner Av Sc Matteo Palumbo PoW
	Ju 87 Damaged; Serg Antonio Sterchele returned to El Merduna safely
155ª Sq/3° Gr CT	CR.42 crash-landed, Serg Valeriano Bolognesi PoW
	CR.42 crash-landed, Serg Augusto Mannu PoW

Sunday, 25 January 1942

Rommel's precarious advance was meeting with immediate success, the unsuspecting and weakened Commonwealth forces falling back all along the line. During the day Axis troops reached Zt Msus, causing the defending ground forces to withdraw towards Charruba, some 40 miles to the north-east, with the Allied fighter squadrons being forced to re-locate to Mechili.

All available aircraft were engaged in covering the army's withdrawal and doing as much as possible to dislocate the Axis advance. Fighter sweeps were undertaken throughout the day, although it was early afternoon before much opposition was met in the air. This commenced when Plt Off Booth and Sgt Phillips of 94 Squadron were scrambled to intercept a reconnaissance Ju 88 over the Mechili area. Phillips caught this 20 miles to the south-east, claiming to have shot it down at 1245. Two more Hurricanes, this time from 238 Squadron, then intercepted four or five Ju 88s over an incoming convoy, claiming one shot down and two damaged. Shortly after this engagement a further reconnaissance Ju 88 was claimed south-east of Barce by Plt Off Weeks of 274 Squadron. He had taken off at once on report of the aircraft's approach, but after first sighting it, lost it in cloud. Spotting it again, he got in two long bursts, but then saw a second fighter attacking, one of two friendly Hurricanes which appeared, all three pilots watching the intruder crash 20 miles south-east of Sidi Barrani. The two who had joined in this combat would seem to have been the 238 Squadron pair. An hour after the successes attributed to the 238 and 274 Squadron pilots, Sgt Smallwood from the former unit encountered yet another Ju 88 over the convoy, reporting that it blew up as a result of his first burst of fire. During these encounters at least two Ju 88s from LG 1 were lost, one from I.Gruppe and one from 12.Staffel.

At much the same time Kittyhawks of 3 RAAF Squadron undertook a strafing attack on MT, pilots claiming four troop carriers and a petrol tanker on fire ten miles north of Agedabia, plus others damaged. Two pilots then spotted a Bf 110 which they claimed shot down between them.

Nine Kittyhawks from 112 Squadron then flew close escort to Blenheims drawn from two squadrons, but during the return flight these were attacked by five Bf 109s of II./JG 27 when north-east of Antelat, Sgt Leu claiming one of the attackers shot down. On this occasion the German pilots claimed four P-40s shot down, two of them by Obfw Schulz, all of which were recorded as falling in Axis-held territory. No corresponding WDAF losses have been discovered, which is most unusual at this point in the fighting. One Blenheim of 11 Squadron was lost during this sortie when it force-landed after one engine was hit by Flak.

During the day, however, 33 Squadron's long-range Hurricanes were again active, strafing MT. Intense Flak shot down one of the unit's aircraft, Flt Lt Nourse losing his life. Beaufighters undertook similar attacks along the Nofilia-Bir El Merduna road, claiming seven vehicles destroyed there. Attacks on the advancing Axis columns continued into the night, 15 Wellingtons bombing traffic on the Agheila-Agedabia road, where three of the bombers descended to low level to allow the turret gunners to indulge in strafing as well (See Chapter 12 – The RAF's Night Bombing Offensive).

Serg Magg Giovanni Tait from 80ª Squadriglia of 17° Gruppo scrambled from Tamet to intercept a reconnaissance aircraft. The interception was unsuccessful and the pilot damaged his MC.202 on landing at Arae Philenorum.

British Claims

94 Sqn	Sgt R.H.Phillips	Hurricane IIb Z5330	Ju 88	20m from Mechili 1245
274 Sqn	Plt Off Weeks	Hurricane IIb Z4000	Ju 88*	20m SE Barce 1400-1445
238 Sqn	Plt Off Jenkins	Hurricane IIc	Ju 88*	convoy patrol 1315-1550
	Plt Off Jenkins	Hurricane IIc	Ju 88 damaged	convoy patrol 1315-1550
	Plt Off Jenkins	Hurricane IIc	½ Ju 88 damaged	convoy patrol 1315-1550
	Plt Off Milne	Hurricane IIc	½ Ju 88 damaged	convoy patrol 1315-1550
	Sgt P.Smallwood	Hurricane IIc	Ju 88	5m S convoy 1445-1545
3 RAAF Sqn	Sgt F.B.Reid	Kittyhawk AK612	} Bf 110	Agedabia area 1450
	Sgt V.F.Curtiss	Kittyhawk AK691		
112 Sqn	Sgt R.M.Leu	Kittyhawk AK637	Bf 109	Agedabia-Mechili 1515-1725
	Sqn Ldr C.R.Caldwell	Kittyhawk AK658	Bf 109 damaged	
RNFS	Lt H.P.Allingham	Hurricane I	} He 111 damaged	off coast
	Sub Lt B.H.C.Nation	Hurricane I		

*Although individual victories were confirmed in both cases, Weeks and Jenkins appear actually to have shared in the destruction of a single Ju 88.

British Casualties

33 Sqn	Hurricane I shot down by Flak; Lt L.B.Nourse KiA
11 Sqn	Blenheim IV V5899, hit by Flak and force-landed; Sgt F.B.Borrett, RAAF, and one injured; Flt Sgt J.Richmond, DFM, KiA

German Claims

4./JG 27	Obfw Alfred Schulze		P-40	NE Antelat 1635
	Obfw Otto Schulz		P-40	NE Antelat 1635
	Obfw Otto Schulz		P-40	15m NE Antelat 1640
6./JG 27	Obgefr Otto Monska		P-40	NE Antelat 1640

German Casualties	
1./LG 1	Ju 88A-4 WNr 5563 L1+DH shot down over sea; Lt Peter Schwartz and three MiA
3./LG 1	Ju 88A-4 WNr 8555 L1+?L damaged by fighters 35%; crash-landed; one of crew WiA
12./LG 1	Ju 88A-5 WNr 4377 L1+CR shot down Mechili; Lt Alf Billert and three MiA
7/ZG 26	Bf 110 damaged 70% by fighter attack at Agedabia; pilot safe but gunner, Uffz Heinz Golisch WiA
Italian Casualties	
80ª Sq/17° Gr CT	MC 202 MM7751 damaged on landing, Serg Magg Giovanni Tait safe

Monday, 26 January 1942

Severe sandstorms again adversely affected efforts to slow down the Axis columns, despite which fighters managed to undertake a number of such attacks during the day. Indeed, it was believed that at least 120 vehicles had been damaged or destroyed and heavy casualties inflicted. 15 MT, AFVs and fuel tankers were seen to have been burnt out, plus a number of troop-carrying vehicles. It was also observed that movement on the Antelat-Zt Msus road which had been heavy during the morning, had been practically brought to a standstill by the afternoon, many vehicles apparently having been abandoned as a result of the strafing attacks.

During one such sortie, Flt Lt Barber and three Sgts of 250 Squadron failed to return, having been forced to land after becoming lost in a dust storm. All were able to take off again later, returning safely to their unit. On another such flight eight of that unit's Tomahawks were strafing when an MC.200 was seen and claimed shot down to the east of Msus by Flg Off John Waddy. The only other hostile aircraft seen during the day was a Bf 110 which escaped after being attacked ineffectively. One of 3 RAAF Squadron's Kittyhawks crash-landed after being hit by Flak, but the pilot, Sgt Mailey, was picked up by another of the unit's pilots and flown safely back to base.

Six S.79 torpedo-bombers of 279ª and 284ª Squadriglie, led by Cap Giulio Marini, took off at 1515 to intercept a British naval force reported to include a battleship, three cruisers and about ten destroyers which had been sighted at 1205 by an Italian reconnaissance aircraft. The first formation of three aircraft, flown by Marini, S.Ten Aligi Strani and S.Ten Alfredo Pulzetti, made the first attack, releasing their torpedoes at one of the cruisers. The crews thought that two hits had been scored, but fire from the vessels severely damaged Strani's and Pulzetti's aircraft. The second flight, led by Cap Oscar Pegna, followed in the first trio almost at once. S.Ten Giovanni Teta claimed to have gained a hit on a second cruiser while Ten Giuseppe Balzarotti released his weapon at the ship already attacked by the first section. In doing so, his S.79 was also badly damaged by return fire. Notwithstanding the damage suffered, all six Italian aircraft regained their base between 1840-1920.

British Claims				
250 Sqn	Plt Off J.L.Waddy	Tomahawk AN444	MC.200	15m W Msus 1515
British Casualties				
3 RAAF Sqn	Kittyhawk AK699 hit by Flak, crash-landed; Sgt W.H.A.Mailey picked up by another Kittyhawk and flown back to base			
Italian Casualties				
279ª Sq AS	S.79 damaged by ships' AA; S.Ten Aligi Strani and crew safe			
	S.79 damaged by ships' AA; S.Ten Alfredo Pulzetti and crew safe			
284ª Sq AS	S.79 damaged by ships' AA; Ten Giuseppe Balzarotti and crew safe			

Tuesday, 27 January 1942

Tactical reconnaissance aircraft reported a substantial force approaching Sceleidima from Zt Msus, but here it split into many individual columns, heading east, north and north-west. While sending part of his force towards Mechili in order to induce the British command into believing that this was the main focus of his advance, Rommel had in fact swung the bulk of his troops northwards to race for Benghazi.

One of 208 Squadron's Hurricanes was intercepted over this area by six Bf 109s. Plt Off Moss managed to evade their attacks, but was subsequently obliged to carry out a crash-landing when his aircraft ran out of fuel. For this sortie Plt Off J.Moss was subsequently awarded a DFC. Stated the recommendation for his award:

" …Moss was detailed to carry out a photographic reconnaissance of the Msus-Antelat area for the Army Commander. When flying at 20,000 ft, having just started his run, he noticed three Me 109s 5,000 ft below him and about three miles away. He continued his run for approximately eight minutes and on completion of the last exposure realised that the enemy aircraft had intercepted him and were bearing to attack. He immediately put his aircraft into a violent turn and spiralled down to 4,000 ft during which time his windscreen and hood iced up and his visibility was restricted almost to a minimum.

"When below 4,000 ft the icing cleared and he found the enemy aircraft still in pursuit. One remained on his tail while the others carried out quarter attacks. Plt Off Moss cleverly evaded them by turning towards the attackers and continued to do this the whole way to Mechili. He realised that his petrol was getting very low and he made for a sandstorm in the direction of Mechili. He lost the enemy aircraft in the sandstorm but their attacks were not immediately broken off as he could see their shots passing to the right and left of him.

"He passed over the satellite landing ground but was unable to land owing to sand. It was now obvious that he would have to force-land owing to lack of petrol so he flew west until clear of tents and motor transport and force-landed with his undercarriage up and without damage to the cameras. He removed the magazines, commandeered a vehicle and returned to the Squadron detachment at Mechili with the photographs."

Six Beaufighters carried out an attack on 60 MT, bunched in small convoys on the road west of Sirte. 12 were claimed to have been destroyed and many more damaged. It was thought at HQ, WS, that the fighters had managed to destroy around 70 vehicles during the day. S.Ten Lorenzo Chellini of 17° Gruppo was scrambled from Tamet in his MC.202 to intercept incoming bombers, on return claiming to have shot down a Beaufighter, although none of these aircraft were recorded as being lost on this date.

With the territory retaken rapidly expanding, the Axis fighter units now began moving forward during the day, I. and II./JG 27 moving from Agheila to Agedabia and Bel Audah, joined in the former location by III.Gruppe which had been further back at Arco Philenorum and Castel Benito. It was to Agedabia also that 6 Gruppo moved during the evening with 19 serviceable MC.202s. Here they were joined by 150° Gruppo, 209ª and 236ª Squadriglie, while 8° Gruppo moved to Agheila and 3° Gruppo to Sidi Ahmur.

Far to the east, on the other side of the lines, a new fighter unit arrived at LG.20, El Daba, to undertake patrol duties. 335 Squadron had formed at Aqir in October, moving to St Jean, Palestine, during December. Equipped with Hurricane Is and commanded by Sqn Ldr X.J.Varvaressos, the unit was composed wholly of Greek personnel.

British Casualties			
208 Sqn	Hurricane crash-landed due to fuel shortage; Plt Off J.Moss safe		
Italian Claims			
72ª Sq/17° Gr CT	S.Ten Lorenzo Chellini	Beaufighter	via Balbia 1400-1430

Wednesday, 28 January 1942

The Axis thrust towards Benghazi proved to be a complete success, and before the day was over the port had been retaken. Two squadrons of Hurricanes and Tomahawks attacked columns heading for the city, at least 50 vehicles including an ammunition truck, being claimed destroyed. The troops they were carrying were also believed to have been killed, but it was to no avail. Fighters attacking in the Sceleidima-Zt Msus area throughout the day also claimed at least six vehicles, five of which were identified as fuel tankers, together with damage to some 40 others. At least 30 troops were thought to have been killed and an Hs 126 damaged on the ground. Three squadrons of Blenheims, all with fighter escorts, attacked MT south-east of El Abiot, 30 miles east of Benghazi; such raids would continue to be carried out throughout the rest of the month.

Flak and other ground fire proved to be the most dangerous adversary at this time, and during the morning three Hurricanes fell to this scourge. Two of the pilots brought down were from 229 Squadron and both returned safely on foot. Sgt Vidler had crash-landed after a bullet struck the glycol cooling system to his aircraft's engine, following which he walked for 30 miles to Mechili from where he returned to his unit two days later. He reported that he had seen Hurricanes strafing Allied troops in error.

The only Luftwaffe casualty at this time was a Bf 110 of III./ZG 26 which crash-landed north of Ghemines. The crew became PoWs, but it appears that the gunner, Ogfr Lepinat, must have been seriously injured or wounded, as he was subsequently reported to have died on 4 February.

With nightfall Axis forces were seen to be moving on Coefia, eight miles north-east of Benghazi to block the Benghazi-Tocra road, where heavy fighting would occur next day. Meanwhile, having completed the move to Agedabia by the early morning of the 28th, 6° Gruppo was ordered to move on to Beleudah landing ground, 25 miles to the south-east, towards the end of the day. The unit's ground echelon had been carried forward in its 'hack' Ca.133 and in an S.82 transport, these aircraft now accompanying the gruppo's fighters to this new base.

British Casualties	
274 Sqn	Hurricane IIb Z2835 shot down by Flak; Sgt Clark
229 Sqn	Hurricane IIc shot down by Flak; Plt Off T.G.Foley returned
	Hurricane IIc shot down by Flak; Sgt Vidler returned on 30th

German Casualties	
III./ZG 26	Bf 110 crash-landed; Obfw Franz Sander/Ogfr Lepinat PoWs; Lepinat died 4 February

Thursday, 29 January 1942

Beaufighters flying up the coast attacked five barges at Ras el Aoli, 23 miles west-north-west of El Agheila, claiming two of these destroyed.

German Casualties	
1./StG 3	Ju 87 shot down by AA SW Sidi Ahmed el Magrun; Uffz Matthias Reh/Obfw Werner Strube
Italian Casualties	
236ª Sq Ass	CR.42 MM4394 Ten Emanuele Spagnoletti KiA, cause not found

Friday, 30 January 1942

A pilot of 238 Squadron patrolling over ships near Tobruk, intercepted an He 111 and claimed to have probably destroyed it.

British Claims				
238 Sqn	Flt Lt C.R.Forsyth	Hurricane I	He 111 probable	convoy patrol 0815-0955

German Casualties	
7./ZG 26	Bf 110 3U+GR WNr 4333 shot down bt AA 12m N Chemines; Obfw Franz Sander and Uffz Günter Lepinat MiA

Saturday, 31 January 1942

Flg Off Davies of 208 Squadron took off at 0820 on a Tac R sortie over the Trigh el Abd. In the Garari area he was attacked by two Bf 109s but escaped these in a dust cloud although his Hurricane had been badly damaged. This caused him to crash-land shortly afterwards, coming down 20 miles south-west of Tengeder, returning to his unit on foot next day. One of the Luftwaffe's reconnaissance aircraft was also lost when a 1.(F)/121 Ju 88 failed to return from a sortie over Cyrenaica. It is believed that this aircraft had been attacked and claimed damaged by Sgt W.G.Eagle, a pilot newly arrived with 274 Squadron.

During the day AHQ recorded that nine unidentified Axis aircraft had attacked El Adem airfield, destroying one Gladiator and seriously damaging a Blenheim and three Hurricanes; 12 other aircraft suffered slight damage. Hurricanes undertook an offensive reconnaissance over the Benghazi area, attacking MT on the Ghemines road, where five lorries were claimed destroyed and casualties inflicted on Axis troops.

By night an RAF raid on Agedabia caused several casualties amongst Italian personnel. Six DICAT (anti-aircraft) gunners were killed; amongst the wounded were two pilots.

British Claims				
274 Sqn	Sgt W.G.Eagle	Hurricane IIb	Ju 88 damaged	Mechili
British Casualties				
208 Sqn	Hurricane shot down; Flg Off K.G.C.Davies returned on foot next day			

German Casualties	
1.(F)/121	Ju 88D-1 WNr 1561 7A+GH MiA E Cyrenaica; Uffz Erich Reber, Lt Hans Köchele and one KiA

Thus the Crusader offensive finally petered out completely, and in some ignominy. Rommel's sudden about face which had so disconcerted XIII Corps had relied not only on the arrival of renewed supplies

A group of Italian pilots being decorated with the *Eisernes Kreuz II Klasse* (Iron Cross, 2nd Class). In the front row, from left to right, are: S.Ten Fausto Filippi, Ten Mario Bellagambi and Magg Antonio Vizzotto (all of 150° Gruppo CT).

and equipment at Tripoli, but also information from 'the good source'. The latter was the US Military Attaché in Cairo, Colonel Bonnert Frank Fellers, whose code for reporting to Washington had been broken by the Italians. This provided Rommel with "vital information on the Middle East battlefields", recalled Hans-Otto Behrendt, a member of his intelligence staff. "In fact, it was stupefying in his openness" regarding British tank losses, the number of tanks operational and overall strength. While much has been made of the benefits to the British of the information derived from the breaking of the Ultra transcripts, intelligence was often a two-way weapon. After the Axis counter-strike had reached the line at Gazala on 30 January, Kesselring was later to record that the offensive had been "…carried out by very weak forces with wonderful enthusiasm, supported in model fashion by the Luftwaffe in Africa. All credit for this success must go to Rommel; he was unsurpassed in leading armoured formations and suchlike raids, provided his nerve did not desert him."

The month ended with some fairly considerable movements of WDAF units. 33 and 73 Squadrons moved to Gazala but 80 Squadron, which had re-equipped with cannon-armed Hurricane IIcs during the month, was forced to withdraw to LG.109 as it was experiencing problems with this armament.

94 Squadron was ordered to move to LG.110 and commence re-equipment with Kittyhawks, while a new Australian Kittyhawk unit, 450 Squadron, moved to LG.012 at Sidi Haneish preparatory to entering operations. However, the TacR unit 237 Squadron moved to El Firdan, off operations.

In taking stock at this time, Italian records show that since 7 February 1941 the Regia Aeronautica had claimed 148 aircraft shot down, 125 of them by fighters. 37 more had been claimed as probables, 28 of them by fighter pilots. Aircraft losses had amounted to 80 in the air, of which only 26 were fighters, and 179 on the ground – 82 being fighters. Nearly 500 aircraft had suffered damage of one sort or another.

At this time Tedder recorded that:

"Mary Coningham and his team were keeping their heads as usual, but were incensed at the Army's defeatist attitude." He confided to his diary: "Our Fighter chaps have been doing some grand work

– they are feeling rather angry about it all. Been talking this evening to see if we cannot pass on some of their anger – and spirit – to the Land Forces. A [Auchinleck] is first rate. He has got fight and leadership, so have a lot of our chaps."

A few days later, following learning of some articles in newspapers at home which were seeking to place the blame for the failure of the army and navy on lack of air support, and advocating an army air force, Tedder, with Auchinleck's approval, wrote to Sir Archibald Sinclair:

"You should know that the RAF in the desert realise that they have saved the Army, both in the recent advance and in the withdrawal, and naturally resent any suggestion that the Army should control them."

He continued:

"The RAF have on this occasion given the Army, at great sacrifice, all the air support and protection required. The German Air Force has interfered little with Army operations. Yet the Army continues to withdraw; therefore, the RAF crews are perplexed and feel that their efforts have been wasted."

Turning to his diary again, he added:

"I told the Secretary of State that during the withdrawal some RAF armoured car crews had driven back nine serviceable tanks abandoned by the Army. This, and similar stories, had naturally circulated, and whether rightly or wrongly, the RAF in the Desert felt that the Army did not know how to use their weapons and were not willing fighters. This impression had been further strengthened by the aggressive action of some RAF armoured cars who took on some German tanks. The spirit of the RAF's personnel in the Desert was: 'Give us some tanks and we will stop this retreating if the Army does not wish to fight.' There was therefore real danger that incessant Press correspondence on the failure to exploit air superiority might lead to strained relations between the Army and RAF."

Since taking over command of WDAF, Coningham had become acutely aware of the phenomenon represented by the constant over-claiming – particularly against the Axis fighters. During December he had confided to Tedder: "…we have practically no marksmen because there is no practical air-to-air firing done until they are thrown into the battle when they are all worked up and so do not know what they are doing. It is then too late, except for the lucky and perhaps more experienced ones who survive." The situation was an unhappy one and one which would, in many ways, become worse during the year to come.

This was but the start of a series of reverses which were to rob the Commonwealth forces of all that had been achieved at considerable loss. The RAF still had many months of costly fighting to come before it began fully to wrest aerial superiority from the Luftwaffe and Regia Aeronautica. The next steps in this long and tortuous journey will be described in Volume 2.

CHAPTER 12

THE RAF's NIGHT BOMBING OFFENSIVE

Whilst closely co-ordinated with events on the ground in the Western Desert (and indeed, when necessary, elsewhere), the activities of the RAF's night bombers very rarely impinged on the direct activities of the units operating by day. Consequently to try and fit these bomber activities into the daily diary treatment of the main actions over the front line areas was considered likely to produce a rather disjointed narrative, upsetting the flow of the description of operations by day without offering a commensurate advantage. The decision was therefore taken to treat this element of aerial activity in much the same way as the coastal and over-sea operations of 201 Group, and the defensive operations over the Nile Delta and Suez Canal areas. In consequence this chapter deals with the growth and operations of the night bomber units of Royal Air Force, Middle East, from the launching of Operation Compass in December 1940.

As has already been described, in June 1940 RAF, Middle East, had available in Egypt only 216 Squadron, equipped with Bristol Bombay bomber-transports to operate by night in the heavy bomber role. Of course, the Blenheim squadrons also undertook such activities on occasion, but these were really an adjunct to their main role as light/medium bombers operating by day.

All that was available for long-range night bombing at the outbreak of war in the Middle East in June 1940 was 216 Squadron with its Bristol Bombay bomber/transports, one of which is about to touch down.

Consequently, on 11 June 1940 ten Bombays, each armed with eight 250lb GP (general purpose) bombs moved forward to El Daba in preparation for an initial raid on Tobruk. In the event this was cancelled, and during the deployment one Bombay (5849) was badly damaged when a Blenheim inadvertently taxied into it.

The first raid by the squadron was undertaken on the night of 14 June when three aircraft, operating from the airfield at Mersa Matruh, bombed Tobruk. Further raids on this port and its harbour continued, the first loss being suffered on 21 June when Flt Lt Wentworth-Smith and his crew in L5850 were reported missing.

To enhance the range of these rather elderly aircraft, long-range tanks were fitted to all operational machines on 22 June, and in July a detachment of six were moved forward to Fuka. On 14 July these raided Tobruk again, but on the return flight, owing to low cloud, Sqn Ldr Taylor became lost.

Next day four Bombays returned from Fuka to Heliopolis, but L5848, flown by Sgt Campbell, force-landed near Lake Maryut, suffering severe damage, although the crew escaped unhurt. Again, this loss was occasioned by bad weather.

Thereafter, while occasional raids continued, the squadron became increasingly involved in its alternative transport role, carrying supplies down to the Imperial forces in East Africa. On 1 October the unit's commanding officer, Wg Cdr S.D.Chichester, handed over to Wg Cdr F.J.Laine.

Throughout this period the other bomber-transport unit in Egypt, 70 Squadron, had operated only in the latter role, its elderly biplane Vickers Valentias not being considered appropriate for bombing duties. On 1 September 1940, however, the first six Vickers Wellington IC heavy bombers arrived at Heliopolis to commence the partial re-equipment of the unit; this initial flight was led by Sqn Ldr R.J.Wells.

70 Squadron moved to a new airfield at Kabrit on 9 September, from where it carried out its first bombing operation with its new aircraft on the 18th – a raid on Benghazi harbour. This target, the main supply base for the Cyrenaican province of Libya, had already been targetted by 216 Squadron's Bombays during the same month, again operating from Fuka. This advanced satellite airfield was also to be employed by the Wellingtons when undertaking the fairly long haul to Benghazi – a target which would become extremely familiar with the whole night-bombing force over the next two years.

Two more Wellingtons arrived on 25 September, a third having crashed on landing at Malta en route, and five days later a further trio arrived. While Benghazi remained the main target for the Wellingtons at this stage, attacks were also flown against Tobruk and the Italian-occupied island of Rhodes – some of these sorties being flown by day.

Following the Italian invasion of Greece in October, a detachment of six Wellingtons was sent to Eleusis on 5 November. Next day these undertook a daylight attack on Valona (Albania), but were subjected to fighter interception, two being shot down and two damaged (see *Air War for Yugoslavia, Greece and Crete 1940-41*). The returning survivors were able to shoot down a Cant.Z.506B en route, but on 8 November these aircraft were all flown back to Egypt. Six more were at once sent to Eleusis to continue operations, and here they remained until 24 November, although all further operations over hostile territory were undertaken by night only.

Meanwhile, as already mentioned in Chapter 3 – Graziani Makes a Move, two more full squadrons of Wellington ICs had been ordered from the United Kingdom to the Middle East, these being 37 Squadron at Feltwell (Wg Cdr W.H.Merton) and 38 Squadron at Marham (Wg Cdr W.P.J.Thompson). Both these units had taken part in early daylight operations over the north German ports during December 1939, which had proved very costly (see *Fledgling Eagles*).

While the air parties set out to fly to Egypt via Gibraltar and Malta, the ground crews of both units, together with those of 73 (Fighter) Squadron, were despatched to Gibraltar aboard a number of vessels including HMT *Franconia* and MVs *New Zealand Star*, *Clan Forbes*, and one other merchant vessel. This small convoy was escorted as far as Gibraltar by the aircraft carrier HMS *Furious* (which was carrying 73 Squadron's Hurricanes for delivery to West Africa), the cruiser HMS *Manchester*, and three destroyers.

At Gibraltar all the RAF personnel went aboard HMS *Manchester* on 25 November, leaving for Egypt at 0700 that morning. Two days later *Manchester*, accompanied by cruisers *Southampton*, *Sheffield*, *Newcastle* and *Berwick*, and supported by the battleships HMS *Renown* and *Ramillies*, encountered units of the Italian fleet. Suddenly the air force men found themselves in the midst of a fairly major naval engagement as 14 salvoes straddled *Manchester*, fortunately without hitting her. One of her own shells, meanwhile, gained a direct hit on an Italian eight-inch gun cruiser.

One of the first squadrons to reach Egypt from the UK to reinforce RAF, Middle East, was 37 Squadron. A Vickers Wellington Ic of this unit is seen here in flight.

As if this excitement was not enough, at 1630 on this day 15 Italian aircraft attacked the carrier HMS *Ark Royal*, which was now in company with the Royal Navy vessels, the AA guns of the fleet going fully into action. Next day came a torpedo attack, two of these missiles passing close behind *Manchester* and exploding in her wake. At 1100 on 28 November Malta was passed and two days later a safe disembarkation followed at Alexandria at the end of an eventful and memorable voyage.

Meanwhile the Wellingtons and their crews had begun arriving at Kabrit some days earlier on 15 November. En route Plt Off D.F.Benbow and his 37 Squadron crew had encountered and claimed to have shot down an Italian seaplane into the sea. Their opponent may have been a Cant.Z.501, MM35468 of 143ª Squadriglia RM from Menelao which was lost off Mersa Matruh, apparently due to a crash-landing following an engine failure at 0945 in the morning, the aircraft breaking in two. The two pilots, Ten Virgilio Lorenzoni and Serg Magg Guerrino Granci were killed, but the rest of the crew survived and were rescued.

From their new base, aircraft were flown to 102 MU at Abu Sueir immediately after arrival to have Vokes filters fitted to their engines to protect them against the desert sand and dust.

Also during November 12 Wellingtons had been flown to Malta from England, where at the start of December these formed a new 148 Squadron at Luqa. From here these aircraft would be able to attack not only targets in Sicily and southern Italy, but also the other major Libyan port/city of Tripoli, which was beyond the range of the Egyptian-based units (see *Malta: the Hurricane Years, 1940-41*). The aircraft here were already operating by mid November, prior to the formation of their squadron, and of the two new units at Kabrit.

The new arrivals in Egypt were ready for operations just in time to take part in the Operation Compass offensive. During the night of 8/9 December, as the Imperial forces in the desert prepared to strike, Wellingtons from all three squadrons raided Regia Aeronautica airfields around Benina, while three of 216 Squadron's Bombays dropped bombs in the Sidi Barrani-Sollum area.

Seven of 37 Squadron's aircraft had flown to Fuka during the day, taking off at 1530 and flying out to sea in formation towards Benghazi. As darkness fell, formation was broken and the aircraft headed in individually to bomb Benina airfield and buildings there. 70 Squadron demonstrated by the manner of

A trio of 37 Squadron Wellington Ics over North Africa.

ts attack one way in which operations over North Africa would tend to differ from those over western Europe. Bombs having been released, pilots then took their aircraft down to low level, allowing the front and rear turret gunners to strafe any suitable targets which they spotted.

Raids on airfields remained the priority over the next few days as the successes on the ground began to gather momentum. Typically, 37 Squadron launched seven bombers to attack El Adem during the night of 10/11 December, four to Derna during 13/14, five to Bardia on 14/15, and nine more to this target on 16/17. Only during the night of 12/13 was any opposition other than AA fire encountered, when over Tobruk docks an unidentified single-engined monoplane attacked one Wellington, but withdrew when fired on by the rear turret gunner.

On 17 and 18 December 37 and 38 Squadrons moved from Kabrit to Shallufa as their new permanent base, leaving only 70 Squadron at the former base. From here this latter unit, led by Wg Cdr E.B.Webb, was again being called upon to exercise some of its efforts over Greece.

At this stage it was believed that 216 Squadron would also soon be re-equipped with Wellingtons. With the heavy night bomber force now so much increased, on 20 December 257 (Heavy Bomber) Wing was set up at Shallufa under the command of Grp Capt L.L.MacLean to administer the two bases and the three resident squadrons, with the intention that 216 Squadron would be added following re-equipment. In the event this was not to happen. The Bombays continued to add their weight to the overall offensive until the middle of December, but thereafter the usefulness of the squadron in the transport role predominated, and it settled down to continue this vital, if more prosaic activity with its existing 'mix' of Bombays and Valentias.

To this point casualties during the North African activities had been effectively nil for the Wellingtons, but during the night of 20/21 December the first loss was suffered – though not to hostile action. Four of 37 Squadron's aircraft had gone out to attack Berka and Benina airfields, but L7865, flown by Plt Off Lax, suffered engine trouble and crashed 30 miles south-east of Sidi Barrani at 0010. All the crew survived this experience unhurt.

On New Year's Day, 1941, 257 Wing was able to co-ordinate a harassing raid on the defences of Bardia, which was about to be assaulted by the advancing ground forces. One Wellington of 37 Squadron, two of 38 Squadron and two of 70 Squadron took part in this attack (see also Chapter 4 – Operation Compass). Eight aircraft were despatched by 38 Squadron to attack Tobruk on 6/7 January, but during this raid one Wellington was hit in three places by AA fire, the rear fuselage and starboard engine suffering severe damage. During the return flight the damaged engine burst into flames and the aircraft crashed into the sea off the Ishaila Rocks, near Sidi Barrani; only the rear gunner of Sgt Clegg's crew survived.

Rhodes again became the target for attack on 15 January, 37 and 38 Squadrons each despatching four Wellingtons to bomb Maritza airfield there. At this stage 37 Squadron experienced a change of command when Wg Cdr Merton was posted to 257 Wing as SASO.

During the night of 30 January 1941 Shallufa was bombed by German aircraft which approached from the direction of Suez between 0430-0530. These aircraft were believed to have been operating from Rhodes, and had dropped magnetic mines (about 20 in number) into the Canal (see more in Chapter 13 – Blitz on Egypt). This event would trigger further bombing both of this island and of Scarpanto, eight 37 Squadron Wellingtons raiding Maritza airfield again on 2 February, several other attacks soon following. It was during a raid on Benghazi by three 38 Squadron aircraft on the night of 14/15, that one Wellington was lost due to technical difficulties..

The extent of the successful advances on the ground now allowed detachments of Wellingtons to be sent forward to operate from El Adem airfield, now in British hands. Six 70 Squadron aircraft moved there on 3 February, but the demands of RAF, Middle East's other responsibilities continued to lead to dissipation of available forces. On 12 February six 37 Squadron aircraft were detached to Greece, four of these flying across the Adriatic Sea from there to attack Brindisi on the 15th. Here it was believed that a seaplane hangar and three aircraft on the ground had been destroyed, although one Wellington was lost during this raid. This was the unit's second loss at this time for during the previous day Plt Off Wright's Wellington had crashed into mountains in Turkey whilst raiding Aegean targets, he and his crew all being killed.

Following intensive operations from Malta, which was now under sustained Luftwaffe air attacks, five of 148 Squadron's Wellingtons and their crews had been ordered to Heliopolis for overhaul and rest. To replace them, five Egypt-based aircraft, one of 37, two of 38 and two of 70 Squadrons, were ordered to the island to operate for a week. En route on 20 February one crew reported seeing wreckage falling into the sea 110 miles south-east of Malta, Flg Off Hough and his 37 Squadron crew being reported missing.

Thursday – Friday, 13/14 February 1941

Friday – Saturday, 14/15 February 1941

Tuesday, 25 February 1941

Malta was indeed now a desperately dangerous place for Wellingtons, and 70 Squadron's T2891 was lost while operating from here over Tripoli, with Plt Off G.H.Green and his crew. Next day a heavy raid destroyed one of the 70 Squadron aircraft on the island, plus six of 148 Squadron's aircraft, seven more being damaged seriously.

0 Sqn	Wellington IC T2891 'O' Plt Off G.H.Green and one KiA; four of crew baled out and PoW
	Wellington IC T2816 'J' destroyed on ground at Luqa

However, the availability of landing grounds ever further to the west occasioned by the advance of the army right to the border of Tripolitania, allowed the attack on Tripoli now to be taken up by 257 Wing's squadrons. On 24 February four of 70 Squadron's El Adem detachment, using Benina as an advanced landing ground, were able to raid the Libyan capital from 6,500-9,000 feet between 0320-0410; this attack was repeated the following night (in company with Malta-based aircraft), and on subsequent nights.

At Shallufa meanwhile, Grp Capt MacLean had been replaced due to illness by the World War I fighter pilot, Grp Capt J.S.T.Fall, DSC, AFC.

During March all of 70 Squadron's aircraft moved up to El Adem, which airfield was also being used increasingly as an advanced base by 38 Squadron, although this latter unit was shortly to move forward itself to an airfield at Great Gambut. During the night of 10/11 March ten aircraft from 37 and 70 Squadrons raided Gadurra, while next day five 70 Squadron aircraft, joined by one from 38 Squadron, flew from El Adem to attack Rhodes. Six more bombers from 37 and 70 Squadrons returned on 12/13, bombing Maritza and Kattavia airfields as well as Gadurra. At the latter target one S.79 was destroyed and four damaged, while a single S.81 suffered damage at Maritza. Severe sandstorms in the desert for two days, 13/14 March, brought a temporary halt to operations there, but when this abated, both units undertook further raids on Tripoli.

Saturday – Sunday, 8/9 March 1941

0 Sqn	Wellington IC T2733 damaged beyond repair in heavy landing after raid on Tripoli; Sgt Fear and crew safe

Following its near-catastrophic losses at Luqa, 148 Squadron (Wg Cdr E.C.Lewis) left Malta for Kabrit, although it was to maintain a detachment of Wellingtons on the island for another month. These were eventually replaced by units of Blenheims from England, which it was felt enjoyed the advantage of being able to operate both by day and by night (see *Malta: the Hurricane Years, 1940-41*).

Shortly after arrival the squadron lost the services of one of its leading personalities, Flt Lt W.N.Perioli, DFC & Bar, when Wellington T2876 'Y' crashed into a wall in a dust storm as he was landing at Heliopolis while ferrying passengers to a conference there. Periolo and the other seven aboard were all injured and the aircraft damaged beyond repair. Perioli was air-lifted home to the UK a few days later.

Monday – Tuesday, 17/18 March 1941

0 Sqn	Wellington IC T2732 engine trouble during raid on Tripoli; overshot on landing, collided with obstacle and damaged beyond repair; Flt Lt R.E. Ridgway and crew safe

38 Squadron returned to Shallufa from Great Gambut on 22/23 March, although the latter airfield continued to be used as a refuelling base.

Sunday, 30 March 1941

48 Sqn	Wellington IC T2890 'E' engine cut after take-off from Gambut; crash-landed on return. Burnt when airfield evacuated

These weeks were to see constant detachments from Egypt, not only to Malta and Greece, but during May to Iraq. The start of April saw 38 Squadron move forward to Great Gambut again for operations during the moon period, which was just beginning, but on 6 April came news of the Axis advance in

Tripolitania, and units began withdrawing almost at once. 70 Squadron was ordered from El Adem to Sidi Aziez, while 257 Wing HQ sought to establish itself at this same airfield to provide operational control of the bombers generally. New orders required advanced landing grounds for 38 and 148 Squadrons to be maintained also at Sidi Aziez, and for 70 Squadron at Capuzzo North. 148 Squadron had just moved up from Kabrit to Bu Amud, but was at once sent back to Capuzzo North as well.

In the midst of all this confusion, 38 Squadron managed to launch further raids on Rhodes, claiming five or six aircraft destroyed on the ground at Maritza. By 7 April all squadrons were moving back toward the Fuka area, but at this stage a series of huge sandstorms driven by 60 mph winds brought most flying to a halt.

Saturday – Sunday, 5/6 April 1941
British Casualties

148 Sqn	Wellington IC R1251 'L' engine cut and crash-landed near Sollum; destroyed by crew of Sgt J.G.Broad-Smith, who survived unhurt

Monday, 7 April 1941
British Casualties

70 Sqn	Wellington IC T2995 crash-landed soon after take-off due to engine failure during sortie to Tobruk; not repaired

148 Squadron now set about reinforcing its remaining detachment on Malta, sending three more Wellingtons to the island on 12 April to bring the number there to nine; three more would follow shortly. Meanwhile, the other units in Egypt were heavily involved in bombing landing grounds which were once more in Axis hands, and attacking concentrations and columns of motor transport. By night on the 13th Wellington 'K' of 70 Squadron bombed and strafed El Adem airfield, where the unit had so recently been based, also attacking the coast road west of Tobruk.

38 Squadron had undertaken a series of similar raids, but was now withdrawing via Fuka Satellite to Sollum and then Shallufa. Here the squadron received a batch of decorations, including six DFCs, one for the commanding officer, Wg Cdr W.P.J.Thompson, plus two DFMs. On 11 April the unit sent a detachment to Eleusis in Greece. The crews remaining at Shallufa launched attacks on Derna, Gazala, El Adem and Capuzzo during the next few days, during which, on the night of 13/14, Flg Off H.W.S.Adams and his crew in R1033 were lost without trace.

Sunday – Monday, 13/14 April 1941
British Casualties

38 Sqn	Wellington IC R1033 Flg Off H.W.S.Adams & crew MiA

Next night four 70 Squadron aircraft raided El Adem, Menastir, Derna and Bu Amud. Crews claimed a hit on a hangar at El Adem, while at Menastir one Axis aircraft was claimed to have been destroyed on the ground by strafing, one more and two probables being claimed at Derna.

Monday, 21 April 1941
British Casualties

38 Sqn	Wellington IC T2993 'E' bombed Burre; aircraft struck off charge, presumably due to damage; Plt Off Slatter and crew safe

27 April brought a further re-organisation in 257 Wing, albeit in some ways a decidedly temporary one. Advanced HQ was to be responsible only for the operational control of forces – now to be four heavy bomber units and three Glenn Martin Maryland squadrons – while Rear HQ was to control all administrative matters in the Western Desert.

A couple of nights after this new arrangement came into force, 70 Squadron lost Wellington T2727, the crew of which became disoriented while returning from a raid on Benghazi, Flg Off B.S.M.Jones, the squadron's longest-serving member, and his co-pilot, Plt Off D.R.Mitchell, being killed when the aircraft flew into the escarpment south of Sollum in low cloud; the other five aboard were all injured. Plt Off C.A.Patten set off to seek help, walking for a day and a half to do so. On 30 April the squadron sent nine aircraft to Shaibah in Iraq to aid in the defence of the Habbaniya base (see *Dust Clouds in the Middle East*)

Monday – Tuesday, 28/29 April 1941

British Casualties

| 70 Sqn | Wellington IC T2727 Flg Off B.S.M.Jones and one KiFA; four injured |

The situation in Iraq was to demand further support, eight 37 Squadron aircraft moving to Aqir, Palestine, on 1 May, more of this unit's bombers flying in to join 70 Squadron at Shaibah next day. On the 1st meanwhile, five of 38 Squadron's Wellingtons undertook raids, but while landing back at Shallufa one of these was totally destroyed by the accidental release of a 40 lb bomb which had hung-up. Plt Off H.W.E.Lane and his crew in N2855 'R' were all killed.

Thursday – Friday, 1/2 May 1941

British Casualties

| 38 Sqn | Wellington IC N2855 'R' destroyed by hung-up 40lb bomb; Plt Off H.W.E. Lane & crew KiFA |

Friday – Saturday, 2/3 May 1941

On 2 May a single aircraft from 148 Squadron attacked Benina, claiming a direct hit on a Ju 52/3m plus one more destroyed by machine-gun fire and several others damaged. 37 Squadron despatched one of its remaining aircraft at Shallufa, R1290 'Y', on a raid but while landing at Fuka Satellite on return the pilot came down on the wrong side of the flarepath and ran into 38 Squadron's N2855 which was fully bombed-up and refuelled – but fortunately with no crew aboard. Both aircraft burst into flames, but the 37 Squadron crew were all able to escape with their lives, although both pilot and co-pilot suffered broken bones and two other members of the crew were burned, one of them seriously.

British Claims

| 148 Sqn | 2 Ju 52/3ms destroyed & 1 damaged |

British Casualties

| 37 Sqn | Wellington IC R1290 'Y'; collided with N2855 on landing; Plt Off L.R.Hewitt & 3 injured |
| 38 Sqn | Wellington IC N2855 destroyed in collision with R1290 |

Sunday – Monday, 4/5 May 1941

This night saw both 37 and 38 Squadrons operating again, one returning crew claiming four aircraft on fire at Kalathos, Rhodes. However, it proved to be a bad night for the 257 Wing squadrons. T2615 'S' of 37 Squadron failed to return from a sortie to Benghazi, one member of Plt Off D.Paterson's crew being killed and the other six all becoming PoWs, including a SAAF Lt who had apparently gone along as a passenger. One of 38 Squadron's aircraft crashed on return from a raid on Benina and was destroyed with the loss of the whole crew.

British Casualties

| 37 Sqn | Wellington IC T2615 'S' Plt Off D.Paterson & 5 PoW; 1 KiA |
| 38 Sqn | Wellington IC W5681 crashed on return from raid; Sgt N.F.Dixon & crew KiFA |

At this time sorties were also being directed over Greece again, where the Luftwaffe now had bases in the south of the country, and supplies were dropped to Allied troops in Crete. Raids on airfields in Greece and the Dodecanese Islands were made by aircraft from all four squadrons during the nights of 12/13 and 13/14 May, while at this time the detached aircraft of 37 and 70 Squadrons returned from Shaibah to rejoin their parent units in Egypt. During one raid on Hassani, Greece, in the early hours of 13 May by a pair of 70 Squadron aircraft, the crews reported having definitely destroyed four aircraft and probably another nine.

Attacks on the Peleponnese airfields continued on 17 May, in support of the forces on Crete, but later in the month that island itself became increasingly the target for attacks as evacuation of the defenders began. According to Italian sources, a Wellington was claimed shot down over Derna by a Bf 110 pilot, but no British losses are recorded as having occurred.

Friday – Saturday, 23/24 May 1941

Six 37 Squadron Wellingtons set off for Maleme on the night of 23/24 May, one of these returning early with technical problems. The raid, however, cost three aircraft. Sgt W.R.Faulkner bombed Maleme airfield, but due to fuel shortage he was obliged to land L7866 'R' at Heraklion airfield which was still in British hands. The aircraft was refuelled, but was then destroyed by strafing Bf 110s. The crew were too late to be evacuated, and all became PoWs.

Meanwhile Sgt H.J.Mew's T2895 'J' failed to return, all the crew being lost, and Sgt G.E.Harris' T2875 'B' came down in the sea 140 miles north of Maaten Bagush when it too ran out of fuel. Harris was fortunate to be able to ditch close to the cruiser HMS *Coventry*, and all the crew were safely picked up.

Four more Wellingtons from 38 Squadron all returned safely, three having bombed Maleme where a Ju 52/3m of KGrzbV 102 was destroyed on the ground, being seen on fire by the crews. Seven 148 Squadron aircraft also attacked Maleme, using anti-submarine bombs. Sqn Ldr R.J.Wells claimed one aircraft destroyed on the ground and a large building demolished, on the strength of which he was awarded an immediate DFC.

British Casualties	
37 Sqn	Wellington IC L7866 'R' Sgt W.R.Faulkner and crew PoW
	Wellington IC T2875 'B' Sgt G.E.Harris and crew picked up by cruiser and safe
	Wellington IC T2895 'J' Sgt H.J.Mew and crew KiA
British Claims	
38 Sqn	Ju 52/3m on ground
148 Sqn	E/a on ground by Sqn Ldr R.J.Wells and crew
German Casualties	
KGrzbV 102	Ju 52/3m destroyed on ground

Monday – Tuesday, 26/27 May 1941

Maleme was again attacked on 26 May when five aircraft were claimed destroyed, while on 27/28th two more Wellingtons were successful here, a Ju 52/3m of KGrzbV 106 and a Bf 109E of III./JG 52 being destroyed. 38 Squadron's Flt Lt D.H.Duder was a further recipient of the DFC.

British Claims	
257 Wg	5 aircraft destroyed on ground

Tuesday – Wednesday, 27/28 May 1941

German Casualties	
KGrzbV 106	Ju 52/3m destroyed on ground
III./JG 52	Bf 109E destroyed on ground

Wednesday – Thursday, 28/29 May 1941

Two 70 Squadron aircraft attacked Scarpanto during the night of 28/29 May, and here a Bf 109E of the recently-arrived III./JG 77 was badly damaged by bomb splinters.

German Casualties	
III./JG 77	Bf 109E badly damaged on ground

Thursday – Friday, 29/30 May 1941

Scarpanto was the target for 37 Squadron next night, three of this unit's aircraft joined by two of 70 Squadron and one of 148 Squadron. An aircraft was seen going down in flames, and this was L7860 'A' of 37 Squadron, Flt Sgt D.D.Strickland and his crew all being killed when the bomber crashed on Efialti airfield, Rhodes. One CR.42 was damaged by bomb splinters at Scarpanto. Two more of this unfortunate unit's aircraft were preparing to take off at Shallufa to attack Maleme again. Sgt J.W.Kenner in W5685 turned across the flarepath just as Sgt H.N.Goodall's W5622 was beginning its take-off run, and crashed into it. In each aircraft the bombs exploded, destroying them both. Goodall and all his crew were injured, he and one other subsequently dying. However, all but one of Kenner's crew died in the explosion, a single injured sergeant surviving.

Benghazi had also been a target during this night, and from this location another Wellington failed to return. An Italian radio broadcast confirmed that Sgt G.Leather and his crew had all become PoWs.

Their 38 Squadron R1388 had been hit by Flak over the target, the starboard engine being put out of action and the port one set on fire; the aircraft crash-landed about 50 miles east of the port.

British Casualties	
37 Sqn	Wellington IC L7860 'A' Flt Sgt D.D.Strickland & crew shot down in flames
	Wellington IC W5685 collided on flarepath on take-off; Flt Sgt J.W.Kenner and three KiFA; one injured
	Wellington IC W5622 Sgt H.N.Goodall and one died of injuries; four injured
38 Sqn	Wellington IC R1388 hit by Flak and crash-landed; Sgt G.Leather & crew PoW
Italian Casualties	
62ª Sq CT	CR.42 damaged on ground

Friday – Saturday, 30/31 May 1941

The recently-decorated Sqn Ldr Wells led seven 148 Squadron aircraft to Heraklion, six completing attacks on this target where fires were seen. A number of Ju 52/3ms had been hit including at least one of I./KGrzbV 1. At Maleme four 38 Squadron crews reported fires and explosions, believing that three aircraft had been destroyed. In fact three KGrzbV 172 Ju 52/3ms were badly damaged, one of which was written off.

Other Wellingtons raided the Greek mainland, striking at the harbour at Piraeus. Here the Bulgarian steamer *Knyaquinya Maria Luisa* (3,821 tons) was hit as she rode at anchor in the harbour entrance. Her deck cargo of drums of benzine caught fire and detonated her main cargo of ammunition. She blew up and in doing so sank two other vessels, the German *Alicante* (2,140 tons) and the Rumanian *Jiul* (3,127 tons); some 200 casualties were caused.

German Casualties	
I./KGrzbV 1	Ju 52/3m destroyed on ground at Heraklion
KGrzbV 172	Ju 52/3m badly damaged on ground and written off at Maleme
	2 Ju 52/3ms badly damaged on ground at Maleme

Saturday – Sunday, 31 May/1 June 1941

Five 37 Squadron Wellingtons raided Maleme while four of 70 Squadron attacked Heraklion. At least ten aircraft were claimed probably destroyed, but many of these were almost certainly already wrecked from the earlier attacks during the German landings.

Tuesday – Wednesday, 3/4 June 1941

During a raid on Benghazi by aircraft of 148 Squadron, Sqn Ldr F.F.Rainford's rear gunner, Sgt Moore, claimed a CR.42 shot down during the return flight.

British Claims	
148 Sqn	CR.42 claimed by Wellington rear gunner

Thursday – Friday, 5/6 June 1941

148 Squadron again attacked Benghazi with five aircraft in bad weather, while one more set out to drop supplies to troops still at liberty in Crete. This latter aircraft, T2981 'G', ditched in the sea about 100 miles north of Sidi Barrani. Flt Lt H.E.Broadsmith's crew were spotted in their dinghy by the crew of a Sunderland flyingboat next day and supplies were dropped to them. However, bad weather prevented a landing to pick them up, and they were not found again.

British Casualties	
148 Sqn	Wellington IC T2981 'G' ditched in sea 100m N Sidi Barrani after dropping supplies on Crete;
	Flt Lt H.E.Broadsmith and crew MiA

Friday – Saturday, 6/7 June 1941

Next night it was 37 Squadron which again reported the loss of one of its aircraft. During another raid on Benghazi, Flg Off McArthur's T2917 'N' was hit by Flak and ditched north of El Daba. This crew were luckier, being picked up by a Sunderland on the 8th.

British Casualties

37 Sqn	Wellington IC T2917 'N' hit by Flak and ditched in sea N El Daba. Flg Off McArthur and crew rescued by flyingboat on 8th; pilot and two of crew injured

Tuesday – Wednesday, 10/11 June 1941

Sgt C.Muller of 70 Squadron undertook an attack on Benghazi in W5654. While being diverted due to fog during the return flight, he attempted to land at Fuka but bellied-in when one engine failed; all the crew were safe.

British Casualties

70 Sqn	Wellington IC W5654 crash-landed when engine failed (possibly due to lack of fuel) during return from raid; Sgt C.Muller and crew safe

Tuesday – Wednesday, 17/18 June 1941

British Casualties

37 Sqn	Wellington IC T2728 crash-landed on return from raid on Benghazi; Plt Off P.S. Fougere and crew safe

Wednesday, 18 June 1941

All Wellington units were ordered to commence attacks on Aleppo and Beirut in support of the invasion of Syria and the Lebanon (see *Dust Clouds in the Middle East*).

Friday – Saturday, 20/21 June 1941

During an attack on Benghazi harbour, 38 Squadron's T2748 'K' suffered an engine failure and subsequently crashed about 100 miles east of the target. Two members of the crew became PoWs, but Sgt C.G.E.Newton and three others were never found, nor was the wreck of their Wellington.

British Casualties

38 Sqn	Wellington IC T2748 'K' crashed 100m E Benghazi due to engine failure. Sgt C.G.E. Newton and three of crew MiA; two members of crew PoW

Sunday – Monday, 22/23 June 1941

British Casualties

37 Sqn	Wellington IC L7846 'J' unable to find Benghazi in cloud and failed to return; Sgt C.T.Fletcher and crew MiA

Tuesday – Wednesday, 24/25 June 1941

Benghazi was the target for 38 Squadron's W5628 'Y'. However, Plt Off R.J.Cooper was obliged to crash-land near Sidi Barrani when one propeller and its reduction gear flew off. The aircraft was damaged beyond repair, but the crew survived unhurt.

British Casualties

38 Sqn	Wellington IC W5628 'Y' crash-landed near Sidi Barrani due to loss of propeller; Plt Off R.J.Cooper and crew safe

Saturday – Sunday, 5/6 July 1941

With the campaign in Syria approaching its conclusion, further raids were launched on Beirut and Aleppo in an effort to hasten the Vichy French decision to cease fighting.

Monday,7 July 1941

In conjunction with the raids on Syria, Flg Off F.C.D.Winser of 148 Squadron took off to attack Aleppo in T2746 'R'. When returning from this raid he encountered bad visibility and flew into the ground, the wrecked and burnt-out aircraft being discovered amongst sand dunes about 55 miles east of Ismailia. All the crew were dead except the rear gunner who had suffered injuries but survived.

That night over Benghazi 70 Squadron's Sgt Cowley suffered an attack on his T2814 by a CR.42. The rear gunner, Sgt Clancy, allowed it to close before firing, whereupon it spun away, although he did not see it crash.

Far to the east this squadron's Plt Off Duigan was also raiding Aleppo when W5660 was attacked by a reported three fighters and he was obliged to jettison his bombs. The rear gunner, Plt Off George Morris, was wounded and his turret put out of action. Nonetheless, he continued to operate the turret manually, claiming one shot down, one probable and one damaged. Duigan was then obliged to crash-land his damaged Wellington on return to base. The French fighter pilots involved were from GC I/7, reportedly suffering no damage to their Morane 406s, though Adj Chef Georges Amarger, who reported intercepting two bombers which he identified as Blenheims, was credited with one shot down. Morris would be awarded a DFC during the following month. The citation stated:

"This officer was rear gunner of an aircraft which was attacked from the rear with cannon and machine gun fire from three enemy fighters while making a run over Nasrulla aerodrome. The enemy's first burst of fire destroyed the hydraulic system of the rear turret and wounded Pilot Officer Morris in the abdomen and right leg. Despite his wounds he operated his turret by hand and fired a long burst into one of the attacking fighters which burst into flames and crashed. The remaining attackers concentrated on the rear turret which was shot to pieces. Pilot Officer Morris, however, continued to keep his guns in action and fired another long burst of fire which, with one from the front gunner, entered another of the enemy fighters and caused it to dive towards the ground. It was probably destroyed. Further bursts from the front and rear guns were fired into the remaining fighter causing it to break off the engagement. Throughout the action Pilot Officer Morris set a splendid example of courage and endurance."

This account shows well how in the heat of both battle and darkness events thought to be seen can be misinterpreted in all good faith.

British Claims

70 Sqn	CR.42 probable	Claimed by Sgt Cowley, rear gunner in T2814, over Benghazi
	MS 406	Claimed by Plt Off G.S.E.Morris, rear gunner in W5660, over Nasrulla, Syria
	MS 406 probable	Claimed by Plt Off G.S.E.Morris, rear gunner and front gunner as above
	MS 406 damaged	Claimed by Plt Off G.S.E.Morris, rear gunner and front gunner as above

British Casualties

148 Sqn	Wellington IC T2746 'R' crashed into ground in bad visibility; Flg Off F.C.D.Winser and four of crew KiA; rear gunner Sgt J.K.Callister badly injured but survived
70 Sqn	Wellington IC W5660 damaged by French fighter and crash-landed; rear gunner, Plt Off G.S.E.Morris, wounded

French Claims

GC I/7	Wellington (claimed as Blenheim) by Adj Chef Georges Amarger over Nasrulla, Syria

Sunday – Monday, 13/14 July 1941

British Casualties

38 Sqn	Wellington IC N2756 'U' MiA from raid on Benghazi; Flt Sgt J.P.Wilkins and crew KiA

Wednesday – Thursday, 16/17 July 1941

Minelaying was now being undertaken by 257 Wing as part of the campaign against the supply port of Benghazi. These operations were codenamed 'Cucumbers'. While engaged on such a sortie, Flt Lt P.A.Ostle's L7864 'T' of 38 Squadron failed to return, the crew all surviving as PoWs.

British Casualties

38 Sqn	Wellington IC L7864 'T' abandoned near Matruh while on minelaying sortie; Flt Lt P.A.Ostle and crew PoW

Thursday, 24 July 1941

Wg Cdr Lewis, 148 Squadron's commanding officer, was now posted to 257 Wing as SASO. His place was taken by Sqn Ldr F.F.Rainford, who was promoted Wg Cdr.

Thursday – Friday, 31 July/1 August 1941

Six Wellingtons attacked shipping at Benghazi, 257 Wing learning that one had force-landed in the sea ten miles north-west of Ras el Milh. This was 37 Squadron's R1067 'A' in the hands of Sgt D.K.Taylor; the whole crew were lost.

On 1 August 108 Squadron which had been disbanded in the UK in April 1940, was reformed at Kabrit with one flight of Wellington ICs. Sqn Ldr B.J.McGinn arrived from 204 Group as temporary commanding officer until Wg Cdr R.J.Wells, DFC, could be posted in from 148 Squadron on the 6th.

With all other diversions of effort now out of the way, 257 Wing's aircraft were almost entirely settled in Egypt for the time being, and were able to concentrate on priority targets of which Benghazi was the pre-eminent. However, regular raids were also made on Bardia, Capuzzo, Crete and Greece, where Eleusis and the Corinth Canal were quite frequent targets.

During the month the first Luftwaffe night fighters arrived in North Africa when Hptmn Peters led the Bf 110s of I./NJG 3 from Greece to Derna. Until this time the Wellingtons had enjoyed a relatively trouble-free time at night, and losses had been low. They were to remain fairly untroubled for a while, as the Bf 110s were initially used mainly for day reconnaissance and strafing missions.

Friday – Saturday, 8/9 August 1941

Indeed, it was against the Corinth Canal that a maximum effort was launched as a result of which it was believed that the waterway was blocked for about a month.

In the meantime 38 Squadron had despatched a detachment to Malta at the start of the month. This was joined by the balance of the unit after the Corinth raid, and here it was to remain until late October. Its priority target was to be Tripoli, the first attack on this port being launched on 18 August.

Sunday – Monday, 17/18 August 1941

Friday – Saturday, 22/23 August 1941

Saturday – Sunday, 30/31 August 1941

During attacks on Tripoli 38 Squadron was to lose but two aircraft, the first of these during the night of 30/31 August. On this occasion Plt Off P.C.F.Mauchlen's X479737 'Z' was reported by Italian sources to have been shot down in flames by a torpedo boat. The pilot and one other member of the crew were killed, the other four becoming PoWs.

Sunday – Monday, 31 August/1 September 1941

Generally, however, this period was to bring considerably fewer operational losses, although it was on the following night that one of these occurred. While raiding Benghazi Z8791 of 148 Squadron failed to return. The burnt-out wreckage of the aircraft together with the bodies of some of Flt Sgt R.T.Gayer's crew were later found by an army patrol 70 or so miles south of Tobruk near Wadi Suissaba on 1 October.

Friday – Saturday, 5/6 September 1941
British Casualties

37 Sqn	Wellington IC T2512 'P' took off from Fuka to raid Derna; did not return; Flg Off R.H.Wheeler and crew MiA

Saturday – Sunday, 6/7 September 1941
British Casualties

148 Sqn	Wellington IC W5683 'U' during raid on Benghazi, force-landed near El Abiot; Plt Off J.A.G.Parker and five PoW

Sunday – Monday, 14/15 September 1941
British Casualties

148 Sqn	Wellington IC Z87724 crashed while taking off to raid Benghazi; Sgt V.V. Skerman and crew KiFA

Monday – Tuesday, 22/23 September 1941
38 Squadron's second loss while operating over Tripoli from Malta was suffered on this date, Sgt R.Secomb and his crew being lost with Z8776.

British Casualties

38 Sqn	Wellington IC Z8776 Sgt R.Secomb and crew KiA

Saturday, 27 September 1941
Whilst at dispersal at LG.09, Flt Lt E.E.C.Tomkins left R1095 'F' of 37 Squadron to get a cushion. While he was so involved a 250lb bomb aboard the Wellington blew up, destroying it and all the rest of the crew. X8684 parked nearby was damaged beyond repair by the explosion, one member of the crew being hurt.

108 Squadron, having completed its formation, had moved to Fayid on 12 September, commencing operations against Benghazi on the 23rd. On 27 September, however, Sqn Ldr G.F.Irving's T2729 'V' did not return from an attack on Rhodes. A radio message was received advising that an engine was failing and that the crew were setting a course for Turkey. Obviously the aircraft failed to make it, apparently coming down in the sea south of Rhodes, where all the crew were lost.

British Casualties

37 Sqn	Wellington IC R1095 'F' bomb exploded aboard when the aircraft was on the ground five members of the crew KiA; pilot, Flt Lt E.E.C.Tomkins, not aboard at time and survived
	Wellington IC X8684 damaged beyond repair by explosion of R1095
108 Sqn	Wellington IC T2729 'V' Sqn Ldr G.F.Irving and crew KiA

Whilst the regular attacks on Benghazi continued into October, the opening nights of that month were to see some resumption of casualties.

Thursday – Friday, 2/3 October 1941
British Casualties

37 Sqn	Wellington IC T2508 'O' swung on take-off; undercarriage collapsed, damaged beyond repair; Sgt L.G.Fuller and crew safe

Friday – Saturday, 3/4 October 1941
37 Squadron's Z8768 'V' suffered an engine fire while returning from the target. Flt Lt H.J.Honour ditched just off the coast at El Daba after the port propeller had fallen off due to an engine fire, the crew paddling ashore in their dinghy.

British Casualties

37 Sqn	Wellington IC Z8768 'V' ditched in sea; Flt Lt H.J.Honour and crew safe

Saturday – Sunday, 4/5 October 1941
Lt C.A.D.Key, SAAF, was pilot of T2626 'X' of 70 Squadron which failed to return from Benghazi. He and his crew became PoWs.

By day on the 5th Z8733 'S' of 148 Squadron suffered an engine fire which led Sgt J.K.Pickering to crash-land 12 miles west of Burg el Arab. Pickering had both his legs broken as a result, but the rest of the crew survived with cuts and bruises.

The squadron recorded at this time that problems were being experienced due to the mix of Wellington ICs and Mark IIs which it was now operating. The former ran on 90 octane fuel, but the latter, powered by Rolls-Royce Merlin inline engines, required 100 octane. For this, additional refuelling bowsers were urgently necessary.

British Casualties

70 Sqn	Wellington IC T2626 'X' Lt C.A.D.Key and crew PoWs
148 Sqn	Wellington IC Z8733 'S' crash-landed after engine fire; pilot, Sgt J.K.Pickering, injured; rest of crew safe

Wednesday – Thursday, 8/9 October 1941

British Casualties

148 Sqn	Wellington II W5594 'R' port engine failed over Benghazi during raid; on return in bad weather starboard engine began to fail; crash-landed and destroyed; Plt Off Cowan and crew safe

During October 70 Squadron attacked oil installations at Piraeus, Greece, whereas on Malta Wellingtons of 104 Squadron began arriving from the UK to relieve 38 Squadron. Both squadrons undertook big raids on Tripoli during the night of 17/18 September, and on Naples (by 24 aircraft) on 20/21. However, 40 Squadron was also beginning to arrive on the island as further reinforcement from the UK, allowing 38 Squadron's nine aircraft to return to Egypt, led by that unit's new commanding officer, Wg Cdr J.D.Rollinson, DFC.

Thursday – Friday, 16/17 October 1941

British Casualties

37 Sqn	Wellington IC T2801 'G' taking off to raid Benghazi, collided with a bowser; aircraft and bowser destroyed; Sgt Carver's crew safe

Friday – Saturday, 17/18 October 1941

British Casualties

37 Sqn	Wellington IC Z8735 'N' ran out of fuel returning from Benghazi and crashed while force-landing; Sgt R.A.Mirre and crew all slightly injured, but safe

Wednesday – Thursday, 29/30 October 1941

148 Squadron's targets were shipping at Candia and at Suda Bay, Crete, during this particular night. Two Wellingtons failed to return, all the crew in Sgt Taranto's Z8330 'S' being killed; in Z8368 'W' only the pilot, Flg Off Canton, survived. He was sheltered by locals for a time, but was eventually captured by German troops and became a PoW.

British Casualties

148 Sqn	Wellington II Z8330 'S' Sgt T.Taranto and crew KiA
	Wellington II Z8368 'W' Flg Off N.E.Canton PoW; five crew KiA

At the start of November 257 Wing was expanded into a new 205 Group at Shallufa, this being warranted by the growing number of heavy bomber squadrons now becoming available.

Saturday – Sunday, 1/2 November 1941

The first operations under the aegis of the new group were not to prove auspicious, due to a complete failure of the signals organisation to warn crews of 148 Squadron returning from a raid on Benghazi that a heavy mist was forming. As a result five of the squadron's aircraft ran short of fuel and crashed or force-landed at LG.104. Three members of the crew of one aircraft were injured and two in each of two others were also hurt.

These were not the night's only losses, for T2543 of 70 Squadron also belly-landed at Kabrit due to an engine failure – fortunately without injury to the crew.

148 Sqn	Wellington II Z8336 'K' damaged beyond repair landing; Sgt H.W.Burr and crew safe
	Wellington II W5556 'H' force-landed and damaged beyond repair; three members of Sgt K.F.D.Attwell's crew injured
	Wellington II Z8332 'C' crashed while force-landing; two members of Plt Off R.B. Milburn's crew seriously injured
	Wellington II Z8348 crash-landed; Sgt Lane's crew safe
	Wellington II Z8349 crashed while force-landing; two members of Sgt A.P. Mayhew's crew seriously injured
70 Sqn	Wellington IC T2543 crash-landed due to engine failure; Sgt Sadd's crew safe

Wednesday –Tuesday, 5/11 November 1941

Raids were steadily getting heavier as more aircraft and units became available, those on 5 November being typical of the increased effort now being expended. On this night 24 Wellingtons – nine from 38 Squadron, eight from 148 Squadron, five from 70 Squadron and two from 108 Squadron – raided Benghazi. 148 Squadron had just taken delivery of some of the first 4,000lb bombs to arrive in the Middle East, these weapons being known as 'Cookies'.

20 Wellingtons from 37 and 108 Squadrons attacked Derna on the 6th, and next night three from 148 Squadron dropped the first 4,000 pounders on Benghazi port. On this occasion seven more of the unit's aircraft carrying 1,000lb and 500lb bombs failed to release these due to bad weather.

At this time 205 Group had received a small additional reinforcement when 90 Squadron arrived from the UK with a handful of Boeing Fortress I four-engined bombers. Disbanded in April 1940, this unit had reformed in the UK in May 1941 to receive the first Fortresses from the USA. This detachment to the Middle East would be renumbered 220 Squadron Detachment at the start of December. This latter unit actually being a UK-based Coastal Command squadron which was still operating Hudsons. In the event the detachment was to do very little, and would transfer to the Far East at the beginning of May 1942, ceasing to be a part of 220 Squadron at that point. Fortress 'H' undertook its first high level daylight attack on Benghazi between 1245-1310 on 8 November, but AN529 'K' which was also to make a similar attack, ran out of fuel and crashed while attempting a force-landing 80 miles west of Fort Maddalena.

British Casualties

90 Sqn Det	Fortress I AN529 'K' crashed while force-landing 80m W Fort Maddalena

As the army prepared for its forthcoming Operation Crusader offensive, targets in mid November became predominantly the Axis airfields at Gazala, Benina, Berka and Derna. Mixed loads of bombs varying from 4lb and 20lb missiles to 500 pounders became the norm. On 11 November for instance 14 aircraft of 37 Squadron, 11 from 108 Squadron and four from 70 Squadron were out attacking such targets.

Wednesday – Thursday, 12/13 November 1941

Benghazi continued to be a priority target despite the increased concentration on the airfields. During the night the port was raided by 148 Squadron, but two of this unit's Wellingtons failed to return; Flt Sgt J.J.Watson (Z8338 'Z') and Sgt R.E.Shears (Z8340 'C') were presumed to have been shot down, both crews being killed. This squadron was to drop several more 4,000 pounders during the month.

British Casualties

38 Sqn	Wellington IC R1139 'M' force-landed during raid on Benghazi; Flg Off J.D.Hall and crew of five PoW
148 Sqn	Wellington II Z8338 'Z' Flt Sgt J.J.Watson and crew KiA
	Wellington II Z8340 'C' Sgt R.E.Shears and crew KiA

Thursday, 13 November 1941
British Casualties

70 Sqn	Wellington IC N2811 'T' crash-landed at LG.104 soon after take-off on Benghazi raid; two members of Sgt G.A.Morley's crew injured

Saturday – Sunday, 15/16 November 1941
British Casualties

37 Sqn	Wellington IC W5626 'Q' failed to return from raid on Bardia; Flg Off P.R.Bellamy and crew KiA

Sunday – Monday, 16/17 November 1941

While no sign had been seen by night of the few Bf 110 night fighters which had arrived at Derna during August, a perhaps more cogent threat was occasioned when six Ju 88C-6 aircraft from 2./NJG 2 flew in to Benghazi from Sicily at this time.

148 Squadron suffered another loss during the Benghazi raid when Z8355 'B' was seen to be hit by Flak and go down in flames; again, all the crew were lost. Flg Off R.H.Gorden, DFC, had been with the squadron for more than a year, and it was recorded that he had been "the most popular and brilliant pilot in the squadron"; all his crew had completed at least 40 operational sorties.

British Casualties

148 Sqn	Wellington II Z8355 'B' Flg Off R.H.Gorden and crew KiA

Tuesday – Wednesday, 18/19 November 1941

108 Squadron undertook 16 sorties against various targets during which 'H' was attacked by fighters identified as Bf 109Fs, slight damage to the fuselage being inflicted by a cannon shell. The squadron noted that Flak and searchlights has become noticeably more active at this time.

British Casualties

108 Sqn	Wellington IC 'H' slightly damaged by fighter attack

Wednesday – Thursday, 19/20 November 1941

Following operations over Derna and Bardia, 38 Squadron was to suffer two losses during this night. T2991 'D' crashed attempting a force-landing at El Imayid and blew up, Sgt F.H.Lewis and his crew all being killed. Sgt Swingler and his crew became lost in Z7871 'F'. After a fruitless search they baled out when fuel was exhausted, coming down near Bahariya Oasis, 250 miles south of Sidi Barrani and 180 miles south of Fuka. They were found and picked up next day by a motor patrol of the Egyptian army.

The night had seen 32 sorties against the Gazala airfields by 37, 70 and 108 Squadrons. The latter unit received news of great portent a few days later – it was to have the first Consolidated Liberator four-engined bombers to reach North Africa.

British Casualties

38 Sqn	Wellington IC T2991 'D' Sgt F.H.Lewis and crew KiFA
	Wellington IC Z8711 'F' Sgt Swingler and crew picked up safely

Friday, 21 November 1941

British Casualties

148 Sqn	Wellington II W5568 destroyed on ground in an air raid

Tuesday – Wednesday, 25/26 November 1941

15 Wellingtons from 148 Squadron and ten from 37 Squadron raided Benghazi, but three losses were suffered. 37 Squadron's Plt Off G.E.Guthrie in Z8798 'L' sent out an SOS nearly four hours after take-off, the aircraft coming down 50 miles east of Benghazi where the crew became PoWs. Z8801 'P' (Sgt L.H.Mellor) suffered engine trouble and was eventually abandoned by the crew 25 miles west of Mersa Matruh; they were picked up next day. 148 Squadron's Z8362 K had one engine cut after take-off and crash-landed near base, two members of Sgt J.B.Starkey's crew being killed.

British Casualties

37 Sqn	Wellington IC Z8798 'L' Plt Off G.E.Guthrie and crew PoW
	Wellington IC Z8801 'P' Sgt L.H.Mellor and crew safe
148 Sqn	Wellington II Z8362 'K'; two members of Sgt J.B.Starkey's crew KiFA

Wednesday – Thursday, 26/27 November 1941

Derna was the target for 17 Wellingtons of 108 Squadron and nine of 38 Squadron in bad weather; 25 tons of bombs were dropped. Z8736 'Q' of the latter unit sent out an SOS but failed to return. Flg Off

R.J.Cooper and his crew were lost.

British Casualties

38 Sqn	Wellington IC Z8736 'Q' Flg Off R.J.Cooper and crew MiA

Saturday, 29 November 1941

Plt Off Ashworth of 38 Squadron flew to Heliopolis in X9690 'W' to lead a pair of Wellesleys to Malta. What the purpose was of the flight of these elderly aircraft to the island at a time when it was again under sustained attack, has not been identified. During the flight at 1237 an enemy aircraft was seen which Ashworth and the Wellesleys passed at low level. The crew of this aircraft fired at them for some time and was seen to be jettisoning considerable cargo. The RAF aircraft then reformed and set course for Malta. At 1420 one Wellesley suddenly streamed clouds of black smoke from the engine and crashed into the sea. The crew managed to get out and into their dinghy, following which Ashworth remained in the area until he saw air-sea rescue arrive, whereupon he completed his flight to Malta.

The Albacores of 826 Squadron continued to carry out night sorties over the Derna-Bardia-Sidi Omar area from LG.75.

British Casualties

Unspecified unit	Wellesley crashed in sea due to engine failure en route to Malta; identity of crew not known

205 Group was considerably aided during the second half of 1941 by the Fairey Albacore torpedo-bombers of the Fleet Air Arm, which specialised in dropping flares over targets to assist in the bombing by RAF Wellingtons.

Sunday – Monday, 30 November/1 December 1941

14 Wellingtons of 37 Squadron and 12 of 148 Squadron operated with Benghazi as the main target. However, 37 Squadron attacked Barce town and airfield, claiming a direct hit on a four-engined aircraft. This unit's Sgt J.C.Smith crashed L7856 'M' at Burg el Arab on return, out of fuel; the crew were not hurt badly.

148 Squadron's W5597 'U' was in the landing circuit at LG.60 on return, but found an aircraft of 37 Squadron on the flarepath. Plt Off W.Astell only spotted this as he was about to land. In attempting to go round again, one wing hit the ground and tore off, the aircraft crashing and bursting into flames. However, although Astell and three other members of the crew were seriously injured, they all survived.

British Casualties

37 Sqn	Wellington IC L7856 'M' Sgt J.C.Smith and crew safe with minor injuries
148 Sqn	Wellington II W5597 'U' Plt Off W.Astell and two of crew injured

During December Liberators began arriving with 108 Squadron, which commenced conversion and training on their new aircraft while continuing to send out Wellingtons on operations. Of note at this time 148 Squadron recorded that their Plt Off L.A.Vaughan was awarded a DFC; he had been a fighter pilot in WWI and was now aged 43. Len Vaughan's citation read:

"This officer air gunner has participated in 54 raids, including 26 against targets in Germany and German-occupied territory. Throughout, he has displayed the utmost keenness for operations which, together with his utter contempt for danger has set a splendid example to all. On one occasion during a mine-laying mission, his aircraft was subjected to fire, at close range, from two anti-aircraft guns. By silencing these guns, Pilot Officer Vaughan performed very valuable work in difficult circumstances. As a qualified gunnery leader, he carried out a great deal of the instruction of new crews, a work in which he shows real ability."

Sunday, 7 December 1941

Both 826 and 815 Squadrons were now operating in support of the Wellingtons. El Adem was now being used as a night operations advanced landing ground for their sorties.

Tuesday – Wednesday, 9/10 December 1941

Z8333 'M' of 148 Squadron set out in the hands of Flg Off D.L.Skinner, DFC, to bomb motor transport. It did not return and was later found in a salt marsh, apparently undamaged, but with the crew all dead.

British Casualties

148 Sqn	Wellington II Z8333 'M' Flg Off D.L.Skinner and crew KiA

Next night Maleme, Crete, was the target for 26 Wellingtons from 38, 108 and 148 Squadrons.

Friday – Saturday, 12/13 December 1941

24 bombers from 37 and 70 Squadrons were sent off to the Derna area where one Axis aircraft was claimed destroyed on the ground. Italian records confirm that an S.79 was destroyed during this attack. However, two Wellingtons were lost here. 37 Squadron's N2780 'E' had been detailed to attack MT, but was damaged by Flak over the target, Sgt Carver then bringing the aircraft down in the sea off Sidi Barrani. Four of the crew, two of whom were injured, got ashore in the dinghy next afternoon, but two others who set off to swim were not seen again.

70 Squadron's X9686 'Z' was shot down, crashing near Martuba. Flg Off K.C.Kitto and his crew were killed.

British Casualties

37 Sqn	Wellington IC N2780 'E' Sgt Carver and one safe; two KiA, two injured
70 Sqn	Wellington IC X9686 'Z' Flg Off K.C.Kitto and crew KiA
Italian Casualties	
19ª Sq BT	S.79 destroyed on ground at Derna

Saturday – Sunday, 13/14 December 1941
15 Wellingtons returned to Derna in very bad weather.

Sunday – Monday, 14/15 December 1941
British Casualties

826 Sqn	Albacore N4319 '4F' FTR from raid on Derna airfield in poor weather; Sub Lt K.W.Jones and two KiA

Tuesday – Wednesday, 16/17 December 1941
The commanding officer of 826 Squadron, Lt Cdr J.W.S.Corbett, set off in Albacore N4362 '4A' to bomb Bachi, refuelling at Bu Amud. Due to clouds over the target, nearby barracks were bombed instead. During the return flight engine failure was experienced, the aircraft being landed on the road three miles from Bu Amud from where it was towed back.

Thursday – Saturday, 18/20 December 1941
By night on the 18th five mine-carrying Wellingtons of 148 Squadron laid ten Cucumbers at the entrance to Benghazi harbour. Next night, 19/20, three more of this unit's aircraft and 12 of 70 Squadron raided Benina. The latter unit's T2987 'O' was shot down by Flak with the loss of Capt L.N.Evans, SAAF, and his crew, while Z8728 'U' crashed on return when an engine failed, Sqn Ldr W.A.A.de Freitas, DFC, and crew all being killed also.

By day 70 Squadron's commanding officer, Wg Cdr G.J.L.Read, AFC, handed the unit over to Wg Cdr J.H.T.Simpson.

British Casualties

70 Sqn	Wellington IC T2987 'O' Capt L.N.Evans, SAAF, and crew KiA
	Wellington IC Z8728 'U' Sqn Ldr W.A.A.de Freitas* and crew KiA

*De Freitas's promotion to Wg Cdr came through at the time of his death, and he was listed thus in casualty records, but still referred to as Sqn Ldr in the unit ORB.

Wednesday, 24 December 1941
11 of 70 Squadron's aircraft were out again, joined by six of 108 Squadron. During this raid 'M' force-landed but both crew and aircraft survived.

Thursday, 25 December 1941
British Casualties

826 Sqn	Albacore N4284 ferrying from Sollum to Bardia, shot down by machine-gun fire from the ground; Sub Lt R.S.Nathan and one safe, but observer KiA

Tuesday – Wednesday, 30/31 December 1941
The end of the year saw a heavy attack on Salamis by 37, 38, 70, 108 and 148 Squadron aircraft. During the month 70 Squadron, the original desert Wellington unit, had undertaken 102 sorties; it was to carry out 70 more in January during which it would drop 154,360lbs of bombs.

Friday – Saturday, 2/3 January 1942
70 Squadron began the new year on a bad note, however, when Sgt Parker returned from a sortie to the Ras Lanuf-Marble Arch (Arae Philenorum) road area in X9987 'P' and was obliged to force-land on a beach 30 miles west of Sidi Barrani. The undercarriage sank into the soft sand causing the aircraft to swing into the sea as the undercarriage struts collapsed. Fortunately, the crew were unharmed.

British Casualties

70 Sqn	Wellington IC X9987 'P' Sgt A.V.Parker and crew safe

Sunday – Monday, 4/5 January 1942
Benghazi was attacked by seven bombers, crews reporting that a small oil dump had been destroyed and an empty hangar set on fire.

Monday – Tuesday, 5/6 January 1942

Axis bombers now struck at Tobruk, nine aircraft attacking first, followed by eight more. Little damage was done, but at Bu Amud a Blenheim was destroyed and a second damaged, damage also being inflicted on five motor vehicles.

Tuesday, 6 January 1942

By this time 108 Squadron's aircrews had decided that the armament fitted to the Liberator II was totally inadequate for a heavy bomber, and modifications were made – including trying to fit a Wellington tail turret to the new aircraft. On this date one Liberator was slated to join six Wellingtons in the first operational use of the aircraft, but this was cancelled due to bad weather.

British Casualties	
148 Sqn	Wellington II Z8363 'F' on return to LG.60 from a raid on Tripoli, flew on to LG.09 due to evacuation; became lost, ran out of fuel and crashed south of El Shaba; Flt Lt D.A.Cracknell and crew safe

Wednesday, 7 January 1942

By this time Rommel's counter-attack following the conclusion of the Crusader thrust was leading to a repeat withdrawal reminiscent of the previous April. 148 Squadron noted that LG.60 was being abandoned, all aircraft moving back to El Adem.

During the day a 37 Squadron Wellington flew a reconnaissance patrol over Capuzzo airfield, carrying six passengers including Lewis G.Merritt, of the US Marine Corps, who would subsequently become a brigadier general in that service. The aircraft was hit by Flak and Sqn Ldr Alexander had to crash-land in territory behind the Axis lines south of the Halfaya Pass. Here the party was rescued safely by the army, although the aircraft was lost.

British Casualties	
37 Sqn	Wellington IC Z8763 two members of Sqn Ldr Alexander's crew injured in crash-landing

205 Group recorded that targets were more diverse during January and that perhaps in consequence, very few losses occurred. The group did make mention of 109 Squadron undertaking special reconnaissance operations. This unit, which had been formed in the UK in December 1940 from the Wireless Intelligence Unit at Boscombe Down, was also Wellington-equipped, but was not sent out to the Middle East, although it appears that some of its aircraft had indeed been detached to this area for electronic counter-measures. Two of them had been shot down, one on 20 or 21 November and one on the 22nd of that month. However, since these losses were suffered during daylight they are dealt with in the main chapters detailing the daytime operations over the Western Desert.

Friday – Saturday, 9/10 January 1942

En route to attack MT on the Buerat-Sirte road, a 37 Squadron aircraft – L7864 'D' – flown by Sgt J.F.R.Morrison, suffered an engine failure, lost height and crash-landed ten miles north-east of El Adem, being damaged beyond repair.

British Casualties	
37 Sqn	Wellington IC L7864 'D' Sgt J.F.R.Morrison and crew safe

Saturday – Sunday, 10/11 January 1942

108 Squadron's first operational Liberator sortie was flown when AL566 'P' in the hands of Wg Cdr Wells, accompanied six of the unit's Wellingtons to attack Tripoli harbour. The squadron recorded that it was more by way of a test flight than a serious operational one.

Prior to dark on Saturday another four-engined bomber had come to grief, however. In 90 Squadron's small detachment of Fortress Is, AN521 suffered an engine fire a few miles north-north-west of Shallufa. The crew baled out, but one man hit the tailplane and was killed; one other failed to survive the experience and two more suffered injuries. This second loss marked the end of the Fortress I's very brief sojourn in North Africa.

Monday, 12 January 1942
British Casualties

148 Sqn   Wellington II Z8347 'L' hit by fire from Flak ship and blew up 30 miles east of Buerat-El Hsun; Plt Off T.F.B.Geary and crew KiA

On 12 January 70 Squadron moved to LG.75, and two days later the detachment of Wellingtons from 104 Squadron which had been operating on Malta since October, were ordered to Kabrit. The parent unit in England had been re-numbered 158 Squadron, so 104 now became 205 Group's sixth heavy bomber squadron.

Another of 108 Squadron's Liberators, AL574, was put to different service on 18 January. 84 Squadron (Blenheims) had been posted to the Far East following the Japanese attack there, and this large aircraft was employed to carry that unit's equipment out to Palembang in Sumatra. Having achieved this chore, it returned safely to its own unit on 25 January.

Tuesday – Wednesday, 20/21 January 1942
One of the few losses of the month occurred during another attack on the submarine base at Salamis. Eight out of the 12 aircraft despatched reached the target, but only two released their bombs, the rest returning with their loads due to the bad weather which interfered with aiming. From this raid 148 Squadron's W5584 'W' failed to return, Sqn Ldr M.E.Abbott, DFC, and his crew being lost.

British Casualties

148 Sqn   Wellington II W5584 'W' Sqn Ldr M.E.Abbott and crew KiA

Saturday, 24 January 1942
British Casualties

828 Sqn   Albacore X8971 (based at Hal Far, Malta) en route from Benghazi to Malta, MiA; Lt V.N.S.Davies and one KiA

Sunday – Monday, 25/26 January 1942
In support of 8th Army, 15 Wellingtons attacked MT columns near Agedabia. Three aircraft machine-gunned these from low level. More such attacks would follow over the next few nights.

Tuesday – Wednesday, 27/28 January 1942
19 Wellingtons were again active over the battle area, four of these going down so that the turret gunners could do some strafing.

As the month drew to a close, the Liberators of 108 Squadron came more fully into use. On 29 January two, AL530 'Q' (Wg Cdr Wells) and AL577 'O' (Flt Lt Alexander) accompanied six of the unit's Wellingtons to attack MT on the Agedabia-Agheila road. Two nights later two of these aircraft again accompanied the Wellingtons on a raid. The great advantage of the Liberator had now become obvious – its very long range capability allowed it to undertake raids base-to-base with no requirement for the use of advanced landing grounds for refuelling.

At the close of January 1942 therefore, as the Western Desert Force withdrew towards its new defensive line in the Gazala area, 205 Group's available resources stood at:

37 Squadron	Wellington IC	Shallufa
38 Squadron	Wellington IC*	Shallufa
70 Squadron	Wellington IC	LG.75
104 Squadron	Wellington II	Kabrit
108 Squadron	Wellington IC/	
	Liberator II	Fayid
148 Squadron	Wellington II *	Kabrit

*During October 1941 the Wellington IIs with which 38 Squadron was partially equipped, were exchanged with 148 Squadron, for that unit's Mark ICs, allowing each unit to be fully equipped with only one version of the aircraft.

It will have been noted, no doubt, that throughout this period no more than one claim had been submitted against British night bombers by night fighters of either the Luftwaffe or Regia Aeronautica. Losses to enemy action, where the cause was identified, were all to Flak or other ground fire. The largest number of losses had occurred due to lack of fuel or engine failures. Between the start of December 1940 and the end of January 1942, however, circa a further 23 Wellingtons had been lost to a variety of accidental or technical causes whilst engaged in other than operational flights. What must have been particularly galling to the command however, was the loss of some 52 further aircraft during their delivery flights from the UK. Although some of the latter were of aircraft heading for Malta, the cumulative effect was none the less similar. It should not be overlooked that losses on Malta had also been heavy, whilst the figures presented in this chapter do not include losses suffered when operating from airfields in Greece or Iraq (for which see other volumes in this series dealing with those areas).

CHAPTER 13

BLITZ ON EGYPT

Initial Attacks

Initial raids on Alexandria and Suez were launched mainly from Italian bases in the Dodecanese Islands, but they proved to be of limited duration or strength.

Saturday, 22 June 1940

Alexandria suffered its first bombing raid during the night of 21/22 June by 12 S.81s of 39° Stormo BT (six from 56° Gruppo and six from 92° Gruppo). These bombers departed their base at Gadurra, Rhodes, between 0030 and 0230; on their approach five of 80 Squadron's Gladiators were scrambled in an effort to intercept. The pilots saw nothing, and had the indignity of being fired on by the city's anti-aircraft defences. However, the gunfire was effective in hitting the bomber flown by Ten Tanrico Chiantia, causing it to crash-land in the sea. The crew survived, and were picked up by a Cant.Z.506B floatplane sent out from Rhodes.

Italian Casualties

201ª Sq/92° Gr/39° St BT   S.81 MM20469 crash-landed in the sea due to AA damage; Ten Tanrico Chiantia and crew picked up safely

Friday, 4 July 1940

Gladiators of 80 Squadron were also in action on this date, six of them intercepting nine S.79s of 34° Gruppo BT from Gadurra, north of Alexandria at 12,000 feet, and flying in formations of five and four. The first section of Gladiators attacked the first five bombers as they were heading for the port, but these at once turned and headed out to sea, soon outdistancing the following fighters. The second Gladiator trio, now 3,000 feet above the second Italian formation, dived to make a stern quarter attack, all concentrating on the bomber on the far right of the formation. The leading pilot expended all his ammunition, but Flg Offs A.A.P.Weller and G.F.Graham continued the chase, believing that they had inflicted substantial damage before they were left behind. Eye-witness accounts indicated that the aircraft may have been sufficiently badly damaged to have been shot down, as it was starting to lag behind the rest of the formation and lose height. In consequence Weller and Graham were credited with a probable victory.

The aircraft from 67ª Squadriglia had indeed been hard hit, the last burst of fire to hit it killing the first pilot, Cap Ugo Pozza, but nonetheless it managed to get back to its home base. Here it was found that one of the gunners, Serg Magg Armando Di Tullio, had continued to man his gun even though critically wounded. He died shortly afterwards; both he and Cap Pozza were awarded the Medaglia d'Oro posthumously. One more bomber had been hit, and three crewmen were wounded, although gunners claimed to have shot down one Gladiator. The result of the resistance put up by the defences was to persuade the Italian command not to carry out any further daylight attacks on Alexandria throughout the next 12 months.

British Claims

80 Sqn	Flg Off A.A.P.Weller	½ S.79 probable	N Alexandria
	Flg Off G.F.Graham	½ S.79 probable	N Alexandria

471

Italian Claims

34° Gr BT	S.79 gunners	Gladiator	over Alexandria

Italian Casualties

67ª Sq/34° Gr/11° St BT   2 S.79s damaged by fighters; Cap Ugo Pozza and Serg Magg Armando Di Tullio KiA; three WiA

Sunday, 7 July 1940

Eight S.81s of 56° Gruppo made a further raid on Alexandria. Intense AA fire hit the bomber flown by Ten Enrico Rallo, which failed to return.

Italian Casualties

222ª Sq/56° Gr/ 39° St BT   S.81 MM 20598 Ten Enrico Rallo and crew FTR from night raid on Alexandria

Tuesday, 16 July 1940

12 S.81s of 39° Stormo, drawn equally from 56° and 92° Gruppo, carried out a further night raid on Alexandria harbour, dropping about 500kg of bombs – some of them with delayed action fuses – between 2130-2200. The crew of S.Ten Carlo Felice Ottaviani became lost due to a navigational error, crash-landing in the sea near the island of Scarpanto. The pilot, being a good swimmer, swam ashore and arranged for the crew to be rescued.

Italian Casualties

222ª Sq/56° Gr/39° Sq BT   S.81 ditched in sea; Ten Carlo Felice Ottaviani and crew safe

Thursday, 25 July 1940

Nine S.81s from 39° Stormo (three from 56° Gruppo and six from 92° Gruppo) raided Alexandria by night.

Saturday, 27 July 1940

S.79s returned to attack Alexandria, but this time by night. Four of these bombers from 42° Gruppo, 12° Stormo BT undertook the raid, their crews claiming hits on wharfs and docks.

Monday, 26 August 1940

During the early hours 39° Stormo BT made a further raid on Alexandria, nine S.81s of 56° Gruppo leaving Maritza, northern Rhodes, between 0030-0120. On this occasion only weak AA gunfire was reported by the crews.

Sunday, 8 September 1940

A dusk raid on Alexandria was now tried, two flights each of four 56° Gruppo S.81s attacking between 1935-2000. This time the AA fire was reported to be very heavy, but this was not what caused two of the bombers to fail to return. Both ran out of fuel and ditched together to the east of Castellorizo island, close to the Turkish coast. The crews of both aircraft were picked up next day by a Cant.Z.506B, with the notable exception of the good swimmer, S.Ten Ottaviani. Trying to repeat his performance of 16 July, he managed to swim to the coast – but here he was captured and interned by the Turks.

Italian Casualties

222ª Sq/56° Gr BT   2 S.81s, MM20636 and MM21229, ditched in the sea due to fuel shortage; crews safe, but S.Ten Carlo
                      Felice Ottaviani interned in Turkey

Following these attacks, a further uneventful sortie was made by nine S.81s from 56° Gruppo and six from 92° Gruppo on 22 October. The last such raid was made six and a half months later on 13 May 1941 by three S.79s with which by that time 92° Gruppo had been re-equipped. On that occasion the crews reported being attacked, for the first time, by night fighters.

AERIAL MINESWEEPING

As explained in Chapter One, 201 Group, which had been set up as a general reconnaissance formation, had been without any squadrons under command at the outbreak of war with Italy, pending the arrival of flyingboats to operate over the Mediterranean generally. Experience early in the war around Britain's coasts had quickly provided evidence of a new and very dangerous threat to shipping – the magnetic mine. It was rapidly discovered that at least a partial answer was the fitting of a 'de-gaussing' ring around the aircraft, attached like a giant hoop to the wingtips and tail. An ancillary engine within the aircraft then provided the energy to send an electric current around this ring, which, when passing over such a mine, would replicate the metal hull of a ship and cause the mine to explode – hopefully harmlessly. Coastal Command in the UK at once equipped some of its aircraft to undertake such duties, and having provided for local defence of this nature, in May 1940 1 GRU (General Reconnaissance Unit) was formed at Manston in Kent to take such technology out to the Middle East, now threatened by imminent Italian involvement in the conflict. Equipped with five modified Wellington Is, the unit flew out at once via Gibraltar, Tunis and Malta, arriving first at Mersa Matruh and then Ismailia.

Rapidly fitted with generators and Gypsy engines to provide the power, this unit's aircraft, commanded by Sqn Ldr J.H.Chaplin, flew their first sorties as early as 14 June 1940, sweeping over Alexandria and Port Said harbours during the next few days. The aircraft deployed to Egypt were L4227, L4235, L4374 and L7771. No magnetic mines were to be found in the area until after the arrival of Luftwaffe aircraft, however, but sweeps over the potentially threatened areas continued. Unfortunately, L4235 was lost when it crashed on landing at Ismailia on 30 July 1940.

As German involvement in the Mediterranean war began to be established, an early strategic target selected for attack was the Suez Canal. In the circumstances of the British advance through Cyrenaica in early 1941, attacks from the available airfields still in Italian hands would require to be made at extreme range, whereas a much more promising base of operations could be found on the Italian-occupied island of Rhodes.

L4374 of 1 GRU, fitted with a 'de-gaussing' ring for aerial minesweeping duties, particularly over the Suez Canal.

Close-up of the de-gaussing ring on a Wellington operated by 1 GRU.

Consequently X.Fliegerkorps began moving an appropriate unit to the area, II./KG 26, led by Maj Bertram von Comiso, being sent from Sicily to undertake the first such attack. Fuel was not available in sufficient quantities in Rhodes, however, but was at Benghazi, although the latter city was about to be occupied by British forces. Consequently, 14 Heinkel He 111s were despatched here in preference to the more conveniently-located island. Three of these bombers were damaged in collisions whilst landing, while three more were retained to undertake post-raid reconnaissance flights. Thus only eight Heinkels remained available to make the actual attack.

Friday – Saturday, 17/18 January 1941

On the afternoon of 17 January, 1941, news was received that a convoy was standing off Suez at the south end of the canal, waiting to sail north. At once, the He 111s were launched by night at half-hour intervals to make the maximum range 700-mile flight to the canal. Four were to search the right bank and four the left, the two quartets flying in opposite directions to each other. Careful fuel control by flying at the most economical cruising speed would be necessary.

The receipt of a weather forecast predicting an unfavourable 40 mph wind required that the ideal altitude at which to undertake the flight would be 12,000 feet. To aid in this difficult mission, the X.Fliegerkorps chief of staff, Maj Martin Harlinghausen, opted to lead the raid in the aircraft flown by Hptmn Robert Kowalewski.

Suez was reached by this first aircraft after a four-hour flight and the aircraft turned north, flying right up the canal and around the Great Bitter Lake. No ships were to be seen, and consequently the following bombers were redirected to alternative targets. Harlinghausen meanwhile ordered Kowalewski to turn back south and repeat the search, but once more nothing was seen and instead some bombs were dropped on the Ismailia ferry. As the Great Bitter Lake was reached again, however, ships were at last spotted, widely dispersed in the lake and at anchor. The remaining bombs were released on one vessel, but missed.

As Kowalewski set course to return, he now encountered a 75 mph headwind, but in the dark no landmarks could be seen; he and his crew thus had no idea how far they still had to fly. After five and a half hours, with fuel virtually exhausted, he crash-landed in the desert on a stretch of ground which proved to be so level that he subsequently realised he could have landed on it successfully with undercarriage down. The aircraft was set on fire and the crew, Harlinghausen included, set off on foot for Benghazi, which they felt could not be far in the distance. In fact it was still 175 miles away.

Oblt Kaupisch in one of the other He 111s had realised that the wind at 12,000 ft was far stronger than anticipated, and had made his return flight at low level and close to the coast. In consequence, his was the only bomber to reach Benghazi that night. All the others made emergency landings in the desert, three of these being destroyed and most of the crews captured by British forces. This unsuccessful raid had been the first incursion over Egypt by the Luftwaffe.

German Casualties

5./KG 26	He 111H-5 WNr 3653 1H+BN Fw Karl Wellenreuther and crew KiA
4./KG 26	He 111H-5 WNr 3848 1H+GM Lt Hans Foller and crew, including Maj Helmut Bertram as observer, KiA
6./KG 26	He 111H-5 WNr 3784 crash-landed 25m W Sollum; two of crew injured

Immediately following the raid, two of 1 GRU's de-gaussing Wellingtons undertook a sweep from the Great Bitter Lake to Port Tewfic, and from Ismailia to Port Said in case any mines had been laid in the canal. Such was not, of course, the case, and nothing was to be found.

This was not to be so at the end of the month, however, for during the night of 30/31 January 1941 mines were indeed dropped into the waters of the canal. At this time 1 GRU's three aircraft had been sent forward to Capuzzo to sweep the coastal harbours newly in British hands. From here they were rushed back to Ismailia on 1 February, commencing sweeps immediately. Results were impressive, and during the first morning sortie two were exploded.

There was a need to move the 25,000-ton *Dominion Monarch*, which was waiting in Lake Tinsah to make its way on to Suez. Sweeps in this area caused no explosions and were just about to be concluded when Sqn Ldr Chaplin ordered that one more sweep by the two Wellingtons involved, should be made. His decision proved to be prescient, and on the final sweep a mine was exploded right in front of *Dominion Monarch* as she entered the canal. Had she been sunk at that point, the canal would have been closed to shipping for about three months.

Next day four more sorties resulted in a further explosion, but on 4 February one of the vagaries of the weapon was to be exhibited. A convoy of 12 ships had passed safely up the canal, but on the 13th, SS *Aglios Georgios* exploded a mine as she passed over it and sank at Kilo 142. Next day SS *Ramree* caused another to blow up at Kilo 83, the blast splitting the vessel in two. The canal pilot aboard managed to move the vessel to the side of the canal before it sank, thus avoiding a major blockage. No less than 24 ships had passed over this particular mine before it finally blew up.

Another attack at 0400 on 22 February laid six mines, one of which exploded prematurely on impact with the water. The Wellingtons were not successful in their subsequent sweeps on this occasion, for the mines proved either to have been 'damped', or to be acoustic, requiring to be swept by more traditional methods.

Further mine-laying raids were made during March 1941, and following one such, Wellington L4374 exploded a mine at Kilo 48.8 on 6 March. Sweeps continued for the next six days without further success. On 26 March 1 GRU moved to Kabrit, but would return to Ismailia in August. By that time command had changed, Chaplin being promoted Wg Cdr and posted to Palestine. His place would be taken by Sqn Ldr D.O.Butler.

Such further raids as were made during the opening months of 1941 were aimed mainly at Alexandria, and were usually flown by elements of the Regia Aeronautica operating in the majority of cases from airfields on the Dodecanese islands of Rhodes and Scarpanto. Responsibility for the defence of the base areas remained in the hands of 252 Wing at Helwan, the initially limited activities of which have already been detailed in earlier chapters. The commanding officer of this wing was Wg Cdr K.B.B.Bing Cross, DFC, who we have already encountered. At the port 971 (Balloon Barrage) Squadron was operating up to 30 balloons by mid January.

During January 1941 a single staffel of He 111s – 2./KG 4 'General Wever' – arrived in Sicily to join X.Fliegerkorps as a specialist minelaying unit, operating mainly around Malta and towards the North African coast. This unit also used airfields on Rhodes as advanced bases on occasion to lay mines between there and Benghazi, and in the Suez Canal. This may have been the unit which despatched four or five aircraft to the latter area during the night of 18/19 February. Another raid, this time with bombs, was undertaken by four aircraft on the night of 10/11 March, targetting the canal and the coast from Port Said to El Arish. Seven Hurricanes were scrambled from Ismailia, but made no interceptions. The raid inflicted little or no significant damage, however.

Meanwhile the British High Command were planning an invasion of the Dodecanese islands, and of the small island of Castelorizzo, which was fairly close to Cyprus, under the codename Operation Mandible. (Full details of this operation may be found in *Air War for Yugoslavia, Greece and Crete, 1940-41*.) While initial planning was in hand, 17 He 111s of II./KG 26 arrived on Rhodes on detachment, together with a few reconnaissance Ju 88s from 1(F)./121. During the night of 30/31 January the Heinkels of the former unit undertook another mining operation in the Suez area, a reported 11 aircraft dropping bombs and mines in the canal area between Ismailia and Suez. They then withdrew via Port Said and Damietta.

At this stage the forces available to 252 Wing remained extremely limited, amounting in reality only to 274 Squadron, although theoretically supported by the Gladiators of 2 and 5 Squadrons of the Royal Egyptian Air Force at Almaza and Suez. These two units would exchange bases in early April.

The events of April both in Libya and in the Balkans brought the potential for a considerably increased threat to the Egyptian hinterland, but initially a threat was what it remained.

Friday, 11 April 1941
Just after midday a Dodecanese-based Cant.Z.1007bis flew a reconnaissance patrol over Alexandria where it was intercepted and shot down by Flg Off 'Sam' Weller and Plt Off Douglas Spence of 274 Squadron. The stricken aircraft came down in the sea 50 miles to the north-north-west of the port, two of the crew of five surviving to be picked up subsequently by a Sunderland, and brought into port to become PoWs.

British Claims

274 Sqn	Flg Off A.A.P.Weller	V7717	}	Cant.Z.1007	60m N Alexandria 1245-1330
	Plt Off D.J.Spence	V7780			

Italian Casualties

172ª Sq Aut RST	Cant.Z.1007bis Ten Giulio Gabella and crew PoWs

Five days after this encounter, 274 Squadron was released to return to the Cyrenaican battleground, its place at Amiriya being taken by 1 SAAF Squadron, newly-arrived from East Africa. A little over a week later 252 Wing noted the arrival at Alexandria of the eight Yugoslav floatplanes from Greece – of which more later.

The fall of Greece towards the end of April led to some significant movements of Luftwaffe units. Already 2./KG 4 had left X.Fliegerkorps to take part in the invasion of Greece, and this unit would not return to the Mediterranean area thereafter. However, the geschwader's II.Gruppe had formed part of Luftflotte 4 for the invasion of the Balkans, and following the occupation of Yugoslavia, would move via Rumania to Gadurra airfield on Rhodes to lay mines in the Alexandria area and in the Suez Canal.

All other German units were for the time being engaged in attacks on Crete, preparatory to the invasion of that island, and to interdicting shipping making for this island with reinforcements. Deeply involved in these activities were X.Fliegerkorps' I. and II./LG 1 and II./KG 26.

Wednesday, 7 May 1941
During the night of 7/8 May 252 Wing recorded that 20 raiders passed Alexandria from the direction of Libya and overflew the Suez Canal, where a number of mines were laid. These were He 111s of II./KG 26, which would appear to have taken advantage of the availability of landing grounds newly-captured in Cyrenaica, to launch their attack from here. As a result of this raid two of the bombers were lost and two more crashed on return, one member of each crew being killed.

German Casualties

4./KG 26	He 111H-5 WNr 3877 crashed on return; one of crew killed
	He 111H-5 crashed on return; one of crew killed
	He 111 H-5 1H+BC WNr3970 lost; Oblt Eberhard Stüwe and crew rescued by Seenot
5./KG 26	He 111 H-5 1H+FN WNr 3885 lost; Oblt Max Voight and crew MiA

Thursday, 8 May 1941

This date saw the departure from 252 Wing for the Western Desert of the recently-arrived 1 SAAF Squadron. For a few days Alexandria was virtually defenceless again, but on 11 May 250 Squadron, which had just undertaken its initial operational sorties over Syria a few days earlier (see *Dust Clouds in the Middle East*), arrived at Amiriya from Aqir (Palestine) with ten new Curtiss Tomahawk fighters.

By this time the Luftwaffe's dispositions for the assault on Crete were in place. These included I. and II./LG 1 and II./KG 26 from X.Fliegerkorps, all of which had moved to Eleusis in Greece to operate as part of VIII.Fliegerkorps. (Details of the invasion of Crete and associated aerial activities may be found in *Air War for Yugoslavia, Greece and Crete, 1940-41*.)

This night's raid, however, had been successful in laying further magnetic mines in the canal, requiring a new programme of sweeps by 1 GRU's aircraft. On 12 May, just after L7771 had passed over a mine at Kilo 87.5 without apparent effect, L4374 flew over the same spot, an explosion occurring on this occasion.

Next day, just as the Tiger convoy was docking at Alexandria (see Chapter 6 –Reverses and Reinforcements), another Italian reconnaissance aircraft, identified as a Cant.Z.1007bis, was intercepted by one of the Tomahawks. However, when the pilot attempted to open fire the guns refused to operate, and no result was obtained. His intended victim had in fact been an S.79 of 175ª Squadriglia flown by Ten Dell'Antonio, whose crew reported being attacked by three Hurricanes.

As mentioned in Chapter 6, 94 Squadron had arrived at Amiriya on 19 April from Aden, but had then moved to Ismailia three days later to provide some direct defence for the Canal Zone. During May this unit was just re-equipping fully with Hurricanes prior to the next raid on this area occurring.

The first unit to be equipped with the Curtiss Tomahawk was 250 Squadron. Initially the unit was based at Maryut, operating in defence of the Alexandria area. Left to right: Plt Off D.A.R.Munro, Flg Off J.Hamlyn, Plt Off Monteith, Flg Off Wolsey, Sgt M.S.Wells, Flt Lt R.F.Martin, Sqn Ldr J.E.Scoular and Chapman (rank and initials unknown), unidentified.

Saturday – Sunday, 17/18 May 1941

On this occasion the attack was made slightly before midnight by 11 Gadurra-based He 111s of II./KG 4 which released both mines and bombs. Two of the raiders were claimed shot down by the AA defences and one by Lt Moolman, a SAAF pilot serving with 94 Squadron. This latter aircraft, flown by Fw Hans Borchers, crashed in flames onto a house in which six Egyptians perished together with the bomber's crew; this proved to be the only damage caused by this particular attack.

British Claims			
94 Sqn	Lt A.H.M.Moolman	Z7479 FZ-U	He 111
German Casualties			
4./KG 4	He 111P-2 WNr 2156 5J+KM Fw Hans Börner and crew MiA		

Friday – Monday, 23/26 May 1941

250 Squadron moved to Maryut on 23 May. Next night two Axis aircraft appeared over Aboukir and Alexandria, but apparently were only involved in a reconnaissance, as no bombs were dropped. However, about a dozen more raided the Suez Canal, dropping 14 mines and nine bombs, although with only minimal effect.

On the 25th 202 Group was reformed to control all units in the Delta and to be responsible for the defence of Egypt. For this role it was headquartered in Cairo.

Thursday, 29 May 1941

Tomahawks joined FAA Fulmars in providing protection for vessels returning from Crete up to 100 miles out to sea. One 250 Squadron pilot lost consciousness when at 25,000 feet, subsequently force-landing his fighter in the sea. Although injured, he was picked up safely by a Sunderland flyingboat.

British Casualties	
250 Sqn	Tomahawk force-landed in sea and lost – not enemy action

Friday – Saturday, 30/31 May 1941

During the night of 30 May four or five bombers raided Alexandria harbour and the surrounding area, mines being laid in the Great Pass and harbour entrance as bombs hit Dekheila airfield. Here some buildings were damaged, two men being killed, two badly injured and three slightly so.

Saturday-Sunday, 31 May/1 June 1941

A similar raid during the following night again saw mines laid in the Great Pass, and 252 Wing's radio transmitter was slightly damaged. The end of the month brought 971 Balloon Squadron under the operational control of this wing. More shipping escorts were flown by Tomahawks and Fulmars on 1 June, this time extending out 120 miles.

Indeed, this day saw the completion of the evacuation of Crete in so far as this could be achieved. Whilst action over the returning vessels continued, an He 111 of II./KG 4 undertook a reconnaissance towards Alexandria. It failed to return and two members of the crew who were subsequently picked up were under the impression that they had been shot down by AA fire. However, it seems possible that this aircraft had fallen to a pair of 806 Squadron Fulmars which had taken off from Aboukir and had intercepted a single bomber which they took to be a Ju 88.

British Claims		
806 Sqn	Lt R.MacDonald-Hall	Ju 88
	Sub Lt G.A.Hogg	
German Casualties		
II./KG 4	He 111 2 of crew survived as PoWs; victim of either AA or 806 Squadron Fulmars	

Following the recent attacks, A Flight of 94 Squadron returned to Amiriya from Ismailia with eight Hurricanes to aid in the defence of the port.

Tuesday – Wednesday, 3/4 June 1941

Again four or five raiders targetted Alexandria, four high explosive bombs and many incendiaries being released. 15 houses and two shops outside the dockyard were damaged, 37 Egyptians being killed and others injured, but no military damage was caused. Two 94 Squadron Hurricanes took off, one of them under the vector control of the aircraft carrier HMS *Formidable*. No interceptions resulted.

The completion of the Allied withdrawal from Crete provided the Luftwaffe with additional airfields from which attacks on the Egyptian base and reinforcement areas might be launched. With this in mind, I. and II./LG 1 moved to Rhodes on 4 June, joining II./KG 26 there. II./KG 4 had despatched it as 4.Staffel to Iraq during May (see *Dust Clouds in the Middle East*), but in July this unit departed the Mediterranean area to take part in operations over Russia. Nearly all the other units of Luftflotte 4 and VIII.Fliegerkorps had already left Greece and Crete for this new front during the early part of June. On 5 June Stab and I./LG 1 moved back to Eleusis in Greece, II.Gruppe to Heraklion, Crete, and III.Gruppe to Derna in Cyrenaica.

250 Squadron's initial aerial victory was the first for the Curtiss fighter anywhere in the world. Flg Off Jack Hamlyn intercepted and shot down a Rhodes-based Cant.Z.1007bis reconnaissance-bomber of 211 near Alexandria on 8 June 1941.

Saturday, 7 June 1941

With nightfall I. and II./LG 1 despatched all serviceable Ju 88s to raid Alexandria where 975 kilos of bombs were dropped, 200 more kilos being released on Suez. 31 Ju 88s reached their targets, most returning to Rhodes where four crashed on landing as did one more which got back to Eleusis. Plenty of AA fire and searchlights were reported by the crews, but no night fighters.

German Casualties	
I./LG 1	Ju 88A-5 damaged 60% WNr 3294
	Ju 88A-5 damaged 40% WNr 5268
	Ju 88A-5 damaged 40% WNr 6226
	Ju 88A-5 damaged 40% WNr 7205
II./LG 1	Ju 88A-5 damaged 80% WNr 8273

Following this raid LG 1's activities were directed towards Syria, where the British invasion had commenced (see *Dust Clouds in the Middle East*).

Sunday, 8 June 1941

During the afternoon two Tomahawks managed to intercept a reconnaissance Cant.Z.1007bis of 211ª Squadriglia which had taken off from Rhodes for a sortie over Alexandria. This was shot down by Flg Off Jack Hamlyn for the first victory to be gained with the new fighter.

British Claims				
250 Sqn	Flg Off J.Hamlyn	AK377	Cant.Z.1007bis	5m NW Alexandria 1540-1625
Italian Casualties				
211ª Sq/50º Gr	Cant.Z.1007bis Ten Onorio Socche and crew KiA; co-pilot Serg Emilio Bianchi baled out; PoW			

479

Tuesday, 10 June 1941

Four Tomahawks were scrambled, two of which were able to intercept a reconnaissance Ju 88 of 2(F)./123. This was attacked by Flg Off Hamlyn and was last seen at sea level with black smoke pouring from both engines.

British Claims

250 Sqn	Flg Off J.Hamlyn	AK351	Ju 88	Alexandria 1130

German Casualties

2(F)./123	Ju 88A-5 WNr 0661 4U+AK Uffz Albert Schwarz (pilot), Oblt Richard Kern (observer) & 2 KiA

Next day 250 Squadron was ordered to the Western Desert to take part in the up-coming Operation Battleaxe. One section of two aircraft was left behind for the defence of Alexandria, although 30 Squadron, which had been reforming at Amiriya on Hurricanes following its return from Crete, now came under 252 Wing's operational control.

Monday – Saturday, 16/21 June 1941

While carrying out a searchlight exercise during the early hours of the 16th, a 94 Squadron Hurricane crashed with fatal results for the pilot. Two nights later seven or eight raiders bombed singly between 0320-0511, but caused little damage. On 19 June 94 Squadron's A Flight returned to Ismailia. On 21 June a bigger raid by an estimated 24-30 bombers maintained a continuous attack on Alexandria from 0310-0510. Six 30 Squadron Hurricanes managed to get off at 0525, but only to find that all the attackers had gone.

Monday – Monday, 23/30 June 1941

A further big raid on Alexandria took place on the 23rd, 16-20 aircraft taking part.

German Casualties

5./KG 26	He 111 H-5 WNr 4086 ditched off Alexandria; Stfw Erich Krame and crew MiA

On the 25th 252 Wing was given control for a single day of a number of Brewster Buffaloes of 805 Squadron, FAA. Two days later, however, the recently-reformed 33 Squadron became available at Amiriya, several of the unit's pilots flying with 30 Squadron.

Two more raids were recorded on 28 and 29 June; during the first of these a reconnaissance Cant.Z.1007bis of 222ª Squadriglia, 56° Gruppo, flown by Ten Sisto Ferrari, had left Rhodes to attempt a sortie over Alexandria. However, before reaching the Egyptian coast it was intercepted by fighters and driven off. On the last day of the month a section of two Tomahawks of 2 SAAF Squadron arrived at Maryut, while 94 Squadron's A Flight again flew over to Amiriya from Ismailia.

The increased threat posed to both Alexandria and the Canal Zone required a division of control to allow concentration in each area as necessary. Consequently, on 1 July 1941 250 Wing, which had previously existed as a bomber wing at Ismailia, was reformed at that base as 250 (Signals) Wing under the command of Sqn Ldr W.F.MacDonald, DFC. The unit was effectively to be a fighter wing, controlling the defence of the Canal Zone. Immediately available, of course, was 94 Squadron, together with the Gladiator-equipped 5 Squadron, Royal Egyptian Air Force, commanded by Flt Lt Mohammed Hasez. 94 Squadron's Hurricanes, therefore, provided 250 Wing's striking arm. These fighters were backed up by three balloon squadrons and four radar stations – AMES(air minstry experimental stations) 204, 219, 254 and 259 – and by sector operations rooms at Port Said and Fayid, manned by 13 and 17 Wireless Operating Units (WOUs). Following the initial formation, the wing was taken over by Grp Capt J.W.Turton-Jones on 19 July.

Just as 94 Squadron was preparing for this new role, its long-serving commanding officer, Wg Cdr W.T.F.Wightman, DFC, departed, handing over to Sqn Ldr H.C.Mayers, DFC. The latter was an experienced fighter pilot, who had served in England with 601 Squadron during 1940 with some notable success. At this stage his new unit had been brought up to strength with an infusion of SAAF pilots, since most of those who had served in Aden and Iraq had been posted to other units forming in the latter area.

For the next year or so 250 and 252 Wings were to carry on their own private night war, almost completely divorced from the main operations over the front line areas in Egypt and Libya.

Tuesday – Friday, 1/11 July 1941

Another raid by 16 bombers took place on 1 July. On this occasion Beaufighters of 272 Squadron attempted to intercept, but without success. Two bombers dropped a couple of bombs near Shallufa on 5 July, while at 2305 that night, following warning of a bigger raid, 15 more attacked Alexandria. Five Hurricanes of 94 Squadron were scrambled, two of these making interceptions, but with indecisive results.

Saturday – Sunday, 5/6 July 1941

According to Ultra reports, seven He 111s of II /KG 26 took off around 1820 on Saturday evening to attack the Suez Canal. Four landed at Eleusis between 0342 and 0553, one had returned early, one stopped off at Rhodes on the way back and one was missing.

German Casualties

./KG 26	He 111H-5 WNr 3876 1H+LP lost; Uffz Kurt Steins and crew MiA
	He 111H-5 WNr 3851 damaged 70%

With the occupation of Syria virtually completed, LG 1's Ju 88s returned to the attack on the Alexandria area during the night of 9/10 July, sending 23 Ju 88s to attack Abu Sueir. On the 11th 94 Squadron's flight again returned to Ismailia. 30 Squadron, which had moved to Edcu on 22 June, now took over responsibility for the night defence of the port. That night (11/12) 52 of LG 1's bombers – 25 from .Gruppe and 27 from II.Gruppe – raided Port Said. On this occasion returning crews reported seeing seven fighters, four of which made ineffectual attacks.

Saturday, 12 July 1941

Some 20 bombers raided the Suez Canal on this date. By day at 1228, a single hostile plot was spotted on the radar 58 miles north of El Daba. This followed the coast for ten miles eastwards at 20,000 feet, then proceeding south for about 30 miles before turning east again and approaching Alexandria. Flt Lt Vernon Woodward of 33 Squadron and Flg Off Crockett of 30 Squadron were scrambled from Amiriya and vectored onto this intruder which proved to be another reconnaissance Ju 88 of 2(F)./123. It dived for the ground when intercepted, pursued by both Hurricanes which caught it 40 miles south-west of their airfield and shot it down in flames.

This was Woodward's last claim, bringing his total to over 21; ten and one shared had been claimed before he was posted with the squadron to Greece, and two had been added since his return. He was at the time the highest-scoring RAF pilot still on operations in the Middle East, but was soon to be posted away on non-operational duties.

British Claims

3 Sqn	Flt Lt V.C.Woodward	Z4268	}	Ju 88	40m SW Amiriya 1250-1410
0 Sqn	Flg Off Crockett	Z4196			

German Casualties

(F)./123	Ju 88 A-5 4U+CK WNr 0531 lost;Fw Josef Verschoth and crew KiA

Monday – Tuesday, 14/29 July 1941

Suez was again raided by about 20 bombers during the night of 13/14 July, and on the 16th 24 LG 1 Ju 88s undertook the fourth raid here in seven days; 18 of the bomber crews reported bombing ships, with the other six releasing their bombs on Port Tewfik. Raiders returned to Alexandria on 19 and 26 July, but on the way back from the latter raid one Ju 88 of 6./LG 1 force-landed on Corfu following an engine fire; the pilot and two members of the crew were killed.

Suez was the target again on 22 and 27 July, a third attack following on the next night. I./LG 1 attacked first, followed an hour later by II Gruppe, 28 bombers in all participating in the raid. The geschwader was then ordered to turn its efforts on Tobruk for the next few nights.

Saturday, 26 July 1941

German Casualties

./LG 1	Ju 88A-5 WNr 5277 force-landed Corfu due to engine fire; Lt Horst Drognitz and two KiFA, one injured

MEANWHILE:

Friday, 18 July 1941

Following action over Syria, 80 Squadron (see *Dust Clouds in the Middle East*) despatched a detachment of Hurricanes to Cyprus, which was now suffering a number of Axis bombing raids. This detachment included a number of 213 Squadron pilots who had been attached to 80 Squadron since their arrival in North Africa. On 18 July one of the 213 Squadron pilots, Flg Off George Westlake, was scrambled during one such attack to intercept four Ju 88s. After seeing nothing initially, he then spotted a pair of these bombers heading west over Morphou Bay. Giving chase, he caught these intruders at low level above some local fishing boats and opened fire. His first burst reportedly caused one of the bombers to blow up and disintegrate in a fireball. Westlake was forced to break away upwards to avoid colliding with the debris, so he did not see his victim crash, also losing sight of the second raider. The occupants of the fishing boats subsequently confirmed the destruction of one bomber, but found no survivors. (No note of such a loss has yet been discovered in Luftwaffe records.)

British Claims

80/213 Sqn	Flg Off G.H.Westlake	Ju 88	Morphou Bay, Cyprus

Next day the 80 Squadron party withdrew, leaving the Hurricanes with the 213 Squadron pilots. The rest of the latter unit then moved in to provide a more permanent defence of the island, which at that stage was considered to be at risk of Axis invasion.

A group of 451 Squadron ground personnel with the tail and rear fuselage of a shot-down Heinkel He 111 bomber.

Sunday – Monday, 3/4 August 1941

An estimated 12-13 bombers raided Suez and Port Said. Again, no interceptions were made, but despite this one of the attackers failed to return. This was an He 111 of II./KG 26.

German Casualties		
I./KG 26	He 111 MiA	

Monday – Tuesday, 4/5 August 1941

Next night another 15 raiders approached, this time to attack Ismailia itself. Lt A.H.M. Moolman had taken off at 0240 for a patrol over the area when he was lucky enough to spot a Ju 88 of I./LG 1 which was held in the searchlights for two minutes. This allowed him to make a telling attack, and L1+BB subsequently force-landed in a lake at Baltion, Ofw Kurt Petermann and his crew being captured. The aircraft was later inspected by the 94 Squadron intelligence officer. Two more bombers fell to the AA defences on this occasion.

British Claims				
4 Sqn	Lt A.H.M.Moolman	Z4498	Ju 88	Ismailia 0300

German Casualties	
./KG 26	He 111H-6 WNr 4197 1H+LN Uffz Erich Meyer and crew MiA
./LG 1	Ju 88A-5 WNr 650 L1+BB Ofw Kurt Petermann and crew PoW
	Ju 88A-5 WNr 6220 L1+AH Fw Erich Mager and crew KiA

Throughout August and September the two main targets received almost nightly raids. These seem to have been strangely ineffective, however, damage in the main being restricted to civilian buildings and local inhabitants. To list every raid would be repetitive, so only those where any matters of note were recorded, are set out below.

Wednesday – Thursday, 6/7 August 1941

Approximately 13 more raiders appeared next night, attacking Suez, 16-25 others raiding Alexandria, Here a dozen houses were destroyed, 14 civilians were killed and 40 injured. Again no interceptions were achieved. But nonetheless Ju 88 L1+SL of 3./LG 1 failed to return to its base with the loss of Oblt Heinrich Böcker and crew who came down at Fethiye, where they were interned; it appears therefore, that they had become lost and landed in Turkey. Raids now became a frequent occurrence, continuing throughout the rest of August.

German Casualties	
./LG 1	Ju 88A WNr 6311 L1+SL Oblt Heinrich Böcker and crew interned in Turkey

Thursday – Friday, 7/8 August 1941

Between 1855 and 1936 30 Ju 88s of I. and II./LG 1 set off to attack shipping in Alexandria harbour. The attack was carried out between 2140-2237 hours, during which the aircraft of Hptmn Hans von Kobylinski, staffelkapitän of 1.Staffel, was brought down. This proved to be one of those situations which give rise to considerable difficulty in deciding just what had occurred. Seven Hurricanes of 30 Squadron had been scrambled to intercept, going off at about 2227. At about 2346 three pilots reported attacking Ju 88s, but claims initially were only for one confirmed and two unconfirmed. Subsequently the squadron noted that German radio admitted the loss of four aircraft on this night, and on the basis of this each of the three claims was apparently confirmed, while one of the pilots seems to have been credited with a second success.

However, 252 Wing in recording that the attacks destroyed about a dozen houses, killing 13 and injuring 40, also noted that a Ju 88 crashed on Lake Maryut due to the pilot having been blinded by searchlights; no mention of the fighter attacks was made.

It seems incredible that a pilot as experienced as von Kobylinski should have been in such a situation at such low level unless he was under sustained attack, but in a letter many years later, he recorded that the aircraft had been hit by AA, but that the gunner had been wounded by a machine-gun bullet; this seems to indicate that the aircraft had been hit by both elements of the defence. The records of LG 1 indicate that his Ju 88 was lost as the result of an aerial combat, but this appears to be the only loss suffered that night. It is surmised therefore that the three Hurricane pilots, who all submitted claims at about the same time, had all attacked the same aircraft, and that von Kobylinski crashed in attempting a force-landing resulting from damage, and that this attempt was thwarted by the effect of the searchlights.

British Claims

30 Sqn	Sgt G.W.Ratledge	Z7005	Ju 88	2346
	SgtR.F.Marrack*	Z4196	Ju 88	2346
	Flt Lt R.T.P.Davidson		Ju 88	2346

*Marrack may subsequently have been credited with a second victory.

German Casualties

1./LG 1	Ju 88A-5 WNr 3232 L1+GB Hptmn Hans von Kobylinski and radio operator Fw Erwin Lehmann PoW; 2 of crew KiA

Friday – Saturday, 8/9 August 1941
Two waves of bombers attacked Ismailia, Port Said and Suez. One Ju 88 was intercepted south of Ismailia by Lt R.B.Palm, SAAF, but escaped before he could open fire.

Sunday – Monday, 10/11 August 1941
During Sunday evening a raid on Alexandria caused 22 casualties, six of them fatal, and demolished several houses. Eleven LG 1 Ju 88s raided Suez, claiming a ship sunk and two damaged; two more of this unit's aircraft bombed Kabrit airfield near Port Said, and one attacked Ismailia.

Monday, 11 August 1941
A pair of 2 SAAF Squadron Tomahawks recently detached to Maryut, departed to join their unit in the Western Desert. They were replaced by three similar aircraft from 112 Squadron.

Wednesday – Thursday, 13/14 August 1941
An estimated 12-15 raiders were overhead from 0234-0525. 14 Hurricanes were scrambled by 94 Squadron and three interceptions followed. Lt J.A.K.D'Alebout, SAAF, reported sighting an aircraft which he identified as a Do 17, and Lts A.P.M.Laurenson and R.B.Palm both encountered Ju 88s. However, all three interceptions proved indecisive.

British Claims

94 Sqn	Lt R.B.Palm	Z4170	Ju 88 Damaged	Ismailia 0430

Friday, 15 August 1941
30 Squadron began forming a Yugoslav flight to take part in the defence of Alexandria.

Friday, 22 August 1941
Seven raiders hit Alexandria, causing some damage to the Electricity and Gas Company's plant. Three people were killed and five injured.

Tuesday, 26 August 1941
About eight bombers attacked Alexandria with one more raiding Aboukir. At the latter location some RAF barracks were hit and damaged, seven airmen being injured.

Since July raids on Cyprus had reduced considerably, but on this date 213 Squadron's Flg Off George Westlake was up on a practice flight in co-operation with the army when a reconnaissance Cant.Z.1007bis appeared over the island. Flying at 6,000 ft, Westlake heard a section being scrambled after "a bandit over Famagusta at 13,000 ft", and being already halfway to that altitude, he gave chase, spotting the Italian aircraft at 18,000 ft, heading south. As he closed in the rear gunner opened fire from about 1,000 yards range, but Westlake carried on to make a quarter attack, firing at the starboard engine. The Cant flicked over and headed downwards rotating, falling apart as it did so. It crashed on the seashore between Cape Greco and Napa, the bodies of the crew being removed by troops of the Royal Scots. This was the first Axis aircraft to be brought down on Cypriot soil.

British Claims

213 Sqn	Flg Off G.H.Westlake	Cant.Z.1007bis	Between Ormidhia and
			Balohaghou 1115

Italian Casualties

172° Sq RST	Cant.Z.1007bis MM23370 (loaned to 210ª Sq BT) missing; T.Col Luigi Gagliani, Ten Pietro Braida and crew MiA

Friday, 29 August 1941

On 29 August 94 Squadron moved to El Ballah, located alongside the canal, a few miles to the north of Ismailia.

Sunday, 31 August 1941

A further indecisive interception of a Ju 88 was made by 94 Squadron's Flg Off A.Darling. Six or seven raiders attacked Alexandria where seven 30 Squadron Hurricanes and a single 272 Squadron Beaufighter took off. Only two interceptions were made, both these proving indecisive. On this date 33 Squadron left 252 Wing on posting to the Western Desert.

Raids were to continue unabated during September, in which month 250 Wing received another WOU and two more radar stations – 261 and 262 AMES. Detachments of Beaufighter IC coastal heavy fighters also arrived, two of these aircraft from 272 Squadron and four from 252 Squadron.

On 6 September 73 Squadron flew in to El Gamil, near Port Said, to strengthen the air defences further. Still commanded by Sqn Ldr Peter Wykeham-Barnes, the squadron was at last receiving a well-earned rest after its trying period of operations in the front line area.

Saturday – Sunday, 6/7 September 1941

Fifteen LG 1 Ju 88s attacked the airfield and supply dump at Abu Sueir during the night of 6/7 September. Two more interceptions were achieved here, bringing 94 Squadron's second and third confirmed successes since joining 250 Wing. Lt J.G.Sandison, SAAF, caught a Ju 88 at 0415 near Tel el Kebir, where it crashed and exploded; two of the crew were seen to bale out, the wing recording that three prisoners were taken, only one member of the crew having been killed.

Meanwhile during a patrol from 2120-2245, Lt E.T.Watkinson, SAAF, attacked another bomber which he was able to claim only as damaged. However, this aircraft, an He 111, crashed in the desert south of Burg el Arab, and its destruction was therefore subsequently confirmed. The identity of this aircraft was provided by an Ultra intercept, which source gives other interesting details.

During early September six FW 200 four-engined reconnaissance-bombers and nine He 111s, all from KG 40, arrived in Greece for operations over the Gulf of Suez area; some aircraft of each type were equipped to drop torpedoes.

Ultra also established that on this particular night 16 He 111s drawn from both II./KG 26 and 8./KG 40 set off to attack Ismailia. A further report advised that another He 111 from 7./KG 40, F8+EP, had force-landed between Sollum and Derna while trying to get back to base from the Nile Delta after one engine had been destroyed, the crew being rescued. This appears to have been the aircraft destroyed by Lt Watkinson.

Meanwhile, aircraft of I./KG 40 (presumably FW 200s) had taken off at 1558 and 1603 on a reconnaissance to the Red Sea. However, at 1625 one of these aircraft crashed into the sea near Cape Sounion and exploded; there were no survivors. The second carried on, attacking a ship in the Gulf of Suez at 2127 on which the crew claimed to have achieved a hit, and landed at Eleusis at 0437. One of these aircraft was F8+GH of 1. Staffel.

British Claims

94 Sqn	Lt J.G.Sandison	Z4710	Ju 88	1m W Abu Sueir camp 0445
	Lt E.T.Watkinson	Z4373	Ju 88 probable Ismailia 2145, 6 September Ju 88 damaged – but later	
			confirmed as an He 111 destroyed Abu Sueir, S Burg el Arab 0425-0510 7 Sept	

German Casualties

6./LG 1	Ju 88A-5 WNr 2182 L1+BP Fw Karl-Heinz Kessler KiA; rest of crew PoW (listed by LG 1 as lost to AA)
7./KG 40	He 111 F8+EP Force-landed between Derna and Sollum with one engine shot out; crew rescued
1./KG 40	FW 200 C-3 F8+GH WNr 007 crashed into sea near Cape Sounion and blew up; Oblt Horst Neumann and crew MiA

Tuesday – Wednesday, 9/10 September 1941

Seven bombers appeared over Ismailia between 0310-0448, no less than 16 Hurricanes being launched by 94 Squadron during this period. There were eight engagements reported, two of which proved inconclusive, but it transpired that the other six pilots had all attacked the same unfortunate Ju 88 – again an aircraft of II./LG 1, flown by Oblt Günther Biesing. Lts Moolman, Watkinson, Gibson, Laurenson, Palm and Garner sent this bomber down to crash in flames ten miles west of Kantara; the crew of four all survived to become PoWs.

LG 1 had attacked both Ismailia and Suez, reporting meeting strong AA fire and 13 night fighters. Apart from the loss of Biesing's aircraft, another 6.Staffel Ju 88 was hit by AA and was forced to return early to Eleusis.

British Claims

94 Sqn	Flg Off Darling	Z4234		E/a Damaged	Ismailia 2345-0050
	Lt A.H.M. Moolman	Z4379	⎫		
	Lt A.P.M.Laurenson	V7486	⎪		
	Lt E.T.Watkinson	Z4373	⎬ Ju 88		Ismailia, 10m W Katara 0425
	Lt D.Gibson	Z4609	⎪		
	Lt R.B.Palm	Z4170	⎪		
	Lt B.R.Garner	Z4247	⎭		

German Casualties

6./LG 1	Ju 88A-5 WNr 6199 slightly damaged; gunner wounded; crash-landed Eleusis, Greece
	Ju 88A-5 WNr 6261 L1+GP Oblt Günther Biesing and crew PoW

Thursday – Friday, 11/12 September 1941

A dozen more raiders – again from LG 1 – came over two nights later between 0236-0523. Of the five interceptions made, three proved inconclusive. However, Sqn Ldr Howard Mayers with Lts J.G.Sandison and H.Smith caught another II./LG 1 Ju 88 – L1+BN of 4.Staffel, flown by Lt Josef Niehaus – which they shot down into the Ataga mountains west of Suez. Three members of the crew were captured, but one was killed in the crash.

British Claims

94 Sqn	Sqn Ldr H.C.Mayers	Z4355	⎫		
	Lt J.G.Sandison	Z4378	⎬ Ju 88	Mountains 10-15m W Suez 0420	
	Lt H.Smith	W9271	⎭		

German Casualties

4./LG 1	Ju 88A-5 WNr 6241 L1+BN Lt Josef Niehaus and crew PoW. Recorded by LG 1 as a loss to AA

Tuesday – Wednesday, 16/17 September 1941

LG 1 recorded that five Ju 88s and an He 111 raided Heliopolis and Aboukir, while 252 Wing noted the first serious attack on Cairo between 0208-0348. Property in Abbasia was damaged, fires were caused at Gamalia, and 39 civilians were killed, another 93 suffering injuries.

On 18 September six of 274 Squadron's Hurricanes arrived at El Khanka under the control of the Heliopolis sector, following the recent raid on the Cairo area. However, on 5 October 112 Squadron's Tomahawks departed for the desert; 30 Squadron was then provided with a single Hurricane IIb specifically to provide daytime interception capability against reconnaissance aircraft, for which the Mark I was no longer considered to be adequate.

September had brought 94 Squadron's recent run of successes to an end. The unit was shortly to go forward to the frontal area, despite still being equipped with elderly Hurricane Is; on 27 October it would depart for LG.103 near Sollum. Its place was taken by a detachment of 213 Squadron from Cyprus which now arrived at Ismailia; 5 Royal Egyptian Air Force Squadron was exchanged for 2 Royal Egyptian Air Force Squadron (Sqn Ldr Salah Sared).

Raids continued into October, but at a reduced rate.

RAF in the Delta

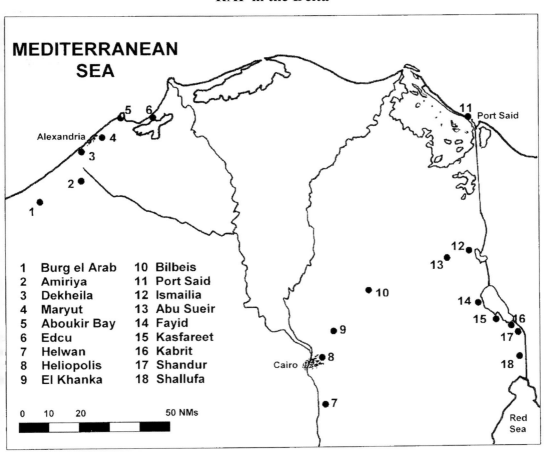

MEDITERRANEAN
SEA

Alexandria

Port Said

Cairo

Red
Sea

1	Burg el Arab	10	Bilbeis
2	Amiriya	11	Port Said
3	Dekheila	12	Ismailia
4	Maryut	13	Abu Sueir
5	Aboukir Bay	14	Fayid
6	Edcu	15	Kasfareet
7	Helwan	16	Kabrit
8	Heliopolis	17	Shandur
9	El Khanka	18	Shallufa

0   10   20   50 NMs

Monday, 6 October 1941

German Casualties

5.KG26   III H-5 1H+JN WNr 4293 lost; Lt Heinrich Menge and crew MiA

On 24 October nine pilots and seven more aircraft from 213 Squadron arrived at Edcu to take over the duties of 30 and 274 Squadrons, both of these units then being ordered to the desert in preparation for the forthcoming major offensive to be launched there in November. Thus 213 Squadron was providing virtually all the fighter defences for both 250 and 252 Wings. However, before the end of October the squadron would be joined by 73 Squadron which had recently augmented its Hurricanes with a number of Tomahawks.

During October Bing Cross, who had been promoted Grp Capt during July, was posted to 204 Group. His place was taken by Grp Capt G.V.Howard, DFC, who arrived from the UK. His stay would not be a long one, for in early January 1942 he was replaced by Grp Capt G.L.Carter, AFC, from HQ, RAF Middle East (and also recently ex-UK); Howard then moved to command AHQ, Iraq.

On 20 October 260 (Balloon) Wing arrived at Ismailia, having just been shipped out from the UK to take over command of all the balloon squadrons in Egypt – including those in 250 and 252 Wings.

These changes coincided with a reduction in the intensity of raids, and few interceptions were to be recorded for several months. However, at this juncture 250 Wing received a very significant reinforcement with the arrival on 27 November of the advanced party of 89 Squadron at Abu Sueir. The unit had been formed in England two months earlier, with Beaufighter IF radar-equipped night fighters. On 24 November four of these fighters, together with two coastal Beaufighter Ics, left Portreath for Gibraltar. A second flight followed two days later, and a third on 30 November. Commanded by Wg Cdr G.A.Stainforth of Schneider Trophy fame, this welcome addition to Middle Eastern establishment would soon be maintaining detachments throughout Egypt and on Malta.

The ground party meanwhile, had left England by sea some time earlier and was now en route for Aboukir. Here it was learned that the aircrafts' arrival had been delayed due to cracked engine bearers having been discovered at Gibraltar, delaying their departure while repairs were undertaken. In consequence, the ground party arrived at Cairo on 4 November, ahead of the air party.

From Gibraltar the aircraft began continuing their flights to Malta at the end of the month, led by the flight commanders, Sqn Ldrs P.M.J.Evans and D.S.Pain. Pain's detachment then reached Dekheila on 6 December. At this stage Wg Cdr Stainforth led out a further flight from England to bring the unit to full strength. Work on the camp at the unit's new base at Abu Sueir was carried out throughout the month, and by 18 December night flying tests were underway. 89 Squadron became formally operational on 10 December, meanwhile, but not until 22 January was the first scramble undertaken due to the disappearance of almost any opposition.

A move was made on 1 February from Abu Sueir to Edcu, and here on 7 February 1942 tests were flown with a captured Bf 110. This was found to be slightly faster than the Beaufighter at or above 15,000 ft, though the advantage switched to the British aircraft at lower altitude. The Messerschmitt was, however, deemed to be the more manoeuvrable of the two at all heights.

MEANWHILE:

Monday, 10 November 1941
At 1315 Tomahawks and a lone Hurricane intercepted an unidentified enemy aircraft 12 miles out to sea at 15,000 feet. Several pilots, including Sgt Wilson who was flying the Hurricane, fired at this intruder which was believed to have been seriously damaged and departed with its starboard engine disabled. Wilson then suffered an engine failure, baling out into the sea from 4,000 feet, He was picked up safely by the trawler SS *Thorgian*.

This engagement was recorded by 252 Wing, but does not appear in the ORBs of either 73 or 213 Squadrons, so the full identity of Sgt Wilson and his unit have not been ascertained – nor has any matching record been found in Axis sources.

British Casualties

252 Wg	Hurricane lost operationally in sea due to engine failure; Sgt Wilson safe

---

Wednesday, 12 November 1941
A small attack by three or four raiders over the Fayoum district from 1732 proved to be one of the most damaging yet. A direct hit struck a mosque with eight houses also destroyed, 64 deaths and nearly 100 injuries resulting.

Meanwhile, with the Crusader operation now in full swing, 73 Squadron, which had been taken over by Sqn Ldr D.H.Ward during October, had been ordered to remain at El Gamil on defensive duties. This did not suit Ward, who sought permission to form a flight of around six experienced pilots with new Hurricanes to move up to the front line area in order to take part in operations there. This was acceded to, and he formed a flight, including himself, Flt Lt R.A.M.'Robin' Johnston, Flg Off T.P.K.Scade, Flg Off R.McDougall, Plt Off R.I. Laing (newly-commissioned) and Lt R.D.'Dormie' Barlow SAAF. This was sent forward as a detachment known as 'The Battle Flight' to operate in the Western Desert. At the end of December 213 Squadron also moved up to LG.90 to the south and west of Alexandria, although a detachment was maintained at El Khanka, north of Cairo.

With the Axis forces driven back into Tripolitania, there were by now no raids on the Canal area, incursions here being limited to single high-flying reconnaissance aircraft – and this would remain the situation until March 1942, by which time the British forces had fallen back again to the Gazala area of Cyrenaica.

Wednesday, 10 December 1941
Two Tomahawks intercepted a Ju 88 attempting to bomb a ship 25 miles north of Alexandria, the pilots claiming to have inficted damage on the bomber.

CHAPTER 14

IN DEFENCE OF TRIPOLI

As was the case with the British base areas in Egypt at Alexandria, around Cairo and in the Nile Delta and Suez Canal areas, Tripoli, the administrative capital of the Tripolitanian province of Libya – and, indeed, of Libya itself – was a major reinforcement and concentration area for the Italian forces in North Africa. It was also beyond the range of the majority of RAF units based in Egypt, and could be reached only occasionally by Vickers Wellington bombers, and then only when they had the advantage of secure forward landing grounds for refuelling en route. Consequently, the air defence of this port and its adjacent airfields, coastline, etc, was as divorced from activities over the main desert battlefront (virtually wherever this happened to have moved to), as was that over the British bases in Egypt.

Tripoli was, however, well within the range of aircraft based on Malta, and it was from here that the majority of operations launched against the port and its facilities had to come. (These operations have been covered in some detail in *Malta: The Hurricane Years, 1940-41*, but at the time of writing that volume, little or no detailed information was available regarding the defensive activities of the Regia Aeronautica. That is no longer the case, and while some additional details in this regard were included at the beginning of *Malta: The Spitfire Year, 1942*, the authors have felt that it is appropriate to provide a fairly detailed account of these operations specifically, particularly having regard to the great importance of Tripoli and the supply route to it to the whole desert story. Sensibly, reference to the two Malta volumes is recommended to aid in understanding the whole picture surrounding the background to most of the matters described here, certainly insofar as the British units involved are concerned.

During the opening months of the war, Malta lacked almost any striking force which might be employed to attack Tripoli, or indeed, any reinforcement and resupply shipping heading for this port from southern Europe. Following the Italian declaration of war on 10 June 1940, two training squadrons of the Fleet Air Arm which had been undertaking their function in the south of France, were withdrawn to Tunisia, and from there the pick of the crews and Fairey Swordfish torpedo-bombers were despatched to Malta to form an operational unit to be known as 830 Squadron. Here the elements of an RAF unit, 3 AACU, which also flew Swordfish, were amalgamated with the Royal Navy unit.

The Swordfish were followed to Malta by a handful of Martin 167F attack bombers, the residue of a French order with the US manufacturer, taken over by the RAF following that nation's withdrawal from the fighting by way of an armistice. Arriving in early September, they formed the basis of 431 Flight, intended to undertake strategic reconnaissance and photographic sorties. Apart from the Swordfish and a few Sunderland flyingboats operating on occasion from Malta, these were the only aircraft with the range to reach Tripoli and return. It was one of these aircraft, in the hands of Flg Off J.H.T.Foxton, which flew the first incursion over Tripoli to reconnoitre the port and its environs.

While the Regia Aeronautica maintained a fairly substantial part of its Aeronautica della Libia in Tripolitania as Comando Settore Ovest, headquartered in Tripoli, most of the units were equipped with bomber or army support aircraft. The sole fighter defence rested in the hands of 13° Gruppo CT (77ª, 78ª and 82ª Squadriglie) equipped with a mixed complement of Fiat CR.32 and 42 biplane fighters. It would be a considerable time before any of the pilots based in this sector were afforded the solid opportunity to intercept and deal effectively with any intruders.

It was from Sicily, however, that the first Italian actions were made to ensure the security of the Tripolitanian base. These occurred immediately on the outbreak of war, and prior to the French capitulation:

RAIDS ON TUNISIA

Thursday, 13 June 1940

The first (and largest) Regia Aeronautica raid on Tunisian targets occurred on this date. 33 S.79s (19 of 36° Stormo BT and 14 of 30° Stormo BT) took off between 0705-0715 from their Sicilian bases at Castelvetrano and Sciacca to bomb El Aouina, Kassar Said and Menzel Temine aerodromes. An S.79 of 192ª Squadriglia swerved in taking off and was so seriously damaged that it had to be written off, although the crew remained unscathed. The formation was led by Gen Giuseppe Barba, commander of 11ª Divisione Aerea; the commanders of both stormi, Col Antonino Serra of 30° and Col Carlo Drago of 36°, also took part in the mission. The escort was provided by 15 CR.42s of 157° Gruppo CT which joined the bombers over Pantelleria, where the fighters had moved earlier from Trapani. Over El Aouina three fighters, identified as Morane Saulnier 406s, attacked the S.79s of 36° Stormo but were intercepted by the escorting CR.42s, the pilots of which claimed two enemy fighters damaged. This claim was apparently later changed to a single aircraft destroyed, because a Morane was credited on this occasion to Serg Magg Teresio Martinoli, the future Regia Aeronautica top-scoring ace. Two fighters, flown by S.Ten Angelo Carminati and Serg Fausto Fiorani failed to return, possibly after a mid-air collision. The bombers got back between 0900 and 1010, but an S.79 of 194ª Squadriglia hit some trees on landing and suffered damage so heavy that it was written off. Again, the crew emerged unscathed.

Italian Claims

384ª Sq/157° Gr CT	Serg Magg Teresio Martinoli	Morane Saulnier 406

Italian Casualties

192ªSq/87°Gr/30°St BT	S.79 MM22128 Ten Luigi Arrighi and crew safe, a/c w/o after a take-off accident
194ªSq/90°Gr/30°St BT	S.79 MM21331 Ten Terzo Mazzotti and crew safe, a/c w/o after a landing accident
386ª Sq/157° Gr CT	CR.42 S.Ten Angelo Carminati KiFA
386ª Sq/157° Gr CT	CR.42 Serg Fausto Fiorani KiFA

Some other rather uneventful raids on Tunisian targets were carried out from Sicily during the days which followed, but the armistice of 24 June between Italy and France put a quick end to these operations.

Monday, 17 June 1940

13° Gruppo CT was ordered to move eastwards to Cyrenaica, leaving just a small section called Nucleo 2° Stormo to defend Tripoli's harbour; this section initially had a strength of just one CR.42 and three CR.32s. Thereafter, the fighter defence of Tripoli would be provided as follows:

Nucleo 2° Stormo	CR.32/CR.42	from 17 June 1940
2° Gruppo CT (150ª, 152ª, 358ª Squadriglie)	G.50bis	5 January-21 April 1941
18° Gruppo CT (83ª, 85ª, 95ª Squadriglie)	CR.42	29 January-23 February 1941
151° Gruppo CT (366ª, 367ª, 368ª Squadriglie)	CR.42	24 February-31 July 1941
374ª Squadriglia CT	MC.200	19 April-31 May 1941
376ª Squadriglia CT	CR.42	1 May-30 August 1941
155° Gruppo CT (351ª, 360ª, 378ª Squadriglie)	G.50bis	25 May-31 August 1941
3° Gruppo CT (153ª, 154ª, 155ª Squadriglie)	CR.42	1 August-28 December 1941
12° Gruppo CT (159ª, 160ª, 165ª Squadriglie)	G.50bis	6 August- year end 1941
23° Gruppo CT (70ª, 74ª, 75ª Squadriglie)	CR.42/MC.200	14-24 December 1941

On Malta, meanwhile, 431 Flight had been brought up to full squadron strength, and would become 69 Squadron on 10 January 1941. The island had by now been quite substantially reinforced, and rendered a much more secure base for offensive operations by aircraft, warships and submarines. To add to its striking power, 148 Squadron had arrived from the United Kingdom at the end of October, bringing in two dozen Wellington bombers. These, however, were not intended purely as a striking force against Tripoli, the targets allocated to its crews including fairly numerous locations in Sicily, as well as some in southern Italy, notably the port and city of Naples.

Saturday, 7 December 1940

Just before the commencement of the Operation Compass attack in the east, the RAF's offensive against the Regia Aeronautica's airfields commenced with a raid by 11 Wellingtons of 148 Squadron from Malta on the Castel Benito area. Three of these bombers had taken off initially and were led by Sqn Ldr A.Golding to attack coastal areas, while three more, led by Sqn Ldr P.S.Foss, attacked Mellaha airfield to the east of the city. Five more Wellingtons then followed at 15-minute intervals to bomb Castel Benito airfield in an effort to stop interceptors taking off. In fact at least two aircraft of the Nucleo 2° Stormo CT which had been left at that airfield to form a 'sezione d'allarme', managed to get into the air, S.Ten Francesco De Seta intercepting Foss's section as they were bombing Mellaha and attacking two of these. He claimed one shot down and the second probably so with Serg Vito Rinaldi; Foss's aircraft was hit and damaged, the rear gunner, Sgt A.Hollingsworth, being wounded. On return to Luqa with the starboard wing and tailplane damaged, the aircraft suffered a burst tyre and swung off the runway. Flg Off P.W.de B.Forsyth's aircraft was also seriously hit and he force-landed on return (see *Malta: The Hurricane Years 1940-41*).

The bomber crews reported that they believed they had destroyed or damaged 29 Italian aircraft on the ground. The Regia Aeronautica recorded heavy damage, including three S.79s and a CR.42 written off at Castel Benito.

British Claims		
148 Sqn	29 aircraft destroyed or damaged on ground in the Benghazi area	
British Casualties		
148 Sqn	Wellington T2838 damaged; Flg Off P.W.deB.Forsyth & crew safe	
	Wellington damaged: Sqn Ldr P.S.Foss & crew returned; rear gunner wounded	
Italian Claims		
2° St CT	S.Ten Francesco De Seta	Wellington
	S.Ten Francesco De Seta }	
	Serg Vito Rinaldi }	Wellington probable
Italian Casualties		
54ª Sq/47° Gr/15° St BT	S.79 destroyed on ground	
13ª Sq/26° Gr/9° St BT	2 S.79s (MM21634 & 22039) destroyed on ground	
?	CR.42 destroyed on ground	
Unspecified units	3 S.79s badly damaged on ground	
	9 S.79s damaged on ground	
	9 CR.42s damaged on ground	
	2 G.50bis damaged on ground	
	2 CR.32s damaged on ground	

Friday, 13 December 1940

Swordfish of 830 Squadron from Malta dive-bombed Tripoli harbour. During this attack K8866 was lost, Sub Lts R.H.Thompson and A.E.Dyer being killed.

British Casualties	
830 Sqn	Swordfish K8866 MiA Tripoli; Sub Lts R.H.Thompson and A.E.Dyer KiA

Sunday – Wednesday, 15/25 December 1940

Following the raids on 7 December, the RAF was mainly engaged in activities over Cyrenaica and the Egyptian frontier area. It was to be two weeks before a further heavy attack was made in Tripolitania. This time the assault came not from Malta, but from the deck of the newly-arrived aircraft carrier, HMS *Illustrious*.

This vessel had been involved in two recent sorties mainly connected with Malta convoys, although on 12 December her Swordfish had bombed transport laagers near Bardia in support of Operation Compass. Following a return to Alexandria to refuel, she had sailed again with the Mediterranean Fleet to attack targets on Rhodes and Stampalia (see *Air War for Yugoslavia, Greece and Crete, 1940-41*). Heading then to Malta, where the battleship HMS *Warspite* put into harbour briefly, the fleet approached Tripoli to interdict the flow of supplies to the Italian forces in Libya. On 21 December nine torpedo-armed Swordfish drawn from the carrier's two squadrons, intercepted a convoy of three merchant vessels off Kerkennah Island, claiming seven hits which sank the 6,511-ton refrigerator ship *Norge* and the 1,926-ton steamer *Peuceta*. Next day 15 Swordfish attacked Tripoli, claiming to have set fire to warehouses and dumps, all save one of the aircraft returning safely to their parent ship. Throughout this particular sortie, which lasted from 15-25 December, no aerial attacks were experienced, and the carrier's fighters were not called upon to fly any defensive operations.

British Casualties

819 Sqn	Swordfish P4075 '5Q'missing; Lt D.C.Garton-Stone, Lt J.H.R.Medlicott-Vereker and NA1 W.E.Sperry KiA

Italian Casualties (21 December)

Unspecified units	S.8 destroyed on ground when three torpedoes being carried, exploded

By this time, however, Operation Compass was already well underway in Cyrenaica, where Italian forces were in retreat and the Regia Aeronautica was in critical need of reinforcement. It was certainly not the ideal moment to seek to strengthen the defences of Tripoli.

Sunday, 9 February 1941
During January 1941 148 Squadron commenced a further series of attacks on Tripoli, and in this it was joined on occasion by 830 Squadron, eight of this unit's Swordfish attacking on 9 February, but losing one aircraft in doing so.

British Casualties

830 Sqn	Swordfish MiA

By now elements of the Luftwaffe's X.Fliegerkorps had arrived in Sicily and had succeeded in seriously damaging HMS *Illustrious*, causing her removal from the Mediterranean. A growing weight of attack on Malta was steadily reducing the ability of her forces to strike back at a time when convoys from Italy were delivering considerable reinforcements of Italian troops and equipment to Tripoli, and also the initial units of the new German Afrika Korps (hence the arrival of the Luftwaffe in the area). Indeed, by late February it was becoming increasingly difficult to maintain any bomber aircraft, destroyer flotillas or submarines at the island, where the defences were fighting for their very lives. 148 Squadron was reinforced on 20 February, but only by two Wellingtons from 70 Squadron in Egypt.

Monday – Tuesday, 24/25 February 1941
On the night of 24/25 February nine Wellingtons raided Tripoli, suffering the loss of one 70 Squadron aircraft, but next day a particularly crippling air raid resulted in the destruction of six of the unit's aircraft and one of those attached from 70 Squadron, with seven more seriously damaged (see also Chapter 12 – The RAF's Night Bombing Offensive).

British Casualties

(Night 24/25th)	
70 Sqn	Wellington Ic T2891 'O' MiA; Plt Off G.H.Green and one KiA; four PoW
(Day 25th)	
148 Sqn	Wellington Ic R1247 'M' destroyed on ground
	Wellington Ic R1381 'U' destroyed on ground
	Wellington Ic R1382 'A' destroyed on ground
	Wellington Ic R1383 'V' destroyed on ground
	Wellington Ic R1384 'B' destroyed on ground
	Wellington Ic T2955 'W' destroyed on ground
70 Sqn	Wellington Ic T2816 'J' destroyed on ground
148 Sqn	7 Wellingtons badly damaged on ground

For the time being this put an end to raids by Wellingtons, but the remaining Swordfish and Marylands (as the M-167Fs were now known) were carefully husbanded.

Sunday, 9 March 1941

Italian Casualties

Unspecified unit	Cant.Z.501 destroyed by bombs at Caramanlis

Tuesday, 18 March 1941

On 18 March nine of the Swordfish, by night as usual, raided the port, suffering a single loss in doing so.

British Casualties

830 Sqn	Swordfish K5939 'Q' force-landed Zarzis, Tunisia; Sub Lt W.E.Grant/LA W.E.J.Thompson interned

With the approach of spring and summer, elements of X.Fliegerkorps were steadily withdrawn from Sicily to return northwards to take part in the forthcoming invasions of the Balkan countries, and then of the Soviet Union. At the same time successful deliveries during April and May of additional Hurricanes for the defences, allowed the offensive power of Malta to commence reinstatement. Interdiction of convoys passing across the Mediterranean had become a very urgent priority, and to achieve this it had become obvious that better results could be accomplished by aircraft operating by day, rather than seeking to find their targets in the dark. Consequently, the decision was taken to detach squadrons of Blenheim IV bombers from Bomber Command's 2 Group in England, to Malta. The first element to arrive, the detached air party of 21 Squadron, flew in during mid April, and on the 27th of that month the seven remaining Wellingtons of 148 Squadron left Luqa for Egypt to make way for the new arrivals. 2 Group's units were to spend the rest of the year engaged in one of the most hazardous and costly enterprises of the war.

It was at this stage that Tripoli's defenders recorded their initial operational losses. During a patrol on 17 April over a convoy off Kerkennah Island, close to the Tunisian coast, two CR.42 pilots from 368ª Squadriglia, 151° Gruppo CT, Cap Giuseppe Zuffi (the unit's commanding officer) and Serg Francesco Bozzi, ran out of fuel and were both obliged to force-land in Tunisia, about six miles from the Libyan border. In doing so, Bozzi managed to somersault his aircraft. Both pilots were released by the French authorities on 22 April and returned to their home airfield.

Italian Casualties

368ª Sq/151° Gr CT	CR.42 force-landed Tunisia; Cap Giuseppe Zuffi released 22 April
	CR.42 force-landed Tunisia; Serg Francesco Bozzi released 22 April

Monday, 21 April 1941

It will be recalled that on 20 April the Mediterranean Fleet was approaching the Tripoli area during a sortie from Alexandria which had already resulted in some aerial engagements further to the east (see Chapter 6 – Reverses and Reinforcements). As night fell the fleet divided, the aircraft carrier HMS *Formidable*, accompanied by the cruisers *Ajax* and *Perth*, drawing away northwards to fly off air support, while three battleships, the cruiser *Gloucester*, and seven covering destroyers headed inshore to carry out a bombardment. During the early hours, Wellingtons from Malta bombed the port and flares were dropped by Swordfish of 830 Squadron. Other Swordfish and Albacores from *Formidable*'s 826 and 829 Squadrons followed to release more flares to assist the naval gunners, and at 0503 fire was opened from a range of 11,000 yards by the 15 inch and six inch guns of the warships. After twenty minutes the fleet changed course to commence withdrawing, continuing to fire for a further 20 minutes until the range had increased to 16,000 yards. Only during this latter phase was any return fire experienced from the shore, which achieved no hits. One Swordfish crashed while landing on the carrier, but the fleet was soon safely away on its return route to Alexandria. Complete surprise had been achieved, but heavy air attack was now anticipated.

Tuesday – Wednesday, 6/7 May 1941

Meanwhile, the Swordfish of 830 Squadron continued to maintain operations from Malta. During the night of 6/7 May three of the unit's aircraft laid mines in Tripoli harbour. On this occasion one Swordfish was hit by AA and its pilot, Lt N.K.Campbell, had to ditch in the sea just off the coast. He and his observer managed to swim ashore, but the TAG (telegraphist/air gunner), Pty Off(A) W.G.T.Welsh, died of the wounds he had suffered.

830 Sqn	Swordfish P4232 ditched after AA hit; Lt N.K.Campbell and Lt G.D.Nutt, both injured and PoWs; Pty Off(A) W.G.T.Welsh died of wounds

Saturday – Sunday, 10/11 May 1941

The Swordfish were out again during the night of 10/11 May, once again laying mines in the harbour as seven Wellingtons, four of them from 148 Squadron, staged through Malta to bomb the port as a diversion.

A few days later two more Blenheim squadrons arrived from England; these were 82 and 139 Squadrons. On their arrival the 21 Squadron detachment appears to have been amalgamated into 82 Squadron, Wg Cdr L.V.E.Atkinson who had been leading the former aircraft now taking over command of 82. Commanding officer of 139 Squadron was Wg Cdr D.W.Scivier, AFC.

Wednesday, 21 May 1941

The defence of the port was enhanced by the arrival from Italy at Castel Benito of 376ª Squadriglia CT with its CR.42s.

Tuesday, 27 May 1941

The two newly-arrived Blenheim squadrons attacked a convoy escorted by six destroyers. Hits were achieved on the steamer *Foscarini* and she was later towed into Tripoli on fire. However, the defensive barrage put up by the destroyers was fierce, and coupled with the explosions of their own bombs at so low a level, two of the six bombers went into the water – a grim indicator of what lay ahead for the anti-shipping units.

British Casualties

82 Sqn	Blenheim IV V6460, possibly brought down by explosions of own bombs; Sgt E.B. Innan and one KiA; one PoW
	Blenheim IV Z6427 'H' possibly brought down by explosions of own bombs; Flt Lt G.M.Fairbairn and crew KiA

Wednesday, 28 May 1941

Next day two more of 139 Squadron's aircraft flew south to Sfax harbour, where they bombed a vessel which was seen to blow up.

At the start of June 7./JG 26, the sole staffel of Bf 109Es in Sicily, which had been playing havoc with the fighters seeking to defend Malta, at last departed, heading for North Africa. This took a considerable pressure off the defenders, and with the Luftwaffe now virtually entirely gone from Sicily, the use of the island as an offensive interdiction base was soon considerably enhanced.

Friday, 30 May 1941

Italian Casualties

145ª Sq RST	Cant.Z.501 MM35579 collided with torpedo-boat *Pleiadi* and destroyed; pilots S.Ten Augusto Sala and M.llo Tullio Pedemonte KiFA

Tuesday, 17 June 1941

Ten Serafino Molinari, 351ª Squadriglia, 155° Gruppo, crashed in his G.50bis during a test flight at Castel Benito, and was killed.

Italian Casualties

351ª Sq/155° Gr CT	G.50bis MM 6357 Pilot Ten Serafino Molinari KiFA at Castel Benito

Friday, 20 June 1941

On this date Flg Off Adrian Warburton of 69 Squadron undertook a sortie to Tripolitania in one of the unit's Marylands, reporting that he had strafed Homs and Misurata airfields, claiming to have set three S.79s on fire there.

British Claims

69 Sqn	Crew of Maryland	3 S.79s destroyed on ground

Italian Casualties

| Unspecified unit | S.81 destroyed on ground at Misurata |
| | 3 S.82s damaged on ground at Misurata |

Sunday, 22 June 1941

By now 82 Squadron was at full strength, following the arrival of more of the unit's Blenheims. On this date six of the unit's aircraft attacked a convoy off Lampedusa which it was quickly realised had an escort of CR.42s. AA fire from the ships was also heavy, and as Sqn Ldr J.Harrison-Broadley approached, the port engine of his bomber was hit and began to burn. His flying speed allowed him to complete his bombing run before he was forced to ditch his stricken aircraft in the sea, and one of his bombs was seen to strike one of the ships. He and his crew were picked up and became prisoners.

Meanwhile, Flt Lt T.J.Watkins, who had survived some of the costly raids which the unit had undertaken in France in 1940, attacked a merchant vessel believed to be of some 6,000 tons displacement, but his Blenheim too was hit as he pressed home his attack, and he was badly wounded in the legs. Nonetheless, hits were obtained before the aircraft was attacked by one of the escorting fighters upon which he manoeuvred to allow his gunner, Sgt E.F.Chandler, to have as good a field of fire as possible. The CR.42 closed in, but Chandler claimed to have shot it down. Watkins then lapsed into unconsciousness as the aircraft headed north. At this point the navigator, Sgt J.S.Sargent, removed him from his seat and took over the controls. Arriving over Malta, Watkins insisted on taking over control again, and in great pain and considerably weakened by loss of blood, he made a successful landing. Subsequently he was awarded a DSO, Harrison-Broadley receiving a DFC, while Chandler and Sargent were both awarded DFMs. In their attack they had seriously damaged the 5,584-ton steamer *Tembien* and the German vessel *Wachtfels*, both of which managed to reach Tripoli with the assistance of tugs.

British Claims

| 82 Sqn | Sgt E.F.Chandler, gunner in Blenheim CR.42 |

British Casualties

| 82 Sqn | Blenheim IV Z6422 shot down; Sqn Ldr J.Harrison-Broadley and crew PoW |
| | Blenheim IV Z9545 damaged; Flt Lt T.J.Walters WiA |

Tuesday, 24 June 1941

A similar sortie to that undertaken by 69 Squadron on 20 June was flown four days later by Flg Off R.Drew, he and his crew engaging in a fight with a CR.42 which attempted to intercept them. This was seen falling away steeply, but no claim was submitted.

82 Squadron was also out again, attacking the convoy which was now in Tripoli harbour. Led by Wg Cdr Atkinson, the Blenheim crews claimed damage to a 20,000-ton liner and a 12,500-ton motor vessel.

Wednesday, 25 June 1941

During the afternoon a long-range Hurricane II which 69 Squadron now used for more hazardous reconnaissance sorties, appeared over four 20,000-ton merchant ships with an escort of seven destroyers to the south-east of Malta. At this time the Italians had begun using four ships of just such displacement to transport troops to Libya to relieve forward elements of the Afrika Korps. These were the liners *Marco Polo, Neptunia, Oceania* and *Vulcania*. On the receipt of the Hurricane pilot's report, a Maryland was at once despatched flown by Flg Off J.R.Bloxham, and with Lt.H.E.H.Pain, 830 Squadron's senior observer, to keep the convoy in view while a Swordfish strike was planned. In order to strike as soon as possible, meanwhile, all available Marylands were armed with two 500lb bombs apiece and sent off to attack. No hits were obtained and one Maryland failed to return, the crew last being heard over the radio reporting that they were bombing the ships. It appears likely that they were shot down by an MC 200 of 10° Gruppo CT, flown by Serg Roberto Steppi who claimed one Blenheim shot down and a second damaged. This unit was not based in the Tripoli area but is believed to have flown this defensive sortie whilst on its way to Cyrenaica.

At 1800 a Swordfish was sent out to shadow the convoy, followed by more armed with torpedoes. Just over an hour later these attacked, claiming several hits which it was thought might have sunk a large transport. In fact the liner *Esperia* reached Tripoli only slightly damaged by air attacks but one of the Swordfish was brought down by AA.

British Casualties		
69 Sqn	Maryland I AR726 missing; Sgt B.P.Hanson and crew MiA	
830 Sqn	Swordfish P3996 'S' shot down by AA; Sub Lt D.A.R.Holmes/LA J.R.Smith KiA	

Italian Claims		
84ª Sq/10º Gr CT	Serg Roberto Steppi	Blenheim over sea
	Serg Roberto Steppi	Blenheim damaged over sea

Saturday, 28 June 1941

Flg Off Bloxham led three Marylands to attack a convoy which had been found off Tripoli. Bombs were dropped and at least one 15,000-ton troopship was reported as being seen on fire.

Sunday, 29 June 1941

82 Squadron's Blenheims sought to attack the ships off Tripoli, but the aircraft flown by Sgt J.A.Cover failed to return. A G.50bis pilot from 155º Gruppo CT engaged on a convoy escort, claimed a British bomber probably shot down. During the day, however, an RAF attack on Castel Benito airfield destroyed two of 151º Gruppo CT's CR.42s and a Ca.133 'hack'.

British Casualties			
82 Sqn	Blenheim IV B MiA; Sgt J.A.Cover and crew KiA		

Italian Claims			
155º Gr CT	Unidentified pilot	Bomber probable	Homs area

Italian Casualties			
151º Gr CT	2 CR.42s destroyed on ground at Sorman		
	Ca.133 destroyed on ground at Sorman		
360ª Sq/155º Gr CT	G.50 MM5977 crash-landed due to fuel shortage; pilot safe		

Tuesday – Wednesday, 1/2 July 1941

At the end of June a detachment of six Wellingtons of 148 Squadron returned to the island from Egypt, led by Sqn Ldr R.J.Wells, DFC. During the night of 1/2 July five of these bombed Tripoli harbour, the crews returning to report that they believed they had hit a vessel estimated to be of 8,000-ton displacement; they had sunk the minesweeper *Eritrea* and damaged the steamer *Sabbia*. Next night they returned, accompanied by eight 830 Squadron Swordfish. Six of the latter carried mines which were sown inside the harbour entrance while two bombed and set on fire the 1,724-ton German steamer *Sparta*.

Wednesday, 3 July 1941

Reconnaissance next day indicated that much congestion of shipping had been caused by the mines, and consequently four 82 Squadron Blenheims were sent out to attack by day. A further reconnaissance then indicated that one vessel of 8,000 tons and one of 3,000 tons had been severely damaged, with a further vessel estimated at 5,000 tons sinking. One of the Marylands operating in the area was flown by Flg Off Drew, who strafed Zuara airfield where he believed he had hit a number of S.81s and set one on fire.

British Claims			
69 Sqn	Flg Off R.Drew	S.81	on ground Zuara

Italian Casualties			
Unspecified unit	S.81 damaged on ground Zuara		

Wednesday, 9 July 1941

Now occurred the most effective interception which the Regia Aeronautica was to undertake during the course of the operations against Tripoli throughout the period under review. On this date 110 Squadron sent seven Blenheims to attack the harbour, where direct hits were claimed on four merchant vessels, one estimated at 12,000 tons, two at 10,000 tons each, and one at 7,000 tons. Fighters had been scrambled in time to intercept the bombers effectively, and at about 1600 hours (Axis time) M.llo Aldo Buvoli from 155º Gruppo CT was cruising over Tripoli in his G.50bis MM6384 at 5,000 ft altitude. He spotted a formation of four Blenheims, followed at a distance by a fifth. He shot down one over the port and a second over the sea at the end of a long chase. Two pilots of 151º Gruppo also intercepted in their CR.42s,

One of the most successful actions against intruders over Tripoli was carried out on 9 July 1941, by M.llo Aldo Buvoli of 378ª Squadriglia, 155° Gruppo CT, who shot down two Blenheims in his G.50bis.

M.llo Paolo Montanari and Serg Ottorino Ambrosi each claiming one Blenheim shot down. Four of the bombers were indeed lost; Sqn Ldr Searle's aircraft was seen to force-land in the sea, Sgt Twist and his crew coming down a few miles north of Tripoli, as did the other two aircraft.

A little later Flg Off Warburton's 69 Squadron Maryland appeared over Tripoli, seeking to ascertain the results of the attack. He was intercepted by M.llo Francesco Fagiolo of 155° Gruppo CT, who claimed either a Blenheim or a Maryland shot down. In this case Warburton managed to escape after his aircraft had been damaged, his gunner claiming the attacking fighter – which he identified as a MC.200 – probably shot down. Fagiolo returned safely.

British Claims			
69 Sqn	Turret gunner in Maryland	MC.200 probable	Tripoli area
British Casualties			
110 Sqn	Blenheim IV Z6449 shot down; Sqn Ldr D.H.Searle and crew KiA		
	Blenheim IV Z9537 shot down; Flt Lt M.E.Potier and one KiA; two of crew PoW		
	Blenheim IV Z9578 shot down; Plt Off W.H.Lowe and crew PoW		
	Blenheim IV Z9533 shot down; Sgt W.H.Twist and crew PoW		
69 Sqn	Maryland I damaged over Tripoli; Flg Off A.Warburton and crew unhurt		
Italian Claims			
378ª Sq/155° Gr CT	M.llo Aldo Buvoli	2 Blenheims	Tripoli
366ª Sq/151° Gr CT	M.llo Paolo Montanari	Blenheim	Tripoli
368ª Sq/151° Gr CT	Serg Ottorino Ambrosi	Blenheim	Tripoli
360ª Sq/155° Gr CT	M.llo Francesco Fagiolo	Blenheim or Maryland	Tripoli

Sunday, 13 July 1941
Two Blenheims were claimed shot down over Tripoli by a CR.42 pilot of 376ª Squadriglia Autonoma CT. No corresponding RAF losses have been found.

Italian Claims			
376ª Sq Aut CT	Ten Aldo Marchetti	2 Blenheims	Tripoli

Tuesday, 15 July 1941

A 69 Squadron Maryland failed to return from an afternoon reconnaissance over Tripolitania, Sgt C.F.Lee and his all-Australian crew being lost.

British Casualties	
69 Sqn	Maryland I AR729 MiA; Sgt C.F.Lee and crew KiA

Wednesday – Thursday, 16/17 July 1941

By night three Swordfish of 830 Squadron arrived over Tripoli, two armed with bombs, while Lt G.M.T.Osborn's aircraft carried a torpedo. Gliding down over the harbour, Osborn spotted a large tanker off the North Mole, released from 250 yards, and gained a hit amidships. The 6,212-ton *Panuco* was damaged sufficiently to make it impossible to unload her whole cargo and she was forced to return to Italy with 6,000 tons of fuel still aboard.

Friday, 18 July 1941

Six Blenheims of 110 Squadron returned to Tripoli, led by Wg Cdr Theo M.Hunt, DFC, this time to bomb a power station. Hunt's aircraft was seen to obtain a direct hit on the target, but during the return flight the formation was attacked by a lone CR.42 of 368ª Squadriglia, 151° Gruppo CT, when ten miles out to sea. Ten Armando Capogrossi opened fire at long range and Hunt's Blenheim at once crashed into the sea.

British Casualties			
110 Sqn	Blenheim IV Z9582 shot down; Wg Cdr T.M.Hunt, DFC, and crew KiA		
Italian Claims			
368ª Sq/151° Gr CT	Ten Armando Capogrossi	Blenheim	Tripoli area

Tuesday, 22 July 1941

During the afternoon Ten Vincenzo Graffeo in a CR.42 of 367ª Squadriglia reported intercepting a Blenheim over Tripoli harbour which he claimed to have damaged.

Italian Claims			
367ª Sq/151° Gr CT	Ten Vincenzo Graffeo	Blenheim damaged	Tripoli harbour

At the end of July the commanding officer of 830 Squadron, Lt Cdr F.D.Howie. who had recently been awarded the DSO, was posted to the AOC's staff, his place within the squadron being taken by Lt H.E.H.Pain, continuing the unit's tradition of appointing observer officers to command. The squadron had been reinforced during a delivery of further aircraft to the island by way of aircraft carrier, and which on this occasion also brought seven new Swordfish. Importantly, two of these were equipped with the recently-developed ASV (air to surface vessel) radar, the first aircraft so fitted to reach Malta. Coupled with the very secret information regularly received by the island's commanders via Ultra, the ability to find and attack shipping by night was thereby considerably enhanced.

Thursday, 31 July 1941

Sgt J.K.Hutt of 69 Squadron flew a morning reconnaissance over Tripoli during which he strafed Zuara airfield, claiming to have set one S.79 on fire and damaged three more. The day also saw the arrival at Sorman of 3° Gruppo CT (153ª, 154ª and 155ª Squadriglie) with 20 CR.42s. A further 13 would subsequently arrive, this unit's primary duty being the defence of Tripoli harbour.

British Claims				
69 Sqn	Sgt J.K.Hutt	Maryland I	S.79	on ground Zuara
	Sgt J.K.Hutt	Maryland I	3 S.79s damaged	on ground Zuara
Italian Casualties				
Unspecified unit	S.79 damaged on ground at Zuara			

Another Blenheim unit, 105 Squadron, had just arrived on Malta at this time, and on this date undertook its first sorties when six aircraft spotted a convoy 50 miles off Pantelleria. Intense AA fire and four patrolling CR.42s dissuaded the crews from attacking, but they were able to report the convoy's presence on their return. At 1000 therefore, Lt A.S.Whitworth of 830 Squadron, flying one of the new ASV-equipped Swordfish with Lt Pain as observer, led four aircraft, all carrying torpedoes, in search of the ships. These were found an hour later, but visibility had worsened and only one hit was thought to have been obtained. It was later confirmed that a 6,000-ton freighter had been badly damaged.

Friday, 1 August 1941
Following the previous day's attack, three more of 105 Squadron's Blenheims were sent out, attacking a ship in Lampedusa harbour, but losing one aircraft to machine-gun fire from the ground.

British Casualties	
105 Sqn	Blenheim IV Z9605 'U' shot down into sea; Flt Lt A.B.Broadley, DFC, and one PoW; Plt Off A.S.Ramsay, DFC, KiA

At the start of August Malta lost the Beaufighters of 272 Squadron which had been operating there, but which now departed for Egypt. Their place was at once taken by 38 Squadron's Wellingtons which flew in from Shallufa, making their first attack on Tripoli by night on 8 August.

Friday, 8 August 1941
During the morning Serg Magg Pietro Scaramucci of 159ª Squadriglia, 12° Gruppo CT claimed a Blenheim probably shot down. No engagement has been found in RAF records.

Italian Claims			
159ª Sq/ 12° Gr CT	Serg Magg Pietro Scaramucci	Blenheim probable	Tripoli area

Thursday – Friday, 14/15 August 1941
During the night nine 830 Squadron Swordfish set off to attack a convoy of five merchant vessels reported to be off Tripoli. Six of the attackers carried torpedoes, two were equipped to drop flares, and the ninth was one of the ASV aircraft, the crew of which sought to control the raid. Two of the ships were claimed seriously damaged by Lt Osborn and Sub Lt Taylor, while an attendant destroyer was also claimed hit by Lt Whitworth. Sailing from Benghazi to Tripoli, the refrigerator vessel *Adua* of 400 tons was sunk near Buerat.

Wednesday, 20 August 1941
Beginning at dawn, two CR.42s of 3° Gruppo and two G.50bis of 155° Gruppo provided escort for a convoy bound for Tripoli. When so engaged, a submarine was seen and was machine gunned by the CR.42 pilots. They had attacked HMS *Unique*, but were unable to stop her torpedoing and sinking the 11,398-ton liner *Esperia* 13 miles off Tripoli at 1030.

Saturday – Sunday, 30/31 August 1941
Raids damaged the tanker *Pozzarica* and sank two mine sweepers during the day, but by night gunners aboard the torpedo boat *Clio* shot down X9737 of 38 Squadron, which fell in flames. Plt Off Mauchlen and one member of his crew were killed, but four others survived as PoWs. (See Chapter 12 – The RAF's Night Bombing Offensive)

Sunday – Monday, 31 August/1 September 1941
By night on the last day of August, 38 Squadron Wellingtons returned to Tripoli, where the 6,630-ton German steamer *Riva* was sunk.

Friday, 5 September 1941
Ten Enzo Bianchi of 155ª Squadriglia, 3° Gruppo was scrambled at night, engaging an unidentified bomber 12 miles north of Tripoli. He attacked this several times and claimed it as probably destroyed.

Italian Claims			
155ª Sq/ 3° Gr CT	Ten Enzo Bianchi	u/i e/a probable	12m N Tripoli

Wednesday – Thursday, 10/11 September 1941

On 10 September a convoy of six merchant vessels and six destroyers left Naples, making for Tripoli. During the afternoon of the following day these ships had reached a point between Pantelleria and Lampedusa, where they were spotted by a 69 Squadron Maryland. At once 830 Squadron prepared for a night strike, five torpedo-armed Swordfish following one of the ASV aircraft to the area of the Tunisian coast where the convoy was being 'shadowed' by the other ASV aircraft. Shortly after midnight the attack began. Claims were made for one ship probably sunk and two more damaged. One Swordfish suffered damage to its tail from AA fire. One of the vessels hit was the 6,476-ton *Caffaro* which was still afloat at daybreak when eight Blenheims from 105 and newly-arrived 107 Squadrons appeared, led by Sqn Ldr B.W.Smithers, although she was to blow up and sink later in the day. The Blenheims attacked at once, but three immediately fell victims to the AA, and a fourth badly damaged, crash-landing on its return to Malta.

With nightfall, the Swordfish were ordered off again, six torpedo-carriers and one ASV aircraft sighting the convoy at about 2300 hours, two hits being claimed on the 6,003-ton *Nicolò Odero*, which was crippled. In support of this attack seven of 38 Squadron's Wellingtons arrived over Tripoli at 0330 and bombed shipping, claiming four hits; crews reported that they had seen two vessels burning. Shortly after this attack, the damaged *Nicolò Odero* blew up.

British Casualties	
105 Sqn	Blenheim IV Z7357 'U' shot down in sea; Sgt F.B.Brandwood and crew picked up from dinghy by submarine *Utmost* next day
	Blenheim IV Z9606 'V' damaged by AA and crash-landed at Luqa on return; Flt Sgt J.Bendall and crew safe; one injured
107 Sqn	Blenheim IV Z750 'G' shot down in sea; Sqn Ldr F.R.H.Charney, DFC, and crew KiA
	Blenheim IV Z9603 'F' shot down in sea; Sgt J.E.Mortimer and crew KiA

Wednesday, 17 September 1941

Four Blenheims made a low-level attack on a large liner in Tripoli harbour. However, two of the bombers flew into wires stretched between the masts of a large schooner which was being towed by a tug, and both crashed, one going into the sea; the other struck the deck of the schooner. One of the crews lost was that which had crash-landed at Luqa five days earlier following the attack on a convoy on that occasion.

British Casualties	
105 Sqn	Blenheim IV P4840 'Y' crashed in sea after striking wire obstacle; Flt Sgt J.Bendall and crew KiA
107 Sqn	Blenheim IV Z7755 'O' crashed on deck of schooner; Plt Off P.E.C.Robinson and crew KiA

Friday, 19 September 1941

Two Blenheims, one each from 105 and 107 Squadrons, attacked some destroyers and a cruiser in Tripoli harbour, claiming hits on the larger vessel.

Monday, 22 September 1941

During a raid on army barracks and an ammunition dump at Homs, a Blenheim of 105 Squadron from Malta flown by the commanding officer, collided with another of the unit's aircraft and was cut in two. It crashed at once near the target, the crew being killed. The second aircraft survived the collision and returned to base.

British Casualties	
105 Sqn	Blenheim IV Z7423 'H' crashed due to collision; Wg Cdr D.W.Scivier, AFC, and two KiFA
	Blenheim IV Z9609 damaged in collision with Z7423, but returned

Wednesday, 24 September 1941

British Casualties	
107 Sqn	Blenheim IV Z9599 shot down by AA during attack on transport on Misurata-Benghazi road; Sqn Ldr T.J.S.Warren, DFC, and two KiA

Thursday, 25 September 1941
Italian fighters claimed a Blenheim probably shot down during the early afternoon, but no matching RAF account has been found.

Italian Claims

393ª Sq/ 160º Gr CT	Serg Vittorio Ghini	Blenheim probable	Tripoli area

Sunday, 28 September 1941
During the day 165ª Squadriglia of 12º Gruppo CT arrived at Castel Benito to bring the unit to its full three-squadriglie strength (159ª, 160ª and 165ª).

Saturday, 4 October 1941
Eight Blenheims from 107 Squadron sought to attack a 6,000-ton merchant ship reported off the Tripolitanian coast. Failing to find this vessel, they targeted instead Zuara airfield. As they approached, AA fire was encountered from a destroyer in the harbour, and four CR.42s were seen in the air. One of these, flown by S.Ten Cesare Ciapetti of 3º Gruppo, followed the Blenheims 50 miles out to sea, gaining hits on Sgt Hamlyn's aircraft and he force-landed his aircraft in the sea, while two other bombers were damaged. The gunners in these aircraft claimed to have damaged the fighter in return. Hamlyn and his crew were picked up a few days later when they were found floating in their dinghy near Djerba on the Tunisian coast, and were interned by the Vichy French authorities there.

British Claims

107 Sqn	Bomber gunners	CR.42 damaged	near Tripoli

British Casualties

107 Sqn	Blenheim IV V5821 shot down; Sgt D.E.Hamlyn and crew rescued and interned in Tunisia
	2 Blenheim IVs damaged

Italian Claims

154ª Sq/3º Gr CT	S.Ten Cesare Ciapetti	Blenheim ditched in sea	Zuara

Tuesday – Wednesday, 7/8 October 1941
105 and 107 Squadrons undertook their first night sorties on this date, attacking a 2,000-ton vessel off Tripoli from 20 feet over the sea, claiming two hits. Swordfish were also out, seeking a convoy of six cargo vessels and escorting destroyers located east of Tripoli. Attacking just before 0200, three pilots claimed hits, Sub Lt Taylor's target, the 6,099-ton *Rialto*, exploding. Two lifeboats were seen leaving the ship and it was later reported to have sunk. However, no Italian ships were reported lost on this date.

During October another 2 Group Blenheim unit arrived at Malta on detachment; this was 18 Squadron. However, at the same time 104 Squadron also arrived from England with Wellingtons. Led by Wg Cdr P.R.Beare, DFC, this unit subsequently relieved the aircraft of 38 Squadron, which would soon return to Egypt. A detachment from 40 Squadron, similarly equipped, also arrived a few days later as did a small detachment of three 'special' Wellington VIIIs from 221 Squadron. Led by Flt Lt A.Spooner, these aircraft (known as 'Roosters') were fitted with ASV, and would join in night operations in conjunction with 830 Squadron. That latter unit also saw a further change of command when Lt Cdr J.G.Hunt arrived to take over from Lt Pain.

Saturday, 11 October 1941
The remnants of 105 Squadron returned to England, but their place was soon taken by 15 new Blenheims flown in by 18 Squadron's crews. 107 Squadron continued to operate meanwhile, and during the day six of the unit's aircraft attacked shipping in the Gulf of Sirte which included a tanker, the cargo vessel *Priaruggia*, and two destroyers. *Priaruggia* was left in flames, but Flg Off Greenhill's Blenheim was seen to be hit in the belly and crashed into the sea. Bombs from Sgt Routh's aircraft were observed to strike a corvette which also burst into flames, but this bomber too then also went down. The loss of Greenhill's aircraft seems to have been almost bizarre. When the attack took place an S.81 of 103ª Squadriglia was on patrol, flown by the unit commander, Cap Antonio Rinaldo. One gunner in this aircraft apparently obtained the hits which brought the British bomber down. The Italians reported that a Canadian NCO who was picked up from the sea, confirmed that this was so. This must have been Sgt C.A.Whidden, who

although rescued, was to die from his injuries on 4 November. The rest of the crew had lost their lives immediately. Routh's aircraft does appear to have been claimed by naval AA gunners. However, although not reported by the returning crews, one of the missing aircraft may have been shot down by Serg Adriano Vezzi of 155ª Squadriglia, 3° Gruppo, who claimed one Blenheim near the Tunisian coast. He then force-landed near Novelmour Castle in Tunisia, without damaging his aircraft. He would return to his unit on 15 October. *Priaruggia* (1,196 tons) made it into harbour at Tripoli, but there she would blow up during the night of the 27th.

British Casualties			
107 Sqn	Blenheim IV Z7618 shot down; Sgt A.D.M.Routh and crew KiA		
	Blenheim IV Z9663 shot down; Flg Off R.A.Greenhill and crew KiA		

Italian Claims			
155ª Sq/3° Gr CT	Serg Adriano Vezzi	Blenheim	off Tunisian coast

Monday, 13 October 1941
By night Ten Egisto Andalò of 154ª Squadriglia, 3° Gruppo CT intercepted an unidentified bomber over Tripoli, making a number of passes at this without apparent result.

That night 830 Squadron Swordfish attacked the 7,933-ton *Bainsizza* south of Lampedusa, leaving her sinking.

Tuesday – Wednesday, 14/15 October 1941
Next night 830 Squadron Swordfish were out again to sink an already damaged cargo vessel that had been torpedoed by a submarine and which was now being towed into port.

Saturday, 18 October 1941
A further reinforcement flight reached Malta from the west on this date, this time including an additional Fleet Air Arm torpedo-bomber unit. This was 828 Squadron, equipped with 11 Fairey Albacores and two Swordfish, one of which was lost en route.

That same evening five 830 Squadron Swordfish were out yet again, this time seeking four merchant vessels and four destroyers which were being shadowed by Flt Lt Spooner's ASV Wellington about 80 miles south-east of Lampedusa. The Wellington crew released flares and two of the Swordfish crews launched torpedoes at the 4,786-ton *Caterina*. Sub Lt S.Campbell passed over the vessel after completing his attack at an altitude of only 2,000 feet, only just avoiding the debris thrown up as she blew up. Another pilot released bombs into the inferno and the ship sank shortly afterwards, damage being claimed to a second freighter.

Wellingtons were also active that night, six of the new arrivals joining 11 from 38 Squadron to raid Tripoli. Two of the 104 Squadron aircraft dropped 4,000lb Cookies on the city for the first time, which were estimated to have caused considerable damage. At the same time a 3,000-ton ship in the harbour was claimed to have suffered a direct hit from one of the smaller bombs released.

Monday, 20 October 1941
During a convoy escort by the CR.42s of 153ª Squadriglia, 3° Gruppo, early in the afternoon, one fighter crashed into the sea for no obvious reason, the pilot being killed.

A Cant.Z.501 flyingboat, MM35430 of 145ª Squadriglia RM flown by Ten Dante Colabucci with Serg Francesco Gibilisco as co-pilot and s.t.v. Pietro Sussi as observer, took off from Tripoli on an anti-submarine patrol. During this sortie a British submarine was spotted and bombed without result.

Italian Casualties	
153ª Sq/3° Gr CT	CR.42 MM7515 crashed in sea; Serg Angelo Zanaria KiFA

Wednesday, 22 October 1941
Six of the newly-arrived 18 Squadron Blenheims raided barracks at Homs, dropping 40lb anti-personnel bombs suspended from parachutes. One of the bombers, flown by Sgt J.D.Woodburn, DFM, collided with some of these dropped by the aircraft ahead. These exploded, destroying the Blenheim and its crew.

Monday, 27 October 1941

A Blenheim was reported to have been intercepted over Tripoli and was claimed to have been damaged. No matching account has been found in RAF records.

Italian Claims

160ª Sq/12° Gr CT	S.Ten Francesco Lisi	Blenheim damaged	Tripoli

Tuesday – Wednesday, 28/29 October 1941

Six Wellingtons of 104 Squadron raided Tripoli; all returned safely.

Wednesday – Thursday, 29/30 October 1941

17 Wellingtons from 104 Squadron and the 40 Squadron detachment attacked Tripoli again, on this occasion the target being railway marshalling yards.

Thursday, 30 October 1941

Again, a claim for a Blenheim damaged during an attack on Tripoli was submitted by 160ª Squadriglia of 12° Gruppo CT. Again, no matching report has been found in RAF records.

Italian Claims

160ª Sq/12° Gr CT	Serg Leopoldo Giovacchini	Blenheim damaged	Tripoli

By the end of October all further Axis sailings to Tripoli had been suspended for the time being. Sinkings during the past five months had exceeded construction and had totalled 270,000 tons throughout the Mediterranean. On the Italy-North Africa supply route, 178,577 tons had been lost, the majority during the August-October period. 24 ships, totalling 101,894 tons had succumbed to attacks by aircraft. The cost to Malta-based Blenheims operating to both north and south, had amounted so far to 35 aircraft and most of their crews. Now, with increased numbers of Wellingtons and RN torpedo-bombers, but fewer Blenheims available, the effort by night was again in the ascendant. However, the night bombers still had to include Naples, Palermo and Brindisi in their timetable, but still retaining Tripoli as their first priority target.

Sunday – Monday, 2/3 November 1941

During the night Wellingtons from both 40 and 104 Squadrons raided Castel Benito airfield. One New Zealand pilot of the former unit, Sgt C.A.Armstrong, pressed home his attacks in such a determined manner that he was immediately awarded a DFM. The citation stated: "…he bombed the aerodrome…, setting aircraft on the ground on fire. He then descended to 200 feet and machine gunned the airfield." However, another of the unit's aircraft became the first clear night fighter victory over the area for the Regia Aeronautica. Several 3° Gruppo CT CR.42s had been scrambled, attacking a number of aircraft. Ten Egisto Andalò claimed one shot down and one probable, a second also being claimed as a probable by another pilot; Andalò was, however, hit and wounded by return fire. On the ground two BR.20 bombers of 98° Gruppo BT were destroyed during the raid, as were five other miscellaneous aircraft. Numerous casualties were suffered, including Ten De Nunzio of 239ª Squadriglia BaT, who was killed.

British Casualties

40 Sqn	Wellington Ic X9763 'U' shot down; Sgt G.D.Colville and crew KiA

Italian Claims

154ª Sq/3° Gr CT	Ten Egisto Andalò	Wellington	Castel Benito
		Wellington probable	Castel Benito
155ª Sq/3° Gr CT	Ten Enzo Bianchi	Wellington probable	Castel Benito

Italian Casualties

154ª Sq/3° Gr CT	CR.42 damaged; Ten Egisto Andalò WiA

Italian Casualties

98° Gr BT	2 BR.20s destroyed on ground at Castel Benito
Unspecified unit	G.50bis destroyed on ground at Castel Benito
	S.79 destroyed on ground at Castel Benito
	S.84 destroyed on ground at Castel Benito
	S.81 destroyed on ground at Castel Benito

German Casualties

Unspecified unit	Ju 87 destroyed on ground at Castel Benito

Wednesday – Thursday, 5/6 November 1941

Three pilots of 154ª Squadriglia, 3° Gruppo, were scrambled to intercept bombers attacking Tripoli. Each pilot claimed one Wellington probably shot down, but no RAF losses of such aircraft were in fact suffered. Return fire hit one CR.42, Serg Magg Petrelli being wounded.

Italian Claims

154ª Sq/3° Gr CT	Ten Elio Broganelli	Wellington probable	Tripoli
	S.Ten Cesare Ciapetti	Wellington probable	Tripoli
	Serg Magg Italo Petrelli	Wellington probable	Tripoli

Italian Casualties

154ª Sq/3° Gr CT	CR.42 damaged; Serg Magg Italo Petrelli WiA

Wednesday, 19 November 1941

From Luqa six Blenheims of 18 Squadron set off on an ill-fated strike against an Axis convoy which had been spotted in the Gulf of Sirte. This comprised the 5,000-ton German freighter *Spezia*, the 2,000-ton Italian *Cadamosto* and a motor-assisted sailing boat, the *Cora*. They were escorted by a single warship, *Centauro*, variously described as a small destroyer or a large torpedo-boat. Whatever its categorisation, the gun crews on this vessel appear to have been extremely well-trained, for when the attack began at 1445, they shot down three of the Blenheims in quick succession, all the crews being lost (see also *Malta: The Hurricane Years, 1940-41*).

British Casualties

18 Sqn	Blenheim IV V606 'U' shot down by ship's AA; Sgt D.W.Buck and two KiA Gulf of Sirte 1445
	Blenheim IV V6492 'P' shot down by ship's AA; Sgt J.H.Woodman and two KiA Gulf of Sirte 1445
	Blenheim IV Z7860 'F' shot down by ship's AA; Sgt H.L.Hanson and two KiA Gulf of Sirte 1445

Sunday, 23 November 1941

Italian Claims

159ª Sq/12° Gr CT	Serg Giuseppe Zardini	Blenheim	Castel Benito 1315

Friday – Saturday, 28/29 November 1941

Five Albacores of 828 Squadron from Malta flew through stormy conditions to target Castel Benito airfield by dive-bombing. One aircraft was hit by AA fire and reportedly fell in flames. Italian records note, however, that the aircraft crash-landed near Suani where the crew of two was captured (see also *Malta: The Hurricane Years, 1940-41*).

British Casualties

828 Sqn	Albacore T9249 shot down near Castel Benito by AA; Sub Lt E.H.Walshe and observer PoW

Italian Casualties

Unspecified unit	S.79 loaded with a torpedo destroyed on the ground at Castel Benito by bombs

Sunday – Monday, 30 November/1 December 1941

By night Flt Lt Spooner in his 221 Squadron Rooster Wellington had spotted two small convoys, each of one freighter and one destroyer. He shadowed both all night until strikes could be launched, finally landing after 11 hours 20 minutes in the air. Meanwhile, the 3,476-ton *Capo Faro* was sunk by six Blenheims of 18 Squadron near the island of Zante.

———

During the morning CR.42s of 155ª Squadriglia, 3° Gruppo CT patrolling over a convoy, engaged Blenheims (possibly the 18 Squadron aircraft), claiming two shot down and a third probably so. No losses have been found.

Italian Claims

155ª Sq/3° Gr CT	S.Ten Bruno Ciapparelli Serg Magg Luigi Modesti Serg Gino Bonato	}	2 Blenheims Blenheim probable	over convoy 1140 over convoy 1140

Tuesday, 2 December 1941

A Beaufighter of 252 Squadron on temporary detachment to Malta, intercepted an S.81 near Tripoli during the day and claimed to have shot it down. Blenheims caught another convoy 70 miles north of Tripoli and damaged the 10,540-ton tanker *Iridio Mantovani*, which was later bombed again and sunk.

British Claims

252 Sqn	Flg Off D.A.Smith	Beaufighter Ic	S.81	near Tripoli

Thursday, 4 December 1941

During the day the 10,000-ton tanker *Reichenfels*, which had taken on 7,000 tons of fuel at Naples, arrived off the North African coast, heading for Tripoli. Spotted by a Maryland, she was at once attacked by Blenheims from 18 and 107 Squadrons, which flew through a blizzard of AA fire and past four escorting Cant.Z.501 flyingboats to get to her. After the attack, the crew were seen to be abandoning ship and one hit was claimed by Sgt D.T.Bone and his crew. One Blenheim was attacked by an Italian fighter and the navigator, Plt Off A.S.Aldrige, was wounded in the back.

British Casualties

18 Sqn	Blenheim IV slightly damaged; Plt Off A.S.Aldridge, navigator, WiA

Friday, 5 December 1941

The two 252 Squadron Beaufighters on Malta patrolled during the day to cover the arrival of Blenheims on their way to the Middle East via Gibraltar and Malta. While so engaged, Flg Off Smith spotted an aircraft which he identified as a BR.20 and which he shot down into the sea, one member of the crew being seen to bale out. This was a reinforcement for 98° Gruppo BT, which was flying from Sicily to Libya; the crew were lost.

British Claims

252 Sqn	Flg Off D.A.Smith	Beaufighter Ic	BR.20	over sea

Italian Casualties

241ª Sq/98° Gr/13° St BT	BR.20 lost on transfer flight from Sicily to Libya; Ten Eugenio Cortinovis and crew MiA

Next day these aircraft would return to Africa. When on Malta their crews had claimed two aircraft shot down and three CR.42s seriously damaged on the ground at Tamet. They had also shot-up eight petrol tankers and a trailer, and damaged several other vehicles. Italian records indicate that no damage to aircraft on the ground at Tamet was recorded at this time.

Saturday, 6 December 1941

Italian Claims

154ªSq/3° Gr CT	S.Ten Guglielmo Russino	Blenheim	Tauorga area 1110

Monday, 8 December 1941

Italian Casualties

Unspecified units	3 S.81s under repair destroyed on ground at Castel Benito by night
	S.82 under repair destroyed on ground at Castel Benito by night
	G.50bis under repair destroyed on ground at Castel Benito by night

Friday, 12 December 1941

Italian Casualties

Unspecified unit   CR.42 destroyed on ground at Castel Benito by bombs

Wednesday, 17 December 1941

Two Blenheims of 107 Squadron took off to attack motor vehicles between Sorman and Zuara. One crashed two miles east of Zuara at 1150, one member of the crew being killed, while the pilot and one other survived as PoWs. It appears that this aircraft was claimed shot down both by a CR.42 pilot of 3° Gruppo CT and by Italian AA gunners.

British Casualties

107 Sqn	Blenheim IV Z9804 FTR; Plt Off F.H.W.Keebe and one PoW; one KiA		

Italian Claims

154ª Sq/3° Gr CT	Ten Luigi Deggiovanni	Blenheim	nr Marsa Zuaga 1345
Italian AA		Blenheim	nr Marsa Zuaga 1345

Monday, 22 December 1941

During air raids on Castel Benito and Mellaha airfields, two Italian and one German aircraft were destroyed.

Italian Casualties

Unspecified unit	MC.200 destroyed on ground by bombs
	G.50bis destroyed on ground by bombs

German Casualties

Unspecified unit	Ju 52/3m destroyed on ground by bombs

Tuesday, 23 December 1941

Serg Magg Gianni Bianchelli in his G.50bis of 159ª Squadriglia, 12° Gruppo CT, reported that on patrolling over the coast near Tripoli, he spotted and pursued a Blenheim which he claimed to have shot down into the sea 30 miles off the coast. No aircraft of this type was reported lost in this area by the RAF.

Italian Claims

159ª Sq/12° Gr CT	Serg Magg Gianni Bianchelli	Blenheim	30m N Tripoli 1430

Wednesday, 24 December 1941

Three Blenheims of 107 Squadron took off from Malta to attack shipping in Zuara harbour. As they swept in the wingtip of Sgt Crossley's aircraft struck a stay on a small schooner which caused it to flip over and crash into the sea. Italian gunners thought that their fire had been the cause of the demise of the aircraft and claimed to have shot it down.

British Casualties

107 Sqn	Blenheim IV Z7848 turned over and crashed into sea after colliding with an obstacle; Sgt E.Crossley and two KiA

Tuesday, 27 January 1942

Italian Casualties

394ª Sq/160° Gr CT   CR.42 MM5671 crash-landed, Serg Renato Tagliani WiA

By now the situation had altered radically as Axis fortunes changed for the better – as will be related in Volume 2.

CHAPTER 15

IN SUPPORT OF THE ROYAL NAVY

As a consequnce of the Greek and Cretan evacuations 201 Group at last began to expand, following calls of increasing urgency from the Royal Navy for more air support from the RAF. This was particularly the case now that no aircraft carrier presence remained in the Eastern Mediterranean. Command was once more in the hands of Grp Capt G.M.Bryer, OBE, AFC.

With the withdrawal from the Balkans, the RAF had become the temporary home of the Greek air force 13 Mira (to be known as 13 [Hellenic] Squadron), equipped with five Avro Ansons (N51, 52, 55, 56 and 61). Also in Egypt were eight Dornier Do 22 and single Sim XIV floatplanes of the Yugoslav 1, 2 and 3 Hidroplanska Komanda; the latter were attached to 230 Squadron as 2 Yugoslav Squadron in June, joining that unit's Sunderlands at their new base at Aboukir. Both these units now came under the direct control of 201 Group. Their obsolescent aircraft would carry out considerable anti-submarine and air-sea rescue work in the eastern reaches of the Mediterranean. The areas of greater danger of hostile aircraft being present continued to fall mainly within the remit of the Sunderlands.

Initially, co-operation with the Royal Navy by the RAF was mainly in the hands of 230 Squadron; one of this unit's Short Sunderland flyingboats has just broken contact with the surface of the sea as it takes off.

Friday, 18 April 1941

A Seagull V catapult amphibian from HMAS *Perth*, A2-17, was reported shot down off Crete by two Ju 88s. The crew survived and were rescued.

Having arrived at Shandur on 21 March, newly equipped with Marylands, 39 Squadron moved to Wadi Natrun on 8 May for strategic reconnaissance sorties; 203 Squadron, with Blenheim IVs, arrived at Kabrit on 30 April to carry out closer range over-sea reconnaissance. This unit would move to LG.101 on 20 June. During earlier operations from Aden and in Iraq, this unit had flown the Mark IVf version of the Blenheim, fitted at unit level with under-fuselage packs containing four .303in machine guns. However, it appears that when brought up to strength with replacement aircraft for this new task, the unit would fly only the standard bomber version with a single wing-mounted gun.

Thursday, 12 June 1941

The Italian submarine *Alagi* (commanding officer Ten Vasc Giulio Contreas) was attacked by an aircraft north-east of Ras Azzaz. The vessel remained on the surface, returning fire, the crew claiming to have inflicted damage on the attacker.

Two units of coastal Beaufighters had been despatched from the UK, these being 252 and 272 Squadrons. The story involved is a tortuous one, but well worthy of setting out here. In April 1941 the two squadrons were both Coastal Command long-range fighter units in the UK. 252, based at Aldergrove in Northern Ireland, had been flying the Beaufighter Ic heavy fighter since the turn of the year, while 272, which had been formed more recently, had just moved to Chivenor, but was still equipped with the older Blenheim If.

At the end of April 15 Beaufighters from 252 Squadron, led by Sqn Ldr R.G.Yaxley, MC, departed from St Eval for the Mediterranean via Gibraltar. One aircraft force-landed at Casablanca where it was interned, and when the remaining 14 departed for Malta on 1 May, one suffered engine trouble and had to return. Although the main body, now 13 strong, reached Malta safely, another pilot was rushed out to Gibraltar, subsequently accompanying the unserviceable aircraft to the island after repairs had been effected. The pilots involved in the operation thus far were:

Sqn Ldr R.G.Yaxley, MC	Flg Off J.B.Holgate	Plt Off J.C.Davidson
Flt Lt W.Riley	Flg Off C.S.H.MacDonald	Sub Lt I.F.Fraser, FAA
Flt Lt R.E.Jay	Flg Off N.E.H.Virgin	Sub Lt V.B.Crane, FAA
Flt Lt J.J.Lowe	Flg Off P.S.Hirst	Sub Lt K.Holme, FAA
Flg Off J.W.Blennerhassett	Flg Off H.Verity	
	Flg Off G.J.Lemar (replacement)	

The main purpose for the movement of this quite strong detachment to Malta was to provide long-range fighter cover for a fast merchant vessel, SS *Parracomb*, which was to make an unescorted dash for Malta carrying 21 crated Hurricanes and various other urgent supplies. The detachment would also remain to provide similar support for the planned Tiger convoy, due to reach the area on 8 May (see Chapter 6 – Reverses and Reinforcements).

In England, meanwhile, 272 Squadron had been reduced to cadre for overseas service, and re-equipped with Beaufighters. It was then ordered to Egypt, arriving at Abu Sueir on 28 May. In Northern Ireland on 14 June the 252 Squadron parent unit of the Malta detachment, was ordered to hand its aircraft to 143 Squadron and effectively pass the squadron number to the Malta detachment.

In the meantime the Malta detachment had enjoyed a very busy time, escorting convoys and undertaking low level attacks on airfields in Sicily and Sardinia. A detachment of eight had even been sent to Crete in mid May to strafe Luftwaffe airfields in southern Greece prior to the aerial invasion of that island by the Germans, and a few days later some of the unit's aircraft had acted as guides, leading Hurricanes which had arrived at Malta from HMS *Ark Royal* and *Furious* (Operation Splice) to North Africa. (Full details of all these operations may be found in *Malta: The Hurricane Years, 1940-41*, and in Chapter 8 – Midsummer Crisis).

Here there is a gap in the records, for although Yaxley and three others had reached North Africa, four had been destroyed on the ground when based on Malta, and four more flew back to the UK on 21 May, loaded with spare aircrew; one of these aircraft crashed into the sea off Eire, the three aboard being saved, but interned.

However, it seems that more new aircraft and crews were sent out, for on 17 June Sqn Ldr Yaxley led eight aircraft to Egypt to join 252 Squadron. At this stage 252 Squadron had no ground staff and the unit's aircraft would be required to be maintained by 272 Squadron for the time being. Therefore the 252 Squadron party was attached to 272 Squadron for operations, and would share a joint Form 540 (operations record book) with this unit. Effectively, therefore, an air party made up largely of 252 Squadron aircrew and aircraft would operate nominally as 272 Squadron for the next six months or so. This has, not surprisingly, led to considerable confusion regarding which Beaufighter units were operating over the Mediterranean at this time.

About 19 July most available Beaufighters were concentrated in 252 Squadron while 272 Squadron flew directly from Edcu, which had become the operational base for the aircraft, to Malta. Here the unit was joined by eight new crews and aircraft directly from the UK.Once more, protection for convoys to Malta was the reason for this further detachment. It appears that the unit now on Malta was led by both Sqn Ldr Yaxley and Sqn Ldr A.W.Fletcher, DFC, the commanding officer of 252 Squadron. Another detachment of 13 aircraft was sent to Malta on 24 September, this time under Fletcher's leadership only.

252 Squadron would become an independent unit again at some stage during the latter months of 1941, and indeed, during the heavy operations in which 272 Squadron was to be involved during November and December, the unit was loaning Beaufighters to that squadron to make good some of its losses. At the start of December 252 was able to detach a pair of aircraft and their crews to Malta, and to begin undertaking operations of its own along the North African coast.

Returning to June, despite the welcome reinforcements arriving at that time, 201 Group lost 228 Squadron when this unit took its Sunderlands to West Africa.

On 18 June a 230 Squadron crew reported spotting the crew of a Wellington in their dinghy. Group records noted that the aircraft in question was P9277, which apparently had been lost a day earlier. A message was sent calling for them to be picked up, but initially they were not to be found. Finally on 27 June the dinghy was again spotted with four men still aboard, and this time they were successfully rescued. It transpired that two other members of the crew had attempted to swim to a destroyer seen some two miles away, but both had been lost. This is a good example of the confusions and frustrations which historians frequently have to unravel. Firstly, no Wellington had been lost on 16, 17 or 18 June. In fact P9277, an OADU aircraft on its way to the Middle East, only departed Malta on the 27th in the hands of Plt Off C.F.Butler, but ditched at 0900 ! It would appear, therefore, that the surviving members of the crew were picked up on the very day that they went into the sea, not some ten days later. There were, however, four crew aboard the dinghy, Plt Off L.H.Campbell-Rogers, RCAF, and Sgt A.D.Cragg having been lost in the circumstances described.

Besides its RAF units, 201 Group also controlled any land-based Fleet Air Arm aircraft within its area, which initially was restricted to 775 Squadron, a fleet requirements unit based at Dekheila which had undertaken target-towing duties with four Blackburn Rocs. Subsequently this unit also received a number of Swordfish, later supplemented with some Albacores, a couple of Fulmars, two Sea Gladiators, and some Queen Bee radio-controlled targets. However, on 1 July two Swordfish of 815 Squadron and six Albacores of 826 and 829 Squadrons arrived to reinforce the existing unit. Initially these aircraft were mainly involved in operations against French shipping seeking to reach Syria (see *Dust Clouds in the Middle East*).

Now able to employ airfields in Cyprus and Palestine as well as Egypt, the group proposed a daily scale of reconnaissance sorties to the Royal Navy. Each sortie using a Beaufighter would fly over 'Area M' with a periodic examination of the harbours on Rhodes. At the same time a Swordfish would undertake a coastal search of Cape Anania to Cape Kelicharia, including the Gulf of Adalya. Another Swordfish would cover Cape Kizliman-Karadash Burnie and return. In the afternoon a Beaufighter or Blenheim would cover the coast from Cape Anamur to the Seven Capes.

Meanwhile, at the start of July 39 Squadron provided a detachment of three Marylands fitted with extra tankage, which were to fly long-range reconnaissance sorties over southern Greece, Crete and the Eastern Mediterranean from Burg el Arab, co-operating with 203 Squadron. 39 Squadron was about to be brought up to strength at this time by the attachment of 2 Free French Flight, led by Lt Col Du Marmier, which was due to arrive from 223 Squadron in the Sudan in order to gain experience of such duties.

From 3-8 July initial daily reconnaissances were made over the Dodecanese and Pelopponese islands by Marylands to commence this vital new service to the navy.

Friday, 4 July 1941

Flg Off R.A.Lewis and his crew in their Maryland undertook a photographic 'run' over Piraeus, Salamis, Eleusis Bay and Kalo. When so engaged an aircraft identified as an S.79 was spotted over Amorgos Island at Rhodes, and this was shot down in flames. This was in fact an S.83 – an executive transport version of the S.79. 41° Gruppo was at this time commanded by T.Col Ettore Muti who was a Fascist party 'big shot', hence having had this aircraft allocated to him. His personal pilot was Cap Paolo Moci which is why the aircraft carried the recognition letters I-MOCI. It was on this occasion being flown by T.Col Fortunato Federigi with Cap Adolfo Rebec as co-pilot from Rhodes to Athens when intercepted, and did indeed fall on the island of Amorgos in flames, the crew of four all perishing.

British Claims

39 Sqn	Flg Off R.A.Lewis	Maryland AH295 'B'	S.79	Amorgos Island, Rhodes

Italian Casualties

205ª Sq/41° Gr Aut	S.83 MM415 I-MOCI; T.Col Fortunato Federigi, Cap Adolfo Rebec and two KiA Amorgos Island, Rhodes

Friday, 11 July 1941

39 Squadron was to claim a further success when the Australian Sgt C.K.Berriman engaged another trimotor, again identified as an S.79, ten miles east of Ras el Milh whilst on a reconnaissance over Cyrenaica. The crew believed that they had shot this aircraft down also. It appears that this may have been an aircraft of 10ª Squadriglia, 27° Gruppo BT, flown by S.Ten Melchiorri, who identified his attacker as a Blenheim and crash-landed at Ras Azzaz.

British Claims

39 Sqn	Sgt C.K.Berriman	Maryland	S.79	near Marsa Luch 1810

Italian Casualties

10ª Sq/28° Gr BT	S.79 crash-landed, S.Ten Luigi Melchiorri and crew safe except for gunner, 1° Av Alessandro Rea who was mortally wounded.

This S.83 I-MOCI, the personal aircraft of T.Col Ettore Muti, was shot down on 4 July 1941 over Amorgos Island by a 39 Squadron Maryland flown by Flg Off R.A.Lewis when undertaking a flight from Rhodes to Athens.

Tuesday, 29 July 1941

39 Squadron's recently successful Flt Lt R.A.Lewis and his crew failed to return from a sortie over Crete on this date. A month later a dinghy was washed ashore in Egypt containing the body of Flt Sgt H.T.Downs and the logbook of Plt Off V.L.Dearman, RAAF, both members of Lewis's crew.

During the day 203 Squadron Blenheim Z6431 'Y' on a patrol between Crete and Libya, spotted and attacked a submarine without effect. On landing the aircraft's undercarriage collapsed. It was subsequently reported that the aircraft had inadvertently run into an attack on four British destroyers being made by Ju 88s.

British Casualties	
39 Sqn	Maryland II AH297 MiA; Flg Off R.A.Lewis and crew KiA
203 Sqn	Blenheim IV Z6431 'Y' destroyed in landing crash at Mersa Matruh on return from attack on submarine; Sgt E.Langston and crew safe

August brought decorations for 39 Squadron, including a DFC for the recently deceased Flt Lt Lewis and another for Flg Off W.M.Lewis, a second pilot of that name within the unit. Sgt S.Sill received a DFM, while the unit's much-respected commanding officer, Wg Cdr Bowman, got a Bar to his DFC.

Friday, 1 August 1941

A Sunderland of 230 Squadron set off in the hands of Flt Lt Brand to patrol over the Gulf of Sollum in conjunction with four destroyers, but this failed to return. The crew had spotted an Italian submarine, *Delfino* (commanded by Cap Corv Alberto Avogadro di Cerrione) north-east of Ras Azzaz, and had attacked this at 1230. Damage inflicted by the flyingboat rendered it impossible to dive, but fire was returned and the aircraft was shot down, four members of the crew being picked up and made PoWs. News of the fate of this aircraft was discovered from an intercepted German radio broadcast.

British Casualties	
230 Sqn	Sunderland L2166 'V' shot down in Gulf of Sollum; Flt Lt Brand and crew PoW

Saturday, 9 August 1941

The crew of Sunderland T9050 'Y' of 230 Squadron, commanded by Flt Lt Milligan, were engaged in searching for the crew of a missing Wellington when they encountered a Do 24 flyingboat. Two engagements followed between the big aircraft, each lasting for about five minutes. Following these the Dornier withdrew, the British crew believing that they had damaged it so severely that it might not have reached its base.

British Claims		
230 Sqn	Sunderland crew	Do 24 badly damaged

Monday, 11 August 1941

During the day HMS *Protector* was torpedoed 40 miles north-west of Port Said, 201 Group recording that the weapon had probably been launched by an aircraft.

Wednesday, 13 August 1941

The Middle East Air Sea Rescue Flight was set up at Kabrit under Flt Lt P.W.Dawson to operate as part of 201 Group. Initially it was equipped with a trio of 'operationally tired' Wellington Ics (T2551, T2829 and T2839), six high-speed launches and a carrier pigeon service. A move was made to LG.39 at Burg el Arab as the unit's operational base on 15 September, but it was not ready to commence operations until eleven days later. The reason for the delay proved to be a rather mundane one – camouflage paint. Having been used by night, the Wellingtons were painted mainly black, but the scheme employed by the RAF's flyingboats was considered more appropriate. However, no copy was available to indicate how this was to be applied, and none of the correct dopes were to be had either. Finally, the aircraft were painted with a mixture of blue, grey and silver dopes. All was finally ready, the first sorties being flown on 29 September searching for a missing 203 Squadron crew.

Meanwhile, during August 815 Squadron returned to Dekheila from Cyprus to re-equip with 12 new Albacores and a pair of ASV-equipped Swordfish. However, within days the unit returned to Lakatamia where it would remain until mid November. Then, as Operation Crusader approached, it would fly to LG.75 at Maaten Bagush to join 826 Squadron in undertaking night operations in co-operation with the army.

Sunday, 17 August 1941
203 Squadron's Blenheim C took off from LG.16 on an anti-shipping patrol. As it returned, both engines cut when the aircraft was flying at low altitude, whereupon Sgt A.Booth managed to ditch into the sea north-west of Sollum Bay. The pilot and wireless operator both escaped, but Plt Off L.A.Smith, who was in the nose of the aircraft at the time of ditching, was lost when the fuselage broke in half and sank.

British Casualties

203 Sqn	Blenheim IV Z9552 'C' crashed in sea due to engine failure; Sgt A.Booth and one safe; Plt Off L.A.Smith KiA

Tuesday, 19 August 1941
On this date Operation Treacle commenced, taking the Polish Brigade to Tobruk by sea to relieve 18th Australian Brigade (see Chapter 9 – Operation Battleaxe for further details of this operation). On this first day 12 vessels were involved, including seven mine-laying cruisers, two store-carrying destroyers and one personnel-carrying destroyer. 203 Squadron Blenheims were engaged on at least two occasions with Ju 88s and Bf 110s, but no losses were suffered, and claims were made by gunners for damage to some of the German raiders.

During August and September 201 Group was to continue to operate from Edcu, Burg el Arab, Dekheila and Aboukir. On 22 August, however, the group was weakened by the despatch of most of its Beaufighters to undertake operations from Malta.

During the first week of the Treacle operations 39 Squadron's Flt Lt J.S.T.Halliday was on one occasion to strafe Axis camps in the Bardia area, while Plt Off Avery evaded a Bf 110 which pursued and attacked his aircraft for ten minutes. On 26 August 39 Squadron recorded that Beaufort torpedo-bombers were to begin replacing the unit's Marylands.

Friday, 22 August 1941
On a reconnaissance to the area between Tobruk and the frontier, a Blenheim flown by Sgt C.K.Berriman of 39 Squadron was shot down by Italian fighters, he and his crew being killed. (See Chapter 9 – Operation Battleaxe for full details.)

The month remained a costly one for 39 Squadron. When taking off, Flg Off B.W.Jeffrey's aircraft collided with a parked Tomahawk, crashed and burst into flames. Two members of the crew got out with only minor injuries, but Jeffrey and the observer were both badly burned. Although the latter survived, Jeffrey ultimately died after five weeks in hospital.

Thursday, 28 August 1941
A Blenheim of 203 Squadron attacked a submarine believed to be Italian – but it proved to be HMS *Tetrach*, which escaped.

Saturday, 30 August 1941
On returning from a reconnaissance another 39 Squadron Maryland was lost when intercepted by 11 Bf 110s on offensive patrol over Bir Sofafi. Flt Lt Halliday and his crew were lost; their aircraft would appear to be that claimed by III./ZG 26 as the unit's 33rd success since arriving in North Africa.

British Casualties

39 Sqn	Maryland II AH367 MiA; Flt Lt J.S.T.Halliday and crew MiA Bir Sofafi		

German Claims

III./ZG 26	U/k pilot(s)	Maryland	Bir Sofafi

Tuesday, 9 September 1941
At this stage the main part of 39 Squadron ceased operations and withdrew to Wadi Natrun to re-equip with Beauforts and commence training for sea reconnaissance/torpedo-bomber operations with 201 Group; a number of Beaufort crews from 86 Squadron in the UK had been posted in for this purpose. However, a detached flight of Marylands remained at Edcu, commanded by Sqn Ldr Hunter, to continue

At the start of September 1941 39 Squadron commenced replacement of its Marylands with Bristol Beaufort torpedo-bombers.

reconnaissances over Athens, Crete and the Dodecanese. The rest of the unit's Marylands were handed to 12 SAAF Squadron, and the crews were temporarily attached to that unit to train its personnel in the reconnaissance role. At this time of change, Wg Cdr Bowman departed for 204 Group headquarters, his place at the head of the squadron being taken by Wg Cdr R.B.Cox from 202 Group.

Monday, 22 September 1941
On this date 55 Squadron was instructed to operate with 201 Group from LG.17. By this time though, the Fleet Air Arm units working within the group had gone, with the exception of 815 Squadron. 826 Squadron had moved forward to Maaten Bagush to operate over the area of the front, while 829 Squadron rejoined HMS *Formidable* as she sailed through the Red Sea on her way to repairs in the USA.

203 Squadron targetted the island of Leros, where a floating dock was located at Portolago Bay. This attack was repeated in the afternoon, but although little damage was inflicted, surprise achieved had been complete.

Tuesday, 23 September 1941
One of 39 Squadron's Marylands from the remaining flight flew a reconnaissance patrol over Leros to photograph the results of the previous day's attacks, but was forced to retreat with its duty unfulfilled when pursued by five fighters identified as Bf 109s.

Wednesday, 24 September 1941
During the month another major convoy was to sail through the Western Mediterranean to Malta, codenamed Halberd. Once again all available Beaufighters were needed to support this operation, mainly through strafing attacks on the Italian airfields in Sardinia. Therefore on 24 September all 13 available 272 Squadron aircraft left again for this area. En route three Belgian pilots, Flg Off Roman, Sgt Le Jeune and Sgt Demoulin spotted a pair of Ju 52/3ms above the Gulf of Bomba, attacking these and claiming damage to both.

On this date a lone Cant.Z.506B floatplane from 170ª Squadriglia RM based at Augusta, Sicily, commenced an early morning reconnaissance patrol over the Central Mediterranean. While so engaged, it was intercepted by a Maryland from the Malta-based 69 Squadron, flown by the intrepid Flg Off Adrian Warburton, who reported its location as being over some ships in the Eastern Ionian Sea (see *Malta: The Hurricane Years, 1940-41*). Warburton's attack forced the Italian pilot, S.Ten Pierluigi Colli, to crash-land the aircraft on the open sea. It also seriously wounded the observer, s.t.v.* Leonardo Madoni and inflicted wounds on two other members of the crew, 1° Av Salvatore Capuano, the radio operator, and 1° Av Enrico Miola, the flight mechanic. Although in a bad state, Madoni managed to ascertain their position and put out a call for rescue. At once another Z.506B, this one from 186ª Squadriglia, was sent off in the hands of Cap Mario Bellotto.

Meanwhile, circling overhead, Warburton saw apparent indications of capitulation, and two men in a dinghy paddling away from the stricken aircraft. He then strafed the Cant.Z. until it sank, but when so engaged, experienced some return fire from the rear turret which led him to believe that the gunner had remained behind, laying an ambush for the Maryland. The aircraft's armourer, Av Sc Luigi Scattolin, was indeed still aboard, attempting to defend it from further damage. This time Warburton's fire holed the floats and it began to sink slowly. At this point Warburton broke off and returned to Malta.

At about 1300 Cap Bellotto arrived overhead, landed and loaded Madoni on board, taking off for Tocra on the Libyan coast; from here he was rushed to the nearest hospital which was at Barce. He died of his wounds a few days later on 4 October, subsequently receiving a posthumous award of the Medaglia d'Oro. A third Cant.Z.506B, this time from 614ª Squadriglia Soccorso, reached the scene at 1620 and picked up the rest of the crew. In the meantime, however, Miola had succumbed to his wounds.

British Claims

69 Sqn	Flg Off A.Warburton	Maryland		Z.506B	Eastern Ionian Sea
272 Sqn	Flg Off C.L.Roman	Beaufighter 'H'			
	Sgt O.G.Le Jeune	Beaufighter 'L'	}	2 Ju 52.3ms damaged	Gulf of Bomba
	Sgt R.J.G.Demoulin	Beaufighter ' R'			

Italian Casualties

170ª Sq RM	Z.506B MM45318 shot down; pilot S.Ten Pierluigi Colli and two of crew rescued; one died of wounds same day;
	observer, s.t.v. Leonardo Madoni, rescued, but died of wounds 4 October 1941

* s.t.v. abbreviation for Sotto Tenente di Vascello, an Italian naval rank equivalent to the Regia Aeronautica's Tenente.

Monday, 29 September 1941
Plt Off Ruxton of 203 Squadron took off early on an anti-shipping patrol. Over the British tanker SS *Tiberio* he spotted a Bf 110 the pilot of which, like the Blenheim crew, had mistaken the vessel for an Italian one and was affording it protection. It seems that the two aircraft became involved in a combat, Ruxton and his crew failing to return and being assumed to have been shot down.

British Casualties

203 Sqn	Blenheim IV Z6445 'Y' MiA; Plt Off T.R.Ruxton and crew KiA

During September 230 Squadron's long-serving commanding officer, Wg Cdr Geoffrey Francis, who had received a DSO to add to the DFC which he had been awarded at the end of the previous year, finally completed his tour, handing over to Wg Cdr T.W.G.Eady.

Wednesday – Thursday, 1/2 October 1941
Taking off from LG.17 at Fuka, Flt Lt Harries' 55 Squadron Blenheim was refuelled at Giarabub from where he departed again at 1630 on an anti-shipping sweep seeking a tanker and three other vessels. Failing to find these, he crossed the coast to bomb and strafe an airfield, but then crashed south-east of Sidi Barrani after running out of fuel. He and one of his crew were killed, but the third survived.

British Casualties

55 Sqn	Blenheim IV V6306 'R' crashed due to fuel shortage; Flt Lt J.A.Harries and one KiA; one survived

39 Squadron had begun operating its Beauforts towards the end of September, engaging mainly in anti-submarine patrol sorties codenamed Plug. For closer and more efficient operations, the unit then moved to Maryut on 10 October, where it was joined by the Maryland flight from Edcu. Together with 203

Squadron, this latter unit now provided all the Mediterranean Sea reconnaissances for RAF, Middle East. At this time too, 815 Squadron received some Albacores to supplement its remaining Swordfish.

Friday, 10 October 1941
Even as these moves were taking place, 203 Squadron lost one of its Blenheims during a reconnaissance towards Crete from LG.101. A radio message announced the aircraft's likely time of return at 1730, but nothing further was heard, Flg Off J.P. Rowntree and his crew being reported missing.

British Casualties

203 Sqn	Blenheim IV Z6403 'L' MiA; Flg Off J.P.Rowntree and crew MiA

Monday, 13 October 1941
Three days later a further Blenheim went down when Flg Off G.Washington took off on a similar reconnaissance from LG.101 at 0700. This time a message was received advising that the aircraft was being 'shadowed' by an enemy machine, but again nothing further was heard. It was presumed that the Blenheim had been shot down. It is possible that some of the aircraft lost at this time had fallen to the Bf 110 pilots of I./NJG 3, since all claims made by III./ZG 26 are available, and several of the losses which have been listed are not included.

British Casualties

203 Sqn	Blenheim IV Z9619 'M' MiA; Flg Off G.Washington and crew MiA

Wednesday, 15 October 1941
Plt Off van der Wate and his 203 Squadron crew claimed to have sunk a submarine on this date.

Thursday, 16 October 1941
201 Group was further reinforced by the Royal Navy with the formation at Dekheila of 700 (Mediterranean) Squadron – actually a detachment of the Fleet Air Arm's main operational testing unit in the United Kingdom. Initially, the unit was equipped with a number of Walrus amphibians – extremely useful for air-sea rescue work – but was to become responsible in the first instance for all disembarked FAA aircraft undertaking primarily duties involved in co-operating with the Mediterranean Fleet.

Sunday, 19 October 1941
Blenheim Z7416 of 55 Squadron departed Fuka at 1355 to sweep to the north-west of Derna. It failed to return from this sortie.

British Casualties

55 Sqn	Blenheim IV Z7415 FTR; 2/Lt J.N.Murphy, SAAF, and crew MiA

Monday, 20 October 1941
The commanding officer of 55 Squadron was shot down by Bf 109s during a sortie over the front line area. This engagement is dealt with in Chapter 9 – Operation Battleaxe for the sake of continuity.

Tuesday, 21 October 1941
At 0950 a 203 Squadron Blenheim crew, led by Wg Cdr A.F.Johnson, spotted the gunboat *Gnat*, which was stationary and down by the bow. She had been torpedoed at 0245 and was badly damaged. Johnson and his crew also observed what they identified as a dark green Sunderland escorted by one Bf 109 and two Bf 110s; what the identity and type of aircraft the flyingboat was has not been discovered. At this point Johnson radioed:

> "am engaging enemy aircraft". Later he reported: "Enemy broken off attack, smoke, slight damage to own aircraft."

The Bf 110s had attacked, one of them three times, but had not been able to inflict more than a few holes in the Blenheim. The rear gunner in the German aircraft was then silenced, black and grey smoke being seen pouring from its starboard engine as it lost height to about ten feet above the sea and made off.

Wednesday, 22 October 1941

In 230 Squadron Ken Garside, who had been involved in one of the unit's earliest engagements with Regia Aeronautica fighters, and who was now a Sqn Ldr, was able to attack a surfaced submarine in his Sunderland W3987. However, the vessel at once crash-dived, and nothing of note was achieved.

Sunday, 2 November 1941

From Maryut two of 39 Squadron's Beauforts took off on a Plug operation during which Plt Off Leaming and his crew spotted and attacked a Ju 52/3m at 500 feet. Three passes were made over a period of eight minutes, the rear gunner being silenced and the trimotor last being seen losing height and pouring smoke from its starboard engine. However, Flt Lt Lenton and his crew in the second aircraft, failed to return; having become lost in an electrical storm, the pilot had force-landed on a beach in Crete.

British Claims		
39 Sqn	Plt Off Leaming and crew	Ju 52/3m damaged
British Casualties		
39 Sqn	Beaufort N1091 force-landed in Crete after getting lost; Flt Lt Lenton and crew PoW	

Saturday, 8 November 1941

Flg Off A.T.Read of 203 Squadron encountered three Ju 52/3ms, attacking one with both front and turret guns. Hits were seen, but no obvious damage.

During the days which followed a great increase in sightings of hostile aircraft – mostly Ju 88s and Ju 52/3ms – occurred, due to the preparations being made by Rommel at this time for his planned offensive against Tobruk.

Sunday, 9 November 1941

A 203 Squadron Blenheim and its crew was reported missing.

British Casualties	
203 Sqn	Blenheim IV Z7708 'K' MiA; Flt Lt P.N.Screeton and crew MiA

Monday, 10 November 1941

The crew of a 203 Squadron Blenheim reported spotting Ju 52/3ms towing gliders.

Thursday, 13 November 1941

Sgt Langton of 203 Squadron in Z6423 attacked a Ju 52/3m from astern. As he did so, he noticed that it was painted with red crosses and immediately broke away.

Friday, 14 November 1941

203 Squadron's Sqn Ldr Scott spotted three Ju 52/3ms towing gliders, escorted by Bf 110s. He then saw many more aircraft – Bf 110s, Ju 87s and He 111s – but all ignored the Blenheim.

During this period submarines were also often seen and attacked, but usually these were able to escape by making crash-dives.

Thursday – Friday, 20/21 November 1941

A Cant.Z.506B from 288ª Squadriglia RM took off from Taranto at 0725 during the morning, but failed to return. It had become engaged with a 69 Squadron Maryland from Malta, flown by Plt Off R.G.Fox over the Corfu-Cephalonia area. Fox attacked four or five times with his front guns, but had to break away when his supply of ammunition expired. As the port engine of the aircraft was seen to be on fire, he claimed the floatplane probably destroyed on his return. During the engagement return fire had hit and damaged the Maryland and on return he had to force-land, suffering slight injury.

He had indeed inflicted critical damage on the Italian aircraft, but it was next day before a message was received indicating that the crew of a Ju 52/3m (1Z+LT) had observed the floatplane being shot down, reportedly by two Blenheims, about 50 miles west of Argostoli. (This message to the naval command at Salonika was also intercepted by Ultra.) At 1145 next day, therefore, the pilot, Ten Fulvio Franchini and observer, t.v.* Mario Loffredo, were picked by a Do 24 flyingboat of III Seenot Athens, and were taken to Piraeus, where they reported that the crew had shot down one of their attackers. The rest of the four members of the crew were listed as missing.

Thursday, 20 November 1941

British Claims

69 Sqn	Plt Off R.G.Fox	Maryland	Z.506B	Corfu-Cephalonia area early a.m.

British Casualties

69 Sqn	Maryland damaged; force-landed on return; Plt Off R.G.Fox slightly injured

Italian Claims

288ª Sq RM	Floatplane gunner	Blenheim		50m W Argostoli

Italian Casualties

288ª Sq RM	Cant.Z.506B MM45341 '290-7' shot down; pilot Ten Fulvio Franchini and observer t.v. Mario Loffredo rescued; four of crew MiA

* t.v. = Tenente di Vascello, equivalent to a Regia Aeronautica Capitano

During 21 November pairs of Fulmars from the RN Fulmar Flight at Dekheila, provided cover for a convoy proceeding towards Tobruk. At dusk six He 111s approached, one at 7,000 feet, the others low over the water. One Fulmar pilot climbed to attack the high aircraft as the other went for the five low aircraft which jettisoned their torpedoes; otherwise, the combat was indecisive.

One of 39 Squadron's Beauforts, recorded as being N1098 flown by Plt Off Cowman, failed to return from a patrol sortie. It had force-landed in the sea due to an engine failure. Although the observer had suffered a severe head injury from which he died, the other members of the crew managed to get into their dinghy in which they were eventually spotted three days later.

Sunday, 23 November 1941

A Sunderland from 230 Squadron was sent to Morphone Bay, Cyprus, where a Russian flyingboat had landed and been beached by the army. This proved to be a GST, the Soviet-built version of the PBY Catalina, which had flown from Sevastapol in the Crimea (under siege by German forces), loaded with the personal belongings of a general. The mechanic had decided that the escape was being cut too fine and he had taken off alone, flying south until nearly out of fuel. His ultimate fate is not recorded, but it is likely that at some stage he would have been returned to his homeland where his desertion was probably not looked upon with any great indulgence!

Monday – Tuesday, 24/25 November 1941

The air-sea rescue unit (minus T2839 which had crash-landed during a training flight on 17 November) had moved to Abu Menas early in the month. Here a message was received from 201 Group that a dinghy had been sighted 30 miles off Sollum. Ten minutes later at 1540 on the 24th came a further message that a second dinghy had been spotted further west.

One Wellington took off at 0815 to begin the search, with orders to make contact with a motor launch which had put to sea from Mersa Matruh. One of the dinghies containing three men was spotted and shadowed, but the launch suffered engine trouble and was unable to proceed further. Instead, a Royal Navy Walrus was ordered to take off early in the afternoon; this it failed to do, although it did manage to get off later. By now the dinghy was reported to be only 25 miles offshore, but while one of the Wellingtons (T2551, flown by Sgt Swift) was shadowing the Walrus, a petrol filler cap on the port wing broke off, causing the wing to have a higher stalling speed than normal.

The pilot continued to remain in the area until darkness fell, then returning to base. On making a left hand circuit preparatory to landing, the Wellington slipped downwards and hit the ground, bursting into flames. The second pilot was thrown clear and survived, but all the rest of the crew were killed. Meanwhile the Walrus had reached the dinghy which contained the 39 Squadron Beaufort crew lost three days earlier. However, it could not take off again due to the increased load of the three survivors, and instead the little amphibian continued taxying for six miles towards the coast.

Wednesday, 26 November 1941

With morning, Sgt Langston in 203 Squadron Blenheim V6465 'B', found the Walrus and directed a launch to it. Two more of the unit's aircraft engaged a flyingboat identified as probably a Do 24 between

Crete and Libya. They engaged this indecisively, although one Blenheim sustained slight damage.

Thursday, 27 November 1941
At last a 'Eureka' boat from Mersa Matruh found the 39 Squadron survivors and the crew of the Walrus and evacuated them.

Friday, 28 November 1941
Sgt Boyce (203 Squadron Blenheim Z6157 'Y') engaged a Ju 52/3m with front and rear guns, but without result.

Sunday, 30 November 1941
Following the loss of the air-sea rescue Wellington on the 25th, a replacement aircraft was now flown up to the unit from 57 RSU. This proved to be an ex-38 Squadron aircraft which had been shot-up and belly-landed, but was otherwise fairly new, having only undertaken about 50 hours flying; it had been held at the RSU for about six months. At the same time two small amphibian aircraft, a Grumman and a Fairchild, were presented to the unit by a US charity, arriving from Geneifa and Heliopolis. It appears that the former aircraft may subsequently have been passed to 1 RAAF Air Ambulance Unit.

Thereafter the unit returned to Burg el Arab during December, moving in January 1942 to El Adem. At the end of the month, following the Axis advance back into central Cyrenaica, it withdrew to Gambut. Here on 10 January the last of the three original Wellingtons would be destroyed in a landing crash.

At the start of December 39 Squadron learned with great sadness that Wg Cdr A.McD. Bowman, DFC & Bar, who had commanded the unit from April 1939-September 1941, had been killed in the desert. In fact he and Grp Capt C.J.S.Dearlove of 204 Group had both died in a non-operational crash on 30 November. The recently-arrived CO, Wg Cdr R.B.Cox, had been overseas for a long period, having previously served in India, and at this time he was posted home to the UK. He would be replaced by Wg Cdr A.J.Mason, who would arrive on 17 December.

Monday, 1 December 1941
A 39 Squadron Beaufort was lost on a Plug sortie. Another, flown by Plt Off Blaby, was attacked by a Ju 88. Finding that the Beaufort could turn more tightly than the Junkers, he engaged it and drove it away. However, the Beaufort had suffered some damage, and subsequently force-landed at Burg el Arab on return.

Following an uneventful morning sortie by three torpedo-carrying S.79s, a further trio were despatched during the afternoon, flown by Giulio Marini, commanding officer of 279ª Squadriglia AS, and by S.Ten Aligi Strani and Giuseppe Coci. Early in the flight a large vessel was spotted, but as the pilots prepared to attack this was seen to be a Red Cross-marked hospital ship, and they veered away. At 1218 three warships were seen heading east, and a low level attack was made by all three bombers, almost simultaneously, Marini and Strani approaching from the north and Coci from the south. Immediately after torpedoes had been released, Marini's aircraft was hit in the right wing by AA fire, but all three crews recorded having obtained hits on what they identified as a *Birmingham*-class cruiser 20 miles north of Marsa Luch. Their victim was actually the destroyer HMS *Jackal*, which suffered heavy damage to its stern. She managed to get back to Alexandria, where she would remain under repair until April 1942. Marini's aircraft had been badly damaged and Strani's was also hit by small calibre machine-gun fire, the former aircraft having to be force-landed, although the latter made it back to base. No members of either crew suffered any injuries.

British Casualties	
39 Sqn	Beaufort W6496 MiA; Sgt Rowbotham and crew MiA
	Beaufort damaged in combat and force-landed at Burg el Arab; Plt Off Blaby and crew safe
Italian Casualties	
279ª Sq AS	S.79 MM93964 damaged by ship's AA and force-landed; Cap Giulio Marini and crew safe
	S.79 MM94076 damaged by ship's AA, but returned safely; S.Ten Aligi Strani and crew safe

Monday, 8 December 1941
A 39 Squadron Beaufort on a reconnaissance encountered and attacked a Ju 88 to the west of Crete. The two fought it out for some time, by the end of which both had suffered damage and broke away. On arrival at base, the Beaufort made a force-landing.

After a successful torpedo mission on 1 December 1941, Cap Giulio Marini, commanding officer of 279ª Squadriglia AS, crash-landed his S.79 which had been damaged by return fire.

Friday – Saturday, 12/13 December 1941

On both dates 55 Squadron, operating under Advanced 201 Group control, were engaged with Luftwaffe fighters over the sea whilst undertaking sorties mainly in the area where aircraft of Air HQ, Western Desert, were operating. Although ostensibly a part of the 201 Group narrative, these have been dealt with in Chapter 10 – Operation Crusader. The same holds for Blenheims of 18 and 107 Squadrons from Malta which appear to have been engaged by North Africa-based Luftwaffe fighters.

Wednesday, 17 December 1941

252 Squadron recorded that four new Beaufighters arrived from the UK for 272 Squadron, but that these were retained on 252's establishment, although all were then loaned to the other unit for its operations over the battle area. These were T4648, 4709, 4720 and 4783.

Friday, 19 December 1941

Three 203 Squadron Blenheims patrolled between Crete and Libya from which one of their number failed to return.

Flt Lt C.S.H.McDonald, who had previously served with 252 Squadron, but had then been posted to 272, returned as temporary commanding officer. Three days later, however, Sqn Ldr A.G.Wincott would arrive to take over this post. Is it possible that this plane was shot down by a Bf 110 of 7./ZG 26, the pilot misidentifying his victim as a Beaufighter?

British Casualties			
203 Sqn	Blenheim IV V6294 'E' FTR Flg Off A.T.Read and crew MiA		
German Claims			
7./ZG 26	Lt Helmut Scheid	Beaufighter	over sea 0840

Saturday, 20 December 1941

Patrolling Blenheims from 203 Squadron encountered Ju 52/3ms on the Crete-Libya route. The crew of 'P' reported attacking two of these transports, believing that they had inflicted some damage on both. 'V' meanwhile, dropped bombs in front of one Junkers, then attacking with guns. Return fire was experienced, one bullet hitting the tail of the RAF aircraft.

Monday, 22 December 1941

Following several months of constant patrols, but without casualties, one of 2 Yugoslav Squadron's Do 22s (DD307) was fired on by a merchant vessel which was being investigated. A cannon shell burst below the cockpit occupied by the observer, Lt Ivkovic, wounding him in the legs. However, Flt Sgt Pishpale, the pilot, got the damaged aircraft back to Alexandria safely.

During the same day Flt Lt S.W.R.Hughes in Sunderland T9071 of 230 Squadron, departed Aboukir for Kalafrana, Malta, carrying both passengers and freight. Three miles north of Ras Amor and about 50 miles north-east of Benghazi, the flyingboat was attacked by two Bf 110s from III./ZG 26 (one of which is believed to have been flown by Obfw Helmut Haugk). During the engagement one of the Zerstörer was claimed probably shot down by Sgt Jacques Dupont, RAAF, after two of the gunners had been wounded. However, the Sunderland had been badly damaged, both starboard engines having been put out of action. Hughes, a New Zealander, force-landed on the sea, the aircraft coming to rest after two bounces. The crew had to spread themselves along the undamaged wing to keep the remaining float in the water since that on the starboard side had been smashed in the landing. In this way the aircraft drifted tail-first until it struck a reef just offshore at Ras Amt, where it stuck, beginning to break up as it was battered by heavy seas.

After two hours the crew and passengers – 20 in all – struggled ashore. Sgt Dupont helped one of the gunners, who had been mortally wounded, into a dinghy, then swimming alongside this in the surging sea. The dinghy capsized, but he held on to his companion and finally got him ashore. Here a group of Italian soldiers approached and surrendered to the British party. However, more Italians then arrived, reversing the situation by taking the flyingboat party prisoner, moving them to a Senussi village where the wounded gunner died and was buried. As it was uncertain whether the British had yet captured Benghazi as part of the Operation Crusader offensive, the parties split up the next day. The group finally reached British lines, having collected some 130 voluntary Italian prisoners along the way. Sgt Dupont was later awarded a DFM for his gallantry on this date (See also *Malta: The Hurricane Years, 1940-41*.)

British Claims		
230 Sqn	Sgt J.Dupont Sunderland gunner	Bf 110 probable
British Casualties		
230 Sqn	Sunderland T9071 ditched on sea after damage by fighters and rendered a complete write-off. One gunner died of	
	wounds; Flt Lt S.W.R.Hughes and rest of crew safe	
2 Yugoslav Sqn	Do 22 DD307 damaged by fire from ship; observer wounded	
German Claims		
III./ZG 26	Sunderland	

Thursday, 25 December 1941

252 Squadron recorded that its Beaufighter, T4720, which was on loan to 272 Squadron, had been lost on this date during a low-level attack on the Agheila road. The latter unit do not seem to have suffered any losses on this date, however, and it is presumed that this was a late report of one of the losses suffered by 272 two days earlier.

Friday, 26 December 1941

British Casualties

39 Sqn	Beaufort N1092; Plt Off L.G.R.Wallington and crew FTR from Rake operation in Crete area

Thursday, 1 January 1942

The still under-strength 252 Squadron recorded the arrival of several new members of aircrew and some new Beaufighters, giving hope that the unit might be able to become operational in the near future.

Friday, 2 January 1942

A Blenheim on reconnaissance attacked a submarine on the surface 165 miles south-west of Sapienza. Three hits were claimed and a large oil patch observed on the surface.

Plt Off F.J.W.Saunders of 39 Squadron was killed when his aircraft was shot down by Flak when flying over Halfaya Pass, where the German garrison was still holding out. The rest of his crew and some passengers aboard were all captured, However, two had been seriously wounded and were at once handed over by the defenders to the besieging forces in order that they might receive hospital treatment. The rest would be freed when Halfaya fell on 15 January.

Sunday, 4 January 1942

The crew of a reconnoitring Blenheim spotted an Italian naval force identified as one battleship, three
cruisers and eight destroyers 100 miles south-west of Sapienza Island, heading south-south-west. Following
this sighting, further aircraft continued shadowing the vessels until next day, when the force, reduced by
the departure of four destroyers, was seen 65 miles east of Tripoli, now proceeding east-north-east.

Wrecked Junkers Ju 52/3m of KGrzbV 1 found at Tmimi airfield by 8th Army troops in January 1942.

Fieseler Fi 156 Storch ambulance aircraft abandoned at Gambut airfield at the end of 1941.

Monday, 5 January 1942

One of 39 Squadron's remaining Marylands undertook a special search over the Gulf of Sirte, sighting a battleship and several other vessels. The aircraft was attacked by fighters, but managed to escape these successfully.

Friday, 9 January 1942

Sunderland W3987 'W' of 230 Squadron flown by Sqn Ldr Garside, was able to attack a surfaced submarine. Following the attack as the vessel went below the surface, a huge bubble was seen, followed by a big oil patch and further bubbles, allowing a claim to be made that a sinking had been achieved.

Saturday – Tuesday, 17/27 January 1942

252 Squadron now commenced a move up to Berka to begin operations, undertaking its first sorties next day. These, being over the forward area, are dealt with earlier (see Chapter 11 – A New Year Dawns – Darkly). On 19 January the detachment moved to El Gobbi, but next day returned to Edcu. Five days later eight Beaufighters were despatched to Bu Amud to provide cover for a convoy. However the weather proved to be very bad and the operation for 26 January was cancelled as the dust storms were so severe. All returned to Edcu next day.

Friday, 23 January 1942

Having spent much of the month training in torpedo dropping, 39 Squadron crews were given the opportunity to test their new skills when a convoy was spotted by a 203 Squadron Blenheim during the morning. The convoy, located 175 miles north-east of Syracuse and heading south, was identified as comprising a large merchant vessel or liner, estimated to be of about 20,000 tons displacement escorted by a battleship, cruisers and destroyers – in total 20-30 vessels attempting to run through to Tripoli.

Following this sighting all available light bombers in Libya and mediums in the Delta, were briefed to attack. Six Blenheims failed to find the target, but the two available Boeing Fortresses had a little more luck. Although one crew failed to see anything of note, that of the other reported near-misses to the battleship and one of the merchant vessels. Six more Blenheims then attacked a reported 24 ships 170 miles north-east of Misurata, but no hits were observed. However, taking off from Berka Satellite, near Benghazi, three Beauforts from 39 Squadron (N1033, N1093 and W6518 flown by Flt Lt Taylor and Plt Offs Grant and Jepson), all loaded with torpedoes, had accompanied Blenheims of 11, 14 and 55 Squadrons. Despite fierce AA fire, all three torpedoes were released at 1,500 yards range, following which a large column of smoke was observed rising from the liner, resulting from a hit it was thought. Indeed, a lucky hit from this considerable distance had been achieved on the liner *Victoria* (13,098 tons).

Further attacks by Wellingtons and Albacores of 826 Squadron followed at night. The crews of the latter aircraft located the convoy 175 miles north-east of Misurata, also launching a torpedo attack during which hits were claimed on a merchant ship of about 20,000 tons (again, *Victoria*), bringing it to a standstill. A destroyer was also reported to have exploded violently. 14 Wellingtons had been sent out to attack, seven of these actually bombing. Two of the crews reported near-misses on merchant vessels, while two others went down low, allowing the turret gunners to strafe two of the escorting destroyers. In one of the Albacores was the commanding officer of 826 Squadron, Lt Cdr Corbett, this aircraft being shot down by the defending fire. The pilot, Lt Jackson, Corbett and one other crewman spent 24 hours afloat in their dinghy before being picked up by an Italian hospital ship and becoming PoWs.

Next day it was noted that the liner was missing from the vessels still in the area, allowing a report that it might have been sunk. *Victoria* had indeed gone down, her destruction subsequently being credited jointly to 39 and 826 Squadrons. However, it proved to be the only success gained with torpedoes for the Beauforts until several months later.

British Casualties

826 Sqn	Albacore T9241 '4A' shot down by AA; Lt J.D.Jackson (pilot), Lt Cdr J.W.S.Corbett and one picked up by Italian hospital ship after 24 hours and PoWs

---

Tuesday, 27 January 1942

230 Squadron's aggressive Sqn Ldr Garside again attacked a surfaced submarine which at once crash-dived. He released depth charges, reporting that his quarrie had possibly been damaged.

Thursday, 29 January 1942

Sqn Ldr Garside was once more able to engage a surfaced submarine, launching a dive attack during which eight 250 lb bombs were dropped, straddling the conning tower. The vessel momentarily disappeared, then the stern was seen to rise vertically from the water, the submarine then sliding out of sight. An oil patch was seen spread over an area 400 yards long by 200 yards wide, and the destruction of this vessel was claimed.

Saturday, 31 January 1942

With extraordinary luck, Sqn Ldr Garside of 230 Squadron found his fourth submarine of the month on the surface, spotting this with the aid of ASV radar. Flying Sunderland W3987 as usual, he again made a dive attack to drop eight 250 lb bombs, but on this occasion four failed to release, the other four over-shooting by 15-20 yards. The front gunner fired on the vessel as the flyingboat dived, members of the vessel's crew on the deck replying with an automatic cannon until the submarine crash-dived.

A few minutes later Garside's crew homed onto yet another ASV contact, but this proved to be a Swordfish, and a head-on collision with this was only narrowly avoided. A message was at once passed to the crew of this aircraft: "Have bombed submarine in vicinity", the crew then watching as the Swordfish dived and released depth charges in the area where flame floats had been dropped by the Sunderland. The intrepid Ken Garside would be awarded a DFC a few months later, by which time he had been promoted Wg Cdr.

At the end of January 39 Squadron's remaining Marylands and crews, together with the detachment commander, Sqn Ldr D.G.Hunter, who was the longest-serving pilot in the unit, were transferred to 203 Squadron to supplement the unit's Blenheims. 39 Squadron then became wholly Beaufort-equipped. However, from these early beginnings 201 Group would soon blossom into a powerful and effective force.

BIBLIOGRAPHY

The Original

Fighters over the Desert Christopher Shores and Hans Ring Neville Spearman 1969

Linked Titles in the Series

Malta: The Hurricane Years, 1940-41 Christopher Shores and Brian Cull with Nicola Malizia
    Grub Street 1987

Air War for Yugoslavia, Greece and Crete, 1940-41 Christopher Shores and Brian Cull with Nicola Malizia
    Grub Street 1987

Dust Clouds in the Middle East; The Air War for East Africa, Iraq, Syria and Madagascar, 1940-42
    Christopher Shores Grub Street 1996

Major Research Titles

Fighter Squadrons of the RAF and Their Aircraft John D.R.Rawlings Macdonald 1969

Bomber Squadrons of the RAF and Their Aircraft Philip Moyes Macdonald 1964

Coastal, Support and Special Squadrons of the RAF and Their Aircraft John D.R.Rawlings Jane's 1982

Royal Air Force Flying Training and Support Units Ray Sturtivant, John Hamlin and James J.Halley
    Air-Britain 1997

*RAF Squadrons; A Comprehensive Record of the Movement and Equipment of all RAF Squadrons and their
    Antecedents Since 1912* Wing Commander C.G. Jefford MBE RAF Airlife 1988

The Squadrons of the Fleet Air Arm Ray Sturtivant Air-Britain 1984

RAF Bomber Losses in the Middle East & Mediterranean, Volume 1: 1939-1942 David Gunby & Pelham
    Temple Midland 2006

The History of the Second World War; The Mediterranean and Middle East, Volumes I, II and III
    Major-General I.S.O.Playfair, CB, DSO, MC and Others HM Stationery Office 1954, 1956 and 1960

Springbok Fighter Victories; SAAF Operations in 1939-1945, Volumes 1 and 2 Michael Schoeman
    Freeworld Publications CC 2002 and 2009

*South African Forces in World War II; Volume 4 –Eagle Strike; The SAAF in Egypt, Cyrenaica, Libya,
    Tunisia, Tripolitania and Madagascar, 1931-1943* James Ambrose Brown Purnell 1974

Die Jagdfliegerverband 1934-1945; Volumes 5, 8/I and 8/II Jochen Prien, Gherhard Stemmer, Peter Rodeike
    and Winfried Bock Struve's Buchdruckerie und Verlag 2003-2004

Bomber Units of the Luftwaffe 1932-1945. Volumes 1 and 2 Henry L.de Zeng IV and Douglas G.Stankey with
    Eddie Creek Chevron Publishing Ltd 2007 and 2008

Dive-Bomber and Ground Attack Units of the Luftwaffe 1933-1945, Volume 1 Henry L. de Zeng IV and
    Douglas G.Stankey Ian Allan Publishing 2009

The Distinguished Flying Cross and How it was Won, 1918-1995, Volumes 1(A-L) and 2(M-Z) Nick and
    Carol Carter Savannah 1998

The Distinguished Flying Medal Register for the Second World War, Volumes 1(A-J) and 2 (K-Z) Ian
    Tavender Savannah 2000

Additional Research Titles

Australia in the War of 1939-1945; Air War Against Germany and Italy, 1939-1943 John Herington
　　Australian War Memorial, Canberra 1954

Desert Warriors; Australian P-40 pilots at war in the Middle East and North Africa, 1941-1943 Russell Brown
　　Banner Books 2000

Kittyhawks over the Sand; The Canadians & RCAF Americans; The Men & The Aircraft Michel Lavigne &
　　W/C James F.Edwards Lavigne Aviation Publications 2002

Hurricanes over the Sands; The Canadians & The RCAF Americans; The Men and the Aircraft, Part One
　　Michel Lavigne & W/C James F.Edwards Lavigne Aviation Publications 2003

Pictorial History of the Mediterranean Air War, Volume One Christopher F. Shores Ian Allan 1972

Hurricanes over Tobruk; The Pivotal Role of the Hurricane in the Defence of Tobruk, January-June 1941
　　Brian Cull with Don Minterne Grub Street 1999

The Bristol Blenheim; a Complete History Graham Warner Crécy Publishing 2002

Desert Air Force at War Chaz Bowyer and Christopher Shores Ian Allan 1981

Aces High; A Tribute to the Most Notable Fighter Pilots of the British and Commonwealth Forces in WWII
　　Christopher Shores and Clive Williams Grub Street 1994

Those Other Eagles: A Tribute to the British.Commonwealth and Free European Fighter Pilots Who Claimed
　　Between Two and Four Victories in Aerial Combat, 1939-1982 Christopher Shores Grub Street 2004

Fleet Air Arm Aircraft 1939 to 1945 Ray Sturtivant ISO, with Mick Burrow Air-Britain 1995

Courage Alone: The Italian Air Force 1940-1943 Chris Dunning Hikoki Publications 1998

Squadron/Unit Histories

Flat Out; The Story of 30 Squadron, Royal Air Force John F.Hamlin Air-Britain 2002

The Flying Camels; The History of No. 45 Squadron, RAF Wg Cdr C.G.Jefford, MBE, BA, RAF(Retd)
　　C.G.Jefford 1995

The History of 73 Squadron; Part 2 November 1940 to September 1943 Don Minterne Tutor Publishing 1997

Strike True; The Story of No. 80 Squadron, Royal Air Force Christopher Shores Air-Britain 1986

Shark Squadron; The History of 112 Squadron, 1917-1975 Robin Brown Crécy Books 1994

A History of 209 Squadron Flight Lieutenant D.S.B.Marr, B.Sc(Eng), RAF Privately published 1966

The Hornet Strikes; The Story of No.213 Squadron, Royal Air Force Frank M.Leeson Air-Britain 1998

The Desert Harassers; Memoirs of 450 (RAAF) Squadron Leonard L.Barton Aston Publications 1991

Bankstown to Berlin; with 451 (RAAF) Squadron, 1941-1946 Leonard L.Barton The Committee of the 451
　　(RAAF) Squadron Association 1996

Theirs is the Glory; The Story of 12 Squadron, SAAF Stuart N.McCreath Widdlecombe and Ogden
　　date unspecified

Per Noctem Per Diem; The Story of 24 Squadron, SAAF E.N.Tucker and P.M.J.McGregor 24 Squadron
　　Album Committee 1961

Die Geschichte des Lehrgeschwaders 1; Band 1 1936-1942 Peter Taghon VDM Heinz Nickel 2004

Pilot Autobiographies or Biographies

Killer Caldwell: Australia's Greatest Fighter Pilot Jeffrey Watson Hodder 2005

Clive Caldwell, Air Ace Kristen Alexander Allen & Unwin 2006

Boy, tales of Childhood, and Going Solo Roald Dahl Penguin Books 1984

Test Pilot Neville Duke Allan Wingate 1953 republished by Grub Street in 1992

The War Diaries of Neville Duke DSO, OBE, DFC (two Bars), AFC, Czech Military Cross, 1941-1944 Edited
　　by Norman Franks Grub Street 1995

Kittyhawk Pilot; Wing Cdr James (Stocky) Edwards J.P.A.Michel Lavign and J.F.(Stocky) Edwards Turner-
　　Walker Publications 1983

Goon in the Block Don Edy Private publication 1961; revised edition 2010

You Live But Once; Bobby Gibbes; Autobiography Wing Commander (Retd) R.H.Gibbes, DSO, DFC
　　& Bar Private publication 1994

Mezze (mee-zay); Little bites of flying, living and golfing Oliver Green Ryan Publishing 1999

A Lot to Fight For; The War Diaries and Letters of S/Ldr J.F.Jackson DFC Private publication by Patricia
　　and Arthur Jackson 2001

Imshi; A Fighter Pilot's Letters to his Mother W.H.Allen & Co Ltd 1943

Messerschmitt Roulette; The Western Desert 1941-42 Wing Commander Geoffrey Morley-Mower DFC, AFC Phalanx Publishing Co Ltd 1993

Woody; A Fighter Pilot's Album Hugh A.Halliday Canav Books 1987

Air Commanders

From Sea to Sky, 1910-1945 Air Chief Marshal Sir Arthur Longmore Geoffrey Bles, 1946

With Prejudice Marshal of the Royal Air Force Lord Tedder Cassell 1966

Coningham; A Biography of Air Marshal Sir Arthur Coningham Vincent Orange Methuen 1990

Straight and Level Air Chief Marshal Sir Kenneth Cross KCB,CBE,DSO,DFC, with Professor Vincent Orange Grub Street 1993

Be Bold Air Chief Marshal Sir Frederick Rosier GCB, CBE, DSO with David Rosier Grub Street 2011

The Memoirs of Field Marshal Kesselring William Kimber and Co Ltd Reprinted by Purnell Book Services Ltd 1974

Ground Commanders

Wavell; Soldier & Statesman Victoria Schofield John Murray 2006

The Forgotten Victor; General Sir Richard O'Connor KT, GCB, DSO, MC John Baynes Brassey's (UK) 1989

Auchinleck; The Lonely Soldier Philip Warner Buchan & Enright Publishers Ltd 1981 Republished by Pen & Sword Military 2006

Armoured Crusader; The Biography of Major-General Sir Percy 'Hobo' Hobart Kenneth Macksey Hutchinson 1967 Republished by Grub Street 2004

Panzer Commander The Memoirs of Colonel Hans von Luck Cassell 2002

Related Books, Ground Operations

The Early Battles of Eighth Army; 'Crusader' to the Alamein Line 1941-1943 Adrian Stewart Leo Cooper 2002

Crusader; The Eighth Army's Forgotten Victory, November 1941-January 1942 Richard Humble Leo Cooper 1987

The Great Tank Scandal; British Armour in the Second World War Part 1 David Fletcher HM Stationery Officer 1989

The Tanks; The History of the Royal Tank Regiment; Volume Two 1939-1945 Captain B.H.Liddell Hart Cassell 1959

Leakey's Luck; A Tank Commander with Nine Lives R.E.A. Leakey with George Forty Sutton Publishing 1999

Tanks Across the Desert; The War Diary of Jake Wardrop George Forty William Kimber & Co Ltd 1981 Republished by Sutton Publishing 2003

Additional Bibliography

La guerra aerea in Africa Settentrionale, Borgiotti, A. and Gori, C., Stem Mucchi, Modena, 1973

Quelli del cavallino rampante, Duma, A., Dell'Ateneo, Roma 1970

Italian Aces of World War 2, Massimello, G. and Apostolo G., Osprey Publishing, Oxford, 2000

L'Aeronautica Italiana nella seconda guerra mondiale, Santoro, G., Ed. Esse, Roma, 1957 Tarantola, E., Il 150°, 151° e 153° Gruppo Caccia, SMA, Roma, 1987

INDEX

Borham, G.H. Sgt 238 Sqn 377,379

Borrett, F.B. Sgt 11 Sqn 442

Bosch, S.L. Lt Col 12 Saaf Sqn 270

Bosman, A.C. Capt 4 Saaf Sqn 334,336,365, 388,389,394,409,414,423,431

Botha, A.J. Lt 1 Saaf Sqn 193,211,212,220

Bothwell, P.R. Flg Off 3 Raaf Sqn 262,342, 345

Bower, P. Sgt 45 Sqn 23,24

Bowerman, R.E. Sgt 24 Saaf Sqn 380

Bowker, N. Flt Lt 112 Sqn 260,264,306,318, 344,352,355,362,363,365,412,427

Bowman, A.Mcd. Wg Cdr 39 Sqn, 204 Grp 191,216,511,513,518

Boyce, Sgt 203 Sqn 518

Boyce, C.D.C. Wg Cdr 84 Sqn 253,282,293

Boyd, A.H. Flg Off 3 Raaf Sqn 77,79,92,93, 102,132, 315

Boyd, O.T. Air Marshal 81

Boyd, 'Jock' Lac 73 Sqn 170

Boyde, A.L. (Or Botde) Sgt 229 Sqn 322

Bradbury, E.A. Flg Off 3 Raaf Sqn 353, 356,436

Braithwaite, T.L. Lt 12 Saaf Sqn 314,315

Brand, Flt Lt 230 Sqn 511

Brandwood, F.B. Sgt 105 Sqn 500

Bray, Sqn Ldr 138,138

Brierley, E.U. Maj 60 Saaf Sqn 292

Briggs, J.L. Plt Off 274 Sqn 221,222

Briggs, P.J. Flg Off 3 Raaf Sqn 394,427

Briggs, T.J.L. 3 Raaf Sqn 356

Britz, J.F. Maj 21 Saaf Sqn 264,269,270

Broadley, A.B. Flt Lt 105 Sqn 499

Broadsmith, H.E Flt Lt 148 Sqn 457

Broad-Smith, J.G. Sgt 148 Sqn 454

Bromwich, H.F. Lt 805 Sqn 381

Brown, A.M. Flt Lt 2 Pru 135,271

Brown, L.O. Grp Capt 202 Grp 11,127, 132,150

Browne, A.G. Sgt 229 Sqn 403,426

Browne, C.D.A. Plt Off 274 Sqn 422

Bruen, J.M. Lt 803 Sqn 169,182,183

Brunton, P.C.F. Sgt 112 Sqn 276

Bryer, G.M. Grp Capt 201 Grp 507

Buchanan, J.K. Wg Cdr 14 Sqn 275,281, 282,293

Buck, D.W. Sgt 18 Sqn 504

Bullot, F.R. Flg Off 55 Sqn 115

Burbery, Flg Off 3 Raaf Sqn 262,264

Burgan, G.S. Plt Off 11 Sqn 350

Burger, H.J.P. Lt 1 Saaf Sqn 187,223

Burney, H.G. Sgt 112 Sqn 306,328,332,407

Burns, C.W.Mcl. Sgt 229 Sqn 360

Burns, J. Flt Sgt 45 Sqn 407

Burr, E.H. 2/Lt 113 Sqn 279

Burr, H.W. Sgt 148 Sqn 463

Burrage, R.I. 2/Lt 11 Sqn 389

Butler, C.F. Plt Off Oadu 509

Butler, D.O. Sqn Ldr 1 Gru 475

Byers, J.A. Flt Lt 451 Sqn 260

Cable, W.O. Sgt 250 Sqn 336,363,365

Caldwell, C.R. Sqn Ldr 250, 112 Sqns 231, 232,233, 234,237,238,243,245,246,252, 253,269,270, 271,275,336,347,350,355, 363,365,388,396,403,404,408,411,424, 428,442

Callister, J.K. Sgt 148 Sqn 459

Cameron, A.C. Sgt 3 Raaf Sqn 276,288,346, 347,352,354,377,379,394,420

Campbell, A.U.M. Lt 39 Sqn 183

Campbell, D. Sqn Ldr 3 Raaf Sqn 117,134, 139,141,144,145,146

Campbell, G.L. Flt Lt 272 Sqn 314,315,336, 346,347,366, 367,368

Campbell, J.C. Flg Off 3 Raaf Sqn 117

Campbell, J.R. Lt Col I/C Retimo, Crete 205

Campbell, N.K. Lt 830 Sqn 493,494

Campbell, S. Sub Lt 830 Sqn 502

Campbell, Sgt 238 Sqn 189

Campbell, Sgt 216 Sqn 449

Campbell-Rogers, Plt Off Oadu 509

Canton, N.E. Flg Off 148 Sqn 462

Canty, M.A. Sgt 250 Sqn 382,384

Carlisle, R. Pty Off 807 Sqn 181,183

Carson, K.F. Sgt 112 Sqn 318,321,322,377, 379,409,426

Carson, Sgt 229 Sqn 400,403,426

Carter, G.L. Grp Capt Hq,Me, 252 Wg 311, 487

Carter, L. Sgt 113 Sqn 64

Carver, Sgt 37 Sqn 462,466

Casbolt, C.E. Sgt 80 Sqn 24

Case, Sgt 229 Sqn 419,420,421

Cash, J.F. Sgt 274 Sqn 245

Castelain, N. Sous Lt 73 Sqn 153,154,157, 158,167

Chadwick, R. Lt 4 Saaf Sqn 341,380,381

Chalkley, G.A. Lt 24 Saaf Sqn 322

Challis, B.W. Sgt 33 Sqn 358,359,407

Chandler, E.F. Sgt 82 Sqn 495

Chantry, R. Sgt 6 Sqn 95

Chaplin, J.H. Wg Cdr 1 Gru 473,475

Chapman, D.R. Sqn Ldr 3 Raaf Sqn 420,421

Chapman, 250 Sqn 477

Charles, G.P. Wg Cdr Xiii Corps Air Adsr 428

Charles, P.S. Flg Off 33 Sqn 358,371,375, 399,400

Charlton, P.N. Sub Lt Rnfs 315,318,319,357

Charney, F.R.H. Sqn Ldr 107 Sqn 500

Chatfield, R.M. Flg Off 73 Sqn 170,172, 218,234

Chatfield, W.T. Pty Off 803 Sqn 183

Cheesman, J.H. Sgt 55 Sqn 203

Chichester, S.D. Wg Cdr 216 Sqn 449

Chinchen, G.T. Flg Off 3 Raaf Sqn 425,426

Cholmely, A.H. Plt Off 80 Sqn 56,57

Christie, A.N. Sgt 112 Sqn 318

Christie, R.H. Sgt 3 Raaf Sqn 362

Christie, R.V. Lt 1 Saaf Sqn 220

Christmas, B.E. Flt Lt 4 Saaf Sqn 423,424

Churcher, T.F. Flg Off 45 Sqn 201,202

Churchill, The Hon W.S. Uk Pm 74,114,178, 179,208,211,257

Cidman, Plt Off 260 Sqn 404

Clancy, Sgt 70 Sqn 458

Clark, D. Sgt 274 Sqn 445

Clarke, B.W. Flg Off 272 Sqn

Clarke, J.H. Sgt 80 Sqn 56,57,94,95

Clarke, R.H. Plt Off 112 Sqn 72,73

Clarke, W.C. Sgt 55 Sqn 63

Clarkson, C.L. Lt 24 Saaf Sqn 220,243

Clarkson, K.H. Lt 4 Saaf Sqn 423

Clegg, W.E. Sgt 38 Sqn 452

Cloete, Flg Off 33 Sqn 405

Clostre, D.H.J. (French) Flg Off 33, 274 Sqns 187,346

Clulee, M.V. Sgt 24 Saaf Sqn 381

Coetzee, I.M. Lt 24 Saaf Sqn 220

Coetzee, O.B. Lt 2 Saaf Sqn 308

Coke, The Hon D.A. Flt Lt 80 Sqn 341,377, 379,432

Cole, R.B. Plt Off 250 Sqn 321,322,336

Coles, ?? The Same Plt Off 250 Sqn 282, 446

Collenette, F.De B. Flt Lt 238 Sqn 336,337

Collins, E.G. Flg Off 45 Sqn 160

Collins, M.W. Wg Cdr 230 Sqn 292

Collingwood, R.J.P. 2/Lt 1 Saaf Sqn 388,403

Collishaw, R. Air Cdr 202 Grp 11,13,23,94, 116,128,129,150,170,202,224,226

Colville, G.D. Sgt 40 Sqn 503

Comfort, A.C. Sgt 80 Sqn 338,341,344,400, 403

Coningham, Sir Arthur Avm Wdaf 244,302, 303,304,311,340, 383,446,447

Conrad, W.A.G. Plt Off 274 Sqn 259,357, 392,394

Conradie, J. Lt 1 Saaf Sqn 225,227,240

Connell, G.R. 2/Lt 1 Saaf Sqn 365,393,394

Cooper, R.J. Plt Off 38 Sqn 458,465

Copeland, W.M. Lt 4 Saaf Sqn 404,423,424

Copley, D.G. Cpl 6 Sqn 142

Corbett, F.S. Lt 21 Saaf Sqn 316,319

Corbett, J.W.S. Lt Cdr 826 Sqn 293,467,522

Cordy, S. Sgt 45 Sqn 187

Cornall, C. Sgt 250 Sqn 282

Corniglion-Molinier, E. (French) Grb 1 293

Costello, A.R. Plt Off 33, 112 Sqns 25,38,39, 40,78

Coston, F. Pty Off 803 Sqn 182,183

Cotton, P.T. Flg Off 208 Sqn 351

Cottingham, L. Flt Sgt 80 Sqn 32,33

Couchman, R.A. Flg Off 33 Sqn 25

Coudray, C.G.M. Wt Off 274 Sqn 201,222, 232

Courcott, P. (French) Lt 24 Saaf Sqn 200, 201,202

Cover, J.A. Sgt 82 Sqn 496

Cowan, Plt Off 148 Sqn 462

Coward, G.C. Sgt 250 Sqn 231,334,337, 388,406,409

Harley, Sgt 45 Sqn 107

Harries, J.A. Flt Lt 55 Sqn 514

Harris, C.W. Plt Off 250 Sqn 436

Harris, G.E. Sgt 37 Sqn 456

Harris, J. Flt Lt 55 Sqn 203

Harris, L. Lt Faa 110

Harrison-Broadley, J. Sqn Ldr 82 Sqn 495

Hart, K.G. Flg Off 250 Sqn 362,370,384, 423,436

Hart, R.C. Flg Off 3 Raaf Sqn 425,436

Harvey, L.W. Sgt 94 Sqn 428,430

Hasez, M. (Egyptian) Flt Lt 5 Reaf Sqn 480

Hatting, T.J. Sgt 12 Saaf Sqn 308

Haupt, D.R. Lt 24 Saaf 381

Hawkins, G.E. Sqn Ldr 33, 274 Sqns 28,87, 167,177,205,216

Hawkins, Pte Sas 397

Hawthorne, T.R. Plt Off 260 Sqn 396

Hay, R.C. Lt 808 Sqn 180,181,183

Haylock, R.A. 272 Sqn 315

Hayter, F.E.G. Flt Lt 6 Sqn 201

Heath, P.R. Sqn Ldr 3 Raaf Sqn 77,79

Hedley, P.M. Lt 1 Saaf Sqn 244,277,278

Hemus, J.F. Sgt 113 Sqn 315

Henderson, G.R. Sub Lt Rnfs 334,336

Henderson, R.W. Sgt 274 Sqn 275

Henley, R.S. Lt 806 Sqn 165,169,182,183, 184,185,186

Herbert, W.L. Lt 1 Saaf Sqn 252,365,366, 370

Hewett, E.W.F. Sgt 80 Sqn 42

Hewitt, L.R. Plt Off 37 Sqn 455

Hickey, W.J. Sqn Ldr 80 Sqn 49,55

Hill, L.S. Lt 806 Sqn 182,183

Hiller, G.E. Sgt 3 Raaf Sqn 266,346,347

Hinde, D.A. Lt 2 Saaf Sqn 275,321,322, 348,359

Hindle, T. Sgt 94 Sqn 379

Hinton, R.V. Sub Lt 805 Sqn 196

Hirst, P.S. Flg Off 252 Sqn 508

Hoare, N.C. Wt Off 229 Sqn 336,347

Hobbis, Sgt 272 Sqn 320,322

Hobbs, J.B. Flt Lt 274 Sqn 222,230,370

Hodge, E. Sgt 6 Sqn 201,202

Hoffe, W.H. Lt 274, 1 Saaf Sqns 234,357, 358

Hogg, G.A. Sub Lt 806 Sqn 64,166,168,478

Hojem, G.C. Lt 1 Saaf Sqn 369,370,403

Holdenby, P. Plt Off 73 Sqn 150

Holgate, J.B. Flg Off 252 Sqn 508

Holland, Flg Off 267 Sqn 138

Holderness, J.B. Flt Lt 229, 6 Sqns 226

Hollenbach, W.N. Lt 24 Saaf Sqn 370

Hollingsworth, A. Sgt 148 Sqn 491

Holliwell, Flg Off 80 Sqn 71,72,73

Holman, F.S. Flg Off 33 Sqn 71,73

Holme, K. Sub Lt 252 Sqn 508

Holmes, D.A.R. Sub Lt 830 Sqn 496

Hone, 451 Sqn

Honor, D.S.G. Wg Cdr 274 Sqn 147,167, 176,177,187,191,197,198,199,200,207, 213,225

Honour, H.J. Flt Lt 37 Sqn 461

Horgan, T.M. Sqn Ldr 80 Sqn 293,320,322, 377,379

Horniman, P.J. Plt Off 229, 73 Sqns 247,250

Hoskins, N. Sgt 14 Sqn 192

Hough, A.G.W. Flg Off 37 Sqn 452

Houston, W.E. Sgt 112 Sqn 389

Howard, G.V. Grp Capt 252 Wg 487

Howard, L.G.T. Pty Off 808 Sqn 180,183

Howell, Flt Lt 31 Sqn 374,375

Howie, F.D. Lt Cdr 830 Sqn 498

Howie, G.R. Wg Cdr 216 Sqn 292

Hudson, R.T. Plt Off 451 Sqn 244

Hughes, A. Sqn Ldr 45 Sqn 314,315

Hughes, S.W.R. Flt Lt 230 Sqn 520

Hulbert, J.C. Sgt 274 Sqn 107

Humphrey, P.C. Plt Off 73 Sqn 150,173

Humphreys, P.H. Flg Off 112 Sqn 306,342, 344,362,389

Humphries, A. Sgt 250 Sqn 269,270

Hunt, J.G. Lt Cdr 830 Sqn 501

Hunt, T.M. Wg Cdr 110 Sqn 498

Hunter, D.G. Sqn Ldr 39 Sqn 512,523

Hustin, Sqn Ldr 45 Sqn 325

Hutchins, C.J.K. Wg Cdr 55 Sqn 259,282,287

Hutchinson, Flt Lt 237 Sqn 324,332

Hutley, W.D. Flt Lt 451 Sqn 264

Hutt, J.K. Sgt 69 Sqn 498

Hutt, P.H.V. Plt Off 274 Sqn 176,177,187, 191

Huxtep, P. Sgt 55 Sqn 166

Iddeson, J.S. 2/Lt 208 Sqn 421

Ingham-Brown, T. Sgt 84 Sqn 348

Inglesby, H. Sgt 33 Sqn 338,341

Innan, E.B. Sgt 82 Sqn 494

Innes-Smith, Flt Sgt 30 Sqn 40,41

Irving, G.F. Sqn Ldr 108 Sqn 461

Ivkovic, (Yugoslavian) Lt 2(Yugo) Sqn 520

Jabin, R. (French) Wt Off Grb 1 350

Jack, M. Air Sgt 21 Saaf Sqn 310

Jackson, E.H.B. Flg Off 3 Raaf Sqn 326,331, 344,393,425

Jackson, J.F. Flg Off 3 Raaf Sqn 93,102,103, 117, 130,131,132,140,143,144,145,148, 159

Jackson, R.E. Lt 4 Saaf Sqn 334,336,431

Jackson, Sgt 272 Sqn 409

Jacquier, P.J.F. (French) Flt Lt 80, 274 Sqns 46,200,201,202

Jarvis, J.A. Plt Off 30 Sqn 54,56,57

Jay, R.E. Flt Lt 252 Sqn 508

Jeffries, R.J.D. Plt Off 112 Sqn 276,315,318, 319,321,322,389

Jeffrey, B.W. Flg Off 39 Sqn 512

Jeffrey, P. Wg Cdr 3 Raaf Sqn, 132,139,157, 159,344,352,353,354,356,377,379

Jenkins, Plt Off 238 Sqn 336,354,442

Jepson, Plt Off 39 Sqn 522

Jeudwine, H.P. Sgt 14 Sqn 197,199

Jewell, W.E. Flg Off 3 Raaf Sqn 145,148, 149,276, 342,345

Jewell, 33 Sqn 317,319

Johns, G.B. Plt Off 229, 73 Sqns 239,244, 336,419,420

Johnson, A.F. Wg Cdr 203 Sqn 292,515

Johnson, A.G. Pty Off 807 Sqn 180,183

Johnson, D.V. Wg Cdr 33 Sqn 15,28,130,174

Johnson, R. Plt Off 14 Sqn 182

Johnson, S.C. Sgt 112 Sqn 396

Johnston, G.R.A.Mcg. Flg Off 73 Sqn 374, 376,378,488

Johnston, R.L. Sub Lt 805, Rnfs 318,344,345

Jonas, R.C. Sqn Ldr 80 Sqn 15

Jones, B.S.M. Flg Off 70 Sqn 454,455

Jones, C.J.C. Lac 228 Sqn 43

Jones, E.G. Flt Lt 80 Sqn 30,49

Jones, H.D. Sqn Ldr 84 Sqn 137

Jones, K.S.P. Capt 24 Saaf Sqn 200

Jones, K.W. Sub Lt 826 Sqn 467

Jones, R.S. Flg Off 3 Raaf Sqn 427

Jones, S.V. 2/Lt 229 Sqn 414

Jones, Lt 45 Sqn 197

Joubert, C.C.O. Plt Off 73 Sqn 150

Joubert, F. Air Sgt 24 Saaf Sqn 248,249

Joubert, F.J. 2/Lt 274 Sqn 93

Judge, J.W.B. Wg Cdr 211 Sqn 15,132,150

Jupp, G.A. Sgt 73 Sqn 235,237

Jury, F.W. Sgt 18 Sqn 394

Kay, N. Sgt 238 Sqn 345,347

Kearney, C.S. Lt 24 Saaf Sqn 206,207,218

Keebe, F.H.W. Plt Off 107 Sqn 506

Keefer, G.C. Plt Off 274 Sqn 259,370,375

Keighley-Peach, C.L. Lt Cdr HMS *Eagle* 34

Keily, G.B. Sqn Ldr 113 Sqn 16,40,41,60

Keith, L.K. Lt 805 Sqn 226,227

Kellett, R. Wg Cdr 11 Sqn 293,370

Kelsall, R.W. Sgt 33 Sqn 305,336,422

Kenner, J.W. Sgt 37 Sqn 456,457

Kent, J.F.S. Plt Off 250 Sqn 231,232,234

Kershaw, R.H.C. Capt 1 Saaf Sqn 317,319, 362,369,370,388

Kerr, G.M. Sgt 274 Sqn 163,164,200,202,207

Key, C.A.D. Lt 70 Sqn 461,462

Kierath, Sgt 33 Sqn 407

Kindersley, A.T.J. Lt 808 Sqn 180,183

Kingon, A.M. Lt 24 Saaf Sqn 369,370

Kings, R.A. Flg Off 238 Sqn 245,347

Kitto, K.C. Flg Off 70 Sqn 466

Kloster, W.G. Flg Off 3 Raaf Sqn 139,141, 145,288,328,332,354

Knappett, R.A. Sgt 238 Sqn 278,279,345,347

Knight, D.E. Flg Off 3 Raaf Sqn 396

Uebele, Lt 2.(H)/14 156
Unger, Otto Uffz 2.(H)/14 220
Unterberger, Josef Oblt 2./Jg 27 396
Ursinus, Günther Fw 2.(H)/14 380

Verschoth, Josef Fw 2.(F)/123 481
Vetter, Rudolf Fw 3./Stg 1 337
Vockelmann, Karl Lt 7./Jg 53 393,394
Vögl, Ferdinand Oblt 4./Jg 27 337
Voigt, Max Oblt 5./Kg 26 182,184,476
Vollmarie, Uffz I./Stg 1 130
Vos, Eberhard Fw 1./Stg 3 394

Wagner, Hans Lt 3./Stg 1 242
Wagner, Max Fw 1./Stg 1 394
Wala, Johann Uffz 7./Zg 26 152
Walchhofer, Johann Uffz 6./Jg 27 440,441
Warnicke, Hans-Joachim Oblt 6./Stg 2 227,
  239
Weber, Fritz Uffz 4./Stg 2 158
Weber, Hermann Lt 9./Zg 26 375
Wegmann, Günther Uffz Iii./Zg 26 384,389
Wegscheider, Anton Uffz 8./Stg 1 155
Wehmeyer, Alfred Lt Iii./Zg 26 133,153,
  341,362
Weist, Gerhard Fw 8./Zg 26 250
Weith, Kurt Oblt 2.(H)/14 152
Wellendorf, Uffz 9./Zg 26 375
Wellenreuther, Karl Fw 5./Kg 26 475
Werner, Uffz 8./Zg 26 250
Werfft, Peter Fw 1./Jg 27 240,252,258
Weskott, Josef Obfw 1./Jg 27 329,332
Wever, Walter General 300
Wiesböck, Friedrich Uffz 8./Zg 26 234
Wiessmann, Bernhard Oblt 4./Lg 1 407
Wilcke, Heinz Gefr 6./Stg 2 146
Wilcke, Wolf-Dietrich Hptmn Stab Iii./Jg 53
  376,384,385
Wimmer, Hans Obfw 3./Stg 1 199
Woethe, Fw Ii./Kg 26 134
Wohlert, Walter Gefr 8./Zg 26 177
Woidich, Franz Obfw 5./Jg 27 320,332
Woldenga, Bernhard Maj Stab/Jg 27 367,368
Wolf, Albert Uffz 6./Stg 2 239
Wünsche, Uffz 8./Zg 26 173
Wüst, Ogfrh Iii./Zg 26 133

Italian Personnel
Abbarchi, Serg Magg Rovero 78ª Sq,
  13° Gr, 2° St Ct 38,39,40
Abello, S.Ten Oscar 70ª Sq, 23° Gr Ct
  103,108
Abrami, Serg Italo 378ª Sq, 155° Gr Ct
  318,219,355
Accardo, Col Fernando Co 8° St Bt 296
Accomazzo, M.Llo Cesare 95 Sq, 18 Gr Ct
  193
Accorsi, M.Llo Giovanni 368ª Sq,
  151° Gr Aut Ct 117,124

Agnelli, S.Ten Carlo 96ª Sq, 9° Gr,
  4ª St Ct 70,71
Aicardi, M.Llo Marco 358ª Sq,
  2° Gr Aut Ct 227
Aimone-Cat, Gen Sa Mario Co 5ª Squadra
  124,298
Aini, T.Col Giuseppe Co 11° Gr,
  13° St Bt 296
Albanese, Cap Nicolò Co 146ª Sq Rm 297
Albertini, S.Ten Carlo 366ª Sq,
  151° Gr Aut Ct 73
Alesi, M.Llo Omero 90ª Sq, 10° Gr,
  4ª St Ct 29,55
Alessandri, M.Llo Giuseppe 150ª Sq,
  2° Gr Aut Ct 111
Alessandrini, Cap Bruno Co 155ª Sq,
  3° Gr Aut Ct 294
Allevi, Ten Umberto 610ª Sq T 294
Ambrosi, Serg Ottorino 368ª Sq,
  151° Gr Aut Ct 497
Ambrosino, 1° Av Luigi 241ª Sq 98°
  Gr Bt 139
Ammannato, Ten Aramis 232ª Sq, 59° Gr,
  41° St Bt 94,96
Ammannato, Cap Athos Co 235ª Sq,
  60° Gr, 41° St Bt 69,99,126
Anceschi, 1° Av Renato 175ª Sq Rst 142
Andalò, Ten Egisto 154ª Sq, 3° Gr Aut Ct
  502,503
Andraghetti, Serg Magg Anselmo 97ª Sq,
  9° Gr, 4ª St Ct 368
Andrei, T.Col Oreste Co 2° Gr Apc 22
Anelli, S.Ten Giuseppe 175ª Sq Rst 112,113
Anelli, Cap Mario Sezione Cinematografica
  230
Angelin, Serg Pietro 57ª Sq, 32° Gr,
  10° St Bt 34
Annoni, Ten Emanuele 96ª Sq, 9° Gr,
  4ª St Ct 55,346,347,358
Anselmino, 1° Av Renato 241ª Sq, 98° Gr Bt
  140
Aramu, Col Mario Co 9° St Bt 53,54,97
Arangino, Ten Piero 372ª Sq, 153° Gr Aut Ct
  235
Arcangeletti, Cap Paolo Co 393ª Sq,
  160° Gr Aut Ct 296
Arrabito, Cap Guglielmo Co 82ª Sq,
  13° Gr, 2° St Ct 21,91,92
Atti, Ten Enea 363ª Sq, 150° Gr Aut Ct 425
Aurili, Ten Giuseppe 84ª Sq, 10° Gr,
  4ª St Ct; 90ª Sq 38,39,43,55,58,86
Avogadro Di Cerrione, Cap Corv Alberto
  Co Delfino 511
Azzaroni, Serg Edoardo 93ª Sq, 8° Gr,
  2° St Ct 26

Bacchi Andreoli, S.Ten Vittorio 71ª Sq,
  17° Gr, 1° St Ct 376
Bacich, Cap Mario Co 93ª Sq, 8° Gr,
  2° St Ct; Co 8° Gr 22,298

Baculo, Cap Calcedonio Co 45ª Sq,
  36° Gr, 33° St Bt 20
Baduel, Cap Sebastiano Co 23ª Sq,
  2° Gr Apc 22
Bagato, Serg Luigi 376ª Sq Aut Ct 322
Bagatta, T.Col Aristide Co 1° Gr Apc 21
Bagnoli, S.Ten Renato 80ª Sq, 17° Gr,
  1° St Ct 363,376,389
Baisi, Cap Aurelio 10ª Sq, 28° Gr,
  8° St Bt 260
Baj, S.Ten Carlo 240ª Sq, 98° Gr Bt 137
Balbo, Maresciallo Italo Governor Of Libya
  30,51
Baldacci, Serg Bruno 353ª Sq, 20° Gr Ct
  237,255
Baldasso, Serg Ido 115ª Sq Oa 66
Baldin, Serg Filippo 82ª Sq, 13° Gr,
  2° St Ct 96
Balestrero, S.Ten Renato 143ª Sq Rm 60
Balzarotti, Ten Giuseppe 284ª Sq,
  131° Gr As 443
Bandini, M.Llo Mario 84ª Sq, 10° Gr,
  4° St Ct 27
Banba, Gen Giuseppe Co 11 Div Aerea 490
Barbani, Ten Umberto 279ª Sq As 252,279
Barbetta, Ten Italo 159ª Sq, 12° Gr,
  50° St As 109,126
Barcaro, S.Ten Giovanni 97ª Sq, 9° Gr,
  4ª St Ct 62,63,347,358,376
Baroni, S.Ten Renato 393ª Sq,
  160° Gr Aut Ct 285
Bartesaghi, Serg Luigi 88ª Sq, 6° Gr,
  1° St Ct 425
Bartoletti, Serg Bruno 90ª Sq, 10° Gr,
  4° St Ct 55,56
Bartolomasi, Serg Renzo 209ª Sq Bat 264
Bartolozzi, Serg Magg Umberto 159ª Sq,
  12° Gr, 50° St Ass 126
Baruffi, Cap Pericle Co 71ª Sq, 17° Gr,
  1° St Ct 298,363
Baschiera, Ten Lanfranco 151ª Sq,
  20° Gr Ct 363
Baschirotto, M.Llo Gian Lino 88ª Sq,
  6° Gr, 1° St Ct 425
Bassi, M.Llo Enrico 236ª Sq Bat 154
Bassi, Cap Francesco Co 3ª Sq, 43° Gr,
  13° St Bt 296
Basso, Serg Leone 77ª Sq, 13° Gr, 2° St Ct
  39,40,60
Bastico, Marshal Ettore Cinc Iaf N.Africa 300
Battagion, Ten Gino 70ª Sq, 23° Gr Ct 106
Battaglia, Ten Carlo 73ª Sq, 9° Gr, 4ª St Ct
  45,70
Baylon, Magg Giuseppe Co 2° Gr Aut Ct
  103,107,109,111,223,225
Beduz, Ten Giovanni 78ª Sq, 13° Gr, 2° St Ct
  39,40,64,65
Beggiato, Ten Guido 81ª Sq, 6° Gr, 1° St Ct
  389

Bellagambi, Ten Mario Co 364ª Sq,
150° Gr Aut Ct 298,446

Bellini, S.Ten Giacomo 216ª Sq, 53° Gr,
34° St Bt 103

Bellocchi, Cap Elio, 284ª Sq, 131° Gr As 433

Belloni, S.Ten Francesco 18ª Sq, 27° Gr,
8°St Bt 144

Bellotto, Cap Mario Co 143ª Sq Rm 22,514

Benedetti, Col Giovanni Co 10° St Bt 21,26

Berghino, M.Llo Rinaldo 20ª Sq, 46° Gr,
15° St Bt 56,57

Bergonzoli, Gen Annibale Co 23° Corpo
D'armata 125

Bernardi, Serg Duilio 393ª Sq,
160° Gr Aut Ct 284

Bernardini, Cap Orazio 279ª Sq As 230

Berni, Magg Ezio Co 45° Gr, 14° St Bt 21

Bertelli, Cap Ermine Co 58ª Sq,
32° Gr, 10° St Bt 21

Berti, Gen Mario Co 10ª Armata 52,54

Bertinelli, Serg Magg Italo 93ª Sq, 8° Gr,
2° St Ct 37

Bevilacqua, Ten Domenico 93ª Sq, 8° Gr,
2° St Ct, Co 77ª Sq, Co 365ª Sq 33,72,73,
298,424,425

Biagetti, S.Ten Vittorio 240° Sq, 98° Gr Bt
137

Bianchelli, Serg Magg Gianni 159ª Sq,
12° Gr Aut Ct 506

Bianchi, Serg Emilio 211ª Sq, 50 Gr Bt 479

Bianchi, Ten Enzo 155ª Sq, 3° Gr Aut Ct
499,503

Bianchi, Magg Luigi Co 155° Gr Ct
148,154,297,337,355,359

Biccolini, Ten Manlio 378ª Sq,
155° Gr Ct 154

Biffani, Serg Magg Guglielmo 73ª Sq,
9° Gr, 4° St Ct 88

Bilancia, Ten Antonio 175ª Sq Rst 54,55

Billi, Serg Danilo 94ª Sq, 8° Gr, 2° St Ct 70

Binetti, S.Ten Giulio 372ª Sq, 153° Gr Aut Ct
240,242

Bissoli, Ten Gioacchino 93ª Sq, 8° Gr, 2° St Ct
23,24,26

Bladelli, Serg Alessandro 90ª Sq, 10° Gr,
4° St Ct 27,38,43

Bobba, Cap Guido Co 74ª Sq, 23° Gr Ct
102,103

Boetto, Cap Armando Co 49ª Sq, 38° Gr,
32° St Bt 180,184

Bogoni, Serg Gino 367 Sq, 151 Gr Ct 89

Bolagna, Serg Magg Riccardo 279ª Sq As 230

Bolognesi, Serg Valeriano 155ª Sq,
3° Gr Aut Ct 441

Bombardini, Serg Alfredo 97ª Sq, 9° Gr,
4° St Ct 358,376

Bonato, Serg Gino 153ª Sq, 3° Gr Aut Ct 505

Bonazza, Serg Aldo 352ª Sq, 20° Gr Ct 363

Bonelli, Serg Magg Otello 352ª Sq,
20° Gr Ct 255,366

Bonfatti, Ten Piero 73ª Sq, 9° Gr,
4° St Ct 89,93,97,98,99

Bonfiglio, Ten Giuseppe 351ª Sq,
155° Gr Ct 355

Bonzano, T.Col Mario Co 20° Gr Ct 254,
255,296,363,366

Bordoni-Bisleri, Ten Franco 95ª Sq, 18° Gr Ct
135,136,156,158,160,212

Borgogno, Cap Luigi Co 352ª Sq, 20° Gr Ct
255,296,366

Borreo, Serg Magg Anano 88ª Sq, 6° Gr,
1° St Ct 425

Bosi, M.Llo Vasco 4ª Sq, 11° Gr,
13° St Bt 335,337

Botta, S.Ten Giuseppe 77ª Sq, 13° Gr,
2° St Ct 77,95

Botto, Magg Ernesto Co 9° Gr, 4° St Ct 34,
35,41,67,68,78,86,87,88,111

Bozzi, Serg Francesco 368ª Sq, 151° Gr Aut Ct
493

Braida, Ten Pietro 210ª Sq, 50° Gr Bt 485

Brambilla, Ten Alfredo 209ª Sq Bat 264

Brambilla, T.Col Bruno Co 17° Gr Ct 298,
363,378,382,384

Bresciani, S.Ten Guido 233ª Sq, 60° Gr,
41° St Bt 99

Brescianini, Cap Venanzio Co 6ª Sq,
44° Gr, 14° St Bt 21

Bressanelli, Cap Luigi Co 55ª Sq,
30° Gr, 10° St Bt 21

Brigadue, S.Ten Dario 37ª Sq Oa 40

Briguglio, Av Sc Sante 3ª Sq, 43° Gr,
13° St Bt 422

Broganelli, Ten Elio 154ª Sq, 3° Gr Aut Ct
184,504

Broilo, Serg Remo 71ª Sq, 17° Gr,
1° St Ct 378,389

Brombini, S.Ten Livio 215ª Sq, 52° Gr,
34° St Bt 106

Bruni, Ten Brunetto 175ª Sq Rst 100

Bulgarelli Cap Loris Co 60ª Sq, 33° Gr Aut Bt
36,57,93

Buogo Serg Egidio 71ª Sq, 17° Gr,
1° St Ct 363,389

Burroni, Ten Mario 168ª Sq, 16° Gr,
50° St Ass 53,57

Buscaglia, Ten Carlo Emanuele 278ª Sq As
58,402

Buvoli, M.Llo Aldo 378ª Sq, 155° Gr Ct 496

Cabassi, Ten Giulio 58ª Sq, 32° Gr,
10°St Bt 36

Caiani, Ten Dario 234ª Sq, 60° Gr,
41° St Bt 94,96

Cainero, Serg Luciano 209ª Sq Bat 264

Calistri, Cap Pietro Co 75ª Sq,
23° Gr Ct 106,107

Callieri, Cap Gino Co 360ª Sq, 155° Gr Ct
148,241,273,296

Callori Di Vignale, S.Ten Raniero 145ª Sq Rm
60

Calosso, Magg Carlo Co 151° Gr Aut Ct 53,
71,72,89,93,94,104

Calzolari, Serg Magg Giulio 19ª Sq,
28° Gr, 8° St Bt 191

Camarda, Cap Domenico Co 79ª Sq, 6° Gr,
1° St Ct 298,386,390

Camerini, Serg Antonio 366ª Sq,
151° Gr Aut Ct 124,125,346,347

Campanini, Serg Nino 82ª Sq, 13° Gr,
2° St Ct

Canè, S.Ten Giuseppe 215ª Sq, 52° Gr,
34° St Bt 106

Cannaviello Magg Vittorio 281ª Sq As 191

Cantarella, Cap Raffaele Co 175ª Sq Rst 294

Cantelli, M.Llo Romolo 160ª Sq, 12° Gr,
50° St Ass 42,414

Cantù, S.Ten Giuseppe 375ª Sq,
160° Gr Aut Ct 345,347

Capelli, Ten Carlo 235ª Sq, 60° Gr,
41° St Bt 70

Capellini, S.Ten Ottorino 71ª Sq,
17° Gr, 1° St Ct 363,376

Capogrossi, Ten Armando 368ª Sq,
151° Gr Aut Ct 498

Caponigro, Serg Magg Ersio 353ª Sq, 255

Caporali, S.Ten Ruggero 91ª Sq, 10° Gr,
4° St Ct 103

Cappa, S.Ten Francesco 280ª Sq As 180,184

Cappellini, Serg Icaro 145ª Sq Rm 60

Capriata, Serg Vinicio 209ª Sq Bat 420,421

Caprini, Cap Antonio 62ª Sq, 29° Gr,
9° St Bt 64

Capuano, 1 Av Salvatore 170 Sq Rm 514

Carabini, Ten Angelo 13ª Sq, 26° Gr,
9° St Bt 76

Caracciolo, Ten Gianni 360ª Sq, 155° Gr Ct
172,253

Caraffa, Ten Italo 175ª Sq Rst 89,91

Cardano, Serg Magg Arturo 94ª Sq, 8° Gr,
2° St Ct 32,33

Cardini, Serg Giuseppe 159ª Sq, 12° Gr,
50° St Ass 126

Carini, Ten Mario 72ª Sq, 17° Gr, 1° St Ct
376

Carmignani, Serg Elio 384ª Sq,
157° Gr Aut Ct 360

Caroli, Serg Magg Luigi 351ª Sq,
155° Gr Ct 164,337

Carrari, Serg Renato 364ª Sq, 150° Gr Aut Ct
436

Casali, Cap Mario Co 218ª Sq,
33° Gr Aut Bt; 244ª Sq 36,296

Casero, Serg Giovanni 91ª Sq, 10° Gr,
4° St Ct 107

Casolla, Ten Francesco 43ª Sq, 35° Gr,
33° St Bt 41

Castro, S.Ten Ivo 215ª Sq, 52° Gr,
34° St Bt 106

Cattani, Serg Dino 152ª Sq, 2° Gr Aut Ct 111,112

Cavalca, Serg Magg Guerrino 154ª Sq, 3° Gr Aut Ct 180

Cazminati, S.Ten Angelo 386ª Sq, 157° Gr Ct 490

Ceard, Ten Vittorio 56ª Sq, 30° Gr, 10° St Bt 47

Ceccacci, Cap Corrado Co 165ª Sq, 12° Gr Aut Ct 294

Ceccaroni, Ten Mendes 209ª Sq Bat 422

Cecchi, Serg Magg Trento 94ª Sq, 8° Gr, 2° St Ct 32,33

Ceccotti, Cap Livio 367ª Sq 151° Gr Aut Ct 123

Celentano, S.Ten Agostino 150ª Sq, 2° Gr Aut Ct 227

Celotto, Cap Antonio Co 219ª Sq, 54° Gr Aut Bt 36

Cenni, Cap Giuseppe Co 239 Sq, Gr Bat 199

Ceoletta, Serg Giovanni Battista 91ª Sq, 10° Gr, 4° St Ct 26,40,41,107

Cerne, Magg Bruno Co 46° Gr, 15° St Bt; Co 15° Gr Oa 20,297

Cerofolini, S.Ten Gilberto 82ª Sq, 13° Gr, 2° St Ct 61,62,77

Cerutti, Cap Alessandro 236ª Sq Aut Bat 294

Cesare, M.Llo Giulio 366ª Sq 151° Gr Aut Ct 99

Cesaro, Serg Elio 152ª Sq, 2° Gr Aut Ct 141

Chellini, S.Ten Lorenzo 72ª Sq, 17° Gr, 1° St Ct 363,444

Chiantia, Ten Tanrico 201ª Sq, 92° Gr, 39° St Bt 471

Chiarini, Ten Guglielmo 82ª Sq, 13° Gr, 2° St Ct 38,60,73,77,86,88,124

Chiarmetta, Serg Cesare 366ª Sq 151° Gr Aut Ct 76,86

Ciapetti, S.Ten Cesare 154ª Sq, 3° Gr Aut Ct 184,501,504

Ciapparelli, S.Ten Bruno 153ª Sq, 3° Gr Aut Ct 505

Cigerza, Ten Giuseppe 1ª Sq, 11° Gr, 13° St Bt 333

Cima, S.Ten Natale 78ª Sq, 13° Gr, 2° St Ct 37,97,98

Cimolini, Cap Oscar 278ª Sq As 166,168

Cirillo, Serg Eraldo 174ª Sq Rst 414

Civale, Cap Giovanni Co 137ª Sq, 73° Gr Oa 22

Civetta, S.Ten Alfredo 88ª Sq, 6° Gr, 1° St Ct 425

Cocchia, Cap Vasc Aldo 204

Coci, S.Ten Giuseppe 279ª Sq As 518

Codignola, Ten Carlo 129ª Sq Oa 306

Colabucci, Ten Dante 145 Sq Rm 502

Colacicchi, T.Col Raffaello Co 151° Gr Aut Ct 104

Colauzzi, Serg Magg Davide 368ª Sq 151° Gr Aut Ct 72,73,90,91,99

Colavolpe, Cap Nicola Co 54° Gr Aut Bt 36

Colli, S.Ten Pierluigi 170ª Sq Rm 514

Collovini, M.Llo Giovanni 81ª Sq, 6° Gr, 1° St Ct 404

Colombo, 1° Av Giacomo 236ª Sq Bat 154

Colombo, S.Ten Roberto 288ª Sq Rm 105,106

Como, S.Ten Cesare 143ª Sq Rm 47,48

Compagnone, Ten Paolo 175ª Sq Rst 98

Contarini, Serg Luigi 90ª Sq, 10° Gr, 4° St Ct 107

Conti, S.Ten Aldo 353ª Sq, 20° Gr Ct 240,242

Conti, Ten Giuseppe 129ª Sq Oa 342,345

Conti, Ten Pierfrancesco 71ª Sq, 17° Gr, 1° St Ct 363,378,390

Conti, Ten Vittorio 385ª Sq, 157° Gr Aut Ct 363

Contreras, Ten Vasc Giulio Co Alagi 508

Copello, Ten Carlo 278ª Sq As 181

Coppi, Col Giovanni Co 14° St Bt 21

Corda, Ten Virgilio 159ª Sq, 12° Gr, 50° St Ass 25,26

Corsi, Serg Magg Ugo 84ª Sq, 10° Gr, 4° St Ct 27

Cortinovis, Ten Eugenio 241 Sq, 98° Gr Bt 505

Costantini, Cap Giuseppe Co 367ª Sq, 151° Gr Aut Ct 298

Cottarelli, S.Ten Sergio 232ª Sq, 59° Gr, 41° St Bt 94,96

Covacovich, Magg Nicola 143ª Sq Rm 64

Covre, Serg Magg Tullio 353ª Sq, 20° Gr Ct 255,363

Crestani, Serg Onorino 84ª Sq, 10° Gr, 4° St Ct 91,92

Crivellini, Ten Laerte 209ª Sq Bat 264

Crociati, Serg Silvio 90ª Sq, 10° Gr, 4° St Ct 30

Cudugnello, Magg Bruno Co 12° Gr, 50° St Ass 20,40,76,294

Cugnasca, Ten Carlo 351ª Sq, 155° Gr Ct 148,150,156,157,158

Curto, Cap Mario Co 234ª Sq, 60° Gr, 41° St Bt 69

D'agostini, Cap Mario Co 94ª Sq, 8° Gr Ct 298

D'agostinis, Cap Giuseppe Co 91ª Sq, 10° Gr, 4° St Ct 22,28,35,45

D'alessio, Ten Antonio 159ª Sq, 12° Gr, 50° St Ass 119

Dall'aglio, Cap Giuseppe Co 78ª Sq, 13° Gr, 2° St Ct 21,71

Dallari, Serg Magg Enrico 73ª Sq, 9° Gr, 4° St Ct 45,88,93

Damiani, M.Llo Rinaldo 97ª Sq, 9° Gr, 4° St Ct 358

D'aurelio, Gen Ba Venceslao Co Settore Centrale 296

Daverio, S.Ten Mario 239ª Sq Bat 214

Davico, Serg Magg Dante 77ª Sq, 13° Gr, 2° St Ct 73

De Bellis, Serg Ernesto 92ª Sq, 8° Gr, 2° St Ct 61,90

De Benedetti, S.Ten Neri 90ª Sq, 10° Gr, 4° St Ct 71,107

De Campo, Ten Valerio 73ª Sq, 9° Gr, 4° St Ct 45,88,93,97,98

De Fraia, S.Ten Nunzio 94ª Sq, 8° Gr, 2° St Ct 32,33

De Francesco, S.Ten Silvio 20ª Sq, 46° Gr, 15° St Bt 56,57

De Mattia, Magg Pietro Co 36° Gr, 33° St Bt 20

De Nunzio, Vladimiro 239ª Sq Bat 503

De Pascale, 1° Av Nazzareno 233ª Sq, 59° Gr, 41° St Bt 99

De Portis, Serg Magg Gastone 162ª Sq Ct 204

De Prato, Cap Tullio Co 150ª Sq, 2° Gr Aut Ct 111

De Seta, Ten Francesco Nucleo 2° St Ct 112, 114,355,491

De Silvestri, Serg Magg Renato 352ª Sq, 20° Gr Ct 255

De Vivo, M.Llo Francesco 159 Sq, 12 Gr, 50° St Ass 100

De Wittemberski, T.Col Ivo Co 98° Gr Bt 137,139,178,294

Deanna, Ten Giuseppe 97ª Sq, 9° Gr, 4° St Ct 402,403

Deggiovanni, Ten Luigi 154ª Sq, 3° Gr Aut Ct 506

Degli Espost, Serg Guido 12ª Sq Apc 347

Del Curto, Ten Ugo 175ª Sq Rst 142

Del Dotto, Ten Fortunato 22ª Sq, 45° Gr, 14° St Bt 88

Del Fabbro, Serg Giovanni 378ª Sq, 155° Gr Ct 256

Del Prete, Cap Giampiero Co 151ª Sq, 20° Gr Ct 255

Della Ciana, Serg Augusto 233ª Sq, 59° Gr, 41° St Bt 99

Dell'antonio, Ten Carlo 175ª Sq Rst 477

Dell'oro, Cap Antonio Co 159ª Sq, 12° Gr, 50° St Ass 20,26,41,47,67

Dentis, M.Llo Carlo 75ª Sq, 23° Gr Ct 119

Dequal, Magg Vincenzo Co 278ª Sq As 46,64

Desideri, M.Llo Giuseppe 375ª Sq, 160° Gr Aut Ct 285

Devoto, S.Ten Bruno 91ª Sq, 10° Gr, 4° St Ct 106

Di Barberino, Gen Ba Raul Co Settore Ovest 20,294

Di Frassineto, Ten Roberto 11ª Sq, 26° Gr, 9° St Bt 73

Di Giglio, S.Ten Giuseppe 145ª Sq Rm 68

Di Luise, Magg Guglielmo 281ª Sq As 191

Marini, Cap Giulio Co 279ª Sq As 251,252, 280,297,402,443,518,519

Marini, Ten Marino 280ª Sq As 180,184

Marinucci, Serg Alvino 152ª Sq, 2° Gr Aut Ct 172

Marsan, Cap Simeone Co 367ª Sq, 151° Gr Aut Ct 53,99

Marsilli, M.Llo Pio 80ª Sq, 17° Gr, 1° St Ct 389

Martina, M.Llo Achi!le 71ª Sq, 17° Gr, 1° St Ct 376

Martinelli, Ten Tullio 378ª Sq, 155° Gr Ct 337,355

Martinoli, Serg Teresio 78ª Sq, 13° Gr, 2° St Ct; 73ª Sq 73,100,107,490

Martissa, Ten Enzo 91ª Sq, 10° Gr, 4° St Ct 27,38,39,44,45

Marzuoli, S.Ten Pasquale 174ª Sq Rst 413, 414

Masenti, Serg Magg Ezio 78ª Sq, 13° Gr, 2° St Ct; 368ª Sq 64,65,116,124

Masi, 1° Av Italo 239ª Sq Bat 214

Masoero, Cap Giovanni 21ª Sq, 46° Gr, 15° St Bt 56,57

Masperi, S.Ten Augusto 2° Gr Apc 113

Mastrodicasa, Ten Gaetano Co Sez Soccorso 297

Maurelli, Serg Francesco 233ª Sq, 59° Gr, 41° St Bt 99

Mauro, Ten Mario 374ª Sq, 153° Gr Aut Ct 355

Mayer-Ziotti, Cap Arturo Co 57ª Sq, 32° Gr, 10° St Bt 21

Mazza, S.Ten Pietro 26ª Sq Apc 124

Mazzetti, T.Col Felice Co 145° Gr Aut T 294

Mechelli, Serg Salvatore 78ª Sq, 13° Gr, 2° St Ct 37

Meille, Cap Valdo Co 233ª Sq, 59° Gr, 41° St Bt 69,99

Melchiorri, S.Ten Luigi 10ª Sq, 28° Gr, 8° St Bt 510

Menaldi, S.Ten Pietro 151ª Sq, 20° Gr Ct 255

Meneghetti, Serg Magg Nello 81ª Sq, 6° Gr, 1° St Ct 404

Menon, Ten Federico 53ª Sq, 47° Gr, 15° St Bt 100

Merlo, Ten Vittorio 353ª Sq, 20° Gr Ct 237

Meroni, S.Ten Pierluigi 60ª Sq, 33° Gr Aut Bt 93

Mezzatesta, S.Ten Giuseppe 160ª Sq 12° Gr, 50° St Ass 118,119

Mezzetti, Ten Felice 372ª Sq, 153° Gr Aut Ct 368,406

Mezzetti, T.Col Vezio Co 6° Gr, 1° St Ct 298, 378,401,402,403

Milazzotto, S.Ten Filippo 174ª Sq Rst 422, 423

Milella, Serg Magg Salvatore 366ª Sq, 151° Gr Aut Ct 104

Minelli, Serg Gustavo 96ª Sq, 9° Gr, 4° St Ct 92,97

Minervino, Cap Giovanni Co 67° Gr Oa 297

Minuto-Rizzo, Cap Oreste Co 357ª Sq, 157° Gr Aut Ct 298

Miolla, 1° Av Enrico 170ª Sq Rm 514

Miotto, Serg Elio 91ª Sq, 10° Gr, 4° St Ct 27,38

Mirrione, Serg Giuseppe 352ª Sq, 20° Gr Ct 255

Moccheggiani, S.Ten Giorgio 60ª Sq, 33° Gr Bt 94

Moci, Cap Paolo 41° Gr Bt 510

Modesti, Serg Magg Luigi 153ª Sq, 3° Gr Aut Ct 505

Modiano, S.Ten Guido 72ª Sq, 17° Gr, 1° St Ct 376

Moioli, Cap Amedeo 280ª Sq As 180

Molinari, Ten Serafino 351ª Sq, 155° Gr Ct 494

Molino, Col Pietro Co 50° St Ass 20

Molteni, Serg Magg Natale 160ª Sq, 12° Gr, 50° St Ass 119

Monaldi, Serg Girolamo 378ª Sq, 155° Gr Ct 355

Mondini, S.Ten Bruno 358ª Sq, 2° Gr Aut Ct 117

Montanari, Ten Fioravante 159ª Sq, 12° Gr, 50° St Ass 109,111

Montanari, M.Llo Paolo 98ª Sq, 7° Gr comb; 366ª Sq 55,347,497

Montanari, Ten Walter 19ª Sq, 28° Gr, 8° St Bt 305

Montazzoli, Ten Costanzo 3ª Sq, 43° Gr, 13° St Bt 422

Montefusco, Cap Mario Co 151ª Sq, 20° Gr Ct 234

Monterumici, Serg Amleto 90ª Sq, 10° Gr, 4° St Ct 30,43

Monti, T.Col Innocenzo Co 3° Gr Aut Ct 180, 294,424

Monti, Cap Luigi Co 84ª Sq, 10° Gr, 4° St Ct 22,27,28,43,45,92

Monti, Serg Nadio 92ª Sq, 8° Gr, 2° St Ct 52,53,69,423,424

Morassutti, Ten Mario 210ª Sq, 50° Gr Bt 192

Moresi, S.Ten Armando 96ª Sq, 9° Gr, 4° St Ct 78

Morettin, Serg Ferruccio 54ª Sq, 47° Gr, 15° St Bt 126

Morino, T.Col Pietro Co 27° Gr, 8° St Bt 296

Moroso, 1° Av Luigi 23ª Sq Apc 25

Munich, Serg Aurelio 375ª Sq, 160° Gr Aut Ct 347

Muraro, Serg Magg Mario 152ª Sq, Gr Aut Ct 109

Muratori, S.Ten Vittorio 92ª Sq, 8° Gr, 2° St Ct; 352ª Sq 61,251,255

Muscinelli, M.Llo Ottorino 358ª Sq, 2° Gr Aut Ct 118,119

Musch, Cap Gerardo Co 56ª Sq, 30° Gr, 10° St Bt 21,47,48

Mussi, Ten Camillo 56ª Sq, 30° Gr, 10° St Bt 47,48

Mussolini, Benito Head Of Italian Government 51,52,57,80

Musumeci, Cap Mario Co 16ª Sq, 2° Gr Apc 22

Muti, T.Col Ettore Co 41° Gr Bt 510

Nanin, Serg Francesco 366ª Sq, 151° Gr Ct 77,87,88

Napoleoni, T.Col Italo Co 26° Gr, 9° St Bt 53,71

Napoli, Col Silvio Co 15° St Bt 20, 26,28, 101

Niclot Doglio, Cap Furio 353ª Sq, 20° Gr Ct; Co 151ª Sq 233,234,296

Nicolai, Cap Nicola Co 136ª Sq, 64° Gr Oa 21

Nioi, Cap Clizio Co 80ª Sq, 17° Gr, 1° St Ct 298,389

Niggi, Cap Maurizio Co 22ª Sq, 45° Gr, 14° St Bt 21

Notari, S.Ten Alfonso 92ª Sq, 8° Gr, 2° St Ct 52.53

Novelli, M.Llo Raffaele 97ª Sq, 9° Gr, 4° St Ct 347,368

Nuti, S.Ten Alfonso 368ª Sq, 151° Gr Aut Ct 119

Oberweger, S.Ten Giorgio 352ª Sq, 20° Gr Ct 255,355

Oblach, S.Ten Giuseppe 73ª Sq, 9° Gr, 4° St Ct 93,99

Ocarso, Cap Dante Co 88ª Sq, 6° Gr, 1° St Ct 298,424,425,426

Olivetti, M.Llo Manlio 96ª Sq, 9° Gr, 4° St Ct 347

Ornani, 1°Av Dino 20ª Sq, 46° Gr, 15° St Bt 35

Ottaviani, Ten Carlo Felice 222ª Sq, 56° Gr, 39° St Bt 472

Ottaviani, Ten Edoardo 1ª Sq, 11° Gr, 13° St Bt 333

Padovani, Cap Piero Co 232ª Sq, 59° Gr, 41° St Bt 69

Pagliacci, Cap Giuseppe Co 44ª Sq, 35° Gr, 33° St Bt 20

Pagliani, S.Ten Romano 358ª Sq, 2° Gr Aut Ct 115

Pagliocchini, T.Col Roberto Co 43° Gr, 13° St Bt 296

Palamidessi, S.Ten Alessandro 209ª Sq Bat 264

Palazzeschi, Ten Antonio 81ª Sq, 6° Gr, 1° St Ct 403

Pallancini, Ten Lorenzo 150ª Sq, 2° Gr Ct 112

Palli, Ten Italo 372ª Sq, 153° Gr Aut Ct 285,331,333

Palli, Ten Ugo 378ª Sq, 155° Gr Ct 256

Palmieri, 1° Av Alfredo 233ª Sq, 59° Gr, 41° St Bt 99

Palumbo, Av Sc Matteo 209ª Sq Bat 441

Panante, Cap Guido 176ª Sq Rst 360

Pandolfi, Ten Bruno 235ª Sq, 60° Gr, 41° St Bt 100

Paolazzi, S.Ten Bruno 96ª Sq, 9° Gr, 4° St Ct 47

Paolini, Serg Ernesto 77ª Sq, 13° Gr, 2° St Ct 73

Paparatti, M.Llo Guido 368ª Sq, 151° Gr Aut Ct 96,119

Pappalepore, Serg Magg Giacomo 159ª Sq, 12° Gr, 50° St Ass 92

Pardi, M.Llo Egeo 374ª Sq, 153° Gr Aut Ct 242,355

Pardini, Serg Pardino 70ª Sq, 23° Gr Ct 108

Paroli, Ten Orfeo 368ª Sq, 151° Gr Aut Ct 88

Pascali, Av Sc Giuseppe 159ª Sq, 12° Gr, 50° St Ass 26

Passini, 1° Av Augusto 209ª Sq Bat 397

Pastorelli, Ten Roberto 60ª Sq, 33° Gr Aut Bt 53,67,294

Patriarca, Serg Magg Antonio 358ª Sq, 2° Gr Aut Ct 115,227

Patrizi, Serg Corrado 84ª Sq, 10° Gr, 4° St Ct 29

Pavan, Serg Ernesto 92ª Sq, 8° Gr, 2° St Ct 26,52,53

Pecchiari, Serg Magg Francesco 352ª Sq, 20° Gr Ct 255,366

Pecoraro, Serg Magg Gregorio 136ª Sq Oa 32

Pedemonte, M.Llo Tullio 145ª Sq Rm 494

Pegna, Cap Oscar 284ª Sq, 131° Gr As 443

Pelo, Ten Stefano 2ª Sq, 45° Gr, 14° St Bt 67

Penzo, Av Sc Flavio 209ª Sq Bat 264

Perdoni, Serg Luciano 84ª Sq, 10° Gr, 4° St Ct 100

Peri, Ten Amelio 67° Gr Oa 103

Perino, Gen Da Egisto 5ª Squadra Chief of Staff 124

Perno, Serg Magg Paolo 159ª Sq, 12° Gr, 50° St Ass 42,90

Perotti, Serg Magg Otello 97ª Sq, 9° Gr, 4° St Ct 88,92,93,358,376,403

Persico, Ten Mario 233ª Sq, 59° Gr, 41° St Bt; Co 5ª Sq 99,296

Perversi, Ten Gianfranco 77ª Sq, 13° Gr, 2° St Ct 72,73

Peselli, S.Ten Mario 372ª Sq, 153° Gr Aut Ct 242,286,287

Peterlini, S.Ten Aldo 216ª Sq, 53° Gr, 34° St Bt 103

Petrellese, Av Sc Alberto 209ª Sq Bat 241,242

Petrelli, Serg Magg Italo 154ª Sq, 3° Gr Aut Ct 504

Petrignani, Serg Spartaco 85ª Sq, 18° Gr Ct 205

Pezzè Ten Vittorio 73ª Sq, 9° Gr, 4° St Ct 34,43,45

Pezzi, Col Enrico Co 41° St Bt 69

Piacentini, Cap Duilio Co 52ª Sq, 27° Gr, 8° St Bt 296

Piazza, S.Ten Amedeo 241ª Sq, 98° Gr Bt 141

Piccaretta, Ten Cesare 10ª Sq, 28° Gr, 8° St Bt 259

Piccolomini, Ranieri 92ª Sq, 8° Gr, 2° St Ct 24,25,28,67,69

Piccone, S.Ten Carlo 394ª Sq, 160° Gr Aut Ct 285

Pillepich, Serg Narciso 84ª Sq, 10° Gr, 4° St Ct 28,55

Pilot, Cap Gualtiero Co 209ª Bat 441

Pinna, Cap Mario Co 74ª Sq, 23° Gr Ct 102, 108

Piovano, Cap Riccardo Co 1ª Sq, 11° Gr, 13° St Bt; Co 239ª Sq Bat 296,355

Piragino, T.Col Armando Co 10° Gr, 4° Stª Ct 22,27,28,35

Pirino, Col Antonio Co 13° St Bt 296

Pisetta, Serg Remo 85ª Sq, 18° Gr Ct 123

Pitaluga, Cap Vincenzo Co 7ª Sq, 44° Gr, 14° St Bt 21

Pittini, 1° Av Ruggero 239ª Sq Bat 234

Pittoni, Cap Egeo 374ª Sq, 153° Gr Ct 262, 264

Pivetti, Ten Loris 607ª Sq T 166

Pivetti, Serg Magg Riccardo 209ª Sq Bat 264

Pizzini, S.Ten Ivo 375ª Sq, 160° Gr Aut Ct 338

Pluda, Cap Mario Co 73ª Sq, 9° Gr, 4° St Ct 78

Poli, Serg Lido 73ª Sq, 9° Gr, 4° St Ct 44, 45

Polizzy, Ten Piero 79ª Sq, 6° Gr, 1° St Ct 400,403

Porro, Gen Sa Felice Co Aeronautica Della Libia 20,30,39,124

Porcarelli, Serg Magg Alfredo 151ª Sq, 20° Gr Ct 255

Porta, Serg Franco 82ª Sq, 13° Gr, 2° St Ct 60,61,62

Possemato, Cap Francesco 19ª Sq, 28° Gr, 8° St Bt 175

Pozza, Cap Ugo 67ª Sq, 34° Gr, 11° St Bt 471

Pozzati, Cap Mario Co 104ª Sq, 1° Gr Apc 21

Pozzati, Serg Vittorio 96ª Sq, 9° Gr, 4° St Ct 78

Pozzi, 1° Av Giovanni 209ª Sq Bat 264

Prati, S.Ten Luigi 90ª Sq, 10° Gr, 4° St Ct; 376ª Sq 92,228

Premrù, Ten Boris 233ª Sq, 59° Gr, 41° St Bt 99

Pretto, S.Ten Stanislao 1ª Sq, 11° Gr, 13° St Bt 272

Profumi, Cap Fortunato Co 2ª Sq, 45° Gr, 14° St Bt 21

Proner, Ten Luigi 98ª Sq, 7° Gr comb 68

Proserpio, S.Ten Mario 374ª Sq, 153° Gr Aut Ct 282

Pucci, Cap Edvige Co 13ª Sq, 26° Gr, 9° St Bt 53

Pugnali, Cap Silvio Co 43ª Sq, 35° Gr, 33° St Bt 20

Pulzetti, S.Ten Alfredo 279ª Sq As 443

Putti, Cap Carlo 284ª Sq, 131° Gr As 433

Putzu, Serg Francesco 97ª Sq, 9° Gr, 4° St Ct 78

Quarantelli, Ten Ezio 209ª Sq Bat 261,264, 420,421

Querci, S.Ten Alvaro 73ª Sq, 9° Gr, 4° St Ct 45

Raffaelli, Gen Ba Ferdinando Co Settore Est 124,296,350,402,401,402

Ragazzini, Cap Giacomo Co 209ª Sq Bat 261, 393

Ragonese, S.Ten Antonio 209ª Sq Bat 245, 261,264

Raimondi, Cap Piero Co 373ª Sq, 153° Gr Aut Ct 297,321,322

Raimondo, Cap Mario 174ª Sq Rst 423

Rallo, Ten Enrico 222ª Sq, 56° Gr, 39° St Bt 472

Ranieri, Ten Guglielmo 279ª Sq As 280,402

Ravizza, Ten Piero 18ª Sq, 28° Gr, 8° St Bt 333

Rea, 1° Av Alessandro 10ª Sq, 28° Gr, 8° St Bt 510

Rebec, Cap Adolfo 205ª Sq, 41° Gr Bt 510

Regnoli, Cap Aldo Co 125ª Sq Oa 297

Reiner, Ten Giulio 73ª Sq, 9° Gr, 4° St Ct 67,68,88,93,97,98

Remorino, Cap Alberto Co 54ª Sq, 47° Gr, 15° St Bt 20

Renzi, M.Llo Norino 73ª Sq, 9° Gr, 4° St Ct 44,45

Revello, Serg Ernesto 157° Gr Ct 371

Revetria, Magg Secondo Co 13° Gr, 2° St Ct 21,77

Riccardi, S.Ten Giuseppe 351ª Sq, 155° Gr Ct 337

Ricci, 1° Av Oscar 209ª Sq Bat 245

Ricci, Serg Rino 152ª Sq, 2° Gr Aut Ct 169

Ricotti, Serg Magg Annibale 368ª Sq, 151° Gr Aut Ct 99,119

Rinaldi, Serg Vito Nucleo 2° St Ct 491

Rinaldo, Cap Antonio 103ª Sq Apc 501

Rivoli, Cap Ugo 280ª Sq As 180

Rizzati, Serg Graziadio 96ª Sq, 9° Gr, 4° St Ct 43,95

Robone, Ten Guido 278ª Sq As 58,166,182

Rocchetta, M.Llo Erberto 372ª Sq,
153° Gr Aut Ct 271

Roggero, Ten Giovanni 60ª Sq,
33° Gr Aut Bt 57

Romagna, Serg Magg Gabriele 72ª Sq,
17° Gr, 1° St Ct 363

Romagnoli, Magg Carlo Co 10° Gr, 4° St Ct
35,41,43,45,101,102,103,106,107

Romandini, M.Llo Vittorio 91ª Sq, 10° Gr,
4° St Ct 27

Romanese, Cap Marco Co 209ª Sq Bat 245,
261,264

Romanini, 1° Av Gianni 278ª Sq As 166

Ronzi, Cap Ferruccio Co 174ª Sq Aut Rst 296

Rosa, Serg Aldo 91ª Sq, 10° Gr, 4° St Ct 45

Rosica, Ten Vasc Gino Co Achille Papa 241

Rosselli, 1° Av 98ª Sq, 7° Gr Ass 68,69

Rossi, S.Ten Bruno 56ª Sq, 30° Gr, 10° St Bt
47

Rossi, T.Col Giuseppe Co 30° Gr, 10° St Bt
21

Rossi, Serg Pasquale 91ª Sq, 10° Gr, 4° St Ct
99

Rossini, S.Ten Gioacchino 10ª Sq, 28° Gr,
8° St Bt 243

Rosso, Serg Alfredo 357ª Sq, 157° Gr Aut Ct
406

Roveda, Cap Riccardo Co 353ª Sq, 20° Gr Ct
255,296,345,366

Rovelli, Ten Luigi 281ª Sq As 413,424

Ruggiero, Ten Giovanni Co 11ª Sq, 26° Gr,
9° St Bt 53

Rusconi, Serg Ambrogio 91ª Sq, 10° Gr,
4° St Ct 107

Russino, S.Ten Guglielmo 154ª Sq,
3° Gr Aut Ct 505

Saccani, Serg Magg Elvio 373ª Sq, 153°
Gr Aut Ct 352

Sacchetti, Ten Raimondo 368ª Sq, 151°
Gr Aut Ct 76

Sagliaschi, M.Llo Ennio 159ª Sq, 12°
Gr, 50° St Ass 90,92

Saiani, Serg Renato 79ª Sq, 6° Gr, 1° St Ct
386,390

Sala, S.Ten Augusto 145ª Sq Rm 494

Salandin, Ten Lino 217ª Sq, 53° Gr, 34° St Bt
108

Salvatore, Serg Magg Massimo 97ª Sq, 9° Gr,
4° St Ct 88,347,364,366

Salvi, S.Ten Eugenio 95ª Sq, 18° Gr Ct 119

Sanguettoli, Serg Giuseppe 74ª Sq, 23° Gr Ct
119

Sant'andrea, Cap Vincenzo Co 160ª Sq,
12° Gr Aut Ct 294

Santavicca, S.Ten Italo 78ª Sq, 13° Gr,
2° St Ct 29

Santonocito, Serg Domenico 84ª Sq, 10° Gr,
4° St Ct 55

Santucci, Serg Aldo 160ª Sq, 12° Gr,
50° St Ass 32

Sappa, Ten Renzo 373ª Sq, 153° Gr Aut Ct
356,358

Sarasino, Serg Franco 97ª Sq, 9° Gr, 4° St Ct
62,68

Sarti, Ten Corrado 160ª Sq, 12° Gr,
50° St Ass 55,56,118,119

Sartof, Ten Sergio 22ª Sq, 45° Gr, 14° St Bt
86,88

Savini, Serg Magg Angelo 90ª Sq, 10° Gr,
4° St Ct 45

Savoia, Ten Giorgio 92ª Sq, 8° Gr, 2° St Ct
28

Scagliarini, M.Llo Bruno 233ª Sq, 59° Gr,
41° St Bt 99

Scagliarini, Cap Giovanni 233ª Sq,
60° Gr, 41° St Bt 96

Scaglioni, Serg Giuseppe 84ª Sq, 10° Gr,
4° St Ct 26,29,40,41

Scandone, Ten Felice 46ª Sq, 36° Gr, 33° St Bt
54

Scaramucci, Serg Magg Pietro 159ª Sq,
12° Gr, 50° St Ass 90,499

Scardapane, Serg Magg Ugo 281ª Sq As 444

Scarpetta, Cap Piergiuseppe Co 384ª Sq,
157° Gr Aut Ct 298

Scattaglia, T.Col Michele Co 35° Gr,
33° St Ct 20

Schiroli, S.Ten Sante 74ª Sq, 23° Gr Ct 108

Sella, Magg Spartaco Co 16° Gr, 50° St Ct 20

Serafini, Cap Bernardino Co 366ª Sq,
151° Gr Aut Ct 53,72,73,123,346,347

Serafino, M.Llo Lorenzo 378ª Sq, 155° Gr Ct
154

Serra, Col Antonio Co 30° St Bt 490

Sgorbati, S.Ten Roberto 88ª Sq, 6° Gr,
1° St Ct 425

Silvestri, Ten Andrea 19ª Sq, 28° Gr, 8° St Bt
407

Silvestri, Gen Ba Fernando Co Settore Est 21

Simionato, M.Llo Olindo 150ª Sq,
2° Gr Aut Ct 227

Simonetti, Serg Magg Michele 353ª Sq,
20° Gr Ct 243

Sinisi, M.Llo Vito 279ª Sq As 230

Sironi, Serg Cesare 70ª Sq, 23° Gr Ct 117

Socche, Ten Onorio 211ª Sq, 50° Gr Bt 479

Solaro, Ten Claudio 70ª Sq, 23° Gr Ct 103,
106,126

Sordini, Cap Alfredo Co 241ª Sq,
98° Gr Bt 141,294

Sorvillo, Ten Eduardo 77ª Sq, 13° Gr,
2° St Ct 95,96

Spada, Av Sc Martino 239ª Sq Bat 366

Spagnoletti, Ten Emanuele 236ª Sq Bat 445

Spagnolini, Cap Riccardo Co 352ª Sq,
155° Gr Ct 297

Spampinato, Serg Magg Pasquale 234ª Sq,
60° Gr, 41° St Bt 96

Sparapani, S.Ten Giuseppe 88ª Sq, 6° Gr,
1° St Ct 425

Speranza, Serg Magg Oreste 23ª Sq Apc 25

Spezzaferri, Cap Mario 278ª Sq As 181

Spigaglia, Ten Alberto 364ª Sq,
150° Gr Aut Ct 428

Spina, Serg Magg Francesco 367ª Sq,
151° Gr Aut Ct 96

Spitzl, Serg Magg Bruno 96ª Sq, 9° Gr,
4° St Ct 70,97,358

Squassoni, Serg Magg Felice 85ª Sq, 18° Gr Ct
185

Stabile, M.Llo Natalino 88ª Sq, 6° Gr,
1° St Ct 389

Stancanelli, Ten Vittorio 233ª Sq, 59° Gr,
41° St Bt 99

Stauble, Serg Sergio 73ª Sq, 9° Gr, 4° St Ct
93

Steffanina, S.Ten Luigi 239ª Sq Bat 366

Steppi, Serg Roberto 84ª Sq, 10° Gr,
4° St Ct 28,55,92,495,396

Sterchele, Serg Antonio 209ª Sq Bat 441

Sterzi, Cap Annibale Co 358ª Sq, 2° Gr Aut Ct
109,117,169,223,224

Strani, S.Ten Aligi 279ª Sq As 280,443,518

Sturla, S.Ten Guido 372ª Sq, 153° Gr Aut Ct
371

Sussi, S.T.V.Pietro 145ª Sq Rm 502

Suster, Cap Vittorio Nucleo Comunicazioni
Lati 112

Tadini, Ten Giovanni 94ª Sq, 8° Gr, 2° St Ct
32,33

Tagliani, Serg Renato 394ª Sq, 160° Gr Aut Ct
506

Tait, Serg Magg Giovanni 80ª Sq, 17° Gr,
1° St Ct 442,443

Talamini, Ten Renato 80ª Sq, 17° Gr, 1° St Ct
376

Tamanini, M.Llo Riccardo 374ª Sq,
153° Gr Aut Ct 277

Tarantini, Serg Magg Luciano 393ª Sq,
160° Gr Aut Ct 313

Tarantola, Serg Magg Ennio 239ª Sq Bat;
151ª Sq Ct 232,233,363,366

Tassinari, M.Llo Federico 151ª Sq,
20° Gr Ct 255

Tassinari, Serg Magg Secondo 372ª Sq,
153° Gr Aut Ct 264

Tattanelli, Cap Bruno Co 378ª Sq, 155° Gr Ct
148,154,157,297,338

Tedeschi, Cap Vincenzo Co 62ª Sq, 29° Gr,
9° St Bt 53

Teja, Cap Salvatore Co 152ª Sq, 2° Gr Aut Ct
169,172

Tellera, Gen Giuseppe Co 10ª Armata 125

Tempo, Av Sc Giuseppe 239ª Sq Bat 212

Tenchini, Ten Terzo 176ª Sq Rst 360

Terracciano, Cap Felice Co 18ª Sq, 27° Gr,
8° St Bt 296

Teta, S.Ten Giovanni 284ª Sq, 131° Gr As
443

Timolina, S.Ten Giuseppe 77ª Sq, 13° Gr,
2° St Ct 77

Tivegna, Magg Angelo Co 47° Gr, 15° St Bt
20

Tobia, S.Ten Renato 176ª Sq Rst 431

Tomaselli, Cap Pio Co 72ª Sq, 17° Gr,
1° St Ct 298,363

Tomelleri, S.Ten Celestino 19ª Sq, 28° Gr,
8° St Bt 286

Tonachella, S.Ten Amedeo 63ª Sq, 29° Gr,
9° St Bt 97

Tonello, Serg Magg Giovanni 374ª Sq,
153° Gr Aut Ct 284

Toni, Ten Armando 6ª Sq, 44° Gr, 14° St Bt
88

Torresi, S.Ten Giulio 77ª Sq, 13° Gr, 2° St Ct
30,38,39,86,88

Tosoni Pittoni, Cap Corv Franco Co Bagnolini
24

Tovazzi, Cap Giuseppe Co 154ª Sq,
3° Gr Aut Ct 294

Tozzi, Serg Magg Mario 79ª Sq, 6° Gr,
1° St Ct 403

Travaglini, Cap Eduardo 13° Gr Ct 95

Trevigni, 1°Av Antonio 53ª Sq, 47° Gr,
15° St Bt 48

Trocca, Cap Bruno Co 604ª Sq T 294

Trolla, S.Ten Ferdinando 232ª Sq, 59° Gr,
41° St Bt 99

Tucceri, Ten Angelo 241ª Sq, 98° Gr Bt
140,141

Tugnoli, Cap Giorgio Co 153ª Sq,
3° Gr Aut Ct 180,184,294

Turchi, Serg Mario 368ª Sq, 151° Gr Aut Ct
72,73,120

Unia, T.Col Carlo Co 32° Gr, 10° St Bt 21

Vaccari, Ten Riccardo 97ª Sq, 9° Gr, 4° St Ct
62,63,76,88

Valle, Serg Magg Antonio 73ª Sq, 9° Gr,
4° St Ct 45,88

Valsania, Ten Domenico 37ª Sq, 67° Gr Oa 34

Vanni, Ten Ivano 160ª Sq, 12° Gr, 50° St Ass
32

Vanni, Cap Vincenzo 91ª Sq, 10° Gr, 4° St Ct
55

Vanz, 1° Av Guido 209ª Sq Bat 394

Vatta, Ten Glauco 71ª Sq, 17° Gr, 1° St Ct
378,389,390

Veneziani, Ten Piero 366ª Sq, 151° Gr Aut Ct
93

Venosta, S.Ten Luigi 56ª Sq, 30° Gr, 10° St Bt
47,48

Venturi, Av Sc Guido 209ª Sq Bat 422

Vercesi, Ten Ambrogio 1ª Sq, 11° Gr,
13° St Bt 333

Vergna, S.Ten Arcadio 18ª Sq, 27° Gr,
8° St Bt 144

Vernesi, Cap Vezio Co 132ª Sq Oa 297

Veronesi, Serg Mario 77ª Sq, 13° Gr, 2° St Ct;
84ª Sq 73,104

Veronesi, Cap Natale Co 374ª Sq,
153° Gr Aut Ct 286,297

Vescovi, Serg Giovanni 352ª Sq, 20° Gr Ct
255

Vezzi, Serg Adriano 153ª Sq, 3° Gr Aut Ct
425,502

Vichi, Ten Francesco 358ª Sq, 2° Gr Aut Ct
109

Vicoli, Ten Luigi 57ª Sq, 32° Gr, 10° St Bt
34,35

Viglione Borghese, Cap Ezio Co 96ª Sq,
9° Gr, 4° St Ct 58,62,63,88,92,93,
298,347,358,376

Villa, Serg Aldo 373ª Sq, 153° Gr Aut Ct 308

Vimercati Sanseverino, Magg Ottaviano Co
Battaglione Sahariano 22

Visconti, Ten Adriano 23ª Sq Apc; 159ª Sq,
12° Gr, 50° St Ass 24,26,56,57,90,126

Visentin, Serg Magg Francesco 352ª Sq,
20° Gr Ct 237,255

Visentin, Ten Gino 57ª Sq, 32° Gr, 10° St Bt
47,48

Vitali, Ten Giuseppe 352ª Sq, 20° Gr Ct 117,
360,361,363

Vizzotto, T.Col Antonio Co 150° Gr Aut Ct
298,424,425,436,446

Weiss, S.Ten Antonino 160ª Sq, 12° Gr,
50° St Ass 31

Zaccaria, Serg Angelo 174ª Sq Rst 423

Zambaldi, Magg Ettore Co 69° Gr Oa 297

Zambelli, Serg Magg Armando 11ª Sq,
26° Gr, 9° St Bt 73

Zanardi, Cap Alfredo Co 167ª Sq, 16° Gr,
50° St Ass 20

Zanaria, Serg Angelo 153ª Sq, 3° Gr Aut Ct
184,502

Zanazzo, Cap Cesare Co 209ª Sq Bat 261,
264,296

Zancristoforo, S.Ten Arrigo 384ª Sq,
157° Gr Aut Ct 363

Zanello, S.Ten Pietro 378ª Sq, 155° Gr Ct
355

Zani, Serg Giuseppe 153ª Sq, 3° Gr Aut Ct
184

Zanni, T.Col Fernando Co 160° Gr Aut Ct
296

Zannier, Cap Martino Nino Co 92ª Sq,
8° Gr, 2° St Ct 22,26,298

Zardini, Serg Giuseppe 159ª Sq, 12° Gr,
50° St Ass 92,337,504

Zavadlal, Ten Bruno 372ª Sq, 153° Gr Aut Ct 286

Zelè, Cap Daniele Co 21ª Sq, 46° Gr, 15° St Bt
20,28

Zolesi, S.Ten Umberto 23ª Sq Apc 25

Zuccarini, S.Ten Gian Mario 77ª Sq,
13° Gr, 2° St Ct 30

Zuffi, Cap Giuseppe E. Co 368ª Sq,
151° Gr Aut Ct 96,119,298,493

British Commonwealth Units

Raf Middle East 11,13,135,178,179,189,
207,211,289,294,432,448

Ahq, Egypt 135

Hq, Western Desert 273,278,279,280,290,
291,292,305,314,395,408

Hq, Cyrenaica 127,150

Western Desert Air Force 303,311,422,423,
424,431,433,437,442,446,447

Groups

2 Group 493,501

201 Group 12,68,290,291,292,507,509,
511,512,513,515,519

202 Group 12,13,15,30,32,47,81,82,104,
127,128,129,132,150,292,478,513

203 Group 84

204 Group 129,150,157,160,177,178,179,
194,200,202,204,211,223,231,232,247,
261,290,460, 484,513,518

205 Group 290,291,292,462,463,468,469

206 Group 289

211 Group 290

Wings

Advanced Wing 11,12

1 (Bomber) Wing 11,12

1 (General Reconnaissance) Wing 12

2 (Bomber) Wing 11

86 Wing 12

232 Wing 291,351

233 Wing 291

234 Wing 291,402

235 Wing 291,292

250 Wing 12,292,480,485,487

251 Wing 12

252 Wing 12,59,66,81,110,124,292,475,
476,480,483,485,487,488

253 Wing 12,284,290,291,293

257 Wing 81,129,290,451,452,453,454,
455,456,458,460,462

258 Wing 81,130,136,141,147,150,172,
174,194,275,283,280,291,293,402,
303,318,332,343,344,379, 402,413,435

259 Wing 291

260 (Balloon) Wing 487

261 Wing 252,277,280,291,305

262 Wing 275,291,293,301,313,332,342,
403,405

263 Wing 291,293,302,440

264 Wing 280,291

265 Wing 280,281,291,309

268 Wing 291

269 Wing 275,280,291,293,402,404,405

270 Wing 280,281,291,293,322,370
272 Wing 291,351
273 Wing 291
3 Saaf Wing 291,293,305,310,314,316,368,
381,383,384,409
Z Wing 147

Squadrons
1 Squadron 75
6 Squadron 16,84,95,127,135,136,137,138,
143,147,148,152,156,160,173,176,177,
191,192,201,202,216,221,222,226,228,
229,230,231,232,234,246,252,265,268
8 Squadron 293,322
11 Squadron 11,81,84,94,95,114,115,179,
209,264,277,285,293,314,318,319,324,
330,331,348,349,350,370,382,384, 385,
389,419,421,442
14 Squadron 11,12,159,162,185,186,192,
194,196,197,198,199,203,216,225,230,
237,275,280,281,282,291,293, 313,
377,379,396,400,414,417,419,427
18 Squadron 391,394,502,503,504,505,519
21 Squadron 493,494
30 Squadron 11,12,16,27,30,40,41,43,55,
56,57,74,179,203,210,225,230,237,291,
293,305,310,351,402,413,422,427,428,
432,480, 481,483,485,586
31 Squadron 292,374,375
33 Squadron 11,12,15,25,26,27,28,29,30,
31,32,33,34,36,38,39,40,41,45,49,50,61,
65,71,72,73,74,75,77,78,81 84,86,87,88,
89,90,91,92,96,97,98,99,100,103,106,107,
109,115,124,125,128,177,186,206,211,
223,225,227,228,245,257,258,259,260,
264,270,271,272,275,277,278,279,280,
281,282,287,291,293,305,307,308,313,
314,316,319,329,331,336,337,341,346,
347,348,358,359,365,366,371,375,385,
389,393,394,399,400,405,406,407,412,
413,422,435,438,440,442,446,480,513,
514,515,519
37 Squadron 65,75,81,84,120,128,179,210,
292,449,450,451,453,455,456,457,458,
460,461,462,463,464,466,467,468,469
38 Squadron 65,75,81,84,120,210,292,449,
451,452,453,454,455,456,457,458,459,
460,461,462,463,464,465,467,469,499,
500,502
39 Squadron 81,84,115,160,161,174,178,
183,191,199,203,206,216,220,222,250,
251,252,280,281,282,292,508,509,510,
511,512,513,514,516,517,518,520, 521,
522
40 Squadron 462,501,503
45 Squadron 11,12,15,23,24,26,30,33,81,84,
88,89,91,92,104,106,107,108,120,124,
137,156,160,174,177,186,187,191,195,
197,199, 201,202,203,204,206,210,211,
216,264,277,279,281,282,284,291,293,

314,315,323,324,331,362,406,407,418
47 Squadron 146,162
55 Squadron 11,12,16,23,24,27,36,37,39,
42,46,50,52,54,63,67,68,70,71,78,84,
94,95,105,106,115,116,123,136,137,
141,146,148,156,160,164,166,167,172,
177,186,197,201,203,204
60 Squadron 11
69 Squadron 207,490,494,495,496,497,498,
500,514,516,517
70 Squadron 11,12,15,16,59,67,74,81,84,
179,210,292,449,450,451,453,454,455,
457,458,459,461,463,464,466,467,469,
492
72 Squadron 481
73 Squadron 75,81,84,94,96,97,98,99,103,
104,105,106,108,109,111,113,115,118,
122,123,124,125,126,127,131,133,134,
138,142,144,145,146,147,148,149,150,
151,152,153,154,155,156,157,158,165,
167,168,169,170,172,173,175,176,178,
185,186,191,192,194,196,199,204,205,
206,211,212,213,214,215,216,218,220,
222,223,228,230,231,232,234,235,237,
238,239,240,243,247,250,253,273,283,
291,292,310,341,351,373,374,375,376,
377,378,446,449,485,487,488
79 Squadron 147
80 Squadron 11,12,13,14,15,24,27,28,29,
30,31,41,43,44,46,47,48,49,50,52,54,55,
56,57,61,66,67,69,70,71,74,179,209,210,
234,285,291,293,302,306,316,320,322,
324,338,340,341,343,344,348,372,375,
377, 378,379,386,389,399,400,403,405,
412,421,428,431,432,446,471,482
82 Squadron 494,495,496
84 Squadron 11,66,70,71,74,137,209,210,
253,280,281,282,291,293,348,400,421,
469
86 Squadron 512
89 Squadron 487,488
90 Squadron 463,468
94 Squadron 162,179,211,258,278,285,291,
293,306,333,336,339,340,341,348,350,
365,371,375,379,382,384,391,392,393,
400,411,421,426,427,428,429,430,439,
442,478,479,480,481,483,485,486
104 Squadron 469,501,502,503
105 Squadron 498,499,500,501
107 Squadron 391,394,500,501,502,505,
506,519
108 Squadron 292,460,461,463,464,466,
467,468,469
109 Squadron 319,322,323,331,344,357,363
110 Squadron 496,497,498
112 Squadron 12,16,30,31,32,33,34,36,38,
39,40,47,48,49,52,54,71,73,77,78,84,
87,97,103,114,115,162,179,186, 210,
245,257,260,264,270,272,275,276,291,
293,301,306,307,310,315,318,319,320,

322,324,325,331,332,342,344,345,346,
352,355,360,362,363,365,366,374,377,
386,388,389,396,399,400,406,407,408,
409,411,412,413,414,420,425,426,427,
430,435,442,484,486
113 Squadron 14,16,23,24,25,27,30,31,32,
33,41,42,52,53,54,56,60,61,62,64,70,71,
72,79,84,88,99,107,113,179,210,216,
217,225,230,231,234,238,241,243,244,
252,253,259,271,277,278,279,280,281,
282,284,285,286,287,291,293,305,307,
308,314,315,389,428
117 Squadron 292
127 Squadron 210
139 Squadron 494
145 Squadron 147
148 Squadron 210,292,450,452,453,454,455,
456,457,458,459,460,462,463,466,467,
468,469, 490,491,492,493,494,496
158 Squadron 469
200 Squadron 189
203 Squadron 162,179,209,212,292,508,511,
512,513,514,515,516,517,518,519,522
208 Squadron 11,12,15,17,34,50,64,69,76,
84,115,116,119,127,135,179,187,209,
210,216,278,291,293,306,318,319,351,
412,417,421,428,430,440,441,443,444,
445
211 Squadron 11,12,15,23,24,26,30,34,35,
37,38,42,53,54,60,62,69,74,94,210
213 Squadron 171,189,190,199,216,217,
222,224,229,292,418,482,485,486,488
216 Squadron 11,14,16,29,36,59,69,74,84,
292,309,310,375,439,440,448,449,450,
451
220 Squadron 287,463
221 Squadron 501,504
223 Squadron 162,226,283,285,292,322,508
228 Squadron 15,32,43,53,60,68,84,207,509
229 Squadron 189,190,199,213,216,223,
224,225,226,227,229,231,238,239,243,
244,247,250,253,256,259,275,276,291,
293,320,322,324,331,333,334,336,337,
345,346,347,351,360,367,368,395,396,
400,403,412,414,419,420,421,426,435,
439,444,445
230 Squadron 15,28,29,32,49,64,69,84,
123,138,146,211,237,283,287,291,292,
314,324,332,341,359,368,370,393,394,
446,507,509,511,514,516,517,520,522,
523
238 Squadron 189,190,217,228,255,259,263,
278,279,282,291,293,306,324,331,333,
334,336,337,345,347,348,351,352,354,
358,359,367,368,377,379,395,396,412,
413,419,420,421, 428,432,443,445
249 Squadron 189
250 Squadron 162,189,215,216,217,223,
224,226,227,230,231,232,233,234,237,
238,240,242,243,245,246,251,252,253,

269,270,271,275,282,283,291,293,301,
315,317,318,319,321,322,333,334,336,
337,347,350,351,355,356,357,358,360,
362,363,364,366,370,376,377,378,382,
384,386,388,389,394,395,396,399,403,
404,405,406,407,408,409,411,412,413,
423,424,426,428,430,432,436,443,477,
478,479,479,480

252 Squadron 189,194,204,205,206,211,224,
254,331,359,425,432,433,485,505,508,
509,519,520

260 Squadron 189,281,291,293,306,310,333,
348,351,378,391,393,394,395,396,400,
404,411,413, 421,426,428,430,431

261 Squadron 189,210

267 Squadron 50,66,67,84,138,148,149,159,
291

272 Squadron 204,217,226,251,252,254,256,
277,283,292,293,308,309,310,311,313,
314,317,318,320,322,331,335,336,337,
341,342,344,345,347,348,353,359,366,
367,368,370,384,385,388,389,393,394,
399,400,405,408,409,410,411,420,421,
431,432,433,481,485,499,508,509,513,
519,520

274 Squadron 13,49,50,54,56,63,75,75,81,
84,86,87,88,89,90,91,92,93,94,95,96,97,
98,99,100,102,107,108,109,110,111,
112,113,115,116,117,118,120,125,126,
134,137,147,160,163,164,165,166,168,
171,173,174,175,176,177,178,185,186,
187,189,191,194,196,197,198,199,200,
201,202,203,204,205,206,207,211,213,
214,215,216,217,218,220,221,223,225,
227,228,230,233,234,245,273,278,283,
291,293,308,311,313,314,315,317,318,
320,322,331,335,336,337,370,372,375,
377,378,392,393,394,395,396,404,407,
413,414,422,440,441,442,445,476, 486

335 Squadron 444

450 Squadron 188,190

451 Squadron 188,234,238,244,254,259,
260,264,268,270,271,272,275,280,291,
293,301,302,306,314,315,318,321,322,
325,347,383,403,432

601 Squadron 480

3 Raaf Squadron 36,49,65,74,77,79,84,
87,89,91,93,97,102,103,116,117,126,
127,130,131,132,133,134,138,139,140,
141,142,143,144,145,147,148,150,154,
156,157,158,159,160,189,257,259,261,
264,266,267,269,275,276,277,278,284,
285,286,293,310,314,315,318,319,323,
329,331,332,344,345,346,347,352,353,
354,355,356,357,375,377,378,379,386,
388,389,392,393,394,395,396,400,413,
414,420,421,424,425,427,428,430,432,
435,436,442,443

10 Raaf Squadron 178

1 Saaf Squadron 162,178,185,186,187,191,

192,193,204,206,211,212,213,214,216,
218,220,223,224,225,227,230,233,234,
238,240,242,244,247,248,252,253,257,
266,267,271,273,279,280,291,293,301,
306,308,314,317,319,344,348,349,350,
357,360,362,364,365,366,367,368,369,
370,372,386,388,389,392,393,394,400,
402,403,404,422,432,441,476, 477

2 Saaf Squadron 162,204,216,220,222,223,
224,239,240,241,244,247,248,249,251,
253,254,255,256,257,261,264,271,272,
275,276,277,279,284,285,286,291,293,
301,308,309,321,322,334,341,344,348,
358,359,360,364,365,366,373,375,377,
378,380,381,386,389,392,393,399,400,
403,404,408,409,411,412,422,424,432,
441,489,484

3 Saaf Squadron 162

4 Saaf Squadron 273,284,291,293,301,302,
314,318,321,322,333,334,336,337,338,
341,365,380,381,382,384,386,388,389,
393,399,400,403,404,408,409,411,412,
414,423,424,431,441

12 Saaf Squadron 161,162,204,230,231,244,
248,250,252,258,260,269,270,272,273,
279,284,285,286,287,291,293,306,307,
308,310,314,315,341,383,384,385,388,
404,405,409,410,513

14 Saaf Squadron 162

21 Saaf Squadron 161,252,264,265,266,270,
279,282,284,285,286,287,291,293,301,
308,310,313,314,316,318,319,325,334,
377,383,384,385,389,399,404,405,409,
432

24 Saaf Squadron 161,162,194,196,199,200,
203,204,205,206,207,214,216,218,220,
225,230,243,244,247,250,252,260,264,
265,283,291,293,309,322,334,337,338,
341,348,368,370,380,381,403,405,408,
409

40 Saaf Squadron 211,301,302,314,321,
403,432

60 Saaf Squadron 162,280,283,290,292

2 (Yugoslav) Squadron 190,292,507,519,520

13 (Hellenic) Squadron 190,292,507

Lorraine Squadron/Grb1 281,282,291,293,
321,350,362,367,406,407,509

Alsace Squadron/Gc 1 173,205,432

2 Reaf Squadron 12,59,476,486

5 Reaf Squadron 12,59,476,480,486

Flights

431 Flight 489,490

1411 (Met) Flight 290

1437 Flight 290,292

Asr Flight 290,292,511,517

K Flight 81,162

X Flight 209,510

Miscellaneous Units

1 Gru 179,292,473,474,475,477

1 Raaf Air Ambulance 292,372,373,374,
375,378,518

1 Pru 13

2 Pru 135,136,203,271,272,291,302,358,359

3 Aacu 489

Raf 2nd Armoured Car Company 80

971(Balloon) Squadron 475,478

Commonwealth Air Training Plan 209

Fleet Air Arm Units

773 Squadron 509

802 Squadron 34

803 Squadron 166,168,169,182,183,210,
245,412

805 Squadron 185,196,210,226,227,240,
245,271,291,310,334,335,337,381,413,
480

806 Squadron 58,60,64,81,165,166,168,169,
182,183,184,185,186,210,228,245,413,478

807 Squadron 180,181,183

808 Squadron 180,181,183

813 Squadron 34

815 Squadron 58,210,466,509,511,515

819 Squadron 58,492

824 Squadron 34,37

826 Squadron 255,293,357,465,466,467,
493,509,512,522

828 Squadron 469,502,504

829 Squadron 493,509

830 Squadron 186,489,491,492,493,494,496,
498,499,500,502

RNFS 244,245,247,249,251,252,256,267,
270,278,280,291,293,310,316,318,319,
320,334,336,337,344,351,356,357,359,
365,376,381,382,386,413,432,442

RN Fulmar Flight 283,291,359,413,517

Operational Training Units/Reserve Pools

70(Middle East) Otu 13,81,289

71 Otu 271,289

73 Otu 289

74 Otu 289

Middle East Pool 289

Training & Reserve Pool 289

Flying Training Schools

4 Fts 13

Air Stores Parks

1 Middle East Asp 12

12 Middle East Asp 12

31 Middle East Asp 12,155,289

32 Asp 13,289

33 Asp 289

34 Asp 289

36 Asp 289

37 Asp 289

38 Asp 289

Air Ministry Experimental Stations
(Radar Stations)
204 Ames 480
216 Ames 134,178,485
219 Ames 480
235 Ames 485
254 Ames 480
259 Ames 480

Maintenance Units
10 Mu 22
101 Mu 12
102 Mu 12,61
103 Mu 12
108 Mu 81

Repair And Salvage Units
51 R & Su 12,289
52 R & Su 289
53 R & Su 13,289
54 R & Su 289
55 R & Su 289
56 R & Su 289
57 R & Su 289,518
58 R & Su 289
59 R & Su 289
61 R & Su 289

Wireless Operating Units
13 Wou 480
17 Wou 480

Personnel Transfer Units
21 Ptc 289
22 Ptc 289
23 Ptc 289
24 Ptc 289

Luftwaffe Units
4.Luftflotte 476,479
Ii. Fliegerkorps 300,301
Viii.Fliegerkorps 477,479
X.Fliegerkorps 209,300,301,474,475,
476,477,492,493
Fliegerführer Afrika 209,300

Fighter Units
7./Jg 26 211,222,225,227,228,229,230,
232,238,239,241,242,243,247,250,267
Stab/Jagdgeschwader 27 299,301,431
I./Jg 27 162,167,170,172,174,175,191,
202,211,214,216,218,220,221,222,237,
238,239,240,245,249,250,258,265,268,
269,270,277,299,316,319,337,346,348,
354,355,363,377,378,392,395,396,402,
423,426,427,428,431,436,440
1./Jg 27 163,164,165,166,168,170,172,
176,187,193,215,220,222,224,227,231,
232,238,240,242,243,249,251,252,253,
255,256,258,260,264,265,270,277,302,
307,308,310,313,315,319,322,324,332,
337,338,341,345,347,348,350,358,366,
369,371,380,384,391,394,409,410,411,
424,427
2./Jg 27 163,169,187,200,202,212,213,
218,221,222,224,227,230,231,232,246,
247,250,253,275,277,278,279,380,381,
382,384,392,394,396,400,403,405,407,
413,414,427,428
3./Jg 27 163,171,172,175,176,177,178,
183,184,187,191,220,222,223,224,227,
231,232,233,234,240,252,253,258,259,
260,264,266,267,270,276,277,280,364,
366,368,371,375,377,380,381,382,384,
392,394,400,403,404,410,421,424,425,
426
Ii./Jg 27 265,266,271,272,273,279,280,
282,287,299,314,322,332,334,335,337,
341,342,345,350,352,363,365,366,378,
380,394,403,405,412,419,421,422,423,
428,429,431,442
4./Jg 27 266,268,272,273,282,309,310,
319,322,332,337,345,350,355,358,363,
366,368,371,374,375,382,384,399,405,
407,422,427,428,442
5./Jg 27 266,272,273,279,302,315,318,321,
332,337,355,358,361,366,367,368,369,
371,377,380,392,394,407,424,431
6./Jg 27 266,278,279,351,366,369,371,419,
422,442
Iii./Jg 27 299,367,376,399,410,411,414,415,
421,431
7./Jg 27 368,407,415,427
8./Jg 27 368,411,412
9./Jg 27 368,389,403,404,411
Iii./Jg 52 456
Stab/Jg 53 300,301
I./Jg 53 300,301
Ii./Jg 53 300,301
Iii./Jg 53 300,366,371,376,380,384,385,
388,396,400
7./Jg 53 376,382,384,389,393,394,396,
399,400,408
8./Jg 53 376,392,394,405
9./Jg 53 376,388,389,391,394,397
Jabost/Jg 53 431
Stab/Jg 77 204,205
Ii./Jg 77 197,198,199,200
5./Jg 77 197,198,199
6./Jg 77 197,199,202
Iii./Jg 77 194,456
8./Jg 77 202
9./Jg 77 195,204
I.(Jagd)/Lehrgeschwader 2 194,195,200,202
I./Zerstörergeschwader 26 121
2./Zg 26 121,206
Iii./Zerstörergeschwader 26 121,122,130,
132,133,137,138,141,142,143,148,151,
152,153,154,156,157,158,160,164,166,
177,205,212,225,227,237,238,248,299,
301,308,310,338,342,344,362,363,373,
389,394,411,415,416,431,444,445,515
7./Zg 26 121,141,149,150,152,157,158,
160,310,341,373,375,445,519
8./Zg 26 121,153,174,177,213,227,233,
234,239,243,247,250,265,310,315,319,
338,341,345,375,385,389,391,394
9./Zg 26 121,141,181,184,310,322,341,
345,347,375,411
I./Nachtjagdgeschwader 2 301,332,337,385,
389,391,392,394,464
Nachtjagdgeschwader 3 244,265,283,460,515

Bomber Units
I./Kampfgeschwader 2 205,206
2./Kg 4 122,475,476
Ii./Kg 4 476,478,479
4./Kg 4 478,479
Ii./Kg 26 115,121,122,133,134,150,152,
205,206,234,299,476,477,481,483,485
4./Kg 26 184,475,476
5./Kg 26 182,184,475,476,480,483,486
6./Kg 26 182,184,475
Iii./Kg 30 134,163
8./Kg 30 164
9./Kg 30 164
I./Kg 40 485
1./Kg 40 485
7./Kg 40 485
8./Kg 40 485
Stab/Kg 54 301
I.Kg 54 301
Stab/Kg 77 301
Ii./Kg 77 301
Iii./Kg 77 301
Stab(Kampf)/Lehrgeschwader 1 122,244,
299,301,330
I./Lg 1 232,299,382,384,431,481,483
1./Lg 1 330,332,443,476,479,483,484
2./Lg 1 431
3./Lg 1 443,483
Ii./Lg 1 122,134,185,203,206,228,232,
299,301,406,476,477,481,483,486
4./Lg 1 279,332,351,354,382,407,486
5./Lg 1 186,253,407
6./Lg 1 253,394,481,485,486
Iii./Lg 1 122,130,132,133,169,185,205,216,
232,234,238,299,301,318,319,337,382,
479
7./Lg 1 185,186,251,308,397
8./Lg 1 169,412,431
9./Lg 1 134,204,287
12./Lg 1 443
Erggr/Lg 1 403
I.Gr 606 301
K.Gr 806 301

Dive-Bomber Units

Stukageschwader 1 121
I./Stg 1 122,130,133,180,212,223,242,
301,310,315,324,333,381,441
1./Stg 1 131,224,332,337,394
2./Stg 1 241,319,333,337
3./Stg 1 199,234,242,333,337,381
Iii./Stg 1 155,156,158,160
7./Stg1 155
8./Stg 1 155
Stab Ii./Stg 2 142,175,176,193,227,361,363
Ii./Stg 2 132,145,149,156,202,212,213,
215,234,238,301,324,332,333,342,352,
441
4./Stg 2 146,158,352,355,409
5./Stg 2 133,143,239,319
6./Stg 2 143,144,146,227,239,333,337
Stab/Stg 3 122,137,253,264,273,301,330,
333,440
I./Stg 3 301,333,342,345,440
1./Stg 3 394
3./Stg 3 345,366,441
Ii./Stg 3 441
4./Stg 3 184
6./Stg 3 333,337
Iii./Stg 3 441

Reconnaissance Units

2.(H)/14 138,149,151,152,155,156,164,
175,186,211,212,220,222,244,266,309,
319,322,335,337,342,345,347,377,380,
426,436
1.(F)/121 122,184,299,380,400,407,445,476
4.(F)/121 205,206
2.(F)/123 148,184,204,205,275,277,287,
299,357,358,377,380,414,415,480,481

Transport Units

Ii./Kgrzbv 1 384,428
Iii./Kgrzbv 1 148,152,457,521
Iv./Kgrzbv 1 153
I./Llg 1 194,195
I./Grzbv 9 166
1./Kgrzbv 9 159
Kgrzbv 40 191
Kgrzbv 60 199,200,202
Kgrzbv 102 375,389
Kgrzbv 104 174
Kgrzbv 105 202
Kgrzbv 106 194,195,197,199,200,456
Kgrzbv 300 384
Kgrzbv 400 384
3./Kgrzbv 400 389
3./Kgrzbv 500 404
Kgrzbv 172 200,202,457
Stab Xi./Flk 200,202

Miscellaneous Units

Kdo.Fl.Ber Afrika 216
St.Fl.Ber.X.Flk 186

Kurier St.Afrika 146,322
Iii./Ln Regt 40 130
Seenotst. 6 166

Prisoner Of War Camps

Stalag Luft Iii 306
Stalag Viia 350

Regia Aeronautica Units

Aeronautica Della Libia 20,30,40
Battaglione Sahariano 22
Comando Settore Centrale 296
Comando Settore Est 20,85,87,296
Comando Settore Ovest 20,84,294
Nucleo 2° Stormo 490,491
Reparto Sperimentale Aerosiluranti 46,47,58
Sezione Cinematografica 230
Sezione Soccorso 297
5ª Squadra Aerea 39,52,53,84,124,294,297,
298,370
1° Stormo Ct 296,297,298,299,346,378,
413,416
2° Stormo Ct 40,52,53,61,77,85,86,98,100,
415
4° Stormo Ct 34,35,42,47,55,56,58,61,62,
76,88,91,92,93,97,98,99,100,102,103,
104,107,109,113,346,415
8° Stormo Bt 144,178,191,243,258,259,260,
264,286,296,305,333,394,407
9° Stormo Bt 37,45,46,53,54,55,64,66,68,
71,73,78,84,95,97,113,491
10° Stormo Bt 21,26,34,35,36,39,40,47,48,
50,53,57,247
11° Stormo Bt 472
12º Stormo Bt 472
13° Stormo Bt 272,296,333,338,341,360,
422,505
14° Stormo Bt 21,53,63,67,71,72,73,85,88,
113
15° Stormo Bt 20,26,28,35,47,48,50,53,65,
84,93,97,98,100,491
30° Stormo Bt 490
32° Stormo Bt 180,184
33° Stormo Bt 20,41,46,47,48,50,53,54,58
34° Stormo Bt 103,104,106,108
36° Stormo Bt 490
37° Stormo Bt 96
39° Stormo Bt 471,472
41° Stormo 69,70,84,92,94,96,99,100,126
50° Stormo Assalto 20,25,31,37,38,41,76,
85,91,92,109,111,112,118,129,126
54° Stormo Ct 118
56° Stormo Ct 120

1° Gruppo Apc 17,21,85
2° Gruppo Apc 16,22,23,85,113
2° Gruppo Autonomo Ct 103,106,107,109,
111,112,113,115,117,118,119,141,164,
169,172,223,224,227,244,490,491

3° Gruppo Autonomo Ct 180,184,294,423,
424,425,426,428,436,440,441,490,499,
501,502,503,504,505,506
6° Gruppo Autonomo Ct 296,298,378,389,
390,400,401,403,404,407,424,425,427,
432,445
7° Gruppo (5° St Ass) 45,55,69
8° Gruppo (2° St Ct) 16,22,23,24,26,28,29,
31,32,33,34,36,37,38,39,53,54,61,67,69,
70,85,89,94,98,298,360,408,415,423,424
9° Gruppo (4° St Ct) 34,35,41,43,45,47,62,
63,67,68,70,71,76,78,85,86,87,88,89,91,
92,93,97,98,99,100,108,111,298,344,345,
346,347,357,358,364,366,368,371,376,
402,403,405,407
10° Gruppo (4° St Ct) 17,22,25,26,27,28,29,
30,34,35,38,39,40,41,43,45,55,56,61,
71,85,92,99,101,102,103,104,106,107,
415,496
11° Gruppo (13° St Bt) 272,273,296,333,338
12° Gruppo (50° St Ass) 17,20,22,26,27,29,
37,40,42,47,56,57,85,90,91,92,109,111,
112,118,119,244,294,337,414,499,501,
503,504,506
13° Gruppo (2° St Ct) 17,21,25,29,30,31,36,
37,38,39,40,60,61,62,64,65,71,72,73,77,
85,87,88,91,92,95,97,98,100,489,490
15º Gruppo Oa 297
16° Gruppo (50° St Ass) 17,20,22,37,47,56,
57,85,90,91,118
17° Gruppo (1° St Ct) 297,298,299,344,346,
363,376,378,382,384,388,389,390,403,
407,413,414,442,443,444
18° Gruppo Ct 119,129,135,136,156,158,
159,160,185,187,193,199,205,212,232,
233,234,241,490
20° Gruppo Ct 120,224,233,234,237,240,
242,243,245,254,255,258,280,285,287,
296,298, 313,315,345,359,360,361,363,
366,382,392,394
22° Gruppo Ct 120
23° Gruppo Ct 100,102,103,106,107,108,
109,111,117,119,126,490
26° Gruppo (9° St Bt) 37,46,53,71,73,76,
84,491
27° Gruppo (8° St Bt) 144,178,296,333
28° Gruppo (8° St Bt) 144,191,243,259,260,
264,286,296,305,394,407,510
29° Gruppo (9° St Bt) 53,64,68,71,73,84,97
30° Gruppo (10° St Bt) 17,21,22,39,40
32° Gruppo (10° St Bt) 17,21,22,35,36
33° Gruppo Autonomo Bt 36,46,53,57,71,
85,86,92,93,94,96
34° Gruppo (11° St Bt) 85,471,472
35° Gruppo (33° St Bt) 17,20,41,50
36° Gruppo (33° St Bt) 17,20,46,54
38° Gruppo (32° St Bt) 184
41° Gruppo Autonomo Bt 510
42° Gruppo Autonomo Bt 92,472
43° Gruppo (13° St Bt) 296,422

44° Gruppo (14° St Bt) 16,21,71,85,88
45° Gruppo (14° St Bt) 16,21,65,67,85,86, 88
46° Gruppo (15° St Bt) 17,20,28,35,56,57, 84
47° Gruppo (15° St Bt) 17,20,22,84,100,491
50° Gruppo Autonomo Bt 192,479
52° Gruppo (34° St Bt) 85,104,106
53° Gruppo (34° St Bt) 85,103,108,191
54° Gruppo Autonomo Bt 36,85
56° Gruppo (39° St Bt) 471,472,480
59° Gruppo (41° St Bt) 69,84,94,96,98,99
60° Gruppo (41° St Bt) 69,70,84,94,96, 98,99,100,126
63° Gruppo Oa 55
64° Gruppo Oa 17,21,84
67° Gruppo Oa 34,84,101,102,103,297
69° Gruppo Oa 297
73° Gruppo Oa 16,22,23,85,89
87° Gruppo (30° St Bt) 490
89° Gruppo (32° St Bt) 184
90° Gruppo (30° St Bt) 490
92° Gruppo (39° St Bt) 471,472
96° Gruppo Bat 151,156,175,178
97° Gruppo Bat 178
98° Gruppo Bt 137,141,173,178,294,360, 503,504,505
114° Gruppo Speciale Bt 85,120
130° Gruppo Autonomo As 184
131° Gruppo Autonomo As 230,433
145° Gruppo Autonomo T 17,294
150° Gruppo Autonomo Ct 298,415,424, 425,428,436,440,446
151° Gruppo Autonomo Ct 53,71,72,76, 78,85,86,87,88,89,91,93,94,96,99,104, 116,117,119,120,123,124,125,142,177, 298,299,346,347,359,360,365,366,371, 376,407,490,493,496,498
153° Gruppo Autonomo Ct 160,235,240,242, 255,256,262,263,264,265,277,284,286, 287,297,298,308,321,322,324,333,337, 351,352,355,356,358,359,360,363,366, 370,371,392,401,407,415
155° Gruppo Autonomo Ct 120,123,148, 152,153,154,156,158,164,172,178,179, 250,251,256,257,273,297,298,310,313, 319,322,333,337,338,353,355,359,490, 494,496,497,499
157° Gruppo Autonomo Ct 287,298,359,360, 361,363,370,371,406,407,415,490
160° Gruppo Autonomo Ct 244,245,268,285, 296,313,341,345,359,360,407,408,501, 506

1ª Squadriglia (11° Gr, 13° St Bt) 272,296, 333,338
2ª Squadriglia (45° Gr, 14° St Bt) 21,67
3ª Squadriglia (43° Gr, 13° St Bt) 296,422
4ª Squadriglia (11° Gr, 13° St Bt) 273,274, 296

5ª Squadriglia (43° Gr, 13° St Bt) 296
6ª Squadriglia (44° Gr, 14° St Bt) 21,88
7ª Squadriglia (44° Gr, 14° St Bt) 21
10ª Squadriglia (28° Gr, 8° St Bt) 144,243, 259,260,296,510
11ª Squadriglia (26° Gr, 9° St Bt) 53,78
12ª Squadriglia (1° Gr Apc) 21,346,347
13ª Squadriglia (26° Gr, 9° St Bt) 37,46,53, 76,491
16ª Squadriglia (2° Gr Apc) 22
18ª Squadriglia (27° Gr, 8° St Bt) 124,144, 296,333
19ª Squadriglia (28° Gr, 8° St Bt) 144,175, 191,231,260,264,286,296,305,308,394, 407
20ª Squadriglia (46° Gr, 15° St Bt) 20,35, 56,57
21ª Squadriglia (46° Gr, 15° St Bt) 20,28, 56,57
22ª Squadriglia (45° Gr, 14° St Bt) 21,86,88
23ª Squadriglia (2° Gr Apc) 22,24,26,123
26ª Squadriglia Apc 124,125
32ª Squadriglia (67° Gr Oa) 297,341,376
37ª Squadriglia (67° Gr Oa) 34
41ª Squadriglia (63° Gr Oa) 55
43ª Squadriglia (35° Gr, 33° St Bt) 20,41
44ª Squadriglia (35° Gr, 33° St Bt) 20,50
45ª Squadriglia (36° Gr, 33° St Bt) 20,46
46ª Squadriglia (36° Gr, 33° St Bt) 20,54
49ª Squadriglia (38° Gr, 32° St Bt) 180
52ª Squadriglia (27° Gr, 8° St Bt) 144,178, 258,296
53ª Squadriglia (47° Gr, 15° St Bt) 20,65,100
54ª Squadriglia (47° Gr, 15° St Bt) 20,126, 491
55ª Squadriglia (30° Gr, 10° St Bt) 21
56ª Squadriglia (30° Gr, 10° St Bt) 21,47
57ª Squadriglia (32° Gr, 10° St Bt) 21,35, 47,48
58ª Squadriglia (32° Gr, 10° St Bt) 21,32, 47,48
59ª Squadriglia (33° Gr Aut Bt) 36,46
60ª Squadriglia (33° Gr Aut Bt) 36,46,53, 57,93,94,96
62ª Squadriglia (29° Gr, 9° St Bt) 53,64,97
63ª Squadriglia (29° Gr, 9° St Bt) 53,68,71, 73,97
67ª Squadriglia (34° Gr, 11° St Bt) 471,472
70ª Squadriglia (23° Gr Ct) 106,107,108, 114,376,490
71ª Squadriglia (17° Gr, 1° St Ct) 297,298, 363,378,389,390,414
72ª Squadriglia (17° Gr, 1° St Ct) 298,363, 376,414,444
73ª Squadriglia (9° Gr, 4° St Ct) 34,43,45, 67,68,70,78,88,89,93,98,99,108,298
74ª Squadriglia (23° Gr Ct) 102,103,108, 111,119,490
75ª Squadriglia (23° Gr Ct) 106,107,108, 114,119,490

76ª Squadriglia (7° Gr, 5° St Ass) 45
77ª Squadriglia (13° Gr, 2° St Ct) 21,31, 32,33,38,39,40,60,72,73,77,86,88,96,489
78ª Squadriglia (13° Gr, 2° St Ct) 21,36,37, 39,40,64,65,73,97,96,489
79ª Squadriglia (6° Gr, 1° St Ct) 298,390, 400,403,426
80ª Squadriglia (17° Gr, 1° St Ct) 298,363, 376,389,414,442,443
81ª Squadriglia (6° Gr, 1° St Ct) 296,298, 389,400,401,403,404,432
82ª Squadriglia (13° Gr, 2° St Ct) 21,25,38, 60,61,62,72,73,77,87,88,91,92,95,96,489
83ª Squadriglia (18° Gr Ct) 159,233,234,490
84ª Squadriglia (10° Gr, 4° St Ct) 22,27, 28,29,39,40,41,44,45,61,91,104,496
85ª Squadriglia (18° Gr Ct) 123,160,185, 205,232,490
86ª Squadriglia (7° Gr, 5° St Ass) 45
88ª Squadriglia (6° Gr, 1° St Ct) 298,299, 389,424,425,426
89ª Squadriglia (1° Gr Apc) 21
90ª Squadriglia (10° Gr, 4° St Ct) 22,25,26, 28,29,30,39,40,41,43,45,55,56,71,86,107
91ª Squadriglia (10° Gr, 4° St Ct) 22,27,28, 30,38,39,40,44,45,55,101,102,103,106
92ª Squadriglia (8° Gr, 2° St Ct) 22,24,25, 26,28,52,53,61,67,69,97,98,298,423,424
93ª Squadriglia (8° Gr, 2° St Ct) 22,23,24, 25,26,31,33,36,37,298
94ª Squadriglia (8° Gr, 2° St Ct) 22,23,24, 31,32,33,70,91,298
95ª Squadriglia (18° Gr Ct) 119,135,136, 158,160,187,193,212,490
96ª Squadriglia (9° Gr, 4° St Ct) 34,43,47, 55,70,71,78,92,95,97,99,298,346,347, 357,358,366,376,403
97ª Squadriglia (9° Gr, 4° St Ct) 34,62,63, 76,78,92,93,298,347,357,358,368,376,403
98ª Squadriglia (7° Gr, 5° St Ass) 45,68,69
99ª Squadriglia Aviazione Sahariana 17,21
103ª Squadriglia Apc 601
104ª Squadriglia (1° Gr Apc) 21
113ª Squadriglia (63° Gr Oa) 55
115ª Squadriglia (67° Gr Oa) 34,66
118ª Squadriglia (69° Gr Oa) 297
122ª Squadriglia (64° Gr Oa) 21
123ª Squadriglia (69° Gr Oa) 297
125ª Squadriglia (67° Gr Oa) 297,347
127ª Squadriglia (73° Gr Oa) 22,89
129ª Squadriglia (67° Gr Oa) 285,297, 306,342,345
132ª Squadriglia (67° Gr Oa) 297
136ª Squadriglia (64° Gr Oa) 21,32,40,41
137ª Squadriglia (73° Gr Oa) 22,61,62,65
141ª Squadriglia Rm 59
143ª Squadriglia Rm 17,22,48,60,64,85
145ª Squadriglia Rm 60,68,85,297,494,502
150ª Squadriglia (2° Gr Aut Ct) 111,112, 164,227,490

151ª Squadriglia (20° Gr Aut Ct) 233,234, 255,285,287,296,363,366

152ª Squadriglia (2° Gr Aut Ct) 109,111, 112,141,164,169,172,490

153ª Squadriglia (3° Gr Aut Ct) 180,184, 294,366,490,502

154ª Squadriglia (3° Gr Aut Ct) 180,184, 294,490,501,502,503,504,505,506

155ª Squadriglia (3° Gr Aut Ct) 294,441, 490,502,503,505

159ª Squadriglia (12° Gr, 5° St Ass) 20,25, 26,40,41,42,55,56,61,67,70,111,112,244, 294,337,490,499,501,504,506

160ª Squadriglia (12° Gr, 5° St Ass) 20,29, 31,32,40,41,42,55,56,61,67,70,111, 112,118,119,244,294,490,501,503

162ª Squadriglia Ct 203,204

165ª Squadriglia (12° Gr) 244,294,414, 490,501

167ª Squadriglia (16° Gr, 5° St Ass) 20,61

168ª Squadriglia (16° Gr, 5° St Ass) 20,57, 61,90,91

170ª Squadriglia Rm 513,514

172ª Squadriglia Autonoma Rst 476,485

174ª Squadriglia Autonoma Rst 268,296, 341,414,422,423

175ª Squadriglia Autonoma Rst 40,54,55, 85,89,91,98,100,112,113,142,181,294,477

176ª Squadriglia Autonoma Rst 314,350, 351,360,388,431

192ª Squadriglia (87° Gr, 30° St Bt) 490

194ª Squadriglia (90° Gr, 30° St Bt) 490

196ª Squadriglia Rm 233,235,297

201ª Squadriglia (92° Gr, 39° St Bt) 471

205ª Squadriglia (41° Gr Aut Bt) 510

209ª Squadriglia (97° Gr Bat) 178,242,245, 260,261,262,264,296,391,394,397,420, 421,422,436,440,441,444

211ª Squadriglia (50° Gr Aut Bt) 479

215ª Squadriglia (52° Gr, 34° St Bt) 106

216ª Squadriglia (53° Gr, 34° St Bt) 103,191

217ª Squadriglia (53° Gr, 34° St Bt) 108, 109,191

218ª Squadriglia (54° Gr Aut Bt) 36

219ª Squadriglia (54° Gr Aut Bt) 36

222ª Squadriglia (56° Gr, 39° St Bt) 472,480

228ª Squadriglia (89° Gr, 32° St Bt) 180

232ª Squadriglia (59° Gr, 41° St Bt) 69,94, 96,99

233ª Squadriglia (59° Gr, 41° St Bt) 69,99

234ª Squadriglia (60° Gr, 41° St Bt) 69,94,96

235ª Squadriglia (60° Gr, 41° St Bt) 69,70, 99,100,126

236ª Squadriglia (96° Gr Bat) 154,175, 294,444,445

239ª Squadriglia (97° Gr Bat) 178,199,212, 214,216,232,234,238,354,355,366,391, 503

240ª Squadriglia (98° Gr Bt) 137,139,140, 178,294

241ª Squadriglia (98° Gr Bt) 137,139,141, 173,294,505

244ª Squadriglia Autonoma Bt 296

272ª Squadriglia (114° Gr Aut Bt) 120

273ª Squadriglia (114° Gr Aut Bt) 120

278ª Squadriglia Autonoma As 46,48,58,64, 68,85,166,168,181,182

279ª Squadriglia Autonoma As 214,230,242, 251,252,279,280,297,402,443,518,519

280ª Squadriglia Autonoma As 180,184

281ª Squadriglia Autonoma As 191,402, 403,414

284ª Squadriglia (131° Gr As) 348,433,443

288ª Squadriglia Rm 105,106,123,516,517

351ª Squadriglia (155° Gr Aut Ct) 120,148, 150,152,156,157,158,164,179,337,363, 490,494

352ª Squadriglia (20° Gr Aut Ct) 251,255, 296,297,361,363,366

353ª Squadriglia (20° Gr Aut Ct) 233,234, 237,240,242,243,255,280,296,345,366

357ª Squadriglia (157° Gr Aut Ct) 287,298, 406,407

358ª Squadriglia (2° Gr Aut Ct) 109,115, 117,118,119,164,169,224,227,490

360ª Squadriglia (155° Gr Aut Ct) 148,154, 157,172,179,241,253,273,274,285,296, 490,496,497

363ª Squadriglia (150° Gr Aut Ct) 298,425

364ª Squadriglia (150° Gr Aut Ct) 298,415, 428,436

365ª Squadriglia (150° Gr Aut Ct) 298,326, 425

366ª Squadriglia (151° Gr Aut Ct) 53,62,63, 72,73,76,78,86,88,89,90,91,93,96,104, 123,124,125,177,298,347,363,366,490, 497

367ª Squadriglia (151° Gr Aut Ct) 53,89, 96,99,123,298,490,498

368ª Squadriglia (151° Gr Aut Ct) 53,72, 73,76,87,88,90,91,96,99,116,117,119, 120,124,125,142,298,490,493,497,498

372ª Squadriglia (153° Gr Aut Ct) 235, 240,242,264,265,285,287,297,333,371

373ª Squadriglia (153° Gr Aut Ct) 297,308, 322,352,356,363,371,406

374ª Squadriglia (153° Gr Aut Ct) 160,242, 263,264,277,282,284,286,297,355,490

375ª Squadriglia (160° Gr Aut Ct) 244,285, 296,341,345,347

376ª Squadriglia Autonoma Ct 228,297, 322,359,415,490,497

378ª Squadriglia (155° Gr Aut Ct) 120,123, 148,151,152,154,157,164,256,257,297, 319,333,337,338,355,361,400,497

384ª Squadriglia (157° Gr Aut Ct) 298,360, 363,490

385ª Squadriglia (157° Gr Aut Ct) 287,298, 363

386ª Squadriglia (157° Gr Aut Ct) 490

393ª Squadriglia (160° Gr Aut Ct) 244,268, 285,296,313,501

394ª Squadriglia (160° Gr Aut Ct) 244,245, 285,296,360,506

600ª Squadriglia (145° Gr T) 294

604ª Squadriglia (145° Gr T) 294,359,360

610ª Squadriglia (145° Gr T) 294

607ª Squadriglia T 165,166

614ª Squadriglia Soccorso 85,514

British Commonwealth Army Units

Western Desert Force 13,120,223,224

8th Army 275,304,324,339,345,432,433

Xiii Corps 128,129,304,306,310,314, 319,321,323,413,424,428,432,435,437, 438,440,445

Xxx Corps 304,306,310,313,314,319,323, 333

I Australian Corps 129

Cyrenaica Command 129

1st Armoured Division 435,436

2nd Armoured Division 65,134,135,142, 143,144,147,148

7th Armoured Division 51,52,80,81,82,91, 125,134,186,220,221,260,313,318,319, 348,399,409,432

1st South African Division 65,334

4th Indian Division 80,82,223

5th Indian Division 65

6th Division 13

6th Australian Division 82,105,116,124,125, 135

7th Australian Division 135,147

New Zealand Division 65,135,319,352,356

4th Armoured Brigade 313

22nd Guards Brigade 186,221

18th Cavalry (India) Army Brigade 246

22nd Armoured Brigade 313,318

29th Indian Infantry Brigade Group 304

Indian Brigade 400

11th Indian Brigade Group 221

Aa Brigade 81

104th Brigade, Royal Horse Artillery 55

Polish Brigade Group (Carpathian Brigade) 135,246

1st King's Royal Rifle Regiment 55,130

1st Royal Northumberland Fusiliers 55

3rd Coldstream Guards 55,276

4th South African Armoured Car Regiment 354

6th South African Armoured Car Regiment 304

7th Royal Tank Regiment 80

Oasis Force 304

7th Hussars 25

11th Hussars 52,67,80,130

King's Dragoon Guards 27,406

25/26 Medium Battery, Royal Artillery 55

German Army Units
Afrika Korps 226,318,356,492,495
3rd Panzer Division 80
5th Light Division 127,135,137,148,187,223
15th Panzer Division 148,187,223
21st Panzer Division 260,318
5th Panzer Regiment 149

Italian Army Units
10ª Armata (10th Army) 51,52,54,55,57,82,
   125,126
1ª Divisione Camicie Nere (Blackshirts)
   '23 Marzo' 52,55,57
1ª Divisione Libica 82
2ª Divisione Libica 82
4ª Divisione Camicie Nere (Blackshirts) 52,82
62ª Divisione 'Marmarica' 52,82
63ª Divisione 'Cirene' 52,82
64ª Divisione 'Catanzaro' 52,82
Divisione 'Ariete' (Armoured) 139,142,148
Divisione 'Bologna' 139
Divisione 'Brescia' 139,142,148
Divisione 'Pavia' 139
Divisione 'Trento' (Mobilised) 134
Raggruppamento Maletti (Maletti's Group)
   52,54,57,82

Royal Navy Vessels
Mediterranean Fleet 29,33,34,35,47,58,68,
   110,165,166,182,188,277,403,515
Force B 204
Force D 191,192,206
Force H 110,179
1st Battle Squadron 179,184,186
3rd Cruiser Squadron 34
5th Destroyer Flotilla 179
1st Submarine Flotilla 12

Aircraft Carriers
HMS *Ark Royal* 179,180,181,182,189,
   259,450,508
HMS *Eagle* 23,33,34,50,57,81,186,226
HMS *Formidable* 165,166,179,182,183,
   186,441,479,493,513
HMS *Furious* 75,96,110,189,259,449,508
HMS *Illustrious* 57,63,68,81,114,121,
   441,491,492
HMS *Glorious* 33,110
HMS *Victorious* 189

Battleships/Battlecruisers
HMS *Barham* 179
HMS *Queen Elizabeth* 179,182
HMS *Ramillies* 449
HMS *Renown* 449
HMS *Valiant* 63,179,180,181
HMS *Warspite* 23,37,63,279,491

Cruisers
HMS *Ajax* 182,493
HMS *Berwick* 449
HMS *Calcutta* (AA Cruiser) 211
HMS *Caledon* 34
HMS *Capetown* 34
HMS *Carlisle* 432
HMS *Coventry* 456
HMS *Euryalis* 314
HMS *Fiji* 179
HMS *Glasgow* 63
HMS *Gloucester* 159,160,179,493
HMS *Kent* 58
HMS *Liverpool* 63,68
HMS *Manchester* 75,449,450
HMS *Naiad* 179,314
HMS *Newcastle* 449
HMS *Orion* 63
HMAS *Perth* 493,508
HMS *Phoebe* 206,252
HMS *Sheffield* 179,449
HMS *Southampton* 114,441
HMAS *Sydney* 29,63
HMS *York* 58,63

Destroyers
HMS *Dainty* 134
HMS *Defender* 196,238
MV *Dumana* (RAF Depot Ship) 12
HMS *Flamingo* 232,238
HMS *Foresight* 180
HMS *Griffin* 248
HMS *Havoc* 242
HMS *Jackal* 248
HMS *Jaguar* 196
HMS *Juno* 192
HMS *Kandahar* 248
HMS *Kipling* 247
HMS *Napier* 206
HMS *Nizam* 206
HMAS *Stuart* 64
HMS *Vendetta* 238,242
HMAS *Waterhen* 232,232

Submarines
HMS *Cachalot* (Minelaying Submarine) 241
HMS *Regent* 113
HMS *Tetrach* 512
HMS *Unique* 499
HMS *Utmost* 500

Miscellaneous
A Lighters 140,277
HMS *Aphis* (Gunboat) 192
HMS *Auckland* (Sloop) 230
HMS *Cricket* (Minesweeper/Gunboat) 232,
   238
HMT *Chalka* (Transport) 175
HMS *Cyclops* (Submarine Depot Ship) 12
HMS *Fareham* (Mine Dredger) 170

HMT *Franconia* (Transport) 449
HMS *Gloxinia* (Corvette) 170
HMS *Gnat* (Gunboat) 515
HMS *Grimsby* (Sloop) 199
HMS *Laton* (Minelayer) 280
HMAS *Parramatta* (Sloop) 230
HMS *Protector* (Fast Net-Laying Boom
   Defence Vessel) 511
HMS *Terror* (Monitor) 132,134

Merchant Vessels
SS *Aglios Georgios* 475
SS *Antiklion* 232
SS *British Lord* (Oiler) 166
SS *Clan Campbell* 179
SS *Clan Chattan* 179
SS *Clan Lamont* 179
SS *Dilwarra* 36,49
SS *Dominion Monarch* 475
SS *Draco* 154,170
MV *Clan Forbes* 443
SS *Helka* 199
SS *Empire Song* 179,182
MV *Miranda Tiberio* 232,514
SS *Tiberio* (Tanker) ? The Same
MV *New Zealand Star* 179,182,449
MV *Parracombe* (Fast MV) 506
MV *Pass Of Halmata* 230,232
SS *Ramree* 475
MV *South Isles* 232
SS *South Seas* (Whaler) 170
SS *Thorgian* (Trawler) 468
SS *Urania* 170

German And Other Axis Vessels
Admiral Hipper (Battlecruiser) 110
Admiral Scheer (Battlecruiser) 110
Alicante (German Freighter) 457
Reichenfels (Tanker) 505
Riva (German Freighter) 499
Spezia (German Freighter) 504
Sparta (German Freighter) 496
Wachtfels (German Freighter) 495
Jiul (Rumanian Freighter) 457
Knyaquinya Maria Luisa (Bulgarian
   Freighter) 457

Italian Vessels
Achille Papa (Torpedo Boat) 241
Adua (Refrigerator Ship) 499
Alagi (Submarine) 508
Aquilone 58
Bainsizza (Freighter) 502
Bagnolini (Submarine) 24
Borea (Destroyer) 58
Cadamosto (Freighter) 504
Caffaro (Freighter) 500
Calipso 50
Capo Faro (Freighter) 504
Caterina (Freighter) 502